TOWARD A MORE PERFECT UNION

INTRODUCTION TO AMERICAN GOVERNMENT

Second Edition

Patrick C. Coaty, Ph.D.

Orange Coast College

Kendall Hunt
publishing company

Kendall Hunt
publishing company

www.kendallhunt.com
Send all inquiries to:
4050 Westmark Drive
Dubuque, IA 52004-1840

CONTENTS

DEDICATION

To Ruby Hernandez Coaty and Jacob Patrick Coaty

Love always creates, it never destroys. In this lies man's only promise—Leo Buscaglia

ACKNOWLEDGMENTS

I would like to thank Janice Samuells and Amanda Smith of Kendall Hunt for helping me with this project. Janice had the idea for a book before I did, and Carrie and her team have helped turn a manuscript into a book. I would like to thank my colleagues at Orange Coast College for being true friends and being available to talk about general political events and listening to my ideas for incorporating original documents into the writing process.

Finally, I would like to thank my wife Ruby, who has given me her love and support. She also gave me insight and valuable assistance in writing this book, and our son Jacob, who is my window to the future and a symbol of my optimism for the challenges we face as a country.

IMAGE FROM DEFENSE VISUAL INFORMATION CENTER

INTRODUCTION

FOR THE STUDENT

The object of this textbook is not so much to supply a person with a complete body of information, as to train students to apply what they learn. So they may be able to have the skills in which they can analyze new ideas and concepts in which they will come in contact with in the future. The Chapters and Original Documents of *Toward a More Perfect Union* are supplied in no specific chronological order. Instead, they are arranged in a power relationship, the beginning chapters deal with the structure of the United States Government and your rights and responsibilities under the United States Constitution. The following chapters explore how leaders are chosen by the people of the United States and finally, we analyze how public policy is formed and implemented. This organization is designed to give the course flexibility for incorporating either: current events or outside articles and/or books. This textbook is designed for a mixed skilled student audience and because of this we start our program with a discussion of study skills.

LECTURE NOTES

Every student will find it to their advantage to take careful notes during lectures. Taking notes as a skill disciplines your mind to condense and remember material; note taking should glue the parts of the course together. Unlike High School, College and University courses should not be viewed as separate sections in which you memorize a chapter of information and then regurgitate for the exam; in college you must see the connections inside the content in order to answer conceptual questions. It is easier if the student takes notes during lectures. Students are also advised to summarize their notes by using headings and marginal catch phrases; this makes it easier to review for exams.

USE OF TEXTBOOKS

Every introductory college course needs to be reinforced by a general textbook. The objective of textbooks is to give the student a connected view of the whole subject, and to furnish an essential body of facts. A good method for reading a textbook is to read the chapters three times. (This is borrowed from Mortimer Adler's *How to Read a Book*). The first time a student views a book they should read the Table of Contents slowly and then quickly scan every page of the book. The second time a student reads a chapter he/she should read it as though you were reading a magazine or a novel. Then, the third time a student should read each paragraph and keep a reading notebook and answer in their words "What is the author saying?" Remember it is important to answer this question in your own words—then after you have done this, you will be able to summarize your reading into a two or three page summary that you will understand. This will prove invaluable for your college career.

In all courses, it is assumed that the students are doing regular reading. No one can expect to follow what goes on in the classroom if you are not prepared by reading the textbook. In college a student should also do extra reading that follows along the course outline. For example in an American Government course students should be reading the newspaper daily, watching daily newscasts and be familiar with the great events of our times.

If a student is serious about achieving success in college these hints are designed to be a starting point for organizing their work.

EXAMINATIONS

If you are organized then there will not be a need to "cram" the night before an exam. Examinations are necessary not so much to test the study habits of the students as to find out how far they are able to apply what they have learned during the course. Examinations test the ability of the student to use critical thinking to highlight the most important concepts in the reading assignments and classroom. The following suggestions may be useful as you prepare for an examination: 1. Come to the exam rested. 2. Read the questions before beginning to write. 3. Studies have shown if a student is prepared for the exam they tend to change correct answers into wrong answers. For Essay Exams: 4. Write legibly; ink is preferred. 5. Arrange and paragraph your work neatly and systematically. 6. Indicate subdivisions of your argument. 7. Budget your time correctly.

Many of you may be aware of these study skills. If you are not, these may help lower your feelings of frustration and alienation that many students feel when they are entering college.

CONCEPTUAL INTRODUCTION

Has the election of Barack Obama changed the attitude of Americans about politics? Has the economic crisis that we have seen since the summer of 2008 shaken people's apathy? Since the election of 2008, the United States government has spent trillions of dollars and most Americans cannot tell you the name of the Representative or Congressman. It is as if we were all playing poker without knowing the rules. "Dealer calls the game." If you play cards or watch poker, you may have heard players call something similar to this during a game. What it means is the dealer gets to lay out the rules of the hand of poker that is being played. Setting the rules is one way to have an advantage over your rivals. The Government is changing the rules. These rules that are being written today will determine if your behavior will be rewarded or punished in the future.

During the last decade everyone was told they should buy a house. We all have friends and relatives who mortgaged their future on the belief that home values would increase eight percent a year forever. Now these unfortunate people have mortgages that are greater than the piece of property they purchased. Some people struggle to pay their mortgages and hope someday the value of their property will increase. Others have cynically stopped paying their mortgage in the hope the Government will come and bail them out. Of course, the government will not. At the time of this writing, General Motors and Chrysler Motors are trying to stay out of bankruptcy. After receiving billions of dollars; it looks like Chrysler will either be merging with the Italian Company FIAT or will not remain in operation. Would the people who bought homes they cannot afford or the managers and dealers in the automobile industry like to fold in their cards? I would bet they would like to. Keep this in mind, when someone tells you government and politics are boring and unimportant.

Generally, if I told you someone is taking a third of your paycheck—then would you be interested in what they did with your money? Of course, you would be. Right now, the government does take an average of thirty percent of the majority of peoples' income. In some counties in California, the sales tax is ten percent on all purchases. The majority of taxes are paid by Americans who earn between 40,000–200,000 dollars a year. Even in a slow economy if you are employed and your spouse is employed you will be paying roughly a third of your paycheck to Washington D.C. and Sacramento. So, is this still boring?

President Obama has called for a program of national service, otherwise known as a military draft. If there was a draft, would you be interested in the criteria used in the selection of military leaders? Would you be interested in the government's plans for your city in order to evacuate you from an attack by terrorists with a weapon of mass destruction? Would the Government be more competent with a new President or would the performance of the Government be the same as it was after Katrina hit New Orleans and the Gulf Coast?

Think of learning about government and politics as a way to conceptualize strategies for your future. Are your life and the rules in which you will live boring? By being in school and reading this book, we know you do not think your future is boring.

One reason people believe the study of politics and governments is unimportant is the government has embedded both the costs and benefits of its actions in our daily lives. In other words, the rules of the game are so embedded we do not think about them. They are the assumptions we accept in order to play. This book is organized to examine the government's role in our society. We will investigate the fundamental structure of the government and the politics that enable people to become leaders of the government and write the rules (laws) that we all must live under. It is our goal to give students and concerned lay readers the analytical insights to understand our system. Not to indoctrinate the reader but have the reader draw their own conclusions. In order for the reader to become an independent and informed member of our society, he or she needs to understand the incentives created by government to create a better life.

To fulfill this objective, our discussion will include fifteen chapters and a series of original historical documents. Each chapter will examine a segment of the system we use to govern ourselves. Starting with Chapter One, which analyzes the challenges you will face in the twenty-first century, including a brief discussion on issues concerning the government and personal behavior. Chapters Two and Three trace the development of the U.S. Constitution. Chapter Four focuses on the important aspects of Civil Rights and Civil Liberties and how our contemporary view of these is often confused. Chapter Five looks at federalism and inter-governmental re-

lations. We have seen how federalism throughout history has been used to shield accountability of government officials in times of emergency and failure. This will complete the formal discussion of the foundational structure of the government of the United States.

We then move to the political traditions that have developed since the ratification of the Constitution. In Chapter Six, we will analyze how we vote and public opinion. This introduces us to a very important level of analysis of the individual. We then widen our scope of analysis in Chapter Seven to people in groups; we study the role and differences of political parties and interest groups. What these groups do is investigated in Chapter Eight when we discuss campaigns and elections. After our treatment of politics, we center our focus on the three branches of government: Congress, the Presidency and the Judiciary—these are covered in Chapters Nine, Ten and Eleven respectively. After our discussion of the interaction of the three branches of the Federal government we will explore the role of the bureaucracy in our society in Chapter Twelve. This is a very important chapter, since the bureaucracy is the facet of government that most people will encounter during their lifetimes. Finally, Chapter Thirteen probes the issues surrounding domestic public policy, followed by Chapter Fourteen, public policy and nuclear weapons and we conclude with Chapter 15. As one can see, the fifteen chapters are divided by some rationale, but these divisions are somewhat arbitrary. We would like to remind the reader to look for connections between the concepts and chapters presented. It is easier to understand the workings of our government if we see it as a connected phenomenon.

Finally, it is more enjoyable to study politics and government if we remember the government was formed by men, albeit, great men. These people sought to change world history and they succeeded. Trying to understand how they wanted to balance the need for citizen participation in politics and the state and at the same time trying to honor the liberty everyone has to opt out of the political process, is with us today. We may be out of balance today, since many people do not vote. They do not choose to vote out of principle, they choose (many times) out of ignorance or laziness. We hope to arm you with reasons to either participate in our system or not to participate, but again, hopefully you reach your own conclusion after some thought and study.

chapter one

POWER AND THE CHALLENGES OF THE TWENTY-FIRST CENTURY

INTRODUCTION

Why are you in college? You go to school to achieve a better life. This entails the use of power. In effect you attend school to learn how to use power. Once you understand power and how it works, you will begin to develop strategies that will give you the capacity for a more fruitful personal and professional life. College can be considered the compression of human experience in order for students to achieve an understanding of our civilization in a short period of time. In this process, you will develop a strategy that balances the costs and benefits of your behavior in the short and long term, also at the same time, incorporating your emotional perspective for you to make choices for you to have a happy existence. Hopefully, by the end of your formal education, this type of thinking becomes second nature. This is the function of critical thinking and the use of theory as a problem solving technique.

Theory is used to give us answers to questions that are accepted as being true. The use of theory

therefore, enables us to learn from the work of others in order to save us time and effort by not forcing us to re-invent the basic principles of our field of study. If we have a problem, and we are aware of a theory that addresses our question, we should use it as a clue in our efforts to solve the problem. Is it better to investigate the great thinkers of human history or listen to the voices produced by popular culture? If you are unfamiliar with the theories produced by the great minds of our civilization you will not have the skills to compare arguments of the former against the latter.

To start our journey on the road to developing our reasoning skills, we have to understand the currency of our analysis. As economists investigate the properties of money and people's behavior around the use of money, in Political Science we use power. Political scientists investigate power and people's behavior surrounding government. Power is the currency our theories and investigations are built on. What makes up the elements of power? How do we define and use it in our investigations? These ques-

5

tions will be addressed in our discussion of the elements of power.

ELEMENTS OF POWER

We define power as the ability to get someone to do what you want them to do. Using this definition, we are all experts in the use of power on a personal level. Look at the relationships inside your family and you will see all sorts of power relationships. Who do you go to if you need something? What are the strategies you have learned when you have to ask your parents for something or you have to tell them bad news? Leo Tolstoy in his novel *Anna Karenina* starts with the statement "Happy families are all alike; every unhappy family is unhappy in its own way."[1] We would argue if you study the power relationships of a family, they are all unique—happy or unhappy. We know of a family where the kids would tell their Mother bad news and she would wait until their Father had eaten dinner before she would tell him. It seemed this simple observation of the man's moods and his wife's understanding of how to use power, created a happier environment for the family.

Generally speaking, the youngest child of a family will have a different relationship with their parents than the oldest child. If you are a middle child you will also have a different relationship with your parents and your siblings. Yes, these things are determined by your personality, economics and other forces inside your family, but our reactions to the environment is caused by our understanding of the power dynamic inside of the family.

What about dating, who has more power a woman or a man? If you measure power by the amount of pain inflicted, then it is easily measured that women have more power than men in the world of dating. This particular torture starts with the average boy entering junior high school and the ritual of asking a girl to a dance. Most boys view the first phone call to a girl's house as sheer terror, especially if her father answers the phone. Even in today's world of cell phones, asking a girl out for a boy remains a nerve racking event. Even when the boy grows up to be a young man and the girl grows up to be a young woman, the power dynamic does not change. The next time you are in a club, look at the single people asking each other for a dance or phone number. You will usually see a group of men standing around in a clump and a group of women. All of a sudden one man will break from the group and walk over to a young woman. You see her smile and his gestures, from behind the guy you see her shake her head no, and he slinks back to his buddies. They jeer at him but in the back of their minds, they know it is part of the game.

Many men have tried to work out a routine that encompasses some sort of mythical "magic line" that enables them to ask a woman out on a date without the nervousness and the feeling that they do not have any power. It is not easy for women either, for men are a fairly clueless lot. When a woman does find a man she wants to go out with, she usually has to do some ridiculous things to communicate to the guy she is interested. However, generally speaking women do have more power in marriage, dating and family relationships. Although this discussion has been a little tongue and cheek, we have used these examples to get you to realize that you do have expertise in getting people to do what you want them to do. Our central theme in this book is to illustrate that you are also involved in a relationship you have largely ignored—and that relationship is between you and the government. So think about this book as a relationship guide. We are going to coach you in how to get the government to do what you want, because as you know the government will try to get you to do what it wants.

The relationship between your family, friends, and lovers is different than your relationship with the government. The former relationships are built on love (or at least our perceived impressions of that emotion). People in our family, who we date and ultimately marry and to a different people who we befriend, these relationships are built on mutual feelings. The relationship between the government and yourself is built on a different power relationship, although the skills you have learned in your personal relationships will help you understand this new relationship—it is based on compliance.

The invention of government was conceived because of the need for people to protect themselves from the forces of anarchy. Anarchy can be defined as the absence of a central enforcement mechanism. In an anarchical environment people have conflict because of the clash of interests. These conflicts are normally settled with violence; therefore, in this environment, people became victims of violence. Soon people learned they could set up organizations such as families and clans that could cooperate. This co-

---

[1] Leo Tolstoy, *Anna Karenina* (New York: The Modern Library, 1993), p. 3.

operation gave way to the first agreement between people to set some sort of limitations to total freedom of action in exchange for limited personal security guarantees.

James Madison is famous for writing: "If men were angels, no government would be necessary."[2] Conflict plays an important role in understanding politics and government. One basic characteristic of humans is that we are never satisfied. This can be a good or bad trait. It can be good, if we use this need to produce and invent. It can be bad if we follow this need to pursue destructive and hurtful behaviors. In terms of changing a political environment from one of anarchy to one of government, this conflict remains. It can be categorized into three different sections. We have conflict because of differences in the beliefs of right and wrong, differences in goals for society, and the distribution of limited resources is the third category of why we have conflict. We will illustrate how these differences are part of our political and governmental structure today.

CONFLICT: DIFFERENCES IN THE BELIEFS OF RIGHT AND WRONG

The major arena of conflict between the belief of right and wrong in the United States today is the area of issues that surround what is called by the media as the Culture Wars. These clashes concern areas of abortion, same sex marriage, and school prayer. The two sides in all of these issues have the same perspectives. One side has a religious element. The interest groups and political party have members who freely and openly believe organized religion has a place in politics. The other side is allied with secular groups who are trying to limit the influence of politics by religion. These two sides have been called "Orthodox" and "Progressive."

The orthodox perspective believes there is an absolute right and wrong way of behavior. These rules of behavior have come from one of the main religions of the world and entail certain universal behaviors. Prohibitions about stealing, killing, abusing others are found in all of the holy books of the mainstream religions of the world. Another common idea that forms this perspective is the existence of good and evil. Evil is part of the world. Religions differ on the nature of evil, however they do not differ that evil is part of the world. Therefore, people

should obey the rules of behavior given to them by religion in order to become closer to God and to fight the effects of the existence of evil.

The progressive perspective believes there is not really an absolute right or wrong. There are behaviors that ensure we live in a civilized society. Again, the prohibitions about stealing and murder, however, progressives will question the environment of which the behavior is performed. You are the captain of your soul. Progressives would argue nothing is absolute. Circumstances and the changing nature of the world entail everyone to choose their behavior. One must look at the sociological, economic and environmental characteristics in order to judge a person's behavior. We see the different perspectives in action when we discuss the major issues in this debate between orthodox and progressive perspectives. By the way, these labels do not represent any inherent value; progressive should not be seen as better than orthodox or vice versa. These labels are just that—labels. Now, let us examine the dynamics of this dichotomy by briefly exploring the issues of abortion, same sex marriage, decency ratings for the media, and school prayer.

ABORTION

The abortion debate has galvanized this battle for the past 35 years. The main question centers on the status of two entities: the woman who is pregnant and the fetus. The group that opposes abortion is called pro-life (orthodox) and the group that supports a woman's right to choose is called pro-choice (progressive).

The orthodox argument is a simple one. The fetus is a human being with all the rights and protections of all of us. At the point of conception is the moment where life begins and that is the point where all of the protections of the state should come into play. This point of view is reinforced by most major religions. They argue abortion is murder. Of course, people who support this idea are not ignorant of the behavior of people in our society. They know people are having sex. However, again the sexual behavior of people is covered in their religious life. They argue, just because someone has erred in their behavior does not give them the right to violate the rights of the unborn child. Furthermore, they contend, there are programs such as adoption that insure an unwanted birth will be placed in a loving home. Therefore, there are viable options to having abortions. If people are educated and are conservative

[2]James Madison, *Federalist Papers No. 51.*

about their sexual lives then it would lessen the need for unwanted pregnancies. Again, if a woman does get pregnant the orthodox school of thought says, then they should not compound the problem by ending the pregnancy. So, you see the outline of the pattern of thinking. Religion (God) gives us rules even on our sexual life. If we follow those rules (sex inside the institution of marriage) that will produce on the whole wanted pregnancies. When you go outside of the rules (casual sex) of the religion then the consequences of breaking the rules will complicate your life. These complications can be unwanted pregnancies, sexual transmitted diseases and other things.

The contrary argument is the pro-choice (progressive) argument. This is also based on a simple principle; that is, the fetus is not an unborn child. The fetus is a collection of cells inside a woman's body. The progressive school of thought always takes into consideration the environment in which the act was taking place. There are few absolutes in the progressive environment. They argue having a baby may be compounding the mistake and ruining two lives (or maybe three if you count the person the woman had sex with). The important thing to the progressive is the ability for a woman to choose for herself. You can see between this discussion about the difference of these two perspectives while there is little or no compromise between these two perspectives. They are diametrically opposed. To the person who believes in the orthodox perspective, there is a way to behave. If you do not behave in that certain way you will have an unhappy life. Sex outside of marriage is usually viewed by religious and the orthodox perspective as wrong for both men and women, but particularly for women. The progressives view sex as a matter of personal choice. Progressives do not care who you have sex with or how you have sex. Progressives argue concerns of pregnancy should not get in the way of a woman's personal freedom to have sex.

Two programs that have a direct outcome of this clash of perspectives are sexual education in the schools and the promise by young people to remain virgins until they are married. Both of these efforts to influence young people are proposed by these two different perspectives. There is very little hope for a progressive to convince a person who follows the orthodox point of view and vice versa. That is why the abortion debate has been going on so long and in some quarters that is why it is so heated. Another issue in which we see these two perspectives fighting is on the issue of same sex marriage.

SAME SEX MARRIAGE

Should the government be in the marriage business? At the time of this writing, the U.S. Senate has voted twice on a Constitutional Amendment to ban same sex marriage. It has failed twice. Gordon Babst has argued the government's intervention in the institution of marriage creates a shadow establishment of religion in the society.[3] This is an argument made by a person who is using the progressive school of thought. He argues the government should not be in the marriage business. The concept of marriage is both a religious and secular institution.

As a secular institution two people (right now a man and woman) go to their local court house, pay a fee, wait a couple of days and say a vow before a judge or justice of the peace, they sign the license and in the eyes of society they are able to live together and enjoy the benefits of marriage. The perks of marriage may include the commingling of economic resources, adoption, inheritance and parental rights and protections. Government has defined the benefits of marriage. These benefits do not change from couple to couple. In the government's eyes, a married couple is a status inside our society.

Marriage as a religious institution is very different depending on the marriage inside the religion you are analyzing. For instance, Catholics believe you are married for as long as you live. Although Catholics do get divorced from the secular institution of marriage they are not allowed to get divorced inside the Church. If a Catholic is married inside the religious institution and does get divorced that person is not supposed to participate in many of the religious sacraments of the Catholic faith. This is different from other religious beliefs who do allow divorce. In Muslim countries polygamy is an accepted practice. Although there are limits to the number of wives a man may have, it is an accepted practice for wealthy Muslims to have more than one wife. This basic observation of marriage in religion underlies the importance marriage has for the people who hold the orthodox perspective. The status of marriage and the ceremony of marriage inside religion is one of the most important differentiations between believers and non-believers.

Progressives will argue the rights and privileges given by the government is a question of civil rights

---

[3]Gordon Albert Babst, *Liberal Constitutionalism, Marriage and Sexual Orientation: A Contemporary Case for Dis-Establishment.* New York: Peter Lang Publishing Co., 2002, p. 66.

and equality. The movement to allow same sex marriage is a movement that is trying to have the economic and societal benefits of marriage to a different category of people who cannot attain the status of marriage. The progressives claim this is a civil rights issue. During the U.S. Senate debate Senator Edward Kennedy called the people who are against same sex marriage bigots and the analogy has been used that if you are against same sex marriage you would have been against the civil rights movement lead by Dr. Martin Luther King, Jr.

Orthodox people would argue first of all that the analogy does not hold. The Civil Rights movement of the 1950s and 1960s has very little to do with the question of same sex marriage. They would say, if you allow everyone the status of marriage, then the effect would be no one is going to be married. You will have a distinction without a difference. Why get married if you can have sex, legal and economic privileges and society's blessing for every relationship. People who are members of a religious community that have their own practices of marriage, look at the movement for same sex marriage as an assault on the essence of marriage.

The debate is couched by both groups that seem to be very difficult to find a compromise. On the economic issues most Americans polled believe long term gay relationships should have some economic rights such as shared employee benefits, the right to visit your partner in the hospital and the right of inheritance of shared property if the one's partner dies. A civil union is what the government is trying to call this compromise. Neither the progressives nor orthodox perspectives are very excited about this solution.

Recently, we have seen law enforcement officials looking for polygamists who have violated the marriage laws. The government contends these polygamists are sexually abusing young girls by having them "married" to older men. If this is true, we can all agree these men should be prosecuted and punished by the full extent of the law. However, let us assume that there are groups of consenting adults (either two women and one man or two men and one woman). Should the government allow this type of marriage? Babst uses the examples of polygamist laws as an example of the shadow establishment of religious institutions in our government. There was a debate among the leaders of the National (Federal) Government and Utah's territorial leaders about the Mormon Church's practice of polygamy. The Mormon Church changed this practice and this allowed Utah to become a state. Marriage laws were the big stumbling block to statehood for Utah. It was the religious people in this instance that changed their practice (since this time the Mormon Church has not practiced polygamy and it is unfair that the media tries to link the Mormon Church with the practice of polygamy we see today).

Orthodox people would counter this comparison to between polygamy and same sex marriage with a recounting of history. Marriage first of all was a religious institution. Marriage gave children legitimacy and property rights that children born outside of marriage did not have. Marriage was also used to pass the ideas of religion from generation to generation; it was not designed to sanction every relationship because it was long term. The orthodox perspective would continue to argue the government co-opted the institution of marriage and now the political forces in society are trying to change it in order to sanction life styles that are not compatible with the original design of marriage.

Assuming people of goodwill, it is very difficult to have compromise when issues are close to people's hearts. If you truly believe something is wrong as we saw in the previous examples the debate can last for decades and people will attempt to get the government to intercede on their behalf. On the issues of same sex marriage and abortion, the progressives have argued the government must insure people have the freedom to act. The social mores of the institutional rules of society must not be enforced. In the next example, school prayer, the progressives are taking the opposite policy position. The progressives want the governmental institution, in this case schools, not to allow the free assembly of students to gather or use institutional resources.

SCHOOL PRAYER

The relationship between religion and government in this country has been outlined in the First Amendment of the U.S. Constitution. The Supreme Court has held that school officials must be neutral in their treatment of religion, showing neither favoritism nor hostility against religious expression. The Court has ruled that there is a "crucial difference between the government speech endorsing religion, which the establishment clause forbids, and private speech endorsing religion which the Free Speech and Free Exercise Clauses protect."

You can see how these rulings would drive people who hold the orthodox perspective scratching their heads. Everyone can agree school officials should not be evangelists in doing their professional duties. However, is it being neutral if you allow students to gather and use school resources for clubs that explore the gay life style and other sexual orientated activities, but, if students want to have a bible study they are not allowed to use a classroom? The orthodox perspective argues the progressives want to protect individual behavior against institutional values when the behavior propels the progressive agenda. When the behavior strengthens the orthodox agenda then institutions must step in and prevent the freedom of choice of students who want to freely assemble and pray.

Progressives counter this argument by talking about the establishment clause of the First Amendment of the Constitution. Religion has to be separated from the institutions of our government. The people in the middle of this debate of course are school officials, no matter what their political beliefs (progressive or orthodox), and the students. The U.S. Department of Education has set forth guidelines that are designed to give educators some idea of what is appropriate in a public school setting. The most famous of these guidelines is the "minute of silence": "If a school has a minute of silence or other quiet periods during the school day, students are free to pray silently, or not pray, during these periods of time. Teachers and other school employees may neither encourage nor discourage students from praying during such periods." The idea of neutrality borders on the ridiculous the orthodox would contend. If you have a minute of silence during the school day how can a teacher encourage or discourage prayer? These rules have become so cumbersome that most school officials have just opted out of allowing students any religious activity on campus.

Progressives argue this is what the Founding Fathers wanted when they wrote the establishment clause. We do not know about that. The end result of the debate on school prayer is the flight of many people who hold any type of religious views from the public school system. In turn, the support for financing public education has dwindled because of this debate.

We have discussed three controversial examples of how people have conflict because of their beliefs in what is right and what is wrong. By illustrating the two schools of thought, the progressive and orthodox we have simplified these complex examples. Individuals may jump from the progressive to the orthodox and back again depending on the issue. As we have said many people may be progressive in their attitude about abortion or sex education and ortho-

dox about same sex marriage and school prayer. Depending on the personal outlook of each individual, there does not have to be consistency on each issue between the two different perspectives.

The next element that contributes to conflict in society is between people with differing perspectives on the objective for society. In other words, what type of society do you want to live in? We analyze how this question also divides people. It relates to issues of justice, opportunity and our understanding of advancement or progress for society.

CONFLICT: OBJECTIVES FOR SOCIETY

Most of us think democracy is a virtue. Societies should have democratic institutions, but let us ask, is more democracy better for our society than less democracy? Most Americans view democracy as a positive characteristic of our society. We want people to participate in the system, but, what if we have a society full of people who do not have a basic understanding of how our system works? Just because someone knows a lot about a particular field of interest does not mean they will necessarily transfer their understanding to other issues. There are arenas where democracy does not work. For example, we have a person who does not know anything about cars. They simply know how to drive a car. They understand how, when you turn the steering wheel the car follows and they understand when you push on the gas pedal, the car goes faster, and finally they know the horn makes noise when you press a button on the steering wheel. The only part they have never heard of is the distributor cap. This person does not know what the distributor cap distributes, but they have heard people talking about the need for distributor caps. One day, this unfortunate person realizes that their car does not run. The car is towed to a mechanic and the mechanic inspects the car. After taking some time the mechanic goes to the car owner and diagnoses the problem. "You need a new transmission," the mechanic says. The car owner says, "No I believe I need new distributor cap. Let's vote on it."

Of course, this example is silly. However, we are constantly discounting expertise in our discussions about government. The media polls people every day and we hear a large selection of our population believe "x" policy is better than "y" policy. Just like our unfortunate car owner, it would be nice to know the context of which the people are being polled. Yes they must be randomly selected, however, the knowledge of the people and the person conducting the interview is never explained to the consumers of the polls. As a general concept, most Americans believe—more democracy the better, yet we tend not to discuss the responsibilities of, or in other words, our duties in a democratic society. Our system of government is based on a Representative Republic because the writers of the Constitution did not want to have a direct democracy. The Founding Fathers believed democracy was essential to the formation of a just society but there had to be limits to the level of democracy people would enjoy.

Former Vice President Al Gore's loss in the 2000 election was not illegal. Many of his supporters were upset because Gore won the popular vote and President Bush won the electoral vote. In the next chapter, we will discuss the dynamics of the Constitution. However, for our purposes right now, this is an example of how the Founding Fathers did not want to have direct voting by the people for the office of President of the United States. Both Bush and Gore knew the rules going into the election, it was a historical fact that this result happened, but it is not evidence of an "illegal election" that many supporters of Gore still claim today. Another concept people view as a goal of society other than democracy is justice.

Do economic issues come under a discussion of justice? Is national healthcare a characteristic of a just society? Does it make a difference if the healthcare system is universal but provides an inadequate level of care for people? Is a guaranteed job a characteristic of a just society? Or does it have to be a job that the person has a choice in pursuing? Is equality of salary and benefits an element of a just society or should a measurement of effort and risk be tied to a person's economic benefits? Is inheritance a characteristic of a just society? When one asks these economic issues as it relates to justice we start to see the fragmentation of how people perceive justice. Justice is defined as "the assignment of merited rewards and punishments."[4] These questions are complicated and have many points of view. It becomes very difficult in our modern society to separate our economic and political lives.

We would like to address the notion of inheritance since the Constitution is quite clear on what the Founding Fathers thought of royalty. The writers of the Constitution outlawed the concept of royalty. A person should be judged on their achievements, not on their ancestors. They viewed a just society was one that had social mobility. It did not matter to what station a person was born if they were talented enough to achieve something they should be able to enjoy that success. Currently, we see a debate in Congress about the repeal of the inheritance tax. Republicans call it a "death tax." They argue it is not just to tax people who are dead. In order to preserve small businesses and farms the government should eliminate this tax. Of course, this argument is quite ridiculous. The government does not tax people, it taxes money. As an example, think about all the taxes you pay in one week. Let us imagine you receive your paycheck on Monday, when you see your pay stub you notice the government (or your employer) has withheld money from your pay even before you get your hands on it. Then everything you purchase with the money you get from your pay is also taxed. Later at the end of the year you must file an income tax, and if you own property, a property tax. Finally, if you managed to save something (most Americans do not) your savings will be taxed. If you believed the advocates of the elimination of the inheritance tax you would think we would tax someone only once. We wish!

As you can see, if we speak generally about economic justice all of us can agree on generalizations. It is when we start to be specific, disagreements and conflict start to emerge. Another discussion of justice can be viewed though our personal habits. Is it better for society to criminalize certain personal habits such as drinking, smoking, prostitution, or gambling? Conflict arises when we get into specifics. We can all agree that liberty is an important concept and a goal for our government. Argument about liberty did spark, and later sustain, the American Revolution. Do people have the liberty to practice behavior that we personally find disgusting? Where does an individual's right end and the ideals of society start? Previously, we have examined the different points of view of the progressive and orthodox schools of thought. We have many laws that are designed to curb individual activity because of the costs to society. Even smoking has been targeted by those who do not wish to pay or to become a victim of passive smoke. Would we be a better society if no one smoked, took drugs or drank alcohol? Maybe. What about eating meat, or trans-fat? Is it a reasonable price of being part of our society to watch what you eat or is it being part of a "nanny-nation"? All of these questions highlight how goals for a society create con-

---

[4]Webster's *Third New International Dictionary*, p. 1228.

flict, and in turn this conflict takes shape as political questions.

CONFLICT: LIMITED RESOURCES AND THE DISTRIBUTION OF THESE RESOURCES

There is a bumper sticker that reads "live simply so others may simply live." We usually find this bumper sticker on luxury sedans. As we stated before, people usually have a difficult time satisfying their appetites. We think to ourselves if only I could earn enough money then I would be happy. When we attain the amount we thought was a great deal of money we find that we are not happy. Then we say, if I can only earn more money then I would be happy, and it goes on and on. We live in a society that is based on consumption. We label simple failures of impulse as addictions. The media even puts the suffix "oholic" on every indulgence such as choc**oholic**, food**oholic** or shop**oholic**, and if you cannot resist a bowl of ice cream, you would be called an ice cream**oholic**. This shows how silly we are and also tends to cheapen the serious problem of addictions.

We use this illustration to show that the conflict over limited resources is an aggregate result of our need or failure in controlling our appetites. Some argue this is a result of capitalism. However, if you study the history of the Soviet Union and other socialist states you would see the drive for consuming was even greater in those societies than in the non-socialist states. In the past, however, especially during the time of multi-ethnic empires of Britain, France and Russia, we did see a drive known as Imperialism.

Imperialism is an economic structure that consists of a mother country (Great Britain or France) and colonies. The mother country produced finished products and colonies supplied the raw materials. The relationship between these two entities was monopolistic and the colonist could not sell their raw materials to other countries outside of their particular empire. To grow economically, an empire had to gain more colonies to serve both as markets and sources of raw material. Near the end of this era, conflict between empires would break out and ultimately the demise of multi-ethnic empires would come after World War II. This economic model is no longer viable and is not practiced by the major economic players in the world. Even though you may have people argue the U.S. has gone to war because of a commodity, or has to expand markets by military conquests, these ideas are very old fashioned.

Knowledge, especially technical knowledge, seems to be the basis for economic development today. Countries that are very small geographically have very developed economies. Countries such as Japan, South Korea and Israel do not have a great deal of resource endowment. What they do have is an educated population that innovates and works to provide the world with consumer goods. Please do not misunderstand—there is still conflict over the distribution of resources. Later in the text when we examine public policy and foreign policy, we will look at the politics of economic policy. However, developed nations do not go to war over the expansion of markets, as they once did. Instead, we see conflict on the distribution of resources when we examine the domestic politics and the development of trade policies.

Everyone wants to have cheap energy, yet no one wants to live next to a recycling plant. Everyone wants plentiful electricity, yet no one wants to live next to a nuclear power plant. This attitude illustrates a political phenomenon that is related to the distribution of resources known as NIMBY, which stands for "not in my back yard." We see every time infrastructure improvements are called for, the wealthy want these improvements in other neighborhoods. The conflict on resources we see in effect every time a Wal-Mart is built. People claim they do not use a Wal-Mart because it threatens the economic viability of the quaint little stores in their neighborhoods, yet, it has been estimated that half the population of America (over 100 million people) shop at Wal-Mart every week. People do not want to live next to a Wal-Mart because of the traffic and the buildings are quite ugly, however, they do like saving on their purchases at Wal-Mart as long as the store is in someone else's neighborhood.

These examples of how conflict is created, either because of differing beliefs of right or wrong, differing goals for society people may have, or disagreement over the distribution of resources controlled by a society, show the need for government. In history there has been tension between the individual and the government. Government's role is to draw the boundaries of people's conflict and to insure the government does not become a tyranny.

The Constitution of the United States is the first document in history that incorporates the protection of the individual. There are two final elements of governmental power: authority and legitimacy. Authority is the right to enforce compliance with decisions made by the government. All of our laws are based on the government's authority to reward and punish people after certain procedures have been followed. The role of authority of the U.S. government is spelled out in the U.S. Constitution. The second property of general government power is the idea of legitimacy. Since the 1960s there has been an increase in the questioning of governmental power being used as illegitimate. If a group disagrees with the policy, they question the right of the government to act. Governmental actions therefore, are judged by a dual standard. Does the government have the authority to act and does the government use the authority in a legitimate way? We will also use this standard to analyze governmental power. However, we will do this with a difference. That difference will be the use of critical thinking in our analysis. Our political discussions today are flooded with personal opinion. Opinions are fine, the problem is they cannot be analyzed. Opinions are for private discussions at the coffee shop. On the other hand, analysis uses arguments. An argument is a premise combined with evidence and drawing a conclusion. We will use arguments to study governmental power.

An example of conspiracy theories and opinions making its way into political analysis is the discussions that surround the 2000 Presidential election. Americans never directly vote for President. The process of electing Presidents is spelled out in the U.S. Constitution (we will discuss this fully in the next chapter). Simply the candidates for President compete against each other to gain the popular vote. The candidate that receives the majority plus one vote will receive the total number of electoral votes. This winner-takes-all system has been part of the electoral system since the ratification of the U.S. Constitution. There have been several amendments to this process, but the winner-takes-all character of the system has been in place for over 200 years.

As we know, the election between former Vice President Al Gore and then Governor George W. Bush was very close. Al Gore received a majority of the popular vote. In states such as California and New York Gore defeated Bush by a very large number. However, it did not matter since all Gore had to do was to defeat Bush by one vote in those states. The Electoral College system was invented to protect small states. Bush defeated Gore in more small states with a smaller margin for victory. There was a question in Florida over counting the votes. After several weeks of state court and federal court hearings the Supreme Court took up the case and ruled in favor of George W. Bush. After the decision of the Supreme Court was announced, many Democrats contended President Bush was an illegitimate President. This is not correct. Bush won the election not because of the popular vote; he won because he and his campaign team's strategy concentrated on the electoral votes of states. Another example people argue is an illegal or illegitimate use of governmental power was the invasion of Iraq in March 2003. Again, the U.S. Constitution delineates the roles of the Congress and President in case of war. The Bush Administration went to Congress. Congress approved military action by what some call giving President Bush a "blank check" on Iraq. The Bush Administration then went to the United Nations Security Council, and the U.N. Security Council voted unanimously to have Iraq comply with the U.N. Security Council's previous resolutions. After the invasion, members of Congress who gave the Executive branch the green light for the invasion came out publicly and acted surprised there was an invasion of Iraq. The opponents of the invasion call the war in Iraq illegal. It was not. It may be the wrong strategic decision, and we can debate about the connection of the Iraq war and the global war on terror, but the Bush Administration did follow the procedure to send forces into combat. Just because you may disagree with the policy does not make the governmental action illegitimate. Illegitimacy comes from abusing the procedures used to construct the governmental policy.

DRUGS, OIL, ILLEGAL IMMIGRATION AND THE WAR ON TERROR: CHALLENGES OF THE TWENTY-FIRST CENTURY

We have established a dichotomy of passing laws and giving law enforcement officials' discretion to enforce the laws. This produces an environment where authority of the government is both questioned and abused. The legal environment and the protection for average people is a foundation of our shared perspective of the legitimate use of force. In every police show on television we see a police officer reading the rights to an accused person. In real life, the police are involved in many personal issues. There should be a national debate on three issues that will challenge our society in the twenty-first century. The objective of this debate should be to design policies that would relate to the realistic behavior of people.

We have laws that are designed to criminalize behavior that young people are routinely doing. Either underage drinking or smoking marijuana is a common experience for young people who graduate high school in this country. Does anyone believe the policy of our "war on drugs" is winning? The question that should be debated by our society is whether we should take the money out of the drug business and legalize drugs and tax and license its use for adults. Instead of spending government resources worrying about whether drugs are coming into this country, maybe the government should inspect the manufacture of drugs and tax it heavily, while at the same time financing educational programs that show the devastating effects drugs have on people, their families and communities. We need to have an honest debate and an honest examination of our policies related to the criminalization of drugs. We need the government to declassify documents and educate all of us the connection between al-Qaeda and drugs. If we could get real evidence about the dimensions of the money al-Qaeda and its allies raise from our appetite for drugs, maybe we could find a real solution to this challenge.

The other addiction we have is oil. In this area, we also need a national debate about the money raised by oil states and al-Qaeda; we have seen the price of oil rise dramatically in the last two years. During World War II, the United States did not trade with countries that supported the enemy. Furthermore, oil was considered a strategic resource and was rationed. Oil conservation, drilling in Alaska or off the coast of the U.S., alternative energy programs, and emergency planning if Iran or terrorists attack the oil infrastructure of the world, should be discussed by all of us. What is not helpful to the discussion are attacks on the oil companies (who do not set the price of their product) or silly conspiracy theories that we are now seeing in Congress and the media.

Congress and the media are also involved in addressing the final issue we should have a rational debate about in the future and that is illegal immigration. Just as with drugs, the criminalization of undocumented workers is not necessarily the result of passing new laws. The country should decide whether to have laws that are enforced or to do away with those laws and have an amnesty program. As long as a person has a passport and the government establishes a database which can be used to identify people who support terrorism, this would not necessarily interfere on the War on Terror. The creation of a permanent underclass in this society who cannot bargain for the minimal protections offered to other workers should be debated. When you criminalize individual activity you do not change that behavior you just put the behavior underground and make the people who do that behavior—criminals. We are not drawing conclusions about these issues, we are bringing them to your attention because we will have to address each of these challenges in the future.

The last challenge we will face is the War on Terror.[5] The leadership of the government, both Democratic and Republican parties, should try to depoliticize the war as much as possible. Both parties have used this political environment to make political points instead of providing leadership. The House and Senate were afraid to vote for a declaration of war after the attacks of September 11, 2001. Instead, they have given the President a blank check and this has created a false impression that the war is a painless exercise. The people who have joined the military and their families are the ones who have suffered in this war. The Congress spends its time voting for funding the war and the rest of the time criticizing the implementation of the war. This has destroyed the unity we enjoyed after September 11th. The President is also guilty of using the war on terror as a political tool to stifle legitimate criticism and debate about the condition of our war effort.

These points are used to illustrate that you have to start thinking about these things. The government and our political leaders are making decisions that will affect your future, as in other relationships in your life. You have to use your understanding of power to make sure your interests are heard and considered by our society. This is one of the goals of this book—to open your minds to the idea that government is dynamic and following what goes on is your responsibility.

CONCLUSION

You are building your future by attending college. We have discussed the reasons why theory is important and how formal education is designed to familiarize you with the skills of critical thinking. We then defined power as the ability to get someone to do what you want them to do. This discussion followed several general examples of how we all use power every day in our lives. Our personal lives are filled with examples of people understanding the use of power and how to obtain more and more power. This chap-

[5]Patrick Coaty, *Understanding the War on Terror*. Dubuque, IA: Kendall/Hunt Publishing, Co., 2006. This book examines the challenges of the war on terror as a supplement to American Government, International Relations, History and Criminal Justice classes who address the challenges of terrorism for our society.

ter expands on the personal dynamics of power and we examine the reasons why we need government. These reasons can be broken down into three broad categories: disagreement stemming from different perspectives between right and wrong, disagreement over the objectives of society and disagreement in how to distribute the limited resources we have on this planet. These three reasons for conflict make it essential to have government.

We illustrated these conflicts with current controversial disagreements that we are having in our political environment. Abortion, same sex marriage, school prayer and other issues were used to illustrate both the division of our society between progressive and orthodox schools of thought and to highlight how government actions are embedded in our daily lives. We finished this chapter with a discussion on the future, the challenges you will face include a call for a rational debate about terrorism, drugs, immigration, and our dependence on oil as a source of energy.

In this chapter, we looked at the future. In the next chapter we will look at the past and analyze the development of the Constitution. We will look at the Founding Fathers and give a brief historical con-

text to the document they gave us. Then we will go through every aspect of the document and explain how this is the rule book of our society. If you understand the U.S. Constitution you will understand not only our government but also our political culture and the way we design our institution in order to give the government the authority to exercise its power in a legitimate way.

TERMS TO REMEMBER

ANARCHY

ORTHODOX

PROGRESSIVE

JUSTICE

IMPERIALISM

NIMBY

AUTHORITY

LEGITIMACY

ARGUMENT

NATION

Power and the Challenges of the Twenty-First Century

TRUE OR FALSE QUESTIONS

1. Theory is not useful, it is just philosophy that does not have any practical purposes for solving today's issues.   T / F

2. Tolstoy wrote in *Anna Karenina* that all happy families are the same.   T / F

3. Generally speaking the youngest child will have a different relationship with their parents than the oldest child.   T / F

4. Power is the ability to get someone to do what you want them to do.   T / F

5. The Introduction does not mention abortion as an issue facing us in politics.   T / F

6. Religion has no role in marriage.   T / F

7. The establishment clause of the U.S. Constitution prevents the establishment of an American Church.   T / F

8. Democracy works all the time for every situation that may cause a problem in our lives.   T / F

9. The United States today is an Imperial power.   T / F

MULTIPLE CHOICE QUESTIONS

10. Economists study money and political scientists study
    a. elections
    b. power
    c. taxes
    d. abortion

11. The invention of government was conceived because of the effects of
    a. anarchy
    b. depression
    c. marriage
    d. hunger

12. Conflict comes from people having a different understanding of right and wrong issues under this classification except
    a. abortion
    b. same sex marriage
    c. school prayer
    d. taxes

13. Orthodox believe in
    a. an absolute right and wrong.
    b. relative values.
    c. you are the captain of your soul.
    d. the environment is important in determining guilt or innocence in a court of law.

14. Conflict comes from people having a different understanding of goals for society except in issues involving
    a. abortion
    b. same sex marriage
    c. school prayer
    d. taxes

15. NIMBY stands for
    a. not in multi-annual yields.
    b. numeric international macroeconomic bivarate yields.
    c. no innocent bystanders yonder.
    d. not in my back yard.

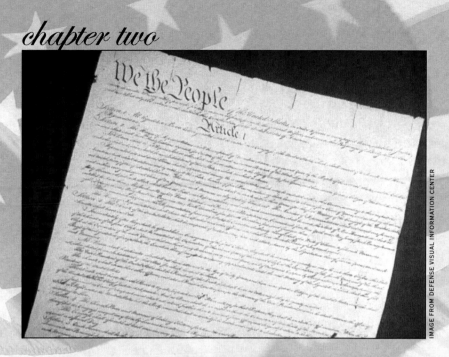

chapter two

IMAGE FROM DEFENSE VISUAL INFORMATION CENTER

THE U.S. CONSTITUTION PART ONE, THE ESTABLISHMENT OF A NEW CENTRAL GOVERNMENT

INTRODUCTION

In 2006, President Bush had the opportunity to appoint a new Chief Justice and a new Associate Justice of the United States Supreme Court. Whenever there is an appointment on the Supreme Court, we see two dominate perspectives shown by Senators who have the responsibility to approve the President's choice. One point of view, stresses the language used by the original writers of the Constitution. These men are sometimes called the Founding Fathers. This school of thought is commonly called the original intent school and is held by mainly conservative politicians. The other perspective believes the Constitution is a living document. When the Founding Fathers wrote a passage, they intended for us to reasonably interpret the passage we are examining. An example often used by scholars of this school of thought is the expansion of the right to vote.[1] The Constitution's original language was quite

limited on who was qualified to vote. Women, minorities and young people were excluded from voting. Yet, in modern times all of these groups have been given the right to vote. The proponents of the living document or interpretative school of thought believe in the expansion of the Constitution to modern life. We see this debate between the original intent and living document schools of thought whenever the President nominates someone to the Supreme Court of the United States.

Many Senators who were involved in the confirmation debates for or against Chief Justice Roberts and Justice Alioto would argue that the two different schools of thought are mutually exclusive: you either use original intent all of the time or you have a living document that can be hammered into any shape the present society wants. In this chapter, we will show, despite political posturing of both political parties, there is common ground between both schools of thought. We will demonstrate how the Founding Fathers wanted to keep their outline of a just society, but also adapt the document so it is relevant and useful to solving problems in our contemporary society.

[1]Thomas E. Patterson, *The Vanishing Voter: Public Involvement In An Age of Uncertainty*. New York: Alfred A. Knopf, 2002, p. 8.

We organize our treatment of the country's founding and writing of the U.S. Constitution into two parts. The first is a brief historical exploration of the personalities and events that will give us a flavor of the period and context to the intent of the Founders. The second part of the chapter will break down the Constitution, illustrating where the language describes the objectives the writers of the Constitution wanted to instill on the future.

AGAINST THE ODDS: SELF GOVERNANCE AND THE EARLY AMERICAN EXPERIENCE

The early Americans found themselves victorious after the Revolutionary War. Peace had brought a thin veneer of social cohesion. There was a problem in post-Revolutionary America. Congress had to maintain an Army to enforce the Treaty of Paris that gave sovereignty to the United States.[2] However, the French Revolution was showing the dangers of having a large standing Army. The Congress finding other priorities was reluctant to pay the soldiers who insured the victory against the British Empire. George Washington had to keep his Army together with limited cooperation from the new government that was formed by the Articles of Confederation.[3] In 1781, the Articles were adopted. Under this system the thirteen states had almost all of the governmental power in the new country. There were two serious shortcomings of this confederation.[4]

The first was the national government could not call on its own military to force compliance of its rulings and keep the domestic peace. The state militia system was the backbone of the military establishment of the nation. This gave state governors a veto on the size and use of military resources available to the national government. Without the power of enforcement, the laws passed by the national government under the articles were largely ignored.

The second challenge of the Articles was on an economic level. After the Revolution, an economic depression hit the United States. There was not a way for the national government to control the production of currency, since each state had the power to print money. This enabled the states to print money at such a speed that inflation was rampant in some states.

Merchants and bankers in one state would not honor payment of debts in different state's currency causing a banking crisis. The elite of each state realized something was wrong with this system. The national government was simply too weak to ever be effective. Remember, the people who lived during this time did not see themselves primarily as Americans, their identity was mainly with their state.

Most people were against a loss of power of their state. They knew the system was not working but they also distrusted other states' ability to govern their lives. By 1787, there was a call to hold a convention in Philadelphia to revise the Articles in order to fix the political structure of the new country. On first appearance, the Philadelphia Convention was not deemed very important. Only five state delegations gathered during the first weeks of the meeting. However, what was striking were the men who were members of those delegations. Most notably, George Washington, the leader who had defeated the British, was in attendance and soon to be elected as the leader of the convention. Ultimately the Virginia delegation would have Thomas Jefferson, James Madison, George Mason and Edmund Randolf among its ranks. It was Randolf who suggested a list of changes to the Articles that became the basis for changing the whole system. Randolf's proposal was called the Virginia Plan.[5]

THE VIRGINIA PLAN

The components of the Virginia Plan included a bicameral legislature with representation determined by the population of the state being represented. There was to be an Executive albeit, the person would be elected from the Legislative branch and the number of people who would be in the Executive was not fully determined. The Judicial branch of this plan would be appointed for life and would have power to veto state actions. This governmental plan gave the advantage to states that have larger populations. The lower house of the legislature would be elected by direct election by the people. The higher house of the legislature would be elected by the state legislatures. The proportion of each state's share of representatives in each house of the legislature would be determined by the population of the state. Therefore, the delegations of large states would dominate both houses of the legislature. This plan also limited

[2]J.M. Roberts, *The New Penguin History of the World*. New York: Penguin Group, 2002, p. 724.

[3]Ibid.

[4]Ibid. p. 725.

[5]Karen O'Connor and Larry J. Sabato, *American Government Continuity and Change*. New York: Longman Inc., 2000, p. 59.

the power of elections directly by the people, granting more power to elites. One can assume to get elected by the legislature of a state you need to have connection that would make you a viable candidate. Ratification of this plan would be by a popular vote. Small states came to complain about the Virginia Plan because of the inherent structural biases against their interests. The smaller states' plan would be nicknamed the New Jersey Plan.[6]

THE NEW JERSEY PLAN

Small states did not have the problems with the Articles of Confederation the large states had, the questions of economic depression, law and order were not as intense with smaller states as it was with larger states. The Legislative branch under the New Jersey Plan would be unicameral. Every state would have the same number of seats in their delegations regardless of population. The executive would be several people, who could be removed by the Legislative branch. The Judicial branch would not have any power over the states under this plan. And finally, the ratification of this plan would be by election of the state legislatures. The Convention had two plans and the members of the Convention were divided into small states and large states. Regional difference, such as north and south, also caused a divide in the convention. How were they going to solve this divide among the delegates of convention?

The Convention had two overarching rules of procedure. First, the proceedings were kept secret. There was not a press corps outside the convention hall. Therefore, leaks of the proceedings and political posturing for public consumption were at a minimum. Secondly, any topic could be discussed as many times as the delegates wanted to talk about them. A vote on a resolution of a topic did not end the discussion of the topic. This rule created an environment that prevented delegates from leaving the convention. Issues were debated and debated. Difficult rivalries between North and South, small and large states, were hammered out and compromises were found because of the ability to debate, discuss and find solutions to these difficult problems.

At the end of the Convention there was a finished product. Not all of the delegates supported the new document. There were several famous men who signed the Declaration of Independence did not support the ratification of the Constitution. Men such as

Patrick Henry and George Mason argued "why did we fight the Revolution to gain our liberty from King George III of England to replace it with an American tyranny." This line of reasoning would later be called the Anti-Federalists. The supporters of the Constitution would counter this argument with the fact that the country needed a stronger central government in order to keep the peace and establish some economic order inside the new country. The debate between the Federalists and Anti-Federalists was captured in the writings of the Founders in the Federalist Papers. In these writings you see some of the greatest examples of critical thinking and rhetoric ever produced in the context of applying political philosophy to issues of everyday governance.

The Federalists won the argument and the Constitution was ratified following the procedures outlined in the document. Next, we will examine the actual text of the Constitution and analyze point by point one of the most important documents ever produced.

THE UNITED STATES CONSTITUTION

The debate between the Federalists and Anti-Federalists can be boiled down to the issue of whether the United States needed a stronger central government. The Federalists thought, in order for the American experiment in self government to last, the central government had to be stronger than the state governments. The Anti-Federalists were concerned with the issues of individual liberty and tyranny. Even after ratification, there was a compromise between these two perspectives. There was an agreement to amend the Constitution to include ten amendments that would be nicknamed the Bill of Rights. After our discussion on the Constitution you can decide for yourself who you agree with, the Federalists or Anti-Federalists.

PREAMBLE

WE THE PEOPLE OF THE UNITED STATES, IN ORDER TO FORM A MORE PERFECT UNION, ESTABLISH JUSTICE, INSURE DOMESTIC TRANQUILITY, PROVIDE FOR THE COMMON DEFENSE, PROMOTE THE GENERAL WELFARE, AND SECURE THE BLESSINGS OF LIBERTY TO OURSELVES AND OUR POSTERITY, DO ORDAIN AND ESTABLISH THIS CONSTITUTION FOR THE UNITED STATES OF AMERICA.

The first three words of the Constitution demonstrates the truly revolutionary experiment the Americans were about to undertake. Since the end of the Greek democracies and the Roman republic, West-

---

[6]Ibid.

ern Civilization had established a different criteria for men to lead their people legitimately. This reasoning was called the Devine Right of Kings. Nations had been established by commonality in three areas: religion, language and race. If you were a member of a nation, you shared the same belief in a religion, you had an understanding of the language used in that particular nation and you had some of the same racial characteristics as the other members in the nation. Even today, most nations are built on these three pillars. Examples include people who are Greek, Japanese, Iranian (Persian) and others.

Most leaders of these nations were some form of King. There was combination between the religion and the state. The religion usually commanded obedience to the leader of the Church and who they deemed as the legitimate ruler of the nation. In Europe, before the Reformation, you see rulers trying to get legitimacy from the leaders of the Catholic Popes in Rome. After the Reformation, kings declared themselves the leaders of their respective national church. The experience of the British Monarch is an example of this change. This merging of national religion and monarchical power were not unique to Europe. In Japan and China, the rationale for obedience to the Emperor was the connection between the ruler and God.

The Devine Right of Kings argument is described as follows: if God has a master plan and that plan must entail the selection of rulers and He is all knowing. Therefore, God has selected the King and because of this selection the transfer of obedience and power from God to the King is legitimate. It was the duty of all the subjects to obey the King as they would obey God. Remember, people during this period were convinced of the existence of an afterlife, both heaven and hell. The most severe punishment a person could receive was ex-communication from their particular religion. This power of course was held by the leader of the church who was also leader of the nation. If you violated the orders of the King you were also violating the orders of God.

In the U.S. Constitution this idea was put aside by three words: "We the People." These words demonstrated a different organizational structure for a nation. This idea was called popular sovereignty. Popular sovereignty is the idea that people have the power to organize the government. The King is not a representative of God's will. The Founding Fathers argued it was not God's will to have a despot control all of the wealth and power of a people. The people had a right to organize the government in any way they saw fit. The use of democratic procedures and

republican values would ensure the rulers that would ultimately wield power would be legitimate. The first three words of the Constitution is a social contract. "We the People" is a phrase that gives everyone the collective right to enter into this agreement. Popular sovereignty is one of the pillars the writers of the Constitution would use to build an American nation.

The next part of the preamble is also very interesting, "in order to form a more perfect Union, establish Justice." Justice is a complicated concept in political philosophy. The writing of the Constitution is the first step in establishing a system of justice because laws must be written down in order for people to have an understanding of the system of government they are living in. This goes together with the concepts of popular sovereignty, the legal system and the ideals of justice must be written down so people can understand the system they are agreeing to live under. Another ingredient of a system of justice is the power of law. The second pillar the Founding Fathers wanted to establish is the rule of law. We are a nation of laws, we have heard this again and again. Rule of law is a system that strives to achieve justice. In the system of laws, everyone is supposed to be treated with the same procedures. Everyone is supposed to be aware of the legal system, and violation of the law will be enforced equally against everyone. This is the ideal. However, this is the second pillar of a nation the Founding Fathers were creating. Popular Sovereignty, Rule of Law would take the place of language, race and religion.

We see today efforts to make English the national language, or others argue the Founding Fathers were incorporating religious values into the Constitution. If we read the preamble, the Founding Fathers did not want to have a society based on public enforcement of language, religion or race. There is a third foundational element the writers of the Constitution wanted to instill in American society. This is in the phrase: "and secure the Blessings of Liberty to ourselves and our Posterity."

What is liberty? Some would say liberty is freedom. Yes, one aspect of liberty is freedom. However, another dimension of liberty is understanding your neighbor also has liberty. This dimension of liberty is tolerance. Tolerance is not acceptance. You can disagree with the behavior of people without violating either their liberty or your liberty. There are practices you may find offensive, liberty does not mean you have to support these behaviors. You can shun the people doing the behavior, you can use your economic power not to support the behavior, and you can ultimately use it as a litmus test in choosing the people you vote for. Today we see a phenomenon of the criminalization of behavior. The Founding Fathers would have probably fought many of the laws we have today on issues such as smoking, drinking, drugs and other laws that violate personal liberty. We can speculate the reaction of the Founding Fathers on laws that have criminalized the use of fireworks, grooming of dogs, the raising of pets and the ability to build on land that you own. We will address many of these laws later.

The main point to remember about the Constitutional preamble is this is a statement of the motivation and promise they sought in changing the Articles of Confederation and building a new society. Using the three pillars of building a nation: Popular Sovereignty, Rule of Law and Tolerance, the Founding Fathers wrote a contract that if you agree with these three principles then you would be able to become a member of this nation, regardless of your religion, race or language. This was truly the greatest innovation of establishing the relationship between government and the governed since the beginning of history. These fifty-two words would change the organizational structure of modern nations and states, by discounting the arguments for racially, religious or linguistic separation of people. Using popular sovereignty, rule of law and tolerance, the United States would be a different type of society; a society that would welcome diversity of thought and personal freedom.

The preamble also sought to address contemporary failures of the Articles of Confederation. The lack of central organization between the states on important issues such as common defense, internal rioting and economic problems were also introduced by the preamble of the Constitution. The organizational structure of the new Federal government would be introduced in the first three articles of the Constitution.

ARTICLE I

Section 1. All legislative Powers herein granted shall be vested in a Congress of the United States, which shall consist of a Senate and a House of Representatives.

Article I of the Constitution starts with the concept the Founding Fathers were the most comfortable with, that is an assembly or a Congress. Even before the Revolution, colonial states had general assemblies. They were residents of the states who could meet and voice their opinions on issues concerning the governing of the colony. By the time of the Revolution and the Declaration of Independence, the practice of a Continental Congress was established and accepted as an agreeable way to organize a procedure to incorporate the different perspectives of the different states. In this section, we also see the incorporation of the great compromise. There are two houses of the Legislative branch—the House of Representatives and the Senate.

Section 2. The House of Representatives shall be composed of Members chosen every second Year by the people of the several States, and the Electors in each State shall have the Qualifications requisite for Electors of the most numerous Branch of the State Legislature.

No Person shall be a Representative who shall not have attained the Age of twenty five Years, and been seven Years a Citizen of the United States, and who shall not, when elected, be an Inhabitant of that State in which he shall be chosen.

Representatives and direct Taxes shall be apportioned among the several States which may be included within this Union, according to their respective numbers, *which shall be determined by adding to the whole Number of free Persons, including those bound to Service for a Term of Years and excluding Indians not taxed, three-fifths of all other Persons.* **The actual Enumeration shall be made within three Years after the first Meeting of the Congress of the United States, and with every subsequent Term of ten Years, in such Manner as they shall by Law direct. The number of Representatives shall not exceed one for every thirty Thousand, but each State shall have at Least one Representative;** *and until such enumeration shall be made, the State of New Hampshire shall be entitled to choose three, Massachusetts eight, Rhode Island and Providence Plantations one, Connecticut five, New York six, New Jersey four, Pennsylvania eight, Delaware one, Maryland six, Virginia ten, North Carolina five, South Carolina five, and Georgia three.*

When vacancies happen in the Representation from any State, the Executive Authority there of shall issue Writs of Election to fill such Vacancies.

The House of Representatives shall chuse their Speaker and other Officers; and shall have the sole Power of Impeachment.

Section 2 of the first Article gives us the procedure to have elections every other year and the qualifications for members of the Legislative branch. A person has to be at least twenty five years old and seven years a citizen of the United States, furthermore, the person has to be an inhabitant of the state he/she is representing when elected. This section also creates the requirement of a census every ten years to distribute the representative between the various states. This section also has the main failure of the document. On the issue of slavery, although no longer a part of the Constitution, this section has the infamous "three-fifths of all other persons." This represents the failure to outlaw slavery and therefore created one of the biggest challenges succeeding generations have had to deal with ever since the issue of slavery and race.

The last part of Section 2 deals exclusively with the House of Representatives. When a Representative leaves his/her seat and there is time on his/her term, for whatever reason, there will be a special election in the district that has lost representation. Section 2 also calls for the election of the leadership of the House of Representatives that includes the Speaker of the House and other officers. The last part of this section gives the House of Representatives the power of Impeachment. Impeachment is the power to indict. The trial of Impeachment takes place in the Senate of the United States. The special and unique properties of the Senate are described in Section 3.

Section 3. The Senate of the United States shall be composed of two Senators from each State, *chosen by the Legislature thereof*, for six years; and each Senator shall have one Vote.

Immediately after they shall be assembled in Consequence of the first Election, they shall be divided as equally as may be into three Classes. The Seats of the Senators of the first Class shall be vacated at the Expiration of the second Year, of the second Class at the expiration of the fourth Year, and of the third Class at the expiration of the sixth Year, so that one-third may be chosen every second Year; *and if Vacancies happen by Resignation or otherwise, during the Recess of the Legislature of any State, the Executive thereof may make temporary Appointments until the next meeting of the legislature, which shall then fill such Vacancies.*

No person shall be a Senator who shall not have attained to the Age of thirty Years, and been nine Years a Citizen of the United States, and who shall not when elected, be an Inhabitant of that State for which he shall be chosen.

The Vice-President of the United States shall be President of the Senate, but shall have no Vote, unless they be equally divided.

The Senate shall choose their other officers, and also a President pro tempore, in the absence of the Vice-President, or when he shall exercise the Office of President of the United States.

The Senate shall have the sole Power to try all impeachments. When sitting for that purpose, they shall be on Oath or Affirmation. When the President of the United States is tried, the Chief Justice shall preside: and no Person shall be convicted without the Concurrence of two-thirds of the members Present.

Judgment in Cases of Impeachment shall not extend further than to removal from the Office, and disqualification to hold and enjoy any Office of honor, Trust or Profit under the United States: but the Party convicted shall nevertheless be liable and subject to Indictment, Trial, Judgment and Punishment, according to Law.

Article I Section 3 describes the role of the United States Senate and the role of the U.S. Vice President, who is President of the Senate. The requirements of the membership in the U.S. Senate include being thirty years old and have been a citizen of the U.S. for nine years. A Senator will serve six years a term and if the Senate seat is vacated the Governor will have the power to appoint a member. Unlike the House of Representatives there is not a special election. The Vice President will not have vote unless there is a tie. Finally, after the House of Representatives impeaches the President the Senate will conduct a hearing presided by the Chief Justice and it will take two-thirds of the Senate to convict. There have been two Presidents who have been tried, both have been acquitted—Presidents William Clinton and Andrew Johnson.

Section 4. The Times, Places and Manner of holding Elections for Senators and Representatives shall be prescribed in each State by the Legislature thereof; but the Congress may at any time by Law make or alter such regulations, except as to the Places of chusing Senators.

The Congress shall assemble at least once in every Year, and such meeting *shall be on the first Monday in December, unless they shall by Law appoint a different Day.*

The State Legislatures determine the nature of elections in our system. The Presidential election of 2000 was decided by the U.S. Supreme Court partly because of this section of the Constitution. The

Florida legislature had a majority of Republican legislators and they had decided the "butterfly" ballot was to be used. The State legislatures and their agents in local governments draw the rules for elections in the United States.

Section 5. Each House shall be Judge of the Elections, Returns and Qualifications of its own Members, and a Majority of each shall constitute a Quorum to do Business; but a smaller Number may adjourn from day to day, and may be authorized to compel the Attendance of absent Members, in such Manner, and under such Penalties as each House may provide.

Each House may determine the Rules of its proceedings, punish its Members for disorderly behavior, and with the Concurrence of two-thirds, expel a Member.

Each House shall keep a Journal of its Proceedings, and from time to time publish the same, excepting such Parts as may in their Judgment require Secrecy; and the Yeas and Nays of the Members of either House on any question shall, at the Desire of one-fifth of those Present, be entered on the Journal.

Neither House, during the Session of Congress, shall, without the Consent of the other, adjourn for more than three days, nor to any other Place than that in which the two Houses shall be sitting.

Section 5 describes the power of the legislators to judge election results and the nature of quorums to be used to conduct everyday business in Congress. It also has remedies for members who are disruptive and requires a publication of their actions by the keeping of a journal of the proceedings, and finally, it establishes a procedure for the legislature to adjoin in an orderly way.

Section 6. The Senators and Representatives shall receive a Compensation for their services, to be ascertained by Law and paid out to the Treasury of the United States. They shall in all Cases, except Treason, Felony and Breach of the Peace, be privileged from Arrest during their Attendance at the Session of their repective Houses, and in going to and returning from the same; and for any Speech or Debate in either House, they shall not be questioned in any other Place.

No Senator or Representatives shall, during the Time for which he was elected, be appointed to any civil office under the Authority of the United States, which shall have been created and the Emoluments whereof shall have been increased, during such time; and no Person holding any Office under the United States, shall be a Member of either House during his Continuance in Office.

Section 6 provides a salary for Congressmen and Senators. Today, Congressmen and Senators earn roughly 150,000 dollars a year. There is a movement by the Democrats in Congress to link their salary with an increase in the Federal minimum wage. Most members of Congress are very successful people. In California and in other states, the costs of campaigning for office can run into the millions of dollars. Why would a person spend millions of dollars to get paid less than two hundred thousand dollars a year?

Believe it or not, most members of Congress are not crooks, they run in order to make decisions that affect all of us. Most members believe they are serving both the country and history. How much should a member of Congress get paid? This is an open question. To many of us, 150,000 dollars a year is a lot of money. Most members of Congress are lawyers, businessmen, and teachers. Would Congress be a better place if other professions were represented? There are a couple of nurses in the House of Representatives and the current Majority Leader of the Senate is a licensed doctor. However, because of this section, members cannot earn outside their salaries, so many of the health professionals who are in Congress have received a cut in pay and work *pro bono* (for free). Would Congress be a better place if there were people who were members of different occupational fields? A good plumber, mechanic, or scientist may help Congress answer some of the different issues it has to face. When the issue of stem cell research comes to the floor of Congress, maybe the Congressional members who have training concerning this field should be listened to more than the ones who have legal training. The Founding Fathers were a mix of professional training that proved to be very helpful in drawing the Constitution. As long as campaigning is so expensive this will bar the average person from running for Congress. This results in people feeling isolated and alienated from their members of Congress.

Section 7. All bills for raising Revenue shall originate in the House of Representatives; but the Senate may propose or concur with Amendments as on other Bills.

Every Bill which shall have passed the House of Representatives and the Senate, shall, before it becomes a Law, be presented to the President of the United States; if he approves he shall sign it, but if not he shall return it with Objections to that House in which it originated, who shall enter the Objections at large on their journal, and proceed to reconsider it. If after such Reconsideration two-thirds of that House shall agree to pass the Bill, it shall be sent, together with the Objections, to the other House, by which it shall likewise be reconsidered, and if approved by two-thirds of that House, it shall become a Law. But in all such Cases the Votes of both Houses shall be determined by Yeas and Nays, and the Names of the Persons voting for and against the Bill shall be entered on the journal of each House respectively. If any Bill shall not be returned by the President within ten Days (Sundays excepted) after it shall have been presented to him, the Same shall be a Law, in like Manner as if he had signed it, unless the Congress by their Adjournment prevent its Return, in which Case it shall not be a Law.

Every Order, Resolution or Vote to which the Concurrence of the Senate and House of Representatives may be necessary (except on a question of Adjournment) shall be presented to the President of the United States; and before the Same shall take Effect, shall be approved by him, or being disapproved by him, shall be repassed by two-thirds of the Senate and House of Representatives, according to the Rules and Limitations prescribed in the Case of a Bill.

Section 7 is a very important description of Congressional power. This procedure remains in use today. How a bill becomes a law is the essence of legislative power in the United States. First of all, bills that deal with raising money must originate in the House of Representatives. Therefore, the House of Representatives has the Appropriation Committee that is very powerful because they have the check book. This section also describes the way a bill becomes a law. It is quite simple, if a bill is passed by a majority of both Senators and Congressmen it goes to the President. If he signs it, the bill becomes a law. If the President does not sign the bill, it is vetoed. Congress can then override the veto by passing the bill with two-thirds majorities. If two-thirds majorities are achieved the bill becomes a law. This procedure is fairly difficult, yet not impossible. President Bush has yet to veto any bills in his six years in office.

Section 8. The Congress shall have Power

To lay and collect Taxes, Duties, Imposts, and Excises to pay the Debts and provide for the common Defense and general Welfare of the United States; but all Duties, Imposts and Excises shall be uniform throughout the United States;

To borrow Money on the credit of the United States;

To regulate Commerce with foreign Nations, and among the several States, and with the Indian tribes;

To establish an uniform Rule of Naturalization, and uniform Laws on the subject of Bankruptcies throughout the United States;

To coin Money, regulate the Value thereof, and of foreign Coin, and fix the Standard of Weights and Measures;

To provide for the Punishment of counterfeiting the Securities and current coin of the United States;

To establish Post Offices and Post Roads;

To promote the Progress of Science and useful Arts by securing for limited Times to Authors and Inventors the exclusive Right to their respective Writings and Discoveries;

To constitute Tribunal inferior to the Supreme Court;

To define and punish Piracies and Felonies committed on the high Seas, and offenses against the Law of Nations;

To declare War, grant Letters of Marque and Reprisal, and make Rules concerning Captures on Land and Water;

To Raise and support Armies, but no Appropriation of Money to that Use shall be for a longer Term than two Years;

To provide and maintain a Navy;

To make rules for the Government and Regulation of the Land and naval Forces;

To provide for calling forth the Militia to execute the Laws of the Union, suppress Insurrections, and repel Invasions;

To provide for organizing, arming and disciplining the Militia, and for governing such Part of them as may be employed in the Service of the United

States, reserving to the States respectively the Appointment of the Officers, and the Authority of training the Militia according to the discipline prescribed by Congress;

To exercise exclusive Legislation in all Cases whatsoever, over such District (not exceeding ten Miles square) as may, by cession of particular States, and the Acceptance of Congress, become the Seat of Government of the United States, and to exercise like Authority over all places purchased by the Consent of the Legislature of the State in which the Same shall be, for Erection of Forts, Magazines, Arsenals, Dock-yards, and other needful Buildings;—And

To make all Laws which shall be necessary and proper for carrying into Execution the foregoing Powers, and all other powers vested by this Constitution in the Government of the United States, or in any Department or Officer thereof.

Section 8 has the expressed and implicit powers of Congress. The first part of the section explicitly gives Congress the power to collect taxes, provide for the defense and general welfare of the United States. The only restriction on Congress in the issuance of taxes is that taxes must be uniform in all of the states. Congress has the expressed power to borrow money, regulate trade and pass laws on immigration. They also have the power to coin money and regulate bankruptcies.

One very interesting aspect of Section 8 is the foresight the Founding Fathers had on the issue of copyright and trademarks. Men like Thomas Jefferson and Benjamin Franklin were inventors. One reason they became revolutionaries was because of the idea the King would own all of the inventions and property of the kingdom. They believed people should benefit from their labor. This was a revolutionary part of the Constitution. In effect it said to the world, give us your thinkers, writers and inventors because if you produce something in the worlds of art or science you own it and shall receive royalties for your efforts. This was a spur to our economic development.

The last part of Section 8 is known as the necessary and proper clause. This entitles Congress to do anything it deems necessary and proper to carry out its duties. People also call this clause the implied powers of Congress. It gives the Legislative branch of government the benefit of the doubt. When you hear someone questioning the powers of Congress to do something, Congress probably does have the power due to this clause.

Section 9. *The Migration or Importation of such persons as any of the States now existing shall think proper to admit, shall not be prohibited by the Congress prior to the Year 1808; but a Tax or duty may be imposed on such importation, not exceeding $10.00 for each person.*

The Privilege of the Writ of Habeas Corpus shall not be suspended, unless when in Cases of Rebellion or Invasion the public Safety may require it.

No Bill of Attainder or ex-post facto Law shall be passed.

No Capitation, or other direct Tax shall be laid, unless in Proportion to the Census or Enumeration herein before directed to be taken.

No Tax or Duty shall be laid on Articles exported from any State.

No Preference shall be given by any Regulation of Commerce or Revenue to the Ports of one State over those of another; nor shall Vessels bound to, or from, one State, be obliged to enter, clear, or pay Duties in another.

No Money shall be drawn from the Treasury, but in Consequence of Appropriations made by Law: and a regular Statement and Account of the receipts and Expenditures of all public Money shall be published from time to time.

No Title of Nobility shall be granted by the United States; and no Person holding any Office or Profit or trust under them, shall, without the Consent of the Congress, accept of any present, Emolument, Office or Title, of any kind whatever, from any King, Prince, or foreign State.

This section has the weak compromise on slavery that was a failure. Although we can look back and see the start of the Civil War happened because of the failure to outlaw slavery in the Constitution. To be fair slavery was dead in the North because it was not profitable and (at this time) dying in the South. Two things happened to revive slavery in the South. The first, was the invention of the cotton engine (or cotton gin) by Eli Whitney. This machine separates the cotton seed from the lint. It is the lint that makes thread and ultimately makes cloth. Before the cotton gin a slave would take eight hours to produce one pound of lint. After the invention, hundreds of pounds of cotton lint could be produced in a single day. This made slavery profitable, because it made large plantations profitable. The other aspect that made slavery profitable was the language in the law outlawing the importation of slaves in 1808. As we know, if you outlaw the importation of something the price of the domestic market increases. Instead of slowing the slave trade, the South was involved in the evil act of setting up slave factories that would force the breeding of people. These two factors could not be foreseen by the Founding Fathers. Having said this there is no doubt the main failure of the Constitution was not ending slavery.

The failure to end slavery is combined in this section with personal protections from the central government and the importance of establishing a meritocracy. The government is barred from jailing people without telling them why they are being jailed, and is prevented from passing ex-post facto laws (ex-post facto is Latin for "after the fact"). Next, the Founding Fathers describe a procedure for the government to tax and spend money. In the last part of this section, the Founding Fathers outlaw titles of nobility. Before the Revolution, men such as Washington, Franklin, and Jefferson wanted to be thought of as English Gentlemen. We know when these men spent time communicating with the English, they soon learned they would never aspire to that status because of where they were born. The lack of merit disturbed them. So they believed you should be judged on what you do in life—the antithesis of this is the noble class. One inherits a title for being born. It is too bad they could not see the same injustice on the issue of slavery. However, they laid open the idea of a society judging a person on their merits, not how they were born. Again, this was a great jump in our understanding of concepts of societal justice.

Section 10. No State shall enter into any Treaty, Alliance, or Confederation; grant Letters of Marque and Reprisal; coin Money; emit Bill of Credit; make any Thing but gold and silver Coin a Tender in Payment of Debts; pass any Bill of Attainder, ex post facto law, or Law impairing the obligations of Contracts, or grant any Title of Nobility.

No State shall, without the Consent of Congress, lay any Imposts or Duties on Imports or Exports, except what may be absolutely necessary for executing its inspection Laws: and the net Produce of all duties and imposts, laid by any State on such Laws shall be subject to the Revision and Control of the Congress.

No State shall, without the consent of Congress, lay any Duty of Tonnage, keep Troops or Ships of war in time of Peace, enter into any Agreement or Compact with another State, or with a foreign Power, or

engage in War, unless actually invaded, or in such imminent Danger as will not admit delay.

We finish our discussion of Article I with the taking away of powers from the States. States lose the power to coin money, go into debt, tax others and have a foreign policy. The Congress of the United States will have this power. As you can see, the Legislative branch of the Federal Government has a great deal of power. The Legislative branch is not the only power grab made by the men who attended the Philadelphia Convention. The Second Article of the Constitution describes the role of the Executive branch. Unlike the Articles of Confederation, there would be an executive in the new government that would have power, yet he would not be a King. This is how the Founding Fathers balanced the existence of an executive without creating a tyrant.

ARTICLE II

Section 1. The executive Power shall be vested in a President of the United States of America. He shall hold his office during the Term of four Years, and, together with the Vice President, chosen for the same Term, be elected as follows: Each State shall appoint, in such Manner as the Legislature thereof may direct, a Number of Electors, equal to the whole Number of Senators and Representatives to which the State may be entitled in the Congress; but no Senator or Representative, or Person holding an Office of Trust or Profit under the United States, shall be appointed an Elector.

The Electors shall meet in their respective States, and vote by Ballot for two Persons, of whom one at least shall not be an inhabitant of the same State with themselves. And they shall make a List of all the Persons voted for, and of the Number of Votes for each: which List they shall sign and certify, and transmit sealed to the Seat of Government of the United States, directed to the President of the Senate. The President of the Senate shall, in the presence of the Senate and House of Representatives, open all the Certificates, and the Votes shall then be counted. The Person having the greatest Number of Votes shall be the President, if such Number be a Majority of the whole number of Electors appointed; and if there be more than one who have such a Majority, and have equal Number of Votes, then the House of Representatives shall immediately chuse by Ballot one of them for President; and if no Person have a Majority, then from the five highest on the List said House shall in like Manner chuse the President. But in chusing the President the Votes shall be taken by States, the Represen-

tation from each State having one Vote; a quorum for this purpose shall consist of a Member of Members from two thirds of the States, and a Majority of all the States shall be necessary to a Choice. In every Case, after the Choice of the President, the person having the greatest Number of Votes of the Electors shall be the Vice President. But if there should remain two or more who have equal Votes, the Senate shall chuse from them by Ballot the Vice President.

The Congress may determine the Time of chusing the Electors and the Day on which they shall give their Votes; which Day shall be the same throughout the United States.

No person except a natural born Citizen, or a Citizen of the United States at the time of the Adoption of this Constitution, shall be eligible to the Office of President; neither shall any Person be eligible to that Office who shall not have attained to the age of thirty-five Years, and been fourteen Years a Resident within the United States.

The executive of the government is called the President of the United States, one must be thirty-five years old and a natural born citizen and be a resident of the United States for fourteen years. These are the only physical requirements for the position.

In cases of the Removal of the President from Office or of his Death, Resignation, or inability to discharge the Powers and Duties of the said Office, the same shall devolve on the Vice President, and the Congress may by law provide for the case of Removal, Death, Resignation, or inability, both of the President and Vice President, declaring what Officer shall then act as President, and such Officer shall act accordingly, until the Disability be removed, or a President shall be elected.

The President shall, at stated Times, receive for his Services, a Compensation, which shall neither be increased nor diminished during the Period for which he shall have been elected, and he shall not receive within that Period any other eumolument from the United States, or any of them.

Compensation for the President is a very strange issue. Today, the President earns roughly 400,000 dollars a year. The raise came after President Clinton left office. His salary was 200,000 dollars. Now, I know that sounds like a lot of money. Let us put it in context. President Grant was paid over 100,000 dollars a year (and that was 1870s money). The President does receive use of a house but food is not provided for his family. His (as of yet we have not had a woman President) wife works for free and must pay

her way on Air Force One. All of the State dinners and banquets we see are paid for by the President. So the question is what does a person do if they are elected President with average means? Harry Truman, Jimmy Carter and Dwight Eisenhower were men who were not wealthy when they were President. What is fair compensation for arguably the most difficult job in the world?

Some contend after the President leaves office he has a great opportunity to become wealthy. This is true, however, people criticized Ronald Reagan for receiving a seven figure honorarium for several speeches in Japan. Soon, we learned he was ill and the criticism soon ended. Former President Truman urged Congress to use the ex-Presidents as a resource, giving them permanent seats in the Senate (without the power of voting) and paying them a pension. Truman argued it was very difficult for an ex-President to earn a living and men of normal wealth would suffer from having served. The pension system was passed, the idea of ex-Presidents as permanent members of the Senate never received much serious consideration. Today, we see former Presidents Bush, Carter, and Clinton trying to live as ex-Presidents. Presidents Carter and Clinton were in debt when they left office.

Before he enter on the Execution of his Office, he shall take the following Oath or Affirmation—"I do solemnly swear (or affirm) that I will faithfully execute the Office of President of the United States, and will to the best of my Ability preserve, protect and defend the Constitution of the United States."

The Presidential oath is an oath to protect the Constitution. Later George Washington would add "so help me God." This unofficial part of the oath has remained as a tradition. The essence of the President's job is to defend the Constitution. This was designed to prevent a President from becoming a dictator, it also serves to remind Presidents that they are not above the law.

Section 2. The President shall be Commander in Chief of the Army and Navy of the United States, and of the Militia of the several States, when called into the actual service of the United States; he may require the Opinion, in writing, or the principal Officer in each of the executive Departments, upon any Subject relating to the Duties of their respective Offices, and he shall have Power to grant Reprieves and Pardons for Offences against the United States, except in Cases of Impeachment.

He shall have Power, by and with the Advice and Consent of the Senate, to make Treaties, provided two-thirds of the Senators present concur; and he shall nominate, other public Ministers and Consuls, Judges of the Supreme Court, and all other Officers of the United States, whose Appointments are not herein otherwise provided for, and which shall be established by Law: but Congress may by Law vest the Appointment of such inferior Officers, as they think proper, in the President alone, in the courts of Law, or in the Heads of Departments.

The President shall have Power to fill up all Vacancies that may happen during the Recess of the Senate, by granting Commissions which shall expire at the end of their next session.

The role of Commander in Chief means the President is the ultimate authority on military issues. Congress has the power to declare war. Once the declaration of war has been approved it is the President who must implement the strategies for winning the war. As Commander in Chief all military personnel are under his command. The President also has the power to engage in foreign relations with other states.

The President also has the power to appoint people to the Federal bureaucracy. His first day in office, the President will have to appoint five to six thousand people to work at the senior levels of the Executive branch. The President with the approval of the Senate also appoints members of the Federal Judiciary.

Section 3. He shall from time to time give to the Congress Information of the State of the Union, and recommend to their Consideration such Measures as he shall judge necessary and expedient; he may on extraordinary Occasions, convene both Houses or either of them, and in Case of Disagreement between them, with Respect to the Time of Adjournment, he may adjourn them to such Time as he shall think proper; he shall receive Ambassadors and other public Ministers; he shall take Care that the Laws be faithfully executed, and shall Commission all the Officers of the United States.

The State of the Union Address given by the President of the United States is one of the rare opportunities to see all of the members of the Government together. The President gives his speech in a joint session of Congress with the Supreme Court looking on. Usually most of the members of the Cabinet are there and it is a night of ceremony and pomp. Sometimes, such as President Bush's address before the Iraqi inva-

sion, the President may say something important (Niger Uranium) that may be examined. However, most of the time, these speeches tend to be a list of proposals that Congress may consider or may not. The State of the Union speech was not a speech for over a hundred years. Thomas Jefferson started a practice of delivering his State of the Union Speech in writing and this was followed until Woodrow Wilson started to give the speech in person.

If you know someone who is an officer in the military, ask them to show you their commission, on it you will see a Presidential signature. The President personally commissions all of the officers in the military. However, their loyalty is not to the person but to the Constitution. They also make an oath similar to the President's to defend this document.

Section 4. The President, Vice President and all civil Officers of the United States shall be removed from Office on Impeachment for, and on Conviction of, Treason, Bribery, or other high Crimes and Misdemeanors.

The President, Vice President and all of the people who work for the Government are not above the law. If they do commit a crime they will be impeached. Again, impeachment is done by the House of Representatives, and the Senate acts to decide innocence or guilt. The issue of impeachment deals only with removal from office. Consequently, Presidents, Vice Presidents or the civil officers of the government would face criminal and civil charges for the acts that lead to their impeachment.

ARTICLE III

Section 1. The judicial Power of the United States shall be vested in one supreme Court, and in such inferior Courts as the Congress may from time to time ordain and establish. The Judges, both of the supreme and inferior Courts, shall hold their Offices during good Behaviour, and shall, at stated Times, receive for their Services a Compensation which shall not be diminished during their Continuance in Office.

Section 2. The judicial Power shall extend to all Cases, in Law and Equity, arising under this Constitution, the Laws of the United States, and Treaties made, or which shall be made, under their Authority; to all Cases affecting Ambassadors, other public Ministers and Consuls; to all Cases of admiralty and maritime Jurisdiction; to Controversies to which the United States shall be a Party; to con-

troversies between two or more States—between Citizens of the same State claiming Lands under grants of different States, and between a State, or the Citizens thereof, and foreign States, Citizens or Subjects.

In all cases affecting Ambassadors, other public Ministers and Counsuls, and those in which a State shall be Party, the supreme Court shall have original Jurisdiction. In all the other Cases before mentioned, the supreme Court shall have appellate Jurisdiction, both as to Law and Fact, with such Exceptions, and under such Regulations, as the Congress shall make.

The Trial of all Crimes, except in cases of Impeachment, shall be by Jury; and such Trial shall be held in the State where said Crimes shall have been committed; but when not committed within any State, the Trial shall be at such Place or Places as the Congress may by Law have directed.

Article III of the Constitution establishes the third branch of government—the Judiciary. Congress and the President pass the laws, it is the Judiciary that interprets the laws that are passed. The main issue facing the judiciary is, do the laws passed by the Congress and President uphold the constitutional principles that are spelled out by the writers of the Constitution. You can think of the Judiciary as the umpires or referees of the constitutional system. They examine both the rule of law and the role our institutions play in our society.

The second part of this section describes the jurisdiction of the courts. Simply, the courts have jurisdiction in all of the cases arising in our society. The Constitution describes the Supreme Court. Congress has established both District Courts that have original jurisdiction and another level of appellate court known as the Federal Appellate Court that also gives plaintiffs and defendants a route to seek justice in the appellate process.

Section 3. Treason against the United States shall consist only in levying War against them or in adhering to their Enemies; giving them Aid and Comfort. No Person shall be convicted of Treason unless on the Testimony of two Witnesses to the same overt Act, or on confession in open Court.

The Congress shall have power to declare the Punishment of Treason, but no Attainder of Treason shall work Corruption of Blood, or Forfeiture except during the Life of the Person Attainted.

This is a continuing demonstration of how the Founding Fathers thought one should be judged by what they do, society should reward and punish people on their own actions. If your father was a traitor, the scorn and punishment would not revert to you (as they do in some societies). In some societies if your ancestors are found to be a traitor, future generations will also be punished. Just as titles of nobility should not be transferred for the benefit of future generations, the corruption of blood should not be attributed to the future generations of people who are found to be guilty of treason. Also, the Founding Fathers wanted treason to be a very difficult crime to prove. As you may know, these men were considered traitors to the English Crown. They saw how kings abused the notion of treason and how many people were punished for treason for simply being on the wrong side of the King. Therefore, the writers wanted a very specific criteria: "shall consist only in levying War against them or in adhering to their enemies; giving them aid or comfort"—only this can be considered treason. Recently, we have heard the charge the media has committed treason. Has the media given aid or comfort to the al-Qaeda? This again is an open question, however, it would be very difficult for the government to prove.

ARTICLE IV

Section 1. Full Faith and Credit shall be given in each State to the public Acts, Records, and judicial Proceedings of every other State. And the Congress may by general laws prescribe the Manner in which such Acts, Records, and Proceedings shall be proved, and the Effect thereof.

Section 2. The Citizens of each State shall be entitled to all Privileges and Immunities of Citizens in the several States.

A Person charged in any State with Treason, Felony, or other Crime, who shall flee from Justice, and be found in another State, shall on Demand of the executive Authority of the State from which he fled, be delivered up to be removed to the State having Jurisdiction of the Crime.

No person held to Service or Labor in one State, under the Laws thereof, escaping into another, shall, in consequence of any Law or Regulation therein, be discharged from such Service or Labor, but shall be delivered up on Claim of the Party to whom such Service or Labor may be due.

Section 3. New States may be admitted by the Congress into this Union; but no new State shall be formed or erected within the Jurisdiction of any other State; nor any State be formed by the Junction of two or more States, or parts of States, without the Consent of the Legislatures of the States concerned as well as of the Congress.

The Congress shall have Power to dispose of and make all needful Rules and Regulations respecting the Territory or other Property belonging to the United States; and nothing in this Constitution shall be so construed as to Prejudice any Claims of the United States, or of any particular State.

Section 4. The United States shall guarantee to every State in this Union a Republican Form of Government, and shall protect each of them against Invasion; and on Application of the Legislature or of the Executive (when the Legislature cannot be convened), against domestic Violence.

This article is known as the full faith and credit article of the Constitution. In this article the Founding Fathers are saying any privilege or law that one citizen of a state enjoys all of the residents of the state, regardless of their residency, must be able to enjoy the same status. Marriage, drivers licenses and business rights were to be uniform. Every State has a republican form of government. This means every state has a Representative branch, Executive and Judicial branches. Most states copy the structure of government outlined in the Constitution. However, Nebraska does a unicameral (one house) legislature and Louisiana uses the Napoleonic legal code of the French tradition.

ARTICLE V

The Congress, whenever two-thirds of both Houses shall deem it necessary, shall propose Amendments to this Constitution, or, on the Application of the Legislatures of two-thirds of the several States, shall call a Convention for proposing Amendments, which, in either Case, shall be valid to all Intents and Purposes, as part of this Constitution, when ratified by the legislatures of three-fourths of the several States, or by Conventions in three-fourths thereof, as the one or the other Mode of Ratification may be proposed by the Congress; Provided *that no Amendment which may be made prior to the Year One thousand eight hundred and eight shall in any Manner affect the first and fourth clauses in the Ninth Section of the first Article; and that*

no State, without its Consent, shall be deprived of its equal suffrage in the Senate.

This article describes the procedures for amending the Constitution. The Founding Fathers believed it was important to have a process that would change the Constitution to reflect the issues of the future. However, they also wanted it difficult enough so changing the Constitution would be a thought out process. There have been examples when political passions have gotten in the way of thoughtful amendments. The passing of prohibition is an example of an amendment that did not work. Most amendments have stood the test of time and have reflected the needs of the Constitution to change with the changing concepts of justice. The expansion of the franchise (voting rights) is an example of amendments that have worked.

ARTICLE VI

All Debts contracted and Engagements entered into, before the Adoption of this Constitution, shall be as valid against the United States under this Constitution, as under the Confederation.

This Constitution, and the Laws of the United States which shall be made in Pursuance thereof; and all Treaties made, or which shall be made, under the Authority of the United States, shall be the supreme Law of the Land; and the judges in every State shall be bound thereby, anything in the Constitution or Laws of any State to the Contrary notwithstanding.

The Senators and Representatives before mentioned, and the Members of the several State Legislatures, and all executive and judicial Officers, both of the United States and of the several States, shall be bound by Oath or Affirmation to support this Constitution; but no religious test shall ever be required as a Qualification to any Office or public Trust under the United States.

All of the debts and contracts that were engaged in under the Articles of Confederation would be honored by the new government established under the Constitution. This is a direct admission that the Articles of Confederation and the Constitution are connected and even though one was a failure, the new government would honor the actions of the previous government in order to minimize economic and political disruption that may have happened if this language had not been included in the Constitution.

ARTICLE VII

The ratification of the Conventions of nine States shall be sufficient for the Establishment of this Constitution between the States so ratifying the Same.

Done in Convention by the Unanimous Consent of the States present, the seventeenth day of September in the Year of our Lord one thousand seven hundred and eighty-seven and of the Independence of the United States of America the twelfth. In WITNESS whereof WE have hereunto subscribed our Names. George Washington and Thirty-Seven Others

The last article of the Constitution explains the ratification process and the votes and names of the Founding Fathers who supported the ratification of the document. There were those who did not support the document and there would be a heated debate but ultimately the Constitution was ratified and George Washington became the first President and John Adams became the first Vice President of the United States.

CONCLUSION

Today there are many revisionist historians who criticize the Constitution as a document written by white males to exploit everyone else. This characterization is more racist and narrow minded than the Founding Fathers ever were. We have showed that the Constitution does have a failure, and this failure nearly cost the country everything. If the Founding Fathers would have ended slavery then one could argue this document would have been perfect. It was not perfect—they did fail in this important aspect.

Where did they succeed? They succeeded in designing a new central government that was built on popular sovereignty, rule of law and tolerance. This was quite a revolutionary leap in how men had organized their nations before the American experiment. Other nations are built on racial, religious and linguistic similarities. The American nation is built on popular sovereignty, rule of law and tolerance.

Popular sovereignty is the argument that individuals are responsible enough to organize their own government. People enter into a social contract to push the effects of anarchy into the international system. Governmental institutions are produced in order to protect the rights of individuals against violence and the cupreous acts of the powerful. In exchange, people agree to live under and obey the authorities that are produced by the institutions. The Devine Right of Kings is an argument that believes authority of the King derives from God, and the people obey the authority of government because it is part of their religious duty, since God picked the person who would become King. In the United States, there is no litmus test of religion in order to serve and participate in governmental institutions. This takes away the power of the government to excommunicate (or in other words send to damnation) people who dissent and disagree with governmental authority, but may be very obedient when it comes to religious practice. This was a great change in power from having the authority flow downward, to having the authority of establishing a sovereign government flow up from the people.

The act of writing a constitution is an awareness that the authority of government comes from the people. In exchange for people to enter into this contract, the writers of the Constitution set for one of their objectives, the establishment of a system of justice. The first step in establishing a system of justice is to write the laws down so everyone is aware of what is legal behavior and what is not. Rule of Law was the second pillar the Founding Fathers established to build a different type of society. Remember under a King there is no law. Monarchies are ruled by men not law.

The third pillar the Founding Fathers wanted to use to build a new American society is tolerance. Tolerance is the ability to mind your own business and respect the liberty of your neighbors. It does not mean you necessarily accept behaviors that you may deem immoral. Personal behaviors (even if they are unhealthful) can be tolerated without being accepted. A person can use their economic and social power to not accept practices that they may tolerate out of the respect honoring a person's liberty.

These three pillars—popular sovereignty, rule of law and tolerance are why the Founding Fathers wrote the Constitution. In this chapter we have analyzed the Constitution as a document that established a more effective central government for the United States. As stated previously, there was a debate about establishing a central government without the protection of freedom to an individual. In the next chapter we will analyze the protections known as the Bill of Rights that were designed to create a list of civil rights and civil liberties to insure Americans live in an environment of liberty.

TERMS TO REMEMBER

POPULAR SOVEREIGNTY
RULE OF LAW
TOLERANCE
FEDERALIST
ANTI-FEDERALIST

The U.S. Constitution Part One, the Establishment of a New Central Government

TRUE OR FALSE QUESTIONS

1. In 2006, President George Bush appointed three members to the Supreme Court.   T / F

2. Democratic Senators use original intent as a criterion for voting on Supreme Court nominees.   T / F

3. There was not an economic dimension to the failure of the Articles of Confederation.   T / F

4. The Massachusetts Plan was known as the great compromise.   T / F

5. Thomas Jefferson was part of the Washington, D.C. delegation.   T / F

6. The Constitution was unanimously ratified after the close of the Constitutional Convention.   T / F

7. The failure of the Articles of Confederation was all economic in origin.   T / F

8. King George III thought the Articles of Confederation were a good idea.   T / F

9. The Founding Fathers wanted a national religion in order to have unity in faith.   T / F

10. The Constitution starts with a preamble.   T / F

MULTIPLE CHOICE QUESTIONS

11. The first three words of the Constitution are
    a. The Constitution of . . .
    b. We the People . . .
    c. United States of . . .
    d. The Preamble of . . .

12. "We the People" illustrates what pillar of American Society?
    a. Democracy
    b. Republicanism
    c. Popular Sovereignty
    d. Elections

13. A system of Justice illustrates another pillar of American Society.
    a. Courts
    b. Rule of Law
    c. Criminalization of behavior
    d. Popular Sovereignty

14. The Blessings of Liberty illustrates another pillar of American Society.
    a. Freedom
    b. Elections
    c. Rule of Law
    d. Tolerance

15. The Devine Right of Kings gives justification to the monarchy using
    a. military force
    b. religion
    c. family ties
    d. language

16. The Legislative powers of the nation are invested in
    a. Congress
    b. President
    c. Supreme Court
    d. Bureaucracy

17. Article I of the Constitution
    a. outlines the power of the President
    b. outlines the power of the Congress
    c. outlines the power of the Supreme Court
    d. outlines the power of the Bureaucracy

18. A person has to be at least this age to serve in House of Representatives
    a. 45
    b. 35
    c. 50
    d. 25

19. Article II of the Constitution outlines the powers of
    a. House of Representatives
    b. Senate
    c. Supreme Court
    d. Presidency

20. Article III of the Constitution outlines the powers of
    a. Supreme Court
    b. Presidency
    c. Congress
    d. Central Intelligence Agency

chapter three

My flag still stands for
FREEDOM

IMAGE FROM DEFENSE VISUAL INFORMATION CENTER

THE BILL OF RIGHTS

INTRODUCTION

"AFTER ALL IT IS MY PRINCIPLE THAT THE WILL OF THE MAJORITY SHOULD ALWAYS PREVAIL. IF THEY APPROVE THE PROPOSED CONVENTION IN ALL ITS PARTS, I SHALL CONCUR CHEERFULLY, IN HOPES THAT THEY WILL AMEND IT WHENEVER THEY SHALL FIND THE WORK WRONG." (THOMAS JEFFERSON IN A LETTER TO JAMES MADISON.)[1]

In the previous chapter, we examined the fabric of the central government of the United States. In this chapter, we examine the ratification process and the amendment process that kept the Constitution a living document. Thomas Jefferson realized the Founding Fathers were not perfect. This document is written by men. Being such, men can make mistakes. Therefore, they created a process in which the country could change the Constitution in order to improve on the goals that were expressed in the preamble of the Constitution. Slavery, expanding the

right to vote to all people over eighteen years of age, and protection from unreasonable searches and seizures are just a few of the corrections our society has made since the adoption of the Constitution.

This chapter will briefly discuss the ratification of the Constitution and then take all of the amendments step by step and explain how they relate to our everyday lives. Just as we did in the previous chapter, we will examine the Amendments to the Constitution giving the original text and then commenting on the mainstream interpretation of the text. The amendment process was truly revolutionary, for it is the first time in history that people will be protected from the excesses of their government.

RATIFICATION OF THE U.S. CONSTITUTION

The adoption of the Constitution by the delegates at the convention in Philadelphia was only the first step in the ratification process. The Founding Fathers believed the second Continental Congress would not

---

[1]Thomas Jefferson, *Writings*. New York: Viking Press, 1984, p. 918.

be amenable to the replacement of the existing central government. To their surprise, the second Continental Congress did pass the Constitution and sent it to the thirteen states for ratification. This is when the ratification debate began.

The issue surrounding the ratification of the Constitution was around the issue of whether the Americans wanted a strong central government. The people who were in favor of a strong central government were called Federalists. The people who were against a strong central government were called anti-Federalists. The anti-Federalists argued that states must be protected against the excesses of a strong central government. The Federalists argued the Union would not survive because of the economic and political challenges facing the new country if a strong national government was not established. This debate was carried on in newspapers and pamphlets which were the mass media of the day.

The famous arguments for ratification are preserved for us in the *Federalist Papers*. These essays were written by Alexander Hamilton and James Madison with a few being written by John Jay. In total, there were eighty-five essays with the most famous being the Federalist paper number 10. The anti-Federalist also published essays. Their main contention that seemed to make sense was the idea that a strong central government would ultimately leave the states in a power vacuum.

In this arrangement of power, the individual would need to be protected and the states would have to be guaranteed in the structure of the government the right to survive. This was the genesis for the idea of amending the Constitution to include a bill of rights to protect the average citizen from tyranny that governments tended to form since the early days of civilization.

From December 1787 to June 1788, the debate preoccupied the political class of the new country. The small states (Delaware and New Jersey) were quick to ratify the new Constitution in order to preserve the agreement of equal representation in the Senate. Pennsylvania was the first large state to ratify the Constitution. The state had a large proportion of Federalists who were organized for victory.

After Pennsylvania's vote, the idea of a bill of rights began to solidify in people's thinking. The Federalists realized this would be another compromise in a litany of compromises that had gotten the process down the road this far, and states started to approve the Constitution. However, they would stipulate they wanted to see the anti-Federalist amendments

in the documents. Massachusetts ratified the Constitution but called for the immediate inclusion of the bill of rights. June 21, 1788, New Hampshire approved the Constitution fulfilling the legal requirement set forth in the document.

Two major states, however, did not vote for the Constitution. Therefore, the viability of the national government was of a great concern. These states, New York and Virginia, also had roughly forty percent of the population of the whole country. It would illustrate the anti-Federalists' worries about tyranny if you imposed the Constitution, even though you fulfilled the legal requirement of ratification. Once Virginia acceded with the reservation of amending the Constitution with a bill of rights, New York followed. The last state to ratify the Constitution was Rhode Island. North Carolina originally defeated the Constitution but after seeing the anti-Federalists amendment approved, they joined the Union.

With the ratification process complete, the Founding Fathers had to craft the amendments. There are two methods to amending the Constitution. The first which has never been tried to amend the Constitution, is there can be a national constitutional convention that can be called at the request of two-thirds of the state legislatures. The method that has been used is a two-third vote in Congress, and three-fourths of state legislatures must approve the amendment before it becomes part of the Constitution.

Now let us examine the actual language of the Amendments that have been produced by the succeeding generations, as in Jefferson's words "in hopes that they will amend it whenever they shall find the work wrong."

THE AMENDMENTS TO THE U.S. CONSTITUTION

AMENDMENT I

Congress shall make no law respecting an establishment of religion, or prohibiting the free exercise thereof; or abridging the freedom of speech, or of the press; or the right of the people to peaceably assemble, and to petition the Government for a redress of grievances.

The first ten amendments to the Constitution are called the Bill of Rights. These were the anti-Federalists amendments that were designed to protect individuals and the state governments against the excesses of a strong central government. As you can see, the first amendment is a recipe for political opposition. The first phrase bans the ability of the leadership of the central government to establish a national religion. The Founding Fathers wanted to prevent the government from using religious power in order to keep people compliant. Although this may not seem very important in our day and age, remember during the 1700s the power of religion was stronger than the power of civil society. Therefore, the first traditional aspect of a nation's common religion is rejected by the Founding Fathers.

The second phrase of the first Amendment gives people the freedom of speech. Under the Constitution, people have the freedom to say what is on their minds. If they do not like the government, they can express their opposition to the personalities and issues addressed by the government. If they do not like their neighbors, people also have the freedom to express this. However, with this freedom also comes responsibility. After hearing what you said about your neighbor it may be very difficult to have a normal relationship with that person. If you believe in racist, sexist, or any other type of hate, you can believe that rubbish, but people also have the freedom to avoid having any contact with you.

As an example, in the summer of 2006 actor Mel Gibson was arrested for driving while intoxicated. He said things that were anti-Semitic and hateful. He later apologized to the Jewish community and argued it was his drinking that was doing the talking. People have the right to accept or not accept his apology. The Disney Corporation suspended contracts with him and Gibson is suffering the consequences of his freedom of speech. Hopefully, he will have a change of heart, but if he wants to believe in hate there is really little any of us can do about it. This is one example of how we have both the freedom of speech and the responsibility of living with the things that we say.

The freedom of speech under the first Amendment is not an unlimited protection. There is a doctrine called a clear and present danger doctrine. This doctrine limits freedom of speech by explaining a person does not have the freedom to cause a clear and present danger to society. The classic example is yelling fire in a crowded theater. By yelling fire, the person speaking is causing a panic that could result in the injury or possible deaths of patrons in the theater. This is clearly not protected speech. The standard for all of the protections in the Bill of Rights is what is reasonable. Would a reasonable person be able to participate in this activity without suffering harm to other people? The second clause in the first amendment, therefore, gives people the right to voice their opposition to the government. Associated with freedom of speech is the freedom of the press. One may be able to voice his or her opposition to the government by themselves. However, for the opposition to turn into a movement, one should have the ability to use the media in the case of the Constitution, the freedom of the press. If I can circulate my ideas in writing or in the broadcast media, then my ability for changing people's minds on the actions of the government will become more powerful. The Founding Fathers used the power of the print media to galvanize the revolutionary spirit in the colonies. They wanted to preserve the power of the media for those who oppose the power and policies of the central government. Now, if you are in opposition to the central government, you cannot be excommunicated from your church, you can articulate your opposition in private speech and in the media. The next section of the First Amendment gives you the protection from governmental interference to meet or assemble people who agree with you.

Freedom of assembly is another very important protection if you are in opposition to a governmental policy. How do you plan a course of action if you are unable to meet? The Founding Fathers again saw this freedom as a necessity in their opposition to the English Crown. Formally, this protection can be seen in the formation of the first Continental Congress and the forming local revolutionary assemblies. This protection also protects small groups to assemble their members and meet. There may be some minor requirements, such as a flag has to be present, or if it is a larger group, fire permits. The government cannot stop a group from meeting. Even hate groups such as the Nazis or Ku Klux Klan have this freedom to assemble. The theory behind this freedom is in the market place of ideas, hate groups are more likely to fail when their ideas are out in the open than if you ban them.

The last part of the recipe for political opposition included in the First Amendment is the ability of individuals and groups to petition the government for a redress of grievances. We see this every day. People writing to their Representative in Congress and in the Senate asking for help to prevent some type of governmental action. This protection also guarantees the right of lobbyists to petition the government. In the recent scandal involving the lobbyist Jack Abramoff, we see how lobbyists influence the elected leaders of the government. Although this scandal and the Enron scandal show how lobbyists do influence governmental activity, there is a basic freedom to voice your grievances against the government that is unique to this country.

The First Amendment, therefore, gives us all of the protections to actively oppose the government. You can see this in the anti-war protests. The activists have used their freedom of speech, press, to assemble and to petition the government to get U.S. troops out of Iraq. Agree with them or not, they have exercised their freedoms that have been guaranteed under the First Amendment.

AMENDMENT II

A well-regulated militia being necessary to the security of a free State, the right of the people to keep and bear arms shall not be infringed.

The Second Amendment to the Constitution has caused a lot of debate and has spawned large organizations that have used the First Amendment to oppose governmental activity on both sides of the gun control debate. If you are an advocate of gun control you look at the language of the Second Amendment and highlight the term "a well regulated militia" and that is the National Guard. One would argue that this protection is outdated since the time for the minutemen is long passed, and members of the National Guard do not take their M-16 assault rifles home with them. If you are an opponent of gun control you tend to highlight the last phrase of the amendment, the right of a people to keep and bear arms shall not be infringed. The debate between gun control advocates and people who want to have the freedom to own guns is a debate much like the abortion debate. That is one of the central issues of political discourse in this country.

AMENDMENT III

No Soldier shall, in time of peace, be quartered in any house without the consent of the Owner, nor in time of war, but in a manner prescribed by law.

The British had a tradition of using the best houses in a city to house the troops. People felt this was a violation of their property rights and so it was a protection for the average person against the excesses of the Army. This amendment has not caused a lot of debate in our political environment.

The next amendments, the Fourth, Fifth and Sixth Amendments, are very important as they protect people who are suspected of violating the law and protects against the police powers of the state.

AMENDMENT IV

The right of the people to be secure in their persons, houses, papers and effects, against unreasonable searches and seizures, shall not be violated, and no Warrants shall issue but upon probable cause, supported by Oath or Affirmation, and particularly describing the place to be searched, and the persons or things to be seized.

We have many laws, especially the laws that deal with drugs that require the police to search people's residences and cars. You are protected from unreasonable searches and seizures, the key concept of this protection is unreasonable. What is reasonable? Remember the standard is what the average person views as reasonable. The police use a criterion known as the chain of causation. How does this chain work? Well, normally the police will stop someone who uses drugs, not on a drug violation, but on a separate violation.

An example could be, a person is stopped because he or she has a headlight and brake light out on their car. Now on the car is a bumper sticker with a marijuana leaf on it.

The person in the car's eyes are bloodshot. He seems to have some sort of cigarette burning in the ashtray. All of these things separately may have an explanation but when you link them together, is it reasonable for the police to have a suspicion on this person's drug use? Maybe, maybe not, what is reasonable? Probable Cause is the criterion used in order to get a search warrant. Let us expand the scenario, the car does not have lights and the person inside the car has a lot of junk food wrappers on the front seat. Again, would that be enough for probable cause? What if the person's speech and motor ability was impaired? The police are trained to look for little things to build the chain of causation in order to get a search warrant. Finally, this amendment does give direction on how a search warrant must be constructed. It must be particular about the places being searched and the things that are going to be seized. The government does have the power to search property, however, this amendment does put some limits on this power.

AMENDMENT V

No person shall be held to answer for a capital, or otherwise infamous crime, unless on a presentment or indictment of a Grand Jury, except in cases arising in the land or naval forces, or in the Militia,

when in actual service in time of War or public danger; nor shall any person be subject for the same offense to be twice put in jeopardy of life or limb; nor shall be compelled in any criminal case to be a witness against himself, nor be deprived of life, liberty, or property, without due process of law; nor shall private property be taken for public use without just compensation.

This is the famous Fifth Amendment. We see it on all of the television shows—"people taking the fifth." The first part of the Fifth Amendment is to outline the procedures the government must fulfill in order to convict someone of a crime. The government must convene a Grand Jury.

The job of the Grand Jury is to determine if there is probable cause for the prosecution to continue. The second part of this amendment gives some exception to the Grand Jury procedure, those being military trials and times of war and public danger. In normal times of peace and security, the Fifth Amendment offers this protection to people who are charged with a serious violation of the law. The government has one chance to convict you of the same crime, this is also known as double jeopardy. The next protection offered people who are charged with a crime is the ability to not be compelled to testify against themselves. If you do not testify, you cannot be forced to be cross-examined. Most lawyers will tell you that their clients talk too much. When a person is charged with a crime they should be aware of this protection and ask for an attorney, and then be quiet. The police have been trained to get people charged to talk. This protection is voluntary and many people do not use it because they believe they can talk their way out of trouble. Usually they cannot, and the information will be used against them. Recently, there has been a heated debate surrounding the last part of this amendment. The power of eminent domain is the power of the government to take private property for public use as long as the private party receives "just" compensation. However, property developers and other interests have been able to use this power for economic development. In the past, eminent domain has been used to build schools, highways, and other public buildings. The Supreme Court has recently ruled that communities are able to build private property such as malls and other businesses. We have seen people fighting to keep their property and the government has used its power to take property from one private interest to another private interest in the name of economic development. Congress and state legislatures are working to change the effect of the Supreme Court ruling. This will be a greater issue in the future.

AMENDMENT VI

In all criminal prosecutions, the accused shall enjoy the right to a speedy and public trial, by an impartial jury of the State and district wherein the crime shall have been committed, which district shall have been previously ascertained by law, and to be informed of the nature and cause of the accusation; to be confronted with the witnesses against him; to have compulsory process for obtaining Witnesses in his favor, and to have the assistance of counsel for his defense.

The Sixth Amendment gives a person charged with a violation of the law a procedure to ensure that they receive a fair trial. A person is entitled to a speedy and public trial. They are to read the charges that are against them and to have competent public representation that will be provided for them even if they cannot afford it. Finally, the lawyers for the defense will have the power to subpoena witnesses that will help their case. These procedures are in place in order to give the defense every resource to mount a defense of the person being charged with a crime.

AMENDMENT VII

In Suits at common law, where the value in controversy shall exceed twenty dollars, the right of trial by jury shall be preserved, and no fact tried by a jury shall be otherwise reexamined in any Court of the United States, than according to the rules of the common law.

The Seventh Amendment places great importance on the power of Juries in courts. Juries are finders of fact in a court of law. Hence, what a jury determines as the facts of a case cannot be appealed. Appellate issues are centered on the actions of the Judge. The Judge determines the issue of law. It is ironic in our society that all of us want to get out of jury duty, we see it as an inconvenient and unrewarding use of our time. Yet, it is one of the most important duties we have in order to preserve the right of defendants to have a fair trial.

AMENDMENT VIII

Excessive bail shall not be required, nor excessive fines imposed, nor cruel and unusual punishments inflicted.

This amendment outlaws the use of excessive bail or cruel and unusual punishment to be administered by the legal system. The criteria for excess bail and cruel punishments is what is deemed as reasonable. These amendments were used to act as a protection from the state if you happen to be involved in the criminal justice system. The next amendments were designed to protect both individuals and the states. After the Civil War, they have become somewhat antiquated and historically, they have not been able to stop the growing power of the central government.

AMENDMENT IX

The enumeration in the Constitution, of certain rights, shall not be construed to deny or disparage others retained by the people.

AMENDMENT X

The powers not delegated to the United States by the Constitution, nor prohibited by it to the States, are reserved to the States respectively, or to the people.

The first ten amendments were called the Bill of Rights. As you can see the Federalists incorporated many of the protections the anti-Federalists wanted during the ratification debate. However, the amendment process did not end there. Our discussion of the further amendments to the Constitution illustrate the different issues and problems that would face the country in the following years after the ratification and implementation of the system took place.

AMENDMENT XI

The Judicial power of the United States shall not be construed to extend to any suit in law or equity, commenced or prosecuted against one of the United States by Citizens of another state, or by Citizens or Subjects of any Foreign State.

AMENDMENT XII

The electors shall meet in their respective States, and vote by ballot for President and Vice-President, one of whom, at least, shall not be an inhabitant of the same state with themselves; they shall name in their ballots the person voted for as President, and in distinct ballots the person voted for as Vice President, and they shall make distinct lists of all persons voted for as President, and of all persons voted for as Vice President, and of the number of votes for each, which lists they shall sign and certify, and transmit sealed to the seat of government of the United States, directed to the President of the Senate; the President of the Senate shall, in the presence of the Senate and House of Representatives, open all the certificates and the votes shall then be counted; the person having the greatest number of votes for President shall be the President, if such number be a majority of the whole number of electors appointed; and if no person have such majority, then from the persons having the highest numbers not exceeding three on the list of those voted for as President, the House of Representatives shall choose immediately, by ballot, the President. But in choosing the President, the votes shall be taken by States, the representation from each State having one vote; a quorum for this purpose shall consist of a member or members from two-thirds of the States, and majority of all States shall be necessary to a choice. And if the House of Representatives shall not choose a President whenever the right of choice shall devolve upon them, before the *fourth day in March* next following then the Vice President shall act as President, as in the case of the death or other constitutional disability of the President. The person having the greatest number of votes as Vice President shall be the Vice President, if such number be a majority of the whole number of electors appointed; and if no person have a majority, then from the two highest numbers on the list the Senate shall choose the Vice President; a quorum for the purpose shall consist of two-thirds of the whole number of Senators, and a majority of the whole number shall be necessary to a choice. But no person constitutionally ineligible to the office of President shall be eligible to that of Vice President of the United States.

The Twelfth Amendment was passed after Thomas Jefferson was elected as Vice President and John Adams was elected President. The problem of course was that Adams and Jefferson had different political agendas. Jefferson was the leading figure against the policies that had been developed by the Federalists. Even though Jefferson had been Washington's Secretary of State, he disagreed philosophically with the ideas of Alexander Hamilton, who was Washington's Secretary of the Treasury, and who is responsible for the economic miracle that happened after the adoption of the Constitution. After this amendment was passed, the Vice President and President would run together as a team. The original procedure was to pick the person who received the highest votes to be President and the second highest to become Vice President. This was changed, and soon after the development of political parties appeared in American political culture.

AMENDMENT XIII

Section 1. Neither slavery nor involuntary servitude, except as a punishment for crime whereof the party shall have been duly convicted, shall exist within the United States, nor any place subject to their jurisdiction.

Section 2. Congress shall have power to enforce this article by appropriate legislation.

The main failure of the Constitution was the inability of the Founding Fathers to find a compromise and outlaw slavery. The Civil War was fought and the North was victorious. The Thirteenth Amendment outlaws slavery in the United States.

AMENDMENT XIV

Section 1. All persons born or naturalized in the United States, and subject to the jurisdiction thereof, are citizens of the United States and of the State wherein they reside. No State shall make or enforce any law which shall abridge the privileges or immunities of citizens of the United States; nor shall any State deprive any person of life, liberty, or property, without due process of law; nor deny to any person within its jurisdiction the equal protection of the laws.

Section 2. Representatives shall be apportioned among the several States according to their respective numbers, counting the whole number of persons in each State excluding Indians not taxed. But when the right to vote at any election for the choice of electors for President and Vice President of the United States, Representatives in Congress, the Executive and Judicial officers of a State, or the members of the Legislature thereof, is denied to any of the male inhabitants of such State, being twenty-one years of age, and citizens of the United States, or in any way abridged, except for participation in rebellion, or other crime, the basis of representation therein shall be reduced in the proportion which the number of male citizens twenty-one years of age in such State.

Section 3. No person shall be a Senator or Representative in Congress, or elector of President or Vice President, or hold any office, civil or military, under the United States, or under any State, who, having previously taken an oath, as a member of Congress, or as an officer of the United States, or as a member of any State legislature, or as an executive or judicial officer of any State, to support the Constitution of the United States, shall have engaged in insurrection or rebellion against the same, or given aid or comfort to the enemies thereof, but Congress may by a vote of two-thirds of each House, remove such disability.

Section 4. The validity of the public debt of the United States, authorized by law, including debts incurred for payment of pensions and bounties for services in suppressing insurrection and rebellion, shall not be questioned. But neither the United States nor any State shall assume or pay any debt or obligation incurred in aid of insurrection or rebellion against the United States, or any claim for the loss or emancipation of any slave, but all such debts, obligations and claims shall be held illegal and void.

Section 5. The Congress shall have power to enforce, by appropriate legislation, the provisions of this article.

There was a debate about the status of ex-slaves. Despite the challenges faced by most ex-slaves, President Lincoln believed it was in the country's best interest to make everyone who had been emancipated citizens. Lincoln said these men have fought for the Union and the Union cannot abandon them. Therefore, all of the freed slaves were to become citizens with all the rights and privileges of any other citizens.

AMENDMENT XV

Section 1. The right of citizens of the United States to vote shall not be denied or abridged by the United States or by any State on account of race, color, or previous condition of servitude.

Section 2. The Congress shall have power to enforce this article by appropriate legislation.

Voting is the key to power in the United States. The Jim Crow laws of the South adopted after the Civil War prevented African-Americans the right to vote in many of the Southern states. This amendment would not be fully enforced until the voting rights act of 1965. Even though it was in the Constitution, law enforcement and government officials failed to enforce this amendment until the civil rights movement of the late 1950s and 1960s.

AMENDMENT XVI

The Congress shall have the power to lay and collect taxes on incomes, from whatever source derived, without apportionment among the several States, and without regard to any census or enumeration.

This amendment legalized the income tax by the Federal Government. Some charlatans will show people an older version of the Constitution and claim the power of the government to lay income taxes is unconstitutional. This was true until the ratification of this amendment in 1913. Today, you must pay your income taxes. Do not be fooled, the income tax is legitimate and legal.

AMENDMENT XVII

The Senate of the United States shall be composed of two Senators from each State, elected by the people thereof, for six years; and each Senator shall have one vote. The electors in each State shall have the qualifications requisite for elector of the most numerous branch of the State legislatures. When vacancies happen in the representation of any State in the Senate, the executive authority of such State shall issue writs of election to fill such vacancies: Provided, that the legislature of any State may empower the executive thereof to make temporary appointments until the people fill the vacancies by election as the legislature may direct. This amendment shall not be so construed as to affect the election or term of any Senator chosen before it becomes valid as part of the Constitution.

During the Progressive Era (1890–1920) there was a drive to have Senators elected by popular vote instead of by the state legislatures. The belief was that the more people could vote for someone there would be a greater incentive for people to participate and become informed citizens. Today, we elect our U.S. Senators.

AMENDMENT XVIII

Section 1. After one year from the ratification of this article the manufacture, sale or transportation of intoxicating liquors within, the importation thereof into, or the exportation thereof from the United States and all territory subject to the jurisdiction thereof for beverage purposes is hereby prohibited.

Section 2. The Congress and the several States shall have concurrent power to enforce this article by appropriate legislation.

Section 3. This article shall be inoperative unless it shall have been ratified as an amendment to the Constitution by the legislatures of the several States, as provided in the Constitution, within seven years from the date of submission hereof to the States by Congress.

This amendment outlawed the use and sale of alcohol. It is probably the second most famous failure of the Constitution. The result of this amendment was an increase in the power and scope of organized crime. We still have not learned the lesson that outlawing something does not necessarily fix a problem. It can make a problem even more complicated and difficult to solve if the government attaches criminal sanctions to a certain behavior, as in this case, drinking. It just forced otherwise law abiding citizens to break the law.

AMENDMENT XIX

The right of citizens of the United States to vote shall not be denied or abridged by the United States or by any State on account of sex. Congress shall have power to enforce this article by appropriate legislation.

The Nineteenth Amendment gave the right to vote to women who are over 21 years of age.

AMENDMENT XX

Section 1. The terms of the President and Vice President shall end at noon on the 20th day of January, and the terms of Senators and Representatives at noon on the 3d day of January, of the years in which such terms would have ended if this article had not been ratified; and the terms of their successors shall then begin.

Section 2. The Congress shall assemble at least once in every year, and such meeting shall begin at noon on the 3d day of January, unless they shall by law appoint a different day.

Section 3. If, at the time fixed for the beginning of the term of the President, the President-elect shall have died, the Vice President-elect shall become President. If a President shall not have been chosen before the time fixed for the beginning of his term, or if the President-elect shall act as President until a President shall have qualified; and the Congress may by law provide for the case wherein neither a President-elect nor a Vice President-elect shall have qualified, declaring who shall then act as President, or the manner in which one who is to act shall be selected, and such person shall act accordingly until a President or Vice President shall have qualified.

Section 4. The Congress may by law provide for the case of the death of any of the persons from whom the House of Representatives may choose a President whenever the rights of choice shall have devolved upon them, and for the case of the death of any of the persons from whom the Senate may choose a Vice President whenever the right of choice shall have devolved upon them.

Section 5. Sections 1 and 2 shall take effect on the 15th day of October following ratification of this article.

Section 6. This article shall be inoperative unless it shall have been ratified as an amendment to the Constitution by the legislatures of three-fourths of the several States within seven years from the date of its submission.

This amendment changes the inauguration date from March 4 to January 21. It also makes clear the succession pattern for the office of the President. In modern times the need to have transition from November to March was not necessary. The change was made in order to have the new President take over the government as a result of the election.

AMENDMENT XXI

Section 1. The eighteenth article of amendment to the Constitution of the United States is hereby repealed.

Section 2. The transportation or importation into any State, Territory, or possession of the United States for delivery or use therein of intoxicating liquors, in violation of the laws thereof, is hereby prohibited.

Section 3. This article shall be inoperative unless it shall have been ratified as an amendment to the Constitution by conventions in the several States, as provided in the Constitution, within seven years from the date of the submission hereof to the States by the Congress.

Prohibition was repealed, during the early years of the Roosevelt Presidency.

AMENDMENT XXII

No person shall be elected to the office of the President more than twice, and no person who has held the office of President, or acted as President, for more than two years of a term to which some other person was elected President shall be elected to the office of the President more than once. But this Article shall not apply to any person holding the office of President when this Article was proposed by the Congress, and shall not prevent any person who may be holding the office of President, or acting as President, during the term within which this Article becomes operative from holding the office of President or acting as President during the remainder of such term.

As a result of President Franklin Roosevelt's four terms. The Republican Party pushed for this amendment limiting Presidents to two terms. The first President who fell under this amendment was Dwight D. Eisenhower. Eisenhower was a Republican, he was so popular that he would probably have been re-elected for a third term. The next President who had a chance at getting reelected for a third term would have been Ronald Reagan. These Republican Presidents although they were old, if it was not for this amendment may have run for a third term. The point is politics through Constitutional Amendments usually have different results than anticipated by the groups and parties who want to change the Constitution.

AMENDMENT XXIII

Section 1. The District constituting the seat of Government of the United States shall appoint in such manner as the Congress may direct: A number of electors of President and Vice President equal to the whole number of Senators and Representatives in Congress to which the District would be entitled if it were a State, but in no event more than the least populous State; they shall be in addition to those appointed by the States, but they shall be considered, for the purposes of the election of President and Vice President, to be electors appointed by a State; and they shall meet in the District and perform such duties as provided by the twelfth article of amendment.

Section 2. The Congress shall have power to enforce this article with appropriate legislation.

The residents of Washington, D.C. are now eligible to vote for President and Vice President, however, they still do not have the representation in Congress. In the House of Representatives there is a delegate from the District of Columbia; however, that member does not have voting powers. Recently, there has been a compromise proposed that Washington, D.C. would have a member of Congress and that person would surely be a Democrat, and the state of Utah would get another member of Congress who would probably become a Republican. This compromise has been presented for the 2006 session. By 2008, this idea had died.

AMENDMENT XXIV (1964)

Section 1. The right of citizens of the United States to vote in any primary or other election for President or Vice President, for electors for President or Vice President, or for Senator or Representative in Congress, shall not be denied or abridged by the United States or any State by reason of failure to pay poll tax or other tax. Section

2. The Congress shall have power to enforce this article by appropriate legislation.

This Amendment made it illegal for political parties and state governments to charge a poll tax which blocked access to the right to vote.

AMENDMENT XXV

Section 1. In case of removal of the President from office or of his death or resignation, the Vice President shall become President.

Section 2. Whenever there is a vacancy in the office of the Vice President, the President shall nominate a Vice President who shall take office upon confirmation by a majority vote of both Houses of Congress.

Section 3. Whenever the President transmits to the President pro tempore of the Senate and the Speaker of the House of Representatives his written declaration that he is unable to discharge the powers and duties of his office, and until he transmits to them a written declaration to the contrary, such powers and duties shall be discharged by the Vice President as Acting President.

Section 4. Whenever the Vice President and a majority of either the principal officers of the executive departments or of such other body as Congress may by law provide, transmit to the President pro tempore of the Senate and the Speaker of the House of Representatives their written declaration that the President is unable to discharge the powers and duties of his office, the Vice President shall immediately assume the powers and duties of the office as Acting President. Thereafter, when the President transmits to the President pro tempore of the Senate and the Speaker of the House of Representatives his written declaration that no inability exists, he shall resume the powers and duties of his office unless the Vice President and a majority of either the principal officers of the executive department or of such other body as Congress may by law provide, transmit within four days to the President pro tempore of the Senate and the Speaker of the House of Representatives their written declaration that the President is unable to discharge the powers and duties of his office. Thereupon Congress shall decide the issue, assembling within forty-eight hours for that purpose if not in session. If the Congress within twenty-one days after receipt of the latter written declaration, or, if Congress is not in session within twenty-one days after Congress is required to assemble, determines by two-thirds vote of both Houses that the President is unable to discharge the powers and duties of his office, the Vice President shall continue to discharge the same as Acting President; otherwise, the President shall resume the powers and duties of his office.

The Twenty-Fifth Amendment set new ground for the succession of the President in case the President is unable to fulfill his duties. This amendment has been invoked several times during the Presidencies of George W. Bush and Ronald Reagan. When these Presidents had to undergo surgeries they had the Vice President stand in as Acting President only for very brief periods, in both cases it was a matter of hours.

AMENDMENT XXVI

Section 1. The right of citizens of the United States, who are eighteen years of age or older, to vote shall not be denied or abridged by the United States or by any State on account of age.

Section 2. The Congress shall have power to enforce this article by appropriate legislation.

The age of voting has been expanded to include eighteen-year-old citizens. The amendment process has expanded the voting franchise. First we saw the extension of voting rights to all men regardless of their race or ethnicity if they were over twenty-one years old. Next, women received the right to vote.

Now the Twenty-Sixth Amendment gave everyone over 18 the right to vote. We will discuss later in this book, the irony of how low voting turnout is for Americans. The Constitution has expanded the number of voters and the turnout of those voters keeps declining.

AMENDMENT XXVII

No law varying the compensation for the services of Senators and Representatives shall take effect until an election of Representatives shall have intervened.

This amendment was a reaction to the pay raises Congress tried to vote for itself. The President and Vice President received a raise after the 2000 election. Simply put, Congress gives itself a raise then there will be an opportunity for people to choose to reelect the Representative. This ensures the people exercise a reaction to when Congress votes itself a pay raise. We have completed our examination of the specific amendments to the Constitution. There are several general conclusions we can discuss. First, specific problems such as alcohol abuse should not be encased in the Constitution. Amendments work when they deal with a strategic and general problem. Secondly, the Amendment process is not a good process if you need to solve a political problem, such as term limits of the Presidency or salary of Congress. And thirdly, the Amendment process is important because it does protect the average citizen from the excesses of the central government. The process has been able to keep the Constitution relevant throughout the more than two centuries it has been the supreme law of the land.

CONCLUSION

The Constitution of the United States is a living document. We have shown this with our discussion of the different amendments that have been passed and one repealed during the lifetime of the document and the Republic. The amending process works and also illustrates the first time in history where a society tried to protect the individual from the excesses of a strong central government. At roughly the same time of the adoption of the Constitution, the French Revolution and the excesses of mass terror and ultimately dictatorship were being witnessed by Americans. The amendment process prevented these excesses in America.

In this chapter, we have gone through every amendment and have seen the original text and some comments about how to interpret the language of the amendments into everyday life. The first ten amendments are known as the Bill of Rights. These amendments protect both the state and individual from unreasonable action of government. The term reasonableness is subjective; however, we can define it as how an average person would react to a particular situation. Underlying the criterion of reasonableness is probable cause. Probable cause or the chain of causation is a system that the police and courts use in order not to act arbitrarily. The average person has protections that shelter them from prosecution. However, these protections are primarily designed to insure innocent people are not wrongly put in prison. The burden of proof to convict someone in our system is on the state. The Amendments to the Constitution provide a procedure everyone acknowledges is weighed in favor of presuming people are innocent. It was designed like this because the police powers of the state are so strong and easily abused.

The Founding Fathers wanted to make it difficult to take someone's liberty away for a violation of the law. Have we strayed from the original intent of the Founding Fathers? We have included the original text of the Constitution in this chapter and in the previous chapter so you can think about this question. The local, state and federal governments produce a large number of laws every year. The California legislature alone passes an average of 1500 laws a year. We have laws that regulate skateboarding, drug use, driving, walking your dog and even what type of paint you can use when you redecorate your house. The explosion of governmental activity since World War II has made a discussion on our protections from the police powers of the state very important.

The Amendment process has produced a legal idea of Civil Liberties. Civil Liberties and Civil Rights are again unique properties of the American system. In the next chapter, we will define and examine these concepts. Now that you understand both sides of the Constitution, the forming of a strong central government, and the protections from that government for the individual and state, we can trace the development of Civil Liberties and Civil Rights.

The Bill of Rights

TRUE OR FALSE QUESTIONS

1. Thomas Jefferson, James Madison and John Adams were anti-Federalists. T / F

2. The *Federalist Papers* gave arguments for ratifying the Constitution. T / F

3. The small states were against ratification. T / F

4. The first ten amendments are called the Bill of Rights. T / F

5. The First Amendment is a recipe for political opposition to the Government. T / F

6. Americans have the freedom to own guns. T / F

7. The Fifth Amendment requires that Americans talk to the police. T / F

8. There are three ways to amend the Constitution. T / F

9. *Federalist No. 10* is not very famous and not very useful in convincing people on the ratification debate. T / F

10. Thomas Jefferson said about the Constitution "in hopes that they will amend it whenever they shall find the work wrong." T / F

MULTIPLE CHOICE QUESTIONS

11. The First Amendment includes protections except for
    a. speech
    b. searches
    c. religion
    d. assembly

12. Lobbying is protected under the
    a. Third Amendment
    b. Second Amendment
    c. First Amendment
    d. Tenth Amendment

13. Protection from unreasonable searches is found in
    a. Second Amendment
    b. First Amendment
    c. Fourth Amendment
    d. Sixth Amendment

14. The Congress has the power to collect income taxes because of
    a. Fifteenth Amendment
    b. First Amendment
    c. Sixteenth Amendment
    d. Fifth Amendment

15. Originally U.S. Senators were selected by State Legislatures however, this was changed by

  a. Sixteenth Amendment
  b. Tenth Amendment
  c. Eighteenth Amendment
  d. Seventeenth Amendment

16. Prohibition was enacted by the passage of the Twenty-Third Amendment which outlawed
  a. marijuana
  b. heroin
  c. ecstasy
  d. beer

17. The limit of people to serve two terms for President was begun by the passage of
  a. Twenty-Second Amendment
  b. Tenth Amendment
  c. Twenty-Fourth Amendment
  d. Second Amendment

18. Women earned the vote by passage of the Twentieth Amendment which passed in
  a. 1930
  b. 1940
  c. 1970
  d. 1920

19. The Fourteenth and Fifteenth Amendments gave voting and citizenship to
  a. ex-slaves who are men
  b. women
  c. 18 year olds
  d. Native Americans

20. How many amendments have there been to the Constitution
  a. 19
  b. 18
  c. 25
  d. 27

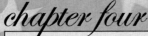

CIVIL RIGHTS AND CIVIL LIBERTIES: THEIR DIFFERENCES

INTRODUCTION

The Americans of the 1780s had a fear of government and a passion for liberty. We can see this in the language that is used in the Constitution. What does it mean for us in the twenty-first century? In the previous chapter, we said the Constitution was a living document with ramifications for our everyday lives. In this chapter, we will trace the development of two important concepts: Civil Rights and Civil Liberties. We first define Civil Rights and trace the development of the concept of Civil Rights using the African-American experience. We then widen our analysis to other groups who are advocating for their Civil Rights. This analysis ends with a discussion on the backlash we see and the challenges we face as a society on issues concerning diversity and Civil Rights. In the second section of this chapter, we define the concept of Civil Liberties.

We examine how the language of the Bill of Rights has been implemented to create a balance between Civil Liberties of the individual and the interests of the community in areas such as security,

order and peace. It is the objective of this chapter to illustrate how the language of the Constitution has been interpreted and refashioned in an effort to achieve one of the goals of the preamble of the Constitution "establish a system of justice." Civil Rights can be thought as a duty of the government to do something in order to give everyone equal protection under the law. There are two types of discrimination, *de jure* means by law or act of the government. The other type of discrimination is called *de facto*, which is discrimination as a matter of fact. We start the discussion of Civil Rights by examining the failure of the Founding Fathers in outlawing slavery and the ramifications of their failure.

CIVIL RIGHTS: A MISCARRIAGE AT BIRTH

Starting with the Constitution, the United States government was enforcing laws that discriminated against African-Americans. If the Founding Fathers would have found a way to eliminate slavery, then the responsibility of race relations may have been addressed by different organizations such as churches or service organizations. However, this is not the case. The Constitution had embedded in it the compromise that insured slavery would be part of the American landscape for another seventy-five years. In Article I, Section 2, there is language that produced the compromise. The "three-fifths of other persons" is the language that set aside the issues of justice for a whole race of people that were living in the United States. Consequently, this language enabled the government of the United States to enforce an entire body of laws that kept people in bondage. Some forget there were laws that prohibited the teaching of slaves to read or write, slave marriages and family relations had no legal bearing, and the legal status of a slave was the same as a piece of property.

The Founding Fathers thought slavery would actually die out in the South as it had in the North. Before the invention of the cotton engine (gin), a slave would spend eight hours and produce a handful of cotton lint (lint is the useful part of the cotton plant that can be made into thread). After Eli Whitney's invention, the machine was able to produce pounds of lint in a matter of hours. The economics of slavery had changed. It was possible to send cotton lint to Europe and keep the textile mills of England supplied. During this period, you have the South believing in a slogan that cotton was king, and because of the need of cotton to Europe, the countries of Europe would recognize and help a southern plan for seceding from the United States.

As slavery started to become profitable in the South, there were people primarily in the North, and also in the beginning primarily Quakers, who started to organize and mobilize a movement that would one day abolish slavery. The country became polarized between the North and the South. The issue of slavery colored all political discussions and the balance between slave state and non-slave state was becoming impossible. At the same time, the government was enforcing the institution of slavery. If you were a run-away slave and found yourself in a free state, it did not matter, you could be caught and returned to your previous condition of slavery. The Supreme Court of the United States weighed in on the issue of run-away slaves with the *Dred Scott* decision.[1] In this decision, the Supreme Court basically said slaves did not have the rights of other Americans.

This political conflict turned into a military conflict with the election of Abraham Lincoln in 1860. The South looked at Lincoln's election as the "radicalization" of the North—meaning the North would now actively seek to abolish slavery or in the worse case, as John Brown had done, to try to arm the slaves in order to have a violent social revolution. Starting with South Carolina, the Southern states started to leave the Union. At the beginning of the Civil War, people believed it would be a short and bloodless war.

It was neither. In the beginning of Lincoln's presidency, he believed he could separate the idea of abolishing slavery and preserving the Union. He was wrong. The Civil War cost thousands of lives and after two years of bitter fighting, Lincoln realized if he asked African-Americans to fight in the war, then he would have to abolish slavery at the end of the conflict. On September 22, 1862 President Lincoln announced the Emancipation Proclamation that ended slavery.[2] This did two things for Lincoln: it again enabled African-Americans to fight for their liberty, and it prevented the European capitals from recognizing the Confederacy. Especially the British (who were against slavery) were not now going to support a country that embedded slavery inside their Constitution. The Confederacy ultimately lost the Civil War and Lincoln was assassinated.

The Constitution was amended to answer the question of the status of the ex-slaves and the failure of the government of the United States to equally protect all of its citizens. A system of justice that was talked about in the preamble of the Constitution, although miscarried at birth, now had a chance to be realized at the end of the bloodiest war America had known.

THE END OF SLAVERY, NOT THE END OF GOVERNMENT SANCTIONED DISCRIMINATION

The end of the Civil War saw the adoption of the Thirteenth Amendment which ended slavery, and the Fourteenth Amendment that gave ex-slaves citizenship and guaranteed them equal protection and due process. The discrimination continued as soon as the war ended. Reconstruction saw the passage of the black codes of 1865–1866.[3] These rules have been

---

[1] Samuel Eliot Morison, *The Oxford History of the American People: Volume Two: 1789 through Reconstruction*. New York: Penguin Group, p. 435.

[2] Ibid.

[3] Ibid. p. 507.

called by some historians similar to the rules that the Nazis perpetrated against the Jews during the years 1933–1945. These codes included restrictions on all aspects of economic, political and civil activity. Unlike the Nazis, the Southern whites did not want to exterminate the ex-Slaves. They wanted to exploit their labor as they had before the war.[4]

In other parts of the United States, people were encouraged to better themselves. Night schools, English language centers and programs to help new immigrants sprang up in order for people to fulfill their version of the American dream. However, in the South from the end of the Civil War to the end of World War II, it was thought that if an African-American was trying to better his or her life through education or through entrepreneurship, the white community looked at the person as being "uppity." This term was still prevalent in the South until recent times.

These attitudes of the South did get codified into law as early as 1883. There is a legal doctrine that is articulated by the Supreme Court. The case of *Plessy v. Ferguson* said that it was acceptable to have different public schools, transportation and other facilities based on race. However, these facilities could be separate but they had to be equal. Sadly, this was the law of the land from the 1880s to 1954.[5]

Plessy highlighted the government's involvement in discrimination against the African-American community we saw in the South until the end of World War II. At the end of the War, three developments happened to bring the issues of the African-American community to the forefront. The first was the internal movement of the African-American community to other parts of the country outside the South, between 1940–1960, the African-American population in northern states trebled.[6] By 1960, New York State had the largest concentration of African-Americans in the country. This created a larger stage for the issues of the Civil Rights movement. By the movement of people, race relations had evolved from a regional issue to a national issue. Concurrently, outside of the United States, the decolonization of the world saw many new nations that were becoming independent that were not controlled by the Europeans or Americans. The contradiction between American ideals and the government treatment of Afri-

can-Americans was made apparent by Soviet and other Communist propaganda. While more and more nations were becoming independent in Africa, Asia and in the Southern Hemisphere, the job of selling America's vision in the Cold War became very difficult. Leaders such as Nassar, Ho Chi Mihn, and Fidel Castro spent a great deal of their time pointing out the difference between the domestic environment of African-Americans and what the United States was saying about human rights and the living conditions of other people around the world.

Finally, and probable most importantly, was the leadership of the African-American community itself. Especially if we examine the period from 1945–1968 when the African-American community, and leaders such as Dr. Martin Luther King, Jr., tried to use tactics developed by Ghandi for Indian independence. King understood the contradiction of the ideals that were written in the U.S. Constitution and the everyday life of injustice the average African-American had to suffer. The Civil Rights movement would have a two track strategy: the first, was to use the federal courts to redress the government enforced or *de jure* discrimination that plagued the everyday life of African-Americans in the South. The second, was to use the average Americans' sense of justice and fairness to stop politically the lock on political power that was enjoyed by, ironically, the Democratic party of the South.

SEPARATE CANNOT BE EQUAL

Thurgood Marshall and the National Association for the Advancement of Colored People (NAACP) pursued the first strategy to rid the United States of this unjust legal doctrine called "separate but equal." Marshall and his fellow lawyers believed, ultimately the legal system of the United States could not survive on this contradiction. Under the Fourteenth Amendment, American society promised the exslaves and their descendants that they would have equal protection under the law.[7] The doctrine of separate but equal made this promise a sham for the African-American community. Their plan was to go to court and challenge the law.

In 1954, in a court case called *Brown v. Board of Education of Topeka,* the Supreme Court ruled that it was unjust to have separate public school systems based on race. The Supreme Court understood that it was an impossibility to have separate but equal.

[4]Ibid.

[5]Samuel Eliot Morison, *The Oxford History of the American People: Volume Three: 1869 through the Death of John F. Kennedy.* New York: Penguin Group, 1972, p. 108.

[6]Ibid.

[7]Ibid. pp. 456–457.

The Supreme Court ordered schools be integrated "with all deliberate speed." Thurgood Marshall had succeeded in demonstrating to the Supreme Court and most Americans the separate but equal doctrine was unjust. The first part of the Civil Rights movement had begun—the effort to integrate public education and other facilities in order to have equal access and equal protection under the law.

At the same time, Dr. Martin Luther King, Jr. was starting to organize political action to integrate public facilities. Under King's leadership, the Civil Rights movement started to use economic and political power in order to change the public accommodations of the South. Many Americans from different regions in the country did not realize the separation of accommodations that all of the Southern states had up until the 1960s. African-Americans could not eat at the same lunch counters, use the same restrooms or seats as whites on buses or other modes of public transportation. Authorities responded to the widespread sit-in movement by arresting people simply for sitting at a lunch counter. The Supreme Court ruled in *Garner v. Louisana* that people who participated in sit-ins at lunch counters was not inherently a disturbance of the peace, and threw out the wholesale arrests. The Civil Rights movement would spread and become a national movement stirring the conscience of northern and western cities as African-Americans tried to agitate for better living and working conditions in other parts of the Country.

Tactics used by the mainstream Civil Rights organizations were peaceful and organized—sit-ins, boycotts, and marches were used to mobilize the African-American community and sympathetic communities to highlight the injustice. While at the same time, these activities brought the issues to the forefront on the public agenda.

THE EFFORT TO END "DE JURE" DISCRIMINATION

In 1957, the U.S. Senate passed the first Civil Rights bill.[8] This bill was engineered by Lyndon Johnson, who at that time was the Majority Leader of the Senate and he had plans to run for President in 1960. The tricks of southern Senators could not prevent a bill, but they did produce a weak law. The law was used to prevent Southern states from creating "second class" citizens, to use President Eisenhower's

words, on his orders to enforce the integration of schools in Little Rock.

During the fall of 1960, Dr. King was arrested in Georgia and sentenced to ten years and hard labor, many in the Civil Rights movement worried that King would get hurt while he was in jail. During the Presidential campaign the Democratic nominee John F. Kennedy called the Georgia Governor to pressure for the release of Dr. King. Richard Nixon who was the Republican nominee and current Vice President was urged by prominent African-Americans such as Jackie Robinson to help the jailed Civil Rights leader. Kennedy acted and Nixon did not. This started a political earthquake in the South.

Roughly for a hundred years from 1860–1960 the South was known to vote Democratic. The South had famous politicians who had made their careers on upholding the evil system of segregation. Two were able to run for the Presidency, Strom Thurmond in 1948 and George Wallace in 1968, who tried to capture the backlash from changes in the political landscape. Both of these efforts were not very serious. The earthquake came when northern Democrats saw the African-American community in large urban centers around the country as a new source for their political power. The thought went that if you capture the urban center you can capture the state. The Democratic party took over the mantle of Civil Rights and became partners with the Civil Rights movement to pass important Civil Rights legislation, especially in the Voting Rights Act of 1964 and the Civil Rights Act of 1968.

The Republican party—the party of Lincoln, that fought the Civil War and freed the slaves, became the party of the South. White Southerners who previously supported segregation became Republicans. The Republican party was identified by Senator Barry Goldwater's (the Republican nominee for President in 1964) "no" vote on the Voting Rights Act of 1964. This led to the image that the Republicans did not identify with the interests of the Civil Rights movement in general and the African-American community specifically.

In 1968, Dr. Martin Luther King, Jr. was assassinated in Memphis, Tennessee. Later in that year, Robert F. Kennedy would be assassinated in California. The death of these two leaders would cement the Civil Rights movement and the Democratic party and in contrast make the Republican party the dominant party in the South. In light of this historical development, the African-American community is the most loyal of the ethnic communities that sup-

---

[8]Robert Carro, *Master of the Senate.*

port the Democratic party. To redress the effects of *de jure* discrimination, plans were made to try to correct the economic problems facing the African-American community. Some thought quotas based on race in college admissions and job placement and government contracting (known as "set asides") would help fund the economic development of the African-American community. By the mid 1970s these programs were established and they were called Affirmative Action.

The heart of the problem of race relations today between the African-American community and the white community is how can a society redress such an evil practice as slavery? One can draw a direct line—between slavery and the government of the United States which directly enforced this institution from 1789–1865. After the Civil War, the government then allowed the Southern States to use their police powers to discriminate against the African-American community from 1865–1964. This is a fact. Even if we take the most conservative estimate of time that the U.S. government has been involved in the enforcement of *de jure* (by law) discrimination against the African-American community, it is 175 years.

After the passing of the important Civil Rights legislation and the assassination of Dr. King, some people thought that race relations in the United States would improve. The problem was discrimination has two forms—*de jure* (meaning by law) and *de facto* (meaning as a matter of fact). The integration of the South was easier since the segregation generated by the South was primarily through legal statute. It was more difficult in the North. School districts including Chicago, Milwaukee, Los Angeles, Omaha and Boston had famous protests when it came to integrating or busing children to different schools in order to obey court ordered de-segregation. Housing, job opportunities and other realities of racial discrimination could not be changed by changing laws.

By the 1980s, there was a backlash against the Civil Rights movement in the North and in the South. During the 1950s and 1960s, Northern urban centers sided with the Civil Rights movement until the African-American communities in the North started to complain about the *de facto* discrimination they were receiving in Northern and Western cities of the country.

Today, one of the biggest challenges facing the United States is the challenge of race relations. The policies of affirmative action and racial quotas are

bankrupt. Contractual set asides have been criticized and have become a vehicle of corruption. The issue, however, must be addressed. If the primary result of *de jure* discrimination as enforced by the United States government is the lack of economic opportunity, how do you redress 175 years of discrimination? Yes, the North did win the Civil War and yes maybe your ancestors did not own slaves. These two arguments are rather silly and irrelevant. The problem is, in the white community, leaders see addressing these issues as a no-win situation. If you challenge affirmative action or have any different ideas about redressing some of the effects of past discrimination, you can be labeled a racist. Some in the African-American community are calling for reparations. This idea is interesting but almost impossible to implement. How do you quantify the truly evil acts our government was involved in? Can you erase the effects of discrimination with a check? Most people believe you cannot. Although most would agree reparations will not be paid, the issues surrounding reparations and the actions of history should be explored and race relations should be at the top of the political agenda, not to get someone elected, but as President Eisenhower said, not have any "second class" citizens.

This thumbnail sketch of the history of discrimination against the African-American community demonstrates the uniqueness of the African-American experience because of the role of the government. Another group that the government used its police powers against was the Native American community. While the Native Americans were not slaves, they were driven from their traditional land and required by the government to move into reservations, where the government acted as a provider of goods, services and acted to squash their culture.

APPROPRIATION OF NATIVE AMERICAN LANDS AND THE TRAIL OF TEARS

As the government enforced slavery on the African-American community, it was also trying to deal with the Nations that preceded the European experience on the North American Continent—the Native Americans. Starting in 1789 and the ratification of the Constitution, Native Americans had a different status. Either they were considered an independent country and had sovereignty (from the early time of the Constitution to the end of the Civil War the U.S. government signed over 70 treaties with the different Native American tribes), or their status was one of second class status inside American society. The first wave of immigration against Native American hunting grounds started in the 1840s with the Gold Rush. It has been reported there were over 100,000 Native Americans in California in 1850.[9] By 1860 there were barely 35,000 an Indian Affairs report said "despoiled the irresistible forced of land of their fathers; with no country on earth to which they can migrate; in the midst of a people with whom they cannot assimilate." Miners and the cattlemen had started to take over the land in the West and in the Great Plains.[10]

The Civil War and the invention of the railroad was the spur that started the great expansion to the West by white settlers. At the end of the Civil War, many rebel soldiers and their families found that their towns were burned down. They had no "country" to go back to. Some moved outside the country to Brazil, or Mexico. Others decided to move to southern states that suffered much less damage such as Texas. Remember most of the population in the North and South were farmers at this time. In the plain states they had land. This was great opportunity compared to living under the military occupation of reconstruction. So, the Civil War uprooted many people who sought to start over and to get away from the domination of the central government.

Another feature of the Civil War was the apparent success for railroads. Congress before the war had considered building a trans-continental railroad, two routes were considered one through the North and one through the South. Once the South left the Union, the northern route was chosen. This route was designed to link the state of California with the other states. California basically lobbied for the railway since it was the only practical way to be part of the other states in the nation. In 1862, the Sioux of the Dakotas went on the warpath after miners had invaded Colorado and white settlers moved along the upper Mississippi valley in Minnesota. The Sioux killed over 1000 white settlers. Retribution was swift and deadly for the next twenty-five years conflict between the Whites and the Native Americans was a constant part of life in the West.

Almost all of the male settlers after the Civil War were army veterans. This meant they knew how to use guns and were used to combat. The Civil War produced a generation of men who were trained and conditioned on the horrendous fields of battle, where it was not uncommon to see 50,000 men being killed on both sides in one day. This training made it possible for the workers who were veterans of the Civil War to be able to put down their picks and pick up a rifle to fight the Native Americans warriors in battle or to destroy their hunting grounds which drove the tribes off the land. On May 10, 1869, the first trans-continental railroad was complete. This facilitated white settlement of the middle part of the United States.

In 1881, President Arthur started the paternalistic relationship that would be adopted by Washington which would culminate in the Dawes Act, which established a policy of trying to break up the reservations. This act tried to get the Plain Native American to start farming. The problem of course was these tribes were hunters. Since the average Native American was not trained in farming, they tended to lease or sell the land the government allotted them. Therefore, in the fifty years after 1887, Native American land holding fell from 138 million acres to 48 million acres.[11] The Native Americans wanted to be left alone, however, they were in the way of railroad, cattle and mining interests. Thomas Jefferson, after he heard the report of Lewis and Clark, thought it would take seven generations by seven generations to settle the West. It actually took less than forty years.

The Native Americans were put in reservations in order to move them out of the way for the expansion of the West. Again, we see the government of the United States actively involved in the manner in which the Native American tribes would be handled. This is again a product of *de jure* discrimination.

There is no question, the Native Americans have been discriminated against. Their Civil Rights were violated, although they were not enslaved, their land was taken and their life style was stolen from them. Even after they were put on reservations, land grabbers found ways to take away their birthright. In 1924, Native Americans were made American citizens. The Civil Rights movement for Native Americans began to crystallize after the publication of the book *Bury My Heart at Wounded Knee* which highlighted the plight of Native Americans. Similar to the African-American Civil Rights movement, there were several strategies—one was litigation. Native American groups have litigated for the right to use peyote for religious use, and have litigated and won damages for land that

---

[9]Samuel Eliot Morison, *The Oxford History of the American People: Volume Three: 1869 through the Death of John F. Kennedy.* New York: Penguin Group, 1974, p. 64.
[10]Ibid.

---

[11]Ibid.

was taken away in Maine. However, the Supreme Court has given States a lot of leeway to deal with the Native American tribes in more bi-lateral relationships. Although the situation is different for Native Americans, there is a realization their Civil Rights have been violated in the past.

The African-American and Native American cases are illustrative of *de jure* discrimination. Their historical experiences were only possible by the involvement of the U.S. government. In the next sections of this chapter, we will examine other groups who call for their rights vis-à-vis governmental discrimination. However, the case of a positive governmental action is less clear. Their arguments are a mixture of *de jure* discrimination and *de facto* discrimination.

THE HISPANIC AND ASIAN EXPERIENCE IN THE U.S.

People who have Spanish as their native language and come from the Western Hemisphere are referred to as Hispanics. The label covers a truly diverse community that includes: Cubans, Mexicans, Puerto Ricans and others from Central and South America. The Cubans and Mexicans are interested in immigration issues. Puerto Ricans are American citizens because Puerto Rico is an American commonwealth. As one can see, there are real differences when one examines specifically the issues that matter to the different Hispanic communities. Traditionally, Mexican-Americans have had low political participation. In the Spring of 2006, there were a series of demonstrations that called for immigration reform and bilingual opportunities. This may signal a change in the attitude of Mexican-Americans especially in the West and Southwest. These rallies in favor of immigration amnesty have also caused a backlash from other communities in which many are calling for English to be the official language of the country. Although laws such as these do not force people to conduct their everyday business in English, it does require the official language of the government to be in English, which could cause disruption to people participating in elections or in petitioning the government about their grievances.

Similar to the Hispanic identification, the label of Asian-American is complex and not very helpful. Some include all communities including the communities of South Asia. Others argue Asian-Americans are only from the far-east. This label is not very helpful. Some groups have been in the country for over

two hundred years such as Chinese-Americans. They have suffered *de facto* discrimination and *de jure* discrimination. While others such as Vietnamese-Americans and Hmong-Americans have emigrated as a result of the fighting in South East Asia. There are some similarities. Most Asian-American communities like Mexican-Americans are reluctant to get involved in politics. There are now some cases where we have elected officials from these groups but there is a reluctance to become politically involved.

Both the Hispanic and Asian Americans are using the federal courts to redress discrimination when it occurs in their communities. The infamous internment of the Japanese was solved by an apology by the United States and a small monetary payment to signify a symbolic reparation. These groups are awakening to their Civil Rights and are becoming more and more politically aware in our society.

GENDER, SAME SEX, AGE DISCRIMINATION AND DISABLED AMERICANS: NEW FRONTIERS IN CIVIL RIGHTS

When the Fourteenth Amendment of the Constitution was passed, some wanted to add the word sex in order to give women the right to vote. The writers of the amendment decided specifically not to include voting rights for women. Women would not get the right to vote until 1920 after another major war. There was governmental action to prevent women from voting, owning property and being paid the same wages as men for the same work. After 1920, women received the right to vote and their voting participation rates are the same as men. Women tend to vote and act politically as their male counterparts. If they are minority women they tend to vote the same as minority men. If they are white women, they tend to vote and participate at the same rate. Political scientists who study voting behavior have concluded gender does not play a big role in determining voting.

During the 1980s and 1990s, there was a large discussion of the gender gap. This said that women would tend to vote more liberally than men, since women are more concerned about domestic issues and welfare issues. This proved not to be the case. Women became active in politics during the early part of the abolitionist movement. Abortion, and gender-based discrimination in the workplace have been the cornerstones of fighting for Civil Rights for women. The key issue in examining discrimination based on gender is whether it was unconstitutional according to the courts.

Another area that is in our discussion of current events and has been reported deeply by the media, is the issue of same sex marriage. We have examined this topic in Chapter One. Is being gay a Civil Right or a personal liberty? The courts have yet to answer this issue. Many who advocate Civil Rights protection for sexual orientation argue it is not a choice, therefore, should be protected from discrimination. Others have countered being gay is a choice, and although people who are gay should be protected from violence and harassment, it is a personal choice that should not be lumped in with other protected classes. Science and the courts are still grappling with this issue. The issue again is whether the government has sanctioned the discrimination or do people have the liberty to discriminate on personal behaviors they might disagree with. The gay community points to the military and discrimination on social policies such as adoption, marriage and sharing of employment benefits. Literally, the jury is still out on this discussion. Our society has not made the decision on Civil Rights for the gay community. A majority of Americans believe the gay community should not be discriminated against when it comes to employment benefits, inheritance of property or access to social services. Most agree to civil unions; however, a majority of Americans in several states have opposed same sex marriage amendments.

The strategy for the gay rights movement has been to use the courts and political activity to bring these issues to the agenda, similar to other Civil Rights groups we have examined. We will see if these groups can successfully convince a majority of voters and judges that being gay should be a Civil Right and protected by governmental action.

Another category is age discrimination. Most of us will become old. At universities and colleges there used to be mandatory retirement rules. The Supreme Court has judged these are unconstitutional—they violate the rights of older workers. Is being old a status that needs governmental protection? This issue, similar to gay rights, has not been settled. With the "baby-boom" generation retiring and requiring more and more resources, you will see the strongest lobbying organization in Washington, D.C., the American Association of Retired People (AARP) get even stronger. They are strong because older people vote, have money, have time to volunteer, and get involved in politics. We may see a confrontation between generations that made the 1960s generation gap look very mild.

Finally, disabled Americans is the final category of Civil Rights we will be discussing. The Americans with Disabilities Act (ADA) has settled this question. Disabled Americans are a protected class under Civil Rights legislation. A public institution must have reasonable accommodations for people with disabilities in order for them to be employed. The interesting thing about the status of disabled American is the number of people who call themselves disabled in America is vastly increasing. The graying of the population makes the increase of people with this status very likely.

We have discussed the various aspects of Civil Rights. Remember, Civil Rights are a governmental obligation to act in order to protect the rights of protected classes against discrimination. Historically, these classes have been based on race, ethnic background, and religious background. Today, the protections have enlarged to encompass disability status and there are movements to include sexual orientation and age. This discussion on Civil Rights began with the failure of the Constitution to end slavery. This examination has developed a spectrum of governmental actions from outright enforcement of the depriving of certain groups' Constitutional rights to a more nuanced governmental action that leaves room for debate. In the next section of this Chapter, we will examine Civil Liberties—those protections against governmental action that are unique to our society.

CIVIL LIBERTIES

Civil Rights are an active duty of the government in order to enable equal protection under the law for different protected groups. We have seen a spectrum of governmental reaction to the enforcement of discrimination and the failure to enforce groups' Civil Rights. The groups we have discussed, have learned to approach their issues with both political activism and legal action. Civil Liberties are different from Civil Rights. Civil Liberties are a government "do not do" list. They are protection against government intrusion in our daily lives. Civil Liberties can be organized into two major sections. Protection from government and protection from the rule of the majority in certain areas of life.

Our Civil Liberties come from the Bill of Rights of the Constitution. We have discussed these in the previous chapter. The first ten amendments are protection from the government and individuals. Many of the Founding Fathers argued the Bill of Rights did not extend to actions of state governments. In 1833, the Supreme Court confirmed this with the case *Barron v Baltimore*.[12] However, after the Civil War and the passage of the Fourteenth Amendment, there has been a constant movement by the Supreme Court to incorporate Civil Liberties into many of the actions of state governments.

We have examined the various freedoms we have under the Bill of Rights. Why are people afraid of government? We have seen how governments' power has grown. In modern times, we see the uniting of technology and political power to create totalitarian systems such as Stalin's Russia and Hitler's Germany. Even more recently the genocide we see in parts of Africa serves as a reminder of the power of the unchecked governmental police power. We have seen people in the former Yugoslavia live peaceably for decades and in the matter of two years rape and reinvent the methods of ethnic cleansing in Europe. Civil Liberties are an effort to prevent genocide and ethnic cleansing in order to prevent governmental powers from being used to such ends. Civil Liberties protect us from the government and the tyranny of the majority. This means that you do have the freedom and the protection to be different from the majority—in your speech, religion, political, civic and private lives. Civil Liberties entail the true nature of democracy—the freedom to be yourself and organize your community as you and members of the particular community wish.

CONCLUSION

Civil Rights and Civil Liberties are guaranteed under the Constitution. However, these two concepts are very different. Civil Rights we have defined as a governmental duty to ensure there is equal protection under the law for everyone, particularly protected groups. These groups include race, ethnic, religious, gender, age, disability and sexual orientation. It is illegal to discriminate against someone on these grounds. Civil Liberties entail the prevention of governmental action. You do have a right to act in ac-

cordance to your own ideas when it comes to speech, religion, press, petitioning the government and being free from unreasonable searches and seizures and other liberties that we have examined in the previous chapter. This difference is very important, and most people—even professional Political Scientists—confuse these two concepts. We have examined the failure of government to insure equal protection under the law to certain racial and ethnic groups. In order to protect this failure of our system, we have seen groups take on both a legal strategy using the courts and the ideals expressed in the Constitution to enforce their rights as Americans and a political strategy in order to highlight the failure to live up to the Founding Fathers ideas.

Civil Liberties are composed of the freedoms we have in order to prevent governmental action against individuals. We may find action by certain individuals and groups to be personally offensive or the government may find them to be inconvenient for implementing governmental policies (such as the ACLU). They are protections for all of us from the growth of governmental power and the intolerance that can be displayed by the majority in every society.

This completes our discussion on Civil Rights and Civil Liberties specifically and the Constitution generally. In the next chapter, we will see how the Founding Fathers and the governmental leaders who followed, implemented and tried to interpret relationship between State government and the Federal government. They did not eliminate the states, this new central government was superimposed on the structure that was already established by tradition and necessity. The relationship between units of government is called Federalism. We will analyze the development of the relationship between local, state and the federal government and how it produces policies that are unique to the American system of government.

TERMS TO REMEMBER

DE JURE DISCRIMINATION
DE FACTO DISCRIMINATION
CIVIL RIGHTS
CIVIL LIBERTIES

[12]Daniel J. Elazar, "Federal-State Cooperation in the Nineteenth-Century United States." *Political Science Quarterly* 79, 1964, pp. 248–265.

Civil Rights and Civil Liberties: Their Differences

TRUE OR FALSE QUESTIONS

1. A Civil Right prevents action from the government.   T / F

2. The Founding Fathers thought slavery would die out by 1860.   T / F

3. Eli Whitney invented the Cotton Engine.   T / F

4. The British wanted to support the Confederacy because of slavery.   T / F

5. The Supreme Court helped enforce slavery and Jim Crow laws.   T / F

6. Martin Luther King, Jr. used economic pressure to change segregation policies in the South.   T / F

7. Civil Rights used non-violent methods to influence policy changes.   T / F

8. The Republican party was the party of Lincoln and therefore supported the Civil Rights bills passed in Congress.   T / F

9. George Wallace and Strom Thurmond both ran for President to try to capture the backlash from the Civil Rights movement.   T / F

10. Slavery was enforced by the government from the adoption of the Constitution to the Civil War.   T / F

MULTIPLE CHOICE QUESTIONS

11. The South needed slaves to work on plantations that grew primarily
    a. corn
    b. barley
    c. cotton
    d. hops

12. The Federal government enforced slavery from 1789 to
    a. 1860
    b. 1861
    c. 1862
    d. 1863

13. Martin Luther King, Jr. organized trying to change the segregation laws of
    a. Southern states
    b. Western states
    c. Northern states
    d. Eastern states

14. School segregation was ended due to the Supreme Court opinion of
    a. *Plessy v. Ferguson*
    b. *Marbury v. Madison*
    c. *Brown v. Board of Education of Topeka*
    d. *Main v. Bleaker*

15. Thurgood Marshall's legal career started when he worked for
    a. his own law office
    b. NAACP
    c. Howard Law School
    d. Supreme Court Law Clerk

16. Segregation that is enforced by law is called
    a. legal
    b. *de jure*
    c. *de facto*
    d. immoral

17. Segregation that is enforced because of conditions or environment is called
    a. *de facto*
    b. legal
    c. immoral
    d. *de jure*

18. The first Civil Rights bill after the Civil War was passed in
    a. 1948
    b. 1950
    c. 1968
    d. 1957

19. The Majority Leader who was responsible for the first Civil Rights bill to become law was from
    a. Texas
    b. Illinois
    c. Wisconsin
    d. New York

20. How many treaties did the Federal government sign with Native American tribes?
    a. 50
    b. 300
    c. 70
    d. 150

chapter five

IMAGE FROM DEFENSE VISUAL INFORMATION CENTER

FEDERALISM:
THE LIMITS OF POWER SHARING

INTRODUCTION

In the previous chapters, we have examined the predicament the Founding Fathers found themselves in with a government that did not work. Then, we saw how they solved the problems of the Articles of Confederation and the ratification process that gave the new country, known as the United States, a government that would help unify the states and produce an American political culture. The Constitution was not written in a vacuum. The Founding Fathers did not replace all of the governments that were in the thirteen states. Instead, they put this governmental structure over the local and state governments that were intact after the American Revolution.

Federalism is the study of this internal dynamic between units of government. In our system there is the Federal government in Washington, D.C. and the fifty state governments, and under the state governments there are counties, towns and usually incorporated cities. The first Federal government used the Constitution and traditions borrowed from the British Crown and the Articles of Confederation as ex-

amples of how different levels of government should interact with one another.

This chapter will examine three traditional forms of Federalism we see in the world. Next, we will trace the Constitutional elements that make Federalism possible. Then, we will describe the evolution of power between the Federal and state governments from the earliest time in the Republic until today. Finally, we will examine the increasing role of the Federal government in the traditional state realms of education, welfare, and public safety. This will enable us to have an understanding of the theoretical underpinnings the Founding Fathers had in mind, combined with the practical applications of these ideas by the generations that followed.

THREE MODELS OF GOVERNMENTAL ORGANIZATION

When we analyze internal governmental relations (Federalism), we can find three definitive models that most countries use. They are: unitary, confederacy, and federal. This classification is useful, since the political structure in a country usually highlights the political culture and the compromises that were formed when the country was trying to organize itself as a state.

The Unitary form of government is the first model we will examine. This form of government is the most popular. It has a centralized power structure, all decisions are made usually in the capital of the country and there is no local decision making. Local governmental units are used to administer the decisions that are made by the central government. Most countries have this form of government. Because most countries come from a monarchial tradition, kings tended to organize the countries they ruled into a convenient centralized structure. Countries such as France, Spain and England have this type (or a slightly modified type) of unitary government. An example of how centralized some of these governments have become is when Vietnam was a colony of France and all of the clocks in Vietnam (known as Indo-China during the French colonization) were set at Paris Central Time. Decisions were made in Paris for all of the colonies regardless of climate, economic standard or distance from Paris. One can see how resentment could build under this type of system. If you study the large multi-ethnic empires of the past, you will read stories about the education system, economic system and political system that caused local people who were a great distance from the capital, to resent and ultimately revolt from these unitary systems of government. Unitary means there is one central government that dominates the country.

The next model, used by countries when organizing their intergovernmental affairs is the confederation model. In this model, the local units dominate over a weak central governmental body. The center is never stronger than its parts. This model is adopted by a country when there are regional power blocks. Each individual unit jealously holds on to power causing (usually) inefficiency and weakness inside the central government of a country. The most famous confederacy is the Confederate States of America. The Southern states during the Civil War were famous for fighting amongst each other. Jefferson Davis, the President of the Confederate States of America constantly complained about his lack of power vis-à-vis President Lincoln. Of course, the Confederate States of America were formed to preserve the idea of State's rights. This made the economic lessons learned from the Founding Fathers lost on most of the Confederate leaders.

Another confederacy is the United Nations (U.N.). It may be more grammatically correct to say, another famous confederacy is the U.N., since sovereign states are the members of the U.N. and the U.N. cannot do anything if the member states do not agree. We hear crackpot ideas about the U.N. becoming a world government, or a U.N. army invading the United States. This would never happen as long as the U.S. or any other permanent member of the U.N. Security Council has a veto. The U.N. cannot do anything that France, Great Britain, Russia, China or the United State does not want the U.N. to do. If you have witnessed the U.N. responses to world crises, you can see how this form of government creates weakness and slow action by the countries and organizations who have adopted this model. Finally, the Articles of Confederation we have talked about in previous chapters of this book. The Founding Fathers had a very difficult time having a central government that was able to protect the peace and regulate the economy. Therefore, they replaced it with the third model of governmental organization—Federalism.

Federalism is a governmental structure that has the division of government articulated usually in a Constitution, or by political tradition. Authority is divided among the governmental units and usually those units have their survival guaranteed. Local units will make decisions about certain governmental functions, and the central, federal or national government will have primacy over other aspects of the government. The fifty United States each have a role in protecting their states and have primary roles in areas such as welfare and education. States usually organize local government into counties, towns, and cities.

Federalism was the practical solution to the issue of governmental reform. The Constitution had rewritten the rules for society at the national level. If the governing elite would have changed structure of the state and local governments, the Founding Fathers would have never succeeded in their effort in building a stronger central government. During this period of history, the state government had the dominant position in the governmental structure. Furthermore, the average person's loyalty was to their state government, not to a national government. Hence, the strapping on of this new central government over the individual state governments was a practical solution to the question of why we have a Federal structure of government.

THE EVOLUTION OF FEDERAL SUPERIORITY

Federalism has gone through different phases throughout the history of the United States. Soon after the ratification of the U.S. Constitution, there was a question of the role of the Congress vis-à-vis the power of the States. The process of the Federal Government[1] dominating over the state government would start as early as 1815 with the Supreme Court of Chief Justice Marshall ruling on the case of *McColloch v. Maryland*. There were two issues the Supreme Court ruled on: first, did the Congress have the power to charter a new U.S. Bank, and second, could a state tax one of the branches of the Bank. Marshall writes "The government of the Union . . . is emphatically and truly a government of the people. In form and substance it emanates from them. Its powers are granted by them, and are to be exercised directly on them and for their benefit." This is the classic definition of national sovereignty—going directly to the power of the people to organize the government as they saw fit. This was a huge power grab by the Supreme Court. What Marshall basically said is the Federal government is superior and the Supreme Court would determine how the Constitution would be interpreted.

On the other issue on the right of a state to tax a federally chartered institution, Marshall goes on to write:

THE GOVERNMENT OF THE UNION, THOUGH LIMITED IN ITS POWERS, IS SUPREME WITHIN ITS SPHERE OF ACTION. . . . WE ADMIT, AS ALL MUST ADMIT, THAT THE POWERS OF THE GOVERNMENT ARE LIMITED, AND THAT ITS LIMITS ARE NOT TO BE TRANSCENDED. BUT WE THINK THE SOUND CONSTRUCTION OF THE CONSTITUTION MUST ALLOW TO THE NATIONAL LEGISLATURE THAT DISCRETION, WITH RESPECT TO THE MEANS BY WHICH THE POWERS IT CONFERS ARE TO BE CARRIED INTO EXECUTION, WHICH WILL ENABLE THAT BODY TO PERFORM THE HIGH DUTIES ASSIGNED TO IT, IN THE MANNER MOST BENEFICIAL TO THE PEOPLE. LET THE END BE LEGITIMATE, LET IT BE WITHIN THE SCOPE OF THE CONSTITUTION, AND ALL MEANS WHICH ARE APPROPRIATE, WHICH ARE PLAINLY ADAPTED TO THAT END, WHICH ARE NOT PROHIBITED, BUT CONSIST WITH THE LETTER OF THE SPIRIT OF THE CONSTITUTION, ARE CONSTITUTIONAL.[2]

This gives enormous power to both the Congress and the Supreme Court. The Supreme Court in *McColloch* has said that although Congress's powers are limited, the limits are not put on by the state governments. The limit to Congress's power is the Constitution. Who can determine the limits of Congressional power is the Supreme Court. Using the power vested in popular sovereignty and the rule of law, Marshall establishes both the power of Congress to go beyond the "necessary and proper" clause in the Constitution and the power of the Supreme Court to interpret what is constitutional. This is the start of the dominance of the Federal government over state governments.

Another important Supreme Court case was *Gibbons v. Ogden*. The dispute in this case was over the regulation of steamboat traffic. New York State had chartered Robert Fulton the exclusive right to have steamboat traffic on the Hudson River. The Congress also chartered a company to run steamboats along the Hudson River.[3] As time went on and the Supreme Court ultimately heard the case, the issue and legal procedures had become very complicated. The Supreme Court used *Gibbons* to answer a basic issue—What is the extent of Congress's power under the commerce clause of the Constitution? The Supreme Court ruled that Congress did have the power to regulate commercial activity and the limits of the Congress under the Constitution, was limited to the specific language of the Constitution. In general, the Supreme Court ruled States did not have any authority to regulate interstate commerce. Specifically, the Court said, the state of New York did not have the power to charter steamboat companies on the Hudson River. This opinion is very important, it not only undercut the power of States, it gave Congress a guide in writing future legislation regarding interstate commerce. Congress would be involved in internal improvements of the transportation network that was designed to bind the nation together.

The Marshall Court had provided the groundwork for the ultimate superiority of the Federal government to overcome the sovereignty of the States. After Marshall's death, the new Court under Chief Justice Taney would backtrack on the idea of the superiority of the Federal government. Taney would author a doctrine called Dual Federalism. Dual Federalism was the belief that there was concurrent sovereignty between the states and the Federal gov-

[1]The term "Federal government" refers to the national government of the United States of America.
[2]Samuel Eliot Morison, *The Oxford History of the American People: Volume 2: 1789 through Reconstruction*. New York: Penguin Group, 1994, p. 134.
[3]Ibid.

ernment. Again, we see the language "separate but equal." Even after the Civil War, in the case *Plessy v. Ferguson* in 1896, the Supreme Court uses this language and permits the states the right to regulate civil rights notwithstanding the Constitutional amendments that passed after the Civil War.

The Supreme Court would try to explain the doctrine of Dual Federalism from the end of the Civil War to the start of the New Deal programs in 1933. It was a difficult thing to do since the doctrine was a failure and had two contradictory arguments. The first, being that the Federal government was superior in terms of regulating interstate commerce and the States had sovereignty when it came to the administration of civil rights and local police powers. This led to a confusing and costly amount of litigation that tried to determine the lines between interstate commerce and intrastate commerce. The New Deal ended the era of Dual Federalism.

The Great Depression lasted from 1929 until the start of World War II in 1941. The four years, from 1929 to 1932, saw unemployment at 25 percent and in the cities soup kitchens and breadlines were a common sight. Factory payrolls in 1931 were half of what they were in 1929. In 1932, Franklin D. Roosevelt was elected to the Presidency. In his inaugural address he stated: "First of all, let me assert my firm belief that the only thing we have to fear is fear itself—nameless, unreasoning, unjustified terror which paralyzes needed efforts to convert retreat into advance."[4] This was the trumpet call to end Dual Federalism.

Roosevelt was going to intervene in the economic and political lives of every American. During the first 100 days of the Roosevelt Administration there would be a record-setting agenda from March 9, 1933–June 16, 1933. Roosevelt and the Congress passed major legislative bills including the Emergency Banking Act, Economy Act, Civilian Conservation Corps, Gold Standard abandonment, Federal Emergency Relief Act, Tennessee Valley Authority and more. The New Deal, as these legislative packages were called, would create the greatest expansion of Federal government activity since the Civil War.

By the middle of the 1930s however, the Supreme Court would rule these acts went beyond the boundaries of the commerce clause. In the *Schechter Poultry* case, the Supreme Court ruled the National Recovery Act was unconstitutional. The court still believed in a limited role of government in economic issues. These justices soon were to die or retire by 1940, and an almost new Supreme Court was picked by Roosevelt. These Justices included: Hugo Black, William O. Douglas and Felix Frankfurter. They believed in the expanded role of government in the economy and changed the doctrine of Dual Federalism.[5]

The Great Depression and World War II that followed forced all levels of government to cooperate. The Federal government led the way; however, state and county governments were responsible for spending the money the Federal government provided. This historic scenario paved the wave for a whole generation to change the way the government worked. Americans looked to government for answers as far reaching as education, real estate, and the economy. Even landing on the moon was a function of government. This reached its climax in the Great Society programs of President Lyndon B. Johnson and the expansion of the Federal bureaucracy under President Richard M. Nixon's Administration. In 1980, when Ronald Reagan became President, he sought to change this arrangement and devised a plan called New Federalism.

New Federalism changed many of the categorical grant programs into less restrictive block grants. In the early 80s the relationship between the Federal government and the state government changed. Funding from the Federal government to local governmental units actually declined during the Reagan Administration. The philosophy of the Reagan Administration was to give some resources for state and local government but have less "strings" attached. This would enable local leaders to spend the money more wisely than if all the decisions were made in Washington, D.C. This sounds like a good idea, but there were issues such as minority rights and corruption on the state and local scale that may hinder this idea.

After President Reagan left office, the budget deficits were so large the Federal government had limited resources to spend on programs. During the Clinton years, the expansion of government continued, it continued with the use of unfunded mandates. These are rules written by the Federal government that must be followed by State governments. Examples of unfunded mandates include clean air and water legislation, access to facilities for disabled Americans and other programs. These unfunded mandates function to restrict the choices states have

[4]Samuel Eliot Morison, *The Oxford History of the American People: Volume 3: 1869 through the Death of John F. Kennedy.* New York: Penguin Group, 1994, p. 294.

[5]Ibid.

in setting priorities in spending. These unfunded mandates, create an environment where the decisions for spending on local and state issues occurs on the Federal level. While at the same time, the Federal government does not have to provide any money to implement these decisions. The use of unfunded mandates is symbolic for the transformation of our system of government. In the beginning of the Constitution, the States were the superior unit of government. People were loyal to their state, their identity was linked to the state they were born in. While today, the Federal government is superior, our state residence is only important when it comes to our drivers license and if we are going to school, if we have to pay in-state tuition. The Federal government has expanded its role in our lives to such an extent that we do not realize when a program is a Federal program or state. In the next section of this chapter, we will examine the expansion of the Federal government in three program areas: education, welfare, and public safety.

THE EXPANSION OF THE FEDERAL GOVERNMENT IN EDUCATION, WELFARE, AND PUBLIC SAFETY

To explain the complexities of Federalism, political scientists used to describe the layers of government as a layer cake. People would react to different levels of governmental action as if the government were in separate layers. This analogy was improved when in modern times, textbooks described the interaction as more as a marble cake with the different levels of government intertwined. While these analogies are simple, they also are illustrative to the expansion of governmental action in our lives. In this section of the chapter, we will trace the actions of government on three areas that used to be the exclusive domain of State governments—education, welfare and public safety. Now the lines between governmental action has blurred and in some cases has become erased.

EDUCATION

The Federal government's first efforts in education came under the land grant legislation passed by Congress in 1862. The Morrill Land Grant Act deeded 30,000 acres for each state to have a state university system. The only requirement for states to have the land is there had to be an agricultural program on the campus. In the United States during the 1860s, farming was the leading occupation. Even today agricul-

tural interests are a powerful lobbying group in Washington. This legislation was considered essential in contributing to the development of democracy and the economy. Before this legislation, there was not a serious college and university system west of the Allegheny Mountains. This land grant was the seed for all of the major state University systems we see in the Midwest and West.

Even though under President Roosevelt's New Deal, participation in education by the Federal government was increased. States were the primary governmental unit when it came to issues of teacher training and local public school administration. Local school board elections were run by county government, and taxes based primarily on property taxes supplied the major portion of public school budgets. The veterans of World War II and Korean War swelled the ranks of universities, colleges and trade schools. This indirect funding of universities caused the number of people participating in some form of higher education to explode. People who had never dreamed of going to college now had the financial opportunity to at least try higher education.

At the same time, as the older veterans were invading campuses, the government was also involved in competing with the Soviet Union in major science programs. After the launch of the first satellite by the Soviet Union, the National Science Foundation established scholarships for people to study science and international studies, especially area studies concerning countries the United States would be competing against Soviet interests in Asia, Africa and South America. Again, the Federal government supplied the money, but the individual State governments, usually by way of a Board of Regents, provided the administration of the programs. After the initial rush of students on campuses during the 1940s, the first babies of the baby boom started college in the early and mid-1960s. This was the highpoint of both Federal funding in specific programs and in hard research areas. After twenty years of Federal money, almost every state had a large University system. States such as California, New York, Wisconsin and Michigan had integrated higher education systems that were designed to serve all of the residents of the state.

On the public school system level, the Federal government was highly involved in changing the nature of public schools. As we examined earlier, starting in the 1950s and going through the 1980s, the Federal government was in an effort to racially integrate the school systems of the South and the North.

The Federal government was also starting the successful Head Start program in which both parents and preschool children would learn the skills they would need to become prepared for Kindergarten. The Federal government through funding and unfunded mandates was getting involved in the day to day administration of local school districts. School districts in Milwaukee, Wisconsin, Chicago, Illinois and Boston, Massachusetts were all under court order to racially integrate their school districts. The Federal government supervised these efforts to change both the racial make up of the school and the property tax system that funded poor and rich districts alike.

The 1970s brought a backlash for the unfunded mandates the Federal government used, but by that time the educational system was addicted to the Federal money. Student grant programs such as the Pell Grants and Student Loans that were federally guaranteed by the Federal government were now the main drivers for funding of both private and public institutions of higher learning. Using these programs the Federal government was funding individuals directly, the administration of the programs would remain in the hands of the State Education system; however, now it would be the student who would determine what kind of funding and what institution they would attend.

The landmark legislation by President George W. Bush has changed the role of the Federal government in the realm of primary and secondary education. "No Child Left Behind" directly involves the Federal and State government in daily activity in the classroom. There are mandatory testing at certain grade levels and schools can be publicly graded on whether their students are getting the skills that are required. If the school has shown to fail, families of students who are assigned to attend the failing school will have the opportunity to receive a voucher to attend a different school. This has made the Federal government the final arbiter on the curriculum that is taught in grade schools and high schools across the country.

During the 1980s, there would be a dramatic decrease in funding programs in higher education. However, President Ronald Reagan's Secretary of Education, William Bennett, would use this new cabinet department to highlight vocational education and the community college systems around the country. Today, we see the Federal government involved in almost every student loan that is written. Putting the choice in student's hands has produced a competitive market place for students. The concern,

however, is the Federal government also has created an educational environment that treats education as if it is a consumer product. Profit institutions have been established and use student loans as a mainstay for their development. There is a question about student retention and the possibility of students being mislead on career potential or having the proper skills to graduate.

As we investigate the Federal government's role in education, we see an increase in unfunded mandates, and providing student loans. We see some defense and space related research, and we see an increase in the visibility of the Federal government on campuses. President Bush has made many visits to community colleges and vocational educational institutions. The Federal government believes these institutions are efficient and effective in changing the socio-economic position of some of the poorest members of our society. In the mid 1990s, community colleges and vocational institutes were assigned a major role in changing and training people who were on welfare.

WELFARE

From the ratification of the Constitution in 1789 to the Great Depression starting in 1929, most Americans believed it was not government's role to help people when the economy failed. Machine politics of the late 1800s through World War I did provide some help for people in need and there were rudimentary governmental programs called "relief." However, most Americans believed helping people through hard times was the role of churches and charities. Although these organizations did their best in helping out, the demand for people in need was too great for traditional solutions during the Great Depression. Starting with the election of Franklin D. Roosevelt, there was a shift in the view of the role of government on all levels when it came to fighting against the Depression.

One of the most controversial and productive programs created was the Works Progress Administration or WPA. This program was responsible for building roads, airports and public buildings such as schools, courthouses, police stations and firehouses. The WPA built enough highway miles to circle the globe 24 times.[6] The program also built enough buildings to furnish every county in the country with ten buildings.

---

[6]Ibid.

There was controversy in the program however, some people argued many of the projects were make-work and politicians used the program to hand out favors. Robert Carro's books on Lyndon Johnson, *A Path to Power and Master of the Senate*, are excellent examples of how Lyndon Johnson used both the WPA program as an administrator (he was the youngest state administrator in the nation) for highway programs and, once elected to Congress, used the New Deal to bring electricity to his rural Texas congressional district.[7] Having said this, the WPA has been looked at as a successful and necessary program that did help the infrastructure of the nation.

The model used by the Federal government was to use local governments to identify projects and help inform people about the opportunity of getting a job. Contractors with political contacts usually were responsible for the actual building of the project, and all of the different levels of government were forced to work together because the needs of the Depression were so great. Following the Great Depression, World War II and the economic boom time of the 1950s, helped bring prosperity to many Americans who could remember getting helped by President Roosevelt's New Deal. As the nation became more prosperous, the attitude of most Americans in the 1960s was for greater governmental funding for issues concerning poverty.

With the assassination of President John Kennedy, the new President Lyndon Johnson began his Great Society programs. In these programs the Federal government sent money through the States to the counties to administer. During the late 1960s, poverty programs called Welfare were regulating many people's lives, especially the urban poor who were living in government housing and receiving a check from the government. The bureaucratic welfare system was employing people to make sure the Welfare recipients were following the draconian rules that had developed, yet the question of generations continuing to be on welfare was a problem. Again during the 1980s and 1990s, the issues surrounding governmental programs on all levels, but specifically on Welfare, was changing the relationship between the local, state and Federal governments.

In 1996, President Clinton and the Republican Congress passed a bill called Welfare Reform. The Federal government had become the largest organization helping the poor in the country. The Federal government was employing thousands of people to administer the Welfare programs and the state and county governments were also employing a huge bureaucratic structure, yet the question remained, was it doing any good? The Welfare Reform Act had three important components—first, it put a limit on increasing the size of the monthly help by increasing the number of children people had, second, it put a time limit of five years total anyone could have for help, and third, it connected governmental help with receiving training and gaining employment.

Even with the reforms of Welfare Reform, there were still a large number of people who criticized the programs. Later in this book we will examine both the nature of bureaucracies and the nature of economic policies that produced the Welfare State as we know it. For our purposes here, we are illustrating how the Federal government has taken over the role of helping poor people in this society that was once performed by churches and charities, then taken over by local "machine party" bosses and local government, and then ultimately dominated by state and local government bureaucracies. The final example of the domination of the Federal government's role in Federalism is in the area of public safety.

PUBLIC SAFETY

Public safety is the primary responsibility of governments. The Federal government traditionally has been responsible for international security, while State and local governments have been responsible for domestic security and the fighting of crime. Since September 11, 2001, the lines between international security and domestic security have blurred. We may debate whether the invasion of Iraq is connected to the War on Terrorism, but one thing is clear, the first responders (police, fire and emergency medical personnel) are on the frontlines of this different type of war.

First responders tend to be local and state employees. The airports are usually run by a local airport authority but the screeners inside airports are part of the new Federal government's Homeland Security Department. As globalization takes place, the Federal government will tend to dominate areas of security that are both international and domestic. Homeland Security, the FBI and CIA are now talking with their state and local counterparts. If a local police officer asks a person their immigration status, is the police officer acting as a Federal law enforcement officer helping the Federal immigration officials or is

---

[7] Robert Carro, *Path to Power and Master of the Senate*.

he a local government employee? This is the next frontier in public safety. What are the boundaries of the different governmental agencies.

In a natural disaster, as we saw in New Orleans in the summer of 2005, the Federal, state and local officials failed. Each governmental unit and political leader blamed the other units as an excuse for their own lack of execution. An article in the *Los Angeles Times* by Greg Krikorian on August 16, 2006, reported on a study done by the RAND Corporation on the effects of a nuclear attack on the port of Long Beach, California. In this simulation, it was estimated that the economic damage would be ten times greater than 9/11 and 60,000 people would die immediately, 150,000 would die after being exposed to radiation.[8] How would the Local, State, and Federal governments react to a catastrophic attack by terrorists? If Hurricane Katrina is any model, the government will fail. States have Homeland Security offices, the Federal government has a Homeland Security Department combined with the CIA and FBI, not counting all of the local first responders. The government changes the organizational boxes; however, according to the 9/11 Commission and several terrorism experts we remain as vulnerable to terrorist attack as we were before the September 11th attacks.

We have seen the role of the Federal government expand in these traditionally local and state roles in the area of education, welfare and public safety. The issues of Federalism goes back to the original arguments surrounding the role of government in our society.

FEDERALISM: THE GOOD, BAD AND UGLY

There are aspects of Federalism that are good. States have the freedom to experiment with policies that hopefully would solve difficult and complex problems such as welfare reform, Medicaid reform and child nutrition. It was the state governments of Wisconsin and Michigan who showed welfare reform was possible. During the Progressive era at the beginning of the previous century, there were Governors of States who experimented with bringing expertise of the state universities and the State government together in order to solve social issues such as labor relations, food and drug inspection, and ending child labor practices. The greatest politicians of this era, Theodore Roosevelt and Woodrow Wilson, were progressive Governors. Think of the different state governments as potential public policy laboratories which have the potential to discover new and ingenious public policy solutions for many of the national problems that face our society. Even the New Deal started as state programs that were put on a grander scale to try to quell the effects of the Great Depression. The division of labor between State and Federal government would be more useful if both were better at communicating with each other in fields that both have expertise such as education, public safety, and welfare reform. Yet, it is difficult to see how states are involved in any policy experimentation in the area of health or higher education costs. Most recently, because of term limits and the lack of political imagination, most states have not been involved with public policy experimentation as they once were.

Federalism also made it possible to have the evil system of segregation in the South. This is the bad aspect of Federalism. Southern state governments were able to prevent and interfere with the African-American's ability to vote by charging poll taxes and having different voting rules for White voters and African-American voters. After roughly one hundred years, the Civil Rights movement started to use the Federal court system to have equal protection under the law. Ultimately, the system did work, but it took a very long time and should have never been allowed to happen.

Finally—the ugly. If you have ever applied for student financial aid using both the Federal and State government's forms, and if you have ever filed your taxes for both the State and Federal governments, then you know the bureaucratic problems a person can have dealing with the different governmental organizations. In California alone, there are over one hundred community colleges, each with its own administration. Local and municipal administration units number into the thousands. Each of these groups are writing rules that you have to follow. Combine those with Federal regulations and the complexities are so great, it is a wonder we build anything in this country.

This is the ugly face of Federalism. Government in this country is the biggest employer. We have set up bureaucracies that have little accountability and, some can be argued, were established for a good reason one hundred years ago, but now are used to make

---

[8]*Los Angeles Times*, August 16, 2006. For a discussion on nuclear terrorism see Patrick C. Coaty, *Understanding the War on Terror.* Dubuque, IA: Kendall/Hunt Publishing Co.

sure people have jobs. We all know the stories that circulate around the end of the year that describe outdated laws that are still on the books and can be enforced. These are all a product of having many levels of government, and each government getting lobbied to do something. We will talk more about this in one of the following chapters on the bureaucracy. We can all admit whether we like government or not, one has to agree that sometimes the rules and the bureaucracy are quite ugly. Another aspect of the ugly nature of Federalism is the way the Federal and State governments fight on the division of powers. As we have gone from the 1990s to today, the increase on unfunded mandates and limitation of State government budgets have left the public with disgust over our leaders inability to solve basic questions concerning the division of power. Protecting the environment, making sure children have healthy food in their schools, and protecting the homeland are all admirable goals, but, the issue of who should pay and what level of government should administer are new issues that the average person does not really care about. However, they are vitally important to the smooth and efficient running of the government. This is the environment we have today surrounding the issues of Federalism.

INTERGOVERNMENTAL RELATIONS AND STATE GOVERNMENTS

State governments are not completely without power in relationship to the Federal government. Although the Federal government has the power of the purse, it can run budget deficits while States cannot. The States do have the power of lobbying Congress. There are seven major lobbying groups[9] that have the power to lobby Congress and the President. These groups have power because their members are local leaders who are able to have grassroots support. These "big seven" intergovernmental associations are able to shape Federal programs in order to have uniform programs in every state and to lobbying about the administration challenges facing state and local government.

Combine this lobbying effort with the lobbying effort of local business and labor organizations and it is apparent there is communication in political terms

---

[9]These seven lobbying groups are: National Governor's Association, Council of State Governments, National Conference of State Legislatures, National League of Cities, National Association of Counties, U.S. Conference of Mayors and the International City/County Management Association.

between the different levels of government. By the late 1990s, the Supreme Court was trying to establish a better balance between the Federal government and the states on issues such as physician-assisted suicide, domestic violence and medical marijuana. It remains very issue specific on what governmental level has jurisdiction on any controversy. In some cases such as physician-assisted suicide and medical marijuana, voters had passed a state initiative but the Supreme Court decided these were unconstitutional because they violated Federal law. If you want to change the system, one has to understand the different dynamics of Federalism and how our intergovernmental system works.

CONCLUSION

In 1789, the Founding Fathers came to the nation with a plan. This plan was designed to create a national or Federal government that would improve the life of average Americans by providing more public safety, economic regulation and protection from international invasion. This was done secretly, most Americans at this time would not call themselves Americans. Their loyalty was usually strongest at the local level, then the county in which they lived, next was the state, and finally after all of the loyalties had been fulfilled, they would serve the nation. In theory, the Constitution has language that prevents it from certain actions and preserves the existence of states. On a practical level, the Federal governmental structure was superimposed over each state government. In many cases this caused confusion on all levels of government. The ratification of the Constitution presented a challenge to the Federal government that is with us today. What is the relationship between the Federal government and the States?

We started our examination of this question by looking at the general political structures of societies. There are three models that have been developed. They are: unitary, confederation, and federal. Unitary is the most common form we see in the world. This is because most countries had a monarchy that administered the government from a capital city to the outer regions of their kingdom. When there was a revolution to overthrow the monarchy the revolutionaries usually kept the structure. France, Britain, and Japan all have unitary governmental structures.

The second model we discussed was the confederation model. This model has a weak central government and the units that make up the underlying structure have more power. Examples of this model include the Confederate States of America and the United Nations. The weakness of this system is the central government's lack of power can inhibit unified action in the event of a natural disaster, war or economic dislocation. A confederation uses the economies of scale that come with the administrating large units. The final disadvantage for this model to work is there can be little or no political disagreement. Once the member units start to disagree on a policy that should be followed by the whole confederation, usually each member has a veto power. Therefore, action is only taken by majority vote or by unanimous decision making.

The third model we analyzed was the federal model. This model was adopted by the United States after the ratification of the Constitution. Germany also has a federal system. The advantage of this system is the central government has more power than the central government in the confederation system. Yet, there also are some procedures to ensure local control is still maintained. In the Federal system, a society has economies of scale in order to fight outside enemies, keep the public order and maintain economic well being. The disadvantages of the Federal system are the members of the society have to pay taxes to many forms of government. The average American has to pay numerous taxes to every governmental jurisdiction. These can range from municipal government, educational district including kindergarten through community college district, water board (if you live in the West), county government, state government and the Federal government. This of course does not include user fees or sales taxes. The high taxes are also combined with the bureaucratic hurdles one faces when they live in a Federal system. If you know someone who is dealing with the State and Federal government, Veteran affairs, Social Security, the state and federal versions of the IRS, or student financial aid, you know the bureaucratic forms and "red tape" you must go through to get anything done. In one of the following chapters we will discuss the skills that are required to live in our bureaucratic society. These advantages and disadvantages were traced with our treatment of the evolution of the role of the Federal government and its growing superiority vis-à-vis the States.

We analyzed the role the Supreme Court played in trying to define the practical and theoretical relationship between the Federal government and the states. Starting with the case *McColloch v. Maryland*, the facts surrounding the case had to deal with the power of the Federal government to charter a Bank of the United States. Even though there is not any language of this power stated in the Constitution, the Supreme Court ruled the Federal government does have power to charter banks. The second issue that the Supreme Court addressed was whether a state could tax the branches of the Federally chartered bank. The court ruled it could not. On the surface one may argue this case was fairly basic, but what makes this case historic was the underlying procedure the court would follow in the future. The Supreme Court said it was their role to interpret the relationship between the Federal government and the States.

The Supreme Court would interpret the Constitution so that other branches such as the Executive and Legislative, could implement their decisions. Before the *McColloch* case it had been an open question who would interpret the Constitution when it came to intergovernmental or federalism cases. Now, it was apparent the Supreme Court would take on this role. The record of the Supreme Court is very mixed when it comes to trying to define Federalism for other branches of government. From the Civil War to the Great Depression, the Supreme Court tried to define a concept they called Dual Federalism. This concept was a failure. It provided the rationale for "separate but equal" which enforce *de jure* discrimination on the African-American community. In addition, it became very burdensome to practically define the difference between interstate commerce and intrastate commerce. The Supreme Court finally gave up on this doctrine by the mid 1930s. During the Great Depression through the 1970s, there was a new concept called cooperative federalism. The Federal government would provide money for programs in education, welfare, infrastructure and other things. The state and local governments would implement the programs. Depression era programs such as the Works Progress Administration (WPA) were examples of cooperative federalism. Cooperative federalism works as long as there is money. In the 1980s, we saw the Federal government could not afford these programs. Instead of funding individual programs, the Federal government started to consolidate its funding into block grants. Also during the 1980s to today, there is an increased amount of unfunded mandates. These are regulations that have to be followed but the Federal government does not provide any funding to follow the regulations. This has caused friction from state and local governments.

Today, we see the Federal government involved in a host of activities in our lives and the states have been diminished in their role. The advantages of Federalism are the states can experiment with public policy ideas. If the policies are effective and successful they can be implemented on a national scale. We saw this during the progressive era and even today with the implementation of welfare reform. Another advantage is the implementation of civil rights across the country. Without the Federal courts, the Civil Rights movement would have had a much harder time because of the corruption of the Southern States' legal systems. It was the Federal court system that started to move us to a system that tried to give equal protection under the law for everyone.

This concludes our examination of the structure of the American system. We have discussed the Constitution, civil rights and civil liberties, and federalism. In the next chapter, we will examine the practical responsibilities we all have as members of our society. We will also analyze the dynamics of voting and public opinion. With your understanding of our system, you now have the tools to investigate the processes we use in picking our leaders on all levels of government.

TERMS TO REMEMBER

FEDERALISM
UNITARY
CONFEDERATION
FEDERAL
CATEGORICAL GRANT
BLOCK GRANT
UNFUNDED MANDATE

chapter 5 | Federalism: The Limits of Power Sharing

TRUE OR FALSE QUESTIONS

1. Federalism is the study of the relationships between governmental units. T / F

2. The Federal system is the most popular system of government. T / F

3. Confederacy system of government is the strongest form of government. T / F

4. Jefferson Davis was the President of the Confederate States of America. T / F

5. The relationship between different levels of government is articulated in a Constitution. T / F

6. States are superior to the central government in the United States. T / F

7. The Great Depression was a problem solved by the State governments. T / F

8. The Morrill Act gave states the land to create a state university. T / F

9. Traditionally state government had superiority in educational policy. T / F

10. Segregation of the South during the hundred years after the Civil War (1864–1959) was possible because of Federalism. T / F

MULTIPLE CHOICE QUESTIONS

11. Countries that have a unitary system of government are all of these except
    a. France
    b. Spain
    c. England
    d. Germany

12. The case of *McColloch v. Maryland* illustrates the concept of
    a. Federal law is the supreme law of the land.
    b. Congress has the responsibility to declare war.
    c. The Treasury has the right to print money.
    d. State universities cannot use race in granting admissions.

13. The case of *Gibbon v. Ogden* helped define the legal concept
    a. Superiority of the Federal government.
    b. The Treasury has the right to print money.
    c. Refines the boundary of interstate commerce versus intrastate commerce.
    d. Congress has the responsibility to declare war.

14. New Federalism was a phrase coined by President
    a. Gerald Ford
    b. Franklin D. Roosevelt
    c. Abraham Lincoln
    d. Ronald Reagan

15. Federal research money was the most plentiful at universities during
    a. 1940s
    b. 1950s
    c. 1930s
    d. 1960s

16. The Head Start Program was part of what liberal Democratic President's program
    a. Franklin D. Roosevelt's New Deal
    b. John F. Kennedy's New Frontier
    c. Lyndon Johnson's Great Society
    d. Woodrow Wilson's Progressive Society

17. The Works Programs Administration (WPA) was part of what liberal Democratic President's program
    a. Franklin D. Roosevelt's New Deal
    b. John F. Kennedy's New Frontier
    c. Lyndon Johnson's Great Society
    d. William Clinton's Bridge to the 21st Century

18. "No Child Left Behind" was the result of legislation from
    a. Franklin Roosevelt
    b. John F. Kennedy
    c. Ronald Reagan
    d. George W. Bush

19. Welfare reform was the result of legislation from
    a. John F. Kennedy
    b. Lyndon Johnson
    c. Woodrow Wilson
    d. William Clinton

20. What is not a model of Federalism?
    a. Unitary
    b. Teritary
    c. Confederal
    d. Federal

POLITICAL PARTICIPATION AND PUBLIC OPINION POLLS

INTRODUCTION

Previously, our analysis has centered around issues concerning the Constitution and Federalism. Now, we start our examination of American politics. Many people are convinced politics is boring and political life has nothing to do with their daily lives. In this chapter, we will analyze how your opinions do reflect the agenda pursued by our leaders and how your right to vote does indirectly determine who runs the government. The Founding Fathers struck a balance when describing the voting procedures to pick members of the legislatures and the executive branch. They did not believe in direct democracy. These men were afraid to let the masses exercise direct political power. This fear was based on two characteristics of early America; literacy was very low at the time of the founding and the idea of popular sovereignty and democracy were very new.[1] To be blunt, the Found-

ing Fathers were not sure of the effect a direct democracy would have on the country.

Therefore, the Founders opted for a republican form of government which provided a safeguard from the passions of people and rule of the mob which was a possibility in a direct democracy. It was a paternalistic view. Remember, the Articles of Confederation were not replaced because the old system had a lack of democratic participation. It was replaced because of issues of public safety and economic regulation. The Constitution as we have discussed, was a compromise between political participation and the need to have a predictable and orderly use of governmental power. The voting system we see today is the main result of this compromise. We never directly vote for President of the United States. Even if you participate in Presidential primaries or state caucuses, in reality you are voting for a slate of delegates that will vote in the party convention that ultimately will pick a presidential candidate. Although today most nominees for the Presidency are well known before the convention, they are not selected by the people,

---

[1]Symbolic of the view for representative democracy was the view put forth by John Adams. Adams had reviewed the literature of how democracies worked up to that time and concluded a nation of equals was impossible, but they strived for a government of laws not men. David McCullough, *John Adams*. New York: Simon and Schuster, 2001, pp. 376, 377.

they are selected indirectly through a delegate system. In the general election, we all know from the previous chapters, that we vote for electors of the Electoral College, therefore, we never vote directly for President of the United States.

Every four years, especially if there is a close election, there are calls for reforming the electoral process, yet, these cries for reform die out when the electoral cycle begins again. In this chapter, we will analyze the properties of public opinion and explore how our opinions are formed. Then, we will examine the science of public opinion polling and the power polls have on agenda setting for the political leaders of our country. Next, we will explore political culture and the relationship between private opinion and public culture. Finally, we will look at voter participation and discuss if voting is your duty or not voting is your right. The objective of this chapter is to highlight the complexities and interactions between private opinions and public actions.

Public opinion polls showed a majority of Americans were in favor of invading Iraq in February 2002. However, the latest polls done show a majority of Americans do not favor the war in Iraq and believe the troops should leave as soon as possible. This change has influenced candidates who are running for the Senate and Congress in the fall of 2006. There has been increased criticism of Senators and Representatives who voted for the invasion of Iraq, yet, today do not support the war. Whether Democratic or Republican, people are not accepting the double game the legislative branch has played on this issue. As we will explain, opinions do not have to be true, they do not have to be based on facts. Opinions are feelings, not arguments. We start our discussion by describing the properties of public opinion.

PUBLIC OPINION DEFINED AND ITS QUALITIES

Public opinion is defined as the collective of individual beliefs shared by some adults in the population. The main difference between public and private opinion is when a person does something to make a particular opinion known in public. Public opinion is expressed either by elections with people voting, or is collected by public opinion polls. The science of public opinion polls is accurate. If you have taken a statistics course you have heard of a theorem called the Central Limit Theorem. This theorem states that if you have random data, the results of your statistical analysis can be generalized to

the whole population.[2] The trick is to have your data set randomly selected. In the past this used to be difficult. However, in today's connected world the availability of cellular telephones makes randomness of data a less problematic situation as it was during the 1948 Presidential campaign.

In 1948, President Harry Truman was running against Thomas Dewey, the Governor of New York.[3] All of the public opinion polls showed Thomas Dewey with a large lead over Harry Truman.[4] Everyone in the country believed Truman was going to lose the election, except Harry Truman. The night of the Presidential election everyone was surprised to see Harry Truman had won the election.[5] The public opinion polls were wrong because the data collection was not random. The polling companies were using telephones to retrieve their data for the polls. The ratio of people owning telephones in 1948 was quite low, only the upper middle class tended to own their own phones in this era. Therefore, the polls tilted toward a Republican victory.

Today, the issue of randomness is not very prevalent since most pollsters understand this problem when determining the validity of a poll. Polls on the Internet do have this problem, since one has to own or have access to a computer that is connected to the Internet. Furthermore, people have the ability to vote more than once on most Internet polls which skews the result of the specific poll. Be careful when you see a poll that is being quoted from an Internet source, they are not scientific and do not fall under the Central Limit Theorem. If you think of a poll as a snapshot of opinion on a given day, then they can be very useful. Just like a piece of fruit after seven days, it is stale. Although it may be stale does not mean that it was inaccurate. People involved in the media and in electoral politics pay attention to polls, some voters also pay attention. If you believe in polls or not, you should understand the properties that characterize public opinion in order to be aware of what everyone else is paying attention to when dealing with both elections or popular culture. Politicians and media use polls but so do marketers in order to sell products. To enable you to be a better consumer of information, we will describe the properties of public opinion.

---

[2]Donald J. Koosis, *A Self Teaching Guide: Statistics.* New York: John Wiley & Sons Inc., 1997, p. 67.

[3]David McCullough, *Truman.* New York: Simon & Schuster, 1992, p. 708.

[4]Ibid. p. 590.

[5]Ibid. pp. 709–719.

PROPERTIES OF PUBLIC OPINION

There are seven important properties which shape public opinion.[6] These properties help us describe and analyze public opinion and determine what people are following, by knowing these properties we can distinguish between a fad or a deep shift in people's attitudes. The seven properties are: intensity, fluidity, permanence, quiescence, relevance, political knowledge and consensus and division.

INTENSITY

How strong a person holds on to a particular opinion describes intensity. Common courtesy used to dictate when you first meet someone you should not talk about religion, politics or race. The idea was it would be impolite to talk about these subjects since people have very intense feelings about opinions that fall into these categories. Some things we have strong opinions about in different stages of life. Music and movies to many young people are very important and they have intense opinions about the music and movies they enjoy. In America, professional sports seems to have taken over as a passion of many people—favorite teams and players are something to fight over. As we see in Europe, their football (soccer) fans have riots when they lose a match. Ironically, in America, we have riots when teams win championships. You may have known someone who has a very strong opinion about something you do not care about at all. When dealing with opinion there really is not a correct or incorrect opinion, opinions are feelings and you have the right to your opinion. It is interesting to see how fast opinions can change. This brings us to the second property of public opinion—fluidity.

FLUIDITY

Public opinion has dual and contradictory properties. On one hand it can be very intense, and on the other, people's opinion can change overnight. It is very fluid. This can be defined as the amount of change in people's feelings on an issue over time. Some things are very fluid. Fashion has a longer twenty year cycle—you see people today wearing clothes from the early 1970s and it has a smaller yearly or seasonal cycle. If you have an intense opinion about being fashionable, then you know how fast styles can change. Entertainment is also very fluid. Movies, television shows, and music all have a very short cycle. If you are interested in movies, you know that most movies have a one weekend life cycle. In politics candidates in Presidential elections can also be very fluid. A candidate makes a mistake or something comes out on his/her background and before they know it, their candidacy will be finished. Depending on the opinion, there are also opinions that are very stable.

STABILITY

Another property of public opinion is stability. There are some opinions that are very stable. Interestingly, the most stable private opinion is your taste in food. If a family immigrates from another country to the United States it takes three or four generations for members of that family to change their eating habits. An example would be, if a family came from Asia sixty years ago, the descendants of those immigrants would still eat food from the country they are ethnically from. Food is one of the last things that becomes assimilated. Of course, one could argue the American diet is a mixture of all of the world's cuisines, but the point of this illustration is opinions may be held for long periods of time. Identity with different ethnic groups and political party affiliation is another example of the property of stability in public opinion. We have examined the African-American experience and the loyalty to the Democratic party that they have exhibited in elections since 1932. This is a very stable opinion.

QUIESCENCE

Quiescence is a property of public opinion which is defined as an opinion which has not yet formed in the minds of people. Usually it will take a defining event or moment to bring a quiescent opinion into the public realm. Pearl Harbor and September 11th were defining moments for people. Before these events some may have had an opinion about Adolf Hitler or Osama Bin Laden respectively, but most people did not. After these events, however, opinions

---

[6]These properties of public opinion and the discussion on voting behavior is information borrowed from numerous American Government Textbooks and Instructors Manuals. These include: Michael Dinneen, *Instructors Manual for American Government and Politics Today: The Essentials 1998–1999 Edition.* New York: West Wadsworth Publishers, 1998, pp. 93–107. Karen O'Connor and Larry J. Sabato, *American Government: Continuity and Change.* New York: New York: Longman Publishing Co., pp. 17–26. Walter E. Volkomer, *American Government.* New York: Pearson, 1975, p. 66. Among others, most American Government texts use this categorization for public opinion and voter's behavior.

about these two for most Americans dramatically changed from one of apathy to one of great determination to defeat these killers. In 1933, most people did not know who Adolf Hitler was, by 1945 everyone knew who he was. In 1989, some people might have known who Bin Laden was, by September 12, 2001 all Americans knew who he was. Opinions can be formed very quickly when defining moments happen. The ability to change opinions quickly is also a property of relevance.

RELEVANCE

This characteristic of public opinion refers to the ability of an opinion to get "critical mass" once an event happens. Immigration became an important issue for most people after the events of spring 2006. Most people before that time did not believe immigration was an important matter. It may have been a personal matter, or even an economic matter. The radio talk show hosts on both sides of the immigration issue have stirred their audiences to where the issue has become an important political topic for the election of 2006. The opinions expressed on this issue have a dynamic mixture of properties including intensity, stability and now relevance.

The Global War on Terror is another issue that people have strong opinions but the opinions can change without much notice. Before September 11th, people did not think Islamic Radicalism (or Islamic Fascists) were important to their daily lives.[7] If people were polled on the important issues of the election that was held in 2000, terrorism was very low on the list. Social Security, abortion and a host of other issues were of greater importance to the electorate. After the attacks, terrorism suddenly became the number one issue on all of the weekly polls taken by media networks and corporations such as the Gallup organization.[8]

POLITICAL KNOWLEDGE

Political knowledge is a property of public opinion that is probably one reason you are reading this book. Somewhere, either in college or for private interest you realize the more you know about our political system the more analysis you can bring to answering some of these difficult questions for yourself. This is

also true of our society. The more a question or issue is examined, people's opinion may change. Problems may be complex even for professionals in the area that is being examined. Issues such as physician-assisted suicide, abortion, stem cell research and even climate change are very complex, so the experts keep changing their opinions. It is believed, if you expose people to the marketplace of ideas, most people will digest the information that they are being exposed to and make the best decisions for their situation. This is why we measure the aggregate of adult opinion for polling purposes.

CONSENSUS AND DIVISION

This is the last property of public opinion. Some issues start with a seriously divided public, and as events turn out, the public becomes more unified. The 1990 Gulf War was an example of this phenomenon. The opposite happened with the Vietnam War and the War in Iraq. In those two conflicts, the public was quite unified until events started to sour people's perceptions of the conflict. Consensus and division can also change overnight such as the reaction to the attack on Pearl Harbor. Before Pearl Harbor, there was a very strong and organized isolationist and pacifist movement in the United States. After December 7, 1941 this movement was dead until the far left of Ralph Nader and the far right of Patrick Buchanan revived it during the 2000 election.

These are the qualities of public opinion on the "macro" level. We see large changes in public opinion and label it with one of these dominant labels. Where do our opinions come from? In the next section of this discussion we will discuss how opinions are formed. The process which changes personal opinion to public opinion is called political socialization. Political socialization is defined as the process in which people get political beliefs. This process takes place on the interpersonal level of interaction. A person may have an opinion and once they share that opinion they will get instant feedback on the appropriateness of that opinion or action. Hand gestures, words, and opinions are all learned. The appropriateness of our actions is taught through our interactions with family, friends and institutions of our society. In the next section we examine the formation of public opinion.

---

[7]Patrick C. Coaty, *Understanding the War on Terror*. Dubuque, IA: Kendall/Hunt Publishing Co., 2006, p. 90.
[8]Ibid.

THE FORMATION OF PUBLIC OPINION

Political socialization takes place on an individual level and on a societal level. We see the appropriateness of language change over the years. Using the word "ass" (usually this word is used to refer to the body part not the animal), was once considered inappropriate for television, radio and polite society. Today, this word is used in common language. The language used in the mass media today would make the most progressive producers of the 1960s turn green. There has been a forty year effort to shock our society. From Elvis Presley shaking his hips on television to the latest version of a hip hop music video, the effort to get people talking has taken a cynical turn. To the point where when Madonna and Britney Spears did their famous kiss no one was shocked. The audience knew it was a stunt. How do we form our opinions? We will list several of the important elements which contribute to the development of our opinions. They include: family, education, peers, religious influence, economic status, political events, leaders, the media and demographic traits. On an individual level these elements contribute to a subconscious encoding that enable people to form opinions.

FAMILY

The early influences of childhood are the most important influence. If you know someone's parent's political affiliation then, you have a very good insight into their political leanings. We know most people fall in love with someone who reminds them of their parents, women tend to marry someone who reminds them of their fathers and men tend to marry someone who reminds them of their mother. This is a simple fact of life. If you are dating someone and you are not married, look at your boyfriend or girlfriend's mother or father, that is who you will end up with. Seriously, most of the time this is just a curious outcome of our biological and anthropological coding. However, in some extreme cases, such as the cycles of domestic violence or child abuse, this coding can be very difficult to break and generations of families have suffered.

The influence of the family is the most dominating feature in forming political opinions. If your parents vote, you will probably vote. If not, you probably will not vote. Families have influence but you are not predestined to repeat the behaviors of your parents. There are other influences that can change your opinions and behavior.

EDUCATION

Education is supposed to change our opinions. The best part of education is trying to take from your family what you like and add different influences. The main objective of going to school is to learn how to think in order to either reject or reinforce the opinions you hold. Education is a process, if you engage in intellectual activity you are bound to change some of your opinions. Examination of long held beliefs is one of the first things one does when they become educated. There are people you may know that have many degrees, but, they have not examined any of their opinions since they left school. Well, we would contend these people may have degrees but they are not educated. Some argue the colleges and universities are trying to indoctrinate students with a certain type of political ideology. While some instructors and professors may try to do this, it is doomed to failure. Once someone is exposed to critical thinking, they should examine all points of view and use the same rigorous methodology on every issue they wish to examine. Therefore, a professor who is trying to ram a political point of view down his/her students' throats will find this actually backfires. Students may regurgitate his/her malpractice in the classroom, but ultimately the students will reject these types of efforts.

PEERS AND PEER GROUP

One of the few measurements we have to predict student success is whether a student is involved in at least one extra-curricular activity. If they have friends who are in school, usually they will be successful in school. People have friends because there is usually something in common with the other person. Music, sports, cars, anything can be a bond of friendship. If you have friends who are not going to college, what do you talk about? Do you say "I just got back from this exciting political science class and I want to share the ideas we were talking about!!" Maybe, but highly unlikely, your friends who are not in college would look at you as if you were crazy. More likely, your friends who are in college would understand your excitement (maybe). Some people have friends and contacts from their high school five years after graduation. Most people lose contact with their high school friends. People's friendships tend to fade because they do not have things in common or the cement that forged the friendship is no longer an important part of their lives.

Peer groups in high school determine to a great extent whether a student will smoke, drink or do drugs. Peer groups determine how you look. What your taste are in music, fashion, and other things. Colleges and universities' peer groups also have a great influence on the behaviors of different students. Colleges and universities are big enough that almost every group is representative and people can pick and choose their peers. Students tend to be more independent in college and many times parents and family members are surprised by the type of peers students pick after high school.

RELIGIOUS ORIENTATION

People who go to church tend to vote more than people who do not attend church. Religious influence is related usually to family influence and peer group. Some people change their religion. Most of the time people share the same religion as their parents and other family members. If they do not, marriage is a major reason for people to convert to another religion. People who belong to religions tend to be more active in their communities and are more aware of issues facing their religion inside and outside the secular community. However, just because someone goes to church does not mean they will be politically conservative. Religious people can be both politically conservative and liberal.

Twenty or thirty years ago, it was possible to identify a person's religion and figure out the probability of his/her political orientation. Jewish people and Catholics tended to vote for Democrats during the 1950s through the 1980s. However, now both these groups are divided down the middle fifty-fifty. John Kerry who is Catholic only received half of the Catholic vote. President Bush's support of Israel has gained support among Jewish voters, the Republicans now receive fifty percent of this group too. Protestants are likely to vote for Republicans, however, even this identification has changed recently.

ECONOMIC STATUS

Economic status or money does not play a great role in determining political opinions. If we have two siblings—one rich, one poor—their political opinions will probably be closer than if we would poll two rich people from different families. Money may change marginal opinions but core beliefs are rarely changed because of economic status. There are some issues that people who are wealthy and poor disagree. Usually, people who are poorer tend to vote more conservatively when it comes to issues of civil liberties and

the rich tend to vote more liberally. On taxes and other economic policies, until recently, the rich were against taxes and the poor were for increasing taxes on the rich. Recently, however, some super rich people including Warren Buffet and William Gates, Sr. (Bill Gates' father) have argued the rich are not taxed enough in this country. We all believe we would be happy if we were rich. Most of us would be the same person and hold most of the same opinions if we were rich or poor.

POLITICAL EVENTS

Political events can have a great impact on opinion formation. The assassination of President Lincoln after victory in the Civil War produced a political climate that produced Republican majorities until the Great Depression. The death of President Roosevelt on the eve of victory in World War II, produced Democratic party dominance until 1980, and the assassination attempt on President Reagan resulted in unifying the country behind him until the Iran-Contra scandal. The attacks of September 11th did give President Bush and the Republican party victories in two elections (2002 and 2004). However, today the invasion of Iraq has produced an anti-war movement that is well defined and at the moment of this writing gaining strength in the Democratic party with the defeat of Senator Joe Lieberman in his Democratic primary to Ned Lamont in the summer of 2006.[9]

All of these political events had a great deal of influence on the generation that lived through the event. One could say the events scarred the political psyche to such a degree, that the opinions and emotions formed during these traumatic events were taken as truth; obvious to the people who lived through the event. World War II veterans had and have a great deal of influence on formation of political opinions.[10] Vietnam veterans, veterans of the Gulf War and the veterans who have fought in the Global War on Terror (Afghanistan and Iraq), have less influence. Why? Is it because there were more veterans of World War II? Was it because the people

---

[9]Ned Lamont did defeat Joe Lieberman in the Primary. However, the latest polls show Lieberman with a ten point lead over Lamont running as an independent candidate. Lieberman did win re-election in November, 2006.

[10]Christopher Matthews, *The Rivalry That Shaped Postwar America: Kennedy & Nixon.* New York: Simon & Schuster, 1996, Chapter One, "World War II Was Their Greatest Campaign Manager," pp. 27–43.

involved in the war were more aware of why they were fighting the war? Did the unity Pearl Harbor produced also open the door to the society not turning the venom of the debate about the war to effect policies and politics that were directed at the veterans? We do not know. One thing we do know is the unity that was inside the country after September 11th was squandered.[11] Today we cannot even agree that the U.S. government was not involved in the attacks. These beliefs in crackpot conspiracies has got to stop if we are going to fight this war together. If you are over ten years old you have lived through the most important political event arguably since Pearl Harbor. Did it change our opinions? We previously said how Pearl Harbor silenced the isolationists movement in this country for fifty years. Did September 11th change our political landscape? Five years ago, we all thought it would. It can be argued the attacks did not increase our knowledge of the importance of understanding the threats posed by our enemies.[12]

LEADERS

The failure of President Bush to mobilize this country for war, the same way Franklin Roosevelt did after Pearl Harbor, is a clear difference in leadership. The two most dramatic political events were taken by the American leadership at the time in two very different directions. Roosevelt had a military draft instituted, mobilized the whole economy (including rationing gas) to fight the war. He said we will fight for unconditional surrender, no matter how long it took. Everyone was involved in defeating the Axis nations. Even kids were mobilized to save their pennies and buy war bonds.

President Bush had a different approach. His administration stated we should all buy consumer goods, the exact opposite Roosevelt had said. President Bush described an Axis of Evil, and did not declare war on those countries. He said this would be a new fifty year conflict, yet he did not get the average person involved in the fight. The Bush Doctrine was designed to defeat any terrorist group that threatened the United States. The U.S. and its allies invaded Afghanistan and Iraq. To be sure, the nature of World War II and the Global War on Terrorism is

different. One thing that is not different is you need people (soldiers) to fight a war and win the peace.

Roosevelt understood to keep people united you had to have everyone involved in fighting a war. Bush thought the threat was self-evident and he would have the unity that he enjoyed for a year after the September 11th attacks throughout his administration and the fighting of the War on Terror. Regrettably, the Bush Administration has not unified the country. We are probably as close to being divided on the war in Iraq as we were during the last stages of Vietnam. President Roosevelt is considered a hero for his leadership. History may prove President Bush was correct in his leadership in fighting the War on Terror by fighting an unpopular war, such as President Harry Truman is considered a hero. Once again, it seems from a leadership point of view, the unity of the war and the implementation of a successful strategy has not been achieved.

MEDIA

Some blame the media and the biases they perceive as the reason President Bush has lost the unity he enjoyed a year after the attacks of September 11th. In forming political opinions, the media tends to reflect our opinions more than create opinions. Television, radio and print media are losing influence when it comes to the power of shaping opinions. The explosion of the "new" media in politics and how online media and blogs have begun to start a media revolution. The revolution may have started, yet these methods have not been decisive in efforts to win elections as of yet.

DEMOGRAPHIC TRAITS

Demographic traits are traits that have a lot of influence on people, yet the individual has little or no control over these properties. Race, gender, age, marital status and geographical location, are traits that effect our opinions. Race in the United States is a very strong measure on predicting voter attitudes. The African-American community overwhelmingly supports the Democratic party. Regardless of socio-economic status most African-American people identify with the Democrats. Asian-Americans and Latinos (Hispanics) are more complicated. Korean-Americans tend to vote for Republicans, while Chinese and Vietnamese are more mixed in their political party identifications. Hispanic voters such as Cubans are identified with the Republicans and

---

[11]Patrick C. Coaty, *Understanding the War on Terror*. Dubuque, IA: Kendall/Hunt Publishing Co., 2006, pp. 130–131.
[12]Ibid.

Puerto Ricans and Mexican-Americans identify with the Democratic party. When a person may have several demographic traits such as race and gender, race trumps the identity hierarchy.

In the 1980s and 1990s there were political consultants who kept on talking about a gender gap. The gap occurs when men and women support different political programs. Supposedly, women were in favor of the programs of the Democratic party and men were identifying with the Republican party. The Democratic nominee Walter Mondale designed his political strategy against President Ronald Reagan on this belief. It did not materialize. Later on, in almost every Presidential election, political consultants (especially for the Democratic party) talk about gender as an important demographic trait. We know it is an important trait. However, in voter identification, there is little proof that gender affects the way people vote. If you have two people of the same race and different gender they tend to vote more similarly than two people of the same gender and different race.

Age is an interesting demographic trait. Young people have always been poor voters. It seems as people mature, pay taxes and have families they tend to become better voters. In 2004, John Kerry ran as the Democratic party's nominee. Like Walter Mondale, he designed a strategy that targeted a group that normally does not vote—young people. He lost because of his assumption that, unlike other elections, young people would vote because of the rising anti-war sentiment. This did not materialize. Older people vote. The government caters to older people because on average, they have more money, more time and they vote more than young people.

As with age, marital status is another interesting demographic characteristic. As people marry, they tend to vote more. Married people tend to share the same opinions. Whether it is on social issues or international issues, a couple tends to share the same perspective (or their opinions tend to merge over time).

The last demographic trait that tends to influence opinion is one that is fading in importance—geographical location. Before the information revolution, opinions were different in the American South, West and East. However, with the massive migration of people inside the United States and dominance of popular culture, for example, there are very few people who are not aware of who Mickey Mouse is, what hip-hop is, or have eaten at McDonald's. Most recently, a television producer was trying to establish a "Real Beverly Hillbilly" program. By the way, *The Beverly Hillbillies* was a 1960s television show that put people

who were poor and isolated in the Appalachian Mountains, and put them in the center of Rodeo Drive. The producers could not do this because they could not find anyone who was authentically isolated from the popular culture of today.

Although all of the demographic traits are important, race, age, and martial status tend to have more influence on the formation of people's opinions than the other traits, such as gender and geographical location. Now that we have analyzed the aspects of public opinion from the perspective of a social scientist, we will now analyze how these opinions form our political culture.

AMERICAN POLITICAL CULTURE

Political culture is composed of a set of opinions and ideas about the nation and government. These opinions are shared by a vast majority of the society and are accepted as legitimate reasons to judge the legitimacy of government, leaders and the distribution of resources. In the United States, these opinions include values such as liberty, equality, justice, religious freedom and duty. These values surround our political discussions when we analyze and create criterion for the debate of important public issues. These touchstones of debate are used to frame our discussions and our perspectives to what is acceptable when we address what the government ought to be doing.

In other countries, ideas about freedom and liberty are alien. They do not believe young people should have the freedom not to follow their parents wishes. Economic or social conditioning offsets any personal desires when it comes to people in some other countries. The idea of privacy is very strange to people who live in the densely populated countries of Asia. Women's rights are foreign to some of the traditional societies of the Middle East and Africa. Our notions of justice and liberty come from our indoctrination in our political culture. There may be some regional, religious or economic similarities that create similar political cultures; however, every state has a unique political culture. One of the reasons it has taken Europe so long to unify has been the differences in political culture. Questions such as abortion have brought trouble in unifying Europe. The Irish may feel differently about this question than a person from the former East Germany. The Irish have had very strict abortion laws, while the policy in the former East Germany was very liberal when it came to a women's right to choose an abortion. This is just one example of how people's perspective on what is right or wrong can get in the way of political arrangements that may make perfect economic and political sense.

American political culture has several foundational values such as liberty, equality, justice, religious freedom, and duty to the community. Europeans complain about the narrowness of the political spectrum in the United States. They say there is not much difference between the Democratic and Republican parties. These people are correct. One reason we have this narrowness is most Americans agree with these values. The disagreement comes when one tries to apply them to current problems or the interpretation of them when we analyze our historical experience.

We have analyzed the three pillars the Founding Fathers tried to build a new society on: popular sovereignty, rule of law, and tolerance. These are incorporated into American political culture. Discussion of liberty has a dimension of both popular sovereignty and tolerance. If people have a right to govern themselves, there has to be a component of liberty in the freedom to discuss the organization of the government they will live under. The relationship between tolerance and liberty we have analyzed in previous chapters stated that one has to respect the liberty of the other person. There are behaviors the community has declared wrong, and has passed laws that prohibit this behavior, even if a law has not been passed. If a person finds the behavior distasteful, they can shun the person exhibiting the offensive behavior. One does not have to accept behavior to respect the other person's liberty.

The idea of respecting a person's liberty goes hand in hand with the idea that we are all equal under the law. American political culture believes that everyone should be given a fair chance to make it in this country. This value of course, comes under the rule of law pillar of the Founding Fathers. We see this in our everyday life. For example, young children learn to stand in line in Kindergarten, no one is immune to waiting their turn in line for a treat. The concept of equality is how many political arguments are carried out. The question of is it fair? Are the resources being distributed equally? Equality is a very valid area of discussion in American politics. The idea of equality is connected also with the issues of rule of law. As with the idea of justice, justice can be thought of as equal protection under the law. More informally, it can be looked at as the idea of getting what one deserves. A system of justice is designed to judge individuals equally without prejudice to any classification.

We hear politicians and pundits talking about how programs are not just. They either reward people who do not deserve to be rewarded or we hear how they unfairly punish the innocent. Whether the discussion is about social welfare programs, defense spending, drug policy or tax policy, we continue to hear the argument put in the terms of political culture and public opinion. Issues and arguments are framed using the values of political culture. Both parties are using the same words, but their meaning is very different. An example is the debate concerning national security. Republicans define national security in terms of military strength and fighting the war on terror. Democrats argue national security issues include healthcare, education and changes in other areas that have nothing to do with the traditional areas of national security. We are not drawing any conclusions, we are merely illustrating the use of the values of political culture. Everyone is going to support national security. National security issues are of primary importance in these times of threat from terrorism. However, one can make an argument, in order to fight a biological terrorist attack we should spend more money on healthcare in order for the healthcare system to provide the help people will need if an attack occurs. It can also be argued more spending has to be made on the educational system since the war on terror requires all people to be aware of the threats posed by our enemy. This awareness has to be taught in the public schools.

These arguments demonstrate the common use of values to influence and change public opinion. Today, however, we see a fatigue among the common person. The average person distrusts the semantic games of both the Republican and Democratic parties.[13] Because of this fatigue, Americans tend not to vote in great numbers, although there is substantial agreement on the values the Founding Fathers displayed in the Constitution, many people have lost faith in their ability to influence events or in influencing any difference among the two political parties.

VOTER PARTICIPATION: WHO VOTES?

There are several arguments. One asks: why is voter participation so low in the United States?[14] Some ar-

---

[13]Thomas E. Patterson, *The Vanishing Voter: Public Involvement in an Age of Uncertainty.* New York: Alfred Knopf, 2002, p. 99.
[14]Ibid.

gue, people do not vote because they are basically happy with the status quo. In other countries such as Australia and Belgium voters who do not vote are taxed. Taxing voters does create participation rate above 95 percent. However, is it a violation of one's liberty to be forced to participate in the electoral process?

In most places in the United States, voting is a two step process. One has to register to vote and then they are qualified to actually vote. People who argue voting participation is low in the United States compare the actual number of voters to the number of people who are eligible to vote in the country. Using this measure, the United States has one of the lowest rates of voting in the industrialized world. The rate of people who are registered is much higher. Voting rights advocates has tried to pass legislation that would make it easier to register. Examples of this legislation are same day registration laws and efforts to use driver's licenses or car registration as a type of voter registration. It may or may not be the difficulty in registration that keeps people from voting. Yes, if you are registered you tend to vote, yet that does not necessarily mean if you have easier registration, more people will vote. A person who registers tends to be a more motivated person, since they have taken the small effort to register.

There have been other ideas that have been advocated such as making election day a holiday. It is argued if people did not have to go to work, they would be free to vote. This is a highly dubious assumption. People who are not motivated to vote for whatever reason, probably will not vote if they have a day off. More likely, people who have a holiday, will probably use the holiday to make other plans. There has also been a suggestion the state hold a million dollar lottery and draw the numbers from people who have voted. This seems to be an interesting idea, except if you have an identification number on your ballot, then your vote is no longer secret. One has to ask the question whether voting in of itself is useful. If it is, then contests or holidays are not important. If it is not, then people should have the power to make up their own minds. Assuming the public institutions have done their job in communicating the importance of voting, then how can we force people to participate in the process?

On average there are about 40 percent of eligible voters on any given election.[15] When people are asked why they did not vote, most give the reason that they were not registered.[16] Of the total of 40 percent, people with more wealth vote more than people who are poor. As discussed earlier, older people vote more than young people, and women and men historically tend to vote at the same rate, although some would argue women tend to support Democratic candidates more often. Women are becoming the majority of adults in the United States, therefore, more attention is being paid to "women's issues." The racial makeup of the electorate is more complicated. African-Americans have a lower percentage of voter turnout, yet they support the Democratic party overwhelmingly. Asian-Americans are not monolithic and neither are Hispanics. The Asian-American community tends to vote for the Republicans if the group has an anti-communist heritage such as the Vietnamese and Korean communities. Other communities tend to vote 50-50 split among party loyalty.

Many Americans no matter what their demographic traits, see divided government as an additional check and balance. We see voters more and more vote for candidates of different parties. This practice is called ticket splitting. A person may vote for a Republican for President, Democrat for Senator and another Republican for the House of Representatives. This phenomenon has coincided with the increase of personal attacks or negative advertising and the increasing weakness of the political parties. Many people do not feel there is any difference between the Democratic and Republican parties. They look at the performance of the elected politicians and their behavior seems to be the same. The average voter does not trust either party to govern. Since the elections of 2004, the Republicans have enjoyed control over the Senate, House of Representatives and the Presidency. There have been tax cuts, but also there has been an incredible increase in governmental spending. Defenders of President Bush and Congress remind us that there is a war going on. Notwithstanding, many of the people who voted for the Republicans wanted less governmental spending. They complain the Republican Congress spends the same way the Democratic Congress did for roughly the sixty years they controlled the Congress. The result of the 2006 midterm elections changed the Congress to Democratic.

This perception builds in apathy when it comes to voting. "Why should I vote, there is no difference be-

---

[15]Ibid.

[16]Thomas E. Patterson, *The Vanishing Voter: Public Involvement in an Age of Uncertainty*. New York: Alfred Knopf, 2002, p. 20–22.

tween the parties," is often heard.[17] This sense of political participation and the role you play in the political process is known as efficacy. Political efficacy is the person's sense that their participation matters. Efficacy can be divided into two categories. Internal efficacy is where a person has a sense of their participation and external efficacy is how a person perceives the reaction of the system to their participation.

Americans have a low sense of external efficacy. They believe if they vote, it really will not change anything. Europeans have even a lower sense of external efficacy than Americans; however, because of laws that promote voting, European's voting participation rates are typically higher than American. One contributing reason for this is in America, there are many more elections than in Europe.

In the United States following the Jacksonian democratic tradition, we tend to have elections for everything. School Board, Water Board, City Council, County Supervisor, State Assembly, State Senator, Governor, U.S. Congressman, U.S. Senator and President are just the main elections we have. Among others, the executive officers that are elected such as the numerous County and City Clerks, Treasurers, and Secretaries. In most jurisdictions Judges and District Attorneys are also elected. The great number of elections held in the United States could have the effect of discounting the importance of elections. Since people who do not participate will have another election to participate in very soon. Two political scientists have studied the different degrees of voter participation and have developed this scale.

Sidney Verba and Norman Nie have developed a six step scale that identifies the dominant trait of participation.

1. **Inactives**—They number around 22 percent of the population and they do not participate in politics at all. People without education or money, African-Americans, the very young and very old and women tend to be in this group.
2. **Voting Specialists**—They comprise 21 percent of the population. They strongly identify with a party. The party connection is the thing that brings them to the polls.
3. **Parochial Participants**—They comprise 4 percent of the population. They tend to have a personal problem or issue that needs governmental intervention. They contact elected officials for assis-

tance. They do not have a strong ideological nor party identification. They tend to be in lower socio-economic status, Catholics and live in cities.
4. **Communalists**—They also compromise 20 percent of the population. These people do not actively participate in electoral politics except for voting. They do participate in civic and social groups to solve problems. Through these activities they are involved in politics but not in an ideological or partisan way. These people tend to be among the higher socio-economic groups.
5. **Campaigners**—This is 15 percent of the population. This group is very active in campaign activity but does very little in civic or social group participation. This group tends to be higher status but Catholics and African-Americans are also campaigners.
6. **Complete Activists**—Eleven percent of the population can be categorized into this group. They are complete participants—voting, campaigning, group membership. This group is affluent and middle aged, and they are highly attuned to politics.[18]

These categories enable us to easily identify the mixture of both voting and participation. We have said the Europeans have a higher rate of voting but, they have a lower rate of participation. Participation is defined as a person doing anything that involves civic groups or political organizations. Giving money, answering a poll or even signing a petition are all acts of participation. One of the great ironies of the American political system is the expansion of the right to vote, yet the percentage of people who vote is very low. In other parts of the world, American soldiers are dying to give people democracy, while in this country we tend to take our democracy for granted. Benjamin Franklin's famous answer to a question: "A lady named Mrs. Powell, asks Dr. Franklin, 'What type of government did you give us?' His response, 'a Republic if you can keep it.'"[19] A person's feeling about voting and participating is a private act that has public overtones. Yes, it is a product of our belief in liberty not to force people to participate in the political process. Yet, our institutions that help form opinions should try to build people's internal efficacy instead of reinforcing feelings of alienation and apathy.

---

[17]Ibid. p. 40.

[18]Verba and Nie, *Political Participation in America*, pp. 56–81.

[19]Walter Isaacson, *Benjamin Franklin: An American Life*. New York: Simon & Schuster, 2003, p. 459.

VOTING IN THE FUTURE

The election of 2000 highlighted the logistical problems we have with voting. The technology that is used (a punch card) is very old technology. Putting a mark on a piece of paper is the most basic technology that has been invented in the process of voting. There has been a movement to install electronic voting machines, but again some believe that this technology can be tampered. Congresswoman McKinney of Georgia blamed her primary loss on electronic voting machines, regardless of the fact that she struck a Capital policeman and was highly incompetent as a Representative for her district. We trust computers with our money, most of us have ATM cards, credit cards, and/or debit cards that let us deposit money or withdraw money from a kiosk the same way electronic voting works.

There is a need to strengthen the methods that we use when we vote. Voter fraud is a concern. Larger concerns are the organizational aspects of our elections. Are the voting booths in convenient places? Some minority communities complain about the number of voting booths in their neighborhoods. Are the elections timed in order to facilitate participation or are our traditional methods just not relevant to the times we live in. In his study, *The Vanishing Voter: Public Involvement in an Age of Uncertainty*,[20] Thomas E. Patterson examined the pattern of voting participation in the United States. He argues that since the 1960s, politics in the United States has become candidate centered, and the tactics such as negative campaigning and the tedium of the long campaign are designed to make sure voters are disgusted and bored so they will stay home.[21]

The status of people who are eligible to vote is also under question for the future. There is nothing in the Constitution that forbids a felon to vote, with the criminalization of behavior such as drug use, many have called for the right to vote to be extended to felons since the United States has one of the highest rates of incarceration in the history of the world. The argument goes—we have more people in prison than the Soviet Union and South Africa under apartheid. An overwhelming proportion of prisoners are held on non-violent drug offenses.[22] Why should

we take away their right to vote? Others counter this argument with the argument that voting is a right, but it is also a privilege, and if a person breaks the law then they should forfeit their right to vote.

Another argument for the future of voting is the right of citizens and non-citizens to vote. Interest groups for undocumented workers are advocating a series of reforms to bring these people into the political process. Some advocates in California have argued that non-citizens with children in the public school system should have the right to vote in local school board races and vote on issues such as property taxes and other local boards that pass laws that touch non-citizens' lives. This controversy is going to be the next big issue we will see, especially in the era of illegal immigration and globalization, where determining who is a citizen and non-citizen in the United States is getting more and more difficult.

An essential question for our democracy is the procedure that opens the door to the voting booth. We have analyzed how opinions and participation are interlocked on a personal level and how this changes the political environment on every level of government from municipal, state and the Federal government. Voting behavior and public opinion are issues that have many facets. Non-participation can be a function of a person's liberty or it can be a function of apathy and ignorance, depending on the case we are analyzing. Voting rights was a major issue in the civil rights movement, yet African-Americans have a very low voter turnout. Is this a result of discrimination of the past or is it because the political environment today does not target African-Americans because of their loyalty to the Democratic party? Hispanic voters are growing, yet their rate of participation does not seem to be growing. Is this because of issues dealing with citizenship or issues dealing with a tradition of low voter turnout? The poor also have a very low turnout. Should there be programs to increase the numbers of lower socio-economic voters to participate? Technology, education, and politics are all influenced by the rate of turnout. Young people do not vote, old people do vote, that is why the government and politicians listen to old people and they are slower to respond to young people.

CONCLUSION

In this chapter, we have analyzed public opinion and how people vote. We have defined public opinion as the collective of individual beliefs shared by some adults in the population. Public opinion is expressed

---

[20]Thomas E. Patterson, *The Vanishing Voter: Public Involvement in an Age of Uncertainty*. New York: Alfred Knopf, 2002.

[21]Ibid. p. 52.

[22]Lawrence M. Friedman, *Law in America: A Short History*. New York: The Modern Library, pp. 116–117.

in either elections or polls that are conducted by public opinion firms. Media groups today take public opinion polls every day. Scientifically, public opinion polls are accurate because of the Central Limit Theorem. This theorem which makes modern statistics possible basically says if you have a random sample you can generalize your findings. Public opinion polls are accurate because of this theorem. They may be accurate but they are also time sensitive. The age of a poll will have significant bearing on its meaning. The shelf life of a poll should be considered the same as danish. The same day it is baked is usually the best time to consume it. Day old is still eatable, but, not the best. Therefore, if the poll is two days old it should be thrown away.

Keeping this in mind, we went on to describe the qualities of public opinion. These qualities are: intensity, fluidity, stability, quiescence, relevance, political knowledge, consensus and division. These qualities enable us to analyze the changes we see in public opinion from one poll to another. Connecting private and public opinion, we described the institutions and social contact that help people form opinions. Overwhelmingly, we know your family is the most dominant agent for the formulation of opinions. Education, peer group, religious influence, occupation, political and leadership also play a role in forming general opinions. Demographic traits also contribute to our differing understanding of the environment around us. After our examination of opinion, we then examined voting behavior.

The Presidential election of 2000 highlighted the problems we have in voting technology. Voting patterns, in general, show the rate of eligible voters has been falling since the 1960s. Usually older, higher income and protestant people vote more than poor, minority and young people. As politics has become more candidate-centered, negative campaigning and the never-ending campaign have lured voters to stay home. The attitude "that they are all crooks" has lowered external efficacy to the point where many Americans do not see the importance of voting. They believe whoever is elected will not serve their interests, so why vote.

By examining patterns of voting behavior in the past, we can determine some future trends that may be highly disturbing to some people. The technology of voting is being re-examined, the use of electronic voting machines has been questioned. This questioning seems somewhat misplaced since economically we trust these types of machines (similar to an ATM machine to handle our money and banking). There are projects being done by both academia and industry to make sure the new electronic voting machines will be reliable and tamper proof.

Another challenge for the future is changing the non-voting status of a large number of people who live in the United States. There have been movements to change the non-voting status of both non-violent felons and non-citizens in the hope of having a democracy that reflects the people who live in the country. These issues are just starting to be debated and the conclusion of where our society will end up on these issues is still in doubt. Finally, the whole discussion of this chapter is encompassed by the idea of political socialization. Shared opinions and acting on those opinions in the voting booth are products of the political culture of the United States. Why it is difficult to have laws than require voter participation is the idea of liberty of people who choose not to participate. Our political culture entitles people to hold opinions and act in ways that may be detrimental to their personal interests. People not voting is one of those types of behaviors. There is an old joke—A poll worker asks a man: "Are voters apathetic or ignorant about voting?" He responds: "I don't know and I don't care." Is it impossible to peer into people's motives? Are they not voting as a positive protest, or are they not voting because they are ignorant of the power of the ballot box? We frankly cannot generalize non-participation of people in the political process.

In the next chapter, we will concentrate on people and organizations that do participate in the electoral process. Our next step in this discussion is to examine the roles of political parties, interest groups and money in our electoral process. How do these groups relate to one another? Furthermore, how do they relate to the voter to be successful? These are the organizations that shape our political environment and draw the context in which the individual responds.

TERMS TO REMEMBER

PUBLIC OPINION

CENTRAL LIMIT THEOREM

POLITICAL SOCIALIZATION

POLITICAL CULTURE

EFFICACY

Political Participation and Public Opinion Polls

TRUE OR FALSE QUESTIONS

1. Public opinion polls are not scientifically based.   T / F

2. Public opinion supported the invasion of Iraq in 2002.   T / F

3. Public opinion polls helped Harry Truman defeat Thomas Dewey in 1948.   T / F

4. There are not any properties of public opinion, people do not think rationally.   T / F

5. Family has very little influence on how people form their opinions.   T / F

6. Friends have the most influence on opinions.   T / F

7. Gender determines voting behavior between men and women.   T / F

8. Race has little or no effect on voting behavior.   T / F

9. American political culture does not have any values.   T / F

10. Forty percent of eligible voters vote on any given election.   T / F

MULTIPLE CHOICE QUESTIONS

11. The Central Limit Theorem helps with
    a. random sampling
    b. counting votes
    c. generalizing results of a poll
    d. proves polling, if done correctly, is scientific

12. Which is not a property of public opinion?
    a. Fluidity
    b. Quiescence
    c. Stability
    d. Bias

13. Which office do we not vote directly for?
    a. House of Representatives
    b. Presidency
    c. Senate
    d. Governor

14. Which group is the most loyal to the Democratic party?
    a. Hispanic Americans
    b. Asian Americans
    c. African-Americans
    d. South Asian-Americans

15. Verba and Nie developed a scale of participation. Which is one of the categories of their scale?
    a. Inactives
    b. Never voted
    c. Always vote
    d. Felons

16. Public opinion polls should be consumed fresh just like
    a. sushi
    b. ham
    c. steak
    d. chicken

17. Which is not a property of public opinion?
    a. Fluidity
    b. Stability
    c. Relevance
    d. Capability

18. Which group is not allowed to vote?
    a. Felons
    b. 18 year olds
    c. Women
    d. Naturalized citizens

19. Voting machines are not used because
    a. they are too expensive.
    b. they can be tampered with through hacking.
    c. they are too complicated.
    d. they use too much electricity.

20. Voting is
    a. a duty.
    b. an obligation.
    c. a private act on a public stage.
    d. a right, but one also has the freedom not to participate.
    e. all of the above.

chapter seven

POLITICAL PARTIES AND INTEREST GROUPS

INTRODUCTION

There is not a provision in the Constitution that calls for the development of political parties. Political parties evolved from the ratification debate on the powers of the Federal government. If you remember, there were the Federalists who advocated a strong central government that could enforce public safety and regulate economic activity. Countering them were the Anti-Federalist who wanted strong state government as a counterbalance to a central government to insure individual liberty.[1] This debate continues even though the party labels may change. There is a basic divide in American politics over the size and power of the Federal government and its role in our daily lives.

In American history this divide has dominated politics resulting in a two party system. Since the Civil War these parties have been the Democrats and

Republicans. There have been attempts to establish third parties in this country. As recently as 2000 there has been Presidential candidates for the Green Party and Reform Party. The former had significant popular support (in the context of third party candidates), and the latter had qualified for public financing for the general election. Are these groups really political parties? In this chapter we will review the definition of a political party, the functions the parties play in our elections and who are the dominant groups in each of the major political parties. Our discussion moves to investigating the role of interest groups and an examination of the major interest groups in American politics today.

Our analysis has been twofold. So far, we have described the governmental structure of our society and the personal activities that result in opinion formation and influence the decision for individuals to vote or not to vote. This discussion on political parties starts our examination of the institutions that play a major role in the flavor of politics we have today. The political environment we have today is a

---

[1] Samuel Eliot Morison, *The Oxford History of the American People: Volume 2: 1789 through Reconstruction*. New York: Penguin Group, 1965, pp. 33–56.

combination of all three of these components; the structure of government, the behavior of individuals and political parties. It is important for us to understand where they are connected and how all three: structure, voting behavior and institutional activities create both the political and social environment in which we live today.

POLITICAL PARTIES: A DEFINITION

A political party is defined as "a group of activists who organize to win elections, to operate the government, and to determine public policy."[2] This definition is very useful to clear the clutter for our analysis. Presently, there are only two political parties in the United States—the Republican and Democratic. Other organizations such as the Green Party, Reform Party, Natural Law Party and the Libertarian party just to name a few are not political parties because they do not win elections. The first component of this definition is a party has to win elections. These groups do not win. Once they start winning elections then we may consider their activities and organization but they have virtually no influence either as a political party or social group in the political process.

The second attribute of a political party are the people who make the "card-carrying" membership of the party—political activists. These are people, who we described in the previous chapter, as campaigners. They are totally engaged in the political process. Their loyalty is to the party winning elections. They really do not care about issues, or candidates. These things may have contributed to their activity at the beginning of their activity but now they are more loyal to the party. Another motive may be their jobs are connected to their party affiliation. Either they have appointments that are contingent on their party winning or are governmental, or union appointments where their party affiliation is not a matter of choice. You will find this in geographic areas that are dominated by one party (Democrats in the old South). The other party will still have members since there are always patronage jobs such as Post-Master or U.S. Attorney that must be filled. Presidents and Senators are usually more inclined to appoint someone who is from their own party. Therefore, these activists are not interested in philosophy or issues, they are only interested in winning elections.

This is why, when you see a candidate change positions, the party members usually go along with the position. The way President Clinton authored Welfare reform and President Bush's change on illegal immigration are just a couple of examples of party members going along with a major change in policy. Although the base of the party (people who identify with the party but are not members) may become discouraged, such as the conservative wing of the Republican party today, or the liberal wing of the Democratic party after September 11th, the activists go along with the changing political environment. So, using our definition, we have narrowed our analysis to political parties who win elections and their membership who are activists.

People join political parties and political parties are formed to operate the government. People are motivated to work in political campaigns, mostly for the opportunity to work inside the government. Political power and prestige are given to political appointments. The government is the largest employer in the country and even though there is civil service[3] the operational base of a political party is very important. It gives the candidates both a pool of talented people to appoint and institutional memory on how the government should work. In his classic book *The Best and the Brightest*, David Halberstam starts this story with the President-Elect John F. Kennedy meeting Robert A. Lovell who was a leading banker and Democratic governmental appointee.[4] He worked with George Marshall in World War II, and later when General Marshall was the Secretary of State. In this meeting described by Halberstam, Kennedy offers him any job in the government. Lovell turns him down; instead he advises or recommends people who are capable but also loyal Democrats.[5] This happens when there is a new President, Congressman, Governor, or State Legislator elected. Once elected, a candidate has to ask: "Who is good and can they help me get re-elected?"

One major problem third parties have is they do not have the experience of having members that have operated inside the government. When Jesse Ventura was elected to the Governorship of Minne-

---

[2]Michael Dinneen, *Instructor's Manual for American Government and Politics Today: The Essentials 1998–1999 Edition*. New York: Wadsworth Publishing Co., 1998, p. 128.

[3]Civil Service is a merit-based hiring and promotion system used by most state governments and the Federal government. However, the highest levels of government are filled by political appointment. On average the first day a new President takes office he has to appoint over five thousand people.

[4]David Halberstam, *The Best and the Brightest*. New York: Ballantine Books, 1992, pp. 1–4.

[5]Ibid.

sota, he appointed people to run his office from both the Democratic and Republican parties because the Reform party did not have anyone who had experience in working at the highest level of state government. What if Ralph Nader had won the Presidency in 2000 or 2004? Who would have been his Secretary of State? Attorney General? Secretary of the Agriculture? It is very difficult to say, because the Green Party does not have members who have been in government. Like Ventura, President Nader would have found himself in very lonely company; there is no one who is a member of the Green party that has worked in the sub-cabinet level of the Executive branch of the Federal government. This is an operational hurdle third parties must overcome if they are to be taken seriously.

Finally, we get to the question of where the party should stand on issues concerning public policy. Issues such as pro-life and pro-choice, high taxes or low taxes, increasing social security or defense spending are questions that may be high in the voters mind, but they are the last thing political party activists are concerned about. "Tell the voters what they want to hear" is what many activists think to themselves when they disagree with one of their candidates. We all know people who are activists, no matter where their party is on an issue, they agree with the party. Activists had to do cartwheels in order to keep ahead of President Clinton on his flip-flops on welfare reform, the Federal government deficit and education reform. Republicans had their own acrobatics when they tried to follow President Reagan's flips on arms control and negotiation with the Soviet Union. Republicans who used to complain about Federal spending are today having a difficult time explaining why the Republican Congress and President Bush have become such large spenders of the taxpayers' money.

The most recent and dramatic example of the public policy agenda taking second place to the belief that we need a candidate who can win was the John Kerry Presidential campaign. During the primaries Kerry argued that Howard Dean could not win because of his opposition to the war. Kerry said the anti-war people should support him because he can win. Howard Dean lost the primaries and John Kerry won the nomination. This tells you the anti-war movement in the Democratic party was more anti-Bush than anti-war, since John Kerry had voted to give President Bush the power to invade Iraq. The Democratic activists used the sentiment of the anti-war movement to try to mobilize voters to their candidate. This ultimately failed and John Kerry lost the 2004 Presidential election. It did succeed in confirming the anti-war credentials of the Democratic party which may serve them in the future. We will see. If in 2008, Hillary Clinton runs for President it will be very interesting to see how the anti-war activists decide to play their hand. Are they Democrats first? Or are they more concerned with the issues surrounding the invasion of Iraq and the War on Terror? If you are an anti-war activist it must be very difficult to support Hillary Clinton since she voted for the war in Iraq and has supported the war since the invasion in 2002.

If the public policy issues are more important to you than the political party then your interest lay in joining an interest group. An interest group is different than a political party. An interest group are people acting together to form coalitions and present action on a particular issue. These groups usually have alliance with lobbying groups and have coalitions inside political parties. An example would be a president of a local Teachers Union would probably also be a member of the Democratic party. Unions are the major interest group inside the Democratic party. It is possible for interest groups to be involved with both political parties if they are powerful enough. The most powerful interest group is the American Association of Retired Persons. They are powerful because their membership is universal (if you reach the age 55 you can join). Older people vote and older people tend to have more money than younger people and older people, because they are retired, tend to have more time to volunteer than other people. This mix of membership and organization makes this group very powerful.[6]

In President Bush's first term, the AARP supported the prescription drug benefit that passed the Congress and the President signed into law. In the beginning of President Bush's second term, President Bush presented a plan that would change Social Security. The AARP was against the plan and the plan died during the first year of the second term of the Bush Presidency. On the prescription drug plan, AARP was with the Republicans and on Social Security they were with the Democrats. Both parties welcome this group's influence and one can see a very similar program on issues concerning retirees between the Democrats and Republicans.

---

[6]Hedrick Smith, *The Power Game: How Washington Works*. New York: Ballantine Books, 1988, p. 240.

Are the Democrats and Republicans different? The Democrats and Republicans have a very similar structure and because of election laws (which they helped to write) the legal restrictions on their actions is also very much the same. On policy issues it seems each party picks a position on an issue regardless of the philosophy behind the issue. If Republicans are pro-life, then why are they in favor of the death penalty? If Democrats are pro-choice then why are they generally against the use of capital punishment? Republicans continue to say they are against governmental solutions for problems, yet since 2000 they have spent money as if they were in favor of government involvement in every segment of our lives, including the Departments of Education and Energy, two departments previous Republican candidates for President said they would disband. President Bush campaigned on and approved greater Federal government involvement in education than any previous President with his "No Child Left Behind Educational Reform Act."

Not to be overly cynical, basically the role of the party is to get elected. In the United States the roles of the two parties is very similar and therefore one has to conclude that the parties are very much the same. This sameness can be seen when we analyze the several functions the Republicans and Democrats serve in order for their members to win elections.

FUNCTIONS OF POLITICAL PARTIES

Political parties serve five functions in the electoral process in the United States. They are: recruiting candidates, organizing and running elections, operating the government, presenting alternative policies to the electorate and providing organized opposition to the party in power. Although political parties' influence on politics has declined since the 1960s, by providing these essential functions, political parties have been able to keep themselves relevant in the political arena. While keeping in mind the candidate centric politics of today, let us examine each of these functions.

RECRUITING CANDIDATES

There are two types of candidates in politics: recruited candidates and self-promoted candidates. Almost all candidates are self-promoted candidates. One of the great things about politics is there is not a structure where a person starts at the bottom of the political ladder and ends up, after years of hard work,

at the top. One day anyone can wake up and say to themselves I think I am going to run for political office. In the modern era, almost every President has been self-promoted.

Right after World War II, there were two recruited candidates. The first was Harry Truman. Truman was not recruited to be a candidate for the Presidency. Instead, he was recruited by President Roosevelt's advisers to be Vice President. President Roosevelt's health was a secret and although people suspected he was very sick as he was running for his fourth term, people suspected but no one spoke of the chances of Roosevelt not living through the fourth term. Truman was recruited because he was from a border state and he was famous for activities of his Truman Commission that investigated waste fraud and abuse from governmental contractors during World War II.[7]

Truman was elected to the Vice Presidency in 1944. Upon President Roosevelt's death he became President. President Truman did run in 1948 and won. He did this out of a sense of personal duty and he wanted to finish the job he had started.[8] However, if he had never been Vice President it is very doubtful that Harry Truman would have been President.

Another President who was recruited to the job was President Eisenhower. Dwight Eisenhower had been an Army officer for most of his life. He was the field commander during the invasion of Europe in World War II. After the war, he had helped implement the Truman Administration's foreign policy in Europe by serving as the first commander of the North Atlantic Treaty Organization (NATO). He was so popular, that Harry Truman in 1948 wrote to Eisenhower offering him the nomination for the Presidency of the Democratic party and Truman would serve again as Vice President. This is an illustration of both Eisenhower's popularity and Truman's patriotism and lack of political ego. Eisenhower turned down Truman's offer and stated in 1948 that he would not run for any office since, in his heart, he remained an Army officer, not a politician.

Events during the next four years would change the General's mind. Even though Eisenhower had helped the Truman Administration post-war policies in Europe, Eisenhower declared he was a Republican.[9]

---

[7]David McCullough, *Truman.* New York: Simon & Schuster, 1992, p. 346.

[8]Ibid.

[9]Fred I. Greenstein, *The Hidden Hand Presidency: Eisenhower as a Leader.* New York: Basic Books, 1982, p. 11.

The Republican party in 1952 had been out of power since the election of Franklin D. Roosevelt in 1933. There was serious concern about the survival of the party if it could not regain power in 1952. Many saw the Republicans as a party that had not been responsive to the issues of modern times. The Republican response to the Great Depression had been to wait and things will get better. The Republican response to the aggressive nature of Imperial Japan and the Nazis had been isolationism and the America First campaign. The victory of President Truman in 1948 to many Republicans seemed to be the last nail in the coffin of the party. Then Eisenhower announced that he was a Republican. According to Steven Ambrose, Eisenhower's decision to enter politics was due to his perception and disappointment of the leadership qualities of both the Democrats and Republicans at this time.

Republican leaders such as Thomas Dewey saw Eisenhower as their best chance to win the Presidency. The Conservative wing of the Republican party led by Senator Robert Taft sought to stop the draft Ike movement. Eisenhower was a war leader and was popular with the common soldier. He was able to translate this popularity into political success after he had been convinced and recruited by the Republicans to run for office. This type of recruitment of candidates is very rare. In recent times, the only candidate that has been recruited was Colin Powell.

Colin Powell was also a successful General who was recruited by both the Democrats and Republicans to run for President. He declared himself to be a Republican, but decided he did not have the "fire in the belly" to run for President. Instead, he endorsed President Bush and became his first Secretary of State. Party recruitment of candidates has become very rare because parties do not have leaders *per se*. The leaders of the national parties are not dictators. Usually, the Chairmen of the Democratic and Republican parties job is to raise money and set the parameters of elections. In many cases the people who hold these jobs are surrogates for candidates who want to control the rule making machinery and who themselves are self promoting candidates for the Presidency. There are many people who would make good candidates, but today, candidates are self-promoting and like Colin Powell, if you cannot promote yourself, parties will not nominate you. The second function of political parties is probably the most important for the sustaining and maintaining of the two party system in this country. The political parties are the bodies that organize and run elections.

ORGANIZING AND RUNNING ELECTIONS

Every county or municipal government in the United States has an election commission. On this commission are representatives of both the Democratic and Republican parties in equal number who set up the rules for the elections. As we read in the Constitution, it is the legislatures who are responsible for organizing elections in each state. Over time, legislatures have found it is easier having input from the two political parties in the country. The reason why your state has a particular primary or caucus on a given day is the result of the legislature working with the county or municipal election commission. Although it is illegal to discriminate against individuals, the rules have been written to discriminate against third party candidates and their organizations.

An example of how both parties work together to set the rules for elections happened in California before the 2004 Presidential election. There was a referendum that asks the legislature to change the primary election system in California. Today, California has a closed primary system (meaning someone has to declare their party membership and is only allowed to vote in their declared party's primary). People voted in California to change this system to an open primary system (an open primary system allows a voter to vote for both party's candidates and "crossover" to vote for anyone people like). Overwhelmingly this initiative won. After the election both parties went to court to prevent the changing of the primary system, from one of closed to one that would be open. They argued the political parties were private membership-based organizations and the picking of a candidate was private business. Being a private organization gave them the right to pick their candidates how they deemed appropriate. The California judges agreed with the parties and California has a closed primary system today. This argument that both political parties are membership-based private organizations probably came as a surprise to many people who supported both parties. It is a prime example of how the political parties write the rules in order for people to stay home.

How does this affect voter turnout? Let us take a person who traditionally votes for the Democrats. However, this election; he is interested in his Congressional race because the seat is open and he favors a Republican who is running in a contested primary. In states that have open primaries, he could vote for the Republican congressional primary race and then vote for Democrats he favors in the other races. When he participates in a closed primary, our voter would have to change his registration, then he can vote for the Republican he wants in Congress, but, he has thrown away his opportunity to vote in any Democratic primary races. This is very difficult and prevents people from voting for the person they think is best regardless of the political party. Well, you can see how political parties do not want people voting in this way. Political parties want voters to vote for their whole slate of candidates.

Other rules the political parties have developed has been the drawing of the legislative districts on all levels of government. The only geographical legislative districts we have in our system are the U.S. Senate. In the Senate, candidates have to run for their seats campaigning in the whole state. Other legislative candidates will have a district that is carved out by a compromise between the two parties. These districts usually have a majority for one party or the other party. This is why being an incumbent legislator is almost a life appointment. The district you represent probably does not have enough voters of the other party or independents to vote you out of office, unless you commit a crime.

Another function of political parties is to write the rules for public financing for elections. Currently, the only public financed election is for the Presidency. The formula for qualifying for federal matching funds requires a party to run in two Presidential elections before you can qualify for funding and have a certain percentage in the polls during the race you are currently running in. The Reform party did qualify; however, there was a disruption in their party when Ross Perot did not seek another candidacy and Patrick Buchanan declared himself a Reform party candidate in order to get the financing. They held a convention in Long Beach California in 2000 and the party split, never to be heard from again. By the way, the Reform party only acquired the qualification for Federal funding because Ross Perot spent millions of dollars of his own money in order to get the party to qualify. It does not seem likely that another billionaire will be willing to spend, to give birth to another political party in the near future.

The Democrats and Republicans have fixed elections in this country. They are able to control the process of who is a candidate, what type of district these candidates run in and how we finance these candidates once they are in the general election. There is nothing sinister or conspiratorial about this system. It is one of the basic functions of the two political parties we have in the United States.

OPERATING THE GOVERNMENT

One of the reasons the parties are able to write the regulation on how we run elections is because the members of the government who are involved in running elections are all members of the two political parties in the United States. As we said previously in our discussion of the definition of a political party, it is the parties that participate in the operation of the government. Most people are volunteering in campaigns because they want to be appointed to a governmental job. Yes, it is true that there are idealists who support candidates because of where they stand on a particular issue or issues. However, most people who are volunteering their expertise are hoping if the candidate wins, they will be able to work either on the candidate's staff, or will be appointed to a position as a reward for supporting the candidate and the party. This relationship between the party, candidate and experts has created a triangle that is very difficult for a third party to break. If a Republican or Democrat wins the Presidency we have a rough idea of who that person will appoint to the important offices in their administration. If a third party wins, we would not have any idea. This was mentioned earlier when we spoke of the appointments of Governor Jesse Ventura in Minnesota. These experts, when they are not in public office, also contribute to the party's institutional memory and strength by providing alternative public policy to the public.

CREATING ALTERNATIVE PUBLIC POLICIES

How would the Democrats fight the War on Terror? How would the Republicans guarantee the civil rights of African-Americans and other protected classes of people? These questions are in the minds of candidates and voters. Why is a person a Republican? Why are they a Democrat? We know a person's family has a great deal to do with their choice of which political party to join. Also, alternative policies help political parties to make a stand and trademark their perspective in easy and memorable ways. In 1960, after eight years of the Eisenhower Administration, John F. Kennedy ran on a platform of more governmental intervention on the problems of American life.[10] He and the Democrats ran on issues that questioned the country's preparedness for national secu-

---

[10]Theodore H. White, *The Making of the President 1960*. New York: Antheneum Publishers, 1961, p. 319.

rity (the famous missile gap) debate and for intervention on the economy. Richard Nixon's campaign in 1968 presented an alternative to the Democrats when he said he was the candidate for the "silent majority." What both Kennedy and Nixon were doing was to present alternative visions that had been prepared by experts who identified with the Party and each candidate.

With the election of President Kennedy we saw the establishment of the Democratic party take back the operations of the government from the Republicans. One exception of this was the CIA director who was replaced after the Bay of Pigs failure. Kennedy brought in people who were young—one of Kennedy's criterion was the person's war experience during World War II, and technocrats, especially the people Kennedy appointed in the departments of Defense and State.[11] Richard Nixon eight years later would appoint Henry Kissinger, Daniel Patrick Moyihan and others who were not loyal to him as a Presidential candidate. Yet these were experts who articulated an alternative policy while the party was out of office and then were appointed to implement their policies once the party gained power.[12]

In 2006, the Democratic party has an opportunity to gain significant electoral progress against the Republicans; however, the Democrats have yet to define an alternative policy for fighting the War on Terror. The Democratic party is in the process of being an anti-war party in a political environment where the country is at war. Their experts are going to have to present a realistic policy on Iraq and the War on Terror if they are going to be able to elect a President in 2008. The Democratic candidate John Kerry lost the election because he was unwilling or unable to articulate a simple and believable policy on the War on Terror. Even today, the people who would be appointed Secretary of State or Secretary of Defense in a democratic administration, have advocated sending troops to Darfur and striking North Korea's missile site. Their recommendations on foreign policy and defense policy seem not to make sense.

The Republicans have enjoyed a majority in both legislative houses and the Presidency since 2004. They have had the opportunity to implement a policy; yet their policies also lack attractiveness to the general public. The lack of imagination coming from the informal experts of both parties shows the institutional weakness of both parties in drawing up alternative policies that are capable of winning elections and solving problems. If the Democrats had a unifying and realistic voice on foreign and strategic issues, their opposition to the Republicans would be much more effective.

PROVIDING ORGANIZED OPPOSITION

It is a simple fact that the United States could not have invaded Iraq without Democratic votes in the U.S Senate and House of Representatives. Democrats called for the removal of the Iraqi Dictator before George W. Bush was elected. Now, Senators such as Hillary Clinton, John Kerry and ex-Senator John Edwards are trying to change this fact. It is very difficult to be against a war that you voted for. Their argument has become, they were in favor of giving the President the power to invade Iraq however, he did not implement the war well. What this tells average voters is the objectives between the Democrats and Republicans were the same. Their opposition to the war is not the fact that the war was wrong, but the fact that the management of the war was incompetent. This is not an alternative public policy. Calling for multilateral diplomacy or changing the margins of a Republican policy will not get either the Democratic base excited or independents who disagree with the Republican policy interested in voting for them.

The Democratic party is becoming very poor at presenting alternative policies. The Republican party is also becoming very poor at instituting public policies that their conservative base can be excited about. The illegal immigration issue could be an issue that the Democrats could use their progressive instincts and co-op conservative voters. Instead, they are mimicking the Republican amnesty program. The Democrats have not called for the arresting of employers who hire illegal immigrants. If you arrest the CEO of Tyson Foods, or other large corporations who hire illegal immigrants, this would win favor of the progressive elements and union members of the Democratic party. It would also divide the Republican party base between conservative (who would favor the arrest of employers) and the business interests (who would be against such an alternative policy). Instead, the Democratic party has made the decision to try to court the illegal immigration lobby, in order to create a future coalition at the expense of the coalition that it built in the past. Will the Democrats be successful at this? Again, the Republicans are also trying to carve out a new coalition that includes the illegal immigration lobby.

[11]David Halberstam, *The Best and the Brightest*. New York: Ballantine Books, 1969, p. 162.
[12]Ibid. p. 664.

As we will see, today both parties seem to be very much the same. The Democrats (because they are in opposition) have not done a very good job at framing issues and differentiating themselves from many of the Republican policies. The Democratic argument seems to be "we will be better managers of the same failed policies." This does not seem to be an exciting alternative that will bring candidates to the party or voters to the voting booth. On issues such as the War on Terror, Iraq, and immigration the Democrats and Republicans have the same policies.

The failure of both the Republican and Democratic parties to address the important issues since the turn of the century has made many people looking past the horizon and envisioning a new political party (or changing one of the existing parties) to reflect a different political perspective. Howard Dean's Presidential campaign in 2004 had a revolutionary element in it. Although he lost, his campaign showed how the new media and anti-war sentiment was growing in this country. There is nothing written in the Constitution that says we have to have two parties that are named Republican and Democrat. We have identified the functions of political parties. When a political party starts to fail at a number of these functions they must reform and change or they will perish.

The Democratic party was changed by Franklin D. Roosevelt, and the Republican party was changed by Barry Goldwater and Ronald Reagan. The rise of a third party is unlikely but possible. More probable is the morphing of one of the major political parties to reflect the dissatisfaction of a majority of Americans in the choices they are able to make when they vote. A party's functions are only part of the equation that brings political victory. In recent times, the parties have become very weak. They have become weak while interest groups and candidates have become stronger.

In the next section of our discussion, we will trace the history of the political parties and the elements of the political environment that contribute to their increased weakness in today's politics.

A BRIEF HISTORY OF THE DEMOCRATIC AND REPUBLICAN PARTIES

The names of the two political parties in the United States have been the same since the Civil War. In spite of this fact, the positions taken and coalitions built by the two parties has differed from 1860 to today. During the Civil War, the Democratic party was the party of succession and the defense of slavery. The party was divided into Northern and Southern Democrats. The identification of the Democratic party with the Confederacy hurt their electoral chances in the North from the end of the Civil War until the end of World War II. On the state level, the Democratic party was very powerful. Depending on the state, there were large political machines that controlled the votes of new immigrants and urban workers. A political machine is a relationship where the local party leader extends jobs, food, apartments—any type of help in exchange for votes. So if your uncle was a policeman and his job was dependent on which party won the election, he would make sure you voted. This relationship made winning elections almost guaranteed by the men who ran the machines called bosses. The Democratic party controlled the large urban centers of the East and Midwest and the Southern States.

The Stock Market Crash of 1929 would provide a unique opportunity for the Democrats. The Great Depression showed the Republican party had run out of ideas and their sixty years of domination of Presidential politics was coming to an end. The Democratic party under President Roosevelt became a very interesting coalition. He was able to combine both politicians who supported the discriminatory laws of the South and the African-American community. The Democrats also had popularity among Catholics, Jews and white Southern Protestants. Also included in Roosevelt's coalition were the Union workers and Progressive activists.

The Democratic party would dominate national politics from 1933 to the early 1980s under the Reagan Administration. The Democratic party during the Civil War was an advocate of states rights by the time President Roosevelt was elected; the Democrats were in favor of increasing the Federal government's role in almost every facet of American life. World War II and the 1950s would see the Democratic party's coalition survive until the challenges of Vietnam and the failure of the Great Society, that was established by Lyndon Johnson. The Democratic party would only see two Presidents elected from 1968 through 2004. The two Presidents would come from the South—Jimmy Carter was elected in 1976 and William Clinton was elected in 1992. Both of these Presidents enjoyed the confidence of both Southerners and people who lived in the large urban centers of the country.

The coalition of the Democratic party in the 1990s consisted of the African-American community (who are the most loyal Democrats as a racial or ethnic group, however, they have a low voter participation rate), union members (because of the change of the economy, union membership is decreasing) and progressive groups such as feminists, environmentalists, anti-war activists, and other groups who would consider their politics progressive. There is a problem with this coalition. Frankly, it is too narrow to get elected. Even with all of the advantages of incumbency, the Democrats lost control of the House of Representatives in 1994 and have recently regained control. Most middle class and non-union workers are not interested in voting for the Democrats. White men especially in the South are not attracted to voting for Democrats. The Democratic party has to find a way, as Howard Dean said, to attract Southern white men who drive pick-up trucks. The Presidential election of 2008 will tell if the Democratic party is able to put together a coalition that will make it a dominant party or just receiving votes because people are dissatisfied with the Republican party.

The Republican party was founded on the eve of the Civil War in order to abolish slavery and to keep states in the Union. The result of the Civil War made modern America. Slavery was eliminated, the South was forced to stay in the Union and the Republican party, the party of Abraham Lincoln, was the party everyone (except Southerners) were loyal to. The Republicans also had bosses and political machines that gave benefits for political loyalty. The dominance of the Republican party from 1860 to the 1920s also created an interesting coalition between progressives and business interests. The African-American community voted for Republicans up to the time Franklin Roosevelt convinced them to join his coalition.

During the Progressive era Republicans, especially President Theodore Roosevelt, understood the government had to be involved in the economic issues facing the country or there would be a revolution. This idea split the Republican coalition when Roosevelt ran for President under the Progressive party banner. This split the Republican vote and Woodrow Wilson was elected. This election changed the Republican party. Most people who were progressives left the Republican party for good. The Republican party had started as a party that was fundamentally against states rights and became a party of the business and conservative interests. By the end of the 1920s, the Republican party would stand for business interests and a hands-off attitude toward regulation and governmental intervention. This is a winning formula in good times, albeit in bad times, it is a po-

litical disaster. The Great Depression would make the Republican party a minority party until the election of Dwight Eisenhower in 1952. The Republicans had been out of power for such a long time that if Eisenhower would not have been elected to the Presidency, there was speculation the party would not survive. Eisenhower picked a young Senator from California by the name of Richard Nixon.

Nixon would build a coalition that would serve the Republican party until the policies of George W. Bush. Nixon realized when he ran for President in 1960, the country had changed and the South was no longer solid for the Democratic party. Civil rights had divided the South and Southern whites were looking for a new party. The Roosevelt coalition was breaking up. The African-American community would stay with the Democrats and the Southern whites would join the Republicans.

This change was revolutionary, the South had been Democratic since before the Civil War and now there was an opening that very few people realized. Nixon and the Republicans would also develop a Western strategy. The invention of air conditioning made living in the West possible. People were leaving the weather of Michigan and Wisconsin to enjoy the pleasant conditions of Phoenix, Denver and Los Angeles. The Democrats thought a strategy that concentrated on the large urban centers of each state would make them a viable party throughout the 1960s through the 1990s. The Democrats catered to urban interests. This proved not to be effective. The Republican's coalition was built to reflect the social mobility of people. Ethnic groups that had supported Franklin Roosevelt and John F. Kennedy were now voting for Gerald Ford and Ronald Reagan.

The Republicans had captured the middle class, while it may have been Democratic policies that gave people the start to enter the middle class. Once they achieved their homes, education and social security, they looked to the Republicans to lower their taxes and get government regulation out of their lives. This message has been repeated since Richard Nixon's first election in 1968. Although conservatives do not consider Richard Nixon a conservative, his understanding of coalition-building and the work done by conservatives in politics in 1964 has dominated politics since.

Since 1960, both political parties have lost influence. Very few Americans would admit being a "party person." Most of us claim to be independent voters even if we never vote for candidates of the other party. The Republican strategy has been to focus on people who vote. They are older people, people who are in the middle class, religious people and finally people who are concerned about national security (from 1960–1989 the Cold War, and from 2000 people concerned about the War on Terror). The Democrats have concentrated their strategies on people who do not vote. In the 1980s there was the strategy to attract women as part of the gender gap, it failed. In the 1990s, President Clinton was responsible for Welfare reform and he succeeded. In 2004 John Kerry tried to recruit young voters to form a winning coalition for the Democratic party, as we know, he also failed.

The dominance of the Republican party since 1968 is a result of convincing people who vote to vote for them. The failure of the Democratic party since 1968 is developing strategies that are aimed at people who do not vote or their rate of voting is too low. This may be changing; the Republican party on immigration may be making a strategic mistake by ostracizing their current base of support in the hope of having a platform for people who may be eligible to vote in the future.

This brief history of the coalitions that form political marriages is just that—very brief. Theodore White's books *The Making of the President, 1960; Making of the President, 1964; and the Making of the President, 1968,* show how these coalitions were formed and how the evolution of candidate-centered politics has eaten away at the influence of political parties in this country. Another group that has taken influence from political parties are interest groups. We continue our analysis of institutions that are engaged by changing our focus to the allies of political parties—interest groups.

THE DEVELOPMENT OF INTERESTS GROUP POLITICS

In electoral campaigns, political parties and candidates cannot do everything on their own. Integral partners of modern politics are Interest Groups. Interest groups provide financial backing, volunteers and contributions that have stepped into the void to the increasing decline of political parties. An interest group is defined as an organized group of people sharing the same objectives, who actively attempt to influence office holders. Today in the United States there are over one hundred thousand interest groups. What do they do? Interest groups have direct and indirect techniques to influence the government, for shorthand we call these techniques lobbying.

The direct techniques of lobbying are a combination of helping frame an issue through expertise and helping people get elected through campaign money. Interest groups hold private meetings with members of Congress. They also testify in front of Congressional committees and executive agencies. Most legislation is written by interest groups. Members of Congress put their names on the legislation, but when they need a draft of the legislation it is written by interest groups. Connected to this, is when a legislator needs facts and statistics about an issue, interest groups again provide the specific information. They also recommend appointments to governmental positions. In this capacity, the interest groups help leaders legislate. In later chapters, we will examine the inner workings of Congress. Before anyone can legislate, they have to get elected. This is where the partnership starts.

Interest groups align themselves usually to political parties and directly to candidates. They do this with campaign assistance. Most interest groups have or encourage volunteers to campaign for endorsed candidates. This endorsement may take the form of a ratings list or may take the form of including the candidates name in their magazine or newsletter. In recent times, the invention of the Political Action Committee (PAC) as a fund raising organization that will distribute campaign contributions to the interest groups' endorsed candidates. PACs have dominated political fund raising. Here is how it works for a typical union (which is a labor interest group).

A member of the union will pay dues that are automatically taken out of his/her paycheck. A portion of the dues are given to the PAC in the case of the AFL-CIO. The PAC is called the Committee on Public Education (COPE). This PAC will then distribute millions of dollars, usually to Democrats. In exchange for campaign money, the PAC will receive access to the candidate once that candidate is elected. It is a circular relationship between candidates, political parties and interest groups. These are the direct techniques.

There are also indirect techniques. These techniques include generating public pressure by having people contact their local members of Congress. This can be done either by shotgun approach—an interest group organized a series of large rallies and protests. This was done in the spring of 2006, when organizers for undocumented workers had a series of protests to demonstrate the number of potential voters that undocumented workers represented. On the other hand, one can use the rifle approach. This approach targets vulnerable members of Congress and constituents are enrolled to act as lobbyists. The American Israeli Political Action Committee is very good at using this approach.[13] They send busloads of people to lobby their own Congressmen. Sometimes it is more effective to have individuals from a member of Congress' home district than it is to have a paid lobbyist. Another indirect technique interest groups use is to form an alliance with other interest groups to increase both their lobbying effort and create critical mass on an issue.[14] Again, using the illegal immigration issue, both labor and management interest groups cooperated and sponsored ways to coordinate and ultimately stop any legislation on immigration reform.

As we stated earlier, there are thousands of interest groups. The formation of interest groups started in the late 1800s–early 1900s with the formation of labor unions and industrial (management) associations. The economic contest between labor and management was the primary catalyst for the formation of early interest groups. After the Civil War, we see the concentration of wealth and power on an industrial scale. These organizations known as Trusts caused great concern since there was not a counterbalance. During the Progressive Era both Theodore Roosevelt and Woodrow Wilson sought to give labor unions more legitimacy in bargaining with management. Elihu Root who was an influential advisor to President Theodore Roosevelt said in a speech to the New York Bar Association in 1912: "The real difficulty appears to be that the new conditions incident to the extraordinary industrial development of the last half-century are continuously and progressively demanding the readjustment of the relations between great bodies of men and the establishment of new legal rights."[15] Root is saying what everyone recognized by 1912, that labor needed to be recognized and needed to be a large organization to compete against large corporate management. From the Progressive era to today, people have felt a need to join groups. In turn, these groups compete to form alliances with political parties to have influence on the government.

Almost every facet of American life has an interest group. The most powerful interest group is the American Association for Retired Persons (AARP). They are the most powerful group because older people vote, they have time, they have money, and the membership is almost universal, most people will live past 55 and are qualified to join. The largest unions are the AFL-CIO (American Federation of Labor), AFSCME (American Federation of State, County and Municipal Employees), the UAW (United Auto Workers) and the Teamsters. The largest management associations are the NAM (The National Association of Manufacturers), U.S. Chamber of Commerce, and the Business Roundtable. There are also professional associations such as the American Medical Association and the American Bar Association. Every professional group has an association.

There are also non-economic groups; these groups can be classified as political groups. These groups include the environmental lobby such as the Sierra Club and Audubon Society and public interest groups such as Common Cause and the Nader Organizations. In addition, in the political category, there are single issue groups such as the National Rifle Association and NOW (National Organization for Women). These groups concentrate their resources on gun rights and abortion respectively. Finally, foreign governments also lobby the government and use these techniques, although lobbyists must register with the Justice Department and ethic committees of both houses. Many former members of Congress are hired to lobby for foreign governments. Whenever a scandal hits the media, the latest is the bribery case of San Diego Congressman Duke Cunningham and lobbyist Jack Abramov, there are calls to restrict lobbying and the access interest groups have in Congress. The problem is lobbying is protected by the Constitution. The First Amendment of the Constitution gives us all the right to petition the government for redress of our grievances. This is what special interest groups do.

There has been legislation passed, and the Legislation Reorganization Act of 1946 requires lobbyists to report expenses and report activities. This act also defines what a lobbyist is—a lobbyist is someone who spends at least 20 percent of their time and earns 5,000 dollars a year from their activities. If a person falls under these criteria, then they are considered a lobbyist and must fulfill the obligations required by law (registering and filling out the forms of a lobbyist). Religious groups and tax exempt groups are not required under this law.

---

[13]Hedrick Smith, *The Power Game: How Washington Works.* New York: Ballantine Books, 1988, pp. 216–231.

[14]Ibid.

[15]Samuel Eliot Morrison, *The Oxford History of the American People, Vol.3: 1869 through the Death of John F. Kennedy.* New York: Meridan Publishing Co., 1994, p. 131.

The structure of the U.S. government invites interest groups, as we noted the Constitution preserves the right of people to lobby the government. It insures that we have pluralism in our approach to governmental regulation. Congress is able to hear from labor and management, industry and environmental groups when they consider legislation. There have been scandals, and sometimes when one party dominates over the institutions, their allied interest groups can also become corrupt. If that is the case, ultimately and hopefully, these groups will be either thrown in jail or thrown out of office. There are some purists who look at interest groups or otherwise known as special interest groups, as a negative in our political life. They also serve a way that individuals can find their collective voices on important issues and be heard.

CONCLUSION

Political parties and interest groups serve the political structure of the society. We have defined political parties as a group of activists who organize: 1) to win elections, 2) to operate the government, and 3) to determine public policy. Interest groups are defined as an organized group of people sharing the same objectives, who actively attempt to influence office holders. Using these definitions we can see the interaction between these two groups. Critics see the decline of political parties as a direct result of the increasing strength of interest groups. The alliance of interest groups and their ability to raise money has given some interest groups an incredible amount of power in our political life. The most powerful interest group in the U.S. is the AARP. This is an organization that has a membership of people over 55 years of age. This group has done a very good job in providing benefits to its members. Its members have also done a very good job in being involved in the election process. Because of their membership's involvement, politicians and candidates listen to the needs and desires of the AARP.

The alliance between interest groups and parties has also had a positive effect on American politics. Interest groups are a way a person with limited resources can pool their resources together and be heard. Whether the issue is abortion rights, environmental issues or work-related issues, a person can join an interest group, pay their dues and have the interest group form a PAC and make an effort to influence the electoral agenda. So, there is a balance between the benefits of collective action and the curse of a concentration of power out of the hands of individuals. Keeping this balance is a crucial aspect of how we organize both elections and the legislative agenda of the Congress.

In our analysis, we started with the "rules of the game" and we applied those rules when we discussed the Constitution and Federalism. We moved further and examined how individuals and groups interplay in our political environment. In the next chapter, we will discuss how political parties, interest groups and individuals interact when we apply the democratic principles and procedures described in the Constitution to actual campaigning and elections. The next chapter discusses how a person gets elected and the dynamics that enable us to elect people to serve in the government.

TERMS TO REMEMBER

POLITICAL PARTY
INTEREST GROUP
CLOSED PRIMARY
OPEN PRIMARY
POLITICAL MACHINE
POLITICAL BOSSES
LOBBYING
POLITICAL ACTION COMMITTEE

Political Parties and Interest Groups

TRUE OR FALSE QUESTIONS

1. There is a provision in the Constitution that calls for the development of political parties. T / F

2. There are several political parties in the United States. T / F

3. Everyone in the United States is a member of a political party. T / F

4. Political philosophy is the most important party function. T / F

5. Harry Truman was a Republican. T / F

6. Dwight Eisenhower was a Republican. T / F

7. Organizing and running elections is not a function of the political parties. T / F

8. Political parties draw legislative districts in states. T / F

9. Political parties operate the government. T / F

10. Interest groups do not lobby the Congress. T / F

MULTIPLE CHOICE QUESTIONS

11. Who was a recruited candidate for the Presidency?
    a. Harry Truman
    b. Dwight Eisenhower
    c. John F. Kennedy
    d. Herbert Hoover

12. Which is a political party in the United States?
    a. Republican
    b. Democrat
    c. Green Party
    d. a. and b.

13. Why do we have only two parties in the United States?
    a. The people want two parties to make the choice easy.
    b. Only two parties consistently win elections.
    c. It reflects the differences in philosophy between Jefferson and Hamilton.
    d. It reflects our differences during the Civil War.

14. The most powerful interest group is
    a. American Federation of Farmers
    b. American Federation of Teachers
    c. American Association of Retired Persons
    d. Chamber of Commerce

15. The last candidate that thought of being recruited for the Presidency was
    a. John Kerry
    b. George W. Bush
    c. Colin Powell
    d. Bill Clinton

16. Thomas Jefferson's party was called
    a. Republican
    b. Democrat
    c. Whig
    d. Democratic-Republicans

17. The Republican party was the anti-slavery party during what war?
    a. World War II
    b. World War I
    c. Civil War
    d. War of 1812

18. George Washington belonged to what party?
    a. Democratic Republicans
    b. Democratic party
    c. Republican party
    d. He was not a member of a party when elected

19. The American Israeli lobbying group is known as
    a. AIPAC
    b. Israel First Committee
    c. American-Israeli Union
    d. Committee to Aid Israel

20. The major business lobbying group is
    a. Chamber of Commerce
    b. Chamber of Industry
    c. Congress of Industry
    d. Industrial Chamber of America

chapter eight

IMAGE FROM DEFENSE VISUAL INFORMATION CENTER

CAMPAIGNS AND ELECTIONS

INTRODUCTION

An election is the process in which we choose our leaders. The period before an election is called a campaign. During the campaign season, we see all of the elements of politics and government that we have examined so far in action. The political environment consists of the ground rules set by the Constitution. Organizing and running the elections is performed by political parties. In addition, political parties and interest groups work to influence the way people think about a candidate or an issue. Finally, after the campaign, people (about 40 percent of eligible voters) go to vote for a candidate. How the political environment operates elections and campaigns is the focus of this chapter. We will specifically look at the organization of campaigns, the legal requirements to become a candidate, how money is regulated in the process, and how the President of the United States is elected.

We have already discussed the relationship between political parties and interest groups. In this chapter, we will watch how different candidates use different strategies in order to make an argument of why they should be elected. The campaign environment does have basic rules, in which if candidates choose to ignore these rules, they run the risk of failure. Examples of candidates violating these rules include: John Kerry's strategy of targeting young people (we know young people do not vote), Walter Mondale's strategy of trying to exploit a gender gap (women do not necessarily vote differently than men), and Al Gore's strategy of picking Joe Lieberman for Vice President (Lieberman came from Connecticut, he did not have the electoral college balance to offset George W. Bush's home state of Texas). All of these candidates tried to innovate and their innovation contributed to their defeat.

Also, there are examples of how candidates innovate on the campaign trail and succeed. President Bill Clinton did not balance his electoral ticket, when he chose Al Gore as his running mate, Gore was from Tennessee and Clinton was from Arkansas. It had been the first time in modern times that two

Southerners were elected President and Vice President. President John F. Kennedy had to innovate in a way that both Protestants and Catholics would vote for him. Later in this chapter, we will show how Kennedy used television as a way to bridge the religious gap he faced. Finally, Richard Nixon and Ronald Reagan were able to manipulate the media in 1968 and 1980 in new ways that foresaw the rise of the political consultant and the use of advertising techniques to make people vote for them, using emotional responses and negative advertising.

The objective of any campaign is winning. You achieve this when your supporters go to the polls and vote and your opponent's supporters stay at home and do not vote. We start our examination of elections with the ground rules provided by the Constitution.

A CONSTITUTIONAL PERSPECTIVE ON CAMPAIGNS AND ELECTIONS

The Constitution created the broad outlines of the political environment by describing the basic procedures that the government must follow in order to have the Constitution address elections at the Federal level. These offices include elections for the House of Representatives, Senate and the President. The Senate and Presidency are elections based on geography. For the Senate, it is individual states and for the President the election is in every state. The House of Representatives has population as its criterion for elections. Therefore, a census must be taken every ten years to distribute representatives amongst the different states that are reflected by a change in population in each state. These reflections are made by the drawing of Congressional Districts that are drawn by the state legislatures.

Eligibility for running in Federal races is also described by the Constitution. If a person wants to run for the House of Representatives, he or she must be twenty-five years old. Moreover, they must have been a citizen of the country for seven years and a resident of the state they are seeking office when elected. Candidates for the Senate must be thirty years old, a citizen for nine years and also a resident of the state when they are elected. A candidate for the Presidency and Vice Presidency must be "a natural born citizen," thirty-five years old and a resident of the United States for fourteen years. These are the basic requirements for office holders. The Constitution does not mention political parties nor does it mention anything about race, education or other personal characteristics of people seeking office.

Although this is changing, people seeking political office tend to be male, white and have a legal education. More women and minorities are getting elected. However, lawyers do dominate as a profession of people who are getting elected.

The Constitution defers to the individual state legislatures on the nature of Congressional and Senatorial elections. However, for the Presidency, the Constitution describes in detail the procedures used in electing a President. The number of electoral college votes each state has is the sum of all of the congressional seats plus two senate seats. This system enables small states to have influence on Presidential campaigns. It also enables geography to play a role in the election. Throughout the history of American elections, a candidate's state of origin has played an important part in planning their strategies to get elected to the Presidency. This is called balancing the ticket. As a result of the Civil War, from 1865 to 1976, a Southerner had not gotten elected to the Presidency on their own. The only Southern Presidents during this era were Vice Presidents who succeeded to the office after the President had died or was killed. Examples include: Andrew Johnson was from Tennessee, he succeeded Abraham Lincoln, Harry Truman was from Missouri (a border state) but his family had supported the confederacy, he succeeded Franklin D. Roosevelt, and Lyndon Johnson was from Texas, he succeeded John F. Kennedy. Since 1976, only candidates with southern roots have been elected as Democrats (Jimmy Carter and Bill Clinton) to the Presidency.

The intent of the Founding Fathers was to balance the needs of small and large states in the electoral process. Over the years, especially after close elections, there is an outcry to change the Electoral College system. The problem is there is not a better way to ensure this compromise. If we only use the popular vote, the small states such as North Dakota will be entirely ignored. The Midwest and South will have little or nothing to say about who is elected President. Others argue the winner-take-all system should be changed to a proportional representation of electoral votes by either congressional district or county. This may be an idea that needs studying; however, because the election cycle is almost continuous, neither Congress, nor the State legislatures have pursued this idea. For now, the system of electing Presidents as described by the Constitution is the system that will be used in the future.

The Constitution also describes who is eligible to vote. There has been a concerted effort to expand the right to vote in the United States. In 1850, there was the elimination of the requirements to own property. In 1870, race as a requirement was eliminated. In 1920, gender requirements were lifted and in 1972 the age was lowered to eighteen. Ironically, as the franchise has been expanded, voter participation has declined. Later in this chapter, we will analyze this phenomenon. These are the properties the Constitution has set forth for the election of Federal office holders, especially the President of the United States. How do you create a system that is viewed as a legitimate reflection of the people's will? Political parties and interest groups have shaped our elections by adding procedures (such as primaries and nominating conventions) that create a bias for candidates who run on one of the two parties in this country. To answer this question we describe the process used to elect our leaders. To do this, we will take three levels of analysis. First, we will examine the individual traits that are important in discerning who should lead. Next, we will examine the nature of primary elections and how one creates a strategy for achieving success at that level. Finally, we will show the differences between a primary campaign and a general election campaign.

GETTING ELECTED: THE CANDIDATES

Previously, we discussed the Constitution's requirement for individuals running for national office. These are fairly general dealing with a person's age and residency. History has taught us there are more qualifications than those of the Constitution.

Generally speaking, most candidates have been men, but this is changing, women have been getting elected in more numbers since the 1990s. Although, there is not a gender gap *per se*, there are a greater number of women candidates who have successfully argued diversity of gender makes a stronger Congress. It will not be too long before we see a woman who is elected President and/or Vice President. The Republicans and Democrats have a substantial number of women candidates who are qualified to fill either of these offices. In 1984, Geraldine Ferraro, Representative from New York State, was the first woman to be nominated for the Vice Presidency. Walter Mondale did this to try to stir up the race and exploit the perceived gender gap that pollsters and journalists were hyping in order to get some excitement in the race. Mondale and Ferraro did lose the race; however, no one blames the loss on the fact that Mondale nominated a woman as his running mate.

In 2000, Elizabeth Dole, the wife of former Majority Leader Bob Dole, did try to run for the Presidency, it was not much of an effort. However, in 2004 she was elected to the U.S. Senate from North Carolina. She has served in Washington from the Reagan Administration and may have an ambition to try for the Presidency again in the future. Other leading Senators who may run for the Presidency include Hillary Clinton, who is the wife of former President Bill Clinton. In 2000 Hillary Clinton was elected to the U.S. Senate from New York and she is running for re-election to the Senate in 2006. As of this writing, she is considered the front runner for the Democratic Party in 2008. However, her vote for supporting the Iraq invasion could leave her potentially weak to the anti-war wing of the Democratic party. There are also several women Governors that could make a serious run for the Presidency or Vice Presidency.

Just as with gender, we have never had a person who is not a white male who has been elected President. Again, this may change very quickly. In 2006, there are several African-American and Latino candidates who may be able to run a serious campaign for President or be selected to become Vice President. Bill Richardson, Governor of New Mexico and former United Nations Ambassador and Obama Barak, Senator from Illinois are two of the leading candidates who do not fit the traditional stereotype of candidates we see running for President and Vice President. On the Republican side, Secretary of State Rice has been touted for a run for President. She has said she is not interested in electoral politics—it is conceivable that even if she does not run for President she could be convinced to be selected as Vice President. There are others in the Republican party, such as Mel Martinez, U.S. Senator from Florida, who also served in the Bush Cabinet that could be selected as a Vice Presidential candidate. There are also numerous Cabinet officials in the Bush Administration that could have a future in electoral politics.

Hopefully, one day we will not look at gender and race, however, today these considerations seem important to some people. Are the voters ready for a woman President or a President from a minority group? Who knows, again hopefully people will vote for the candidates that reflect their preferences on issues and image and not hold a person's gender, race or religion against them.

With the decline of political parties and the growth of Political Action Committees, the personality of the candidate, or the perceived personality of the candidate, seems to have taken hold as the most important aspect of a candidacy. One of the reasons Al Gore was defeated in the Presidential election of 2000 was he was perceived as a phony or weird. He seemed too staged, his debate performances were contrived. Of course every campaign is staged, however, Gore's campaign strategy and his personality made him lose the 2000 election.

Americans want their Presidents to be different things at the same time. We want a President to be "one of us." Yet, we also want him to be better than ourselves. Americans vote for candidates who are basically wealthy, and yet, they want candidates who understand you have to use cash to pay at McDonalds' and know how a scanning machine works at the supermarket.[1] Presidents, Senators, and Congressmen have had this difficult balancing act since the early years of the Republic. Theodore Roosevelt and Franklin D. Roosevelt came from privileged backgrounds, yet their life experiences created the image of a person who had battled in life and won. Theodore Roosevelt's battle happened when he went out to the frontier and became a cowboy and later, a war hero during the Spanish-American War in Cuba. Soon after the war with Spain, Roosevelt became Governor of New York, Vice President and succeeded to the Presidency after the assassination of President McKinley (he was the youngest man ever to have that office at age 43).

Franklin D. Roosevelt's battle with polio, although hidden, gave him an empathy with people who were suffering. Roosevelt would be the longest serving President from 1933–1944 (he was elected to four terms and died soon after being inaugurated for the fourth term). Other Presidents such as Abraham Lincoln and Bill Clinton grew up poor but became President because of their genius for politics and overall intelligence. There is no recipe for how a person's personality will affect their chances for being elected. If one would compare the personalities of Presidents since 1960 you would see their personalities are quite different.[2] No matter what a President or other candidate's personality is, there are two aspects of getting elected they must master—the primary and general election. We will concentrate on elections on the Presidential level; however, today elections for Congress also have the same elements as Presidential elections.

GETTING ON THE BALLOT, CAUCUSES, AND PRIMARY ELECTIONS

When someone decides to run for office, in most States and for most offices the first thing the person has to do is to gather signatures of registered voters. These signatures demonstrate the candidate has enough popularity and is a real person in order to get on the ballot. This first step is designed to limit the number of candidates on the ballot. In campaigns that are state-wide the required number of signatures can be at least 20,000–50,000. In some states, there are businesses candidates can hire to collect signatures at a dollar a signature. In other cases political parties or interest groups will organize their members to collect signatures. If you are a new candidate and you do not have these options, it can be a daunting challenge to get on the ballot. After getting your name on the ballot if there is another person who wants to participate in the election, then there is a primary.

A primary is a test of different candidates who want to represent their particular party. It is a practice election that enables the party to determine which candidate can gather more votes. Primaries can be "open" or "closed" depending on the rules that are passed by the party in each state. An open primary enables voters who are not registered as declared party members of the party to participate in the primary. A closed primary restricts the participation of voters to those who registered under a particular party label. The closed primary is designed to prevent crossover voting. Crossover voting is where voters whose allegiance is with the other party vote for a weaker candidate in order to give their candidate an easier time in the general election. Closed primaries are only possible when a person who registers to vote decides what party's primary they want to participate in. Open primaries tend to help voter participation since the voters can be involved in all of the interesting races. Closed primaries do prevent crossover, however, they also tend to limit participation. A growing problem is as more Americans see themselves as independents, and if they register as such, they are not eligible to vote in a closed primary.

When there is unequal party representation sometimes the primaries are more heated and have

---

[1]President Reagan during a campaign stop took his McDonalds' food without paying for it, causing one of the workers to object. President Bush when visiting a supermarket was intrigued by the scanners during the campaign of 1992.

[2]Presidents from 1960–2006 include John F. Kennedy, Lyndon B. Johnson, Richard Nixon, Gerald Ford, Jimmy Carter, Ronald Reagan, George H. Bush, Bill Clinton, George W. Bush.

more interesting candidates than during the general election. Congressional Districts have been drawn to have "safe" Republican and Democratic districts. The legislature is responsible for drawing legislative representative districts for both State and Federal offices. Usually both parties can make a deal, so that even if the popularity of each party is lopsided there will be a couple of safe districts for the minority party in order for there to be agreement for re-districting plan. This process takes place every ten years. This is why legislative districts have no bearing on city boundary, county boundaries or demographic facts on the ground. The critical criterion is the number of registered voters that can have their party membership measured.

Theoretically, primaries are designed to guarantee the voters have input on which candidate will represent the party in the general election. During the Progressive Era, primaries were invented to prevent the domination of boss politics from having total control of the political process. Over the years, as primaries have grown and political bosses have faded, most legislative races involve a primary. The other procedure to pick candidates to represent a party is a caucus. In legislative races, primaries are used more than caucuses.

A party caucus is where people meet in a room and publicly and physically get together and pledge their support for the candidate of their choice. The most famous caucus are the Iowa caucuses for President. These are thought to be by many, the first step in winning the Presidency. The caucuses in Iowa are organized that everyone who wants to participate goes to a neighborhood school gym or other public place. The organizers then give a physical space where people have to stand and be counted, it may be a corner of a large room or it may be different rooms in a school, church or other public building. Primaries are used more than caucuses in the elections for legislative candidates.

In the Presidential campaign, after the Iowa caucuses, there are a series of primaries and caucuses. Caucuses usually have a lower priority after Iowa. New Hampshire traditionally has been the first primary. Other states have tried to move their primaries forward in an effort to have more influence on the selection process, plus they would like to have the increased revenue that can be created in the state if there is an important primary contest. Iowa and New Hampshire have a great deal of influence on the early selection of candidates. Some argue these two states have undue influence since both are small

and have very limited minority representation. Bill Clinton and George W. Bush are the only two Presidents in modern times who have not won the New Hampshire primary but have been elected. Starting in 1960, with the Presidential election of John F. Kennedy, candidates began to realize they did not have to wait on the party bosses to get nominated for the Presidency. If they could raise the money and have the organization, they could run in a series of primaries to collect delegates. These delegates would be pledged to the candidate and the candidate could get the nomination at the convention without paying attention to the people who traditionally ran the political parties and selected Presidential candidates.

Before 1960, party leaders and delegates would meet at political conventions. These were gatherings that had two important jobs, to write the party platform that set down a set of principles that the party stands for and will run on. The other mission of the convention is to pick a candidate for President and Vice President. One of the most famous conventions was the Republican Convention that selected Abraham Lincoln as President. Leaders of the party would gather and sort out the strengths and weaknesses of each person who wanted to be President. This process would produce candidates who were not revolutionary; however, they did produce candidates that (sometimes in spite of the bosses) produced progressive policies. Woodrow Wilson and William Jennings Bryan, and Theodore Roosevelt (for Vice President) were some candidates who were picked by conventions. Conventions used to be thought of as exciting national showcases for the two political parties and would have gavel to gavel television coverage. Currently, the two party national conventions have been turned into long boring campaign commercials in which the television networks only give a couple of hours at the end of the convention to have the nominees deliver their acceptance speeches.

The primary process narrows the number of candidates of the political parties to two nominees. After years of convincing the activists of the party, the candidate will represent the activist point of view. The nominee must now appeal to the average American voter, who does not share the same interest as people who identify with the party's rank and file. Now everything the candidate and his family will do is considered open game for the media and the candidate's opponent. The general election rarely turns on issues. In modern times, the campaign for the Presidency centers on the question, does the average American like this person? Will they like the spouse and children of the Candidate? Personality or perceived personality is now the major factor in determining the result of the general election.

The three phases of a campaign: primary campaign, convention and general election campaign are designed to have a candidate thoroughly vetted before he/she becomes President of the United States. Party bosses used to be in charge of this process. Today, the media and negative advertisements provide most of our information about the candidates who run for President. Next, we analyze two concrete historical elections that have influenced the elections we have today. Two of the most important elections were the Presidential election of 1960 and the Congressional election of 1974. In 1960, a relatively unknown Senator from Massachusetts used television, organization and an unlimited amount of money, to jump the line for the Oval Office. Four years later we would see the first inkling of the Republican party turning away from its progressive past and becoming the Conservative Party of the United States. The Presidential election of 1960 introduced the country to leaders who would dominate Presidential politics for twenty years and the Congressional election of 1974 would produce leaders that remain in Congress today. These are the reasons why we will be examining these important modern elections. Let's start when politics seemed exciting to young people—the election of 1960.

TWO KEY ELECTIONS 1960 AND 1974

THE PRESIDENTIAL ELECTION OF 1960

The young men who went to war in World War II, came back with a drive to make up for the four years lost during the war. The veterans of this era were politically aware and benefited from the most generous veteran program that the government ever gave people for serving their country.[3] The experience of World War I taught governments that if you have a generation of idle veterans who were trained to follow orders and use weapons it could be a potent force for revolution.[4] Revolutions in Germany (both the

communists and Nazis) had a core of veterans that populated their street armies. The Soviet Union was formed by the Bolsheviks who recruited sailors and soldiers from the Imperial Army and Trotsky, the Red Army's creator and commander, used the Tsar's Officer Corps when he could, either by kidnapping their families for ransom or by using some other incentive. It was veterans who came home from the war and started to question authority. After World War II, the G.I. bill was introduced and passed by Congress in an effort to slow the veterans impact on the economy by slowing their reintroduction into the work force by offering them education programs of all kinds.

There were men who fought in World War II who already had their educations. Men such as John F. Kennedy, Richard Nixon, Bob Dole and Gerald Ford had contemplated political careers as soon as they were out of the military. All of these men were elected to Congress as young veterans. In 1948, John Kennedy and Richard Nixon would be fast friends having offices that were close to one another and sharing the same committee assignments and ironically the same ambitions. Twelve years later, these two men would be in contention for the Presidency.[5]

Richard Nixon was a Junior Senator from California when Dwight D. Eisenhower picked him to be his Vice President.[6] Nixon had made a name for himself as a member of the House Un-American Activities Committee (HUAC). The difference between Richard Nixon and Senator Joseph McCarthy was that Nixon actually did catch a Soviet agent, Alger Hiss. He was a Soviet agent that worked in the U.S. State Department. The famous case called the Pumpkin Papers. Later examination of the Soviet Archives, shows Hiss was an agent. Nixon parlayed his record to the Senate Seat and to the Vice Presidency. There as Vice President, Nixon served eight years and stood as Eisenhower's successor. He would easily win the Republican nomination. He would have trouble finding a suitable Vice Presidential running-mate (Governor of New York Nelson Rockefeller would not accept his invitation). He picked former Senator of Massachusetts Henry Cabot-Lodge. Kennedy had defeated Cabot-Lodge for his Senate seat in 1952.[7]

[3]Christopher Matthews, *The Rivalry that Shaped Postwar America: Kennedy & Nixon.* New York: Simon & Schuster, 1996, p. 27.

[4]David McCullough, *Truman.* New York: Simon & Schuster, 1992, p. 548.

[5]Christopher Matthews, *The Rivalry that Shaped Postwar America: Kennedy & Nixon.* New York: Simon & Schuster, 1996, p. 133.

[6]Theodore H. White, *The Making of the President 1960.* New York: Antheneum Publishers, 1961, p. 180.

[7]Ibid.

John F. Kennedy actually gave money to Richard Nixon to defeat Helen Douglas for the U.S. Senate in 1950. He was in the Senate in 1952 and was planning a Presidential race in 1960. In 1956 he tried to have the Vice Presidential nomination under Adlai Stevenson, but he was considered too young and too Catholic. After 1956, Kennedy and his team realized they would have to develop a strategy that would earn them the Democratic nomination. Democrats had controlled Congress since 1933 and they were the dominant party during the 1940s through the 1960s. The leading candidates for the Presidency before 1960 were Lyndon B. Johnson who was the Senator from Texas and Majority Leader. Hubert H. Humphrey, the Senator from Minnesota was considering a run for the White House. Stuart Symington, the Senator from Missouri had the backing of ex-President Harry Truman.

These Senators would dominate Presidential politics for the next twenty years. Except for Symington, Nelson Rockefeller, Richard Nixon, John F. Kennedy, Lyndon Johnson and Hubert Humphrey would all become Vice President. Nixon, Kennedy and Johnson would ultimately become President of the United States.

How did Kennedy get the nomination? Kennedy was not going to wait his turn to run for the Presidency.[8] He was the son of a wealthy and famous man, Joseph P. Kennedy, who was going to spend a great deal in order to have a Catholic elected President. John Kennedy's campaign did not have to worry about fund raising. They would by-pass the Democratic party leadership by running in the primaries and actively recruit delegates to the Democratic party Convention in Los Angeles. He planned to have the first modern campaign with the use of modern logistics such as airplanes and television.

The first test in 1960 was the New Hampshire primary where Kennedy won easily, being from New England. At this time most politicians did not realize how important the primaries would become. The first real challenge for the Kennedy campaign would be the Wisconsin primary. In this primary Kennedy and Humphrey would face off. If Kennedy won, he could demonstrate that his appeal was not just a regional basis. If he lost, his quest for the Presidency would be over. Kennedy's campaign invaded the eleven congressional districts of Wisconsin. Kennedy visited small Wisconsin cities.[9] Years later, people

would tell the Author, how they had met John Kennedy and it was the most exciting point in their lives.[10] Hubert Humphrey was the Senator from next door, many people supported his liberal views in the northwestern region of the state. Wisconsin has a large Catholic population in the southeastern urban part of the state, but the northwest section has a large population of Protestants. Wisconsin would serve as a test for Kennedy to see if he could attract non-Catholics.

The Humphrey campaign was outspent and outmanned. His campaign did have a folksy appeal and the feeling of a local running for office. Primary election night approached and many of the pundits were calling for a sweep for Kennedy. This was not to be. Basically, Kennedy won the primary but he lost to Humphrey many of the congressional districts in the western and northwestern part of the state. Humphrey although he technically lost, viewed the results as a victory. There would have to be another test for Kennedy to prove the country would vote for a Catholic. This test would be the primary of West Virginia.

West Virginia is a state known for coal mines and is part of the country that is referred to as the "bible belt." The Kennedy's were seen as alien and the Catholic religion was seen as strange. The contest between Humphrey and Kennedy would concentrate on the labor unions and the common coal miner. This primary would determine who would go on in the Presidential campaign, the defeated candidate would go home. Kennedy won the primary. The West Virginia primary from Kennedy's point of view proved he could get Protestant support. Other Democrats were not so sure.

By the time of the Convention Kennedy had looked like he had the nomination sewed up. However, the U-2 incident had erupted and the Soviet Union had captured Francis Gary Powers and had berated the Eisenhower Administration.[11] The tensions in the Cold War were getting high and people questioned Kennedy's experience and maturity for such an important role. Other candidates such as Lyndon Johnson and Stuart Symington were gathering momentum. Their strategies would be to stop Kennedy on the first round of balloting for the nomination. This would release the pledged delegates and then anyone could get the nomination. Kennedy would have to get the nomination on the first ballot

[8]Ibid. p. 48.
[9]Ibid. p. 93.

[10]Patrick C. Coaty—personal recollections growing up in Wisconsin.
[11]Theodore H. White, *The Making of the President 1960*. New York: Antheneum Publishers, 1961, p. 180.

or his campaigning and hard work from the previous four years would be thrown away.

Ultimately, what we see in the 1960 primary campaign is the decrease in a candidate's reliance on party leadership's endorsement and the increase in a direct strategy of convincing voters to vote for you. This contributed to the undermining of party leaders throughout the country. State party leaders had very little say about who would represent the party as the Presidential nominee, if the state had a primary. Kennedy won the nomination because he was willing to bypass the party leadership and go directly to the voters in New Hampshire, Wisconsin and West Virginia.

After the Republicans and Democrats had their conventions, the two nominees, Richard Nixon and John F. Kennedy would start the general campaign. Richard Nixon would pledge to campaign in every state. The number of states had expanded to fifty in 1959, with the inclusion of Hawaii and Alaska.[12] This may have been a good rhetorical message but it was a terrible strategy. Presidential elections are not really one big election, they are fifty little elections, with the winner of every state earning the total electoral votes. A candidate who wins a majority of the votes wins the election. Popular votes only count to determine who is the winner of the state's electoral votes. Near the end of the campaign, Nixon would have to go to Alaska, while Kennedy was campaigning in New York.

Nixon's strategy was to paint Kennedy as an inexperienced legislator, a President we would have to train, is how he put it. The turning point of the election was the use of television and the first Presidential debate. Television was a relatively new invention in 1960. It had exploded on the American scene. In 1950, there were roughly four million televisions in America, by 1960 there were over 44 million.[13] The Kennedy campaign understood the power of advertising and particularly the power of television from the beginning. The Nixon campaign underestimated the power of personal appeal and a candidate's need to look relaxed and in control.

Vice President Nixon had been a trained debater all of his life, he was a lawyer and had the skills of a world class debater. He was going to debate Kennedy and show to the world how unfit he was to be President. Kennedy's strategy was different, he was going to talk to the American people, he did not have to debate Nixon directly, he was going to show the people through the use of television, that he was ready (or at least as ready as Nixon) for the Presidency.[14]

Several things happened to Nixon, first he had been sick. Because of this he had lost weight and looked drawn and tired. Secondly, he only used a little bit of makeup called "lazy shave," which under the camera lights made him appear very pale. Finally, he wore a gray suit which made his body blend in to the gray background of the television studio. Kennedy wore a dark blue suit and had professional makeup artists work on his appearance. If people saw the debate on television, they thought Kennedy had won the debate, if they heard the debate on radio they thought Nixon had won. Television and the effects of personal appearance had become a major criterion for electing leaders.

His performance during the debates had closed the maturity gap that Nixon had tried to put into people's minds. Side by side comparisons showed that Kennedy could hold his own against Nixon. These two men had very similar careers as we have said, they both were elected to the Congress and met again in the Presidential general election. Nixon is a relatively young man also (he is less than fifty years old). The race became very close and by the time of election night all of the elements of a new political era had become apparent. The weakness of political bosses, the increasing strength of candidates and the start of the perpetual campaign for President and finally, even though Kennedy did not have to worry about financing—money and television would become the dominant part of politics in the campaigns that followed.

The result of the 1960 campaign gave Kennedy a close victory. Nixon would later become President after another defeat when he ran for Governor of California in 1962. The election of John F. Kennedy to the Presidency showed if a person had enough money and ran early in the primaries he could bend the political establishment to his needs. This lesson was not lost on the young people who were being introduced to politics who supported both Kennedy on the Democratic side and Nixon on the Republican side. Fourteen years later, these young people would be elected to Congress using many of the techniques first introduced by the Kennedy campaign.

---

[12]Ibid. p. 208.

[13]Theodore H. White, *The Making of the President 1960*. New York: Antheneum Publishers, 1961, p. 279.

[14]Ibid.

THE CONGRESSIONAL ELECTION OF 1974

As World War II was a defining event for the generation that gave us John F. Kennedy and Richard Nixon, Vietnam and Watergate were two defining moments for the baby boom generation. The country had lowered the voting age to 18 in 1971 and the military draft had ended. President Nixon had resigned during the summer of 1974 and the Republicans would face a dramatic loss, there would be young people elected in Congress including Tom Downing who was just 25 and George Miller, a California Congressmen who was elected at 28. Miller, as of this writing is still in Congress and as the Democrats won control of the House of Representatives, he will become a very powerful member with over thirty years of service in the House.[15] He is just an example of how the people who were elected in 1974 are still in Congress, they came in as young reformers and have stayed until now they are in their fifties and sixties.

The opportunity came for these candidates in 1973 as a result of the Vietnam War and Watergate. Also the military draft and the lowering of the voting age contributed to the political hurricane that wiped out the old order in Congress. The candidates who were running as Democrats that year did not see themselves as beholden to the Democratic party. They ran their campaigns as individual candidates with individual power centers. The campaign techniques introduced by the Kennedy campaign were adapted and perfected by these new Congressional candidates.[16] The techniques are direct mail, candidate's performances, television advertising and perpetual fund raising. The Kennedy candidacy showed everyone that a legislative record is not important when running for office.

The personal touch and personality were more important than how a candidate votes for issues. With the introduction of computers it became possible for personalized letters from candidates to thousands of individuals. In the early seventies people were impressed if they received a personal letter from a candidate for Congress, especially if the letter had personal information and issues that are of concern to the individual. This technique is called narrowcasting. The election of 1974 showed that people responded to direct mail. Candidates and interest groups used this technique for fund raising and getting the vote out.[17] Today, we all receive "junk mail" so this technique has lost most of its power. It remains a very strong tool for charities and interest groups who are trying to raise funds but, it has lost a lot of its power since most people know the candidate is not sitting down and writing a personal letter. It was and remains a technique that once elected, does keep Congressmen in office.

Letters are good, but shaking the hands of constituents and talking directly to service organizations such as the Lions Club and Rotary Clubs remain an important aspect of a campaign. The Congressmen who won office in 1974 understood that you can loose your office by ignoring the local issues that face your congressional district. That is why Congressmen travel to their district every weekend to attend the important events such as county fairs, parades and other civic meetings. Nothing is better than having the candidate meet a group of people and convince them to support them.

Probably the most important campaign technique that was adopted from the 1960 campaign was the use of television. Similar to direct mail, television enables a campaign to go directly into a person's home. Television has a threefold objective. First is to let people know your candidate's name. Second is to produce negative campaign advertisements in order to bash your opponent. Finally, to get others (not your supporters) to stay home. Sometimes in campaign language a television campaign is called the air war. This is the main campaign technique used today.

Television requires candidates have huge campaign budgets. A candidate does not have to have any type of campaign organization except a television team. The candidate needs to have a commercial production team, advertising buy team that schedules the running of the commercials and the money to pay for the commercials we see during the popular television shows. Starting in 1974, these techniques have been adopted and institutionalized into the daily life of members of Congress.

Television advertising can be categorized into four types of commercials. Positive commericial, negative commercial, contrast commercial and inoculation commercial. A positive ad is usually used to introduce the candidate to the electorate or it trumpets the accomplishments of the candidate and

[15]Hedrick Smith, *The Power Game: How Washington Works.* New York: Ballentine Books,1988, p. 119.
[16]Ibid.
[17]Ibid. p. 46.

it gives positive reasons why people should support the candidate. The sponsorship of positive advertising usually is financed by the candidate's campaign or sympathetic interest groups. The negative commercial is the opposite, it uses opposition research (when a candidate runs for office his or her whole life must be researched, and issues can be opened up by interviewing old associates, and in the case of lawyers or other professionals, old clients and business associates). This opposition research is used for negative advertisements. Even if the candidate has not done anything wrong, things can be slanted to look as if the opposition candidate is someone no one would support. This has a twofold objective, the first is to turn off the people who have not made up their minds on who to support and secondly, it may discourage voter turnout by confusing the issues for the voter. Negative commercials are very effective in turning people off to the electoral process. One hears the comment; that they are all crooks, or I do not want to vote for any of them. Negative commercials are a major reason good and accomplished people do not want to run for political office.

A milder form of a negative commercial is the contrast advertisement; this commercial will try to make a comparison between issues or candidates. Of course, the contrast has a bias toward the camp that produced the commercial. The fourth type of commercial that has developed in modern campaigns is the inoculation commercial that tries to bring up a negative issue of the candidate, but it puts a positive context on the issue. This can be very difficult and can backfire, since the campaign is admitting a negative fact about the candidate. These television techniques are very effective and these commercials have become the dominant political technique of our era.

As the broadcast television audience becomes smaller, new media has not played a major impact on elections yet. In the Presidential election of 2004 Howard Dean used the Internet to raise a substantial amount of money, yet when it came time to organize in the Iowa caucus he failed, and of course gave the "I have a scream speech,"[18] doomed his chances for the New Hampshire primary. The potential for podcasting and personal attack commercials aimed at individuals has the potential to be a dominant political technique. However, it has not proven yet to be effective.

---

[18]In this speech Governor Howard Dean describes how he is going to run in the different primaries and end up in Washington, D.C. and he screams "Yeeea!" This is how it became known as the "I have a scream speech."

The issue of television advertising and campaign finance reform are hand in hand. Television has made campaigning too expensive for the average person to ever dream of participating in politics. In 2004, the average congressional campaign in California cost seven million dollars. The odds of someone of average means (not average ability) to generate that much money is greater than a person of average height to become a player in the National Basketball Association. Television has been the instrument that has run the cost of running for election out of the reach of most people.

Reformers have concentrated on the "supply side" of campaign finance reform. We will not have reform until the billions of dollars spent on television, usually at the local market level, is changed by either giving all candidates free air time or by banning television commercials in political campaigns. The British have campaigns that are limited in time and ban broadcast advertising. There are issues of freedom of speech, the Supreme Court has ruled that a person spending their own money cannot be restricted in the amount they are able to spend, since spending is considered part of political speech which is protected under the Constitution. In order to have more competitive elections, we may want to consider the British example or other ideas that may make politics more interesting to more people than those who are interested in it today.

CONCLUSION

Elections and campaigns are the procedures we use to elect our leaders. There are two main periods in most elections, the primary election and the general election. Building on our discussion of political parties and interest groups, we see the efforts of individuals who want to serve in the government put themselves through a strenuous vetting process that in theory enables people to vote for the most desirable candidate. In reality, we see how the campaign for President in 1960 and the Congressional campaign of 1974 have shaped the campaigns and elections we have today. The dominance of personal politics and television has alienated many people from the political process.

John F. Kennedy's campaign for President illustrated to everyone that a person with enough money and support does not have to wait their turn. If you have the will to expose yourself to the primary and caucus voter, you may be able to wrestle control of the party apparatus and turn a junior U.S. Senator into the President of the United States. The congressional elections of 1974 illustrated the campaign techniques of direct mailing, personal presentations to your district, television commercials, and permanent fund raising will enable a person to be in Congress for their lifetime—something the Founding Fathers did not intend. Many of the Congressmen who were elected in 1974 have been re-elected as late as 2006. These techniques, it can be argued, has created a permanent class of legislators that has indirectly contributed to the continued alienation of people to the political process.

Recently, we have seen reformers trying to end the inherent expense of electoral campaigns. After political scandals, legislation was introduced and passed that has the intention of controlling political spending. Maybe we should examine the role of television, especially local television, and the billions of dollars candidates spend on commercials. The candidates spend the money because these commercials are effective and in our society the most efficient way to have a large number of people recognize and remember your name in the voting booth. In the next chapter, we will analyze the permanency of Congress and how the phenomenon developed of our feelings toward Congress. Typically, Americans love their Representative in Congress but despise the actions of the whole Congress. This seemingly collective split personality that Americans have will be examined in the next chapter on Congress.

TERMS TO REMEMBER

ELECTION

CAMPAIGN

CROSSOVER VOTING

PARTY CAUCUS

CONVENTION

NEGATIVE ADVERTISEMENT

POSITIVE ADVERTISEMENT

CONTRAST ADVERTISEMENT

INOCULATION ADVERTISEMENT

Campaigns and Elections

TRUE OR FALSE QUESTIONS

1. An election is a process in which we choose our leaders.   T / F

2. The Presidential election is not a geographically based election.   T / F

3. The Constitution provides detailed rules for organizing an election.   T / F

4. Balancing a ticket for the Presidency and Vice Presidency refers to gender.   T / F

5. The Constitution describes who is eligible to vote.   T / F

6. John F. Kennedy was the youngest man ever to be elected to the Presidency.   T / F

7. Theodore Roosevelt was the youngest man ever to be elected to the Presidency.   T / F

8. Party Bosses decide who is going to be on the ballot.   T / F

9. We directly vote for the President of the United States.   T / F

10. We do not directly vote for the President of the United States.   T / F

MULTIPLE CHOICE QUESTIONS

11. Which of the following is not used by parties to pick candidates?
    a. Primaries
    b. Caucuses
    c. Conventions
    d. Telethons

12. The Iowa Caucus is important because
    a. demographically Iowa is the most similar to the U.S.
    b. it is last.
    c. it is in the Midwest.
    d. it is first.

13. New Hampshire is an important primary because
    a. it is last.
    b. it is first.
    c. it is in the Midwest.
    d. it is in the East.

14. National Party Conventions are important because
    a. they are last.
    b. they are first.
    c. the party leaders can get together and pick a candidate.
    d. they are not important except for the acceptance speech.

15. A Candidate's first step in running for office is
    a. gathering signatures for qualifying to be put on the ballot.
    b. raising money.
    c. talking to party leaders.
    d. making television commercials.

16. PAC stands for
    a. Pacific Association of Commerce
    b. Political Association of California
    c. Political Action of Citizens
    d. Political Action Committee

17. PACs usually
    a. raise money.
    b. provide volunteers.
    c. recruit candidates.
    d. a. and b.

18. Since World War II, the most important Presidential election has been (in political terms)
    a. 1948
    b. 1960
    c. 1984
    d. 2000

19. The most important aspect of American campaigning today is
    a. billboards
    b. television commercials
    c. direct mail
    d. campaign buttons

20. The most important Congressional Campaign since World War II has been
    a. 1974
    b. 1994
    c. 1964
    d. 2004

chapter nine

CONGRESS—FORUM OF THE NATION

INTRODUCTION

We have traced the development of the American political environment starting with the Constitution and the related elements of how Americans elect their leaders. In this chapter, and in the following three chapters, we analyze the institutions of the government that socialize the people we elect to serve in Washington, D.C. This chapter concentrates on the Congress and its functions. We start with the Constitutional roots of the institution. Next, we describe the leadership and committee structure that enables Congress to get something accomplished. Congress is usually judged by the passing of legislation, therefore, we will examine the law making function of Congress. Then, we will explore the many functions individual members of Congress must master in order to be effective and get re-elected. Finally, we will investigate the interaction of the Legislative branch with the Executive branch.

Throughout American history there has been a forum in which people debated and tried to find compromises on issues that pressed communities. At first, it was the town hall meetings and colonial assemblies. During the American Revolution it was the Continental Congress and after victory, there was the Congress under the Articles of Confederation. The Founding Fathers agreed there had to be a Legislative branch in order to have a representation in government of the popular will.[1] Congress has been the forum of airing popular sentiment since 1789. So, it is logical to start our analysis with the Constitutional foundations of Congress.

CONSTITUTIONAL ROOTS OF CONGRESS

The greatest achievement of the Constitution in many respects was the compromise that resulted in a bicameral legislative Congress.[2] The great compro-

---

[1]Samuel Eliot Morison, *The Oxford History of the American People, Volume 2: 1789 through Reconstruction.* Penguin Books, 1965, p. 33.
[2]Ibid.

mise, as it was called, made it possible for large states to have a greater voice in the House of Representatives and ensure smaller states would not be railroaded by having equal representation in the U.S. Senate.[3] The writers of the Constitution understood this compromise would make it possible to have issues that would separate states based on population, region or political inclination, to debate and try to work on issues that would entail compromises in order to have a unified country.

The Founding Fathers were concerned about the historical problem of having such a large piece of land governed by a republic. The only experiments in democracy and a republican form of government were in the ancient world, and all of these experiments failed when the civilizations grew larger. They split on factionalism, and dictators were able to take control of governments when it seemed the democracies and republics had failed.[4] The compromise inside the Constitution was designed to have a forum so that all parties would feel they have a fair chance to have their position heard by the nation.

The power of Congress is addressed in the First Article, section 8, in which the Founding Fathers wrote the expressed powers Congress was responsible for and the necessary and proper clause that gave Congress the power to implement laws, that it saw as necessary and proper to carry out the expressed responsibilities that are in the Constitution. We have examined these powers in previous chapters. However, it is important to note, the Founding Fathers wanted the Legislative branch to be powerful. The Congress was not designed to rubber stamp the President.

In many areas such as declaring war, issues of impeachment, and passing laws Congress has the primary power in the Constitution, the President has a secondary role. However, if the Congress does not use the power, as in the case of not declaring war after the September 11th attacks, then the other branches of the government will take over the power vacuum created by the lack of action.[5] The tradition of a strong Congress has been with us since the Civil War.

During the Civil War, President Lincoln had more power than any President since Washington. After his assassination, the Radical Republicans, as they were known in Congress, took over and tried to impeach President Andrew Johnson.[6] The members of Congress wanted a harsh reconstruction of the South and sent the Union Army to occupy the South. After World War I, Woodrow Wilson had taken great steps to mobilize the country and achieve victory.[7] However, again, it was the Congressional leadership that led the fight against the Treaty of Versailles and membership of the United States in the League of Nations.[8] It has only been since the end of World War II that the Presidency has seemed to loom larger than the Congress. In our times, the immediacy of threats from terrorists, financial market crashes and world events, make many Americans look to the White House, but in reality it is the Congress that has the real power.

The Constitution gives the Congress the power to tax and spend the people's money. It is the Congress that funds all of the policies the President proposes. If you want to change policies such as free trade, war on terror, or the environmental policies of the United States, the most effective approach to policy change is to change members of Congress. It is more difficult to change the composition of Congress since it is difficult to focus on more than five hundred people, but the Congress, as a collective body, received more power from the Constitution than the President.

How is this power spread around Congress? In the next section of this chapter, we will discuss the leadership of Congress and the role of committees in determining the legislative agenda of Congress.

COMMITTEE STRUCTURE AND LEADERSHIP IN CONGRESS

The House of Representatives and the Senate are deliberative bodies that discuss laws and issues regarding the public interest of the people of the United States. One organizational structure that is very important to Congress are committees. In both the House of Representatives and the Senate, there are four types of committees: standing committees, joint committees, conference committees, and select committees. Standing committees are committees that were formed and are carried over from previous Congresses. These committees are usually the most

[3] Ibid. p. 37.

[4] David McCullough, *John Adams*. New York: Simon & Schuster, 2001, p. 560.

[5] Patrick C. Coaty, *Understanding the War on Terror*. Dubuque, IA: Kendall/Hunt Publishing Co., 2006, p. 2.

[6] Samuel Eliot Morison, *The Oxford History of the American People, Volume 2: 1789 through Reconstruction*. New York: Meridan Book, 1965, pp. 516–517.

[7] Arthur Walworth, *Woodrow Wilson*. Baltimore, MD: Penguin Books, 1958, Book II, p. 86.

[8] Ibid.

powerful and members want to serve on these committees. Standing committees in the House of Representatives include the Appropriations and Ways and Means committees. These committees deal with how the government collects and spends tax dollars. In the Senate the standing committees include Armed Services, Budget and Judiciary. Armed Services and Judiciary committees get a lot of attention when there is a military crisis or a Presidential appointment to the Supreme Court.

Joint committees are committees that have a membership included in both houses of Congress. These committees are formed to investigate certain issues or conduct special studies. There have been joint committees on Economic Development and Taxation that are examples of joint committees in the 106th Congress. Conference committees also have members from both the House of Representatives and the Senate, however, these committees try to work out differences in legislation that has been passed by both Houses. The Congress has to agree on shared language in order to send legislation to the President. When there is a difference in the bills that have been passed, the conference committee is made up of Congressmen and Senators who served on the committees that had original consideration of the bill. Therefore, depending on the bill, individual membership on the conference committee will change.

The fourth type of committee is called select, ad hoc or sometimes special committee, this type of committee is formed for a specific duty. A select committee has investigated the events behind the Pearl Harbor and 9/11 attacks, the assassinations of John F. Kennedy, Martin Luther King, Jr. and Robert Kennedy, and the Watergate scandal. The committees can have a great deal of publicity and in some cases being on a select committee has made the political career of a heretofore unknown Congressman or Senator. If something happens that shocks the nation, the Congress will respond by organizing a select committee. This does not mean only scandals are the subject of select committees. Sometimes, an interest group or members of Congress will want to investigate a certain issue and form a select committee.

These are the four broad categories of committees Congress uses to sort out issues, legislations and egos of members. Behind the broad committees are subcommittees. Subcommittees is where the real work may get done. In private, the members of the subcommittee work on the legislation and work out compromises between interests and members. The vast majority of bills will be sent into committees where a subcommittee will work on it and the bill never again is considered by the Congress. If the leadership of the committee does not want a bill to pass, they will just refuse to hold hearings on the committee and it will die.

Congressional leadership is earned with a combination of seniority and popularity inside a member's party caucus. A party caucus is the gathering of all party members in order to work out strategy, pick Congressional leaders and organize their functions inside Congress.

Historically, there have been two party caucuses, the party in the majority elects the Speaker of the House and the Majority Leader of the Senate. These two leaders are the face of each institution. In the House, to help the Speaker of the House, there is the Majority Leader, Majority Whip and the minority (other party's leaders) these include the Minority Leader and Minority Whip. On the Senate side, the equivalent to the Speaker is the Majority Leader of the Senate. The Majority Leader's counterpart is the Minority Leader of the Senate, below them are the Senate Whip of each party.

There have been strong Congressional leaders in Congress, Republican Speaker of the House Joe Cannon who controlled the House of Representatives from 1903–1910 was an example of a very strong Speaker. Overt power for the Speaker of the House has led to members revolting and trying to limit the Speaker's power. Sam Rayburn, Democrat of Texas, was a very powerful Speaker. He was Speaker from the New Deal to his death in the early 1960s. He relied on informal powers of persuasion and the old adage you reward friends and punish enemies.[9] Newt Gingrich was the last powerful Speaker of the House the nation has had. He changed the institutional power of the Speaker in exchange for this increase in power. He agreed only to be Speaker for eight years. After scandal, Gingrich resigned from Congress and his expected successor also resigned due to a personal scandal. Dennis Hassert, a little known cautious politician from Illinois, has been Speaker of the House. Even though he is third in line for the Presidency, very few people know who he is. In January 2007, Nancy Pelosi will become the new Speaker.

The leadership of Congress helps make Congress work. In the Constitution, Congress's main duty is to use its power to make laws. To make a law, Congress has to pass legislation. This process is described in

---

[9]Robert A. Caro, *Lyndon Johnson: Master of the Senate*. New York: Vintage Books, 2003, p. 401.

Section 7 of Article One. We move our discussion to this process of how a bill becomes a law.

CONGRESS' LAW-MAKING FUNCTION

The Constitution's version of how a bill becomes a law is the skeletal procedure of how Congress works. A bill becomes a law by having both houses of Congress cast a majority of votes and the President signs the bill. If the President uses his veto, Congress can override the veto by voting two-thirds majority and the bill becomes a law. This is the basic procedure the Constitution gives the Congress.

A more complicated procedure has developed over the years. Although the Constitutional outlines have been followed, there are interest groups, local interests and events that help drive the writing of legislation and define the law-making function of Congress more completely. Generically, the formal process of how a bill becomes a law has a nine step process for a Congressman.

★　A member will write a bill.
★　The bill will be sent to a subcommittee.
★　If it survives there it will go to the full committee.
★　If it is approved there, it will be sent to the House Rules Committee.
★　If it is approved there, then it would go to the full House.
★　If it is approved there, then it will go to the Senate.
★　Floor leaders in the Senate will have to approve it.
★　Then if there are any difference between the House version and the Senate version then it will have to go to the Conference Committee.
★　And then to the President.

As you can see the odds of a bill becoming a law in the formal description is quite remote. This nine step process does not take into account the personalities and the politics that may surround an idea that some want to become law. In real life it is much more complicated.

There are many interesting real life examples of how difficult it is to have a bill become a law. Hedrick Smith's book *The Power Game: How Washington Works* describes the passing of the 1986 tax reform package from the point of view of Congressional staff, politicians and lobbyists.[10] Robert Caro

in his biography of Lyndon B. Johnson, *Master of the Senate*, describes the simple procedure of bringing the Civil Rights Bill of 1957 off the Senate calendar and bring it to the floor:

> NEITHER KNOWLAND NOR THE DOUGLAS GROUP SEEMED TO UNDERSTAND—AND IF NIXON UNDERSTOOD, HE DID NOT DISCLOSE WHAT HE UNDERSTOOD—THAT THE EXISTENCE OF SUFFICIENT VOTES TO PASS THE BILL SIMPLY MEANT THAT NO VOTE WOULD BE ALLOWED ON THE BILL, NOT EVEN ON THE MOTION TO BRING IT TO THE FLOOR.[11]

The Senate in the 1950s was controlled by Southern Democrats who refused to have any civil rights legislation, even as with the case in the 1957 legislation, a majority of Senators wanted to support the bill.[12] This gives one an idea of how difficult it is to pass a bill into law even if the law is designed to help fulfill the promise of the Constitution.

The men and women who made their political careers in Congress had to be very patient as this illustration shows. Meaningful civil rights legislation was not enacted until 1964.[13] They also had to balance national and local interests. We have to look at the individual to understand fully the law-making function of Congress. How do people keep their constituents happy and at the same time acquire national power? In the next section of the chapter we examine the many roles of an average member of Congress.

THE ROLES OF A MEMBER OF CONGRESS

People who live in populous states sometimes have an uneven perception of the importance of Congressmen. If you are from California and there are forty-three members of the House of Representatives and two Senators you may think being a Congressman is not an important office, but just an introductory position. You are one of a large delegation and your importance in the system is not that great. This could not be farther from the truth. Congressmen are important, even if you are one member out of four hundred and fifty-two, they are important. On the other hand, if you live in a small state, you may have one member of Congress and two U.S. Senators. Everyone will be aware of the member of Congress, and on some important is-

---

[10]Hedrick Smith, *The Power Game: How Washington Works*. New York: Ballantine Books, 1988, Chapter 7, p. 119.

[11]Robert A. Caro, *Lyndon Johnson: Master of the Senate*. New York: Vintage Books, 2003, p. 928.
[12]Ibid.
[13]Ibid.

sues, being the only member of a delegation may give you a great amount of influence.

No matter what type of state you come from, being in Congress is an awesome responsibility and most members of Congress are highly successful honorable people. Their functions in office can be broken down into six different and related functions. These functions include: law making, service to constituents, representing the constituents, conflict resolution function, and public education. These functions reinforce the perception of the voters that their Congressman is doing a good job for them.

We have discussed in general, the law making function. Specifically, it is very difficult for a new member of Congress to have much influence on legislation. The egos and turf battles of long established members usually get in the way of getting famous by writing legislation. It has happened but it is very rare. Another part of the law making function is voting on bills. This establishes a track record and votes that seem to make sense now, several years later may torpedo future campaign plans. The Democratic Senators who voted for the invasion of Iraq is a good example of how their votes may affect their chances at getting the Democratic nomination in 2008. Many members of Congress try to specialize on specific legislative products. Sam Nunn, the former Democratic Senator from Georgia was a specialist on national defense, the Congress looked to him when there was legislation concerning the Defense Department. Former Senator Warren Rudman from New Hampshire was an expert on tax legislation. During his time in the Senate, he made a name for himself by fighting the Federal deficits by writing a piece of legislation. This again is very rare for newly elected members of the legislative branch.[14]

Most members of Congress make a political reputation for themselves by providing services to their constituents. This work can be labeled as either ombudsmen work or case work. As an ombudsmen, a Congressman will investigate complaints of constituents they have against the federal bureaucracy. People may need help if one of their relatives has been treated unfairly by the IRS or there is a bureaucrat that is abusing his local power. If you have problems with the Federal government and it concerns abuses by the bureaucracy, your Congressmen is a good person to contact. The other part of the service to constituents is what Congressional staffers call

case work. This is the run of the mill work members of Congress do. If you have problems with getting Grandma's social security check or her prescription benefit from medicare, your Congressman is a very good place to start getting answers. Members of Congress realize the service function of their jobs is very important. Once you help someone, they tend to be grateful when the election time comes. So if you do have problems with the Federal government, write to your member of Congress.

The next function a member of Congress performs is the representative function. There are different strategies different members of Congress use when they try to represent their districts. Some members who have expertise in an area try to be a trustee to the district. They will try to filter the information citizens have on an issue and bring their expertise to convince the people who live in their district, that this is the correct direction on a particular issue. Others try to be an instructed delegate. These are members who are constantly polling their districts and trying to follow instead of lead on issues concerning the Federal government. It is understandable especially if you are a new member of Congress to keep the pulse of public opinion in your district. However, there are many members of Congress who do not take a stand on any issue unless it has shown to be popular in their districts. The problem is the average person is not as fully informed on these issues as a member of Congress. That is why we see some in Congress tend to change their minds when circumstances change.

The last part of the representative function for members of Congress, is they are the chief representative of the political party in their districts or states. This function is called being a politico. It is the responsibility of the member of Congress to sell their Party's position on various issues to their constituents. The Republicans at the time of this writing have done a terrible job in this function. The Republicans lost control of the House of Representatives and the Senate. The Democrats have also done a very bad job in articulating reasons why voters should vote for them. The political debate many times turns on local issues. However, since the attacks on 9/11 the War on Terrorism and the war in Iraq have dominated the debate and both Democrats and Republican members of Congress do not seem to have an articulated strategy for victory in either of these areas. The failure of a Congressman to be a politico usually means the person will not be re-elected if his or her party is in power. This year, 2006 could look a lot like 1974 if the Re-

[14]Hedrick Smith, *The Power Game: How Washington Works.* New York: Ballantine Books, 1988, pp. 660–661.

publicans are not careful. The difference between 2006 and 1974 is the Democratic party has not developed a clear and cogent plan on what they would do differently. Remember, the President could not have invaded Iraq without the votes from Democratic members of Congress.

The next function a member of Congress has to master is the oversight function. When we hear of scandals by the Federal bureaucracy or private business, such as the Enron scandal—it is Congress' job to investigate and create legislation that will prevent these scandals in the future. During World War II, Senator Harry Truman from Missouri established the Truman Committee that oversaw the government contracts that were being rewarded as a result of the war effort.[15] He traveled across the country looking for waste, abuse and fraud by government contractors.[16] The scandals that surround the equipment of our army in Iraq and the failed relief efforts by the government to help people after Hurricane Katrina have not been investigated by Congress. It is Congress' responsibility to have oversight on the Federal bureaucracy. Again, they can have oversight because they have the power of the purse. They are the ones who determine how money is spent.

As in Katrina or on the September 11th attacks, one Federal bureaucracy will try to blame another part of the Federal bureaucracy on its failure to act effectively. It is the function of Congress to step in and investigate and determine how to settle conflicts inside the government. During the investigation of the terrorist attacks of September 11th, the Federal Bureau of Investigation and the Central Intelligence Agency were quarreling about who was responsible for the failure of intelligence that prevented authorities from realizing an attack was being planned.[17] The Congress investigated and tried to write rules and regulations that hopefully will prevent such attacks in the future. The famous blame game that went on after Katrina illustrates the conflict between agencies can take an immature path. Name calling and sheer incompetence still plagues the recovery effort in New Orleans. FEMA, the Coast Guard and Army Corps of Engineers have all looked to Congress in an effort to reduce the interagency conflict that has showed itself since the storm.

The last function a member of Congress has is the public education function. This function can be the Congressman communicating to his or her constituency. A member of Congress does not have to pay for postage. They simply have to sign their name on top of an envelope and it will be delivered by the Postal service. This is called the franking privilege. It is worth more than a million dollars a year and is one of the reasons incumbents stay in Congress. The other side of this function is you can ask your member of Congress about research the Federal government is doing about any topic and you will receive a packet of information. Also every non-classified document and non-classified testimony Congress produces is available to people either on line or at libraries across the country.

This is a great resource for people who believe in conspiracies. You can use the Freedom of Information Act to request all the documents the government has on area 51, alien abductions or anything else you may read in the tabloid newspapers that are in the grocery store. Also most libraries will have the Congressional record so you can read what your Congressman has said regarding issues that are important to you. It is in the government's interest generally and your member of Congress specifically to give you all of the information you desire. Seriously, even if you do not believe in conspiracies, the public education function of Congress can be an effective research tool for students who are interested in cutting edge research done by scientists in all fields in which the government has sponsored research.

These functions of Congress: the lawmaking function, service to constituents, the representative function, oversight, conflict resolution, and public education functions are all ways members of Congress get re-elected. These functions all contribute to the average person's feeling that they love their Congressman but hate Congress. Next, we examine the difference between the Senate and the House of Representatives. These differences are largely spelled out in the Constitution and they affect the personality of the two different institutions that make up the Legislative branch of our government.

INSTITUTIONAL DIFFERENCES BETWEEN THE SENATE AND THE HOUSE OF REPRESENTATIVES

The Founding Fathers developed key institutional differences between the House of Representatives and the Senate. The House of Representatives was

---

[15]David McCullough, *Truman.* New York: Simon & Schuster, 1992, p. 254.

[16]Ibid.

[17]Lee Hamilton, Thomas Kean, et al. *The 9/11 Commission Report.* Washington, DC: Government Printing Office, 2003, p. 399.

supposed to be a vehicle that absorbed the passion of the people. Instead of revolution, people were supposed to change their government by elections. The House has elections every two years in order to have new members that express the different needs and interests of the electorate. The Senate was to be a more mature political institution. Members were to be elected every six years and the age requirement was five years greater than in the House of Representatives. If you look at the Legislative branch as a motor, the Senate was to act as a governor that prevented the passions of the people from accelerating change too fast.

One can see this difference when we compare the rules on debates in each body. In the House of Representatives the rules are very constricting for members to discuss their positions on the floor of the House. Since there are 435 members of the House of Representatives the leadership has to limit the time each member is given on debates. When the Iraq War was being considered, each member of the House received five minutes of time to make a speech on one of the most important issues that has reached Congress in the past five years. In comparison Senators have unlimited privileges to speak on issues on the Senate floor. A favorite tactic is if a Senator does not want to have an issue on the floor of the Senate, he or she will employ the filibuster. A filibuster allows the Senator to monopolize the Senate for as long as he or she can physically control the floor of the Senate. This was used most skillfully during the 1950s when the Democrats of the South blocked Civil Rights legislation by filibustering the issue.[18] This difference between the House of Representatives and the Senate during the early years of the Republic when public speaking was important, gave an advantage to Senators over Representatives as better orators.

Senators are famous for their speeches: Everett Dirksen, Stephen Douglas, Daniel Webster all made their reputations on the Senate floor. Abraham Lincoln, whose previous Federal office had been as a member of the House of Representatives, did not get a reputation as a great public speaker until he had left the House of Representatives. The House does not lend itself to great dramatic moments on the floor as the Senate does. Some have called the Senate the greatest deliberative body ever invented. The Senators know their role is to question, debate and question again any issue of importance that may have been passed hastily by the House of Representatives.

Since World War I it has been very difficult for a member of the House of Representatives to become President of the United States. The Senate has more prestige, since there are only two Senators from each state; people tend to know who their Senators are. It is rare for Senators to become President. John F. Kennedy, Lyndon B. Johnson and Richard Nixon were the last Senators to become President. Both Nixon and Johnson were Vice President before assuming the office of the President. Gerald Ford, although not elected, was the last member of the House of Representatives to become President. Ford, of course, also served as Vice President before he was elevated to the Presidency. We have had candidates from both the House of Representatives and the Senate. However it is very difficult for members of the House to have a national following since their exposure to both electoral organization and fund raising tends to be limited to their congressional districts. Richard Gephardt was the last serious candidate from the House of Representatives to try a run for the Presidency.

The odds are a bit better for Senators, especially Senators from larger states. We have discussed the innovations John F. Kennedy had to implement to become President. He was the last Senator to become elected to the Presidency directly from the Senate. The last Senator to earn the nomination of a political party was John Kerry who was the Democratic party nominee in 2004. The last Vice President we had that came directly from the Senate was Al Gore, when he ran with Bill Clinton.

Senators such as Al Gore, Bob Dole, John Kerry, and Lyndon Johnson (in 1960) look to the average American as too inside Washington. It is very difficult to run a campaign that tries to convince people you are going to change the way Washington works, if you are one of the power brokers and have lived in the Senate for thirty years. Bob Dole tried to become Vice President and President since he was nominated in 1976 for the Vice Presidency to run with Gerald Ford. They lost. Even today, Dole's wife Elizabeth is a Senator from North Carolina and she has run for President in 2000 and is considered a candidate for the Vice Presidency every four years. Even if the candidate has been considered a Presidential personality, such as Senator Edward Kennedy, it is very difficult to translate popularity into organizational effectiveness. Kennedy ran against President Jimmy Carter in 1980 and lost significantly. We will continue our dis-

---

[18]Robert A. Caro, *The Years of Lyndon Johnson: Master of the Senate.* New York: Vintage Books, 2003, pp. 182–185.

cussion on the Presidency in the next chapter, but to gain the White House from the Senate is easier than being in the House of Representatives, but it remains very difficult.

These institutional differences were part of the design of the Founding Fathers. There were also things the writers of the Constitution could not have envisioned, such as the modern personal power centers and the development of the perpetual campaign. Because of this, the re-election rate to the House of Representatives is actually larger than the re-election rate for Senators. If one can get elected to the House of Representatives it can literally be a life time appointment. While Senators, because they are more public, the election is geographically based and they run every six years, tend to lose more often than their House of Representative counterparts. The average re-election rate in Congress is 97.7 percent. The incumbents that lose their seats are usually Senators, not Representatives unless the Representative is redistricted or touched personally by scandal.

CONGRESSIONAL REDISTRICTING

Assuming a member of Congress does not have a problem with a scandal, changes in Congressional districts is the other major contributor to a defeat of incumbents. Every ten years the census is taken by the Government as required by the Constitution. If there is a population shift, or a political party shift (when one party replaces the other in the state legislature or in a State Governor's office) a member of Congress may face a change in their Congressional district. This happened in Texas after the 2000 census. Texas was a Republican state, yet, the majority of the Congressional delegation was Democratic. So, the state legislature (with the help of former House Majority Leader Tom Delay) re-wrote the Congressional districts of the state.

It is the state legislature that re-apportions or draws the Congressional districts. Normally, there is agreement between the parties to draw "safe" Congressional districts. To include a majority in each district so that the elections are fairly predictable and the advantage is given to incumbents of both parties. This is why some analysts have commented that there are two parties in this country: incumbents and challengers. The criterion for drawing districts is the party makeup in the district or sometimes these are called majority-minority districts. This arrangement makes sense for the two political parties. It ensures each party keeps its number of seats in a given state. For example, let us

say we are State Legislators in a State that is roughly 40 percent Republican and 60 percent Democratic. If you are a Republican, the population of your support may be concentrated in two or three areas. Would you rather have one or two safe Congressional seats or the possibility of losing all of the Congressional races by slim margins because the districts do not concentrate your voting power? The Democrats, on the other hand, do not have to work to freeze out the Republicans. They may agree to create two safe seats for the Republicans in order to have eight safe seats for themselves. It is logical from a political party perspective, but there are other criteria the legislature has to use in order to have the Constitutional rule of one man one vote upheld. Racial minorities, and others have fought that the parties have to include other demographic information in deciding how to reapportion the Congressional districts every ten years.

One tradition the courts have changed is the aspect of geography. Congressional districts have to reflect the demographic properties of the area, not the geography. If an urban center has always had a Congressional district and it is bordered by a geographic feature, maybe a river, lake, or some other type of barrier, the legislatures cannot use the physical features of the area to keep the district inside the urban area. The use of physical features to form Congressional districts was used in the South to have an unequal urban-rural ratio of representation.

Currently, there have been Supreme Court decisions that have outlined the procedure to be used in re-writing Congressional districts. The districts cannot be drawn to dilute minority groups' strengths and they cannot be drawn with obvious racial purposes. When legislatures draw and re-draw Congressional districts they must also keep in mind the enforcement of the Voting Rights Act of 1965. As long as a state legislature follows these general guidelines, they can draw the map as they see fit. If a member of Congress does not have a following in the legislature or a powerful member of the state legislature wants to become a member of Congress, a Congressman can wake up and find their district has been changed. In some instances, as what happened in Texas, two Democratic incumbents had to run against each other in a primary in order to preserve their status as members of Congress. This is one of the reasons the Democrats started to investigate Majority Leader of the House of Representatives Tom DeLay, because he was responsible with working with the Texas Republicans in the Texas legislature to turn the Texas House delegation from a marginally Democratic delegation to a Republican delegation by re-drawing and defeating ten Democratic incumbents. The particular re-districting plan has been working its way in the court system. One can see how this dramatic change can cause consternation on the part of the party that had its members replaced. Although it may represent a more accurate dispersal of Congressional districts, usually, parties try to cooperate on these matters since no one knows when they will be a minority party trying to preserve a small number of safe seats in Congress.

We have examined how Congress works from the individual perspective and from an institutional perspective. Next, we will analyze the relationship between the Congress and the President. What institution has gained in power and how has the relationship between these two branches of government changed since the end of World War II to today.

CONGRESS AND THE PRESIDENT, A UNIQUELY AMERICAN DANCE

Many Presidents have never served in Congress. Theodore Roosevelt, Woodrow Wilson, Franklin Roosevelt, Dwight Eisenhower, and George W. Bush never were Congressmen or Senators from their states. Other Presidents such as John F. Kennedy and Richard Nixon served a very short time in both the House of Representatives and the Senate until the Presidential bug bit them to seek higher office. On the other hand, many members in Congress have served more than thirty years. Some Representatives in the House have served more than forty years. Their attitudes can be summed up as they have seen Presidents come and go; but we are the permanent members of our institution.

The Constitution calls for the Executive and Legislative branches of government to have their own spheres of influence on the laws and policies that are set forth. At the initial stages of the Republic, the Congress tended to have a more dominant position on policy than the President. Since World War II however, the President has taken the lead on many policy issues and is the center of the American political environment.

Even before World War II, President Franklin Roosevelt led Congress. He understood the Congress wanted to do something in the dire emergencies that were the Great Depression and World War II. Members of Congress could report that they were doing something to fight the economic hardship or the aggression of dictators when they passed legislation in favor of Roosevelt's agenda. It also did not hurt when the money was spent in their home districts for projects such as rural electrification and highway beautification and other infrastructure investments. Presidents author the central proposals in their budgets and State of the Union Addresses but, it is Congress who ultimately decides on how the money is spent.

From 1933 to 1994, the Democratic party dominated Congress. They had the majority of both the Senate and House of Representatives for almost sixty years with a few interruptions during the 1950s. President Roosevelt enjoyed a majority in the Congress. Harry Truman did have to deal with Republican majorities in the late 1940s and early 1950s. President Eisenhower did have Republican majorities for some of his time in the White House, but overall, the Congress was a Democratic majority for most of the twentieth century. This created for Republican Presidents a bigger challenge. How do you curb the investigative powers of Congress if the other party controls Congress? From the Watergate scandal to the impeachment of Bill Clinton, if the other party has a majority in Congress, it can distract the nation and keep Presidents pre-occupied by looking for ways to hinder the objectives of the President.

The impeachment process is a way to remove a President and other Federal officials. Although no President has ever been removed from office by being impeached, two have been impeached—Presidents Johnson and Clinton. President Nixon resigned when he was threatened by impeachment. There are eight steps in impeaching a President; the first step is the resolution. The resolution is sent to the House Judiciary Committee were it is considered. Then the Committee votes on the resolution if this passes. The next step is the whole House of Representatives votes on the resolution. If this passes, the House will hold impeachment hearings and after the hearing there will be a report. The whole House again votes on each article of impeachment. Simple majority vote is needed to send the articles of impeachment to the Senate. Then there is an Impeachment Trial in the Senate that is conducted by the Chief Justice of the United States. After all of this, there is a vote by the full Senate and two-thirds majority of the Senators must agree to convict the President. If this happens then the President will be impeached. As the Constitution says, impeachment only means the removal of the President from office. This process is a very extreme process, it is designed to be difficult so that when the opposition party loses a Presidential election but they remain in the majority, they cannot just remove a President.

In the two impeachment trials the Senate has conducted, both failed to achieve a two-thirds majority in the Senate. As with Representatives and Senators, if they can keep away from scandal or breaking the law, it is very difficult to remove someone from office once they are elected. In normal times, the relationship between Congress and the President is adversarial. The Congress is very good at deliberating on issues, articulating local views and getting federal dollars to member's home districts. The President is the only elected officer who is elected (although indirectly) by all of the American people. He has to have a national perspective in selling his programs to Congress. This different perspective causes different friction between the two institutions. This is exactly what the Founding Fathers intended when they wrote the First and Second Articles of the Constitution.

The Founding Fathers may have anticipated the friction between the Executive and Legislative branches of government. They did not anticipate the competition and explosive growth both branches have engaged in since the Great Depression. The need for experts and staff have grown all out of proportion. Members of Congress today have multi-million dollar budgets to fund staff and hire experts in all of the fields that their political activities touch on. Many Senators have advisers that rival the President. There is a Congressional Budget Office and Economic Advisors that compete with the Executive branch. The staff of the Armed Services and Intelligence Committees are experts in foreign and national security issues. These people compete against the experts in the CIA and State Department.

Since it is Congress that spends tax money, they have put themselves in a position to hire as many (if not more) staff members as the Presidents. Although, these staff members are not well known and they usually do not talk in front of television cameras. They have a great deal of influence on how laws are written and how members of Congress treat a certain issue. Members of Congress are so busy on the three days a week they are in Washington, D.C., that many rely totally on their staff. The members of Congress are political experts on how to get re-elected, they are not experts on issues. Even though they may want to have a certain expertise on a certain issue, they are too over-scheduled to follow any one issue. It is the staff that writes the legislation, does the case work and edits the final newsletters trumpeting the Congressman's latest accomplishments. The power of

staff is illustrated by the story of Lyndon B. Johnson. As a young staffer to a Congressmen, he was able to work the bureaucracy of the pre-World War II Washington establishment. He was elected to his own seat at the age of 28 and he complained that he had more power when he was a Congressional secretary than as a member.

Issues are more complex and varied and the demand of the perpetual campaign have made members of Congress beholden to staff. Congress has a dual struggle on its hands to try to compete with the President on issues such as the War on Terror, the economy and social security, and at the same time trying to hold on to power from members of the staff of the Congressional bureaucracy. For Congress to look serious to the American people they have to look as if they are leading a serious policy and political agenda. If the majority of the members of Congress are in the same party as the President this may be easier. If the majority of the members are of the opposite party, this means that a dual or opposite center of gravity has to be created in Congress to compete with the President. The Democrats have majorities in the House of Representatives and the Senate starting in January 2007, we will see if they are able to create this counter-balance.

CONCLUSION

In this chapter, we have analyzed the Congress from two levels of analysis. First, from an institutional level. We examined the role of the Congress that was described in the Constitution and how through history the roles between the House of Representatives and the Senate were defined. The Constitution gives the Legislative branch of government powers that are enumerated such as the power to spend money and declare war. The Congress also has the necessary and proper clause in which the power of Congress can be used to implement the expressed powers any way it wants as long as the Supreme Court does not strike the law down as unconstitutional.

We then examined the many steps on how a bill becomes a law. The outline again was in the Constitution. However, our discussion showed how difficult it is to pass legislation and how equally difficult it is to make a name for yourself just concentrating on the legislative process. The next part of the chapter described the many roles Congressmen have. These roles include the challenges of getting re-elected. The perpetual campaign has made Congress a Tuesday–Thursday club, because all of the members of the

House of Representatives tend to leave Washington for long weekends at their home districts.

The members are not vacationing on these long weekends, they are reporting to the people of their district. They are participating in the public education function of members, which happens to coincide with the personal campaigning and fund raising members of Congress must do in order to get re-elected. Then we examined how incumbency and the drawing of districts affects the chances of members of Congress to get re-elected. Incumbents have a 97.7 percent chance of re-election if they are not entangled with a scandal or if their Congressional districts are not re-drawn by the state legislature.[19] Finally, we examined the problem of staff and the competition the Legislative branch has with the Executive branch. Although the Founding Fathers wanted there to be friction and competition, since the attacks of 9/11, members of Congress from both parties have failed to articulate a clear strategy for leadership on many of the vital issues we face today.

The next chapter will focus on the Presidency and how that branch of the government has developed since the ratification of the Constitution. We will examine the explosive growth in the Office of the Presidency and see if the Presidency has turned into a pseudo monarchy as the Founding Fathers feared. We will also share some historic insights on how the men who held the job of President fared and how some of our most recent Presidents used a combination of personality and intellect to lead the country out of some very serious crises.

TERMS TO REMEMBER

NECESSARY AND PROPER CLAUSE

STANDING COMMITTEE

JOINT COMMITTEE

CONFERENCE COMMITTEE

SELECT COMMITTEE

VETO

FRANKING PRIVILEGE

FILIBUSTER

---

[19]Hedrick Smith, *The Power Game: How Washington Works*. New York: Ballantine Books, 1988, p. 123.

Congress—Forum of the Nation

TRUE OR FALSE QUESTIONS

1. Senators have a two year term of office.   T / F

2. A person must be 30 years old to be a Representative in the House of Representatives.   T / F

3. A person must be 30 years old to be a Senator.   T / F

4. Congressmen pay for their postage.   T / F

5. After the Civil War, the Congress was more powerful than the President.   T / F

6. After World War II, the Congress was more powerful than the President.   T / F

7. The Republican party has always had a majority in Congress.   T / F

8. The leader of the Senate is known as the Speaker.   T / F

9. There has never been a woman Speaker of the House.   T / F

10. The first African-American Senator was elected in 2000.   T / F

MULTIPLE CHOICE QUESTIONS

11. Which is not a committee in Congress?
    a. Joint Committee
    b. Standing Committee
    c. Select Committee
    d. Adjunct Committee

12. The leader of the Senate is called
    a. Speaker
    b. Majority Leader
    c. Majority Whip
    d. Chief

13. Congress gets its power from the Constitution in
    a. Article I, Section 7
    b. Article I, Section 8
    c. Article II, Section 7
    d. Article II, Section 8

14. Congress gets its law-making function from
    a. Article I, Section 7
    b. Article I, Section 8
    c. Article II, Section 7
    d. Article II, Section 8

15. The Speaker is leader of the
    a. Senate
    b. Republicans
    c. Democrats
    d. House of Representatives

16. The most famous Majority Leader of the Senate since World War II is
    a. John F. Kennedy
    b. Richard Nixon
    c. Lyndon B. Johnson
    d. Gerald Ford

17. How many steps are there in how a bill becomes a law?
    a. Three
    b. Seven
    c. Six
    d. Nine

18. How many U.S. Senators are there?
    a. 435
    b. 98
    c. 100
    d. 50

19. How many Representatives to the House are there?
    a. 100
    b. 98
    c. 50
    d. 435

20. A filibuster is a tactic used by
    a. the House of Representatives to pick a speaker.
    b. the President to stop a bill from becoming a law.
    c. the Speaker to assign committee assignments.
    d. the Senate to postpone a vote on a bill.

chapter ten

THE PRESIDENCY

INTRODUCTION

The Articles of Confederation failed because there was lack of executive control over the different states. The Constitution rectified this mistake by establishing an Executive branch of government. The executive was called the President of the United States. Contrary to the establishment of Congress, the Presidency was controversial. Many of the Founding Fathers believed it was not necessary to have an executive to run the Federal government. They became the Anti-Federalists. These members believed it was ill-advised to substitute the English tyranny with an American tyrant. The President was viewed by some as an American version of the King of England. This was the minority point of view, yet some had questions to the powers and procedures needed to select a President. The Presidency is a unique office, it changes with the person who occupies it; also it changes the people who serve in, what some have called, the most powerful office in the world.

In this chapter, we will examine both sides of the Presidency, the institutional requirements and restrictions each man has faced as President. Futhermore, we will discuss the interesting personalities that have occupied the office, concentrating on the Presidents who have built the institution to what it is today. The organization of this chapter includes the personal qualifications of who can be President of the United States, the different functions of the President, different types of Presidential power and its abuses, the organization of the executive branch of the Federal government and we finish our discussion with a discussion on Presidential leadership in a time of war. Since the beginning of the Republic there have only been white men elected to the Presidency. It is our firm belief that in the next two or three elections there will be either a racial minority or a woman (or both) elected to either the Vice Presidency or Presidency. Since that has not happened yet, we will use the pronoun "he" when talking about the Presidency, since this is historically accurate. As we will see, the personal qualifications of becoming President in the Constitution did not restrict people on the basis of gender or race.

PERSONAL REQUIREMENTS FOR THE PRESIDENCY

The Constitution has very basic requirements for becoming President: the person must be a natural-born citizen of the United States, 35-years-old and been a resident for 14 years. The residency requirement was used because during the late 1700s people may have been gone from the country for long periods of time, especially if they were involved in international diplomacy or business. The writers of the Constitution wanted a person to have been in the country for a while before they tried to run for the Presidency. The other requirements are quite self-explanatory. Plus, the President has to be older than 35-years-old. President Theodore Roosevelt was the youngest man ever to become President at 43. President John F. Kennedy was also 43 (but a little older than Theodore Roosevelt), he was the youngest man ever to be elected to the Presidency. We also forget Franklin D. Roosevelt was a young 49-year-old man when he was elected. The oldest Presidents were Ronald Reagan and Dwight D. Eisenhower, Reagan was 69 when he was elected, Eisenhower was 63.

Professionally, a large majority of Presidents have been lawyers. Some were farmers and two were military officers. What is surprising when you look at their backgrounds is how many Presidents never served in the Congress, 16 out of the 43 Presidents we have had never served in either the House of Representatives or the Senate. One could conclude from this American's like to elect Presidents who are outsiders. There has been one Catholic elected to the Presidency, the rest have been of various Protestant religious traditions. Since the Civil War there has been a geographic bias. There has been two Presidents from the deep South, Presidents Carter and Clinton, and if we are technical about their residences three Presidents from Texas: Lyndon Johnson, George H. Bush and George W. Bush. Although George H. Bush and George W. Bush were born outside of Texas they consider themselves Texans. The majority of Presidents after the Civil War have come from States that fought for the Union.

The men who occupied the White House were very different, some were born in very modest circumstances, and some were born to incredible wealth. How they started their road to the White House may have been different, but once elected, no matter their background, they belong to an exclusive club of men who must lead the nation. In times of crises, it is the President who the country looks to for confidence, leadership and solutions. No matter what political party the President leads or his political philosophy, he must be able to perform the different functions of the Presidency.

THE FUNCTIONS OF THE PRESIDENT

In a famous quip, Franklin D. Roosevelt said to the famous actor Orson Welles, "Orson, we are the two greatest actors in America." At times, it does appear the President must be a magician trying to do tricks in order to lead the emotions of a nation. There are five major categories of Presidential functions, they are: Chief of State, Chief Executive, Commander-in-Chief, Chief Diplomat, and Chief Legislator. These different functions many times overlap. It is difficult to divide where a role of Chief Diplomat and Commander-in-Chief separate especially in relationship to the modern Presidency, where a President might order a military strike in order to pressure diplomatic negotiations on a particular state. The first function the President has had since the ratification of the Constitution was Chief of State.

CHIEF OF STATE

The President of the United States symbolizes the sovereignty of the country. The person who occupies the Presidency uses things such as: the Presidential Seal, the White House, Air Force One, limousines, Camp David—all of the things Hollywood is attracted to when they film a movie or a television show about the Presidency. In reality, these things are symbolic extensions of the power of the United States.

The modern Presidential Seal and Flag were designed by President Harry Truman in 1945. He changed the direction of the eagle's head, as Truman said when he showed the design for the first time "This new flag faces the eagle toward the staff," Truman explained, "which is looking to the front all the time when you are on the march, and also has him looking at the olive branch for peace instead of the arrows for war."[1] Why would a President of the United States worry about the eagle on the flag and seal? Truman understood the importance of the sym-

---

[1]David McCullough, *Truman*. New York: Simon & Schuster, 1992, p. 474.

bolism and historic message he wanted to present to the world. Not only were these symbols graphically and fashionably important, they also contributed to the debate between the United States and the Soviet Union during the Cold War on ideology. The office of the President is the personification of the power of the United States and the recognition that he represents all of the people of the United States. Philosophically, of course the country was founded on the concept of popular sovereignty. However, just as Kings and Queens have their sovereignty encased in crowns and scepters, the sovereignty of the United States is encased in the office of the President. These symbols are also very handy when trying to use the Presidential power to convince other leaders either foreign or domestic. They are connected to the person who holds the office of the Presidency, even if the President goes on a local trip.

When President Ronald Reagan went to Tennessee to open the World's Fair in Knoxville, Hedrick Smith explains the great trouble the bureaucracy went through to make sure it was secure.[2] The Secret Service inspected the town, put agents in the small choir at the local church and deputized every police officer in the town. They even sent the food the President was going to be served back to Washington, D.C. to make sure it was not poisoned. The symbols of sovereignty went to a little town in Tennessee as if it was a foreign capital of a major power. Unlike in other countries, there is no difference between the role of the Chief of State and the Chief Executive in the United States. Sometimes the symbols of office do make it easier to intimidate others in the government in order to administer the largest bureaucracy of the country—the Federal government. The President is the Chief Executive of a trillion dollar enterprise and the largest employer in the United States.

CHIEF EXECUTIVE

In England, the role of Chief of State and Chief Executive are divided and held by two different people. The Queen is England's Chief of State and the Prime Minister is the British Chief Executive. In the United States, we combine these two functions. This has advantages in protocol and in the exercise of Presidential power. As Chief Executive the President is responsible to administer and enforce all the laws, treaties and court orders produced by the U.S. government. However, he lacks the command power that everyone thinks a President has. Instead, as Chief Executive, the President must use his powers of persuasion. If you remember our definition of power as the ability of a person to get you to do what you want them to do, the campaign for the Presidency is a marathon of trying to persuade the whole country to vote for you to the office.

It does not get any easier once you have been elected. Presidential leadership is the ability to get people to do something that may not be in their interest but the President deems the right thing to do. We see this most clearly when there is a path the President wants the country to take yet, for whatever reason, the country is not ready to follow the President. Jon Meacham in his book *Franklin and Winston: An Intimate Portrait of an Epic Friendship* describes President Franklin D. Roosevelt's dilemma in trying to convince the American public to join forces with England to fight Nazi Germany. "Roosevelt's sympathies were clear . . . Yet Roosevelt faced a public that, by and large, could not see what good came of forays into affairs of seemingly faraway places."[3] This was observed by Eleanor Roosevelt, the President's wife, during a visit of the King and Queen of England to the United States. Even in his capacity of Chief of State (since the British Monarchs have no political power) Roosevelt was trying to create contacts with the English since he foresaw the British would be in trouble. People forget, how strong the isolationist movement was in the United States before Pearl Harbor. The President in this case, Roosevelt, could not command the people to get ready for a World War, he had to persuade and try to mobilize the country on the margins. The visit we have talked about was in 1938. It would take Roosevelt three years to outwardly fight the threat he saw in 1938.

Once the attack at Pearl Harbor happened, the country was mentally prepared to follow a strong President. Hence due to his preparing the country before Pearl Harbor, President Roosevelt became the greatest war Chief Executive since Abraham Lincoln. The United States had a very small standing army and a slightly better equipped Navy. Within eighteen months the Army was invading North Africa and within a total of four years of the American victory was achieved.[4] The world has never seen a country

---

[2]Hedrick Smith, *The Power Game: How Washington Works*. New York: Ballantine Books, 1988, pp. 5–9.

[3]Jon Meacham, *Franklin and Winston: An Intimate Portrait of an Epic Friendship*. New York: Random House, 2004, p. 37.
[4]Ibid.

mobilize for war as fast as the United States had at the end of Pearl Harbor. It was Roosevelt's power of persuasion and perception to seize an opportunity that made it possible for the isolationists to be converted overnight in fighting the war.

Compare Roosevelt's power of persuasion and leadership in a war environment to that of Lyndon B. Johnson's. After 1964, President Johnson was elected in his own right as President of the United States. Similar to Roosevelt's record, Johnson wanted to expand social programs and also fight a war in Vietnam. Johnson's Defense Secretary Robert McNamara convinced Johnson the war would be a fast strategic victory against the North Vietnamese, Chinese Communists and ultimately the Russians. David Halberstam describes the environment before the 1964 elections in his classic book *The Best and the Brightest*

> IN 1964 THE LEADERSHIP, CONFIDENT OF ITSELF AND ITS PROFESSIONALISM, HELD BACK ON MAKING DECISIONS ON VIETNAM AND ALLOWED THE BUREAUCRACY TO PLAN FOR WAR. THERE WERE SIGNS OF THIS IN EARLY 1964; INDEED, IF YOU PUT THE SIGNS TOGETHER IN RETROSPECT, THEY WERE LARGELY NEGATIVE. HOWEVER, THAT ALL SEEMED MORE OBVIOUS LATER; THEY WERE WELL CONCEALED AT THE TIME. AT THE TIME, THE POLITICAL MEN AROUND THE PRESIDENT WERE BUSY PLANNING FOR HIS ELECTION CAMPAIGN, AND FOR THE GREAT SOCIETY TO COME AND THEY WERE SURE THAT VIETNAM WAS SOMEHOW A STUMBLING BLOCK OVER WHICH THEY WOULD NOT STUMBLE, THAT JOHNSON, IN THE WORDS OF THE SPEECHES BEING WRITTEN, WANTED NO WIDER WAR, THAT HE WOULD, AS HE HIMSELF THOUGHT, REASON WITH THE OTHER SIDE.[5]

President Johnson thought he could postpone the decision to fight the war until after the 1964 election. Even after the election there was never a truthful moment where the President tried to be very frank with the American people and give them the true struggle and sacrifice they would have to make to achieve victory. A simple way to test if a President is being successful in communicating his war aims is the question: "Why are we fighting?" If people are asking this question, the President has failed as the Chief Execute in a war environment. We are not talking about the military capacity of a President. We are talking about the power to persuade the public, Congress, and the bureaucracy to mobilize to fight a war. We will never know, because it was a path not taken. If the leaders in the Johnson Administration

and Johnson himself were to accurately communicate to the American people and to have an authentic declaration of war passed by the Congress, the mindset of the country would have been different. We do know, people, both Republicans and Democrats, thought they were promised an easy or at least a competent leadership in fighting in Vietnam. Johnson and then Nixon saw support evaporate because they anticipated victory without mobilization, and victory did not materialize. The same failure can be said about President Bush's handling of the War in Iraq. Again, President Bush did get United Nations approval and the approval of Congress to attack Iraq. However, the American people were told the war would be short. They were also told Saddam was an unpopular tyrant and the Iraqi people would treat our occupation as heroes, and there would not be an insurgency. There are many reasons why we are having problems with Iraq. One crucial reason is the President failed and has yet to be frank, about future plans and has not described the sacrifices that have to be made in order to have a victory in Iraq and on the War on Terror.[6]

Outside of the area of mobilizing civilians in the country for war, the role of Chief Executive is very difficult because of the large size of the Federal government. Also as power floats to other players, the President must be cognizant of interpersonal relationships and the understanding that all politics is personal.[7] This is where some of the roles between Chief of State and Chief Executive merge. A better label may be Salesman and Chief. The symbols of a Chief of State can help the President sell a program or a perception. The seal of the President is a symbol of the sovereignty of the United States, yet Presidents have it on everything from towels, matchbooks and napkins on Air Force One. Why do they put the seal on everything? Because they use these souvenirs as tokens of goodwill.[8]

Again, if the President is the Chief Salesman, how do you convince someone to listen to your point of view on an issue? Especially if the person is a Congressman or Senator. You can threaten them or you can ask them to bring two or three of their largest local contributors over to have a picture taken with you. When there was the Presidential Yacht the *Se-*

---

[5]David Halberstam, *The Best and the Brightest*. New York: Ballantine Books, 1969, p. 306.

[6]For a more complete discussion of the War on Terrorism and preemptive war, see Patrick C. Coaty, *Understanding the War on Terror*. Dubuque, IA: Kendall/Hunt Publishing Co., pp. 117–130.

[7]Hedrick Smith, *The Power Game: How Washington Works*. New York: Ballantine Books, 1988, p. 6.

[8]Ibid. pp. 7–8.

quoia, Harry Truman would sail up the Potomac River and have drinks with Congressional leaders and their wives. How do you think a Congressmen or Senator would react if you invited them to the White House for a State Dinner with Hollywood celebrities and the elite of Washington? They would tend to at least listen to the President's point of view on an issue. Yes, I know it may sound simplistic but our leaders are people and people do respond to kind gestures.

Again, we are not saying a conservative Congressman will give up his politics because a liberal President gives him a ride on Air Force One. What we are saying is by combining the roles of Chief of State, those symbols and being the Chief Executive you can persuade people to listen to you.[9] Washington is a city that moves on trust, according to David Gergen, longtime Presidential advisor.[10] If you are in Washington for any length of time you have to relate to others on a personal level.

This was President Jimmy Carter's failure. He saw the symbols of the Chief of State as an unnecessary luxury. He sold the Presidential Yacht and painted the Presidential limousine a beige color (black was too imperial) and tried to de-imperialize the Presidency.[11] Carter's Presidency failed on the shoals of personal relations. He may be a brilliant man, but politics and power are built on doing little favors for people. Presidential favors such as having a picture with the President in the Oval Office, meeting a Congressman's favorite contributor, cooperative staff relations with other governmental agencies. Jimmy Carter was famous for not doing these things. According to the Speaker of the House Thomas P. O'Neill, the Carter Administration at the Staff level would not speak with other members on Congressional staffs.[12] Although rationally, the Carter Administration may have been correct on many issues, especially on energy policy. No one wanted to follow them.

The Reagan Administration on the other hand, was very good at doing these favors for friends and opponents alike. So at the end of the day you may have disagreed with the policies of the Reagan Administration, but you liked President Reagan and in some instances this influenced the political environment surrounding his Presidency. Not every successful President can trace it to a friendly personality dishing out personal favors.[13] As the Chief Executive, the President must also be feared.

Robert Dallek in his biography of President Lyndon Johnson describes a meeting between President Johnson and the Governor of Alabama George Wallace on enforcing the voting rights of African-Americans in that state.

> BUT LYNDON WANTED WALLACE TO UNDERSTAND THAT HE WAS THE GREAT PERSUADER, WHO WOULD BEND WALLACE AND THE SOUTH TO HIS WILL . . .
>
> AFTER NEARLY THREE HOURS OF HAMMERING AT THE GOVERNOR, JOHNSON APPEALED TO HIS SENSE OF HISTORY. HE URGED WALLACE NOT TO "THINK ABOUT 1968; YOU THINK ABOUT 1988. YOU AND ME, WE'LL BE DEAD AND GONE THEN, GEORGE. NOW YOU'VE GOT A LOT OF POOR PEOPLE DOWN THERE IN ALABAMA, A LOT OF IGNORANT PEOPLE. YOU CAN DO A LOT FOR THEM, GEORGE. YOUR PRESIDENT WILL HELP YOU. WHAT DO YOU WANT AFTER YOU DIE? DO YOU WANT A GREAT . . . BIG . . . MARBLE MONUMENT THAT READS, 'GEORGE WALLACE—HE BUILT? . . . OR DO YOU WANT A LITTLE PIECE OF SCRAWNY PINE BOARD LYING ACROSS THAT HARSH, CALICHE SOIL, THAT READS 'GEORGE WALLACE—HE HATED?'" AFTER THEIR MEETING, WALLACE REMARKED: "HELL, IF I'D STAYED IN THERE MUCH LONGER, HE'D HAVE HAD ME COMING OUT FOR CIVIL RIGHTS."[14]

In 1964, Johnson believed his opponent Republican Senator Barry Goldwater would try to capitalize on the backlash from civil rights in the South. He had manipulated George Wallace to ask for Federal troops in order to stop the bloodshed (the police attacking civil rights workers) and try to enforce the voting laws in the South. This is a great example of how the President as the Chief Executive must enforce laws, treaties and court orders.

A less dramatic example of the President as the Chief Executive are appointment powers the President has. The day the President is elected he must appoint approximately 5,000 people his first day. Every President has to lean on the political party apparatus to provide lists of potential candidates for executive and bureaucratic positions. The American tradition of the spoils system introduced by Andrew Jackson, means the winner gets the spoils. By run-

---

[9]Hedrick Smith, *The Power Game: How Washington Works.* New York: Ballantine Books, 1988, pp. 461–465.

[10]David Gergen was a Presidential advisor to Presidents Nixon, Ford, Reagan and Clinton. Hedrick Smith, *The Power Game: How Washington Works.* New York: Ballantine Books, p. 466.

[11]Ibid.

[12]Ibid. p. 462.

[13]Hedrick Smith, *The Power Game: How Washington Works.* New York: Ballantine Books, 1988, p. 462.

[14]Robert Dalleck, *Flawed Giant: Lyndon Johnson and His Times 1961–1973.* New York: Oxford University Press, 1998, p. 217.

ning for an election and winning, a President wins the right to appoint people to run the government. If you remember, this is part of our definition of a political party.

However, the Civil Service reforms introduced during the Progressive Era, limits the Presidential appointment powers to senior level positions. President Richard Nixon would complain the bureaucracy was appointed by Democrats, therefore, was slow in implementing his policies. President Reagan had the Air Traffic Controllers Strike early in his career in which he fired all of the air traffic controllers who went on strike and broke the Union known as PATCO. He replaced the controllers with military controllers who temporarily ran the traffic in the airport until replacements were hired. Reagan argued the strike was illegal and he was enforcing the law. It was in reality a hard core message to other public unions that Reagan would not tolerate striking public workers. Again, another irony of Presidents, Reagan had served as the President of the Screen Actors Guild, a powerful union which started his career in politics, a former union President was responsible for breaking unions.

Of course in 1984, when President Reagan was running for re-election, all of the Unions except for the Teamsters, endorsed Walter Mondale. By using either the stick or the carrot, Presidents have to be able to convince others in the government and people outside the government that they are in control and they are the Chief Executive of the Federal government. It does not matter if the President personally knows all of the intricacies of the different policies and programs they must administer. Presidential leadership is essentially the ability to get people to do what you want them to do, which happens to be our definition of power. The President has the potential to be the most powerful man in the world. However, if the President does not use the power, then someone else will take it since power floats to people who are willing to use it. One of the challenges a President faces is not how they treat their enemies, but what they do for their friends and people who try to associate themselves to their administrations.

Presidents tend to have scandals over who they pardon, give jobs to, or let into their inner circle. President Clinton has his famous scandals: white water and Lewinsky. He also had a damaging scandal, when on the last days of his administration he pardoned numerous people who were connected to his fund raising for his Presidential library. No one can

criticize him for giving his brother a pardon (Roger Clinton was a felon from a drug conviction), but he gave Marc Rich, a man who traded with the Iranian regime during a time an American boycott was being enforced for tax evasion. Rich's ex-wife had raised funds for the Clinton library and there seemed to have been a lack of judgment, meaning President Clinton did not anticipate the public outcry by the pardon. President George H. Bush on his last days as President pardoned many of the main people who were being investigated on the Iran-Contra scandal, preventing an investigation that may have brought out more information on the reasons we had such simplistic and unrealistic policies regarding the Iranian regime.[15] Pardons were designed for Presidential action in order to reverse an injustice or failure of the justice system. As the chief law enforcement officer of the United States, the President must have this power, however, they should be very careful when they use it.

COMMANDER-IN-CHIEF

The Revolutionaries who won independence from Great Britain distrusted the military. They read history and concluded democracies are an experiment that are short lived and usually doomed. They had witnessed the experience of the French Revolution and the death of the French Republic as it was replaced by Napoleon. The Founding Fathers had concluded, one of the ingredients that foiled democratic experiments was an established military class.[16] This is why they wrote in the Constitution that the budgets for the Navy and Army were to be on a two year cycle. If a Napoleon would try to replace the Constitution (even though it would violate this person's oath) the last resort was to starve the Army of its resources. Another institution that was to prevent an American dictatorship was making the President Commander-in-Chief of the military. What this essentially does is make every General and Admiral a subordinate of the President.

On September 2006, the Thai Army had its 32nd coup d'etat against the elected government of Thailand. The King of Thailand was in favor of the coup leaders, and the transfer of power seems to be blood-

---

[15]For an excellent and concise history of U.S.-Iranian policy see: Kenneth M. Pollack, *The Persian Puzzle: The Conflict Between Iran and America.* New York: Random House, 2004.

[16]David McCullough, *John Adams.* New York: Simon & Schuster, 2001, on titles 408.

less. Nevertheless, the military replaced an elected government. The Pakistani President Musharrif is a product of a military coup, he replaced a democratically elected Prime Minister and has yet to step down. The Founding Fathers had a great deal of foresight when they made the President Commander-in-Chief and gave control of the military to civilians.

Commander-in-Chief can be defined as the President who has the ultimate authority in all things concerning the military. It is in this role that the President does not have to use his powers of persuasion. He can give orders to military officers and as long as the orders are legal the military is required to follow the orders. In our history, we have had two Presidents who were graduates of West Point, and one who was a graduate of Annapolis (Naval Academy). The role of Commander-in-Chief has become greater because of the threat of nuclear weapons and the War on Terror. The country, if attacked, needs to have its leadership intact and ready at any moment to command a military response to threats that are posed by the outside world.

The President also can use the military for internal insurrection and securing public order. Presidents Eisenhower, Kennedy, Johnson and George H. Bush all sent troops into cities to enforce either court orders or to stop rioting in major cities. Most of us, however, see the role as Commander-in-Chief as the President acting in our behalf on issues dealing with the military.

Throughout the history of the United States, the President has had a fairly free hand when it comes to policies dealing with the military. The Congress does pass the budget for the military but it is the President who commands the different forces, commissions the officers and even recommends officers for senior rank (with Senate approval). When the country finds itself at war, the country instinctively turns to the President.

On Sunday, September 25, 2006, President Clinton complained on an interview program that although he failed to kill Osama Bin Laden, he had tried.[17] Yes, the attacks of September 11th did change everything; however, the Clinton Administration did not view military policy as important. He viewed issues legalistically. He could have made the same arguments that President Bush made after September 11th after the first World Trade Center attack, instead he viewed it as a criminal event. He also viewed other attacks as crimes. The embassy bombings in Kenya

and Tanzania by al-Qaeda, and the attack on the USS Cole by al-Qaeda were treated by civil authorities by President Clinton, not by military.[18] We can analyze this approach, but for better or worse it was the approach President Clinton chose after Osama Bin Laden declared war on the United States in 1996. President Clinton did use military force in the Balkans. David Halberstam writes the relationship between the Clinton Administration and the Department of Defense were strained:

> CLINTON HAD BEEN AWARE FROM THE START OF THE DOUBTS ABOUT HIM AMONG THE MILITARY. BEFORE HE COULD FUNCTION EFFECTIVELY AS [P]RESIDENT, HE KNEW HE WOULD HAVE TO OVERCOME AT LEAST SOME OF THOSE DOUBTS, AND HE HAD WORKED HARD TO DO THAT. HE UPGRADED HIS PERSONAL BEHAVIOR IN DEALING WITH THEM AND HAD USED ALL OF HIS CONSIDERABLE TALENTS AND CHARM IN PERSONAL MEETINGS TO DIMINISH WHATEVER LINGERING STEREOTYPES THEY MIGHT HAVE OF HIM . . . HE COULD BE JUST AS TOUGH AND HARD-NOSED AS NECESSARY. HE CONSTANTLY REACHED OUT TO THEM . . .[19]

Did the relationship between the Defense Department and the Clinton Administration color their response to the attacks by al-Qaeda? We do not know. What we do know is the Commander-in-Chief role was not used very well by the Clinton Administration.

In contrast to President Clinton's relationship with the Army, President Harry Truman was very comfortable in the role of Commander-in-Chief and in keeping civilian control over the military. He understood the importance of retaining civilian control over the military. After World War I, the Truman Administration reorganized the old War Department and made the reforms that we now have in the Defense Department. After World War II, the legends who won the war: George Marshall, Dwight Eisenhower, Douglas MacArthur, and Omar Bradley and others were still alive and in the cases of MacArthur, Bradley and Eisenhower still in the Army. These men and the U.S. Army had tremendous prestige among the American people. MacArthur had won the Congressional Medal of Honor for his escape from the Philippines. Marshall had been Chief of Staff under Roosevelt and was the architect for victory and Eisenhower and Bradley had defeated Hitler. Truman had been a Captain in the Army during World War I, and had

---

[17]*Fox News Sunday* with Chris Wallace aired September 25, 2006.

[18]Patrick C. Coaty, *Understanding the War on Terror*. Dubuque, IA: Kendall/Hunt Publishing Co., p. 124.

[19]David Halberstam, *War in a Time of Peace*. New York: 2001, p. 417.

worked a little with Marshall in his efforts as a Senator and Vice President.

In 1950, the North Koreans invaded South Korea. From the beginning of the invasion, Truman reacted as if it was war. On one hand, but did not want an expansion of the conflict to World War III on the other.[20] Truman understood the question of civilian control of the military. Marshall and Bradley knew that MacArthur had overstepped the bounds of this relationship when he sent a letter to Republican Speaker of the House Joe Cannon.[21]

In the letter, MacArthur stated the problems with Truman's policies and the need to strive for total victory instead of a stalemate on the Korean Peninsula.[22] Truman knew he would have "the biggest fight of his administration" according to Dean Acheson, but it was the only way to relieve the situation of an insubordinate general. Even the military had become disenchanted with MacArthur, therefore, it did make it easier to relieve him of command.[23]

Truman's actions were at the time considered deeply unpopular. Remember during the early defeats of World War II, the government had built MacArthur up as the hero of the Pacific (awarding him the Medal of Honor after his escape from the Philippines). After World War II, he controlled the occupation of Japan, writing for the Japanese their Constitution and instituting such progressive ideas as equality for women and recognizing labor unions. Finally, even during the Korean War, MacArthur showed the world his military ingenuity by successfully repelling the North Korean invasion from the Southern part of the Peninsula by invading the port of Inchon. However, MacArthur's ideas of letting Chiang Kai-Shek send troops from Taiwan to Korea (especially after the Chinese Communists entered the war) would have spread the war, exactly what Stalin wanted.[24] Truman fired MacArthur, and he addressed a joint session of Congress in which his famous "old soldiers never die—they just fade away" speech. The Constitutional question of ignoring policies that are made by the President was the real reason MacArthur was relieved of command.

The Founding Fathers understood history, they knew societies especially those that have recently had victory in a tough war, will shower the generals with glory. This glory will be reflected as infallibility, and sometimes as with the French Revolution, a general may be tempted to take control of the government. This is why they made the President the Commander-in-Chief of the armed forces.

As Commander-in-Chief of the military, it is the President who once given the permission to attack by the Congress must implement the military strategy for victory. Today, we see the issues concerning the War on Terror in both Afghanistan and Iraq as the President's responsibility. Has Congress shirked its responsibility by not declaring war against the states that sponsor terrorism? Probably, but the President did not ask for a declaration of war. The role of the President as Commander-in-Chief ultimately makes the environment facing the military on the ground his responsibility. President Bush has picked his counter-terrorism strategy as pre-emptive war. In the beginning the majority of American people agreed with this strategy. Now, he faces increasing opposition to the plans he has implemented. People are not opposed to Congressional action which enabled President Bush to go into Iraq, instead they hold the President accountable.[25] Whether it is fair or not, only history can judge. It is the way our system is designed—the President is the Commander-in-Chief. He is the ultimate authority in all military matters. Linked to the President's role as Commander-in-Chief is the President's duties as the Chief Diplomat of the United States.

CHIEF DIPLOMAT

The foreign policy of the United States is almost exclusively the President's realm. Whether in times of peace or war, the President is the chief architect of foreign policy which makes the President the nation's Chief Diplomat. The President has the State Department and National Security Council to run the day to day administration of foreign policy. However, there are some decisions that only the President has authority to handle. Decisions such as recognizing other sovereign states is a Presidential decision,

---

[20]Truman did not have to respond the way he did. When the Soviet Union invaded Afghanistan President Carter did not respond at all in a conventional military way, he boycotted the Olympics in Moscow in 1980 and tried economic sanctions and some small covert actions.

[21]David McCullough, *Truman*. New York: Simon & Schuster, 1992, pp. 838–839.

[22]Ibid.

[23]Ibid.

[24]Patrick C. Coaty, *Understanding the War on Terror*. Dubuque, IA: Kendall/Hunt Publishing Co., 2006, p. 48.

[25]Patrick C. Coaty, *Understanding the War on Terror*. Dubuque, IA: Kendall/Hunt Publishing Co., 2006, p. 212.

and the negotiation of treaties are also a President's prerogative. The nation and other branches of the government turn to the President when there is a crisis and his role of Commander-in-Chief and Chief Diplomat combine in order for there to be an American solution to a crisis.

We see this throughout history. Presidents are judged by how they handle crises. Many historians look at the successful crises such as Kennedy's Cuban Missile Crisis, or George H. Bush's reaction to the invasion of Kuwait by Saddam Hussein. However, it can also be noteworthy to analyze how a President grows in the office when he is tested early in his Presidency. The Bay of Pigs showed President Kennedy had to become the Chief Diplomat very fast. In Chris Matthews book he describes a scene between Nixon and Kennedy: Nixon suggested that he would invade Cuba, Kennedy reminded Nixon if he went in that would open the door to West Berlin for the Soviet Union.[26] Kennedy goes on to explain (in the locker room fashion) to Nixon, that "It is really true that foreign affairs is the only important issue for a president. Who gives a shit if the minimum wage is $1.15 or $1.25 in comparison to something like this."[27] In June of that year, the Soviet Union had established the German Democratic Republic and signed a treaty willing to defend its sovereignty. In August, the Soviets would build the Berlin Wall. Kennedy as the Chief Diplomat said, "It's not a very nice solution, but a wall is a hell of a lot better than a war."[28] The Bay of Pigs made Kennedy lean more on diplomacy than on military in this crisis. Later in his Presidency, however, during the Cuban Missile Crisis he would also use diplomacy and the military with his quarantine strategy.

Putting both military and diplomatic power in the office of the Presidency gives the occupant of the office a tool box that can be used in crises; however, there are some Presidents who have hesitated in using the military or engaging in diplomacy. When someone is in the Presidency who leans on one tool more than the other it tends to weaken their ability in both. The last function the President must master is the role as Chief Legislator. It is the President who signs the bills that makes them law. It is he who holds the responsibility for being the check against the power of Congress.

CHIEF LEGISLATOR

Franklin D. Roosevelt and Lyndon B. Johnson were the two most prolific Presidents when it came to signing legislation. Roosevelt passed bills to help the country out of the Great Depression and Johnson signed bills in order to shape the country under his vision for a Great Society. The President's first act when he is playing Chief Legislator is the State of the Union Address.

The State of the Union Address is the only time when all three branches of government are in the Capitol.[29] In the speech, the President usually gives Congress a "laundry list" of objectives and proposals he would like to see passed during the legislative year. Of course, getting the legislation passed may be a totally different matter. As we stated earlier, depending on the President's skills with members of Congress, a President can use favors or punishments. Lyndon Johnson was the most powerful Senate Majority Leader the country had ever seen. Now as President, he would try to direct strategies for the passage of his program. Most Presidents do not know the intimate institutional details like Johnson did. This was one reason Johnson holds the record for the most laws passed by any President.

Today, President Bush has yet to wield his veto for the first six years of his Administration. This may be because the President has enjoyed a Republican Congress up to his first term and half of the second term. Or it could be the President believes in big government programs. President Bush and the Republican Congress tend to be working together, much like President Johnson and his Democratic Congress did in the middle of the 1960s. The use of the veto is very powerful. President Gerald Ford's short Administration showed how a President who wants to curb governmental programs and spending can use the veto effectively even if the Congress is held by the other party. Ford was criticized a great deal for the use of the veto, however, as we discussed earlier, it is very difficult to get a bill passed the first time. It is almost impossible to have the Congress override the veto if the President has any power in his role as Chief Legislator.

These different roles we have described—Chief of State, Chief Executive, Commander-in-Chief, Chief Diplomat, Chief Legislator are all mixed. The best Presidents we have had used the different tools

---

[26]Christopher Matthews, *The Rivalry That Shaped Postwar America: Kennedy & Nixon.* New York: Simon & Schuster, 1996, p. 199.

[27]Ibid.

[28]Ibid. p. 203.

---

[29]Usually, one cabinet member is not in the building for security and continuity of government issues.

for different issues and crises. In the next section of the chapter, we will examine how these roles are played in three different areas, borrowed by Hedrick Smith's *The Power Game*.[30] In this book, Smith writes, the President, in order to be effective in the long run, must master the agenda game, image game and coalition game. These three "games" are what the American people see when we see the President in action.

PRESIDENTIAL POWER IN ACTION

The President is the only person in government that is indirectly elected by everyone. It is the President's duty to look after the affairs of the American people as a whole. When he decides to propose legislation in the State of the Union Address or to stop legislation with his veto, he should be thinking about the effects of the legislation on the country as a whole. This is a unique position held by the President. Most Presidents have understood their unique position in the government. In this part of our analysis of Presidential power, we will look at three overarching tasks he must master: agenda setting, coalition forming and media manipulation. Most Presidents have been good at one or two of these tasks, while the great Presidents have been able to master all three.

Presidents have put forth issues that may not have been apparent to Americans when they first approach the issue. Harry Truman talked about civil rights, Jimmy Carter introduced us to the problems of reliance on foreign oil and Ronald Reagan tried to create a missile defense system that would change the power structure of the world. What a President decides to concentrate on will contribute to the determination of whether history will view their Presidencies as successes or failures. Even if a President has the insight to lead on certain problems that may seem off in the horizon, he has to make sure the people are willing to address the issue. Failures in setting the agenda for an Administration includes President Carter's agenda, where he cluttered the legislative agenda by sending up water reform, energy reform, pension reform and all sorts of other legislative initiatives. By not focusing and prioritizing both Congress and the country, Carter was bound to fail.[31] The Reagan Administration was determined to learn from Carter's mistakes.

"WE DREW THREE BROAD CONCLUSIONS," DAVID GERGEN SAID. "ONE: IN THE FIRST ONE HUNDRED DAYS, YOU HAVE A CHANCE TO DEFINE YOUR PERSONA AS PRESIDENT, TO FORM ANEW IN THE PUBLIC MIND WHO YOU ARE AND WHAT YOUR CHARACTER IS. TWO: THIS IS THE CRITICAL TIME FOR SETTING THE THEMES AND AGENDA FOR YOUR ENTIRE PRESIDENCY. REMEMBER, IKE WENT TO KOREA TO BEGIN TO MAKE PEACE DURING HIS TRANSITION. CARTER'S AGENDA WAS DIFFUSE. AND THREE: THE FIRST ONE HUNDRED DAYS WAS A TIME WHEN YOU WERE VULNERABLE TO A GRIEVOUS MISTAKE THAT WOULD HAUNT YOU, LIKE KENNEDY'S BAY OF PIGS. YOU HAVE TO AVOID GETTING INTO MISCHIEF."[32]

As Gergen points out, agenda setting may be one of the most important things a President is able to do. President George W. Bush in his first term (before the September 11th attacks) had an economic agenda that stressed tax cuts and a foreign policy that was a mix of free trade and backing away from the commitments made during the Clinton era. Of course the attacks of September 11th changed his agenda until his re-election. The start of President Bush's second term we see how important an agenda is, while the War on Terror is raging, he says the most important issue facing the country is Social Security reform. This highlighted what many of Bush's critics have said, that he was disengaged in the real issues that confronted people. Bush might be correct that Social Security has to be changed in order to accommodate the "baby boom," however, he ran his re-election campaign on the issue of who can fight the War on Terror more effectively, himself or Senator John Kerry.

Shortly after the election, Bush surprises everyone by saying he is going to use his political capital in reforming Social Security. This change in priority paralyzed both the Congress and his administration. President Bush's second term is unable to control the agenda on issues such as the War on Terror, Iraq, or even Social Security. Presidents who are elected to a second term tend to have problems maintaining the discipline that Gergen explains to Hedrick Smith. If we use as examples the last three Presidents that have been elected to second terms we see they have not kept out of mischief. President Nixon had Watergate, President Reagan had Iran-Contra, and President Clinton was impeached. In all of these cases, the Presidents had trouble with setting the agenda with the second term. President Bush has also had problems prioritizing and getting a new message

---

[30]Hedrick Smith, *The Power Game: How Washington Works*. New York: Ballantine Books, 1988, pp. 329–392.

[31]Hedrick Smith, *The Power Game: How Washington Works*. New York: Ballantine Books, 1988, p. 343.

[32]Ibid. p. 344.

to the public. Social Security reform may be an important issue, but when soldiers are dying in Iraq and the threat of terrorism, the idea that we should take for granted our retirement strikes many Americans as absurd. It was an agenda setting mistake that still haunts the second Bush administration.

Exercising Presidential power does not entail setting the agenda and then sitting back waiting for solutions to problems. The second part of our discussion includes the roles Presidents have in manipulating the media. In other words, getting their message to the American people. Just as setting the agenda controls what people are talking about, handling the media is a way to control how people think in terms of the issues facing the President.

Walter Cronkite, CBS news anchor during the 1960s and 1970s, made a commentary that said "To say we are closer to victory is to believe in the face of the evidence, the optimists who have been wrong in the past. To suggest we are on the edge of defeat is to yield to unreasonable pessimism. To say that we are mired in stalemate seems the only realistic, yet unsatisfactory conclusion." After hearing this, President Johnson was quoted as saying "if I've lost Cronkite, I've lost Middle America."[33] Was Vietnam won or lost on the television screens of America? That is a question that historians will have to deal with and not one that we are equipped to answer here. However, Presidential influence on the media can create an environment for success or failure.

President Carter had the bad luck of coming into office after Watergate. The media was hyper-sensitive to be seen as being controlled or influenced by the President. Vietnam and Watergate showed to the members of the press that they had an important function in acting as a watchdog on the President. Some of these people talked in terms of themselves being a "fourth estate" or fourth branch of government. The media during President Carter's administration was not in the mood for being agreeable. Carter, as we have discussed earlier, was not one to try to influence the media with small personal favors. Instead, he tried to debate the media. Television is not a place where a President can debate issues on the merits. As we saw with the 1960 election, complicated issues such as the energy crisis or the hostage crisis were not sensitive to happy pictures. Carter continually looked as if the job of President was bigger than he could handle. Carter became a subject of

open ridicule, just as Nixon and Johnson before him by the press. In one of the final episodes of President Carter's administration, there were media reports President Carter was attacked by a rabbit and he saved himself by hitting the animal with a wooden oar. This, of course, cost Carter most of the credibility he had. If a man could not defend himself against a rabbit, how could he deal with the Soviet Union or the Iranians.[34]

President Reagan was a much better salesman than President Carter. The Reagan media team knew that in our time pictures are more important than text. We are a generation that reacts to graphics. A television announcer can talk about how two leaders are not getting along, but there are pictures of both of them happy, shaking hands and toasting each other we tend to believe the pictures. Reagan was the oldest President we have ever had, however, because he was in such good physical shape, all the media people had to do was to show Reagan chopping wood or riding his horse and all of the voices calling Reagan old would go away. The proof was in the pictures. The Carter Administration did not understand this, President Carter is a man who is also trying to improve himself, this is admirable. However, when President Carter took up long distance running, the wire photographs of a President running a half marathon was something that did not project power and comfort with the job.

The image game with the heavy emphasis started with John F. Kennedy. However, all Presidents have tried to influence their coverage by the press. The President has to use both favors and punishments when dealing with the press. The media needs access to Administration officials as much as the President needs to have good press. Therefore, if there is something such as the Iran-Contra scandal or other types of bad news, the President's media advisors have several strategies that they can resort to. The first is limiting access of administration officials. Suddenly, no one shows up to be guests on the Sunday talk shows. Or, right before deadline, the administration can put "spin" on the story in order to try to put the best light possible on the piece of bad news. Or finally, the President's media people will try to run the story outside of the Administration. When a story comes from the White House it has a certain credibility. As in the Iran-Contra scandal, the White House media experts did not comment on the daily story, instead

[33]Robert Dallek, *Flawed Giant: Lyndon Johnson and His Times 1961–1973*. New York: Oxford University Press, 1998, p. 506.

[34]Hedrick Smith, *The Power Game: How Washington Works*. New York: Ballantine Books, 1988, p. 424.

they referred to the special counsel's office who was investigating the scandal.

These tools are not evil or bad, manipulating the media is something that is done by everyone who deals with public policy. Having a positive image of the President is one way to make the President's job easier to handle. If the media people for the President are effective, they tell the truth, however, they try to accentuate the positive aspects of that truth. This is a very important part of Presidential leadership. President Carter and Johnson started their administrations with high ratings in public approval. Carter was perceived as a good man who had come in to reform Washington, President Johnson had tried to heal the wounds of a Presidential assassination. Both would find they failed even though they tried to have the media understand their role as President.

President Reagan succeeded in understanding the perception of success builds and increases a power. Most people think President Reagan is responsible for the end of the Cold War, while in fact President George H. Bush was in power and is largely responsible for the peaceful re-uniting of Germany. In politics perception is reality if not checked by facts and analysis. Image is important, that is why we see movie stars being considered for public office. President Reagan showed how successful actors can be in public life. But, there comes a time when image alone will not enable you to govern. The third function a President must master is building a coalition that can pass the legislation needed for success.

The Democratic party that controlled Congress and the Presidency from 1933 to 1968, included civil rights workers and white southerners who opposed any civil rights legislation. This coalition known as the Roosevelt coalition put together these opposing groups in order to run the government and the country. Reagan's coalition was made up of Southern Democrats or otherwise known as Reagan Democrats, Conservatives, small and large business people, and people who attend church. Both Roosevelt and Reagan were able to create alliances where there had not been agreement before. Reagan was able to convince both union members (not union leadership) and management that he was trying to help everyone with his tax cuts. He invoked the image of John F. Kennedy (who had previously passed a tax cut) in order to have his 1981 budget and tax cuts passed.

Today, the issue of illegal immigration has the potential of tearing the Republican party apart. If a Democratic candidate would take a tough stand on the employers who break the law they may be able to break the alliance between the business men who hire illegal immigrants and the conservatives who believe the country is being "invaded" by undocumented workers. A Democratic President who would promise the "perp walk" for employers would get support from the anti-business progressives of the Democratic party and conservatives who want tough legislative acts to stop illegal immigration. Coalition people bringing people who appear to have nothing in common is the way Presidents use their power.

President Clinton also produced an alliance between Republican conservatives and moderates in the Democratic party to produce welfare reform. Even though President Clinton complained privately about "triangulation" he used it to co-op the Republican dominated Congress in 1994 to ensure his victory in 1996. Effective Presidents look for a way to be the main salesmen for their programs. Presidents such as Roosevelt, Johnson, Reagan and Clinton have made coalitions that produced legislation that revolutionized the political environment when they were in office. Ineffective Presidents such as Jimmy Carter and George H. Bush (when it came to domestic policy) could not produce the lasting coalition that could be translated into political power.[35] In all of the aspects of Presidential power setting agendas, managing the media and creating coalitions takes a mixture of tools available to the President. Very few have been great at all three, some have been good at one or two, Lyndon Johnson holds the record of legislative accomplishment but ultimately failed because he lied to the press. Jimmy Carter's failure at the agenda game plagued his administration throughout his tenure as President, and George H. Bush probably lost re-election when he failed to manage the conservatives in the Republican when he said no new taxes and then went on to raise taxes. A President has to be able to mix all types of contradictory political aims in order to convince different people with different objectives to vote and follow his program.

CONCLUSION

Harry Truman once described the job of the President is to get people to do what is right. He went on to explain the President is the only person in government who is responsible to everyone. Senators and Congressmen have their constituents, the media and

---

[35]Ibid. p. 425.

interest groups have their members and shareholders that they are responsible to. It is the President's job to have a vision for the country as a whole. In this chapter, we have examined the constitutional requirements for a person to be elected President. We then explored the different roles the President must perform. They include Chief of State, Chief Executive, Commander-in-Chief, Chief Diplomat, and Chief Legislator. At the same time the President must master three aspects of power, the setting of the agenda for the country, managing the media, and building a coalition in order to garner support for his program. We have demonstrated how the President must persuade both people in government and outside government. If he is effective in applying his message through the media, and if he can persuade people, his agenda reflects the pressing business of the nation and he looks as if he is in control by using the symbols of his office in the media, then he may be on his way to becoming a successful President. The idea that a President can command people is not accurate in today's government. The President has to be the ultimate salesman to be successful in the Presidency today.

TERMS TO REMEMBER

COMMANDER-IN-CHIEF

COUP DE ETAT

CHIEF OF STATE

CHIEF EXECUTIVE

The Presidency

TRUE OR FALSE QUESTIONS

1. The President serves one six-year term.   T / F

2. The President can serve as many terms as he can.   T / F

3. The President has to be a white male.   T / F

4. The President has to be married.   T / F

5. The President has to be at least 35 years old.   T / F

6. The President has to be a resident of the country for 14 years.   T / F

7. The President and Vice President must come from different states.   T / F

8. The President is Chief of State just like the British Prime Minister.   T / F

9. President Kennedy was the youngest man ever to serve as President.   T / F

10. The President has the power to appoint all of the workers in the Federal government.   T / F

MULTIPLE CHOICE QUESTIONS

11. Which President served in Congress before he was elected?
    a. Dwight Eisenhower
    b. Woodrow Wilson
    c. Lyndon Johnson
    d. Ronald Reagan

12. Which President was a Governor before he was elected?
    a. George W. Bush
    b. George H.W. Bush
    c. Jeb Bush
    d. John F. Kennedy

13. Which is a function of the President?
    a. Commander in Chief
    b. Chief of Protocol
    c. Chief Spender
    d. Indian Chief

14. Which is not a function of the President?
    a. Chief of State
    b. Chief Executive
    c. Politico
    d. Head of a Church

15. The President's use of Air Force One is a function of the
    a. Chief Executive
    b. Foreign Policy Chief
    c. Party Chief
    d. Chief of State

16. The President has the power to
    a. declare war
    b. tax people
    c. coin money
    d. give pardons

17. Which is not part of the President's power game?
    a. Agenda game
    b. Coalition game
    c. Image game
    d. Party game

18. Civilian control of the military is an example of the President's role as
    a. Chief of State
    b. Chief Diplomat
    c. Commander in Chief
    d. Chief Executive

19. Presidents U.S. Grant and Dwight Eisenhower both graduated from West Point. What President graduated from the Naval Academy?
    a. Franklin D. Roosevelt
    b. John F. Kennedy
    c. Gerald Ford
    d. Jimmy Carter

20. Which President has won the Nobel Peace Prize while in office?
    a. Richard Nixon
    b. John F. Kennedy
    c. Theodore Roosevelt
    d. Jimmy Carter

21. How many terms did Franklin Roosevelt serve?
    a. 1
    b. 2
    c. 3
    d. 4

chapter eleven

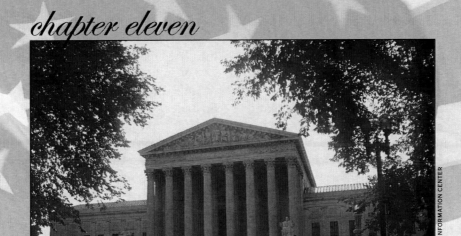

THE JUDICIARY

INTRODUCTION

We have examined the formation of the Constitution, the behavior of people, leaders and institutions that set the rules and environment for your daily life. In previous chapters, we have discussed the importance of popular sovereignty and tolerance. Now our discussion will turn more specifically to the concept of rule of law. In this chapter, we will examine the workings of the Supreme Court and the development of the legal system in the United States. The Third Article of the Constitution stipulates that there will be a Supreme Court and the Congress will have the power to establish inferior courts in order to have an efficient and effective judicial system. Has Congress succeeded in having a court system that reflects our need for litigation?

In America, law has substituted the unifying effects of a shared language, religion, ethnic or racial background. Our belief in the rule of law is supposed to make the United States a Nation as well as a State. We said earlier when we examined the Con-

stitution, the Founding Fathers were trying an experiment that was truly revolutionary. In this chapter we will analyze the Supreme Court and briefly introduce the elements of the American legal system. The legal system does have flaws, and one of the major flaws of the system is the increasing use of criminal law to control people's habits. One brief example of the changing of legal norms in our society from that of our ancestors in the late 1800s is the change in how the legal system views drugs and sex. Roughly one hundred years ago, sex outside of marriage was criminalized in many states and opium was legally produced and consumed. Today, our legal system has the opposite norm. Today opium and its byproducts are outlawed and sex with a person over the age of consent is considered legal.[1] This is not to suggest people were more tolerant of drugs, they were not, but they did not look to the law as a device to

---

[1]Lawrence M. Friedman, *Law in America: A Short History.* New York: Modern Library Paperback Edition, 2004, p. 102.

stop drug addiction, they looked to other institutions such as the family, community and religion to solve the problem of drug addiction. Today our political leaders and the voters believe if they pass laws the problem will be solved. Some of the laws we have today simply do not make any sense—the drinking age, outlawing of cell phones while driving, smoking laws and speed limits are a few examples of laws that simply have not changed people's behaviors. How can we have a nation built on rule of law if the whole society continually breaks laws it does not agree with?

We have so many laws that the police and the courts have to sort out and prioritize the laws that are being enforced. Do you drive the speed limit when every one else is speeding or do you go with the flow of traffic? Do young people drink wine when they are under 21 even though it is with their family and they are home? Do you use your cell phone when driving to contact someone in an emergency? Technically, in California all of these things are illegal. Yet, we can set out good reasons why we are individually breaking the law. However, it is very bad if collectively we all decide to ignore the law. Police find themselves being selective when it comes to stopping cars—who is safe, what do the people inside the car look like (yes, racial profiling is illegal) but young men, especially if there are more than three, statistically are involved in more crime than three old ladies in a car. In this chapter, we will dissect the legal system and we will show the relationship between the Supreme Court and the other political institutions in the country. To start this discussion, we will connect this chapter with the previous chapter by talking about how Presidents appoint Justices to the Supreme Court. Then we will discuss the development of the legal system throughout American history, and then finally, we will describe the general ways the Supreme Court carries out its business. The law fascinates some, bores others, yet it touches all of our lives. Laws can ruin a young person's potential, and it can also insure a young person to get the opportunity they have earned. The objective of this chapter is to show the political discussion we have had does not happen in a vacuum. The leaders who get elected are sent to Washington, D.C. and they pass laws. These laws are then enforced and interpreted in ways that may not have been intended by the original writers of the legislation. In turn, these laws may change the lives of all Americans who normally would not have broken the laws but the laws were so unreasonable that it forces a generation to get used

to violating the law. Prohibition, although not mis-interpreted, made honest law-abiding Americans into law breakers for simply having a drink.

We all seem to recognize that prohibition was a terrible mistake yet, we keep on making the same mistakes. Once you make something illegal, you make it profitable. Whether it is greenhouse gases, marijuana or cell phones, by prohibiting their use you have essentially made a black market for the product, and in doing so made the production or in the case of greenhouse emissions, the disposal of the product, a business.

If you make cheeseburgers illegal all of a sudden they will be ten dollars apiece instead of a dollar apiece. We know this is true, however, we simply cannot help ourselves. Our politicians have to run for re-election by saying they have passed laws and if the law bans behaviors that we find distasteful any-way, we ignore the effect it will have on our liberty. The dynamic between liberty and tolerance is under threat since people and special interest groups are trying to ban all types of behavior, not because it hurts someone, but because we may hurt ourselves in the future with the "bad" behavior. We start with the political aspects of this discussion and move to the legal. How do we get Supreme Court Justices and what are their general qualifications? This question will be answered in the next section of the chapter.

PRESIDENTIAL APPOINTMENTS TO THE JUDICIARY

The most important appointment a President can make is an appointment to the Supreme Court. If a President nominates a person in their forties or early fifties, that person can remain on the Court for over thirty years (assuming the person serves until they are eighty). The ironic thing about giving someone lifetime tenure on the highest court in the land is, once the choice is made and the nominee is con-firmed by the Senate, there are no longer any checks to the person's behavior. Therefore, the President that may have appointed them may be long gone and the political culture may have turned upside down by the time they are retired. This is true of Justice Stevens, he was appointed by President Ford. At the time of his appointment it was believed that he would be a conservative Justice, however, today he is considered one of the more liberal Justices on the Court.

Why do some Justices change? Do they deliber-ately mislead the Presidents and Senators who appointed them to the Supreme Court? No, they do not. Presidents cannot anticipate the nature of the cases the Justices will hear in twenty or thirty years. People change, situations change, and even though a President may know how a Justice will act on a number of issues, the law is changing and it is impossible to know in actuality how a Justice will vote on any given case. As the late Chief Justice Rehnquist has written:

THUS HISTORY TEACHES US, I THINK, THAT EVEN A "STRONG" PRESIDENT DETERMINED TO LEAVE HIS MARK ON THE COURT—SUCH AS LINCOLN OR FRANKLIN ROOSEVELT—IS APT TO BE ONLY PARTIALLY SUCCESSFUL. NEITHER THE PRESIDENT NOR HIS APPOINTEES CAN FORESEE WHAT ISSUES WILL COME BEFORE THE COURT DURING THE TENURE OF THE APPOINTEES, AND IT MAY BE THAT NONE HAS THOUGHT VERY MUCH ABOUT THESE ISSUES. EVEN THOUGH THEY AGREE ON THE PROPER RESOLUTION OF CURRENT CASES, THEY MAY WELL DISAGREE ON FUTURE CASES INVOLVING OTHER QUESTIONS WHEN, AS JUDGES THEY STUDY BRIEFS AND HEAR ARGUMENTS. LONGEVITY OF THE APPOINTEES, OR UNTIMELY DEATHS SUCH AS THOSE OF MURPHY OR RUTLEDGE, MAY ALSO FRUSTRATE A PRESIDENT'S EXPECTATIONS; SO ALSO MAY THE PERSONAL ANTAGONISMS DEVELOPED BETWEEN STRONG-WILL APPOINTEES OF THE SAME PRESIDENT.[2]

As with people who try to influence the behavior of their heirs once they have died by writing conditions in their wills, Presidents cannot interfere with the behavior of Justices once the President has selected a person to serve on the Supreme Court. However, as Rehnquist writes, depending on the personalities of the people on the Court, the cases and arguments that are developed during the person's tenure and basically the Justice's conscience are the elements that make up a judicial career.

Justices are human and so are Presidents. In modern times there seems to be two types of appointments Presidents try to make. One is the rewarding of a long term friend or loyal supporter to be on the Supreme Court, the other is, making a historic choice such as the first person of a racial, ethnic or religious group ever to serve on the land's highest court. President Roosevelt is famous for his plan to pack the Court that was defeated by the Senate after his landslide victory in 1936. He would later appoint eight Justices during his twelve years in the Presidency. President Lyndon Johnson's manipulation of people to get his friend on the Court is one of the most interesting from a human relations point of view.

Justice Arthur Goldberg had been appointed to the Supreme Court by President Kennedy. Lyndon Johnson wanted to appoint his friend Abe Fortas to the Supreme Court. However, there were no openings. Johnson tried to convince Goldberg to become his Secretary of Heath, Education and Welfare. Goldberg had said he was happy on the Court.[3] Adlai Stevenson, the United Nations Ambassador died in July of that year. Here was Johnson's chance. He went to Goldberg and offered him the United Nations Ambassadorship.

A Justice of the Supreme Court has much more independence and prestige than a United Nations Ambassador. How did Johnson convince Goldberg to resign in order to appoint his friend Abe Fortas? Johnson had a three pronged strategy to get Goldberg to resign the Supreme Court for the U.N. Ambassadorship. First, he would hint that as an Ambassador to the U.N. he would be in contention to become Vice President.[4] Henry Cabot-Lodge was President Eisenhower's U.N. Ambassador when Richard Nixon had picked him as his running mate in 1960. The second prong of the argument was a promise, as U.N. Ambassador, Goldberg would have influence on foreign policy especially in trying to solve the Vietnam War. And the third prong of the strategy was to promise Goldberg the opportunity to help underdeveloped nations and the poor.

Goldberg resigns from the Supreme Court and Johnson was able to appoint his friend Abe Fortas to Associate Justice of the Supreme Court. Arthur Goldberg did not have the influence he sought and of course was not selected to serve as Johnson's Vice President in 1964. The lesson is if you are ever on the Supreme Court, do not resign. Johnson loved being seen as a great persuader.[5] He had succeeded in creating a Supreme Court vacancy that was not there and he had succeeded in appointing his life-long friend to the Court.

AS JOHNSON AND FORTAS RECOUNTED THE STORY, THE PRESIDENT WOULDN'T TAKE "NO" FOR AN ANSWER. ON JULY 28, JOHNSON ASKED FORTAS TO COME TO THE WHITE HOUSE, WHERE HE TOLD HIM HE WAS ABOUT TO ANNOUNCE THE SENDING OF 50,000 TROOPS TO VIETNAM AND

[2]William H. Rehnquist, *The Supreme Court*. New York: Random House, 2001, pp. 220–221.

[3]Robert Dallek, *Flawed Giant: Lyndon Johnson and His Times 1961–1973*. New York: Oxford University Press, 1998, p. 234.

[4]Ibid.

[5]Ibid.

HIS APPOINTMENT TO THE COURT. FORTAS NEEDED TO FOLLOW THE LEAD OF THESE MEN BY MAKING A SACRIFICE FOR HIS COUNTRY. JOHNSON REMEMBERED THAT FORTAS NOW GAVE IN AND ACCOMPANIED THE PRESIDENT TO A PRESS CONFERENCE. "THAT WAS THE ONLY WAY I MANAGED TO GET HIM ON THE COURT," JOHNSON SAID. FORTAS COMPLAINED THAT JOHNSON INFORMED HIM OF HIS INTENTION ONLY ON THE WAY TO THE PRESS CONFERENCE AND NEVER EVEN GAVE HIM THE CHANCE TO RESPOND.[6]

Is this a believable story? Maybe, what we know is Lyndon Johnson was able to convince an Associate Justice to leave the Supreme Court. Did Johnson lie to both Fortas and Goldberg? Yes, of course. However, the point is Johnson succeeded in making history where other Presidents had failed. Roosevelt, Lincoln and other great Presidents were unable to create vacancies on the Supreme Court Johnson did. Johnson did appoint old friends to the Court; he also made historic appointments to the Supreme Court.

Again, it was a manipulation that enabled Johnson to appoint Thurgood Marshall, the first African-American on the Supreme Court. Tom Clark was an Associate Justice of the Supreme Court. Johnson wanted to make his son Ramsey Clark Attorney General of the United States. However, Johnson said there would be a conflict of interest if Justice Clark remained on the Court. So Justice Clark resigned his position on the Supreme Court in order for his son Ramsey Clark to become Attorney General. Before this, Johnson had to convince Thurgood Marshall to resign as a Federal District Court Judge in order to become U.S. Solicitor General. Again, the power of persuasion Presidents must have. Can you imagine giving up a life-time appointment and the independence of being a Federal Judge (not including a cut in salary) to become the top lawyer in the government? Johnson had been specific every meeting he had with Marshall that there was not going to be any *quid pro quo*. Marshall should not count on an appointment to the Supreme Court just because he had agreed to become Solicitor General. Johnson did appoint Marshall but it took over twenty-three months in order for him to engineer another appointment.[7]

Johnson's performance was historic and he would later get into trouble by trying to appoint Fortas to the Chief Justice position near the end of his Presidency. However, the Marshall appointment did add to the legacy of President Johnson as a champion of civil rights. These two examples also show how personalities affect history. If Arthur Goldberg had not been ambitious and sensitive to issues of foreign policy, Fortas would not have been able to be on the Supreme Court. And if Tom Clark had not been ambitious for his son Ramsey, Thurgood Marshall may not have been appointed either. Johnson had the ability to create these vacancies which was a very rare talent indeed. Yet, even with the talent to manipulate vacancies, once a person is appointed, the President who appoints them becomes a historical footnote.

Supreme Court Justices and Federal Judges try to decide decisions on a methodology called legal reasoning. No matter if a Judge or Justice is considered liberal or conservative, if they are professional, they will try to couch their decisions on the foundations of accepted legal principles. Although new reasoning is introduced from time to time, when interpreting the Constitution and the legal system, Judges and Justices are supposed to be looking backward at the previous decisions of their predecessors. In the next part of the chapter we will explain two types of law in the American legal system. The first is partially borrowed from the English, called Common Law, and the second is produced by cooperation of the Executive and Legislative branches of the government, called statutory law. We will see how these two categories of laws coincide in our system and influence our lives.

THE ENGLISH COMMON LAW AND STATUTORY LAW

The British have had a tradition of courts. The examples of these courts were used in their colonies. Australia, Canada, the United States (in colonial times) all had courts that used the English Common Law. There were differences between the Courts in England and the Courts that were established in the United States. In England, less than two percent of the people owned almost all the land in the country.[8] In the United States there were no great landlords. The Courts were designed to establish and settle disputes concerned over land.

The Common Law is sometimes called Judge made law. The law is determined by the principle of *stare decisis* meaning "the previous decision stands." In Common Law, Judges hear cases and they base their decisions are determined on the previous deci-

---

[6]Ibid. p. 235.
[7]Ibid. p. 440.

[8]Lawrence M. Freidman, *Law in America: A Short History*. New York: The Modern Library, 2004, p. 30.

sions that judges ruled on similar cases. Each case has a set of facts, an issue, rule of law that applies to the issue and a conclusion. During colonial times many of the cases that came to judges dealt with property and the question of who owns the property. Blackstone's *Commentaries on the Laws of England*, became a best seller in the United States because it gave a basic structure of how cases should be settled in the tradition of English Common Law.[9] Remember there were not many formal law schools in the United States. Even up to the middle of the 1800s many lawyers did not go to law school. We can see examples of the common law when we see television programs such as *Judge Judy* or *The People's Court*. If you watch these shows you will see there is a defendant and a plaintiff. There is a fact situation that usually deals with an ex-roommate, ex-boyfriend or girlfriend or people lending money to one another. Then the Judge will hear each side and the Judge will render a decision based usually on *stare decisis*. Two hundred years ago, in a little more serious fashion, this is how the common law was carried out between people who lived in jurisdictions that recognized the English Common Law.

Stare decisis in underdeveloped areas such as colonies for an empire performs useful functions. It is efficient, all of the judges are using the same methodology in reviewing cases. Lawyers are trained to present cases in a certain way, and they can guess in most cases how the Judge will determine a case. This enables lawyers to advise clients if their case is weak to abandon their case, or if it is strong to bring it to court. Therefore, lawyers can act as gatekeepers for the courts. So only the stronger cases may be heard when a judge goes from town to town on the circuit. *Stare decisis* is also uniform. If all of the judges are using the same case books, and assuming they are being rational and reasonable, the decisions are going to be roughly the same. This gives courts on average, a generally uniform scope of decisions depending on the type of cases the judges are hearing. The efficiency and uniformity of the Common Law insured the laws were stable and predictable. Remember in the wilderness of Colonial America, to have a stable and predictable legal system was very useful, since people would be able to understand the ramifications of their actions, they could carve out agreements that were enforceable by the courts.

The second type of law we have in the United States is statutory law. These laws are the laws the Congress and the state legislatures pass. The first part of statutory law of course, is a constitution. A constitution gives the general organization of the government be it on the national, state, or local level. It set outs the general powers of the different bodies under the government, and in the case of the U.S. Constitution, has limits on the central government. Constitutions also describe the procedure used to pass laws, in the U.S. Constitution it is Article I Section 7. This procedure is still used today when Congress and the President pass a law.

These are the two different types of law we see in the United States. Statutory and Common Law are used in our system. Judges know both of these systems and even the Supreme Court follows *stare decisis*. The Supreme Court follows the previous decisions of earlier Supreme Courts. In the next section of our discussion, we will talk about the most important case that allowed the Supreme Court to be the interpreters of the Constitution. It has been said the decision of *Marbury v. Madison* has been the linchpin of Constitutional Law in the United States since 1803.[10]

"MARBURY V. MADISON" AND THE CONCEPT OF JUDICIAL REVIEW

The power of the Supreme Court to interpret the Constitution comes from the opinion cited in *Marbury vs. Madison*.[11] The facts revolve around the loss of the Presidency by the Federalists and the election of Thomas Jefferson. During the period between the election of the new President and the swearing in of the new President (usually called lame duck period) Adams had appointed new Judges. Marbury was one of the judges that had been appointed in a round of appointments called the midnight hour appointments. Madison was the Secretary of State under Thomas Jefferson, the new Republican Administration. In order for a new appointment to become official, the certificate of the appointment had to have the Great Seal of the United States affixed to the certificate, this was done by the Secretary of State.

Unluckily for Marbury, his certificate was not completed until the swearing in of the new President. Marbury sued to have the seal affixed and to take his office as a district judge. The Supreme Court according to the late Chief Justice Rehnquist had four legal issues to adjudicate.

[9]Ibid. p. 31.

[10]William H. Rehnquist, *The Supreme Court*. New York: Vintage Books, 2001, p. 35.

[11]Ibid.

DOES MARBURY HAVE A LEGAL RIGHT TO THE POSITION OF JUSTICE OF THE PEACE FOR THE DISTRICT OF COLUMBIA, AND THENCE TO THE COMMISSION WHICH BESTOWS OR ESTABLISHES THAT RIGHT? (2) IF HE HAS SUCH A RIGHT, DOES THE LAW GIVE HIM A REMEDY? (3) IS A WRIT OF MANDAMUS A PROPER REMEDY IN THIS CASE? (4) MAY SUCH A WRIT OF MANDAMUS ISSUE FROM THE SUPREME COURT IN THIS CASE?[12]

Chief Justice Marshall does answer these four legal questions. However, the important part of this decision for our purposes is the fact that Marshall in his opinion declared the part of the Judiciary Act of 1789 unconstitutional. It was this law that Marbury relied on to file his case with the Supreme Court as an original jurisdiction forum. The Supreme Court in this case argued the Constitution states the Supreme Court will be an appellate court. Again Chief Justice Rehnquist describes the difference between courts of original jurisdiction and appellate jurisdiction. "Original jurisdiction means the power to hear and decide a lawsuit in the first instance, while appellate jurisdiction means the authority to review the judgment of another court."[13] The Supreme Court said because they are an appellate court and not a court of original jurisdiction the Judiciary Act of 1789 was unconstitutional. In the future it would be the Supreme Court that would have Judicial Review over the Constitution. According to Marshall the Congress cannot give different jurisdictions to the Supreme Court. Marshall writes:

THE GOVERNMENT OF THE UNITED STATES IS OF THE LATTER DESCRIPTION. THE POWERS OF THE LEGISLATURE ARE DEFINED AND LIMITED; AND THAT THOSE LIMITS MAY NOT BE MISTAKEN, OR FORGOTTEN, THE CONSTITUTION IS WRITTEN. TO WHAT PURPOSE ARE POWERS LIMITED, AND TO WHAT PURPOSE IS THAT LIMITATION COMMITTED TO WRITING, IF THESE LIMITS MAY, AT ANY TIME, BE PASSED BY THOSE INTENDED TO BE RESTRAINED? THE DISTINCTION BETWEEN A GOVERNMENT WITH LIMITED AND UNLIMITED POWERS IS ABOLISHED, IF THOSE LIMITS DO NOT CONFINE THE PERSONS ON WHOM THEY ARE IMPOSED, AND IF ACTS PROHIBITED AND ACTS ALLOWED ARE OF EQUAL OBLIGATION.[14]

In other words, regardless of what happens to poor Marbury, the Supreme Court would be the branch of the Federal government that would put constitutional limits on the other two branches of government. Chief Justice Marshall was signaling to the country that it would be the Supreme Court who would act as the referee between the Executive and Legislative branches of government in the future. The Supreme Court would interpret the Constitution in cases that would be on appellate jurisdiction for the most part. The Supreme Court would articulate the Constitutional limits on the other branches of government and on society as a whole.

This idea of Judicial Review has kept the Constitution a relevant document. It has also prevented the Congress or President to manipulate constitutional principles in order for political ends. The question arises however, if the Founding Fathers anticipated this arrangement. According to the *Federalist Papers*, Alexander Hamilton and James Madison felt the Judiciary branch would be the weakest of the three branches.[15] Chief Justice Marshall and the *Marbury v. Madison* decision would change this landscape and make the Supreme Court as important as the other branches. Some suggest the Supreme Court is more powerful than the other branches since its members serve for life and they are not elected. Be it as it may, the power of the Supreme Court lays in the fact the American people believe the government should be governed by the limits imposed on it by the Constitution and the people who interprets these limits are the Supreme Court.

What are the procedures the Supreme Court uses to hear a case? *Marbury v. Madison* may be one of the most famous cases, but the Supreme Court hears hundreds of cases every term. How do they decide which cases to hear? We turn our discussion to a description of the procedures used by the Supreme Court. The biggest challenge of examining the action of the Supreme Court is that the conferences and other aspects of the Supreme Court are secret. There are no elections and no requirements to have the actions of the Supreme Court opened up to the public. Therefore, we can only use the published writings of "insiders" of the court who give us a small porthole into the workings of the Judiciary branch of the government.

HOW THE SUPREME COURT DECIDES TO HEAR A CASE

In *Marbury v. Madison*, Chief Justice Marshall basically said to Marbury the Supreme Court is not a

[12]Ibid. p. 29.

[13]William H. Rehnquist, *The Supreme Court*. New York: Vintage Books, 2001, p. 31.

[14]Ibid. p. 32.

[15]Alexander Hamilton, James Madison, and John Jay, *The Federalist Papers*. New York: Mentor Book, 1961, pp. 310, 465, 484.

court of original jurisdiction. What does this mean? It means generally, there are two types of courts in the United States. Courts that have original jurisdiction and courts that have appellate jurisdiction. Original jurisdiction are the courts that are dramatized on television and in the movies. They have juries and a judge and call witnesses to ascertain the information concerning the issues before the court. The Judge and Jury have different functions in a court of original jurisdiction. The Jury is the finder of fact. This means the Jury decides the facts of a trial. If they determine a defendant is at a place at a certain time then the defendant is there no matter what type of evidence to the contrary. The Jury's findings cannot be appealed. Once the facts of a case have been established, they do not change.

The Judge is the finder of law. The Judge determines the legal issues, and frames the legal remedies for the Jury to deliberate on. The actions of the Judge are the issues that can be appealed. The Appeals Court and the Supreme Court are only investigating errors in the law. The first step in the appellate process is the acceptance of a petition for *certiorari*.

The Supreme Court will receive about seven thousand petitions for *certiorari* and they will choose about one hundred cases to review each term.[16] When a petition for *certiorari* has been accepted, there is not a call for witnesses or juries. The Supreme Court (and other appellate courts) simply ask for the court record, combining the court record with written briefs supplied by the lawyers for each side, and then oral arguments. The Supreme Court will then vote on them in conference and prepare written opinions supporting the results reached by the majority votes. There is room to publish opinions of separate justices and opinions of dissenting justices.

The process that has the most publicity is the oral argument. One of the interesting points of the 2000 Presidential election is the Supreme Court released an audio recording of the oral arguments. This was truly fantastic since it gave everyone a chance to hear some of the country's top lawyers in the country's highest court. Again Rehnquist has written about this: "Lawyers often ask me whether oral argument really makes a difference. . . . Speaking for myself, I think it does make a difference. In a significant minority of the cases in which I have heard oral argument, I have left the bench feeling differently about a case than I did when I came on the bench."[17] After oral arguments, in

roughly a two week period, the Justices will meet in a conference. The Justices are the only people allowed in the room. Law clerks, staff and others are not allowed in the conference room when the Justices are deciding on cases.[18] After a vote is taken, if the Chief Justice is in the majority, he will assign a Justice to write an opinion on the case.

The Supreme Court basically has a three step process in which it hears cases. They pick a case through the petition for *certiorari*. They read the record of the case, read the briefs and hear oral arguments, then they conference vote on the case and write an opinion. If Justices disagree they then write dissenting opinions. Of all the branches in the Federal government, the Supreme Court and its power of Judicial Review is pretty closed to the average American. One can ask for Congresses records and the Presidents minutes of meetings using the Freedom of Information Act. However, the Supreme Court is not open to the press or to the average American. It is a confidential body, although members claim they do not "log roll" votes (the process in Congress where one trades a vote on one issue for a colleague's vote on another) we do not know the particulars of how different Justices decide.

Some commentators use labels such as original construction, or conservative or liberal. Even if the Justice is a member of a particular school of thought, many times in particular cases, Justices will vote in a manner they deem the most appropriate regardless of any record of consistency or label. As an example of the scope of Judicial Review in our system, there are an average of 150 Federal laws that are declared unconstitutional every year and over 1,000 state laws declared unconstitutional. It is just not the Supreme Court that declares laws unconstitutional. Next, we are going to examine the structure of the court system today.

TODAY'S COURT SYSTEM

When discussing today's court system, one has to think in terms of a four by four matrix between criminal and civil law and state and Federal jurisdiction. Most crimes are tried by state law, unless there is an element of the crime that will fall into Federal jurisdiction. These elements include a Federal question that deals with the U.S. Constitution, the violation of Federal laws or treaties, diversity of citizenship and the case must exceed 75,000 dollars between citizens of

---

[16]William H. Rehnquist, *The Supreme Court*. New York: Vintage Books, 2001, p. 224.
[17]Ibid. p. 243.

[18]Ibid. p. 257.

different states. Since most states (except Louisiana) have the tradition of English Common Law and then have fifty different statute laws, we will concentrate our discussion on the Federal courts. However, most states have imitated the three different levels of the Federal court system.

The Federal courts of original jurisdiction are called District Courts. These are the courts that establish the court record. There are Judges, juries and lawyers—one can think of this court as the bottom of a layer cake. The next level is the U.S. Court of Appeals. These courts will look at the errors of the trial judge. They are a personal first chance at changing the result of the District Court. Similar to the Supreme Court, the Appellate Court will only ask for the record and will adjudicate only errors in the law. Then, on top of the cake is the U.S. Supreme Court. These three levels of courts are designed to give people every opportunity to have errors corrected. Many Justices have complained about the volume of cases that are in the system. As our society has become more litigious and we criminalize more activities, the weight of having a system of justice that is manageable falls on the shoulders of the Justices and their support network.

The sheer numbers described by Chief Justice Rehnquist shows there is a great amount of work done by the nine Supreme Court Justices and their three or four law clerks. The great number of cases goes throughout the whole system. Jury trials and appeals are time consuming and expensive. How does court system manage? At least in the criminal cases, the plea-bargain has been replaced by a trial. Lawrence M. Freidman of Stanford University states:

WHAT REPLACED TRIAL BY JURY? BY AND LARGE, IT WAS THE GUILTY PLEA. THE DEFENDANT DID NOT GO TO TRIAL, BECAUSE HE ADMITTED HE WAS GUILTY; THIS REMOVED THE NEED FOR A JURY, AND FOR THE COURTROOM BATTLE OF THE LAWYERS. OVER TIME, MORE AND MORE DEFENDANTS PLEADED GUILTY. SOME OF THESE DEFENDANTS GAVE UP THE STRUGGLE NO DOUBT BECAUSE THEY FELT ASHAMED AND REPENTANT; BUT FOR THE VAST MAJORITY, THE GUILTY PLEAS WAS PART OF A DEAL—PART OF THE PROCESS OF PLEA BARGAINING. . . . THE DEFENDANT AGREED TO PLEAD GUILTY; IN EXCHANGE, THE PROSECUTOR AGREED TO DROP SOME CHARGES, OR TO KNOCK DOWN SOME CHARGES FROM FELONY TO MISDEMEANOR.[19]

Friedman goes on to write in the twentieth century that in some courthouses ninety percent of all felony convictions come by plea bargaining.[20] Plea bargaining is a management tool for some prosecutors. However, courts are over burdened because we are a litigious society that tries to remedy everything through the court system. Maybe we should re-think some of our strategies for dealing with societal problems if we cannot afford the time and effort to have trials by jury. Plea bargaining aside the growth of the Federal Judiciary has been explosive since the founding. The last four Presidents have appointed an average of 202 Judges during their terms.[21] All Federal Judges are lawyers, what else do they have in common when they are appointed?

Most people who have been appointed to Federal judgeships have had other political experience, either they have worked on campaigns or they were elected themselves. Their ages are typically in the late forties and they are reasonably well-off financially, with roughly 70 percent stating their net worth is more than 200,000 dollars.[22] Seventy-two percent of the appointees are white and 19 percent are African-American and 6.6 percent are Hispanic. About half had previous experiences as judges and a third were prosecutors.[23] One-third of the appointees were female and two-thirds were male. Probably the most important criteria used by Presidents to appoint judges, besides being a lawyer, is the political party affiliation of the appointees. Most Presidents appoint members of their own party roughly 88–90 percent of the time. Once a person is appointed they must be confirmed by the Senate.

THE CONFIRMATION PROCESS BY THE SENATE

The Constitution instructs the President to appoint Judges with the advise and consent of the Senate. Traditionally, these hearings were low key and the appointee did not testify in front of the Senate until Felix Frankfurter did in early 1939.[24] However, this changed as the Federal courts became more involved in the daily activities of Americans. President

[19]Lawrence M. Friedman, *Law in America: A Short History.* New York: The Modern Library, 2004, p. 93.

[20]Ibid.
[21]Sheldon Goldman and Elliot E. Slotnick, "Clinton's First Term *Judiciary: Many Bridges to Cross.*" *Judicature* (May–June 1997), p. 261.
[22]Ibid.
[23]Ibid.
[24]William H. Rehnquist, *The Supreme Court.* New York: Vintage Books, 2001, p. 136.

Ronald Reagan nominated Robert H. Bork to be on the Supreme Court. This was not the first politically opposed appointment, but it was different because it was interest groups that thwarted the nomination of Robert Bork. These interest groups (in the Bork case it was democratic and pro-life interest groups) threatened political retribution if Senators supported his nomination. We have seen on the Democratic and Republican sides of the aisle in the Senate, where an appointee is on the issue of abortion seems to trump all other legal issues.

Robert Bork was defeated, but Presidents and their staff learned the new environment an appointee to the Federal courts would have to face. If the person was a legal professor or some other type of legal scholar and had written many articles about the Constitution, this person may be at a disadvantage than someone who did not have a paper trail. The abortion question which Chief Justice Roberts has called settled law seems to be a litmus test for democratic support, but this may also be a religious test which is unconstitutional.

Does the abortion issue disqualify Catholics, Mormons, Muslims, and members of other mainstream religious traditions who are basically pro-life? Can a Hispanic person become a Federal Judge? If they are members of the Catholic Church, many Democratic Senators would not vote for them if they were pro-life. On the other hand, what about a woman who has had an abortion, can she be a Federal Judge? Many Republicans may find having an abortion may be a disqualification. Abortion and the interest groups that surround this issue have used Federal appointments since the naming of Robert Bork as a fund raiser and a reason for existence. The Senators should look at the whole person when nominated, not where they stand on this issue that has been clearly decided law for thirty years. Both Democratic and Republican Senators should put this issue in perspective and stop treating appointees as if they were cast members in a reality television show. We are losing the best people because of the difficulty and exposure appointees have in the confirmation process. Yes, they are appointed for life. Yes, it is the Senators duty to ask penetrating legal questions before the body confirms a lifetime appointment. However, the Senators do not have the right or responsibility to question a person's integrity and embarrass their family just because your party lost the previous Presidential election.

As with the recent appointment of President Bush, the interest groups investigated whether Chief Justice Roberts' used his influence when adopting his children, or another case when Justice Alioto was a member of a Princeton alumni group that some of the members where accused of racist language. The Senators tried to besmirch Alioto's reputation to the point where his wife broke down and started to weep. These examples are not extraordinary and illustrate how special interest money controls Senators of both parties in the confirmation process.

The Supreme Court and the other Federal courts are not all powerful. There are checks and balances for this third branch of the government as well as the Legislative and executive branches. In the last part of our examination of the judiciary, we will explore some of these checks on the power of the courts in the United States.

LIMITS ON THE JUDICIARY

There are limits to the power of the judiciary just as there are limits to the other two branches of the Federal government. *Stare decisis* is a framework that limits the power of Judges and to a lesser extent Justices.[25] The legal reasoning of these people must make sense to other judges. Although it may seem to lay people that Judges are just making things up, the constraints on individual judges by *stare decisis* is quite real. Outside the legal community there are other limits on the power of the Judicial branch.

Congress can pass new laws and change the Constitution if there is some action taken by the Supreme Court that people find offensive. Amendments to the Constitution though rare cannot be ignored by the Supreme Court. We have discussed in the earlier chapters on the Constitution how remedies such as this usually are not good politics Prohibition comes to mind as a bad use of changing the Constitution for political ends. It is possible to limit the Supreme Court by changing the Constitution. Changing the laws are also ways to limit the power of the Supreme Court. The Supreme Court will only challenge the constitutionality of a law if there is a case. There has to be a controversy surrounding the law. The Supreme Court does not offer preliminary opinions on the constitutionality of a bill being considered in Congress. As we have said, over 150 laws a year are determined unconstitutional by the Supreme Court. Many more laws are passed by Congress and are never reviewed by the Supreme Court.

---

[25]*Stare decisis* has less effect of Justices because they have the final word on interpreting the Constitution.

Another check on the Judicial branch is the Executive branch. The President has the power to appoint Justices and Judges. Starting with the appointment of Chief Justice Marshall by John Adams, this can be the mainstay of a President's legacy. As an example of the importance of the power of appointment, John Marshall would serve as Chief Justice for thirty-four years.[26] Of all the problems facing George W. Bush today, he may well be remembered for his appointments of Chief Justice Roberts and Justice Alioto more than anything else. Similar to Chief Justice Marshall, who was 45-years-old when appointed, Chief Justice Roberts was 50 when he was appointed, and assuming a normal life span he may well be on the court 30–40 years from now.

The other executive check on the Supreme Court is lack of enforcement power. President Lincoln simply ignored the Supreme Court rulings during the early days of the Civil War. Lincoln had suspended the writ of habeas corpus and Chief Justice Taney ruled it was not appropriate for the President to unilaterally suspend this Constitutional right. Lincoln simply ignored Taney saying:

> MUST [THE LAWS] BE ALLOWED TO FINALLY FAIL OF EXECUTION EVEN HAD IT BEEN PERFECTLY CLEAR THAT BY THE USE OF THE MEANS NECESSARY TO THEIR EXECUTION SOME SINGLE LAW, MADE IN SUCH EXTREME TENDERNESS OF THE CITIZEN'S LIBERTY THAT PRACTICALLY IT RELIEVES MORE OF THE GUILTY THAN OF THE INNOCENT, SHOULD TO A VERY LIMITED EXTENT BE VIOLATED? TO STATE THE QUESTION MORE DIRECTLY, ARE ALL THE LAWS BUT ONE TO GO UNEXECUTED, AND THE GOVERNMENT ITSELF GO TO PIECES LEST THAT ONE BE VIOLATED.[27]

Taney was ridiculed and rebuked, the author of the *Dred Scott* decision was also held in contempt for his lack of support and understanding of the crisis faced by Lincoln. Lincoln simply ignored the Supreme Court. This is an extreme example but even in modern times, people have tried to persuade Presidents to ignore Supreme Court rulings.

President Eisenhower decided to enforce the Court's ruling in desegregating schools in Little Rock, Arkansas, but the Court had little recourse if he had decided not to send troops. However, for a hundred years before, the Supreme Court ruled that separate could not be equal, segregation lived in the South, and the amendments for equal protection under the law—the motto of the Supreme Court Building was ignored. Put quite simply, if Presidents do not want to enforce the rulings of the Supreme Court, the Supreme Court does not have any recourse except for their power of persuasion and the perception by the American people that the Supreme Court does has the legitimate right to interpret the Constitution and have its rulings enforced by the Executive branch of the government.

The third limit on the power of the Supreme Court is quite limited since the Justices are independent of elections and politics once appointed. However, public opinion does influence a Justice's sense of what is appropriate. No matter how insulated they are, they remain members of our society with family and friends. They also read the same newspapers and watch the same television programs as we all do. This does limit their actions a little. Although many Justices would not admit any outside influences have influenced a change in their legal reasoning, it was Chief Justice Warren who, as Attorney General of California, was responsible for convincing Roosevelt to intern Japanese-Americans; was the same man who started the legal implementation of integration in the South.

CONCLUSION

When the Founding Fathers wrote the Constitution many of them wrote in the *Federalist Papers*, how they believed the third branch of the Federal government would be the weakest branch. Today we see the Judiciary is not a mere afterthought or a weak stepchild of the Constitution. We have examined the two types of law used in the United States: the Common Law and Statutory Law. We explained how the Common Law was borrowed from England and is sometimes called "judge made law." The Courts used in the Common Law system did not contain juries, judges determined the facts and the law of the case. Common Law cases are showcased today on television, in which the judge usually scolds plaintiffs and defendants before rendering decisions for prize money.

The other type of law used in this country is Statutory Law. Starting with the Constitution (either Federal or state) statutory law is the law produced by the actions of both the Legislative and Executive branches of government. The Constitution describes the organization of the government, the procedures used to produce laws and the limits of power the gov-

---

[26]David McCullough, *John Adams*. New York: Simon and Schuster, 2001, p. 560.

[27]William H. Rehnquist, *The Supreme Court*. New York: Vintage Books, 2001, p. 67.

ernment has vis-à-vis individuals. Statutory law is made by the different state legislatures and the Federal government.

We went on to examine how Presidents appoint Judges and Justices, who are engaged in the interpretation of both the Common Law and Statutory Law. This chapter illustrates the importance of judicial appointments to Presidential legacies. President Adams who appointed Chief Justice Marshall, was rightfully proud of this last minute appointment, while Johnson and Eisenhower were more remorseful in their appointments to the Supreme Court. Chief Justice Marshall can be considered the greatest Chief Justice ever because he was the one who determined it was the role of the Supreme Court to interpret the Constitution. In the case *Marbury v. Madison*, Chief Justice Marshall concluded a portion of the Judiciary Act of 1789 was unconstitutional. Having done this, he contended the Supreme Court was the only branch of the Federal government that had the power to determine what was constitutional and what was not constitutional. This was not foreseen by the Founding Fathers and was a tremendous power grab and made the Judiciary the powerful branch we see today. After tracing how the Supreme Court developed the power for Judicial Review, we then explored the daily working of the Supreme Court.

The Supreme Court is the only institution (beside classified operations) that is not open to the public or the press. The Justices of the Supreme Court are appointed for life and are isolated from the political environment that surrounds other institutions in Washington, D.C. Having this freedom and independence from politics is designed to have Justices and Federal Judges use their legal reasoning and experience to find decisions that help contribute to the system of justice the Founding Fathers set out in the preamble of the Constitution. This chapter completes our examination of the three branches of government set out in the Constitution.

The Legislative, Executive and Judiciary branches of the Government provide a system of checks and balances that are designed to protect our individual liberty. However, there is another organization that has power over our lives and it is not included in the Constitution. Bureaucracies, both private and public, have power that keeps growing and does not have a check or balance against it. In the next chapter, we will examine the power of the Federal Bureaucracy and how with the growth of laws and regulations our liberty is being threatened by the increase of the Federal Bureaucracy and our privacy is being threatened by the expansive growth of private bureaucracies. An example of the spread of bureaucratic regulation and litigation in society is the widespread use of social security numbers and the issues of both privacy and immigration that stem out of the need for the government to keep track of who we are, what we are doing and how we pay taxes. Our discussion moves to the issues and problems of dealing with the bureaucratization of our society.

TERMS TO REMEMBER

STARE DECISIS

DEFENDANT

PLAINTIFF

COMMON LAW

STATUTORY LAW

ORIGINAL JURISDICTION

APPELLATE JURISDICTION

JUDICIAL REVIEW

 **The Judiciary**

TRUE OR FALSE QUESTIONS

1. America has one set of laws called Common Law.　　　　　　　　　　　T / F

2. The President appoints Supreme Court Justices every four years.　　　T / F

3. Justices serve six year terms.　　　　　　　　　　　　　　　　　　T / F

4. The Constitution requires a Justice of the Supreme Court be a lawyer.　T / F

5. Chief Justice Marshall was the first Chief Justice of the Supreme Court.　T / F

6. The Supreme Court is the last bastion of democracy in our system.　　T / F

7. A Justice must be a male.　　　　　　　　　　　　　　　　　　　　T / F

8. Each Justice is elected every four years.　　　　　　　　　　　　　T / F

9. *Stare decisis* is Latin for the previous decision must stand.　　　　　T / F

10. Common law and statutory law are the type of law you see on the courtroom programs on day time television.　　　　　　　　　　　　　　　　　　　　T / F

MULTIPLE CHOICE QUESTIONS

11. The first African-American Justice appointed to the Supreme Court was
    a. Warren Burger
    b. Thurgood Marshall
    c. Hugo Black
    d. Robert Thomas

12. The Supreme Court Case that was instrumental in giving them the power to interpret the Constitution was
    a. *Gibbons*
    b. *Roe v. Wade*
    c. *Marbury v. Madison*
    d. *Plessy*

13. Who was not a Chief Justice of the United States?
    a. Warren Burger
    b. William Rehnquist
    c. John Roberts
    d. Abe Fortas

14. The Supreme Court works with _____ to settle the law.
    a. House of Representatives
    b. President
    c. Senate
    d. No one

15. Which is not a Federal Court?
    a. District
    b. Appeals
    c. Supreme
    d. Criminal

16. The Supreme Court gets its power in the Constitution from
    a. Article I
    b. Article II
    c. Article III
    d. Article IV

17. The first step for the Supreme Court to hear a case is to write a(n)
    a. legal opinion
    b. legal brief
    c. legal memo
    d. *certiorari*

18. Justices call upon _____ to decide a case.
    a. juries
    b. evidence
    c. the Police
    d. the Court record

19. Which is not part of the three step process the Supreme Court uses in hearing a case?
    a. Petition for *certiorari*
    b. Read the record of the case
    c. Call the jury
    d. Hear oral arguments

20. What is not a limit on the Judiciary?
    a. Congress can change the Constitution
    b. Congress can write a new law
    c. Presidential veto
    d. The President can ignore the ruling

chapter twelve

THE BUREAUCRACY

INTRODUCTION

We have described and examined the various aspects of the political environment of the United States. There are three branches of government enshrined in the U.S. Constitution: the Legislative, Executive, and Judicial branches. We now turn our analytical lens to another aspect of government—the bureaucracy. The Founding Fathers believed a small efficient bureaucracy should be inside the Executive branch of government. However, we will see through time, Presidents have felt the bureaucracy is not responsive to their administration's political or regulatory goals. Congress at times has sought to control or reform the bureaucracy, but again we will see how many times this too has failed.

The bureaucracy is important since it is the part of the Federal government that people come in contact with. It is the face of the government that more often than not are not understanding, charges fines and punishments and has the power to take your freedom, possessions, and determine if you are suc-

cessful in life or a failure. Governmental departments such as the Internal Revenue Service, Federal Bureau of Investigation, Drug Enforcement Agency and Social Security Administration are just four of the many governmental departments that may affect your everyday life. In this chapter, we will define and discuss the concept of a bureaucracy and the models that scholars have developed in order to predict the behavior of these organizations. We then look at the historical development of the Federal bureaucracy and the different challenges faced by Congress and the President in trying to reform and rein in the bureaucracy. We then describe today's bureaucratic structure and the problems it was designed to handle. Next, we profile the type of people who populate the bureaucracy and if they do a good job for the taxpayers. Finally, we examine the role of private bureaucracies in our society, and the challenges facing the average individual in the fight to keep our privacy from both the public and private bureaucracies that have ever increasing power in our society.

The first step in our discussion is to define what is a bureaucracy? For our purposes, a bureaucracy is any organization that has regulations or policies that has to be enforced. This enforcement requires some type of organizational structure and this structure is called a bureaucracy. Under this definition, there are many bureaucracies, the police and fire departments are obvious bureaucracies. There are other bureaucracies that people even in their professions, do not think they are bureaucrats.

Professors (especially those in public institutions) are bureaucrats. Each Professor is a specialist in their chosen academic discipline. They are hired by an institution to certify that students have spent the required hours in a classroom (or in front of a computer), read the required amount of material and have been tested in that material for a specified number of credits and the credits are graded usually on a letter scale between A–F. These credits are then collected by the records office and it becomes a permanent record of a student's time spent at the institution. The record is called a transcript.

Why is it, that almost every class you have taken since graduating high school has the same basic organization and components (syllabus, textbook, some type of presentation and exams)? Is it because the nature of the class in higher education is dictated to the Professor through (in our case) state law? The California Education Code is specific that each Professor must have a textbook and a syllabus that describes the nature of the class. Furthermore, the Education Code also requires Professors to have a written assignment and a means of objective evaluation for the students. Sometimes students and professors complain about the environment that is produced by having these requirements. Students complain about textbooks and professors complain about grading. Just as the Department of Motor Vehicles (DMV) employee must make sure the form you fill out for your driver's license is correct. Professors must also enforce state law in order for you to have your credits transferred to other institutions of higher learning. Once you have read this chapter, you will see many more bureaucracies, both in government and in other private institutions.

We start the analysis with a description of the different theoretical models developed to try to understand the nature of bureaucracies. Early social scientists believed the explosive growth and power of bureaucracies would ultimately become the primary threat to individual liberty in the world. These models are an attempt to understand and sometimes predict the nature of bureaucracies in order to prevent the widespread abuse of organizational power against individuals. These models are early efforts in the fields of sociology, anthropology and political science.

FOUR UNIVERSAL PROPERTIES OF BUREAUCRACIES AND UNDERSTANDING BUREAUCRATIC MODELS

Max Weber was the father of sociology. His early work centered on the German bureaucracy of the 1800s. During this period in Germany, the state was monarchical and militaristic. Weber studied the German bureaucracy because he feared it was bureaucracies that would ultimately destroy the human spirit. Weber's studies indicated that all bureaucracies have four universal properties. First, they are all hierarchical.

When you go visit a bureaucratic office, either to renew your driver's license at the DMV, or you have to go to the courthouse to pay a parking or traffic ticket, or when you try to change your schedule at your school's records office, you will see a bank of windows designed to serve the individuals who need the bureaucratic services being offered. Look behind the window and usually you will see desks behind the person interfacing with the public. There are usually people working, talking and carrying on. These people at the desks are usually supervising the people at the windows. Now, if you can look further you may see another row of desks or offices, these are symbols of the supervisors who are in charge of supervising the people at the desks and so on.

This hierarchy can become frustrating when you have a problem, and the person you are dealing with at the window is inexperienced or does not care about your problem. To make our point, think of the airport as a typical bureaucracy. If you have ever missed a flight you know how frustrating it can be to deal with the first level of employees. Sometimes, the person at the ticket counter cannot help you (or does not care to help). You ask to see a supervisor, why? You ask to see a supervisor because there is an assumption the supervisor has either more experience or more power to change your situation and either find a more convenient flight or compensate you with some type of upgrade. Of course this rarely works, because the person you are talking to really does not have more power, or experience, or freedom to change your situation. The frustration builds and you end up waiting—exasperated with your experience.

On the other side of the counter, what are the employees thinking about? The people at the window are thinking: in fifteen minutes, I get my break;

in three months I get my vacation and in three years I hope to have one of the desks of a supervisor. The supervisor is thinking: in three hours, I get lunch, in three months, the worker at the window will take a vacation and I have to fill her time schedule and in six years I hope to get an office. Nothing in the reward structure of the airport bureaucracy rewards employees to get you on a more convenient flight. Furthermore, there are probably rules that prevent the supervisor to upgrade you or to put you on an empty flight (overbooking is a common practice for airlines). The frustration grows for the customer because they have to use their ticket, yet, we all know the incentive structure and the hierarchy are designed not to fix the problem.

We see this not only in the little problems of a person missing a flight at the airport. The nature of hierarchy causes organizations to grow exponentially and inefficiently to the point where the organization cannot complete the original problem it was created to solve.

The second property Weber saw in all bureaucracies was the role of specialization. Again, using the DMV as an example, when you go to the DMV office you notice different stations for things such as filling out the forms for license renewals, vehicle registration, pictures, information and others. Employees are trained to do a certain job. They become specialists in their particular station. So, the person in charge of taking the driver's license pictures only works in that area. It does not matter if no one needs a picture in the beginning of the day (assuming the picture is one of the last things in the procedure of getting a new driver's license). As a result, that person may sit around for an hour or so after the doors have opened to the DMV station. The person does not do other jobs that may be needed; they are in charge of pictures. Usually you see people with seniority work out a niche for themselves. We know of a mailman who worked twenty years until he earned a specialized route at one of the high rise buildings. He was so proud of his accomplishment, because it meant that he no longer had to deal with the weather, all of his work was inside the building. He moved a "Laz-y-boy" chair into the mailroom of the building and spent twenty more happy years working his specialized route. As with the Post Office or the DMV, these specialized jobs are encapsulated inside the bureaucracy. It becomes frustrating for outsiders when we see people not engaged in serving the public because at a particular point of time (usually when we are in line) we see people being engaged in not serving us.

Specialization usually requires some type of unique knowledge, but sometimes it can be based on seniority or favoritism. Specialization can cause logjams in the bureaucracy. These logjams can produce opportunities for people to exercise their power even though they may not be in the formal hierarchy. Because of specialization, jobs that may not pay a lot or may not have a great deal of social prestige may have a great deal of power. So when you start a new job, be aware of the people who hold these positions and be nice to them. The first position that has the potential to have a great deal of power, are secretaries. Although, in both private and public organizations they are becoming more rare, secretaries (especially if they have been with their bosses for a long time), control the paper flow to your boss and to your boss's boss. If you want your paperwork for anything to be handled in an efficient way, try to be polite and responsive to the secretaries in your organization.

Janitors or maintenance workers are another group of people who has great power over your comfort and productivity in your job. Always be considerate to the people who pick up after you. Specialization enables janitors to decide which job is a priority, so if a pipe is leaking some strange green liquid on to your desk, and you were just rude to the janitor, they may tell you to put a bucket under the leak and they will get to it. While if you have a professional and polite relationship with them, they will fix your leak right away. The third job that in many organizations that have power that belies their status are parking lot attendants, especially if you drive a nice car. You want someone who would notice someone standing around your car or acting strange around your car.

Now of course you should be professional and polite to everyone when you start a new job. However, sometimes people think because they have more prestige and/or make more money than these people in these positions that they can ignore them. Bureaucratic specialization can make these people very powerful in special circumstances. So, after you read this book, remember one thing, remember to be nice to secretaries, janitors and parking lot attendants. Specialization is possible because of the necessity of bureaucracies to have the duties of employees written down. Job descriptions are an attempt to set down in writing the responsibilities of everyone who works for a bureaucracy. This brings us to the next universal property of bureaucracy. Weber called this Rules and Regulations.

Decisions in bureaucracies are based on rules and regulations promulgated by the people in authority. Our society is full of simple rules and regulations that there are not supposed to be any exceptions, these are called laws. In bureaucracies there are rules and regulations that drive the decision making process. Trying to get a job in the bureaucracy is a very good example of how rules and regulations dictate who gets hired to work in the bureaucracy. Take a simple position as a clerk in the post office. The first thing the Post Office must do is to administer a test for the position. There are rules about how many days and what media is required to give the public notice that a postal exam will be given on a certain date. A person cannot just show up on the day of the exam, they must first follow the procedure of registering for the exam. This registration could be weeks, if not months, before the day of the exam. Then, on the day of the exam, the applicant to take the exam must provide sufficient documentation—usually a driver's license, military identification card, birth certificate to prove they are who they say they are.

The applicant has not taken the test yet, however, if they fail in any of the previous steps they are deemed ineligible to take the test. This is a way bureaucracies, not just the Post Office, test people to see if they follow directions but it also is an inexpensive and fair way to eliminate many of the candidates before they have even taken the test for the postal clerk position. Rules and regulations are at the heart of our examination of bureaucracies. On face value, rules and regulations are considered objective and neutral. This brings us to the fourth characteristic of bureaucracies—neutrality.

Bureaucrats are supposed to be neutral to a person's background, social networks or other aspects that may influence a bureaucrat's decisions in their role of enforcing rules and regulations. No one is supposed to be given preferential treatment in the decision making process. Being neutral has advantages but it also has, in extreme cases, disadvantages. The bureaucracy will not consider outside factors that may have influenced a certain person's situation. Depending on the issue being considered, issues of justice are sometimes outside the decision making procedures. On issues such as college admissions, deciding job applications or credit scores, bureaucrats make decisions after they have applied their procedures with as much neutrality as can possibly be administered. It is impossible to consider millions of credit applications if there is not a credit score assigned to each of us.

However, many people who suffer through divorce or some other type of disaster may have a low score, but they may be good credit risks. Because of the volume of the number of applications, being neu-

tral is the only way bureaucratic decisions can be made in an efficient way. These four properties of bureaucracies—Hierarchy, Specialization, Rules and Regulations, and Neutrality are found in different degrees in every bureaucracy around the world. Next, we will describe the different theoretical models that have developed to understand how these four properties interact and exacerbate the societal forces on the people who have to deal with bureaucracies in everyday life. The four models we will explore are the Weberian Model, the Acquisitive Model, the Monopolistic Model, and the Garbage Can Model. We start with Weber's analysis of how the properties he identified related to each other.

WEBER'S BUREAUCRATIC MODEL

As we have stated earlier, Max Weber's interest in bureaucracies came from his experience in living in modern Germany before and during World War I. Weber foresaw the increasing power of the bureaucracy and how with this power, if left unchecked, the lives of people would be crushed in order to serve the needs of the bureaucracy. Although Weber believed in a strong state, and was a German nationalist, he was not a Nazi. In the Weberian model, it is hierarchical, and power flows from the top to the bottom. Decisions are based on technical considerations and the focus of decision making is centered on rational unbiased decision making. Taken to the extreme, you can see how a bureaucracy can be turned to a genocidal instrument that we have seen in Hitler's Germany, Pol Pot's Cambodia, Stalin's Russia, Mao's China, and Kim Jong Il's North Korea. Weber's perception of the bureaucracy is that it is essential to insure the state survives. However, if the bureaucracy does not have a foundation of justice, then the powers at the top of the bureaucracy can set rules and regulations that force and enable common workers inside the bureaucracy to genocidal crimes. A more economic perspective of bureaucratic models is the Acquisitive Model.

ACQUISITIVE MODEL

The assumptions used in this model contend the bureaucrats do not make decisions in a neutral vacuum. They make decisions that serve the interest of the bureaucracy. Each part of the bureaucracy is concerned with protecting their "turf" and building bureaucratic fiefdoms in which the leaders of the organization keep on expanding their influence and their organizations continue to seek new goals for the organization. An example of this behavior is the adaptation of both the Central Intelligence Agency (CIA), Defense Intelligence Agency (DIA) and the Federal Bureau of Investigation (FBI) following the attacks on September 11th. According to an ex-Commander of the National Security Agency, William E. Odom, in his book *Fixing Intelligence for a More Secure America* illustrates the problems the bureaucrats in both the FBI and CIA had in changing their organizations after the collapse of the Soviet Union and before the September 11th attacks.

STRUCTURAL PROBLEMS AFFLICT NOT ONLY INTELLIGENCE COLLECTION BUT ALSO INTELLIGENCE ANALYSIS. DURING THE COLD WAR THIS WAS CONSPICUOUS IN THE CONTINUING DEBATE BETWEEN THE CIA AND DEFENSE INTELLIGENCE AGENCY (DIA) ON ESTIMATES OF SOVIET MILITARY CAPABILITIES. THE GROSS UNDERESTIMATE OF SOVIET MILITARY EXPENDITURES CAN BE EXPLAINED LARGELY AS THE RESULT OF COMPETITION THAT CAUSED EACH OF THESE AGENCIES TO BE LESS CONCERNED WITH THE TRUTH OF MATTERS IN THE SOVIET UNION THAN WITH PROVING THE OTHER WRONG IN THE EYES OF CONGRESS. THE NEEDS OF EXECUTIVE BRANCH POLICYMAKERS, FOR WHOM THIS INTELLIGENCE WAS PRIMARILY PRODUCED, TENDED TO BE SECONDARY IN BOTH AGENCIES CALCULATIONS. THE HANDLING OF INTELLIGENCE ANALYSIS ON AL-QAEDA IN THE WEEKS AND DAYS LEADING UP TO THE EVENTS OF 11 SEPTEMBER 2001 OFFERS ANOTHER EXAMPLE OF PROBLEMS OF BOTH ANALYSIS AND DISTRIBUTION OF INTELLIGENCE. THE FBI'S JEALOUSY OVER ITS COUNTERINTELLIGENCE TURF, NOT ONLY VIS-À-VIS THE CIA BUT ALSO VIS-À-VIS THE MILITARY SERVICES' COUNTERINTELLIGENCE ANALYSIS (AS WELL AS OPERATIONS), IS A SIMILAR SYMPTOM OF STRUCTURAL PROBLEMS.[1]

Odom's comments illustrate the Acquisitive Model's assumptions, that the bureaucrats will primarily protect their position inside the organization and secondarily, protect the existence of the organization. Even on issues such as life and death, the bureaucracy does not have the capacity to change according to this ex-General's analysis. What was the bureaucratic response to the attacks on September 11th that caught all of the "professional analysts" by surprise? They established another department (Homeland Security) with another counter-intelligence unit. This behavior would bear out the importance of the Acquisitive Model. The next model takes even a more negative perspective of bureaucracies than the Acquisitive Model, this is the Monopolistic Model.

---

[1]William E. Odom, *Fixing Intelligence for a More Secure America*. New Haven: Yale University Press, 2003, p. 5.

MONOPOLISTIC MODEL

In this model, monopolies such as the DMV or Post Office provide services that are monopolies. Because of the lack of competition, these bureaucracies grow inefficient and unable to provide a high quality service.

If you are a resident of your state, you cannot get your driver's license or car registration from other states or private businesses. They are a monopoly. The common person does not have a choice whether they are going to drive or not. Therefore, they must pay the fees, stand in line and do whatever the bureaucrats at the DMV demand. The Post Office is another monopoly. If you want to mail a letter the post office, by law, is the only organization that has the right to do this. With the advent of email and other forms of communication, people are not so dependent on the Post Office. However, next holiday season when you are waiting in line at the Post Office and there is only one clerk at the counter—remember, using the Monopoly model's analysis, there is not an incentive for the Post Office to provide another clerk to get the line moving. The last model we are going to discuss is called the Garbage Can Model.

GARBAGE CAN MODEL

This model is the most negative of all the models. This model basically discounts any type of model building by scholars who study bureaucracies. They claim there is very little rational decision making made in bureaucracies. Basically, the leadership of bureaucracies try things and very little analysis is done to see if the policies are effective or not. New leadership will bring different policies and these policies are either accepted practice or fought by managers and workers. The regulations are added and in this process, a monstrosity of policies and ineffectiveness consume the average person's time and energy.

Bureaucracies are intended to enforce rules and regulations. People do not ask why the government is involved in licensing different professions, cars, and even marriages. These models help us explain how our society has become more and more bureaucratic. In the next section of this chapter we will describe the historical growth of the Federal bureaucracy. This is important since the only time the average person has to deal with the government is through the bureaucracy.

GROWTH AND ORGANIZATION OF THE FEDERAL BUREAUCRACY

In 1789, the Federal bureaucracy was extremely small. President Washington had three departments: State, War and the Treasury. Although small, some would argue with General Knox at the War Department, Thomas Jefferson at the State Department, and Alexander Hamilton at the Treasury Department, may have been one of the most talented Cabinets a President has ever put together. How was it possible for the Federal bureaucracy to grow to the point where today the Federal government is the largest employer in the economy?

If one were to chart the growth of the Federal bureaucracy, one would see there is a significant growth of government during times of war. [2] When the war ends the government does shrink but not to the point before the war. Wars have been traditionally financed through the selling of bonds and the taxing of people. During World War I the number of government employees spiked to 700,000 and by 1920 the number had dropped to half a million.[3] During World War II there were over 3.5 million people who worked for the government. Because the war effort was universal, everyone was involved in working for victory. By 1955 the number of employees had fallen to 2.5 million but before the war (1940) the number was one million. The number of government employees has stayed around 2.5 million people since 2000.

The Federal government has been able to afford all of these workers because of the invention of the personal income tax. The ratification of the XVI Amendment in 1913 has given the Federal government a powerful money machine. The income tax has made the hiring of professional bureaucrats possible.

Starting with the President's Cabinet, there are fifteen different departments. The last one was Department of Homeland Security. Here is a list of the departments by Seniority.

DEPARTMENT

STATE

DEFENSE

TREASURY

JUSTICE

AGRICULTURE

INTERIOR

TRANSPORTATION

COMMERCE

LABOR

HEALTH AND HUMAN SERVICES

HOUSING AND URBAN DEVELOPMENT

ENERGY

EDUCATION

VETERAN'S AFFAIRS

HOMELAND SECURITY

These different departments are the President's Cabinet. The largest department is Health and Human Services. This department takes about 70 percent of the Federal budget. Social Security and Medicare are under this budget and as we get older as a country this department is going to be growing larger and larger.

Along with the departments there are Independent Regulatory Agencies such as the General Services Administration (GSA) and the National Aeronautics and Space Administration (NASA). The directors of these agencies are appointed by the President but they are not part of a Cabinet Department. Furthermore, there are independent regulatory commissions such as the Federal Communication Commission (FCC) that is designed to formulate and regulate rules regarding specific areas designed to protect the public interest. And, finally, there are independent governmental corporation and quasi-governmental corporations. Amtrak, Tennessee Valley Authority (TVA) and the Post Office are all government corporations. Quasi-governmental Corporations include Fannie Mae, Freddie Mac and Sallie Mae, the mortgage and student loan guarantor corporations that play a part in financial markets. These four types of general bureaucratic organizations make up the majority of Federal governments bureaucratic organization. Now, we will examine how we populate these organizations with all the people and expertise that is needed in order to have the bureaucracy work. No matter what your perspective is on the bureaucracy, it could not do anything if people were unwilling to work for the Federal government.

There are two different ways to get to work for the Federal government: Political appointments and Civil Service. Political appointments are usually at the senior or more professional level of the government. We previously discussed the President's and Senate's role in the appointment of Federal Justices and Judges. The other type of appointment is through the Civil Service. Starting in 1883 with the

---

[2]U.S. Department of Commerce, Bureau of the Census, Historical State of U.S.: Colonial Through 1970 (Washington, D.C.: U.S. Government Printing Office, 1975)

[3]Ibid.

Pendleton Act, the Civil Service, was established in order to have a professional and non-political workforce to serve in the government. The establishment of the Civil Service Commission was essential in providing the rules and regulations needed for the government to try to reform and move away from the spoils system initiated by Andrew Jackson.[4] In 1939, there was another reform called the Hatch Act that limited the political activities of Federal employees. The Hatch Act insulated Federal employees from the pressure of politics. Some states, such as Louisiana, required state employees to kick back a portion of their paychecks to the political party in power. This practice was outlawed by the Hatch Act.

The Federal government employs over 100,000 types of workers, and the Post Office is the largest single Federal employer, with over one quarter of the total work force of the Federal government working for the Post Office. In higher position, the Civil Service requires a person fill out an application called form 171. This form is fairly complicated but it is a standard form for being employed by the government. Then there is usually a writing requirement called KSAs. KSA stand for Knowledge, Skills and Abilities. These essays are designed to give the applicant and the selection board an opportunity to have the applicant explain his or her skill set for the position being advertised.

Although, the reforms may have gotten rid of overt politics, there is an inside game to getting a job in the Federal government. Networking and interning inside the bureaucracy remains a very useful thing to do if you are looking for a career inside the bureaucracy. There is a website, usajobs.com, that a person can look for employment and internship opportunities that are offered through the bureaucracy. How do these individuals create an organization and how does this organization relate with the other branches of the government to serve the public? In the next section of the chapter, we will explore the relationships formed by the different mechanisms used to enforce the different policies and procedures that are used by the different aspects of the government. These different relationships have been called iron triangles.

BUREAUCRATIC POLICY IMPLEMENTATION—IRON TRIANGLES

The interaction of the bureaucracy, Congress and interest groups has been known as an iron triangle. It sets the criteria for people to be hired inside the bureaucracy, how Congressmen are assigned to certain committees and why are certain think tanks, large corporations and lobbyist listened to and others are not. This relationship is called an iron triangle because people and money that are inside the triangle have influence on policy, while other Congressmen, interest groups and bureaucratic agents outside the triangle have very little influence on policy. Most scholars and journalists have concentrated on the iron triangle that centers on the Armed Services Committee in Congress, large governmental defense contractors and the branches of the Armed Forces, when discussing the classic iron triangle relationship.[5] However, the relationship described by the analogy of iron triangle happens in all aspects of governmental policy. There is a lobby for old people—AARP (American Association for Retired Persons), governmental agencies—Social Security, Medicare, and large corporations, and Congressional committees on the aged. This is also a powerful iron triangle.

By the way, two-thirds of the Federal government's budget goes to the issues dealing with social programs, only a third goes to defense spending. Keeping this in mind, and since we are at war, let us look at the most studied iron triangle—that of the Pentagon and military contractors.

The defense iron triangle has an advantage. Instead of just issuing checks as the Department of Health and Human Services does for Social Security, the Pentagon actually pays to have things: shoes, weapons, jeeps, food, toilets, all the things that are in a modern city are also on a Nimitz Class Air Craft Carrier. This advantage is the reason how Pentagon can reward Congressmen with jobs in their districts. As Hedrick Smith writes:

"THE MILITARY SERVICES WANT MORE MONEY THAN THEY CAN AFFORD, AND THE PENTAGON WANTS MORE MONEY THAN THE COUNTRY CAN AFFORD," A LONGTIME PRO-DEFENSE SENATE COMMITTEE STAFFER OBSERVED TO ME. "THE SENATOR OR HOUSE MEMBER WANTS MORE FOR HIS DISTRICT THAN THE BUDGET CAN AFFORD. EACH PARTY IS MOTIVATED BY GREED. THE

---

[4]The spoils system was a practice that gave the President unlimited appointment power. Every four years, if there was a party change, every worker would be replaced by workers who were loyal to the party in charge. This system built up party identification and party loyalty. But the institutional memory lost every four years and the problems with corruption offset any political advantage.

---

[5]Hedrick Smith, *The Power Game: How Washington Work*. Ballantine Books, 1988, p. 173.

INTERESTS OF THE SERVICE AND THE CONTRAC-
TORS IS TO START NEW PROGRAMS AND NOT TO
WORRY ABOUT EFFICIENCY. CONTRACTORS LIKE
TO STRETCH OUT PRODUCTION OF WEAPONS
BECAUSE THEY CAN EMPLOY MORE PEOPLE FOR
YEARS. AND CONGRESSMEN LIKE TO STRETCH
OUT PROGRAMS IN THEIR DISTRICTS FOR THE
SAME REASON AND BECAUSE CONGRESS HATES
TO TAKE RESPONSIBILITY FOR KILLING ANY
WEAPONS SYSTEM.[6]

Smith goes on to describe an extraordinary performance of a military weapons analyst who fought the iron triangle in order to give evidence to the military chain of command that an anti-aircraft missile system did not work.[7] The glue to the iron triangle is money and jobs. Liberals, Democrats and Conservative Republicans in Congress all try to get jobs for their congressional districts. The people in uniform who test the weapons, become advocates for the weapons system. If the weapons gets in the inventory it is considered a success and the person may have a future with a defense contractor as an Analyst. Finally, in order to have the greatest influence in Congress and in the Bureaucracy, defense contractors try to sub-contract money all over the country. An example of this is the B-1 Bomber, when President Carter tried to scrap the program, Rockwell the contractor had spread the sub-contracting business to 48 states.[8] The spread of these contracts caused the Congress to continue the program and purchase B-1s that are used today.

People and money are what the bureaucracy needs, more and more contracts that increase the need for workers that influence Congressional action. This relationship has us building bureaucratic systems that may not reflect the reality today. As of this writing, the U.S. forces in Iraq number 140,000. We have spent trillions of dollars on weapons and the military since the end of the Vietnam War. When the Soviet Union existed the military-industrial complex, as President Eisenhower called it, said we need a large conventional force. Today, there seems to be no outcry of the performance of this equipment. Our brave soldiers scramble for scrap steel to armor their humvees. Our enemy kills our soldiers with rocket propelled grenades (RPGs) or improvised explosive devices (IEDs). These weapons cut through their vehicles like they are civilian cars. The Pentagon Iron Triangle, when it does not test fairly its vehicles and weapons systems and when it makes mistakes in the procurement of the items

needed for our troops, causes them to be killed. Instead of protesting our involvement in Iraq, we wish someone would point out how it is possible for our convoys to be blown up. If we would have gone to war against the Soviet Union, did the military planners think we would not have needed convoys and they would not have figured out how to produced IEDs? The failure of the bureaucracy to create a fighting force that can be victorious in the war we face today is the real tragedy of our experience in Iraq.

To be fair we have seen many times the failure of the bureaucracy. The FBI and CIA were asleep before September 11th, the Food and Drug Administration did not anticipate the *e. coli* outbreak of spinach that killed 13 people and made hundreds sick, and the military was not prepared for the North Korean nuclear test nor for the insurgency in Iraq.[9] Now the vast majority of people who work in the bureaucracy and are members of the different iron triangles are honest and hard working people. However, in this system if something is broken or if you have a different perspective, the bureaucratic incentive structure is such that it probably will not be fixed until there is a disaster. We finish our discussion of bureaucracy by examining the spread of bureaucracies to the international arena. Specifically, we examine the United Nations Security Council and its relevance to preventing and securing peace in the post-Cold War Age.

THE RELEVANCE OF THE UNITED NATIONS SECURITY COUNCIL

On a Sunday evening in early October 2006, the North Koreans claimed to have tested a nuclear weapon. The Americans, South Koreans, Japanese, Chinese, Russians and North Koreans had been discussing the ramification of introducing nuclear weapons to the Korean Peninsula for over six years. A week later, the international community, as represented by the Permanent Members of the United Nations (U.N.) Security Council has yet to vote on a meaningful resolution. Is the bureaucracy that was founded after World War II still able to prevent major conflict?

The U.N. Security Council socializes each Permanent Member by providing a permanent forum to

---

[6]Ibid. p. 174.
[7]Ibid. p. 175.
[8]Ibid.

[9]For a complete report of the incompetency of military for the invasion of Iraq planning please see: Michael G. Gordon, Bernard E. Trainor, *Cobra II: The Inside Story of the Invasion and Occupation of Iraq*, New York: Panethon Books, 2006. For CIA and FBI incompetence see William E. Odom, *Fixing Intelligence for a More Secure America*. New Haven: Yale University Press, 2003.

discuss the resolution of disputes between states. This socialization includes both public and private consultations. The interaction takes the form of meetings and resolutions. Votes on the U.N. Security Council resolutions become part of the recorded behavior of each Permanent Member. Similar to Congress, once the resolutions are passed, the U.N. bureaucracy will take the steps necessary to implement the resolutions if their member countries give the U.N. the resources and mandates. The U.N. Security Council Resolutions do have the power of international law.

The U.N. Charter envisioned the role of international law as a device that would put some limits on the choices the strong powers would have in following their own national objectives. Tae Jin Kahng investigated the nature of disputes handled by the U.N. Security Council and the role played by international law.[10] The U.N. has a permanent bureaucracy; however, they do not have a permanent armed force that is in their control.[11] The founding of the U.N. and the participation of the members of the U.N. shows after World War II, states understood that total war was no longer a winning option, due to the nuclear capacity of all the Permanent Members. International law and the role of an international bureaucracy that could mediate and have peacekeeping abilities became more important in settling conflicts by the formation of legal precedents and conventions.[12]

With the change in the international environment and the end of the non-proliferation regime, will the U.N. bureaucracy have to become permanent and more professional on issues such as terrorism, weapons of mass destruction and the spread of nuclear technology? As the globe becomes smaller, is there a role for an international bureaucracy that can have the scientific know-how and the resources to be able to track important issues such as global warming, migration, pandemics and terrorism, without the interference of political considerations? In 1990, Arthur Stein wrote that in the post-Cold War, international environment conflict and cooperation are no longer separate, instead the two appear together in many of the problem areas around the globe.[13]

Another study showed that the Permanent Members of the Security Council are cooperating, while at the same time regional powers and local groups are in conflict.[14] The major powers such as the U.S., China, and Russia, seem to have economic interests that are in common, yet on political issues such as proliferation of nuclear weapons in North Korea there is serious division. It looks at the time of this writing that the U.N. is demonstrating it does not have the power nor will to reform its bureaucracy to make a difference in the international environment.

PRIVATE BUREAUCRACIES

Whether on the international or domestic level, the power to enforce rules and regulations is not only the realm of government. Today, the power of marketing, advertising and business intelligence, enable private concerns know more about our behavior than the government does. Credit card companies can change your interest rate when they learn you have been late on your car payment. If you move to a different area, your car insurance can go higher (car insurance is based on zip code and your driving record). If you have traveled, you know the credit card companies will contact you if they see a pattern of spending that is not typical of your normal habits. All of this information is collected and archived and used to formulate your credit history and credit score.

Being a private bureaucracy does not make the bureaucracy more efficient nor does it negate the models that we have discussed previously. Microsoft and IBM's bureaucracies do not enforce laws but they do enforce such rules and regulations as warranties and the way they do business. The next time you buy a product and have a problem with the warranty, try calling their customer support. What you will find is the same attitude of the worker who works at the Post Office or the DMV. That is of course assuming you actually get to speak with a person.

The private bureaucracies keep tabs on people in order to build a profile of your habits. Every time you are on the Internet, someone is keeping track of the website you are surfing on. We mentioned earlier the Senate Confirmation hearing of Supreme Court nominee Robert H. Bork. During these hearings, someone subpoenaed his video rental account and started asking him about the movies he rented. After this episode Congress passed a law protecting the privacy of peo-

[10]Tae Jin Kahng, *Law, Politics and the Security Council: An Inquiry into the Handling of the Legal Questions Involved in International Disputes and Situations.* The Hauge: Martinus Nijoff Press, 1964, p. 14.

[11]Originally, the U.N. Charter did call for a military force. However, the Permanent Members of the Security Council never implemented this provision of the charter.

[12]Patrick C. Coaty, *The End of Irrelevance: A Study of the U.N. Security Council's Permanent Members Position and Behavior in the Post-Cold War Era.* Claremont, CA: Unpublished Dissertation, p. 51.

[13]Arthur A. Stein, *Why Nations Cooperate: Circumstance and Choice in International Relations.* Ithaca: Cornell University Press, 1990, p. 12.

[14]Patrick C. Coaty, *The End of Irrelevance: A Study of the U.N. Security Council's Permanent Members Position and Behavior in the Post-Cold War Era.* Claremont, CA: Unpublished Dissertation, p. 146.

ple's video accounts. The information this private bureaucracy has potentially could be abuse easier than governmental records. Identity theft is a major concern. We hear news stories about lap top computers being lost or information accounts being hacked into. Congress and the public bureaucracy does use the information gathered by this private bureaucracy to solve crimes and to have surveillance (to fight the War on Terror, phone companies were cooperating with the government to give phone records of suspected terrorists). Recently, a Chief Executive Officer has been charged with a crime because they hired private detectives to gather private information on the Board of Directors. They were trying to access the information the private bureaucracy had on the members of the Board. Their mistake was they lied about who they were in order to get around the privacy regulations and laws that the private companies had put into place. The private investigators posed as either governmental officials or potential employers doing background investigations.

The collection of data and the enforcement of rules and regulations based on the data are recent phenomena because of the information revolution. A number, either a social security number or credit score number, are very powerful codes that enable a person in this country to work, get a loan, or even travel. These numbers are so powerful there is a black market in forged social security cards and other personal identification documents.

The protection of personal information is a new frontier of civil liberties, especially if people learn that their information is worth money and they have not given their consent for their profiles to be sold. Again, this should be on the political agenda, but has yet to be taken seriously by interest groups, politicians or the public bureaucrats.

CONCLUSION

In this chapter, we have defined bureaucracies as any organization that enforces rules and policies. We began by discussing the ways the Federal government enforces its laws and regulations. Starting in 1789, with three governmental departments (State, Treasury and War) the President's Cabinet is now over 15 departments with the last one, the Department of Homeland Security added as a result of the failure of the government to protect its citizens from the September 11th attacks.

We then described Max Weber's model of bureaucracy and the universal characteristics every bu-

reaucracy has, they are: Hierarchy, Specialization, Rules and Regulations, and Neutrality. Using these four characteristics, we then analyzed four models of bureaucracies and observations that lead scholars to categorize the dominant behaviors we find in bureaucracies. We then explored two areas that are new to the study of bureaucracies, the establishment of an international bureaucracy to fight trans-national issues such as terrorism, health, and immigration. We saw how the U.N. is an international bureaucracy. However, with the latest challenges by North Korea and Iran, it seems the U.N. Security Council may be losing its relevance in the post-Cold War world. Furthermore, we explored the new challenge of civil liberties posed by the establishment of private bureaucracy. These bureaucracies collect personal data and then report this data to credit agencies and banks. The use of the Internet for shopping and surfing gives marketers a profile of who uses and how the product is being used. This can create a challenge to privacy.

Health records and genetic information once in these bureaucracies could prevent someone from finding employment or getting health care. We seem to have put a lot of power in the hands of bureaucrats either public or private, yet they are not elected and their accountability as proven by the Hewlitt-Packard case can be abused. The power of the bureaucracy has the potential to take our civil liberties away as much as any terrorist, yet it does not seem to be on the political radar as of yet.

This completes our analysis of the institutions that form our government. The following two chapters will describe how public policy is formed on the international stage and on the domestic stage. We have described all of the machinery of the government. Now, imagine it is similar to describing a car. Now, we will turn the key and see how all the parts run. Think of public policy as the output of all the machinery we have spent describing in the previous chapters.

TERMS TO REMEMBER

BUREAUCRACY
WEBERIAN MODEL
ACQUISITIVE MODEL
MONOPOLISTIC MODEL
CIVIL SERVICE
KEYNESIANISM
MONETARISTS
SUPPLY SIDE ECONOMICS

The Bureaucracy

TRUE OR FALSE QUESTIONS

1. The bureaucracy does not touch our daily lives.   T / F

2. Social Security is not part of the bureaucracy.   T / F

3. Bureaucracy cares about your personal circumstances.   T / F

4. Bureaucracies only exist in government.   T / F

5. There are four universal properties of bureaucracies.   T / F

6. One of the properties of bureaucracies is they are democratic.   T / F

7. Merit is a property of bureaucratic management.   T / F

8. The Department of Motor Vehicles is not a bureaucracy.   T / F

9. Your credit card company is a bureaucracy.   T / F

10. Max Weber is famous for studying bureaucracies.   T / F

MULTIPLE CHOICE QUESTIONS

11. Which is not a property of bureaucracies?
    a. Hierarchical
    b. Neutral
    c. Specialization
    d. Democratic

12. Which is a model of bureaucracies?
    a. Garbage can model
    b. Garbage in model
    c. Garbage disposal model
    d. Garbage bag model

13. The acquisitive model's premise is
    a. bureaucracies get smaller as they get older
    b. bureaucracies get bigger as they get older
    c. bureaucracies become more efficient as they get older
    d. bureaucracies become more inefficient as they get older

14. The monopolistic model's premise is
    a. bureaucracies get smaller as they get older
    b. bureaucracies get bigger as they get older
    c. bureaucracies become more efficient as they get older
    d. bureaucracies become more inefficient as they get older

15. Which is not a bureaucracy?
    a. Police
    b. Fire department
    c. Army
    d. None of the above

16. In 1789 there were how many departments in the Cabinet?
    a. Two
    b. Seven
    c. Five
    d. Three

17. The spoils system started under the Presidency of
    a. John F. Kennedy
    b. Chester Arthur
    c. Andrew Jackson
    d. Abraham Lincoln

18. The Pendleton Act was designed to create
    a. Department of Fashion
    b. Bureau of Standards
    c. Civil Service
    d. Department of Health for Children

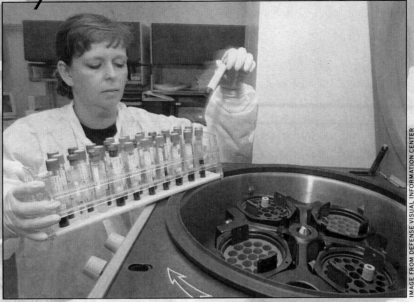

chapter thirteen

IMAGE FROM DEFENSE VISUAL INFORMATION CENTER

THE PUBLIC POLICY PROCESS: DOMESTIC POLICY

INTRODUCTION

The previous chapters have described the political environment, including the three different branches of government, the bureaucracy, the role of interest groups and political parties. In this chapter, we examine what happens when all of the parts of government are put together. As with a student who is studying medicine or automotive mechanics, once a person understands the constituent parts of the system they are studying, then they can turn the engine on or study the body in action. That is our objective in this chapter. We will describe the different aspects of the public policy process. Using Medicare as an issue, we will see how this program was introduced by Harry Truman and fifteen years later how it became a Federal program under President Johnson; and later, under President George W. Bush, how Medicare has become one of the biggest programs and biggest challenges facing domestic policy makers. Then we will introduce three schools of economic thought —Keynesianism, Monetarism and Supply Side Eco-

nomics. These different economic philosophies have a great deal of influence on where one stands on whether the government should be involved in regulating the economy.

We will also examine the relationship between young people and the media. How can the public policy process work if young people are not interested in politics? We did discuss voter participation of young people in a previous chapter, however, we examine the behavior of media consumption of young people. How can an issue be on the public agenda if a whole segment of the population is not aware of a problem. This chapter is organized into two main parts. First, we will briefly examine the patterns of media consumption by young people and compare it to other generations. This data was used originally for explaining young people's voting behavior. We are using it to explain the formation of attitudes in relation to young people's understanding the formation of public policy.

Then, we will trace the nine steps of the public policy process and show that there is a "chicken and egg" problem with young people's attitude toward government. The issues that concern young people do not get on the public policy agenda because they do not vote. Or, is it the other way around, that because the public policy process does not address the issues of concern by young people, therefore, they do not vote? This question cannot be answered in this chapter. It can, however, be introduced for the reader to consider this questions and come to their own conclusion. We start, with an examination of the media consumption of young people.

NEWSPAPER AND TELEVISION VIEWING PATTERNS BY GENERATION

We have discussed the importance of television on politics starting with the election of John F. Kennedy in 1960. Even in Kennedy's era, newspapers and magazines were more influential than television. In this era, people who were born in 1937 were asked in 1957 if they read the newspaper every day. Over 70 percent of twenty-year-olds in 1957 read a newspaper every day.[1] By 2004, the rate had dropped to 20 percent of twenty-year-olds read a newspaper everyday.[2] If only 20 percent of young people are reading the newspaper every day, can we assume they get their news from television? Not really, there seems to be less "water-cooler" shows in which all of us see on television. Young people use remotes and DVDs more than older people. If there is a preemption of network television programming young people will use alternative programming options, either turning to a cable station that is not showing the political programming or putting on a DVD.[3] As the media evolves into narrowcasting and we all have 500 channels to choose from, shows that capture the country as a whole will become extinct. When there is a Presidential news conference, speech or a political national convention, young people seem to turn the channel thinking that this programming is for older people.

Thomas Mann, executive director of the American Political Science Association, talks about the attitude change of Congressmen in their use of the media:

IN THE OLD DAYS, IT WAS SHOW HORSES VERSUS WORKHORSES IN CONGRESS . . . IF YOU WANTED TO GET SOMETHING DONE, YOU HAD TO WORK INSIDE THE LEGISLATURE. AND THE SHOW HORSES WERE JUST POSTURING TO THE PUBLIC. THAT'S CHANGED. NOW, IT'S SEEN THAT PLAYING THE MEDIA IS AN IMPORTANT RESOURCE IN PASSING LEGISLATION. SERIOUS MEMBERS UNDERSTAND THAT THEY HAVE TO SELL THEIR STORY OUTSIDE OF THE INSTITUTION TO HAVE AN IMPACT INSIDE IT.[4]

Even though we live in an era that politicians are more media savvy, it seems young people are one step ahead of them in manipulating the media to their tastes and avoiding all of the programming that is designed to help people understand the public policy process.

Would this change if there were a military draft? During the 1960s, every campus became a center of political activity and opposition to the draft. Since most young men had an obligation to serve involuntarily in the military, they had a vested interest in following what the government policies would be concerning the Vietnam War, the military, and veteran affairs. There was a draft bill introduced by the Democrats in 2004, however, there does not seem to have been a spike in young people's interest in political events. John Kerry thought there would be an anti-draft, anti-war increase in voter turnout for the 2004 election. There was an increase from 28 percent in 2000 to 41 percent but this increase in participation did not translate itself into victory for John Kerry. Political scientists and politicians make an assumption that because a person is young they support the Democratic Party. Martin Wattenberg of the University of California writes that:

FIRST, BECAUSE OF THEIR OPENNESS TO NEW POLICY APPROACHES, THEY SHOULD BE MORE SUSCEPTIBLE TO THE APPEALS OF THIRD-PARTY CANDIDATES. SECOND, GIVEN THAT THEIR POLICY STANDS ARE GENERALLY MORE IN LINE WITH LIBERAL PRINCIPLES THAN ARE THEIR ELDERS', THEY SHOULD BE MORE LIKELY TO HAVE SUPPORTED THE DEMOCRATS IN RECENT ELECTIONS.[5]

Wattenberg makes the same mistake that the John Kerry campaign made when addressing the issue of voting behavior and media tastes of young people. They assume if they can get young people to vote, then they will support Democrats. If you look at the turnout according to Wattenberg's book, you see voting turnout of people under 21 increased from 28–42

---

[1]Martin P. Wattenberg, *Is Voting for Young People?* New York: Pearson/Longman, 2007, p. 16.
[2]Ibid.
[3]Ibid. p. 45.

[4]Hedrick Smith, *The Power Game: How Washington Works*. New York: Balantine Books, 1988, p. 525.
[5]Martin P. Wattenberg, *Is Voting for Young People?* New York: Pearson/Longman, 2007, p. 149.

percent. He then goes on to examine the results in both Florida in 2000 and Ohio in 2004. The results are, President Bush received 40 percent of the vote by this age group in 2000 in Florida and in Ohio he received 42 percent.[6] The conclusion made is if more young people would have voted then the Democrats would have won. This conclusion is not necessarily accurate. We know that family is the dominant factor when determining opinions and behavior. During the 1960s, older people were liberal Democrats and their children were also liberal Democrats. The changes in the country that occurred during the 1970s and 1980s made the Republican party the majority party in the 1990s. Therefore, we would contend, using Wattenberg's own evidence on how young people consume media, that their opinions would be more influenced by their families. Furthermore, even if young people would have voted more, it is not conclusive that they would support liberal Democrats. Keep in mind, it was young voters who supported Goldwater in 1964, Reagan in 1980 and they grew up to participate in the "Republican Revolution" in 1994. On college campuses, there are groups of young people who are politically active for the College Republicans. Finally, Wattenberg examines young people's support for third party candidates and concludes young people support third party candidates more than their older counterparts. If young people on the whole are more liberal than older voters then how come only two percent supported Ralph Nader's candidacy in 2000 and even less in 2004?

This conclusion by the academics and political strategists is a projection of their own wishful thinking. They are discounting the affect of family, religion and other influences. *Is Voting for Young People?* is a fine book, however, the conclusion that young people (if they voted) would have made Al Gore President or John Kerry President, is like saying the Los Angeles Clippers would have won the National Basketball Championship if "Shaq" was on the team. Maybe, but he is not on the Clippers, therefore, the conclusion is not supported by the evidence. Young people (under 21) did turnout more in 2004 than in 2000 but President Bush still won.

Maybe young people have a poor voting participation rate and use the media differently than older people because they are satisfied with the way the public policy process addresses issues. If I am satisfied with the political process, either out of ignorance or because my needs are being met and the needs of

my family are being met, then that might be the motive to ignore politics and be more concerned with entertainment.[7]

Again, Wattenberg concludes this generation is one of the most politically ignorant ever. He draws the connection between formal education and supporting President Bush's second term.

> I WOULD ARGUE THAT THE LACK OF ATTENTION YOUNG ADULTS CURRENTLY PAY TO MAINSTREAM MEDIA HAS LED THEM TO MISS OUT ON MANY HIGHLY CONSEQUENTIAL POLITICAL STORIES. IT SHOULD BE NOTED THAT TWO OF THE 2004 STORIES THAT YOUNG ADULTS PAID RELATIVELY LITTLE ATTENTION TO COMPARED TO THE ELDERLY WERE: 1) REPORTS THAT WEAPONS OF MASS DESTRUCTION HAD NOT BEEN FOUND IN IRAQ; AND 2) REPORTS ABOUT THE CONDITION OF THE U.S. ECONOMY.[8]

We would contend younger people are more sophisticated consumers of the media. What Wattenberg calls the "mainstream media" according to your personal political perspective is no longer mainstream. As an example, depending on who you ask, the economy in 2004 was expanding. So if young people were not ignoring the reports on the economy, would they have supported the Republicans generally and President Bush more specifically in 2004? These conclusions demonstrate the perception divide between young people and older people.

Having pointed out the problems with the conclusions presented, we contend the media environment has changed and there is narrow casting. We also contend young people are not paying attention to the traditional forms of media, however, they are sophisticated consumers of the media, and they may well be satisfied consumers of political information from other sources such as family, peers and other factors that we discussed in earlier chapters. This may change if there is another terrorist attack, or if the economy goes into recession, or there is a call for a military draft.

We have to remember that America is a free country, for young people as well as old. Both have the right not to participate in the political environment. Of course, they do so at their own peril. In the next section of this chapter, we analyze how public policy is formed, keeping in mind that a majority of young people have traditionally not participated in this process even when there was a military draft and

---

[6]Ibid. p. 151.

[7]Martin P. Wattenberg, *Is Voting for Young People?* New York: Pearson/Longman, 2007, p. 72. The stories young people paid attention to in 2004 were the following: the Summer Olympics in Athens, release of the movie *Fahrenheit 9/11* and the release of the movie *The Passion of the Christ.* Page 73.

[8]Ibid. pp. 74–75.

they fought to lower the voting age to 18.[9] The demise of the young voters and their political knowledge from the golden era of campus radicals so many academics hark back to is just not a reality (if you use their own data). The public policy process has endured and will continue to endure. Would we like to see more young people using the media to gain political knowledge? Of course. Is it a sign that our political institutions are weakening? Not necessarily. We would contend as we have in previous chapters it may be that our young people have been trained to ignore laws, therefore, when they think of the public policy process they do not realize they do have the power to change things. Maybe this could be an issue of low internal political efficacy. Either way, the media consumption of young people are different and their tastes are not necessarily reflected in the public policy process. Given the background of the behavior of young people, we now turn our attention to the nine steps of the public policy process.

THE NINE STEPS OF THE PUBLIC POLICY PROCESS

The reason we started this chapter on the public policy process, with a discussion on the way young people view the meeting and their role in the political environment, is to preface our examination with the public policy process to show many of the things we will examine, for different reasons, fail to apply to 60 percent of the young people in our society. Yet, policies and law promulgated by the government affects 100 percent of the young people in this country. We contend it is not the amount of formal education that other authors look at, it is the content of education that has failed the young people of our country. We hope this examination of the nine step process will help contribute to the political understanding of the reader, in order to close the gap previously discussed.

The public policy process entails nine steps, these steps include:

1. A crisis occurs.
2. Placement of the problem on the national agenda.
3. The problem becomes a national issue.
4. A plea for action.
5. Debate and compromise on the type of action that should take place.
6. The placement of the issues in the formal framework of government.
7. Implementation.
8. Effects of the implementation.
9. Evaluation of the public policy.

We will use the development of the Medicare program to illustrate the relationship of all these steps with the political dynamics we have learned about in previous chapters. We start with step one: a crisis occurs.

A CRISIS OCCURS

The need for government medical coverage for Americans was introduced by President Harry Truman.[10] Truman and the New Deal Democrats saw the need during the Great Depression for people to get medical care. After the assassination of John F. Kennedy, Lyndon B. Johnson saw a crisis. In the early 1960s, three-fourths of the causes of deaths of Americans came from heart attacks, strokes or cancer.[11] Johnson throughout his career had been an advocate of getting the finest health care to everyone. Johnson also had a personal history with these diseases, his father had died of a heart attack, his mother from cancer, and he had his own heart attack when he was 46.[12] Johnson's first move was to call a task force that was going to tackle heart disease, strokes and cancer. The commission said there could be substantial advancement in conquering if 2.8 billion dollars would be invested in research, as had been done in conquering polio and infectious diseases early in the century.[13]

Robert Dallek shows how Johnson changed gears from a program to fight the causes of death in the United States to a campaign promise for a health benefit for older Americans.

PARTLY RESPONDING TO OPINION SURVEYS BY POLLSTER OLIVER QUAYLE OF THE MOST IMPORTANT ELECTION YEAR ISSUES, JOHNSON PUBLICLY MADE MEDICARE A HIGH LEGISLATIVE PRIORITY IN THE 1965 CONGRESSIONAL TERM. IN NOVEMBER, ON THE EVE OF THE ELECTION, WHEN ASKED BY A REPORTER WHETHER MEDICARE WOULD BE A "MUST" BILL NEXT YEAR, JOHNSON ANSWERED: "JUST TOP OF THE LIST."[14]

---

[9]Martin P. Wattenberg, *Is Voting for Young People?* New York: Pearson/ Longman, 2007, p. 99. Voter turnout in 1972 for people under 21 was 48 percent, in 1976 it dropped to 38 percent, and in 2000 it continued to drop to 28 percent.

[10]David McCullough, *Truman.* Simon & Schuster, 1992, p. 990.

[11]Robert Dallek, *Flawed Giant: Lyndon Johnson and His Times 1961–1973.* New York: Oxford University Press, 1998, p. 204.

[12]Ibid.

[13]Ibid.

[14]Ibid. p. 205.

Johnson started with the crisis created when people die of heart attacks, strokes and cancer, and because of politics and public opinion polls, the idea of healthcare for elderly was placed on the national agenda. That is the second step in the public policy process.

PLACEMENT OF THE PROBLEM ON THE NATIONAL AGENDA

After the 1964 election, the Democrats controlled the Executive and Legislative branches. Except for Franklin D. Roosevelt's famous first one hundred days, President Johnson used his political capital to tackle problems and put issues on the national agenda. Johnson would propose hundreds of programs in an umbrella phrase called the "Great Society." He would also fight the Vietnam War. Americans saw government as an engine for progress, not a source of their problems. With President Johnson and the liberal congressional landslide of the mid-1960s, the issue of Medicare had become a national issue, with senior citizens and unions rallying for passage of the bill. This takes us to the third step.

THE PROBLEM BECOMES A NATIONAL ISSUE

The advantage of people who advocated a program for the elderly was there are old people everywhere in the country. North, south, east and west—even though we were demographically a different country in the 1960s, almost everyone had grandparents or elderly relatives who needed healthcare. The labor unions who were also at the height of their power (this is when the U.S. still had a large manufacturing lead over other countries in the world) allied themselves with the government to advocate solving this national issue.[15]

In the case of Medicare, after Harry Truman introduced the problem and John F. Kennedy tried to rally the issue before his death, it was Lyndon Johnson who took this issue from a crisis, to placement on the national agenda to a public policy program in a matter of months. This takes us to step four and five in the public policy process: a public policy response and debate and compromise on the proposed action.

A PLEA FOR ACTION

We have said, President Johnson made Medicare a national issue by putting it on top of his agenda and making it a personal campaign. He urged his Cabinet secretaries to make Medicare an important issue for the election in 1964 and the midterm elections of 1966. Stories of how the elderly were suffering and needed help were making the airways and there was a plea for action by the government to create a solution. President Johnson and the Congressional leadership drafted a bill. However, this bill did have some opposition. This takes us to step five: debate and compromise.

DEBATE AND COMPROMISE ON THE ACTION

The Chairman of Ways and Means Committee during this period was a Congressman named Wilbur Mills. He was opposed to the Medicare program on the grounds that the country could not afford to give healthcare to all the people who would become elderly in the future. The baby boom generation, who were just children and teenagers at this time would grow and the ability of the country to provide universal healthcare for everyone over 65 or 72 or whatever the age, worried Wilbur Mills. Throughout the history of Medicare as an issue, Wilbur Mills had opposed the idea.[16] Mills was also not very sensitive to Johnson's pressure. He had a safe seat in Congress and had a conservative majority in his committee.[17] Then the Democratic landslide and the dominance of liberal politics happened in 1964.

Wilbur Mills was a political realist. He realized his conservative majority of the committee was gone. He no longer had the leverage to block the bill. This brings us to the sixth step in the public policy process.

THE PLACEMENT OF THE ISSUE IN THE FORMAL HALLS OF GOVERNMENT

President Johnson had won where other Democratic Presidents had failed. In President Johnson's State of the Union Address he put it this way:

---

[15]Ibid. p. 206.

[16]Ibid. p. 206.

[17]Remember, this is before the election of 1974. Chairmen of committees, especially the Ways and Means Committee, had a great deal of power. They could kill a bill very easily and Wilbur Mills had done that to all of the forms of Medicare that had been introduced before.

SINCE "FOUR OUT OF FIVE PERSONS 65 OR OLDER HAVE A DISABILITY OR CHRONIC DIS-EASE," SINCE HOSPITAL STAYS AND COSTS FOR FOLKS OVER SIXTY-FIVE ARE TWICE WHAT THEY ARE FOR YOUNGER PEOPLE, SINCE "ALMOST HALF OF THE ELDERLY HAVE NO HEALTH INSUR-ANCE AT ALL" AND SINCE "THE AVERAGE RE-TIRED COUPLE CANNOT AFFORD THE COST OF ADEQUATE HEALTH PROTECTION UNDER PRIVATE HEALTH INSURANCE," THE PRESIDENT ASKED THAT SOCIAL SECURITY "BE EXTENDED TO FINANCE THE COST OF BASIC HEALTH SERVICES" THROUGH "REGULAR, MODEST CONTRIBUTIONS DURING WORKING YEARS."[18]

Johnson was so confident of Medicare's passing that it was the first legislative bill of the new Congress, it was H.R. 1 and S. 1.[19] Although Medicare was responsible for covering seniors, it did not cover doctor's fees. After quick passage the next step comes into place, that of implementation.

IMPLEMENTATION

This is one of the most important steps. If the law that is passed by Congress is not effective, then the whole idea of government as a solution becomes moot. Putting what Johnson called for in his State of the Union Address had to be put in practical policies. Wilbur Mills helped draft the legislation that would provide 60 days of hospital coverage and 240 days of home health visits and 180 days of skilled nursing home care for recipients of Social Security. In order to foil Republican and interest group counterattacks, Mills suggested that Medicare be changed to a three layer cake: hospital care, a voluntary insurance program for doctor's bills and an expanded program for the poor. The expansion guaranteed support from the Congress.

After ten years in existence, Medicare is one of the most popular programs that the Johnson Administration and his Great Society produced.[20] Johnson was even able to get the American Medical Association to support Medicare, something Harry Truman was unable to do when he called for universal healthcare in 1948.[21] Now the law is in place and has been implemented. The next step is to study the effects of the implementation.

THE EFFECTS OF THE IMPLEMENTATION

Although Medicare was a very popular program through the 1970s, it has also been a demographic time bomb. To enlist the support of the medical community there were no real controls put on the government's reimbursement policy. As Dallek reports on the effects of implementation:

THE RESULTS OF THIS GENEROSITY WERE STAGGERING INCREASES IN MEDICAL COSTS TO THE ENTIRE SOCIETY. WHERE TOTAL MEDICARE EXPENDITURES WERE 3.5 BILLION IN THE FIRST YEAR OF THE PROGRAM, THEY HAD RISEN TO 144 BILLION BY 1993, DESPITE REPEATED ATTEMPTS BY THE GOVERNMENT TO REIN THEM IN. THE APPROXIMATELY 5 PERCENT OF GROSS NATIONAL PRODUCT AMERICAN'S SPENT ON HEALTH CARE IN 1965 HAD INCREASED THREEFOLD BY THE EARLY NINETIES.[22]

President Reagan during the 1980s saw the rising costs and the effort to reform Medicare and Social Security, and was punished by the voters every time there was any effort to trim the costs to the government. The final step in the public policy process is evaluation.

EVALUATION OF THE PUBLIC POLICY

Almost everyone agrees that the Medicare program is an imperfect solution to a problem that is being faced by other developed nations such as Japan and the countries of Western Europe. The problem is of course that older people vote much more than young people. The reality of politics in the United States is, Medicare is seen as an entitlement in which older Americans (even if they are wealthy or have private insurance) will not give up. Therefore, the evaluation process if very difficult for a popular program that has political punch. Presidents have set up "blue ribbon commissions"[23] to study the long term health of both Social Security and Medicare. Their findings are that the system will be bankrupt if a combination of procedures, such as smaller benefits and larger taxes, are not implemented. Very little has been done to change the nature and the problems of Medicare.

---

[18]Robert Dallek, *Flawed Giant: Lyndon Johnson and His Times 1961–1973*. New York: Oxford University Press, 1998, p. 207.

[19]Ibid.

[20]Ibid. p. 210.

[21]Ibid.

---

[22]Ibid.

[23]Blue Ribbon Commission is a label used for a commission with experts and retired political leaders who recommend public policies in a political vacuum. Some of the commissions have a great deal of influence such as the 9/11 Commission. However most reports are very good in evaluating public policy but, they do deal with the political reality of majoritarian politics.

On a popular program such as Medicare, we see the nine steps of the public policy process may take very little time as a result of public demand and popular support. However, the last two steps, understanding the implementation of the policy and evaluating the policy can take decades and provide many unintended problems for future policy makers. Democracies have a problem that is known as majoritarian politics.

This type of political decision making has two contradictory demands on political leaders, people demand more services and less taxes. This of course creates incredible financial strain on the public institutions. We all pay Social Security taxes, and we all expect to retire at 65. As the baby-boom generation gets older, the baby-boomers who were born in 1941–1942 are now close to retirement age. During the next twenty or so years, the largest generation ever produced will start to pull money out of the Social Security and Medicare programs.

President Roosevelt, when he envisioned Social Security picked 65 because of the German retirement plan that was created in the 1800s by Otto Von Bismarck. In the 1800s, very few people made it to 65 and fewer still lived to be in their 80s. The baby-boom generation will be retiring at 65 and probably live another thirty years in retirement. This means the younger person we talked about earlier in the chapter will be paying more and more for the baby-boom worker. Will this make today's young person a voter, it really does not matter, since the baby-boomers have the numbers and, in our society, majority rules.

This tension between generations has caused great consternation for political leaders. In 2004 after being re-elected, President George W. Bush tried his hand at Social Security reform. Similar to President Johnson, President Bush tried to use his office to bring attention to the crisis that will happen to Social Security in the future. Flush with victory, he tried to condense the first four steps in the public policy process in the first weeks of his second term.

Where President Johnson succeeded and President Bush failed, were the Congress and the country were not prepared to talk about Social Security. President Bush's campaign in 2004 centered around issues that were related to the War on Terror. After his victory he suddenly changed the course of the national discussion away from the War on Terror to Social Security. The failure to lead and manipulate the media and public opinion to show there was an immediate threat to Social Security and that it would trump the importance of the War on Terror or Iraq was wrongheaded.

This mistake has seemed to plague President Bush's second administration. The Social Security reform act was a failure. We could say it did not get past the third or fourth step in the process. Step 3—the problem becomes a national issue or step 4 a plea for action is wanted, never happened in 2004 and 2005. Today, every time President Bush attempts to bring up the issue of Social Security reform the press charges him with trying to change the subject from the problems the country is having in Iraq, Afghanistan, Iran or North Korea.

We see in this examination of the public policy process that it takes the persuasion of the President, the cooperation of Congress, the implementation of the law by the bureaucracy and finally acceptance by interest groups and the public to have major programs established in order to attempt to solve problems. Especially in the domestic policy realm, where people's education, home mortgages, retirement checks and healthcare are the dominant issues. Majoritarian politics creates an environment where politicians try to give us programs and skirt the costs to either other groups who are in the minority or to groups that will have to pay in the future. In the case of Medicare and Social Security, political leaders have done both.

Presidents since Ronald Reagan have tried to change the dynamics of the debate between the people who are paying Social Security taxes and the people who are receiving the checks. To no avail, since the people who are retired argue Social Security was an insurance policy and they paid the premiums all of their working lives so it really is not their problem if the system is going broke. Young workers realize in thirty years from now there will be no way they can retire at 65. The Social Security and Medicare reform of the Bush Administration shows the weakness of the public policy process. Our leaders cannot change programs unless there is a crisis and the public calls for action. We seem not to be able to fix things or reform things until they collapse. Since the establishment of these programs, they have been evaluated and Presidents and Congresses have tried to change the programs. However, the iron triangles of programs and the beneficiaries who receive checks so far have been able to stop any changes in these programs. Whether or not a politician, interest group or individual was for Medicare or against it had a lot to do with what type of economic philosophy they had.

Did they believe in Social Darwinism, where the government has a very small role in regulating the economy and providing social services? This was the dominant belief in the 1800s before the development of economics as a science. Today, there are three major schools of thought in economics and they contribute to our understanding of how government should regulate the economy. They are: Keynesianism, Monetarism, and Supply Side. In the next part of the chapter, we will compare and contrast these three schools and the political economic philosophy spawned by their assumptions and conclusions.

ECONOMIC PHILOSOPHY AND GOVERNMENT REGULATION

The government's involvement in regulating the economy has two broad policy categories—fiscal policy and monetary policy. Fiscal policy are those laws and regulations that deal with trade, taxes and revenue. How the government budgets its money and what behaviors are rewarded and what behaviors are punished are all under the fiscal policy of the Federal government. As an example under fiscal policy, we reward people buying houses—interest rates for mortgages are tax deductible. Also, we punish people for buying luxury cars—there is a luxury car tax. Laws such as these are known as fiscal policy.

Monetary policy is handled by the Federal Reserve. The Federal Reserve is an independent government agency that was established to oversee and control interest rates and money supply. It is the Treasury Department that is responsible for the printing of money. It is the Federal Reserve who determines the monetary policy of money. So, if a country is going to have loose credit or tight credit (otherwise known as credit liquidity) or low or high interest rates, this is the responsibility of the Federal Reserve. The Federal Reserve was instituted by Congress and President Woodrow Wilson. It consists of regional banks and then there is a central board in Washington, D.C. The leader of the Federal Reserve is appointed by the President and confirmed by the Senate, but has a different term than the President (seven years) and he or she is entirely independent of the Executive branch.

One can see the difference between fiscal and monetary policy. The Congress plays a very big role in determining fiscal policy. Remember it is Congress that has the true budgetary power in fiscal policy matters. Neither the President nor Congress has a great deal of direct power over monetary policy. That was taken away from them with the establishment of the Federal Reserve. Keeping this difference between

fiscal and monetary policies in your mind, let us explore the three dominant schools of thought in economics. We will start with the Keynesians.

KEYNESIAN ECONOMIC PHILOSOPHY

John Maynard Keynes was an economic pioneer who helped the British fund their efforts in World War I by speculating in the currency markets of Europe and handing the profits to the War Department. His books were very influential. In one he predicted the economic consequences of the Treaty of Versailles would contribute to another world war. During his lifetime and after, his influence on economic thinking was revolutionary.

Keynes major contribution to economic philosophy is the role of government in regulating economic activities. Before Keynes, the most influential book on economics and government's role in economics was the *Wealth of Nations* by Adam Smith. In this book Smith wrote of the magic of the hidden hand of capitalism, in which people are greedy and selfish to get rich and this in turn benefits societies. If people accumulate capital then they provide the benefits of economic development, the classic hidden hand. Smith's conclusion is government should do very little to interfere with the economic life of its citizens.

Keynes disagreed fundamentally with this idea. He argued instead of a hidden hand generating economic development, the government must be able to regulate and normalize the business cycle in a country. Let us say that the business cycle has the shape of sine wave. There is a peak and a valley. Keynes contended it was government's job to change the sine wave with its peaks and valleys to a straight line. So when the economy is at a peak, the government should have a strict monetary policy and tax consumption in order to slow demand. The government should save the money in special funds. So when the economy turns and the business cycle ends up in a valley (called a recession or depression depending on the severity of the valley) the government then has resources to lower taxes and deficit spending in order to create demand again and keep the economy on an even level.

The crisis of the Great Depression was a valley that Keynesianism seemed perfect to explain. The policies of the New Deal were designed with Keynes' ideas in mind. All the programs Roosevelt and the Congress passed under the National Recovery Act were designed to get money into the hands of people, so that the demand for goods could recover and a normal economy would return. The role of the Federal government in the economic health of the country since the Great Depression has been an accepted feature of American life since the Depression. Richard Nixon in his first term, demonstrated that he was also a Keynesian with one of his domestic policy experts Daniel Patrick Moynihan (who would later become a Senator from New York). He had established economic regulation in areas of the environment, clean air bill and affirmative action to end the dual school system in the South.[24]

The problem with Keynesian economic philosophy was the government in good times never seemed to balance its budget and save for bad times. Because of politics, government taxed and spent, creating an economic environment that over-heated and caused inflation. Inflation in the late 1960s to the early 1980s seemed to be an insurmountable problem. People were earning more, but their buying power was considerably less in the late 1960s compared to the mid-1980s. Even today, if you are a person who works as a "blue collar" employee, your wages have been stagnant, as measured by the amount of purchasing power (the products you are able to buy) your wages provide.[25] The height of purchasing power for blue collar workers was in the late 60s to early 70s. Inflation was the great weakness of Keynesianism. There was a new school of economic theory that was gaining popularity during the 1960s and early 1970s. This was monetarism.

MONETARISM

Milton Friedman was the philosophical father of the monetarists' school of thought. Monetarists believe government should not regulate the economy. Instead they argue that inflation is created when there is too much money chasing too few products. Monetarists watch the supply of money, and argue the ability for government to print money should be limited to the percentage of growth in the economy. They also argue the role of government in regulating the economy should be very limited in order to have a natural business cycle, and let people take risks and get rewarded. Monetarists have gained a great deal of power and in-

fluence during the 1990s since Alan Greenspan, the former Chairman of the Federal Reserve was reportedly a Monetarist. Greenspan and the Presidents he served under were able to have both low unemployment and low inflation. This was quite an extraordinary achievement. Usually if there is low unemployment inflation is generated because wages are increased because of excess demand for labor. Of course, there is the problem of the twin deficits—the trade deficit and the Federal government deficit. These are two areas that Monetarists have worried will bring the American economy to its knees.

The deficits lower the value of the dollar in the foreign currency markets and thus, make consumer goods more expensive for the average family, therefore, driving up inflation. Again the Monetarists worry more about inflation than other economic phenomenon. The third school of economic thought has to deal with supply side economics that President Reagan made popular during the 1980s.

SUPPLY SIDE ECONOMICS

Arthur Laffer was the father of this school of thought. He invented the Laffer Curve which measures the marginal rate of taxation compared to government revenue. People who hold this school of thought believe, the more the government cuts taxes the more revenue government receives because tax receipts increase due to people earning more money. This is true if the marginal rate of taxation (the amount of tax you have to pay on an extra dollar earned) is high. If let us say, the marginal rate of taxation is 90 percent, then a person may not work to earn that extra dollar, since 90 cents will go to the government. However, if the government reduces the marginal rate to 50 cents then a person may want to earn the extra money. In turn the person will use the money to purchase more goods (paying more sales tax) or pay more income tax (by earning more overtime). The problem with this school of thought is the marginal rate has to be relatively high for this relationship to work. If the marginal rate is low, then the lowering of the marginal rate does not stimulate economic activity nor does government revenue increase.

These three schools coincide with the type of public policy perception people have. If you are a liberal you tend to believe in Keynesian economics which calls for a high level of governmental intervention in the economy. If you consider yourself either a Supply Sider or Monetarist you would like a limited amount of government intervention in

---

[24]Christopher Mathews, *The Rivalry that Shaped Postwar America: Kennedy & Nixon*. New York: Simon & Schuster, 1996, p. 288.

[25]While in our service-oriented economy, this label has lost some of its descriptive power, blue collar means people who use physical labor in areas such as manufacturing. White collar are executives and professionals.

people's economic life. This usually means you tend to be a political conservative. Of course there are levels of conservatism and liberalism and there are also different degrees of how people identify with these three economic schools of thought. These three schools of economic thought and the two political labels of conservative and liberal are useful categorizations not for drawing conclusions on people's motives for advocating certain public policies. Calling someone a name or labeling someone is not a substitute for a strong argument.

CONCLUSION

In this chapter, we have put all of the elements that you have learned from the previous chapters and observed how they interacted. We started with a discussion that centered around the behavior of young people and how they consumed the media differently than their elders. We then described the public policy process using the passage of Medicare as an example of how a bill becomes a law and how it is implemented. The nine steps of the public policy procedure was described and we saw how an issue becomes a national problem and there is a plea for action. Ultimately, the government will respond if there is the political will to do something from the public, interest groups and political leaders. We have examined the relationships between Presidential action, Congressional action and the changes that come out of compromises between these two. Medicare, although very popular with older Americans, has the potential of bankrupting the country and becoming a terrible burden on young people.

President Bush has tried to persuade the country to deal with these issues. However, it is very difficult for a President to move too fast away from the public on certain issues. We saw how President Carter tried to formulate a rational policy for energy conservation, and how President Roosevelt was ahead of the public on helping the British fight Nazi Germany. President Bush may be ahead of the country

on Social Security and Medicare, but in this chapter we saw how President Johnson originally wanted a program to fund the elimination of heart disease, strokes and cancer, and when he was unable to politically achieve this, he switched to helping older Americans gain health care.

President Johnson had to compromise with Wilbur Mills, who was a conservative. Mills believed in a different role of the government than did President Johnson. Johnson was a Keynesian, while Mills believed in little or no government intervention. After we described the public policy and Medicare, we then continued with a description of the three dominant economic schools of thought that political leaders hold and argue when they are advocating a public policy. The three schools of thought are Keynesian, Monetarist, and Supply Side. We discussed the presumptions and conclusions of each of the schools of thought and how they relate to leaders and groups political ideology. Today, we have seen some issues such as Social Security start out as an important part of President Bush's second term.

President Bush seems to have given up on any type of domestic reform. He seems to be concentrating his remaining political capital with the issues that surround foreign policy. In the next chapter, we will examine the public policy process on issues surrounding atomic weapons. Although we will see the same interaction of governmental organizations, atomic policy is different because of the anarchic nature of the international environment and the ability of states to use violence as a public policy.

TERMS TO REMEMBER

MAJORITARIAN POLITICS
SOCIAL DARWINISM
FISCAL POLICY
MONETARY POLICY

The Public Policy Process: Domestic Policy

TRUE OR FALSE QUESTIONS

1. Eighty percent of young people read a newspaper every day.   T / F

2. Ninety percent of young people vote on important issues to themselves.   T / F

3. Forty percent of young people voted for John Kerry for President in 2004.   T / F

4. Young voters made George W. Bush President in 2000.   T / F

5. Young voters are always liberal.   T / F

6. Young voters are always religious.   T / F

7. There are ten steps to public policy.   T / F

8. Implementation is a step of the public policy process.   T / F

9. Evaluation is not a step in the public policy process.   T / F

10. A crisis spurs the government into forming a public policy.   T / F

MULTIPLE CHOICE QUESTIONS

11. Which is not a step in the public policy process?
    a.   Placement on the national agenda
    b.   A plea for action
    c.   Debate and action
    d.   Television advertisements

12. President Johnson wanted a program to fight
    a.   Alzheimer's disease
    b.   cancer
    c.   heart attacks and strokes
    d.   b. and c.

13. Medicare became a public policy because Johnson failed to
    a.   get political support for his program to fight premature death.
    c.   get the funding for doctors bills.
    c.   did not create an environment for a crisis.
    d.   spend time on his program to fight cancer, heart attacks and strokes.

14. The first President to bring Medicare to the attention of the American people was
    a.   Lyndon Johnson
    b.   Dwight D. Eisenhower
    c.   Bill Clinton
    d.   Harry Truman

15. An advantage of advocating a program for old people is
    a. they die.
    b. they get sick.
    c. they have money.
    d. everyone will become a member of this class.

16. Medicare became an important issue in the election of
    a. 1960
    b. 1948
    c. 1964
    d. 1974

17. Sixty-five as a retirement age was originally picked by Otto Von Bismarck and adopted by
    a. Herbert Hoover
    b. Franklin D. Roosevelt
    c. Lyndon Johnson
    d. Richard Nixon

18. The major problem with Medicare is
    a. people are getting more healthy.
    b. it is a demographic time bomb.
    c. experimental treatments are not covered.
    d. there is no problem with Medicare.

19. What did not contribute to the failure of President Bush's failed Social Security Reform Act?
    a. The War on Terror is taking too much of the President's time.
    b. Social Security does not need reform.
    c. He did not campaign on the issue so it caught everyone off guard.
    d. AARP did not support the bill.

20. The President who holds the record for most legislation passed is
    a. Franklin D. Roosevelt
    b. George Washington
    c. Lyndon Johnson
    d. Abraham Lincoln

21. The economic school of thought that calls for governmental intervention is
    a. Monetarism
    b. Supply side
    c. Conservative
    d. Keynesianism

chapter fourteen

IMAGE FROM DEFENSE VISUAL INFORMATION CENTER

PUBLIC POLICY AND NUCLEAR WEAPONS

INTRODUCTION

On October 9, 2006, the Democratic Peoples Republic of Korea (North Korea) tested an atomic weapon. The test has taken the international community by surprise and has essentially scrapped the so called "six-party talks."[1] North Korea is the latest country to have developed these weapons. Pakistan, India and probably Israel are also countries that have developed this weapons capacity, causing a continuing crisis of the failure of the Non-Proliferation Treaty (NPT) regime. This chapter will examine the development of public policy as it relates to the development of nuclear weapons and how these weapons have become, for some countries, a badge of state pride and achievement.

Atomic bombs have been a focus point that has merged domestic and foreign policies. This chapter is organized into four sections. First, we will discuss the

history of the development of the first atomic weapons and their use by the United States. Next, we examine the strategic policy of Mutually Assured Destruction during the Cold War, which created a reliance on nuclear weapons by the United States and how succeeding Presidential administrations tried but failed to change the strategic policies of the U.S. Then, we will explore how the Cold War policies and practices have proven not to be very effective in the post-Cold War international environment. Finally, we will discuss the challenges facing the United States as countries that are known to support terrorism, develop their own atomic arsenals. The possibility of nuclear weapons started with a physicist Leo Szilard walking across the street and envisioning the possibility of a nuclear chain reaction.[2] We start our examination of public policy and atomic weapons with the development and use of atomic weapons by the United States.

---

[1]The six parties include: China, Russia, North Korea, South Korea, Japan and the United States.

[2]Richard Rhodes, *Dark Sun: The Making of the Hydrogen Bomb*. New York : Simon & Schuster, 1995, p. 582.

THE UNITED STATES AND THE DEVELOPMENT OF NUCLEAR WEAPONS

On October 9, 1941, 67 years earlier than the atomic test of North Korea, President Franklin Roosevelt made the decision to have his chief of defense research, Vannevar Bush, to investigate the idea of pursuing an atomic device.[3] Roosevelt understood that Bush would use all of his bureaucratic resources to pursue what would become the weapon that provided a victory over the Japanese. This was two months before the Pearl Harbor attack and with this decision, the U.S. was on its way to developing atomic weapons:

THUS, TWO MONTHS BEFORE PEARL HARBOR, THE PRESIDENT OF THE UNITED STATES BECAME THE FIRST POLITICAL LEADER TO SET HIS COUNTRY FIRMLY ON A COURSE THAT COULD LEAD TO A BOMB. THIS DECISION DID NOT DETERMINE THE OUTCOME OF THE EFFORT, BUT, IT DID DETERMINE THAT THE EFFORT WOULD BE MADE. TWO MONTHS LATER THIS DETERMINATION WAS HARDENED BEYOND FURTHER ARGUMENT BY THE OUTBREAK OF OPEN WAR WITH JAPAN AND GERMANY.[4]

In June 1940, President Roosevelt was to form an atomic partnership with Great Britain. The agreement was the classic 50-50 partnership.[5] The two countries agreed to merge their efforts and the results would be shared equally. Later this arrangement would be altered. However, for the time being, the two countries would give resources to change a scientific theory into a weapon that would possibly contribute to ending the war.

In December 1942, Enrico Fermi and others achieved the first sustainable nuclear chain reaction, the half way point to making an atomic bomb.[6] We have said Congress' role in wartime is to declare war and budget enough money for the President to execute the war. In World War II, and especially when we examine the public policy surrounding the Manhattan Project, we see vast sums of money being invested. Not only were hundreds of millions of dollars being invested in areas such as Oak Ridge, Tennessee (for uranium enrichment) but also a special theoretical physics laboratory was being erected in the

desert of New Mexico.[7] Los Alamos was originally a boys school that the government bought for 440,000 dollars. The University of California was contracted to operate the secret installation.[8] At Los Alamos, the government would recruit some of the best physicists to work on the atomic bomb. Unlike recent war efforts, during World War II, people were recruited and universities and colleges supported the war effort. Richard Rhodes writes:

WHAT WE WERE TRYING TO DO, WRITES JOHN MANLEY, THE UNIVERSITY OF ILLINIOS PHYSICIST WORKING WITH OPPENHEIMER THEN, "WAS BUILD A NEW LABORATORY IN THE WILDS OF NEW MEXICO WITH NO INITIAL EQUIPMENT EXCEPT THE LIBRARY OF HORATIO ALGER BOOKS OR WHATEVER IT WAS THAT THOSE BOYS IN THE RANCH SCHOOL READ, AND THE PACK EQUIPMENT THAT THEY USED GOING HORSEBACK RIDING, NONE OF WHICH HELPED US VERY MUCH IN GETTING NEUTRON PRODUCING ACCELERATORS."[9]

Everyone who went to Los Alamos knew it was going to be primitive, yet they also knew some of the most talented people would be there, and if they succeeded they would be making history. Oppenheimer, the director of the Los Alamos, knew who the world's leading scientists were and he went to recruit as many of them as possible. On July 16, 1945, with the cooperative effort of the military, universities, and corporations the first atomic explosion was successfully achieved.[10]

There has been a lot of things written over the decision to end World War II by using atomic bombs. Here are some facts about President Truman's decision to end the war.

ANOTHER ESTIMATE AT THE PENTAGON INCLUDED THE INVASION OF BOTH SOUTHERN AND NORTHERN KYUSHU, AS WELL AS JAPAN PROPER ("THE DECISIVE INVASION"), AND THE COST OF THIS PLAN CAME TO 220,000 CASUALTIES, NEARLY A QUARTER OF A MILLION MEN. BUT A MEMORANDUM OF JUNE 4, 1945, WRITTEN BY GENERAL THOMAS HANDY OF MARSHALL'S STAFF, IN LISTING THE ADVANTAGES OF MAKING PEACE WITH JAPAN, SAID AMERICA WOULD SAVE NO LESS THAN 500,000 TO 1 MILLION LIVES BY AVOIDING THE INVASION ALTOGETHER—WHICH SHOWS THAT FIGURES OF SUCH MAGNITUDE WERE THEN IN USE AT THE HIGHEST LEVELS.[11]

[3] McGeorge Bundy, *Danger and Survival: Choices about the Bomb in the First Fifty-Years.* New York: Random House, 1988, p. 3.

[4] Ibid.

[5] Jon Meacham, *Franklin and Winston: An Intimate Portrait of an Epic Friendship.* New York: Random House, 2003, p. 183.

[6] Samuel Eliot Morison, *The Oxford History of the American People.* New York: Penguin Books, 1965, p. 407.

[7] Richard Rhodes, *The Making of the Atomic Bomb.* New York: Simon & Schuster, 1986, p. 407.

[8] Ibid.

[9] Ibid. p. 452.

[10] Samuel Eliot Morison, *The Oxford History of the American People.* New York: Penguin Books, 1965, p. 407.

[11] David McCullough, *Truman.* New York: Simon & Schuster, 1992, p. 401.

Before the decision to drop the atomic weapons, an invasion would have cost at least 220,000 American soldiers' lives and maybe as much a one million lives would be lost. This does not even count Japanese lives which have been estimated at triple the American casuality rate. The speculation of revisionist historians, who complain about Truman's decision, are simply Monday morning quarterbacks, who do not understand war or politics. Truman had in his power the ability to stop the killings of Americans, Chinese, Vietnamese, Englishmen, French and Russians. There were also estimates that after the invasion and victory, Japan would be such a tinderbox that there would be a need for an occupation army of over two million men.[12]

Stephen Ambrose writes the strongest argument against using the bomb was the Japanese were ready to surrender. However, this is not true. The Japanese were still in control of one of the largest empires the world had ever seen. Imperial Japan's empire stretched three-quarters of the globe. After the battle of Okinawa, Prime Minister Suzuki only suggested the war would end if Japan continued to control almost all of Vietnam, Manchuria and Korea.[13] The revisionist historians do not talk about the political impossibility of accepting this position to the American public. Who remembered the Bataan Death March, Pearl Harbor and the thousands of Americans killed in the bloody battles on the small islands of the Pacific War?[14] The mistakes some scholars make are they assume the occupation would have been the same if there would have been a surrender without the atomic bomb. Again Ambrose puts it very well:

THE [JAPANESE] GENERALS HAD NO ANSWER TO THE ATOMIC BOMB. THEY COULD NOT EVADE THE FACT THAT THEY WERE DEFEATED AND COULD OFFER NO ALTERNATIVE TO THE GOVERNMENT SAVE A SUICIDAL RESISTANCE WHICH THE EMPEROR REFUSED TO CONTEMPLATE.[15]

Ambrose's research shows the results of the atomic attacks reported by American movies, radio and newspapers, which described the utter hell that is the result of atomic attack. This had a great impact on public opinion. People who were demanding blood, were shocked and decided the Japanese had been punished for starting the war. On the other hand, most people did not feel Germany had been punished enough for their role in World War II, especially since the stories of the concentration camps were starting to be more known.[16]

Speculation is just that—speculation. Truman did drop the atomic bomb and the Japanese did surrender. The era of atomic weapons was at hand. For the first five years the United States would have a monopoly on the technology to create atomic weapons. The Soviet Union did declare war on Japan. However, they did not occupy Japan, so Japan was spared the division of its land. The Koreans and Vietnamese would not be so fortunate. All of the elements of government were involved in fighting World War II and producing the atomic bomb.

President Truman did tell Joseph Stalin of the existence of the bomb, and Stalin seemed to know the existence of the new American bomb. It has been substantiated that Stalin did have a ring of spies at Los Alamos, as a consequence of the Anglo-American agreement to share their efforts in discovering the secrets of the atomic weapon. The spies were led by a British scientist name Klaus Fuchs, who had been sending diagrams and secret information to the Soviets since the beginning of his time in Los Alamos. The Rosenbergs and Fuchs were involved in spying and giving the secrets that enabled the Soviets to have atomic weapons much faster than any analyst believed possible.[17] The report of Stalin's reaction after the meeting with Truman (according to Marshal Georgy Zhukov) was to "tell Kurchatov to hurry up the work,"[18] using all of their resources including plans stolen from Los Alamos.[19] On September 23, 1949, President Truman announced the Soviets had succeeded in developing their own atomic bomb. The American monopoly was over. How was the public policy apparatus going to respond? In the next section we analyze the development of the public policies surrounding the Cold War and atomic weapons.

[12]Steven E. Ambrose, *Americans at War*. New York: Berkley Books, 1998, p. 129.

[13]Ibid.

[14]A Gallup poll taken on May 29, 1945 revealed that 33 percent of all Americans wanted Hirohito executed as a war criminal—Steven E. Ambrose, *Americans at War*. New York: Berkley Books, 1998, p. 130.

[15]Ibid. p. 132

[16]Ibid.

[17]See Richard Rhodes, *Dark Sun: The Making of the Hydrogen Bomb*. New York: Simon & Schuster, 1995.

[18]David McCullough, *Truman*. New York: Simon & Schuster: 1992, p. 443.

[19]Igor Vasilievich Kurchatov was the father of the Soviet nuclear program. He documents how the Soviet program received intelligence reports on American and British research. Richard Rhodes, *Dark Sun: The Making of the Hydrogen Bomb*. New York: Simon & Schuster, 1995.

PLAYING CHICKEN: ATOMIC WEAPONS, THE KOREAN WAR AND THE CUBAN MISSILE CRISIS

The first concrete policy reaction of the U.S. to the announcement of the successful Soviet atomic tests was an increase in the production of uranium and plutonium in order to build more bombs.[20] The nuclear arms race between the two Superpowers had begun. The Soviet Union was consolidating its control of Eastern Europe. Furthermore, the American people were shocked by the Communists takeover of China and the alliance between the Soviet Union and the People's Republic of China. In this context, we analyze two major conflicts during this period, where the use of atomic weapons was directly threatened by the United States and/or the Soviet Union. These two episodes were the Korean War (1950–1953) and the Cuban Missile Crisis (October 1962).

EISENHOWER'S THREAT OF ATOMIC WEAPONS IN KOREA

There were three phases of the Korean War, first was the initial invasion of South Korea. The second phase was the brilliant landing at Inchon and the Americans occupying almost all of North Korea. And, the third phase was the Chinese intervention into the war.

The Korean War started as a shock to the United States. Much like the Pearl Harbor attack, the U.S. was not prepared for war in Asia. The U.S. Army had grown soft in occupation duty in Japan and was caught ill-prepared, and ill-equipped to fight the North Koreans. North Korea had been successful sending U.N. Troops[21] south along the Korean Peninsula to a small area around the port city of Pusan. Being caught ill-prepared, the U.S. sent emergency troops to try to stem the tide and stop the North Koreans.

The second phase of the war was a complete reversal of fortunes for the North Koreans. General MacArthur was the commanding general and he did a brilliant invasion through the city of Inchon. Outflanking the North Koreans, MacArthur went all the way through North Korea to the Chinese border at the Yalu River. This daring strategy by MacArthur

was rested on the assumption the Chinese would not intervene.[22]

The third phase started in late November 1950. The Chinese intervened in Korea, sending over 200,000 troops and sending the U.N. forces all the way back past the 38th parallel. MacArthur was fired by Truman. General Matthew Ridgway took back Seoul in March 24, 1951.[23] By the time Ridgway was in command there were 365,000 troops in Korea, and the Korean War had become a stalemate. Harry Truman had decided not to run for a third term as President. The new President was Dwight D. Eisenhower. Eisenhower had campaigned on the pledge to go to Korea, and end the war in a quick and honorable fashion. The Truman Administration had ruled out the use of atomic weapons fearing even the use of even tactical weapons could not be limited and could lead to an escalation of the conflict. Eisenhower had no public position in this regard. He made it known to the Chinese and Russians that if he had to, he would not hesitate to use the American nuclear arsenal.

Americans play poker, Russians and Chinese play chess. The question of an Eisenhower bluff is pretty certain, if you look at what Eisenhower had written in his memoirs:

THE LACK OF PROGRESS IN THE LONG-STALEMATED TALKS—THEY WERE THEN RECESSED—AND THE NEARLY STALEMATED WAR BOTH DEMANDED, IN MY OPINION, DEFINITE MEASURES ON OUR PART TO PUT AN END TO THESE INTOLERABLE CONDITIONS. ONE POSSIBILITY WAS TO LET THE COMMUNIST AUTHORITIES UNDERSTAND THAT, IN THE ABSENCE OF SATISFACTORY PROGRESS, WE INTENDED TO MOVE DECISIVELY WITHOUT INHIBITION IN OUR USE OF WEAPONS, AND WOULD NO LONGER BE RESPONSIBLE FOR CONFINING HOSTILITIES TO THE KOREAN PENINSULA. WE WOULD NOT BE LIMITED BY ANY WORLD WIDE GENTLEMAN'S AGREEMENT. IN INDIA AND IN THE FORMOSA STRAIT AREA, AND AT THE TRUCE NEGOTIATIONS AT PANMUNJOM, WE DROPPED THE WORD, DISCREETLY, OF OUR INTENTION. WE FELT QUITE SURE IT WOULD REACH SOVIET AND CHINESE COMMUNIST EARS.

SOON THE PROSPECTS FOR ARMISTICE NEGOTIATIONS SEEMED TO IMPROVE.[24]

It seems that Eisenhower had bluffed, and had been successful in convincing the other side in the

[20]Richard Rhodes, *The Making of the Atomic Bomb*. New York: Simon & Schuster, 1986, p. 767.

[21]Harry Truman used the new U.N. Security Council to pass a chapter 7 resolution to have international troops fight in Korea. This procedure was done this way in order not to have it appear as if it was an American war. Of course, most of the troops were Americans.

[22]Samuel Eliot Morison, *The Oxford History of the American People, Volume Three: 1869 through the Death of John F. Kennedy*. New York: Penguin Books, 1965, p. 436.

[23]Ibid. p. 438.

[24]Quoted in McGeorge Bundy, *Danger and Survival: Choices about the Bomb in the First Fifty Years*. New York: Random House, 1988, p. 239.

Korean War that the United States had their fill of this war and would end it by a show of overwhelming force.[25]

It is unclear if the signals were received in China. It has been suggested the death of Stalin in March of that year was probably the deciding factor in whether the Communists could have signed an armistice. McGeorge Bundy, President Kennedy's National Security Advisor, had conversations with Chinese leaders and friends. He claims these people "had been told by Zhou En-lai himself that Stalin's death was what made the armistice possible."[26] Zhou En-lai was in charge of China's foreign policy, and in Bundy's quote at the time was considered the established opinion in China and Russia in the 1980s before the end of the Cold War.

For our purposes, whether Eisenhower's strategy or the death of Joseph Stalin was the real reason for the change in atmosphere at the conference table to end the Korean War is unimportant. The public policy structure of the United States believed President Eisenhower's threats had made the difference. This perception would be kept with the people and institutions that create policy and implement strategies in times of crisis. After the Korean War, there was an overdependence by the United States on the use of nuclear weapons.

The American people did not want to support a large military establishment. After World War II, a large army that had been built was de-mobilized. The Korean War showed the U.S. Army was ill-prepared to fight a limited or proxy war in Europe or Asia. The United States started to set up different mutual defense treaties that surrounded the Soviet Union. This policy was called "containment," a policy that was coined by the scholar and diplomat George Kennan. Kennan thought containment meant competing with the Soviet Union on every level in trying to contain their ideas, technology, culture and military. However, the public policy establishment concentrated on containment of the Soviet influence in a military and nuclear arms race.

Combined with containment, the strategy of Mutually Assured Destruction or MAD was developed. The assumptions of this strategy are simple. The policy planners believed the Soviet Union's leaders were rational and they did not want to commit suicide. Therefore, the policy states that if the Soviet Union attacks any country that the United States had signed a defense treaty with (and the attack uses atomic weapons) the United States will respond by using its nuclear weapons, thereby guaranteeing the destruction of the Soviet Union.

The Eisenhower Administration and the American people thought this strategy was fundamentally sound. It made it possible not to have to spend money on a large standing army and it deterred the Russians and their allies from adventures, such as an invasion of Western Europe. The combination of containment and MAD was the basis of American foreign policy throughout the Cold War. Coinciding with American Presidential elections, about every four years, there would be a crisis in order for the Russian leadership to test the American leadership in their resolve to use or implement the doctrine of MAD.

After the Korean War, Eisenhower's Presidency was a period of peace and American prosperity. The United States was the number one country in almost everything. Manufacturing was not challenged by the economies of Asia, although the U.S. relied on Japanese manufacturing to support their forces in Korea and the German challenge had not developed (especially in luxury goods and cars). Eisenhower had served two terms and the election of 1960 brought John F. Kennedy into the White House. We have talked about the Kennedy-Nixon election. Now the Russians would test Kennedy in the closest thing the United States and the Soviet Union ever came to implementing mutually assured destruction. The Cuban Missile Crisis of October 1962.

CUBAN MISSILE CRISIS

The Kennedy Administration had already failed one test against the Russians. The Bay of Pigs was a disaster which cost the CIA director his job and gave the Russians the belief that Kennedy was indecisive. It also made Castro a special Kennedy nemesis. At the same time, President Kennedy's Secretary of Defense Robert McNamara was trying to wean the American public and public policy machinery away from the strategy of mutually assured destruction to a strategy called flexible response. When McNamara first came into office, he was instructed to build missiles since Kennedy had campaigned that there was a ballistic missile gap with the Soviet Union. This was not the case. In his classic book on how the United States went into Vietnam, David Halberstam writes how McNamara was especially prepared for the Cuban Missile Crisis because he had been trying to change

---

[25] In the three years of the Korean War the U.S. lost about 50,000 men. Compare this with the roughly 50,000 men the United States lost in Vietnam in seventeen years.

[26] McGeorge Bundy, *Danger and Survival: Choices about the Bomb in the First Fifty Years.* New York: Random House, 1988, p. 241.

U.S. policy vis-à-vis the Soviet Union since he first took the position of Secretary of Defense.

IT WAS HE [DANIEL ELLSBERG] THOUGHT, AN IMPRESSIVE PERFORMANCE, NOT JUST BECAUSE OF MCNAMARA'S ALMOST EMOTIONAL ABHORRENCE OF THE WEAPONS BUT BECAUSE HE UNDERSTOOD THE DANGERS OF HIS SITUATION: [MCNAMARA] HE HAD TO KEEP HIS FEELINGS HIDDEN, FOR IF THE CHIEFS, OR CONGRESS FOUND OUT HOW HE FELT HE WOULD BE FINISHED AS SECRETARY OF DEFENSE. THE WHOLE MIGHT OF AMERICA WAS CONCENTRATED ON NUCLEAR WEAPONS, AND WE HAD SOLD THE IDEA OF NUCLEAR RETALIATION TO THE EUROPEANS; IF THE WORD GOT OUT THE SECRETARY'S NEGATIVE ATTITUDE, IT WOULD MEAN THAT THE UNITED STATES WAS VIRTUALLY DISARMED, SO OF COURSE HE WOULD NOT BE ABLE TO STAY IN OFFICE.[27]

Because of his abhorrence to the use of nuclear weapons, and the reliance of the American military and diplomatic public policy apparatus on these weapons, McNamara started to educate and reform the Pentagon and the Europeans. He did this by forming a group called the Nuclear Planning Group. This committee consisted of his European counterparts, Defense Ministers and Secretaries of Defense usually are dependent on their military advisers. The Ministers are politicians and usually are not managers. McNamara's experience was as the CEO of Ford Motor Corporation and before World War II, he taught at Harvard's Business School and was supposed to be a genius when it came to statistics and applied management techniques. Halberstam goes on to describe the rules McNamara used to educate the Defense Ministers of Europe

NO PREPARED PAPERS OR SET SPEECHES WERE ALLOWED, AND THEY COULD NOT TURN TO THEIR GENERALS WHO THEN TURNED TO THEIR COLONELS. THEY CAME TO THE MEETINGS, ONLY ONE PERSON FROM EACH COUNTRY AT THE TABLE, AND ONLY FOUR OTHERS WERE ALLOWED IN THE ROOM, HE [MCNAMARA] HATED CROWDS. AT FIRST IT DID NOT WORK TOO WELL BECAUSE MCNAMARA OVERWHELMED THEM, HE WAS TOO STRONG A PRESENCE, BUT GRADUALLY HE FORCED THEM TO TAKE POLITICAL RESPONSIBILITY FOR DEFENSE POSITIONS, AND EQUALLY IMPORTANT, BUILD SKILLED PROFESSIONAL STAFFS WHICH COULD CHALLENGE THE TECHNICAL THINKING OF THE MILITARY AT THE LOWER LEVELS, POINT BY POINT, SO THEY COULD NOT BE FORCED INTO BLIND CHOICES AT THE HIGHEST LEVELS.[28]

McNamara was trying to take the "hair trigger" off the nuclear forces of the United States. The problem was, up to this time, nuclear weapons had not been used since World War II and they appeared a cheap and effective way to prevent aggression.

The Bay of Pigs debacle and McNamara's efforts to change the dominant military strategy of the United States did not give the Kennedy Administration great credibility with the Joint Chiefs of Staff of the Armed Forces, especially the Air Force, who was the prime architect of the idea of strategic bombing. Changing the perception of the bureaucracy, and setting new assumptions in the public policy apparatus is like turning an eighteen wheel truck, it must be done slowly and carefully. McNamara's first effort found resistance.

I HAVE SPOKEN ON A NUMBER OF OCCASIONS OF THE DECLINING RELATIVE VALUE OF OUR NUCLEAR SUPERIORITY. I AM CONTINUALLY SURPRISED AT THE COMPLAINTS WHICH SUCH STATEMENTS AROUSE, AS THOUGH THE PROBLEM WOULD GO AWAY IF WE STOPPED TALKING ABOUT IT. YET OF COURSE WE ARE NOT TALKING ABOUT A POLICY . . . IT IS NOT A POLICY WHICH WE CAN CHOOSE TO FOLLOW OR NOT TO FOLLOW, BUT A FACT OF LIFE AND A FACT WHICH WE CAN IGNORE ONLY AT GREAT PERIL TO OUR NATIONAL SECURITY. THE INCREASING NUMBERS OF SURVIVABLE MISSILES IN THE HANDS OF BOTH THE UNITED STATES AND THE SOVIET UNION ARE A FACT OF LIFE. NEITHER SIDE TODAY POSSESSES A FORCE WHICH CAN SAVE ITS COUNTRY FROM SEVERE DAMAGE IN A NUCLEAR EXCHANGE. NEITHER SIDE CAN REALISTICALLY EXPECT TO ACHIEVE SUCH A FORCE IN THE FORESEEABLE FUTURE. AND THESE, TOO, ARE FACTS OF LIFE.[29]

The largest obstacle to McNamara's effort to change the strategic policy of the U.S. was the military. Especially in Chief of Staff Air Force General LeMay. He believed McNamara was turning his back on the tried and tested strategy of Mutually Assured Destruction. Furthermore, it was LeMay who commanded the bomber force that was responsible for the destruction of Japan during World War II and was the personality behind the Strategic Air Command that McNamara was rejecting as well. This debate turned practical in October of 1962.

The Soviet gambit to put missiles into Cuba was a response to the perception that Kennedy did not have the experience, or in Khrushchev's perception, the maturity to respond to this type of crisis. He would put the missiles in and then when they were

---

[27]David Halberstam, *The Best and the Brightest*. New York: Ballantine Books, 1969, p. 243.
[28]Ibid.

[29]McGeorge Bundy, *Danger and Survival: Choices about the Bomb in the First Fifty Years*. New York: Random House, 1988, p. 546.

operational, he would announce it to the world. What could the Americans do? The Soviets did not count on the fact the installation of missiles would be discovered by the intelligence overflights of Cuba.[30] For the next fourteen days, most authors and scholars who have studied this believe, the world came as close at it ever got to a nuclear exchange during the Cold War.

This is why probably the Cuban Missile Crisis is one of the most studied crises ever in American political science. The elements of the crisis were—the Soviet Union had tried to put nuclear missiles inside its client state of Cuba. This would shorten the warning time the United States had if a Soviet first strike missile attack to 25 minutes to less than five minutes to hit Washington, D.C. If the Soviets were aiming for Florida, the warning would be even less than five minutes. McGeorge Bundy was a participant in the crisis and he writes the number one objective of the Administration was to have the missiles removed from Cuba.

WITHIN FORTY-EIGHT HOURS A SINGLE OBJECTIVE OF OUR POLICY HAD BEEN IDENTIFIED: THE REMOVAL OF THE MISSILES. MOREOVER, WE HAD REDUCED OUR OPTIONS TO TWO: A CONVENTIONAL AIR STRIKE ON THE MISSILE SITES, AND A NAVAL QUARANTINE ON THE DELIVERY OF OFFENSIVE WEAPONS.

THE MISSILES MUST BE REMOVED. THIS WAS THE PRESIDENT'S IMMEDIATE AND FIRM DETERMINATION, AND IT WAS THE TEST AGAINST WHICH OTHER OPTIONS FELL AWAY, EITHER BECAUSE THEY OFFERED TOO LITTLE HOPE, OR BECAUSE IN A SITUATION WHICH ALREADY APPEARED DANGEROUS BEYOND THE EXPERIENCE OF ANY OF US, THEY DEMANDED TOO MUCH.[31]

Kennedy's Administration had learned something from the crises they had faced. They tried to present the President with all of the options possible. This had not been done before the Bay of Pigs in Cuba. So, they discussed how they could implement a plan that would get rid of the missiles. The questions of the survivability of the Castro regime or any other issue that interfered with the objective of getting the missiles out of Cuba would be avoided.[32]

Kennedy considered a "surgical air strike" but he, McNamara and the Attorney General Robert Kennedy did not trust the implementation of this policy.

McNamara's previous problems with General LeMay made the argument for a military strike also weaker. Kennedy chose to use a naval blockade. On Monday, October 22, 1962, Kennedy would address the nation and the world. Kennedy outlined his seven initial steps he would take as a response to the Soviet move.

1. strict naval quarantine on offensive weapons;
2. increased surveillance and readiness for further action that would be justified if offensive Soviet preparations continued;
3. announcement that any nuclear missile launched from Cuba against any part of the hemisphere would be treated "as an attack by the Soviet Union on the United States," requiring full retaliatory response upon the Soviet Union;
4. reinforcement of the base at Guantanamo and evacuation of dependents of military personnel;
5. an appeal for support to the Organization of American States;
6. the calling of an emergency meeting of the United Nations Security Council and
7. a call on Khrushchev "to halt and eliminate this clandestine, reckless, and provocative threat to world peace."[33]

The Kennedy speech had to communicate to the public that the Soviet missiles were a real and present danger. Almost everyone understood the geography involved and the disadvantage the United States would be in if the Soviets were allowed to have strategic missiles inside of Cuba. The famous "debate" at the U.N. Security Council, in which Ambassador Adlai Stevenson cornered Soviet Ambassador Valerian Zorin was by asking whether the Soviets had put missiles in Cuba. When Zorin refused to answer Stevenson's question, he had the evidence wheeled before the cameras and the world.

The Soviets would remove the missiles in Cuba and the Americans would remove missiles from Turkey (in secret). The ending of the crisis came in a Soviet radio broadcast: "The Soviet Government . . . has given a new order to dismantle the arms which you describe as offensive, and to crate and return them to the Soviet Union."[34] This ended the most important aspects of the crisis.

The result of the Cuban Missile Crisis brought Robert McNamara's lesson home to everyone. The

---

[30]McGeorge Bundy, *Danger and Survival: Choices about the Bomb in the First Fifty Years*. New York: Random House, 1988, p. 404.

[31]McGeorge Bundy, *Danger and Survival: Choices about the Bomb in the First Fifty Years*. New York: Random House, 1988, p. 397.

[32]Ibid.

[33]Ibid. p. 404.

[34]Ibid. p. 406.

United States was no longer going to be able to have a sufficient nuclear superiority vis-à-vis the Soviet Union. Mutually Assured Destruction was a strategic doctrine that would be in the back of leaders' minds. It was not a substitute for conventional, well thought out discussions between the United States and the Soviet Union. There were procedures implemented and a status-quo worked on by the Superpowers.

Kennedy was assassinated in 1963, and Khrushchev was removed from office shortly after the missile crisis. Even though the Americans and the Soviets were trying to work out their issues dealing with an arms race, there were new players ready to join the nuclear club. How would they react once they achieve the status of being a nuclear power?

October 16, 1964, the People's Republic of China (China) detonated its first nuclear weapon, the Chinese road to becoming a nuclear power started by the lessons learned in Korea.[35] China during the 1950s and 1960s was a very impoverished country (it is not China of today), the United States did not recognize China and by the mid-1960s the alliance between the Soviet Union and China was almost over.

The United States now had a third country that had nuclear weapons, yet this country was not recognized by the U.S. Furthermore, China and the U.S. were involved in a limited war in Vietnam. China was a communist power however, they sought an independent road from the Soviet Union. So, during the mid-1960s the three main nuclear powers (France and Great Britain were also nuclear powers by this time), all disagreed with each other.

The result of the Soviets' concern over the development of a Chinese atomic weapon caused major movement by the Soviet Union and the U.S. to agree to the Non-Proliferation Treaty.[36] This treaty would be one of the pillars that the Soviet Union and the United States would rely on to stop the spread of nuclear weapons. The United States would work with the Soviet Union to have a non-proliferation treaty. However, the U.S. would also end China's isolation by having Richard Nixon visit and de facto recognition of the regime and let China become a Permanent Member of the United Nations Security Council.

By 1973, President Nixon had been in office for four years, and he was now trying to get the public policy machinery away from the reliance of Mutually Assured Destruction. The nuclear arsenals of both the Soviet Union and the United States would be a counterforce to insure no leader would strike first. Henry Kissinger, President Nixon's National Security Advisor stressed the need for the United States to develop their conventional forces.

[T]HE STRATEGIC ARSENALS OF THE TWO SIDES FIND THEIR PRINCIPLE PURPOSE IN MATCHING AND DETERRING THE FORCES OF THE OPPONENT AND IN MAKING CERTAIN THAT THIRD COUNTRIES PERCEIVE NO INEQUALITY. IN NO POSTWAR CRISIS HAS AN AMERICAN PRESIDENT COME CLOSE TO CONSIDERING THE USE OF STRATEGIC NUCLEAR WEAPONS. THERE WAS, IN SHORT, NO MORE URGENT TASK FOR AMERICAN DEFENSE POLICY THAN TO INCREASE SUBSTANTIALLY THE CAPACITY FOR LOCAL RESISTANCE. AMERICAN DEFENSE POLICY HAD ANNOUNCED THIS GOAL SINCE THE EARLY 1960s, BUT THE NECESSARY STRENGTHENING OF CONVENTIONAL AND TACTICAL NUCLEAR FORCES HAD BEEN PREVENTED BY THE VIETNAM WAR AND THE RESULTING ANTI-MILITARY MOOD.[37]

Similar to Kissinger's notion of a counter strike nuclear force, the China's nuclear policy was also one of counter strike. The closest the Soviet Union ever got to using nuclear weapons was probably during the 1969 border clashes with the Chinese.

Although Nixon did tell the Soviets the United States would defend China if the Soviets used their nuclear arsenal, the Chinese had also developed a counterforce to the United States and the Soviet Union. The Chinese declared "Should a handful of war maniacs dare to raid China's strategic sites, . . . that will be war, that will be aggression, and the 700 million Chinese people will rise up in resistance and use revolutionary war to eliminate the war of aggression."[38] As we know, the Soviet Union did not attempt a first strike against China. However, the Chinese did understand their weakness and after this incident was more inclined to ally itself with the United States against the Soviet Union until the end of the Cold War.

The nuclear powers tried to keep the technology away from other countries. During the Cold War the Soviet Union and the United States primarily would police the ambitions of countries that would try to get nuclear weapons. By using the Non-Proliferation Treaty and the Nuclear Test Ban Treaty and the International Atomic Energy Agency, it was hoped these

[35]John Wilson Lewis and Xue Litai, *China Builds the Bomb*. Stanford, CA: Stanford University Press, 1988, p. 10.

[36]Robert Dallek, *Flawed Giant: Lyndon Johnson and His Times 1961–1973*. New York: Oxford University Press, 1998, p. 437.

[37]Henry A. Kissinger, *Years of Upheaval*. Boston: Little, Brown and Co., 1982, p. 1000.

[38]John Wilson Lewis and Xue Litai, *China Builds the Bomb*. Stanford, CA: Stanford University Press, 1988, p. 216.

agreements and the nuclear protection of each Superpower to its respective client states, would prevent other countries from turning into nuclear powers.

It was the Federal Public Policy structure that enabled the United States to be the first state with a nuclear weapon. The dropping of the first atomic weapons on Japan to end World War II, convinced most Americans that these weapons would curtail any aggressor in the future. After the Soviet Union tested its atomic weapons, the United States created doctrines of Containment and Mutually Assured Destruction. The United States throughout the 1950s and 1960s relied too heavily on this strategy at the expense of the difficult task of creating and maintaining effective conventional military structures. The Korean War and the Cuban Missile Crisis showed the limits of atomic weapons during the Cold War. These limits also included the assumption that the leaders of nuclear powers are rational.

The lessons learned from the Korean War and the Cuban Missile Crisis reinforced the necessity of not relying on atomic weapons. People as diverse as Robert McNamara, Henry Kissinger, John F. Kennedy, Lyndon Johnson and Richard Nixon all tried to move the foreign policy bureaucracy away from the strategic concept of Mutually Assured Destruction and all failed. President Ronald Reagan would change the policies of containment and MAD with a bold proposal and the promise to the public policy establishment of increased funding.

President Ronald Reagan in 1979, before he was elected to the Presidency, went on a visit to the North American Defense Command (NORAD). He was briefed by the Commander of NORAD and they discussed what would happen if the Soviets launched a missile against the United States.

WELL, HILL [NORAD COMMANDER] REPLIED "WE WOULD PICK IT UP RIGHT AFTER IT WAS LAUNCHED, AND THE OFFICIALS OF THE CITY WOULD BE ALERTED THAT THEIR CITY WOULD BE HIT BY A NUCLEAR BOMB IN TEN OR FIFTEEN MINUTES. THAT'S ALL WE CAN DO. WE CAN'T STOP IT."

DISBELIEF SPREAD OVER REAGAN'S FACE. FLYING HOME TO CALIFORNIA WITH ANDERSON [REAGAN'S DOMESTIC POLICY AIDE] . . . OBVIOUSLY THINKING AHEAD, HE TURNED TO THE DILEMMA OF A PRESIDENT ONCE A SOVIET ATTACK WAS LAUNCHED. THE POLICY OPTIONS HE WOULD HAVE WOULD BE TO PRESS THE BUTTON OR DO NOTHING. REAGAN SAID STARKLY "THEY ARE BOTH BAD."[39]

The paradox Reagan describes is exactly the problem that President Eisenhower had in Korea, and President Kennedy had in the Cuban Missile Crisis. The challenge was how does one change the public policy process?

President Reagan did this by creating a new public policy environment. Some Conservatives say President Reagan is responsible for the collapse of the Soviet Union. Reagan (the argument goes) spent them into history by building up the conventional forces in the first term and then announced the Strategic Defense Initiative (SDI). SDI was a new idea that said to the military to try to build a defensive weapon against intercontinental ballistic missiles (ICBM). There is some evidence of this argument, however, most analysts and historians argue the collapse of the Soviet Union was a natural result of the break up of large multi-ethnic empires. Whatever the case, we do see a movement by the public policy establishment away from Mutually Assured Destruction and toward the development of a defense.

This movement was created because the Reagan and Bush Administrations have put resources to reward people working on SDI, and the collapse of the Soviet Union made the defense establishment find a way to keep the funding of their strategic assets from decreasing. Why do you need strategic weapons if the Soviet Union no longer exists and the Russians are creating a democracy? Well, SDI would be the new mantra to the public policy establishment, even though the technology is not developed. We will see the new challenge is not an atomic weapon from a missile, but, the proliferation of nuclear technology by states and non-state actors and the effort to keep this technology out of the hands of terrorists.

PUBLIC POLICY AND PROLIFERATION IN THE POST-COLD WAR ENVIRONMENT

The Strategic Defense Initiative would not be part of the practical solution to nuclear weapons for the next twenty or thirty years.[40] India and Pakistan have tested and confirmed they have nuclear weapons. The sanctions against these countries have been fairly mild, and as late as 2006, the United States has concluded a treaty with India that will give the Indians access to American technology for both weapons development and for energy use. Pakistan, as the result of a military coup, is a nuclear country that has

---

[39]Hedrick Smith, *The Power Game: How Washington Really Works.* New York: Ballantine Books, 1988, p. 604.

[40]As of this writing they are still trying to test the technology.

a population that favors terrorism and is actively helping the Taliban to attack coalition forces in Afghanistan.[41] The United States supports President Musharraf in an effort to prevent a Muslim radical takeover of the government. The Pakistanis also created another problem.

Their leading nuclear scientist A.Q. Khan was engaged in selling nuclear plans to Iran and North Korea, and there are reports of al-Qaeda having the blueprints for an atomic weapon.[42] We have this problem because the Non-Proliferation Treaty has failed. It failed when countries such as India and Pakistan developed their atomic weapons. In addition, it failed when countries did not "confirm nor deny" they had atomic weapons, such as Israel.

In 1974, the Central Intelligence Agency had concluded the Israelis had produced atomic weapons. The Central Intelligence Agency stated in their report:

> WE BELIEVE THAT ISRAEL HAS ALREADY PRODUCED NUCLEAR WEAPONS. OUR JUDGEMENT IS BASED ON ISRAELI ACQUISITION OF LARGE QUANTITIES OF URANIUM, PARTLY BY CLANDESTINE MEANS; THE AMBIGUOUS NATURE OF ISRAELI EFFORTS IN THE FIELD OF URANIUM ENRICHMENT, AND ISRAEL'S LARGE INVESTMENT IN A COSTLY MISSILE SYSTEM DESIGNED TO ACCOMMODATE NUCLEAR WARHEADS. WE DO NOT EXPECT ISRAELIS TO PROVIDE CONFIRMATION OF WIDESPREAD SUSPICIONS OF THEIR CAPABILITY, EITHER BY NUCLEAR TESTING OR BY THREATS OF USE, SHORT OF A GRAVE THREAT TO THE NATION'S EXISTENCE.[43]

The United States estimated that Israel had atomic weapons, but, did not do anything to punish Israel. In 1986, a British newspaper had an extensive account of the Israeli program. The United States did not act in any way to the development of the Israeli nuclear weapons. The Carter Administration stated American policy assuming Israel was not a nuclear power because it said so.[44] Even though the CIA had assessments and evidence that it was the Israelis that had introduced nuclear weapons in the Middle East. Again, the public policy apparatus was not reacting to the question of proliferation *per se*, it was reacting to proliferation by perceived enemies of the United States.

We are not arguing the United States is somehow responsible for proliferation, or if the policy had been different, the world would not have this challenge in the post-Cold War environment. What we are arguing, the United States cannot have it both ways. The United States cannot have the power to reduce the planet to ashes using nuclear weapons and then turn around and condemn proliferation efforts. The United States strategic posture has changed from a modified form of Mutual Assured Destruction to a mix of missile defense, and if that fails, then the United States will use Mutual Assured Destruction.

As the Soviet Union collapsed and its allies lost the Soviet nuclear protection, countries started to worry about their relationship with the United States. After the attacks on September 11th, the United States started to tell countries, in this fight you are either for us or against us. What happens if you are countries like North Korea and Iran? Neither country is protected by Russian or Chinese nuclear weapons. President Bush became even more specific with these two countries. In his State of the Union address in 2002, President Bush called on the states of the world to fight countries such as North Korea and Iran, calling them the Axis of Evil.[45] A new strategic approach would be devised by the Bush Administration called preventive war or the Bush Doctrine.

Similar to President Reagan, President Bush said the attacks on September 11, 2001 present a historic opportunity to change international politics. The Administration has argued that, the first fundamental concept of the Bush Doctrine is the establishment of democratic states. This is designed to make the world more stable. Democracies reflect the will of the people. Tyrants disregard international agreements, coerce their neighbors and oppress their citizens, while democracies tend not to engage in these behaviors.[46] By invading Iraq and implementing a democratic process that will produce a government, a "reverse domino effect" will take place. Case in point: the recent events in Lebanon have been used as evidence that there is a change in the political climate in the Middle East. The Bush Administration has argued, once an individual is part of a democracy, extremist politics as expounded by terrorists will lose much of their attractiveness. Radicalism will decline because their perceived grievances that extremism is

---

[41]Sebastian Junger, "America's Forgotten War." *Vanity Fair*, April, 2006, p. 218.

[42]Patrick C. Coaty, *Understanding the War on Terror* (Dubuque, IA: Kendall/Hunt Publishing Co., 2006, p. 78.

[43]McGeorge Bundy, *Danger and Survival: Choices about the Bomb in the First Fifty Years.* New York: Random House, 1988, p. 507.

[44]Ibid.

[45]Patrick C. Coaty, "The War Next Door: The Bush Doctrine and Iranian State Building," *Vaseteh: Journal of the European Society for Iranian Studies.* Rome: University of Rome, 2005, vol. 1 no. 1:11.

[46]Robert Jervis, "Understanding the Bush Doctrine." *Political Science Quarterly*, 118, no. 3, Fall 2003, p. 369.

built on will be addressed through the democratic process.[47] It is the hope that there is a connection between democracy and the behavior of states and individuals, but the jury is still out.

The second fundamental concept of the Bush Doctrine is that the international environment has changed and with this change comes serious threats to America. The most serious threat Americans face is the ability of a terrorist organization to obtain weapons of mass destruction.[48] This threat would result in the killing of thousands, if not tens of thousands of innocent people. This threat is real. The Anarchical Vulnerability that is felt by Americans needs to be answered by the government. In the past, it was believed Anarchical Vulnerability was diffused by conflict or deterrence.[49] For example, conflict was used after the Americans were attacked by Imperial Japan, the Americans mobilized to defeat the Axis in World War II. Deterrence was used after the shock of discovering missiles in Cuba. The Bush Doctrine presumes the policies of deterrence do not work on this new enemy. The use of suicide bombers illustrates the traditional incentive of self-preservation does not apply in the War on Terror.[50] Therefore, to counter this intersection of rogue states and terrorist organizations, the ability to conduct a preventive war has been developed.[51] Preventive war implies among other things, a high degree of confidence that the future will be bleak unless action is taken. It is a policy that inherently rests on speculation—but that is not new. What is new, however, is that the Bush Doctrine rests on unilateral action premised on speculation. We can all agree that in the face of a clear and present danger (like the evidence of a weapon of mass destruction in a major city), the government's primary duty is to protect its citizens. The real issue is what happens when the danger is not clear and present?

The idea of preventive war is problematic in three ways: first, because information of the threat deals with future events, it is very difficult to be certain of the threat; second, even information on past capabilities, as in the case of Saddam Hussein's development of Weapons of Mass Destruction, behaviors may be difficult to ascertain; and, third, unless

challengers are conclusively deterred by the first preventive war, another may be engaged in,[52] thereby creating an environment of serial preventive wars which, by their nature, would not prevent future attacks.[53] Furthermore, faced with this degree of uncertainty of analysis, doubt and uncertainty of the threat will be created. This, in turn, causes political opposition to form that will hamper a unified front. Because of this opposition, national leaders will not force strong action.[54] Ultimately, because of the lack of strong analysis and strong leadership, preventive wars create an environment of unilateralism.

The third fundamental concept of the Bush Doctrine is the maintenance of American hegemony. America is the only state in the international community that can provide both a military and a cultural response to the challenges of the War on Terror. Realists have criticized this concept. Neo-Realists argue no state is unique. Neo-Realists contend the American perception of uniqueness comes from the lack of a balancing power in the international environment today. Some authors in this school of thought contend the United States is not a *status-quo* power due to this fear of the future. Even though the Bush Administration claims to be Realist in its foreign policy, observers have said the notion of changing governments (a fundamental objective of preventive war) is really Wilsonian or Liberal.[55] Critics of the Bush Doctrine have argued the proliferation of nuclear programs in North Korea and Iran are examples of states trying to balance (or deter) the United States. As Robert Jervis stated in his discussion of Realist critics of the Bush Doctrine: "Amid the debate about [what] these [nuclear] weapons can accomplish, everyone agrees that they can deter invasion, which makes them very attractive to a state who fear they may be in American gun sights."[56]

The Bush Doctrine has created a very real, worrisome result of unintended consequences. Hence, the change in American foreign policy due to this combination of optimism and fear may have created a perception by suspected nations that the only way

---

[47]Ibid. p. 366.

[48]Ibid. p. 369.

[49]Chris J. Dolan, "The Bush Doctrine and U.S. Intervention." *American Diplomacy*, 9, no. 2, 2004, p. 4.

[50]Robert Jervis, "Understanding the Bush Doctrine." *Political Science Quarterly*, 118, no. 3, Fall 2003, p. 369.

[51]Ibid. p. 373.

[52]Ibid. p. 376.

[53]For a more detailed discussion on the Bush Doctrine and Iranian state building see: Patrick C. Coaty, "The War Next Door: The Bush Doctrine and Iranian State Building." *Vaseteh: Journal of the European Society for Iranian Studies*, Rome: University of Rome, 2005, vol. 1, no.1: pp. 11–35.

[54]Ibid.

[55]Chris J. Dolan, "The Bush Doctrine and U.S. Intervention." *American Diplomacy* 9, no. 2, 2004, p. 4.

[56]Robert Jervis, "Understanding the Bush Doctrine." *Political Science Quarterly*, 118, no. 3, Fall 2003, p. 387.

to deter the United States is through developing a nuclear weapon. Iran's actions seem consistent with this view. Is the development of a nuclear weapon or other programs we see the North Koreans and Iranians doing rational? It was a combination of naiveté or hubris to believe the North Koreans and the Iranians would not respond to this labeling as an enemy to the United States. The Iranians and North Koreans have had years to respond to the Bush speech.

We know the answer of the North Koreans. They have developed atomic weapons as both an export product and as a prestige enhancing device for the regime. They are now nominally an atomic power. They seem to think that after achieving this technological success that countries (especially the United States) have to negotiate with them on a one-to-one basis. Their perception is based on the experiences of the other countries that have proliferated especially Israel, India, Pakistan and China. North Korea's neighbor, Japan, is in the process of changing its strategic outlook as a result of the North Korean nuclear test. Even though the United States has reiterated its defense obligation if Japan is attacked, now that the threat is from a country such as North Korea, it seems the Japanese will probably have no choice but to re-examine their strategic strategy as it deals with nuclear weapons.

The Iranians appear to be several steps behind the North Koreans. Some believe the North Koreans test could be a type of trade show to show off their product to would be buyers such as the Iranians. One thing we do know as of this writing, it looks as though the Bush Doctrine and the arguments that were made for invading Iraq have failed. It also looks as if the democratization of the Middle East is also failing with the war between the Israelis and Hezbollah in the summer of 2006.

We have seen a new development in the post-Cold War, that states are pursuing nuclear weapons in order to prevent an invasion by the United States or other power. The Bush Doctrine was intended to prevent countries from developing weapons of mass destruction and giving them to terrorist groups. Instead, it has been interpreted as, develop weapons of mass destruction as fast as you can. Similar to Joseph Stalin's reaction to President Truman's announcement at the Potsdam Conference at the end of World War II.

One last wrinkle in the new strategic environment from the Cold War to the post-Cold War is Mutually Assured Destruction does not work with an enemy who uses suicide as a major attack device. The fear of most analysts is not an ICBM launched from North Korea or Iran. It is a terrorist group of suicide bombers equipped with an atomic device or dirty bomb in a van inside a city. The terrorists do not have any intention of surviving the attack, so what would an American President do? Our public policy apparatus and our political leaders have failed in outlining this nightmare. Mutually Assured Destruction does not work if the enemy is not deterred by their own death.[57]

CONCLUSION

The public policy process concerning nuclear weapons has several themes. First, the lessons of the United States having nuclear superiority throughout the end of World War II and the Cold War, gave rise to two strategic doctrines called Containment and Mutually Assured Destruction. These strategic options did not give Presidents enough choices when crises occurred. The policy choice seemed to be: use nuclear weapons or do nothing.

Several times, the world was close to a nuclear exchange of weapons. All of these scenarios involved the Soviet Union. Two of them the Korean War and the Cuban Missile Crisis, involved an American President implying he would use nuclear weapons to change the behavior of the Soviet Union.

In our discussion, we have shown even though the Presidents wanted different strategies, the lack of willingness of the American people to support a large conventional military force and the stubbornness of the public policy apparatus made the strategic doctrines of the Cold War live on much longer than was necessary. As long as each side of the Cold War had nuclear weapons deterrence, the problem of nuclear proliferation was to be policed by the Superpowers by several treaties including the Non-Proliferation Treaty and the Nuclear Test Ban treaty. Furthermore, the International Atomic Energy Agency was also used to inspect states that may try to cheat on the treaties.

President Reagan also tried to change his options and he came up with the Strategic Defense Initiative. Reagan promised the public policy apparatus funding for increased conventional military and a new vision that would replace MAD. Soon after

---

[57]For a more detailed discussion of nuclear terrorism see Patrick C. Coaty, *Understanding the War on Terror.* Dubuque, IA: Kendall/Hunt Publishing Co., 2006, pp. 112–114.

leaving office, the Soviet Union collapsed creating opportunities for the United States to re-examine its strategic policies.

The collapse of the Soviet Union resulted in many countries not having a nuclear deterrent. Combined with the terrorist attacks of September 11th and the issue of nuclear proliferation has become front and center on the world stage. President Bush in 2002 restructured the strategic thinking of the United States by highlighting countries that were known sponsors of terrorism and working on weapons programs. He called these countries the Axis of Evil. These countries included Iraq, Iran and North Korea. After the American invasion of Iraq, Iran and North Korea set to get nuclear weapons technology as fast as they could. The world watched and did nothing. The problem with the so called Bush Doctrine is the United States does not have the conventional military capacity nor the political will to force Iran or North Korea to give up its nuclear ambitions. In this chapter, we have shown how the public policy process has failed to give Presidents the tools to have a more effective nuclear policy. We also examined the unintended effect of the Bush Doc-

trine. If you have nuclear weapons, the United States will not pressure you. Countries such as Pakistan or Israel are new nuclear powers with the status of American allies. However, if you are trying to achieve nuclear weapons, then we reserve the right to invade your country. All this did was put Iran and North Korea on notice to get nuclear weapons no matter what the cost.

TERMS TO REMEMBER

NUCLEAR CHAIN REACTION

LOS ALAMOS

CUBAN MISSILE CRISIS

MUTUALLY ASSURED DESTRUCTION (MAD)

NUCLEAR PLANNING GROUP

NAVAL QUARANTINE

STRATEGIC DEFENSE INITIATIVE

PREVENTIVE WAR

CONTAINMENT

Public Policy and Nuclear Weapons

TRUE OR FALSE QUESTIONS

1. North Korea does not have an atomic bomb.   T / F

2. South Korea does not have an atomic bomb.   T / F

3. NPT stands for the Nuclear Power Treaty.   T / F

4. Great Britain and the United States formed a partnership to develop nuclear power.   T / F

5. Klaus Fuchs was a spy for the Soviet Union.   T / F

6. President Johnson was the first President to drop an atomic bomb.   T / F

7. Nuclear bombs were used in Vietnam.   T / F

8. Nuclear bombs are being used in Iraq.   T / F

9. The United States used atomic bombs in World War II because Japan is an Asian country.   T / F

10. The Iranians and Israelis have atomic weapons.   T / F

MULTIPLE CHOICE QUESTIONS

11. MAD stands for
    a. Mutually Assured Destruction
    b. Mutually Assumed Destruction
    c. Momentarily Assured Destruction
    d. Militarily Assumed Destruction

12. Leo Szilard was
    a. the scientist who first conceived the possibility of a nuclear chain reaction.
    b. was the first director of Los Alamos.
    c. was from Germany.
    d. was Harry Truman's Secretary of War.

13. Henry Stimson was
    a. the scientist who first conceived the possibility of a nuclear chain reaction.
    b. was the first director of Los Alamos.
    c. was from Germany.
    d. was Harry Truman's Secretary of War.

14. The government bought Los Alamos for
    a. 2 million dollars
    b. 1 million dollars
    c. 550,000 dollars
    d. 440,000 dollars

15. Who was contracted to run Los Alamos?
    a. Army
    b. Navy
    c. Air Force
    d. University of California

16. If the United States would not have dropped the atomic bombs on Japan it has been estimated the occupation force after the invasion of Japan would have numbered
    a. 100,000
    b. 300,000
    c. 1 million
    d. 2 million

17. The United States also used atomic weapons in Korea
    a. because of Eisenhower's bluff.
    b. because MacArthur had to fight the Chinese Communists.
    c. the U.S. did not use atomic weapons in Korea.
    d. because the North Koreans used atomic weapons first.

18. Robert McNamara was John F. Kennedy's
    a. Secretary of State
    b. Secretary of Defense
    c. National Security Advisor
    d. U.N. Ambassador

19. Americans play poker, Russians play
    a. soccer
    b. bridge
    c. chess
    d. roulette

20. The closest the Russians and Americans came to a nuclear conflict during the Cold War was during the
    a. Berlin Crisis.
    b. Korean War.
    c. Cuban Missile Crisis.
    d. Soviet Invasion of Afghanistan.

chapter fifteen

IMAGE FROM DEFENSE VISUAL INFORMATION CENTER

CONCLUSION: NOW YOU KNOW

INTRODUCTION

We started this book with an analogy of the power of the dealer in a hand of poker. One of the main themes of this book is the power of understanding the rules before you play the game of life. Our educational system and popular culture have sent a message that somehow government and politics is boring and for old people. This book has been an attempt to challenge the outdated messages you have been receiving from the media, academia, and even your family and friends. Our objective has been to lay out the issues and systems for your own analysis. If you are able to discern for yourself the reason why you are acting in a certain way, then we will be successful in our effort to help you analyze the American system of government.

The Constitution was the starting point of our analysis. We began by reading and examining the original text of the document. In the Constitution we saw how the Founding Fathers provided a blue-print for the development of our society. They believed in an experiment of self government that at its foundation had three universal principles. These principles are: popular sovereignty, rule of law and tolerance. We have examined all three of the principles in the context of the relationship between the individual and the state. First, we created a context for our analysis by reviewing the issues that have made news in the media and the issues our leaders have been talking about in the recent elections. Then, we examined the Constitution as a document that protected each of us from the power of the Federal government. The effort to write the document and have a Bill of Rights designed for this purpose were the early efforts of the Founding Fathers to create a system of justice. Finally, we explained how one cannot enjoy the fruits of liberty without the understanding of tolerance. We defined tolerance as different from acceptance. We can disagree on people's behavior. There are behaviors that most of us can

205

disagree with. However, that does not mean a person should not have the liberty to pursue those behaviors nor does it mean a person should not suffer the consequences of their actions doing such behaviors. Should the state be involved in issues that police personal behavior even if those behaviors can hurt the person doing them?

We have discussed issues such as smoking bans, policing a person's sexual preferences, and eating behaviors. We have tried to highlight the idea that there are other ways to show that you disagree with a certain behavior than by outlawing it. A person can shun behaviors they do not agree with, or they can use their economic power not to support any corporations or institutions that support a behavior they disagree with. We have shown that liberty cannot be a commodity that one person enjoys at the expense of others. It has a very delicate property that all of us must be aware of to preserve it.

Next, we discussed the difference between civil liberties and civil rights. Civil liberties can be thought of as a government "do not do" list. In the Constitution these are specific prohibitions on actions taken by the government. The freedom of religion is an example of a civil liberty. A civil right is an obligation of the government to be engaged and set down laws and procedures that insure people are treated equally. The Civil Rights movement made famous by Martin Luther King, Jr., was a movement that demanded the government act to have equal protection under the law for all people. We discussed how important the Civil Rights movement is in protecting all of our rights. This distinction is important so we can analyze and make decisions, keeping in mind the great ideas of Martin Luther King, Jr. and the Founding Fathers. Yes, the Constitution did fail in the early years by allowing slavery. However, we have discussed the reasoning and the failed compromise that was produced. The issue of race relations is one of the biggest challenges all of us face. It is our hope our examination of this issue in the context of understanding the distinctions between civil liberties and civil rights, contribute to a better understanding and some common ground in which we can start a discussion of mutual respect and tolerance in order to work out these issues for future generations.

After our examination of the personal protections afforded to us by the Constitution and the successes and failures of those protections for members of our society, we analyzed the intergovernmental relations between the different layers of our government. The different models of Federalism has been discussed including the increasing federal role in the policy areas of education and economic development. The different types of federal aid and mandates was also examined and discussed to give us a better understanding of the institutional effectiveness of the government. So, when we decide to vote for an increase in the Federal government's activities in a certain area, we will understand how it will affect our local and state governments.

This completed our discussion of the basic structure of the government. We then turned our attention to the politics and procedures used to select the people who represent us inside this structure. We examined the properties of public opinion and polling. In this chapter, we explained the science behind statistical analysis of random sampling and showed how public opinion polls are similar to fresh bread, they should be used the same day. If they are older than a day or two the information becomes as stale as week old bread. Then we analyzed the properties of public opinions and briefly discussed the ways individuals determine and form their own opinions. After we understood how people form opinions, we then explored the uniquely American exercise of campaigns and elections. In chapter 8, we discussed two significant elections—the 1960 Presidential election and the 1974 Congressional election. These elections were prototypical of the elections we have today. The idea of the candidate as the personal power center at the expense of the party has been a constant theme throughout the modern period of elections. We then went on to discuss the roles of the party and briefly how after 1960 television has become the essential tool for campaigns. This, in turn, has created an insatiable appetite for money by candidates in order for them to afford commercials that introduce them to the voters or attack their opponents in negative advertisements.

After our discussion of the way we select our leaders, we then analyzed the branches of government: the Congress, which is the Legislative branch, the Presidency, which is the Executive branch, and the Supreme Court, which is the Judiciary. All of these branches were written into the Constitution. In our analysis we showed how these branches interact with each other and how they have grown. Included in this discussion was the rising power of the bureaucracy. This is not a branch of government (it is included in the Executive branch), but, for many it is the only part of the government they will deal with. The properties of the bureaucracy were defined and we distinguished between private and public bureaucracies so that you would understand this distinction and be aware of the private information you give to these bureaucracies.

After all of this, we put all of the parts of government and politics together and observed the public policy process. In the final two chapters we saw how the government selects a problem to be dealt with on the domestic front. We used the Medicare program to illustrate how government serves people who vote (older people) and ignore people who do not vote (younger people). Then we showed how Medicare started as a program to have research on the three leading causes of death at the time, heart disease, strokes and cancer. The politics were not there to spend 2.5 billion dollars on a research program, so President Johnson and Congress decided to create Medicare. Medicare and the funding of Medicare is another challenge we will face as a society in the coming years. Finally, we discussed the role of nuclear weapons in shaping our domestic and foreign policies since their first use and development during World War II.

We saw how the public policy process did not serve the needs of the President in creating options for his use in times of crisis. The Congress, bureaucracy and the American people saw nuclear weapons (as long as they were not used) as a cheap and easy way to stop aggression by other nations. During the Cold War, when the world was divided by two Superpowers each having their own nuclear umbrella to shield their allies. The strategic doctrine of Mutually Assured Destruction was unruly but reasonable. However, after the collapse of the Soviet Union many countries lost their protection and did not have the confidence of the successor states to provide protection from nuclear powers (primarily the United States).

President Bush's State of the Union address marked this fundamental weakness of these states by issuing a warning against Iraq, Iran and North Korea about pursuing nuclear weapons or weapons of mass destruction. The problem for the United States was we had not punished countries that joined the nuclear club, therefore North Korea and Iran especially viewed having nuclear weapons as a means of deterring the United States from pursuing a policy of regime change. As of October 9, 2006, North Korea successfully tested an atomic weapon, therefore becoming a member of the nuclear club and sowing the seeds for a crisis with the United States. The United States has already warned North Korea, if they sell their technology to another state or non-state actor and they successfully attack the United States with a North Korean weapon, the United States will view it as an attack by North Korea and respond. Nuclear proliferation is another challenge you will face in the future.

We wrote this book in order to give you the analytical tools for you to make your own conclusions on issues such as nuclear proliferation, Medicare, and other challenges you will face in the future. Having read this book, you will have a greater understanding of how the government works, and why the rules are written in a certain way. It is our hope that now you will take a seat at the poker table and when the dealer sets down the rules you will have an increased understanding of how to play the cards you have been dealt.

IMAGE FROM DEFENSE VISUAL INFORMATION CENTER

HISTORICAL DOCUMENTS

100 Milestone Documents

The following is a list of 100 milestone documents, compiled by the National Archives and Records Administration, and drawn primarily from its nationwide holdings. The documents chronicle United States history from 1776 to 1965.

Lee Resolution (1776)

Declaration of Independence (1776)

Articles of Confederation (1777)

Treaty of Alliance with France (1778)

Original Design of the Great Seal
  of the United States (1782)

Treaty of Paris (1783)

Virginia Plan (1787)

Northwest Ordinance (1787)

Constitution of the United States (1787)

Federalist Papers, No. 6, No. 10, No. 37, and No.
  51 (1787–1788)

President George Washington's First Inaugural
  Speech (1789)

Federal Judiciary Act (1789)

Bill of Rights (1791)

Patent for Cotton Gin (1794)

President George Washington's Farewell Address
  (1796)

Alien and Sedition Acts (1798)

Jefferson's Secret Message to Congress Regarding
  the Lewis and Clark Expedition (1803)

Louisiana Purchase Treaty (1803)

Marbury v. Madison (1803)

Treaty of Ghent (1814)

McCulloch v. Maryland (1819)

Missouri Compromise (1820)

Monroe Doctrine (1823)

Gibbons v. Ogden (1824)

President Andrew Jackson's Message to Congress
  "On Indian Removal" (1830)

Treaty of Guadalupe Hidalgo (1848)

Compromise of 1850 (1850)

Kansas-Nebraska Act (1854)

Dred Scott v. Sanford (1857)

Telegram Announcing the Surrender
  of Fort Sumter (1861)

Homestead Act (1862)

Pacific Railway Act (1862)

Morrill Act (1862)

Emancipation Proclamation (1863)

War Department General Order 143: Creation of
  the U.S. Colored Troops (1863)

Gettysburg Address (1863)

Wade-Davis Bill (1864)

President Abraham Lincoln's Second Inaugural
  Address (1865)

Articles of Agreement Relating to the Surrender
  of the Army of Northern Virginia (1865)

13th Amendment to the U.S. Constitution:
  Abolition of Slavery (1865)

Check for the Purchase of Alaska (1868)

Treaty of Fort Laramie (1868)

14th Amendment to the U.S. Constitution:
  Civil Rights (1868)

15th Amendment to the U.S. Constitution:
  Voting Rights (1870)

Act Establishing Yellowstone National Park (1872)

Thomas Edison's Patent Application
  for the Light Bulb (1880)

Chinese Exclusion Act (1882)

Pendleton Act (1883)

Interstate Commerce Act (1887)

Dawes Act (1887)

Sherman Anti-Trust Act (1890)

Plessy v. Ferguson (1896)

De Lôme Letter (1898)

Joint Resolution to Provide for Annexing the
  Hawaiian Islands to the United States (1898)

Platt Amendment (1903)

Theodore Roosevelt's Corollary to the Monroe
  Doctrine (1905)

16th Amendment to the U.S. Constitution:
  Federal Income Tax (1913)

17th Amendment to the U.S. Constitution: Direct Election of U.S. Senators (*1913*)

Keating-Owen Child Labor Act of 1916 (*1916*)

Zimmermann Telegram (*1917*)

Joint Address to Congress Leading to a Declaration of War Against Germany (*1917*)

President Woodrow Wilson's 14 Points (*1918*)

19th Amendment to the U.S. Constitution: Women's Right to Vote (*1920*)

Boulder Canyon Project Act (*1928*)

Tennessee Valley Authority Act (*1933*)

National Industrial Recovery Act (*1933*)

National Labor Relations Act (*1935*)

Social Security Act (*1935*)

President Franklin Roosevelt's Radio Address Unveiling the Second Half of the New Deal (*1936*)

President Franklin Roosevelt's Annual Message (Four Freedoms) to Congress (*1941*)

Lend-Lease Act (*1941*)

Executive Order 8802: Prohibition of Discrimination in the Defense Industry (*1941*)

Joint Address to Congress Leading to a Declaration of War Against Japan (*1941*)

Executive Order 9066: Resulting in the Relocation of Japanese (*1942*)

General Dwight D. Eisenhower's Order of the Day (*1944*)

Servicemen's Readjustment Act (*1944*)

Manhattan Project Notebook (*1945*)

Surrender of Germany (*1945*)

United Nations Charter (*1945*)

Surrender of Japan (*1945*)

Truman Doctrine (*1947*)

Marshall Plan (*1948*)

Press Release Announcing U.S. Recognition of Israel (*1948*)

Executive Order 9981: Desegregation of the Armed Forces (*1948*)

Armistice Agreement for the Restoration of the South Korean State (*1953*)

Senate Resolution 301: Censure of Senator Joseph McCarthy (*1954*)

Brown v. Board of Education (*1954*)

National Interstate and Defense Highways Act (*1956*)

Executive Order 10730: Desegregation of Central High School (*1957*)

President Dwight D. Eisenhower's Farewell Address (*1961*)

President John F. Kennedy's Inaugural Address (*1961*)

Executive Order 10924: Establishment of the Peace Corps (*1961*)

Transcript of John Glenn's Official Communication with the Command Center (*1962*)

Aerial Photograph of Missiles in Cuba (*1962*)

Test Ban Treaty (*1963*)

Official Program for the March on Washington (*1963*)

Civil Rights Act (*1964*)

Tonkin Gulf Resolution (*1964*)

Social Security Act Amendments (*1965*)

Voting Rights Act (*1965*)

The Lee Resolution

Resolved, That these United Colonies are, and of right ought to be, free and independent States, that they are absolved from all allegiance to the British Crown, and that all political connection between them and the State of Great Britain is, and ought to be, totally dissolved.

That it is expedient forthwith to take the most effectual measures for forming foreign Alliances.

That a plan of confederation be prepared and transmitted to the respective Colonies for their consideration and approbation.

The Declaration of Independence

When in the Course of human events it becomes necessary for one people to dissolve the political bands which have connected them with another and to assume among the powers of the earth, the separate and equal station to which the Laws of Nature and of Nature's God entitle them, a decent respect to the opinions of mankind requires that they should declare the causes which impel them to the separation.

We hold these truths to be self-evident, that all men are created equal, that they are endowed by their Creator with certain unalienable Rights, that among these are Life, Liberty and the pursuit of Happiness.—That to secure these rights, Governments are instituted among Men, deriving their just powers from the consent of the governed,—That whenever any Form of Government becomes destructive of these ends, it is the Right of the People to alter or to abolish it, and to institute new Government, laying its foundation on such principles and organizing its powers in such form, as to them shall seem most likely to effect their Safety and Happiness. Prudence, indeed, will dictate that Governments long established should not be changed for light and transient causes; and accordingly all experience hath shewn that mankind are more disposed to suffer, while evils are sufferable than to right themselves by abolishing the forms to which they are accustomed. But when a long train of abuses and usurpations, pursuing invariably the same Object evinces a design to reduce them under absolute Despotism, it is their right, it is their duty, to throw off such Government, and to provide new Guards for their future security.—Such has been the patient sufferance of these Colonies; and such is now the necessity which constrains them to alter their former Systems of Government. The history of the present King of Great Britain is a history of repeated injuries and usurpations, all having in direct object the establishment of an absolute Tyranny over these States. To prove this, let Facts be submitted to a candid world.

He has refused his Assent to Laws, the most wholesome and necessary for the public good.

He has forbidden his Governors to pass Laws of immediate and pressing importance, unless suspended in their operation till his Assent should be obtained; and when so suspended, he has utterly neglected to attend to them.

He has refused to pass other Laws for the accommodation of large districts of people, unless those people would relinquish the right of Representation in the Legislature, a right inestimable to them and formidable to tyrants only.

He has called together legislative bodies at places unusual, uncomfortable, and distant from the depository of their Public Records, for the sole purpose of fatiguing them into compliance with his measures.

He has dissolved Representative Houses repeatedly, for opposing with manly firmness his invasions on the rights of the people.

He has refused for a long time, after such dissolutions, to cause others to be elected, whereby the Legislative Powers, incapable of Annihilation, have returned to the People at large for their exercise; the State remaining in the mean time exposed to all the dangers of invasion from without, and convulsions within.

He has endeavoured to prevent the population of these States; for that purpose obstructing the Laws for Naturalization of Foreigners; refusing to pass others to encourage their migrations hither, and raising the conditions of new Appropriations of Lands.

He has obstructed the Administration of Justice by refusing his Assent to Laws for establishing Judiciary Powers.

He has made Judges dependent on his Will alone for the tenure of their offices, and the amount and payment of their salaries.

He has erected a multitude of New Offices, and sent hither swarms of Officers to harass our people and eat out their substance.

He has kept among us, in times of peace, Standing Armies without the Consent of our legislatures.

He has affected to render the Military independent of and superior to the Civil Power.

He has combined with others to subject us to a jurisdiction foreign to our constitution, and unacknowledged by our laws; giving his Assent to their Acts of pretended Legislation:

For Quartering large bodies of armed troops among us:

For protecting them, by a mock Trial, from punishment for any Murders which they should commit on the Inhabitants of these States:

For cutting off our Trade with all parts of the world:

For imposing Taxes on us without our Consent:

For depriving us in many cases, of the benefit of Trial by Jury:

For transporting us beyond Seas to be tried for pretended offences:

For abolishing the free System of English Laws in a neighbouring Province, establishing therein an Arbitrary government, and enlarging its Boundaries so as to render it at once an example and fit instrument for introducing the same absolute rule into these Colonies:

For taking away our Charters, abolishing our most valuable Laws, and altering fundamentally the Forms of our Governments:

For suspending our own Legislatures, and declaring themselves invested with power to legislate for us in all cases whatsoever.

He has abdicated Government here, by declaring us out of his Protection and waging War against us.

He has plundered our seas, ravaged our Coasts, burnt our towns, and destroyed the lives of our people.

He is at this time transporting large Armies of foreign Mercenaries to compleat the works of death, desolation and tyranny, already begun with circumstances of Cruelty & perfidy scarcely paralleled in the most barbarous ages, and totally unworthy the Head of a civilized nation.

He has constrained our fellow Citizens taken Captive on the high Seas to bear Arms against their Country, to become the executioners of their friends and Brethren, or to fall themselves by their Hands.

He has excited domestic insurrections amongst us, and has endeavoured to bring on the inhabitants of our frontiers, the merciless Indian Savages whose known rule of warfare, is an undistinguished destruction of all ages, sexes and conditions.

In every stage of these Oppressions We have Peti-

tioned for Redress in the most humble terms: Our repeated Petitions have been answered only by repeated injury. A Prince, whose character is thus marked by every act which may define a Tyrant, is unfit to be the ruler of a free people.

Nor have We been wanting in attentions to our British brethren. We have warned them from time to time of attempts by their legislature to extend an unwarrantable jurisdiction over us. We have reminded them of the circumstances of our emigration and settlement here. We have appealed to their native justice and magnanimity, and we have conjured them by the ties of our common kindred to disavow these usurpations, which would inevitably interrupt our connections and correspondence. They too have been deaf to the voice of justice and of consanguinity. We must, therefore, acquiesce in the necessity, which denounces our Separation, and hold them, as we hold the rest of mankind, Enemies in War, in Peace Friends.

We, therefore, the Representatives of the United States of America, in General Congress, Assembled, appealing to the Supreme Judge of the world for the rectitude of our intentions, do, in the Name, and by Authority of the good People of these Colonies, solemnly publish and declare, That these United Colonies are, and of Right ought to be Free and Independent States, that they are Absolved from all Allegiance to the British Crown, and that all political connection between them and the State of Great Britain, is and ought to be totally dissolved; and that as Free and Independent States, they have full Power to levy War, conclude Peace, contract Alliances, establish Commerce, and to do all other Acts and Things which Independent States may of right do. And for the support of this Declaration, with a firm reliance on the protection of Divine Providence, we mutually pledge to each other our Lives, our Fortunes and our sacred Honor.

– John Hancock

New Hampshire:
Josiah Bartlett, William Whipple, Matthew Thornton

Massachusetts:
John Hancock, Samuel Adams, John Adams, Robert Treat Paine, Elbridge Gerry

Rhode Island:
Stephen Hopkins, William Ellery

Connecticut:
Roger Sherman, Samuel Huntington, William Williams, Oliver Wolcott

New York:
William Floyd, Philip Livingston, Francis Lewis, Lewis Morris

New Jersey:
Richard Stockton, John Witherspoon, Francis Hopkinson, John Hart, Abraham Clark

Pennsylvania:
Robert Morris, Benjamin Rush, Benjamin Franklin, John Morton, George Clymer, James Smith, George Taylor, James Wilson, George Ross

Delaware:
Caesar Rodney, George Read, Thomas McKean

Maryland:
Samuel Chase, William Paca, Thomas Stone, Charles Carroll of Carrollton

Virginia:
George Wythe, Richard Henry Lee, Thomas Jefferson, Benjamin Harrison, Thomas Nelson, Jr., Francis Lightfoot Lee, Carter Braxton

North Carolina:
William Hooper, Joseph Hewes, John Penn

South Carolina:
Edward Rutledge, Thomas Heyward, Jr., Thomas Lynch, Jr., Arthur Middleton

Georgia:
Button Gwinnett, Lyman Hall, George Walton

The Articles of Confederation

To all to whom these Presents shall come, we, the undersigned, Delegates of the States affixed to our Names, send greeting: Whereas the Delegates of the United States of America in Congress assembled, did on the fifteenth day of November, in the year of our Lord one thousand seven hundred and seventy seven, and in the second year of the Independence of America, agree to certain articles of Confederation and perpetual Union between the states of New Hampshire, Massachusetts bay, Rhode Island and Providence Plantations, Connecticut, New York, New Jersey, Pennsylvania, Delaware, Maryland, Virginia, North Carolina, South Carolina, and Georgia, in the words following, viz. Articles of Confederation and perpetual Union between the States of New Hampshire, Massachusetts bay, Rhode Island and Providence Plantations, Connecticut, New York, New Jersey, Pennsylvania, Delaware, Maryland, Virginia, North Carolina, South Carolina, and Georgia.

Article I. The stile of this confederacy shall be, "The United States of America."

Article II. Each State retains its sovereignty, freedom, and independence, and every power, jurisdiction, and right, which is not by this confederation, expressly delegated to the United States, in Congress assembled.

Article III. The said States hereby severally enter into a firm league of friendship with each other, for their common defence, the security of their liberties, and their mutual and general welfare, binding themselves to assist each other against all force offered to, or attacks made upon them, or any of them, on account of religion, sovereignty, trade, or any other pretence whatever.

Article IV. The better to secure and perpetuate mutual friendship and intercourse among the people of the different States in this union, the free inhabitants of each of these States, paupers, vagabonds, and fugitives from justice excepted, shall be entitled to all privileges and immunities of free citizens in the several States; and the people of each State shall have free ingress and regress to and from any other State, and shall enjoy therein all the privileges of trade and commerce, subject to the same duties, impositions, and restrictions, as the inhabitants thereof respectively; provided that such restrictions shall not extend so far as to prevent the removal of property imported into any State, to any other State, of which the owner is an inhabitant; provided also, that no imposition, duties, or restriction, shall be laid by any State on the property of the United States, or either of them.

If any person guilty of, or charged with, treason, felony, or other high misdemeanor in any State, shall flee from justice, and be found in any of the united States, he shall, upon demand of the governor or executive power of the State from which he fled, be delivered up, and removed to the State having jurisdiction of his offence.

Full faith and credit shall be given, in each of these States, to the records, acts, and judicial proceedings of the courts and magistrats of every other State.

Article V. For the more convenient management of the general interests of the united States, delegates shall be annually appointed in such manner as the legislature of each State shall direct, to meet in Congress on the first Monday in November, in every year, with a power reserved to each State to recall its delegates, or any of them, at any time within the year, and to send others in their stead, for the remainder of the year.

No State shall be represented in Congress by less than two, nor by more than Seven Members; and no person shall be capable of being delegate for more than three years, in any term of Six years; nor shall any person, being a delegate, be capable of holding any office under the united States, for which he, or another for his benefit, receives any salary, fees, or emolument of any kind.

Each State shall maintain its own delegates in a meeting of the States, and while they act as members of the committee of the States.

In determining questions in the united States in Congress assembled, each State shall have one vote.

Freedom of speech and debate in Congress shall not be impeached or questioned in any Court or place out of Congress; and the members of Congress shall be protected in their persons from arrests and imprisonments during the time of their going to and from, and attendance on, Congress, except for treason, felony or breach of the peace.

Article VI. No State, without the consent of the united States, in congress assembled, shall send any embassy to, or receive any embassy from, or enter into any conference, agreement, alliance, or treaty, with any King, prince or State; nor shall any person holding any office of profit or trust under the united States, or any of them, accept of any present, emolument, office, or title of any kind whatever, from any king, prince, or foreign State; nor shall the united States, in congress assembled, or any of them, grant any title of nobility.

No two or more States shall enter into any treaty, confederation, or alliance whatever, between them, without the consent of the united States, in Congress assembled, specifying accurately the purposes for which the same is to be entered into, and how long it shall continue.

No State shall lay any imposts or duties, which may interfere with any stipulations in treaties, entered into by the united States, in congress assembled, with any king, prince, or State, in pursuance of any treaties already proposed by congress to the courts of France and Spain.

No vessels of war shall be kept up in time of peace, by any State, except such number only as shall be deemed necessary by the united States, in congress assembled, for the defence of such State, or its trade; nor shall any body of forces be kept up, by any State, in time of peace, except such number only as, in the judgment of the united States, in congress assembled, shall be deemed requisite to garrison the forts necessary for the defence of such State; but every State shall always keep up a well-regulated and disciplined militia, sufficiently armed and accounted, and shall provide and constantly have ready for use, in public stores, a due number of field-pieces and tents, and a proper quantity of arms, ammunition, and camp equipage.

No State shall engage in any war without the consent of the united States, in congress assembled, unless such State be actually invaded by enemies, or shall have received certain advice of a resolution being formed by some nation of Indians to invade such State, and the danger is so imminent as not to admit of a delay till the united States, in congress assembled, can be consulted; nor shall any State grant commissions to any ships or vessels of war, nor letters of marque or reprisal, except it be after a declaration of war by the united States, in congress assembled, and then only against the kingdom or State, and the subjects thereof, against which war has been so declared, and under such regulations as shall be established by the united States, in congress assembled, unless such State be infested by pirates, in which case

vessels of war may be fitted out for that occasion, and kept so long as the danger shall continue, or until the united States, in congress assembled, shall determine otherwise.

Article VII. When land forces are raised by any State, for the common defence, all officers of or under the rank of colonel, shall be appointed by the legislature of each State respectively by whom such forces shall be raised, or in such manner as such State shall direct, and all vacancies shall be filled up by the State which first made appointment.

Article VIII. All charges of war, and all other expenses that shall be incurred for the common defence or general welfare, and allowed by the united States, in congress assembled, shall be defrayed out of a common treasury, which shall be supplied by the several States, in proportion to the value of all land within each State, granted to, or surveyed for, any person, as such land and the buildings and improvements thereon shall be estimated, according to such mode as the united States, in congress assembled, shall, from time to time, direct and appoint. The taxes for paying that proportion shall be laid and levied by the authority and direction of the legislatures of the several States, within the time agreed upon by the united States, in congress assembled.

Article IX. The united States, in congress assembled, shall have the sole and exclusive right and power of determining on peace and war, except in the cases mentioned in the sixth Article, of sending and receiving ambassadors; entering into treaties and alliances, provided that no treaty of commerce shall be made, whereby the legislative power of the respective States shall be restrained from imposing such imposts and duties on foreigners, as their own people are subjected to, or from prohibiting the exportation or importation of any species of goods or commodities whatsoever; of establishing rules for deciding, in all cases, what captures on land or water shall be legal, and in what manner prizes taken by land or naval forces in the service of the united Sates, shall be divided or appropriated; of granting letters of marque and reprisal in times of peace; appointing courts for the trial of piracies and felonies committed on the high seas; and establishing courts; for receiving and determineing finally appeals in all cases of captures; provided that no member of congress shall be appointed a judge of any of the said courts.

The united States, in congress assembled, shall also be the last resort on appeal, in all disputes and differences now subsisting, or that hereafter may arise between two or more States concerning boundary, jurisdiction, or any other cause whatever; which authority shall always be exercised in the manner following. Whenever the legislative or executive authority, or lawful agent of any State in controversy with another, shall present a petition to congress, stating the matter in question, and praying for a hearing, notice thereof shall be given, by order of congress, to the legislative or executive authority of the other State in controversy, and a day assigned for the appearance of the parties by their lawful agents, who shall then be directed to appoint, by joint consent, commissioners or judges to constitute a court for hearing and determining the matter in question: but if they cannot agree, congress shall name three persons out of each of the united States, and from the list of such persons each party shall alternately strike out one, the petitioners beginning, until the number shall be reduced to thirteen; and from that number not less than seven, nor more than nine names, as congress shall direct, shall, in the presence of congress, be drawn out by lot, and the persons whose names shall be so drawn, or any five of them, shall be commissioners or judges, to hear and finally determine the controversy, so always as a major part of the judges, who shall hear the cause, shall agree in the determination: and if either party shall neglect to attend at the day appointed, without showing reasons which congress shall judge sufficient, or being present, shall refuse to strike, the congress shall proceed to nominate three persons out of each State, and the secretary of congress shall strike in behalf of such party absent or refusing; and the judgment and sentence of the court, to be appointed in the manner before prescribed, shall be final and conclusive; and if any of the parties shall refuse to submit to the authority of such court, or to appear or defend their claim or cause, the court shall nevertheless proceed to pronounce sentence, or judgment, which shall in like manner be final and decisive; the judgment or sentence and other proceedings being in either case transmitted to congress, and lodged among the acts of congress, for the security of the parties concerned: provided that every commissioner, before he sits in judgment, shall take an oath to be administered by one of the judges of the Supreme or Superior court of the State where the cause shall be tried, "well and truly to hear and determine the matter in question, according to the best of his judgment, without favour, affection, or hope of reward:" Provided, also, that no State shall be deprived of territory for the benefit of the united States.

All controversies concerning the private right of soil claimed under different grants of two or more States, whose jurisdictions as they may respect such lands, and the States which passed such grants are adjusted, the said grants or either of them being at the same time claimed to have originated antecedent to such settlement of jurisdiction, shall, on the petition of either party to the congress of the united States, be finally determined, as near as may be, in the same manner as is before prescribed for deciding disputes respecting territorial jurisdiction between different States.

The united States, in congress assembled, shall also have the sole and exclusive right and power of regulating the alloy and value of coin struck by their own authority, or by that of the respective States fixing the standard of weights and measures throughout the united States; regulating the trade and managing all affairs with the Indians, not members of any of the States; provided that the legislative right of any State, within its own limits, be not infringed or violated; establishing and regulating post-offices from one State to another, throughout all the United States, and exacting such postage on the papers passing through the same, as may be requisite to defray the expenses of the said office; appointing all officers of the land forces in the service of the united States, excepting regimental officers; appointing all the officers of the naval forces, and commissioning all officers whatever in the service of the united States; making rules for the government and regulation of the said land and naval forces, and directing their operations.

The united States, in congress assembled, shall have authority to appoint a committee, to sit in the recess of congress, to be denominated, "A Committee of the States," and to consist of one delegate from each State; and to appoint such other committees and civil officers as may be necessary for managing the general affairs of the united States under their direction; to appoint one of their number to preside; provided that no person be allowed to serve in the office of president more than one year in any term of three years; to ascertain the necessary sums of money to be raised for the service of the united States, and to appropriate and apply the same for defraying the public expenses; to borrow money or emit bills on the credit of the united States, transmitting every half year to the respective States an account of the sums of money so borrowed or emitted; to build and equip a navy; to agree upon the number of land forces, and to make requisitions from each State for its quota, in proportion to the number of white inhabitants in such State, which requisition shall be binding; and thereupon the Legislature of each State shall appoint the regimental officers, raise the men, and clothe, arm, and equip them, in a soldier-like manner, at the expense of the united States; and the officers and men so clothed, armed, and equipped, shall march to the place appointed, and within the time agreed on by the united States, in congress assembled; but if the united States, in congress assembled, shall, on consideration of circumstances, judge proper that any State should not raise men, or should raise a smaller number than its quota, and that any other State should raise a greater number of men than the quota thereof, such extra number shall be raised, officered, clothed, armed, and equipped in the same manner as the quota of such State, unless the Legislature of such State shall judge that such extra number cannot be safely spared out of the same, in which case they shall raise, officer, clothe, arm, and equip, as many of such extra number as they judge can be safely spared. And the officers and men so clothed, armed, and equipped, shall march to the place appointed, and within the time agreed on by the united States in congress assembled.

The united States, in congress assembled, shall never engage in a war, nor grant letters of marque and reprisal in time of peace, nor enter into any treaties or alliances, nor coin money, nor regulate the value thereof nor ascertain the sums and expenses necessary for the defence and welfare of the united States, or any of them, nor emit bills, nor borrow money on the credit of the united States, nor appropriate money, nor agree upon the number of vessels of war to be built or purchased, or the number of land or sea forces to be raised, nor appoint a commander in chief of the army or navy, unless nine States assent to the same, nor shall a question on any other point, except for adjourning from day to day, be determined, unless by the votes of a majority of the united States in congress assembled.

The congress of the united States shall have power to adjourn to any time within the year, and to any place within the united States, so that no period of adjournment be for a longer duration than the space of six months, and shall publish the journal of their proceedings monthly, except such parts thereof relating to treaties, alliances, or military operations, as in their judgment require secrecy; and the yeas and nays of the delegates of each State, on any question, shall be entered on the journal, when it is desired by any delegate; and the delegates of a State, or any of them, at his or their request, shall be furnished with a transcript of the said journal, except such parts as are above excepted, to lay before the legislatures of the several States.

Article X. The committee of the States, or any nine of them, shall be authorized to execute, in the recess of congress, such of the powers of congress as the united States, in congress assembled, by the consent of nine States, shall, from time to time, think expedient to vest them with; provided that no power be delegated to the said committee, for the exercise of which, by the articles of confederation, the voice of nine States, in the congress of the united States assembled, is requisite.

Article XI. Canada acceding to this confederation, and joining in the measures of the united States, shall be admitted into, and entitled to all the advantages of this union: but no other colony shall be admitted into the same, unless such admission be agreed to by nine States.

Article XII. All bills of credit emitted, monies borrowed, and debts contracted by or under the authority of congress, before the assembling of the united States, in pursuance of the present confederation, shall be deemed and considered as a charge against the united States, for payment and satisfaction whereof the said United States and the public faith are hereby solemnly pledged.

Article XIII. Every State shall abide by the determinations of the united States, in congress assembled, on all questions which by this confederation are submitted to them. And the articles of this confederation shall be inviolably observed by every State, and the Union shall be perpetual; nor shall any alteration at any time hereafter be made in any of them, unless such alteration be agreed to in a congress of the united States, and be afterwards confirmed by the legislatures of every State.

And Whereas it hath pleased the Great Governor of the World to incline the hearts of the legislatures we respectively represent in congress, to approve of, and to authorize us to ratify the said articles of confederation and perpetual union, Know Ye, that we, the undersigned delegates, by virtue of the power and authority to us given for that purpose, do, by these presents, in the name and in behalf of our respective constituents, fully and entirely ratify and confirm each and every of the said articles of confederation and perpetual union, and all and singular the matters and things therein contained. And we do further solemnly plight and engage the faith of our respective constituents, that they shall abide by the determinations of the united States, in congress assembled, on all questions which by the said confederation are submitted to them; and that the articles thereof shall be inviolably observed by the States we respectively represent, and that the Union shall be perpetual. In witness whereof, we have hereunto set our hands, in Congress. Done at Philadelphia, in the State of Pennsylvania, the ninth day of July, in the year of our Lord one thousand seven hundred and seventy eight, and in the third year of the Independence of America.

The Treaty of Alliance with France

TREATY OF ALLIANCE

The most Christian King and the United States of North America, to wit, New Hampshire, Massachusetts Bay, Rhodes island, Connecticut, New York, New Jersey, Pennsylvania, Delaware, Maryland, Virginia, North Carolina, South Carolina, and Georgia, having this Day concluded a Treaty of amity and Commerce, for the reciprocal advantage of their Subjects and Citizens have thought it necessary to take into consideration the means of strengthening those engagements and of rondring them useful to the safety and tranquility of the two parties, particularly in case Great Britain in Resentment of that connection and of the good correspondence which is the object of the said Treaty, should break the Peace with france, either by direct hostilities, or by hindring her commerce and navigation, in a manner contrary to the Rights of Nations, and the Peace subsisting between the two Crowns; and his Majesty and the said united States having resolved in that Case to join their Councils and efforts against the Enterprises of their common Enemy, the respective Plenipotentiaries, impower'd to concert the Clauses & conditions proper to fulfil the said Intentions, have, after the most mature Deliberation, concluded and determined on the following Articles.

ART. 1.

If War should break out betwan france and Great Britain, during the continuance of the present War betwan the United States and England, his Majesty and the said united States, shall make it a common cause, and aid each other mutually with their good Offices, their Counsels, and their forces, according to the exigence of Conjunctures as becomes good & faithful Allies.

ART. 2.

The essential and direct End of the present defensive alliance is to maintain effectually the liberty, Sovereignty, and independance absolute and unlimited of the said united States, as well in Matters of Gouvernement as of commerce.

ART. 3.

The two contracting Parties shall each on its own Part, and in the manner it may judge most proper, make all the efforts in its Power, against their common Ennemy, in order to attain the end proposed.

ART. 4.

The contracting Parties agree that in case either of them should form any particular Enterprise in which the concurrence of the other may be desired, the Party whose concurrence is desired shall readily, and with good faith, join to act in concert for that Purpose, as far as circumstances and its own particular Situation will permit; and in that case, they shall regulate by a particular Convention the quantity and kind of Succour to be furnished, and the Time and manner of its being brought into action, as well as the advantages which are to be its Compensation.

ART. 5.

If the united States should think fit to attempt the Reduction of the British Power remaining in the Northern Parts of America, or the Islands of Bermudas, those Countries or Islands in case of Success, shall be confederated with or dependent upon the said united States.

ART. 6.

The Most Christian King renounces for ever the possession of the Islands of Bermudas as well as of any part of the continent of North america which before the treaty of Paris in 1763. or in virtue of that Treaty, were acknowledged to belong to the Crown of Great Britain, or to the united States heretofore called British Colonies, or which are at this Time or have lately been under the Power of The King and Crown of Great Britain.

ART. 7.

If his Most Christian Majesty shall think proper to attack any of the Islands situated in the Gulph of

Mexico, or near that Gulph, which are at present under the Power of Great Britain, all the said Isles, in case of success, shall appertain to the Crown of france.

ART. 8.

Neither of the two Parties shall conclude either Truce or Peace with Great Britain, without the formal consent of the other first obtain'd; and they mutually engage not to lay down their arms, until the Independence of the united states shall have been formally or tacitly assured by the Treaty or Treaties that shall terminate the War.

ART. 9.

The contracting Parties declare, that being resolved to fulfil each on its own Part the clauses and conditions of the present Treaty of alliance, according to its own power and circumstances, there shall be no after claim of compensation on one side or the other whatever may be the event of the War.

ART. 10.

The Most Christian King and the United states, agree to invite or admit other Powers who may have received injuries from England to make common cause with them, and to accede to the present alliance, under such conditions as shall be freely agreed to and settled between all the Parties.

ART. 11.

The two Parties guarantee mutually from the present time and forever, against all other powers, to wit, the united states to his most Christian Majesty the present Possessions of the Crown of france in America as well as those which it may acquire by the future Treaty of peace: and his most Christian Majesty guarantees on his part to the united states, their liberty, Sovereignty, and Independence absolute, and unlimited, as well in Matters of Government as commerce and also their Possessions, and the additions or conquests that their Confederation may obtain during the war, from any of the Dominions now or here-

tofore possessed by Great Britain in North America, conformable to the 5th & 6th articles above written, the whole as their Possessions shall be fixed and assured to the said States at the moment of the cessation of their present War with England.

ART. 12.

In order to fix more precisely the sense and application of the preceding article, the Contracting Parties declare, that in case of rupture between france and England, the reciprocal Guarantee declared in the said article shall have its full force and effect the moment such War shall break out and if such rupture shall not take place, the mutual obligations of the said guarantee shall not commence, until the moment of the cessation of the present War between the united states and England shall have ascertained the Possessions.

ART. 13.

The present Treaty shall be ratified on both sides and the Ratifications shall be exchanged in the space of six months, sooner if possible.

In faith where of the respective Plenipotentiaries, to wit on the part of the most Christian King Conrad Alexander Gerard royal syndic of the City of Strasbourgh & Secretary of his majestys Council of State and on the part of the United States Benjamin Franklin Deputy to the General Congress from the State of Pensylvania and President of the Convention of the same state, Silas Deane heretofore Deputy from the State of Connecticut & Arthur Lee Councellor at Law have signed the above Articles both in the French and English Languages declaring Nevertheless that the present Treaty was originally composed and concluded in the French Language, and they have hereunto affixed their Seals.

Done at Paris, this sixth Day of February, one thousand seven hundred and seventy eight.

C. A. GERARD
B FRANKLIN
SILAS DEANE
ARTHUR LEE

The Original Design of the Great Seal of the United States

The Great Seal of the United States is the symbol of our sovereignty as a nation. Its obverse is used on official documents to authenticate the signature of the President and it appears on proclamations, warrants, treaties, and commissions of high officials of the government. The Great Seal's design, used as our national coat of arms, is also used officially as decoration on military uniform buttons, on plaques above the entrances to U.S. embassies an consulates, and in other places. Both the obverse and the less familiar reverse, which is never used as a seal, are imprinted on the one-dollar bill.

The history of the Great Seal begins with the day of our founding as a nation. The Continental Congress appointed a committee to design a seal for the United States on July 4, 1776, just a few hours after they adopted the Declaration of Independence. The committee members—Benjamin Franklin, Thomas Jefferson, and John Adams—prepared a very complicated design that was promptly tabled by Congress. However, one prominent feature of their design appeared in the design that was originally adopted—the motto E Pluribus Unum, "Out of Many, One."

In 1780, a second committee—James Lovell of Massachusetts and John Morin Scott and William Churchill Houston of Virginia—developed a second design, but it was also tabled by Congress. Like the first design, the second had elements that were later incorporated into the final seal, including the olive branch, the constellation of 13 stars, and the shield with red and white stripes on a blue field.

A third committee was appointed in May of 1782. This committee's design employed the eagle for the first time, in the crest.

Early in 1782, Congress referred the three designs to Secretary of the Continental Congress Charles Thompson. Thompson made a fourth design that was revised by William Barton, a Philadelphia student of heraldry. Thompson submitted a written description of his final version to the Continental Congress that described the design and explained its symbolism. The Continental Congress approved this design on June 20, 1782.

(Information excerpted from *The Great Seal of the United States*. National Archives and Records Administration: Washington, DC, 1986.)

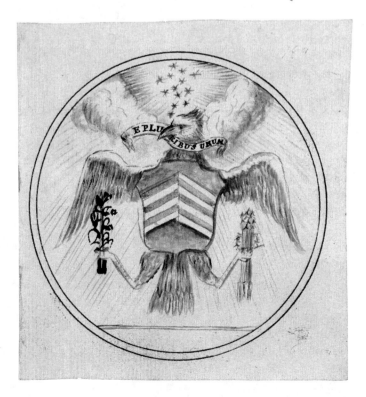

The Treaty of Paris

THE DEFINITIVE TREATY OF PEACE 1783

In the name of the most holy and undivided Trinity.

It having pleased the Divine Providence to dispose the hearts of the most serene and most potent Prince George the Third, by the grace of God, king of Great Britain, France, and Ireland, defender of the faith, duke of Brunswick and Lunebourg, archtreasurer and prince elector of the Holy Roman Empire etc., and of the United States of America, to forget all past misunderstandings and differences that have unhappily interrupted the good correspondence and friendship which they mutually wish to restore, and to establish such a beneficial and satisfactory intercourse, between the two countries upon the ground of reciprocal advantages and mutual convenience as may promote and secure to both perpetual peace and harmony; and having for this desirable end already laid the foundation of peace and reconciliation by the Provisional Articles signed at Paris on the 30th of November 1782, by the commissioners empowered on each part, which articles were agreed to be inserted in and constitute the Treaty of Peace proposed to be concluded between the Crown of Great Britain and the said United States, but which treaty was not to be concluded until terms of peace should be agreed upon between Great Britain and France and his Britannic Majesty should be ready to conclude such treaty accordingly; and the treaty between Great Britain and France having since been concluded, his Britannic Majesty and the United States of America, in order to carry into full effect the Provisional Articles above mentioned, according to the tenor thereof, have constituted and appointed, that is to say his Britannic Majesty on his part, David Hartley, Esqr., member of the Parliament of Great Britain, and the said United States on their part, John Adams, Esqr., late a commissioner of the United States of America at the court of Versailles, late delegate in Congress from the state of Massachusetts, and chief justice of the said state, and minister plenipotentiary of the said United States to their high mightinesses the States General of the United Netherlands; Benjamin Franklin, Esqr., late delegate in Congress from the state of Pennsylvania, president of the convention of the said state, and minister plenipotentiary from the United States of America at the court of Versailles; John Jay, Esqr., late president of Congress and chief justice of the state of New York, and minister plenipotentiary from the said United States at the court of Madrid; to be plenipotentiaries for the concluding and signing the present definitive treaty; who after having reciprocally communicated their respective full powers have agreed upon and confirmed the following articles.

ARTICLE 1:

His Brittanic Majesty acknowledges the said United States, viz., New Hampshire, Massachusetts Bay, Rhode Island and Providence Plantations, Connecticut, New York, New Jersey, Pennsylvania, Delaware, Maryland, Virginia, North Carolina, South Carolina and Georgia, to be free sovereign and independent states, that he treats with them as such, and for himself, his heirs, and successors, relinquishes all claims to the government, propriety, and territorial rights of the same and every part thereof.

ARTICLE 2:

And that all disputes which might arise in future on the subject of the boundaries of the said United States may be prevented, it is hereby agreed and declared, that the following are and shall be their boundaries, viz.; from the northwest angle of Nova Scotia, viz., that nagle which is formed by a line drawn due north from the source of St. Croix River to the highlands; along the said highlands which divide those rivers that empty themselves into the river St. Lawrence, from those which fall into the Atlantic Ocean, to the northwesternmost head of Connecticut River; thence down along the middle of that river to the forty-fifth degree of north latitude; from thence by a line due west on said latitude until it strikes the river Iroquois or Cataraquy; thence along the middle of said river into Lake Ontario; through the middle of said lake until it strikes the communication by water between that lake and Lake Erie; thence along the middle of said communication into Lake Erie, through the middle of said lake until it arrives at the water communication between that lake and Lake Huron; thence along the middle of said water communication into Lake Huron, thence through the middle of said lake to the water communication between that lake and Lake Superior; thence through Lake Superior northward of the Isles Royal and Phelipeaux to the Long Lake; thence through the middle of said Long Lake and the water communication between it and the Lake of the Woods, to the said Lake of the Woods; thence through the said lake to the most northwesternmost point thereof, and from thence on a due west course to the river Mississippi; thence by a line to be drawn along the middle of the said river Mississippi until it shall intersect the northernmost part of the thirty-first degree of north latitude, South, by a line to be drawn due east from the determination of the line last mentioned in the latitude of thirty-one degrees of the equator, to the middle of the river Apalachicola or Catahouche; thence along the middle thereof to its junction with the Flint River, thence straight to the head of Saint Mary's River; and thence down along the middle of Saint Mary's River to the Atlantic Ocean; east, by a line to be drawn along the middle of the river Saint Croix, from its mouth in the Bay of Fundy to its source, and from its source directly north to the aforesaid highlands which divide the rivers that fall into the Atlantic Ocean from those which fall into the river Saint Lawrence; comprehending all islands within twenty leagues of any part of the shores of the United States, and lying between lines to be drawn due east from the points where the aforesaid boundaries between Nova Scotia on the one part and East Florida on the other shall, respectively, touch the Bay of Fundy and the Atlantic Ocean, excepting such islands as now are or heretofore have been within the limits of the said province of Nova Scotia.

ARTICLE 3:

It is agreed that the people of the United States shall continue to enjoy unmolested the right to take fish of every kind on the Grand Bank and on all the other banks of Newfoundland, also in the Gulf of Saint Lawrence and at all other places in the sea, where the inhabitants of both countries used at any time heretofore to fish. And also that the inhabitants of the United States shall have liberty to take fish of every kind on such part of the coast of Newfoundland as British fishermen shall use, (but not to dry or cure the same on that island) and also on the coasts, bays and creeks of all other of his Brittanic Majesty's dominions in America; and that the American fish-ermen shall have liberty to dry and cure fish in any of the unsettled bays, harbors, and creeks of Nova Scotia, Magdalen Islands, and Labrador, so long as the same shall remain unsettled, but so soon as the same or either of them shall be settled, it shall not be lawful for the said fishermen to dry or cure fish at such settlement without a previous agreement for that purpose with the inhabitants, proprietors, or possessors of the ground.

ARTICLE 4:

It is agreed that creditors on either side shall meet with no lawful impediment to the recovery of the full value in sterling money of all bona fide debts heretofore contracted.

ARTICLE 5:

It is agreed that Congress shall earnestly recommend it to the legislatures of the respective states to provide for the restitution of all estates, rights, and properties, which have been confiscated belonging to real British subjects; and also of the estates, rights, and properties of persons resident in districts in the possession on his Majesty's arms and who have not borne arms against the said United States. And that persons of any other decription shall have free liberty to go to any part or parts of any of the thirteen United States and therein to remain twelve months unmolested in their endeavors to obtain the restitution of such of their estates, rights, and properties as may have been confiscated; and that Congress shall also earnestly recommend to the several states a reconsideration and revision of all acts or laws regarding the premises, so as to render the said laws or acts perfectly consistent not only with justice and equity but with that spirit of conciliation which on the return of the blessings of peace should universally prevail. And that Congress shall also earnestly recommend to the several states that the estates, rights, and properties, of such last mentioned persons shall be restored to them, they refunding to any persons who may be now in possession the bona fide price (where any has been given) which such persons may have paid on purchasing any of the said lands, rights, or properties since the confiscation.

And it is agreed that all persons who have any interest in confiscated lands, either by debts, marriage settlements, or otherwise, shall meet with no lawful impediment in the prosecution of their just rights.

ARTICLE 6:

That there shall be no future confiscations made nor any prosecutions commenced against any person or persons for, or by reason of, the part which he or they may have taken in the present war, and that no person shall on that account suffer any future loss or damage, either in his person, liberty, or property; and that those who may be in confinement on such charges at the time of the ratification of the treaty in America shall be immediately set at liberty, and the prosecutions so commenced be discontinued.

ARTICLE 7:

There shall be a firm and perpetual peace between his Brittanic Majesty and the said states, and between the subjects of the one and the citizens of the other, wherefore all hostilities both by sea and land shall from henceforth cease. All prisoners on both sides shall be set at liberty, and his Brittanic Majesty shall with all convenient speed, and without causing any destruction, or carrying away any Negroes or other property of the American inhabitants, withdraw all his armies, garrisons, and fleets from the said United States, and from every post, place, and harbor within the same; leaving in all fortifications, the American artilery that may be therein; and shall also order and cause all archives, records, deeds, and papers belonging to any of the said states, or their citizens, which in the course of the war may have fallen into the hands of his officers, to be forthwith restored and delivered to the proper states and persons to whom they belong.

ARTICLE 8:

The navigation of the river Mississippi, from its source to the ocean, shall forever remain free and open to the subjects of Great Britain and the citizens of the United States.

ARTICLE 9:

In case it should so happen that any place or territory belonging to Great Britain or to the United States should have been conquered by the arms of either from the other before the arrival of the said Provisional Articles in America, it is agreed that the same shall be restored without difficulty and without requiring any compensation.

ARTICLE 10:

The solemn ratifications of the present treaty expedited in good and due form shall be exchanged between the contracting parties in the space of six months or sooner, if possible, to be computed from the day of the signatures of the present treaty. In witness whereof we the undersigned, their ministers plenipotentiary, have in their name and in virtue of our full powers, signed with our hands the present definitive treaty and caused the seals of our arms to be affixed thereto.

Done at Paris, this third day of September in the year of our Lord, one thousand seven hundred and eighty-three.

D. HARTLEY (SEAL)
JOHN ADAMS (SEAL)
B. FRANKLIN (SEAL)
JOHN JAY (SEAL)

The Virginia Plan

State of the resolutions submitted to the consideration of the House by the honorable Mr. Randolph, as altered, amended, and agreed to, in a Committee of the whole House.

1. Resolved that it is the opinion of this Committee that a national government ought to be established consisting of a Supreme Legislative, Judiciary, and Executive.

2. Resolved that the national Legislature ought to consist of Two Branches.

3. Resolved that the members of the first branch of the national Legislature ought to be elected by the People of the several States for the term of Three years. to receive fixed stipends, by which they may be compensated for the devotion of their time to public service to be paid out of the National Treasury. to be ineligible to any Office established by a particular State or under the authority of the United-States (except those peculiarly belonging to the functions of the first branch) during the term of service, and under the national government for the space of one year after it's expiration.

4. Resolved that the members of the second Branch of the national Legislature ought to be chosen by the individual Legislatures to be of the age of thirty years at least. to hold their offices for a term sufficient to ensure their independency, namely seven years to receive fixed stipends, by which they may be compensated for the devotion of their time to public service—to be paid out of the National Treasury to be ineligible to any office established by a particular State, or under the authority of the United States (except those peculiarly belonging to the functions of the second branch) during the term of service, and under the national government, for the space of one year after it's expiration.

5. Resolved that each branch ought to possess the right of originating acts.

6. Resolved that the national Legislature ought to be empowered to enjoy the legislative rights vested in Congress by the confederation—and moreover to legislate in all cases to which the separate States are incompetent: or in which the harmony of the United States may be interrupted by the exercise of individual legislation to negative all laws passed by the several States contravening, in the opinion of the national Legislature, the articles of union, or any treaties subsisting under the authority of the union.

7. Resolved that the right of suffrage in the first branch of the national Legislature ought not to be according to the rule established in the articles of confederation: but according to some equitable ratio of representation—namely, in proportion to the whole number of white and other free citizens and inhabitants of every age, sex, and condition including those bound to servitude for a term of years, and three fifths of all other persons not comprehended in the foregoing description, except Indians, not paying taxes in each State.

8. Resolved that the right of suffrage in the second branch of the national Legislature ought to be according to the rule established for the first.

9. Resolved that a national Executive be instituted to consist of a single person to be chosen by the National Legislature for the term of seven years. with power to carry into execution the national Laws, to appoint to Offices in cases not otherwise provided for to be ineligible a second time, and to be removable on impeachment and conviction of malpractice or neglect of duty to receive a fixed stipend, by which he may be compensated for the devotion of his time to public service to be paid out of the national Treasury.

10. Resolved that the national executive shall have a right to negative any legislative act: which shall not be afterwards passed unless by two third parts of each branch of the national Legislature.

11. Resolved that a national Judiciary be established to consist of One Supreme Tribunal. The Judges of which to be appointed by the second Branch of the National Legislature to hold their offices during good behaviour to receive, punctually, at stated times, a fixed compensation for their services: in which no encrease or diminution shall be made so as to affect the persons actually in office at the time of such encrease or diminution.

12. Resolved That the national Legislature be empowered to appoint inferior Tribunals.

13. Resolved that the jurisdiction of the national Judiciary shall extend to cases which respect the collection of the national revenue: impeachments of any national officers: and questions which involve the national peace and harmony.

14. Resolved that provision ought to be made for the admission of States, lawfully arising within the limits of the United States, whether from a voluntary junction of government and territory, or otherwise, with the consent of a number of voices in the national Legislature less than the whole.

15. Resolved that provision ought to be made for the continuance of Congress and their authorities until a given day after the reform of the articles of Union shall be adopted; and for the completion of all their engagements.

16. Resolved that a republican constitution, and its existing laws, ought to be guaranteed to each State by the United States.

17. Resolved that provision ought to be made for the amendment of the articles of Union, whensoever it shall seem necessary.

18. Resolved that the Legislative, Executive, and Judiciary powers within the several States ought to be bound by oath to support the articles of Union.

19. Resolved that the amendments which shall be offered to the confederation by the Convention, ought at a proper time or times, after the approbation of Congress to be submitted to an assembly or assemblies of representatives, recommended by the several Legislatures, to be expressly chosen by the People to consider and decide thereon.

Received this sheet from the President of the United States, with the journals of the general Convention, March 19th, 1796.

Timothy Pickering
Secy of State

State of the Resolutions submitted by Mr. Randolph to the Consideration of the House, as altered, amended and agreed to in a committee of the whole House.

Received from the President of the U. States, March 19, 1796. by

Timothy Pickering
Secy of State

The Northwest Ordinance

An Ordinance for the government of the Territory of the United States northwest of the River Ohio.

Section 1. Be it ordained by the United States in Congress assembled, That the said territory, for the purposes of temporary government, be one district, subject, however, to be divided into two districts, as future circumstances may, in the opinion of Congress, make it expedient.

Sec 2. Be it ordained by the authority aforesaid, That the estates, both of resident and nonresident proprietors in the said territory, dying intestate, shall descent to, and be distributed among their children, and the descendants of a deceased child, in equal parts; the descendants of a deceased child or grandchild to take the share of their deceased parent in equal parts among them: And where there shall be no children or descendants, then in equal parts to the next of kin in equal degree; and among collaterals, the children of a deceased brother or sister of the intestate shall have, in equal parts among them, their deceased parents' share; and there shall in no case be a distinction between kindred of the whole and half blood; saving, in all cases, to the widow of the intestate her third part of the real estate for life, and one third part of the personal estate; and this law relative to descents and dower, shall remain in full force until altered by the legislature of the district. And until the governor and judges shall adopt laws as hereinafter mentioned, estates in the said territory may be devised or bequeathed by wills in writing, signed and sealed by him or her in whom the estate may be (being of full age), and attested by three witnesses; and real estates may be conveyed by lease and release, or bargain and sale, signed, sealed and delivered by the person being of full age, in whom the estate may be, and attested by two witnesses, provided such wills be duly proved, and such conveyances be acknowledged, or the execution thereof duly proved, and be recorded within one year after proper magistrates, courts, and registers shall be appointed for that purpose; and personal property may be transferred by delivery; saving, however to the French and Canadian inhabitants, and other settlers of the Kaskaskies, St. Vincents and the neighboring villages who have heretofore professed themselves citizens of Virginia, their laws and customs now in force among them, relative to the descent and conveyance, of property.

Sec. 3. Be it ordained by the authority aforesaid, That there shall be appointed from time to time by Congress, a governor, whose commission shall continue in force for the term of three years, unless sooner revoked by Congress; he shall reside in the district, and have a freehold estate therein in 1,000 acres of land, while in the exercise of his office.

Sec. 4. There shall be appointed from time to time by Congress, a secretary, whose commission shall continue in force for four years unless sooner revoked; he shall reside in the district, and have a freehold estate therein in 500 acres of land, while in the exercise of his office. It shall be his duty to keep and preserve the acts and laws passed by the legislature, and the public records of the district, and the proceedings of the governor in his executive department, and transmit authentic copies of such acts and proceedings, every six months, to the Secretary of Congress: There shall also be appointed a court to consist of three judges, any two of whom to form a court, who shall have a common law jurisdiction, and reside in the district, and have each therein a freehold estate in 500 acres of land while in the exercise of their offices; and their commissions shall continue in force during good behavior.

Sec. 5. The governor and judges, or a majority of them, shall adopt and publish in the district such laws of the original States, criminal and civil, as may be necessary and best suited to the circumstances of the district, and report them to Congress from time to time: which laws shall be in force in the district until the organization of the General Assembly therein, unless disapproved of by Congress; but afterwards the Legislature shall have authority to alter them as they shall think fit.

Sec. 6. The governor, for the time being, shall be commander in chief of the militia, appoint and commission all officers in the same below the rank of general officers; all general officers shall be appointed and commissioned by Congress.

Sec. 7. Previous to the organization of the general assembly, the governor shall appoint such magistrates and other civil officers in each county or township, as he shall find necessary for the preservation of the peace and good order in the same: After the general assembly shall be organized, the powers and duties of the magistrates and other civil officers shall be regulated and defined by the said assembly; but all magistrates and other civil officers not herein otherwise directed, shall during the continuance of this temporary government, be appointed by the governor.

Sec. 8. For the prevention of crimes and injuries, the laws to be adopted or made shall have force in all parts of the district, and for the execution of process, criminal and civil, the governor shall make proper divisions thereof; and he shall proceed from time to time as circumstances may require, to lay out the parts of the district in which the Indian titles shall have been extinguished, into counties and townships, subject, however, to such alterations as may thereafter be made by the legislature.

Sec. 9. So soon as there shall be five thousand free male inhabitants of full age in the district, upon giving proof thereof to the governor, they shall receive authority, with time and place, to elect a representative from their counties or townships to represent them in the general assembly: Provided, That, for every five hundred free male inhabitants, there shall be one representative, and so on progressively with the number of free male inhabitants shall the right of representation increase, until the number of representatives shall amount to twenty five; after which, the number and proportion of representatives shall be regulated by the legislature: Provided, That no person be eligible or qualified to act as a representative unless he shall have been a citizen of one of the United States three years, and be a resident in the district, or unless he shall have resided in the district three years; and, in either case, shall likewise hold in his own right, in fee simple, two hundred acres of land within the same; Provided, also, That a freehold in fifty acres of land in the district, having been a citizen of one of the states, and being resident in the district, or the like freehold and two years residence in the district, shall be necessary to qualify a man as an elector of a representative.

Sec. 10. The representatives thus elected, shall serve for the term of two years; and, in case of the death of a representative, or removal from office, the governor shall issue a writ to the county or township for which he was a member, to elect another in his stead, to serve for the residue of the term.

Sec. 11. The general assembly or legislature shall consist of the governor, legislative council, and a house of representatives. The Legislative Council shall consist of five members, to continue in office five years, unless sooner removed by Congress; any three of whom to be a quorum: and the members of the Council shall be nominated and appointed in the following manner, to wit: As soon as representatives shall be elected, the Governor shall appoint a time and place for them to meet together; and, when met, they shall nominate ten persons, residents in the district, and each possessed of a freehold in five hundred acres of land, and return their names to Congress; five of whom Congress shall appoint and commission to serve as aforesaid; and, whenever a vacancy shall happen in the council, by death or removal from office, the house of representatives shall nominate two persons, qualified as aforesaid, for each vacancy, and return their names to Congress; one of whom congress shall appoint and commission for the residue of the term. And every five years, four months at least before the expiration of the time of service of the members of council, the said house shall nominate ten persons, qualified as aforesaid, and return their names to Congress; five of whom Congress shall appoint and commission to serve as members of the council five years, unless sooner removed. And the governor, legislative council, and house of representatives, shall have authority to make laws in all cases, for the good government of the district, not repugnant to the principles and articles in this ordinance established and declared. And all bills, having passed by a majority in the house, and by a majority in the council, shall be referred to the governor for his assent; but no bill, or legislative act whatever, shall be of any force without his assent. The governor shall have power to convene, prorogue, and dissolve the general assembly, when, in his opinion, it shall be expedient.

Sec. 12. The governor, judges, legislative council, secretary, and such other officers as Congress shall appoint in the district, shall take an oath or affirmation of fidelity and of office; the governor before the president of congress, and all other officers before the Governor. As soon as a legislature shall be formed in the district, the council and house assembled in one room, shall have authority, by joint ballot, to elect a delegate to Congress, who shall have a seat in Congress, with a right of debating but not voting during this temporary government.

Sec. 13. And, for extending the fundamental principles of civil and religious liberty, which form the basis whereon these republics, their laws and constitutions are erected; to fix and establish those principles as the basis of all laws, constitutions, and governments, which forever hereafter shall be formed in the said territory: to provide also for the establishment of States, and permanent government therein, and for their admission to a share in the federal councils on an equal footing with the original States, at as early periods as may be consistent with the general interest:

Sec. 14. It is hereby ordained and declared by the authority aforesaid, That the following articles shall be considered as articles of compact between the original States and the people and States in the said territory and forever remain unalterable, unless by common consent, to wit:

Art. 1. No person, demeaning himself in a peaceable and orderly manner, shall ever be molested on account of his mode of worship or religious sentiments, in the said territory.

Art. 2. The inhabitants of the said territory shall always be entitled to the benefits of the writ of habeas corpus, and of the trial by jury; of a proportionate representation of the people in the legislature; and of judicial proceedings according to the course of the common law. All persons shall be bailable, unless for capital offenses, where the proof shall be evident or the presumption great. All fines shall be moderate; and no cruel or unusual punishments shall be inflicted. No man shall be deprived of his liberty or property, but by the judgment of his peers or the law of the land; and, should the public exigencies make it necessary, for the common preservation, to take any person's property, or to demand his particular services, full compensation shall be made for the same. And, in the just preservation of rights and property, it is understood and declared, that no law ought ever to be made, or have force in the said territory, that shall, in any manner whatever, interfere with or affect private contracts or engagements, bona fide, and without fraud, previously formed.

Art. 3. Religion, morality, and knowledge, being necessary to good government and the happiness of mankind, schools and the means of education shall forever be encouraged. The utmost good faith shall always be observed towards the Indians; their lands and property shall never be taken from them without their consent; and, in their property, rights, and liberty, they shall never be invaded or disturbed, unless in just and lawful wars authorized by Congress; but laws founded in justice and humanity, shall from time to time be made for preventing wrongs being done to them, and for preserving peace and friendship with them.

Art. 4. The said territory, and the States which may be formed therein, shall forever remain a part of this Confederacy of the United States of America, subject to the Articles of Confederation, and to such alterations therein as shall be constitutionally made; and to all the acts and ordinances of the United States in Congress assembled, conformable thereto. The inhabitants and settlers in the said territory shall be subject to pay a part of the federal debts contracted or to be contracted, and a proportional part of the expenses of government, to be apportioned on them by Congress according to the same common rule and measure by which apportionments thereof shall be made on the other States; and the taxes for paying their proportion shall be laid and levied by the authority and direction of the legislatures of the district or districts, or new States, as in the original States, within the time agreed upon by the United States in Congress assembled. The legislatures of those districts or new States, shall never interfere with the primary disposal of the soil by the United States in Congress assembled, nor with any regulations Congress may find necessary for securing the title in such soil to the bona fide purchasers. No tax shall be imposed on lands the property of the United States; and, in no case, shall nonresident proprietors be taxed higher than residents. The navigable waters leading into the Mississippi and St. Lawrence, and the carrying places between the same, shall be common highways and forever free, as well to the inhabitants of the said territory as to the citizens of the United States, and those of any other States that may be admitted into the confederacy, without any tax, impost, or duty therefor.

Art. 5. There shall be formed in the said territory, not less than three nor more than five States; and the boundaries of the States, as soon as Virginia shall alter her act of cession, and consent to the same, shall become fixed and established as follows, to wit: The western State in the said territory, shall be bounded by the Mississippi, the Ohio, and Wabash Rivers; a direct line drawn from the Wabash and Post Vincents, due North, to the territorial line between the United States and Canada; and, by the said territorial line, to the Lake of the Woods and Mississippi. The middle State shall be bounded by the said direct line, the Wabash from Post Vincents to the Ohio, by the Ohio, by a direct line, drawn due north from the mouth of the Great Miami, to the said territorial line, and by the said territorial line. The eastern State shall be bounded by the last mentioned direct line, the Ohio, Pennsylvania, and the said territorial line: Provided, however, and it is further understood and declared, that the boundaries of these three States shall be subject so far to be altered, that, if Congress shall hereafter find it expedient, they shall have authority to form one or two States in that part of the said territory which lies north of an east and west line drawn through the southerly bend or extreme of Lake Michigan. And, whenever any of the said States shall have sixty thousand free inhabitants therein, such State shall be admitted, by its delegates, into the Congress of the United States, on an equal footing with the original States in all respects whatever, and shall be at liberty to form a permanent constitution and State government: Provided, the constitution and government so to be formed, shall be republican, and in conformity to the principles contained in these articles; and, so far as it can be consistent with the general interest of the confederacy, such admission shall be allowed at an earlier period, and when there may be a less number of free inhabitants in the State than sixty thousand.

Art. 6. There shall be neither slavery nor involuntary servitude in the said territory, otherwise than in the punishment of crimes whereof the party shall have been duly convicted: Provided, always, That any person escaping into the same, from whom labor or service is lawfully claimed in any one of the original States, such fugitive may be lawfully reclaimed and conveyed to the person claiming his or her labor or service as aforesaid.

Be it ordained by the authority aforesaid, That the resolutions of the 23rd of April, 1784, relative to the subject of this ordinance, be, and the same are hereby repealed and declared null and void.

Done by the United States, in Congress assembled, the 13th day of July, in the year of our Lord 1787, and of their soveriegnty and independence the twelfth.

The Constitution of the United States

We the People of the United States, in Order to form a more perfect Union, establish Justice, insure domestic Tranquility, provide for the common defence, promote the general Welfare, and secure the Blessings of Liberty to ourselves and our Posterity, do ordain and establish this Constitution for the United States of America.

ARTICLE. I.

SECTION. 1.

All legislative Powers herein granted shall be vested in a Congress of the United States, which shall consist of a Senate and House of Representatives.

SECTION. 2.

The House of Representatives shall be composed of Members chosen every second Year by the People of the several States, and the Electors in each State shall have the Qualifications requisite for Electors of the most numerous Branch of the State Legislature.

No Person shall be a Representative who shall not have attained to the Age of twenty five Years, and been seven Years a Citizen of the United States, and who shall not, when elected, be an Inhabitant of that State in which he shall be chosen.

Representatives and direct Taxes shall be apportioned among the several States which may be included within this Union, according to their respective Numbers, which shall be determined by adding to the whole Number of free Persons, including those bound to Service for a Term of Years, and excluding Indians not taxed, three fifths of all other Persons. The actual Enumeration shall be made within three Years after the first Meeting of the Congress of the United States, and within every subsequent Term of ten Years, in such Manner as they shall by Law direct. The Number of Representatives shall not exceed one for every thirty Thousand, but each State shall have at Least one Representative; and until such enumeration shall be made, the State of New Hampshire shall be entitled to chuse three, Massachusetts eight, Rhode-Island and Providence Plantations one, Connecticut five, New-York six, New Jersey four, Pennsylvania eight, Delaware one, Maryland six, Virginia ten, North Carolina five, South Carolina five, and Georgia three.

When vacancies happen in the Representation from any State, the Executive Authority thereof shall issue Writs of Election to fill such Vacancies.

The House of Representatives shall chuse their Speaker and other Officers; and shall have the sole Power of Impeachment.

SECTION. 3.

The Senate of the United States shall be composed of two Senators from each State, **chosen by the Legislature** thereof for six Years; and each Senator shall have one Vote.

Immediately after they shall be assembled in Consequence of the first Election, they shall be divided as equally as may be into three Classes. The Seats of the Senators of the first Class shall be vacated at the Expiration of the second Year, of the second Class at the Expiration of the fourth Year, and of the third Class at the Expiration of the sixth Year, so that one third may be chosen every second Year; **and if Vacancies happen by Resignation, or otherwise, during the Recess of the Legislature of any State, the Executive thereof may make temporary Appointments until the next Meeting of the Legislature, which shall then fill such Vacancies.**

No Person shall be a Senator who shall not have attained to the Age of thirty Years, and been nine Years a Citizen of the United States, and who shall not, when elected, be an Inhabitant of that State for which he shall be chosen.

The Vice President of the United States shall be President of the Senate, but shall have no Vote, unless they be equally divided.

The Senate shall chuse their other Officers, and also a President pro tempore, in the Absence of the Vice President, or when he shall exercise the Office of President of the United States.

The Senate shall have the sole Power to try all Impeachments. When sitting for that Purpose, they shall be on Oath or Affirmation. When the President of the United States is tried, the Chief Justice shall preside: And no Person shall be convicted without the Concurrence of two thirds of the Members present.

Judgment in Cases of Impeachment shall not extend further than to removal from Office, and disqualification to hold and enjoy any Office of honor, Trust or Profit under the United States: but the Party convicted shall nevertheless be liable and subject to Indictment, Trial, Judgment and Punishment, according to Law.

SECTION. 4.

The Times, Places and Manner of holding Elections for Senators and Representatives, shall be prescribed in each State by the Legislature thereof; but the Congress may at any time by Law make or alter such Regulations, except as to the Places of chusing Senators.

The Congress shall assemble at least once in every Year, and such Meeting shall **be on the first Monday in December**, unless they shall by Law appoint a different Day.

SECTION. 5.

Each House shall be the Judge of the Elections, Returns and Qualifications of its own Members, and a Majority of each shall constitute a Quorum to do Business; but a smaller Number may adjourn from day to day, and may be authorized to compel the Attendance of absent Members, in such Manner, and under such Penalties as each House may provide.

Each House may determine the Rules of its Proceedings, punish its Members for disorderly Behaviour, and, with the Concurrence of two thirds, expel a Member.

Each House shall keep a Journal of its Proceedings, and from time to time publish the same, excepting such Parts as may in their Judgment require Secrecy; and the Yeas and Nays of the Members of either House on any question shall, at the Desire of one fifth of those Present, be entered on the Journal.

Neither House, during the Session of Congress, shall, without the Consent of the other, adjourn for more than three days, nor to any other Place than that in which the two Houses shall be sitting.

SECTION. 6.

The Senators and Representatives shall receive a Compensation for their Services, to be ascertained by Law, and paid out of the Treasury of the United States. They shall in all Cases, except Treason, Felony and Breach of the Peace, be privileged from Arrest during their Attendance at the Session of their respective Houses, and in going to and returning from the same; and for any Speech or Debate in either House, they shall not be questioned in any other Place.

No Senator or Representative shall, during the Time for which he was elected, be appointed to any civil Office under the Authority of the United States, which shall have been created, or the Emoluments whereof shall have been encreased during such time; and no Person holding any Office under the United States, shall be a Member of either House during his Continuance in Office.

SECTION. 7.

All Bills for raising Revenue shall originate in the House of Representatives; but the Senate may propose or concur with Amendments as on other Bills.

Every Bill which shall have passed the House of Representatives and the Senate, shall, before it become a Law, be presented to the President of the United States: If he approve he shall sign it, but if not he shall return it, with his Objections to that House in which it shall have originated, who shall enter the Objections at large on their Journal, and proceed to reconsider it. If after such Reconsideration two thirds of that House shall agree to pass the Bill, it shall be sent, together with the Objections, to the other House, by which it shall likewise be reconsidered, and if approved by two thirds of that House, it shall become a Law. But in all such Cases the Votes of both Houses shall be determined by yeas and Nays, and the Names of the Persons voting for and against the Bill shall be entered on the Journal of each House respectively. If any Bill shall not be returned by the President within ten Days (Sundays excepted) after it shall have been presented to him, the Same shall be a Law, in like Manner as if he had signed it, unless the Congress by their Adjournment prevent its Return, in which Case it shall not be a Law.

Every Order, Resolution, or Vote to which the Concurrence of the Senate and House of Representatives may be necessary (except on a question of Adjournment) shall be presented to the President of the United States; and before the Same shall take Effect, shall be approved by him, or being disapproved by him, shall be repassed by two thirds of the Senate and House of Representatives, according to the Rules and Limitations prescribed in the Case of a Bill.

SECTION. 8.

The Congress shall have Power To lay and collect Taxes, Duties, Imposts and Excises, to pay the Debts and provide for the common Defence and general Welfare of the United States; but all Duties, Imposts and Excises shall be uniform throughout the United States;

To borrow Money on the credit of the United States;

To regulate Commerce with foreign Nations, and among the several States, and with the Indian Tribes;

To establish an uniform Rule of Naturalization, and uniform Laws on the subject of Bankruptcies throughout the United States;

To coin Money, regulate the Value thereof, and of foreign Coin, and fix the Standard of Weights and Measures;

To provide for the Punishment of counterfeiting the Securities and current Coin of the United States;

To establish Post Offices and post Roads;

To promote the Progress of Science and useful Arts, by securing for limited Times to Authors and Inventors the exclusive Right to their respective Writings and Discoveries;

To constitute Tribunals inferior to the supreme Court;

To define and punish Piracies and Felonies committed on the high Seas, and Offences against the Law of Nations;

To declare War, grant Letters of Marque and Reprisal, and make Rules concerning Captures on Land and Water;

To raise and support Armies, but no Appropriation of Money to that Use shall be for a longer Term than two Years;

To provide and maintain a Navy;

To make Rules for the Government and Regulation of the land and naval Forces;

To provide for calling forth the Militia to execute the Laws of the Union, suppress Insurrections and repel Invasions;

To provide for organizing, arming, and disciplining, the Militia, and for governing such Part of them as may be employed in the Service of the United States, reserving to the States respectively, the Appointment of the Officers, and the Authority of training the Militia according to the discipline prescribed by Congress;

To exercise exclusive Legislation in all Cases whatsoever, over such District (not exceeding ten Miles square) as may, by Cession of particular States, and the Acceptance of Congress, become the Seat of the Government of the United States, and to exercise like Authority over all Places purchased by the Consent of the Legislature of the State in which the Same shall be, for the Erection of Forts, Magazines, Arsenals, dock-Yards, and other needful Buildings;— And

To make all Laws which shall be necessary and proper for carrying into Execution the foregoing Powers, and all other Powers vested by this Constitution in the Government of the United States, or in any Department or Officer thereof.

SECTION. 9.

The Migration or Importation of such Persons as any of the States now existing shall think proper to admit, shall not be prohibited by the Congress prior to the Year one thousand eight hundred and eight, but a Tax or duty may be imposed on such Importation, not exceeding ten dollars for each Person.

The Privilege of the Writ of Habeas Corpus shall not be suspended, unless when in Cases of Rebellion or Invasion the public Safety may require it.

No Bill of Attainder or ex post facto Law shall be passed.

No Capitation, or other direct, Tax shall be laid, **unless in Proportion to the Census or enumeration herein before directed to be taken**.

No Tax or Duty shall be laid on Articles exported from any State.

No Preference shall be given by any Regulation of Commerce or Revenue to the Ports of one State over those of another; nor shall Vessels bound to, or from, one State, be obliged to enter, clear, or pay Duties in another.

No Money shall be drawn from the Treasury, but in Consequence of Appropriations made by Law; and a regular Statement and Account of the Receipts and Expenditures of all public Money shall be published from time to time.

No Title of Nobility shall be granted by the United States: And no Person holding any Office of Profit or Trust under them, shall, without the Consent of the Congress, accept of any present, Emolument, Office, or Title, of any kind whatever, from any King, Prince, or foreign State.

SECTION. 10.

No State shall enter into any Treaty, Alliance, or Confederation; grant Letters of Marque and Reprisal; coin Money; emit Bills of Credit; make any Thing but gold and silver Coin a Tender in Payment of Debts; pass any Bill of Attainder, ex post facto Law, or Law impairing the Obligation of Contracts, or grant any Title of Nobility.

No State shall, without the Consent of the Congress, lay any Imposts or Duties on Imports or Exports, except what may be absolutely necessary for executing it's inspection Laws: and the net Produce of all Duties and Imposts, laid by any State on Imports or Exports, shall be for the Use of the Treasury of the United States; and all such Laws shall be subject to the Revision and Controul of the Congress.

No State shall, without the Consent of Congress, lay any Duty of Tonnage, keep Troops, or Ships of War in time of Peace, enter into any Agreement or Compact with another State, or with a foreign Power, or engage in War, unless actually invaded, or in such imminent Danger as will not admit of delay.

ARTICLE. II.

SECTION. 1.

The executive Power shall be vested in a President of the United States of America. He shall hold his Office during the Term of four Years, and, together with the Vice President, chosen for the same Term, be elected, as follows:

Each State shall appoint, in such Manner as the Legislature thereof may direct, a Number of Electors, equal to the whole Number of Senators and Representatives to which the State may be entitled in the Congress: but no Senator or Representative, or Person holding an Office of Trust or Profit under the United States, shall be appointed an Elector.

The Electors shall meet in their respective States, and vote by Ballot for two Persons, of whom one at least shall not be an Inhabitant of the same State with themselves. And they shall make a List of all the Persons voted for, and of the Number of Votes for each; which List they shall sign and certify, and transmit sealed to the Seat of the Government of the United States, directed to the President of the Senate. The President of the Senate shall, in the Presence of the Senate and House of Representatives, open all the Certificates, and the Votes shall then be counted. The Person having the greatest Number of Votes shall be the President, if such Number be a Majority of the whole Number of Electors appointed; and if there be more than one who have such Majority, and have an equal Number of Votes, then the House of Representatives shall immediately chuse by Ballot one of them for President; and if no Person have a Majority, then from the five highest on the List the said House shall in like Manner chuse the President. But in chusing the President, the Votes shall be taken by States, the Representation from each State having one Vote; A quorum for this purpose shall consist of a Member or Members from two thirds of the States, and a Majority of all the States shall be necessary to a Choice. In every Case, after the Choice of the President, the Person having the greatest Number of Votes of the Electors shall be the Vice President. But if there should remain two or more who have equal Votes, the Senate shall chuse from them by Ballot the Vice President.

The Congress may determine the Time of chusing the Electors, and the Day on which they shall give their Votes; which Day shall be the same throughout the United States.

No Person except a natural born Citizen, or a Citizen of the United States, at the time of the Adoption of this Constitution, shall be eligible to the Office of President; neither shall any Person be eligible to that Office who shall not have attained to the Age of thirty five Years, and been fourteen Years a Resident within the United States.

In Case of the Removal of the President from Office, or of his Death, Resignation, or Inability to discharge the Powers and Duties of the said Office,

the Same shall devolve on the Vice President, and the Congress may by Law provide for the Case of Removal, Death, Resignation or Inability, both of the President and Vice President, declaring what Officer shall then act as President, and such Officer shall act accordingly, until the Disability be removed, or a President shall be elected.

The President shall, at stated Times, receive for his Services, a Compensation, which shall neither be increased nor diminished during the Period for which he shall have been elected, and he shall not receive within that Period any other Emolument from the United States, or any of them.

Before he enter on the Execution of his Office, he shall take the following Oath or Affirmation:—"I do solemnly swear (or affirm) that I will faithfully execute the Office of President of the United States, and will to the best of my Ability, preserve, protect and defend the Constitution of the United States."

SECTION. 2.

The President shall be Commander in Chief of the Army and Navy of the United States, and of the Militia of the several States, when called into the actual Service of the United States; he may require the Opinion, in writing, of the principal Officer in each of the executive Departments, upon any Subject relating to the Duties of their respective Offices, and he shall have Power to grant Reprieves and Pardons for Offences against the United States, except in Cases of Impeachment.

He shall have Power, by and with the Advice and Consent of the Senate, to make Treaties, provided two thirds of the Senators present concur; and he shall nominate, and by and with the Advice and Consent of the Senate, shall appoint Ambassadors, other public Ministers and Consuls, Judges of the supreme Court, and all other Officers of the United States, whose Appointments are not herein otherwise provided for, and which shall be established by Law: but the Congress may by Law vest the Appointment of such inferior Officers, as they think proper, in the President alone, in the Courts of Law, or in the Heads of Departments.

The President shall have Power to fill up all Vacancies that may happen during the Recess of the Senate, by granting Commissions which shall expire at the End of their next Session.

SECTION. 3.

He shall from time to time give to the Congress Information of the State of the Union, and recommend to their Consideration such Measures as he shall judge necessary and expedient; he may, on extraordinary Occasions, convene both Houses, or either of them, and in Case of Disagreement between them, with Respect to the Time of Adjournment, he may adjourn them to such Time as he shall think proper; he shall receive Ambassadors and other public Ministers; he shall take Care that the Laws be faithfully executed, and shall Commission all the Officers of the United States.

SECTION. 4.

The President, Vice President and all civil Officers of the United States, shall be removed from Office on Impeachment for, and Conviction of, Treason, Bribery, or other high Crimes and Misdemeanors.

ARTICLE III.

SECTION. 1.

The judicial Power of the United States shall be vested in one supreme Court, and in such inferior Courts as the Congress may from time to time ordain and establish. The Judges, both of the supreme and inferior Courts, shall hold their Offices during good Behaviour, and shall, at stated Times, receive for their Services a Compensation, which shall not be diminished during their Continuance in Office.

SECTION. 2.

The judicial Power shall extend to all Cases, in Law and Equity, arising under this Constitution, the Laws of the United States, and Treaties made, or which shall be made, under their Authority;—to all Cases affecting Ambassadors, other public Ministers and Consuls;—to all Cases of admiralty and maritime Jurisdiction;—to Controversies to which the United States shall be a Party;—to Controversies between two or more States;—**between a State and Citizens of another State;**—between Citizens of different States;—between Citizens of the same State claiming Lands under Grants of different States, and between a State, or the Citizens thereof, and foreign States, Citizens or Subjects.

In all Cases affecting Ambassadors, other public Ministers and Consuls, and those in which a State shall be Party, the supreme Court shall have original Jurisdiction. In all the other Cases before mentioned, the supreme Court shall have appellate Jurisdiction, both as to Law and Fact, with such Exceptions, and under such Regulations as the Congress shall make.

The Trial of all Crimes, except in Cases of Impeachment, shall be by Jury; and such Trial shall be held in the State where the said Crimes shall have been committed; but when not committed within any State, the Trial shall be at such Place or Places as the Congress may by Law have directed.

SECTION. 3.

Treason against the United States, shall consist only in levying War against them, or in adhering to their Enemies, giving them Aid and Comfort. No Person shall be convicted of Treason unless on the Testimony of two Witnesses to the same overt Act, or on Confession in open Court.

The Congress shall have Power to declare the Punishment of Treason, but no Attainder of Treason shall work Corruption of Blood, or Forfeiture except during the Life of the Person attainted.

ARTICLE. IV.

SECTION. 1.

Full Faith and Credit shall be given in each State to the public Acts, Records, and judicial Proceedings of every other State. And the Congress may by general Laws prescribe the Manner in which such Acts, Records and Proceedings shall be proved, and the Effect thereof.

SECTION. 2.

The Citizens of each State shall be entitled to all Privileges and Immunities of Citizens in the several States.

A Person charged in any State with Treason, Felony, or other Crime, who shall flee from Justice, and be found in another State, shall on Demand of the executive Authority of the State from which he fled, be delivered up, to be removed to the State having Jurisdiction of the Crime.

No Person held to Service or Labour in one State, under the Laws thereof, escaping into another, shall, in Consequence of any Law or Regulation therein, be discharged from such Service or Labour, but shall be delivered up on Claim of the Party to whom such Service or Labour may be due.

SECTION. 3.

New States may be admitted by the Congress into this Union; but no new State shall be formed or erected within the Jurisdiction of any other State; nor any State be formed by the Junction of two or more States, or Parts of States, without the Consent of the Legislatures of the States concerned as well as of the Congress.

The Congress shall have Power to dispose of and make all needful Rules and Regulations respecting the Territory or other Property belonging to the United States; and nothing in this Constitution shall be so construed as to Prejudice any Claims of the United States, or of any particular State.

SECTION. 4.

The United States shall guarantee to every State in this Union a Republican Form of Government, and shall protect each of them against Invasion; and on Application of the Legislature, or of the Executive (when the Legislature cannot be convened), against domestic Violence.

ARTICLE. V.

The Congress, whenever two thirds of both Houses shall deem it necessary, shall propose Amendments to this Constitution, or, on the Application of the Legislatures of two thirds of the several States, shall call a Convention for proposing Amendments, which, in either Case, shall be valid to all Intents and Purposes, as Part of this Constitution, when ratified by the Legislatures of three fourths of the several States, or by Conventions in three fourths thereof, as the one or the other Mode of Ratification may be proposed by the Congress; Provided that no Amendment which may be made prior to the Year One thousand eight hundred and eight shall in any Manner affect the first and fourth Clauses in the Ninth Section of the first Article; and that no State, without its Consent, shall be deprived of its equal Suffrage in the Senate.

ARTICLE. VI.

All Debts contracted and Engagements entered into, before the Adoption of this Constitution, shall be as valid against the United States under this Constitution, as under the Confederation.

This Constitution, and the Laws of the United States which shall be made in Pursuance thereof; and all Treaties made, or which shall be made, under the Authority of the United States, shall be the supreme Law of the Land; and the Judges in every State shall be bound thereby, any Thing in the Constitution or Laws of any State to the Contrary notwithstanding.

The Senators and Representatives before mentioned, and the Members of the several State Legislatures, and all executive and judicial Officers, both of the United States and of the several States, shall be bound by Oath or Affirmation, to support this Constitution; but no religious Test shall ever be required as a Qualification to any Office or public Trust under the United States.

ARTICLE. VII.

The Ratification of the Conventions of nine States, shall be sufficient for the Establishment of this Constitution between the States so ratifying the Same.

The Word, "the," being interlined between the seventh and eighth Lines of the first Page, the Word "Thirty" being partly written on an Erazure in the fifteenth Line of the first Page, The Words "is tried" being interlined between the thirty second and thirty third Lines of the first Page and the Word "the" being interlined between the forty third and forty fourth Lines of the second Page.

Attest William Jackson Secretary

Done in Convention by the Unanimous Consent of the States present the Seventeenth Day of September in the Year of our Lord one thousand seven hundred and Eighty seven and of the Independence of the United States of America the Twelfth In witness whereof We have hereunto subscribed our Names,

Go. Washington
President and deputy from Virginia

Delaware
Geo: Read
Gunning Bedford jun
John Dickinson
Richard Bassett
Jaco: Broom

Maryland
James McHenry
Dan of St Thos. Jenifer
Danl. Carroll

Virginia
John Blair
James Madison Jr.

North Carolina
Wm. Blount
Richd. Dobbs Spaight
Hu Williamson

South Carolina
J. Rutledge
Charles Cotesworth Pinckney
Charles Pinckney
Pierce Butler

Georgia
William Few
Abr Baldwin

New Hampshire
John Langdon
Nicholas Gilman

Massachusetts
Nathaniel Gorham
Rufus King

Connecticut
Wm. Saml. Johnson
Roger Sherman

New York
Alexander Hamilton

New Jersey
Wil: Livingston
David Brearley
Wm. Paterson
Jona: Dayton

Pennsylvania
B Franklin
Thomas Mifflin
Robt. Morris
Geo. Clymer
Thos. FitzSimons

Jared Ingersoll
James Wilson
Gouv Morris

ARTICLES in addition to, and Amendment of the Constitution of the United States of America, proposed by Congress, and ratified by the Legislatures of the several States, pursuant to the Fifth Article of the original Constitution.

AMENDMENT I (1791)

Congress shall make no law respecting an establishment of religion, or prohibiting the free exercise thereof; or abridging the freedom of speech, or of the press; or the right of the people peaceably to assemble, and to petition the Government for a redress of grievances.

AMENDMENT II (1791)

A well regulated Militia, being necessary to the security of a free State, the right of the people to keep and bear Arms, shall not be infringed.

AMENDMENT III (1791)

No Soldier shall, in time of peace be quartered in any house, without the consent of the Owner, nor in time of war, but in a manner to be prescribed by law.

AMENDMENT IV (1791)

The right of the people to be secure in their persons, houses, papers, and effects, against unreasonable searches and seizures, shall not be violated, and no Warrants shall issue, but upon probable cause, supported by Oath or affirmation, and particularly describing the place to be searched, and the persons or things to be seized.

AMENDMENT V (1791)

No person shall be held to answer for a capital, or otherwise infamous crime, unless on a presentment or indictment of a Grand Jury, except in cases arising in the land or naval forces, or in the Militia, when in actual service in time of War or public danger; nor shall any person be subject for the same offence to be twice put in jeopardy of life or limb; nor shall be compelled in any criminal case to be a witness against himself, nor

be deprived of life, liberty, or property, without due process of law; nor shall private property be taken for public use, without just compensation.

AMENDMENT VI (1791)

In all criminal prosecutions, the accused shall enjoy the right to a speedy and public trial, by an impartial jury of the State and district wherein the crime shall have been committed, which district shall have been previously ascertained by law, and to be informed of the nature and cause of the accusation; to be confronted with the witnesses against him; to have compulsory process for obtaining witnesses in his favor, and to have the Assistance of Counsel for his defence.

AMENDMENT VII (1791)

In Suits at common law, where the value in controversy shall exceed twenty dollars, the right of trial by jury shall be preserved, and no fact tried by a jury, shall be otherwise re-examined in any Court of the United States, than according to the rules of the common law.

AMENDMENT VIII (1791)

Excessive bail shall not be required, nor excessive fines imposed, nor cruel and unusual punishments inflicted.

AMENDMENT IX (1791)

The enumeration in the Constitution, of certain rights, shall not be construed to deny or disparage others retained by the people.

AMENDMENT X (1791)

The powers not delegated to the United States by the Constitution, nor prohibited by it to the States, are reserved to the States respectively, or to the people.

AMENDMENT XI (1798)

The Judicial power of the United States shall not be construed to extend to any suit in law or equity, commenced or prosecuted against one of the United States by Citizens of another State, or by Citizens or Subjects of any Foreign State.

AMENDMENT XII (1804)

The Electors shall meet in their respective states and vote by ballot for President and Vice-President, one of whom, at least, shall not be an inhabitant of the same state with themselves; they shall name in their ballots the person voted for as President, and in distinct ballots the person voted for as Vice-President, and they shall make distinct lists of all persons voted for as President, and of all persons voted for as Vice-President, and of the number of votes for each, which lists they shall sign and certify, and transmit sealed to the seat of the government of the United States, directed to the President of the Senate; — the President of the Senate shall, in the presence of the Senate and House of Representatives, open all the certificates and the votes shall then be counted; — The person having the greatest number of votes for President, shall be the President, if such number be a majority of the whole number of Electors appointed; and if no person have such majority, then from the persons having the highest numbers not exceeding three on the list of those voted for as President, the House of Representatives shall choose immediately, by ballot, the President. But in choosing the President, the votes shall be taken by states, the representation from each state having one vote; a quorum for this purpose shall consist of a member or members from two-thirds of the states, and a majority of all the states shall be necessary to a choice. [And if the House of Representatives shall not choose a President whenever the right of choice shall devolve upon them, before the fourth day of March next following, then the Vice-President shall act as President, as in case of the death or other constitutional disability of the President. —] The person having the greatest number of votes as Vice-President, shall be the Vice-President, if such number be a majority of the whole number of Electors appointed, and if no person have a majority, then from the two highest numbers on the list, the Senate shall choose the Vice-President; a quorum for the purpose shall consist of two-thirds of the whole number of Senators, and a majority of the whole number shall be necessary to a choice. But no person constitutionally ineligible to the office of President shall be eligible to that of Vice-President of the United States.

AMENDMENT XIII (1865)

SECTION 1.

Neither slavery nor involuntary servitude, except as a punishment for crime whereof the party shall have been duly convicted, shall exist within the United States, or any place subject to their jurisdiction.

SECTION 2.

Congress shall have power to enforce this article by appropriate legislation.

AMENDMENT XIV (1868)

SECTION 1.

All persons born or naturalized in the United States, and subject to the jurisdiction thereof, are citizens of the United States and of the State wherein they reside. No State shall make or enforce any law which shall abridge the privileges or immunities of citizens of the United States; nor shall any State deprive any person of life, liberty, or property, without due process of law; nor deny to any person within its jurisdiction the equal protection of the laws.

SECTION 2.

Representatives shall be apportioned among the several States according to their respective numbers, counting the whole number of persons in each State, excluding Indians not taxed. But when the right to vote at any election for the choice of electors for President and Vice-President of the United States, Representatives in Congress, the Executive and Judicial officers of a State, or the members of the Legislature thereof, is denied to any of the male inhabitants of such State, being twenty-one years of age, and citizens of the United States, or in any way abridged, except for participation in rebellion, or other crime, the basis of representation therein shall be reduced in the proportion which the number of such male citizens shall bear to the whole number of male citizens twenty-one years of age in such State.

SECTION 3.

No person shall be a Senator or Representative in Congress, or elector of President and Vice-President, or hold any office, civil or military, under the United States, or under any State, who, having previously taken an oath, as a member of Congress, or as an officer of the United States, or as a member of any State legislature, or as an executive or judicial officer of any State, to support the Constitution of the

United States, shall have engaged in insurrection or rebellion against the same, or given aid or comfort to the enemies thereof. But Congress may by a vote of two-thirds of each House, remove such disability.

SECTION 4.

The validity of the public debt of the United States, authorized by law, including debts incurred for payment of pensions and bounties for services in suppressing insurrection or rebellion, shall not be questioned. But neither the United States nor any State shall assume or pay any debt or obligation incurred in aid of insurrection or rebellion against the United States, or any claim for the loss or emancipation of any slave; but all such debts, obligations and claims shall be held illegal and void.

SECTION 5.

The Congress shall have the power to enforce, by appropriate legislation, the provisions of this article.

AMENDMENT XV (1870)

SECTION 1.

The right of citizens of the United States to vote shall not be denied or abridged by the United States or by any State on account of race, color, or previous condition of servitude—

SECTION 2.

The Congress shall have the power to enforce this article by appropriate legislation.

AMENDMENT XVI (1913)

The Congress shall have power to lay and collect taxes on incomes, from whatever source derived, without apportionment among the several States, and without regard to any census or enumeration.

AMENDMENT XVII (1913)

The Senate of the United States shall be composed of two Senators from each State, elected by the people thereof, for six years; and each Senator shall have one vote. The electors in each State shall have the qualifications requisite for electors of the most numerous branch of the State legislatures.

When vacancies happen in the representation of any State in the Senate, the executive authority of such State shall issue writs of election to fill such vacancies: *Provided,* That the legislature of any State may empower the executive thereof to make temporary appointments until the people fill the vacancies by election as the legislature may direct.

This amendment shall not be so construed as to affect the election or term of any Senator chosen before it becomes valid as part of the Constitution.

AMENDMENT XVIII (1919)

SECTION 1.

After one year from the ratification of this article the manufacture, sale, or transportation of intoxicating liquors within, the importation thereof into, or the exportation thereof from the United States and all territory subject to the jurisdiction thereof for beverage purposes is hereby prohibited.

SECTION 2.

The Congress and the several States shall have concurrent power to enforce this article by appropriate legislation.

SECTION 3.

This article shall be inoperative unless it shall have been ratified as an amendment to the Constitution by the legislatures of the several States, as provided in the Constitution, within seven years from the date of the submission hereof to the States by the Congress.

AMENDMENT XIX (1920)

The right of citizens of the United States to vote shall not be denied or abridged by the United States or by any State on account of sex.

Congress shall have power to enforce this article by appropriate legislation.

AMENDMENT XX (1933)

SECTION 1.

The terms of the President and the Vice President shall end at noon on the 20th day of January, and the terms of Senators and Representatives at noon on the 3d day of January, of the years in which such terms would have ended if this article had not been ratified; and the terms of their successors shall then begin.

Section 2.

The Congress shall assemble at least once in every year, and such meeting shall begin at noon on the 3d day of January, unless they shall by law appoint a different day.

Section 3.

If, at the time fixed for the beginning of the term of the President, the President elect shall have died, the Vice President elect shall become President. If a President shall not have been chosen before the time fixed for the beginning of his term, or if the President elect shall have failed to qualify, then the Vice President elect shall act as President until a President shall have qualified; and the Congress may by law provide for the case wherein neither a President elect nor a Vice President shall have qualified, declaring who shall then act as President, or the manner in which one who is to act shall be selected, and such person shall act accordingly until a President or Vice President shall have qualified.

Section 4.

The Congress may by law provide for the case of the death of any of the persons from whom the House of Representatives may choose a President whenever the right of choice shall have devolved upon them, and for the case of the death of any of the persons from whom the Senate may choose a Vice President whenever the right of choice shall have devolved upon them.

Section 5.

Sections 1 and 2 shall take effect on the 15th day of October following the ratification of this article.

Section 6.

This article shall be inoperative unless it shall have been ratified as an amendment to the Constitution by the legislatures of three-fourths of the several States within seven years from the date of its submission.

Amendment XXI (1933)

Section 1.

The eighteenth article of amendment to the Constitution of the United States is hereby repealed.

Section 2.

The transportation or importation into any State, Territory, or Possession of the United States for delivery or use therein of intoxicating liquors, in violation of the laws thereof, is hereby prohibited.

Section 3.

This article shall be inoperative unless it shall have been ratified as an amendment to the Constitution by conventions in the several States, as provided in the Constitution, within seven years from the date of the submission hereof to the States by the Congress.

Amendment XXII (1951)

Section 1.

No person shall be elected to the office of the President more than twice, and no person who has held the office of President, or acted as President, for more than two years of a term to which some other person was elected President shall be elected to the office of President more than once. But this Article shall not apply to any person holding the office of President when this Article was proposed by Congress, and shall not prevent any person who may be holding the office of President, or acting as President, during the term within which this Article becomes operative from holding the office of President or acting as President during the remainder of such term.

Section 2.

This article shall be inoperative unless it shall have been ratified as an amendment to the Constitution by the legislatures of three-fourths of the several States within seven years from the date of its submission to the States by the Congress.

AMENDMENT XXIII (1961)

SECTION 1.

The District constituting the seat of Government of the United States shall appoint in such manner as Congress may direct:

A number of electors of President and Vice President equal to the whole number of Senators and Representatives in Congress to which the District would be entitled if it were a State, but in no event more than the least populous State; they shall be in addition to those appointed by the States, but they shall be considered, for the purposes of the election of President and Vice President, to be electors appointed by a State; and they shall meet in the District and perform such duties as provided by the twelfth article of amendment.

SECTION 2.

The Congress shall have power to enforce this article by appropriate legislation.

AMENDMENT XXIV (1964)

SECTION 1.

The right of citizens of the United States to vote in any primary or other election for President or Vice President, for electors for President or Vice President, or for Senator or Representative in Congress, shall not be denied or abridged by the United States or any State by reason of failure to pay poll tax or other tax.

SECTION 2.

The Congress shall have power to enforce this article by appropriate legislation.

AMENDMENT XXV (1967)

SECTION 1.

In case of the removal of the President from office or of his death or resignation, the Vice President shall become President.

SECTION 2.

Whenever there is a vacancy in the office of the Vice President, the President shall nominate a Vice President who shall take office upon confirmation by a majority vote of both Houses of Congress.

SECTION 3.

Whenever the President transmits to the President pro tempore of the Senate and the Speaker of the House of Representatives his written declaration that he is unable to discharge the powers and duties of his office, and until he transmits to them a written declaration to the contrary, such powers and duties shall be discharged by the Vice President as Acting President.

SECTION 4.

Whenever the Vice President and a majority of either the principal officers of the executive departments or of such other body as Congress may by law provide, transmit to the President pro tempore of the Senate and the Speaker of the House of Representatives their written declaration that the President is unable to discharge the powers and duties of his office, the Vice President shall immediately assume the powers and duties of the office as Acting President.

Thereafter, when the President transmits to the President pro tempore of the Senate and the Speaker of the House of Representatives his written declaration that no inability exists, he shall resume the powers and duties of his office unless the Vice President and a majority of either the principal officers of the executive department or of such other body as Congress may by law provide, transmit within four days to the President pro tempore of the Senate and the Speaker of the House of Representatives their written declaration that the President is unable to discharge the powers and duties of his office. Thereupon Congress shall decide the issue, assembling within forty-eight hours for that purpose if not in session. If the Congress, within twenty-one days after receipt of the latter written declaration, or, if Congress is not in session, within twenty-one days after Congress is required to assemble, determines by two-thirds vote of both Houses that the President is unable to discharge the powers and duties of his office, the Vice President shall continue to discharge the same as Acting President; otherwise, the President shall resume the powers and duties of his office.

AMENDMENT XXVI (1971)

SECTION 1.

The right of citizens of the United States, who are eighteen years of age or older, to vote shall not be denied or abridged by the United States or by any State on account of age.

SECTION 2.

The Congress shall have power to enforce this article by appropriate legislation.

AMENDMENT XXVII (1992)

No law, varying the compensation for the services of the Senators and Representatives, shall take effect, until an election of representatives shall have intervened.

Federalist Paper No. 6

ALEXANDER HAMILTON

To the People of the State of New York:

THE three last numbers of this paper have been dedicated to an enumeration of the dangers to which we should be exposed, in a state of disunion, from the arms and arts of foreign nations. I shall now proceed to delineate dangers of a different and, perhaps, still more alarming kind—those which will in all probability flow from dissensions between the States themselves, and from domestic factions and convulsions. These have been already in some instances slightly anticipated; but they deserve a more particular and more full investigation.

A man must be far gone in Utopian speculations who can seriously doubt that, if these States should either be wholly disunited, or only united in partial confederacies, the subdivisions into which they might be thrown would have frequent and violent contests with each other. To presume a want of motives for such contests as an argument against their existence, would be to forget that men are ambitious, vindictive, and rapacious. To look for a continuation of harmony between a number of independent, unconnected sovereignties in the same neighborhood, would be to disregard the uniform course of human events, and to set at defiance the accumulated experience of ages.

The causes of hostility among nations are innumerable. There are some which have a general and almost constant operation upon the collective bodies of society. Of this description are the love of power or the desire of pre-eminence and dominion—the jealousy of power, or the desire of equality and safety. There are others which have a more circumscribed though an equally operative influence within their spheres. Such are the rivalships and competitions of commerce between commercial nations. And there are others, not less numerous than either of the former, which take their origin entirely in private passions; in the attachments, enmities, interests, hopes, and fears of leading individuals in the communities of which they are members. Men of this class, whether the favorites of a king or of a people, have in too many instances abused the confidence they possessed; and assuming the pretext of some public motive, have not scrupled to sacrifice the national tranquillity to personal advantage or personal gratification.

The celebrated Pericles, in compliance with the resentment of a prostitute,[1] at the expense of much of the blood and treasure of his countrymen, attacked, vanquished, and destroyed the city of the SAMNIANS. The same man, stimulated by private pique against the MEGARENSIANS,[2] another nation of Greece, or to avoid a prosecution with which he was threatened as an accomplice of a supposed theft of the statuary Phidias,[3] or to get rid of the accusations prepared to be brought against him for dissipating the funds of the state in the purchase of popularity,[4] or from a combination of all these causes, was the primitive author of that famous and fatal war, distinguished in the Grecian annals by the name of the PELOPONNESIAN war; which, after various vicissitudes, intermissions, and renewals, terminated in the ruin of the Athenian commonwealth.

The ambitious cardinal, who was prime minister to Henry VIII., permitting his vanity to aspire to the triple crown,[5] entertained hopes of succeeding in the acquisition of that splendid prize by the influence of the Emperor Charles V. To secure the favor and interest of this enterprising and powerful monarch, he precipitated England into a war with France, contrary to the plainest dictates of policy, and at the hazard of the safety and independence, as well of the kingdom over which he presided by his counsels, as of Europe in general. For if there ever was a sovereign who bid fair to realize the project of universal monarchy, it was the Emperor Charles V., of whose intrigues Wolsey was at once the instrument and the dupe.

The influence which the bigotry of one female,[6] the petulance of another,[7] and the cabals of a third,[8] had in the contemporary policy, ferments, and pacifications, of a considerable part of Europe, are topics that have been too often descanted upon not to be generally known.

To multiply examples of the agency of personal considerations in the production of great national events, either foreign or domestic, according to their direction, would be an unnecessary waste of time. Those who have but a superficial acquaintance with the sources from which they are to be drawn, will themselves recollect a variety of instances; and those who have a tolerable knowledge of human nature will not stand in need of such lights to form their opinion either of the reality or extent of that agency. Perhaps, however, a reference, tending to illustrate the general principle, may with propriety be made to a case which has lately happened among ourselves. If Shays had not been a DESPERATE DEBTOR, it is much to be doubted whether Massachusetts would have been plunged into a civil war.

But notwithstanding the concurring testimony of experience, in this particular, there are still to be found visionary or designing men, who stand ready to advocate the paradox of perpetual peace between the States, though dismembered and alienated from each other. The genius of republics (say they) is pacific; the spirit of commerce has a tendency to soften the manners of men, and to extinguish those inflammable humors which have so often kindled into wars. Commercial republics, like ours, will never be disposed to waste themselves in ruinous contentions with each other. They will be governed by mutual interest, and will cultivate a spirit of mutual amity and concord.

Is it not (we may ask these projectors in politics) the true interest of all nations to cultivate the same benevolent and philosophic spirit? If this be their true interest, have they in fact pursued it? Has it not, on the contrary, invariably been found that momentary passions, and immediate interest, have a more active and imperious control over human conduct than general or remote considerations of policy, utility or justice? Have republics in practice been less addicted to war than monarchies? Are not the former administered by MEN as well as the latter? Are there not aversions, predilections, rivalships, and desires of unjust acquisitions, that affect nations as well as kings? Are not popular assemblies frequently subject to the impulses of rage, resentment, jealousy, avarice, and of other irregular and violent propensities? Is it not well known that their determinations are often governed by a few individuals in whom they place confidence, and are, of course, liable to be tinctured by the passions and views of those individuals? Has commerce hitherto done anything more than change the objects of war? Is not the love of wealth as domineering and enterprising a passion as that of power or glory? Have there not been as many wars founded upon commercial motives since that has become the prevailing system of nations, as were before occasioned by the cupidity of territory or dominion? Has not the spirit of commerce, in many instances, administered new incentives to the appetite, both for the one and for the other? Let experience, the least fallible guide of human opinions, be appealed to for an answer to these inquiries.

Sparta, Athens, Rome, and Carthage were all republics; two of them, Athens and Carthage, of the commercial kind. Yet were they as often engaged in wars, offensive and defensive, as the neighboring monarchies of the same times. Sparta was little better than a wellregulated camp; and Rome was never sated of carnage and conquest.

Carthage, though a commercial republic, was the aggressor in the very war that ended in her destruction. Hannibal had carried her arms into the heart of Italy and to the gates of Rome, before Scipio, in turn, gave him an overthrow in the territories of Carthage, and made a conquest of the commonwealth.

Venice, in later times, figured more than once in wars of ambition, till, becoming an object to the other Italian states, Pope Julius II. found means to accomplish that formidable league,[9] which gave a deadly blow to the power and pride of this haughty republic.

The provinces of Holland, till they were overwhelmed in debts and taxes, took a leading and conspicuous part in the wars of Europe. They had furious contests with England for the dominion of the sea, and were among the most persevering and most implacable of the opponents of Louis XIV.

In the government of Britain the representatives of the people compose one branch of the national legislature. Commerce has been for ages the predominant pursuit of that country. Few nations, nevertheless, have been more frequently engaged in war; and the wars in which that kingdom has been engaged have, in numerous instances, proceeded from the people.

There have been, if I may so express it, almost as many popular as royal wars. The cries of the nation and the importunities of their representatives have, upon various occasions, dragged their monarchs into war, or continued them in it, contrary to their inclinations, and sometimes contrary to the real interests of the State. In that memorable struggle for superiority between the rival houses of AUSTRIA and BOURBON, which so long kept Europe in a flame, it is well known that the antipathies of the English against the French, seconding the ambition, or rather the avarice, of a favorite leader,[10] protracted the war beyond the limits marked out by sound policy, and for a considerable time in opposition to the views of the court.

The wars of these two last-mentioned nations have in a great measure grown out of commercial considerations,—the desire of supplanting and the fear of being supplanted, either in particular branches of traffic or in the general advantages of trade and navigation.

From this summary of what has taken place in other countries, whose situations have borne the nearest resemblance to our own, what reason can we have to confide in those reveries which would seduce us into an expectation of peace and cordiality between the members of the present confederacy, in a state of separation? Have we not already seen enough of the fallacy and extravagance of those idle theories which have amused us with promises of an exemption from the imperfections, weaknesses and evils incident to society in every shape? Is it not time to awake from the deceitful dream of a golden age, and to adopt as a practical maxim for the direction of our political conduct that we, as well as the other inhabitants of the globe, are yet remote from the happy empire of perfect wisdom and perfect virtue?

Let the point of extreme depression to which our national dignity and credit have sunk, let the inconveniences felt everywhere from a lax and ill administration of government, let the revolt of a part of the State of North Carolina, the late menacing disturbances in Pennsylvania, and the actual insurrections and rebellions in Massachusetts, declare—!

So far is the general sense of mankind from corresponding with the tenets of those who endeavor to lull asleep our apprehensions of discord and hostility between the States, in the event of disunion, that it has from long observation of the progress of society become a sort of axiom in politics, that vicinity or nearness of situation, constitutes nations natural enemies. An intelligent writer expresses himself on this subject to this effect: "NEIGHBORING NATIONS (says he) are naturally enemies of each other unless their common weakness forces them to league in a CONFEDERATE REPUBLIC, and their constitution prevents the differences that neighborhood occasions, extinguishing that secret jealousy which disposes all states to aggrandize themselves at the expense of their neighbors."[11] This passage, at the same time, points out the EVIL and suggests the REMEDY.

PUBLIUS.

1. Aspasia, vide "Plutarch's Life of Pericles."
2. Ibid.
3. Ibid.
4. Ibid. Phidias was supposed to have stolen some public gold, with the connivance of Pericles, for the embellishment of the statue of Minerva.
5. P Worn by the popes.
6. Madame de Maintenon.
7. Duchess of Marlborough.
8. Madame de Pompadour.
9. The League of Cambray, comprehending the Emperor, the King of France, the King of Aragon, and most of the Italian princes and states.
10. The Duke of Marlborough.
11. Vide "Principes des Negociations" par l'Abbe de Mably.

Federalist Paper No. 10

JAMES MADISON

To the People of the State of New York:

AMONG the numerous advantages promised by a wellconstructed Union, none deserves to be more accurately developed than its tendency to break and control the violence of faction. The friend of popular governments never finds himself so much alarmed for their character and fate, as when he contemplates their propensity to this dangerous vice. He will not fail, therefore, to set a due value on any plan which, without violating the principles to which he is attached, provides a proper cure for it. The instability, injustice, and confusion introduced into the public councils, have, in truth, been the mortal diseases under which popular governments have everywhere perished; as they continue to be the favorite and fruitful topics from which the adversaries to liberty derive their most specious declamations. The valuable improvements made by the American constitutions on the popular models, both ancient and modern, cannot certainly be too much admired; but it would be an unwarrantable partiality, to contend that they have as effectually obviated the danger on this side, as was wished and expected. Complaints are everywhere heard from our most considerate and virtuous citizens, equally the friends of public and private faith, and of public and personal liberty, that our governments are too unstable, that the public good is disregarded in the conflicts of rival parties, and that measures are too often decided, not according to the rules of justice and the rights of the minor party, but by the superior force of an interested and overbearing majority. However anxiously we may wish that these complaints had no foundation, the evidence, of known facts will not permit us to deny that they are in some degree true. It will be found, indeed, on a candid review of our situation, that some of the distresses under which we labor have been erroneously charged on the operation of our governments; but it will be found, at the same time, that other causes will not alone account for many of our heaviest misfortunes; and, particularly, for that prevailing and increasing distrust of public engagements, and alarm for private rights, which are echoed from one end of the continent to the other. These must be chiefly, if not wholly, effects of the unsteadiness and injustice with which a factious spirit has tainted our public administrations.

By a faction, I understand a number of citizens, whether amounting to a majority or a minority of the whole, who are united and actuated by some common impulse of passion, or of interest, adversed to the rights of other citizens, or to the permanent and aggregate interests of the community.

There are two methods of curing the mischiefs of faction: the one, by removing its causes; the other, by controlling its effects.

There are again two methods of removing the causes of faction: the one, by destroying the liberty which is essential to its existence; the other, by giving to every citizen the same opinions, the same passions, and the same interests.

It could never be more truly said than of the first remedy, that it was worse than the disease. Liberty is to faction what air is to fire, an aliment without which it instantly expires. But it could not be less folly to abolish liberty, which is essential to political life, because it nourishes faction, than it would be to wish the annihilation of air, which is essential to animal life, because it imparts to fire its destructive agency.

The second expedient is as impracticable as the first would be unwise. As long as the reason of man continues fallible, and he is at liberty to exercise it, different opinions will be formed. As long as the connection subsists between his reason and his self-love, his opinions and his passions will have a reciprocal influence on each other; and the former will be objects to which the latter will attach themselves. The diversity in the faculties of men, from which the rights of property originate, is not less an insuperable obstacle to a uniformity of interests. The protection of these faculties is the first object of government. From the protection of different and unequal faculties of acquiring property, the possession of different degrees and kinds of property immediately results; and from the influence of these on the sentiments and views of the respective proprietors, ensues a division of the society into different interests and parties.

The latent causes of faction are thus sown in the nature of man; and we see them everywhere brought into different degrees of activity, according to the different circumstances of civil society. A zeal for different opinions concerning religion, concerning government, and many other points, as well of speculation as of practice; an attachment to different leaders ambitiously contending for pre-eminence and power; or to persons of other descriptions whose fortunes have been interesting to the human passions, have, in turn, divided mankind into parties, inflamed them with mutual animosity, and rendered them much more disposed to vex and oppress each other than to co-operate for their common good. So strong is this propensity of mankind to fall into mutual animosities, that where no substantial occasion presents itself, the most frivolous and fanciful distinctions have been sufficient to kindle their unfriendly passions and excite their most violent conflicts. But the most common and durable source of factions has been the various and unequal distribution of property. Those who hold and those who are without property have ever formed distinct interests in society. Those who are creditors, and those who are debtors, fall under a like discrimination. A landed interest, a manufacturing interest, a mercantile interest, a moneyed interest, with many lesser interests, grow up of necessity in civilized nations, and divide them into different classes, actuated by different sentiments and views. The regulation of these various and interfering interests forms the principal task of modern legislation, and involves the spirit of party and faction in the necessary and ordinary operations of the government.

No man is allowed to be a judge in his own cause, because his interest would certainly bias his judgment, and, not improbably, corrupt his integrity. With equal, nay with greater reason, a body of men are unfit to be both judges and parties at the same time; yet what are many of the most important acts of legislation, but so many judicial determinations, not indeed concerning the rights of single persons, but concerning the rights of large bodies of citizens? And what are the different classes of legislators but advocates and parties to the causes which they determine? Is a law proposed concerning private debts? It is a question to which the creditors are parties on one side and the debtors on the other. Justice ought to hold the balance between them. Yet the parties are, and must be, themselves the judges; and the most numerous party, or, in other words, the most powerful faction must be expected to prevail. Shall domestic manufactures be encouraged, and in what degree, by restrictions on foreign manufactures? are questions which would be differently decided by the landed and the manufacturing classes, and probably by neither with a sole regard to justice and the public good. The apportionment of taxes on the various descriptions of property is an act which seems to require the

most exact impartiality; yet there is, perhaps, no legislative act in which greater opportunity and temptation are given to a predominant party to trample on the rules of justice. Every shilling with which they overburden the inferior number, is a shilling saved to their own pockets.

It is in vain to say that enlightened statesmen will be able to adjust these clashing interests, and render them all subservient to the public good. Enlightened statesmen will not always be at the helm. Nor, in many cases, can such an adjustment be made at all without taking into view indirect and remote considerations, which will rarely prevail over the immediate interest which one party may find in disregarding the rights of another or the good of the whole.

The inference to which we are brought is, that the CAUSES of faction cannot be removed, and that relief is only to be sought in the means of controlling its EFFECTS.

If a faction consists of less than a majority, relief is supplied by the republican principle, which enables the majority to defeat its sinister views by regular vote. It may clog the administration, it may convulse the society; but it will be unable to execute and mask its violence under the forms of the Constitution. When a majority is included in a faction, the form of popular government, on the other hand, enables it to sacrifice to its ruling passion or interest both the public good and the rights of other citizens. To secure the public good and private rights against the danger of such a faction, and at the same time to preserve the spirit and the form of popular government, is then the great object to which our inquiries are directed. Let me add that it is the great desideratum by which this form of government can be rescued from the opprobrium under which it has so long labored, and be recommended to the esteem and adoption of mankind.

By what means is this object attainable? Evidently by one of two only. Either the existence of the same passion or interest in a majority at the same time must be prevented, or the majority, having such coexistent passion or interest, must be rendered, by their number and local situation, unable to concert and carry into effect schemes of oppression. If the impulse and the opportunity be suffered to coincide, we well know that neither moral nor religious motives can be relied on as an adequate control. They are not found to be such on the injustice and violence of individuals, and lose their efficacy in proportion to the number combined together, that is, in proportion as their efficacy becomes needful.

From this view of the subject it may be concluded that a pure democracy, by which I mean a society consisting of a small number of citizens, who assemble and administer the government in person, can admit of no cure for the mischiefs of faction. A common passion or interest will, in almost every case, be felt by a majority of the whole; a communication and concert result from the form of government itself; and there is nothing to check the inducements to sacrifice the weaker party or an obnoxious individual. Hence it is that such democracies have ever been spectacles of turbulence and contention; have ever been found incompatible with personal security or the rights of property; and have in general been as short in their lives as they have been violent in their deaths. Theoretic politicians, who have patronized this species of government, have erroneously supposed that by reducing mankind to a perfect equality in their political rights, they would, at the same time, be perfectly equalized and assimilated in their possessions, their opinions, and their passions.

A republic, by which I mean a government in which the scheme of representation takes place, opens a different prospect, and promises the cure for which we are seeking. Let us examine the points in which it varies from pure democracy, and we shall comprehend both the nature of the cure and the efficacy which it must derive from the Union.

The two great points of difference between a democracy and a republic are: first, the delegation of the government, in the latter, to a small number of citizens elected by the rest; secondly, the greater number of citizens, and greater sphere of country, over which the latter may be extended.

The effect of the first difference is, on the one hand, to refine and enlarge the public views, by passing them through the medium of a chosen body of citizens, whose wisdom may best discern the true interest of their country, and whose patriotism and love of justice will be least likely to sacrifice it to temporary or partial considerations. Under such a regulation, it may well happen that the public voice, pronounced by the representatives of the people, will be more consonant to the public good than if pronounced by the people themselves, convened for the purpose. On the other hand, the effect may be inverted. Men of factious tempers, of local prejudices, or of sinister designs, may, by intrigue, by corruption, or by other means, first obtain the suffrages, and then betray the interests, of the people. The question resulting is, whether small or extensive republics are more favorable to the election of proper guardians of the public weal; and it is clearly decided in favor of the latter by two obvious considerations:

In the first place, it is to be remarked that, however small the republic may be, the representatives must be raised to a certain number, in order to guard against the cabals of a few; and that, however large it may be, they must be limited to a certain number, in order to guard against the confusion of a multitude. Hence, the number of representatives in the two cases not being in proportion to that of the two constituents, and being proportionally greater in the small republic, it follows that, if the proportion of fit characters be not less in the large than in the small republic, the former will present a greater option, and consequently a greater probability of a fit choice.

In the next place, as each representative will be chosen by a greater number of citizens in the large than in the small republic, it will be more difficult for unworthy candidates to practice with success the vicious arts by which elections are too often carried; and the suffrages of the people being more free, will be more likely to centre in men who possess the most attractive merit and the most diffusive and established characters.

It must be confessed that in this, as in most other cases, there is a mean, on both sides of which inconveniences will be found to lie. By enlarging too much the number of electors, you render the representatives too little acquainted with all their local circumstances and lesser interests; as by reducing it too much, you render him unduly attached to these, and too little fit to comprehend and pursue great and national objects. The federal Constitution forms a happy combination in this respect; the great and aggregate interests being referred to the national, the local and particular to the State legislatures.

The other point of difference is, the greater number of citizens and extent of territory which may be brought within the compass of republican than of democratic government; and it is this circumstance principally which renders factious combinations less to be dreaded in the former than in the latter. The smaller the society, the fewer probably will be the distinct parties and interests composing it; the fewer the distinct parties and interests, the more frequently will a majority be found of the same party; and the smaller the number of individuals composing a majority, and the smaller the compass within which they are placed, the more easily will they concert and execute their plans of oppression. Extend the sphere, and you take in a greater variety of parties and interests; you make it less probable that a majority of the whole will have a common motive to invade the rights of other citizens; or if such a common motive exists, it will be more difficult for all who feel it to discover their own strength, and to act in unison with each other. Besides other impediments, it may be remarked that, where there is a consciousness of unjust or dishonorable purposes, communication is always checked by distrust in proportion to the number whose concurrence is necessary.

Hence, it clearly appears, that the same advantage which a republic has over a democracy, in controlling the effects of faction, is enjoyed by a large over a small republic,—is enjoyed by the Union over the States composing it. Does the advantage consist in the substitution of representatives whose enlightened views and virtuous sentiments render them superior to local prejudices and schemes of injustice? It will not be denied that the representation of the Union will be most likely to possess these requisite endowments. Does it consist in the greater security afforded by a greater variety of parties, against the event of any one party being able to outnumber and oppress the rest? In an equal degree does the increased variety of parties comprised within the Union, increase this security. Does it, in fine, consist in the greater obstacles opposed to the concert and accomplishment of the secret wishes of an unjust and interested majority? Here, again, the extent of the Union gives it the most palpable advantage.

The influence of factious leaders may kindle a flame within their particular States, but will be unable to spread a general conflagration through the other States. A religious sect may degenerate into a political faction in a part of the Confederacy; but the variety of sects dispersed over the entire face of it must secure the national councils against any danger from that source. A rage for paper money, for an abolition of debts, for an equal division of property, or for any other improper or wicked project, will be less apt to pervade the whole body of the Union than a particular member of it; in the same proportion as such a malady is more likely to taint a particular county or district, than an entire State.

In the extent and proper structure of the Union, therefore, we behold a republican remedy for the diseases most incident to republican government. And according to the degree of pleasure and pride we feel in being republicans, ought to be our zeal in cherishing the spirit and supporting the character of Federalists.

PUBLIUS.

Federalist Paper No. 37

JAMES MADISON

To the People of the State of New York:

IN REVIEWING the defects of the existing Confederation, and showing that they cannot be supplied by a government of less energy than that before the public, several of the most important principles of the latter fell of course under consideration. But as the ultimate object of these papers is to determine clearly and fully the merits of this Constitution, and the expediency of adopting it, our plan cannot be complete without taking a more critical and thorough survey of the work of the convention, without examining it on all its sides, comparing it in all its parts, and calculating its probable effects.

That this remaining task may be executed under impressions conducive to a just and fair result, some reflections must in this place be indulged, which candor previously suggests.

It is a misfortune, inseparable from human affairs, that public measures are rarely investigated with that spirit of moderation which is essential to a just estimate of their real tendency to advance or obstruct the public good; and that this spirit is more apt to be diminished than promoted, by those occasions which require an unusual exercise of it. To those who have been led by experience to attend to this consideration, it could not appear surprising, that the act of the convention, which recommends so many important changes and innovations, which may be viewed in so many lights and relations, and which touches the springs of so many passions and interests, should find or excite dispositions unfriendly, both on one side and on the other, to a fair discussion and accurate judgment of its merits. In some, it has been too evident from their own publications, that they have scanned the proposed Constitution, not only with a predisposition to censure, but with a predetermination to condemn; as the language held by others betrays an opposite predetermination or bias, which must render their opinions also of little moment in the question. In placing, however, these different characters on a level, with respect to the weight of their opinions, I wish not to insinuate that there may not be a material difference in the purity of their intentions. It is but just to remark in favor of the latter description, that as our situation is universally admitted to be peculiarly critical, and to require indispensably that something should be done for our relief, the predetermined patron of what has been actually done may have taken his bias from the weight of these considerations, as well as from considerations of a sinister nature. The predetermined adversary, on the other hand, can have been governed by no venial motive whatever. The intentions of the first may be upright, as they may on the contrary be culpable. The views of the last cannot be upright, and must be culpable. But the truth is, that these papers are not addressed to persons falling under either of these characters. They solicit the attention of those only, who add to a sincere zeal for the happiness of their country, a temper favorable to a just estimate of the means of promoting it.

Persons of this character will proceed to an examination of the plan submitted by the convention, not only without a disposition to find or to magnify faults; but will see the propriety of reflecting, that a faultless plan was not to be expected. Nor will they barely make allowances for the errors which may be chargeable on the fallibility to which the convention, as a body of men, were liable; but will keep in mind, that they themselves also are but men, and ought not to assume an infallibility in rejudging the fallible opinions of others.

With equal readiness will it be perceived, that besides these inducements to candor, many allowances ought to be made for the difficulties inherent in the very nature of the undertaking referred to the convention.

The novelty of the undertaking immediately strikes us. It has been shown in the course of these papers, that the existing Confederation is founded on principles which are fallacious; that we must consequently change this first foundation, and with it the superstructure resting upon it. It has been shown, that the other confederacies which could be consulted as precedents have been vitiated by the same erroneous principles, and can therefore furnish no other light than that of beacons, which give warning of the course to be shunned, without pointing out that which ought to be pursued. The most that the convention could do in such a situation, was to avoid the errors suggested by the past experience of other countries, as well as of our own; and to provide a convenient mode of rectifying their own errors, as future experiences may unfold them.

Among the difficulties encountered by the convention, a very important one must have lain in combining the requisite stability and energy in government, with the inviolable attention due to liberty and to the republican form. Without substantially accomplishing this part of their undertaking, they would have very imperfectly fulfilled the object of their appointment, or the expectation of the public; yet that it could not be easily accomplished, will be denied by no one who is unwilling to betray his ignorance of the subject. Energy in government is essential to that security against external and internal danger, and to that prompt and salutary execution of the laws which enter into the very definition of good government. Stability in government is essential to national character and to the advantages annexed to it, as well as to that repose and confidence in the minds of the people, which are among the chief blessings of civil society. An irregular and mutable legislation is not more an evil in itself than it is odious to the people; and it may be pronounced with assurance that the people of this country, enlightened as they are with regard to the nature, and interested, as the great body of them are, in the effects of good government, will never be satisfied till some remedy be applied to the vicissitudes and uncertainties which characterize the State administrations. On comparing, however, these valuable ingredients with the vital principles of liberty, we must perceive at once the difficulty of mingling them together in their due proportions. The genius of republican liberty seems to demand on one side, not only that all power should be derived from the people, but that those intrusted with it should be kept in dependence on the people, by a short duration of their appointments; and that even during this short period the trust should be placed not in a few, but a number of hands. Stability, on the contrary, requires that the hands in which power is lodged should continue for a length of time the same. A frequent change of men will result from a frequent return of elections; and a frequent change of measures from a frequent change of men: whilst energy in government requires not only a certain duration of power, but the execution of it by a single hand.

How far the convention may have succeeded in this part of their work, will better appear on a more accurate view of it. From the cursory view here taken, it must clearly appear to have been an arduous part.

Not less arduous must have been the task of marking the proper line of partition between the authority of the general and that of the State governments. Every man will be sensible of this difficulty, in proportion as he has been accustomed to contemplate and discriminate objects extensive and complicated in their nature. The faculties of the mind itself have never yet been distinguished and defined, with satisfactory precision, by all the efforts of the most acute and metaphysical philosophers. Sense, perception, judgment, desire, volition, memory, imagination, are found to be separated by such delicate shades and minute gradations that their boundaries have eluded the most subtle investigations, and remain a pregnant source of ingenious disquisition and controversy. The boundaries between the great kingdom of nature, and, still more, between the various provinces, and lesser portions, into which they are subdivided, afford another illustration of the same important truth. The most sagacious and laborious naturalists have never yet succeeded in tracing with certainty the line which separates the district of vegetable life from the neighboring region of unorganized matter, or which marks the ermination of the former and the commencement of the animal empire. A still greater obscurity lies in the distinctive characters by which the objects in each of these great departments of nature have been arranged and assorted.

When we pass from the works of nature, in which all the delineations are perfectly accurate, and appear to be otherwise only from the imperfection of the eye which surveys them, to the institutions of man, in which the obscurity arises as well from the object itself as from the organ by which it is contemplated, we must perceive the necessity of moderating still further our expectations and hopes from the efforts of human sagacity. Experience has instructed us that no skill in the science of government has yet been able to discriminate and define, with sufficient certainty, its three great provinces the legislative, executive, and judiciary; or even the privileges and powers of the different legislative branches. Questions daily occur in the course of practice, which prove the obscurity which reins in these subjects, and which puzzle the greatest adepts in political science.

The experience of ages, with the continued and combined labors of the most enlightened legislatures and jurists, has been equally unsuccessful in delineating the several objects and limits of different codes of laws and different tribunals of justice. The precise extent of the common law, and the statute law, the maritime law, the ecclesiastical law, the law of corporations, and other local laws and customs, remains still to be clearly and finally established in Great Britain, where accuracy in such subjects has been more industriously pursued than in any other part of the world. The jurisdiction of her several courts, general and local, of law, of equity, of admiralty, etc., is not less a source of frequent and intricate discussions, sufficiently denoting the indeterminate limits by which they are respectively circumscribed. All new laws, though penned with the greatest technical skill, and passed on the fullest and most mature deliberation, are considered as more or less obscure and equivocal, until their meaning be liquidated and ascertained by a series of particular discussions and adjudications. Besides the obscurity arising from the complexity of objects, and the imperfection of the human faculties, the medium through which the conceptions of men are conveyed to each other adds a fresh embarrassment. The use of words is to express ideas. Perspicuity, therefore, requires not only that the ideas should be distinctly formed, but that they should be expressed by words distinctly and exclusively appropriate to them. But no language is so copious as to supply words and phrases for every complex idea, or so correct as not to include many equivocally denoting different ideas. Hence it must happen that however accurately objects may be discriminated in themselves, and however accurately the discrimination may be considered, the definition of them may be rendered inaccurate by the inaccuracy of the terms in which it is delivered. And this unavoidable inaccuracy must be greater or less, according to the complexity and novelty of the objects defined. When the Almighty himself condescends to address mankind in their own language, his meaning, luminous as it must be, is rendered dim and doubtful by the cloudy medium through which it is communicated.

Here, then, are three sources of vague and incorrect definitions: indistinctness of the object, imperfection of the organ of conception, inadequateness of the vehicle of ideas. Any one of these must produce a certain degree of obscurity. The convention, in delineating the boundary between the federal and State jurisdictions, must have experienced the full effect of them all.

To the difficulties already mentioned may be added the interfering pretensions of the larger and smaller States. We cannot err in supposing that the former would contend for a participation in the government, fully proportioned to their superior wealth and importance; and that the latter would not be less tenacious of the equality at present enjoyed by them. We may well suppose that neither side would entirely yield to the other, and consequently that the struggle could be terminated only by compromise. It is extremely probable, also, that after the ratio of representation had been adjusted, this very compromise must have produced a fresh struggle between the same parties, to give such a turn to the organization of the government, and to the distribution of its powers, as would increase the importance of the branches, in forming which they had respectively obtained the greatest share of influence. There are features in the Constitution which warrant each of these suppositions; and as far as either of them is well founded, it shows that the convention must have been compelled to sacrifice theoretical propriety to the force of extraneous considerations.

Nor could it have been the large and small States only, which would marshal themselves in opposition to each other on various points. Other combinations, resulting from a difference of local position and policy, must have created additional difficulties. As every State may be divided into different districts, and its citizens into different classes, which give birth to contending interests and local jealousies, so the different parts of the United States are distinguished from each other by a variety of circumstances, which produce a like effect on a larger scale. And although this variety of interests, for reasons sufficiently explained in a former paper, may have a salutary influence on the administration of the government when formed, yet every one must be sensible of the contrary influence, which must have been experienced in the task of forming it.

Would it be wonderful if, under the pressure of all these difficulties, the convention should have been forced into some deviations from that artificial structure and regular symmetry which an abstract view of the subject might lead an ingenious theorist to bestow on a Constitution planned in his closet or in his imagination? The real wonder is that so many difficulties should have been surmounted, and surmounted with a unanimity almost as unprecedented as it must have been unexpected. It is impossible for any man of candor to reflect on this circumstance without partaking of the astonishment. It is impossible for the man of pious reflection not to perceive in it a finger of that Almighty hand which has been so frequently and signally extended to our relief in the critical stages of the revolution.

We had occasion, in a former paper, to take notice of the repeated trials which have been unsuccessfully made in the United Netherlands for reforming the baneful and notorious vices of their constitution. The history of almost all the great councils and consultations held among mankind for reconciling their discordant opinions, assuaging their mutual jealousies, and adjusting their respective interests, is a history of factions, contentions, and disappointments, and may be classed among the most dark and degraded pictures which display the infirmities and depravities of the human character. If, in a few scattered instances, a brighter aspect is presented, they serve only as exceptions to admonish us of the general truth; and by their lustre to darken the gloom of the adverse prospect to which they are contrasted. In revolving the causes from which these exceptions result, and applying them to the particular instances before us, we are necessarily led to two important conclusions. The first is, that the convention must have enjoyed, in a very singular degree, an exemption from the pestilential influence of party animosities the disease most incident to deliberative bodies, and most apt to contaminate their proceedings. The second conclusion is that all the deputations composing the convention were satisfactorily accommodated by the final act, or were induced to accede to it by a deep conviction of the necessity of sacrificing private opinions and partial interests to the public good, and by a despair of seeing this necessity diminished by delays or by new experiments.

PUBLIUS.

Federalist Paper No. 51

TO THE PEOPLE OF THE STATE OF NEW YORK:

TO WHAT expedient, then, shall we finally resort, for maintaining in practice the necessary partition of power among the several departments, as laid down in the Constitution? The only answer that can be given is, that as all these exterior provisions are found to be inadequate, the defect must be supplied, by so contriving the interior structure of the government as that its several constituent parts may, by their mutual relations, be the means of keeping each other in their proper places. Without presuming to undertake a full development of this important idea, I will hazard a few general observations, which may perhaps place it in a clearer light, and enable us to form a more correct judgment of the principles and structure of the government planned by the convention.

In order to lay a due foundation for that separate and distinct exercise of the different powers of government, which to a certain extent is admitted on all hands to be essential to the preservation of liberty, it is evident that each department should have a will of its own; and consequently should be so constituted that the members of each should have as little agency as possible in the appointment of the members of the others. Were this principle rigorously adhered to, it would require that all the appointments for the supreme executive, legislative, and judiciary magistracies should be drawn from the same fountain of authority, the people, through channels having no communication whatever with one another. Perhaps such a plan of constructing the several departments would be less difficult in practice than it may in contemplation appear. Some difficulties, however, and some additional expense would attend the execution of it. Some deviations, therefore, from the principle must be admitted. In the constitution of the judiciary department in particular, it might be inexpedient to insist rigorously on the principle: first, because peculiar qualifications being essential in the members, the primary consideration ought to be to select that mode of choice which best secures these qualifications; secondly, because the permanent tenure by which the appointments are held in that department, must soon destroy all sense of dependence on the authority conferring them.

It is equally evident, that the members of each department should be as little dependent as possible on those of the others, for the emoluments annexed to their offices. Were the executive magistrate, or the judges, not independent of the legislature in this particular, their independence in every other would be merely nominal. But the great security against a gradual concentration of the several powers in the same department, consists in giving to those who administer each department the necessary constitutional means and personal motives to resist encroachments of the others. The provision for defense must in this, as in all other cases, be made commensurate to the danger of attack. Ambition must be made to counteract ambition. The interest of the man must be connected with the constitutional rights of the place. It may be a reflection on human nature, that such devices should be necessary to control the abuses of government. But what is government itself, but the greatest of all reflections on human nature? If men were angels, no government would be necessary. If angels were to govern men, neither external nor internal controls on government would be necessary. In framing a government which is to be administered by men over men, the great difficulty lies in this: you must first enable the government to control the governed; and in the next place oblige it to control itself.

A dependence on the people is, no doubt, the primary control on the government; but experience has taught mankind the necessity of auxiliary precautions. This policy of supplying, by opposite and rival interests, the defect of better motives, might be traced through the whole system of human affairs, private as well as public. We see it particularly displayed in all the subordinate distributions of power, where the constant aim is to divide and arrange the several offices in such a manner as that each may be a check on the other that the private interest of every individual may be a sentinel over the public rights. These inventions of prudence cannot be less requisite in the distribution of the supreme powers of the State. But it is not possible to give to each department an equal power of self-defense. In republican government, the legislative authority necessarily predominates. The remedy for this inconveniency is to divide the legislature into different branches; and to render them, by different modes of election and different principles of action, as little connected with each other as the nature of their common functions and their common dependence on the society will admit. It may even be necessary to guard against dangerous encroachments by still further precautions. As the weight of the legislative authority requires that it should be thus divided, the weakness of the executive may require, on the other hand, that it should be fortified.

An absolute negative on the legislature appears, at first view, to be the natural defense with which the executive magistrate should be armed. But perhaps it would be neither altogether safe nor alone sufficient. On ordinary occasions it might not be exerted with the requisite firmness, and on extraordinary occasions it might be perfidiously abused. May not this defect of an absolute negative be supplied by some qualified connection between this weaker department and the weaker branch of the stronger department, by which the latter may be led to support the constitutional rights of the former, without being too much detached from the rights of its own department? If the principles on which these observations are founded be just, as I persuade myself they are, and they be applied as a criterion to the several State constitutions, and to the federal Constitution it will be found that if the latter does not perfectly correspond with them, the former are infinitely less able to bear such a test.

There are, moreover, two considerations particularly applicable to the federal system of America, which place that system in a very interesting point of view. First. In a single republic, all the power surrendered by the people is submitted to the administration of a single government; and the usurpations are guarded against by a division of the government into distinct and separate departments. In the compound republic of America, the power surrendered by the people is first divided between two distinct governments, and then the portion allotted to each subdivided among distinct and separate departments. Hence a double security arises to the rights of the people. The different governments will control each other, at the same time that each will be controlled by itself. Second. It is of great importance in a republic not only to guard the society against the oppression of its rulers, but to guard one part of the society against the injustice of the other part. Different interests necessarily exist in different classes of citizens. If a majority be united by a common interest, the rights of the minority will be insecure.

There are but two methods of providing against this evil: the one by creating a will in the community independent of the majority that is, of the society itself; the other, by comprehending in the society so many separate descriptions of citizens as will render an unjust combination of a majority of the whole very improbable, if not impracticable. The first method prevails in all governments possessing an hereditary or self-appointed authority. This, at best, is but a precarious security; because a power independent of the society may as well espouse the unjust views of the major, as the rightful interests of the minor party, and may possibly be turned against both parties. The second method will be exemplified in the federal republic of the United States. Whilst all authority in it will be derived from and dependent on the society, the society itself will be broken into so many parts, interests, and classes of citizens, that the rights of individuals, or of the minority, will be in little danger from interested combinations of the majority.

In a free government the security for civil rights must be the same as that for religious rights. It consists in the one case in the multiplicity of interests, and in the other in the multiplicity of sects. The degree of security in both cases will depend on the number of interests and sects; and this may be presumed to depend on the extent of country and number of people comprehended under the same government. This view of the subject must particularly recommend a proper federal system to all the sincere and considerate friends of republican government, since it shows that in exact proportion as the territory of the Union may be formed into more circumscribed Confederacies, or States oppressive combinations of a majority will be facilitated: the best security, under the republican forms, for the rights of every class of citizens, will be diminished: and consequently the stability and independence of some member of the government, the only other security, must be proportionally increased. Justice is the end of government. It is the end of civil society. It ever has been and ever will be pursued until it be obtained, or until liberty be lost in the pursuit. In a society under the forms of which the stronger faction can readily unite and oppress the weaker, anarchy may as truly be said to reign as in a state of nature, where the weaker individual is not secured against the violence of the stronger; and as, in the latter state, even the stronger individuals are prompted, by the uncertainty of their condition, to submit to a government which may protect the weak as well as themselves; so, in the former state, will the more powerful factions or parties be gradnally induced, by a like motive, to wish for a government which will protect all parties, the weaker as well as the more powerful.

It can be little doubted that if the State of Rhode Island was separated from the Confederacy and left to itself, the insecurity of rights under the popular form of government within such narrow limits would be displayed by such reiterated oppressions of factious majorities that some power altogether independent of the people would soon be called for by the voice of the very factions whose misrule had proved the necessity of it. In the extended republic of the United States, and among the great variety of interests, parties, and sects which it embraces, a coalition of a majority of the whole society could seldom take place on any other principles than those of justice and the general good; whilst there being thus less danger to a minor from the will of a major party, there must be less pretext, also, to provide for the security of the former, by introducing into the government a will not dependent on the latter, or, in other words, a will independent of the society itself. It is no less certain than it is important, notwithstanding the contrary opinions which have been entertained, that the larger the society, provided it lie within a practical sphere, the more duly capable it will be of self-government. And happily for the RE-PUBLICAN CAUSE, the practicable sphere may be carried to a very great extent, by a judicious modification and mixture of the FEDERAL PRINCIPLE.

PUBLIUS.

President George Washington's First Inaugural Speech

FELLOW CITIZENS OF THE SENATE AND OF THE HOUSE OF REPRESENTATIVES:

Among the vicissitudes incident to life no event could have filled me with greater anxieties than that of which the notification was transmitted by your order, and received on the 14th day of the present month. On the one hand, I was summoned by my Country, whose voice I can never hear but with veneration and love, from a retreat which I had chosen with the fondest predilection, and, in my flattering hopes, with an immutable decision, as the asylum of my declining years—a retreat which was rendered every day more necessary as well as more dear to me by the addition of habit to inclination, and of frequent interruptions in my health to the gradual waste committed on it by time. On the other hand, the magnitude and difficulty of the trust to which the voice of my country called me, being sufficient to awaken in the wisest and most experienced of her citizens a distrustful scrutiny into his qualifications, could not but overwhelm with despondence one who (inheriting inferior endowments from nature and unpracticed in the duties of civil administration) ought to be peculiarly conscious of his own deficiencies. In this conflict of emotions all I dare aver is that it has been my faithful study to collect my duty from a just appreciation of every circumstance by which it might be affected. All I dare hope is that if, in executing this task, I have been too much swayed by a grateful remembrance of former instances, or by an affectionate sensibility to this transcendent proof of the confidence of my fellow citizens, and have thence too little consulted my incapacity as well as disinclination for the weighty and untried cares before me, my error will be palliated by the motives which mislead me, and its consequences be judged by my country with some share of the partiality in which they originated.

Such being the impressions under which I have, in obedience to the public summons, repaired to the present station, it would be peculiarly improper to omit in this first official act my fervent supplications to that Almighty Being who rules over the universe, who presides in the councils of nations, and whose providential aids can supply every human defect, that His benediction may consecrate to the liberties and happiness of the people of the United States a Government instituted by themselves for these essential purposes, and may enable every instrument employed in its administration to execute with success the functions allotted to his charge. In tendering this homage to the Great Author of every public and private good, I assure myself that it expresses your sentiments not less than my own, nor those of my fellow citizens at large less than either. No people can be bound to acknowledge and adore the Invisible Hand which conducts the affairs of men more than those of the United States. Every step by which they have advanced to the character of an independent nation seems to have been distinguished by some token of providential agency; and in the important revolution just accomplished in the system of their united government the tranquil deliberations and voluntary consent of so many distinct communities from which the event has resulted can not be compared with the means by which most governments have been established without some return of pious gratitude, along with an humble anticipation of the future blessings which the past seem to presage. These reflections, arising out of the present crisis, have forced themselves too strongly on my mind to be suppressed. You will join with me, I trust, in thinking that there are none under the influence of which the proceedings of a new and free government can more auspiciously commence.

By the article establishing the executive department it is made the duty of the President "to recommend to your consideration such measures as he shall judge necessary and expedient." The circumstances under which I now meet you will acquit me from entering into that subject further than to refer to the great constitutional charter under which you are assembled, and which, in defining your powers, designates the objects to which your attention is to be given. It will be more consistent with those circumstances, and far more congenial with the feelings which actuate me, to substitute, in place of a recommendation of particular measures, the tribute that is due to the talents, the rectitude, and the patriotism which adorn the characters selected to devise and adopt them. In these honorable qualifications I behold the surest pledges that as on one side no local prejudices or attachments, no separate views nor party animosities, will misdirect the comprehensive and equal eye which ought to watch over this great assemblage of communities and interests, so, on another, that the foundation of our national policy will be laid in the pure and immutable principles of private morality, and the preeminence of free government be exemplified by all the attributes which can win the affections of its citizens and command the respect of the world. I dwell on this prospect with every satisfaction which an ardent love for my country can inspire, since there is no truth more thoroughly established than that there exists in the economy and course of nature an indissoluble union between virtue and happiness; between duty and advantage; between the genuine maxims of an honest and magnanimous policy and the solid rewards of public prosperity and felicity; since we ought to be no less persuaded that the propitious smiles of Heaven can never be expected on a nation that disregards the eternal rules of order and right which Heaven itself has ordained; and since the preservation of the sacred fire of liberty and the destiny of the republican model of government are justly considered, perhaps, as deeply, as finally, staked on the experiment entrusted to the hands of the American people.

Besides the ordinary objects submitted to your care, it will remain with your judgment to decide how far an exercise of the occasional power delegated by the fifth article of the Constitution is rendered expedient at the present juncture by the nature of objections which have been urged against the system, or by the degree of inquietude which has given birth to them. Instead of undertaking particular recommendations on this subject, in which I could be guided by no lights derived from official opportunities, I shall again give way to my entire confidence in your discernment and pursuit of the public good; for I assure myself that whilst you carefully avoid every alteration which might endanger the benefits of an united and effective government, or which ought to await the future lessons of experience, a reverence for the characteristic rights of freemen and a regard for the public harmony will sufficiently influence your deliberations on the question how far the former can be impregnably fortified or the latter be safely and advantageously promoted.

To the foregoing observations I have one to add, which will be most properly addressed to the House of Representatives. It concerns myself, and will therefore be as brief as possible. When I was first honored with a call into the service of my country, then on the eve of an arduous struggle for its liberties, the light in which I contemplated my duty required that I should renounce every pecuniary compensation. From this resolution I have in no instance departed; and being still under the impressions which produced it, I must decline as inapplicable to myself any share in the personal emoluments which may be indispensably included in a permanent provision for the executive department, and must accordingly pray that the pecuniary estimates for the station in which I am placed may during my continuance in it be limited to such actual expenditures as the public good may be thought to require.

Having thus imparted to you my sentiments as they have been awakened by the occasion which brings us together, I shall take my present leave; but not without resorting once more to the benign Parent of the Human Race in humble supplication that, since He has been pleased to favor the American people with opportunities for deliberating in perfect tranquillity, and dispositions for deciding with unparalleled unanimity on a form of government for the security of their union and the advancement of their happiness, so His divine blessing may be equally conspicuous in the enlarged views, the temperate consultations, and the wise measures on which the success of this Government must depend.

The Federal Judiciary Act

Congress of the United States, begun and held at the City of New York on Wednesday the fourth of March one thousand seven hundred and eighty nine.

CHAP. XX.–An Act to establish the Judicial Courts of the United States.

SECTION 1. Be it enacted by the Senate and House of Representatives of the United States of America in Congress assembled, That the supreme court of the United States shall consist of a chief justice and five associate justices, any four of whom shall be a quorum, and shall hold annually at the seat of government two sessions, the one commencing the first Monday of February, and the other the first Monday of August. That the associate justices shall have precedence according to the date of their commissions, or when the commissions of two or more of them bear date on the same day, according to their respective ages.

SEC. 2. And be it further enacted, That the United States shall be, and they hereby are divided into thirteen districts, to be limited and called as follows, to wit: one to consist of that part of the State of Massachusetts which lies easterly of the State of New Hampshire, and to be called Maine District; one to consist of the State of New Hampshire, and to be called New Hampshire District; one to consist of the remaining part of the State of Massachusetts, and to be called Massachusetts district; one to consist of the State of Connecticut, and to be called Connecticut District; one to consist of the State of New York, and to be called New York District; one to consist of the State of New Jersey, and to be called New Jersey District; one to consist of the State of Pennsylvania, and to be called Pennsylvania District; one to consist of the State of Delaware, and to be called Delaware District; one to consist of the State of Maryland, and to be called Maryland District; one to consist of the State of Virginia, except that part called the District of Kentucky, and to be called Virginia District; one to consist of the remaining part of the State of Virginia, and to be called Kentucky District; one to consist of the State of South Carolina, and to be called South Carolina District; and one to consist of the State of Georgia, and to be called Georgia District.

SEC. 3. And be it further enacted, That there be a court called a District Court, in each of the afore mentioned districts, to consist of one judge, who shall reside in the district for which he is appointed, and shall be called a District Judge, and shall hold annually four sessions, the first of which to commence as follows, to wit: in the districts of New York and of New Jersey on the first, in the district of Pennsylvania on the second, in the district of Connecticut on the third, and in the district of Delaware on the fourth, Tuesdays of November next; in the districts of Massachusetts, of Maine, and of Maryland, on the first, in the district of Georgia on the second, and in the districts of New Hampshire, of Virginia, and of Kentucky, on the third Tuesdays of December next; and the other three sessions progressively in the respective districts on the like Tuesdays of every third calendar month afterwards, and in the district of South Carolina, on the third Monday in March and September, the first Monday in July, and the second Monday in December of each and every year, commencing in December next; and that the District Judge shall have power to hold special courts at his discretion. That the stated District Court shall be held at the places following, to wit: in the district of Maine, at Portland and Pownalsborough alternately, beginning at the first; in the district of New Hampshire, at Exeter and Portsmouth alternately, beginning at the first; in the district of Massachusetts, at Boston and Salem alternately, beginning at the first; in the district of Connecticut, alternately at Hartford and New Haven, beginning at the first; in the district of New York, at New York; in the district of New Jersey, alternately at New Brunswick and Burlington, beginning at the first; in the district of Pennsylvania, at Philadelphia and York Town alternately, beginning at the first; in the district of Delaware, alternately at Newcastle and Dover, beginning at the first; in the district of Maryland, alternately at Baltimore and Easton, beginning at the first; in the district of Virginia, alternately at Richmond and Williamsburgh, beginning at the first; in the district of Kentucky, at Harrodsburgh; in the district of South Carolina, at Charleston; and in the district of Georgia, alternately at Savannah and Augusta, beginning at the first; and that the special courts shall be held at the same place in each district as the stated courts, or in districts that have two, at either of them, in the discretion of the judge, or at such other place in the district, as the nature of the business and his discretion shall direct. And that in the districts that have but one place for holding the District Court, the records thereof shall be kept at that place; and in districts that have two, at that place in each district which the judge shall appoint.

SEC. 4. And be it further enacted, That the before mentioned districts, except those of Maine and Kentucky, shall be divided into three circuits, and be called the eastern, the middle, and the southern circuit. That the eastern circuit shall consist of the districts of New Hampshire, Massachusetts, Connecticut and New York; that the middle circuit shall consist of the districts of New Jersey, Pennsylvania, Delaware, Maryland and Virginia; and that the southern circuit shall consist of the districts of South Carolina and Georgia, and that there shall be held annually in each district of said circuits, two courts, which shall be called Circuit Courts, and shall consist of any two justices of the Supreme Court, and the district judge of such districts, any two of whom shall constitute a quorum: Provided, That no district judge shall give a vote in any case of appeal or error from his own decision; but may assign the reasons of such his decision.

SEC. 5. And be it further enacted, That the first session of the said circuit court in the several districts shall commence at the times following, to wit: in New Jersey on the second, in New York on the fourth, in Pennsylvania on the eleventh, in Connecticut on the twenty-second, and in Delaware on the twenty-seventh, days of April next; in Massachusetts on the third, in Maryland on the seventh, in South Carolina on the twelfth, in New Hampshire on the twentieth, in Virginia on the twenty-second, and in Georgia on the twenty-eighth, days of May next, and the subsequent sessions in the respective districts on the like days of every sixth calendar month afterwards, except in South Carolina, where the session of the said court shall commence on the first, and in Georgia where it shall commence on the seventeenth day of October, and except when any of those days shall happen on a Sunday, and then the session shall commence on the next day following. And the sessions of the said circuit court shall be held in the district of New Hampshire, at Portsmouth and Exeter alternately, beginning at the first; in the district of Massachusetts, at Boston; in the district of Connecticut, alternately at Hartford and New Haven, beginning at the last; in the district of New York, alternately at New York and Albany, beginning at the first; in the district of New Jersey, at Trenton; in the district of Pennsylvania, alternately at Philadelphia and Yorktown, beginning at the first; in the district of Delaware, alternately at New Castle and Dover, beginning at the first; in the district of Maryland, alternately at Annapolis and Easton, beginning at the first; in the district of Virginia, alternately at Charlottesville and Williamsburgh, beginning at the first; in the district of South Carolina, alternately at Columbia and Charleston, beginning at the first; and in the district of Georgia, alternately at Savannah and Augusta, beginning at the first. And the circuit courts shall have power to hold special sessions for the trial of criminal causes at any other time at their discretion, or at the discretion of the Supreme Court.

SEC. 6. And be it further enacted, That the Supreme Court may, by any one or more of its justices being present, be adjourned from day to day until a quorum be convened; and that a circuit court may also be adjourned from day to day by any one of its judges, or if none are present, by the marshal of the district until a quorum be convened; and that a district court, in case of the inability of the judge to attend at the commencement of a session, may by virtue of a written order from the said judge, directed to the marshal of the district, be adjourned by the said marshal to such day, antecedent to the next stated session of the said court, as in the said order shall be appointed; and in case of the death of the said judge, and his vacancy not being supplied, all process, pleadings and proceedings of what nature soever, pending before the said court, shall be continued of course until the next stated session after the appointment and acceptance of the office by his successor.

SEC. 7. And be it [further] enacted, That the Supreme Court, and the district courts shall have power to appoint clerks for their respective courts, and that the clerk for each district court shall be clerk also of the circuit court in such district, and each of the said clerks shall, before he enters upon the execution of his office, take the following oath or affirmation, to wit: "I, A. B., being appointed clerk of   , do solemnly swear, or affirm, that I will truly and faithfully enter and record all the orders, decrees, judgments and proceedings of the said court, and that I will faithfully and impartially discharge and perform all the duties of my said office, according to the best of my abilities and understanding. So help me God." Which words, so help me God, shall be omitted in all cases where an affirmation is admitted instead of an oath. And the said clerks shall also severally give bond, with sufficient sureties, (to be approved of by the Supreme and district courts respectively) to the United States, in the sum of two thousand dollars, faithfully to discharge the duties of his office, and seasonably to record the decrees, judgments and determinations of the court of which he is clerk.

SEC. 8. And be it further enacted, That the justices of the Supreme Court, and the district judges, before they proceed to execute the duties of their respective offices, shall take the following oath or affirmation, to wit: "I, A. B., do solemnly swear or affirm, that I will administer justice without respect to persons, and do equal right to the poor and to the rich, and that I will faithfully and impartially discharge and perform all the duties incumbent on me as, according to the best of my abilities and understanding, agreeably to the constitution, and laws of the United States. So help me God."

SEC. 9. And be it further enacted, That the district courts shall have, exclusively of the courts of the several States, cognizance of all crimes and offences that shall be cognizable under the authority of the United States, committed within their respective districts, or upon the high seas; where no other punishment than whipping, not exceeding thirty stripes, a fine not exceeding one hundred dollars, or a term of imprisonment not exceeding six months, is to be inflicted; and shall also have exclusive original cognizance of all civil causes of admiralty and maritime jurisdiction, including all seizures under laws of impost, navigation or trade of the United States, where the seizures are made, on waters which are navigable from the sea by vessels of ten or more tons burthen, within their respective districts as well as upon the high seas; saving to suitors, in all cases, the right of a common law remedy, where the common law is competent to give it; and shall also have exclusive original cognizance of all seizures on land, or other waters than as aforesaid, made, and of all suits for penalties and forfeitures incurred, under the laws of the United States. And shall also have cognizance, concurrent with the courts of the several States, or the circuit courts, as the case may be, of all causes where an alien sues for a tort only in violation of the law of nations or a treaty of the United States. And shall also have cognizance, concurrent as last mentioned, of all suits at common law where the United States sue, and the matter in dispute amounts, exclusive of costs, to the sum or value of one hundred dollars.

And shall also have jurisdiction exclusively of the courts of the several States, of all suits against consuls or vice-consuls, except for offences above the description aforesaid. And the trial of issues in fact, in the district courts, in all causes except civil causes of admiralty and maritime jurisdiction, shall be by jury.

SEC. 10. And be it further enacted, That the district court in Kentucky district shall, besides the jurisdiction aforesaid, have jurisdiction of all other causes, except of appeals and writs of error, hereinafter made cognizable in a circuit court, and shall proceed therein in the same manner as a circuit court, and writs of error and appeals shall lie from decisions therein to the Supreme Court in the same causes, as from a circuit court to the Supreme Court, and under the same regulations. And the district court in Maine district shall, besides the jurisdiction herein before granted, have jurisdiction of all causes, except of appeals and writs of error herein after made cognizable in a circuit court, and shall proceed therein in the same manner as a circuit court: And writs of error shall lie from decisions therein to the circuit court in the district of Massachusetts in the same manner as from other district courts to their respective circuit courts.

SEC. 11. And be it further enacted, That the circuit courts shall have original cognizance, concurrent with the courts of the several States, of all suits of a civil nature at common law or in equity, where the matter in dispute exceeds, exclusive of costs, the sum or value of five hundred dollars, and the United States are plaintiffs, or petitioners; or an alien is a party, or the suit is between a citizen of the State where the suit is brought, and a citizen of another State. And shall have exclusive cognizance of all crimes and offences cognizable under the authority of the United States, except where this act otherwise provides, or the laws of the United States shall otherwise direct, and concurrent jurisdiction with the district courts of the crimes and offences cognizable therein. But no person shall be arrested in one district for trial in another, in any civil action before a circuit or district court. And no civil suit shall be brought before either of said courts against an inhabitant of the United States, by any original process in any other district than that whereof he is an inhabitant, or in which he shall be found at the time of serving the writ, nor shall any district or circuit court have cognizance of any suit to recover the contents of any promissory note or other chose in action in favour of an assignee, unless a suit might have been prosecuted in such court to recover the said contents if no assignment had been made, except in cases of foreign bills of exchange. And the circuit courts shall also have appellate jurisdiction from the district courts under the regulations and restrictions herein after provided.

SEC. 12. And be it further enacted, That if a suit be commenced in any state court against an alien, or by a citizen of the state in which the suit is brought against a citizen of another state, and the matter in dispute exceeds the aforesaid sum or value of five hundred dollars, exclusive of costs, to be made to appear to the satisfaction of the court; and the defendant shall, at the time of entering his appearance in such state court, file a petition for the removal of the cause for trial into the next circuit court, to be held in the district where the suit is pending, or if in the district of Maine to the district court next to be holden therein, or if in Kentucky district to the district court next to be holden therein, and offer good and sufficient surety for his entering in such court, on the first day of its session, copies of said process against him, and also for his there appearing and entering special bail in the cause, if special bail was originally requisite therein, it shall then be the duty of the state court to accept the surety, and proceed no further in the cause, and any bail that may have been originally taken shall be discharged, and the said copies being entered as aforesaid, in such court of the United States, the cause shall there proceed in the same manner as if it had been brought there by original process. And any attachment of the goods or estate of the defendant by the original process, shall hold the goods or estate so attached, to answer the final judgment in the same manner as by the laws of such state they would have been holden to answer final judgment, had it been rendered by the court in which the suit commenced. And if in any action commenced in a state court, the title of land be concerned, and the parties are citizens of the same state, and the matter in dispute exceeds the sum or value of five hundred dollars, exclusive of costs, the sum or value being made to appear to the satisfaction of the court, either party, before the trial, shall state to the court and make affidavit if they require it, that he claims and shall rely upon a right or title to the land, under a grant from a state other than that in which the suit is pending, and produce the original grant or an exemplification of it, except where the loss of public records shall put it out of his power, and shall move that the adverse party inform the court,

whether he claims a right or title to the land under a grant from the state in which the suit is pending; the said adverse [party] shall give such information, or otherwise not be allowed to plead such grant, or give it in evidence upon the trial, and if he informs that he does claim under such grant, the party claiming under the grant first mentioned may then, on motion, remove the cause for trial to the next circuit court to be holden in such district, or if in the district of Maine, to the court next to be holden therein; or if in Kentucky district, to the district court next to be holden therein; but if he is the defendant, shall do it under the same regulations as in the before-mentioned case of the removal of a cause into such court by an alien; and neither party removing the cause, shall be allowed to plead or give evidence of any other title than that by him stated as aforesaid, as the ground of his claim; and the trial of issues in fact in the circuit courts shall, in all suits, except those of equity, and of admiralty, and maritime jurisdiction, be by jury.

SEC. 13. And be it further enacted, That the Supreme Court shall have exclusive jurisdiction of all controversies of a civil nature, where a state is a party, except between a state and its citizens; and except also between a state and citizens of other states, or aliens, in which latter case it shall have original but not exclusive jurisdiction. And shall have exclusively all such jurisdiction of suits or proceedings against ambassadors, or other public ministers, or their domestics, or domestic servants, as a court of law can have or exercise consistently with the law of nations; and original, but not exclusive jurisdiction of all suits brought by ambassadors, or other public ministers, or in which a consul, or vice consul, shall be a party. And the trial of issues in fact in the Supreme Court, in all actions at law against citizens of the United States, shall be by jury. The Supreme Court shall also have appellate jurisdiction from the circuit courts and courts of the several states, in the cases herein after specially provided for; and shall have power to issue writs of prohibition to the district courts, when proceeding as courts of admiralty and maritime jurisdiction, and writs of mandamus, in cases warranted by the principles and usages of law, to any courts appointed, or persons holding office, under the authority of the United States.

SEC. 14. And be it further enacted, That all the before-mentioned courts of the United States, shall have power to issue writs of scire facias, habeas corpus, and all other writs not specially provided for by statute, which may be necessary for the exercise of their respective jurisdictions, and agreeable to the principles and usages of law. And that either of the justices of the supreme court, as well as judges of the district courts, shall have power to grant writs of habeas corpus for the purpose of an inquiry into the cause of commitment.——Provided, That writs of habeas corpus shall in no case extend to prisoners in gaol, unless where they are in custody, under or by colour of the authority of the United States, or are committed for trial before some court of the same, or are necessary to be brought into court to testify.

SEC. 15. And be it further enacted, That all the said courts of the United States, shall have power in the trial of actions at law, on motion and due notice thereof being given, to require the parties to produce books or writings in their possession or power, which contain evidence pertinent to the issue, in cases and under circumstances where they might be compelled to produce the same by the ordinary rules of proceeding in chancery; and if a plaintiff shall fail to comply with such order, to produce books or writings, it shall be lawful for the courts respectively, on motion, to give the like judgment for the defendant as in cases of nonsuit; and if a defendant shall fail to comply with such order, to produce books or writings, it shall be lawful for the courts respectively on motion as aforesaid, to give judgment against him or her by default.

SEC. 16. And be it further enacted, That suits in equity shall not be sustained in either of the courts of the United States, in any case where plain, adequate and complete remedy may be had at law.

SEC. 17. And be it further enacted, That all the said courts of the United States shall have power to grant new trials, in cases where there has been a trial by jury for reasons for which new trials have usually been granted in the courts of law; and shall have power to impose and administer all necessary oaths or affirmations, and to punish by fine or imprisonment, at the discretion of said courts, all contempts of authority in any cause or hearing before the same; and to make and establish all necessary rules for the orderly conducting business in the said courts, provided such rules are not repugnant to the laws of the United States.

SEC. 18. And be it further enacted, That when in a circuit court, judgment upon a verdict in a civil action shall be entered, execution may on motion of either party, at the discretion of the court, and on such conditions for the security of the adverse party as they may judge proper, be stayed forty-two days from the time of entering judgment, to give time to file in the clerk's office of said court, a petition for a new trial. And if such petition be there filed within said term of forty-two days, with a certificate thereon from either of the judges of such court, that he allows the same to be filed, which certificate he may make or refuse at his discretion, execution shall of course be further stayed to the next session of said court. And if a new trial be granted, the former judgment shall be thereby rendered void.

SEC. 19. And be it further enacted, That it shall be the duty of circuit courts, in causes in equity and of admiralty and maritime jurisdiction, to cause the facts on which they found their sentence or decree, fully to appear upon the record either from the pleadings and decree itself, or a state of the case agreed by the parties, or their counsel, or if they disagree by a stating of the case by the court.

SEC. 20. And be it further enacted, That where in a circuit court, a plaintiff in an action, originally brought there, or a petitioner in equity, other than the United States, recovers less than the sum or value of five hundred dollars, or a libellant, upon his own appeal, less than the sum or value of three hundred dollars, he shall not be allowed, but at the discretion of the court, may be adjudged to pay costs.

SEC. 21. And be it further enacted, That from final decrees in a district court in causes of admiralty and maritime jurisdiction, where the matter in dispute exceeds the sum or value of three hundred dollars, exclusive of costs, an appeal shall be allowed to the next circuit court, to be held in such district. Provided nevertheless, That all such appeals from final decrees as aforesaid, from the district court of Maine, shall be made to the circuit court, next to be holden after each appeal in the district of Massachusetts.

SEC. 22. And be it further enacted, That final decrees and judgments in civil actions in a district court, where the matter in dispute exceeds the sum or value of fifty dollars, exclusive of costs, may be reexamined, and reversed or affirmed in a circuit court, holden in the same district, upon a writ of error, whereto shall be annexed and returned therewith at the day and place therein mentioned, an authenticated transcript of the record, an assignment of errors, and prayer for reversal, with a citation to the adverse party, signed by the judge of such district court, or a justice of the Supreme Court, the adverse party having at least twenty days' notice. And upon a like process, may final judgments and decrees in civil actions, and suits in equity in a circuit court, brought there by original process, or removed there from courts of the several States, or removed there by appeal from a district court where the matter in dispute exceeds the sum or value of two thousand dollars, exclusive of costs, be re-examined and reversed or affirmed in the Supreme Court, the citation being in such case signed by a judge of such circuit court, or justice of the Supreme Court, and the adverse party having at least thirty days' notice. But there shall be no reversal in either court on such writ of error for error in ruling any plea in abatement, other than a plea to the jurisdiction of the court, or such plea to a petition or bill in equity, as is in the nature of a demurrer, or for any error in fact. And writs of error shall not be brought but within five years after rendering or passing the judgment or decree complained of, or in case the person entitled to such writ of error be an infant, feme covert, non compos mentis, or imprisoned, then within five years as aforesaid, exclusive of the time of such disability. And every justice or judge signing a citation on any writ of error as aforesaid, shall take good and sufficient security, that the plaintiff in error shall prosecute his writ to effect, and answer all damages and costs if he fail to make his plea good.

SEC. 23. And be it further enacted, That a writ of error as aforesaid shall be a supersedeas and stay execution in cases only where the writ of error is served, by a copy thereof being lodged for the adverse party in the clerk's office where the record remains, within ten days, Sundays exclusive, after rendering the judgment or passing the decree complained of. Until the expiration of which term of ten days, executions shall not issue in any case where a writ of error may be a supersedeas; and whereupon such writ of error the Supreme or a circuit court shall affirm a judgment or decree, they shall adjudge or decree to the respondent in error just damages for his delay, and single or double costs at their discretion.

SEC. 24. And be it further enacted, That when a judgment or decree shall be reversed in a circuit court, such court shall proceed to render such judgment or pass such decree as the district court should have rendered or passed; and the Supreme Court shall do the same on reversals therein, except where the reversal is in favour of the plaintiff, or petitioner in the original suit, and the damages to be assessed, or matter to be decreed, are uncertain, in which case they shall remand the cause for a final decision. And the Supreme Court shall not issue execution in causes that are removed before them by writs of error, but shall send a special mandate to the circuit court to award execution thereupon.

SEC. 25. And be it further enacted, That a final judgment or decree in any suit, in the highest court of law or equity of a State in which a decision in the suit could be had, where is drawn in question the validity of a treaty or statute of, or an authority exercised under the United States, and the decision is against their validity; or where is drawn in question the validity of a statute of, or an authority exercised under any State, on the ground of their being repugnant to the constitution, treaties or laws of the United States, and the decision is in favour of such their validity, or where is drawn in question the construction of any clause of the constitution, or of a treaty, or statute of, or commission held under the United States, and the decision is against the title, right, privilege or exemption specially set up or claimed by either party, under such clause of the said Constitution, treaty, statute or commission, may be re-examined and reversed or affirmed in the Supreme Court of the United States upon a writ of error, the citation being signed by the chief justice, or judge or chancellor of the court rendering or passing the judgment or decree complained of, or by a justice of the Supreme Court of the United States, in the same manner and under the same regulations, and the writ shall have the same effect, as if the judgment or decree complained of had been rendered or passed in a circuit court, and the proceeding upon the reversal shall also be the same, except that the Supreme Court, instead of remanding the cause for a final decision as before provided, may at their discretion, if the cause shall have been once remanded before, proceed to a final decision of the same, and award execution. But no other error shall be assigned or regarded as a ground of reversal in any such case as aforesaid, than such as appears on the face of the record, and immediately respects the before mentioned questions of validity or construction of the said constitution, treaties, statutes, commissions, or authorities in dispute.

SEC. 26. And be it further enacted, That in all causes brought before either of the courts of the United States to recover the forfeiture annexed to any articles of agreement, covenant, bond, or other speciality, where the forfeiture, breach or non-performance shall appear, by the default or confession of the defendant, or upon demurrer, the court before whom the action is, shall render judgment therein for the plaintiff to recover so much as is due according to equity. And when the sum for which judgment should be rendered is uncertain, the same shall, if either of the parties request it, be assessed by a jury.

SEC. 27. And be it further enacted, That a marshal shall be appointed in and for each district for the term of four years, but shall be removable from office at pleasure, whose duty it shall be to attend the district and circuit courts when sitting therein, and also the Supreme Court in the District in which that court shall sit. And to execute throughout the district, all lawful precepts directed to him, and issued under the authority of the United States, and he shall have power to command all necessary assistance in the execution of his duty, and to appoint as there shall be occasion, one or more deputies, who shall be removable from office by the judge of the district court, or the circuit court sitting within the district, at the pleasure of either; and before he enters on the duties of his office, he shall become bound for the faithful performance of the same, by himself and by his deputies before the judge of the district court to the United States, jointly and severally, with two good and sufficient sureties, inhabitants and freeholders of such district, to be approved by the district judge, in the sum of twenty thousand dollars, and shall take before said judge, as shall also his deputies, before they enter on the duties of their appointment, the following oath of office: "I, A. B., do solemnly swear or affirm, that I will faithfully execute all lawful precepts directed to the marshal of the district of under the authority of the United States, and true returns make, and in all things well and truly, and without malice or partiality, perform the duties of the office of marshal (or marshal's deputy, as the case may be) of the district of   , during my continuance in said office, and take only my lawful fees. So help me God."

SEC. 28. And be it further enacted, That in all causes wherein the marshal or his deputy shall be a party, the writs and precepts therein shall be directed to such disinterested person as the court, or any justice or judge thereof may appoint, and the person so appointed, is hereby authorized to execute and return the same. And in case of the death of any marshal, his deputy or deputies shall continue in office, unless otherwise specially removed; and shall execute the same in the name of the deceased, until another mar-

shal shall be appointed and sworn: And the defaults or misfeasances in office of such deputy or deputies in the mean time, as well as before, shall be adjudged a breach of the condition of the bond given, as before directed, by the marshal who appointed them; and the executor or administrator of the deceased marshal shall have like remedy for the defaults and misfeasances in office of such deputy or deputies during such interval, as they would be entitled to if the marshal had continued in life and in the exercise of his said office, until his successor was appointed, and sworn or affirmed: And every marshal or his deputy when removed from office, or when the term for which the marshal is appointed shall expire, shall have power notwithstanding to execute all such precepts as may be in their hands respectively at the time of such removal or expiration of office; and the marshal shall be held answerable for the delivery to his successor of all prisoners which may be in his custody at the time of his removal, or when the term for which he is appointed shall expire, and for that purpose may retain such prisoners in his custody until his successor shall be appointed and qualified as the law directs.

SEC. 29. And be it further enacted, That in cases punishable with death, the trial shall be had in the county where the offence was committed, or where that cannot be done without great inconvenience, twelve petit jurors at least shall be summoned from thence. And jurors in all cases to serve in the courts of the United States shall be designated by lot or otherwise in each State respectively according to the mode of forming juries therein now practised, so far as the laws of the same shall render such designation practicable by the courts or marshals of the United States; and the jurors shall have the same qualifications as are requisite for jurors by the laws of the State of which they are citizens, to serve in the highest courts of law of such State, and shall be returned as there shall be occasion for them, from such parts of the district from time to time as the court shall direct, so as shall be most favourable to an impartial trial, and so as not to incur an unnecessary expense, or unduly to burthen the citizens of any part of the district with such services. And writs of venire facias when directed by the court shall issue from the clerk's office, and shall be served and returned by the marshal in his proper person, or by his deputy, or in case the marshal or his deputy is not an indifferent person, or is interested in the event of the cause, by such fit person as the court shall specially appoint for that purpose, to whom they shall administer an oath or affirmation that he will truly and impartially serve and return such writ. And when from challenges or otherwise there shall not be a jury to determine any civil or criminal cause, the marshal or his deputy shall, by order of the court where such defect of jurors shall happen, return jurymen de talibus circumstantibus sufficient to complete the pannel; and when the marshal or his deputy are disqualified as aforesaid, jurors may be returned by such disinterested person as the court shall appoint.

SEC. 30. And be it further enacted, That the mode of proof by oral testimony and examination of witnesses in open court shall be the same in all the courts of the United States, as well in the trial of causes in equity and of admiralty and maritime jurisdiction, as of actions at common law. And when the testimony of any person shall be necessary in any civil cause depending in any district in any court of the United States, who shall live at a greater distance from the place of trial than one hundred miles, or is bound on a voyage to sea, or is about to go out of the United States, or out of such district, and to a greater distance from the place of trial than as aforesaid, before the time of trial, or is ancient or very infirm, the deposition of such person may be taken de bene esse before any justice or judge of any of the courts of the United States, or before any chancellor, justice or judge of a supreme or superior court, mayor or chief magistrate of a city, or judge of a county court or court of common pleas of any of the United States, not being of counsel or attorney to either of the parties, or interested in the event of the cause, provided that a notification from the magistrate before whom the deposition is to be taken to the adverse party, to be present at the taking of the same, and to put interrogatories, if he think fit, be first made out and served on the adverse party or his attorney as either may be nearest, if either is within one hundred miles of the place of such caption, allowing time for their attendance after notified, not less than at the rate of one day, Sundays exclusive, for every twenty miles travel. And in causes of admiralty and maritime jurisdiction, or other cases of seizure when a libel shall be filed, in which an adverse party is not named, and depositions of persons circumstanced as aforesaid shall be taken before a claim be put in, the like notification as aforesaid shall be given to the person having the agency or possession of the property libelled at the time of the capture or seizure of the same, if known to the libellant. And every person deposing as aforesaid shall be carefully examined and cautioned, and sworn or affirmed to testify the whole truth, and

shall subscribe the testimony by him or her given after the same shall be reduced to writing, which shall be done only by the magistrate taking the deposition, or by the deponent in his presence. And the depositions so taken shall be retained by such magistrate until he deliver the same with his own hand into the court for which they are taken, or shall, together with a certificate of the reasons as aforesaid of their being taken, and of the notice if any given to the adverse party, be by him the said magistrate sealed up and directed to such court, and remain under his seal until opened in court. And any person may be compelled to appear and depose as aforesaid in the same manner as to appear and testify in court. And in the trial of any cause of admiralty or maritime jurisdiction in a district court, the decree in which may be appealed from, if either party shall suggest to and satisfy the court that probably it will not be in his power to produce the witnesses there testifying before the circuit court should an appeal be had, and shall move that their testimony be taken down in writing, it shall be so done by the clerk of the court. And if an appeal be had, such testimony may be used on the trial of the same, if it shall appear to the satisfaction of the court which shall try the appeal, that the witnesses are then dead or gone out of the United States, or to a greater distance than as aforesaid from the place where the court is sitting, or that by reason of age, sickness, bodily infirmity or imprisonment, they are unable to travel and appear at court, but not otherwise. And unless the same shall be made to appear on the trial of any cause, with respect to witnesses whose depositions may have been taken therein, such depositions shall not be admitted or used in the cause. Provided, That nothing herein shall be construed to prevent any court of the United States from granting a dedimus potestatem to take depositions according to common usage, when it may be necessary to prevent a failure or delay of justice, which power they shall severally possess, nor to extend to depositions taken in perpetuam rei memoriam, which if they relate to matters that may be cognizable in any court of the United States, a circuit court on application thereto made as a court of equity, may, according to the usages in chancery direct to be taken.

SEC. 31. And be it [further] enacted, That where any suit shall be depending in any court of the United States, and either of the parties shall die before final judgment, the executor or administrator of such deceased party who was plaintiff, petitioner, or defendant, in case the cause of action doth by law survive, shall have full power to prosecute or defend any such suit or action until final judgment; and the defendant or defendants are hereby obliged to answer thereto accordingly; and the court before whom such cause may be depending, is hereby empowered and directed to hear and determine the same, and to render judgment for or against the executor or administrator, as the case may require. And if such executor or administrator having been duly served with a scire facias from the office of the clerk of the court where such suit is depending, twenty days beforehand, shall neglect or refuse to become a party to the suit, the court may render judgment against the estate of the deceased party, in the same manner as if the executor or administrator had voluntarily made himself a party to the suit. And the executor or administrator who shall become a party as aforesaid, shall, upon motion to the court where the suit is depending, be entitled to a continuance of the same until the next term of the said court. And if there be two or more plaintiffs or defendants, and one or more of them shall die, if the cause of action shall survive to the surviving plaintiff or plaintiffs, or against the surviving defendant or defendants, the writ or action shall not be thereby abated; but such death being suggested upon the record, the action shall proceed at the suit of the surviving plaintiff or plaintiffs against the surviving defendant or defendants.

SEC. 32. And be it further enacted, That no summons, writ, declaration, return, process, judgment, or other proceedings in civil causes in any of the courts of the United States, shall be abated, arrested, quashed or reversed, for any defect or want of form, but the said courts respectively shall proceed and give judgment according as the right of the cause and matter in law shall appear unto them, without regarding any imperfections, defects, or want of form in such writ, declaration, or other pleading, return, process, judgment, or course of proceeding whatsoever, except those only in cases of demurrer, which the party demurring shall specially sit down and express together with his demurrer as the cause thereof. And the said courts respectively shall and may, by virtue of this act, from time to time, amend all and every such imperfections, defects and wants of form, other than those only which the party demurring shall express as aforesaid, and may at any time permit either of the parties to amend any defect in the process or pleadings, upon such conditions as the said courts respectively shall in their discretion, and by their rules prescribe.

SEC. 33. And be it further enacted, That for any crime or offence against the United States, the offender may, by any justice or judge of the United States, or by any justice of the peace, or other magistrate of any of the United States where he may be found agreeably to the usual mode of process against offenders in such state, and at the expense of the United States, be arrested, and imprisoned or bailed, as the case may be, for trial before such court of the United States as by this act has cognizance of the offence. And copies of the process shall be returned as speedily as may be into the clerk's office of such court, together with the recognizances of the witnesses for their appearance to testify in the case; which recognizances the magistrate before whom the examination shall be, may require on pain of imprisonment. And if such commitment of the offender, or the witnesses shall be in a district other than that in which the offence is to be tried, it shall be the duty of the judge of that district where the delinquent is imprisoned, seasonably to issue, and of the marshal of the same district to execute, a warrant for the removal of the offender, and the witnesses, or either of them, as the case may be, to the district in which the trial is to be had. And upon all arrests in criminal cases, bail shall be admitted, except where the punishment may be death, in which cases it shall not be admitted but by the supreme or a circuit court, or by a justice of the supreme court, or a judge of a district court, who shall exercise their discretion therein, regarding the nature and circumstances of the offence, and of the evidence, and the usages of law. And if a person committed by a justice of the supreme or a judge of a district court for an offence not punishable with death, shall afterwards procure bail, and there be no judge of the United States in the district to take the same, it may be taken by any judge of the supreme or superior court of law of such state.

SEC. 34. And be it further enacted, That the laws of the several states, except where the constitution, treaties or statutes of the United States shall otherwise require or provide, shall be regarded as rules of decision in trials at common law in the courts of the United States in cases where they apply.

SEC. 35. And be it further enacted, That in all courts of the United States, the parties may plead and manage their own causes personally or by assistance of such counsel or attorneys at law as by the rules of the said courts respectively shall be permitted to manage and conduct causes therein. And there shall be appointed in each district a meet person learned in the law to act as attorney for the United States in such district, who shall be sworn or affirmed to the faithful execution of his office, whose duty it shall be to prosecute in such district all delinquents for crimes and offences, cognizable under the authority of the United States, and all civil actions in which the United States shall be concerned, except before the supreme court in the district in which that court shall be holden. And he shall receive as compensation for his services such fees as shall be taxed therefor in the respective courts before which the suits or prosecutions shall be. And there shall also be appointed a meet person, learned in the law, to act as attorney-general for the United States, who shall be sworn or affirmed to a faithful execution of his office; whose duty it shall be to prosecute and conduct all suits in the Supreme Court in which the United States shall be concerned, and to give his advice and opinion upon questions of law when required by the President of the United States, or when requested by the heads of any of the departments, touching any matters that may concern their departments, and shall receive such compensation for his services as shall by law be provided.

Frederick Augustus Muhlenberg, Speaker of the House of Representatives

John Adams, Vice-President of the United States, and President of the Senate

APPROVED, September the Twenty fourth, 1789. George Washington, President of the United States

The Bill of Rights

Congress of the United States begun and held at the City of New York, on Wednesday the fourth of March, one thousand seven hundred and eighty nine.

THE Conventions of a number of the States, having at the time of their adopting the Constitution, expressed a desire, in order to prevent misconstruction or abuse of its powers, that further declaratory and restrictive clauses should be added: And as extending the ground of public confidence in the Government, will best ensure the beneficent ends of its institution.

RESOLVED by the Senate and House of Representatives of the United States of America, in Congress assembled, two thirds of both Houses concurring, that the following Articles be proposed to the Legislatures of the several States, as amendments to the Constitution of the United States, all, or any of which Articles, when ratified by three fourths of the said Legislatures, to be valid to all intents and purposes, as part of the said Constitution; viz.

ARTICLES in addition to, and Amendment of the Constitution of the United States of America, proposed by Congress, and ratified by the Legislatures of the several States, pursuant to the fifth Article of the original Constitution.

Article the first . . . After the first enumeration required by the first article of the Constitution, there shall be one Representative for every thirty thousand, until the number shall amount to one hundred, after which the proportion shall be so regulated by Congress, that there shall be not less than one hundred Representatives, nor less than one Representative for every forty thousand persons, until the number of Representatives shall amount to two hundred; after which the proportion shall be so regulated by Congress, that there shall not be less than two hundred Representatives, nor more than one Representative for every fifty thousand persons.

Article the second . . . No law, varying the compensation for the services of the Senators and Representatives, shall take effect, until an election of Representatives shall have intervened.

Article the third . . . Congress shall make no law respecting an establishment of religion, or prohibiting the free exercise thereof; or abridging the freedom of speech, or of the press; or the right of the people peaceably to assemble, and to petition the Government for a redress of grievances.

Article the fourth . . . A well regulated Militia, being necessary to the security of a free State, the right of the people to keep and bear Arms, shall not be infringed.

Article the fifth . . . No Soldier shall, in time of peace be quartered in any house, without the consent of the Owner, nor in time of war, but in a manner to be prescribed by law.

Article the sixth . . . The right of the people to be secure in their persons, houses, papers, and effects, against unreasonable searches and seizures, shall not be violated, and no Warrants shall issue, but upon probable cause, supported by Oath or affirmation, and particularly describing the place to be searched, and the persons or things to be seized.

Article the seventh . . . No person shall be held to answer for a capital, or otherwise infamous crime, unless on a presentment or indictment of a Grand Jury, except in cases arising in the land or naval forces, or in the Militia, when in actual service in time of War or public danger; nor shall any person be subject for the same offence to be twice put in jeopardy of life or limb; nor shall be compelled in any criminal case to be a witness against himself, nor be deprived of life, liberty, or property, without due process of law; nor shall private property be taken for public use, without just compensation.

Article the eighth . . . In all criminal prosecutions, the accused shall enjoy the right to a speedy and public trial, by an impartial jury of the State and district wherein the crime shall have been committed, which district shall have been previously ascertained by law, and to be informed of the nature and cause of the accusation; to be confronted with the witnesses against him; to have compulsory process for obtaining witnesses in his favor, and to have the Assistance of Counsel for his defence.

Article the ninth . . . In Suits at common law, where the value in controversy shall exceed twenty dollars, the right of trial by jury shall be preserved, and no fact tried by a jury, shall be otherwise re-examined in any Court of the United States, than according to the rules of the common law.

Article the tenth . . . Excessive bail shall not be required, nor excessive fines imposed, nor cruel and unusual punishments inflicted.

Article the eleventh . . . The enumeration in the Constitution, of certain rights, shall not be construed to deny or disparage others retained by the people.

Article the twelfth . . . The powers not delegated to the United States by the Constitution, nor prohibited by it to the States, are reserved to the States respectively, or to the people.

ATTEST,

Frederick Augustus Muhlenberg, Speaker of the House of Representatives
John Adams, Vice-President of the United States, and President of the Senate

John Beckley, Clerk of the House of Representatives.
Sam. A Otis Secretary of the Senate

Patent for Cotton Gin

The cotton gin is a device for removing the seeds from cotton fiber. Such machines have been around for centuries. Eli Whitney's machine of 1794, however, was the first to clean short-staple cotton, and a single device could produce up to fifty pounds of cleaned cotton in a day. This made cotton a profitable crop for the first time.

After this invention, the yield of raw cotton doubled each decade after 1800. Demand was fueled by other inventions of the Industrial Revolution, such as the machines to spin and weave it and the steamboat to transport it. By mid-century America was growing three-quarters of the world's supply of cotton, most of it shipped to England or New England where it was manufactured into cloth. During this time tobacco fell in value, rice exports at best stayed steady, and sugar began to thrive, but only in Louisiana. At mid-century the South provided three-fifths of America's exports—most of it in cotton.

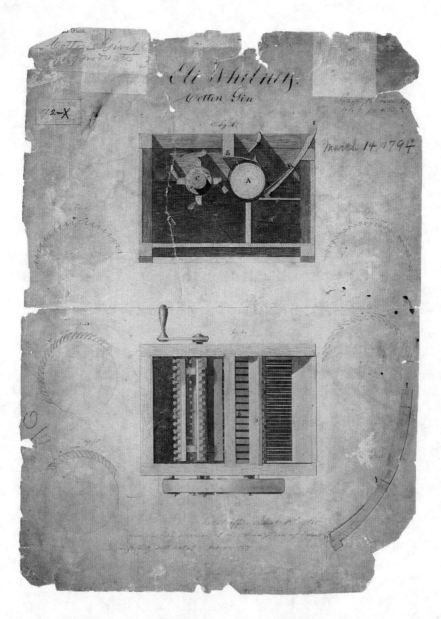

President George Washington's Farewell Address

Friends and Fellow Citizens:

The period for a new election of a citizen to administer the executive government of the United States being not far distant, and the time actually arrived when your thoughts must be employed in designating the person who is to be clothed with that important trust, it appears to me proper, especially as it may conduce to a more distinct expression of the public voice, that I should now apprise you of the resolution I have formed, to decline being considered among the number of those out of whom a choice is to be made.

I beg you, at the same time, to do me the justice to be assured that this resolution has not been taken without a strict regard to all the considerations appertaining to the relation which binds a dutiful citizen to his country; and that in withdrawing the tender of service, which silence in my situation might imply, I am influenced by no diminution of zeal for your future interest, no deficiency of grateful respect for your past kindness, but am supported by a full conviction that the step is compatible with both.

The acceptance of, and continuance hitherto in, the office to which your suffrages have twice called me have been a uniform sacrifice of inclination to the opinion of duty and to a deference for what appeared to be your desire. I constantly hoped that it would have been much earlier in my power, consistently with motives which I was not at liberty to disregard, to return to that retirement from which I had been reluctantly drawn. The strength of my inclination to do this, previous to the last election, had even led to the preparation of an address to declare it to you; but mature reflection on the then perplexed and critical posture of our affairs with foreign nations, and the unanimous advice of persons entitled to my confidence, impelled me to abandon the idea.

I rejoice that the state of your concerns, external as well as internal, no longer renders the pursuit of inclination incompatible with the sentiment of duty or propriety, and am persuaded, whatever partiality may be retained for my services, that, in the present circumstances of our country, you will not disapprove my determination to retire.

The impressions with which I first undertook the arduous trust were explained on the proper occasion. In the discharge of this trust, I will only say that I have, with good intentions, contributed towards the organization and administration of the government the best exertions of which a very fallible judgment was capable. Not unconscious in the outset of the inferiority of my qualifications, experience in my own eyes, perhaps still more in the eyes of others, has strengthened the motives to diffidence of myself; and every day the increasing weight of years admonishes me more and more that the shade of retirement is as necessary to me as it will be welcome. Satisfied that if any circumstances have given peculiar value to my services, they were temporary, I have the consolation to believe that, while choice and prudence invite me to quit the political scene, patriotism does not forbid it.

In looking forward to the moment which is intended to terminate the career of my public life, my feelings do not permit me to suspend the deep acknowledgment of that debt of gratitude which I owe to my beloved country for the many honors it has conferred upon me; still more for the steadfast confidence with which it has supported me; and for the opportunities I have thence enjoyed of manifesting my inviolable attachment, by services faithful and persevering, though in usefulness unequal to my zeal. If benefits have resulted to our country from these services, let it always be remembered to your praise, and as an instructive example in our annals, that under circumstances in which the passions, agitated in every direction, were liable to mislead, amidst appearances sometimes dubious, vicissitudes of fortune often discouraging, in situations in which not unfrequently want of success has countenanced the spirit of criticism, the constancy of your support was the essential prop of the efforts, and a guarantee of the plans by which they were effected. Profoundly penetrated with this idea, I shall carry it with me to my grave, as a strong incitement to unceasing vows that heaven may continue to you the choicest tokens of its beneficence; that your union and brotherly affection may be perpetual; that the free Constitution, which is the work of your hands, may be sacredly maintained; that its administration in every department may be stamped with wisdom and virtue; that, in fine, the happiness of the people of these States, under the auspices of liberty, may be made complete by so careful a preservation and so prudent a use of this blessing as will acquire to them the glory of recommending it to the applause, the affection, and adoption of every nation which is yet a stranger to it.

Here, perhaps, I ought to stop. But a solicitude for your welfare, which cannot end but with my life, and the apprehension of danger, natural to that solicitude, urge me, on an occasion like the present, to offer to your solemn contemplation, and to recommend to your frequent review, some sentiments which are the result of much reflection, of no inconsiderable observation, and which appear to me all-important to the permanency of your felicity as a people. These will be offered to you with the more freedom, as you can only see in them the disinterested warnings of a parting friend, who can possibly have no personal motive to bias his counsel. Nor can I forget, as an encouragement to it, your indulgent reception of my sentiments on a former and not dissimilar occasion.

Interwoven as is the love of liberty with every ligament of your hearts, no recommendation of mine is necessary to fortify or confirm the attachment.

The unity of government which constitutes you one people is also now dear to you. It is justly so, for it is a main pillar in the edifice of your real independence, the support of your tranquility at home, your peace abroad; of your safety; of your prosperity; of that very liberty which you so highly prize. But as it is easy to foresee that, from different causes and from different quarters, much pains will be taken, many artifices employed to weaken in your minds the conviction of this truth; as this is the point in your political fortress against which the batteries of internal and external enemies will be most constantly and actively (though often covertly and insidiously) directed, it is of infinite moment that you should properly estimate the immense value of your national union to your collective and individual happiness; that you should cherish a cordial, habitual, and immovable attachment to it; accustoming yourselves to think and speak of it as of the palladium of your political safety and prosperity; watching for its preservation with jealous anxiety; discountenancing whatever may suggest even a suspicion that it can in any event be abandoned; and indignantly frowning upon the first dawning of every attempt to alienate any portion of our country from the rest, or to enfeeble

the sacred ties which now link together the various parts.

For this you have every inducement of sympathy and interest. Citizens, by birth or choice, of a common country, that country has a right to concentrate your affections. The name of American, which belongs to you in your national capacity, must always exalt the just pride of patriotism more than any appellation derived from local discriminations. With slight shades of difference, you have the same religion, manners, habits, and political principles. You have in a common cause fought and triumphed together; the independence and liberty you possess are the work of joint counsels, and joint efforts of common dangers, sufferings, and successes.

But these considerations, however powerfully they address themselves to your sensibility, are greatly outweighed by those which apply more immediately to your interest. Here every portion of our country finds the most commanding motives for carefully guarding and preserving the union of the whole.

The North, in an unrestrained intercourse with the South, protected by the equal laws of a common government, finds in the productions of the latter great additional resources of maritime and commercial enterprise and precious materials of manufacturing industry. The South, in the same intercourse, benefiting by the agency of the North, sees its agriculture grow and its commerce expand. Turning partly into its own channels the seamen of the North, it finds its particular navigation invigorated; and, while it contributes, in different ways, to nourish and increase the general mass of the national navigation, it looks forward to the protection of a maritime strength, to which itself is unequally adapted. The East, in a like intercourse with the West, already finds, and in the progressive improvement of interior communications by land and water, will more and more find a valuable vent for the commodities which it brings from abroad, or manufactures at home. The West derives from the East supplies requisite to its growth and comfort, and, what is perhaps of still greater consequence, it must of necessity owe the secure enjoyment of indispensable outlets for its own productions to the weight, influence, and the future maritime strength of the Atlantic side of the Union, directed by an indissoluble community of interest as one nation. Any other tenure by which the West can hold this essential advantage, whether derived from its own separate strength, or from an apostate and unnatural connection with any foreign power, must be intrinsically precarious.

While, then, every part of our country thus feels an immediate and particular interest in union, all the parts combined cannot fail to find in the united mass of means and efforts greater strength, greater resource, proportionably greater security from external danger, a less frequent interruption of their peace by foreign nations; and, what is of inestimable value, they must derive from union an exemption from those broils and wars between themselves, which so frequently afflict neighboring countries not tied together by the same governments, which their own rival ships alone would be sufficient to produce, but which opposite foreign alliances, attachments, and intrigues would stimulate and embitter. Hence, likewise, they will avoid the necessity of those overgrown military establishments which, under any form of government, are inauspicious to liberty, and which are to be regarded as particularly hostile to republican liberty. In this sense it is that your union ought to be considered as a main prop of your liberty, and that the love of the one ought to endear to you the preservation of the other.

These considerations speak a persuasive language to every reflecting and virtuous mind, and exhibit the continuance of the Union as a primary object of patriotic desire. Is there a doubt whether a common government can embrace so large a sphere? Let experience solve it. To listen to mere speculation in such a case were criminal. We are authorized to hope that a proper organization of the whole with the auxiliary agency of governments for the respective subdivisions, will afford a happy issue to the experiment. It is well worth a fair and full experiment. With such powerful and obvious motives to union, affecting all parts of our country, while experience shall not have demonstrated its impracticability, there will always be reason to distrust the patriotism of those who in any quarter may endeavor to weaken its bands.

In contemplating the causes which may disturb our Union, it occurs as matter of serious concern that any ground should have been furnished for characterizing parties by geographical discriminations, Northern and Southern, Atlantic and Western; whence designing men may endeavor to excite a belief that there is a real difference of local interests and views. One of the expedients of party to acquire influence within particular districts is to misrepresent the opinions and aims of other districts. You cannot shield yourselves too much against the jealousies and heartburnings which spring from these misrepresentations; they tend to render alien to each other those who ought to be bound together by fraternal affection. The inhabitants of our Western country have lately had a useful lesson on this head; they have seen, in the negotiation by the Executive, and in the unanimous ratification by the Senate, of the treaty with Spain, and in the universal satisfaction at that event, throughout the United States, a decisive proof how unfounded were the suspicions propagated among them of a policy in the General Government and in the Atlantic States unfriendly to their interests in regard to the Mississippi; they have been witnesses to the formation of two treaties, that with Great Britain, and that with Spain, which secure to them everything they could desire, in respect to our foreign relations, towards confirming their prosperity. Will it not be their wisdom to rely for the preservation of these advantages on the Union by which they were procured? Will they not henceforth be deaf to those advisers, if such there are, who would sever them from their brethren and connect them with aliens?

To the efficacy and permanency of your Union, a government for the whole is indispensable. No alliance, however strict, between the parts can be an adequate substitute; they must inevitably experience the infractions and interruptions which all alliances in all times have experienced. Sensible of this momentous truth, you have improved upon your first essay, by the adoption of a constitution of government better calculated than your former for an intimate union, and for the efficacious management of your common concerns. This government, the offspring of our own choice, uninfluenced and unawed, adopted upon full investigation and mature deliberation, completely free in its principles, in the distribution of its powers, uniting security with energy, and containing within itself a provision for its own amendment, has a just claim to your confidence and your support. Respect for its authority, compliance with its laws, acquiescence in its measures, are duties enjoined by the fundamental maxims of true liberty. The basis of our political systems is the right of the people to make and to alter their constitutions of government. But the Constitution which at any time exists, till changed by an explicit and authentic act of the whole people, is sacredly obligatory upon all. The very idea of the power and the right of the people to establish government presupposes the duty of every individual to obey the established government.

All obstructions to the execution of the laws, all combinations and associations, under whatever plausible character, with the real design to direct, control, counteract, or awe the regular deliberation and action of the constituted authorities, are destructive of this fundamental principle, and of fatal tendency. They serve to organize faction, to give it an artificial and extraordinary force; to put, in the place of the delegated will of the nation the will of a party, often a small but artful and enterprising minority of the community; and, according to the alternate triumphs of different parties, to make the public administration the mirror of the ill-concerted and incongruous projects of faction, rather than the organ of consistent and wholesome plans digested by common counsels and modified by mutual interests.

However combinations or associations of the above description may now and then answer popular ends, they are likely, in the course of time and things, to become potent engines, by which cunning, ambitious, and unprincipled men will be enabled to subvert the power of the people and to usurp for themselves the reins of government, destroying afterwards the very engines which have lifted them to unjust dominion.

Towards the preservation of your government, and the permanency of your present happy state, it is requisite, not only that you steadily discountenance irregular oppositions to its acknowledged authority, but also that you resist with care the spirit of innovation upon its principles, however specious the pretexts. One method of assault may be to effect, in the forms of the Constitution, alterations which will impair the energy of the system, and thus to undermine what cannot be directly overthrown. In all the changes to which you may be invited, remember that time and habit are at least as necessary to fix the true character of governments as of other human institutions; that experience is the surest standard by which to test the real tendency of the existing constitution of a country; that facility in changes, upon the credit of mere hypothesis and opinion, exposes to perpetual change, from the endless variety of hypothesis and opinion; and remember, especially, that for the efficient management of your common interests, in a country so extensive as ours, a government of as much vigor as is consistent with the perfect security of liberty is indispensable. Liberty itself will find in such a government, with powers properly distributed and adjusted, its surest guardian. It is, indeed, little else than a name, where the government is too feeble to withstand the enterprises of faction, to confine each member of the society within the limits prescribed by the laws, and to maintain all in the secure

and tranquil enjoyment of the rights of person and property.

I have already intimated to you the danger of parties in the State, with particular reference to the founding of them on geographical discriminations. Let me now take a more comprehensive view, and warn you in the most solemn manner against the baneful effects of the spirit of party generally.

This spirit, unfortunately, is inseparable from our nature, having its root in the strongest passions of the human mind. It exists under different shapes in all governments, more or less stifled, controlled, or repressed; but, in those of the popular form, it is seen in its greatest rankness, and is truly their worst enemy.

The alternate domination of one faction over another, sharpened by the spirit of revenge, natural to party dissension, which in different ages and countries has perpetrated the most horrid enormities, is itself a frightful despotism. But this leads at length to a more formal and permanent despotism. The disorders and miseries which result gradually incline the minds of men to seek security and repose in the absolute power of an individual; and sooner or later the chief of some prevailing faction, more able or more fortunate than his competitors, turns this disposition to the purposes of his own elevation, on the ruins of public liberty.

Without looking forward to an extremity of this kind (which nevertheless ought not to be entirely out of sight), the common and continual mischiefs of the spirit of party are sufficient to make it the interest and duty of a wise people to discourage and restrain it.

It serves always to distract the public councils and enfeeble the public administration. It agitates the community with ill-founded jealousies and false alarms, kindles the animosity of one part against another, foments occasionally riot and insurrection. It opens the door to foreign influence and corruption, which finds a facilitated access to the government itself through the channels of party passions. Thus the policy and the will of one country are subjected to the policy and will of another.

There is an opinion that parties in free countries are useful checks upon the administration of the government and serve to keep alive the spirit of liberty. This within certain limits is probably true; and in governments of a monarchical cast, patriotism may look with indulgence, if not with favor, upon the spirit of party. But in those of the popular character, in governments purely elective, it is a spirit not to be encouraged. From their natural tendency, it is certain there will always be enough of that spirit for every salutary purpose. And there being constant danger of excess, the effort ought to be by force of public opinion, to mitigate and assuage it. A fire not to be quenched, it demands a uniform vigilance to prevent its bursting into a flame, lest, instead of warming, it should consume.

It is important, likewise, that the habits of thinking in a free country should inspire caution in those entrusted with its administration, to confine themselves within their respective constitutional spheres, avoiding in the exercise of the powers of one department to encroach upon another. The spirit of encroachment tends to consolidate the powers of all the departments in one, and thus to create, whatever the form of government, a real despotism. A just estimate of that love of power, and proneness to abuse it, which predominates in the human heart, is sufficient to satisfy us of the truth of this position. The necessity of reciprocal checks in the exercise of political power, by dividing and distributing it into different depositaries, and constituting each the guardian of the public weal against invasions by the others, has been evinced by experiments ancient and modern; some of them in our country and under our own eyes. To preserve them must be as necessary as to institute them. If, in the opinion of the people, the distribution or modification of the constitutional powers be in any particular wrong, let it be corrected by an amendment in the way which the Constitution designates. But let there be no change by usurpation; for though this, in one instance, may be the instrument of good, it is the customary weapon by which free governments are destroyed. The precedent must always greatly overbalance in permanent evil any partial or transient benefit, which the use can at any time yield.

Of all the dispositions and habits which lead to political prosperity, religion and morality are indispensable supports. In vain would that man claim the tribute of patriotism, who should labor to subvert these great pillars of human happiness, these firmest props of the duties of men and citizens. The mere politician, equally with the pious man, ought to respect and to cherish them. A volume could not trace all their connections with private and public felicity. Let it simply be asked: Where is the security for property, for reputation, for life, if the sense of religious obligation desert the oaths which are the instruments of investigation in courts of justice? And let us with caution indulge the supposition that morality can be maintained without religion. Whatever may be conceded to the influence of refined education on minds of peculiar structure, reason and experience both forbid us to expect that national morality can prevail in exclusion of religious principle.

It is substantially true that virtue or morality is a necessary spring of popular government. The rule, indeed, extends with more or less force to every species of free government. Who that is a sincere friend to it can look with indifference upon attempts to shake the foundation of the fabric?

Promote then, as an object of primary importance, institutions for the general diffusion of knowledge. In proportion as the structure of a government gives force to public opinion, it is essential that public opinion should be enlightened.

As a very important source of strength and security, cherish public credit. One method of preserving it is to use it as sparingly as possible, avoiding occasions of expense by cultivating peace, but remembering also that timely disbursements to prepare for danger frequently prevent much greater disbursements to repel it, avoiding likewise the accumulation of debt, not only by shunning occasions of expense, but by vigorous exertion in time of peace to discharge the debts which unavoidable wars may have occasioned, not ungenerously throwing upon posterity the burden which we ourselves ought to bear. The execution of these maxims belongs to your representatives, but it is necessary that public opinion should co-operate. To facilitate to them the performance of their duty, it is essential that you should practically bear in mind that towards the payment of debts there must be revenue; that to have revenue there must be taxes; that no taxes can be devised which are not more or less inconvenient and unpleasant; that the intrinsic embarrassment, inseparable from the selection of the proper objects (which is always a choice of difficulties), ought to be a decisive motive for a candid construction of the conduct of the government in making it, and for a spirit of acquiescence in the measures for obtaining revenue, which the public exigencies may at any time dictate.

Observe good faith and justice towards all nations; cultivate peace and harmony with all. Religion and morality enjoin this conduct; and can it be, that good policy does not equally enjoin it? It will be worthy of a free, enlightened, and at no distant period, a great nation, to give to mankind the magnanimous and too novel example of a people always guided by an exalted justice and benevolence. Who can doubt that, in the course of time and things, the fruits of such a plan would richly repay any temporary advantages which might be lost by a steady adherence to it? Can it be that Providence has not connected the permanent felicity of a nation with its virtue? The experiment, at least, is recommended by every sentiment which ennobles human nature. Alas! is it rendered impossible by its vices?

In the execution of such a plan, nothing is more essential than that permanent, inveterate antipathies against particular nations, and passionate attachments for others, should be excluded; and that, in place of them, just and amicable feelings towards all should be cultivated. The nation which indulges towards another a habitual hatred or a habitual fondness is in some degree a slave. It is a slave to its animosity or to its affection, either of which is sufficient to lead it astray from its duty and its interest. Antipathy in one nation against another disposes each more readily to offer insult and injury, to lay hold of slight causes of umbrage, and to be haughty and intractable, when accidental or trifling occasions of dispute occur. Hence, frequent collisions, obstinate, envenomed, and bloody contests. The nation, prompted by ill will and resentment, sometimes impels to war the government, contrary to the best calculations of policy. The government sometimes participates in the national propensity, and adopts through passion what reason would reject; at other times it makes the animosity of the nation subservient to projects of hostility instigated by pride, ambition, and other sinister and pernicious motives. The peace often, sometimes perhaps the liberty, of nations, has been the victim.

So likewise, a passionate attachment of one nation for another produces a variety of evils. Sympathy for the favorite nation, facilitating the illusion of an imaginary common interest in cases where no real common interest exists, and infusing into one the enmities of the other, betrays the former into a participation in the quarrels and wars of the latter without adequate inducement or justification. It leads also to concessions to the favorite nation of privileges denied to others which is apt doubly to injure the nation making the concessions; by unnecessarily parting with what ought to have been retained, and by exciting jealousy, ill will, and a disposition to retaliate, in the parties from whom equal privileges are withheld. And it gives to ambitious, corrupted, or deluded citizens (who devote themselves to the favorite nation), facility to betray or sacrifice the interests of their own country, without odium, sometimes even with popularity; gilding, with the appearances

of a virtuous sense of obligation, a commendable deference for public opinion, or a laudable zeal for public good, the base or foolish compliances of ambition, corruption, or infatuation.

As avenues to foreign influence in innumerable ways, such attachments are particularly alarming to the truly enlightened and independent patriot. How many opportunities do they afford to tamper with domestic factions, to practice the arts of seduction, to mislead public opinion, to influence or awe the public councils? Such an attachment of a small or weak towards a great and powerful nation dooms the former to be the satellite of the latter.

Against the insidious wiles of foreign influence (I conjure you to believe me, fellow citizens) the jealousy of a free people ought to be constantly awake, since history and experience prove that foreign influence is one of the most baneful foes of republican government. But that jealousy to be useful must be impartial; else it becomes the instrument of the very influence to be avoided, instead of a defense against it. Excessive partiality for one foreign nation and excessive dislike of another cause those whom they actuate to see danger only on one side, and serve to veil and even second the arts of influence on the other. Real patriots who may resist the intrigues of the favorite are liable to become suspected and odious, while its tools and dupes usurp the applause and confidence of the people, to surrender their interests.

The great rule of conduct for us in regard to foreign nations is in extending our commercial relations, to have with them as little political connection as possible. So far as we have already formed engagements, let them be fulfilled with perfect good faith. Here let us stop. Europe has a set of primary interests which to us have none; or a very remote relation. Hence she must be engaged in frequent controversies, the causes of which are essentially foreign to our concerns. Hence, therefore, it must be unwise in us to implicate ourselves by artificial ties in the ordinary vicissitudes of her politics, or the ordinary combinations and collisions of her friendships or enmities.

Our detached and distant situation invites and enables us to pursue a different course. If we remain one people under an efficient government the period is not far off when we may defy material injury from external annoyance; when we may take such an attitude as will cause the neutrality we may at any time resolve upon to be scrupulously respected; when belligerent nations, under the impossibility of making acquisitions upon us, will not lightly hazard the giving us provocation; when we may choose peace or war, as our interest, guided by justice, shall counsel.

Why forego the advantages of so peculiar a situation? Why quit our own to stand upon foreign ground? Why, by interweaving our destiny with that of any part of Europe, entangle our peace and prosperity in the toils of European ambition, rivalship, interest, humor or caprice?

It is our true policy to steer clear of permanent alliances with any portion of the foreign world; so far, I mean, as we are now at liberty to do it; for let me not be understood as capable of patronizing infidelity to existing engagements. I hold the maxim no less applicable to public than to private affairs, that honesty is always the best policy. I repeat it, therefore, let those engagements be observed in their genuine sense. But, in my opinion, it is unnecessary and would be unwise to extend them. Taking care always to keep ourselves by suitable establishments on a respectable defensive posture, we may safely trust to temporary alliances for extraordinary emergencies.

Harmony, liberal intercourse with all nations, are recommended by policy, humanity, and interest. But even our commercial policy should hold an equal and impartial hand; neither seeking nor granting exclusive favors or preferences; consulting the natural course of things; diffusing and diversifying by gentle means the streams of commerce, but forcing nothing; establishing (with powers so disposed, in order to give trade a stable course, to define the rights of our merchants, and to enable the government to support them) conventional rules of intercourse, the best that present circumstances and mutual opinion will permit, but temporary, and liable to be from time to time abandoned or varied, as experience and circumstances shall dictate; constantly keeping in view that it is folly in one nation to look for disinterested favors from another; that it must pay with a portion of its independence for whatever it may accept under that character; that, by such acceptance, it may place itself in the condition of having given equivalents for nominal favors, and yet of being reproached with ingratitude for not giving more. There can be no greater error than to expect or calculate upon real favors from nation to nation. It is an illusion, which experience must cure, which a just pride ought to discard.

In offering to you, my countrymen, these counsels of an old and affectionate friend, I dare not hope they will make the strong and lasting impression I could wish; that they will control the usual current of the passions, or prevent our nation from running the course which has hitherto marked the destiny of nations. But, if I may even flatter myself that they may be productive of some partial benefit, some occasional good; that they may now and then recur to moderate the fury of party spirit, to warn against the mischiefs of foreign intrigue, to guard against the impostures of pretended patriotism; this hope will be a full recompense for the solicitude for your welfare, by which they have been dictated.

How far in the discharge of my official duties I have been guided by the principles which have been delineated, the public records and other evidences of my conduct must witness to you and to the world. To myself, the assurance of my own conscience is, that I have at least believed myself to be guided by them.

In relation to the still subsisting war in Europe, my proclamation of the twenty-second of April, 1793, is the index of my plan. Sanctioned by your approving voice, and by that of your representatives in both houses of Congress, the spirit of that measure has continually governed me, uninfluenced by any attempts to deter or divert me from it.

After deliberate examination, with the aid of the best lights I could obtain, I was well satisfied that our country, under all the circumstances of the case, had a right to take, and was bound in duty and interest to take, a neutral position. Having taken it, I determined, as far as should depend upon me, to maintain it, with moderation, perseverance, and firmness.

The considerations which respect the right to hold this conduct, it is not necessary on this occasion to detail. I will only observe that, according to my understanding of the matter, that right, so far from being denied by any of the belligerent powers, has been virtually admitted by all.

The duty of holding a neutral conduct may be inferred, without anything more, from the obligation which justice and humanity impose on every nation, in cases in which it is free to act, to maintain inviolate the relations of peace and amity towards other nations.

The inducements of interest for observing that conduct will best be referred to your own reflections and experience. With me a predominant motive has been to endeavor to gain time to our country to settle and mature its yet recent institutions, and to progress without interruption to that degree of strength and consistency which is necessary to give it, humanly speaking, the command of its own fortunes.

Though, in reviewing the incidents of my administration, I am unconscious of intentional error,

I am nevertheless too sensible of my defects not to think it probable that I may have committed many errors. Whatever they may be, I fervently beseech the Almighty to avert or mitigate the evils to which they may tend. I shall also carry with me the hope that my country will never cease to view them with indulgence; and that, after forty five years of my life dedicated to its service with an upright zeal, the faults of incompetent abilities will be consigned to oblivion, as myself must soon be to the mansions of rest.

Relying on its kindness in this as in other things, and actuated by that fervent love towards it, which is so natural to a man who views in it the native soil of himself and his progenitors for several generations, I anticipate with pleasing expectation that retreat in which I promise myself to realize, without alloy, the anticipate with pleasing expectation that retreat in which I promise myself to realize, without alloy, the sweet enjoyment of partaking, in the midst of my fellow citizens, the benign influence of good laws under a free government, the ever favorite object of my heart, and the happy reward, as I trust, of our mutual cares, labors, and dangers.

United States
19th September, 1796

Geo. Washington

The Alien and Sedition Acts

FIFTH CONGRESS OF THE UNITED STATES:
At the Second Session,
Begun and help at the city of Philadelphia, in the state of Pennsylvania, on Monday, the thirteenth of November, one thousand seven hundred and ninety-seven.

AN ACT CONCERNING ALIENS.

SECTION 1. Be it enacted by the Senate and the House of Representatives of the United States of America in Congress assembled, That it shall be lawful for the President of the United States at any time during the continuance of this act, to order all such aliens as he shall judge dangerous to the peace and safety of the United States, or shall have reasonable grounds to suspect are concerned in any treasonable or secret machinations against the government thereof, to depart out of the territory of the United Slates, within such time as shall be expressed in such order, which order shall be served on such alien by delivering him a copy thereof, or leaving the same at his usual abode, and returned to the office of the Secretary of State, by the marshal or other person to whom the same shall be directed. And in case any alien, so ordered to depart, shall be found at large within the United States after the time limited in such order for his departure, and not having obtained a license from the President to reside therein, or having obtained such license shall not have conformed thereto, every such alien shall, on conviction thereof, be imprisoned for a term not exceeding three years, and shall never after be admitted to become a citizen of the United States. Provided always, and be it further enacted, that if any alien so ordered to depart shall prove to the satisfaction of the President, by evidence to be taken before such person or persons as the President shall direct, who are for that purpose hereby authorized to administer oaths, that no injury or danger to the United Slates will arise from suffering such alien to reside therein, the President may grant a license to such alien to remain within the United States for such time as he shall judge proper, and at such place as he may designate. And the President may also require of such alien to enter into a bond to the United States, in such pe-nal sum as he may direct, with one or more sufficient sureties to the satisfaction of the person authorized by the President to take the same, conditioned for the good behavior of such alien during his residence in the United States, and not violating his license, which license the President may revoke, whenever he shall think proper.

SEC. 2. And be it further enacted, That it shall be lawful for the President of the United States, whenever he may deem it necessary (for the public safety, to order to be removed out of the territory thereof, any alien who mayor shall be in prison in pursuance of this act; and to cause to be arrested and sent out of the United States such of those aliens as shall have been ordered to depart therefrom and shall not have obtained a license as aforesaid, in all cases where, in the opinion of the President, the public safety requires a speedy removal. And if any alien so removed or sent out of the United Slates by the President shall voluntarily return thereto, unless by permission of the President of the United States, such alien on conviction thereof, shall be imprisoned so long as, in the opinion of the President, the public safety may require.

SEC. 3. And be it further enacted, That every master or commander of any ship or vessel which shall come into any port of the United States after the first day of July next, shall immediately on his arrival make report in writing to the collector or other chief officer of the customs of such port, of all aliens, if any, on board his vessel, specifying their names, age, the place of nativity, the country from which they shall have come, the nation to which they belong and owe allegiance, their occupation and a description of their persons, as far as he shall be informed thereof, and on failure, every such master and commander shall forfeit and pay three hundred dollars, for the payment whereof on default of such master or commander, such vessel shall also be holden, and may by such collector or other officer of the customs be detained. And it shall be the duty of such collector or other officer of the customs, forthwith to transmit to the office of the department of state true copies of all such returns.

SEC. 4. And be it further enacted, That the circuit and district courts of the United States, shall respectively have cognizance of all crimes and offences against this act. And all marshals and other officers of the United States are required to execute all precepts and orders of the President of the United States issued in pursuance or by virtue of this act.

SEC. 5. And be it further enacted, That it shall be lawful for any alien who may be ordered to be removed from the United States, by virtue of this act, to take with him such part of his goods, chattels, or other property, as he may find convenient; and all property left in the United States by any alien, who may be removed, as aforesaid, shall be, and remain subject to his order and disposal, in the same manner as if this act had not been passed.

SEC. 6. And be it further enacted, That this act shall continue and be in force for and during the term of two years from the passing thereof.

Jonathan Dayton, Speaker of the House of Representatives.
TH. Jefferson, Vice President of the United States and President of the Sentate.

I Certify that this Act did originate in the Sentate.
Attest, Sam. A. Otis, Secretary

APPROVED, June 25, 1798.
John Adams
President of the United States.

AN ACT RESPECTING ALIEN ENEMIES

SECTION 1. Be it enacted by the Senate and House of Representatives of the United States of America in Congress assembled, That whenever there shall be a declared war between the United States and any foreign nation or government, or any invasion or predatory incursion shall be perpetrated, attempted, or threatened against the territory of the United States, by any foreign nation or government, and the President of the United States shall make public proclamation of the event, all natives, citizens, denizens, or subjects of the hostile nation or government, being males of the age of fourteen years and upwards, who shall be within the United States, and not actually naturalized, shall be liable to be apprehended, restrained, secured and removed, as alien enemies. And the President of the United States shall be, and he is hereby authorized, in any event, as aforesaid, by his proclamation thereof, or other public act, to direct the conduct to be observed, on the part of the United States, towards the aliens who shall become liable, as aforesaid; the manner and degree of the restraint to which they shall be subject, and in what cases, and upon what security their residence shall be permitted, and to provide for the removal of those, who, not being permitted to reside within the United States, shall refuse or neglect to depart therefrom; and to establish any other regulations which shall be found necessary in the premises and for the public safety: Provided, that aliens resident within the United States, who shall become liable as enemies, in the manner aforesaid, and who shall not be chargeable with actual hostility, or other crime against the public safety, shall be allowed, for the recovery, disposal, and removal of their goods and effects, and for their departure, the full time which is, or shall be stipulated by any treaty, where any shall have been between the United States, and the hostile nation or government, of which they shall be natives, citizens, denizens or subjects: and where no such treaty shall have existed, the President of the United States may ascertain and declare such reasonable time as may be consistent with the public safety, and according to the dictates of humanity and national hospitality.

SEC. 2. And be it further enacted, That after any proclamation shall be made as aforesaid, it shall be the duty of the several courts of the United States, and of each state, having criminal jurisdiction, and of the several judges and justices of the courts of the United States, and they shall be, and are hereby respectively, authorized upon complaint, against any alien or alien enemies, as aforesaid, who shall be resident and at large within such jurisdiction or district, to the danger of the public peace or safety, and contrary to the tenor or intent of such proclamation, or other regulations which the President of the United States shall and may establish in the premises, to cause such alien or aliens to be duly apprehended and convened before such court, judge or justice; and after a full examination and hearing on such complaint and sufficient cause therefor appearing, shall and may order such alien or aliens to be removed out of the territory of the United States, or to give sureties of their good behaviour, or to be otherwise restrained, conformably to the proclamation or regulations which shall and may be established as aforesaid, and may imprison, or otherwise secure such alien or aliens, until the order which shall and may be made, as aforesaid, shall be performed.

SEC. 3. And be it further enacted, That it shall be the duty of the marshal of the district in which any alien enemy shall be apprehended, who by the President of the United States, or by order of any court, judge or justice, as aforesaid, shall be required to depart, and to be removed, as aforesaid, to provide therefor, and to execute such order, by himself or his deputy, or other discreet person or persons to be employed by him, by causing a removal of such alien out of the territory of the United States; and for such removal the marshal shall have the warrant of the President of the United States, or of the court, judge or justice ordering the same, as the case may be.

APPROVED, July 6, 1798.

FIFTH CONGRESS OF THE UNITED STATES: AT THE SECOND SESSION,

Begun and help at the city of Philadelphia, in the state of Pennsylvania, on Monday, the thirteenth of November, one thousand seven hundred and ninety-seven.

AN ACT IN ADDITION TO THE ACT, ENTITLED "AN ACT FOR THE PUNISHMENT OF CERTAIN CRIMES AGAINST THE UNITED STATES."

SECTION 1. Be it enacted by the Senate and House of Representatives of the United States of America, in Congress assembled, That if any persons shall unlawfully combine or conspire together, with intent to oppose any measure or measures of the government of the United States, which are or shall be directed by proper authority, or to impede the operation of any law of the United States, or to intimidate or prevent any person holding a place or office in or under the government of the United States, from undertaking, performing or executing his trust or duty, and if any person or persons, with intent as aforesaid, shall counsel, advise or attempt to procure any insurrection, riot, unlawful assembly, or combination, whether such conspiracy, threatening, counsel, advice, or attempt shall have the proposed effect or not, he or they shall be deemed guilty of a high

misdemeanor, and on conviction, before any court of the United States having jurisdiction thereof, shall be punished by a fine not exceeding five thousand dollars, and by imprisonment during a term not less than six months nor exceeding five years; and further, at the discretion of the court may be holden to find sureties for his good behaviour in such sum, and for such time, as the said court may direct.

SEC. 2. And be it farther enacted, That if any person shall write, print, utter or publish, or shall cause or procure to be written, printed, uttered or published, or shall knowingly and willingly assist or aid in writing, printing, uttering or publishing any false, scandalous and malicious writing or writings against the government of the United States, or either house of the Congress of the United States, or the President of the United States, with intent to defame the said government, or either house of the said Congress, or the said President, or to bring them, or either of them, into contempt or disrepute; or to excite against them, or either or any of them, the hatred of the good people of the United States, or to stir up sedition within the United States, or to excite any unlawful combinations therein, for opposing or resisting any law of the United States, or any act of the President of the United States, done in pursuance of any such law, or of the powers in him vested by the constitution of the United States, or to resist, oppose, or defeat any such law or act, or to aid, encourage or abet any hostile designs of any foreign nation against United States, their people or government, then such person, being thereof convicted before any court of the United States having jurisdiction thereof, shall be punished by a fine not exceeding two thousand dollars, and by imprisonment not exceeding two years.

SEC. 3. And be it further enacted and declared, That if any person shall be prosecuted under this act, for the writing or publishing any libel aforesaid, it shall be lawful for the defendant, upon the trial of the cause, to give in evidence in his defence, the truth of the matter contained in publication charged as a libel. And the jury who shall try the cause, shall have a right to determine the law and the fact, under the direction of the court, as in other cases.

SEC. 4. And be it further enacted, That this act shall continue and be in force until the third day of March, one thousand eight hundred and one, and no longer: Provided, that the expiration of the act shall not prevent or defeat a prosecution and punishment of any offence against the law, during the time it shall be in force.

Jonathan Dayton,
Speaker of the House of Representatives.

Theodore Sedgwick,
President of the Senate pro tempore.

I Certify that this Act did originate in the Senate.
Attest, Sam. A. Otis, Secretary

APPROVED, July 14, 1798 John Adams
President of the United States.

Jefferson's Secret Message to Congress Regarding the Lewis and Clark Expedition

Confidential

Gentlemen of the Senate, and of the House of Representatives:

As the continuance of the act for establishing trading houses with the Indian tribes will be under the consideration of the Legislature at its present session, I think it my duty to communicate the views which have guided me in the execution of that act, in order that you may decide on the policy of continuing it, in the present or any other form, or discontinue it altogether, if that shall, on the whole, seem most for the public good.

The Indian tribes residing within the limits of the United States, have, for a considerable time, been growing more and more uneasy at the constant diminution of the territory they occupy, although effected by their own voluntary sales: and the policy has long been gaining strength with them, of refusing absolutely all further sale, on any conditions; insomuch that, at this time, it hazards their friendship, and excites dangerous jealousies and perturbations in their minds to make any overture for the purchase of the smallest portions of their land. A very few tribes only are not yet obstinately in these dispositions. In order peaceably to counteract this policy of theirs, and to provide an extension of territory which the rapid increase of our numbers will call for, two measures are deemed expedient. First: to encourage them to abandon hunting, to apply to the raising stock, to agriculture and domestic manufacture, and thereby prove to themselves that less land and labor will maintain them in this, better than in their former mode of living. The extensive forests necessary in the hunting life, will then become useless, and they will see advantage in exchanging them for the means of improving their farms, and of increasing their domestic comforts. Secondly: to multiply trading houses among them, and place within their reach those things which will contribute more to their domestic comfort, than the possession of extensive, but uncultivated wilds. Experience and reflection will develop to them the wisdom of exchanging what they can spare and we want, for what we can spare and they want. In leading them to agriculture, to manufactures, and civilization; in bringing together their and our settlements, and in preparing them ultimately to participate in the benefits of our governments, I trust and believe we are acting for their greatest good. At these trading houses we have pursued the principles of the act of Congress, which directs that the commerce shall be carried on liberally, and requires only that the capital stock shall not be diminished. We consequently undersell private traders, foreign and domestic, drive them from the competition; and thus, with the good will of the Indians, rid ourselves of a description of men who are constantly endeavoring to excite in the Indian mind suspicions, fears, and irritations towards us. A letter now enclosed, shows the effect of our competition on the operations of the traders, while the Indians, perceiving the advantage of purchasing from us, are soliciting generally, our establishment of trading houses among them. In one quarter this is particularly interesting. The Legislature, reflecting on the late occurrences on the Mississippi, must be sensible how desirable it is to possess a respectable breadth of country on that river, from our Southern limit to the Illinois at least; so that we may present as firm a front on that as on our Eastern border. We possess what is below the Yazoo, and can probably acquire a certain breadth from the Illinois and Wabash to the Ohio; but between the Ohio and Yazoo, the country all belongs to the Chickasaws, the most friendly tribe within our limits, but the most decided against the alienation of lands. The portion of their country most important for us is exactly that which they do not inhabit. Their settlements are not on the Mississippi, but in the interior country. They have lately shown a desire to become agricultural; and this leads to the desire of buying implements and comforts. In the strengthening and gratifying of these wants, I see the only prospect of planting on the Mississippi itself, the means of its own safety. Duty has required me to submit these views to the judgment of the Legislature; but as their disclosure might embarrass and defeat their effect, they are committed to the special confidence of the two Houses.

While the extension of the public commerce among the Indian tribes, may deprive of that source of profit such of our citizens as are engaged in it, it might be worthy the attention of Congress, in their care of individual as well as of the general interest, to point, in another direction, the enterprise of these citizens, as profitably for themselves, and more usefully for the public. The river Missouri, and the Indians inhabiting it, are not as well known as is rendered desirable by their connexion with the Mississippi, and consequently with us. It is, however, understood, that the country on that river is inhabited by numerous tribes, who furnish great supplies of furs and peltry to the trade of another nation, carried on in a high latitude, through an infinite number of portages and lakes, shut up by ice through a long season. The commerce on that line could bear no competition with that of the Missouri, traversing a moderate climate, offering according to the best accounts, a continued navigation from its source, and possibly with a single portage, from the Western Ocean, and finding to the Atlantic a choice of channels through the Illinois or Wabash, the lakes and Hudson, through the Ohio and Susquehanna, or Potomac or James rivers, and through the Tennessee and Savannah, rivers. An intelligent officer, with ten or twelve chosen men, fit for the enterprise, and willing to undertake it, taken from our posts, where they may be spared without inconvenience, might explore the whole line, even to the Western Ocean, have conferences with the natives on the subject of commercial intercourse, get admission among them for our traders, as others are admitted, agree on convenient deposits for an interchange of articles, and return with the information acquired, in the course of two summers. Their arms and accoutrements, some instruments of observation, and light and cheap presents for the Indians, would be all the apparatus they could carry, and with an expectation of a soldier's portion of land on their return, would constitute the whole expense. Their pay would be going on, whether here or there. While other civilized nations have encountered great expense to enlarge the boundaries of knowledge by undertaking voyages of discovery, and for other literary purposes, in various parts and directions, our nation seems to owe to the same object, as well as to its own interests, to explore this, the only line of easy communication across the continent, and so directly traversing our own part of it. The interests of commerce place the principal object within the constitutional powers and care of Congress, and that it should incidentally advance the geographical knowledge of our own continent, cannot be but an additional gratification. The nation claiming the territory, regarding this as a literary pursuit, which is in the habit of permitting within its dominions, would not be disposed to view it with jealousy, even if the expiring state of its interests there did not render it a matter of indifference. The appropriation of two thousand five hundred dollars, "for the purpose of extending the external commerce of the United States," while understood and considered by the Executive as giving the legislative sanction, would cover the undertaking from notice, and prevent the obstructions which interested individuals might otherwise previously prepare in its way.

TH. Jefferson
Jan. 18. 1803.

The Louisiana Purchase Treaty

Note: The three documents transcribed here are the treaty of cession and two conventions, one for the payment of 60 million francs ($11,250,000), the other for claims American citizens had made against France for 20 million francs ($3,750,000).

TREATY BETWEEN THE UNITED STATES OF AMERICA AND THE FRENCH REPUBLIC

The President of the United States of America and the First Consul of the French Republic in the name of the French People desiring to remove all Source of misunderstanding relative to objects of discussion mentioned in the Second and fifth articles of the Convention of the 8th Vendémiaire an 9 (30 September 1800) relative to the rights claimed by the United States in virtue of the Treaty concluded at Madrid the 27 of October 1795, between His Catholic Majesty & the Said United States, & willing to Strengthen the union and friendship which at the time of the Said Convention was happily reestablished between the two nations have respectively named their Plenipotentiaries to wit The President of the United States, by and with the advice and consent of the Senate of the Said States; Robert R. Livingston Minister Plenipotentiary of the United States and James Monroe Minister Plenipotentiary and Envoy extraordinary of the Said States near the Government of the French Republic; And the First Consul in the name of the French people, Citizen Francis Barbé Marbois Minister of the public treasury who after having respectively exchanged their full powers have agreed to the following Articles.

ARTICLE I

Whereas by the Article the third of the Treaty concluded at St Ildefonso the 9th Vendémiaire an 9 (1st October) 1800 between the First Consul of the French Republic and his Catholic Majesty it was agreed as follows.

"His Catholic Majesty promises and engages on his part to cede to the French Republic six months after the full and entire execution of the conditions and Stipulations herein relative to his Royal Highness the Duke of Parma, the Colony or Province of Louisiana with the Same extent that it now has in the hand of Spain, & that it had when France possessed it; and Such as it Should be after the Treaties subsequently entered into between Spain and other States."

And whereas in pursuance of the Treaty and particularly of the third article the French Republic has an incontestible title to the domain and to the possession of the said Territory—The First Consul of the French Republic desiring to give to the United States a strong proof of his friendship doth hereby cede to the United States in the name of the French Republic for ever and in full Sovereignty the said territory with all its rights and appurtenances as fully and in the Same manner as they have been acquired by the French Republic in virtue of the above mentioned Treaty concluded with his Catholic Majesty.

ART: II

In the cession made by the preceeding article are included the adjacent Islands belonging to Louisiana all public lots and Squares, vacant lands and all public buildings, fortifications, barracks and other edifices which are not private property.—The Archives, papers & documents relative to the domain and Sovereignty of Louisiana and its dependances will be left in the possession of the Commissaries of the United States, and copies will be afterwards given in due form to the Magistrates and Municipal officers of such of the said papers and documents as may be necessary to them.

ART: III

The inhabitants of the ceded territory shall be incorporated in the Union of the United States and admitted as soon as possible according to the principles of the federal Constitution to the enjoyment of all these rights, advantages and immunities of citizens of the United States, and in the mean time they shall be maintained and protected in the free enjoyment of their liberty, property and the Religion which they profess.

ART: IV

There Shall be Sent by the Government of France a Commissary to Louisiana to the end that he do every act necessary as well to receive from the Officers of his Catholic Majesty the Said country and its dependances in the name of the French Republic if it has not been already done as to transmit it in the name of the French Republic to the Commissary or agent of the United States.

ART: V

Immediately after the ratification of the present Treaty by the President of the United States and in case that of the first Consul's shall have been previously obtained, the commissary of the French Republic shall remit all military posts of New Orleans and other parts of the ceded territory to the Commissary or Commissaries named by the President to take possession—the troops whether of France or Spain who may be there shall cease to occupy any military post from the time of taking possession and shall be embarked as soon as possible in the course of three months after the ratification of this treaty.

ART: VI

The United States promise to execute Such treaties and articles as may have been agreed between Spain and the tribes and nations of Indians until by mutual consent of the United States and the said tribes or nations other Suitable articles Shall have been agreed upon.

ART: VII

As it is reciprocally advantageous to the commerce of France and the United States to encourage the communication of both nations for a limited time in the country ceded by the present treaty until general arrangements relative to commerce of both nations may be agreed on; it has been agreed between the contracting parties that the French Ships coming directly from France or any of her colonies loaded only with the produce and manufactures of France or her Said Colonies; and the Ships of Spain coming directly from Spain or any of her colonies loaded only with the produce or manufactures of Spain or her

Colonies shall be admitted during the Space of twelve years in the Port of New Orleans and in all other legal ports of entry within the ceded territory in the Same manner as the Ships of the United States coming directly from France or Spain or any of their Colonies without being Subject to any other or greater duty on merchandize or other or greater tonnage than that paid by the citizens of the United States.

During that Space of time above mentioned no other nation Shall have a right to the Same privileges in the Ports of the ceded territory—the twelve years Shall commence three months after the exchange of ratifications if it Shall take place in France or three months after it Shall have been notified at Paris to the French Government if it Shall take place in the United States; It is however well understood that the object of the above article is to favour the manufactures, Commerce, freight and navigation of France and of Spain So far as relates to the importations that the French and Spanish Shall make into the Said Ports of the United States without in any Sort affecting the regulations that the United States may make concerning the exportation of the produce and merchandize of the United States, or any right they may have to make Such regulations.

ART: VIII

In future and for ever after the expiration of the twelve years, the Ships of France shall be treated upon the footing of the most favoured nations in the ports above mentioned.

ART: IX

The particular Convention Signed this day by the respective Ministers, having for its object to provide for the payment of debts due to the Citizens of the United States by the French Republic prior to the 30th Sept. 1800 (8th Vendémiaire an 9) is approved and to have its execution in the Same manner as if it had been inserted in this present treaty, and it Shall be ratified in the same form and in the Same time So that the one Shall not be ratified distinct from the other.

Another particular Convention Signed at the Same date as the present treaty relative to a definitive rule between the contracting parties is in the like manner approved and will be ratified in the Same form, and in the Same time and jointly.

ART: X

The present treaty Shall be ratified in good and due form and the ratifications Shall be exchanged in the Space of Six months after the date of the Signature by the Ministers Plenipotentiary or Sooner if possible.

In faith whereof the respective Plenipotentiaries have Signed these articles in the French and English languages; declaring nevertheless that the present Treaty was originally agreed to in the French language; and have thereunto affixed their Seals.

Done at Paris the tenth day of Floreal in the eleventh year of the French Republic; and the 30th of April 1803.

Robt R Livingston [seal]
Jas. Monroe [seal]
Barbé Marbois [seal]

A CONVENTION BETWEEN THE UNITED STATES OF AMERICA AND THE FRENCH REPUBLIC

The President of the United States of America and the First Consul of the French Republic in the name of the French people, in consequence of the treaty of cession of Louisiana which has been Signed this day; wishing to regulate definitively every thing which has relation to the Said cession have authorized to this effect the Plenipotentiaries, that is to say the President of the United States has, by and with the advice and consent of the Senate of the Said States, nominated for their Plenipotentiaries, Robert R. Livingston, Minister Plenipotentiary of the United States, and James Monroe, Minister Plenipotentiary and Envoy Extraordinary of the Said United States, near the Government of the French Republic; and the First Consul of the French Republic, in the name of the French people, has named as Pleniopotentiary of the Said Republic the citizen Francis Barbé Marbois: who, in virtue of their full powers, which have been exchanged this day, have agreed to the followings articles:

ART: 1

The Government of the United States engages to pay to the French government in the manner Specified in the following article the sum of Sixty millions of francs independant of the Sum which Shall be fixed by another Convention for the payment of the debts due by France to citizens of the United States.

ART: 2

For the payment of the Sum of Sixty millions of francs mentioned in the preceeding article the United States shall create a Stock of eleven millions, two hundred and fifty thousand Dollars bearing an interest of Six percent per annum payable half yearly in London Amsterdam or Paris amounting by the half year to three hundred and thirty Seven thousand five hundred Dollars, according to the proportions which Shall be determined by the french Govenment to be paid at either place: The principal of the Said Stock to be reimbursed at the treasury of the United States in annual payments of not less than three millions of Dollars each; of which the first payment Shall commence fifteen years after the date of the exchange of ratifications:—this Stock Shall be transferred to the government of France or to Such person or persons as Shall be authorized to receive it in three months at most after the exchange of ratifications of this treaty and after Louisiana Shall be taken possession of the name of the Government of the United States.

It is further agreed that if the french Government Should be desirous of disposing of the Said Stock to receive the capital in Europe at Shorter terms that its measures for that purpose Shall be taken So as to favour in the greatest degree possible the credit of the United States, and to raise to the highest price the Said Stock.

ART: 3

It is agreed that the Dollar of the United States Specified in the present Convention shall be fixed at five francs 3333/100000 or five livres eight Sous tournois.

The present Convention Shall be ratified in good and due form, and the ratifications Shall be exchanged the Space of Six months to date from this day or Sooner it possible.

In faith of which the respective Plenipotentiaries have Signed the above articles both in the french and english languages, declaring nevertheless that the present treaty has been originally agreed on and written in the french language; to which they have hereunto affixed their Seals.

Done at Paris the tenth of Floreal eleventh year of the french Republic 30th April 1803.

Robt R Livingston [seal]
Jas. Monroe [seal]
Barbé Marbois [seal]

CONVENTION BETWEEN THE UNITED STATES OF AMERICA AND THE FRENCH REPUBLIC

The President of the United States of America and the First Consul of the French Republic in the name of the French People having by a Treaty of this date terminated all difficulties relative to Louisiana, and established on a Solid foundation the friendship which unites the two nations and being desirous in complyance with the Second and fifth Articles of the Convention of the 8th Vendémiaire ninth year of the French Republic (30th September 1800) to Secure the payment of the Sums due by France to the citizens of the United States have respectively nominated as Plenipotentiaries that is to Say The President of the United States of America by and with the advise and consent of their Senate Robert R. Livingston Minister Plenipotentiary and James Monroe Minister Plenipotentiary and Envoy Extraordinary of the Said States near the Government of the French Republic: and the First Consul in the name of the French People the Citizen Francis Barbé Marbois Minister of the public treasury; who after having exchanged their full powers have agreed to the following articles.

ART: 1

The debts due by France to citizens of the United States contracted before the 8th Vendémiaire ninth year of the French Republic (30th September 1800) Shall be paid according to the following regulations with interest at Six per Cent; to commence from the period when the accounts and vouchers were presented to the French Government.

ART: 2

The debts provided for by the preceeding Article are those whose result is comprised in the conjectural note annexed to the present Convention and which, with the interest cannot exceed the Sum of twenty millions of Francs. The claims comprised in the Said note which fall within the exceptions of the following articles, Shall not be admitted to the benefit of this provision.

ART: 3

The principal and interests of the Said debts Shall be discharged by the United States, by orders drawn by their Minister Plenipotentiary on their treasury,

these orders Shall be payable Sixty days after the exchange of ratifications of the Treaty and the Conventions Signed this day, and after possession Shall be given of Louisiana by the Commissaries of France to those of the United States.

ART: 4

It is expressly agreed that the preceding articles Shall comprehend no debts but Such as are due to citizens of the United States who have been and are yet creditors of France for Supplies for embargoes and prizes made at Sea, in which the appeal has been properly lodged within the time mentioned in the Said Convention 8th Vendémiaire ninth year, (30th Sept 1800).

ART: 5

The preceding Articles Shall apply only, First: to captures of which the council of prizes Shall have ordered restitution, it being well understood that the claimant cannot have recourse to the United States otherwise than he might have had to the Government of the French republic, and only in case of insufficiency of the captors—2d the debts mentioned in the Said fifth Article of the Convention contracted before the 8th Vendémiaire an 9 (30th September 1800) the payment of which has been heretofore claimed of the actual Government of France and for which the creditors have a right to the protection of the United States;—the Said 5th Article does not comprehend prizes whose condemnation has been or Shall be confirmed: it is the express intention of the contracting parties not to extend the benefit of the present Convention to reclamations of American citizens who Shall have established houses of Commerce in France, England or other countries than the United States in partnership with foreigners, and who by that reason and the nature of their commerce ought to be regarded as domiciliated in the places where Such house exist.—All agreements and bargains concerning merchandize, which Shall not be the property of American citizens, are equally excepted from the benefit of the said Conventions, Saving however to Such persons their claims in like manner as if this Treaty had not been made.

ART: 6

And that the different questions which may arise under the preceding article may be fairly investigated, the Ministers Plenipotentiary of the United

States Shall name three persons, who Shall act from the present and provisionally, and who shall have full power to examine, without removing the documents, all the accounts of the different claims already liquidated by the Bureaus established for this purpose by the French Republic, and to ascertain whether they belong to the classes designated by the present Convention and the principles established in it or if they are not in one of its exceptions and on their Certificate, declaring that the debt is due to an American Citizen or his representative and that it existed before the 8th Vendémiaire 9th year (30 September 1800) the debtor shall be entitled to an order on the Treasury of the United States in the manner prescribed by the 3d Article.

ART: 7

The Same agents Shall likewise have power, without removing the documents, to examine the claims which are prepared for verification, and to certify those which ought to be admitted by uniting the necessary qualifications, and not being comprised in the exceptions contained in the present Convention.

ART: 8

The Same agents Shall likewise examine the claims which are not prepared for liquidation, and certify in writing those which in their judgement ought to be admitted to liquidation.

ART: 9

In proportion as the debts mentioned in these articles Shall be admitted they Shall be discharged with interest at Six per Cent: by the Treasury of the United States.

ART: 10

And that no debt shall not have the qualifications above mentioned and that no unjust or exorbitant demand may be admitted, the Commercial agent of the United States at Paris or such other agent as the Minister Plenipotentiary or the United States Shall think proper to nominate shall assist at the operations of the Bureaus and cooperate in the examinations of the claims; and if this agent Shall be of the opinion that any debt is not completely proved, or if he shall judge that it is not comprised in the principles of the fifth article above mentioned, and if notwithstanding his opinion the Bureaus established

by the french Government should think that it ought to be liquidated, he shall transmit his observations to the board established by the United States, who, without removing documents, shall make a complete examination of the debt and vouchers which Support it, and report the result to the Minister of the United States.—The Minister of the United States Shall transmit his observations in all Such cases to the Minister of the treasury of the French Republic, on whose report the French Government Shall decide definitively in every case.

The rejection of any claim Shall have no other effect than to exempt the United States from the payment of it, the French Government reserving to itself, the right to decide definitively on Such claim So far as it concerns itself.

ART: 11

Every necessary decision Shall be made in the course of a year to commence from the exchange of ratifications, and no reclamation Shall be admitted afterwards.

ART: 12

In case of claims for debts contracted by the Government of France with citizens of the United States Since the 8th Vendémiaire 9th year/30 September 1800 not being comprised in this Convention may be pursued, and the payment demanded in the Same manner as if it had not been made.

ART: 13

The present convention Shall be ratified in good and due form and the ratifications Shall be exchanged in Six months from the date of the Signature of the Ministers Plenipotentiary, or Sooner if possible.

In faith of which, the respective Ministers Plenipotentiary have signed the above Articles both in the french and english languages, declaring nevertheless that the present treaty has been originally agreed on and written in the french language, to which they have hereunto affixed their Seals.

Done at Paris, the tenth of Floreal, eleventh year of the French Republic.
30th April 1803.

Robt R Livingston [seal]
Jas. Monroe [seal]
Barbé Marbois [seal]

Marbury v. Madison

CHIEF JUSTICE MARSHALL DELIVERED THE OPINION OF THE COURT.

At the last term on the affidavits then read and filed with the clerk, a rule was granted in this case, requiring the Secretary of State to show cause why a mandamus should not issue, directing him to deliver to William Marbury his commission as a justice of the peace for the county of Washington, in the district of Columbia.

No cause has been shown, and the present motion is for a mandamus. The peculiar delicacy of this case, the novelty of some of its circumstances, and the real difficulty attending the points which occur in it, require a complete exposition of the principles on which the opinion to be given by the court is founded. . . .

In the order in which the court has viewed this subject, the following questions have been considered and decided:

1st. Has the applicant a right to the commission he demands?

2d. If he has a right, and that right has been violated, do the laws of his country afford him a remedy?

3d. If they do afford him a remedy, is it a mandamus issuing from this court?

The first object of inquiry is—1st. Has the applicant a right to the commission he demands? . . .

It [is] decidedly the opinion of the court, that when a commission has been signed by the president, the appointment is made; and that the commission is complete, when the seal of the United States has been affixed to it by the secretary of state. . . .

To withhold his commission, therefore, is an act deemed by the court not warranted by law, but violative of a vested legal right.

This brings us to the second inquiry; which is 2dly. If he has a right, and that right has been violated, do the laws of his country afford him a remedy?

The very essence of civil liberty certainly consists in the right of every individual to claim the protection of the laws, whenever he receives an injury. One of the first duties of government is to afford that protection. [The] government of the United States has been emphatically termed a government of laws, and not of men. It will certainly cease to deserve this high appellation, if the laws furnish no remedy for the violation of a vested legal right. . . .

By the constitution of the United States, the President is invested with certain important political powers, in the exercise of which he is to use his own discretion, and is accountable only to his country in his political character, and to his own conscience. To aid him in the performance of these duties, he is authorized to appoint certain officers, who act by his authority and in conformity with his orders.

In such cases, their acts are his acts; and whatever opinion may be entertained of the manner in which executive discretion may be used, still there exists, and can exist, no power to control that discretion. The subjects are political. They respect the nation, not individual rights, and being entrusted to the executive, the decision of the executive is conclusive. . . .

But when the legislature proceeds to impose on that officer other duties; when he is directed peremptorily to perform certain acts; when the rights of individuals are dependent on the performance of those acts; he is so far the officer of the law; is amenable to the laws for his conduct; and cannot at his discretion sport away the vested rights of others.

The conclusion from this reasoning is, that where the heads of departments are the political or confidential agents of the executive, merely to execute the will of the President, or rather to act in cases in which the executive possesses a constitutional or legal discretion, nothing can be more perfectly clear than that their acts are only politically examinable. But where a specific duty is assigned by law, and individual rights depend upon the performance of that duty, it seems equally clear, that the individual who considers himself injured, has a right to resort to the laws of his country for a remedy. . . .

It is, then, the opinion of the Court [that Marbury has a] right to the commission; a refusal to deliver which is a plain violation of that right, for which the laws of his country afford him a remedy.

It remains to be enquired whether,

3dly. He is entitled to the remedy for which he applies. This depends on—1st. The nature of the writ applied for, and,

2dly. The power of this court.

1st. The nature of the writ. . . .

This, then, is a plain case for a mandamus, either to deliver the commission, or a copy of it from the record; and it only remains to be enquired,

Whether it can issue from this court.

The act to establish the judicial courts of the United States authorizes the Supreme Court "to issue writs of mandamus in cases warranted by the principles and usages of law, to any courts appointed, or persons holding office, under the authority of the United States."

The Secretary of State, being a person holding an office under the authority of the United States, is precisely within the letter of the description; and if this court is not authorized to issue a writ of mandamus to such an officer, it must be because the law is unconstitutional, and therefore incapable of conferring the authority, and assigning the duties which its words purport to confer and assign.

The constitution vests the whole judicial power of the United States in one Supreme Court, and such inferior courts as congress shall, from time to time, ordain and establish. This power is expressly extended to all cases arising under the laws of the United States; and, consequently, in some form, may be exercised over the present case; because the right claimed is given by a law of the United States.

In the distribution of this power it is declared that "the Supreme Court shall have original jurisdiction in all cases affecting ambassadors, other public ministers and consuls, and those in which a state shall be a party. In all other cases, the Supreme Court shall have appellate jurisdiction."

It has been insisted, at the bar, that as the original grant of jurisdiction, to the supreme and inferior courts, is general, and the clause, assigning original jurisdiction to the Supreme Court, contains no negative or restrictive words, the power remains to the legislature, to assign original jurisdiction to that court in other cases than those specified in the article which has been recited; provided those cases belong to the judicial power of the United States.

If it had been intended to leave it in the discretion of the legislature to apportion the judicial power between the supreme and inferior courts according to the will of that body, it would certainly have been useless to have proceeded further than to have defined the judicial power, and the tribunals in which it should be vested. The subsequent part of the section is mere surplusage, is entirely without meaning, if such is to be the construction. If congress remains at liberty to give this court appellate jurisdiction, where the constitution has declared their jurisdiction shall be original; and original jurisdiction where the constitution has declared it shall be appellate; the distribution of jurisdiction, made in the constitution, is form without substance.

Affirmative words are often, in their operation, negative of other objects than those affirmed; and in this case, a negative or exclusive sense must be given to them or they have no operation at all.

It cannot be presumed that any clause in the constitution is intended to be without effect; and, therefore, such a construction is inadmissible, unless the words require it.

If the solicitude of the convention, respecting our peace with foreign powers, induced a provision that the supreme court should take original jurisdiction in cases which might be supposed to affect them; yet the clause would have proceeded no further than to provide for such cases, if no further restriction on the powers of congress had been intended. That they should have appellate jurisdiction in all other cases, with such exceptions as congress might make, is no restriction; unless the words be deemed exclusive of original jurisdiction.

When an instrument organizing fundamentally a judicial system, divides it into one supreme, and so many inferior courts as the legislature may ordain and establish; then enumerates its powers, and proceeds so far to distribute them, as to define the jurisdiction of the supreme court by declaring the cases in which it shall take original jurisdiction, and that in others it shall take appellate jurisdiction; the plain import of the words seems to be, that in one class of cases its jurisdiction is original, and not appellate; in the other it is appellate, and not original. If any other construction would render the clause inoperative, that is an additional reason for rejecting such other construction, and for adhering to their obvious meaning.

To enable this court, then, to issue a mandamus, it must be shown to be an exercise of appellate jurisdiction, or to be necessary to enable them to exercise appellate jurisdiction.

It has been stated at the bar that the appellate jurisdiction may be exercised in a variety of forms, and that if it be the will of the legislature that a mandamus should be used for that purpose, that will must be obeyed. This is true, yet the jurisdiction must be appellate, not original.

It is the essential criterion of appellate jurisdiction, that it revises and corrects the proceedings in a cause already instituted, and does not create that cause. Although, therefore, a mandamus may be directed to courts, yet to issue such a writ to an officer for the delivery of a paper, is in effect the same as to sustain an original action for that paper, and, therefore, seems not to belong to appellate, but to original jurisdiction. Neither is it necessary in such a case as this, to enable the court to exercise its appellate jurisdiction.

The authority, therefore, given to the Supreme Court, by the act establishing the judicial courts of the United States, to issue writs of mandamus to public officers, appears not to be warranted by the constitution; and it becomes necessary to enquire whether a jurisdiction, so conferred, can be exercised.

The question, whether an act, repugnant to the constitution, can become the law of the land, is a question deeply interesting to the United States; but happily, not of an intricacy proportioned to its interest. It seems only necessary to recognize certain principles, supposed to have been long and well established, to decide it.

That the people have an original right to establish, for their future govern-ment, such principles as, in their opinion, shall most conduce to their own happiness, is the basis on which the whole American fabric has been erected. The exercise of this original right is a very great exertion; nor can it, nor ought it, to be frequently repeated. The principles, therefore, so established, are deemed fundamental. And as the authority from which they proceed is supreme, and can seldom act, they are designed to be permanent.

This original and supreme will organizes the government, and assigns to different departments their respective powers. It may either stop here, or establish certain limits not to be transcended by those departments.

The government of the United States is of the latter description. The powers of the legislature are defined and limited; and that those limits may not be mistaken, or forgotten, the constitution is written. To what purpose are powers limited, and to what purpose is that limitation committed to writing, if these limits may, at any time, be passed by those intended to be restrained? The distinction between a government with limited and unlimited powers is abolished, if those limits do not confine the persons on whom they are imposed, and if acts prohibited and acts allowed, are of equal obligation. It is a proposition too plain to be contested, that the constitution controls any legislative act repugnant to it; or, that the legislature may alter the constitution by an ordinary act.

Between these alternatives there is no middle ground. The constitution is either a superior, paramount law, unchangeable by ordinary means, or it is on a level with ordinary legislative acts, and, like other acts, is alterable when the legislature shall please to alter it.

If the former part of the alternative be true, then a legislative act contrary to the constitution is not law: if the latter part be true, then written constitutions are absurd attempts, on the part of the people, to limit a power in its own nature illimitable.

Certainly all those who have framed written constitutions contemplate them as forming the fundamental and paramount law of the nation, and consequently, the theory of every such government must be, that an act of the legislature, repugnant to the constitution, is void.

This theory is essentially attached to a written constitution, and is, consequently, to be considered, by this court, as one of the fundamental principles of our society. It is not therefore to be lost sight of in the further consideration of this subject.

If an act of the legislature, repugnant to the constitution, is void, does it, notwithstanding its invalidity, bind the courts, and oblige them to give it effect? Or, in other words, though it be not law, does it constitute a rule as operative as if it was a law? This would be to overthrow in fact what was established in theory; and would seem, at first view, an absurdity too gross to be insisted on. It shall, however, receive a more attentive consideration.

It is emphatically the province and duty of the judicial department to say what the law is. Those who apply the rule to particular cases, must of necessity expound and interpret that rule. If two laws conflict with each other, the courts must decide on the operation of each.

So if a law be in opposition to the constitution; if both the law and the constitution apply to a particular case, so that the court must either decide that case conformably to the law, disregarding the constitution; or conformably to the constitution, disregarding the law; the court must determine which of these conflicting rules governs the case. This is of the very essence of judicial duty.

If, then, the courts are to regard the constitution, and the constitution is superior to any ordinary act of the legislature, the constitution, and not such ordinary act, must govern the case to which they both apply.

Those then who controvert the principle that the constitution is to be considered, in court, as a paramount law, are reduced to the necessity of maintaining that the courts must close their eyes on the constitution, and see only the law.

This doctrine would subvert the very foundation of all written constitutions. It would declare that an act which, according to the principles and theory of our government, is entirely void, is yet, in practice, completely obligatory. It would declare that if the legislature shall do what is expressly forbidden, such act, notwithstanding the express prohibition, is in reality effectual. It would be giving to the legislature a practical and real omnipotence, with the same breath which professes to restrict their powers within narrow limits. It is prescribing limits, and declaring that those limits may be passed at pleasure.

That it thus reduces to nothing what we have deemed the greatest improvement on political institutions—a written constitution—would of itself be sufficient, in America, where written constitutions have been viewed with so much reverence, for rejecting the construction. But the peculiar expressions of the constitution of the United States furnish additional arguments in favour of its rejection.

The judicial power of the United States is extended to all cases arising under the constitution.

Could it be the intention of those who gave this power, to say that in using it the constitution should not be looked into? That a case arising under the constitution should be decided without examining the instrument under which it arises?

This is too extravagant to be maintained.

In some cases, then, the constitution must be looked into by the judges. And if they can open it at all, what part of it are they forbidden to read or to oey?

There are many other parts of the constitution which serve to illustrate this subject.

It is declared that "no tax or duty shall be laid on articles exported from any state." Suppose a duty on the export of cotton, of tobacco, or of flour; and a suit instituted to recover it. Ought judgment to be rendered in such a case? Ought the judges to close their eyes on the constitution, and only see the law?

The constitution declares that "no bill of attainder or ex post facto law shall be passed." If, however, such a bill should be passed, and a person should be prosecuted under it; must the court condemn to death those victims whom the constitution endeavors to preserve?

"No person," says the constitution, "shall be convicted of treason unless on the testimony of two witnesses to the same overt act, or on confession in open court."

Here the language of the constitution is addressed especially to the courts. It prescribes, directly for them, a rule of evidence not to be departed from. If the legislature should change that rule, and declare one witness, or a confession out of court, sufficient for conviction, must the constitutional principle yield to the legislative act?

From these, and many other selections which might be made, it is apparent, that the framers of the constitution contemplated that instrument as a rule for the government of courts, as well as of the legislature. Why otherwise does it direct the judges to take an oath to support it? This oath certainly applies, in an especial manner, to their conduct in their official character. How immoral to impose it on them, if they were to be used as the instruments, and the knowing instruments, for violating what they swear to support!

The oath of office, too, imposed by the legislature, is completely demonstrative of the legislative opinion on this subject. It is in these words: "I do solemnly swear that I will administer justice without respect to persons, and do equal right to the poor and to the rich; and that I will faithfully and impartially discharge all the duties incumbent on me as _____, according to the best of my abilities and understanding, agreeably to the constitution, and laws of the United States." Why does a Judge swear to discharge his duties agreeably the constitution of the United States, if that constitution forms no rule for his government? If it is closed upon him, and cannot be inspected by him?

If such be the real state of things, this is worse than solemn mockery. To prescribe, or to take this oath, becomes equally a crime.

It is also not entirely unworthy of observation that in declaring what shall be the supreme law of the land, the constitution itself is first mentioned; and not the laws of the United States generally, but those only which shall be made in pursuance of the constitution, have that rank.

Thus, the particular phraseology of the constitution of the United States confirms and strengthens the principle, supposed to be essential to all written constitutions, that a law repugnant to the constitution is void; and that courts, as well as other departments, are bound by that instrument.

The rule must be discharged.

The Treaty of Ghent

TREATY OF PEACE AND AMITY BETWEEN HIS BRITANNIC MAJESTY AND THE UNITED STATES OF AMERICA.

His Britannic Majesty and the United States of America desirous of terminating the war which has unhappily subsisted between the two Countries, and of restoring upon principles of perfect reciprocity, Peace, Friendship, and good Understanding between them, have for that purpose appointed their respective Plenipotentiaries, that is to say, His Britannic Majesty on His part has appointed the Right Honourable James Lord Gambier, late Admiral of the White now Admiral of the Red Squadron of His Majesty's Fleet; Henry Goulburn Esquire, a Member of the Imperial Parliament and Under Secretary of State; and William Adams Esquire, Doctor of Civil Laws: And the President of the United States, by and with the advice and consent of the Senate thereof, has appointed John Quincy Adams, James A. Bayard, Henry Clay, Jonathan Russell, and Albert Gallatin, Citizens of the United States; who, after a reciprocal communication of their respective Full Powers, have agreed upon the following Articles.

ARTICLE THE FIRST.

There shall be a firm and universal Peace between His Britannic Majesty and the United States, and between their respective Countries, Territories, Cities, Towns, and People of every degree without exception of places or persons. All hostilities both by sea and land shall cease as soon as this Treaty shall have been ratified by both parties as hereinafter mentioned. All territory, places, and possessions whatsoever taken by either party from the other during the war, or which may be taken after the signing of this Treaty, excepting only the Islands hereinafter mentioned, shall be restored without delay and without causing any destruction or carrying away any of the Artillery or other public property originally captured in the said forts or places, and which shall remain therein upon the Exchange of the Ratifications of this Treaty, or any Slaves or other private property; And all Archives, Records, Deeds, and Papers, either of a public nature or belonging to private persons, which in the course of the war may have fallen into the hands of the Officers of either party, shall be, as far as may be practicable, forthwith restored and delivered to the proper authorities and persons to whom they respectively belong. Such of the Islands in the Bay of Passamaquoddy as are claimed by both parties shall remain in the possession of the party in whose occupation they may be at the time of the Exchange of the Ratifications of this Treaty until the decision respecting the title to the said Islands shall have been made in conformity with the fourth Article of this Treaty. No disposition made by this Treaty as to such possession of the Islands and territories claimed by both parties shall in any manner whatever be construed to affect the right of either.

ARTICLE THE SECOND.

Immediately after the ratifications of this Treaty by both parties as hereinafter mentioned, orders shall be sent to the Armies, Squadrons, Officers, Subjects, and Citizens of the two Powers to cease from all hostilities: and to prevent all causes of complaint which might arise on account of the prizes which may be taken at sea after the said Ratifications of this Treaty, it is reciprocally agreed that all vessels and effects which may be taken after the space of twelve days from the said Ratifications upon all parts of the Coast of North America from the Latitude of twenty three degrees North to the Latitude of fifty degrees North, and as far Eastward in the Atlantic Ocean as the thirty sixth degree of West Longitude from the Meridian of Greenwich, shall be restored on each side:—that the time shall be thirty days in all other parts of the Atlantic Ocean North of the Equinoctial Line or Equator:—and the same time for the British and Irish Channels, for the Gulf of Mexico, and all parts of the West Indies:—forty days for the North Seas for the Baltic, and for all parts of the Mediterranean—sixty days for the Atlantic Ocean South of the Equator as far as the Latitude of the Cape of Good Hope—ninety days for every other part of the world South of the Equator, and one hundred and twenty days for all other parts of the world without exception.

ARTICLE THE THIRD.

All Prisoners of war taken on either side as well by land as by sea shall be restored as soon as practicable after the Ratifications of this Treaty as hereinafter mentioned on their paying the debts which they may have contracted during their captivity. The two Contracting Parties respectively engage to discharge in specie the advances which may have been made by the other for the sustenance and maintenance of such prisoners.

ARTICLE THE FOURTH.

Whereas it was stipulated by the second Article in the Treaty of Peace of one thousand seven hundred and eighty three between His Britannic Majesty and the United States of America that the boundary of the United States should comprehend "all Islands within twenty leagues of any part of the shores of the United States and lying between lines to be drawn due East from the points where the aforesaid boundaries between Nova Scotia on the one part and East Florida on the other shall respectively touch the Bay of Fundy and the Atlantic Ocean, excepting such Islands as now are or heretofore have been within the limits of Nova Scotia, and whereas the several Islands in the Bay of Passamaquoddy, which is part of the Bay of Fundy, and the Island of Grand Menan in the said Bay of Fundy, are claimed by the United States as being comprehended within their aforesaid boundaries, which said Islands are claimed as belonging to His Britannic Majesty as having been at the time of and previous to the aforesaid Treaty of one thousand seven hundred and eighty three within the limits of the Province of Nova Scotia: In order therefore finally to decide upon these claims it is agreed that they shall be referred to two Commissioners to be appointed in the following manner: viz: One Commissioner shall be appointed by His Britannic Majesty and one by the President of the United States, by and with the advice and consent of the Senate thereof, and the said two Commissioners so appointed shall be sworn impartially to examine and decide upon the said claims according to such evidence as shall be laid before them on the part of His Britannic Majesty and of the United States respectively. The said Commissioners shall meet at St Andrews in the Province of New Brunswick, and shall have power to adjourn to such other place or places as they shall think fit. The said Commissioners shall by a declaration or report under their hands and seals decide to which of the two Contracting parties the several Islands aforesaid do respectely belong in conformity with the true intent of the said Treaty of Peace of one thousand seven hundred and eighty three. And if the said Commissioners shall agree in their decision both parties shall consider such decision as final and conclusive. It is further agreed that in the event of the two Commissioners differing upon all or any of the matters so referred to them, or in the event of both or either of the said Commissioners refusing or declining or wilfully omitting to act as such, they shall make jointly or separately a report or reports as well to the Government of His Britannic Majesty as to that of the United States, stating in detail the points on which they differ, and the grounds upon which their respective opinions have been formed, or the grounds upon which they or either of them have so refused declined or omitted to act. And His Britannic Majesty and the Government of the United States hereby agree to refer the report or reports of the said Commissioners to some friendly Sovereign or State to be then named for that purpose, and who shall be requested to decide on the differences which may be stated in the said report or reports, or upon the report of one Commissioner together with the grounds upon which the other Commissioner shall have refused, declined or omitted to act as the case may be. And if the Commissioner so refusing, declining, or omitting to act, shall also wilfully omit to state the grounds upon which he has so done in such manner that the said statement may be referred to such friendly Sovereign or State together with the report of such other Commissioner, then such Sovereign or State shall decide ex parse upon the said report alone. And His Britannic Majesty and the Government of the United States engage to consider the decision of such friendly Sovereign or State to be final and conclusive on all the matters so referred.

ARTICLE THE FIFTH.

Whereas neither that point of the Highlands lying due North from the source of the River St Croix, and designated in the former Treaty of Peace between the two Powers as the North West Angle of Nova Scotia, nor the North Westernmost head of Connecticut River has yet been ascertained; and whereas that part of the boundary line between the Dominions of the two Powers which extends from the source of the River st Croix directly North to the above mentioned North West Angle of Nova Scotia, thence along the said Highlands which divide those Rivers that empty themselves into the River St Lawrence from those which fall into the Atlantic Ocean to the North Westernmost head of Connecticut River, thence down along the middle of that River to the forty fifth degree of North Latitude, thence by a line due West on said latitude until it strikes the River Iroquois or Cataraquy, has not yet been surveyed: it is agreed that for these several purposes two Commissioners shall be appointed, sworn, and authorized to act exactly in the manner directed with respect to those mentioned in the next preceding Article unless otherwise specified in the present Article. The said Commissioners shall meet at se Andrews in the Province of New Brunswick, and shall have power to adjourn to such other place or places as they shall think fit. The said Commissioners shall have power to ascertain and determine the points above mentioned in conformity with the provisions of the said Treaty of Peace of one thousand seven hundred and eighty three, and shall cause the boundary aforesaid from the source of the River St Croix to the River Iroquois or Cataraquy to be surveyed and marked according to the said provisions. The said Commissioners shall make a map of the said boundary, and annex to it a declaration under their hands and seals certifying it to be the true Map of the said boundary, and particularizing the latitude and longitude of the North West Angle of Nova Scotia, of the North Westernmost head of Connecticut River, and of such other points of the said boundary as they may deem proper. And both parties agree to consider such map and declaration as finally and conclusively fixing the said boundary. And in the event of the said two Commissioners differing, or both, or either of them refusing, declining, or wilfully omitting to act, such reports, declarations, or statements shall be made by them or either of them, and such reference to a friendly Sovereign or State shall be made in all respects as in the latter part of the fourth Article is contained, and in as full a manner as if the same was herein repeated.

ARTICLE THE SIXTH.

Whereas by the former Treaty of Peace that portion of the boundary of the United States from the point where the fortyfifth degree of North Latitude strikes the River Iroquois or Cataraquy to the Lake Superior was declared to be "along the middle of said River into Lake Ontario, through the middle of said Lake until it strikes the communication by water between that Lake and Lake Erie, thence along the middle of said communication into Lake Erie, through the

middle of said Lake until it arrives at the water communication into the Lake Huron; thence through the middle of said Lake to the water communication between that Lake and Lake Superior:" and whereas doubts have arisen what was the middle of the said River, Lakes, and water communications, and whether certain Islands lying in the same were within the Dominions of His Britannic Majesty or of the United States: In order therefore finally to decide these doubts, they shall be referred to two Commissioners to be appointed, sworn, and authorized to act exactly in the manner directed with respect to those mentioned in the next preceding Article unless otherwise specified in this present Article. The said Commissioners shall meet in the first instance at Albany in the State of New York, and shall have power to adjourn to such other place or places as they shall think fit. The said Commissioners shall by a Report or Declaration under their hands and seals, designate the boundary through the said River, Lakes, and water communications, and decide to which of the two Contracting parties the several Islands lying within the said Rivers, Lakes, and water communications, do respectively belong in conformity with the true intent of the said Treaty of one thousand seven hundred and eighty three. And both parties agree to consider such designation and decision as final and conclusive. And in the event of the said two Commissioners differing or both or either of them refusing, declining, or wilfully omitting to act, such reports, declarations, or statements shall be made by them or either of them, and such reference to a friendly Sovereign or State shall be made in all respects as in the latter part of the fourth Article is contained, and in as full a manner as if the same was herein repeated.

ARTICLE THE SEVENTH.

It is further agreed that the said two last mentioned Commissioners after they shall have executed the duties assigned to them in the preceding Article, shall be, and they are hereby, authorized upon their oaths impartially to fix and determine according to the true intent of the said Treaty of Peace of one thousand seven hundred and eighty three, that part of the boundary between the dominions of the two Powers, which extends from the water communication between Lake Huron and Lake Superior to the most North Western point of the Lake of the Woods;—to decide to which of the two Parties the several Islands lying in the Lakes, water communications, and Rivers forming the said boundary do respectively belong in conformity with the true intent of the said Treaty of Peace of one thousand seven hundred and eighty three, and to cause such parts of the said boundary as require it to be surveyed and marked. The said Commissioners shall by a Report or declaration under their hands and seals, designate the boundary aforesaid, state their decision on the points thus referred to them, and particularize the Latitude and Longitude of the most North Western point of the Lake of the Woods, and of such other parts of the said boundary as they may deem proper. And both parties agree to consider such designation and decision as final and conclusive. And in the event of the said two Commissioners differing, or both or either of them refusing, declining, or wilfully omitting to act, such reports, declarations or statements shall be made by them or either of them, and such reference to a friendly Sovereign or State shall be made in all respects as in the latter part of the fourth Article is contained, and in as full a manner as if the same was herein revealed.

ARTICLE THE EIGHTH.

The several Boards of two Commissioners mentioned in the four preceding Articles shall respectively have power to appoint a Secretary, and to employ such Surveyors or other persons as they shall judge necessary. Duplicates of all their respective reports, declarations, statements, and decisions, and of their accounts, and of the Journal of their proceedings shall be delivered by them to the Agents of His Britannic Majesty and to the Agents of the United States, who may be respectively appointed and authorized to manage the business on behalf of their respective Governments. The said Commissioners shall be respectively paid in such manner as shall be agreed between the two contracting parties, such agreement being to be settled at the time of the Exchange of the Ratifications of this Treaty. And all other expenses attending the said Commissions shall be defrayed equally by the two parties. And in the case of death, sickness, resignation, or necessary absence, the place of every such Commissioner respectively shall be supplied in the same manner as such Commissioner was first appointed; and the new Commissioner shall take the same oath or affirmation and do the same duties. It is further agreed between the two contracting parties that in case any of the Islands mentioned in any of the preceding Articles, which were in the possession of one of the parties prior to the commencement of the present war between the two Countries, should by the decision of any of the Boards of Commissioners aforesaid, or of the Sovereign or State so referred to, as in the four next preceding Articles contained, fall within the dominions of the other party, all grants of land made previous to the commencement of the war by the party having had such possession, shall be as valid as if such Island or Islands had by such decision or decisions been adjudged to be within the dominions of the party having had such possession.

ARTICLE THE NINTH.

The United States of America engage to put an end immediately after the Ratification of the present Treaty to hostilities with all the Tribes or Nations of Indians with whom they may be at war at the time of such Ratification, and forthwith to restore to such Tribes or Nations respectively all the possessions, rights, and privileges which they may have enjoyed or been entitled to in one thousand eight hundred and eleven previous to such hostilities. Provided always that such Tribes or Nations shall agree to desist from all hostilities against the United States of America, their Citizens, and Subjects upon the Ratification of the present Treaty being notified to such Tribes or Nations, and shall so desist accordingly. And His Britannic Majesty engages on his part to put an end immediately after the Ratification of the present Treaty to hostilities with all the Tribes or Nations of Indians with whom He may be at war at the time of such Ratification, and forthwith to restore to such Tribes or Nations respectively all the possessions, rights, and privileges, which they may have enjoyed or been entitled to in one thousand eight hundred and eleven previous to such hostilities. Provided always that such Tribes or Nations shall agree to desist from all hostilities against His Britannic Majesty and His Subjects upon the Ratification of the present Treaty being notified to such Tribes or Nations, and shall so desist accordingly.

ARTICLE THE TENTH.

Whereas the Traffic in Slaves is irreconcilable with the principles of humanity and Justice, and whereas both His Majesty and the United States are desirous of continuing their efforts to promote its entire abolition, it is hereby agreed that both the contracting parties shall use their best endeavours to accomplish so desirable an object.

ARTICLE THE ELEVENTH.

This Treaty when the same shall have been ratified on both sides without alteration by either of the contracting parties, and the Ratifications mutually exchanged, shall be binding on both parties, and the Ratifications shall be exchanged at Washington in the space of four months from this day or sooner if practicable. In faith whereof, We the respective Plenipotentiaries have signed this Treaty, and have hereunto affixed our Seals.

Done in triplicate at Ghent the twenty fourth day of December one thousand eight hundred and fourteen.

GAMBIER. [Seal]
HENRY GOULBURN [Seal]
WILLIAM ADAMS [Seal]
JOHN QUINCY ADAMS [Seal]
J. A. BAYARD [Seal]
H. CLAY. [Seal]
JON. RUSSELL [Seal]
ALBERT GALLATIN [Seal]

McCulloch v. Maryland

CHIEF JUSTICE MARSHALL DELIVERED THE OPINION OF THE COURT.

In the case now to be determined, the defendant, a sovereign State, denies the obligation of a law enacted by the legislature of the Union, and the plaintiff, on his part, contests the validity of an act which has been passed by the legislature of that State. The constitution of our country, in its most interesting and vital parts, is to be considered; the conflicting powers of the government of the Union and of its members, as marked in that constitution, are to be discussed; and an opinion given, which may essentially influence the great operations of the government. No tribunal can approach such a question without a deep sense of its importance, and of the awful responsibility involved in its decision. But it must be decided peacefully, or remain a source of hostile legislation, perhaps of hostility of a still more serious nature; and if it is to be so decided, by this tribunal alone can the decision be made. On the Supreme Court of the United States has the constitution of our country devolved this important duty.

The first question made in the cause is, has Congress power to incorporate a bank?

It has been truly said that this can scarcely be considered as an open question, entirely unprejudiced by the former proceedings of the nation respecting it. The principle now contested was introduced at a very early period of our history, has been recognized by many successive legislatures, and has been acted upon by the judicial department, in cases of peculiar delicacy, as a law of undoubted obligation. . . .

The power now contested was exercised by the first Congress elected under the present constitution. The bill for incorporating the bank of the United States did not steal upon an unsuspecting legislature, and pass unobserved. Its principle was completely understood, and was opposed with equal zeal and ability. After being resisted, first in the fair and open field of debate, and afterwards in the executive cabinet, with as much persevering talent as any measure has ever experienced, and being supported by arguments which convinced minds as pure and as intelligent as this country can boast, it became a law. The original act was permitted to expire; but a short experience of the embarrassments to which the refusal to revive it exposed the government, convinced those who were most prejudiced against the measure of its necessity, and induced the passage of the present law. It would require no ordinary share of intrepidity to assert that a measure adopted under these circumstances was a bold and plain usurpation, to which the constitution gave no countenance.

These observations belong to the cause; but they are not made under the impression that, were the question entirely new, the law would be found irreconcilable with the constitution.

In discussing this question, the counsel for the State of Maryland have deemed it of some importance, in the construction of the constitution, to consider that instrument not as emanating from the people, but as the act of sovereign and independent States. The powers of the general government, it has been said, are delegated by the States, who alone are truly sovereign; and must be exercised in subordination to the States, who alone possess supreme dominion.

It would be difficult to sustain this proposition. The Convention which framed the constitution was indeed elected by the State legislatures. But the instrument, when it came from their hands, was a mere proposal, without obligation, or pretensions to it. It was reported to the then existing Congress of the United States, with a request that it might "be submitted to a convention of delegates, chosen in each State by the people thereof, under the recommendation of its legislature, for their assent and ratification." This mode of proceeding was adopted; and by the convention, by Congress, and by the State legislatures, the instrument was submitted to the people. They acted upon it in the only manner in which they can act safely, effectively, and wisely, on such a subject, by assembling in convention. It is true, they assembled in their several States—and where else should they have assembled? No political dreamer was ever wild enough to think of breaking down the lines which separate the States, and of compounding the American people into one common mass. Of consequence, when they act, they act in their States. But the measures they adopt do not, on that account, cease to be the measures of the people themselves, or become the measures of the State governments.

From these conventions the constitution derives its whole authority. The government proceeds directly from the people; is "ordained and established" in the name of the people; and is declared to be ordained, "in order to form a more perfect union, establish justice, ensure domestic tranquility, and secure the blessings of liberty to themselves and to their posterity." The assent of the States, in their sovereign capacity, is implied in calling a convention, and thus submitting that instrument to the people. But the people were at perfect liberty to accept or reject it; and their act was final. It required not the affirmance, and could not be negatived, by the State governments. The constitution, when thus adopted, was of complete obligation, and bound the State sovereignties. . . . of this fact on the case), is, emphatically, and truly, a government of the people. In form and in substance it emanates from them. Its powers are granted by them, and are to be exercised directly on them, and for their benefit.

This government is acknowledged by all to be one of enumerated powers. The principle, that it can exercise only the powers granted to it, [is] now universally admitted. But the question respecting the extent of the powers actually granted, is perpetually arising, and will probably continue to arise, as long as our system shall exist. . . .

Among the enumerated powers, we do not find that of establishing a bank or creating a corporation. But there is no phrase in the instrument which, like the articles of confederation, excludes incidental or implied powers; and which requires that everything granted shall be expressly and minutely described. Even the 10th amendment, which was framed for the purpose of quieting the excessive jealousies which had been excited, omits the word "expressly," and declares only that the powers "not delegated to the United States, nor prohibited to the States, are reserved to the States or to the people"; thus leaving the question, whether the particular power which may become the subject of contest has been delegated to the one government, or prohibited to the other, to depend on a fair construction of the whole instrument. The men who drew and adopted this amendment had experienced the embarrassments resulting from the insertion of this word in the articles of confederation, and probably omitted it to avoid those embarrassments. A constitution, to contain an accurate detail of all the subdivisions of which its great powers will admit, and of all the means by which they may be carried into execution, would partake of the prolixity of a legal code, and could scarcely be embraced by the human mind. It would probably never be understood by the public. Its nature, therefore, requires, that only its great outlines should be marked, its

important objects designated, and the minor ingredients which compose those objects be deduced from the nature of the objects themselves. That this idea was entertained by the framers of the American constitution, is not only to be inferred from the nature of the instrument, but from the language. Why else were some of the limitations, found in the ninth section of the 1st article, introduced? It is also, in some degree, warranted by their having omitted to use any restrictive term which might prevent its receiving a fair and just interpretation. In considering this question, then, we must never forget that it is a constitution we are expounding.

Although, among the enumerated powers of government, we do not find the word "bank," or "incorporation," we find the great powers to lay and collect taxes; to borrow money; to regulate commerce; to declare and conduct a war; and to raise and support armies and navies. The sword and the purse, all the external relations, and no inconsiderable portion of the industry of the nation, are entrusted to its government. It can never be pretended that these vast powers draw after them others of inferior importance, merely because they are inferior. Such an idea can never be advanced. But it may with great reason be contended, that a government, entrusted with such ample powers, on the due execution of which the happiness and prosperity of the nation so vitally depends, must also be entrusted with ample means for their execution. The power being given, it is the interest of the nation to facilitate its execution. It can never be their interest, and cannot be presumed to have been their intention, to clog and embarrass can never be their interest, and cannot be presumed to have been their intention, to clog and embarrass its execution by withholding the most appropriate means. . . . require it) which would impute to the framers of that instrument, when granting these powers for the public good, the intention of impeding their exercise by withholding a choice of means? If, indeed, such be the mandate of the constitution, we have only to obey; but that instrument does not profess to enumerate the means by which the powers it confers may be executed; nor does it prohibit the creation of a corporation, if the existence of such a being be essential to the beneficial exercise of those powers. It is, then, the subject of fair inquiry, how far such means may be employed.

It is not denied, that the powers given to the government imply the ordinary means of execution. That, for example, of raising revenue, and applying it to national purposes, is admitted to imply the power of conveying money from place to place, as the exigencies of the nation may require, and of employing the usual means of conveyance. But it is denied that the government has its choice of means; or, that it may employ the most convenient means, if, to employ them, it be necessary to erect a corporation. . . .

The government which has a right to do an act, and has imposed on it the duty of performing that act, must, according to the dictates of reason, be allowed to select the means; and those who contend that it may not select any appropriate means, that one particular mode of effecting the object is excepted, take upon themselves the burden of establishing that exception. . . . The power of creating a corporation, though appertaining to sovereignty, is not like the power of making war, or levying taxes, or of regulating commerce, a great substantive and independent power, which cannot be implied as incidental to other powers, or used as a means of executing them. It is never the end for which other powers are exercised, but a means by which other objects are accomplished. . . . The power of creating a corporation is never used for its own sake, but for the purpose of effecting something else. No sufficient reason is, therefore, perceived, why it may not pass as incidental to those powers which are expressly given, if it be a direct mode of executing them.

But the constitution of the United States has not left the right of Congress to employ the necessary means, for the execution of the powers conferred on the government, to general reasoning. To its enumeration of powers is added that of making "all laws which shall be necessary and proper for carrying into execution the foregoing powers, and all other powers vested by this constitution, in the government of the United States, or in any department thereof."

The counsel for the State of Maryland have urged various arguments, to prove that this clause, though in terms a grant of power, is not so in effect; but is really restrictive of the general right, which might otherwise be implied, of selecting means for executing the enumerated powers. . . .

Almost all compositions contain words, which, taken in their rigorous sense, would convey a meaning different from that which is obviously intended. It is essential to just construction, that many words which import something excessive should be understood in a more mitigated sense—in that sense which common usage justifies. The word "necessary" is of this description. It has not a fixed character peculiar to itself. It admits of all degrees of comparison; and

is often connected with other words, which increase or diminish the impression the mind receives of the urgency it imports. A thing may be necessary, very necessary, absolutely or indispensably necessary. To no mind would the same idea be conveyed by these several phrases. This comment on the word is well illustrated by the passage cited at the bar, from the 20th section of the 1st article of the constitution. It is, we think, impossible to compare the sentence which prohibits a State from laying "imposts, or duties on imports or exports, except what may be absolutely necessary for executing its inspection laws," with that which authorizes Congress "to make all laws which shall be necessary and proper for carrying into execution" the powers of the general government, without feeling a conviction that the convention understood itself to change materially the meaning of the word "necessary," by prefixing the word "absolutely." This word, then, like others, is used in various senses; and, in its construction, the subject, the context, the intention of the person using them, are all to be taken into view.

Let this be done in the case under consideration. The subject is the execution of those great powers on which the welfare of a nation essentially depends. It must have been the intention of those who gave these powers, to insure, as far as human prudence could insure, their beneficial execution. This could not be done by confiding the choice of means to such narrow limits as not to leave it in the power of Congress to adopt any which might be appropriate, and which were conducive to the end. This provision is made in a constitution intended to endure for ages to come, and, consequently, to be adapted to the various crises of human affairs. To have prescribed the means by which government should, in all future time, execute its powers, would have been to change, entirely, the character of the instrument, and give it the properties of a legal code. It would have been an unwise attempt to provide, by immutable rules, for exigencies which, if foreseen at all, must have been seen dimly, and which can be best provided for as they occur. To have declared that the best means shall not be used, but those alone without which the power given would be nugatory, would have been to deprive the legislature of the capacity to avail itself of experience, to exercise its reason, and to accommodate its legislation to circumstances. If we apply this principle of construction to any of the powers of the government, we shall find it so pernicious in its operation that we shall be compelled to discard it. . . .

The result of the most careful and attentive consideration bestowed upon this clause is, that if it does not enlarge, it cannot be construed to restrain the powers of Congress, or to impair the rights of the legislature to exercise its best judgment in the selection of measures to carry into execution the constitutional powers of the government. If no other motive for its insertion can be suggested, a sufficient one is found in the desire to remove all doubts respecting the right to legislate on that vast mass of incidental powers which must be involved in the constitution, if that instrument be not a splendid bauble.

We admit, as all must admit, that the powers of the government are limited, and that its limits are not to be transcended. But we think the sound construction of the constitution must allow to the national legislature that discretion, with respect to the means by which the powers it confers are to be carried into execution, which will enable that body to perform the high duties assigned to it, in the manner most beneficial to the people. Let the end be legitimate, let it be within the scope of the constitution, and all means which are appropriate, which are plainly adapted to that end, which are not prohibited, but consist with the letter and spirit of the constitution, are constitutional. . . .

Should Congress, in the execution of its powers, adopt measures which are prohibited by the constitution; or should Congress, under the pretext of executing its powers, pass laws for the accomplishment of objects not entrusted to the government; it would become the painful duty of this tribunal, should a case requiring such a decision come before it, to say that such an act was not the law of the land. But where the law is not prohibited, and is really calculated to effect any of the objects entrusted to the government, to undertake here to inquire into the degree of its necessity, would be to pass the line which circumscribes the judicial department, and to tread on legislative ground. This court disclaims all pretensions to such a power.

After this declaration, it can scarcely be necessary to say that the existence of State banks can have no possible influence on the question. No trace is to be found in the constitution of an intention to create a dependence of the government of the Union on those of the States, for the execution of the great powers assigned to it. Its means are adequate to its ends; and on those means alone was it expected to rely for the accomplishment of its ends. To impose on it the necessity of resorting to means which it cannot control, which another government may furnish or withhold, would render its course precarious, the result of its measures uncertain, and create a dependence on other governments, which might disappoint its most important designs, and is incompatible with the language of the constitution. But were it otherwise, the choice of means implies a right to choose a national bank in preference to State banks, and Congress alone can make the election.

After the most deliberate consideration, it is the unanimous and decided opinion of this Court, that the act to incorporate the Bank of the United States is a law made in pursuance of the constitution, and is a part of the supreme law of the land. . . .

It being the opinion of the Court, that the act incorporating the bank is constitutional; and that the power of establishing a branch in the State of Maryland might be properly exercised by the bank itself, we proceed to inquire—

2. Whether the State of Maryland may, without violating the constitution, tax that branch?

That the power of taxation is one of vital importance; that it is retained by the States; that it is not abridged by the grant of a similar power to the government of the Union; that it is to be concurrently exercised by the two governments: are truths which have never been denied. But, such is the paramount character of the constitution, that its capacity to withdraw any subject from the action of even this power, is admitted. The States are expressly forbidden to lay any duties on imports or exports, except what may be absolutely necessary for executing their inspection laws. If the obligation of this prohibition must be conceded, the same paramount character would seem to restrain, as it certainly may restrain, a State from such other exercise of this power; as is in its nature incompatible with, and repugnant to, the constitutional laws of the Union. . . .

On this ground the counsel for the bank place its claim to be exempted from the power of a State to tax its operations. There is no express provision for the case, but the claim has been sustained on a principle which so entirely pervades the constitution, is so intermixed with the materials which compose it, so interwoven with its web, so blended with its texture, as to be incapable of being separated from it, without rending it into shreds.

This great principle is, that the constitution and the laws made in pursuance thereof are supreme; that they control the constitution and laws of the respective States, and cannot be controlled by them. From this, which may be almost termed an axiom, other propositions are deduced as corollaries, on the truth or error of which, and on their application to this case, the cause has been supposed to depend. These are, 1st. that a power to create implies a power to preserve. 2nd. That a power to destroy, if wielded by a different hand, is hostile to, and incompatible with these powers to create and to preserve. 3d. That where this repugnancy exists, that authority which is supreme must control, not yield to that over which it is supreme. . . .

That the power of taxing by the States may be exercised so as to destroy it, is too obvious to be denied. But taxation is said to be an absolute power, which acknowledges no other limits than those expressly prescribed in the constitution, and like sovereign power of every other description, is trusted to the discretion of those who use it. But the very terms of this argument admit that the sovereignty of the State, in the article of taxation itself, is subordinate to, and may be controlled by, the constitution of the United States. How far it has been controlled by that instrument must be a question of construction. In making this construction, no principle not declared, can be admissible, which would defeat the legitimate operations of a supreme government. It is of the very essence of supremacy to remove all obstacles to its action within its own sphere, and so to modify every power vested in subordinate governments, as to exempt its own operations from their own influence. This effect need not be stated in terms. It is so involved in the declaration of supremacy, so necessarily implied in it, that the expression of it could not make it more certain. We must, therefore, keep it in view while construing the constitution.

The argument on the part of the State of Maryland is, not that the States may directly resist a law of Congress, but that they may exercise their acknowledged powers upon it, and that the constitution leaves them this right in the confidence that they will not abuse it.

Before we proceed to examine this argument, and to subject it to the test of the constitution, we must be permitted to bestow a few considerations on the nature and extent of this original right of taxation, which is acknowledged to remain with the States. It is admitted that the power of taxing the people and their property is essential to the very existence of government, and may be legitimately exercised on the objects to which it is applicable, to the utmost extent to which the government may choose to carry it. The only security against the abuse of this power, is found in the structure of the government itself. In imposing a tax the legislature acts upon its constituents. . . .

The sovereignty of a State extends to everything which exists by its own authority, or is so introduced by its permission; but does it extend to those means which are employed by Congress to carry into execution powers conferred on that body by the people of the United States? We think it demonstrable that it does not. Those powers are not given by the people of a single State. They are given by the people of the United States, to a government whose laws, made in pursuance of the constitution, are declared to be supreme. Consequently, the people of a single State cannot confer a sovereignty which will extend over them.

If we measure the power of taxation residing in a State, by the extent of sovereignty which the people of a single State possess, and can confer on its government, we have an intelligible standard, applicable to every case to which the power may be applied. We have a principle which leaves the power of taxing the people and property of a State unimpaired; which leaves to a State the command of all its resources, and which places beyond its reach, all those powers which are conferred by the people of the United States on the government of the Union, and all those means which are given for the purpose of carrying those powers into execution. We have a principle which is safe for the States, and safe for the Union. We are relieved, as we ought to be, from clashing sovereignty; from interfering powers; from a repugnancy between a right in one government to pull down what there is an acknowledged right in another to build up; from the incompatibility of a right in one government to destroy what there is a right in another to preserve. We are not driven to the perplexing inquiry, so unfit for the judicial department, what degree of taxation is the legitimate use, and what degree may amount to the abuse of the power. The attempt to use it on the means employed by the government of the Union, in pursuance of the constitution, is itself an abuse, because it is the usurpation of a power which the people of a single State cannot give.

We find, then, on just theory, a total failure of this original right to tax the means employed by the government of the Union, for the execution of its powers. The right never existed, and the question whether it has been surrendered, cannot arise.

But, waiving this theory for the present, let us resume the inquiry, whether this power can be exercised by the respective States, consistently with a fair construction of the constitution?

That the power to tax involves the power to destroy; that the power to destroy may defeat and render useless the power to create; that there is a plain repugnance, in conferring on one government a power to control the constitutional measures of another, which other, with respect to those very measures, is declared to be supreme over that which exerts the control, are propositions not to be denied. But all inconsistencies are to be reconciled by the magic of the word CONFIDENCE. Taxation, it is said, does not necessarily and unavoidably destroy. To carry it to the excess of destruction would be an abuse, to presume which, would banish that confidence which is essential to all government.

But is this a case of confidence? Would the people of any one State trust those of another with a power to control the most insignificant operations of their State government? We know they would not. Why, then, should we suppose that the people of any one State should be willing to trust those of another with a power to control the operations of a government to which they have confided their most important and most valuable interests? In the legislature of the Union alone, are all represented. The legislature of the Union alone, therefore, can be trusted by the people with the power of controlling measures which concern all, in the confidence that it will not be abused. This, then, is not a case of confidence, and we must consider it as it really is.

If we apply the principle for which the State of Maryland contends, to the constitution generally, we shall find it capable of changing totally the character of that instrument. We shall find it capable of arresting all the measures of the government, and of prostrating it at the foot of the States. The American people have declared their constitution, and the laws made in pursuance thereof, to be supreme; but this principle would transfer the supremacy, in fact, to the States.

If the States may tax one instrument, employed by the government in the execution of its powers, they may tax any and every other instrument. They may tax the mail; they may tax the mint; they may tax patent rights; they may tax the papers of the custom house; they may tax judicial process; they may tax all the means employed by the government, to an excess which would defeat all the ends of government. This was not intended by the American people. They did not design to make their government dependent on the States. . . .

The Court has bestowed on this subject its most deliberate consideration. The result is a conviction that the States have no power, by taxation or otherwise, to retard, impede, burden, or in any manner control, the operations of the constitutional laws enacted by Congress to carry into execution the powers vested in the general government. This is, we think, the unavoidable consequence of that supremacy which the constitution has declared.

We are unanimously of opinion, that the law passed by the legislature of Maryland, imposing a tax on the Bank of the United States, is unconstitutional and void.

This opinion does not deprive the States of any resources which they originally possessed. It does not extend to a tax paid by the real property of the bank, in common with the other real property within the State, nor to a tax imposed on the interest which the citizens of Maryland may hold in this institution, in common with other property of the same description throughout the State. But this is a tax on the operations of the bank, and is, consequently, a tax on the operation of an instrument employed by the government of the Union to carry its powers into execution. Such a tax must be unconstitutional.

The Missouri Compromise

An Act to authorize the people of the Missouri territory to form a constitution and state government, and for the admission of such state into the Union on an equal footing with the original states, and to prohibit slavery in certain territories.

Be it enacted by the Senate and House of Representatives of the United States of America, in Congress assembled, That the inhabitants of that portion of the Missouri territory included within the boundaries herein after designated, be, and they are hereby, authorized to form for themselves a constitution and state government, and to assume such name as they shall deem proper; and the said state, when formed, shall be admitted into the Union, upon an equal footing with the original states, in all respects whatsoever.

SEC. 2. And be it further enacted, That the said state shall consist of all the territory included within the following boundaries, to wit: Beginning in the middle of the Mississippi river, on the parallel of thirty-six degrees of north latitude; thence west, along that parallel of latitude, to the St. Francois river; thence up, and following the course of that river, in the middle of the main channel thereof, to the parallel of latitude of thirty-six degrees and thirty minutes; thence west, along the same, to a point where the said parallel is intersected by a meridian line passing through the middle of the mouth of the Kansas river, where the same empties into the Missouri river, thence, from the point aforesaid north, along the said meridian line, to the intersection of the parallel of latitude which passes through the rapids of the river Des Moines, making the said line to correspond with the Indian boundary line; thence east, from the point of intersection last aforesaid, along the said parallel of latitude, to the middle of the channel of the main fork of the said river Des Moines; thence down arid along the middle of the main channel of the said river Des Moines, to the mouth of the same, where it empties into the Mississippi river; thence, due east, to the middle of the main channel of the Mississippi river; thence down, and following the course of the Mississippi river, in the middle of the main channel thereof, to the place of beginning: Provided, The said state shall ratify the boundaries aforesaid. And provided also, That the said state shall have concurrent jurisdiction on the river Mississippi, and every other river bordering on the said state so far as the said rivers shall form a common boundary to the said state; and any other state or states, now or hereafter to be formed and bounded by the same, such rivers to be common to both; and that the river Mississippi, and the navigable rivers and waters leading into the same, shall be common highways, and for ever free, as well to the inhabitants of the said state as to other citizens of the United States, without any tax, duty impost, or toll, therefor, imposed by the said state.

SEC. 3. And be it further enacted, That all free white male citizens of the United States, who shall have arrived at the age of twenty-one years, and have resided in said territory: three months previous to the day of election, and all other persons qualified to vote for representatives to the general assembly of the said territory, shall be qualified to be elected and they are hereby qualified and authorized to vote, and choose representatives to form a convention, who shall be apportioned amongst the several counties as follows:

From the county of Howard, five representatives. From the county of Cooper, three representatives. From the county of Montgomery, two representatives. From the county of Pike, one representative. From the county of Lincoln, one representative. From the county of St. Charles, three representatives. From the county of Franklin, one representative. From the county of St. Louis, eight representatives. From the county of Jefferson, one representative. From the county of Washington, three representatives. From the county of St. Genevieve, four representatives. From the county of Madison, one representative. From the county of Cape Girardeau, five representatives. From the county of New Madrid, two representatives. From the county of Wayne, and that portion of the county of Lawrence which falls within the boundaries herein designated, one representative.

And the election for the representatives aforesaid shall be holden on the first Monday, and two succeeding days of May next, throughout the several counties aforesaid in the said territory, and shall be, in every respect, held and conducted in the same manner, and under the same regulations as is prescribed by the laws of the said territory regulating elections therein for members of the general assembly, except that the returns of the election in that portion of Lawrence county included in the boundaries aforesaid, shall be made to the county of Wayne, as is provided in other cases under the laws of said territory.

SEC. 4. And be it further enacted, That the members of the convention thus duly elected, shall be, and they are hereby authorized to meet at the seat of government of said territory on the second Monday of the month of June next; and the said convention, when so assembled, shall have power and authority to adjourn to any other place in the said territory, which to them shall seem best for the convenient transaction of their business; and which convention, when so met, shall first determine by a majority of the whole number elected, whether it be, or be not, expedient at that time to form a constitution and state government for the people within the said territory, as included within the boundaries above designated; and if it be deemed expedient, the convention shall be, and hereby is, authorized to form a constitution and state government; or, if it be deemed more expedient, the said convention shall provide by ordinance for electing representatives to form a constitution or frame of government; which said representatives shall be chosen in such manner, and in such proportion as they shall designate; and shall meet at such time and place as shall be prescribed by the said ordinance; and shall then form for the people of said territory, within the boundaries aforesaid, a constitution and state government: Provided, That the same, whenever formed, shall be republican, and not repugnant to the constitution of the United States; and that the legislature of said state shall never interfere with the primary disposal of the soil by the United States, nor with any regulations Congress may find necessary for securing the title in such soil to the bona fide purchasers; and that no tax shall be imposed on lands the property of the United States; and in no case shall non-resident proprietors be taxed higher than residents.

SEC. 5. And be it further enacted, That until the next general census shall be taken, the said state shall be entitled to one representative in the House of Representatives of the United States.

SEC. 6. And be it further enacted, That the following propositions be, and the same are hereby, offered to the convention of the said territory of Missouri, when formed, for their free acceptance or rejection, which, if accepted by the convention, shall be obligatory upon the United States:

First. That section numbered sixteen in every township, and when such section has been sold, or otherwise disposed of, other lands equivalent thereto, and as contiguous as may be, shall be granted to the state for the use of the inhabitants of such township, for the use of schools.

Second. That all salt springs, not exceeding twelve in number, with six sections of land adjoining to each, shall be granted to the said state for the use of said state, the same to be selected by the legislature of the said state, on or before the first day of January, in the year one thousand eight hundred and twenty-five; and the same, when so selected, to be used under such terms, conditions, and regulations, as the legislature of said state shall direct: Provided, That no salt spring, the right whereof now is, or hereafter shall be, confirmed or adjudged to any individual or individuals, shall, by this section, be granted to the said state: And provided also, That the legislature shall never sell or lease the same, at anyone time, for a longer period than ten years, without the consent of Congress.

Third. That five per cent of the net proceeds of the sale of lands lying within the said territory or state, and which shall be sold by Congress, from and after the first day of January next, after deducting all expenses incident to the same, shall be reserved for making public roads and canals, of which three fifths shall be applied to those objects within the state, under the direction of the legislature thereof; and the other two fifths in defraying, under the direction of Congress, the expenses to be incurred in making of a road or roads, canal or canals, leading to the said state.

Fourth. That four entire sections of land be, and the same are hereby, granted to the said state, for the purpose of fixing their seat of government thereon; which said sections shall, under the direction of the legislature of said state, be located, as near as may be, in one body, at any time, in such townships and ranges as the legislature aforesaid may select, on any of the public lands of the United States: Provided, That such locations shall be made prior to the public sale of the lands of the United States surrounding such location.

Fifth. That thirty-six sections, or one entire township, which shall be designated by the President of the United States, together with the other lands heretofore reserved for that purpose, shall be reserved for the use of a seminary of learning, and vested in the legislature of said state, to be appropriated solely to the use of such seminary by the said legislature: Provided, That the five foregoing propositions herein offered, are on the condition that the convention of the said state shall provide, by an ordinance, irrevocable without the consent or the United States, that every and each tract of land sold by the United States, from and after the first day of January next, shall remain exempt from any tax laid by order or under the authority of the state, whether for state, county, or township, or any other purpose whatever, for the term of five years from and after the day of sale; And further, That the bounty lands granted, or hereafter to be granted, for military services during the late war, shall, while they continue to be held by the patentees, or their heirs remain exempt as aforesaid from taxation for the term of three year; from and after the date of the patents respectively.

SEC. 7. And be it further enacted, That in case a constitution and state government shall be formed for the people of the said territory of Missouri, the said convention or representatives, as soon thereafter as may be, shall cause a true and attested copy of such constitution or frame of state government, as shall be formed or provided, to be transmitted to Congress.

SEC. 8. And be it further enacted. That in all that territory ceded by France to the United States, under the name of Louisiana, which lies north of thirty-six degrees and thirty minutes north latitude, not included within the limits of the state, contemplated by this act, slavery and involuntary servitude, otherwise than in the punishment of crimes, whereof the parties shall have been duly convicted, shall be, and is hereby, forever prohibited: Provided always, That any person escaping into the same, from whom labour or service is lawfully claimed, in any state or territory of the United States, such fugitive may be lawfully reclaimed and conveyed to the person claiming his or her labour or service as aforesaid.

APPROVED, March 6, 1820.

The Monroe Doctrine

Note: The Monroe Doctrine was expressed during President Monroe's seventh annual message to Congress, December 2, 1823:

. . . At the proposal of the Russian Imperial Government, made through the minister of the Emperor residing here, a full power and instructions have been transmitted to the minister of the United States at St. Petersburg to arrange by amicable negotiation the respective rights and interests of the two nations on the northwest coast of this continent. A similar proposal has been made by His Imperial Majesty to the Government of Great Britain, which has likewise been acceded to. The Government of the United States has been desirous by this friendly proceeding of manifesting the great value which they have invariably attached to the friendship of the Emperor and their solicitude to cultivate the best understanding with his Government. In the discussions to which this interest has given rise and in the arrangements by which they may terminate the occasion has been judged proper for asserting, as a principle in which the rights and interests of the United States are involved, that the American continents, by the free and independent condition which they have assumed and maintain, are henceforth not to be considered as subjects for future colonization by any European powers. . .

It was stated at the commencement of the last session that a great effort was then making in Spain and Portugal to improve the condition of the people of those countries, and that it appeared to be conducted with extraordinary moderation. It need scarcely be remarked that the results have been so far very different from what was then anticipated. Of events in that quarter of the globe, with which we have so much intercourse and from which we derive our origin, we have always been anxious and interested spectators. The citizens of the United States cherish sentiments the most friendly in favor of the liberty and happiness of their fellow men on that side of the Atlantic. In the wars of the European powers in matters relating to themselves we have never taken any part, nor does it comport with our policy to do so. It is only when our rights are invaded or seriously menaced that we resent injuries or make preparation for our defense. With the movements in this hemisphere we are of necessity more immediately connected, and by causes which must be obvious to all enlightened and impartial observers. The political system of the allied powers is essentially different in this respect from that of America. This difference proceeds from that which exists in their respective Governments; and to the defense of our own, which has been achieved by the loss of so much blood and treasure, and matured by the wisdom of their most enlightened citizens, and under which we have enjoyed unexampled felicity, this whole nation is devoted. We owe it, therefore, to candor and to the amicable relations existing between the United States and those powers to declare that we should consider any attempt on their part to extend their system to any portion of this hemisphere as dangerous to our peace and safety. With the existing colonies or dependencies of any European power we have not interfered and shall not interfere. But with the Governments who have declared their independence and maintain it, and whose independence we have, on great consideration and on just principles, acknowledged, we could not view any interposition for the purpose of oppressing them, or controlling in any other manner their destiny, by any European power in any other light than as the manifestation of an unfriendly disposition toward the United States. In the war between those new Governments and Spain we declared our neutrality at the time of their recognition, and to this we have adhered, and shall continue to adhere, provided no change shall occur which, in the judgement of the competent authorities of this Government, shall make a corresponding change on the part of the United States indispensable to their security.

The late events in Spain and Portugal shew that Europe is still unsettled. Of this important fact no stronger proof can be adduced than that the allied powers should have thought it proper, on any principle satisfactory to themselves, to have interposed by force in the internal concerns of Spain. To what extent such interposition may be carried, on the same principle, is a question in which all independent powers whose governments differ from theirs are interested, even those most remote, and surely none of them more so than the United States. Our policy in regard to Europe, which was adopted at an early stage of the wars which have so long agitated that quarter of the globe, nevertheless remains the same, which is, not to interfere in the internal concerns of any of its powers; to consider the government de facto as the legitimate government for us; to cultivate friendly relations with it, and to preserve those relations by a frank, firm, and manly policy, meeting in all instances the just claims of every power, submitting to injuries from none. But in regard to those continents circumstances are eminently and conspicuously different.

It is impossible that the allied powers should extend their political system to any portion of either continent without endangering our peace and happiness; nor can anyone believe that our southern brethren, if left to themselves, would adopt it of their own accord. It is equally impossible, therefore, that we should behold such interposition in any form with indifference. If we look to the comparative strength and resources of Spain and those new Governments, and their distance from each other, it must be obvious that she can never subdue them. It is still the true policy of the United States to leave the parties to themselves, in hope that other powers will pursue the same course. . . .

Gibbons v. Ogden

GIBBONS v. OGDEN, 22 U.S. 1 (1824).
[DECIDED MARCH 2, 1824]

Mr. Chief Justice MARSHALL delivered the opinion of the Court, and, after stating the case, proceeded as follows:

The appellant contends that this decree is erroneous because the laws which purport to give the exclusive privilege it sustains are repugnant to the Constitution and laws of the United States. They are said to be repugnant: first, to that clause in the Constitution which authorizes Congress to regulate commerce; second, to that which authorizes Congress to promote the progress of science and useful arts.

As preliminary to the very able discussions of the Constitution which we have heard from the bar, and as having some influence on its construction, reference has been made to the political situation of these states, anterior to its formation. It has been said that they were sovereign, were completely independent, and were connected with each other only by a league. This is true. But, when these allied sovereigns converted their league into a government, when they converted their congress of ambassadors, deputed to deliberate on their common concerns, and to recommend measures of general utility, into a legislature, empowered to enact laws on the most interesting subjects, the whole character in which the states appear underwent a change; the extent of which must be determined by a fair consideration of the instrument by which that change was effected.

This instrument contains an enumeration of powers expressly granted by the people to their government. It has been said that these powers ought to be construed strictly. But why ought they to be so construed? Is there one sentence in the Constitution which gives countenance to this rule? In the last of the enumerated powers, that which grants, expressly, the means for carrying all others into execution, Congress is authorized *to make all laws which shall be necessary and proper* for the purpose. But this limitation on the means which may be used is not extended to the powers which are conferred; nor is there one sentence in the Constitution, which has been pointed out by the gentlemen of the bar, or which we have been able to discern, that prescribes this rule. We do not, therefore, think ourselves justified in adopting it.

What do gentlemen mean by a strict construction? If they contend only against that enlarged construction which would extend words beyond their natural and obvious import, we might question the application of the term, but should not controvert the principle. If they contend for that narrow construction which, in support of some theory not to be found in the Constitution, would deny to the government those powers which the words of the grant, as usually understood, import, and which are consistent with the general views and objects of the instrument; for that narrow construction, which would cripple the government, and render it unequal to the objects for which it is declared to be instituted, and to which the powers given, as fairly understood, render it competent; then we cannot perceive the propriety of this strict construction, nor adopt it as the rule by which the Constitution is to be expounded. As men whose intentions require no concealment generally employ the words which most directly and aptly express the ideas they intend to convey, the enlightened patriots who framed our Constitution, and the people who adopted it, must be understood to have employed words in their natural sense, and to have intended what they have said.

If, from the imperfection of human language, there should be serious doubts respecting the extent of any given power, it is a well-settled rule that the objects for which it was given, especially when those objects are expressed in the instrument itself, should have great influence in the construction. We know of no reason for excluding this rule from the present case. The grant does not convey power which might be beneficial to the grantor, if retained by himself, or which can inure solely to the benefit of the grantee, but is an investment of power for the general advantage in the hands of agents selected for that purpose; which power can never be exercised by the people themselves, but must be placed in the hands of agents, or lie dormant. We know of no rule for construing the extent of such powers other than is given by the language of the instrument which confers them, taken in connection with the purposes for which they were conferred.

The words are: *Congress shall have power to regulate commerce with foreign nations, and among the several states, and with the Indian tribes.* The subject to be regulated is commerce; and our Constitution being, as was aptly said at the bar, one of enumeration and not of definition, to ascertain the extent of the power it becomes necessary to settle the meaning of the word.

Commerce, undoubtedly, is traffic, but it is something more—it is intercourse. It describes the commercial intercourse between nations, and parts of nations, in all its branches, and is regulated by prescribing rules for carrying on that intercourse. The mind can scarcely conceive a system for regulating commerce between nations which shall exclude all laws concerning navigation, which shall be silent on the admission of the vessels of the one nation into the ports of the other, and be confined to prescribing rules for the conduct of individuals in the actual employment of buying and selling or of barter. If commerce does not include navigation, the government of the Union has no direct power over that subject, and can make no law prescribing what shall constitute American vessels, or requiring that they shall be navigated by American seamen.

Yet this power has been exercised from the commencement of the government, has been exercised with the consent of all, and has been understood by all to be a commercial regulation. All America understands, and has uniformly understood, the word *commerce* to comprehend navigation.

The word used in the Constitution, then, comprehends, and has been always understood to comprehend, navigation within its meaning; and a power to regulate navigation is as expressly granted as if that term had been added to the word *commerce*. To what commerce does this power extend? The Constitution informs us to commerce *with foreign nations, and among the several states, and with the Indian tribes.* It has, we believe, been universally admitted that these words comprehend every species of commercial intercourse between the United States and foreign nations. No sort of trade can be carried on between this country and any other to which this power does not extend. It has been truly said that commerce, as the word is used in the Constitution, is a unit, every part of which is indicated by the term. If this be the admitted meaning of the word in its application to foreign nations, it must carry the same meaning throughout the sentence and remain a unit, unless there be some plain intelligible cause which alters it.

The subject to which the power is next applied is to commerce *among the several states.* The word *among* means intermingled with. A thing which is among others is intermingled with them. Commerce among the states cannot stop at the external boundary line of each state, but may be introduced into the interior. It is not intended to say that these words comprehend that commerce which is completely internal, which is carried on between man and man in a state, or between different parts of the same state, and which does not extend to or affect other states. Such a power would be inconvenient and is certainly unnecessary. Comprehensive as the word *among* is, it may very properly be restricted to that commerce which concerns more states than one. The phrase is not one which would probably have been selected to indicate the completely interior traffic of a state, because it is not an apt phrase for that purpose; and the enumeration of the particular classes of commerce to which the power was to be extended would not have been made had the intention been to extend the power to every description. The enumeration presupposes something not enumerated; and that something, if we regard the language or the subject of the sentence, must be the exclusively internal commerce of a state.

The genius and character of the whole government seem to be that its action is to be applied to all the external concerns of the nation and to those internal concerns which affect the states generally; but not to those which are completely within a particular state, which do not affect other states, and with which it is not necessary to interfere for the purpose of executing some of the general powers of the government. The completely internal commerce of a state, then, may be considered as reserved for the state itself.

But, in regulating commerce with foreign nations, the power of Congress does not stop at the jurisdictional lines of the several states. It would be a very useless power if it could not pass those lines. The commerce of the United States with foreign nations is that of the whole United States. Every district has a right to participate in it. The deep streams which penetrate our country in every direction pass through the interior of almost every state in the Union, and furnish the means of exercising this right. If Congress has the power to regulate it, that power must be exercised whenever the subject exists. If it exists within the states, if a foreign voyage may commence or terminate at a port within a state, then the power of Congress may be exercised within a state.

This principle is, if possible, still more clear, when applied to commerce *among the several states*. They either join each other, in which case they are separated by a mathematical line, or they are remote from each other, in which case other states lie between them. What is commerce *among* them, and how is it to be conducted? Can a trading expedition between two adjoining states commence and terminate outside of each? And if the trading intercourse be between two states remote from each other, must it not commence in one, terminate in the other, and probably pass through a third? Commerce among the states must, of necessity, be commerce with the states. In the regulation of trade with the Indian tribes, the action of the law, especially, when the Constitution was made, was chiefly within a state.

The power of Congress, then, whatever it may be, must be exercised within the territorial jurisdiction of the several states. The sense of the nation on this subject is unequivocally manifested by the provisions made in the laws for transporting goods by land between Baltimore and Providence, between New York and Philadelphia, and between Philadelphia and Baltimore.

We are now arrived at the inquiry—What is this power? It is the power to regulate, that is, to prescribe the rule by which commerce is to be governed. This power, like all others vested in Congress, is complete in itself, may be exercised to its utmost extent, and acknowledges no limitations other than are prescribed in the Constitution. These are expressed in plain terms and do not affect the questions which arise in this case, or which have been discussed at the bar. If, as has always been understood, the sovereignty of Congress, though limited to specified objects, is plenary as to those objects, the power over commerce with foreign nations and among the several states is vested in Congress as absolutely as it would be in a single government, having in its constitution the same restrictions on the exercise of the power as are found in the Constitution of the United States.

The wisdom and the discretion of Congress, their identity with the people, and the influence which their constituents possess at elections are, in this as in many other instances, as that, for example, of declaring war, the sole restraints on which they have relied to secure them from its abuse. They are the restraints on which the people must often rely solely in all representative governments. The power of Congress, then, comprehends navigation within the limits of every state in the Union so far as that navigation may be, in any manner, connected with *commerce with foreign nations, or among the several States, or with the Indian tribes*. It may, of consequence, pass the jurisdiction line of New York, and act upon the very waters to which the prohibition now under consideration applies.

But it has been urged with great earnestness that, although the power of Congress to regulate commerce with foreign nations and among the several states be coextensive with the subject itself, and have no other limits than are prescribed in the Constitution, yet the states may severally exercise the same power within their respective jurisdictions. In support of this argument, it is said that they possessed it as an inseparable attribute of sovereignty before the formation of the Constitution, and still retain it, except so far as they have surrendered it by that instrument; that this principle results from the nature of the government, and is secured by the Tenth Amendment; that an affirmative grant of power is not exclusive, unless in its own nature it be such that the continued exercise of it by the former possessor is inconsistent with the grant, and that this is not of that description.

The appellant, conceding these postulates except the last, contends that full power to regulate a particular subject implies the whole power and leaves no residuum; that a grant of the whole is incompatible with the existence of a right in another to any part of it. Both parties have appealed to the Constitution, to legislative acts, and judicial decisions; and have drawn arguments from all these sources to support and illustrate the propositions they respectively maintain.

In discussing the question, whether this power is still in the states, in the case under consideration, we may dismiss from it the inquiry, whether it is surrendered by the mere grant to Congress, or is retained until Congress shall exercise the power. We may dismiss that inquiry because it has been exercised, and the regulations which Congress deemed it proper to make are now in full operation. The sole question is—Can a state regulate commerce with foreign nations and among the states while Congress is regulating it?

The counsel for the respondent answer this question in the affirmative, and rely very much on the restrictions in the 10th Section as supporting their opinion. They say, very truly, that limitations of a power furnish a strong argument in favor of the existence of that power, and that the section which prohibits the states from laying duties on imports or exports proves that this power might have been exercised had it not been expressly forbidden; and, consequently that any other commercial regulation, not expressly forbidden, to which the original power of the state was competent, may still be made.

That this restriction shows the opinion of the Convention, that a state might impose duties on exports and imports, if not expressly forbidden, will be conceded; but that it follows, as a consequence from this concession, that a state may regulate commerce with foreign nations and among the states cannot be admitted.

It has been contended by the counsel for the appellant that, as the word *to regulate* implies in its nature full power over the thing to be regulated, it excludes, necessarily, the action of all others that would perform the same operation on the same thing. That regulation is designed for the entire result, applying to those parts which remain as they were, as well as to those which are altered. It produces a uniform whole, which is as much disturbed and deranged by changing what the regulating power designs to leave untouched as that on which it has operated. There is great force in this argument, and the court is not satisfied that it has been refuted.

Since, however, in exercising the power of regulating their own purely internal affairs, whether of trading or police, the states may sometimes enact laws, the validity of which depends on their interfering with, and being contrary to, an act of Congress passed in pursuance of the Constitution, the court will enter upon the inquiry, whether the laws of New York, as expounded by the highest tribunal of that state, have, in their application to this case, come into collision with an act of Congress, and deprived a citizen of a right to which that act entitles him. Should this collision exist, it will be immaterial whether those laws were passed in virtue of a concurrent power *to regulate commerce with foreign nations and among the several states*, or in virtue of a power to regulate their domestic trade and police.

In one case and the other the acts of New York must yield to the law of Congress; and the decision sustaining the privilege they confer against a right given by a law of the Union must be erroneous. This opinion has been frequently expressed in this court, and is founded as well on the nature of the government as on the words of the Constitution. In argument, however, it has been contended that, if a law passed by a state in the exercise of its acknowledged sovereignty comes into conflict with a law passed by Congress in pursuance of the Constitution, they affect the subject and each other like equal opposing powers.

But the framers of our Constitution foresaw this state of things and provided for it by declaring the supremacy not only of itself but of the laws made in pursuance of it. The nullity of any act inconsistent with the Constitution is produced by the declaration that the Constitution is supreme law. The appropriate application of that part of the clause which confers the same supremacy on laws and treaties is to such acts of the state legislatures as do not transcend their powers, but though enacted in the execution of acknowledged state powers, interfere with, or are contrary to, the laws of Congress, made in pursuance of the Constitution or some treaty made under the authority of the United States. In every such case, the act of Congress or the treaty is supreme; and the law of the state, though enacted in the exercise of powers not controverted, must yield to it.

DECREE

This court is of opinion that so much of the several laws of the state of New York as prohibits vessels, licensed according to the laws of the United States, from navigating the waters of the state of New York, by means of fire or steam, is repugnant to the said Constitution and void. This court is, therefore, of opinion that the decree of the court of New York for the trial of impeachments and the correction of errors, affirming the decree of the chancellor of that state is erroneous and ought to be reversed, and the same is hereby reversed and annulled. And this court doth further direct, order, and decree that the bill of the said Aaron Ogden be dismissed, and the same is hereby dismissed accordingly.

President Andrew Jackson's Message to Congress 'On Indian Removal'

ANDREW JACKSON'S ANNUAL MESSAGE

It gives me pleasure to announce to Congress that the benevolent policy of the Government, steadily pursued for nearly thirty years, in relation to the removal of the Indians beyond the white settlements is approaching to a happy consummation. Two important tribes have accepted the provision made for their removal at the last session of Congress, and it is believed that their example will induce the remaining tribes also to seek the same obvious advantages.

The consequences of a speedy removal will be important to the United States, to individual States, and to the Indians themselves. The pecuniary advantages which it promises to the Government are the least of its recommendations. It puts an end to all possible danger of collision between the authorities of the General and State Governments on account of the Indians. It will place a dense and civilized population in large tracts of country now occupied by a few savage hunters. By opening the whole territory between Tennessee on the north and Louisiana on the south to the settlement of the whites it will incalculably strengthen the southwestern frontier and render the adjacent States strong enough to repel future invasions without remote aid. It will relieve the whole State of Mississippi and the western part of Alabama of Indian occupancy, and enable those States to advance rapidly in population, wealth, and power. It will separate the Indians from immediate contact with settlements of whites; free them from the power of the States; enable them to pursue happiness in their own way and under their own rude institutions; will retard the progress of decay, which is lessening their numbers, and perhaps cause them gradually, under the protection of the Government and through the influence of good counsels, to cast off their savage habits and become an interesting, civilized, and Christian community.

What good man would prefer a country covered with forests and ranged by a few thousand savages to our extensive Republic, studded with cities, towns, and prosperous farms embellished with all the improvements which art can devise or industry execute, occupied by more than 12,000,000 happy people, and filled with all the blessings of liberty, civilization and religion?

The present policy of the Government is but a continuation of the same progressive change by a milder process. The tribes which occupied the countries now constituting the Eastern States were annihilated or have melted away to make room for the whites. The waves of population and civilization are rolling to the westward, and we now propose to acquire the countries occupied by the red men of the South and West by a fair exchange, and, at the expense of the United States, to send them to land where their existence may be prolonged and perhaps made perpetual. Doubtless it will be painful to leave the graves of their fathers; but what do they more than our ancestors did or than our children are now doing? To better their condition in an unknown land our forefathers left all that was dear in earthly objects. Our children by thousands yearly leave the land of their birth to seek new homes in distant regions. Does Humanity weep at these painful separations from everything, animate and inanimate, with which the young heart has become entwined? Far from it. It is rather a source of joy that our country affords scope where our young population may range unconstrained in body or in mind, developing the power and facilities of man in their highest perfection. These remove hundreds and almost thousands of miles at their own expense, purchase the lands they occupy, and support themselves at their new homes from the moment of their arrival. Can it be cruel in this Government when, by events which it can not control, the Indian is made discontented in his ancient home to purchase his lands, to give him a new and extensive territory, to pay the expense of his removal, and support him a year in his new abode? How many thousands of our own people would gladly embrace the opportunity of removing to the West on such conditions! If the offers made to the Indians were extended to them, they would be hailed with gratitude and joy.

And is it supposed that the wandering savage has a stronger attachment to his home than the settled, civilized Christian? Is it more afflicting to him to leave the graves of his fathers than it is to our brothers and children? Rightly considered, the policy of the General Government toward the red man is not only liberal, but generous. He is unwilling to submit to the laws of the States and mingle with their population. To save him from this alternative, or perhaps utter annihilation, the General Government kindly offers him a new home, and proposes to pay the whole expense of his removal and settlement.

The Treaty of Guadalupe Hidalgo

TREATY OF PEACE, FRIENDSHIP, LIMITS, AND SETTLEMENT BETWEEN THE UNITED STATES OF AMERICA AND THE UNITED MEXICAN STATES CONCLUDED AT GUADALUPE HIDALGO, FEBRUARY 2, 1848; RATIFICATION ADVISED BY SENATE, WITH AMENDMENTS, MARCH 10, 1848; RATIFIED BY PRESIDENT, MARCH 16, 1848; RATIFICATIONS EXCHANGED AT QUERETARO, MAY 30, 1848; PROCLAIMED, JULY 4, 1848.

IN THE NAME OF ALMIGHTY GOD

The United States of America and the United Mexican States animated by a sincere desire to put an end to the calamities of the war which unhappily exists between the two Republics and to establish Upon a solid basis relations of peace and friendship, which shall confer reciprocal benefits upon the citizens of both, and assure the concord, harmony, and mutual confidence wherein the two people should live, as good neighbors have for that purpose appointed their respective plenipotentiaries, that is to say: The President of the United States has appointed Nicholas P. Trist, a citizen of the United States, and the President of the Mexican Republic has appointed Don Luis Gonzaga Cuevas, Don Bernardo Couto, and Don Miguel Atristain, citizens of the said Republic; Who, after a reciprocal communication of their respective full powers, have, under the protection of Almighty God, the author of peace, arranged, agreed upon, and signed the following: Treaty of Peace, Friendship, Limits, and Settlement between the United States of America and the Mexican Republic.

ARTICLE I

There shall be firm and universal peace between the United States of America and the Mexican Republic, and between their respective countries, territories, cities, towns, and people, without exception of places or persons.

ARTICLE II

Immediately upon the signature of this treaty, a convention shall be entered into between a commissioner or commissioners appointed by the General-in-chief of the forces of the United States, and such as may be appointed by the Mexican Government, to the end that a provisional suspension of hostilities shall take place, and that, in the places occupied by the said forces, constitutional order may be reestablished, as regards the political, administrative, and judicial branches, so far as this shall be permitted by the circumstances of military occupation.

ARTICLE III

Immediately upon the ratification of the present treaty by the Government of the United States, orders shall be transmitted to the commanders of their land and naval forces, requiring the latter (provided this treaty shall then have been ratified by the Government of the Mexican Republic, and the ratifications exchanged) immediately to desist from blockading any Mexican ports and requiring the former (under the same condition) to commence, at the earliest moment practicable, withdrawing all troops of the United States then in the interior of the Mexican Republic, to points that shall be selected by common agreement, at a distance from the seaports not exceeding thirty leagues; and such evacuation of the interior of the Republic shall be completed with the least possible delay; the Mexican Government hereby binding itself to afford every facility in its power for rendering the same convenient to the troops, on their march and in their new positions, and for promoting a good understanding between them and the inhabitants. In like manner orders shall be despatched to the persons in charge of the custom houses at all ports occupied by the forces of the United States, requiring them (under the same condition) immediately to deliver possession of the same to the persons authorized by the Mexican Government to receive it, together with all bonds and evidences of debt for duties on importations and on exportations, not yet fallen due.

Moreover, a faithful and exact account shall be made out, showing the entire amount of all duties on imports and on exports, collected at such custom houses, or elsewhere in Mexico, by authority of the United States, from and after the day of ratification of this treaty by the Government of the Mexican

Republic; and also an account of the cost of collection; and such entire amount, deducting only the cost of collection, shall be delivered to the Mexican Government, at the city of Mexico, within three months after the exchange of ratifications.

The evacuation of the capital of the Mexican Republic by the troops of the United States, in virtue of the above stipulation, shall be completed in one month after the orders there stipulated for shall have been received by the commander of said troops, or sooner if possible.

ARTICLE IV

Immediately after the exchange of ratifications of the present treaty all castles, forts, territories, places, and possessions, which have been taken or occupied by the forces of the United States during the present war, within the limits of the Mexican Republic, as about to be established by the following article, shall be definitely restored to the said Republic, together with all the artillery, arms, apparatus of war, munitions, and other public property, which were in the said castles and forts when captured, and which shall remain there at the time when this treaty shall be duly ratified by the Government of the Mexican Republic. To this end, immediately upon the signature of this treaty, orders shall be despatched to the American officers commanding such castles and forts, securing against the removal or destruction of any such artillery, arms, apparatus of war, munitions, or other public property. The city of Mexico, within the inner line of intrenchments surrounding the said city, is comprehended in the above stipulation, as regards the restoration of artillery, apparatus of war, & c.

The final evacuation of the territory of the Mexican Republic, by the forces of the United States, shall be completed in three months from the said exchange of ratifications, or sooner if possible; the Mexican Government hereby engaging, as in the foregoing article to use all means in its power for facilitating such evacuation, and rendering it convenient to the troops, and for promoting a good understanding between them and the inhabitants.

If, however, the ratification of this treaty by both parties should not take place in time to allow the embarcation of the troops of the United States to be completed before the commencement of the sickly season, at the Mexican ports on the Gulf of Mexico, in such case a friendly arrangement shall be entered into between the General-in-Chief of the said troops and the Mexican Government, whereby healthy and otherwise suitable places, at a distance from the ports not exceeding thirty leagues, shall be designated for the residence of such troops as may not yet have embarked, until the return of the healthy season. And the space of time here referred to as, comprehending the sickly season shall be understood to extend from the first day of May to the first day of November.

All prisoners of war taken on either side, on land or on sea, shall be restored as soon as practicable after the exchange of ratifications of this treaty. It is also agreed that if any Mexicans should now be held as captives by any savage tribe within the limits of the United States, as about to be established by the following article, the Government of the said United States will exact the release of such captives and cause them to be restored to their country.

ARTICLE V

The boundary line between the two Republics shall commence in the Gulf of Mexico, three leagues from land, opposite the mouth of the Rio Grande, otherwise called Rio Bravo del Norte, or Opposite the mouth of its deepest branch, if it should have more than one branch emptying directly into the sea; from thence up the middle of that river, following the deepest channel, where it has more than one, to the point where it strikes the southern boundary of New Mexico; thence, westwardly, along the whole southern boundary of New Mexico (which runs north of the town called Paso) to its western termination; thence, northward, along the western line of New Mexico, until it intersects the first branch of the river Gila; (or if it should not intersect any branch of that river, then to the point on the said line nearest to such branch, and thence in a direct line to the same); thence down the middle of the said branch and of the said river, until it empties into the Rio Colorado; thence across the Rio Colorado, following the division line between Upper and Lower California, to the Pacific Ocean.

The southern and western limits of New Mexico, mentioned in the article, are those laid down in the map entitled "Map of the United Mexican States, as organized and defined by various acts of the Congress of said republic, and constructed according to the best authorities. Revised edition. Published at New

York, in 1847, by J. Disturnell," of which map a copy is added to this treaty, bearing the signatures and seals of the undersigned Plenipotentiaries. And, in order to preclude all difficulty in tracing upon the ground the limit separating Upper from Lower California, it is agreed that the said limit shall consist of a straight line drawn from the middle of the Rio Gila, where it unites with the Colorado, to a point on the coast of the Pacific Ocean, distant one marine league due south of the southernmost point of the port of San Diego, according to the plan of said port made in the year 1782 by Don Juan Pantoja, second sailing master of the Spanish fleet, and published at Madrid in the year 1802, in the atlas to the voyage of the schooners Sutil and Mexicana; of which plan a copy is hereunto added, signed and sealed by the respective Plenipotentiaries.

In order to designate the boundary line with due precision, upon authoritative maps, and to establish upon the ground landmarks which shall show the limits of both republics, as described in the present article, the two Governments shall each appoint a commissioner and a surveyor, who, before the expiration of one year from the date of the exchange of ratifications of this treaty, shall meet at the port of San Diego, and proceed to run and mark the said boundary in its whole course to the mouth of the Rio Bravo del Norte. They shall keep journals and make out plans of their operations; and the result agreed upon by them shall be deemed a part of this treaty, and shall have the same force as if it were inserted therein. The two Governments will amicably agree regarding what may be necessary to these persons, and also as to their respective escorts, should such be necessary.

The boundary line established by this article shall be religiously respected by each of the two republics, and no change shall ever be made therein, except by the express and free consent of both nations, lawfully given by the General Government of each, in conformity with its own constitution.

ARTICLE VI

The vessels and citizens of the United States shall, in all time, have a free and uninterrupted passage by the Gulf of California, and by the river Colorado below its confluence with the Gila, to and from their possessions situated north of the boundary line defined in the preceding article; it being understood that this passage is to be by navigating the Gulf of California and the river Colorado, and not by land, without the express consent of the Mexican Government.

If, by the examinations which may be made, it should be ascertained to be practicable and advantageous to construct a road, canal, or railway, which should in whole or in part run upon the river Gila, or upon its right or its left bank, within the space of one marine league from either margin of the river, the Governments of both republics will form an agreement regarding its construction, in order that it may serve equally for the use and advantage of both countries.

ARTICLE VII

The river Gila, and the part of the Rio Bravo del Norte lying below the southern boundary of New Mexico, being, agreeably to the fifth article, divided in the middle between the two republics, the navigation of the Gila and of the Bravo below said boundary shall be free and common to the vessels and citizens of both countries; and neither shall, without the consent of the other, construct any work that may impede or interrupt, in whole or in part, the exercise of this right; not even for the purpose of favoring new methods of navigation. Nor shall any tax or contribution, under any denomination or title, be levied upon vessels or persons navigating the same or upon merchandise or effects transported thereon, except in the case of landing upon one of their shores. If, for the purpose of making the said rivers navigable, or for maintaining them in such state, it should be necessary or advantageous to establish any tax or contribution, this shall not be done without the consent of both Governments.

The stipulations contained in the present article shall not impair the territorial rights of either republic within its established limits.

ARTICLE VIII

Mexicans now established in territories previously belonging to Mexico, and which remain for the future within the limits of the United States, as defined by the present treaty, shall be free to continue where they now reside, or to remove at any time to the Mexican Republic, retaining the property which they possess in the said territories, or disposing thereof, and removing the proceeds wherever they please, without their being subjected, on this account, to any contribution, tax, or charge whatever.

Those who shall prefer to remain in the said territories may either retain the title and rights of Mexican citizens, or acquire those of citizens of the United States. But they shall be under the obligation to make their election within one year from the date of the exchange of ratifications of this treaty; and those who shall remain in the said territories after the expiration of that year, without having declared their intention to retain the character of Mexicans, shall be considered to have elected to become citizens of the United States.

In the said territories, property of every kind, now belonging to Mexicans not established there, shall be inviolably respected. The present owners, the heirs of these, and all Mexicans who may hereafter acquire said property by contract, shall enjoy with respect to it guarantees equally ample as if the same belonged to citizens of the United States.

ARTICLE IX

The Mexicans who, in the territories aforesaid, shall not preserve the character of citizens of the Mexican Republic, conformably with what is stipulated in the preceding article, shall be incorporated into the Union of the United States and be admitted at the proper time (to be judged of by the Congress of the United States) to the enjoyment of all the rights of citizens of the United States, according to the principles of the Constitution; and in the mean time, shall be maintained and protected in the free enjoyment of their liberty and property, and secured in the free exercise of their religion without restriction.

ARTICLE X

[Stricken out]

ARTICLE XI

Considering that a great part of the territories, which, by the present treaty, are to be comprehended for the future within the limits of the United States, is now occupied by savage tribes, who will hereafter be under the exclusive control of the Government of the United States, and whose incursions within the territory of Mexico would be prejudicial in the extreme, it is solemnly agreed that all such incursions shall be forcibly restrained by the Government of the United States whensoever this may be necessary; and that when they cannot be prevented, they shall be punished by the said Government, and satisfaction for the same shall be exacted all in the same way, and with equal diligence and energy, as if the same incursions were meditated or committed within its own territory, against its own citizens.

It shall not be lawful, under any pretext whatever, for any inhabitant of the United States to purchase or acquire any Mexican, or any foreigner residing in Mexico, who may have been captured by Indians inhabiting the territory of either of the two republics; nor to purchase or acquire horses, mules, cattle, or property of any kind, stolen within Mexican territory by such Indians.

And in the event of any person or persons, captured within Mexican territory by Indians, being carried into the territory of the United States, the Government of the latter engages and binds itself, in the most solemn manner, so soon as it shall know of such captives being within its territory, and shall be able so to do, through the faithful exercise of its influence and power, to rescue them and return them to their country or deliver them to the agent or representative of the Mexican Government. The Mexican authorities will, as far as practicable, give to the Government of the United States notice of such captures; and its agents shall pay the expenses incurred in the maintenance and transmission of the rescued captives; who, in the mean time, shall be treated with the utmost hospitality by the American authorities at the place where they may be. But if the Government of the United States, before receiving such notice from Mexico, should obtain intelligence, through any other channel, of the existence of Mexican captives within its territory, it will proceed forthwith to effect their release and delivery to the Mexican agent, as above stipulated.

For the purpose of giving to these stipulations the fullest possible efficacy, thereby affording the security and redress demanded by their true spirit and intent, the Government of the United States will now and hereafter pass, without unnecessary delay, and always vigilantly enforce, such laws as the nature of the subject may require. And, finally, the sacredness of this obligation shall never be lost sight of by the said Government, when providing for the removal of the Indians from any portion of the said territories, or for its being settled by citizens of the United States; but, on the contrary, special care shall then be taken not to place its Indian occupants under the necessity of seeking new homes, by committing those invasions which the United States have solemnly obliged themselves to restrain.

ARTICLE XII

In consideration of the extension acquired by the boundaries of the United States, as defined in the fifth article of the present treaty, the Government of the United States engages to pay to that of the Mexican Republic the sum of fifteen millions of dollars.

Immediately after the treaty shall have been duly ratified by the Government of the Mexican Republic, the sum of three millions of dollars shall be paid to the said Government by that of the United States, at the city of Mexico, in the gold or silver coin of Mexico. The remaining twelve millions of dollars shall be paid at the same place, and in the same coin, in annual installments of three millions of dollars each, together with interest on the same at the rate of six per centum per annum. This interest shall begin to run upon the whole sum of twelve millions from the day of the ratification of the present treaty by—the Mexican Government, and the first of the installments shall be paid at the expiration of one year from the same day. Together with each annual installment, as it falls due, the whole interest accruing on such installment from the beginning shall also be paid.

ARTICLE XIII

The United States engage, moreover, to assume and pay to the claimants all the amounts now due them, and those hereafter to become due, by reason of the claims already liquidated and decided against the Mexican Republic, under the conventions between the two republics severally concluded on the eleventh day of April, eighteen hundred and thirty-nine, and on the thirtieth day of January, eighteen hundred and forty-three; so that the Mexican Republic shall be absolutely exempt, for the future, from all expense whatever on account of the said claims.

ARTICLE XIV

The United States do furthermore discharge the Mexican Republic from all claims of citizens of the United States, not heretofore decided against the Mexican Government, which may have arisen previously to the date of the signature of this treaty; which discharge shall be final and perpetual, whether the said claims be rejected or be allowed by the board of commissioners provided for in the following article, and whatever shall be the total amount of those allowed.

ARTICLE XV

The United States, exonerating Mexico from all demands on account of the claims of their citizens mentioned in the preceding article, and considering them entirely and forever canceled, whatever their amount may be, undertake to make satisfaction for the same, to an amount not exceeding three and one-quarter millions of dollars. To ascertain the validity and amount of those claims, a board of commissioners shall be established by the Government of the United States, whose awards shall be final and conclusive; provided that, in deciding upon the validity of each claim, the boa shall be guided and governed by the principles and rules of decision prescribed by the first and fifth articles of the unratified convention, concluded at the city of Mexico on the twentieth day of November, one thousand eight hundred and forty-three; and in no case shall an award be made in favour of any claim not embraced by these principles and rules.

If, in the opinion of the said board of commissioners or of the claimants, any books, records, or documents, in the possession or power of the Government of the Mexican Republic, shall be deemed necessary to the just decision of any claim, the commissioners, or the claimants through them, shall, within such period as Congress may designate, make an application in writing for the same, addressed to the Mexican Minister of Foreign Affairs, to be transmitted by the Secretary of State of the United States; and the Mexican Government engages, at the earliest possible moment after the receipt of such demand, to cause any of the books, records, or documents so specified, which shall be in their possession or power (or authenticated copies or extracts of the same), to be transmitted to the said Secretary of State, who shall immediately deliver them over to the said board of commissioners; provided that no such application shall be made by or at the instance of any claimant, until the facts which it is expected to prove by such books, records, or documents, shall have been stated under oath or affirmation.

ARTICLE XVI

Each of the contracting parties reserves to itself the entire right to fortify whatever point within its territory it may judge proper so to fortify for its security.

ARTICLE XVII

The treaty of amity, commerce, and navigation, concluded at the city of Mexico, on the fifth day of April, A. D. 1831, between the United States of America and the United Mexican States, except the additional article, and except so far as the stipulations of the said treaty may be incompatible with any stipulation contained in the present treaty, is hereby revived for the period of eight years from the day of the exchange of ratifications of this treaty, with the same force and virtue as if incorporated therein; it being understood that each of the contracting parties reserves to itself the right, at any time after the said period of eight years shall have expired, to terminate the same by giving one year's notice of such intention to the other party.

ARTICLE XVIII

All supplies whatever for troops of the United States in Mexico, arriving at ports in the occupation of such troops previous to the final evacuation thereof, although subsequently to the restoration of the custom houses at such ports, shall be entirely exempt from duties and charges of any kind; the Government of the United States hereby engaging and pledging its faith to establish and vigilantly to enforce, all possible guards for securing the revenue of Mexico, by preventing the importation, under cover of this stipulation, of any articles other than such, both in kind and in quantity, as shall really be wanted for the use and consumption of the forces of the United States during the time they may remain in Mexico. To this end it shall be the duty of all officers and agents of the United States to denounce to the Mexican authorities at the respective ports any attempts at a fraudulent abuse of this stipulation, which they may know of, or may have reason to suspect, and to give to such authorities all the aid in their power with regard thereto; and every such attempt, when duly proved and established by sentence of a competent tribunal, They shall be punished by the confiscation of the property so attempted to be fraudulently introduced.

ARTICLE XIX

With respect to all merchandise, effects, and property whatsoever, imported into ports of Mexico, whilst in the occupation of the forces of the United States, whether by citizens of either republic, or by citizens or subjects of any neutral nation, the following rules shall be observed:

(1) All such merchandise, effects, and property, if imported previously to the restoration of the custom houses to the Mexican authorities, as stipulated for in the third article of this treaty, shall be exempt from confiscation, although the importation of the same be prohibited by the Mexican tariff.

(2) The same perfect exemption shall be enjoyed by all such merchandise, effects, and property, imported subsequently to the restoration of the custom houses, and previously to the sixty days fixed in the following article for the coming into force of the Mexican tariff at such ports respectively; the said merchandise, effects, and property being, however, at the time of their importation, subject to the payment of duties, as provided for in the said following article.

(3) All merchandise, effects, and property described in the two rules foregoing shall, during their continuance at the place of importation, and upon their leaving such place for the interior, be exempt from all duty, tax, or imposts of every kind, under whatsoever title or denomination. Nor shall they be there subject to any charge whatsoever upon the sale thereof.

(4) All merchandise, effects, and property, described in the first and second rules, which shall have been removed to any place in the interior, whilst such place was in the occupation of the forces of the United States, shall, during their continuance therein, be exempt from all tax upon the sale or consumption thereof, and from every kind of impost or contribution, under whatsoever title or denomination.

(5) But if any merchandise, effects, or property, described in the first and second rules, shall be removed to any place not occupied at the time by the forces of the United States, they shall, upon their introduction into such place, or upon their sale or consumption there, be subject to the same duties which, under the Mexican laws, they would be required to pay in such cases if they had been imported in time of peace, through the maritime custom houses, and had there paid the duties conformably with the Mexican tariff.

(6) The owners of all merchandise, effects, or property, described in the first and second rules, and existing in any port of Mexico, shall have the right to reship the same, exempt from all tax, impost, or contribution whatever.

With respect to the metals, or other property, exported from any Mexican port whilst in the occupation of the forces of the United States, and previously to the restoration of the custom house at such port, no person shall be required by the Mexican authorities, whether general or state, to pay any tax, duty, or contribution upon any such exportation, or in any manner to account for the same to the said authorities.

ARTICLE XX

Through consideration for the interests of commerce generally, it is agreed, that if less than sixty days should elapse between the date of the signature of this treaty and the restoration of the custom houses, conformably with the stipulation in the third article, in such case all merchandise, effects and property whatsoever, arriving at the Mexican ports after the restoration of the said custom houses, and previously to the expiration of sixty days after the day of signature of this treaty, shall be admitted to entry; and no other duties shall be levied thereon than the duties established by the tariff found in force at such custom houses at the time of the restoration of the same. And to all such merchandise, effects, and property, the rules established by the preceding article shall apply.

ARTICLE XXI

If unhappily any disagreement should hereafter arise between the Governments of the two republics, whether with respect to the interpretation of any stipulation in this treaty, or with respect to any other particular concerning the political or commercial relations of the two nations, the said Governments, in the name of those nations, do promise to each other that they will endeavour, in the most sincere and earnest manner, to settle the differences so arising, and to preserve the state of peace and friendship in which the two countries are now placing themselves, using, for this end, mutual representations and pacific negotiations. And if, by these means, they should not be enabled to come to an agreement, a resort shall not, on this account, be had to reprisals,

aggression, or hostility of any kind, by the one republic against the other, until the Government of that which deems itself aggrieved shall have maturely considered, in the spirit of peace and good neighbourship, whether it would not be better that such difference should be settled by the arbitration of commissioners appointed on each side, or by that of a friendly nation. And should such course be proposed by either party, it shall be acceded to by the other, unless deemed by it altogether incompatible with the nature of the difference, or the circumstances of the case.

ARTICLE XXII

If (which is not to be expected, and which God forbid) war should unhappily break out between the two republics, they do now, with a view to such calamity, solemnly pledge themselves to each other and to the world to observe the following rules; absolutely where the nature of the subject permits, and as closely as possible in all cases where such absolute observance shall be impossible:

(1) The merchants of either republic then residing in the other shall be allowed to remain twelve months (for those dwelling in the interior), and six months (for those dwelling at the seaports) to collect their debts and settle their affairs; during which periods they shall enjoy the same protection, and be on the same footing, in all respects, as the citizens or subjects of the most friendly nations; and, at the expiration thereof, or at any time before, they shall have full liberty to depart, carrying off all their effects without molestation or hindrance, conforming therein to the same laws which the citizens or subjects of the most friendly nations are required to conform to. Upon the entrance of the armies of either nation into the territories of the other, women and children, ecclesiastics, scholars of every faculty, cultivators of the earth, merchants, artisans, manufacturers, and fishermen, unarmed and inhabiting unfortified towns, villages, or places, and in general all persons whose occupations are for the common subsistence and benefit of mankind, shall be allowed to continue their respective employments, unmolested in their persons. Nor shall their houses or goods be burnt or otherwise destroyed, nor their cattle taken, nor their fields wasted, by the armed force into whose power, by the events of war, they may happen to

fall; but if the necessity arise to take anything from them for the use of such armed force, the same shall be paid for at an equitable price. All churches, hospitals, schools, colleges, libraries, and other establishments for charitable and beneficent purposes, shall be respected, and all persons connected with the same protected in the discharge of their duties, and the pursuit of their vocations.

(2) In order that the fate of prisoners of war may be alleviated all such practices as those of sending them into distant, inclement or unwholesome districts, or crowding them into close and noxious places, shall be studiously avoided. They shall not be confined in dungeons, prison ships, or prisons; nor be put in irons, or bound or otherwise restrained in the use of their limbs. The officers shall enjoy liberty on their paroles, within convenient districts, and have comfortable quarters; and the common soldiers shall be dispose (in cantonments, open and extensive enough for air and exercise and lodged in barracks as roomy and good as are provided by the party in whose power they are for its own troops. But if any office shall break his parole by leaving the district so assigned him, or any other prisoner shall escape from the limits of his cantonment after they shall have been designated to him, such individual, officer, or other prisoner, shall forfeit so much of the benefit of this article as provides for his liberty on parole or in cantonment. And if any officer so breaking his parole or any common soldier so escaping from the limits assigned him, shall afterwards be found in arms previously to his being regularly exchanged, the person so offending shall be dealt with according to the established laws of war. The officers shall be daily furnished, by the party in whose power they are, with as many rations, and of the same articles, as are allowed either in kind or by commutation, to officers of equal rank in its own army; and all others shall be daily furnished with such ration as is allowed to a common soldier in its own service; the value of all which supplies shall, at the close of the war, or at periods to be agreed upon between the respective commanders, be paid by the other party, on a mutual adjustment of accounts for the subsistence of prisoners; and such accounts shall not be mingled with or set off against any others, nor the balance due on them withheld, as a compensation or reprisal for any cause whatever, real or pretended Each party shall be allowed to keep a commissary of prisoners, appointed by itself, with every cantonment of prisoners, in possession of the other; which commissary shall see the prisoners as often as he pleases; shall be allowed to receive, exempt from all duties a taxes, and to distribute, whatever comforts may be sent to them by their friends; and shall be free to transmit his reports in open letters to the party by whom he is employed. And it is declared that neither the pretense that war dissolves all treaties, nor any other whatever, shall be considered as annulling or suspending the solemn covenant contained in this article. On the contrary, the state of war is precisely that for which it is provided; and, during which, its stipulations are to be as sacredly observed as the most acknowledged obligations under the law of nature or nations.

ARTICLE XXIII

This treaty shall be ratified by the President of the United States of America, by and with the advice and consent of the Senate thereof; and by the President of the Mexican Republic, with the previous approbation of its general Congress; and the ratifications shall be exchanged in the City of Washington, or at the seat of Government of Mexico, in four months from the date of the signature hereof, or sooner if practicable. In faith whereof we, the respective Plenipotentiaries, have signed this treaty of peace, friendship, limits, and settlement, and have hereunto affixed our seals respectively. Done in quintuplicate, at the city of Guadalupe Hidalgo, on the second day of February, in the year of our Lord one thousand eight hundred and forty-eight.

N. P. TRIST
LUIS P. CUEVAS
BERNARDO COUTO
MIGL. ATRISTAIN

The Compromise of 1850

Note: The six documents transcribed here are Henry Clay's Resolution and the five statutes approved by Congress. The acts called for the admission of California as a "free state," provided for a territorial government for Utah and New Mexico, established a boundary between Texas and the United States, called for the abolition of slave trade in Washington, DC, and amended the Fugitive Slave Act.

CLAY'S RESOLUTIONS JANUARY 29, 1850

It being desirable, for the peace, concord, and harmony of the Union of these States, to settle and adjust amicably all existing questions of controversy between them arising out of the institution of slavery upon a fair, equitable and just basis: therefore,

1. Resolved, That California, with suitable boundaries, ought, upon her application to be admitted as one of the States of this Union, without the imposition by Congress of any restriction in respect to the exclusion or introduction of slavery within those boundaries.

2. Resolved, That as slavery does not exist by law, and is not likely to be introduced into any of the territory acquired by the United States from the republic of Mexico, it is inexpedient for Congress to provide by law either for its introduction into, or exclusion from, any part of the said territory; and that appropriate territorial governments ought to be established by Congress in all of the said territory, not assigned as the boundaries of the proposed State of California, without the adoption of any restriction or condition on the subject of slavery.

3. Resolved, That the western boundary of the State of Texas ought to be fixed on the Rio del Norte, commencing one marine league from its mouth, and running up that river to the southern line of New Mexico; thence with that line eastwardly, and so continuing in the same direction to the line as established between the United States and Spain, excluding any portion of New Mexico, whether lying on the east or west of that river.

4. Resolved, That it be proposed to the State of Texas, that the United States will provide for the payment of all that portion of the legitimate and bona fide public debt of that State contracted prior to its annexation to the United States, and for which the duties on foreign imports were pledged by the said State to its creditors, not exceeding the sum of dollars, in consideration of the said duties so pledged having been no longer applicable to that object after the said annexation, but having thenceforward become payable to the United States; and upon the condition, also, that the said State of Texas shall, by some solemn and authentic act of her legislature or of a convention, relinquish to the United States any claim which it has to any part of New Mexico.

5. Resolved, That it is inexpedient to abolish slavery in the District of Columbia whilst that institution continues to exist in the State of Maryland, without the consent of that State, without the consent of the people of the District, and without just compensation to the owners of slaves within the District.

6. But, resolved, That it is expedient to prohibit, within the District, the slave trade in slaves brought into it from States or places beyond the limits of the District, either to be sold therein as merchandise, or to be transported to other markets without the District of Columbia.

7. Resolved, That more effectual provision ought to be made by law, according to the requirement of the constitution, for the restitution and delivery of persons bound to service or labor in any State, who may escape into any other State or Territory in the Union. And,

8. Resolved, That Congress has no power to promote or obstruct the trade in slaves between the slaveholding States; but that the admission or exclusion of slaves brought from one into another of them, depends exclusively upon their own particular laws.

An Act proposing to the State of Texas the Establishment of her Northern and Western Boundaries, the Relinquishment by the said State of all Territory claimed by her exterior to said boundaries, and of all her Claims upon the United States, and to establish a territorial Government for New Mexico.

Be it enacted by the Senate and House of Representatives of the United States of America in Congress assembled, That the following propositions shall be, and the same hereby are, offered to the State of Texas, which, when agreed to by the said State, in an act passed by the general assembly, shall be binding and obligatory upon the United States, and upon the said State of Texas: Provided, The said agreement by the said general assembly shall be given on or before the first day of December, eighteen hundred and fifty:

FIRST. The State of Texas will agree that her boundary on the north shall commence at the point at which the meridian of one hundred degrees west from Greenwich is intersected by the parallel of thirty-six degrees thirty minutes north latitude, and shall run from said point due west to the meridian of one hundred and three degrees west from Greenwich; thence her boundary shall run due south to the thirty-second degree of north latitude; thence on the said parallel of thirty-two degrees of north latitude to the Rio Bravo del Norte, and thence with the channel of said river to the Gulf of Mexico.

SECOND. The State of Texas cedes to the United States all her claim to territory exterior to the limits and boundaries which she agrees to establish by the first article of this agreement.

THIRD. The State of Texas relinquishes all claim upon the United States for liability of the debts of Texas, and for compensation or indemnity for the surrender to the United States of her ships, forts, arsenals, custom houses, custom house revenue, arms and munitions of war, and public buildings with their sites, which became the property of the United States at the time of the annexation.

FOURTH. The United States, in consideration of said establishment of boundaries, cession of claim—, to territory, and relinquishment of claims, will pay to the State of Texas the sum of ten millions of dollars in a stock bearing five per cent interest, and redeemable at the end of fourteen years, the interest payable half-yearly at the treasury of the United States.

FIFTH. Immediately after the President of the United States shall have been furnished with an authentic copy of the act of the general assembly of Texas accepting these propositions, he shall cause the stock to be issued in favor of the State of Texas, as

provided for in the fourth article of this agreement: Provided, also, That no more than five millions of said stock shall be issued until the creditors of the State holding bonds and other certificates of stock of Texas for which duties on imports were specially pledged, shall first file at the treasury of the United States releases of all claim against the United States for or on account of said bonds or certificates in such form as shall be prescribed by the Secretary of the Treasury and approved by the president of the United States: Provided, That nothing herein contained shall be construed to impair or qualify any thing contained in the third article of the second section of the "joint resolution for annexing Texas to the United States," approved March first, eighteen hundred and forty-five; either as regards the number of States that may hereafter be formed out of the State of Texas, or otherwise.

SEC. 2. And be it further enacted, That all that portion of the Territory of the United States bounded as follows: Beginning at a point in the Colorado River where the boundary line with the republic of Mexico crosses the same; thence eastwardly with the said boundary line to the Rio Grande; thence following the main channel of said river the parallel of the thirty-second degree of north latitude; thence east with said degree to its intersection with the one hundred and third degree of longitude west of Greenwich; thence north with said degree of longitude to the parallel of thirty-eighth degree of north latitude; thence west with said parallel to the summit of the Sierra Madre; thence south with the crest of said mountains to the thirty-seventh parallel of north latitude; thence west with said parallel to its intersection with the boundary line of the State of California; thence with said boundary line to the place of beginning be, and the same is hereby, erected into a temporary government, by the name of the Territory of New Mexico: Provided, That nothing in this act contained shall be construed to inhibit the government of the United States from dividing said Territory into two or more Territories, in such manner and at such times as Congress shall deem convenient and proper, or from attaching any portion thereof to any other Territory or State: And provided, further, That, when admitted as a State, the said Territory, or any portion of the same, shall be received into the Union, with or without slavery, as their constitution may prescribe at the time of their admission.

SEC. 3. And be it further enacted, That the executive power and authority in and over said Territory of

New Mexico shall be vested in, a governor, who shall hold his office for four years, and until his successor shall be appointed and qualified, unless sooner removed by the President of the United States. The governor shall reside within said Territory, shall be commander-in-chief of the militia thereof, shall perform the duties and receive the emoluments of superintendent of Indian affairs, and shall approve all laws passed by the legislative assembly before they shall take effect; he may grant pardons for offences against the laws of said Territory, and reprieves for offences against the laws of the United States, until the decision of the President can be made known thereon he shall commission all officers who shall be appointed to office under the laws of the said Territory, and shall take care that the laws be faithfully executed.

SEC. 4. And be it further enacted, That there shall be a secretary of said Territory, who shall reside therein, and hold his office for four years, unless sooner removed by the President of the United States; he shall record and preserve all the laws and proceedings of the legislative assembly hereinafter constituted and all the acts and proceedings of the governor in his executive department; he shall transmit one copy of the laws and one copy of the executive proceedings, on or before the first day of December in each year, to the President of the United States, and, at the same time, two copies of the laws to the Speaker of the House of Representatives and the President of the Senate, for the use of Congress. And, in case of the death, removal, resignation, or other necessary absence of the governor from the Territory, the secretary shall have, and he is hereby authorized and required to execute and perform all the powers and duties of the governor during such vacancy or necessary absence, or until another governor shall be duly appointed to fill such vacancy.

SEC. 5. And be it further enacted, That the legislative power and authority of said Territory shall be vested in the governor and a legislative assembly. The legislative assembly shall consist of a Council and House of Representatives. The Council shall consist of thirteen members, having the qualifications of voters as hereinafter prescribed, whose term of service shall continue two years. The House of Representatives shall consist of twenty-six members, possessing the same qualifications as prescribed for members of the Council, and whose term of service shall continue one year. An apportionment shall be made, as nearly equal as practicable, among the several counties or districts, for the election of the

Council and House of Representatives, giving to each section of the Territory representation in the ratio of its population, (Indians excepted,) as nearly as may be. And the members of the Council and of the House of Representatives shall reside in, and be inhabitants of, the district for which they may be elected respectively. Previous to the first election, the governor shall cause a census or enumeration of the inhabitants of the several counties and districts of the Territory to be taken, and the first election shall be held at such time and places, and be conducted in such manner, as the governor shall appoint and direct; and he shall, at the same time, declare the number of the members of the Council and House of Representatives to which each of the counties or districts shall be entitled under this act. The number of persons authorized to be elected having the highest number of votes in each of said Council districts, for members of the Council, shall be declared by the governor to be duly elected to the Council; and the person or persons authorized to be elected having the greatest number of votes for the House of Representatives, equal to the number to which each county or district shall be entitled, shall be declared by the governor to be duly elected members of the House of Representatives: Provided, That in case of a tie between two or more persons voted for, the governor shall order a new election to supply the vacancy made by such tie. And the persons thus elected to the legislative assembly shall meet at such place and on such day as the governor shall appoint; but thereafter, the time, place, and manner of holding and conducting all elections by the people, and the apportioning the representation in the several counties or districts to the Council and House of Representatives according to the population, shall be prescribed by law, as well as the day of the commencement of the regular sessions of the legislative assembly: Provided, That no one session shall exceed the term of forty days.

SEC. 6. And be it further enacted, That every free white male inhabitant, above the age of twenty-one years, who shall have been a resident of said Territory at the time of the passage of this act, shall be entitled to vote at the first election, and shall be eligible to any office within the said Territory; but the qualifications of voters and of holding office, at all subsequent elections, shall be such as shall be prescribed by the legislative assembly: Provided, That the right of suffrage, and of holding office, shall be exercised only by citizens of the United States, including those recognized as citizens by the treaty with the republic of Mexico, concluded February second, eighteen hundred and forty-eight.

SEC. 7. And be it further enacted, That the legislative power of the Territory shall extend to all rightful subjects of legislation, consistent with the Constitution of the United States and the provisions of this act; but no law shall be passed interfering with the primary disposal of the soil; no tax shall be imposed upon the property of the United States; nor shall the lands or other property of non-residents be taxed higher than the lands or other property of residents. All the laws passed by the legislative assembly and governor shall be submitted to the Congress of the United States, and, if disapproved, shall be null and of no effect.

SEC. 8. And be it further enacted, That all township, district, and county officers not herein otherwise provided for, shall be appointed or elected, as the case may be, in such manner as shall be provided by the governor and legislative assembly of the Territory of New Mexico. The governor shall nominate, and, by and with the advice and consent of the legislative Council, appoint, an officers not herein otherwise provided for; and in the first instance the governor alone may appoint all said officers, who shall hold their offices until the end of the first session of the legislative assembly, and shall lay off the necessary districts for members of the Council and House of Representatives, and all other officers.

SEC. 9. And be it further enacted, That no member of the legislative assembly shall hold, or be appointed to, any office which shall have been created, or the salary or emoluments of which shall have been increased while he was a member, during the term for which he was elected, and for one year after the expiration of such term; and no person holding a commission or appointment under the United States, except postmasters, shall be a member of the legislative assembly, or shall hold any office under the government of said Territory.

SEC. 10. And be it further enacted, That the judicial power of said Territory shall be vested in a Supreme Court, District Courts, Probate Courts, and in justices of the peace. The Supreme Court shall consist of a chief justice and two associate justices, any two of whom shall constitute a quorum, and who shall hold a term at the seat of government of said Territory annually, and they shall hold their offices during the period of four years. The said Territory shall be divided into three judicial districts, and a District Court shall be held in each of said districts by one of the justices of the Supreme Court, at such time and place as may be prescribed by law; and the said judges shall, after their appointments, respectively, reside in the districts which shall be assigned them. The jurisdiction of the several courts herein provided for, both appellate and original, and that of the Probate Courts and of justices of the peace, shall be as limited by law: Provided, That justices of the peace shall not have jurisdiction of any matter in controversy when the title or boundaries of land may be in dispute, or where the debt or sum claimed shall exceed one hundred dollars; and the said Supreme and District Courts, respectively, shall possess chancery as well as common law jurisdiction. Each District Court, or the judge thereof, shall appoint its clerk, who shall also be the register in chancery, and shall keep his office at the place where the court may be held. Writs of error, bills of exception, and appeals, shall be allowed in all cases from the final decisions of said District Courts to the Supreme Court, under such regulations as may be prescribed by law, but in no case removed to the Supreme Court shall trial by jury be allowed in said court. The Supreme Court, or the justices thereof, shall appoint its own clerk, and every clerk shall hold his office at the pleasure of the court for which he shall have been appointed. Writs of error and appeals from the final decisions of said Supreme Court shall be allowed, and may be taken to the Supreme Court of the United States, in the same manner and under the same regulations as from the Circuit Courts of the United States, where the value of the property or the amount in controversy, to be ascertained by the oath or affirmation of either party, or other competent witness, shall exceed one thousand dollars; except only that in all cases involving title to slaves, the said writs of error or appeals shall be allowed and decided by the said Supreme Court without regard to the value of the matter, property, or title in controversy; and except also that a writ of error or appeal shall also be allowed to the Supreme Court of the United States from the decision of the said Supreme Court created by this act, or of any judge thereof, or of the District Courts created by this act, or of any judge thereof, upon any writ of habeas corpus involving the question of personal freedom; and each of the said District Courts shall have and exercise the same jurisdiction in all cases arising under the Constitution and laws of the United States as is vested in the Circuit and District Courts of the United States; and the said Supreme and District Courts of the said Territory, and the respective judges thereof, shall and may grant writs of habeas corpus in all cases in which the same are grantable by the judges of the United States in the District of Columbia; and the first six days of every term of said courts, or so much thereof as shall be necessary, shall be appropriated to the trial of causes arising under the said Constitution and laws; and writs of error and appeals in all such cases shall be made to the Supreme Court of said Territory, the same as in other cases. The said clerk shall receive in all such cases the same fees which the clerks of the District Courts of Oregon Territory now receive for similar services.

SEC. 11. And be it further enacted, That there shall be appointed an attorney for said Territory, who shall continue in office for four years, unless sooner removed by the President, and who shall receive the same fees and salary as the attorney of the United States for the present Territory of Oregon. There shall also be a marshal for the Territory appointed, who shall hold his office for four years, unless sooner removed by the president, and who shall execute all processes issuing from the said courts when exercising their jurisdiction as Circuit and District Courts of the United States: he shall perform the duties, be subject to the same regulation and penalties, and be entitled to the same fees as the marshal of the District Court of the United States for the present Territory of Oregon, and shall, in addition, be paid two hundred [dollars] annually as a compensation for extra services.

SEC. 12. And be it further enacted, That the governor secretary, chief justice and associate justices, attorney and marshal shall be nominated, and, by and with the advice and consent of the Senate, appointed by the President of the United States. The governor and secretary, to be appointed as aforesaid, shall, before they act as such, respectively take an oath or affirmation, before the district judge, or some justice of the peace in the limits of said Territory, duly authorized to administer oaths and affirmations by the laws now in force therein, or before the chief justice or some associate justice of the Supreme Court of the United States, to support the Constitution of the United States, and faithfully to discharge the duties of their respective offices; which said oaths, when so taken, shall be certified by the person by whom the same shall have been taken, and such certificates shall be received and recorded by the said secretary among the executive proceedings; and the chief justice and associate justices, and all other civil officers in said Territory, before they act as such, shall

take a like oath or affirmation, before the said governor or secretary, or some judge or justice of the peace of the Territory, who may be duly commissioned and qualified, which said oath or affirmation shall be certified and transmitted, by the person taking the same, to the secretary, to be by him recorded as aforesaid; and afterwards, the like oath or affirmation shall be taken, certified, and recorded, in such manner and form as may be prescribed by law. The governor shall receive an annual salary of fifteen hundred dollars as governor, and one thousand dollars as superintendent of Indian affairs. The chief justice and associate justices shall each receive an annual salary of eighteen hundred dollars. The secretary shall receive an annual salary of eighteen hundred dollars. The said salaries shall be paid quarter-yearly, at the treasury of the United States. The members of the legislative assembly shall be entitled to receive three dollars each per day during their attendance at the sessions thereof, and three dollars each for every twenty miles' travel in going to and returning from the said sessions, estimated according to the nearest usually travelled route. There shall be appropriated annually the sum of one thousand dollars, to be expended by the governor, to defray the contingent expenses of the Territory; there shall also be appropriated annually a sufficient sum to be expended by the secretary of the Territory, and upon an estimate to be made by the Secretary of the Treasury of the United States, to defray the expenses of the legislative assembly, the printing of the laws, and other incidental expenses; and the secretary of the Territory shall annually account to the Secretary of the Treasury of the United States for the manner in which the aforesaid sum shall have been expended.

SEC. 13. And be it further enacted, That the legislative assembly of the Territory of New Mexico shall hold its first session at such time and place in said Territory as the Governor thereof shall appoint and direct; and at said first session, or as soon thereafter as they shall deem expedient, the governor and legislative assembly shall proceed to locate and establish the seat of government for said Territory at such place as they may deem eligible; which place, however, shall thereafter be subject to be changed by the said governor and legislative assembly.

SEC. 14. And be it further enacted, That a delegate to the House of Representatives of the United States, to serve during each Congress of the United States, may be elected by the voters qualified to elect members of the legislative assembly, who shall be entitled to the same rights and privileges as are exercised and enjoyed by the delegates from the several other Territories of the United States to the said House of Representatives. The first election shall be held at such time and places, and be conducted in such manner, as the governor shall appoint and direct; and at all subsequent elections, the times, places, and manner of holding the elections shall be prescribed by law. The person having the greatest number of votes shall be declared by the governor to be duly elected, and a certificate thereof shall be given accordingly: Provided, That such delegate shall receive no higher sum for mileage than is allowed by law to the delegate from Oregon.

SEC. 15. And be it further enacted, That when the lands in said Territory shall be surveyed under the direction of the government of the United States, preparatory to bringing the same into market, sections numbered sixteen and thirty-six in each township in said Territory shall be, and the same are hereby, reserved for the purpose of being applied to schools in said Territory, and in the States and Territories hereafter to be erected out of the same.

SEC. 16. And be it further enacted, That temporarily and until otherwise provided by law, the governor of said Territory may define the judicial districts of said Territory, and assign the judges who may be appointed for said Territory to the several districts, and also appoint the times and places for holding courts in the several counties or subdivisions in each of said judicial districts, by proclamation to be issued by him; but the legislative assembly, at their first or any subsequent session, may organize, alter, or modify such judicial districts, and assign the judges, and alter the times and places of holding the courts, as to them shall seem proper and convenient.

SEC. 17. And be it further enacted, That the Constitution, and all laws of the United States which are not locally inapplicable, shall have the same force and effect within the said Territory of New Mexico as elsewhere within the United States.

SEC. 18. And be it further enacted, That the provisions of this act be, and they are hereby, suspended until the boundary between the United States and the State of Texas shall be adjusted; and when such adjustment shall have been effected, the President of the United States shall issue his proclamation, declaring this act to be in full force and operation, and shall proceed to appoint the officers herein provided to be appointed in and for said Territory.

SEC. 19. And be it further enacted, That no citizen of the United States shall be deprived of his life, liberty, or property, in said Territory, except by the judgment of his peers and the laws of the land.

APPROVED, September 9, 1850.

AN ACT FOR THE ADMISSION OF THE STATE OF CALIFORNIA INTO THE UNION.

Whereas the people of California have presented a constitution and asked admission into the Union, which constitution was submitted to Congress by the President of the United States, by message dated February thirteenth, eighteen hundred and fifty, and which, on doe examination, is found to be republican in its form of government:

Be it enacted by the Senate and House of Representatives of the United States of America in Congress assembled, That the State of California shall be one, and is hereby declared to be one, of the United States of America, and admitted into the Union on an equal footing with the original States in all respects whatever.

SEC. 2. And be it further enacted, That, until the representatives in Congress shall be apportioned according to an actual enumeration of the inhabitants of the United States, the State of California shall be entitled to two representatives in Congress.

SEC. 3. And be it further enacted, That the said State of California is admitted into the Union upon the express condition that the people of said State, through their legislature or otherwise, shall never interfere with the primary disposal of the public lands within its limits, and shall pass no law and do no act whereby the title of the United States to, and right to dispose of, the same shall be impaired or questioned; and that they shall never lay any tax or assessment of any description whatsoever upon the public domain of the United States, and in no case shall non-resident proprietors, who are citizens of the United States, be taxed higher than residents; and that all the navigable waters within the said State shall be common highways, and forever free, as well to the inhabitants of said State as to the citizens of the United States, without any tax, impost, or duty therefor: Provided, That nothing herein contained shall be construed as recognizing or rejecting the propositions tendered by the people of California as articles of compact in the ordinance adopted by the convention which formed the constitution of that State.

APPROVED, September 9, 1850.

AN ACT TO ESTABLISH A TERRITORIAL GOVERNMENT FOR UTAH.

Be it enacted by the Senate and House of Representatives of the United States of America in Congress assembled, That all that part of the territory of the United States included within the following limits, to wit: bounded on the west by the State of California, on the north by the Territory of Oregon, and on the east by the summit of the Rocky Mountains, and on the south by the thirty-seventh parallel of north latitude, be, and the same is hereby, created into a temporary government, by the name of the Territory of Utah; and, when admitted as a State, the said Territory, or any portion of the same, shall be received into the Union, with or without slavery, as their constitution may prescribe at the time of their admission: Provided, That nothing in this act contained shall be construed to inhibit the government of the United States from dividing said Territory into two or more Territories, in such manner and at such times as Congress shall deem convenient and proper, or from attaching any portion of said Territory to any other State or Territory of the United States.

SEC. 2. And be it further enacted, That the executive power and authority in and over said Territory of Utah shall be vested in a governor, who shall hold his office for four years, and until his successor shall be appointed and qualified, unless sooner removed by the President of the United States. The governor shall reside within said Territory, shall be commander-in-chief of the militia thereof, shall perform the duties and receive the emoluments of superintendent of Indian affairs, and shall approve all laws passed by the legislative assembly before they shall take effect: he may grant pardons for offences against the laws of said Territory, and reprieves for offences against the laws of the United States, until the decision of the President can be made known thereon; he shall commission all officers who shall be appointed to office under the laws of the said Territory, and shall take care that the laws be faithfully executed.

SEC. 3. And be it further enacted, That there shall be a secretary of said Territory, who shall reside therein, and hold his office for four years, unless sooner removed by the President of the United States: he shall record and preserve all the laws and proceedings of the legislative assembly hereinafter constituted, and all the acts and proceedings of the governor in his executive department; he shall transmit one copy of the laws and one copy of the executive proceedings, on or before the first day of December in each year, to the President of the United States, and, at the same time, two copies of the laws to the Speaker of the House of Representatives, and the President of the Senate, for the use of Congress. And in the case of the death, removal, resignation, or other necessary absence of the governor from the Territory, the secretary shall have, and he is hereby authorized and required to execute and perform, all the powers and duties of the governor during such vacancy or necessary absence, or until another governor shall be duly appointed to fill such vacancy.

SEC. 4. And be it further enacted, That the legislative power and authority of said Territory shall be vested in the governor and a legislative assembly. The legislative assembly shall consist of a Council and House of Representatives. The Council shall consist of thirteen members, having the qualifications of voters as hereinafter prescribed, whose term of service shall continue two years. The House of Representatives shall consist of twenty-six members, possessing the same qualifications as prescribed for members of the Council, and, whose term of service shall continue one year. An apportionment shall be made, as nearly equal as practicable, among the several counties or districts, for the election of the Council and House of Representatives, giving to each section of the Territory representation in the ratio of its population, Indians excepted, as nearly as may be. And the members of the Council and of the House of Representatives shall reside in, and be inhabitants of, the district for which they may be elected respectively. Previous to the first election, the governor shall cause a census or enumeration of the inhabitants of the several counties and districts of the Territory to be taken, and the first election shall be held at such time and places, and be conducted in such manner, as the governor shall appoint and direct; and he shall, at the same time, declare the number of members of the Council and House of Representatives to which each of the counties or districts shall be entitled under this act. The number of persons authorized to be elected having the highest number of votes in each of said Council districts for members of the Council, shall be declared by the governor to be duly elected to the Council; and the person or persons authorized to be elected having the highest number of votes for the House of Representatives, equal to the number to which each county or district shall be entitled, shall be declared by the governor to be duly elected members or the House of Representatives: Provided, That in case of a tie between two or more persons voted for, the governor shall order a new election to supply the vacancy made by such a tie. And the persons thus elected to the legislative assembly shall meet at such place, and on such day, as the governor shall appoint; but thereafter, the time, place, and manner of holding and conducting all elections by the people, and the apportioning the representation in the several counties or districts to the Council and House of Representatives, according to population, shall be prescribed by law, as well as the day of the commencement of the regular sessions of the legislative assembly: Provided That no one session shall exceed the term of forty days.

SEC. 5. And be it further enacted, That every free white male inhabitant above the age of twenty-one years, who shall have been a resident or said Territory at the time of the passage of this act, shall he entitled to vote at the first election, and shall be eligible to any office within the said Territory; but the qualifications of voters and of holding office, at all subsequent elections, shall be such as shall be prescribed by the legislative assembly: Provided, That the right of suffrage and of holding office shall be exercised only by citizens of the United States, including those recognized as citizens by the treaty with the republic of Mexico, concluded February second, eighteen hundred and forty-eight.

SEC. 6. And be it further enacted, That the legislative power of said Territory shall extend to all rightful subjects of legislation, consistent with the Constitution of the United States and the provisions of this act; but no law shall be passed interfering with the primary disposal of the soil; no tax shall be imposed upon the property of the United States; nor shall the lands or other property of non-residents be taxed higher than the lands or other property of residents. All the laws passed by the legislative assembly and governor shall be submitted to the Congress of the United States, and, if disapproved, shall be null and of no effect.

SEC. 7. And be it further enacted, That all township, district, and county officers, not herein other-wise provided for, shall be appointed or elected, as the case may be, in such manner as shall be provided by the governor and legislative assembly of the territory of Utah. The governor shall nominate, and, by and with the advice and consent of the legislative Council, appoint all officers not herein otherwise provided for; and in the first instance the governor alone may appoint all said officers, who shall hold their offices until the end of the first session of the legislative assembly, and shall layoff the necessary districts for members of the Council and House of Representatives, and all other offices.

SEC. 8. And be it further enacted, That no member of the legislative assembly shall hold or be appointed to any office which shall have been created, or the salary or emoluments of which shall have been increased while he was a member, during the term for which he was elected, and for one year after the expiration of such term; and no person holding a commission or appointment under the United States, except postmasters, shall be a member of the legislative assembly, or shall hold any office under the government of said Territory.

SEC. 9. And be it further enacted, That the judicial power of said Territory shall be vested in a Supreme Court, District Courts, Probate Courts, and in justices of the peace. The Supreme Court shall consist of a chief justice and two associate justices, any two of whom shall constitute a quorum, and who shall hold a term at the Beat of government of said Territory annually, and they shall hold their offices during the period of four years. The said Territory shall be divided into three judicial districts, and a District Court shall be held in each of said districts by one of the justices of the Supreme Court, at such time and place as may be prescribed by law; and the said judges shall, after their appointments, respectively, reside in the districts which shall be assigned them. The jurisdiction of the several courts herein provided for, both appellate and original, and that of the Probate Courts and of justices of the peace, shall be as limited by law: Provided, That justices of the peace shall not have jurisdiction of any matter in controversy when the title or boundaries of land may be in dispute, or where the debt or sum claimed shall exceed one hundred dollars; and the said Supreme and District Courts, respectively, shall possess chancery as well as common law jurisdiction. Each District Court, or the judge thereof, shall appoint its clerk, who shall also be the register in chancery, and shall keep his office at the place where the court may be held. Writs of error, bills of exception, and appeals shall be allowed in all cases from the final decisions of said District Courts to the Supreme Court, under such regulations as may be prescribed by law; but in no case removed to the Supreme Court shall trial by jury be allowed in said court. The Supreme Court, or the justices thereof, shall appoint its own clerk, and every clerk shall hold his office at the pleasure of the court for which he shall have been appointed. Writs of error, and appeals from the final decisions of said Supreme Court, shall be allowed, and may be taken to the Supreme Court of the United States, in the same manner and under the same regulations as from the Circuit Courts of the United States, where the value of the property or the amount in controversy, to be ascertained by the oath or affirmation of either party, or other competent witness, shall exceed one thousand dollars, except only that, in all cases involving title to slaves, the said writs of error or appeals shall be allowed and decided by the said Supreme Court, without regard to the value of the matter, property, or title in controversy; and except also, that a writ of error or appeal shall also be allowed to the Supreme Court of the United States, from the decisions of the said Supreme Court created by this act or of any judge thereof or of the District Courts created by this act or of any judge thereof, upon any writ of habeas corpus involving the question of personal freedom; and each of the said District Courts shall have and exercise the same jurisdiction in all cases arising under the Constitution and laws of the United States as is vested in the Circuit and District Courts of the United States; and the said Supreme and District Courts of the said Territory, and the respective judges thereof shall and may grant writs of habeas corpus in all cases in which the same are granted by the judges of the United States in the District of Columbia; and the first six days of every term of said courts, or so much thereof as shall be necessary shall be appropriated to the trial of causes arising under the said Constitution and laws; and writs of error and appeal, in all such cases, shall be made to the Supreme Court of said Territory, the same as in other cases. The said clerk shall receive in all such cases the same fees which the clerks of the District Courts of Oregon Territory now receive for similar services.

SEC. 10. And be it further enacted, That there shall be appointed an attorney for said Territory, who shall continue in office for four years, unless sooner removed by the President, and who shall receive the same fees and salary as the attorney of the United States for the present Territory of Oregon. There shall also be a marshal for the Territory appointed, who shall hold his office for four years, unless sooner removed by the President, and who shall execute all processes issuing from the said courts, when exercising their jurisdiction as Circuit and District Courts of the United States: he shall perform the duties, be subject to the same regulation and penalties, and be entitled to the same fees as the marshal of the District Court of the United States for the present Territory of Oregon; and shall, in addition, be paid two hundred dollars annually as a compensation for extra services.

SEC. 11. And be it further enacted, That the governor, secretary, chief justice and associate justices, attorney and marshal, shall be nominated, and, by and with the advice and consent of the Senate, appointed by the President of the United States. The governor and secretary to be appointed as aforesaid shall, before they act as such respectively, take an oath or affirmation, before the district judge, or some justice of the peace in the limits of said Territory, duly authorized to administer oaths and affirmations by the laws now in force therein or before the chief justice or some associate justice of the Supreme Court of the United States, to support the Constitution of the United States, and faithfully to discharge the duties of their respective offices; which said oaths, when so taken, shall be certified by the person by whom the same shall have been taken, and such certificates shall be received and recorded by the said secretary among the executive proceedings; and the chief justice and associate justices, and all other civil officers in said Territory, before they act as such, shall take a like oath or affirmation, before the said governor or secretary, or some judge or justice of the peace of the Territory who may be duly commissioned and qualified, which said oath or affirmation shall be certified and transmitted, by the person taking the same, to the secretary, to be by him recorded as aforesaid; and afterwards, the like oath or affirmation shall be taken, certified, and recorded, in such manner and form as may he prescribed by law. The governor shall receive an annual salary of fifteen hundred dollars as governor, and one thousand dollars as superintendent of Indian affairs. The chief justice and associate justices shall each receive an annual salary of eighteen hundred dollars. The secretary shall receive an annual salary of eighteen hundred dollars. The said salaries shall be paid quarter-yearly, at the treasury of the United States. The members of the legislative assembly shall be entitled to receive three dollars each per day during their attendance at the sessions thereof, and three dollars each for twenty miles' travel, in going to and returning from the said sessions, estimated according to the nearest usually travelled route. There shall be appropriated annually the sum of one thousand dollars, to be expended by the governor, to defray the contingent expenses of the Territory. There shall also be appropriated, annually, a sufficient sum, to be expended by the secretary of the Territory, and upon an estimate to be made by the Secretary of the Treasury of the United States, to defray the expenses of the legislative assembly, the printing of the laws, and other incidental expenses; and the secretary of the Territory shall annually account to the Secretary of the Treasury of the United States for the manner in which the aforesaid sum shall have been expended.

SEC. 12. And be it further enacted, That the legislative assembly of the Territory of Utah shall hold its first session at such time and place in said Territory as the governor thereof shall appoint and direct; and at said first session, or as soon thereafter as they shall deem expedient, the governor and legislative assembly shall proceed to locate and establish the seat of government for said Territory at such place as they may deem eligible; which place, however, shall thereafter be, subject to be changed by the said governor and legislative assembly. And the sum of twenty thousand dollars, out of any money in the treasury not otherwise appropriated, is hereby appropriated and granted to said Territory of Utah to be applied by the governor and legislative assembly to the erection of suitable public buildings at the seat of government.

SEC. 13. And be it further enacted, That a delegate to the House of Representatives of the United States, to serve during each Congress of the United States, may be elected by the voters qualified to elect members of the legislative assembly, who shall be entitled to the same rights and privileges as are exercised and enjoyed by the delegates from the several other Territories of the United States to the said House of Representatives. The first election shall be held at such time and places, and be conducted in such manner, as the governor shall appoint and direct; and at all subsequent elections, the times, places, and manner of holding the elections shall be prescribed by law. The person having the greatest number of votes shall be declared by the governor to be duly elected, and a certificate thereof shall be given accordingly: Provided, That said delegate shall receive no higher sum for mileage than is allowed by law to the delegate from Oregon.

SEC. 14. And be it further enacted, That the sum or five thousand dollars be, and the same is hereby, appropriated out of any moneys in the treasury not otherwise appropriated, to be expended by and under the direction of the said governor of the territory of Utah, in the purchase of a library, to be kept at the seat of government for the use of the governor, legislative assembly, judges of the Supreme Court, secretary, marshal, and attorney of said Territory, and such other persons, and under such regulations, as shall be prescribed by law.

SEC. 15. And be it further enacted, That when the lands in the said Territory shall be surveyed under the direction of the government of the United States preparatory to bringing the same into market, sections numbered sixteen and thirty-six in each township in said Territory shall be, and the same are hereby, reserved for the purpose of being applied to schools in said Territory, and in the States and Territories hereafter to be erected out of the same.

SEC. 16. And be it further enacted, That temporarily, and until otherwise provided by law, the governor of said Territory may define the judicial districts of said Territory, and assign the judges who maybe appointed for said Territory to the several districts, and also appoint the times and places for holding courts in the several counties or subdivisions in each of said judicial districts, by proclamation to be issued by him; but the legislative assembly, at their first or any subsequent session, may organize, alter, or modify such judicial districts, and assign the judges, and alter the times and places of holding the courts, as to them shall seem proper and convenient.

SEC.17. And be it further enacted, That the Constitution and laws of the United States are hereby extended over and declared to be in force in said Territory of Utah, so far as the same, or any provision thereof, may be applicable.

APPROVED, September 9, 1850.

AN ACT TO AMEND, AND SUPPLEMENTARY TO, THE ACT ENTITLED "AN ACT RESPECTING FUGITIVES FROM JUSTICE, AND PERSONS ESCAPING FROM THE SERVICE OF THEIR MASTERS," APPROVED FEBRUARY TWELFTH, ONE THOUSAND SEVEN HUNDRED AND NINETY-THREE.

Be it enacted by the Senate and House of Repsentatives of the United States of America in congress assembled, That the persons who have been, or may hereafter be, appointed commissioners, in virtue of any act of Congress, by the Circuit Courts of the United States and who, in consequence of such appointment, are authorized to exercise the powers that any justice of the peace, or other magistrate of any of the United States, may exercise in respect to offenders for any crime or offence against the United States, by arresting, imprisoning, or bailing the same under and by virtue of the thirty-third section of the act of the twenty-fourth of September seventeen hundred and eighty-nine, entitled "An Act to establish the Judicial courts of the United States," shall be, and are hereby, authorized and required to exercise and discharge all the powers and duties conferred by this act.

SEC. 2. And be it further enacted, That the Superior Court of each organized Territory of the United States shall have the same power to appoint commissioners to take acknowledgements of bail and affidavits and to take depositions of witnesses in civil causes, which is now possessed by the Circuit Court of the United States; and all commissioners who shall hereafter be appointed for such purposes by the Superior Court of any organized Territory of the United States, shall possess all the powers, and exercise all the duties, conferred by law upon the commissioners appointed by the Circuit Courts of the United States for similar purposes, and shall moreover exercise and discharge all the powers and duties conferred by this act.

SEC. 3. And be it further enacted, That the Circuit Courts of the United States, and the Superior Courts of each organized Territory of the United States, shall from time to time enlarge the number of commissioners, with a view to afford reasonable facilities to reclaim fugitives from labor, and to the prompt discharge of the duties imposed by this act.

SEC. 4. And be it further enacted, That the commissioners above named shall have concurrent jurisdiction with the judges of the Circuit and District Courts of the United States, in their respective circuits and districts within the several States, and the judges of the Superior Courts of the Territories, severally and collectively, in term time and vacation; and shall grant certificates to such claimants, upon satisfactory proof being made, with authority to take and remove such fugitives from service or labor, under the restrictions herein contained, to the State or Territory from which such persons may have escaped or fled.

SEC. 5. And be it further enacted, That it shall be the duty of all marshals and deputy marshals to obey and execute all warrants and precepts issued under the provisions of this act, when to them directed; and should any marshal or deputy marshal refuse to receive such warrant, or other process, when tendered, or to use all proper means diligently to execute the same, he shall, on conviction thereof, be fined in the sum of one thousand dollars, to the use of such claimant, on the motion of such claimant, by the Circuit or District Court for the district of such marshal; and after arrest of such fugitive, by such marshal or his deputy, or whilst at any time in his custody under the provisions of this act, should such fugitive escape, whether with or without the assent of such marshal or his deputy, such marshal shall be liable, on his official bond, to be prosecuted for the benefit of such claimant, for the full value of the service or labor of said fugitive in the State, Territory, or District whence he escaped: and the better to enable the said commissioners, when thus appointed, to execute their duties faithfully and efficiently, in conformity with the requirements of the Constitution of the United States and of this act, they are hereby authorized and empowered, within their counties respectively, to appoint, in writing under their hands, anyone or more suitable persons, from time to time, to execute all such warrants and other process as may be issued by them in the lawful performance of their respective duties; with authority to such commissioners, or the persons to be appointed by them, to execute process as aforesaid, to summon and call to their aid the bystanders, or posse comitatus of the proper county, when necessary to ensure a faithful observance of the clause of the Constitution referred to, in conformity with the provisions of this act; and all good citizens are hereby commanded to aid and assist in the prompt and efficient execution of this law, whenever their services may he required, as aforesaid, for that purpose; and said warrants shall run, and be executed by said officers, anywhere in the State within which they are issued.

SEC. 6. And be it further enacted, That when a person held to service or labor in any State or Territory of the United States, has heretofore or shall hereafter escape into another State or Territory of the United States, the person or persons to whom such service or labor may be due, or his, her, or their agent or attorney, duly authorized, by power of attorney, in writing, acknowledged and certified under the seal of some legal officer or court of the State or Territory in which the same may be executed, may pursue and reclaim such fugitive person, either by procuring a warrant from some one of the courts, judges, or commissioners aforesaid, of the proper circuit, district, or county, for the apprehension of such fugitive from service or labor, or by seizing and arresting such fugitive, where the same can be done without process, and by taking, or causing such person to be taken, forthwith before such court, judge, or commissioner, whose duty it shall be to hear and determine the case of such claimant in a summary manner; and upon satisfactory proof being made, by deposition or affidavit, in writing, to be taken and certified by such court, judge, or commissioner, or by other satisfactory testimony, duly taken and certified by some court, magistrate, justice of the peace, or other legal officer authorized to administer an oath and take depositions under the laws of the State or Territory from which such person owing service or labor may have escaped, with a certificate of such magistracy or other authority, as aforesaid, with the seal of the proper court or officer thereto attached, which seal shall be sufficient to establish the competency of the proof, and with proof, also by affidavit, of the identity of the person whose service or labor is claimed to be due as aforesaid, that the person so arrested does in fact owe service or labor to the person or persons claiming him or her, in the State or Territory from which such fugitive may have escaped as aforesaid, and that said person escaped, to make out and deliver to such claimant, his or her agent or attorney, a certificate setting forth the substantial facts as to the service or labor due from such fugitive to the claimant, and of his or her escape from the State or Territory in which such service or labor was due, to the State or Territory in which he or she was arrested, with authority to such claimant, or his or her agent or attorney, to use such reasonable force and restraint as may be necessary, under the circumstances of the case, to take and remove such fugitive person back to the State or Territory whence he or she may have escaped as aforesaid. In no trial or hearing under this act shall the testimony of such alleged fugitive be admitted in evidence; and the certificates in this and the first [fourth] section mentioned, shall be conclusive of the right of the person or persons in whose favor granted, to remove such fugitive to the State or Territory from which he escaped, and shall prevent all molestation of such person or persons by any process issued by any court judge, magistrate, or other person whomsoever.

SEC. 7. And be it further enacted, That any person who shall knowingly and willingly obstruct, hinder, or prevent such claimant, his agent or attorney, or any person or persons lawfully assisting him, her, or them, from arresting such a fugitive from service or labor, either with or without process as aforesaid, or shall rescue, or attempt to rescue such fugitive from service or labor, from the custody of such claimant, his or her agent or attorney, or other person or persons lawfully assisting as aforesaid, when so arrested, pursuant to the authority herein given and declared; or shall aid, abet, or assist such person so owing service or labor as aforesaid, directly or indirectly, to escape from such claimant, his agent or attorney, or other person or persons legally authorized as aforesaid; or shall harbor or conceal such fugitive, so as to prevent the discovery and arrest of such person, after notice or knowledge of the fact that such person was a fugitive from service or labor as aforesaid, shall, for either of said offences, be subject to a fine not exceeding one thousand dollars, and imprisonment not exceeding six months, by indictment and conviction before the District Court of the United States for the district in which such offence may have been committed, or before the proper court of criminal jurisdiction, if committed within anyone of the organized Territories of the United States; and shall moreover forfeit and pay, by way of civil damages to the party injured by such illegal conduct, the sum of one thousand dollars, for each fugitive so lost as aforesaid, to be recovered by action of debt, in any of the District or Territorial Courts aforesaid, within whose jurisdiction the said offence may have been committed.

SEC. 8. And be it further enacted, That the marshals, their deputies, and the clerks of the said District and Territorial Courts, shall be paid, for their services, the like fees as may be allowed to them for similar services in other cases; and where such services are rendered exclusively in the arrest, custody, and delivery of the fugitive to the claimant, his or her agent or attorney, or where such supposed fugitive may be discharged out of custody for the want of sufficient proof as aforesaid, then such fees are to be paid in the whole by such claimant, his agent or attorney; and in all cases where the proceedings are before a commissioner, he shall be entitled to a fee of ten dollars in full for his services in each case, upon the delivery of the said certificate to the claimant, his or her agent or attorney; or a fee of five dollars in cases where the proof shall not, in the opinion of such commissioner, warrant such certificate and delivery, inclusive of all services incident to such arrest and examination, to be paid, in either case, by the claimant, his or her agent or attorney The person or persons authorized to execute the process to be issued by such commissioners for the arrest and detention of fugitives from service or labor as aforesaid, shall also be entitled to a fee of five dollars each for each person he or they may arrest and take before any such commissioner as aforesaid, at the instance and request of such claimant, with such other fees as may be deemed reasonable by such commissioner for such other additional services as may be necessarily performed by him or them; such as attending at the examination, keeping the fugitive in custody, and providing him with food and lodging during his detention, and until the final determination of such commissioner; and, in general, for performing such other duties as may be required by such claimant, his or her attorney or agent, or commissioner in the premises, such fees to be made up in conformity with the fees usually charged by the officers of the courts of justice within the proper district or county, as near as may be practicable, and paid by such claimants, their agents or attorneys, whether such supposed fugitives from service or labor be ordered to be delivered to such claimants by the final determination of such commissioners or not.

SEC. 9. And be it further enacted, That, upon affidavit made by the claimant of such fugitive, his agent or attorney, after such certificate has been issued, that he has reason to apprehend that such fugitive will be rescued by force from his or their possession before he can be taken beyond the limits of the State in which the arrest is made, it shall be the duty of the officer making the arrest to retain such fugitive in his custody, and to remove him to the State whence he fled, and there to deliver him to said claimant, his agent, or attorney. And to this end, the officer aforesaid is hereby authorized and required to employ so many persons as he may deem necessary to overcome such force, and to retain them in his service so long

as circumstances may require. The said officer and his assistants, while so employed, to receive the same compensation, and to be allowed the same expenses, as are now allowed by law for transportation of criminals, to be certified by the judge of the district within which the arrest is made, and paid out of the treasury of the United States.

SEC. 10. And be it further enacted, That when any person held to service or labor in any State or Territory, or in the District of Columbia, shall escape therefrom, the party to whom such service or labor shall be due, his, her, or their agent or attorney, may apply to any court of record therein, or judge thereof in vacation, and make satisfactory proof to such court, or judge in vacation, of the escape aforesaid, and that the person escaping owed service or labor to such party. Whereupon the court shall cause a record to be made of the matters so proved, and also a general description of the person so escaping, with such convenient certainty as may be; and a transcript of such record, authenticated by the attestation of the clerk and of the seal of the said court, being produced in any other State, Territory, or district in which the person so escaping may be found, and being exhibited to any judge, commissioner, or other officer authorized by the law of the United States to cause persons escaping from service or labor to be delivered up, shall be held and taken to be full and conclusive evidence of the fact of escape, and that the service or labor of the person escaping is due to the party in such record mentioned. And upon the production by the said party of other and further evidence if necessary, either oral or by affidavit, in addition to what is contained in the said record of the identity of the person escaping, he or she shall be delivered up to the claimant. And the said court, commissioner, judge, or other person authorized by this act to grant certificates to claimants of fugitives, shall, upon the production of the record and other evidences aforesaid, grant to such claimant a certificate of his right to take any such person identified and proved to be owing service or labor as aforesaid, which certificate shall authorize such claimant to seize or arrest and transport such person to the State or Territory from which he escaped: Provided, That nothing herein contained shall be construed as requiring the production of a transcript of such record as evidence as aforesaid. But in its absence the claim shall be heard and determined upon other satisfactory proofs, competent in law.

APPROVED, September 18, 1850.

An Act to suppress the Slave Trade in the District of Columbia.

Be it enacted by the Senate and House of Representatives of the United States of America in Congress assembled, That from and after the first day of January, eighteen hundred and fifty-one, it shall not be lawful to bring into the District of Columbia any slave whatever, for the purpose of being sold, or for the purpose of being placed in depot, to be subsequently transferred to any other State or place to be sold as merchandize. And if any slave shall be brought into the said District by its owner, or by the authority or consent of its owner, contrary to the provisions of this act, such slave shall thereupon become liberated and free.

SEC. 2. And be it further enacted, That it shall and may be lawful for each of the corporations of the cities of Washington and Georgetown, from time to time, and as often as may be necessary, to abate, break up, and abolish any depot or place of confinement of slaves brought into the said District as merchandize, contrary to the provisions of this act, by such appropriate means as may appear to either of the said corporations expedient and proper. And the same power is hereby vested in the Levy Court of Washington county, if any attempt shall be made, within its jurisdictional limits, to establish a depot or place of confinement for slaves brought into the said District as merchandize for sale contrary to this act.

APPROVED, September 20, 1850.

Kansas-Nebraska Act

AN ACT TO ORGANIZE THE TERRITORIES OF NEBRASKA AND KANSAS.

Be it enacted by the Senate and House of Representatives of the United States of America in Congress assembled, That all that part of the territory of the United States included within the following limits, except such portions thereof as are hereinafter expressly exempted from the operations of this act, to wit: beginning at a point in the Missouri River where the fortieth parallel of north latitude crosses the same; then west on said parallel to the east boundary of the Territory of Utah, the summit of the Rocky Mountains; thence on said summit northwest to the forty-ninth parallel of north latitude; thence east on said parallel to the western boundary of the territory of Minnesota; thence southward on said boundary to the Missouri River; thence down the main channel of said river to the place of beginning, be, and the same is hereby, created into a temporary government by the name of the Territory Nebraska; and when admitted as a State or States, the said Territory or any portion of the same, shall be received into the Union with without slavery, as their constitution may prescribe at the time of the admission: Provided, That nothing in this act contained shall be construed to inhibit the government of the United States from dividing said Territory into two or more Territories, in such manner and at such tin as Congress shall deem convenient and proper, or from attaching a portion of said Territory to any other State or Territory of the United States: *Provided further,* That nothing in this act contained shall construed to impair the rights of person or property now pertaining the Indians in said Territory, so long as such rights shall remain unextinguished by treaty between the United States and such Indians, or include any territory which, by treaty with any Indian tribe, is not, without the consent of said tribe, to be included within the territorial line or jurisdiction of any State or Territory; but all such territory shall excepted out of the boundaries, and constitute no part of the Territory of Nebraska, until said tribe shall signify their assent to the President of the United States to be included within the said Territory of Nebraska or to affect the authority of the government of the United States make any regulations respecting such Indians, their lands, property, or other rights, by treaty, law, or otherwise, which it would have been competent to the government to make if this act had never passed.

SEC. 2. *And Be it further enacted,* That the executive power and authority in and over said Territory of Nebraska shall be vested in a Governor who shall hold his office for four years, and until his successor shall be appointed and qualified, unless sooner removed by the President of the United States. The Governor shall reside within said Territory, and shall be commander-in-chief of the militia thereof. He may grant pardons and respites for offences against the laws of said Territory, and reprieves for offences against the laws of the United States, until the decision of the President can be made known thereon; he shall commission all officers who shall be appointed to office under the laws of the said Territory, and shall take care that the laws be faithfully executed.

SEC. 3. *And Be it further enacted,* That there shall be a Secretary of said Territory, who shall reside therein, and hold his office for five years, unless sooner removed by the President of the United States; he shall record and preserve all the laws and proceedings of the Legislative Assembly hereinafter constituted, and all the acts and proceedings of the Governor in his executive department; he shall transmit one copy of the laws and journals of the Legislative Assembly within thirty days after the end of each session, and one copy of the executive proceedings and official correspondence semi-annually, on the first days of January and July in each year to the President of the United States, and two copies of the laws to the President of the Senate and to the Speaker of the House of Representatives, to be deposited in the libraries of Congress, and in or case of the death, removal, resignation, or absence of the Governor from the Territory, the Secretary shall be, and he is hereby, authorized and required to execute and perform all the powers and duties of the Governor during such vacancy or absence, or until another Governor shall be duly appointed and qualified to fill such vacancy.

SEC 4. *And be it further enacted,* That the legislative power and authority of said Territory shall be vested in the Governor and a Legislative Assembly. The Legislative Assembly shall consist of a Council and House of Representatives. The Council shall consist of thirteen members, having the qualifications of voters, as hereinafter prescribed, whose term of service shall continue two years. The House of Representatives shall, at its first session, consist of twenty-six members, possessing the same qualifications as prescribed for members of the Council, and whose term of service shall continue one year. The number of representatives may be increased by the Legislative Assembly, from time to time, in proportion to the increase of qualified voters: *Provided,* That the whole number shall never exceed thirty nine. An apportionment shall be made, as nearly equal as practicable, among the several counties or districts, for the election of the council and representatives, giving to each section of the Territory representation in the ratio of its qualified voters as nearly as may be. And the members of the Council and of the House of Representatives shall reside in, and be inhabitants of, the district or county, or counties for which they may be elected, respectively. Previous to the first election, the Governor shall cause a census, or enumeration of the inhabitants and qualified voters of the several counties and districts of the Territory, to be taken by such persons and in such mode as the Governor shall designate and appoint; and the persons so appointed shall receive a reasonable compensation therefor. And the first election shall be held at such time and places, and be conducted in such manner, both as to the persons who shall superintend such election and the returns thereof, as the Governor shall appoint and direct; and he shall at the same time declare the number of members of the Council and House of Representatives to which each of the counties or districts shall be entitled under this act. The persons having the highest number of legal votes in each of said council districts for members of the Council, shall be declared by the Governor to be duly elected to the Council; and the persons having the highest number of legal votes for the House of Representatives, shall be declared by the Governor to be duly elected members of said house: *Provided,* That in case two or more persons voted for shall have an equal number of votes, and in case a vacancy shall otherwise occur in either branch of the Legislative Assembly, the Governor shall order a new election; and the persons thus elected to the Legislative Assembly shall meet at such place and on such day as the Governor shall appoint; but thereafter, the time, place, and manner of holding and conducting all elections by the people, and the apportioning the representation in the several counties or districts to the Council and House of Representatives, according to the number of qualified voters, shall be prescribed by law, as well as the day of the commencement of the regular sessions of the Legislative Assembly: *Provided,*

That no session in any one year shall exceed the term of forty days, except the first session, which may continue sixty days.

SEC. 5. *And be it further enacted,* That every free white male inhabitant above the age of twenty-one years who shall be an actual resident of said Territory, and shall possess the qualifications hereinafter prescribed, shall be entitled to vote at the first election, and shall be eligible to any office within the said Territory; but the qualifications of voters, and of holding office, at all subsequent elections, shall be such as shall be prescribed by the Legislative Assembly: *Provided,* That the right of suffrage and of holding office shall be exercised only by citizens of the United States and those who shall have declared on oath their intention to become such, and shall have taken an oath to support the Constitution of the United States and the provisions of this act: And provided further, That no officer, soldier, seaman, or marine, or other person in the army or navy of the United States, or attached to troops in the service of the United States, shall be allowed to vote or hold office in said Territory, by reason of being on service therein.

SEC. 6. *And Be it further enacted,* That the legislative power of the Territory shall extend to all rightful subjects of legislation consistent with the Constitution of the United States and the provisions of this act; but no law shall be passed interfering with the primary disposal of the soil; no tax shall be imposed upon the property of the United States; nor shall the lands or other property of non-residents be taxed higher than the lands or other property of residents. Every bill which shall have passed the Council and House of Representatives of the said Territory shall, before it become a law, be presented to the Governor of the Territory; if he approve, he shall sign it; but if not, he shall return it with his objections to the house in which it originated, who shall enter the objections at large on their journal, and proceed to reconsider it. If, after such reconsideration two thirds of that house shall agree to pass the bill, it shall be sent, together with the objections, to the other house, by which it shall likewise be reconsidered, and if approved by two thirds of that house, it shall become a law. But in all such cases the votes of both houses shall be determined by yeas and nays, to be entered on the journal of each house respectively. If any bill shall not be returned by the Governor within three days (Sundays excepted) after it shall have been presented to him, the same shall be a law in like manner as if he had signed it, unless the Assembly, by adjournment, prevents its return, in which case it shall not be a law.

SEC. 7. *And be it further enacted,* That all township, district, and county officers, not herein otherwise provided for, shall be appointed or elected, as the case may be, in such manner as shall be provided by the Governor and Legislative Assembly of the Territory of Nebraska. The Governor shall nominate, and, by and with the advice and consent of the Legislative Council, appoint all officers not herein otherwise provided for; and in the first instance the Governor alone may appoint all said officers, who shall hold their offices until the end of the first session of the Legislative Assembly; and shall lay off the necessary districts for members of the Council and House of Representatives, and all other officers.

SEC. 8. *And be it further enacted,* That no member of the Legislative Assembly shall hold, or be appointed to, any office which shall have been created, or the salary or emoluments of which shall have been increased, while he was a member, during the term for which he was elected, and for one year after the expiration of such term; but this restriction shall not be applicable to members of the first Legislative Assembly; and no person holding a commission or appointment under the United States, except Postmasters, shall be a member of the Legislative Assembly, or hold any office under the government of said Territory.

SEC. 9. *And be it further enacted,* That the judicial power of said Territory shall be vested in a Supreme Court, District Courts, Probate Courts, and in Justices of the Peace. The Supreme Court shall consist of a chief justice and two associate justices, any two of whom shall constitute a quorum, and who shall hold a term at the seat of government of said Territory annually, and they shall hold their offices during the period of four years, and until their successor shall be appointed and qualified. The said Territory shall be divided into three judicial districts, and a district court shall be held in each of said districts by one of the justices of the Supreme Court, at such times and places as may be prescribed by of law; and the said judges shall, after their appointments, respectively, reside in the districts which shall be assigned them. The jurisdiction of the several courts herein provided for, both appellate and original, and that of the probate courts and of justices of the peace, shall be as limited by law: *Provided,* That justices of

the peace shall not have jurisdiction of any matter in controversy when the title or boundaries of land may be in dispute, or where the debt or sum claimed shall exceed one hundred dollars; and the said supreme and districts courts, respectively, shall possess chancery as well as common law jurisdiction. Each District Court, or the judge thereof, shall appoint its clerk, who shall also be the register in chancery, and shall keep his office at the place where the court may, be held. Writs of error, bills of exception, and appeals, shall be allowed in all cases from the final decisions of said district courts to the Supreme Court, under such regulations as may be prescribed by law; but in no case removed to the Supreme Court shall trial by jury be allowed in said court. The Supreme Court, or the justices thereof, shall appoint its own clerk, and every clerk shall hold his office at the pleasure of the court for which he shall have been appointed. Writs of error, and appeals from the final decisions of said Supreme Court, shall be allowed, and may be taken to the Supreme Court of the United States, in the same manner and under the same regulations as from the circuit courts of the United States, where the value of the property, or the amount in controversy, to be ascertained by the oath or affirmation of either party, or other competent witness, shall exceed one thousand dollars; except only that in all cases involving title to slaves, the said writs of error, or appeals shall be allowed and decided by the said Supreme Court, without regard to the value of the matter, property, or title in controversy; and except also that a writ of error or appeal shall also be allowed to the Supreme Court of the United States, from the decision of the said Supreme Court created by this act, or of any judge thereof, or of the district courts created by this act, or of any judge thereof, upon any writ of habeas corpus, involving the question of personal freedom: *Provided,* that nothing herein contained shall be construed to apply to or affect the provisions to the "act respecting fugitives from justice, and persons escaping from the service of their masters," approved February twelfth, seventeen hundred and ninety-three, and the "act to amend and supplementary to the aforesaid act," approved September eighteen, eighteen hundred and fifty; and each of the said district courts shall have and exercise the same jurisdiction in all cases arising under the Constitution and Laws of the United States as is vested in the Circuit and District Courts of the United States; and the said Supreme and District Courts of the said Territory, and the respective judges thereof, shall and may grant writs of habeas corpus in all cases in which the same are granted by the judges of the United States in the District of Columbia; and the first six days of every term of said courts, or so much thereof as shall be necessary, shall be appropriated to the trial of causes arising under the said constitution and laws, and writs of error and appeal in all such cases shall be made to the Supreme Court of said Territory, the same as in other cases. The said clerk shall receive in all such cases the same fees which the clerks of the district courts of Utah Territory now receive for similar services.

SEC. 10. *And Be it further enacted,* That the provisions of an act entitled "An act respecting fugitives from justice, and persons escaping from the service of their masters," approved February twelve, seventeen hundred and ninety-three, and the provisions of the act entitled "An act to amend, and supplementary to, the aforesaid act," approved September eighteen, eighteen hundred and fifty, be, and the same are hereby, declared to extend to and be in full force within the limits of said Territory of Nebraska.

SEC. 11. *And be it further enacted,* That there shall be appointed an Attorney for said Territory, who shall continue in office for four years, and until his successor shall be appointed and qualified, unless sooner removed by the President, and who shall receive the same fees and salary I as the Attorney of the United States for the present Territory of Utah. There shall also be a Marshal for the Territory appointed, who shall hold his office for four years, and until his successor shall be appointed and qualified, unless sooner removed by the President, and who shall execute all processes issuing from the said courts when exercising their jurisdiction as Circuit and District Courts of the United States; he shall perform the duties, be subject to the same regulation and penalties, and be entitled to the same fees, as the Marshal of the District Court of the United States for the present Territory of Utah, and shall, in addition, be paid two hundred dollars annually as a compensation for extra services.

SEC. 12. *And be it further enacted,* That the Governor, Secretary, Chief Justice, and Associate Justices, Attorney and Marshal, shall be nominated, and, by and with the advice and consent of the Senate, appointed by the President of the United States. The Governor and a Secretary to be appointed as aforesaid, shall, before they act as such, respectively take an oath or affirmation before the District Judge or some Justice of the Peace in the limits of said Terri-

tory, duly authorized to administer oaths and affirmations by the laws now in force therein, or before the Chief Justice, or some Associate Justice of the Supreme Court of the United States, to support the Constitution of the United States, and faithfully to discharge the duties of their respective offices, which said oaths, when so taken, shall be certified by the person by whom the same shall have been taken; and such certificates shall be received and recorded by the said Secretary among the Executive proceedings; and the Chief Justice and Associate Justices, and all other civil officers in said Territory, before they act as such, shall take a like oath or affirmation before the said Governor or Secretary, or some Judge or Justice of the Peace of the Territory, who may be duly commissioned and qualified, which said oath or affirmation shall be certified and transmitted by the person taking the same to the Secretary, to be by him recorded as aforesaid; and, afterwards, the like oath or affirmation shall be taken, certified, and recorded, in such manner and form as may be prescribed by law. The Governor shall receive an annual salary of two thousand five hundred dollars. The Chief Justice and Associate Justices shall each receive an annual salary of two thousand dollars. The Secretary shall receive an annual salary of two thousand dollars. The said salaries shall be paid quarter-yearly, from the dates of the respective appointments, at the Treasury of the United States; but no such payment shall be made until said officers shall have entered upon the duties of their respective appointments. The members of the Legislative Assembly shall be entitled to receive three dollars each per day during their attendance at the sessions thereof, and three dollars each for every twenty miles' travel in going to and returning from the said sessions, estimated according to the nearest usually travelled route; and an additional allowance of three dollars shall be paid to the presiding officer of each house for each day he shall so preside. And a chief clerk, one assistant clerk, a sergeant-at-arms, and doorkeeper, may be chosen for each house; and the chief clerk shall receive four dollars per day, and the said other officers three dollars per day, during the session of the Legislative Assembly; but no other officers shall be paid by the United States: *Provided,* That there shall be but one session of the legislature annually, unless, on an extraordinary occasion, the Governor shall think proper to call the legislature together. There shall be appropriated, annually, the usual sum, to be expended by the Governor, to defray the contingent expenses of the Territory, including the salary of a clerk of the Executive Department; and there shall also be appropriated, annually, a sufficient sum, to be expended by the Secretary of the Territory, and upon an estimate to be made by the Secretary of the Treasury of the United States, to defray the expenses of the Legislative Assembly, the printing of the laws, and other incidental expenses; and the Governor and Secretary of the Territory shall, in the disbursement of all moneys intrusted to them, be governed solely by the instructions of the Secretary of the Treasury of the United States, and shall, semi-annually, account to the said Secretary for the manner in which the aforesaid moneys shall have been expended; and no expenditure shall be made by said Legislative Assembly for objects not specially authorized by the acts of Congress, making the appropriations, nor beyond the sums thus appropriated for such objects.

SEC. 13. *And be it further enacted*, That the Legislative Assembly of the Territory of Nebraska shall hold its first session at such time and place in said Territory as the Governor thereof shall appoint and direct; and at said first session, or as soon thereafter as they shall deem expedient, the Governor and Legislative Assembly shall proceed to locate and establish the seat of government for said Territory at such place as they may deem eligible; which place, however, shall thereafter be subject to be changed by the said Governor and Legislative Assembly.

SEC. 14. *And be it further enacted*, That a delegate to the House of Representatives of the United States, to serve for the term of two years, who shall be a citizen of the United States, may be elected by the voters qualified to elect members of the Legislative Assembly, who shall be entitled to the same rights and privileges as are exercised and enjoyed by the delegates from the several other Territories of the United States to the said House of Representatives, but the delegate first elected shall hold his seat only during the term of the Congress to which he shall be elected. The first election shall be held at such time and places, and be conducted in such manner, as the Governor shall appoint and direct; and at all subsequent elections the times, places, and manner of holding the elections, shall be prescribed by law. The person having the greatest number of votes shall be declared by the Governor to be duly elected; and a certificate thereof shall be given accordingly. That the Constitution, and all Laws of the United States which are not locally inapplicable, shall have the

same force and effect within the said Territory of Nebraska as elsewhere within the United States, except the eighth section of the act preparatory to the admission of Missouri into the Union approved March sixth, eighteen hundred and twenty, which, being inconsistent with the principle of non-intervention by Congress with slaves in the States and Territories, as recognized by the legislation of eighteen hundred and fifty, commonly called the Compromise Measures, is hereby declared inoperative and void; it being the true intent and meaning of this act not to legislate slavery into any Territory or State, nor to exclude it therefrom, but to leave the people thereof perfectly free to form an regulate their domestic institutions in their own way, subject only to the Constitution of the United States: *Provided*, That nothing herein contained shall be construed to revive or put in force any law or regulation which may have existed prior to the act of sixth March, eighteen hundred and twenty, either protecting, establishing, prohibiting, or abolishing slavery.

SEC. 15. *And Be it further enacted*, That there shall hereafter be appropriated, as has been customary for the Territorial governments, sufficient amount, to be expended under the direction of the said Governor of the Territory of Nebraska, not exceeding the sums heretofore appropriated for similar objects, for the erection of suitable public buildings at the seat of government, and for the purchase of a library, to be kept at the seat of government for the use of the Governor, Legislative Assembly, Judges of the Supreme Court, Secretary, Marshal, and Attorney of said Territory, and such other persons, and under such regulations as shall be prescribed by law.

SEC. 16. *And be it further enacted*, That when the lands in the said Territory shall be surveyed under the direction of the government of the United States, preparatory to bringing the same into market, section; numbered sixteen and thirty-six in each township in said Territory shall be, and the same are hereby, reserved for the purpose of being applied to schools in said Territory, and in the States and Territories hereafter to be erected out of the same.

SEC. 17. *And be it further enacted*, That, until otherwise provided by law, the Governor of said Territory may define the Judicial Districts of said Territory, and assign the judges who may be appointed for said Territory to the several districts; and also appoint the times and places for holding courts in the several counties or subdivisions in each of said Judicial Districts by proclamation, to be issued by him; but the Legislative Assembly, at their first or any subsequent session, may organize, alter, or modify such Judicial Districts, and assign the judges, and alter the times and places of holding the courts, as to them shall seem proper and convenient.

SEC. 18. *And be it further enacted,* That all officers to be appointed by the President, by and with the advice and consent of the Senate, for the Territory of Nebraska, who, by virtue of the provisions of any law now existing, or which may be enacted during the present Congress, are required to give security for moneys that may be intrusted with them for disbursement, shall give such security, at such time and place, and in such manner, as the Secretary of the Treasury may prescribe.

SEC. 19. *And be it further enacted,* That all that part of the Territory of the United States included within the following limits, except such portions thereof as are hereinafter expressly exempted from the operations of this act, to wit, beginning at a point on the western boundary of the State of Missouri, where the thirty-seventh parallel of north latitude crosses the same; thence west on said parallel to the eastern boundary of New Mexico; thence north on said boundary to latitude thirty-eight; thence following said boundary westward to the east boundary of the Territory of Utah, on the summit of the Rocky Mountains; thence northward on said summit to the fortieth parallel of latitude, thence east on said parallel to the western boundary of the State of Missouri; thence south with the western boundary of said State to the place of beginning, be, and the same is hereby, created into a temporary government by the name of the Territory of Kansas; and when admitted as a State or States, the said Territory, or any portion of the same, shall be received into the Union with or without slavery, as their Constitution may prescribe at the time of their admission: *Provided,* That nothing in this act contained shall be construed to inhibit the government of the United States from dividing said Territory into two or more Territories, in such manner and at such times as Congress shall deem convenient and proper, or from attaching any portion of said Territory to any other State or Territory of the United States: *Provided* further, That nothing in this act contained shall be construed to impair the rights of person or property now pertaining to the Indians in said Territory, so long as such rights shall

remain unextinguished by treaty between the United States and such Indians, or to include any territory which, by treaty with any Indian tribe, is not, without the consent of said tribe, to be included within the territorial limits or jurisdiction of any State or Territory; but all such territory shall be excepted out of the boundaries, and constitute no part of the Territory of Kansas, until said tribe shall signify their assent to the President of the United States to be included within the said Territory of Kansas, or to affect the authority of the government of the United States to make any regulation respecting such Indians, their lands, property, or other rights, by treaty, law, or otherwise, which it would have been competent to the government to make if this act had never passed.

SEC. 20. *And be it further enacted,* That the executive power and authority in and over said Territory of Kansas shall be vested in a Governor, who shall hold his office for four years, and until his successor shall be appointed and qualified, unless sooner removed by the President of the United States. The Governor shall reside within said Territory, and shall be commander-in-chief of the militia thereof. He may grant pardons and respites for offences against the laws of said Territory, and reprieves for offences against the laws of the United States, until the decision of the President can be made known thereon; he shall commission all officers who shall be appointed to office under the laws of the said Territory, and shall take care that the laws be faithfully executed.

SEC. 21. *And be it further enacted,* That there shall be a Secretary of said Territory, who shall reside therein, and hold his office for five years, unless sooner removed by the President of the United States; he shall record and preserve all the laws and proceedings of the Legislative Assembly hereinafter constituted, and all the acts and proceedings of the Governor in his Executive Department; he shall transmit one copy of the laws and journals of the Legislative Assembly within thirty days after the end of each session, and one copy of the executive proceedings and official correspondence semi-annually, on the first days of January and July in each year, to the President of the United States, and two copies of the laws to the President of the Senate and to the Speaker of the House of Representatives, to be deposited in the libraries of Congress; and, in case of the death, removal, resignation, or absence of the Governor from the Territory, the Secretary shall be, and he is hereby, authorized and required to execute and perform all the powers and duties of the Governor during such vacancy or absence, or until another Governor shall be duly appointed and qualified to fill such vacancy.

SEC. 22. *And be it further enacted,* That the legislative power and authority of said Territory shall be vested in the Governor and a Legislative Assembly. The Legislative Assembly shall consist of a Council and House of Representatives. The Council shall consist of thirteen members, having the qualifications of voters, as hereinafter prescribed, whose term of service shall continue two years. The House of Representatives shall, at its first session, consist of twenty-six members possessing the same qualifications as prescribed for members of the Council, and whose term of service shall continue one year. The number of representatives may be increased by the Legislative Assembly, from time to time, in proportion to the increase of qualified voters: *Provided,* That the whole number shall never exceed thirty-nine. An apportionment shall be made, as nearly equal as practicable, among the several counties or districts, for the election of the Council and Representatives, giving to each section of the Territory representation in the ratio of its qualified voters as nearly as may be. And the members of the Council and of the House of Representatives shall reside in, and be inhabitants of, the district or county, or counties, for which they may be elected, respectively. Previous to the first election, the Governor shall cause a census, or enumeration of the inhabitants and qualified voters of the several counties and districts of the Territory, to be taken by such persons and in such mode as the Governor shall designate and appoint; and the persons so appointed shall receive a reasonable compensation therefor. And the first election shall be held at such time and places, and be conducted in such manner, both as to the persons who shall superintend such election and the returns thereof, as the Governor shall appoint and direct; and he shall at the same time declare the number of members of the Council and House of Representatives to which each of the counties or districts shall be entitled under this act. The persons having the highest number of legal votes in each of said Council Districts for members of the Council, shall be declared by the Governor to be duly elected to the Council; and the persons having the highest number of legal votes for the House of Representatives, shall be declared by the Governor to be duly elected members of said house: Provided, That in case two or

more persons voted for shall have an equal number of votes, and in case a vacancy shall otherwise occur in either branch of the Legislative Assembly, the Governor shall order a new election; and the persons thus elected to the Legislative Assembly shall meet at such place and on such day as the Governor shall appoint; but thereafter, the time, place, and manner of holding and conducting all elections by the people, and the apportioning the representation in the several counties or districts to the Council and House of Representatives, according to the number of qualified voters, shall be prescribed by law, as well as the day of the commencement of the regular sessions of the Legislative Assembly: *Provided,* That no session in any one year shall exceed the term of forty days, except the first session, which may continue sixty days.

SEC. 23. *And be it further enacted,* That every free white male inhabitant above the age of twenty-one years, who shall be an actual resident of said Territory, and shall possess the qualifications hereinafter prescribed, shall be entitled to vote at the first election, and shall be eligible to any office within the said Territory; but the qualifications of voters, and of holding office, at all subsequent elections, shall be such as shall be prescribed by the Legislative Assembly: *Provided,* That the right of suffrage and of holding office shall be exercised only by citizens of the United States, and those who shall have declared, on oath, their intention to become such, and shall have taken an oath to support the Constitution of the United States and the provisions of this act: And, provided further, That no officer, soldier, seaman, or marine, or other person in the army or navy of the United States, or attached to troops in the service of the United States, shall be allowed to vote or hold office in said Territory by reason of being on service therein.

SEC. 24. *And be it further enacted,* That the legislative power of the Territory shall extend to all rightful subjects of legislation consistent with the Constitution of the United States and the provisions of this act; but no law shall be passed interfering with the primary disposal of the soil; no tax shall be imposed upon the property of the United States; nor shall the lands or other property of non-residents be taxed higher than the lands or other properly of residents. Every bill which shall have passed the Council and House of Representatives of the said Territory shall, before it become a law, be presented to the Governor of the Territory; if he approve, he shall sign it; but if not, he shall return it with his objections to the house in which it originated, who shall enter the objections at large on their journal, and proceed to reconsider it. If, after such reconsideration, two thirds of that house shall agree to pass the bill, it shall be sent, together with the objections, to the other house, by which, it shall likewise be reconsidered, and, if approved by two thirds of that house, it shall become a law. But in all such cases the votes of both houses shall be determined by yeas and nays, to be entered on the journal of each house, respectively. If any bill shall not be returned by the Governor within three days (Sundays excepted) after it shall have been presented to him, the same shall be a law in like manner as if he had signed it, unless the Assembly, by adjournment, prevent its return, in which case it shall not be a law.

SEC. 25. *And be it further enacted,* That all township, district, and; county officers, not herein otherwise provided for, shall be appointed or elected as the case may be, in such manner as shall be provided by the Governor and Legislative Assembly of the Territory of Kansas. The Governor shall nominate, and, by and with the advice and consent of the Legislative Council, appoint all officers not herein otherwise provided for; and, in the first instance, the Governor alone may appoint all said officers, who shall hold their offices until the end of the first session of the Legislative Assembly; and shall lay off the necessary districts for members of the Council and House of Representatives, and all other officers.

SEC. 26. *And be it further enacted,* That no member of the Legislative Assembly shall hold, or be appointed to, any office which shall have been created, or the salary or emoluments of which shall have been increased, while he was a member, during the term for which he was elected, and for one year after the expiration of such term; but this restriction shall not be applicable to members of the first Legislative Assembly; and no person holding a commission or appointment under the United States, except postmasters, shall be a member of the Legislative Assembly, or shall hold any office under the government of said Territory.

SEC. 27. *And be it further enacted,* That the judicial power of said Territory shall be vested in a supreme court, district courts, probate courts, and in justices of the peace. The Supreme Court shall Consist of chief justice and two associate justices, any two of whom shall constitute a quorum, and who shall hold

a term at the seat of government of said Territory annually; and they shall hold their offices during the period of four years, and until their successors shall be appointed and qualified. The said Territory shall be divided into three judicial districts, and a district court shall be held in each of said districts by one of the justices of the Supreme Court, at such times and places as may be prescribed by law; and the said judges shall, after their appointments, respectively, reside in the districts which shall be assigned them. The jurisdiction of the several courts herein provided for, both appellate and original, and that of the probate courts and of justices of the peace, shall be as limited by law: *Provided,* That justices of the peace shall not have jurisdiction of any matter in controversy when the title or boundaries of land may be in dispute, or where the debt or sum claimed shall exceed one hundred dollars; and the said supreme and district courts, respectively, shall possess chancery as well as common law jurisdiction. Said District Court, or the judge thereof, shall appoint its clerk, who shall also be the register in chancery, and shall keep his office at the place where the court may be held. Writs of error, bills of exception, and appeals shall be allowed in all cases from the final decisions of said district courts to the Supreme Court, under such regulations as may be prescribed by law; but in no case removed to the Supreme Court shall trial by jury be allowed in said court. The Supreme Court, or the justices thereof, shall appoint its own clerk, and every clerk shall hold his office at the pleasure of the court for which he shall have been appointed. Writs of error, and appeals from the final decisions of said supreme court, shall be allowed, and may be taken to the Supreme Court of the United States, in the same manner and under the same regulations as from the Circuit Courts of the United States, where the value of the property, or the amount in controversy, to be ascertained by the oath or affirmation of either party, or other competent witness, shall exceed one thousand dollars; except only that in all cases involving title to slaves, the said writ of error or appeals shall be allowed and decided by said supreme court, without regard to the value of the matter, property, or title in controversy; and except also that a writ of error or appeal shall also be allowed to the Supreme Court of the United States, from the decision of the said supreme court created by this act, or of any judge thereof, or of the district courts created by this act, or of any judge thereof, upon any writ of habeas corpus, involving the question of personal freedom: *Provided,* That nothing herein contained shall be construed to apply to or affect the provisions of the "act respecting fugitives from justice, and persons escaping from the service of their masters," approved February twelfth, seventeen hundred and ninety-three, and the act to amend and supplementary to the aforesaid act," approved September eighteenth, eighteen hundred and fifty; and each of the said district courts shall have and exercise the same jurisdiction in all cases arising under the Constitution and laws of the United States as is vested in the Circuit and District Courts of the United States; and the said supreme and district courts of the said Territory, and the respective judges thereof, shall and may grant writs of habeas corpus in all cases in which the same are granted by the judges of the United States in the District of Columbia; and the first six days of every term of said courts, or so much thereof as may be necessary, shall be appropriated to the trial of causes arising under the said Constitution and laws, and writs of error and appeal in all such cases shall be made to the Supreme Court of said Territory, the same as in other cases. The said clerk shall receive the same fees in all such cases, which the clerks of the district courts of Utah Territory now receive for similar services.

SEC. 28. *And be it further enacted,* That the provisions of the act entitled "An act respecting fugitives from justice, and persons escaping from, the service of their masters," approved February twelfth, seventeen hundred and ninety-three, and the provisions of the act entitled "An act to amend, and supplementary to, the aforesaid act," approved September eighteenth, eighteen hundred and fifty, be, and the same are hereby, declared to extend to and be in full force within the limits of the said Territory of Kansas.

SEC. 29. *And be it further enacted,* That there shall be appointed an attorney for said Territory, who shall continue in office for four years, and until his successor shall be appointed and qualified, unless sooner removed by the President, and who shall receive the same fees and salary as the Attorney of the United States for the present Territory of Utah. There shall also be a marshal for the Territory appointed, who shall hold his office for four years, and until his successor shall be appointed and qualified, unless sooner removed by the President, and who shall execute all processes issuing from the said courts where exercising their jurisdiction as Circuit and District Courts of the United States; he shall perform the duties, be subject to the same regulations and penalties, and be entitled to the same fees, as the Marshal of the Dis-

trict Court of the United States for the present Territory of Utah, and shall, in addition, be paid two hundred dollars annually as a compensation for extra services.

SEC. 30. *And be it further enacted,* That the Governor, Secretary, Chief Justice, and Associate Justices, Attorney, and Marshal, shall be nominated, and, by and with the advice and consent of the Senate, appointed by the President of the United States. The Governor and Secretary to be appointed as aforesaid shall, before they act as such, respectively take an oath or affirmation before the district judge or some justice of the peace in the limits of said Territory, duly authorized to administer oaths and affirmations by the laws now in force therein, or before the Chief Justice or some Associate Justice of the Supreme Court of the United States, to support the Constitution of the United States, and faithfully to discharge the duties of their respective offices, which said oaths, when so taken, shall be certified by the person by whom the same shall have been taken; and such certificates shall be received and recorded by the said secretary among the executive proceedings; and the Chief Justice and Associate Justices, and all other civil officers in said Territory, before they act as such, shall take a like oath or affirmation before the said Governor or Secretary, or some Judge or Justice of the Peace of the Territory who may be duly commissioned and qualified, which said oath or affirmation shall be certified and transmitted by the person taking the same to the Secretary, to be by him recorded as aforesaid; and, afterwards, the like oath or affirmation shall be taken, certified, and recorded, in such manner and form as may be prescribed by law. The Governor shall receive an annual salary of two thousand five hundred dollars. The Chief Justice and Associate Justices shall receive As an annual salary of two thousand dollars. The Secretary shall receive an annual salary of two thousand dollars. The said salaries shall be paid quarter-yearly, from the dates of the respective appointments, at the Treasury of the United States; but no such payment shall be made until said officers shall have entered upon the duties of their respective appointments. The members of the Legislative Assembly shall be entitled to receive three dollars each per day during their attendance at the sessions thereof, and three dollars each for every twenty miles' travel in going to and returning from the said sessions, estimated according to the nearest usually travelled route; and an additional allowance of three dollars shall be paid to the presiding officer of each house for each day he shall so preside. And a chief clerk, one assistant clerk, a sergeant at arms, and door keeper, may be chosen for each house; and the chief clerk shall receive four dollars per day, and the said other officers three dollars per day, during the session of the Legislative Assembly; but no to other officers shall be paid by the United States: Provided, That there shall be but one session of the Legislature annually, unless, on an extraordinary occasion, the Governor shall think proper to call the Legislature together. There shall be appropriated, annually, the usual sum, to be expended by the Governor, to defray the contingent expenses of the Territory, including the salary of a clerk of the Executive Department and there shall also be appropriated, annually, a sufficient sum, to be expended by the Secretary of the Territory, and upon an estimate to be made by the Secretary of the Treasury of the United States, to defray the expenses of the Legislative Assembly, the printing of the laws, and other incidental expenses; and the Governor and Secretary of the Territory shall, in the disbursement of all moneys intrusted to them, be governed solely by the instructions of the secretary of the Treasury of the United States, and shall, semi-annually, account to the said secretary for lit the manner in which the aforesaid moneys shall have been expended; and no expenditure shall be made by said Legislative Assembly for objects not specially authorized by the acts of Congress making the appropriations, nor beyond the sums thus appropriated for such objects.

SEC. 31. *And be it further enacted,* That the seat of government of said Territory is hereby located temporarily at Fort Leavenworth; and that such portions of the public buildings as may not be actually used and needed for military purposes, may be occupied and used, under the direction of the Governor and Legislative Assembly, for such public purposes as may be required under the provisions of this act.

SEC. 32. *And be it further enacted,* That a delegate to the House of Representatives of the United States, to serve for the term of two years, who shall be a citizen of the United States, may be elected by the voters qualified to elect members of the Legislative Assembly, who shall be entitled to the same rights and privileges as are exercised and enjoyed by the delegates from the several other Territories of the United States to the said House of Representatives, but the delegate first elected shall hold his seat only during the term of the Congress to which he shall be elected. The first election shall be held at such time and places, and be conducted in such manner, as the

Governor shall appoint and direct; and at all subsequent elections, the times, places, and manner of holding the elections shall be prescribed by law. The person having the greatest number of votes shall be declared by the Governor to be duly elected, and a certificate thereof shall be given accordingly. That the Constitution, and all laws of the United States which are not locally inapplicable, shall have the same force and effect within the said Territory of Kansas as elsewhere within the United States, except the eighth section of the act preparatory to the admission of Missouri into the Union, approved March sixth, eighteen hundred and twenty, which, being inconsistent with the principle of non-intervention by Congress with slavery in the States and Territories, as recognized by the legislation of eighteen hundred and fifty, commonly called the Compromise Measures, is hereby declared inoperative and void; it being the true intent and meaning of this act not to legislate slavery into any Territory or State, nor to exclude it therefrom, but to leave the people thereof perfectly free to form and regulate their domestic institutions in their own way, subject only to the Constitution of the United States: *Provided,* That nothing herein contained shall be construed to revive or put in force any law or regulation which may have existed prior to the act of sixth of March, eighteen hundred and twenty, either protecting, establishing, prohibiting, or abolishing slavery.

SEC. 33. *And be it further enacted;* That there shall hereafter be appropriated, as has been customary for the territorial governments, a sufficient amount, to be expended under the direction of the said Governor of the Territory of Kansas, not exceeding the sums heretofore appropriated for similar objects, for the erection of suitable public buildings at the seat of government, and for the purchase of a library, to be kept at the seat of government for the use of the Governor, Legislative Assembly, Judges of the Supreme Court, Secretary, Marshal, and Attorney of said Territory, and such other persons, and under such regulations, as shall be prescribed by law.

SEC. 34. *And be it further enacted,* That when the lands in the said Territory shall be surveyed under the direction of the government of the United States, preparatory to bringing the same into market, sections numbered sixteen and thirty-six in each township in said Territory shall be, and the same are hereby, reserved for the purpose of being applied to schools in said Territory, and in the States and Territories hereafter to be erected out of the same.

SEC. 35. *And be it further enacted,* That, until otherwise provided by law, the Governor of said Territory may define the Judicial Districts of said Territory, and assign the judges who may be appointed for said Territory to the several districts; and also appoint the times and places for holding courts in the several counties or subdivisions in each of said judicial districts by proclamation, to be issued by him; but the Legislative Assembly, at their first or any subsequent session, may organize, alter, or modify such judicial districts, and assign the judges, and alter the times and places of holding the courts as to them shall seem proper and convenient.

SEC. 36. *And be it further enacted,* That all officers to be appointed by the President, by and with the advice and consent of the Senate, for the Territory of Kansas, who, by virtue of the provisions of any law now existing, or which may be enacted during the present Congress, are required to give security for moneys that may be intrusted with them for disbursement, shall give such security, at such time and place, and in such manner as the Secretary of the Treasury may prescribe.

SEC. 37. *And be it further enacted,* That all treaties, laws, and other, engagements made by the government of the United States with the Indian tribes inhabiting the territories embraced within this act, shall be faithfully and rigidly observed, notwithstanding any thing contained in this act; and that the existing agencies and superintendencies of said Indians be continued with the same powers and duties which are now prescribed by law, except that the President of the United States may, at his discretion, change the location of the office of superintendent.

Approved, May 30, 1854.

Dred Scott v. Sanford

DECEMBER TERM, 1856.
DRED SCOTT VERSUS JOHN F. A. SANDFORD.
DRED SCOTT, PLAINTIFF IN ERROR, v. JOHN F. A. SANDFORD.

I.

1. Upon a writ of error to a Circuit Court of the United States, the transcript of the record of all the proceedings in the case is brought before this court, and is open to its inspection and revision.

2. When a plea to the jurisdiction, in abatement, is overruled by the court upon demurrer, and the defendant pleads in bar, and upon these pleas the final judgment of the court is in his favor—if the plaintiff brings a writ of error, the judgment of the court upon the plea in abatement is before this court, although it was in favor of the plaintiff—and if the court erred in overruling it, the judgment must be reversed, and a mandate issued to the Circuit Court to dismiss the case for want of jurisdiction.

3. In the Circuit Courts of the United States, the record must show that the case is one in which by the Constitution and laws of the United States, the court had jurisdiction—and if this does not appear, and the court gives judgment either for plaintiff or defendant, it is error, and the judgment must be reversed by this court—and the parties cannot by consent waive the objection to the jurisdiction of the Circuit Court.

4. A free negro of the African race, whose ancestors were brought to this country and sold as slaves, is not a "citizen" within the meaning of the Constitution of the United States.

5. When the Constitution was adopted, they were not regarded in any of the States as members of the community which constituted the State, and were nut numbered among its "people or citizen." Consequently, the special rights and immunities guarantied to citizens do not apply to them. And not being "citizens" within the meaning of the Constitution, they are not entitled to sue in that character in a court of the United States, and the Circuit Court has not jurisdiction in such a suit.

6. The only two clauses in the Constitution which point to this race, treat them as persons whom it was morally lawful to deal in as articles of property and to hold as slaves.

7. Since the adoption of the Constitution of the United States, no state can by any subsequent law make a foreigner or any other description of persons citizens of the United States, nor entitle them to the rights and privileges secured to citizens by that instrument.

8. A State, by its laws passed since the adoption of the Constitution, may put a foreigner or any other description of persons upon a footing with its own citizens, as to all the rights and privileges enjoyed by them within its dominion, and by its laws. But that will not make him a citizen of the United States, nor entitle him to sue in its courts, nor to any of the privileges and immunities of a citizen in another State.

9. The change in public opinion and feeling in relation to the African race, which has taken place since the adoption of the Constitution, cannot change its construction and meaning, and it must be construct and administered now according to its true meaning and intention when it was formed and adopted.

10. The plaintiff having admitted, by his demurrer to the plea in abatement, that his ancestors were imported from Africa and sold as slaves, he is not a citizen of the Slate of Missouri according to the Constitution of the United States, and was not entitled to sue in that character in the Circuit Court.

11. This being the case, the judgment of the court below, in favor of the plaintiff of the plea in abatement, was erroneous.

II.

1. But if the plea in abatement is not brought up by this writ of error, the objection to the citizenship of the plaintiff is still apparent on the record, as he himself, in making oct his case, states that he is of African descent, was born a slave, and claims that he and his family became entitled to freed in by being taken by their owner to reside in a territory where slavery is prohibited by act of Congress—and that, in addition to this claim, he

himself became entitled to freedom being taken to Rock Island, in the State of Illinois and being free when he was brought back to Missouri, he was by the laws of that State a citizen.

2. If, therefore, the facts he states do not give him or his family a right to freedom, the plaintiff is still a slave, and not entitled in sue as a "citizen," and the judgment of the Circuit Court was erroneous on that ground also, without any reference to the plea in abatement.

3. The Circuit Court can give no judgment for plaintiff or defendant in a case where it has not jurisdiction, no matter whether there be a plea in abatement or not. And unless it appears upon the face of the record, when brought here by writ of error, that the Circuit Court had jurisdiction, the judgment must be reversed. The case of Capron *v.* Van Noorden (2 Cranch, 126) examined, and the principles thereby decided, reaffirmed.

4. When the record, as brought here by writ of error, does not show that the Circuit Court had jurisdiction, this court has jurisdiction to revise and correct the error, like any other error in the court below. It does not and cannot dismiss the case for want of jurisdiction here; for that would leave the erroneous judgment of the court below in full force, and the party injured without remedy. But it must reverse the judgment, and, as in any other case of reversal, send a mandate to the Circuit Court to conform its judgment to the opinion of this court.

5. The difference of the jurisdiction in this court in the cases of writs of error to State courts and to Circuit Courts of the United States, pointed out; and the mistakes made as to the jurisdiction of this court in the latter case, by confounding it with its limited jurisdiction in the former.

6. If the court reverses a judgment upon the ground that it appears by a particular port of the record that the Circuit Court had not jurisdiction, it does not take away the jurisdiction of this court to examine into and correct, by a reversal of the judgement, any other errors, either as to the jurisdiction or any other matter, where it appears from other parts of the tenor that the Circuit Court had fallen into error. On the contrary, it is the daily and familiar practice of this court to reverse on several grounds, where more than one error appears to have been committed. And the error of a Circuit Court in its jurisdiction stands on the same ground, and is to be treated in the same manner as any other error upon which its judgment is founded.

7. The decision, therefore, that the judgment of the Circuit Court upon the plea in abatement is erroneous, is no reason why the alleged error apparent in the exception should not also be examined, and the judgment reversed on that ground also, if it disclosed a want of jurisdiction in the Circuit Court. It is often the duty of this court, after having decided that a particular decision of the Circuit Court was erroneous, to examine into other alleged errors, and to correct them if they are found to exist. And this has been uniformly done by this court, when the questions are in any degree connected with the controversy, and the silence of the court might cremate doubts which would lead to further and useless litigation.

III.

1. The facts upon which the plaintiff relies did not give him his freedom, and make him a citizen of Missouri.

2. The clause in the Constitution authorising Congress to make all needful rules and regulations for the government of the territory and other property of the United States, applies only to territory within the chartered limits of some one of the States when they were colonies of Great Britain, and which was surrendered by the British Government to the old Confederation of the States, in the treaty of peace. It does not apply to territory acquired by the present Federal Government, by treaty or conquest, from a foreign nation. The case of the American and Ocean Insurance Companies *v.* Canter (1 Peters, 511) referred to and examined, showing that the decision in this case is not in conflict with that opinion, and that the court did not, in the case referred to, decide upon the construction of the clause of the Constitution above mentioned, because the case before them did not make it necessary to decide the question.

3. The United States, under the present Constitution, cannot acquire territory to be held as a colony to be governed at its will and pleasure. But it may acquire territory which, at the time, has not a population that fits it to become a State, and still govern it as a Territory until it has a population which, in the judgment of Congress, entitles it to be admitted as a State of the Union.

4. During the time it remains a Territory, Congress may legislate over it within the scope of its constitutional powers in relation to citizens of the United States—and may establish a Territorial

Government—and the form of this local Government must be regulated by the discretion of Congress, but with powers not exceeding those which Congress itself, by the Constitution, is authorized to exercise over citizens of the United States, in respect to their rights of persons or rights of property.

IV.

1. The territory thus acquired, is acquired by the people of the United States for their common and equal benefit, through their agent and trustee, the Federal Government. Congress can exercise no power over the rights of persons or property of a citizen in the Territory which is prohibited by the Constitution. The Government and the citizen, whenever the Territory is open to settlement, both enter it with their respective rights defined and limited by the Constitution.

2. Congress have no right to prohibit the citizens of any particular State or States from taking up their home there, while it permits citizens of other States to do so. Nor has it a right to give privileges to one class of citizens which it refuses to another. The territory is acquired for their equal and common benefit—and if open to any, it must be open to all upon equal and the same terms.

3. Every citizen has a right to take with him into the Territory any article of property which the Constitution of the United States recognises as property.

4. The Constitution of the United States recognises slaves as property, and pledges the Federal Government to protect it. And Congress cannot exercise any more authority over property of that description than it may constitutionally exercise over property of any other kind.

5. The act of Congress, therefore, prohibiting a citizen of the United States from taking with him his slaves when he removes to the Territory in question to reside, is an exercise of authority over private property which is not warranted by the Constitution—and the removal of the plaintiff, by his owner, to that Territory, gave him no title to freedom.

V.

1. The plaintiff himself acquired no title to freedom by being taken, by his owner, to Rock Island, in Illinois, and brought back to Missouri. This court

has heretofore decided that the *status* or condition of a person of African descent depended on the laws of the State in which he resided.

2. It has been settled by the decisions of the highest court in Missouri, that by the laws of that State, a slave does not become entitled to his freedom, where the owner takes him to reside in a State where slavery is not permitted, and afterwards brings him back to Missouri. Conclusion. It follows that it is apparent upon the record that the court below erred in its judgment on the plea in abatement and also erred in giving judgment for the defendant, when the exception shows that the plaintiff was not a citizen of the United States. And as the Circuit Court had no jurisdiction, either in the case stated in the plea in abatement, or in the one stated in the exception, its judgment in favor of the defendant is erroneous, and must be reversed.

This case was brought up, by writ of error, from the Circuit Court of the United States for the district of Missouri.

It was an action of trespass *vi et armis* instituted in the Circuit Court by Scott against Sandford.

Prior to the institution of the present suit, an action was brought by Scott for his freedom in the Circuit Court of St. Louis county, (State court,) where there was a verdict and judgment in his favor. On a writ of error to the Supreme Court of the State, the judgment below was reversed, and the case remanded to the Circuit Court, where it was constituted to await the decision of the case now in question.

The declaration of Scott contained three counts: one, that Sandford had assaulted the plaintiff; one that he had assaulted Harriet Scott, his wife; and one, that he had assaulted Eliza Scott and Lizzie Scott, his children.

Sandford appeared, and filed the following plea:

Dred Scott v. John F. A. Sandford. *Plea to the Jurisdiction of the Court.*

April Term, 1854.

And the said John F. A. Sandford, in his own proper person, comes and says that this court ought not to have or take further cognizance of the action aforesaid, because he says that said cause of action, and each and every of them, (if any such have accrued to the said Dred Scott,) accrued to the said Dred Scott out of the jurisdiction of this court, and exclusively within the jurisdiction of the courts of the State of Missouri, for that, to wit; the said plaintiff, Dred Scott, is not a citizen of the State of Missouri, as alleged in his declaration, because he is a negro of African descent; his ancestors were of pure African blood, and were brought into this country and sold as negro slaves, and this the said Sandford is ready to verify. Wherefore he prays judgment whether this court can or will take farther cognizance of the action aforesaid.

John F. A. Sandford.

To this plea there was a demurrer in the usual form, which was argued in April, 1854, when the court gave judgment that the demurrer should be sustained.

In May, 1854, the defendant, in pursuance of an agreement between counsel, and with the leave of the court, pleaded in bar of the action:

1. Not guilty.
2. That the plaintiff was a negro slave, the lawful property of the defendant, and, as such, the defendant gently laid his hands upon him, and thereby had only restrained him, as the descendant had a right to do.
3. That with respect to the wife and daughters of the plaintiff, in the second and third counts of the declaration mentioned, the defendant had, as to them, only acted in the same manner, and in virtue of the same legal right.

In the first of these pleas, the plaintiff joined issue; and to the second and third filed replications alleging that the defendant, of his own wrong and without the cause in his second and third pleas alleged, committed the trespasses, &c.

The counsel then filed the following agreed statement of facts, viz:

In the year 1834, the plaintiff was a negro slave belonging to Dr. Emerson, who was a surgeon in the army of the United States. In that year, 1834, said Dr. Emerson took the plaintiff from the State of Missouri to the military post at Rock Island in the State of Illinois, and held him there as a slave until the month of April or May, 1836, At the time last mentioned, said Dr. Emerson removed the plaintiff from said military post at Rock Island to the military post at Fort Snelling, situate on the west bank of the Mississippi river, in the Territory known as Upper Lousiana, acquired by the United States of France, and situated north of the latitude of thirty-six degrees thirty minutes north, and north of the State of Missouri. Said Dr. Emerson held the plaintiff in slavery at said Fort Snelling, from said last-mentioned date until the year 1838.

In the year 1835, Harriet who is named in the second count of the plaintiff's declaration, was the negro slave of Major Taliaferro, who belonged to the army of the United States. In that year, 1835, said Major Taliaferro took said Harriet to said Fort Snelling, a military post, situated as herein before stated, and kept her there as a slave until the year 1836, and then sold and delivered her as a slave at said Fort Snelling unto the said Dr. Emerson hereinbefore named. Said Dr. Emerson held said Harriet in slavery at said Fort Snelling until the year 1838.

In the year 1836, the plaintiff and said Harriet, at said Fort Snelling, with the consent of said Dr. Emerson, who then claimed to be their master and owner, intermarried, and took each other for husband and wife. Eliza and Lizzie, named in the third count of the plaintiff's declaration, are the fruit of that marriage. Eliza is about fourteen years old, and was born on board the steamboat Gipsey, north of the north line of the State of Missouri, and upon the river Mississippi. Lizzie is about seven years old, and was born in the State of Missouri, at the military post called Jefferson Barracks.

In the year 1838, said Dr. Emerson removed the plaintiff and said Harriet and their said daughter Eliza, from said Fort Snelling to the State of Missouri, where they have ever since resided.

Before the commencement of this suit, said Dr. Emerson sold and conveyed the plaintiff, said Harriet, Eliza, and Lizzie, to the defendant, as slaves, and the defendant has ever since claimed to hold them and each of them as slaves.

At the times mentioned in the plaintiff's declaration, the defendant claiming to be owner as aforesaid, laid his hands upon said plaintiff, Harriet, Eliza and Lizzie, and imprisoned them, doing in this respect, however, no more than what he might lawfully do if they were of right his slaves at such times.

Further proof may be given on the trial for either party.

It is agreed that Dred Scott brought suit for his freedom in the Circuit Court of St. Louis county; that there was a verdict and judgment in his favor; that on a writ of error to the Supreme Court, the judgment below was reversed, and the same remanded to the Circuit Court, where is has been continued to await the decision of this case.

In May 1854, the cause went before a jury who found the following verdict, viz: "As to the first issue joined in this case, we of the jury find the defendant not guilty; and as to the issue secondly above joined, we of the jury find that before and at the time when,

&c., in the first count mentioned, the said Dred Scott was a negro slave, the lawful property of the defendant; and as to the issue thirdly above joined, we, the jury, find that before and at the time when, &c., in the second and third counts mentioned, the said Harriet, wife of said Dred Scott, and Eliza and Lizzie, the daughters of the said Dred Scott, were negro slaves, the lawful properly of the defendant."

Whereupon the court gave judgment for the defendant.

After an ineffectual motion for a new trial, the plaintiff filed the following bill of exceptions.

On the trial of this cause by the jury, the plaintiff, to maintain the issues on his part, read to the jury the following agreed statement of facts, (see agreement above.) No further testimony was given to the jury by either party. Thereupon the plaintiff moved the court to give to the jury the following instruction, viz:

"That upon the facts agreed to by the parties, they ought to find for the plaintiff. The court refused to give such instruction to the jury, and the plaintiff, to such refusal, then and there duly excepted."

The court then gave the following instruction to the jury, on motion of the defendant:

"The jury are instructed, that upon the facts In this case, the law is with the defendant" The plaintiff excepted to this instruction.

Upon these exceptions, the case came up to this court.

It was argued at December term, 1855, and ordered to be reargued at the present term.

It was now argued by Mr. *Blair* and Mr. *G. F. Curtis* for the plaintiff in error, and by Mr. *Geyer* and Mr. *Johnson* for the defendant in error.

Mr. Chief Justice TANEY delivered the opinion of the court.

This case has been twice argued. After the argument of the last term, differences of opinion were found to exist among the members of the court; and as the questions in controversy are of the highest importance, and the court was at that time much pressed by the ordinary business of the term, it was deemed advisable to continue the case, and direct a reargument on some of the points, in order that we might have an opportunity of giving to the whole subject a more deliberate consideration. It has accordingly been again argued by counsel, and considered by the court; and I now proceed to deliver its opinion.

There are two leading questions presented by the record:

1. Had the Circuit Court of the United States jurisdiction to hear and determine the case between these parties? And
2. If it had jurisdiction, is the judgment it has given erroneous or not?

The plaintiff in error, who was also the plaintiff in the court below, was, with his wife and children, held as slaves by the defendant, in the state of Missouri; and he brought this action in the circuit court of the United States for that district, to assert the title of himself and his family to freedom.

The declaration is in the form usually adopted in that State to try questions of this description, and contains the averment necessary to give the court jurisdiction; that he and the defendant are citizens of different States; that is, that he is a citizen of Missouri, and the defendant a citizen of New York.

The defendant pleaded in abatement to the jurisdiction of the court, that the plaintiff was not a citizen of the State of Missouri, as alleged in his declaration, being a negro of African descent, whose ancestors were of pure African blood, and who were brought into this country and sold as slaves.

To this plea the plaintiff demurred, and the defendant joined in demurrer. The court overruled the plea, and gave judgment that the defendant should answer over. And he therefore put in sundry pleas in bar, upon which issues were joined; and at the trial the verdict and judgment were in his favor. Whereupon the plaintiff brought this writ of error.

Before we speak of the pleas in bar, it will be proper to dispose of the questions which have arisen on the plea in abatement.

That plea denies the right of the plaintiff to sue in a court of the United States, for the reasons therein stated.

If the question raised by it is legally before us, and the court should be of opinion that the facts stated in it disqualify the plaintiff from becoming a citizen, in the sense in which that word is used in the Constitution of the United States, then the judgment of the Circuit Court is erroneous and must be reversed.

It is suggested, however, that this plea is not before us; and that as the judgment in the court below on this plea was in favor of the plaintiff, he does not seek to reverse it, or bring it before the court for revision by his writ of error; and also that the defendant waived this defeats by pleading over, and thereby admitted the jurisdiction of the court.

But in making this objection, we think the peculiar and limited jurisdiction of courts of the United States has not been adverted to. This peculiar and limited jurisdiction has made it necessary, in these courts, to adopt different rules and principles of pleading, so far as jurisdiction is concerned, from those which regulate courts of common law in England, and in the different states of the Union which have adopted the common-law rules.

In these last-mentioned courts, where their character and rank are analogous to that of a Circuit Court of the United States; in other words, where they are what the law terms courts of general jurisdiction; they are presumed to have jurisdiction, unless the contrary appears. No averment in the pleadings of the plaintiff is necessary, in order to give jurisdiction. If the defendant objects to it, he must plead it specially, and unless the fact On which he relics is found to be true by a jury, or admitted to be true by the plaintiff, the jurisdiction Cannot be disputed in an appellate court.

Now, it is not necessary to inquire whether in courts of that description a party who pleads over in bar, when a plea to the jurisdiction has been ruled against him, does or does not waive his plea; nor whether upon a judgment in his favor on the pleas in bar, and a writ of error brought by the plaintiff, the question upon the plea in abatement would be open for revision in the appellate court. Cases that may have been decided in such courts, or rules that may have been laid down by common-law pleaders, can have no influence in the decision in this court. Because, under the Constitution and laws of the United States, the rules which govern the pleadings in its courts, in questions of jurisdiction, stand on different principles and are regulated by different laws.

This difference arises, as we have said, from the peculiar character of the Government of the United States. For although it is sovereign and supreme in its appropriate sphere of action, yet it does not possess all the powers which usually belong to the sovereignty of a nation. Certain specified powers, enumerated in the Constitution, have been conferred upon it; and neither the legislative, executive, nor judicial departments of the Government can lawfully exercise any authority beyond the limits marked out by the Constitution. And in regulating the judicial department, the cases in which the courts of the United States shall have jurisdiction are particularly and specifically enumerated and defined; and they are not authorized to take cognizance of any case which does not come within the description therein specified. Hence, when a plaintiff sues in a court of the United States, it is necessary that he should show, in his pleadings, that the suit he briars is within the jurisdiction of the court, and that he is entitled to sue there. And if he omits to do this, and should, by any oversight of the Circuit Court, obtain a judgment in his favor, the judgment would be reversed in the appellate court for want of jurisdiction in the court below. The jurisdiction would not be presumed, as in the case of a common-law English or State court, unless the contrary appeared. But the record, when it comes before the appellate court, must show, affirmatively, that the inferior court had authority, under the Constitution, to hear and determine the case. And if the plaintiff claims a right to sue in a Circuit Court of the United States, under that provision of the Constitution which gives jurisdiction in controversies between citizens of discreet States, he must distinctly aver in his pleadings that they are citizens of different States; add he cannot maintain his suit without showing that fact in the pleadings.

This point was decided in the case of Bingham v. Cabot, (in 3 Dall., 382), and ever since adhered to by the court. And in Jackson v. Ashton (8 Pet., 148), it was held that the objection to which it was open could not be waived by the opposite party, because consent of parties could not give jurisdiction.

It is needless to accumulate cases on this subject. Those already referred to, and the cases of Capron v. Van Noorden, (in 2 Cr, 126), and Montalet v. Murray; (4 Cr., 46), are sufficient to show the rule of which we have spoken. The case of Capron v. Van Noorden strikingly illutrates the difference between a common-law court and a court of the United States.

If, however, the fact of citizenship is averred in the declaration, and the defendant does not deny it, and put it in issue by pica in abatement, he cannot offer evidence at the trial to disprove it, and consequently cannot avail himself of the objection in the appellate court, unless the defect should be apparent in some other part of the record. For if there is no plea in abatement, and the want of jurisdiction does not appear in any other part of the transcript brought up by the writ of error, the undisputed averment of citizenship in the declaration must be taken in this court to be true. In this case, the citizenship is averred, but it is denied by the defendant in the manner required by the rules of pleading, and the fact upon which the denial is based is admitted by the demurrer. And, if the plea and demurrer, and judgment of the court below upon it, are before us upon this record, the question to be decided is, whether the facts stated in the plea are sufficient to show that the plaintiff is not entitled to sue as a citizen in a court of the United States.

We think they are before us. The plea in abatement and the judgment of the court upon it, are a part of the judicial proceedings in the Circuit Court, and are there recorded as such; and a writ of error always brings up to the superior court the whole record of the proceedings in the court below. And in the case of the United States v Smith (11 Wheat., 172,) this court said, that the case being brought up by writ of error, the whole record was under the consideration of this court. And this being the case in the present instance, the plea in abatement is necessarily under consideration; and it becomes, therefore, our duty to decide whether the facts stated in the plea are or are not sufficient to show that the plaintiff is not entitled to sue as a citizen in a court of the United States.

This is certainly a very serious question, and one that now for the first time has been brought for decision before this court. But it is brought here by those who have a right to bring it, and it is our duty to meet it and decide it.

The question is simply this: Can a negro whose ancestors were imported into this country, and sold as slaves, become a member of the political community formed and brought into existence by the Constitution of the United States, and as such become entitled to all the rights and privileges and immunities guaranteed to the citizen? One of which rights is the privilege of suing in a court of the United States in the cases specified in the Constitution.

It will be observed, that the plea applies to that class of persons only whose ancestors were negroes of the African race, and imported into this country, and sold and held as slaves. The only matter in issue before the court, therefore, is, whether the descendants of such slaves, when they shall be emancipated, or who are born of parents who had become free before their birth, are citizens of a State, in the sense in which the word citizen is used in the Constitution of the United States. And this being the only matter in dispute on the pleadings, the court must be understood as speaking in this opinion of that class only, that dispute on the pleadings, the court must be understood as speaking in this opinion of that class only, that is, of those persons who are the descendants of Africans who were imported into this country, and sold as slaves.

The situation of this population was altogether unlike that of the Indian race. The latter, it is true, formed no part of the colonial communities, and never amalgamated with them in social connections or in government. But although they were uncivilized, they were yet a free and independent people, associated together in nations or tribes, and governed by their own laws. Many of these political communities were situated in territories to which the white race claimed the ultimate right of dominion. But that claim was acknowledged to be subject to the right of the Indians to occupy it as long as they thought proper, and neither the English nor colonial Governments claimed or exercised any dominion over the tribe or nation by whom it was occupied, nor claimed the right to the possession of the territory, until the tribe or nation consented to cede it. These Indian Governments were regarded and treated as foreign Governments, as much so as if an ocean had separated the red man from the white; and their freedom has constantly been acknowledged, from the time of the first emigration to the English colonies to the present day, by the different Governments which succeeded each other. Treaties have beeen negotiated with them, and their alliance sought for in war; and the people who compose these Indian political communities have always been treated as foreigners not living under our Government. It is true that the course of events has brought the Indian tribes within the limits of the United States under subjection to the white race; and it has been found necessary, for their sake as well as our own, to regard them as in a state of pupilage, and to legislate to a certain extent over them and the territory they occupy. But they may, without doubt, like the subjects of any other foreign Government, be naturalized by the authority of Congress, and become citizens of a State, and of the United States; and if an individual should leave his nation or tribe, and take up his abode among the white population, he would be entitled to all the rights and privileges which would belong to an emigrant from any other foreign people.

We proceed to examine the case as presented by the pleadings.

The words "people of the United States" and "citizens" are synonymous terms, and mean the same thing. They both describe the political body who, according to our republican institutions, form the sovereignty, and who hold the power and conduct the Government through their representatives. They are what we familiarly call the "sovereign people," and every citizen is one of this people and a constituent member of this sovereignty. The question before us is, whether the class of persons described in the plea in abatement compose a portion of this people, and are constituent members of this sovereignty? We think they are not, and that they are not included, and were not intended to be included, under the word "citizens" in the Constitution, and can therefore claim none of the rights and privileges which that instrument provides for and secures to citizens of the United States. On the contrary, they were at that time considered as a subordinate and inferior class of beings, who had been subjugated by the dominant race, and, whether emancipated or not, yet remained subject to their authority, and had no rights or privileges but such as those who held the power and the government might choose to grant them.

It is not the province of the court to decide upon the justice or injustice, the policy or impolicy, of these laws. The decision of that question belonged to the political or law-making power; to those who formed the sovereignty and framed the Constitution. The duty of the court is, to interpret the instrument they have framed, with the best lights we can obtain on the subject, and to administer it as we find it, according to its true intent and meaning when it was adopted.

In discussing this question, we must not confound the rights of citizenship which a State may confer within its own limits, and the rights of citizenship as a member of the Union. It does not by any means follow, because he has all the rights and privileges of a citizen of a State, that he must be a citizen of the United States. He may have all the rights and privileges of the citizen of a State, and yet not be entitled to the rights and privileges of a citizen in any other State. For, previous to the adoption of the Constitution of the United States, every State had the undoubted right to confer on whomsoever it pleased the character of citizen, and to endow him with all its rights. But this character of course was confined to the boundaries of the State, and gave him no rights or privileges in other States beyond those secured to him by the laws of nations and the comity of States. Nor have the several States surrendered the power of conferring these rights and privileges by adopting the Constitution of the United States. Each State may still confer them upon an alien, or any one it thinks proper, or upon any class or description of persons; yet he would not be a citizen in the sense in which that word is used in the Constitution of the United States, nor entitled to sue as such in one of its courts, nor to the privileges and

immunities of a citizen in the other States. The rights which he would acquire would be restricted to the State which gave them. The Constitution has conferred on Congress the right to establish an uniform rule of naturalization, and this right is evidently exclusive, and has always been held by this court to be so. Consequently, no State, since the adoption of the Constitution, can by naturalizing an alien invest him with the rights and privileges secured to a citizen of a State under the Federal Government, although, so far as the State alone was concerned, he would undoubtedly be entitled to the rights of a citizen, and clothed with all the rights and immunities which the Constitution and laws of the State attached to that character.

It is very clear, therefore, that no State can, by any act or law of its own, passed since the adoption of the Constitution, introduce a new member into the political community created by the Constitution of the United States. It cannot make him a member of this community by making him a member of its own. And for the same reason it cannot introduce any person or description of persons, who were not intended to be embraced in this new political family, which the Constitution brought into existence, but were intended to be excluded from it.

The question then arises, whether the provisions of the Constitution, in relation to the personal rights and privileges to which the citizen of a State should be entitled, embraced the negro African race, at that time in this country, or who might afterwards be imported, who had then or should afterwards be made free in any State; and to put it in the power of a single State to make him a citizen of the United States, and endue him with the tall rights of citizenship in every other State without their consent? Does the Constitution of the United States act upon him whenever he shall be made free under the laws of a State, and raised there to the rank of a citizen, and immediately clothe him with all the privileges of a citizen in every other State, and in its own courts?

The court think the affirmative of these propositions cannot be maintained. And if it cannot, the plaintiff in error could not be a citizen of the State of Missouri, within the meaning of the Constitution of the United States, and, consequently, was not entitled to sue in its courts.

It is true, every person, and every class and description of persons, who were at the time of the adoption of the Constitution recognized as citizens in the several States, became also citizens or this new political body; but none other; it was formed by them, and for them and their posterity, but for no one else. And the personal rights and privileges guarantied to citizens of this new sovereignty were intended to embrace those only who were then members of the several State communities, or who should afterwards by birthright or otherwise become members, according to the provisions of the Constitution and the principles on which it was founded. It was the union of those who were at that time members of distinct and separate political communities into one political family, whose power, for certain specified purposes, was to extend over the whole territory of the United States. And it gave to each citizen rights and privileges outside of his State which he did not before possess, and placed him in every other State upon a perfect equality with its own citizens as to rights of person and rights of property; it made him a citizen of the United States.

It becomes necessary, therefore, to determine who were citizens of the several States when the Constitution was adopted. And in order to do this, we must recur to the governments and institutions of the thirteen colonies, when they separated from Great Britain and formed new sovereignties, and took their places in the family of independent nations. We must enquire who, at that time, were recognized as the people or citizens of a State, whose rights and liberties had been outraged by the English Government; and who declared their independence, and assumed the powers of Government to defend their rights by force of arms.

In the opinion of the court, the legislation and histories of the times, and the language used in the Declaration of Independence, show, that neither the class of persons who had been imported as slaves, nor their descendants, whether they had become free or not, were then acknowledged as a part of the people, nor intended to be included in the general words used in that memorable instrument.

It is difficult at this day to realize the state of public opinion in relation to that unfortunate race, which prevailed in the civilized and enlightened portions of the world at the time of the Declaration of Independence, and when the Constitution of the United States was framed and adopted. But the public history of every European nation displays it in a manner too plain to be mistaken.

They had for more than a century before been regarded as beings of an inferior order, and altogether unfit to associate with the white race, either in social or political relations; and so far inferior, that they had no rights which the white man was bound to re-

spect; and that the negro might justly and lawfully be reduced to slavery for his benefit. He was bought and sold, and treated as an ordinary article of merchandise and traffic, whenever a profit could be made by it. The opinion was at that time fixed and universal in the civilized portion of the white race. It was regarded as an axiom in morals as well as in politics, which no one thought of disputing, or supposed to be open to dispute; and men in every grade and position in society daily and habitually acted upon it in their private pursuits, as well as in matters of public concern; without doubting for a moment the correctness of this opinion.

And in no nation was this opinion here firmly fixed or more uniformly acted upon than by the English Government and English people. They not only seized them on the coast of Africa, and sold them or held them in slavery for their own use; but they took them as ordinary articles of merchandise to every country where they could make a profit on them, and were far more extensively engaged in this commerce, than any other nation in the world.

The opinion thus entertained and acted upon in England was naturally impressed upon the colonies they founded on this side of the Atlantic. And, accordingly, a negro of the African race was regarded by them as an article of property, and held, and bought and sold as such, in every one of the thirteen colonies which united in the Declaration of Independence, and afterwards formed the Constitution of the United States. The slaves were more or less numerous in the different colonies, as slave labor was found more or less profitable. But no one seems to have doubted the correctness of the prevailing opinion of the time.

The legislation of the different colonies furnishes positive and indisputable proof of this fact.

It would be tedious, in this opinion, to enumerate the various laws they passed upon this subject. It will be sufficient, as a sample of the legislation which then generally prevailed throughout the British colonies, to give the laws of two of them; one being still a large slaveholding State, and the other the first State in which slavery ceased to exist.

The province of Maryland, in 1717, (ch. 13, s. 5,) passed a law declaring "that if any free negro or mulatto intermarry with any white woman, or if any white man shall intermarry with any negro or mulatto woman, such negro or mulatto shall become a slave during life, excepting mulattoes born of white women, who, for such intermarriage, shall only become servants for seven years, to be disposed of as the justices of the county court, where such marriage so happens, shall think fit; to be applied by them towards the support of a public school within the said county. And any white man or white woman who shall intermarry as aforesaid, with any negro or mulatto, such white man or white woman shall become servants during the term of seven years, and shall be disposed of by the justices as aforesaid, and be applied to the uses aforesaid."

The other colonial law to which we refer was passed by Massachusetts in 1705, (chap. 6.) It is entitled "An act for the better preventing of a spurious and mixed issue," &c.; and it provides, that "if any negro or mulatto shall presume to smite or strike any person of the English or other Christian nation, such negro or mulatto shall be severely whipped, at the discretion of the justices before whom the offender shall be convicted."

And "that none of her Majesty's English or Scottish subjects, nor of any other Christian nation, within this province, shall contract matrimony with any negro or mulatto; nor shall any person, duly authorised to solemnize marriage, presume to join any such in marriage, on pain of forfeiting the sum of fifty pounds; one moiety thereof to her Majesty, for and towards the support of the Government within this province, and the other moiety to him or them that shall inform and sue for the same in any of her Majesty's courts of record within the province, by bill, plaint, or information."

We give both of these laws in the words used by the respective legislative bodies, because the language in which they are framed, as well as the provisions contained in them, show, too plainly to be misunderstood, the degraded condition of this unhappy race. They were still in force when the Revolution began, and are a faithful index to the state of feeling towards the class of persons of whom they speak, and of the position they occupied throughout the thirteen colonies, in the eyes and thoughts of the men who framed the Declaration of Independence and established the State Constitutions and Governments. They show that a perpetual and impassable barrier was intended to be erected between the white race and the one which they had reduced to slavery, and governed as subjects with absolute and despotic power, and which they then looked upon as so far below them in the scale of created beings, that intermarriages between white persons and negroes or mulattoes were regarded as unnatural and immoral, and punished as crimes, not only in the parties, but in the person who joined them in marriage. And no distinc-

tion in this respect was made between the free negro or mulatto and the slave, but this stigma, of the deepest degradation, was fixed upon the whole race.

We refer to these historical facts for the purpose of showing the fixed opinions concerning that race, upon which the statesmen of that day spoke and acted. It is necessary to do this, in order to determine whether the general terms used in the Constitution of the United States, as to the rights of man and the rights of the people, was intended to include them, or to give to them or their posterity the benefit of any of its provisions.

The language of the Declaration of Independence is equally conclusive:

It begins by declaring "that when in the course of human events it becomes necessary for one people to dissolve the political bands which have connected them with another, and to assume among the powers of the earth the separate and equal station to which the laws of nature and nature's God entitle them, a decent respect for the opinions of mankind requires that they should declare the causes which impel them to the separation."

It then proceeds to say: "We hold these truths to be self-evident: that all men are created equal; that they are endowed by their Creator with certain unalienable rights; that among them is life, liberty, and the pursuit of happiness; that to secure these rights, Governments are instituted, deriving their just powers from the consent of the governed."

The general words above quoted would seem to embrace the whole human family, and if they were used in a similar instrument at this day would be so understood. But it is too clear for dispute, that the enslaved African race were not intended to be included, and formed no part of the people who framed and adopted this declaration; for if the language, as understood in that day, would embrace them, the conduct of the distinguished men who framed the Declaration of Independence would have been utterly and flagrantly inconsistent with the principles they asserted; and instead of the sympathy of mankind, to which they so confidently appealed, they would have deserved and received universal rebuke and reprobation.

Yet the men who framed this declaration were great men—high in literary acquirements—high in their sense of honor, and incapable of asserting principles inconsistent with those on which they were acting. They perfectly understood the meaning of the language they used, and how it would be understood by others; and they knew that it would not in any part of the civilized world be supposed to embrace the negro race, which by common consent, had been excluded from civilized Governments and the family of nations, and doomed to slavery. They spoke and acted according to the then established doctrines and principles, and in the ordinary language of the day, and no one misunderstood them. The unhappy black race were separated from the white by indelible marks, and laws long before established, and were never thought of or spoken of except as property, and when the claims of the owner or the profit of the trader were supposed to need protection.

This state of public opinion had undergone no change when the Constitution was adopted, as is equally evident from its provisions and language.

The brief preamble sets forth by whom it was formed, for what purposes, and for whose benefit and protection. It declares that it is formed by the *people* of the United States; that is to say, by those who were members of the different political communities in the several States; and its great object is declared to be to secure the blessings of liberty to themselves and their posterity. It speaks in general terms of the *people* of the United States, and of *citizens* of the several States, when it is providing for the exercise of the powers granted or the privileges secured to the citizen. It does not define what description of persons are intended to be included under these terms, or who shall be regarded as a citizen and one of the people. It uses them as terms so well understood, that no farther description or definition was necessary.

But there are two clauses in the Constitution which point directly and specifically to the negro race as a separate class of persons, and show clearly that they were not regarded as a portion of the people or citizens of the Government then formed.

One of these clauses reserves to each of the thirteen States the right to import slaves until the year 1808, if it thinks proper. And the importation which it thus sanctions was unquestionably of persons of the race of which we are speaking, as the traffic in slaves in the United States had always been confined to them. And by the other provision the States pledge themselves to each other to maintain the right of property of the master, by delivering up to him any slave who may have escaped from his service, and be found within their respective territories. By the first above-mentioned clause, therefore, the right to purchase and hold this property is directly sanctioned and authorized for twenty years by the people who framed the Constitution. And by the second, they pledge themselves to maintain and uphold the right

of the master in the manner specified, as long as the Government they then formed should endure. And these two provisions show, conclusively, that neither the description of persons therein referred to, nor their descendants, were embraced in any of the other provisions of the Constitution; for certainly these two clauses were not intended to confer on them or their posterity the blessings of liberty, or any of the personal rights so carefully provided for the citizen.

No one of that race had ever migrated to the United States voluntarily; all of them had been brought here as articles of merchandise. The number that had been emancipated at that time were but few in comparison with those held in slavery; and they were identified in the public mind with the race to which they belonged, and regarded as a part of the slave population rather than the free. It is obvious that they were not even in the minds of the framers of the Constitution when they were conferring special rights and privileges upon the citizens of a state in every other part of the Union.

Indeed, when we look to the condition of this race in the several States at the time, it is impossible to believe that these rights and privileges were intended to be extended to them.

It is very true, that in that portion of the Union where the labor of the negro race was found to be unsuited to the climate and unprofitable to the master, but few slaves were held at the time of the Declaration of Independence; and when the Constitution was adopted, it had entirely worn out in one of them, and measures had been taken for its gradual abolition in several others. But this change had not been produced by any change of opinion in relation to this race; but because it was discovered, from experience, that slave labor was unsuited to the climate and productions of these States: for some of the States, where it had ceased or nearly ceased to exist, were actively engaged in the slave trade, procuring cargoes on the coast of Africa, and transporting, them for sale to those parts of the Union where their labor was found to be profitable, and suited to the climate and productions, And this tragic was openly carried on, and fortunes accumulated by it, without reproach from the people of the States where they resided. And it can hardly be supposed that, in the States where it was then countenanced in its worst form—that is, in the seizure and transportation—the people could have regarded those who were emancipated as entitled to equal rights with themselves.

And we may here again refer, in support of this proposition, to the plain and unequivocal language of the laws of the several States, some passed after the Declaration of Independence and before the Constitution was adopted, and some since the Government went into operation.

We need not refer, on this point, particularly to the laws of the present slaveholding States. Their statute books are full of provisions in relation to this class, in the same spirit with the Maryland law which we have before quoted. They have continued to treat them as an inferior class, and to subject them to strict police regulations, drawing a broad line of distinction between the citizen and the slave races, and leg slating in relation to them upon the same principle which prevailed at the time of the Declaration of Independence. As relates to these States, it is too plain for argument, that they have never been regarded as a part of the people or citizens of the State, nor supposed to possess any political rights which the dominant race might not withhold or grant at their pleasure. And as long ago as 1822, the Court of Appeals of Kentucky decided that free negroes and mulattoes were not citizens within the meaning of the Constitution of the United States; and the correctness of this decision is recognized, canal the same doctrine affirmed, in 1 Meigs's Tenn. Reports, 331.

And if we turn to the legislation of the States where slavery had worn out, or measures taken for its speedy abolition, we shall find the same opinions and principles equally fixed and equally acted upon.

Thus, Massachusetts, in 1786 passed a law similar to the colonial one of which we have spoken. The law of 1786, like the law of 1705, forbids the marriage of any white person with any negro, Indian, or mulatto, and inflicts a penalty of fifty pounds upon any one who shall join them in marriage; and declares all such marriages absolutely null and void, and degrades thus the unhappy issue of the marriage by fixing upon it the stain of bastardy. And this mark of degradation was renewed and again impressed upon the race, in the careful and deliberate preparation of their revised code published in 1836. This code forbids any person from joining in marriage any white person with any Indian, negro, or mulatto, and subjects the party who shall, offend, in this respect, to imprisonment, not exceeding six months in the common jail, or to hard labor, and to a fine of not less than fifty nor more than two hundred dollars; and like the law of 1786, it declares the marriage to be absolutely null and void. It will be seen that the punishment is increased by the code upon the person who shall marry them, by adding imprisonment to a pecuniary penalty.

So, too, in Connecticut. We refer more particularly to the legislation of this State, because it was not only among the first to put an end to slavery within its own territory, but was the first to fix a mark of reprobation upon the African slave trade. The law last mentioned was passed in October, 1758, about nine months after the State had ratified and adopted the present Constitution of the United States; and by that law it prohibited its own citizens, under severe penalties, from engaging in the trade, and declared all policies of insurance on the vessel or cargo made in the State to be null and void. But up to the time of the adoption of the Constitution, there is nothing in the legislation of the State indicating any change of opinion as to the relative rights and position of the white and black races in this country, or indicating that it meant to place the latter, when free, upon a level with its citizens. And certainly nothing which would have led the slaveholding States to suppose that Connecticut designed to claim for them, under the new Constitution, the equal rights and privileges and rank of citizens in every other State.

The first step taken by Connecticut upon this subject was as early as 1774, when it passed an act forbidding the further importation of slaves Into the State. But the section containing the prohibition is introduced by the following preamble:

"And whereas the increase of slaves in this State is injurious to the poor, and inconvenient."

This recital would appear to have been carefully introduced, in order to prevent any misunderstanding of the motive which induced the Legislature to pass the law, and places it distinctly upon the interest and convenience of the white population—excluding the inference that it might have been intended in any degree for the benefit of the other.

And in the act of 1784, by which the issue of slaves, born after the time therein mentioned, were to be free at a certain age, the section is again introduced by a preamble assigning a similar motive for the act. It is in these words:

"Whereas sound policy requires that the abolition of slavery should be effected as soon as may be consistent with the rights of individuals, and the public safety and welfare"—showing that the right of property in the master was to be protected, and that the measure was one of policy, and to prevent the injury and inconvenience, to the whites, of a slave population in the State.

And still further pursuing its legislation, we find that in the same statute passed in 1774, which prohibited the further importation of slaves into the State, there is also a provision by which any negro, Indian, or mulatto servant, who was found wandering out of the town or place to which he belonged, without a written pass such as is therein described, was made liable to be seized by any one, and taken before the next authority to be examined and delivered up to his master—who was required to pay the charge which had accrued thereby. And a subsequent section of the same law provides, that if any free negro shall travel without such pass, and shall be stopped, seized, or taken up, he shall pay all charges arising thereby. And this law was in full operation when the Constitution of the United States was adopted, and was not repealed till 1797. So that up to that time free negroes and mulattoes were associated with servants and slaves in the police regulations established by the laws of the State.

And again, in 1833, Connecticut passed another law, which made it penal to set up or establish any school in that State for the instruction of persons of the African race not inhabitants of the State, or to instruct or teach in any such school or institution, or board or harbor for that purpose, any such person, without the previous consent in writing of the civil authority of the town in which such school or institution might be.

And it appears by the case of Crandall *v.* the State, reported in 10 Conn. Rep., 340, that upon an information filed against Prudence Crandall for a violation of this law, one of the points raised in the defence was, that the law was a violation of the Constitution of the United States; and that the persons instructed, although of the African race, were citizens of other States, and therefore entitled to the rights and privileges of citizens in the State of Connecticut. But Chief Justice Dagget, before whom the case was tried, held, that persons of that description were not citizens of a State, within the meaning of the word citizen in the Constitution of the United States, and were not therefore entitled to the privileges and immunities of citizens in other States.

The case was carried up to the Supreme Court of Errors of the State, and the question fully argued there. But the case went off upon another point, and no opinion was expressed on this question.

We have made this particular examination into the legislative and judicial action of Connecticut, because, from the early hostility it displayed to the slave trade on the coast of Africa, we may expect to find the laws of that State as lenient and favorable to the subject race as those of any other State in the Union; and if we find that at the time the Constitution was adopted, they were not even there raised to the rank of citizens, but were still held and treated as property, and the laws relating to them passed with reference altogether to the interest and convenience of the white race, we shall hardly find them elevated to a higher rank anywhere else.

A brief notice of the laws of two other States, and we shall pass on to other considerations.

By the laws of New Hampshire, collected and finally passed in 1815, no one was permitted to be enrolled in the militia of the State but free white citizens; and the same provision is found in a subsequent collection of the laws, made in 1855. Nothing could more strongly mark the entire repudiation of the African race. The alien is excluded, because, being born in a foreign country, he cannot be a member of the community until he is naturalized. But why are the African race, born in the State, not permitted to share in one of the highest duties of the citizen? The answer is obvious; he is not, by the institutions and laws of the State, numbered among its people. He forms no part of the sovereignty of the State and is not therefore called on to uphold and defend it.

Again, in 1822, Rhode Island, in its revised code, passed a law forbidding persons who were authorized to join persons in marriage, from joining in marriage any white person with any negro, Indian, or mulatto, under the penalty of two hundred dollars, and declaring all such marriages absolutely null and void; and the same law was again re-enacted in its revised code of 1844. So that, down to the last-montioned period, the strongest mark of inferiority and degradation was fastened upon the African race in that State.

It would be impossible to enumerate and compress in the space usually allotted to an opinion of a court, the various laws, marking the condition of this race, which were passed from time to time after the Revolution, and before and since the adoption of the Constitution of the United States. In addition to those already referred to, it is sufficient to say, that Chancellor Kent, whose accuracy and research no one will question, states in the sixth edition of his Commentaries (published in 1848, 2 vols., 258, note *b,*) that in no part of the country except Maine, did the African race, in point of fact, participate equally with the whites in the exercise of civil and political rights.

The legislation of the States therefore shows, in a manner not to be mistaken, the inferior and subject condition of that race at the time the Constitution was adopted, and long afterwards, throughout the thirteen States by which that instrument was framed;

and it is hardly consistent with the respect due to these States, to suppose that they regarded at that time, as fellow citizens and members of the sovereignty, a class of beings whom they had thus stigmatized; whom, as we are bound, out of respect to the State sovereignties, to assume they had deemed it just and necessary thus to stigmatize, and upon whom they had impressed such deep and enduring marks of inferiority and degradation; or, that when they met in convention to form the Constitution, they looked upon them as a portion of their constituents, or designed to include them in the provisions so carefully inserted for the security and protection of the liberties and rights of their citizens. It cannot be supposed that they intended to secure to them rights, and privileges, and rank, in the new political body throughout the Union, which every one of them denied within the limits of its own dominion. More especially, it cannot be believed that the large slaveholding States regarded them as included in the word citizens, or would have consented to a Constitution which might compel them to receive them in that character from another State. For if they were so received, and entitled to the privileges and immunities of citizens, it would exempt them from the operation of the special laws and from the police regulations which they considered to be necessary for their own satiety. It would give to persons of the negro race, who were recognized as citizens in any one State of the Union, the right to enter every other State whenever they pleased, singly or in companies, without pass or passport, and without obstruction, to sojourn there as long as they pleased, to go where they pleased at every hour of the day or night without molestation, unless they committed some violation of law for which a white man would be punished; and it would give them the full liberty of speech in public and in private upon all subjects upon which its own citizens might speak; to hold public meetings upon political affairs, and to keep and carry arms wherever they went. And all of this would be done in the face of the subject race of the same color, both free and slaves, and inevitably producing discontent and insubordination among them, and endangering the peace and safety of the State.

It is impossible, it would seem, to believe that the great men of the slaveholding States, who took so large a share in framing the Constitution of the United States, and exercised so much influence in procuring its adoption, could have been so forgetful or regardless of their own safety and the safety of those who trusted and confided in them.

Besides, this want of foresight and care would have been utterly inconsistent with the caution displayed in providing for the admission of new members into this political family. For, when they gave to the citizens of each State the privileges and immunities of citizens in the several States, they at the same time took from the several States the power of naturalization, and confined that power exclusively to the Federal Government. No State was willing to permit another State to determine who should or should not be admitted as one of its citizens, and entitled to demand equal rights and privileges with their own people, within their own territories. The right of naturalization was therefore, with one accord, surrendered by the States, and confided to the Federal Government. And this power granted to Congress to establish an uniform rule of *naturalization* is, by the well understood meaning of the word, confined to persons born in a foreign country, under a foreign Government. It is not a power to raise to the rank of a citizen any one born in the United States, who from birth or parentage, by the laws of the country, belongs to an inferior and subordinate class. And when we find the States guarding themselves from the indiscreet or improper admission by other States of emigrants from other countries, by giving the power exclusively to Congress, we cannot fail to see that they could never have left with the States a much more important power—that is, the power of transforming into citizens a numerous class of persons, who in that character would be much more dangerous to the peace and safety of a large portion of the Union, than the few foreigners one of the States might improperly naturalize.

The Constitution upon its adoption obviously took from the States all power by any subsequent legislation to introduce as a citizen into the political family of the United States any one, no matter where he was born, or what might be his character or condition; and it gave to Congress the power to confer this character upon those only who were born outside of the dominions of the United States. And no law of a State, therefore, passed since the Constitution was adopted, can give any right of citizenship outside of its own territory.

A clause similar to the one in the Constitution, in relation to the rights and immunities of citizens of one State in the other States, was contained in the Articles of Confederation. But there is a difference of language, which is worthy of note. The provision in the Articles of Confederation was "that the *free inhabitants* of each of the States, paupers, vagabonds, and fugitives from justice, excepted, should be entitled to all the privileges and immunities of free citizens in the several States."

It will be observed, that under this Confederation, each State had the right to decide for itself, and in its own tribunals, whom it would acknowledge as a free inhabitant of another State. The term *free inhabitant*, in the generality of its terms, would certainly include one of the African race who had been manumitted. But no example, we think, can be found of his admission to all the privileges of citizenship in any State of the Union after these Articles were formed, and while they continued in force. And, notwithstanding the generality of the words "free inhabitants," it is very clear that, according to their accepted meaning in that day, they did not include the African race, whether free or not: for the fifth section of the ninth article provides that Congress should have the power "to agree upon the number of land forces to be raised, and to make requisitions from each State for its quota in proportion to the number of *white* inhabitants in such State, which requisition should be binding."

Words could hardly have been used which more strongly mark the line of distinction between the citizen and the subject; the free and the subjugated races. The latter were not even counted when the inhabitants of a State were to be embodied in proportion to its numbers for the general defence. And it cannot for a moment be supposed, that a class of persons thus separated and rejected from those who formed the sovereignty of the States, were yet intended to be included under the words "free inhabitants," in the preceding article, to whom privileges and immunities were so carefully secured in every State.

But although this clause of the Articles of Confederation is the same in principle with that inserted in the Constitution, yet the comprehensive word *inhabitant*, which might be construed to include an emancipated slave, is omitted; and the privilege is confined to *citizens* of the State. And this alteration in words would hardly have been made, unless a different meaning was intended to be conveyed, or a possible doubt removed. The just and fair inference is, that as this privilege was about to be placed under the protection of the General Government, and the words expounded by its tribunals, and all power in relation to it taken from the State and its courts, it was deemed prudent to describe with precision and caution the persons to whom this high privilege was given—and the worn *citizen* was on that account substituted for the words *free inhabitant*. The word citizen excluded, and no doubt intended to exclude, foreigners who had not become citizens of some one of the States when the Constitution was adopted; and also every description of persons who were not fully recognised as citizens in the several States. This, upon any fair construction of the instruments to which we have referred, was evidently the object and purpose of this change of words.

To all this mass of proof we have still to add, that Congress has repeatedly legislated upon the same construction of the Constitution that we have given. Three laws, two of which were passed almost immediately after the Government went into operation, will be abundantly sufficient to show this. The two first are particularly worthy of notice, because many of the men who assisted in framing the Constitution, and took an active part in procuring its adoption, were then in the halls of legislation, and certainly understood what they meant when they used the words "people of the United States" and "citizen" in that well-considered instrument.

The first of these acts is the naturalization law, which was passed at the second session of the first Congress. March 26, 1790, and confines the right of becoming citizens "*to aliens being free white persons*"

Now, the Constitution does not limit the power of Confess in this respect to white persons. And they may, if they think proper, authorize the naturalization of any one of any color, who was born trader allegiance to another Government. But the language of the law above quoted, shows that citizenship at that time was perfectly understood to be confined to the white race; and that they alone constituted the sovereignty in the government.

Congress might, as we before said, have authorized the naturalization of Indians, because they were aliens and foreigners. But, in their then untutored and savage state, no one would have thought of admitting them as citizens in a civilized community. And, moreover, the atrocities they had but recently committed, when they were the allies of Great Britain in the Revolutionary war, were yet fresh in the recollection of the people of the United States, and they were even then guarding themselves against the threatened renewal of Indian hostilities. No one supposed then that any Indian would ask for, or was capable of enjoying the privileges of an American citizen, and the word white was not used with any particular reference to them.

Neither was it used with any reference to the African race imported into or born in this country;

because Congress had no power to naturalize them, and therefore there was no necessity for using particular words to exclude them.

It would seem to have been used merely because it followed out the line of division which the Constitution has drawn between the citizen race, who formed and held the Government, and the African race, which they held in subject on and slavery, and governed at their own pleasure.

Another of the early laws of which we have spoken, is the first militia law, which was passed in 1792, at the first session of the second Congress. The language of this law is equally plain and significant with the one just mentioned. It directs that every "free able-bodied white male citizen" shall be enrolled in the militia. The word *white* is evidently used to exclude the African race, and the word "citizen" to exclude unnaturalized foreigners; the latter forming no part of the sovereignty, owing it no allegiance, and therefore under no obligation to defend it. The African race, however, born in the country, did owe allegiance to the Government, whether they were slaves or free; but it is repudiated and rejected from the duties and obligations of citizenship in marked language.

The third act to which we have alluded is even still more decisive; it was passed as late as 1813, (2 Stat, 809,) and it provides: "that from and after the termination of the war in which the United States are now engaged with Great Britain, it shall not be lawful to employ, on board of any public or private vessels of the United States, any person or persons except citizens of the United States, or persons of color, natives of the United States."

Here the line of distinction is drawn in express words. Persons of color, in the judgment of Congress, were not included in the word citizens, and they are described as another and different class of persons, and authorized to be employed, if born in the United States.

And even as late as 1820, (chap. 104, sec. 8,) in the charter to the city of Washington, the corporation is authorized "to restrain and prohibit the nightly and other disorderly meetings of slaves, free negroes, and mulattoes," thus associating them together in its legislation; and after prescribing the punishment that may be inflicted on the slaves, proceeds in the following words: "And to punish such free negroes and mulattoes by penalties not exceeding twenty dollars for any one offence; and in case of the inability of any such free negro or mulatto to pay any such penalty and cost thereon, to cause him or her to be confined to labor for any time not exceeding six calendar months." And in a subsequent part of the same section, the act authorizes the corporation "to prescribe the terms and conditions upon which free negroes and mulattoes may reside in the city."

This law, like the laws of the States, shows that this class of persons were governed by special legislation directed expressly to them, and always connected with provisions for the government of slaves, and not with those for the government of free white citizens. And after such an uniform course of legislation as we have stated, by the colonies, by the States, and by Congress, running through a period of more than a century, it would seem that to call persons thus marked and stigmatized, "citizens" of the United States, "fellow citizens," a constituent part of the sovereignty, would be an abuse of terms, and not calculated to exalt the character or an American citizen in the eyes of other nations.

The conduct of the Executive Department of the Government has been in perfect harmony upon this subject with this course of legislation. The quotation was brought officially before the late William Wirt, when he was the Attorney General of the United States, in 1821, and he decided that the words "citizens of the United States" were used in the acts of Congress in the same sense as in the Constitution; and that free persons of color were not citizens, within the meaning of the Constitution and laws; and this opinion has been confirmed by that of the late Attorney General, Caleb Cushing, in a recent case, and acted upon by the Secretary of State, who refused to grant passports to them as "citizens of the United States."

But it is said that a person may be a citizen, and entitled to that character, although he does not possess all the rights which may belong to other citizens; as, for example, the right to vote, or to hold particular offices; and that yet, when he goes into another State, he is entitled to be recognized there as a citizen, although the State may measure his rights by the rights which it allows to persons of a like character or class resident in the State, and refuse to him the full rights of citizenship.

This argument overlooks the language of the provision in the Constitution of which we are speaking.

Undoubtedly, a person may be a citizen, that is, a member of the community who form the sovereignty, although he exercises no share of the political power, and is incapacitated from holding particular office. Women and minors, who form a part of the political family, cannot vote; and when a property qualification is required to vote or hold a particular office, those who have not the necessary qualification cannot vote or hold the office, yet they are citizens.

So, too, a person may be entitled to vote by the law of the State, who is not a citizen even of the State itself. And in some of the States of the Union foreigners not naturalized are allowed to vote. And the State may give the right to free negroes and mulattoes, but that does not make them citizens of the State, and still less of the United States. And the provision in the Constitution giving privileges and immunities in other States, does not apply to them.

Neither does it apply to a person who, being the citizen of a State, migrates to another State. For then he becomes subject to the laws of the State in which he lives, and he is no longer a citizen of the State from which he removed. And the State in which he resides may then, unquestionably, determine his *status* or condition, and place him among the class of persons who are not recognized as citizens, but belong to an inferior and subject race; and may deny him the privileges and immunities enjoyed by its citizens.

But so far as mere rights of persons are concerned, the provision in question is confined to citizens of a State who are temporarily in another State without taking up their residence there. It gives them no political rights in the State, as to voting or holding office, or in any other respect. For a citizen of one State has no right to participate in the government of another. But if he ranks as a citizen in the State to which he belongs, within the meaning of the Constitution of the United States, then, whenever he goes into another State, the Constitution clothes him, as to the rights of person, with all the privileges and immunities which belong to citizens of the State. And if persons of the African race are citizens of a State, and of the United States, they would be entitled to all these privileges and immunities in every State, and the State could not restrict them; for they would hold these privileges and immunities under the paramount authority of the Federal Government, and its courts would be bound to maintain and enforce them, the Constitution and laws of the State to the contrary notwithstanding. And if the States could limit or restrict them, or place the party in an inferior grade, this clause of the Constitution would be unmeaning, and could have no operation; and would give no rights to the citizen when in another State. He would have none but what the State itself

chose to allow him. This is evidently not the construction or meaning of the clause in question. It guaranties rights, to the citizen, and the State cannot withhold them. And these rights are of a character and weald lead to consequences, which make it absolutely certain that the African race were not included under the name of citizens of a State, and were not in the contemplation of the framers of the Constitution when these privileges and immunities were provided for the protection of the citizen in other States.

The case of Legrand *v.* Darnall (2 Peters, 664) has been referred to for the purpose of showing that this court has decided that the descendant of a slave may sue as a citizen in a court of the United States; but the case itself shows that the question did not arise and could not have arisen in the case.

It appears from the report, that Darnall was born in Maryland, and was the son of a white man by one of his slaves, and his father executed certain instruments to manumit him, and devised to him some landed property in the State. This property Darnall afterwards sold to Legrand, the appellant, who gave his notes for the purchase money. But becoming afterwards apprehensive that the appellee had not been emancipated according to the laws of Maryland, he refused to pay the notes until he could be better satisfied as to Darnall's right to convey. Darnall, in the mean time, had taken up his residence in Pennsylvania, and brought suit on the notes, and recovered judgment in the Circuit Court for the district of Maryland.

The whole proceeding, as appears by the report, was an amicable one; Legrand being perfectly willing to pay the money, if he could obtain a title, and Darnall not wishing him to pay unless he could make him a good one. In point of fact, the whole proceeding was under the direction of the counsel who argued the case for the appellee, who was the mutual friend of the parties, and confided in by both of them, and whose only object was to have the rights of both parties established by judicial decision in the most speedy and least expensive manner.

Legrand, therefore, raised no objection to the jurisdiction of the court in the suit at law, because he was himself anxious to obtain the judgment of the court upon his title. Consequently, there was nothing in the record before the court to show that Darnell, who was of African descent, and the usual judgment and award of execution was entered. And Legrand thereupon filed his bill on the equity side of the Circuit Court, stating that Darnall was born a slave, and had not been legally emancipated, and could not therefore take the land devised to him, nor make Legrand a good title; and praying an injunction to restrain Darnall from proceeding to execution on the judgment, which was granted. Darnall answered, averring in his answer that he was a free man, and capable of conveying a good title. Testimony was taken on this point, and at the hearing the Circuit Court was of opinion that Darnall was a free man and his title good, and dissolved the injunction and dismissed the bill; and that decree was affirmed here, upon the appeal of Legrand.

Now, it is difficult to imagine how any question about the citizenship of Darnall, or his right to sue in that character, can be supposed to have arisen or been decided in that case. The fact that he was of African descent was first brought before the court upon the bill in equity. The suit at law had then passed into judgment and award of execution, and the Circuit Court, as a court of law, had no longer any authority over it. It was a valid and legal judgment, which the court that rendered it had not the power to reverse or set aside. And unless it had jurisdiction as a court of equity to restrain him from using its process as a court of law, Darnall, if he thought proper, would have been at liberty to proceed on his judgment, and compel the payment of the money, although the allegations in the bill were true, and he was incapable of making a title. No other court could have enjoined him, for certainly no State equity court could interfere in that way with the judgment of a Circuit Court of the United States.

But the Circuit Court as a court of equity certainly had equity jurisdiction over its own judgment as a court of law, without regard to the character of the parties; and had not only the right, but it was its duty—no matter who were the parties in the judgment—to prevent them from proceeding to enforce it by execution, if the court was satisfied that the money was not justly and equitably due. The ability of Darnall to convey did not depend upon his citizenship, but upon his title to freedom. And if he was free, he could hold and convey property, by the laws of Maryland, although he was not a citizen. But if he was by law still a slave, he could not. It was therefore the duty of the court, sitting as a court of equity in the latter case, to prevent him from using its process, as a court of common law, to compel the payment of the purchase money, when it was evident that the purchaser must lose the land. But if he was free, and could make a title, it was equally the duty of the court not to suffer Legrand to keep the land, and

refuse the payment of the money, upon the ground that Darnall was incapable of suing or being sued as a citizen in a court of the United States. The character or citizenship of the parties had no connection with the question of jurisdiction, and the matter in dispute had no relation to the citizenship of Darnall. Nor is such a question alluded to in the opinion of the Court.

Besides, we are by no means prepared to say that there are not many cases, civil as well as criminal, in which a Circuit Court of the United States may exercise jurisdiction, although one of the African race is a party; that broad question is not before the court. The question with which we are now dealing is, whether a person of the African race can be a citizen of the United States, and become thereby entitled to a special privilege, by virtue of his title to that character, and which, under the Constitution, no one but a citizen can claim. It is manifest that the case of Legrand and Darnall has no bearing on that question, and can have no application to the case now before the court.

This case, however, strikingly illustrates the consequences that would follow the construction of the Constitution which would give the power contended for to a State. It would in effect give it also to an individual. For if the father of young Darnall had manumitted him in his lifetime, and sent him to reside in a State which recognized him as a citizen, he might have visited and sojourned in Maryland when he pleased, and as long as he pleased, as a citizen of the United States; and the State officers and tribunals would be compelled, by the paramount authority of the Constitution, to receive him and treat him as one of its citizens, exempt from the laws and police of the State in relation to a person of that description, and allow him to enjoy all the rights and privileges of citizenship without respect to the laws of Maryland, although such laws were deemed by it absolutely essential to its own safety.

The only two provisions which point to them and include them, treat them as property, and make it the duty of the Government to protect it; no other power, in relation to this race, is to be found in the Constitution; and as it is a Government of special, delegated, powers, no authority beyond these two provisions can be constitutionally exercised. The Government of the United States had no right to interfere for any other purpose but that of protecting the rights of the owner, leaving it altogether with the several States to deal with this race, whether emancipated or not, as each State may think justice, humanity, and the interests and safety of society, require. The States evidently intended to reserve this power exclusively to themselves.

No one, we presume, supposes that any change in public opinion or feeling, in relation to this unfortunate race, in the civilized nations of Europe or in this country, should induce the court to give to the words of the Constitution a more liberal construction in their favor than they were intended to bear when the instrument was framed and adopted. Such an argument would be altogether inadmissible in any tribunal called on to interpret it. If any of its provisions are deemed unjust, there is a mode prescribed in the instrument itself, by which it may be amended; but while it remains unaltered, it must be construed now as it was understood at the time of its adoption. It is not only the same in words, but the same in meaning, and delegates the same powers to the Government, and reserves and secures the same rights and privileges to the citizen; and as long as it continues to exist in its present form, it speaks not only in the same words, but with the same meaning and intent with which it spoke when it came from the hands of its framers, and was voted on and adopted by the people of the United States. Any other rule of construction would abregate the judicial character of this court, and make it the mere reflex of the popular opinion or passion of the day. This court was not created by the Constitution for such purposes. Higher and graver trusts have been confided to it, and it must not falter in the path of duty.

What the construction was at that time, we think can hardly admit of doubt. We have the language of the Declaration of Independence and of the Articles of Confederation, in addition to the plain words of the Constitution itself; we have the legislation of the different States, before, about the time, and since, the Constitution Was adopted; we have the legislation of Congress, from the time of its adoption to a recent period; and we have the constant and uniform action of the Executive Department, all concurring together, and leading to the same result. And if anything in relation to the construction of the Constitution can be regarded as settled, it is that which we now give to the word "citizen" and the word "people."

And upon a full and careful consideration of the subject, the court is of opinion, that, upon the facts stated in the plea in abatement, Dred Scott was not a citizen of Missouri within the meaning of the Constitution of the United States, and not entitled as such to sue in its courts; and, consequently, that the Circuit Court had no jurisdiction of the case, and that the judgment on the plea in abatement is erroneous.

We are aware that doubts are entertained by some of the members of the court, whether the plea in abatement is legally before the court upon this writ of error: but if that plea is regarded as waived, or out of the case upon any other ground, yet the question as to the jurisdiction of the Circuit Court is presented on the face of the bill of exception itself, taken by the plaintiff at the trial; for he admits that he and his wife were born slaves, but endeavors to make out his title to freedom and citizenship by showing that they were taken by their owner to certain places, hereinafter mentioned, where slavery could not by law exist, and that they thereby became free, and upon their return to Missouri became citizens of that State.

Now, if the removal of which he speaks did not give them their freedom, then by his own admission he is still a slave; and whatever opinions may be entertained in favor of the citizenship of a free person of the African race, no one supposes that a slave is a citizen of the State or of the United States. If, therefore, the acts done by his owner did not make them free persons, he is still a slave, and certainly incapable of suing in the character of a citizen.

The principle of law is too well serried to be disputed, that a court can give no judgment for either party, where it has no jurisdiction; and if, upon the showing of Scott himself, it appeared that he was still a slave, the case ought to have been dismissed, and the judgment against him and in favor of the defendant for costs, is, like that on the plea in abatement, erroneous, and the suit ought to have been dismissed by the Circuit Court for want of jurisdiction in that court.

But, before we proceed to examine this part of the case, it may be proper to notice an objection taken to the judicial authority of this court to decide it; and it has been said, that as this court has decided against the jurisdiction of the Circuit Court on the plea in abatement, it has no right to examine any question presented by the exception; and that anything it may say upon that part of the case will be extrajudicial, and mere obiter dicta.

This is a manifest mistake; there can be no doubt as to the jurisdiction of this court to revise the judgment of a Circuit Court, and to reverse it for any error apparent on the record, whether it be the error of giving judgment in a case over which it had no jurisdiction, or any other material error; and this, too, whether there is a plea in abatement or not.

The objection appears to have arisen from confounding writs of error to a State court, with writs of error to a Circuit Court of the United States. Undoubtedly, upon a writ of error to a State court, unless the record shows a case that gives jurisdiction, the case must be dismissed for want of jurisdiction in *this court*. And if it is dismissed on that ground, we have no right to examine and decide upon any question presented by the bill of exception, or any other part of the record. But writs of error to a State court, and to a Circuit Court of the United States, are regulated by different laws, and stand upon entirely different principles. And in a writ of error to a Circuit Court of the United States, the whole record is before this court for examination and decision; and if the sum in controversy is large enough to give jurisdiction, it is not only the right, but it is the judicial duty of the court, to examine the whole case as presented by the record; and if it appears upon its face that any material error or errors have been committed by the court below, it is the duty of this court to reverse the judgment, and remand the case. And certainly an error in passing a judgment upon the merits in favor of either party, in a case which it was not authorized to try, and over which it had no jurisdiction, is as grave an error as a court can commit.

The plea in abatement is not a plea to the jurisdiction of this court, but to the jurisdiction of the Circuit Court. And it appears by the record before us, that the Circuit Court committed an error, in deciding that it had jurisdiction, upon the facts in the case, admitted by the pleadings. It is the duty of the appellate tribunal to correct this error; but that could not be done by dismissing the case for want of jurisdiction here—for that would leave the erroneous judgment in full force, and the injured party without remedy. And the appellate court therefore exercises the power for which alone appellate courts are constituted, by reversing the judgment of the court below for this error. It exercises its proper and appropriate jurisdiction over the judgment and proceedings of the Circuit Court, as they appear upon the record brought up by the writ of error.

The correction of one error in the court below does not deprive the appellate court of the power of examining further into the record, and correcting any other material errors which may have been committed by the inferior court. There is certainly no rule of law—nor any practice—nor any decision of a court—which even questions this power in the appellate tribunal. On the contrary, it is the daily practice of this court, and of all appellate courts where they reverse the judgment of an inferior court for error, to correct by its opinions whatever errors may appear on the record material to the case; and they have always held it to be their duty to do so where the silence of the court might lead to misconstruction or future controversy, and the point has been relied on by either side, and argued before the court.

In the case before us, we have already decided that the Circuit Court erred in deciding that it had jurisdiction upon the facts admitted by the pleadings. And it appears that, in the further progress of the case, it acted upon the erroneous principle it had decided on the pleadings, and gave judgment for the defendant, where, upon the facts admitted in the exception, it had no jurisdiction.

We are at a loss to understand upon what principle of law applicable to appellate jurisdiction, it can be supposed that this court has not judicial authority to correct the last-mentioned error, because they had before corrected the former; or by what process of reasoning it can be made out, that the error of an inferior court in actually pronouncing judgment for one of the parties, in a case in which it had no jurisdiction, cannot be looked into or corrected by this court, because we have decided a similar question presented in the pleadings. The last point is distinctly presented by the facts contained in the plaintiff's own bill of exceptions, which he himself brings here by this writ of error. It was the point which chiefly occupied the attention of the counsel on both sides in the argument—and the judgment which this court must render upon both errors is precisely the same. It must, in each of them, exercise jurisdiction over the judgment, and reverse it for the errors committed by the court below; and issue a mandate to the Circuit Court to conform its judgment to the opinion pronounced by this court, by dismissing the case for want of jurisdiction in the Circuit Court. This is the constant and invariable practice of this court, where it reverses a judgment for want of jurisdiction in the Circuit Court.

It can scarcely be necessary to pursue such a question further. The want of jurisdiction in the court below may appear on the record without any plea in abatement. This is familiarly the case where a court or chancery has exercised jurisdiction in a case where the plaintiff had a plain and adequate remedy at law, and it so appears by the transcript when brought here by appeal. So also where it appears that a court of admiralty has exercised jurisdiction in a case belonging exclusively to a court of common law. In these cases there is no plea in abatement. And for the same reason, and upon the same principles, where the defect of jurisdiction is patent on the record, this court is bound to reverse the judgment, although the defendant has not pleaded in abatement to the jurisdiction of the inferior court.

The cases of Jackson *v.* Ashton and of Capron *v.* Van Noorden, to which we have referred in a previous part of this opinion, are directly in point. In the last-mentioned case, Capron brought an action against Van Noorden in a Circuit Court of the United States, without showing, by the usual averments of citizenship, that the court had jurisdiction. There was no plea in abatement put in, and the parties went to trial upon the merits. The court gave judgment in favor of the defendant with costs. The plaintiff thereupon brought his writ of error, and this court reversed the judgment given in favor of the defendant, and remanded the case with directions to dismiss it, because it did not appear by the transcript that the Circuit Court had jurisdiction.

The case before us still more strongly imposes upon this court the duty of examining whether the court below has not committed an error, in taking jurisdiction and giving a judgment for costs in favor of the defendant; for in Capron *v.* Van Noorden the judgment was reversed because it did *not appear* that the parties were citizens of different States. They might or might not be. But in this case it *does appear* that the plaintiff was born a slave; and if the facts upon which he relies have not made him free, then it appears affirmatively on the record that he is not a citizen, and consequently his suit against Sandford was not a suit between citizens of different States, and the court had no authority to pass any judgment between the parties. The suit ought, in this view of it, to have been dismissed by the Circuit Court, and its judgment in favor of Sandford is erroneous, and must be reversed.

It is true that the result either way, by dismissal or by a judgment for the defendant, makes very little, if any, difference in a pecuniary or personal point of view to either party. But the fact that the result would be very nearly the same to the parties in either form of judgment, would not justify this court in sanctioning an error in the judgment which is patent on the record, and which if sanctioned, might be drawn into precedent, and lead to serious mischief and injustice in some future suit.

We proceed, therefore, to inquire whether the facts relied, on by the plaintiff entitled him to his freedom. The case, as he himself states it, on the record brought here by his writ of error, is this:

The plaintiff was a negro slave, belonging to Dr. Emerson, who was a surgeon in the army of the United States. In the year 1834, he took the plaintiff from the State of Missouri to the military post at Rock Island, in the State of Illinois, and held him there as a slave until the month of April or May, 1836. At the time last mentioned, said Dr. Emerson removed the plaintiff from said military post at Rock Island to the military post at Fort Snelling, situate on the west bank of the Mississippi river, in the territory known as Upper Louisiana, acquired by the United States of France and situate north of the latitude of thirty-six degrees thirty minutes north, and north of the State of Missouri. Said Dr. Emerson held the plaintiff in slavery at said Fort Shelling, from said last-mentioned date until the year 1838.

In the year 1835, Harriet, who is named in the second count of the plaintiff's declaration, was the negro slave of Major Taliaferro, who belonged to the army of the United States. In that year, 1835, said Major Taliaferro took said Harriet to said Fort Shelling, a military post, situated as hereinbefore stated, and kept her there as a slave until the year 1836, and then sold and delivered her as a slave, at said Fort Snelling, unto the said Dr. Emerson hereinbefore named. Said Dr. Emerson held said Harriet in slavery at said Fort Snelling until the year 1838.

In the year 1836, the plaintiff and Harriet intermarried, at Fort Snelling, with the consent of Dr. Emerson, who then claimed to be their master and owner. Eliza and Lizzie, named in the third comet of the plaintiff's declaration, are the fruit of that marriage. Eliza is about fourteen years old, and was born on board the steamboat Gipsey, north of the north line of the State of Missouri, and upon the river Mississippi. Lizzie is about seven years old, and was born in the State of Missouri, at the military post called Jefferson Barracks.

In the year 1838, said Dr. Emerson removed the plaintiff and said Harriet, and their said daughter Eliza, from said Fort Snelling to the State of Missouri, where they have ever since resided.

Before the commencement of this suit, said Dr. Emerson sold and conveyed the plaintiff, and Harriet, Eliza, and Lizzie, to the defendant, as slaves, and the defendant has ever since claimed to hold them, and each of them, as slaves.

In considering this part of the controversy, two questions arise: 1. Was he, together with his family, free in Missouri by reason of the stay in the territory of the United States hereinbefore mentioned? And,

2. If they were not, is Scott himself free by reason of his removal to Rock Island, in the State of Illinois, as stated in the above admissions?

We proceed to examine the first question.

The act of Congress, upon which the plaintiff relies, declares that slavery and involuntary servitude, except as a punishment for crime shall be forever prohibited in all that part of the territory ceded by France, under the name of Louisiana, which lies north of thirty-six degrees thirty minutes north latitude, and not included within the limits of Missouri. And the difficulty which meets us at the threshold of this part of the inquiry is, whether Congress was authorised to pass this law under any of the powers granted to it by the Constitution; for if the authority is not given by that instrument, it is the duty of this court to declare it void and inoperative, and incapable of conferring freedom upon any one who is held as a slave under the laws of any one of the States.

The counsel for the plaintiff has laid much stress upon that article in the Constitution which confers on Congress the power "to dispose of and make all needful rules and regulations respecting the territory or other property belonging to the United States;" but, in the judgment of the court, that provision has no hearing on the present controversy, and the power there given, whatever it may be, is confined, and was intended to be confined, to the territory which at that time belonged to, or was claimed by, the United States, and was within their boundaries as settled by the treaty with Great Britain, and can have no influence upon a territory afterwards acquired from a foreign Government. It was a special provision for a known and particular territory, and to meet a present emergency, and nothing more.

A brief summary of the history of the times, as well as the careful and measured terms in which the article is framed, will show the correctness of this proposition.

It will be remembered that, from the commencement of the Revolutionary war, serious difficulties existed between the States, in relation to the disposition of large and unsettled territories which were included in the chartered limits of some of the States. And some of the other States, and more especially Maryland, which had no unsettled lands, insisted that as the unoccupied lands, if wrested from Great Britain, would owe their preservation to the common purse and the common sword, the money arising from them ought to be applied in just proportion among the several States to pay the expenses of the war, and ought not to be appropriated to the use of the State in whose chartered limits they might happen to lie, to the exclusion of the other State, by whose combined efforts and common expense the territory was defended and preserved against the claim of the British Government.

These difficulties caused much uneasiness during the war, while the issue was in some degree doubtful, and the future boundaries of the United States yet to be defined by treaty, if we achieved our independence.

The majority of the Congress of the Confederation obviously concurred in opinion with the State of Maryland, and desired to obtain from the States which claimed it a cession of this territory, in order that Congress might raise money on this security to carry on the war. This appears by the resolution passed on the 6th of September, 1780, strongly urging the States to cede these lands to the United States, both for the sake of peace and union among themselves and to maintain the public credit; and this was followed by the resolution of October 10th, 1780, by which Congress pledged itself, that if the lands were ceded, as recommended by the resolution above mentioned, they should be disposed of for the common benefit of the United States, and be settled and formed into distinct republican States, which should become members of the Federal Union, and have the same rights of sovereignty, and freedom and independence, as other States.

But these difficulties became much more serious after peace took place, and the boundaries of the United States were established. Every State, at that time, felt severely the pressure of its war debt; but in Virginia, and some other States, there were large territories of unsettled lands, the sale of which would enable them to discharge their obligations without much inconvenience; while other States, which had no such resource, saw before them many years of heavy and burdensome taxation; and the latter insisted, for the reasons before stated, that these unsettled lands should be treated as the common property of the States, and the proceeds applied to their common benefit.

The letters from the statesmen of that day will show bow much this controversy occupied their thoughts, and the dangers that were apprehended from it. It was the disturbing element of the time, and fears were entertained that it might dissolve the Confederation by which the States were then united.

These fears and dangers were, however, at once removed, when the State of Virginia, in 1784, voluntarily ceded to the United States the immense tract of country lying northwest of the river Ohio and which was within the acknowledged limits of the State. The only object of the State, in making this cession, was to put an end to the threatening and exciting controversy, and to enable the Congress of that time to dispose of the lands, and appropriate the proceeds as a common fund for the common benefit of the States. It was not ceded because it was inconvenient to the State to hold and govern it, nor from any expectation that it could be better or more conveniently governed by the United States.

The example of Virginia was soon afterwards followed by other States, and, at the time of the adoption of the Constitution all of the States, similarly situated, had ceded their unappropriated lands, except North Carolina and Georgia. The main object for which these cessions were desired and made, was on account of their money value, and to put an end to a dangerous controversy, as to who was justly entitled to the proceeds when the land should be sold. It is necessary to bring this part of the history of these cessions thus distinctly into view, because it will enable us the better to comprehend the phraseology of the article in the Constitution, so often referred to in the argument.

Undoubtedly the powers of sovereignty and the eminent domain were ceded with the land. This was essential, in order to make it effectual, and to accomplish its objects. But it must be remembered that, at that time, there was no Government of the United States in existence with enumerated and limited powers; what was then called the United States, were thirteen separate, sovereign, independent States, which had entered into a league or confederation for their mutual protection and advantage, and the Congress of the United States was composed of the representatives of these separate sovereignties, meeting together, as equals, to discuss and decide on certain measures which the States, by the Articles of Confederation, had agreed to submit to their decision. But this Confederation had none of the attributes of sovereignty in legislative, executive, or judicial power. It was little more than a congress of ambassadors, authorised to represent separate nations, in matters in which they had a common concern.

It was this congress that accepted the cession from Virginia. They had no power to accept it under the Articles of Confederation. But they had an undoubted right, as independent sovereignties, to accept any cession of territory for their common benefit, which all of them assented to; and it is equally

clear that as their common property, and having no superior to control them, they had the right to exercise absolute dominion over it, subject only to the restrictions which Virginia had imposed in her act of cession. There was, as we have said, no Government of the United States then in existence with special enumerated and limited powers. The territory belonged to sovereignties, who, subject to the limitations above mentioned, had a right to establish any form of Government they pleased, by compact or treaty among themselves, and to regulate rights of person and rights of property in the territory, as they might deem proper. It was by a Congress, representing the authority of these several and separate sovereignties, and acting under their authority and command (but not from any authority derived from the Articles of Confederation,) that the instrument usually called the ordinance of 1787 was adopted; regulating in much detail the principles and the laws by which this territory should be governed; and among other provisions, slavery is prohibited in it. We do not question the power of the States by agreement among themselves, to pass this ordinance, nor its obligatory force in the territory, while the confederation or league of the States in their separate sovereign character continued to exist.

This was the state of things when the Constitution of the United States was formed. The territory ceded by Virginia belonged to the several confederated States as common property, and they had united in establishing in it a system of government and jurisprudence, in order to prepare it for admission as States, according to the terms of the cession. They were about to dissolve this federative Union, and to surrender a portion of their independent sovereignty to a new Government, which, for certain purposes, would make the people of the several States one people, and which was to be supreme and controlling within its sphere of action throughout the United States; but this Government was to be carefully limited in its powers, and to exercise no authority beyond those expressly granted by the Constitution, or necessarily to be implied from the language of the instrument, and the objects it was intended to accomplish; and as this league of States would, upon the adoption of the new Government, cease to have any power over the territory, and the ordinance they had agreed upon be incapable of execution and a mere nullity, it was obvious that some provision was necessary to give the new Government sufficient power to enable it to carry into effect the objects for which it was ceded, and the compacts and agreements which the States had made with each other in the exercise of their powers of sovereignty. It was necessary that the lands should be sold to pay the war debt; that a Government and system of jurisprudence should be maintained in it, to protect the citizens of the United States who should migrate to the territory, In their rights of person and of property. It was also necessary that the new Government, about to be adopted, should be authorized to maintain the claim of the United States to the unappropriated lands in North Carolina and Georgia, which had not then been ceded, but the cession of which was confidently anticipated upon some terms that would be arranged between the General Government and these two States. And, moreover, there were many articles of value besides this property in land such as arms military stores, munitions, and ships of war, which were the common property of the States, when acting in their independent characters as confederates, which neither the new Government nor any one else would have a right to take possession of, or control without authority from them; and it was to place these things under the guardianship and protection of the new Government, and to clothe it with the necessary powers, that the clause was inserted in the Constitution which gives Congress the power "to dispose of and make all needful rules and regulations respecting the territory or other property belonging to the United States." It was intended for a specific purpose, to provide for the things we have mentioned. It was to transfer to the new Government the property then held in common by the States, and to give to that Government power to apply it to the objects for which it had been destined by mutual agreement among the States before their league was dissolved. It applied only to the property which the States held in common at that time, and has no reference whatever to any territory or other property which the new sovereignty might afterwards itself acquire.

The language used in the clause, the arrangement and combination of the powers, and the somewhat unusual phraseology it uses, when it speaks of the political power to be exercised in the government of the territory, all indicate the design and meaning of the clause to be such as we have mentioned. It does not speak of any territory, nor of *Territories*, but uses language which, according to its legitimate meaning, points to a particular thing. The power is given in relation only to the territory of the United States—that is, to a territory then in existence, and then known or claimed as the territory of the United States. It begins its enumeration of powers by that of disposing, in other words, making sale of the lands, or raising money from them, which, as we have already said, was the main object of the cession, and which is accordingly the first thing provided for in the article. It then gives the power which was necessarily associated with the disposition and sale of the lands—that is, the power of making needful rules and regulations respecting the territory. And whatever construction may now be given to these words, every one, we think, must admit that they are not the words usually employed by statesmen in giving supreme power of legislation. They are certainly very unlike the words used in the power granted to legislate over territory which the new Government might afterwards itself obtain by cession from a State, either for its seat of Government, or for forts, magazines, arsenals, dock yards, and other needful buildings.

And the same power of making needful rules respecting the territory is, in precisely the same language, applied to the *other* property belonging to the United States—associating the power over the territory in this respect with the power over movable or personal property—that is, the ships, arms, and munitions of war, which then belonged in common to the State sovereignties. And it will hardly be said, that this power, in relation to the last-mentioned objects, was deemed necessary to be thus specially given to the new Government, in order to authorize it to make needful rules and regulations respecting the ships it might itself build, or arms and munitions of war it might itself manufacture or provide for the public service.

No one, it is believed, would think a moment of deriving the power of Congress to make needful rules and regulations in relation to property of this kind from this clause of the Constitution. Nor can it, upon any fair construction, be applied to any property, but that which the new Government was about to receive from the confederated States. And if this be true as to this property, it must be equally true and limited as to the territory, which is so carefully and precisely coupled with it—and like it referred to as property in the power granted. The concluding words of the clause appear to render this construction irresistible; for, after the provisions we have mentioned, it proceeds to say, "that nothing in the Constitution shall be so construed as to prejudice any claims of the United States, or of any particular State."

Now, as we have before said, all of the States, except North Carolina and Georgia, had made the cession before the Constitution was adopted, according to the resolution of Congress of October 10, 1780, the claims of other States, that the unappropriated lands in these two States should be applied to the common benefit, in like manner, was still insisted on, but refused by the States. And this member of the clause in question evidently applies to them, and can apply to nothing else. It was to exclude the conclusion that either party, by adopting the Constitution, would surrender what they deemed their rights. And when the latter provision relates so obviously to the unappropriated lands not yet ceded by the States, and the first clause makes provision for those then actually ceded, it is impossible, by any just rule of construction, to make the first provision general, and extend to all territories, which the Federal Government might in any way afterwards acquire, when the latter is plainly and unequivocally confined to a particular territory; which was a part of the same controversy, and involved in the same dispute and depended upon the same principles. The union of the two provisions in the same clause shows that they were kindred subjects; and that the whole clause is local, and relates only to lands, within the limits of the United States, which had been or then were claimed by a State; and that no other territory was in the mind of the framers of the Constitution, or intended to be embraced in it. Upon any other construction it would be impossible to account for the insertion of the last provision in the place where it is found, or to comprehend why, or for what object, it was associated with the previous provision.

This view of the subject is confirmed by the manner in which the present Government of the United States dealt with the subject as soon as it came into existence. It must be borne in mind that the same States that formed the Confederation also formed and adopted the new Government, to which so large a portion of their former sovereign powers were surrendered. It must also be borne in mind that all of these same States which had then ratified the new Constitution were represented in the Congress which passed the first law for the government of this territory; and many of the members of that legislative body had been deputies from the States under the Confederation—had united in adopting the ordinance of 1787, and assisted in forming the new Government under which they were then acting, and whose powers they were then exercising. And it is obvious from the law they passed to carry into effect the principles and provisions of the ordinance that they regarded it as the act of the States done in the exercise of their legitimate powers at the time. The

new Government took the territory as it found it, and in the condition in which it was transferred, and did not attempt to undo anything that had been done. And, among the earliest laws passed under the new Government, is one reviving the ordinance of 1787, which had become inoperative and a nullity upon the adoption of the Constitution. Tiffs law introduces no new form or principles for its government, but recite, in the preamble, that it is passed in order that this ordinance may continue to have full effect, and proceeds to make only those rules and regulations which were needful to adapt it to the new Government, into whose hands the power had fallen. It appears, therefore, that this Congress regarded the purposes to which the land in this Territory was to be applied, and the form of government and principles of jurisprudence which were to prevail there, while it remained in the Territorial State, as already determined on by the States when they had full power and right to make the decision; and that the new Government, having received it in this condition, ought to carry substantially into effect the plans and principles which had been previously adopted by the States, and which, no doubt, the States anticipated when they surrendered their power to the new Government. And if we regard this clause of the Constitution as pointing to this Territory, with a Territorial Government already established in it, which had been ceded to the States for the purposes hereinbefore mentioned—every word in it is perfectly appropriate and easily understood, and the provisions it contains are in perfect harmony with the objects for which it was ceded, and with the condition of its government as a Territory at the time. We can, then, easily account for the manner in which the first Congress legislated on the subject—and can also understand why this power over the territory was associated in the same clause with the other property of the United States, and subjected to the like power of making needful rules and regulations. But if the clause is construed in the expanded sense contended for, so as to embrace any territory acquired from a foreign nation by the present Government, and to give it in such territory a despotic and unlimited power over persons and property, such as the confederated States might exercise in their common property, it would he difficult to account for the phraseology used, when compared with other grants of power—and also for its association with the other provisions in the same clause.

The Constitution has always been remarkable for the felicity of its arrangement of different subjects, and the perspicuity and appropriateness of the language it uses. But if the clause is construed to extend to territory acquired by the present Government from a foreign nation, outside of the limits of any charter from the British Government to a colony, it would be difficult to say, why it was deemed necessary to give the Government the power to sell any vacant lands belonging to the sovereignty which might be found within it; and if this was necessary, why the grant of this power should precede the power to legislate over it and establish a Government there; and still more difficult to say, why it was deemed necessary so specially and particularly to grant the power to make needful rules and regulations in relation to any personal or movable property it might acquire there. For the words, *other property,* necessarily, by every known rule of interpretation, must mean property of a different description from territory or land. And the difficulty would perhaps be insurmountable in endeavoring to account for the last member of the sentence, which provides that "nothing in this Constitution shall be so construed as to prejudice any claims of the United States or any particular State," or to say how any particular State could have claims in or to a territory ceded by a foreign Government, or to account for associating this provision with the preceding provisions of the clause, with which it would appear to have no connection.

The words "needful rules and regulations" would seem, also, to have been cautiously used for some definite object. They are not the words usually employed by statesmen when they mean to give the powers of sovereignty, or to establish a Government, or to authorise its establishment. Thus, in the law to renew and keep alive the ordinance of 1787, and to re-establish the Government, the title of the law is: "An act to provide for the government of the territory northwest of the river Ohio." And in the Constitution, when granting the power to legislate over the territory that may be selected for the seat of Government independently of a State, it does not say Congress shall have power "to make all needful rules and regulations respecting the territory"; but it declares that "Congress shall have power to exercise exclusive legislation in all cases whatsoever over such District (not exceeding, ten miles square) as may, by cession of particular States and the acceptance of Congress, become the seat of the Government of the United States.

The words "rules and regulations" are usually employed in the Constitution in speaking of same particular specified power which it means to confer

on the Government, and not, as we have seen, when granting general powers of legislation. As, for example, in the particular power to Congress "to make rules for the government and regulation of the land and naval forces, or the particular and specific power to regulate commerce"; "to establish an uniform *rule* of naturalization"; "to coin money and *regulate* the value thereof." And to construe the words of which we are speaking as a general and unlimited grant of sovereignty over territories which the Government might afterwards acquire, is to use them in a sense and for a purpose for which they were not used in any other part of the instrument. But if confined to a particular Territory, in which a Government and laws had already been established, but which would require some alterations to adapt it to the new Government, the words are peculiarly applicable and appropriate for that purpose.

The necessity of this special provision in relation to property and the rights or property held in common by the confederated States, is illustrated by the first clause of the sixth article. This clause provides that "all debts, contracts, and engagements entered into before the adoption of this Constitution, shall be as valid against the United States under this Government as under the Confederation." This provision like the one under consideration, was indispensable if the new Constitution was adopted. The new Government was not a mere change in a dynasty, or in a form of government, leaving the nation or sovereignty the same, and clothed with all the right, and bound by all the obligations of the preceding one. But, when the present United States came into existence under the new Government, it was a new political body, a new nation, then for the first time taking its place in the family of nations. It took nothing by succession from the Confederation. It had no right, as its successor, to any property or rights of property which it had acquired, and was not liable for any of its obligations. It was evidently viewed in this light by the framers of the Constitution. And as the several States would cease to exist in their former confederated character upon the adoption of the Constitution, and could not, in that character, again assemble together, special provisions were indispensable to transfer to the new Government the property and rights which at that time they held in common; and at the same time to authorize it to lay taxes and appropriate money to pay the common debt which they had contracted; and this power could only be given to it by special provisions in the Constitution. The clause in relation to the territory and other property of the United States provided for the first, and the clause last quoted provides for the other. They have no connection with the general powers and rights of sovereignty delegated to the new Government, and can neither enlarge nor diminish them. They were inserted to meet a present emergency, and not to regulate its powers as a Government.

Indeed, a similar provision was deemed necessary, in relation to treaties made by the Confederation; and when in the clause next succeeding the one of which we have last spoken, it is declared that treaties shall be the supreme law of the land, care is taken to include, by express words, the treaties made by the confederated States. The language is: "and all treaties made, or which shall be made, under the authority of the United States, shall be the supreme law of the land."

Whether, therefore, we take the particular clause in question, by itself, or in connection with the other provisions of the Constitution, we think it clear, that it applies only to the particular territory of which we have spoken, and cannot, by any just rule of interpretation, be extended to territory which the new Government might afterwards obtain from a foreign nation. Consequently, the power which Congress may have lawfully exercises in this Territory, while it remained under a Territorial Government, and which may have been sanctioned by judicial decision, can furnish no justification and no argument to support a similar exercise of power over territory afterwards acquired by the Federal Government. We put aside, therefore, any argument, drawn from precedents, showing the extent of the power which the General Government exercised over slavery in this Territory, as altogether inapplicable to the case before us.

But the case of the American and Ocean Insurance Companies v. Canter (1 Pet., 511) has been quoted as establishing a different construction of this clause of the Constitution. There is, however, not the slightest conflict between the opinion now given and the one referred to; and it is only by taking a single sentence out of the latter and separating it from the context, that even an appearance of conflict can be shown. We need not comment on such a mode of expounding an opinion of the court. Indeed it most commonly misrepresents instead of expounding it. And this is fully exemplified in the case referred to, where, if one sentence is taken by itself, the opinion would appear to be in direct conflict with that now given; but the words which immediately follow that sentence show that the court, did not mean to decide the point, but merely affirmed the power of Congress to establish a Government in the Territory, leaving it an open question, whether that power was derived from this clause in the Constitution, or was to be necessarily referred item a power to acquire territory by cession from a foreign Government. The opinion on this part of the case is short, and we give the whole of it to show how well the selection of a single sentence is calculated to mislead.

The passage referred to is in page 542, in which the court in speaking of the power of Congress to establish a Territorial Government in Florida until it should become a State, uses the following language:

"In the mean time Florida continues to be a Territory of the United States, governed by that clause of the Constitution which empowers Congress to make all needful rules and regulations respecting the territory or other property of the United States. Perhaps the power of governing a Territory belonging to the United States, which has not, by becoming a State, acquired the means of self government, may result, necessarily, from the facts that it is not within the jurisdiction of any particular State, and is within the power and jurisdiction of the United States. The right to govern may be the inevitable consequence of the right to acquire territory. *Whichever may be the source from which the power is derived, the possession of it is unquestionable*."

It is thus clear, from the whole opinion on this point, that the court did not mean to decide whether the power was derived from the clause in the Constitution, or was the necessary consequence of the right to acquire, They do decide that the power in Congress is unquestionable, and in this we entirely concur, and nothing will be found in this opinion to the contrary. The power stands firmly on the latter alternative put by the court—that is, as "*the inevitable consequence of the right to acquire territory*."

And what still more clearly demonstrates that the court did not mean to decide the question, but leave it open for future consideration, is the fact that the case was decided in the Circuit Court by Mr. Justice Johnson, and his decision was affirmed by the Supreme Court. His opinion at the circuit is given in full in a note to the case, and in that opinion he states, in explicit terms, that the clause of the Constitution applies only to the territory then within the limits of the United States and not to Florida, which had been acquired by cession from Spain. This part of his opinion will be found in the note in page 517 of the report. But he does not dissent from the opinion of the Supreme Court; thereby showing that, in his judgment as well as that of the court, the case before them did not call for a decision on that particular point, and the court abstained from deciding it. And in a part of its opinion subsequent to the passage we have quoted, where the court speak of the legislative power of Congress in Florida, they still speak with the same reserve. And in page 546, speaking of the power of Congress to authorise the Territorial Legislature to establish courts there, the court say: "They are legislative courts, created in virtue of the general right of sovereignty which exists in the Government, or in virtue of that clause which enables Congress to make all needful rules and regulations respecting the territory belonging to the United States."

It has been said that the construction given to this clause is new, and now for the first time brought forward. The case of which we are speaking, and which has been so much discussed, shows that the fact is otherwise. It shows that precisely the same question came before Mr. Justice Johnson, at his circuit, thirty years ago—was fully considered by him, and the same construction given to the clause in the Constitution which is now given by this court. And that upon an appeal from his decision the same question was brought before this court, but was not decided because a decision upon it was not required by the case before the court.

There is another sentence in the opinion which has been commented on, which even in a still more striking manner shows how one may mislead or be misled by taking out a single sentence from the opinion of a court, and leaving out of view what precedes and follows. It is in page 546, near the close of the opinion, in which the court say: "In legislating for them," (the territories of the United States,) "Congress exercises the combined powers of the General and or a State Government." And it is said, that as a State may unquestionably prohibit slavery within its territory, this sentence decides in effect that Congress may do the same in a territory of the United States, exercising there the powers of a State, as well as the power of the General Government.

The examination of this passage in the case referred to, would be more appropriate when we come to consider in another part of this opinion what power Congress can constitutionally exercise in a Territory, over the rights of person or rights of property of a citizen. But, as it is in the same case with the passage we have before commented on, we dispose of it now, as it will save the court from the necessity of referring again to the case. And it will be seen upon reading the page in which this sentence is found, that it has no reference whatever to the power of Congress over rights of person or rights of property—but relates altogether to the power of establishing judicial tribunals to administer the laws constitutionally passed, and defining the jurisdiction they may exercise.

The law of Congress establishing a Territorial Government in Florida, provided that the Legislature of the Territory should have legislative powers over "all rightful objects of legislation; but no law should be valid which was inconsistent with the laws and Constitution of the United States."

Under the power thus conferred, the Legislature of Florida passed an act, erecting a tribunal at Key West to decide cases of salvage., And in the case of which we are speaking, the question arose whether the Territorial Legislature could be authorised by Congress to establish such a tribunal, with such powers; and one of the parties, among other objections, insisted that Congress could not under the Constitution authorise the Legislature of the Territory to establish such a tribunal with such powers, but that it must be established by Congress itself; and that a sale of cargo made under its order, to pay salvors, was void, as made without legal authority, and passed no property to the purchaser.

It is in disposing of this objection that the sentence relied on occurs, and the court begins that part of the opinion by stating with great precision the point, which they are about to decide.

They say: "It has been contended that by the Constitution of the United States, the judicial power of the United States extends to all cases of admiralty and maritime jurisdiction; and that the whole of the judicial power must be vested 'in one Supreme Court, and in such inferior courts as Congress shall from time to time ordain and establish.' Hence it has been argued that Congress cannot vest admiralty jurisdiction in courts created by the Territorial Legislature."

And after thus clearly stating the point before them, and which they were about to decide, they proceed to show that these Territorial tribunals were not constitutional courts, but merely legislative, and that Congress might, therefore, delegate the power to the Territorial Government to establish the court in question; and they conclude that part of the opinion in the following words: "Although admiralty jurisdiction can be exercised in the States in those courts only which are established in pursuance of the third article of the Constitution, the same limitation does not extend to the Territories. In legislating for them, Congress exercises the combined powers of the General and State Governments."

Thus it will be seen by these quotations from the opinion that the court, after stating the question it was about to decide in a manner too plain to be misunderstood, proceeded to decide it, and announced, as the opinion of the tribunal, that in organizing the judicial department of the Government in a Territory of the United States, Congress does not act under, and is not restricted by the third article in the Constitution, and is not bound in a Territory to ordain and establish courts in which the judges hold their offices during good behaviour, but may exercise the discretionary power which a State exercises in establishing its judicial department, and regulating the jurisdiction of its courts, and may authorize the Territorial Government to establish, or may itself establish, courts in which the judges hold their offices for a term of years only; and may vest in them judicial power upon subjects confided to the judiciary of the United States. And in doing this, Congress undoubtedly exercises the combined power of the General and a State Government. It exercises the discretionary power of a State Government in authorizing the establishment of a court in which the judges hold their appointments for a term of years only, and not during good behaviour; and it exercises the power of the General Government in investing that court with admiralty jurisdiction, over which the General Government had exclusive jurisdiction in the Territory.

No one, we presume, will question the correctness of that opinion; nor is there anything in conflict with it in the opinion now given. The point decided in the case cited has no relation to the question now before the court. That depended on the construction of the third article of the Constitution, in relation to the judiciary of the United States, and the power which Congress might exercise in a Territory in organizing the judicial department of the Government. The case before us depends upon other and different provisions of the Constitution, altogether separate and apart from the one above mentioned. The question as to what courts Congress may ordain or establish in a Territory to administer laws which the Constitution authorizes it to pass, and what laws it is or is not authorized by the Constitution to pass, are widely different—are regulated by different and separate articles of the Constitution, and stand upon different principles. And we are satisfied that no one who reads attentively the page in Peters's Reports to which we have referred, can suppose that the attention of the court was drawn to a moment to the question now before this court, or that it meant in that

case to say that Congress had a right to prohibit a citizen of the United States from taking any property which he lawfully held into a Territory of the United States.

This brings us to examine by what provision of the Constitution the present Federal Government, under its delegated and restricted powers, is authorized to acquire territory outside of the original limits of the United States, and what powers it may exercise therein over the person or property of a citizen of the United States, while it remains a Territory, and until it shall be admitted as one of the States of the Union.

There is certainly no power given by the Constitution to the Federal Government to establish or maintain colonies bordering on the United States or at a distance, to be ruled and governed at its own pleasure; nor to enlarge its territorial limits in any way, except by the admission of new States. That power is plainly given; and if a new State is admitted, it needs no further legislation from Congress, because the Constitution itself defines the relative rights and powers, and duties of the State, and the citizens of the State and the Federal Government. But no power is given to acquire a Territory to be held and governed permanently in that character.

And indeed the power exercised by Congress to acquire territory and establish a Government there, according to its own unlimited discretion, was viewed with great jealousy by the leading statesmen of the day. And in the Federalist, (No. 38,) written by Mr. Madison he speaks of the acquisition of the Northwestern Territory by the confederated States, by the cession from Virginia, and the establishment of a Government there, as an exercise of power not warranted by the Articles of Confederation, and dangerous to the liberties of the people. And he urges the adoption of the Constitution as a security and safeguard against such an exercise of power.

We do not mean, however, to question the power of Congress in this respect. The power to expand the territory of the United States by the admission of new States is plainly given; and in the construction of this power by all the departments of the Government, it has been held to authorize the acquisition of territory, not fit for admission at the time but to be admitted as soon as its population and situation would entitle it to admission. It is acquired to become a State, and not to be held as a colony and governed by Congress with absolute authority; and as the propriety of admitting a new State is committed to the south discretion of Congress, the power to acquire territory for that purpose, to be held by the United States until it is in a suitable condition to become a State upon an equal footing with the other States, must rest upon the same discretion. It is a question for the political department of the Government, and not the judicial: and whatever the political department of the Government shall recognize as within the limits of the United States, the judicial department is also bound to recognize, and to administer in it the laws of the United States, so far as they apply, and to maintain in the Territory the authority and rights of the Government, and also the personal rights and rights of property of individual citizens, as secured by the Constitution. All we mean to say on this point is, that, as there is no express regulation in the Constitution defining the power which the General Government may exercise over the person or property of a citizen in a Territory thus acquired, the court must necessarily look to the provisions and principles of the Constitution, and its distribution of powers, for the rules and principles by which its decision must be governed.

Taking this rule to guide us, it may be safely assumed that citizens of the United States who migrate to a Territory belonging to the people of the United States, cannot be ruled as mere colonists, dependent upon the will of the General Government, and to be governed by any laws it may think proper to impose. The principle upon which our Governments rest, and upon which alone they continue to exist, is the union of States, sovereign and independent within their own limits in their internal and domestic concerns, and bound together as one people by a General Government, possessing certain enumerated and restricted powers, delegated to it by the people of the several States, and exercising supreme authority within the scope of the powers granted to it, throughout the dominion of the United States. A power, therefore, in the General Government to obtain and hold colonies and dependent territories, over which they might legislate without restriction, would be inconsistent with its own existence in its present form. Whatever it acquires, it acquires for the benefit of the people of the several States who created it. It is their trustee acting for them and charged with the duty of promoting the interests of the whole people of the whole Union in the exercise of the powers specifically granted.

At the time when the Territory in question was obtained by cession from France, it contained no population fit to be associated together and admitted as a State; and it therefore was absolutely necessary to hold possession of it, as a Territory belonging to the United States, until it was settled and inhabited by a civilized community capable of self-government, and in a condition to be admitted on equal terms with the other States as a member of the Union. But, as we have before said, it was acquired by the General Government, as the representative and trustee of the people of the United States, and it must therefore be held in that character for their common and equal benefit; for it was the people of the several States, acting through their agent and representative, the Federal Government, who in fact acquired the Territory in question, and the Government holds it for their common use until it shall be associated with the other States as a member of the Union.

But until that time arrives, it is undoubtedly necessary that some Government should be established in order to organize society, and to protect the inhabitants in their persons and property; and as the people of the United States could act in this matter only through the Government which represented them, and through which they spoke and acted when the Territory was obtained, it was not only within the scope of its powers, but it was its duty to pass such laws and establish such a Government as would enable those by whose authority they acted to reap the advantages anticipated from us acquisition, and to gather there a population which would enable it to assume the position to which it was destined among the States of the Union. The power to acquire necessarily carries with it the power to preserve and apply to the purposes for which it was acquired. The form of government to be established necessarily rested in the discretion of Congress. It was their duty to establish the one that would behest suited for the protection and security of the citizens of the United States, and other inhabitants who might be authorized to take up their abode there, and that must always depend upon the existing condition of the Territory, as to the number and character of its inhabitants, and their situation in the Territory. In some cases a Government consisting of persons appointed by the Federal Government, would best subserve the interests of the Territory, when the inhabitants were few and scattered, and new to one another. In other instances, it would be more advisable to commit the powers of self-government to the people who had settled in the Territory, as being the most competent to determine what was best for their own interests. But some form of civil authority would be absolutely necessary to organize and preserve civilized society, and prepare it to become a State; and what is the best form must always depend on the condition of the territory at the time, and the choice of the mode must depend upon the exercise of a discretionary power by Congress, acting within the scope of its constitutional authority, and not infringing upon the rights of person or rights of property of the citizen who might go there to reside, or for any other lawful purpose. It was acquired by the exercise of this discretion, and it must be held and governed in like manner, until it is fitted to be a State.

But the power of Congress over the person or property of a citizen can never be a more discretionary power under our Constitution and form of Government. The powers of the Government and the rights and privileges of the citizen are regulated and plainly defined by the Constitution itself. And when the Territory becomes a part of the United States the Federal Government enters into possession in the character impressed upon it by those who created it. It enters upon it with its powers over the citizen strictly defined, and limited by the Constitution, from which it derives its own existence, and by virtue of which alone it continues to exist and act as a Government and sovereignty. It has no power of any kind beyond it; and it cannot, when it enters a Territory of the United States put off its character, and assume discretionary or despotic powers which the Constitution has denied to it. It cannot create for itself a new character separated from the citizens of the United States and the duties it owes them under the provisions of the Constitution. The Territory being a part of the United States, the Government and the citizen both enter it under the authority of the Constitution, with their respective rights defined and marked out; and the Federal Government can exercise no power over his person or property, beyond what that instrument confers, nor lawfully deny any right which it has reserved.

A reference to a few of the provisions of the Constitution will illustrate this proposition.

For example, no one, we presume, will contend that Congress can make any law in a Territory respecting the establishment of religion, or the free exercise thereof, or abridging the freedom of speech or of the press, or the right of the people of the Territory peaceably to assemble, and to petition the Government top the redress of grievances.

Nor can Congress deny to the people the right to keep and bear arms, nor the right to trial by jury, nor compel any one to be a witness against himself in a criminal proceeding.

These powers, and others, in relation to rights of person, which it is not necessary here to enumerate, are, in express and positive terms, denied to the General Government; and the rights of private property have been guarded with equal care. Thus the rights of property are united with the rights of person, and placed on the same ground by the fifth amendment to the Constitution, which provides that no person shall be deprived of life, liberty, and property, without due process of law. And an act of Congress which deprives a citizen of the United States of his liberty or property, merely because he came himself or brought his property into a particular Territory of the United States, and who had committed no offence against the laws, could hardly be dignified with the name of due process of law.

So, too, it will hardly be contended that Congress could by law quarter a soldier in a house in a Territory without the consent of the owner, in time of peace; nor in time of war. But in a manner prescribed by law. Nor could they by law forfeit the property of a citizen in a Territory who was convicted of treason, for a longer period than the life of the person convicted; nor take private property for public use without just compensation.

The powers over person and property of which we speak are not only not granted to Congress, but are in express terms denied, and they are forbidden to exercise them. And this prohibition is not confined to the States but the words are general and extend to the whole territory over which the Constitution gives it power to legislate, including those portions of it remaining under Territorial Government, as well as that covered by States. It is a total absence of power everywhere within the dominion of the United States and places the citizens of a Territory so far as these rights are concerned, on the same footing with citizens of the States, and guards them as firmly and plainly against any inroads which the General Government might attempt, under the plea of implied or incidental powers. And if Congress itself cannot do this—if it is beyond the powers conferred on the Federal Government—it will be admitted, we presume, that it could not authorise a Territorial Government to exercise them. It could confer no power on any local Government, established by its authority, to violate the provisions of the Constitution.

It seems, however to be supposed, that there is a difference between property in a slave and other property, and that different rules may be applied to it in expounding the Constitution of the United States. And the laws add usages of nations, and the writings of eminent jurists upon the relation of master and slave and their mutual rights and duties, and the powers which Governments may exercise over it, have been dwelt upon in the argument.

But in considering the question before us, it must be borne in mind that there is no law of nations standing between the people of the United States and their Government, and interfering with their relation to each other. The powers of the Government, and the rights of the citizen under it, are positive and practical regulations plainly written down. The people of the United States have delegated to it certain enumerated powers, and forbidden it to exercise others. It has no power over the person or property of a citizen but what the citizens of the United States have granted. And no laws or usages of other nations, or reasoning of statesmen or jurists upon the relations of master and slave, can enlarge the powers of the Government, or take from the citizens the rights they have reserved. And if the Constitution recognizes the right of property of the master in a slave, and makes no distinction between that description of property and other property owned by a citizen, no tribunal acting under the authority of the United States, whether it it be legislative, executive, or judicial, has a right to draft such a distinction, or deny to it the benefit of the provisions and guarantees which have been provided for the protection of private property against the encroachments of the Government.

Now, as we have already said in an earlier part of this opinion, upon a different point, the right of property in a slave is distinctly and expressly affirmed in the Constitution. The right to traffic in it, like an ordinary article of merchandise and property was guarantied to the citizens of the United States, in every State that might desire it, for twenty years. And the Government in express terms is pledged To protect it in all future time, if the slave escapes from his owner. This is done in plain words—too plain to be misunderstood. And no word can be found in the Constitution which gives Confess a greater power over slave property, or which entitles property of that kind to less protection than property of any other description. The only power conferred is the power coupled with the duty of guarding and protecting the owner in his rights.

Upon these considerations, it is the opinion of the court that the act of Congress which prohibited a citizen from holding and owning property of this kind in the territory of the United States north of the line therein mentioned, is not warranted by the Constitution, and is therefore void; and that neither Dred Scott himself, nor any of his family, were made free by being carried into this territory; even if they had been carried there by the owner, with the intention of becoming a permanent resident.

We have so far examined the case as it stands under the Constitution of the United States, and the powers thereby delegated to the Federal Government.

But there is another point in the case which depends on State power and State law. And it is contended, on the part of the plaintiff, that he is made free by being taken to Rock Island, in the State of Illinois, independently of his residence in the territory of the United States; and being so made free, he was not again reduced to a state of slavery by being brought back to Missouri.

Our notice of this part of the case will be very brief; for the principle on which it depends was decided in this court, upon much consideration in the case of Strader et al. *v.* Graham, reported in 10th Howard, 82. In that case, the slaves had been taken from Kentucky to Ohio, with the consent of the owner, and afterwards brought back to Kentucky. And this court held that their *status* or condition, as free or slave, depended upon the laws of Kentucky, when they were brought back into that State, and not of Ohio; and that this court had no jurisdiction to revise the judgment of a State court upon its own laws. This was the point directly before the court, and the decision that this court had not jurisdiction turned upon it, as will be seen by the report of the case.

So in this case. As Scott was a slave when taken into the State of Illinois by his owner, and was there held as such, and brought back in that character, his *status*, as free or slave, depended on the laws of Missouri, and not of Illinois.

It has, however, been urged in the argument, that by the laws of Missouri he was free on his return, and that this case, therefore, cannot be governed by the case of Strader et al. *v.* Graham, where it appeared, by the laws of Kentucky, that the plaintiffs continued to be slaves on their return from Ohio. But whatever doubts or opinions may, at one time have been entertained upon this subject, we are satisfied, upon a careful examination of all the cases decided in the State courts of Missouri referred to, that it is now firmly settled by the decisions of the highest court in the State, that Scott and his family upon their return were not free, but were, by the laws of Missouri, the property of the defendant; and that the Circuit Court of the United States had no jurisdiction, when, by the laws of the State, the plaintiff was a slave, and not a citizen.

Moreover, the plaintiff, it appears, brought a similar action against the defendant in the State Court of Missouri, claiming the freedom of himself and his family upon the same grounds and the same evidence upon which he relies in the case before the court. The case was carried before the Supreme Court of the State; was fully argued there; and that court decided that neither the plaintiff nor his family were entitled to freedom, and were still the slaves of the defendant; and reversed the judgment of the inferior State court, which had given a different decision. If the plaintiff supposed that this judgment of the Supreme Court of the State was erroneous and that this court had jurisdiction to revise and reverse it, the only mode by which he could legally bring it before this court was by writ of error directed to the Supreme Court of the State, requiring it to transmit the record to this court. If this had been done, it is too plain for argument that the writ must have been dismissed for want of jurisdiction in this court. The case of Strader and others *v.* Graham is directly in point; and, indeed, independent of any decision, the language of the 25th section of the act of 1789 is too clear and precise to admit of controversy.

But the plaintiff did not pursue the mode prescribed by law for bringing the judgment of a State court before this court for revision, but suffered the case to be remanded to the inferior State court, where it is still continued, and is, by agreement of parties, to await the judgment of this court on the point. All of this appears on the record before us and by the printed report of the case.

And while the case is yet open and pending in the inferior State court, the plaintiff goes into the Circuit Court of the United States, upon the same case and the same evidence, and against the same party, and proceeds to judgment, and then brings here the same case from the Circuit Court, which the law would not have permitted him to bring directly from the State court. And if this court takes jurisdiction in this form, the result, so far as the rights of the respective parties are concerned, is in every respect substantially the same as if it had in open violation of law entertained jurisdiction over the judgment of the State court upon a writ of error, and revised and revered its judgment upon the ground that its opinion upon the question of law was erroneous. It would ill become this court to sanction such an attempt to evade the law, or to exercise an appellate power in this circuitous way, which it is forbidden to exercise in the direct and regular and invariable forms of judicial proceedings.

Upon the whole, therefore, it is the judgment of this court, that it appears by the record before us that the plaintiff in error is not a citizen of Missouri, in the sense in which that word is used in the Constitution; and that the Circuit Court of the United States, for that reason, had no jurisdiction in the case, and could give no judgment in it. Its judgment for the defendant must, consequently, be reversed, and a mandate issued, directing the suit to be dismissed for want of jurisdiction.

Telegram Announcing the Surrender of Fort Sumter

On April 10, 1861, Brig. Gen. Pierre G.T. Beauregard, in command of the provisional Confederate forces at Charleston, SC, demanded the surrender of the U.S. garrison of Fort Sumter in Charleston Harbor. Garrison commander Robert Anderson refused. On April 12, Confederate batteries opened fire on the fort, which was unable to reply effectively. At 2:30 p.m., April 13, Major Anderson surrendered Fort Sumter, evacuating the garrison on the following day. The bombardment of Fort Sumter was the opening engagement of the American Civil War. From 1863 to 1865, the Confederates at Fort Sumter withstood a 22-month siege by Union forces. During this time, most of the fort was reduced to brick rubble.

S.S. BALTIC. OFF SANDY HOOK APR. EIGHTEENTH. TEN THIRTY A.M. . VIA

NEW YORK. . HON. S. CAMERON. SECY. WAR. WASHN. HAVING DEFENDED

FORT SUMTER FOR THIRTY FOUR HOURS UNTIL THE QUARTERS WERE EN

TIRELY BURNED THE MAIN GATES DESTROYED BY FIRE. THE GORGE WALLS

SERIOUSLY INJURED. THE MAGAZINE SURROUNDED BY FLAMES AND ITS

DOOR CLOSED FROM THE EFFECTS OF HEAT . FOUR BARRELLS AND THREE

CARTRIDGES OF POWDER ONLY BEING AVAILABLE AND NO PROVISIONS

REMAINING BUT PORK. I ACCEPTED TERMS OF EVACUATION OFFERED BY

GENERAL BEAUREGARD BEING ON SAME OFFERED BY HIM ON THE ELEV

ENTH INST. PRIOR TO THE COMMENGEMENT OF HOSTILITIES AND MARCHED

OUT OF THE FORT SUNDAY AFTERNOON THE FOURTEENTH INST. WITH

COLORS FLYING AND DRUMS BEATING. BRINGING AWAY COMPANY AND

PRIVATE PROPERTY AND SALUTING MY FLAG WITH FIFTY GUNS. ROBERT

ANDERSON. MAJOR FIRST ARTILLERY. COMMANDING.

The Homestead Act

CHAP. LXXV. —AN ACT TO SECURE HOMESTEADS TO ACTUAL SETTLERS ON THE PUBLIC DOMAIN.

Be it enacted by the Senate and House of Representatives of the United States of America in Congress assembled, That any person who is the head of a family, or who has arrived at the age of twenty-one years, and is a citizen of the United States, or who shall have filed his declaration of intention to become such, as required by the naturalization laws of the United States, and who has never borne arms against the United States Government or given aid and comfort to its enemies, shall, from and after the first January, eighteen hundred and sixty-three, be entitled to enter one quarter section or a less quantity of unappropriated public lands, upon which said person may have filed a preemption claim, or which may, at the time the application is made, be subject to preemption at one dollar and twenty-five cents, or less, per acre; or eighty acres or less of such unappropriated lands, at two dollars and fifty cents per acre, to be located in a body, in conformity to the legal subdivisions of the public lands, and after the same shall have been surveyed: Provided, That any person owning and residing on land may, under the provisions of this act, enter other land lying contiguous to his or her said land, which shall not, with the land so already owned and occupied, exceed in the aggregate one hundred and sixty acres.

SEC. 2. And be it further enacted, That the person applying for the benefit of this act shall, upon application to the register of the land office in which he or she is about to make such entry, make affidavit before the said register or receiver that he or she is the head of a family, or is twenty-one years or more of age, or shall have performed service in the army or navy of the United States, and that he has never borne arms against the Government of the United States or given aid and comfort to its enemies, and that such application is made for his or her exclusive use and benefit, and that said entry is made for the purpose of actual settlement and cultivation, and not either directly or indirectly for the use or benefit of any other person or persons whomsoever; and upon filing the said affidavit with the register or receiver,

and on payment of ten dollars, he or she shall thereupon be permitted to enter the quantity of land specified: Provided, however, That no certificate shall be given or patent issued therefor until the expiration of five years from the date of such entry; and if, at the expiration of such time, or at any time within two years thereafter, the person making such entry; or, if he be dead, his widow; or in case of her death, his heirs or devisee; or in case of a widow making such entry, her heirs or devisee, in case of her death; shall. prove by two credible witnesses that he, she, or they have resided upon or cultivated the same for the term of five years immediately succeeding the time of filing the affidavit aforesaid, and shall make affidavit that no part of said land has been alienated, and that he has borne rue allegiance to the Government of the United States; then, in such case, he, she, or they, if at that time a citizen of the United States, shall be entitled to a patent, as in other cases provided for by law: And provided, further, That in case of the death of both father and mother, leaving an Infant child, or children, under twenty-one years of age, the right and fee shall ensure to the benefit of said infant child or children; and the executor, administrator, or guardian may, at any time within two years after the death of the surviving parent, and in accordance with the laws of the State in which such children for the time being have their domicil, sell said land for the benefit of said infants, but for no other purpose; and the purchaser shall acquire the absolute title by the purchase, and be entitled to a patent from the United States, on payment of the office fees and sum of money herein specified.

SEC. 3. And be it further enacted, That the register of the land office shall note all such applications on the tract books and plats of, his office, and keep a register of all such entries, and make return thereof to the General Land Office, together with the proof upon which they have been founded.

SEC. 4. And be it further enacted, That no lands acquired under the provisions of this act shall in any event become liable to the satisfaction of any debt or debts contracted prior to the issuing of the patent therefor.

SEC. 5. And be it further enacted, That if, at any time after the filing of the affidavit, as required in the second section of this act, and before the expiration of the five years aforesaid, it shall be proven, after due notice to the settler, to the satisfaction of the register of the land office, that the person having filed such affidavit shall have actually changed his or her residence, or abandoned the said land for more than six months at any time, then and in that event the land so entered shall revert to the government.

SEC. 6. And be it further enacted, That no individual shall be permitted to acquire title to more than one quarter section under the provisions of this act; and that the Commissioner of the General Land Office is hereby required to prepare and issue such rules and regulations, consistent with this act, as shall be necessary and proper to carry its provisions into effect; and that the registers and receivers of the several land offices shall be entitled to receive the same compensation for any lands entered under the provisions of this act that they are now entitled to receive when the same quantity of land is entered with money, one half to be paid by the person making the application at the time of so doing, and the other half on the issue of the certificate by the person to whom it may be issued; but this shall not be construed to enlarge the maximum of compensation now prescribed by law for any register or receiver: Provided, That nothing contained in this act shall be so construed as to impair or interfere in any manner

whatever with existing preemption rights: And provided, further, That all persons who may have filed their applications for a preemption right prior to the passage of this act, shall be entitled to all privileges of this act: Provided, further, That no person who has served, or may hereafter serve, for a period of not less than fourteen days in the army or navy of the United States, either regular or volunteer, under the laws thereof, during the existence of an actual war, domestic or foreign, shall be deprived of the benefits of this act on account of not having attained the age of twenty-one years.

SEC. 7. And be it further enacted, That the fifth section of the act entitled "An act in addition to an act more effectually to provide for the punishment of certain crimes against the United States, and for other purposes," approved the third of March, in the year eighteen hundred and fifty-seven, shall extend to all oaths, affirmations, and affidavits, required or authorized by this act.

SEC. 8. And be it further enacted, That nothing in this act shall be construed as to prevent any person who has availed him or herself of the benefits of the first section of this act, from paying the minimum price, or the price to which the same may have graduated, for the quantity of land so entered at any time before the expiration of the five years, and obtaining a patent therefor from the government, as in other cases provided by law, on making proof of settlement and cultivation as provided by existing laws granting preemption rights.

APPROVED, May 20, 1862.

The Pacific Railway Act

CHAP. CXX.—AN ACT TO AID IN THE CONSTRUCTION OF A RAILROAD AND TELEGRAPH LINE FROM THE MISSOURI RIVER TO THE PACIFIC OCEAN, AND TO SECURE TO THE GOVERNMENT THE USE OF THE SAME FOR POSTAL, MILITARY, AND OTHER PURPOSES.

Be it enacted by the Senate and House of Representatives of the United States of America in Congress assembled, That Walter S. Burgess, William P. Blodget, Benjamin H. Cheever, Charles Fosdick Fletcher, of Rhode Island; Augustus Brewster, Henry P. Haven, Cornelius S. Bushnell, Henry Hammond, of Connecticut; Isaac Sherman, Dean Richmond, Royal Phelps, William H. Ferry, Henry A. Paddock, Lewis J. Stancliff, Charles A. Secor, Samuel R. Campbell, Alfred E. Tilton, John Anderson, Azariah Boody, John S. Kennedy, H. Carver, Joseph Field, Benjamin F. Camp, Orville W. Childs, Alexander J. Bergen, Ben. Holliday, D. N. Barney, S. De Witt Bloodgood, William H. Grant, Thomas W. Olcott, Samuel B. Ruggles, James B. Wilson, of New York; Ephraim Marsh, Charles M. Harker, of New Jersey; John Edgar Thompson, Benjamin Haywood, Joseph H. Scranton, Joseph Harrison, George W. Cass, John H. Bryant, Daniel J. Morell, Thomas M. Howe, William F. Johnson, Robert Finney, John A. Green, E. R. Myre, Charles F. Wells, junior, of Pennsylvania; Noah L. Wilson, Amasa Stone, William H. Clement, S. S. L'Hommedieu, John Brough, William Dennison, Jacob Blickinsderfer, of Ohio; William M. McPherson, R. W. Wells, Willard P. Hall, Armstrong Beatty, John Corby, of Missouri; S. J. Hensley, Peter Donahue, C. P. Huntington, T. D. Judah, James Bailey, James T. Ryan, Charles Hosmer, Charles Marsh, D. O. Mills, Samuel Bell, Louis McLalle, George W. Mowe, Charles McLaughlin, Timothy Dame, John R. Robinson, of California; John Atchison and John D. Winters, of the Territory of Nevada; John D. Campbell, R. N. Rice, Charles A. Trowbridge, and Ransom Gardner, Charles W. Penny, Charles T. Gorham, William McConnell, of Michigan; William F. Coolbaugh, Lucius H. Langworthy, Hugh T. Reid, Hoyt Sherman, Lyman Cook, Samuel R. Curtis, Lewis A. Thomas, Platt Smith, of Iowa; William B. Ogden, Charles G. Hammond, Henry Farnum, Amos C. Babcock, W. Seldon Gale, Nehemiah Bushnell and Lorenzo Bull, of Illinois; William H. Swift, Samuel T. Dana, John Bertram, Franklin S. Stevens, Edward R. Tinker, of Massachusetts; Franklin Gorin, Laban J. Bradford, and John T. Levis, of Kentucky; James Dunning, John M. Wood, Edwin Noyes, Joseph Eaton, of Maine; Henry H. Baxter, George W. Collamer, Henry Keyes, Thomas H. Canfield, of Vermont; William S. Ladd, A. M. Berry, Benjamin F. Harding, of Oregon; William Bunn, junior, John Catlin, Levi Sterling, John Thompson, Ellhu L. Phillips, Walter D. McIndoe, T. B. Stoddard, E. H. Brodhead, A. H. Virgin, of Wisconsin; Charles Paine, Thomas A. Morris, David C. Branham, Samuel Hanna, Jonas Votaw, Jesse L. Villiams, Isaac C. Elston, of Indiana; Thomas Swan, Chauncey Brooks, Edward Wilkins, of Maryland; Francis R. E. Cornell, David Blakely, A. D. Seward, Henry A. Swift, Dwight Woodbury, John McKusick, John R. Jones, of Minnesota; Joseph A. Gilmore, Charles W. Woodman, of New Hampshire; W. H. Grimes, J. C. Stone, Chester Thomas, John Kerr, Werter R. Davis, Luther C. Challiss, Josiah Miller, of Kansas; Gilbert C. Monell and Augustus Kountz, T. M. Marquette, William H. Taylor, Alyin Saunders, of Nebraska; John Evans, of Colorado; together with commissioners to be appointed by the Secretary of the Interior, and all persons who shall or may be associated with them, and their successors, are hereby created and erected into a body corporate and politic in deed and in law, by the name, style, and title of "The Union Pacific Railroad Company;" and by that name shall have perpetual succession, and shall be able to sue and to be sued, plead and be impleaded, defend and be defended, in all courts of law and equity within the United States, and may make and have a common seal; and the said corporation is hereby authorized and empowered to layout, locate, construct, furnish, maintain, and enjoy a continuous railroad and telegraph, with the appurtenances, from a point on the one hundredth meridian of longitude west from Greenwich, between the south margin of the valley of the Republican River and the north margin of the valley of the Platte River, in the Territory of Nebraska, to the western boundary of Nevada Territory, upon the route and terms hereinafter provided, and is hereby vested with all the powers, privileges, and immunities necessary to carry into effect the purposes of this act as herein set forth. The capital stock of said company shall consist of one hundred thousand shares of one thousand dollars each, which shall be subscribed for and held in not more than two hundred shares by anyone person, and shall be transferable in such manner as the by-laws of said corporation shall provide. The persons hereinbefore named, together with those to be appointed by the Secretary of the Interior, are hereby constituted and appointed commissioners, and such body shall be called the Board of Commissioners of the Union Pacific Railroad and Telegraph Company, and twenty-five shall constitute a quorum for the transaction of business. The first meeting of said board shall be held at Chicago at such time as the commissioners from Illinois herein named shall appoint, not more than three nor less than one month after the passage of this act, notice of which shall be given by them to the other commissioners by depositing a call thereof in the post office at Chicago, post paid, to their address at least forty days before said meeting, and also by publishing said notice in one daily newspaper in each of the cities of Chicago and Saint Louis. Said board shall organize by the choice from its number of a president, secretary, and treasurer, and they shall require from said treasurer such bonds as may be deemed proper, and may from time to time increase the amount thereof as they may deem proper. It shall be the duty of said board of commissioners to open books, or cause books to be opened, at such times and in such principal cities in the United States as they or a quorum of them shall determine, to receive subscriptions to the capital stock of said corporation, and a cash payment of ten per centum on all subscriptions, and to receipt therefor. So soon as two thousand shares shall be in good faith subscribed for, and ten dollars per share actually paid into the treasury of the company, the said president and secretary of said board of commissioners shall appoint a time and place for the first meeting of the subscribers to the stock of said company, and shall give notice thereof in at least one newspaper in each State in which subscription books have been opened at least thirty days previous to the day of meeting, and such subsribers as shall attend the meeting so called, either in person or by proxy, shall then and there elect by ballot not less than thirteen directors for said corporation; and in such election each share of said capital shall entitle the owner thereof to one vote. The president and secretary of the board of commissioners shall act as inspectors of said election, and shall certify under their hands the names of the directors elected at said meeting; and

the said commissioners, treasurer, and secretary shall then deliver over to said directors all the properties, subscription books and other books in their possession, and thereupon the duties of said commissioners, and the officers previously appointed by them shall cease and determine forever, and thereafter the stockholders shall constitute said body politic and corporate. At the time of the first and each triennial election of directors by the stockholders two additional directors shall be appointed by the President of the United States, who shall act with the body of directors, and to be denominated directors on the part of the government; any vacancy happening in the government directors at any time may be filled by the President of the United States. The directors to be appointed by the President shall not be stockholders in the Union Pacific Railroad Company. The directors so chosen shall, as soon as may be after their election, elect from their own number a president and vice-president, and shall also elect a treasurer and secretary. No person shall be a director in said company unless he shall be a bona fide owner of at least five shares of stock in the said company, except the two directors to be appointed by the President as aforesaid. Said company, at any regular meeting of the stockholders called for that purpose, shall have power to make by-laws, rules, and regulations as they shall deem needful and proper, touching the disposition of the stock, property, estate, and effects of the company, not inconsistent herewith, the transfer of shares, the term of office, duties, and conduct of their officers and servants, and all matters whatsoever which may appertain to the concerns of said company; and the said board of directors shall have power to appoint such engineers, agents, and subordinates as may from time to time be necessary to carry into effect the object of this act, and to do all acts and things touching the location and construction of said road and telegraph. Said directors may require payment of subscriptions to the capital stock, after due notice, at such times and in such proportions as they shall deem necessary to complete the railroad and telegraph within the time in this act prescribed. Said president, vice-president, and directors shall hold their office for three years, and until their successors are duly elected and qualified, or for such less time as the by-laws of the corporation may prescribe; and a majority of said directors shall constitute a quorum for the transaction of business. The secretary and treasurer shall give such bonds, with such security, as the said board shall from time to time require, and shall hold their offices at the will and pleasure of the directors. Annual meetings of the stockholders of the said corporation, for the choice of officers (when they are to be chosen) and for the transaction of annual business, shall be holden at such time and place and upon such notice as may be prescribed in the by-laws.

SEC. 2. And he it further enacted, That the right of way through the public lands be, and the same is hereby, granted to said company for the construction of said railroad and telegraph line; and the right, power, and authority is hereby given to said company to take from the public lands adjacent to the line of said road, earth, stone, timber, and other materials for the construction thereof; said right of way is granted to said railroad to the extent of two hundred feet in width on each side of said railroad where it may pass over the public lands, including all necessary grounds for stations, buildings, workshops, and depots, machine shops, switches, side tracks, turntables, and, water stations. The United States shall extinguish as rapidly as may be the Indian titles to all lands falling under the operation of this act and required for the said right of way and; grants hereinafter made.

SEC 3. And be it further enacted, That there be, and is hereby, granted to the said company, for the purpose of aiding in the construction, of said railroad and telegraph line, and to secure the safe and speedy transportation of the mails, troops, munitions of war, and public stores thereon, every alternate section of public land, designated by odd numbers, to the amount of five alternate sections per mile on each side of said railroad, on the line thereof, and within the limits often miles on each side of said railroad, not sold, reserved, or otherwise disposed of by the United States, and to which a preemption or homestead claim may not have attached, at the time the line of said road is definitely fixed: Provided, That all mineral lands shall be excepted from the operation of this act; but where the same shall contain timber, the timber thereon is hereby granted to said company. And all such lands, so granted by this section, which shall not be sold or disposed of by said company within three years after the entire road shall have been completed, shall be subject to settlement and preemption, like other lands, at a price not exceeding one dollar and twenty-five cents per acre, to be paid to said company.

SEC. 4. And be it further enacted, That whenever said company shall have completed forty consecutive miles of any portion of said railroad and telegraph line, ready for the service contemplated by this act, and supplied with all necessary drains, culverts, viaducts, crossings, sidings, bridges, turnouts, watering places, depots, equipments, furniture, and all other appurtenances of a first class railroad, the rails and all the other iron used in the construction and equipment of said road to be American manufacture of the best quality, the President of the United States shall appoint three commissioners to examine the same and report to him in relation thereto; and if it shall appear to him that forty consecutive miles of said railroad and telegraph line have been completed and equipped in all respects as required by this act, then, upon certificate of said commissioners to that effect, patents shall issue conveying the right and title to said lands to said company, on each side of the road as far as the same is completed, to the amount aforesaid; and patents shall in like manner issue as each forty miles of said railroad and telegraph line are completed, upon certificate of said commissioners. Any vacancies occurring in said board of commissioners by death, resignation, or otherwise, shall be filled by the President of the United States: Provided, however, That Do such commissioners shall be appointed by the President of the United States unless there shall be presented to him a statement, verified on oath by the president of said company, that such forty miles have been completed, in the manner required by this act, and setting forth with certainty the points where such forty miles begin and where the same end; which oath shall be taken before a judge of a court of record.

SEC. 5. And be it further enacted, That for the purposes herein mentioned the Secretary of the Treasury shall, upon the certificate in writing of said commissioners of the completion and equipment of forty consecutive miles of said railroad and telegraph, in accordance with the provisions of this act, issue to said company bonds of the United States of one thousand dollars each, payable in thirty years after date, bearing six per centum per annum interest (said interest payable semi-annually,) which interest may be paid in United States treasury notes or any other money or currency which the United States have or shall declare lawful money and a legal tender, to the amount of sixteen of said bonds per mile for such section of forty miles; and to secure the repayment to the United States, as hereinafter provided, of the amount of said bonds so issued and delivered to said company, together with all interest thereon which shall have been paid by the United States, the issue of said bonds and delivery to the company shall ipso facto constitute a first mortgage on the whole line of the railroad and telegraph, together with the rolling stock, fixtures and property of every kind and description, and in consideration of which said bonds may be issued; and on the refusal or failure of said company to redeem said bonds, or any part of them, when required so to do by the Secretary of the Treasury, in accordance with the provisions of this act the said road, with all the rights, functions, immunities, and appurtences thereunto belonging, and also all lands granted to the said company by the United States, which, at the time of said default, shall remain in the ownership of the said company, may be taken possession of by the Secretary of the Treasury, for the use and benefit of the United States: Provided, this section shall not apply to that part of any road now constructed.

SEC. 6. And be it further enacted, That the grants aforesaid are made upon condition that said company shall pay said bonds at maturity, and shall keep said railroad and telegraph line in repair and use, and shall at all times transmit despatches over said telegraph line, and transport mails, troops, and munitions of war, supplies, and public storage upon said railroad for the government, whenever required to do so by any department, thereof, and that the government shall at all times have the preference in the use of the same for all the purposes aforesaid, (at fair and reasonable rates of compensation, not to exceed the amounts paid by private parties for the same kind of service;) and all compensation for services rendered for the government shall be applied to the payment of said bonds and interest until the whole amount is fully paid. Said company may also pay the United States, wholly or in part, in the same or other bonds, treasury notes, or other evidences of debt against the United States, to be allowed at par; and after said road is completed, until said bonds and interest are paid, at least five per centum of the net earnings of said road "shall also be annually applied to the payment thereof.

SEC. 7. And be it further enacted, That said company shall file their assent to this act, under the seal of said company, in the Department of the Interior, within one year after the passage of this act, and shall complete said railroad and telegraph from the point of beginning, as herein provided, to the western boundary of Nevada Territory before the first day of July, one thousand eight hundred and seventy-four: Provided, That within two years after the passage of

this act said company shall designate the general route of said road, as near as may be, and shall file a map of the same in the Department of the Interior, whereupon the Secretary of the Interior shall cause the lands within fifteen miles of said designated route or routes to be withdrawn from preemption, private entry, and sale; and when any portion of said route shall be finally located, the Secretary of the Interior shall cause the said lands hereinbefore granted to be surveyed and set off as fast as may be necessary for the purposes herein named: Provided, That in fixing the point of connection of the main trunk with the eastern connections, it shall be fixed at the most practicable point for the construction of the Iowa and Missouri branches, as hereinafter provided.

SEC. 8. And be it further enacted, That the line of said railroad and telegraph shall commence at a point on the one hundredth meridian of a longitude west from Greenwich, between the south margin of the valley of the Republican River and the north margin of the valley of the Platte River, in the Territory of Nebraska, at a point to be fixed by the President of the United States, after actual surveys; thence running westerly upon the most direct, central, and practicable route, through the territories of the United States, the western boundary of the Territory of Nevada, there to meet and connect with the line of the Central Pacific Railroad Company of California.

SEC. 9. And be it further enacted, That the Leavenworth, Pawnee, and Western Railroad Company of Kansas are hereby authorized to construct a railroad and telegraph line, from the Missouri River, at the mouth of the Kansas River, on the south side thereof, so as to connect with the Pacific railroad of Missouri, to the aforesaid point, on the one hundredth meridian of longitude west from Greenwich, as herein provided, upon the same terms and conditions in all respects as are provided in this act for the construction of the railroad and telegraph line first mentioned, and to meet and connect with the same at the meridian of longitude aforesaid; and in case the general route or line of road from the Missouri River to the Rocky Mountains should be so located as to require a departure northwardly from the proposed line of said Kansas railroad before it reaches the meridian of longitude aforesaid, the location of said Kansas road shall be made so as to conform thereto; and said railroad through Kansas shall be so located between the mouth of the Kansas River, as aforesaid, and the aforesaid point, on the one hundredth meridian of longitude, that the several railroads from Missouri and Iowa, herein authorized to connect with the same, can make connection within the limits prescribed in this act, provided the same can be done without deviating from the general direction of the whole line to the Pacific coast. The route in Kansas, west of the meridian of Fort Riley, to the aforesaid point, on the one hundredth meridian of longitude, to be subject to the approval of the President of the United States, and to be determined by him on actual survey. And said Kansas company may proceed to build said railroad to the aforesaid point, on the one hundredth meridian of longitude west from Greenwich, in the territory of Nebraska. The Central Pacific Railroad Company of California, a corporation existing under the laws of the State of California, are hereby authorized to construct a railroad and telegraph line from the Pacific coast, at or near San Francisco, or the navigable waters of the Sacramento River, to the eastern boundary of California, upon the same terms and conditions, in all respects, as are contained in this act for the construction of said railroad and telegraph line first mentioned, and to meet and connect with the first mentioned railroad and telegraph line on the eastern boundary of California. Each of said companies shall file their acceptance of the conditions of this act in the Department of the Interior within six months after the passage of this act.

SEC. 10. And be it further enacted, That the said company chartered, by the State of Kansas shall complete one hundred miles of their said road, commencing at the mouth of the Kansas River as aforesaid, within two years after filing their assent to the conditions of this act, as herein provided, and one hundred miles per year thereafter until the whole is completed; and the said Central Pacific Railroad Company of California shall complete fifty miles of their said road within two years after filing their assent to the provisions of this act, as herein provided, and fifty miles per year thereafter until the whole is completed; and after completing their roads, respectively, said companies, or either of them, may unite upon equal terms with the first-named company in constructing so much of said railroad and telegraph line and branch railroads and telegraph lines in Luis act hereinafter mentioned, through the Territories from the State of California to the Missouri River, as shall then remain to be constructed, on the same terms and conditions as provided in this act in relation to the said Union Pacific Railroad Company.

And the Hannibal and St. Joseph Railroad, the Pacific Railroad Company of Missouri, and the first-named company, or either of them, on filing their assent to this act, as aforesaid, may unite upon equal terms, under this act, with the said Kansas company, in constructing said railroad and telegraph, to said meridian of longitude, with the consent of the said State of Kansas; and in case said first-named company shall complete their line to the eastern boundary of California before it is completed across said State by the Central Pacific Railroad Company of California, said first-named company is hereby authorized to continue in constructing the same through California, with the consent of said State, upon the terms mentioned in this act, until said roads shall meet and connect, and the whole line of said railroad and telegraph is completed; and the Central Pacific Railroad Company of California, after completing its road across said State, is authorized to continue the construction of said railroad and telegraph through the Territories of the United States to the Missouri River, including the branch roads specified in this act, upon the routes hereinbefore and hereinafter indicated, on the terms and conditions provided in this act in relation to the said Union Pacific Railroad Company, until said roads shall meet and connect, and the whole line of said railroad and branches and telegraph is completed.

SEC. 11. And be it further enacted, That for three hundred miles of said road most mountainous and difficult of construction, to wit: one hundred and fifty miles westwardly from the eastern base of the Rocky Mountains, and one hundred and fifty miles eastwardly from the western, base of the Sierra Nevada mountains, said points to be fixed by the President of the United States, the bonds to be issued to aid in the construction thereof shall be treble the number per mile hereinbefore provided, and the same shall be issued, and the lands herein granted be set apart, upon the construction of every twenty miles thereof, upon the certificate of the commissioners as aforesaid that twenty consecutive miles of the same are completed and between the sections last named of one hundred and fifty miles each, the bonds to be issued to aid in the construction thereof shall be double the number per mile first mentioned, and the same shall be issued, and the lands herein granted be set apart, upon the construction of every twenty miles thereof, upon the certificate of the commissioners as aforesaid that twenty consecutive miles of the same are completed: Provided, That no more than fifty thousand of said bonds shall be issued under this act to aid in constructing the main line of said railroad and telegraph.

SEC. 12. And be it further enacted, That whenever the route of said railroad shall cross the boundary of any State or Territory, or said meridian of longitude, the two companies meeting or uniting there shall agree upon its location at that point, with reference to the most direct and practicable through route, and in case of difference between them as to said location the President of the United States shall determine the said location; the companies named in each State and Territory to locate the road across the same between the points so agreed upon, except as herein provided. The track upon the entire line of railroad and branches shall be of uniform width, to be determined by the President of the United States, so that, when completed, cars can be run from the Missouri River to the Pacific coast; the grades and curves shall not exceed the maximum grades and curves of the Baltimore and Ohio railroad; the whole line of said railroad and branches and telegraph shall be operated and used for all purposes of communication, travel, and transportation, so far as the public and government are concerned, as one connected, continuous line; and the companies herein named in Missouri, Kansas, and California, filing their assent to the provisions of this act, shall receive and transport all iron rails, chairs, spikes, ties, timber, and all materials required for constructing and furnishing said first-mentioned line between the aforesaid point, on the one hundredth meridian of longitude and western boundary of Nevada Territory, whenever the same is required by said first-named company, at cost, over that portion of the roads of said companies constructed under the provisions of this act.

SEC. 13. And be it further enacted, That the Hannibal and Saint Joseph Railroad Company of Missouri may extend its roads from Saint Joseph, via Atchison, to connect and unite with the road through Kansas, upon filing its assent to the provisions of this act, upon the same terms and conditions, in all respects for one hundred miles in length next to the Missouri River, as are provided in this act for the construction of the railroad and telegraph line first mentioned, and may for this purpose use any railroad charter which has been or may be granted by the legislature of Kansas; Provided, That if actual survey shall render it desirable, the said company may construct their road, with the consent of the Kansas legislature, on the most direct and practicable

route west from St. Joseph, Missouri, so as to connect and unite with the road leading from the western boundary of Iowa at any point east of the one hundredth meridian of west longitude, or with the main trunk road at said point; but in no event shall lands or bonds be given to said company, as herein directed, to aid in the construction of their said road for a greater distance than one hundred miles. And the Leavenworth, Pawnee, and Western Railroad Company of Kansas may construct their road from Leavenworth to unite with the road through Kansas.

SEC. 14. And be it further enacted, That the said Union Pacific Railroad Company is hereby authorized and required to construct a single line of railroad and telegraph from a point on the western boundary of the State of Iowa, to be fixed by the President of the United States, upon the most direct and practicable route, to be subject to his approval, so as to form a connection with the lines of said company at some point on the one hundredth meridian of longitude aforesaid, from the point of commencement on the western boundary of the State of Iowa, upon the same terms and conditions, in all respects, as are contained in this act for the construction of the said railroad and telegraph first mentioned; and the said Union Pacific Railroad Company shall complete one hundred miles of the road and telegraph in this section provided for, in two years after filing their assent to the conditions of this act, as by the terms of this act required, and at the rate of one hundred miles per year thereafter, until the whole is completed: Provided, That a failure upon the part of said company to make said connection in the time aforesaid, and to perform the obligations imposed on said company by this section and to operate said road in the same manner as the main line shall be operated, shall forfeit to the government of the United States all the rights, privileges, and franchises granted to and conferred upon said company by this act. And whenever there shall be a line of railroad completed through Minnesota or Iowa to Sioux City, then the said Pacific Railroad Company is hereby authorized and required to construct a railroad and telegraph from Said Sioux City upon the most direct and practicable route to a point on, and so as to connect with, the branch railroad and telegraph in this section hereinbefore mentioned, or with the said Union Pacific Railroad, said point of junction to be fixed by the President of the United States, not further west than the one hundredth meridian of longitude aforesaid, and on the same terms and conditions as provided in this act for the construction of the Union Pacific Railroad as aforesaid, and to complete the same at the rate of one hundred miles per year; and should said company fail to comply with the requirements of this act in relation to the said Sioux City railroad and telegraph, the said company shall suffer the same forfeitures prescribed in relation to the Iowa branch railroad and telegraph hereinbefore mentioned.

SEC. 15. And be it further enacted, That any other railroad company now incorporated, or hereafter to be incorporated, shall have the right to connect their road with the road and branches provided for by this act, at such places and upon such just and equitable terms as the President of the United States may prescribe. Wherever the word company is used in this act it shall be construed to embrace the words their associates, successors, and assigns, the same as if the words had been properly added thereto.

SEC. 16. And be it further enacted, That at any time after the passage of this act all of the railroad companies named herein, and assenting hereto, or any two or more of them, are authorized to form themselves into one consolidated company; notice of such consolidation, in writing, shall be filed in the Department of the Interior, and such consolidated company shall thereafter proceed to construct said railroad and branches and telegraph line upon the terms and conditions provided in this act.

SEC. 17. And be it further enacted, That in case said company or companies shall fail to comply with the terms and conditions of this act, by not completing said road and telegraph and branches within a reasonable time, or by not keeping the same in repair and use, but shall permit the same, for an unreasonable time, to remain unfinished, or out of repair, and unfit for use, Congress may pass any act to insure the speedy completion of said road and branches, or put the same in repair and use, and may direct the income of said railroad and telegraph line to be thereafter devoted to the use of the United States, to repay all such expenditures caused by the default and neglect of such company or companies: Provided, That if said roads are not completed, so as to form a continuous line of railroad, ready for use, from the Missouri River to the navigable waters of the Sacramento River, in California, by the first day of July, eighteen hundred and seventy-six, the whole of all of said railroads before mentioned and to be constructed under the provisions of this act, together with all their furniture, fixtures, rolling stock, machine shops, lands, tenements, and hereditaments, and property of every kind and character, shall be

forfeited to and be taken possession of by the United States: Provided, That of the bonds of the United States in this act provided to be delivered for any and all parts of the roads to be constructed east of the one hundredth meridian of west longitude from, Greenwich, and for any part of the road west of the west foot of the Sierra Nevada mountain, there shall be reserved of each part and installment twenty-five per centum, to be and remain in the United States treasury, undelivered, until said road and all parts thereof provided for in this act are entirely completed; and of all the bonds provided to be delivered for the said road, between the two points aforesaid, there shall be reserved out of each installment fifteen per centum, to be and remain in the treasury until the whole of the road provided for in this act is fully completed; and if the said road or any part thereof shall fail of completion at the time limited therefor in this act, then and in that case the said part of said bonds so reserved shall be forfeited to the United States.

SEC. 18. And be it further enacted, That whenever it appears that the net earnings of the entire road and telegraph, including the amount allowed for services rendered for the United States, after deducting all, expenditures, including repairs, and the furnishing, running, and managing of said road, shall exceed ten per centum upon its cost, exclusive of the five per centum to be paid to the United States, Congress may reduce the rates of fare thereon, if unreasonable in amount, and may fix and establish the same by law. And the better to accomplish the object of this act, namely, to promote the public interest and welfare by the construction of said railroad and telegraph line, and keeping the same in working order, and to secure to the government at all times (but particularly in time of war) the use and benefits of the same for postal, military and other purposes, Congress may, at any time, having due regard for the rights of said companies named herein, add to, alter, amend, or repeal this act.

SEC. 19. And be it further enacted, That the several railroad companies herein named are authorized to enter into an arrangement with the Pacific Telegraph Company, the Overland Telegraph Company, and the California State Telegraph Company, so that the present line of telegraph between the Missouri River and San Francisco may be moved upon or along the line of said railroad and branches as fast as said roads and branches are built; and if said arrangement be entered into and the transfer of said telegraph line be made in accordance therewith to the line of said railroad and branches, such transfer shall, for all purposes of this act, be held and considered a fulfillment on the part of said railroad companies of the provisions of this act in regard to the construction of said line of telegraph. And, in case of disagreement, said telegraph companies are authorized to remove their line of telegraph along and upon the line of railroad herein contemplated without prejudice to the rights of said railroad companies named herein.

SEC. 20. And he it further enacted, That the corporation hereby created and the roads connected therewith, under the provisions of this act, shall make to the Secretary of the Treasury an annual report wherein shall be set forth.

First. The names of the stockholders and their places of residence, so far as the same can be ascertained;

Second. The names and residences of the directors, and all other officers of the company;

Third. The amount of stock subscribed, and the amount thereof actually paid in;

Fourth. A description of the lines of road surveyed, of the lines thereof fixed upon for the construction of the road, and the cost of such surveys;

Fifth. The amount received from passengers on the road;

Sixth. The amount received for freight thereon;

Seventh. A statement of the expense of said road and its fixtures;

Eighth. A statement of the indebtedness of said company, setting forth the various kinds thereof. Which report shall be sworn to by the president of the said company, and shall be presented to the Secretary of the Treasury on or before the first day of July in each year.

APPROVED, July 1, 1862.

The Morrill Act

CHAP. CXXX.—AN ACT DONATING PUBLIC LANDS TO THE SEVERAL STATES AND TERRITORIES WHICH MAY PROVIDE COLLEGES FOR THE BENEFIT OF AGRICULTURE AND MECHANIC ARTS.

Be it enacted by the Senate and House of Representatives of the United States of America in Congress assembled, That there be granted to the several States, for the purposes hereinafter mentioned, an amount of public land, to be apportioned to each State a quantity equal to thirty thousand acres for each senator and representative in Congress to which the States are respectively entitled by the apportionment under the census of eighteen hundred and sixty: *Provided,* That no mineral lands shall be selected or purchased under the provisions of this Act.

SEC. 2. *And be it further enacted,* That the land aforesaid, after being surveyed, shall be apportioned to the several States in sections or subdivisions of sections, not less than one quarter of a section; and whenever there are public lands in a State subject to sale at private entry at one dollar and twenty-five cents per acre, the quantity to which said State shall be entitled shall be selected from such lands within the limits of such State, and the Secretary of the Interior is hereby directed to issue to each of the States in which there is not the quantity of public lands subject to sale at private entry at one dollar and twenty-five cents per acre, to which said State may be entitled under the provisions of this act, land scrip to the amount in acres for the deficiency of its distributive share: said scrip to be sold by said States and the proceeds thereof applied to the uses and purposes prescribed in this act, and for no other use or purpose whatsoever: *Provided,* That in no case shall any State to which land scrip may thus be issued be allowed to locate the same within the limits of any other State, or of any Territory of the United States, but their assignees may thus locate said land scrip upon any of the unappropriated lands of the United States subject to sale at private entry at one dollar and twenty-five cents, or less, per acre: *And provided, further,* That not more than one million acres shall be located by such assignees in any one of the States: *And provided, further,* That no such location shall be made before one year from the passage of this Act.

SEC. 3. *And be it further enacted,* That all the expenses of management, superintendence, and taxes from date of selection of said lands, previous to their sales, and all expenses incurred in the management and disbursement of the moneys which may be received therefrom, shall be paid by the States to which they may belong, out of the Treasury of said States, so that the entire proceeds of the sale of said lands shall be applied without any diminution whatever to the purposes hereinafter mentioned.

SEC. 4. And be it further enacted, That all moneys derived from the sale of the lands aforesaid by the States to which the lands are apportioned, and from the sales of land scrip hereinbefore provided for, shall be invested in stocks of the United States, or of the States, or some other safe stocks, yielding not less than five per centum upon the par value of said stocks; and that the moneys so invested shall constitute a perpetual fund, the capital of which shall remain forever undiminished, (except so far as may be provided in section fifth of this act,) and the interest of which shall be inviolably appropriated, by each State which may take and claim the benefit of this act, to the endowment, support, and maintenance of at least one college where the leading object shall be, without excluding other scientific and classical studies, and including military tactics, to teach such branches of learning as are related to agriculture and the mechanic arts, in such manner as the legislatures of the States may respectively prescribe, in order to promote the liberal and practical education of the industrial classes in the several pursuits and professions in life.

SEC. 5. *And be it further enacted,* That the grant of land and land scrip hereby authorized shall be made on the following conditions, to which, as well as to the provisions hereinbefore contained, the previous assent of the several States shall be signified by legislative acts:

First. If any portion of the fund invested, as provided by the foregoing section, or any portion of the interest thereon, shall, by any action or contingency, be diminished or lost, it shall be replaced by the State to which it belongs, so that the capital of the fund shall remain forever undiminished; and the annual interest shall be regularly applied without diminution to the purposes mentioned in the fourth section of this act, except that a sum, not exceeding ten per centum upon the amount received by any State under the provisions of this act may be expended for the purchase of lands for sites or experimental farms, whenever authorized by the respective legislatures of said States.

Second. No portion of said fund, nor the interest thereon, shall be applied, directly or indirectly, under any pretence whatever, to the purchase, erection, preservation, or repair of any building or buildings.

Third. Any State which may take and claim the benefit of the provisions of this act shall provide, within five years from the time of its acceptance as provided in subdivision seven of this section, at least not less than one college, as described in the fourth section of this act, or the grant to such State shall cease; and said State shall be bound to pay the United States the amount received of any lands previously sold; and that the title to purchasers under the State shall be valid.

Fourth. An annual report shall be made regarding the progress of each college, recording any improvements and experiments made, with their cost and results, and such other matters, including State industrial and economical statistics, as may be supposed useful; one copy of which shall be transmitted by mail [free] by each, to all the other colleges which may be endowed under the provisions of this act, and also one copy to the Secretary of the Interior.

Fifth. When lands shall be selected from those which have been raised to double the minimum price, in consequence of railroad grants, they shall be computed to the States at the maximum price, and the number of acres proportionally diminished.

Sixth. No State while in a condition of rebellion or insurrection against the government of the United States shall be entitled to the benefit of this act.

Seventh. No State shall be entitled to the benefits of this act unless it shall express its acceptance thereof by its legislature within three years from July 23, 1866:

Provided, That when any Territory shall become a State and be admitted into the Union, such new State shall shall be entitled to the benefits of the said act of July two, eighteen hundred and sixty-two, by expressing the acceptance therein required within three years from the date of its admission into the Union, and providing the college or colleges within five years after such acceptance, as prescribed in this act.

SEC. 6. And be it further enacted, That land scrip issued under the provisions of this act shall not be subject to location until after the first day of January, one thousand eight hundred and sixty-three.

SEC. 7. *And be it further enacted,* That the land officers shall receive the same fees for locating land scrip issued under the provisions of this act as is now allowed for the location of military bounty land warrants under existing laws: *Provided,* their maximum compensation shall not be thereby increased.

SEC. 8. *And be it further enacted,* That the Governors of the several States to which scrip shall be issued under this act shall be required to report annually to Congress all sales made of such scrip until the whole shall be disposed of, the amount received for the same, and what appropriation has been made of the proceeds.

The Emancipation Proclamation

BY THE PRESIDENT OF THE UNITED STATES OF AMERICA: A PROCLAMATION.

Whereas, on the twenty-second day of September, in the year of our Lord one thousand eight hundred and sixty-two, a proclamation was issued by the President of the United States, containing, among other things, the following, to wit:

"That on the first day of January, in the year of our Lord one thousand eight hundred and sixty-three, all persons held as slaves within any State or designated part of a State, the people whereof shall then be in rebellion against the United States, shall be then, thenceforward, and forever free; and the Executive Government of the United States, including the military and naval authority thereof, will recognize and maintain the freedom of such persons, and will do no act or acts to repress such persons, or any of them, in any efforts they may make for their actual freedom.

"That the Executive will, on the first day of January aforesaid, by proclamation, designate the States and parts of States, if any, in which the people thereof, respectively, shall then be in rebellion against the United States; and the fact that any State, or the people thereof, shall on that day be, in good faith, represented in the Congress of the United States by members chosen thereto at elections wherein a majority of the qualified voters of such State shall have participated, shall, in the absence of strong countervailing testimony, be deemed conclusive evidence that such State, and the people thereof, are not then in rebellion against the United States."

Now, therefore I, Abraham Lincoln, President of the United States, by virtue of the power in me vested as Commander-in-Chief, of the Army and Navy of the United States in time of actual armed rebellion against the authority and government of the United States, and as a fit and necessary war measure for suppressing said rebellion, do, on this first day of January, in the year of our Lord one thousand eight hundred and sixty-three, and in accordance with my purpose so to do publicly proclaimed for the full period of one hundred days, from the day first above mentioned, order and designate as the States and parts of States wherein the people thereof respectively, are this day in rebellion against the United States, the following, to wit:

Arkansas, Texas, Louisiana, (except the Parishes of St. Bernard, Plaquemines, Jefferson, St. John, St. Charles, St. James Ascension, Assumption, Terrebonne, Lafourche, St. Mary, St. Martin, and Orleans, including the City of New Orleans) Mississippi, Alabama, Florida, Georgia, South Carolina, North Carolina, and Virginia, (except the forty-eight counties designated as West Virginia, and also the counties of Berkley, Accomac, Northampton, Elizabeth City, York, Princess Ann, and Norfolk, including the cities of Norfolk and Portsmouth[)], and which excepted parts, are for the present, left precisely as if this proclamation were not issued.

And by virtue of the power, and for the purpose aforesaid, I do order and declare that all persons held as slaves within said designated States, and parts of States, are, and henceforward shall be free; and that the Executive government of the United States, including the military and naval authorities thereof, will recognize and maintain the freedom of said persons.

And I hereby enjoin upon the people so declared to be free to abstain from all violence, unless in necessary self-defence; and I recommend to them that, in all cases when allowed, they labor faithfully for reasonable wages.

And I further declare and make known, that such persons of suitable condition, will be received into the armed service of the United States to garrison forts, positions, stations, and other places, and to man vessels of all sorts in said service.

And upon this act, sincerely believed to be an act of justice, warranted by the Constitution, upon military necessity, I invoke the considerate judgment of mankind, and the gracious favor of Almighty God.

In witness whereof, I have hereunto set my hand and caused the seal of the United States to be affixed.

Done at the City of Washington, this first day of January, in the year of our Lord one thousand eight hundred and sixty three, and of the Independence of the United States of America the eighty-seventh.

By the President: ABRAHAM LINCOLN
WILLIAM H. SEWARD, Secretary of State.

War Department General Order 143:
Creation of the U.S. Colored Troops

GENERAL ORDERS, No. 143
WAR DEPARTMENT, ADJUTANT GENERAL'S OFFICE,
Washington, May 22, 1863.

I—A Bureau is established in the Adjutant General's Office for the record of all matters relating to the organization of Colored Troops, An officer, will be assigned to the charge of the Bureau, with such number of clerks as may be designated by the Adjutant General.

II—Three or more field officers will be detailed as Inspectors to supervise the organization of colored troops at such points as may be indicated by the War Department in the Northern and Western States.

III—Boards will be convened at such posts as may be decided upon by the War Department to examine applicants for commissions to command colored troops, who, on Application to the Adjutant General, may receive authority to present themselves to the board for examination.

IV— No persons shall be allowed to recruit for colored troops except specially authorized by the War Department; and no such authority will be given to persons who have not been examined and passed by a board; nor will such authority be given any one person to raise more than one regiment.

V—The reports of Boards will specify the grade of commission for which each candidate is fit, and authority to recruit will be given in accordance. Commissions will be issued from the Adjutant General's Office when the prescribed number of men is ready for muster into service.

VI—Colored troops maybe accepted by companies, to be afterward consolidated in battalions and regiments by the Adjutant General. The regiments will be numbered seriatim, in the order in which they are raised, the numbers to be determined by the Adjutant General. They will be designated: "——Regiment of U. S. Colored Troops."

VII—Recruiting stations and depots will be established by the Adjutant General as circumstances shall require, and officers will be detailed to muster and inspect the troops.

VIII—The non-commissioned officers of colored troops may be selected and appointed from the best men of their number in the usual mode of appointing non-commissioned officers. Meritorious commissioned officers will be entitled to promotion to higher rank if they prove themselves equal to it.

IX—All personal applications for appointments in colored regiments, or for information concerning them, must be made to the Chief of the Bureau; all written communications should be addressed to the Chief of the Bureau, to the care of the Adjutant General,

BY ORDER OF THE SECRETARY OF WAR:
E. D. TOWNSEND, Assistant Adjutant General.

The Gettysburg Address

ABRAHAM LINCOLN

Four score and seven years ago our fathers brought forth on this continent, a new nation, conceived in Liberty, and dedicated to the proposition that all men are created equal.

Now we are engaged in a great civil war, testing whether that nation, or any nation so conceived, and so dedicated, can long endure. We are met on a great battlefield of that war. We have come to dedicate a portion of that field, as a final resting place for those who here gave their lives that that nation might live. It is altogether fitting and proper that we should do this.

But, in a larger sense, we can not dedicate—we can not consecrate—we can not hallow—this ground. The brave men, living and dead, who struggled here, have consecrated it, far above our poor power to add or detract. The world will little note, nor long remember what we say here, but it can never forget what they did here. It is for us the living, rather, to be dedicated here to the unfinished work which they who fought here have thus far so nobly advanced. It is rather for us to be here dedicated to the great task remaining before us—that from these honored dead we take increased devotion to that cause for which they gave the last full measure of devotion—that we here highly resolve that these dead shall not have died in vain—that this nation, under God, shall have a new birth of freedom—and that government of the people, by the people, for the people, shall not perish from the earth.

The Wade-Davis Bill

A BILL TO GUARANTEE TO CERTAIN STATES WHOSE GOVERNMENTS HAVE BEEN USURPED OR OVERTHROWN A REPUBLICAN FORM OF GOVERNMENT.

Be it enacted by the Senate and House of Representatives of the United States of America in Congress assembled, That in the states declared in rebellion against the United States, the President shall, by and with the advice and consent of the Senate, appoint for each a provisional governor, whose pay and emoluments shall not exceed that of a brigadier-general of volunteers, who shall be charged with the civil administration of such state until a state government therein shall be recognized as hereinafter provided.

SEC. 2. And be it further enacted, That so soon as the military resistance to the United States shall have been suppressed in any such state, and the people thereof shall have sufficiently returned to their obedience to the constitution and the laws of the United States, the provisional governor shall direct the marshal of the United States, as speedily as may be, to name a sufficient number of deputies, and to enroll all white male citizens of the United States, resident in the state in their respective counties, and to request each one to take the oath to support the constitution of the United States, and in his enrolment to designate those who take and those who refuse to take that oath, which rolls shall be forthwith returned to the provisional governor; and if the persons taking that oath shall amount to a majority of the persons enrolled in the state, he shall, by proclamation, invite the loyal people of the state to elect delegates to a convention charged to declare the will of the people of the state relative to the reestablishment of a state government subject to, and in conformity with, the constitution of the United States.

SEC. 3. And be it further enacted, That the convention shall consist of as many members as both houses of the last constitutional state legislature, apportioned by the provisional governor among the counties, parishes, or districts of the state, in proportion to the white population, returned as electors, by the marshal, in compliance with the provisions of this act. The provisional governor shall, by proclamation, declare the number of delegates to be elected by each county, parish, or election district; name a day of election not less than thirty days thereafter; designate the places of voting in each county, parish, or

district, conforming as nearly as may be convenient to the places used in the state elections next preceding the rebellion; appoint one or more commissioners to hold the election at each place of voting, and provide an adequate force to keep the peace during the election.

SEC. 4. And be it further enacted, That the delegates shall be elected by the loyal white male citizens of the United States of the age of twenty-one years, and resident at the time in the county, parish, or district in which they shall offer to vote, and enrolled as aforesaid, or absent in the military service of the United States, and who shall take and subscribe the oath of allegiance to the United States in the form contained in the act of congress of July two, eighteen hundred and sixty-two; and all such citizens of the United States who are in the military service of the United States shall vote at the headquarters of their respective commands, under such regulations as may be prescribed by the provisional governor for the taking and return of their votes; but no person who has held or exercised any office, civil or military, state or confederate, under the rebel usurpation, or who has voluntarily borne arms against the United States, shall vote, or be eligible to be elected as delegate, at such election.

SEC. 5. And be it further enacted, That the said commissioners, or either of them, shall hold the election in conformity with this act, and, so far as may be consistent therewith, shall proceed in the manner used in the state prior to the rebellion. The oath of allegiance shall be taken and subscribed on the poll book by every voter in the form above prescribed, but every person known by or proved to, the commissioners to have held or exercised any office, civil or military, state or confederate, under the rebel usurpation, or to have voluntarily borne arms against the United States, shall be excluded, though he offer to take the oath; and in case any person who shall have borne arms against the United States shall offer to vote he shall be deemed to have borne arms voluntarily unless he shall prove the contrary by the testimony of a qualified voter. The poll book, showing the name and oath of each voter, shall be returned to the provisional governor by the commissioners of election or the one acting, and the provisional governor shall canvass such returns, and declare the person having the highest number of votes elected.

SEC. 6. And be it further enacted, That the provisional governor shall, by proclamation, convene the delegates elected as aforesaid, at the capital of the state, on a day not more than three months after the election, giving at least thirty days' notice of such day. In case the said capital shall in his judgment be unfit, he shall in his proclamation appoint another place. He shall preside over the deliberations of the convention, and administer to each delegate, before taking his seat in the convention, the oath of allegiance to the United States in the form above prescribed.

SEC. 7. And be it further enacted, That the convention shall declare, on behalf of the people of the state, their submission to the constitution and laws of the United States, and shall adopt the following provisions, hereby prescribed by the United States in the execution of the constitutional duty to guarantee a republican form of government to every state, and incorporate them in the constitution of the state, that is to say:

First. No person who has held or exercised any office, civil or military, except offices merely ministerial, and military offices below the grade of colonel, state or confederate, under the usurping power, shall vote for or be a member of the legislature, or governor.

Second. Involuntary servitude is forever prohibited, and the freedom of all persons is guaranteed in said state.

Third. No debt, state or confederate, created by or under the sanction of the usurping power, shall be recognized or paid by the state.

SEC. 8. And be it further enacted, That when the convention shall have adopted those provisions, it shall proceed to re-establish a republican form of government, and ordain a constitution containing those provisions, which, when adopted the convention shall by ordinance provide for submitting to the people of the state, entitled to vote under this law, at an election to be held in the manner prescribed by the act for the election of delegates; but at a time and place named by the convention, at which election the said electors, and none others, shall vote directly for or against such constitution and form of state government, and the returns of said election shall be made to the provisional governor, who shall canvass the same in the presence of the electors, and if a majority of the votes cast shall be for the constitution and form of government, he shall certify the same, with a copy thereof, to the President of the United States, who, after obtaining the assent of congress, shall, by proclamation, recognize the government so established, and none other, as the constitutional government of the state, and from the date of such recognition, and not before, Senators and Representatives, and electors for President and Vice President may be elected in such state, according to the laws of the state and of the United States.

SEC. 9. And be it further enacted, That if the convention shall refuse to reestablish the state government on the conditions aforesaid, the provisional governor shall declare it dissolved; but it shall be the duty of the President, whenever he shall have reason to believe that a sufficient number of the people of the state entitled to vote under this act, in number not less than a majority of those enrolled, as aforesaid, are willing to reestablish a state government on the conditions aforesaid, to direct the provisional governor to order another election of delegates to a convention for the purpose and in the manner prescribed in this act, and to proceed in all respects as hereinbefore provided, either to dissolve the convention, or to certify the state government reestablished by it to the President.

SEC. 10. And be it further enacted, That, until the United States shall have recognized a republican form of state government, the provisional governor in each of said states shall see that this act, and the laws of the United States, and the laws of the state in force when the state government was overthrown by the rebellion, are faithfully executed within the state; but no law or usage whereby any person was heretofore held in involuntary servitude shall be recognized or enforced by any court or officer in such state, and the laws for the trial and punishment of white persons shall extend to all persons, and jurors shall have the qualifications of voters under this law for delegates to the convention. The President shall appoint such officers provided for by the laws of the state when its government was overthrown as he may find necessary to the civil administration of the slate, all which officers shall be entitled to receive the fees and emoluments provided by the state laws for such officers.

SEC. 11. And be it further enacted, That until the recognition of a state government as aforesaid, the provisional governor shall, under such regulations as he may prescribe, cause to be assessed, levied, and collected, for the year eighteen hundred and sixty-four, and every year thereafter, the taxes provided by the laws of such state to be levied during the fiscal year preceding the overthrow of the state government thereof, in the manner prescribed by the laws of the state, as nearly as may be; and the officers appointed, as aforesaid, are vested with all powers of levying and collecting such taxes, by distress or sale, as were vested in any officers or tribunal of the state government aforesaid for those purposes. The proceeds of such taxes shall be accounted for to the provisional governor, and be by him applied to the expenses of the administration of the laws in such state, subject to the direction of the President, and the surplus shall be deposited in the treasury of the United States to the credit of such state, to be paid to the state upon an appropriation therefor, to be made when a republican form of government shall be recognized therein by the United States.

SEC. 12. And be it further enacted, that all persons held to involuntary servitude or labor in the states aforesaid are hereby emancipated and discharged therefrom, and they and their posterity shall be forever free. And if any such persons or their posterity shall be restrained of liberty, under pretence of any claim to such service or labor, the courts of the United States shall, on habeas corpus, discharge them.

SEC. 13. And be it further enacted, That if any person declared free by this act, or any law of the United States, or any proclamation of the President, be restrained of liberty, with intent to be held in or reduced to involuntary servitude or labor, the person convicted before a court of competent jurisdiction of such act shall be punished by fine of not less than fifteen hundred dollars, and be imprisoned not less than five nor more than twenty years.

SEC. 14. And be it further enacted, That every person who shall hereafter hold or exercise any office, civil or military, except offices merely ministerial, and military offices below the grade of colonel, in the rebel service, state or confederate, is hereby declared not to be a citizen of the United States.

BY THE PRESIDENT OF THE UNITED STATES: A PROCLAMATION:

WHEREAS, at the late session, congress passed a bill to "guarantee to certain states, whose governments have been usurped or overthrown, a republican form of government, " a copy of which is hereunto annexed;

And whereas the said bill was presented to the President of the United States for his approval less than one hour before the sine die adjournment of said session, and was not signed by him;

And whereas the said bill contains, among other things, a plan for restoring the states in rebellion to their proper practical relation in the Union, which plan expresses the sense of congress upon that subject, and which plan it is now thought fit to lay before the people for their consideration;

Now, therefore, I, ABRAHAM LINCOLN, President of the United States, do proclaim, declare, and make known, that, while I am (as I was in December last, when by proclamation I propounded a plan for restoration) unprepared by a formal approval of this bill, to be inflexibly committed to any single plan of restoration; and, while I am also unprepared to declare that the free state constitutions and governments already adopted and installed in Arkansas and Louisiana shall be set aside and held for nought, thereby repelling and discouraging the loyal citizens who have set up the same as to further effort, or to declare a constitutional competency in congress to abolish slavery in states, but am at the same time sincerely hoping and expecting that a constitutional amendment abolishing slavery throughout the nation may be adopted, nevertheless I am truly satisfied with the system for restoration contained in the bill as one very proper plan for the loyal people of any state choosing to adopt it, and that I am, and at all times shall be, prepared to give the executive aid and assistance to any such people, so soon as the military resistance to the United States shall have been suppressed in any such state, and the people thereof shall have sufficiently returned to their obedience to the constitution and the laws of the United States, in which cases military governors will be appointed, with directions to proceed according to the bill.

In testimony whereof; I have hereunto set my hand, and caused the seal of the United States to be affixed.

Done at the city of Washington this eighth day of July, in the year of our [L S.] Lord one thousand eight hundred and sixty-four, and of the Independence of the United States the eighty-ninth.

ABRAHAM LINCOLN.
By the President :

WILLIAH H. SEWARD, Secretary of State.

President Abraham Lincoln's Second Inaugural Address

Fellow Countrymen

At this second appearing to take the oath of the presidential office, there is less occasion for an extended address than there was at the first. Then a statement, somewhat in detail, of a course to be pursued, seemed fitting and proper. Now, at the expiration of four years, during which public declarations have been constantly called forth on every point and phase of the great contest which still absorbs the attention, and engrosses the enerergies of the nation, little that is new could be presented. The progress of our arms, upon which all else chiefly depends, is as well known to the public as to myself; and it is, I trust, reasonably satisfactory and encouraging to all. With high hope for the future, no prediction in regard to it is ventured.

On the occasion corresponding to this four years ago, all thoughts were anxiously directed to an impending civil war. All dreaded it—all sought to avert it. While the inaugeral address was being delivered from this place, devoted altogether to saving the Union without war, insurgent agents were in the city seeking to destroy it without war—seeking to dissole the Union, and divide effects, by negotiation. Both parties deprecated war; but one of them would make war rather than let the nation survive; and the other would accept war rather than let it perish. And the war came.

One eighth of the whole population were colored slaves, not distributed generally over the Union, but localized in the Southern part of it. These slaves constituted a peculiar and powerful interest. All knew that this interest was, somehow, the cause of the war. To strengthen, perpetuate, and extend this interest was the object for which the insurgents would rend the Union, even by war; while the government claimed no right to do more than to restrict the territorial enlargement of it. Neither party expected for the war, the magnitude, or the duration, which it has already attained. Neither anticipated that the cause of the conflict might cease with, or even before, the conflict itself should cease. Each looked for an easier triumph, and a result less fundamental and astounding. Both read the same Bible, and pray to the same God; and each invokes His aid against the other. It may seem strange that any men should dare to ask a just God's assistance in wringing their bread from the sweat of other men's faces; but let us judge not that we be not judged. The prayers of both could not be answered; that of neither has been answered fully. The Almighty has His own purposes. "Woe unto the world because of offences! for it must needs be that offences come; but woe to that man by whom the offence cometh!" If we shall suppose that American Slavery is one of those offences which, in the providence of God, must needs come, but which, having continued through His appointed time, He now wills to remove, and that He gives to both North and South, this terrible war, as the woe due to those by whom the offence came, shall we discern therein any departure from those divine attributes which the believers in a Living God always ascribe to Him? Fondly do we hope—fervently do we pray—that this mighty scourge of war may speedily pass away. Yet, if God wills that it continue, until all the wealth piled by the bondman's two hundred and fifty years of unrequited toil shall be sunk, and until every drop of blood drawn with the lash, shall be paid by another drawn with the sword, as was said three thousand years ago, so still it must be said "the judgments of the Lord, are true and righteous altogether."

With malice toward none; with charity for all; with firmness in the right, as God gives us to see the right, let us strive on to finish the work we are in; to bind up the nation's wounds; to care for him who shall have borne the battle, and for his widow, and his orphan to do all which may achieve and cherish a just, and a lasting peace, among ourselves, and with all nations.

[Endorsed by Lincoln:]

Original manuscript of second Inaugeral presented to Major John Hay.

A. Lincoln April 10, 1865

Articles of Agreement Relating to the Surrender of the Army of Northern Virginia

APPOMATTOX COURT HOUSE VIRGINIA APRIL 10, 1865

Agreement entered into this day in regard to the surrender of the Army of Northern Virginia to the United States Authorities.

1st The troops shall march by Brigades and Detachments to a designated point, stock their Arms, deposit their flags, Sabres, Pistols, etc. and from thence march to their homes under charge of their Officers, superintended by their respective Division and Corps Commanders, Officers, retaining their side Arms, and the authorized number of private horses.

2. All public horses and public property of all kinds to be turned over to Staff Officers designated by the United States Authorities.

3. Such transportation as may be agreed upon as necessary for the transportation of the Private baggage of Officers will be allowed to accompany the Officers, to be turned over at the end of the trip to the nearest U.S. Quarter Masters, receipts being taken for the same.

4. Couriers and Wounded men of the artillery and Cavalry whose horses are their own private property will be allowed to retain them.

5. The surrender of the Army of Northern Virginia shall be construed to include all the forces operating with that Army on the 8th inst., the date of commencement of negociation for surrender, except such bodies of Cavalry as actually made their escape previous to the surrender, and except also such forces of Artillery as were more than Twenty (20) miles from Appomattox Court House at the time of Surrender on the 9th inst.

[Endorsements]

13th Amendment to the U.S. Constitution: Abolition of Slavery

AMENDMENT XIII

SECTION 1.

Neither slavery nor involuntary servitude, except as a punishment for crime whereof the party shall have been duly convicted, shall exist within the United States, or any place subject to their jurisdiction.

SECTION 2.

Congress shall have power to enforce this article by appropriate legislation.

Passed by Congress January 31, 1865. Ratified December 6, 1865.

Note: A portion of Article IV, section 2, of the Constitution was superseded by the 13th amendment.

Check for the Purchase of Alaska

(Note: This is a transcription of the English text of the Treaty of Cession.)

March 30, 1867

Treaty concerning the Cession of the Russian Possessions in North America by his Majesty the Emperor of all the Russias to the United States of America; Concluded March 30, 1867; Ratified by the United States May 28, 1867; Exchanged June 20, 1867; Proclaimed by the United States June 20, 1867.

BY THE PRESIDENT OF THE UNITED STATES OF AMERICA A PROCLAMATION.

Whereas a treaty between the United States of America and his Majesty the Emperor of all the Russias was concluded and signed by their respective plenipotentiaries at the city of Washington, on the thirtieth day of March, last, which treaty, being in English and French languages, is, word for word as follows:

(the French version is omitted for brevity)

The United States of America and His Majesty the Emperor of all the Russias, being desirous of strengthening, if possible, the good understanding which exists between them, have, for that purpose, appointed as their Plenipotentiaries: the President of the United States, William H. Seward, Secretary of State; and His Majesty the Emperor of all the Russias, the Privy Councillor Edward de Stoeckl, his Envoy Extraordinary and Minister Plenipotentiary to the United States.

And the said Plenipotentiaries, having exchanged their full powers, which were found to be in due form, have agreed upon and signed the following articles:

ARTICLE I.

His Majesty the Emperor of all the Russias agrees to cede to the United States, by this convention, immediately upon the exchange of the ratifications thereof, all the territory and dominion now possessed by his said Majesty on the continent of America and in the adjacent islands, the same being contained within the geographical limits herein set forth, to wit: The eastern limit is the line of demarcation between the Russian and the British possessions in North America, as established by the convention between Russia and Great Britain, of February 28 16, 1825, and described in Articles III and IV of said convention, in the following terms:

"Commencing from the southernmost point of the island called Prince of Wales Island, which point lies in the parallel of 54 degrees 40 minutes north latitude, and between the 131st and the 133d degree of west longitude, (meridian of Greenwich,) the said line shall ascend to the north along the channel called Portland channel, as far as the point of the continent where it strikes the 56th degree of north latitude; from this last-mentioned point, the line of demarcation shall follow the summit of the mountains situated parallel to the coast as far as the point of intersection of the 141st degree of west longitude, (of the same meridian;) and finally, from the said point of intersection, the said meridian line of the 141st degree, in its prolongation as far as the Frozen ocean. "IV. With reference to the line of demarcation laid down in the preceding article, it is understood -

"1st. That the island called Prince of Wales Island shall belong wholly to Russia," (now, by this cession, to the United States.)

"2d. That whenever the summit of the mountains which extend in a direction parallel to the coast from the 56th degree of north latitude to the point of intersection of the 141st degree of west longitude shall prove to be at the distance of more than ten marine leagues from the ocean, the limit between the British possessions and the line of coast which is to belong to Russia as above mentioned (that is to say, the limit to the possessions ceded by this convention) shall be formed by a line parallel to the winding of the coast, and which shall never exceed the distance of ten marine leagues therefrom."

The western limit within which the territories and dominion conveyed, are contained, passes through a point in Behring's straits on the parallel of sixty-five degrees thirty minutes north latitude, at its intersection by the meridian which passes midway between the islands of Krusenstern, or Ignalook, and the island of Ratmanoff, or Noonarbook, and proceeds due north, without limitation, into the same Frozen ocean. The same western limit, beginning at the same initial point, proceeds thence in a course nearly southwest through Behring's straits and Behring's sea, so as to pass midway between the northwest point of the island of St. Lawrence and the southeast point of Cape Choukotski, to the meridian of one hundred and seventy-two west longitude; thence, from the intersection of that meridian, in a southwesterly direction, so as to pass midway between the island of Attou and the Copper island of the Kormandorski couplet or group in the North Pacific ocean, to the meridian of one hundred and ninety-three degrees west longitude, so as to include in the territory conveyed the whole of the Aleutian islands east of that meridian.

ARTICLE II.

In the cession of territory and dominion made by the preceding article are included the right of property in all public lots and squares, vacant lands, and all public buildings, fortifications, barracks, and other edifices which are not private individual property. It is, however, understood and agreed, that the churches which have been built in the ceded territory by the Russian government, shall remain the property of such members of the Greek Oriental Church resident in the territory, as may choose to worship therein. Any government archives, papers, and documents relative to the territory and dominion aforesaid, which may be now existing there, will be left in the possession of the agent of the United States; but an authenticated copy of such of them as may be required, will be, at all times, given by the United States to the Russian government, or to such Russian officers or subjects as they may apply for.

ARTICLE III.

The inhabitants of the ceded territory, according to their choice, reserving their natural allegiance, may return to Russia within three years; but if they should prefer to remain in the ceded territory, they, with the exception of uncivilized native tribes, shall be admitted to the enjoyment of all the rights, advantages, and immunities of citizens of the United States, and shall be maintained and protected in the free enjoyment of their liberty, property, and religion. The uncivilized tribes will be subject to such laws and regu-

lations as the United States may, from time to time, adopt in regard to aboriginal tribes of that country.

ARTICLE IV.

His Majesty the Emperor of all the Russias shall appoint, with convenient despatch, an agent or agents for the purpose of formally delivering to a similar agent or agents appointed on behalf of the United States, the territory, dominion, property, dependencies and appurtenances which are ceded as above, and for doing any other act which may be necessary in regard thereto. But the cession, with the right of immediate possession, is nevertheless to be deemed complete and absolute on the exchange of ratifications, without waiting for such formal delivery.

ARTICLE V.

Immediately after the exchange of the ratifications of this convention, any fortifications or military posts which may be in the ceded territory shall be delivered to the agent of the United States, and any Russian troops which may be in the territory shall be withdrawn as soon as may be reasonably and conveniently practicable.

ARTICLE VI.

In consideration of the cession aforesaid, the United States agree to pay at the treasury in Washington, within ten months after the exchange of the ratifications of this convention, to the diplomatic representative or other agent of his Majesty the Emperor of all the Russias, duly authorized to receive the same, seven million two hundred thousand dollars in gold. The cession of territory and dominion herein made is hereby declared to be free and unencumbered by any reservations, privileges, franchises, grants, or possessions, by any associated companies, whether corporate or incorporate, Russian or any other, or by any parties, except merely private individual property holders; and the cession hereby made, conveys all the rights, franchises, and privileges now belonging to Russia in the said territory or dominion, and appurtenances thereto.

ARTICLE VII.

When this convention shall have been duly ratified by the President of the United States, by and with the advice and consent of the Senate, on the one part, and on the other by his Majesty the Emperor of all the Russias, the ratifications shall be exchanged at Washington within three months from the date hereof, or sooner if possible.

In faith whereof, the respective plenipotentiaries have signed this convention, and thereto affixed the seals of their arms.

Done at Washington, the thirtieth day of March, in the year of our Lord one thousand eight hundred and sixty-seven.

[L. S.] WILLIAM H. SEWARD.
[L. S.] EDOUARD DE STOECKL.

And whereas the said Treaty has been duly ratified on both parts, and the respective ratifications of the same were exchanged at Washington on this twentieth day of June, by William H. Seward, Secretary of State of the United States, and the Privy Counsellor Edward de Stoeckl, the Envoy Extraordinary of His Majesty the Emperor of all the Russias, on the part of their respective governments, Now, therefore, be it known that I, Andrew Johnson, President of the United States of America, have caused the said Treaty to be made public, to the end that the same and every clause and article thereof may be observed and fulfilled with good faith by the United States and the citizens thereof.

In witness whereof, I have hereunto set my hand, and caused the seal of the United States to be affixed.

Done at the city of Washington, this twentieth day of June in the year of our Lord one thousand eight hundred and sixty-seven, and of the Independence of the United States the ninety-first.

[L.S.] ANDREW JOHNSON By the President: William H Seward, Secretary of State

The Treaty of Fort Laramie

ARTICLES OF A TREATY MADE AND CONCLUDED BY AND BETWEEN

Lieutenant General William T. Sherman, General William S. Harney, General Alfred H. Terry, General O. O. Augur, J. B. Henderson, Nathaniel G. Taylor, John G. Sanborn, and Samuel F. Tappan, duly appointed commissioners on the part of the United States, and the different bands of the Sioux Nation of Indians, by their chiefs and headmen, whose names are hereto subscribed, they being duly authorized to act in the premises.

ARTICLE I.

From this day forward all war between the parties to this agreement shall for ever cease. The government of the United States desires peace, and its honor is hereby pledged to keep it. The Indians desire peace, and they now pledge their honor to maintain it.

If bad men among the whites, or among other people subject to the authority of the United States, shall commit any wrong upon the person or property of the Indians, the United States will, upon proof made to the agent, and forwarded to the Commissioner of Indian Affairs at Washington city, proceed at once to cause the offender to be arrested and punished according to the laws of the United States, and also reimburse the injured person for the loss sustained.

If bad men among the Indians shall commit a wrong or depredation upon the person or property of nay one, white, black, or Indian, subject to the authority of the United States, and at peace therewith, the Indians herein named solemnly agree that they will, upon proof made to their agent, and notice by him, deliver up the wrongdoer to the United States, to be tried and punished according to its laws, and, in case they willfully refuse so to do, the person injured shall be reimbursed for his loss from the annuities, or other moneys due or to become due to them under this or other treaties made with the United States; and the President, on advising with the Commissioner of Indian Affairs, shall prescribe such rules and regulations for ascertaining damages under the provisions of this article as in his judgment may be proper, but no one sustaining loss while violating the provisions of this treaty, or the laws of the United States, shall be reimbursed therefor.

ARTICLE II.

The United States agrees that the following district of country, to wit, viz: commencing on the east bank of the Missouri river where the 46th parallel of north latitude crosses the same, thence along low-water mark down said east bank to a point opposite where the northern line of the State of Nebraska strikes the river, thence west across said river, and along the northern line of Nebraska to the 104th degree of longitude west from Greenwich, thence north on said meridian to a point where the 46th parallel of north latitude intercepts the same, thence due east along said parallel to the place of beginning; and in addition thereto, all existing reservations of the east back of said river, shall be and the same is, set apart for the absolute and undisturbed use and occupation of the Indians herein named, and for such other friendly tribes or individual Indians as from time to time they may be willing, with the consent of the United States, to admit amongst them; and the United States now solemnly agrees that no persons, except those herein designated and authorized so to do, and except such officers, agents, and employees of the government as may be authorized to enter upon Indian reservations in discharge of duties enjoined by law, shall ever be permitted to pass over, settle upon, or reside in the territory described in this article, or in such territory as may be added to this reservation for the use of said Indians, and henceforth they will and do hereby relinquish all claims or right in and to any portion of the United States or Territories, except such as is embraced within the limits aforesaid, and except as hereinafter provided.

ARTICLE III.

If it should appear from actual survey or other satisfactory examination of said tract of land that it contains less than 160 acres of tillable land for each person who, at the time, may be authorized to reside on it under the provisions of this treaty, and a very considerable number of such persons hsall be disposed to comence cultivating the soil as farmers, the United States agrees to set apart, for the use of said Indians, as herein provided, such additional quantity of arable land, adjoining to said reservation, or as near to the same as it can be obtained, as may be required to provide the necessary amount.

ARTICLE IV.

The United States agrees, at its own proper expense, to construct, at some place on the Missouri river, near the centre of said reservation where timber and water may be convenient, the following buildings, to wit, a warehouse, a storeroom for the use of the agent in storing goods belonging to the Indians, to cost not less than $2,500; an agency building, for the residence of the agent, to cost not exceeding $3,000; a residence for the physician, to cost not more than $3,000; and five other buildings, for a carpenter, farmer, blacksmith, miller, and engineer each to cost not exceeding $2,000; also, a school house, or mission building, so soon as a sufficient number of children can be induced by the agent to attend school, which shall not cost exceeding $5,000.

The United States agrees further to cause to be erected on said reservation, near the other buildings herein authorized, a good steam circular saw mill, with a grist mill and shingle machine attached to the same, to cost not exceeding $8,000.

ARTICLE V.

The United States agrees that the agent for said Indians shall in the future make his home at the agency building; that he shall reside among them, and keep an office open at all times for the purpose of prompt and diligent inquiry into such matters of complaint by and against the Indians as may be presented for investigation under the provisions of their treaty stipulations, as also for the faithful discharge of other duties enjoined on him by law. In all cases of depredation on person or property he shall cause the evidence to be taken in writing and forwarded, together with his findings, to the Commissioner of Indian Affairs, whose decision, subject to the revision of the Secretary of the Interior, shall be binding on the parties to this treaty.

ARTICLE VI.

If any individual belonging to said tribes of Indians, or legally incorporated with them, being the head of a family, shall desire to commence farming, he shall have the privilege to select, in the presence and with the assistance of the agent then in charge, a tract of land within said reservation, not exceeding three hundred and twenty acres in extent, which tract, when so selected, certified, and recorded in the "Land Book" as herein directed, shall cease to be held in common, but the same may be occupied and held in the exclusive possession of the person selecting it, and of his family, so long as he or they may continue to cultivate it.

Any person over eighteen years of age, not being the head of a family, may in like manner select and cause to be certified to him or her, for purposes of cultivation, a quantity of land, not exceeding eighty acres in extent, and thereupon be entitled to the exclusive possession of the same as above directed.

For each tract of land so selected a certificate, containing a description thereof and the name of the person selecting it, with a certificate endorsed thereon that the same has been recorded, shall be delivered to the party entitled to it, by the agent, after the same shall have been recorded by him in a book to be kept in his office, subject to inspection, which said book shall be known as the "Sioux Land Book."

The President may, at any time, order a survey of the reservation, and, when so surveyed, Congress shall provide for protecting the rights of said settlers in their improvements, and may fix the character of the title held by each. The United States may pass such laws on the subject of alienation and descent of property between the Indians and their descendants as may be thought proper. And it is further stipulated that any male Indians over eighteen years of age, of any band or tribe that is or shall hereafter become a party to this treaty, who now is or who shall hereafter become a resident or occupant of any reservation or territory not included in the tract of country designated and described in this treaty for the permanent home of the Indians, which is not mineral land, nor reserved by the United States for special purposes other than Indian occupation, and who shall have made improvements thereon of the value of two hundred dollars or more, and continuously occupied the same as a homestead for the term of three years, shall be entitled to receive from the United States a patent for one hundred and sixty acres of land including his said improvements, the same to be in the form of the legal subdivisions of the surveys of the public lands. Upon application in writing, sustained by the proof of two disinterested witnesses, made to the register of the local land office when the land sought to be entered is within a land district, and when the tract sought to be entered is not in any land district, then upon said application and proof being made to the Commissioner of the General Land Office, and the right of such Indian or Indians to enter such tract or tracts of land shall accrue and be perfect from the date of his first improvements thereon, and shall continue as long as be continues his residence and improvements and no longer. And any Indian or Indians receiving a patent for land under the foregoing provisions shall thereby and from thenceforth become and be a citizen of the United States and be entitled to all the privileges and immunities of such citizens, and shall, at the same time, retain all his rights to benefits accruing to Indians under this treaty.

ARTICLE VII.

In order to insure the civilization of the Indians entering into this treaty, the necessity of education is admitted, especially of such of them as are or may be settled on said agricultural reservations, and they, therefore, pledge themselves to compel their children, male and female, between the ages of six and sixteen years, to attend school, and it is hereby made the duty of the agent for said Indians to see that this stipulation is strictly complied with; and the United States agrees that for every thirty children between said ages, who can be induced or compelled to attend school, a house shall be provided, and a teacher competent to teach the elementary branches of an English education shall be furnished, who will reside among said Indians and faithfully discharge his or her duties as a teacher. The provisions of this article to continue for not less than twenty years.

ARTICLE VIII.

When the head of a family or lodge shall have selected lands and received his certificate as above directed, and the agent shall be satisfied that he intends in good faith to commence cultivating the soil for a living, he shall be entitled to receive seeds and agricultural implements for the first year, not exceeding in value one hundred dollars, and for each succeeding year he shall continue to farm, for a period of three years more, he shall be entitled to receive seeds and implements as aforesaid, not exceeding in value twenty-five dollars. And it is further stipulated that such persons as commence farming shall receive instruction from the farmer herein provided for, and whenever more than one hundred persons shall en-

ter upon the cultivation of the soil, a second blacksmith shall be provided, with such iron, steel, and other material as may be needed.

ARTICLE IX.

At any time after ten years fro the making of this treaty, the United States shall have the privilege of withdrawing the physician, farmer, blacksmith, carpenter, engineer, and miller herein provided for, but in case of such withdrawal, an additional sum thereafter of ten thousand dollars per annum shall be devoted to the education of said Indians, and the Commissioner of Indian Affairs shall, upon careful inquiry into their condition, make such rules and regulations for the expenditure of said sums as will best promote the education and moral improvement of said tribes.

ARTICLE X.

In lieu of all sums of money or other annuities provided to be paid to the Indians herein named under any treaty or treaties heretofore made, the United States agrees to deliver at the agency house on the reservation herein named, on or before the first day of August of each year, for thirty years, the following articles, to wit:

For each male person over 14 years of age, a suit of good substantial woollen clothing, consisting of coat, pantaloons, flannel shirt, hat, and a pair of home-made socks.

For each female over 12 years of age, a flannel shirt, or the goods necessary to make it, a pair of woollen hose, 12 yards of calico, and 12 yards of cotton domestics.

For the boys and girls under the ages named, such flannel and cotton goods as may be needed to make each a suit as aforesaid, together with a pair of woollen hose for each.

And in order that the Commissioner of Indian Affairs may be able to estimate properly for the articles herein named, it shall be the duty of the agent each year to forward to him a full and exact census of the Indians, on which the estimate from year to year can be based.

And in addition to the clothing herein named, the sum of $10 for each person entitled to the beneficial effects of this treaty shall be annually appropriated for a period of 30 years, while such persons roam and hunt, and $20 for each person who engages in farming, to be used by the Secretary of the Interior in the purchase of such articles as from time to time the condition and necessities of the Indians may indicate to be proper. And if within the 30 years, at any time, it shall appear that the amount of money needed for clothing, under this article, can be appropriated to better uses for the Indians named herein, Congress may, by law, change the appropriation to other purposes, but in no event shall the amount of the appropriation be withdrawn or discontinued for the period named. And the President shall annually detail an officer of the army to be present and attest the delivery of all the goods herein named, to the Indians, and he shall inspect and report on the quantity and quality of the goods and the manner of their delivery. And it is hereby expressly stipulated that each Indian over the age of four years, who shall have removed to and settled permanently upon said reservation, one pound of meat and one pound of flour per day, provided the Indians cannot furnish their own subsistence at an earlier date. And it is further stipulated that the United States will furnish and deliver to each lodge of Indians or family of persons legally incorporated with the, who shall remove to the reservation herein described and commence farming, one good American cow, and one good well-broken pair of American oxen within 60 days after such lodge or family shall have so settled upon said reservation.

ARTICLE XI.

In consideration of the advantages and benefits conferred by this treaty and the many pledges of friendship by the United States, the tribes who are parties to this agreement hereby stipulate that they will relinquish all right to occupy permanently the territory outside their reservations as herein defined, but yet reserve the right to hunt on any lands north of North Platte, and on the Republican Fork of the Smoky Hill river, so long as the buffalo may range thereon in such numbers as to justify the chase. And they, the said Indians, further expressly agree:

1st. That they will withdraw all opposition to the construction of the railroads now being built on the plains.

2d. That they will permit the peaceful construction of any railroad not passing over their reservation as herein defined.

3d. That they will not attack any persons at home, or travelling, nor molest or disturb any wagon trains, coaches, mules, or cattle belonging to the people of the United States, or to persons friendly therewith.

4th. They will never capture, or carry off from the settlements, white women or children.

5th. They will never kill or scalp white men, nor attempt to do them harm.

6th. They withdraw all pretence of opposition to the construction of the railroad now being built along the Platte river and westward to the Pacific ocean, and they will not in future object to the construction of railroads, wagon roads, mail stations, or other works of utility or necessity, which may be ordered or permitted by the laws of the United States. But should such roads or other works be constructed on the lands of their reservation, the government will pay the tribe whatever amount of damage may be assessed by three disinterested commissioners to be appointed by the President for that purpose, one of the said commissioners to be a chief or headman of the tribe.

7th. They agree to withdraw all opposition to the military posts or roads now established south of the North Platte river, or that may be established, not in violation of treaties heretofore made or hereafter to be made with any of the Indian tribes.

ARTICLE XII.

No treaty for the cession of any portion or part of the reservation herein described which may be held in common, shall be of any validity or force as against the said Indians unless executed and signed by at least three-fourths of all the adult male Indians occupying or interested in the same, and no cession by the tribe shall be understood or construed in such manner as to deprive, without his consent, any individual member of the tribe of his rights to any tract of land selected by him as provided in Article VI of this treaty.

ARTICLE XIII.

The United States hereby agrees to furnish annually to the Indians the physician, teachers, carpenter, miller, engineer, farmer, and blacksmiths, as herein contemplated, and that such appropriations shall be made from time to time, on the estimate of the Secretary of the Interior, as will be sufficient to employ such persons.

ARTICLE XIV.

It is agreed that the sum of five hundred dollars annually for three years from date shall be expended in presents to the ten persons of said tribe who in the judgment of the agent may grow the most valuable crops for the respective year.

ARTICLE XV.

The Indians herein named agree that when the agency house and other buildings shall be constructed on the reservation named, they will regard said reservation their permanent home, and they will make no permanent settlement elsewhere; but they shall have the right, subject to the conditions and modifications of this treaty, to hunt, as stipulated in Article XI hereof.

ARTICLE XVI.

The United States hereby agrees and stipulates that the country north of the North Platte river and east of the summits of the Big Horn mountains shall be held and considered to be unceded. Indian territory, and also stipulates and agrees that no white person or persons shall be permitted to settle upon or occupy any portion of the same; or without the consent of the Indians, first had and obtained, to pass through the same; and it is further agreed by the United States, that within ninety days after the conclusion of peace with all the bands of the Sioux nation, the military posts now established in the territory in this article named shall be abandoned, and that the road leading to them and by them to the settlements in the Territory of Montana shall be closed.

ARTICLE XVII.

It is hereby expressly understood and agreed by and between the respective parties to this treaty that the execution of this treaty and its ratification by the United States Senate shall have the effect, and shall be construed as abrogating and annulling all treaties and agreements heretofore entered into between the respective parties hereto, so far as such treaties and agreements obligate the United States to furnish and provide money, clothing, or other articles of property to such Indians and bands of Indians as become parties to this treaty, but no further.

In testimony of all which, we, the said commissioners, and we, the chiefs and headmen of the Brule band of the Sioux nation, have hereunto set our hands and seals at Fort Laramie, Dakota Territory, this twenty-ninth day of April, in the year one thousand eight hundred and sixty-eight.

N. G. TAYLOR,
W. T. SHERMAN,
Lieutenant General
WM. S. HARNEY,
Brevet Major General U.S.A.
JOHN B. SANBORN,
S. F. TAPPAN,
C. C. AUGUR,
Brevet Major General
ALFRED H. TERRY,
Brevet Major General U.S.A.
Attest:
A. S. H. WHITE, Secretary.

Executed on the part of the Brule band of Sioux by the chiefs and headman whose names are hereto annexed, they being thereunto duly authorized, at Fort Laramie, D. T., the twenty-ninth day of April, in the year A. D. 1868.

MA-ZA-PON-KASKA, his X mark, Iron Shell.
WAH-PAT-SHAH, his X mark, Red Leaf.
HAH-SAH-PAH, his X mark, Black Horn.
ZIN-TAH-GAH-LAT-WAH, his X mark, Spotted Tail.
ZIN-TAH-GKAH, his X mark, White Tail.
ME-WAH-TAH-NE-HO-SKAH, his X mark, Tall Man.
SHE-CHA-CHAT-KAH, his X mark, Bad Left Hand.
NO-MAH-NO-PAH, his X mark, Two and Two.
TAH-TONKA-SKAH, his X mark, White Bull.
CON-RA-WASHTA, his X mark, Pretty Coon.
HA-CAH-CAH-SHE-CHAH, his X mark, Bad Elk.
WA-HA-KA-ZAH-ISH-TAH, his X mark, Eye Lance.
MA-TO-HA-KE-TAH, his X mark, Bear that looks behind.
BELLA-TONKA-TONKA, his X mark, Big Partisan.
MAH-TO-HO-HONKA, his X mark, Swift Bear.
TO-WIS-NE, his X mark, Cold Place.
ISH-TAH-SKAH, his X mark, White Eye.
MA-TA-LOO-ZAH, his X mark, Fast Bear.
AS-HAH-HAH-NAH-SHE, his X mark, Standing Elk.
CAN-TE-TE-KI-YA, his X mark, The Brave Heart.
SHUNKA-SHATON, his X mark, Day Hawk.
TATANKA-WAKON, his X mark, Sacred Bull.
MAPIA SHATON, his X mark, Hawk Cloud.
MA-SHA-A-OW, his X mark, Stands and Comes.
SHON-KA-TON-KA, his X mark, Big Dog.
Attest:
ASHTON S. H. WHITE, Secretary of Commission.

GEORGE B. WITHS, Phonographer to Commission.
GEO. H. HOLTZMAN.
JOHN D. HOWLAND.
JAMES C. O'CONNOR.
CHAR. E. GUERN, Interpreter.
LEON T. PALLARDY, Interpreter.
NICHOLAS JANIS, Interpreter.

Executed on the part of the Ogallalla band of Sioux by the chiefs and headmen whose names are hereto subscribed, they being thereunto duly authorized, at Fort Laramie, the 25th day of May, in the year A. D. 1868.
TAH-SHUN-KA-CO-QUI-PAH, his mark, Man-afraid-of-his-horses.
SHA-TON-SKAH, his X mark, White Hawk.
SHA-TON-SAPAH, his X mark, Black Hawk.
EGA-MON-TON-KA-SAPAH, his X mark, Black Tiger
OH-WAH-SHE-CHA, his X mark, Bad Wound.
PAH-GEE, his X mark, Grass.
WAH-NON SAH-CHE-GEH, his X mark, Ghost Heart.
COMECH, his X mark, Crow.
OH-HE-TE-KAH, his X mark, The Brave.
TAH-TON-KAH-HE-YO-TA-KAH, his X mark, Sitting Bull.
SHON-KA-OH-WAH-MEN-YE, his X mark, Whirlwind Dog.
HA-KAH-KAH-TAH-MIECH, his X mark, Poor Elk.
WAM-BU-LEE-WAH-KON, his X mark, Medicine Eagle.
CHON-GAH-MA-HE-TO-HANS-KA, his X mark, High Wolf.
WAH-SECHUN-TA-SHUN-KAH, his X mark, American Horse.
MAH-KAH-MAH-HA-MAK-NEAR, his X mark, Man that walks under the ground.
MAH-TO-TOW-PAH, his X mark, Four Bears.
MA-TO-WEE-SHA-KTA, his X mark, One that kills the bear.
OH-TAH-KEE-TOKA-WEE-CHAKTA, his X mark, One that kills in a hard place.
TAH-TON-KAH-TA-MIECH, his X mark, The Poor Bull.
OH-HUNS-EE-GA-NON-SKEN, his X mark, Mad Shade.
SHAH-TON-OH-NAH-OM-MINNE-NE-OH-MINNE, his X mark, Whirling hawk.
MAH-TO-CHUN-KA-OH, his X mark, Bear's Back.
CHE-TON-WEE-KOH, his X mark, Fool Hawk.
WAH-HOH-KE-ZA-AH-HAH, his X mark,
EH-TON-KAH, his X mark, Big Mouth.

MA-PAH-CHE-TAH, his X mark, Bad Hand.
WAH-KE-YUN-SHAH, his X mark, Red Thunder.
WAK-SAH, his X mark, One that Cuts Off.
CHAH-NOM-QUI-YAH, his X mark, One that Presents the Pipe.
WAH-KE-KE-YAN-PUH-TAH, his X mark, Fire Thunder.
MAH-TO-NONK-PAH-ZE, his X mark, Bear with Yellow Ears.
CON-REE-TEH-KA, his X mark, The Little Crow.
HE-HUP-PAH-TOH, his X mark, The Blue War Club.
SHON-KEE-TOH, his X mark, The Blue Horse.
WAM-BALLA-OH-CONQUO, his X mark, Quick Eagle.
TA-TONKA-SUPPA, his X mark, Black Bull.
MOH-TOH-HA-SHE-NA, his X mark, The Bear Hide.
Attest:
S. E. WARD.
JAS. C. O'CONNOR.
J. M. SHERWOOD.
W. C. SLICER.
SAM DEON.
H. M. MATHEWS.
JOSEPH BISS
NICHOLAS JANIS, Interpreter.
LEFROY JOTT, Interpreter.
ANTOINE JANIS, Interpreter.

Executed on the part of the Minneconjou band of Sioux by the chiefs and headmen whose names are hereunto subscribed, they being thereunto duly authorized.

HEH-WON-GE-CHAT, his X mark, One Horn.
OH-PON-AH-TAH-E-MANNE, his X mark, The Elk that Bellows Walking.
HEH-HO-LAH-ZEH-CHA-SKAH, his X mark, Young White Bull.
WAH-CHAH-CHUM-KAH-COH-KEEPAH, his X mark, One that is Afraid of Shield.
HE-HON-NE-SHAKTA, his X mark, The Old Owl.
MOC-PE-A-TOH, his X mark, Blue Cloud.
OH-PONG-GE-LE-SKAH, his X mark, Spotted Elk.
TAH-TONK-KA-HON-KE-SCHUE, his X mark, Slow bull.
SHONK-A-NEE-SHAH-SHAH-ATAH-PE, his X mark, The Dog Chief.
MA-TO-TAH-TA-TONK-KA, his X mark, Bull Bear.
WOM-BEH-LE-TON-KAH, his X mark, The Big Eagle.
MATOH, EH-SCHNE-LAH, his X mark, The Lone Bear.

MA-TOH-OH-HE-TO-KEH, his X mark, The Brave Bear.

EH-CHE-MA-KEH, his X mark, The Runner.

TI-KI-YA, his X mark, The Hard.

HE-MA-ZA, his X mark, Iron Horn.

Attest:

JAS. C O'CONNOR,

WM. D. BROWN,

NICHOLAS JANIS,

ANTOINE JANIS,

Interpreters.

Executed on the part of the Yanctonais band of Sioux by the chiefs and headmen whose names are hereto subscribed, they being thereunto duly authorized:

MAH-TO-NON-PAH, his X mark, Two Bears.

MA-TO-HNA-SKIN-YA, his X mark, Mad Bear.

HE-O-PU-ZA, his X mark, Louzy.

AH-KE-CHE-TAH-CHE-KA-DAN, his X mark, Little Soldier.

MAH-TO-E-TAN-CHAN, his X mark, Chief Bear.

CU-WI-TO-WIA, his X mark, Rotten Stomach.

SKUN-KA-WE-TKO, his X mark, Fool Dog.

ISH-TA-SAP-PAH, his X mark, Black Eye.

IH-TAN-CHAN, his X mark, The Chief.

I-A-WI-CA-KA, his X mark, The One who Tells the Truth.

AH-KE-CHE-TAH, his X mark, The Soldier.

TA-SHI-NA-GI, his X mark, Yellow Robe.

NAH-PE-TON-KA, his X mark, Big Hand.

CHAN-TEE-WE-KTO, his X mark, Fool Heart.

HOH-GAN-SAH-PA, his X mark, Black Catfish.

MAH-TO-WAH-KAN, his X mark, Medicine Bear.

SHUN-KA-KAN-SHA, his X mark, Red Horse.

WAN-RODE, his X mark, The Eagle.

CAN-HPI-SA-PA, his X mark, Black Tomahawk.

WAR-HE-LE-RE, his X mark, Yellow Eagle.

CHA-TON-CHE-CA, his X mark, Small Hawk, or Long Fare.

SHU-GER-MON-E-TOO-HA-SKA, his X mark, Fall Wolf.

MA-TO-U-TAH-KAH, his X mark, Sitting Bear.

HI-HA-CAH-GE-NA-SKENE, his X mark, Mad Elk.

Arapahoes.

LITTLE CHIEF, his X mark.

TALL BEAR, his X mark.

TOP MAN, his X mark.

NEVA, his X mark.

THE WOUNDED BEAR, his X mark.

WHIRLWIND, his X mark.

THE FOX, his X mark.

THE DOG BIG MOUTH, his X mark.

SPOTTED WOLF, his X mark.

SORREL HORSE, his X mark.

BLACK COAL, his X mark.

BIG WOLF, his X mark.

KNOCK-KNEE, his X mark.

BLACK CROW, his X mark.

THE LONE OLD MAN, his X mark.

PAUL, his X mark.

BLACK BULL, his X mark.

BIG TRACK, his X mark.

THE FOOT, his X mark.

BLACK WHITE, his X mark.

YELLOW HAIR, his X mark.

LITTLE SHIELD, his X mark.

BLACK BEAR, his X mark.

WOLF MOCASSIN, his X mark.

BIG ROBE, his X mark.

WOLF CHIEF, his X mark.

Witnesses:

ROBERT P. MCKIBBIN,

Captain 4th Infantry, and Bvt. Lieut. Col. U. S. A., Commanding Fort Laramie.

WM. H. POWELL,

Brevet Major, Captain 4th Infantry.

HENRY W. PATTERSON,

Captain 4th Infantry.

THEO E. TRUE,

Second Lieutenant 4th Infantry.

W. G. BULLOCK.

FORT LARAMIE, WYOMING TERRITORY
November 6, 1868.

MAH-PI-AH-LU-TAH, his X mark, Red Cloud.

WA-KI-AH-WE-CHA-SHAH, his X mark, Thunder Man.

MA-ZAH-ZAH-GEH, his X mark, Iron Cane.

WA-UMBLE-WHY-WA-KA-TUYAH, his X mark, High Eagle.

KO-KE-PAH, his X mark, Man Afraid.

WA-KI-AH-WA-KOU-AH, his X mark, Thunder Flying Running.

Witnessess:

W. MCE. DYE,

Brevet Colonel U. S. Army, Commanding.

A. B. CAIN,

Captain 4th Infantry, Brevet Major U. S. Army.

ROBT. P. MCKIBBIN,

Captain 4th Infantry, Bvt. Lieut. Col. U. S. Army.

JNO. MILLER,

Captain 4th Infantry.

G. L. LUHN,

First Lieutenant 4th Infantry, Bvt. Capt. U. S. Army.

H. C. SLOAN,

Second Lieutenant 4th Infantry.

14th Amendment to the U.S. Constitution: Civil Rights

AMENDMENT XIV

SECTION 1.

All persons born or naturalized in the United States, and subject to the jurisdiction thereof, are citizens of the United States and of the State wherein they reside. No State shall make or enforce any law which shall abridge the privileges or immunities of citizens of the United States; nor shall any State deprive any person of life, liberty, or property, without due process of law; nor deny to any person within its jurisdiction the equal protection of the laws.

SECTION 2.

Representatives shall be apportioned among the several States according to their respective numbers, counting the whole number of persons in each State, excluding Indians not taxed. But when the right to vote at any election for the choice of electors for President and Vice-President of the United States, Representatives in Congress, the Executive and Judicial officers of a State, or the members of the Legislature thereof, is denied to any of the male inhabitants of such State, being twenty-one years of age, and citizens of the United States, or in any way abridged, except for participation in rebellion, or other crime, the basis of representation therein shall be reduced in the proportion which the number of such male citizens shall bear to the whole number of male citizens twenty-one years of age in such State.

SECTION 3.

No person shall be a Senator or Representative in Congress, or elector of President and Vice-President, or hold any office, civil or military, under the United States, or under any State, who, having previously taken an oath, as a member of Congress, or as an officer of the United States, or as a member of any State legislature, or as an executive or judicial officer of any State, to support the Constitution of the United States, shall have engaged in insurrection or rebellion against the same, or given aid or comfort to the enemies thereof. But Congress may by a vote of two-thirds of each House, remove such disability.

SECTION 4.

The validity of the public debt of the United States, authorized by law, including debts incurred for payment of pensions and bounties for services in suppressing insurrection or rebellion, shall not be questioned. But neither the United States nor any State shall assume or pay any debt or obligation incurred in aid of insurrection or rebellion against the United States, or any claim for the loss or emancipation of any slave; but all such debts, obligations and claims shall be held illegal and void.

SECTION 5.

The Congress shall have the power to enforce, by appropriate legislation, the provisions of this article.

15th Amendment to the U.S. Constitution: Voting Rights

FORTIETH CONGRESS OF THE UNITED STATES OF AMERICA;

At the third Session, Begun and held at the city of Washington, on Monday, the seventh day of December, one thousand eight hundred and sixty-eight.

A Resolution Proposing an amendment to the Constitution of the United States.

Resolved *by the Senate and House of Respresentatives of the United States of America in Congress assembled,* (two-thirds of both Houses concurring) that the following article be proposed to the legislature of the several States as an amendment to the Constitution of the United States which, when ratified by three-fourths of said legislatures shall be valid as part of the Constitution, namely:

ARTICLE XV.

Section 1. The right of citizens of the United States to vote shall not be denied or abridged by the United States or by any State on account of race, color, or previous condition of servitude—

Section 2. The Congress shall have the power to enforce this article by appropriate legislation.

An Act Establishing Yellowstone National Park

FORTY-SECOND CONGRESS OF THE UNITED STATES OF AMERICA;

At the Second Session, Begun and held at the City of Washington, on Monday, the Fourth day of December, one thousand eight hundred and seventy-one.

AN ACT TO SET APART A CERTAIN TRACT OF LAND LYING NEAR THE HEADWATERS OF THE YELLOWSTONE RIVER AS A PUBLIC PARK.

Be it enacted by the Senate and House of Representatives of the United States of America in Congress assembled, That the tract of land in the Territories of Montana and Wyoming, lying near the headwaters of the Yellowstone River, and described as follows, to wit, commencing at the junction of Gardiner's river with the Yellowstone river, and running east to the meridian passing ten miles to the eastward of the most eastern point of Yellowstone lake; thence south along said meridian to the parallel of latitude passing ten miles south of the most southern point of Yellowstone lake; thence west along said parallel to the meridian passing fifteen miles west of the most western point of Madison lake; thence north along said meridian to the latitude of the junction of Yellowstone and Gardiner's rivers; thence east to the place of beginning, is hereby reserved and withdrawn from settlement, occupancy, or sale under the laws of the United States, and dedicated and set apart as a public park or pleasuring ground for the benefit and enjoyment of the people; and all persons who shall locate or settle upon or occupy the same, or any part thereof, except as hereinafter provided, shall be considered trespassers and removed therefrom.

SEC 2. That said public park shall be under the exclusive control of the Secretary of the Interior, whose duty it shall be, as soon as practicable, to make and publish such rules and regulations as he may deem necessary or proper for the care and management of the same. Such regulations shall provide for the preservation, from injury or spoliation, of all timber, mineral deposits, natural curiosities, or wonders within said park, and their retention in their natural condition. The Secretary may in his discretion, grant leases for building purposes for terms not exceeding ten years, of small parcels of ground, at such places in said park as shall require the erection of buildings for the accommodation of visitors; all of the proceeds of said leases, and all other revenues that may be derived from any source connected with said park, to be expended under his direction in the management of the same, and the construction of roads and bridlepaths therein. He shall provide against the wanton destruction of the fish and game found within said park, and against their capture or destruction for the purposes of merchandise or profit. He shall also cause all persons trespassing upon the same after the passage of this act to be removed therefrom, and generally shall be authorized to take all such measures as shall be necessary or proper to fully carry out the objects and purposes of this act.

Thomas Edison's Patent Application for the Light Bulb

(Transcription of Thomas A. Edison's application letter for the Patent on an Improvement in Electric Lamps.)

To the Honorable Commissioner of Patents:

Your Petitioner Thomas A. Edison of Menlo Park in the State of New Jersey prays that Letters Patent may be granted to him for the invention of an Improvement in Electric Lamps and in the method of manufacturing the same set forth in the annexed specification. (Case no. 186).

And further prays that you will recognize Lemuel W. Serrell, of the City of New York, N.Y., as his Attorney, with full power of substitution and revocation, to prosecute this application, to make alterations and amendments therein, to receive the Patent, and to transact all business in the Patent Office connected Therewith.

1879

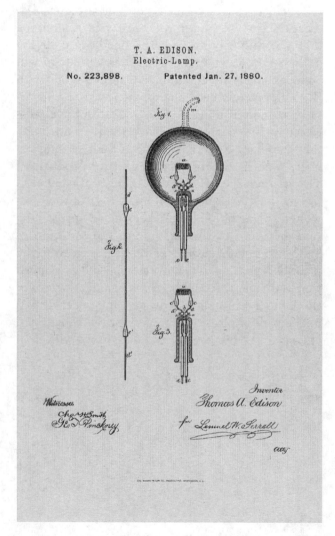

The Chinese Exclusion Act

AN ACT TO EXECUTE CERTAIN TREATY STIPULATIONS RELATING TO CHINESE.

Whereas in the opinion of the Government of the United States the coming of Chinese laborers to this country endangers the good order of certain localities within the territory thereof: Therefore,

Be it enacted by the Senate and House of Representatives of the United States of America in Congress assembled, That from and after the expiration of ninety days next after the passage of this act, and until the expiration of ten years next after the passage of this act, the coming of Chinese laborers to the United States be, and the same is hereby, suspended; and during such suspension it shall not be lawful for any Chinese laborer to come, or having so come after the expiration of said ninety days to remain within the United States.

SEC. 2. That the master of any vessel who shall knowingly bring within the United States on such vessel, and land or permit to be landed, any Chinese laborer, from any foreign port or place, shall be deemed guilty of a misdemeanor, and on conviction thereof shall be punished by a fine of not more than five hundred dollars for each and every such Chinese laborer so brought, and maybe also imprisoned for a term not exceeding one year.

SEC. 3. That the two foregoing sections shall not apply to Chinese laborers who were in the United States on the seventeenth day of November, eighteen hundred and eighty, or who shall have come into the same before the expiration of ninety days next after the passage of this act, and who shall produce to such master before going on board such vessel, and shall produce to the collector of the port in the United States at which such vessel shall arrive, the evidence hereinafter in this act required of his being one of the laborers in this section mentioned; nor shall the two foregoing sections apply to the case of any master whose vessel, being bound to a port not within the United States, shall come within the jurisdiction of the United States by reason of being in distress or in stress of weather, or touching at any port of the United States on its voyage to any foreign port or place: Provided, That all Chinese laborers brought on such vessel shall depart with the vessel on leaving port.

SEC. 4. That for the purpose of properly identifying Chinese laborers who were in the United States on the seventeenth day of November eighteen hundred and eighty, or who shall have come into the same before the expiration of ninety days next after the passage of this act, and in order to furnish them with the proper evidence of their right to go from and come to the United States of their free will and accord, as provided by the treaty between the United States and China dated November seventeenth, eighteen hundred and eighty, the collector of customs of the district from which any such Chinese laborer shall depart from the United States shall, in person or by deputy, go on board each vessel having on board any such Chinese laborers and cleared or about to sail from his district for a foreign port, and on such vessel make a list of all such Chinese laborers, which shall be entered in registry books to be kept for that purpose, in which shall be stated the name, age, occupation, last place of residence, physical marks of peculiarities, and all facts necessary for the identification of each of such Chinese laborers, which books shall be safely kept in the custom house.; and every such Chinese laborer so departing from the United States shall be entitled to, and shall receive, free of any charge or cost upon application therefor, from the collector or his deputy, at the time such list is taken, a certificate, signed by the collector or his deputy and attested by his seal of office, in such form as the Secretary of the Treasury shall prescribe, which certificate shall contain a statement of the name, age, occupation, last place of residence, persona description, and facts of identification of the Chinese laborer to whom the certificate is issued, corresponding with the said list and registry in all particulars. In case any Chinese laborer after having received such certificate shall leave such vessel before her departure he shall deliver his certificate to the master of the vessel, and if such Chinese laborer shall fail to return to such vessel before her departure from port the certificate shall be delivered by the master to the collector of customs for cancellation. The certificate herein provided for shall entitle the Chinese laborer to whom the same is issued to return to and re-enter the United States upon producing and delivering the same to the collector of customs of the district at which such Chinese laborer shall seek to re-enter; and upon delivery of such certificate by such Chinese laborer to the collector of customs at the time of re-entry in the United States said collector shall cause the same to be filed in the custom house anti duly canceled.

SEC. 5. That any Chinese laborer mentioned in section four of this act being in the United States, and desiring to depart from the United States by land, shall have the right to demand and receive, free of charge or cost, a certificate of identification similar to that provided for in section four of this act to be issued to such Chinese laborers as may desire to leave the United States by water; and it is hereby made the duty of the collector of customs of the district next adjoining the foreign country to which said Chinese laborer desires to go to issue such certificate, free of charge or cost, upon application by such Chinese laborer, and to enter the same upon registry books to be kept by him for the purpose, as provided for in section four of this act.

SEC. 6. That in order to the faithful execution of articles one and two of the treaty in this act before mentioned, every Chinese person other than a laborer who may be entitled by said treaty and this act to come within the United States, and who shall be about to come to the United States, shall be identified as so entitled by the Chinese Government in each case, such identity to be evidenced by a certificate issued under the authority of said government, which certificate shall be in the English language or (if not in the English language) accompanied by a translation into English, stating such right to come, and which certificate shall state the name, title or official rank, if any, the age, height, and all physical peculiarities, former and present occupation or profession, and place of residence in China of the person to whom the certificate is issued and that such person is entitled, conformably to the treaty in this act mentioned to come within the United States. Such certificate shall be prima-facie evidence of the fact set forth therein, and shall be produced to the collector of customs, or his deputy, of the port in the district in the United States at which the person named therein shall arrive.

SEC. 7. That any person who shall knowingly and falsely alter or substitute any name for the name written in such certificate or forge any such certificate, or knowingly utter any forged or fraudulent certificate, or falsely personate any person named in any such certificate, shall be deemed guilty of a misdemeanor; and upon conviction thereof shall be fined in a sum not exceeding one thousand dollars, and imprisoned in a penitentiary for a term of not more than five years.

SEC. 8. That the master of any vessel arriving in the United States from any foreign port or place shall, at the same time he delivers a manifest of the cargo, and if there be no cargo, then at the time of making a report of the entry of the vessel pursuant to law, in addition to the other matter required to be reported, and before landing, or permitting to land, any Chinese passengers, deliver and report to the collector of customs of the district in which such vessels shall have arrived a separate list of all Chinese passengers taken on board his vessel at any foreign port or place, and all such passengers on board the vessel at that time. Such list shall show the names of such passengers (and if accredited officers of the Chinese Government traveling on the business of that government, or their servants, with a note of such facts), and the names and other particulars, as shown by their respective certificates; and such list shall be sworn to by the master in the manner required by law in relation to the manifest of the cargo. Any willful refusal or neglect of any such master to comply with the provisions of this section shall incur the same penalties and forfeiture as are provided for a refusal or neglect to report and deliver a manifest of the cargo.

SEC. 9. That before any Chinese passengers are landed from any such line vessel, the collector, or his deputy, shall proceed to examine such passenger, comparing the certificate with the list and with the passengers; and no passenger shall be allowed to land in the United States from such vessel in violation of law.

SEC. 10. That every vessel whose master shall knowingly violate any of the provisions of this act shall be deemed forfeited to the United States, and shall be liable to seizure and condemnation in any district of the United States into which such vessel may enter or in which she may be found.

SEC. 11. That any person who shall knowingly bring into or cause to be brought into the United States by land, or who shall knowingly aid or abet the same, or aid or abet the landing in the United States from any vessel of any Chinese person not lawfully entitled to enter the United States, shall be deemed guilty of a misdemeanor, and shall, on conviction thereof, be fined in a sum not exceeding one thousand dollars, and imprisoned for a term not exceeding one year.

SEC. 12. That no Chinese person shall be permitted to enter the United States by land without producing to the proper officer of customs the certificate in this act required of Chinese persons seeking to land from a vessel. And any Chinese person found unlawfully within the United States shall be caused to be removed therefrom to the country from whence he came, by direction of the President of the United States, and at the cost of the United States, after being brought before some justice, judge, or commissioner of a court of the United States and found to be one not lawfully entitled to be or remain in the United States.

SEC. 13. That this act shall not apply to diplomatic and other officers of the Chinese Government traveling upon the business of that government, whose credentials shall be taken as equivalent to the certificate in this act mentioned, and shall exempt them and their body and household servants from the provisions of this act as to other Chinese persons.

SEC. 14. That hereafter no State court or court of the United States shall admit Chinese to citizenship; and all laws in conflict with this act are hereby repealed.

SEC. 15. That the words "Chinese laborers," wherever used in this act shall be construed to mean both skilled and unskilled laborers and Chinese employed in mining.

Approved, May 6, 1882.

The Pendleton Act

AN ACT TO REGULATE AND IMPROVE THE CIVIL SERVICE OF THE UNITED STATES.

Be it enacted by the Senate and House of Representatives of the United States of America in Congress assembled, That the President is authorized to appoint, by and with the advice and consent of the Senate, three persons, not more than two of whom shall be adherents of thc same party, as Civil Service Commissioners, and said three commissioners shall constitute the United States Civil Service Commission. Said commissioners shall hold no other official place under the United States.

The President may remove any commissioner; and any vacancy in the position of commissioner shall be so filled by the President, by and with the advice and consent of the Senate, as to conform to said conditions for the first selection of commissioners.

The commissioners shall each receive a salary of three thousand five hundred dollars a year. And each of said commissioners shall be paid his necessary traveling expenses incurred in the discharge of his duty as a commissioner.

SEC. 2. That it shall be the duty of said commissioners:

FIRST. To aid the President, as he may request, in preparing suitable rules for carrying this act into effect, and when said rules shall have been promulgated it shall be the duty of all officers of the United States in the departments and offices to which any such rules may relate to aid, in all proper ways, in carrying said rules, and any modifications thereof; into effect.

SECOND. And, among other things, said rules shall provide and declare, as nearly as the conditions of good administration will warrant, as follows:

First, for open, competitive examinations for testing the fitness of applicants for the public service now classified or to be classified hereunder. Such examinations shall be practical in their character, and so far as may be shall relate to those matters which will fairly test the relative capacity and fitness of the persons examined to discharge the duties of the service into which they seek to be appointed.

Second, that all the offices, places, and employments so arranged or to be arranged in classes shall be filled by selections according to grade from among those graded highest as the results of such competitive examinations.

Third, appointments to the public service aforesaid in the departments at Washington shall be apportioned among the several States and Territories and the District of Columbia upon the basis of population as ascertained at the last preceding census. Every application for an examination shall contain, among other things, a statement, under oath, setting forth his or her actual bona fide residence at the time of making the application, as well as how long he or she has been a resident of such place.

Fourth, that there shall be a period of probation before any absolute appointment or employment aforesaid.

Fifth, that no person in the public service is for that reason under any obligations to contribute to any political fund, or to render any political service, and that he will not be removed or otherwise prejudiced for refusing to do so.

Sixth, that no person in said service has any right to use his official authority or influence to coerce the political action of any person or body.

Seventh, there shall be non-competitive examinations in all proper cases before the commission, when competent persons do not compete, after notice has been given of the existence of the vacancy, under such rules as may be prescribed by the commissioners as to the manner of giving notice.

Eighth, that notice shall be given in writing by the appointing power to said commission of the persons selected for appointment or employment from among those who have been examined, of the place of residence of such persons, of the rejection of any such persons after probation, of transfers, resignations, and removals and of the date thereof, and a record of the same shall be kept by said commission. And any necessary exceptions from said eight fundamental provisions of the rules shall be set forth in connection with such rules, and the reasons therefor shall be stated in the annual reports of the commission.

THIRD. Said commission shall, subject to the rules that may be made by the President, make regulations for, and have control of, such examinations, and, through its members or the examiners, it shall supervise and preserve the records of the same; and said commission shall keep minutes of its own proceedings.

FOURTH. Said commission may make investigations concerning the facts, and may report upon all matters touching the enforcement and effects of said rules and regulations, and concerning the action of any examiner or board of examiners hereinafter provided for, and its own subordinates, and those in the public service, in respect to the execution of this act.

FIFTH. Said commission shall make an annual report to the President for transmission to Congress, showing its own action, the rules and regulations and the exceptions thereto in force, the practical effects thereof, and any suggestions it may approve for the more effectual accomplishment of the purposes of this act.

SEC. 3. That said commission is authorized to employ a chief examiner, a part of whose duty it shall be, under its direction, to act with the examining boards, so far as practicable, whether at Washington or elsewhere, and to secure accuracy, uniformity, and justice in all their proceedings, which shall be at all times open to him. The chief examiner shall be entitled to receive a salary at the rate of three thousand dollars a year, and he shall be paid his necessary traveling expenses incurred in the discharge of his duty. The commission shall have a secretary, to be appointed by the President, who shall receive a salary of one thousand six hundred dollars per annum. It may, when necessary, employ a stenographer, and a messenger, who shall be paid, when employed, the former at the rate of one thousand six hundred dollars a year, and the latter at the rate of six hundred dollars a year. The commission shall, at Washington, and in one or more places in each State and Territory where examinations are to take place, designate and select a suitable number of persons, not less than three, in the official service of the United States, residing in said State or Territory, after consulting the head of the department or office in which such persons serve, to be members of boards of examiners, and may at any time substitute any other person in said service living in such State or Territory in the place of anyone so selected. Such boards of examiners shall be so located as to make it reasonably convenient and inexpensive for applicants to attend before them; and where there are persons to be examined in any State or Territory, examinations shall be held therein at least twice in each year. It shall be the duty of the collector, postmaster, and other officers of the United States at any place outside of the District of Columbia where examinations are directed by the President or by said board to be held, to allow the reasonable use of the public buildings for holding such examinations, and in all proper ways to facilitate the same.

SEC. 4. That it shall be the duty of the Secretary of the Interior to cause suitable and convenient rooms and accommodations to be assigned or provided, and to be furnished, heated, and lighted, at the city of Washington, for carrying on the work of said commission and said examinations, and to cause the necessary stationery and other articles to be supplied, and the necessary printing to be done for said commission.

SEC. 5. That any said commissioner, examiner, copyist, or messenger, or any person in the public service who shall willfully and corruptly, by himself or in co-operation with one or more other persons, defeat, deceive, or obstruct any person in respect of his or her right of examination according to any such rules or regulations, or who shall willfully, corruptly, and falsely mark, grade, estimate, or report upon the examination or proper standing of any person examined hereunder, or aid in so doing, or who shall willfully and corruptly make any false representations concerning the same or concerning the person examined, or who shall willfully and corruptly furnish to any person any special or secret information for the purpose of either improving or injuring the prospects or chances of any person so examined, or to be examined, being appointed, employed, or promoted, shall for each such offense be deemed guilty of a misdemeanor, and upon conviction thereof, shall be punished by a fine of not less than one hundred dollars, nor more than one thousand dollars, or by imprisonment not less than ten days, nor more than one year, or by both such fine and imprisonment.

SEC. 6. That within sixty days after the passage of this act it shall be the duty of the Secretary of the Treasury, in as near conformity as may be to the classification of certain clerks now existing under the one hundred and sixty-third section of the Revised

Statutes to arrange in classes the several clerks and persons employed by the collector, naval officer, surveyor, and appraisers, or either of them, or being in the public service, at their respective offices in each customs district where the whole number of said clerks and persons shall be all together as many as fifty. And thereafter, from time to time, on the direction of the President, said Secretary shall make the like classification or arrangement of clerks and persons so employed, in connection with any said office or offices, in any other customs district. And, upon like request, and for the purposes of this act, said Secretary shall arrange in one or more of said classes, or of existing classes, any other clerks, agents, or persons employed under his department in any said district not now classified; and every such arrangement and classification upon being made shall be reported to the President.

Second. Within said sixty days it shall be the duty of the Postmaster General, in general conformity to said one hundred and sixty-third section, to separately arrange in classes the several clerks and persons employed, or in the public service at each post office, or under any postmaster of the United States, where the whole number of said clerks and persons shall together amount to as many as fifty. And thereafter, from time to time, on the direction of the President, it shall be the duty of the Postmaster General to arrange in like classes the clerks and persons so employed in the postal service in connection with any other post office; and every such arrangement and classification upon being made shall be reported to the President.

Third. That from time to time said Secretary, the Postmaster General, and each of the heads of departments mentioned in the one hundred and fifty-eighth section of the Revised Statutes, and each head of an office, shall, on the direction of the President, and for facilitating the execution of this act, respectively revise any then existing classification or arrangement of those in their respective departments and offices, and shall, for the purposes of the examination herein provided for, include in one or more of such classes, so far as practicable, subordinate places, clerks, and officers in the public service pertaining to their respective departments not before classified for examination.

SEC. 7. That after the expiration of six months from the passage of this act no officer or clerk shall be appointed, and no person shall be employed to enter or be promoted in either of the said classes now existing, or that may be arranged hereunder pursuant to said rules, until he has passed an examination, or is shown to be specially exempted from such examination in conformity herewith. But nothing herein contained shall be construed to take from those honorably discharged from the military or naval service any preference conferred by the seventeen hundred and fifty-fourth section of the Revised Statutes, nor to take from the President any authority not inconsistent with this act conferred by the seventeen hundred and fifty-third section of said statutes; nor shall any officer not in the executive branch of the government, or any person merely employed as a laborer or workman, be required to be classified hereunder; nor, unless by direction of the Senate, shall any person who has been nominated for confirmation by the Senate be required to be classified or to pass an examination.

SEC. 8. That no person habitually using intoxicating beverages to excess shall be appointed to, or retained in, any office, appointment, or employment to which the provisions of this act are applicable.

SEC. 9. That whenever there are already two or more members of a family in the public service in the grades covered by this act, no other member of such family shall be eligible to appointment to any of said grades.

SEC. 10. That no recommendation of any person who shall apply for office or place under the provisions of this act which may be given by any Senator or member of the House of Representatives, except as to the character or residence of the applicant, shall be received or considered by any person concerned in making any examination or appointment under this act.

SEC. 11. That no Senator, or Representative, or Territorial Delegate of the Congress, or Senator, Representative, or Delegate elect, or any officer or employee of either of said houses, and no executive, judicial, military, or naval officer of the United States, and no clerk or employee of any department, branch or bureau of the executive, judicial, or military or naval service of the United States, shall, directly or indirectly, solicit or receive, or be in any manner concerned ill soliciting or receiving, any assessment, subscription, or contribution for any political purpose whatever, from any officer, clerk, or employee of the United States, or any department, branch, or bureau thereof, or from any person receiving any salary or compensation from moneys derived from the Treasury of the United States.

SEC. 12. That no person shall, in any room or building occupied in the discharge of official duties by any officer or employee of the United States mentioned in this act, or in any navy yard, fort, or arsenal, solicit in any manner whatever, or receive any contribution of money or any other thing of value for any political purpose whatever.

SEC. 13. No officer or employee of the United States mentioned in this act shall discharge, or promote, or degrade, or in manner change the official rank or compensation of any other officer or employee, or promise or threaten so to do, for giving or withholding or neglecting to make any contribution of money or other valuable thing for any political purpose.

SEC. 14. That no officer, clerk, or other person in the service of the United States shall, directly or indirectly, give or hand over to any other officer, clerk, or person in the service of the United States, or to any Senator or Member of the House of Representatives, or Territorial Delegate, any money or other valuable thing on account of or to be applied to the promotion of any political object whatever.

SEC. 15. That any person who shall be guilty of violating any provision of the four foregoing sections shall be deemed guilty of a misdemeanor, and shall, on conviction thereof, be punished by a fine not exceeding five thousand dollars, or by imprisonment for a term not exceeding three years, or by such fine and imprisonment both, in the discretion of the court.

Approved, January sixteenth, 1883.

The Interstate Commerce Act

FORTY-NINTH CONGRESS OF THE UNITED STATES OF AMERICA; AT THE SECOND SESSION, BEGUN AND HELD AT THE CITY OF WASHINGTON ON MONDAY, THE SIXTH DAY OF DECEMBER, ONE THOUSAND EIGHT HUNDRED AND EIGHTY-SIX

AN ACT TO REGULATE COMMERCE.

Be it enacted by the Senate and House of Representatives of the United States of America in Congress assembled, That the provisions of this act shall apply to any common carrier or carriers engaged in the transportation of passengers or property wholly by railroad, or partly by railroad and partly by water when both are used, under a common control, management, or arrangement, for a continuous carriage or shipment, from one State or Territory of the United States, or the District of Columbia, to any other State or Territory of the United States, or the District of Columbia, or from any place in the United States to an adjacent foreign country, or from any place in the United States through a foreign country to any other place in the United States, and also to the transportation in like manner of property shipped from any place in the United States to a foreign country and carried from such place to a port of trans-shipment, or shipped from a foreign country to any place in the United States and carried to such place from a port of entry either in the United States or an adjacent foreign country: *Provided, however,* That the provisions of this act shall not apply to the transportation of passengers or property, or to the receiving, delivering, storage, or handling of property, wholly within one State, and not shipped to or from a foreign country from or to any State or Territory as aforesaid.

The term "railroad" as used in this act shall include all bridges and ferries used or operated in connection with any railroad, and also all the road in use by any corporation operating a railroad, whether owned or operated under a contract, agreement, or lease; and the term "transportation" shall include all instrumentalities of shipment or carriage.

All charges made for any service rendered or to be rendered in the transportation of passengers or property as aforesaid, or in connection therewith, or for the receiving, delivering, storage, or handling of such property, shall be reasonable and just; and every unjust and unreasonable charge for such service is prohibited and declared to be unlawful.

Sec. 2. That if any common carrier subject to the provisions of this act shall, directly or indirectly, by any special rate, rebate, drawback, or other device, charge, demand, collect, or receive from any person or persons a greater or less compensation for any service rendered, or to be rendered, in the transportation of passengers or property, subject to the provisions of this act, than it charges, demands, collects, or receives from any other person or persons for doing for him or them a like and contemporaneous service in the transportation of a like kind of traffic under substantially similar circumstances and conditions, such common carrier shall be deemed guilty of unjust discrimination, which is hereby prohibited and declared to be unlawful.

Sec. 3. That it shall be unlawful for any common carrier subject to the provisions of this act to make or give any undue or unreasonable preference or advantage to any particular person, company, firm, corporation, or locality, or any particular description of traffic, in any respect whatsoever, or to subject any particular person, company, firm, corporation, or locality, or any particular description of traffic, to any undue or unreasonable prejudice or disadvantage in any respect whatsoever.

Every common carrier subject to the provisions of this act shall according to their respective powers, afford all reasonable, proper, and equal facilities for the interchange of traffic between their respective lines, and for the receiving, forwarding, and delivering of passengers and property to and from their several lines and those connection therewith, and shall not discriminate in their rates and charges between such connecting lines; but this shall not be construed as requiring any such common carrier to give the use of its tracks or terminal facilities to another carrier engaged in like business.

Sec. 4. That it shall be unlawful for any common carrier subject to the provisions of this act to charge or receive any greater compensation in the aggregate for the transportation of passengers or of like kind of property, under substantially similar circumstances and conditions, for a shorter than for a longer distance over the same line, in the same direction, the shorter being included within the longer distance; but this shall not be construed as authorizing any common carrier within the terms of this act to charge and receive as great compensation for a shorter as for a longer distance: *Provided, however,* That upon application to the Commission appointed under the provisions of this act, such common carrier may, in special cases, after investigation by the Commission, be authorized to charge less for longer than for shorter distances for the transportation of passengers or property; and the Commission may from time to time prescribe the extent to which such designated common carrier may be relieved from the operation of this section of this act.

Sec. 5. That it shall be unlawful for any common carrier subject to the provisions of this act to enter into any contract, agreement, or combination with any other common carrier or carriers for the pooling of freights of different and competing railroads, or to divide between them the aggregate or net proceeds of the earnings of such railroads, or any portion thereof; and in any case of an agreement for the pooling of freights as aforesaid, each day of its continuance shall be deemed a separate offense.

Sec. 6. That every common carrier subject to the provisions of this act shall print and keep for public inspection schedules showing the rates and fares and charges for the transportation of passengers and property which any such common carrier has established and which are in force at the time upon its railroad, as defined by the first section of this act. The schedules printed as aforesaid by any such common carrier shall plainly state the places upon its railroad between which property and passengers will be carried, and shall contain the classification of freight in force upon such railroad, and shall also state separately the terminal charges and any rules or regulations which in any wise change, affect, or determine any part or the aggregate of such aforesaid rates and fares and charges. Such schedules shall be plainly printed in large type, of at least the size of ordinary pica, and copies for the use of the public shall be kept in every depot or station upon any such railroad, in such places and in such form that they can be conveniently inspected.

Any common carrier subject to the provisions of this act receiving freight in the United States to be carried through a foreign country to any place in the United States shall also in like manner print and keep for public inspection, at every depot where such freight is received for shipment, schedules showing the through rates established and charged by such common carrier to all points in the United States beyond the foreign country to which it accepts freight for shipment; and any freight shipped from the United States through a foreign country into the United States, the through rate on which shall not have been made public as required by this act, shall, before it is admitted into the United States from said foreign country, be subject to customs duties as if said freight were of foreign production; and any law in conflict with this section is hereby repealed.

No advance shall be made in the rates, fares, and charges which have been established and published as aforesaid by any common carrier in compliance with the requirements of this section, except after ten days' public notice, which shall plainly state the changes proposed to be made in the schedule then in force, and the time when the increased rates, fares, or charges will go into effect; and the proposed changes shall be shown by printing new schedules, or shall be plainly indicated upon the schedules in force at the time and kept for public inspection. Reductions in such published rates, fares, or charges may be made without previous public notice; but whenever any such reduction is made, notice of the same shall immediately be publicly posted and the changes made shall immediately be made public by printing new schedules, or shall immediately be plainly indicated upon the schedules at the time in force and kept for public inspection.

And when any such common carrier shall have established and published its rates, fares, and charges in compliance with the provisions of this section, it shall be unlawful for such common carrier to charge, demand, collect, or receive from any person or persons a greater or less compensation for the transportation of passengers or property, or for any services in connection therewith, than is specified in such published schedule of rates, fares, and charges as may at the time be in force.

Every common carrier subject to the provisions of this act shall file with the Commission hereinafter provided for copies of its schedules of rates, fares, and charges which have been established and published in compliance with the requirements of this section, and shall promptly notify said Commission of all changes made in the same. Every such common carrier shall also file with said Commission copies of all contracts, agreements, or arrangements with other common carriers in relation to any traffic affected by the provisions of this act to which it may be a party. And in cases where passengers and freight pass over continuous lines or routes operated by more than one common carrier, and the several common carriers operating such lines or routes establish joint tariffs of rates or fares or charges for such continuous lines or routes, copies of such joint tariffs shall also, in like manner, be filed with said Commission. Such joint rates, fares, and charges on such continuous lines so filed as aforesaid shall be made public by such common carriers when directed by said Commission, in so far as may, in the judgment of the Commission, be deemed practicable; and said Commission shall from time to time prescribe the measure of publicity which shall be given to such rates, fares, and charges, or to such part of them as it may deem it practicable for such common carriers to publish, and the places in which they shall be published; but no common carrier party to any such joint tariff shall be liable for the failure of any other common carrier party thereto to observe and adhere to the rates, fares, or charges thus made and published.

If any such common carrier shall neglect or refuse to file or publish its schedules or tariffs of rates, fares, and charges as provided in this section, or any part of the same, such common carrier shall, in addition to other penalties herein prescribed, be subject to a writ of mandamus, to be issued by any circuit court of the United States in the judicial district wherein the principal office of said common carrier is situated or wherein such offense may be committed, and if such common carrier be a foreign corporation, in the judicial circuit wherein such common carrier accepts traffic and has an agent to perform such service, to compel compliance with the aforesaid provisions of this section; and such writ shall issue in the name of the people of the United States, at the relation of the Commissioners appointed under the provisions of this act; and failure to comply with its requirements shall be punishable as and for a contempt; and the said Commissioners, as complainants, may also apply, in any such circuit of the United States, for a writ of injunction against such common carrier, to restrain such common carrier from receiving or transporting property among the several States and Territories of the United States, or between the United States and adjacent foreign countries, or between ports of transshipment and of entry and the several States and Territories of the United States, as mentioned in the first section of this act, until such common carrier shall have complied with the aforesaid provisions of this section of this act.

Sec. 7. That it shall be unlawful for any common carrier subject to the provisions of this act to enter into any combination, contract, or agreement, expressed or implied, to prevent, by change of time schedule, carriage in different cars, or by other means or devices, the carriage of freights from being continuous from the place of shipment to the place of destination; and no break of bulk, stoppage, or interruption made by such common carrier shall prevent the carriage of freights from being and being treated as one continuous carriage from the place of shipment to the place of destination, unless such break, stoppage, or interruption was made in good faith for some necessary purpose, and without any intent to avoid or unnecessarily interrupt such continuous carriage or to evade any of the provisions of this act.

Sec. 8. That in case any common carrier subject to the provisions of this act shall do, cause to be done, or permit to be done any act, matter, or thing in this act prohibited or declared to be unlawful, or shall omit to do any act, matter, or thing in this act required to be done, such common carrier shall be liable to the person or persons injured thereby for the full amount of damages sustained in consequence of any such violation of the provisions of this act, together with a reasonable counsel or attorney's fee, to be fixed by the court in every case of recovery, which attorney's fee shall be taxed and collected as part of the costs in the case.

Sec. 9. That any person or persons claiming to be damaged by any common carrier subject to the provisions of this act may either make complaint to the Commission as hereinafter provided for, or may bring suit in his or their own behalf for the recovery of the damages for which such common carrier may be liable under the provisions of this act, in any district or circuit court of the United States of competent jurisdiction; but such person or persons shall not have the right to pursue both of said remedies, and must in each case elect which one of the two methods of procedure herein provided for he or they will adopt. In any such action brought for the recovery of damages the court before which the same shall be pending may compel any director, officer, receiver, trustee, or agent of the corporation or company defendant in such suit to attend, appear, and testify in such case, and may compel the production of the books and papers of such corporation or company party to any such suit; the claim that any such testimony or evidence may tend to criminate the person giving such evidence shall not excuse such witness from testifying, but such evidence or testimony shall not be used against such person on the trial of any criminal proceeding.

Sec. 10. That any common carrier subject to the provisions of this act, or, whenever such common carrier is a corporation, any director or officer thereof, or any receiver, trustee, lessee, agent, or person acting for or employed by such corporation, who, alone or with any other corporation, company, person, or party, shall willfully do or cause to be done, or shall willingly suffer or permit to be done, any act, matter, or thing in this act prohibited or declared to be unlawful, or who shall aid or abet therein, or shall willfully omit or fail to do any act, matter, or thing in this act required to be done, or shall cause or willingly suffer or permit any act, matter, or thing so directed or required by this act to be done not to be so done, or shall aid or abet any such omission or failure, or shall be guilty of any infraction of this act, or shall aid or abet therein, shall be deemed guilty of a misdemeanor, and shall, upon conviction thereof in any district court of the United States within the jurisdiction of which such offense was committed, be subject to a fine of not to exceed five thousand dollars for each offense.

Sec. 11. That a Commission is hereby created and established to be known as the Inter-State Commerce Commission, which shall be composed of five Commissioners, who shall be appointed by the President, by and with the advice and consent of the Senate. The Commissioners first appointed under this act shall continue in office for the term of two, three, four, five, and six years, respectively, from the first day of January, anno Domini eighteen hundred and eighty-seven, the term of each to be designated by the President; but their successors shall be appointed for terms of six years, except that any person chosen to fill a vacancy shall be appointed only for the unexpired term of the Commissioner whom he shall succeed. Any Commissioner may be removed by the President for inefficiency, neglect of duty, or malfeasance in office. Not more than three of the Commissioners shall be appointed from the same political party. No person in the employ of or holding any official relation to any common carrier subject to the provisions of this act, or owning stock or bonds thereof, or who is in any manner pecuniarily inter-

ested therein, shall enter upon the duties of or hold such office. Said Commissioners shall not engage in any other business, vocation, or employment. No vacancy in the Commission shall impair the right of the remaining Commissioners to exercise all the powers of the Commission.

Sec. 12. That the Commission hereby created shall have authority to inquire into the management of the business of all common carriers subject to the provisions of this act, and shall keep itself informed as to the manner and method in which the same is conducted, and shall have the right to obtain from such common carriers full and complete information necessary to enable the Commission to perform the duties and carry out the objects for which it was created; and for the purposes of this act the Commission shall have power to require the attendance and testimony of witnesses and the production of all books, papers, tariffs, contracts, agreements, and documents relating to any matter under investigation, and to that end may invoke the aid of any court of the United States in requiring the attendance and testimony of witnesses and the production of books, papers, and documents under the provisions of this section.

And any of the circuit courts of the United States within the jurisdiction of which such inquiry is carried on may, in case of contumacy or refusal to obey a subpoena issued to any common carrier subject to the provisions of this act, or other person, issue an order requiring such common carrier or other person to appear before said Commission (and produce books and papers if so ordered) and give evidence touching the matter in question; and any failure to obey such order of the court may be punished by such court as a contempt thereof. The claim that any such testimony or evidence may tend to criminate the person giving such evidence shall not excuse such witness from testifying; but such evidence or testimony shall not be used against such person on the trial of any criminal proceeding.

Sec. 13. That any person, firm, corporation, or association, or any mercantile, agricultural, or manufacturing society, or any body politic or municipal organization complaining of anything done or omitted to be done by any common carrier subject to the provisions of this act in contravention of the provisions thereof, may apply to said Commission by petition, which shall briefly state the facts; whereupon a statement of the charges thus made shall be forwarded by the Commission to such common carrier, who shall be called upon to satisfy the complaint or to answer the same in writing within a reasonable time, to be specified by the Commission. If such common carrier, within the time specified, shall make reparation for the injury alleged to have been done, said carrier shall be relieved of liability to the complainant only for the particular violation of law thus complained of. If such carrier shall not satisfy the complaint within the time specified, or there shall appear to be any reasonable ground for investigating said complaint, it shall be the duty of the Commission to investigate the matters complained of in such manner and by such means as it shall deem proper.

Said Commission shall in like manner investigate any complaint forwarded by the railroad commissioner or railroad commission of any State or Territory, at the request of such commissioner or commission, and may institute any inquiry on its own motion in the same manner and to the same effect as though complaint had been made.

No complaint shall at any time be dismissed because of the absence of direct damage to the complainant.

Sec. 14. That whenever an investigation shall be made by said Commission, it shall be its duty to make a report in writing in respect thereto, which shall include the findings of fact upon which the conclusions of the Commission are based, together with its recommendation as to what reparation, if any, should be made by the common carrier to any party or parties who may be found to have been injured; and such findings so made shall thereafter, in all judicial proceedings, be deemed prima facie evidence as to each and every fact found.

All reports of investigations made by the Commission shall be entered of record, and a copy thereof shall be furnished to the party who may have complained, and to any common carrier that may have been complained of.

Sec. 15. That if in any case in which an investigation shall be made by said Commission it shall be made to appear to the satisfaction of the Commission, either by the testimony of witnesses or other evidence, that anything has been done or omitted to be done in violation of the provisions of this act, or of any law cognizable by said Commission, by any common carrier, or that any injury or damage has been sustained by the party or parties complaining, or by other parties aggrieved in consequence of any

such violation, it shall be the duty of the Commission to forthwith cause a copy of its report in respect thereto to be delivered to such common carrier, together with a notice to said common carrier to cease and desist from such violation, or to make reparation for the injury so found to have been done, or both, within a reasonable time, to be specified by the Commission; and if, within the time specified, it shall be made to appear to the Commission that such common carrier has ceased from such violation of law, and has made reparation for the injury found to have been done, in compliance with the report and notice of the Commission, or to the satisfaction of the party complaining, a statement to that effect shall be entered of record by the Commission, and the said common carrier shall thereupon be relieved from further liability or penalty for such particular violation of law.

Sec. 16. That whenever any common carrier, as defined in and subject to the provisions of this act, shall violate or refuse or neglect to obey any lawful order or requirement of the Commission in this act named, it shall be the duty of the Commission, and lawful for any company or person interested in such order or requirement, to apply, in a summary way, by petition, to the circuit court of the United States sitting in equity in the judicial district in which the common carrier complained of has its principal office, or in which the violation or disobedience of such order or requirement shall happen, alleging such violation or disobedience, as the case may be; and the said court shall have power to hear and determine the matter, on such short notice to the common carrier complained of as the court shall deem reasonable; and such notice may be served on such common carrier, his or its officers, agents, or servants, in such manner as the court shall direct; and said court shall proceed to hear and determine the matter speedily as a court of equity, and without the formal pleadings and proceedings applicable to ordinary suits in equity, but in such manner as to do justice in the premises; and to this end such court shall have power, if it think fit, to direct and prosecute, in such mode and by such persons as it may appoint, all such inquiries as the court may think needful to enable it to form a just judgment in the matter of such petition; and on such hearing the report of said Commission shall be prima facie evidence of the matters therein stated; and if it be made to appear to such court, on such hearing or on report of any such person or persons, that the lawful order or requirement of said Commission drawn in question has been violated or disobeyed, it shall be lawful for such court to issue a writ of injunction or other proper process, mandatory or otherwise, to restrain such common carrier from further continuing such violation or disobedience of such order or requirement of said Commission, and enjoining obedience to the same; and in case of any disobedience of any such writ of injunction or other proper process, mandatory or otherwise, it shall be lawful for such court to issue writs of attachment, or any other process of said court incident or applicable to writs of injunction or other proper process, mandatory or otherwise, against such common carrier, and if a corporation, against one or more of the directors, officers, or agents of the same, or against any owner, lessee, trustee, receiver, or other person failing to obey such writ of injunction or other proper process, mandatory or otherwise; and said court may, if it shall think fit, make an order directing such common carrier or other person so disobeying such writ of injunction or other proper process, mandatory or otherwise, to pay such sum of money not exceeding for each carrier or person in default the sum of five hundred dollars for every day after a day to be named in the order that such carrier or other person shall fail to obey such injunction or other proper process, mandatory or otherwise; and such moneys shall be payable as the court shall direct, either to the party complaining, or into court to abide the ultimate decision of the court, or into the Treasury; and payment thereof may, without prejudice to any other mode of recovering the same, be enforced by attachment or order in the nature of a writ of execution, in like manner as if the same had been recovered by a final decree in personam in such court. When the subject in dispute shall be of the value of two thousand dollars or more, either party to such proceeding before said court may appeal to the Supreme Court of the United States, under the same regulations now provided by law in respect of security for such appeal; but such appeal shall not operate to stay or supersede the order of the court or the execution of any writ or process thereon; and such court may, in every such matter, order the payment of such costs and counsel fees as shall be deemed reasonable. Whenever any such petition shall be filed or presented by the Commission it shall be the duty of the district attorney, under the direction of the Attorney General of the United States, to prosecute the same; and the costs and expenses of such prosecution shall be paid out of the appropriation for the expenses of the courts of the United States. For the purposes of this act, excepting its penal provisions, the circuit courts of the United States shall be deemed to be always in session.

Sec. 17. That the Commission may conduct its proceedings in such manner as will best conduce to the proper dispatch of business and to the ends of justice. A majority of the Commission shall constitute a quorum for the transaction of business, but no Commissioner shall participate in any hearing or proceeding in which he has any pecuniary interest. Said Commission may, from time to time, make or amend such general rules or orders as may be requisite for the order and regulation of proceedings before it, including forms of notices and the service thereof, which shall conform, as nearly as may be, to those in use in the courts of the United States. Any party may appear before said Commission and be heard, in person or by attorney. Every vote and official act of the Commission shall be entered of record, and its proceedings shall be public upon the request of either party interested. Said Commission shall have an official seal, which shall be judicially noticed. Either of the members of the Commission may administer oaths and affirmations.

Sec. 18. That each Commissioner shall receive an annual salary of seven thousand five hundred dollars, payable in the same manner as the salaries of judges of the courts of the United States. The Commission shall appoint a secretary, who shall receive an annual salary of three thousand five hundred dollars, payable in like manner. The Commission shall have authority to employ and fix the compensation of such other employees as it may find necessary to the proper performance of its duties, subject to the approval of the Secretary of the Interior.

The Commission shall be furnished by the Secretary of the Interior with suitable offices and all necessary office supplies. Witnesses summoned before the Commission shall be paid the same fees and mileage that are paid witnesses in the courts of the United States.

All of the expenses of the Commission, including all necessary expenses for transportation incurred by the Commissioners, or by their employees under their orders, in making any investigation in any other places than in the city of Washington, shall be allowed and paid, on the presentation of itemized vouchers therefor approved by the chairman of the Commission and the Secretary of the Interior.

Sec. 19. That the principal office of the Commission shall be in the city of Washington, where its general sessions shall be held; but whenever the convenience of the public or of the parties may be promoted or delay or expense prevented thereby, the Commission may hold special sessions in any part of the United States. It may, by one or more of the Commissioners, prosecute any inquiry necessary to its duties, in any part of the United States, into any matter or question of fact pertaining to the business of any common carrier subject to the provisions of this act.

Sec. 20. That the Commission is hereby authorized to require annual reports from all common carriers subject to the provisions of this act, to fix the time and prescribe the manner in which such reports shall be made, and to require from such carriers specific answers to all questions upon which the Commission may need information. Such annual reports shall show in detail the amount of capital stock issued, the amounts paid therefor, and the manner of payment for the same; the dividends paid, the surplus fund, if any, and the number of stockholders; the funded and floating debts and the interest paid thereon; the cost and value of the carrier's property, franchises, and equipment; the number of employees and the salaries paid each class; the amounts expended for improvements each year, how expended, and the character of such improvements; the earnings and receipts from each branch of business and from all sources; the operating and other expenses; the balances of profit and loss; and a complete exhibit of the financial operations of the carrier each year, including an annual balance sheet. Such reports shall also contain such information in relation to rates or regulations concerning fares or freights, or agreements, arrangements, or contracts with other common carriers, as the Commission may require; and the said Commission may, within its discretion, for the purpose of enabling it the better to carry out the purposes of this act, prescribe (if in the opinion of the Commission it is practicable to prescribe such uniformity and methods of keeping accounts) a period of time within which all common carriers subject to the provisions of this act shall have, as near as may be, a uniform system of accounts, and the manner in which such accounts shall be kept.

Sec. 21. That the Commission shall, on or before the first day of December in each year, make a report to the Secretary of the Interior, which shall be by him transmitted to Congress, and copies of which shall be distributed as are the other reports issued from the Interior Department. This report shall contain such information and data collected by the Commission as may be considered of value in the determination of questions connected with the regulation of commerce, together with such recommendations as to additional legislation relating thereto as the Commission may deem necessary.

Sec. 22. That nothing in this act shall apply to the carriage, storage, or handling of property free or at reduced rates for the United States, State, or municipal governments, or for charitable purposes, or to or from fairs and expositions for exhibition thereat, or the issuance of mileage, excursion, or commutation passenger tickets; nothing in this act shall be construed to prohibit any common carrier from giving reduced rates to ministers of religion; nothing in this act shall be construed to prevent railroads from giving free carriage to their own officers and employees, or to prevent the principal officers of any railroad company or companies from exchanging passes or tickets with other railroad companies for their officers and employees; and nothing in this act contained shall in any way abridge or alter the remedies now existing at common law or by statute, but the provisions of this act are in addition to such remedies: *Provided*, That no pending litigation shall in any way be affected by this act.

Sec. 23. That the sum of one hundred thousand dollars is hereby appropriated for the use and purposes of this act for the fiscal year ending June thirtieth, anno Domini eighteen hundred and eighty-eight, and the intervening time anterior thereto.

Sec. 24. That the provisions of sections eleven and eighteen of this act, relating to the appointment and organization of the Commission herein provided for, shall take effect immediately, and the remaining provisions of this act shall take effect sixty days after its passage.

Approved, February 4, 1887.

[Endorsements]

The Dawes Act

FORTY-NINTH CONGRESS OF THE UNITED STATES OF AMERICA; AT THE SECOND SESSION,

Begun and held at the City of Washington on Monday, the sixth day of December, one thousand eight hundred and eight-six.

An Act to provide for the allotment of lands in severalty to Indians on the various reservations, and to extend the protection of the laws of the United States and the Territories over the Indians, and for other purposes.

Be it enacted by the Senate and House of Representatives of the United States of America in Congress assembled, That in all cases where any tribe or band of Indians has been, or shall hereafter be, located upon any reservation created for their use, either by treaty stipulation or by virtue of an act of Congress or executive order setting apart the same for their use, the President of the United States be, and he hereby is, authorized, whenever in his opinion any reservation or any part thereof of such Indians is advantageous for agricultural and grazing purposes, to cause said reservation, or any part thereof, to be surveyed, or resurveyed if necessary, and to allot the lands in said reservation in severalty to any Indian located thereon in quantities as follows:

To each head of a family, one-quarter of a section;

To each single person over eighteen years of age, one-eighth of a section;

To each orphan child under eighteen years of age, one-eighth of a section; and

To each other single person under eighteen years now living, or who may be born prior to the date of the order of the President directing an allotment of the lands embraced in any reservation, one-sixteenth of a section:

Provided, That in case there is not sufficient land in any of said reservations to allot lands to each individual of the classes above named in quantities as above provided, the lands embraced in such reservation or reservations shall be allotted to each individual of each of said classes pro rata in accordance with the provisions of this act: And provided further,

That where the treaty or act of Congress setting apart such reservation provides the allotment of lands in severalty in quantities in excess of those herein provided, the President, in making allotments upon such reservation, shall allot the lands to each individual Indian belonging thereon in quantity as specified in such treaty or act: And provided further, That when the lands allotted are only valuable for grazing purposes, an additional allotment of such grazng lands, in quantities as above provided, shall be made to each individual.

Sec. 2. That all allotments set apart under the provisions of this act shall be selected by the Indians, heads of families selecting for their minor children, and the agents shall select for each orphan child, and in such manner as to embrace the improvements of the Indians making the selection where the improvements of two or more Indians have been made on the same legal subdivision of land, unless they shall otherwise agree, a provisional line may be run dividing said lands between them, and the amount to which each is entitled shall be equalized in the assignment of the remainder of the land to which they are entitled under his act: Provided, That if any one entitled to an allotment shall fail to make a selection within four years after the President shall direct that allotments may be made on a particular reservation, the Secretary of the Interior may direct the agent of such tribe or band, if such there be, and if there be no agent, then a special agent appointed for that purpose, to make a selection for such Indian, which selection shall be allotted as in cases where selections are made by the Indians, and patents shall issue in like manner.

Sec. 3. That the allotments provided for in this act shall be made by special agents appointed by the President for such purpose, and the agents in charge of the respective reservations on which the allotments are directed to be made, under such rules and regulations as the Secretary of the Interior may from time to time prescribe, and shall be certified by such agents to the Commissioner of Indian Affairs, in duplicate, one copy to be retained in the Indian Office and the other to be transmitted to the Secretary of the Interior for his action, and to be deposited in the General Land Office.

Sec. 4. That where any Indian not residing upon a reservation, or for whose tribe no reservation has been provided by treaty, act of Congress, or executive order, shall make settlement upon any surveyed or unsurveyed lands of the United States not otherwise appropriated, he or she shall be entitled, upon application to the local land office for the district in which the lands are located, to have the same allotted to him or her, and to his or her children, in quantities and manner as provided in this act for Indians residing upon reservations; and when such settlement is made upon unsurveyed lands, the grant to such Indians shall be adjusted upon the survey of the lands so as to conform thereto; and patents shall be issued to them for such lands in the manner and with the restrictions as herein provided. And the fees to which the officers of such local land office would have been entitled had such lands been entered under the general laws for the disposition of the public lands shall be paid to them, from any moneys in the Treasury of the United States not otherwise appropriated, upon a statement of an account in their behalf for such fees by the Commissioner of the General Land Office, and a certification of such account to the Secretary of the Treasury by the Secretary of the Interior.

Sec. 5. That upon the approval of the allotments provided for in this act by the Secretary of the Interior, he shall cause patents to issue therefor in the name of the allottees, which patents shall be of the legal effect, and declare that the United States does and will hold the land thus allotted, for the period of twenty-five years, in trust for the sole use and benefit of the Indian to whom such allotment shall have been made, or, in case of his decease, of his heirs according to the laws of the State or Territory where such land is located, and that at the expiration of said period the United States will convey the same by patent to said Indian, or his heirs as aforesaid, in fee, discharged of said trust and free of all charge or incumbrance whatsoever: Provided, That the President of the United States may in any case in his discretion extend the period. And if any conveyance shall be made of the lands set apart and allotted as herein provided, or any contract made touching the same, before the expiration of the time above mentioned, such conveyance or contract shall be absolutely null and void: Provided, That the law of de-

scent and partition in force in the State or Territory where such lands are situate shall apply thereto after patents therefor have been executed and delivered, except as herein otherwise provided; and the laws of the State of Kansas regulating the descent and partition of real estate shall, so far as practicable, apply to all lands in the Indian Territory which may be allotted in severalty under the provisions of this act: And provided further, That at any time after lands have been allotted to all the Indians of any tribe as herein provided, or sooner if in the opinion of the President it shall be for the best interests of said tribe, it shall be lawful for the Secretary of the Interior to negotiate with such Indian tribe for the purchase and release by said tribe, in conformity with the treaty or statute under which such reservation is held, of such portions of its reservation not allotted as such tribe shall, from time to time, consent to sell, on such terms and conditions as shall be considered just and equitable between the United States and said tribe of Indians, which purchase shall not be complete until ratified by Congress, and the form and manner of executing such release prescribed by Congress: Provided however, That all lands adapted to agriculture, with or without irrigation so sold or released to the United States by any Indian tribe shall be held by the United States for the sale purpose of securing homes to actual settlers and shall be disposed of by the United States to actual and bona fide settlers only tracts not exceding one hundred and sixty acres to any one person, on such terms as Congress shall prescribe, subject to grants which Congress may make in aid of education: And provided further, That no patents shall issue therefor except to the person so taking the same as and homestead, or his heirs, and after the expiration of five years occupancy therof as such homestead; and any conveyance of said lands taken as a homestead, or any contract touching the same, or lieu thereon, created prior to the date of such patent, shall be null and void. And the sums agreed to be paid by the United States as purchase money for any portion of any such reservation shall be held in the Treasury of the United States for the sole use of the tribe or tribes Indians; to whom such reservations belonged; and the same, with interest thereon at three per cent per annum, shall be at all times subject to appropriation by Congress for the education and civilization of such tribe or tribes of Inians or the members thereof. The patents aforesaid shall be recorded in the General Land Office, and afterward delivered, free of charge, to the allottee entitled thereto. And if any religious society or other organization is now occupying any of the public lands to which this act is applicable, for religious or educational work among the Indians, the Secretary of the Interior is hereby authorized to confirm such occupation to such society or organization, in quantity not exceeding one hundred and sixty acres in any one tract, so long as the same shall be so occupied, on such terms as he shall deem just; but nothing herein contained shall change or alter any claim of such society for religious or educational purposes heretofore granted by law. And hereafter in the employment of Indian police, or any other employes in the public service among any of the Indian tribes or bands affected by this act, and where Indians can perform the duties required, those Indians who have availed themselves of the provisions of this act and become citizens of the United States shall be preferred.

Sec. 6. That upon the completion of said allotments and the patenting of the lands to said allottees, each and every number of the respective bands or tribes of Indians to whom allotments have been made shall have the benefit of and be subject to the laws, both civil and criminal, of the State or Territory in which they may reside; and no Territory shall pass or enforce any law denying any such Indian within its jurisdiction the equal protection of the law. And every Indian born within the territorial limits of the United States to whom allotments shall have been made under the provisions of this act, or under any law or treaty, and every Indian born within the territorial limits of the United States who has voluntarily taken up, within said limits, his residence separate and apart from any tribe of Indians therein, and has adopted the habits of civilized life, is hereby declared to be a citizen of the United States, and is entitled to all the rights, privileges, and immunities of such citizens, whether said Indian has been or not, by birth or otherwise, a member of any tribe of Indians within the territorial limits of the United States without in any manner affecting the right of any such Indian to tribal or other property.

Sec. 7. That in cases where the use of water for irrigation is necessary to render the lands within any Indian reservation available for agricultural purposes, the Secretary of the Interior be, and he is hereby, authorized to prescribe such rules and regulations as he may deem necessary to secure a just and equal distribution thereof among the Indians residing upon any such reservation; and no other appropriation or grant of water by any riparian proprietor shall permitted to the damage of any other riparian proprietor.

Sec. 8. That the provisions of this act shall not extend to the territory occupied by the Cherokees, Creeks, Choctaws, Chickasaws, Seminoles, and Osage, Miamies and Peorias, and Sacs and Foxes, in the Indian Territory, nor to any of the reservations of the Seneca Nation of New York Indians in the State of New York, nor to that strip of territory in the State of Nebraska adjoining the Sioux Nation on the south added by executive order.

Sec. 9. That for the purpose of making the surveys and resurveys mentioned in section two of this act, there be, and hereby is, appropriated, out of any moneys in the Treasury not otherwise appropriated, the sum of one hundred thousand dollars, to be repaid proportionately out of the proceeds of the sales of such land as may be acquired from the Indians under the provisions of this act.

Sec. 10. That nothing in this act contained shall be so canstrued to affect the right and power of Congress to grant the right of way through any lands granted to an Indian, or a tribe of Indians, for railroads or other highways, or telegraph lines, for the public use, or condemn such lands to public uses, upon making just compensation.

Sec. 11. That nothing in this act shall be so construed as to prevent the removal of the Southern Ute Indians from their present reservation in Southwestern Colorado to a new reservation by and with consent of a majority of the adult male members of said tribe.

Approved, February, 8, 1887.

[Endorsements]

The Sherman Anti-Trust Act

FIFTY-FIRST CONGRESS OF THE UNITED STATES OF AMERICA, AT THE FIRST SESSION, BEGUN AND HELD AT THE CITY OF WASHINGTON ON MONDAY, THE SECOND DAY OF DECEMBER, ONE THOUSAND EIGHT HUNDRED AND EIGHTY-NINE.

AN ACT TO PROTECT TRADE AND COMMERCE AGAINST UNLAWFUL RESTRAINTS AND MONOPOLIES.

Be it enacted by the Senate and House of Representatives of the United States of America in Congress assembled,

Sec. 1. Every contract, combination in the form of trust or otherwise, or conspiracy, in restraint of trade or commerce among the several States, or with foreign nations, is hereby declared to be illegal. Every person who shall make any such contract or engage in any such combination or conspiracy, shall be deemed guilty of a misdemeanor, and, on conviction thereof, shall be punished by fine not exceeding five thousand dollars, or by imprisonment not exceeding one year, or by both said punishments, at the discretion of the court.

Sec. 2. Every person who shall monopolize, or attempt to monopolize, or combine or conspire with any other person or persons, to monopolize any part of the trade or commerce among the several States, or with foreign nations, shall be deemed guilty of a misdemeanor, and, on conviction thereof; shall be punished by fine not exceeding five thousand dollars, or by imprisonment not exceeding one year, or by both said punishments, in the discretion of the court.

Sec. 3. Every contract, combination in form of trust or otherwise, or conspiracy, in restraint of trade or commerce in any Territory of the United States or of the District of Columbia, or in restraint of trade or commerce between any such Territory and another, or between any such Territory or Territories and any State or States or the District of Columbia, or with foreign nations, or between the District of Columbia and any State or States or foreign nations, is hereby declared illegal. Every person who shall make any such contract or engage in any such combination or conspiracy, shall be deemed guilty of a misdemeanor, and, on conviction thereof, shall be punished by fine not exceeding five thousand dollars, or by imprison-

ment not exceeding one year, or by both said punishments, in the discretion of the court.

Sec. 4. The several circuit courts of the United States are hereby invested with jurisdiction to prevent and restrain violations of this act; and it shall be the duty of the several district attorneys of the United States, in their respective districts, under the direction of the Attorney General, to institute proceedings in equity to prevent and restrain such violations. Such proceedings may be by way of petition setting forth the case and praying that such violation shall be enjoined or otherwise prohibited. When the parties complained of shall have been duly notified of such petition the court shall proceed, as soon as may be, to the hearing and determination of the case; and pending such petition and before final decree, the court may at any time make such temporary restraining order or prohibition as shall be deemed just in the premises.

Sec. 5. Whenever it shall appear to the court before which any proceeding under section four of this act may be pending, that the ends of justice require that other parties should be brought before the court, the court may cause them to be summoned, whether they reside in the district in which the court is held or not; and subpoenas to that end may be served in any district by the marshal thereof.

Sec. 6. Any property owned under any contract or by any combination, or pursuant to any conspiracy (and being the subject thereof) mentioned in section one of this act, and being in the course of transportation from one State to another, or to a foreign country, shall be forfeited to the United States, and may be seized and condemned by like proceedings as those provided by law for the forfeiture, seizure, and condemnation of property imported into the United States contrary to law.

Sec. 7. Any person who shall be injured in his business or property by any other person or corporation by reason of anything forbidden or declared to be unlawful by this act, may sue therefor in any circuit court of the United States in the district in which the defendant resides or is found, without respect to the amount in controversy, and shall recover three fold the damages by him sustained, and the costs of suit, including a reasonable attorney's fee.

Sec. 8. That the word "person," or " persons," wherever used in this act shall be deemed to include corporations and associations existing under or authorized by the laws of either the United States, the laws of any of the Territories, the laws of any State, or the laws of any foreign country.

Approved, July 2, 1890.

[Endorsements]

Plessy v. Ferguson

(Transcription of the Judgement of the Supreme Court of the United States in *Plessy v. Ferguson*.)

Supreme Court of the United States,
No. 210, October Term, 1895.

Homer Adolph Plessy, Plaintiff in Error, vs.
J.H. Ferguson, Judge of Section "A"
Criminal District Court for the Parish of Orleans

In Error to the Supreme Court of the State of Louisiana

This cause came on to be heard on the transcript of the record from the Supreme Court of the State of Louisiana, and was argued by counsel.

On consideration whereof, It is now here ordered and adjudged by this Court that the judgement of the said Supreme Court, in this cause, be and the same is hereby, affirmed with costs.

per Mr. Justice Brown,
May 18, 1896.

Dissenting: Mr. Justice Harlan
(Transcription of Opinion of the Supreme Court of the United States in *Plessy v. Ferguson*.)

U.S. SUPREME COURT
PLESSY v. FERGUSON, 163 U.S. 537 (1896)

163 U.S. 537
PLESSY v. FERGUSON. No. 210.
May 18, 1896.

This was a petition for writs of prohibition and certiorari originally filed in the supreme court of the state by Plessy, the plaintiff in error, against the Hon. John H. Ferguson, judge of the criminal district court for the parish of Orleans, and setting forth, in substance, the following facts:

That petitioner was a citizen of the United States and a resident of the state of Louisiana, of mixed descent, in the proportion of seven-eighths Caucasian and one-eighth African blood; that the mixture of colored blood was not discernible in him, and that he was entitled to every recognition, right, privilege, and immunity secured to the citizens of the United States of the white race by its constitution and laws; that on June 7, 1892, he engaged and paid for a first-class passage on the East Louisiana Railway, from New Orleans to Covington, in the same state, and thereupon entered a passenger train, and took possession of a vacant seat in a coach where passengers of the white race were accommodated; that such railroad company was incorporated by the laws of Louisiana as a common carrier, and was not authorized to distinguish between citizens according to their race, but, notwithstanding this, petitioner was required by the conductor, under penalty of ejection from said train and imprisonment, to vacate said coach, and occupy another seat, in a coach assigned by said company for persons not of the white race, and for no other reason than that petitioner was of the colored race; that, upon petitioner's refusal to comply with such order, he was, with the aid of a police officer, forcibly ejected from said coach, and hurried off to, and imprisoned in, the parish jail of New Orleans, and there held to answer a charge made by such officer to the effect that he was guilty of having criminally violated an act of the general assembly of the state, approved July 10, 1890, in such case made and provided.

The petitioner was subsequently brought before the recorder of the city for preliminary examination, and committed for trial to the criminal district court for the parish of Orleans, where an information was filed against him in the matter above set forth, for a violation of the above act, which act the petitioner affirmed to be null and void, because in conflict with the constitution of the United States; that petitioner interposed a plea to such information, based upon the unconstitutionality of the act of the general assembly, to which the district attorney, on behalf of the state, filed a demurrer; that, upon issue being joined upon such demurrer and plea, the court sustained the demurrer, overruled the plea, and ordered petitioner to plead over to the facts set forth in the information, and that, unless the judge of the said court be enjoined by a writ of prohibition from further proceeding in such case, the court will proceed to fine and sentence petitioner to imprisonment, and thus deprive him of his constitutional rights set forth in his said plea, notwithstanding the unconstitutionality of the act under which he was being prosecuted;

that no appeal lay from such sentence, and petitioner was without relief or remedy except by writs of prohibition and certiorari. Copies of the information and other proceedings in the criminal district court were annexed to the petition as an exhibit.

Upon the filing of this petition, an order was issued upon the respondent to show cause why a writ of prohibition should not issue, and be made perpetual, and a further order that the record of the proceedings had in the criminal cause be certified and transmitted to the supreme court.

To this order the respondent made answer, transmitting a certified copy of the proceedings, asserting the constitutionality of the law, and averring that, instead of pleading or admitting that he belonged to the colored race, the said Plessy declined and refused, either by pleading or otherwise, to admit that he was in any sense or in any proportion a colored man.

The case coming on for hearing before the supreme court, that court was of opinion that the law under which the prosecution was had was constitutional and denied the relief prayed for by the petitioner (Ex parte Plessy, 45 La. Ann. 80, 11 South. 948); whereupon petitioner prayed for a writ of error from this court, which was allowed by the chief justice of the supreme court of Louisiana.

Mr. Justice Harlan dissenting.

A. W. Tourgee and S. F. Phillips, for plaintiff in error.

Alex. Porter Morse, for defendant in error.

Mr. Justice BROWN, after stating the facts in the foregoing language, delivered the opinion of the court.

This case turns upon the constitutionality of an act of the general assembly of the state of Louisiana, passed in 1890, providing for separate railway carriages for the white and colored races. Acts 1890, No. 111, p. 152.

The first section of the statute enacts 'that all railway companies carrying passengers in their coaches in this state, shall provide equal but separate accommodations for the white, and colored races, by providing two or more passenger coaches for each passenger train, or by dividing the passenger coaches by a partition so as to secure separate accommodations: provided, that this section shall not be construed to apply to street railroads. No person or persons shall be permitted to occupy seats in coaches, other than the ones assigned to them, on account of the race they belong to.'

By the second section it was enacted 'that the officers of such passenger trains shall have power and

are hereby required to assign each passenger to the coach or compartment used for the race to which such passenger belongs; any passenger insisting on going into a coach or compartment to which by race he does not belong, shall be liable to a fine of twenty-five dollars, or in lieu thereof to imprisonment for a period of not more than twenty days in the parish prison, and any officer of any railroad insisting on assigning a passenger to a coach or compartment other than the one set aside for the race to which said passenger belongs, shall be liable to a fine of twenty-five dollars, or in lieu thereof to imprisonment for a period of not more than twenty days in the parish prison; and should any passenger refuse to occupy the coach or compartment to which he or she is assigned by the officer of such railway, said officer shall have power to refuse to carry such passenger on his train, and for such refusal neither he nor the railway company which he represents shall be liable for damages in any of the courts of this state.'

The third section provides penalties for the refusal or neglect of the officers, directors, conductors, and employees of railway companies to comply with the act, with a proviso that 'nothing in this act shall be construed as applying to nurses attending children of the other race.' The fourth section is immaterial.

The information filed in the criminal district court charged, in substance, that Plessy, being a passenger between two stations within the state of Louisiana, was assigned by officers of the company to the coach used for the race to which he belonged, but he insisted upon going into a coach used by the race to which he did not belong. Neither in the information nor plea was his particular race or color averred.

The petition for the writ of prohibition averred that petitioner was seven-eights Caucasian and one-eighth African blood; that the mixture of colored blood was not discernible in him; and that he was entitled to every right, privilege, and immunity secured to citizens of the United States of the white race; and that, upon such theory, he took possession of a vacant seat in a coach where passengers of the white race were accommodated, and was ordered by the conductor to vacate said coach, and take a seat in another, assigned to persons of the colored race, and, having refused to comply with such demand, he was forcibly ejected, with the aid of a police officer, and imprisoned in the parish jail to answer a charge of having violated the above act.

The constitutionality of this act is attacked upon the ground that it conflicts both with the thirteenth amendment of the constitution, abolishing slavery, and the fourteenth amendment, which prohibits certain restrictive legislation on the part of the states.

1. That it does not conflict with the thirteenth amendment, which abolished slavery and involuntary servitude, except a punishment for crime, is too clear for argument. Slavery implies involuntary servitude, a state of bondage; the ownership of mankind as a chattel, or, at least, the control of the labor and services of one man for the benefit of another, and the absence of a legal right to the disposal of his own person, property, and services. This amendment was said in the Slaughter House Cases, 16 Wall. 36, to have been intended primarily to abolish slavery, as it had been previously known in this country, and that it equally forbade Mexican peonage or the Chinese coolie trade, when they amounted to slavery or involuntary servitude, and that the use of the word 'servitude' was intended to prohibit the use of all forms of involuntary slavery, of whatever class or name. It was intimated, however, in that case, that this amendment was regarded by the statesmen of that day as insufficient to protect the colored race from certain laws which had been enacted in the Southern states, imposing upon the colored race onerous disabilities and burdens, and curtailing their rights in the pursuit of life, liberty, and property to such an extent that their freedom was of little value; and that the fourteenth amendment was devised to meet this exigency.

So, too, in the Civil Rights Cases, 109 U.S. 3, 3 Sup. Ct. 18, it was said that the act of a mere individual, the owner of an inn, a public conveyance or place of amusement, refusing accommodations to colored people, cannot be justly regarded as imposing any badge of slavery or servitude upon the applicant, but only as involving an ordinary civil injury, properly cognizable by the laws of the state, and presumably subject to redress by those laws until the contrary appears. 'It would be running the slavery question into the ground,' said Mr. Justice Bradley, 'to make it apply to every act of discrimination which a person may see fit to make as to the guests he will entertain, or as to the people he will take into his coach or cab or car, or admit to his concert or theater, or deal with in other matters of intercourse or business.'

A statute which implies merely a legal distinction between the white and colored races—a distinction which is founded in the color of the two races, and which must always exist so long as white men are distinguished from the other race by color—has no tendency to destroy the legal equality of the two races, or re-establish a state of involuntary servitude. Indeed, we do not understand that the thirteenth amendment is strenuously relied upon by the plaintiff in error in this connection.

2. By the fourteenth amendment, all persons born or naturalized in the United States, and subject to the jurisdiction thereof, are made citizens of the United States and of the state wherein they reside; and the states are forbidden from making or enforcing any law which shall abridge the privileges or immunities of citizens of the United States, or shall deprive any person of life, liberty, or property without due process of law, or deny to any person within their jurisdiction the equal protection of the laws.

The proper construction of this amendment was first called to the attention of this court in the Slaughter House Cases, 16 Wall. 36, which involved, however, not a question of race, but one of exclusive privileges. The case did not call for any expression of opinion as to the exact rights it was intended to secure to the colored race, but it was said generally that its main purpose was to establish the citizenship of the negro, to give definitions of citizenship of the United States and of the states, and to protect from the hostile legislation of the states the privileges and immunities of citizens of the United States, as distinguished from those of citizens of the states. The object of the amendment was undoubtedly to enforce the absolute equality of the two races before the law, but, in the nature of things, it could not have been intended to abolish distinctions based upon color, or to enforce social, as distinguished from political, equality, or a commingling of the two races upon terms unsatisfactory to either. Laws permitting, and even requiring, their separation, in places where they are liable to be brought into contact, do not necessarily imply the inferiority of either race to the other, and have been generally, if not universally, recognized as within the competency of the state legislatures in the exercise of their police power. The most common instance of this is connected with the establishment of separate schools for white and colored children, which have been held to be a valid exercise of the legislative power even by courts of states where the political rights of the colored race have been longest and most earnestly enforced.

One of the earliest of these cases is that of Roberts v. City of Boston, 5 Cush. 198, in which the supreme judicial court of Massachusetts held that the general school committee of Boston had power to make provision for the instruction of colored children in separate schools established exclusively for them, and to prohibit their attendance upon the other schools. 'The great principle,' said Chief Justice Shaw, 'advanced by the learned and eloquent advocate for the plaintiff [Mr. Charles Sumner], is that, by the constitution and laws of Massachusetts, all persons, without distinction of age or sex, birth or color, origin or condition, are equal before the law. . . . But, when this great principle comes to be applied to the actual and various conditions of persons in society, it will not warrant the assertion that men and women are legally clothed with the same civil and political powers, and that children and adults are legally to have the same functions and be subject to the same treatment; but only that the rights of all, as they are settled and regulated by law, are equally entitled to the paternal consideration and protection of the law for their maintenance and security.' It was held that the powers of the committee extended to the establishment of separate schools for children of different ages, sexes and colors, and that they might also establish special schools for poor and neglected children, who have become too old to attend the primary school, and yet have not acquired the rudiments of learning, to enable them to enter the ordinary schools. Similar laws have been enacted by congress under its general power of legislation over the District of Columbia (sections 281–283, 310, 319, Rev. St. D. C.), as well as by the legislatures of many of the states, and have been generally, if not uniformly, sustained by the courts. State v. McCann, 21 Ohio St. 210; Lehew v. Brummell (Mo. Sup.) 15 S. W. 765; Ward v. Flood, 48 Cal. 36; Bertonneau v. Directors of City Schools, 3 Woods, 177, Fed. Cas. No. 1,361; People v. Gallagher, 93 N. Y. 438; Cory v. Carter, 48 Ind. 337; Dawson v. Lee, 83 Ky. 49.

Laws forbidding the intermarriage of the two races may be said in a technical sense to interfere with the freedom of contract, and yet have been universally recognized as within the police power of the state. State v. Gibson, 36 Ind. 389.

The distinction between laws interfering with the political equality of the negro and those requiring the separation of the two races in schools, theaters, and railway carriages has been frequently drawn by this court. Thus, in Strauder v. West Virginia, 100 U.S. 303, it was held that a law of West Virginia limiting to white male persons 21 years of age, and citizens of the state, the right to sit upon juries, was a discrimination which implied a legal inferiority in civil society, which lessened the security of the right of the colored race, and was a step towards reducing them to a condition of servility. In-

deed, the right of a colored man that, in the selection of jurors to pass upon his life, liberty, and property, there shall be no exclusion of his race, and no discrimination against them because of color, has been asserted in a number of cases. Virginia v. Rivers, 100 U.S. 313; Neal v. Delaware, 103 U.S. 370 ; ush v. Com., 107 U.S. 110, 1 Sup. Ct. 625; Gibson v. Mississippi, 162 U.S. 565, 16 Sup. Ct. 904. So, where the laws of a particular locality or the charter of a particular railway corporation has provided that no person shall be excluded from the cars on account of color, we have held that this meant that persons of color should travel in the same car as white ones, and that the enactment was not satisfied by the company providing cars assigned exclusively to people of color, though they were as good as those which they assigned exclusively to white persons. Railroad Co. v. Brown, 17 Wall. 445.

Upon the other hand, where a statute of Louisiana required those engaged in the transportation of passengers among the states to give to all persons traveling within that state, upon vessels employed in that business, equal rights and privileges in all parts of the vessel, without distinction on account of race or color, and subjected to an action for damages the owner of such a vessel who excluded colored passengers on account of their color from the cabin set aside by him for the use of whites, it was held to be, so far as it applied to interstate commerce, unconstitutional and void. Hall v. De Cuir, 95 U.S. 485. The court in this case, however, expressly disclaimed that it had anything whatever to do with the statute as a regulation of internal commerce, or affecting anything else than commerce among the states.

In the Civil Rights Cases, 109 U.S. 3, 3 Sup. Ct. 18, it was held that an act of congress entitling all persons within the jurisdiction of the United States to the full and equal enjoyment of the accommodations, advantages, facilities, and privileges of inns, public conveyances, on land or water, theaters, and other places of public amusement, and made applicable to citizens of every race and color, regardless of any previous condition of servitude, was unconstitutional and void, upon the ground that the fourteenth amendment was prohibitory upon the states only, and the legislation authorized to be adopted by congress for enforcing it was not direct legislation on matters respecting which the states were prohibited from making or enforcing certain laws, or doing certain acts, but was corrective legislation, such as might be necessary or proper for counteracting and redressing the effect of such laws or acts. In delivering the opinion of the court, Mr. Justice Bradley observed that the fourteenth amendment 'does not invest congress with power to legislate upon subjects that are within the domain of state legislation, but to provide modes of relief against state legislation or state action of the kind referred to. It does not authorize congress to create a code of municipal law for the regulation of private rights, but to provide modes of redress against the operation of state laws, and the action of state officers, executive or judicial, when these are subversive of the fundamental rights specified in the amendment. Positive rights and privileges are undoubtedly secured by the fourteenth amendment; but they are secured by way of prohibition against state laws and state proceedings affecting those rights and privileges, and by power given to congress to legislate for the purpose of carrying such prohibition into effect; and such legislation must necessarily be predicated upon such supposed state laws or state proceedings, and be directed to the correction of their operation and effect.'

Much nearer, and, indeed, almost directly in point, is the case of the Louisville, N. O. & T. Ry. Co. v. State, 133 U.S. 587, 10 Sup. Ct. 348, wherein the railway company was indicted for a violation of a statute of Mississippi, enacting that all railroads carrying passengers should provide equal, but separate, accommodations for the white and colored races, by providing two or more passenger cars for each passenger train, or by dividing the passenger cars by a partition, so as to secure separate accommodations. The case was presented in a different aspect from the one under consideration, inasmuch as it was an indictment against the railway company for failing to provide the separate accommodations, but the question considered was the constitutionality of the law. In that case, the supreme court of Mississippi (66 Miss. 662, 6 South. 203) had held that the statute applied solely to commerce within the state, and, that being the construction of the state statute by its highest court, was accepted as conclusive. 'If it be a matter,' said the court (page 591, 133 U. S., and page 348, 10 Sup. Ct.), 'respecting commerce wholly within a state, and not interfering with commerce between the states, then, obviously, there is no violation of the commerce clause of the federal constitution. . . . No question arises under this section as to the power of the state to separate in different compartments interstate passengers, or affect, in any manner, the privileges and rights of such passengers. All that we can consider is whether the state has the power to require that railroad trains within her lim-

its shall have separate accommodations for the two races. That affecting only commerce within the state is no invasion of the power given to congress by the commerce clause.'

A like course of reasoning applies to the case under consideration, since the supreme court of Louisiana, in the case of State v. Judge, 44 La. Ann. 770, 11 South. 74, held that the statute in question did not apply to interstate passengers, but was confined in its application to passengers traveling exclusively within the borders of the state. The case was decided largely upon the authority of Louisville, N. O. & T. Ry. Co. v. State, 66 Miss. 662, 6 South, 203, and affirmed by this court in 133 U.S. 587, 10 Sup. Ct. 348. In the present case no question of interference with interstate commerce can possibly arise, since the East Louisiana Railway appears to have been purely a local line, with both its termini within the state of Louisiana. Similar statutes for the separation of the two races upon public conveyances were held to be constitutional in Railroad v. Miles, 55 Pa. St. 209; Day v. Owen 5 Mich. 520; Railway Co. v. Williams, 55 Ill. 185; Railroad Co. v. Wells, 85 Tenn. 613; 4 S. W. 5; Railroad Co. v. Benson, 85 Tenn. 627, 4 S. W. 5; The Sue, 22 Fed. 843; Logwood v. Railroad Co., 23 Fed. 318; McGuinn v. Forbes, 37 Fed. 639; People v. King (N. Y. App.) 18 N. E. 245; Houck v. Railway Co., 38 Fed. 226; Heard v. Railroad Co., 3 Inter St. Commerce Com. R. 111, 1 Inter St. Commerce Com. R. 428.

While we think the enforced separation of the races, as applied to the internal commerce of the state, neither abridges the privileges or immunities of the colored man, deprives him of his property without due process of law, nor denies him the equal protection of the laws, within the meaning of the fourteenth amendment, we are not prepared to say that the conductor, in assigning passengers to the coaches according to their race, does not act at his peril, or that the provision of the second section of the act that denies to the passenger compensation in damages for a refusal to receive him into the coach in which he properly belongs is a valid exercise of the legislative power. Indeed, we understand it to be conceded by the state's attorney that such part of the act as exempts from liability the railway company and its officers is unconstitutional. The power to assign to a particular coach obviously implies the power to determine to which race the passenger belongs, as well as the power to determine who, under the laws of the particular state, is to be deemed a white, and who a colored, person. This question, though indicated in the brief of the plaintiff in error, does not properly arise upon the record in this case, since the only issue made is as to the unconstitutionality of the act, so far as it requires the railway to provide separate accommodations, and the conductor to assign passengers according to their race.

It is claimed by the plaintiff in error that, in an mixed community, the reputation of belonging to the dominant race, in this instance the white race, is 'property,' in the same sense that a right of action or of inheritance is property. Conceding this to be so, for the purposes of this case, we are unable to see how this statute deprives him of, or in any way affects his right to, such property. If he be a white man, and assigned to a colored coach, he may have his action for damages against the company for being deprived of his so-called 'property.' Upon the other hand, if he be a colored man, and be so assigned, he has been deprived of no property, since he is not lawfully entitled to the reputation of being a white man.

In this connection, it is also suggested by the learned counsel for the plaintiff in error that the same argument that will justify the state legislature in requiring railways to provide separate accommodations for the two races will also authorize them to require separate cars to be provided for people whose hair is of a certain color, or who are aliens, or who belong to certain nationalities, or to enact laws requiring colored people to walk upon one side of the street, and white people upon the other, or requiring white men's houses to be painted white, and colored men's black, or their vehicles or business signs to be of different colors, upon the theory that one side of the street is as good as the other, or that a house or vehicle of one color is as good as one of another color. The reply to all this is that every exercise of the police power must be reasonable, and extend only to such laws as are enacted in good faith for the promotion of the public good, and not for the annoyance or oppression of a particular class. Thus, in Yick Wo v. Hopkins, 118 U.S. 356, 6 Sup. Ct. 1064, it was held by this court that a municipal ordinance of the city of San Francisco, to regulate the carrying on of public laundries within the limits of the municipality, violated the provisions of the constitution of the United States, if it conferred upon the municipal authorities arbitrary power, at their own will, and without regard to discretion, in the legal sense of the term, to give or withhold consent as to persons or places, without regard to the competency of the persons applying or the propriety of the places selected for the carrying on of the business. It was held to be

a covert attempt on the part of the municipality to make an arbitrary and unjust discrimination against the Chinese race. While this was the case of a municipal ordinance, a like principle has been held to apply to acts of a state legislature passed in the exercise of the police power. Railroad Co. v. Husen, 95 U.S. 465; Louisville & N. R. Co. v. Kentucky, 161 U.S. 677, 16 Sup. Ct. 714, and cases cited on page 700, 161 U. S., and page 714, 16 Sup. Ct.; Daggett v. Hudson, 43 Ohio St. 548, 3 N. E. 538; Capen v. Foster, 12 Pick. 485; State v. Baker, 38 Wis. 71; Monroe v. Collins, 17 Ohio St. 665; Hulseman v. Rems, 41 Pa. St. 396; Osman v. Riley, 15 Cal. 48.

So far, then, as a conflict with the fourteenth amendment is concerned, the case reduces itself to the question whether the statute of Louisiana is a reasonable regulation, and with respect to this there must necessarily be a large discretion on the part of the legislature. In determining the question of reasonableness, it is at liberty to act with reference to the established usages, customs, and traditions of the people, and with a view to the promotion of their comfort, and the preservation of the public peace and good order. Gauged by this standard, we cannot say that a law which authorizes or even requires the separation of the two races in public conveyances is unreasonable, or more obnoxious to the fourteenth amendment than the acts of congress requiring separate schools for colored children in the District of Columbia, the constitutionality of which does not seem to have been questioned, or the corresponding acts of state legislatures.

We consider the underlying fallacy of the plaintiff's argument to consist in the assumption that the enforced separation of the two races stamps the colored race with a badge of inferiority. If this be so, it is not by reason of anything found in the act, but solely because the colored race chooses to put that construction upon it. The argument necessarily assumes that if, as has been more than once the case, and is not unlikely to be so again, the colored race should become the dominant power in the state legislature, and should enact a law in precisely similar terms, it would thereby relegate the white race to an inferior position. We imagine that the white race, at least, would not acquiesce in this assumption. The argument also assumes that social prejudices may be overcome by legislation, and that equal rights cannot be secured to the negro except by an enforced commingling of the two races. We cannot accept this proposition. If the two races are to meet upon terms of social equality, it must be the result of natural affinities, a mutual appreciation of each other's merits, and a voluntary consent of individuals. As was said by the court of appeals of New York in People v. Gallagher, 93 N. Y. 438, 448: 'This end can neither be accomplished nor promoted by laws which conflict with the general sentiment of the community upon whom they are designed to operate. When the government, therefore, has secured to each of its citizens equal rights before the law, and equal opportunities for improvement and progress, it has accomplished the end for which it was organized, and performed all of the functions respecting social advantages with which it is endowed.' Legislation is powerless to eradicate racial instincts, or to abolish distinctions based upon physical differences, and the attempt to do so can only result in accentuating the difficulties of the present situation. If the civil and political rights of both races be equal, one cannot be inferior to the other civilly or politically. If one race be inferior to the other socially, the constitution of the United States cannot put them upon the same plane.

It is true that the question of the proportion of colored blood necessary to constitute a colored person, as distinguished from a white person, is one upon which there is a difference of opinion in the different states; some holding that any visible admixture of black blood stamps the person as belonging to the colored race (State v. Chavers, 5 Jones [N. C.] 1); others, that it depends upon the preponderance of blood (Gray v. State, 4 Ohio, 354; Monroe v. Collins, 17 Ohio St. 665); and still others, that the predominance of white blood must only be in the proportion of three-fourths (People v. Dean, 14 Mich. 406; Jones v. Com., 80 Va. 544). But these are questions to be determined under the laws of each state, and are not properly put in issue in this case. Under the allegations of his petition, it may undoubtedly become a question of importance whether, under the laws of Louisiana, the petitioner belongs to the white or colored race.

The judgment of the court below is therefore affirmed.

Mr. Justice BREWER did not hear the argument or participate in the decision of this case.

Mr. Justice HARLAN dissenting.

By the Louisiana statute the validity of which is here involved, all railway companies (other than streetrailroad companies) carry passengers in that state are required to have separate but equal accommodations for white and colored persons, 'by providing two or more passenger coaches for each passenger train, or by dividing the passenger coaches by a partition so as to secure separate accommodations.' Under this statute, no colored person is permitted to occupy a seat in a coach assigned to white persons; nor any white person to occupy a seat in a coach assigned to colored persons. The managers of the railroad are not allowed to exercise any discretion in the premises, but are required to assign each passenger to some coach or compartment set apart for the exclusive use of is race. If a passenger insists upon going into a coach or compartment not set apart for persons of his race, he is subject to be fined, or to be imprisoned in the parish jail. Penalties are prescribed for the refusal or neglect of the officers, directors, conductors, and employees of railroad companies to comply with the provisions of the act.

Only 'nurses attending children of the other race' are excepted from the operation of the statute. No exception is made of colored attendants traveling with adults. A white man is not permitted to have his colored servant with him in the same coach, even if his condition of health requires the constant personal assistance of such servant. If a colored maid insists upon riding in the same coach with a white woman whom she has been employed to serve, and who may need her personal attention while traveling, she is subject to be fined or imprisoned for such an exhibition of zeal in the discharge of duty.

While there may be in Louisiana persons of different races who are not citizens of the United States, the words in the act 'white and colored races' necessarily include all citizens of the United States of both races residing in that state. So that we have before us a state enactment that compels, under penalties, the separation of the two races in railroad passenger coaches, and makes it a crime for a citizen of either race to enter a coach that has been assigned to citizens of the other race.

Thus, the state regulates the use of a public highway by citizens of the United States solely upon the basis of race.

However apparent the injustice of such legislation may be, we have only to consider whether it is consistent with the constitution of the United States.

That a railroad is a public highway, and that the corporation which owns or operates it is in the exercise of public functions, is not, at this day, to be disputed. Mr. Justice Nelson, speaking for this court in New Jersey Steam Nav. Co. v. Merchants' Bank, 6 How. 344, 382, said that a common carrier was in the exercise 'of a sort of public office, and has public duties to perform, from which he should not be permitted to exonerate himself without the assent of the parties concerned.' Mr. Justice Strong, delivering the judgment of this court in Olcott v. Supervisors, 16 Wall. 678, 694, said: 'That railroads, though constructed by private corporations, and owned by them, are public highways, has been the doctrine of nearly all the courts ever since such conveniences for passage and transportation have had any existence. Very early the question arose whether a state's right of eminent domain could be exercised by a private corporation created for the purpose of constructing a railroad. Clearly, it could not, unless taking land for such a purpose by such an agency is taking land for public use. The right of eminent domain nowhere justifies taking property for a private use. Yet it is a doctrine universally accepted that a state legislature may authorize a private corporation to take land for the construction of such a road, making compensation to the owner. What else does this doctrine mean if not that building a railroad, though it be built by a private corporation, is an act done for a public use?' So, in Township of Pine Grove v. Talcott, 19 Wall. 666, 676: 'Though the corporation [a railroad company] was private, its work was public, as much so as if it were to be constructed by the state.' So, in Inhabitants of Worcester v. Western R. Corp., 4 Metc. (Mass.) 564: 'The establishment of that great thoroughfare is regarded as a public work, established by public authority, intended for the public use and benefit, the use of which is secured to the whole community, and constitutes, therefore, like a canal, turnpike, or highway, a public easement.' 'It is true that the real and personal property, necessary to the establishment and management of the railroad, is vested in the corporation; but it is in trust for the public.'

In respect of civil rights, common to all citizens, the constitution of the United States does not, I think, permit any public authority to know the race of those entitled to be protected in the enjoyment of such rights. Every true man has pride of race, and under appropriate circumstances, when the rights of others, his equals before the law, are not to be affected, it is his privilege to express such pride and to take such action based upon it as to him seems proper. But I deny that any legislative body or judicial tribunal may have regard to the race of citizens when the civil rights of those citizens are involved. Indeed, such legislation as that here in question is inconsistent not only with that equality of rights which pertains to citizenship, national and state, but with the personal liberty enjoyed by every one within the United States.

The thirteenth amendment does not permit the withholding or the deprivation of any right necessarily inhering in freedom. It not only struck down the institution of slavery as previously existing in the United States, but it prevents the imposition of any burdens or disabilities that constitute badges of slavery or servitude. It decreed universal civil freedom in this country. This court has so adjudged. But, that amendment having been found inadequate to the protection of the rights of those who had been in slavery, it was followed by the fourteenth amendment, which added greatly to the dignity and glory of American citizenship, and to the security of personal liberty, by declaring that 'all persons born or naturalized in the United States, and subject to the jurisdiction thereof, are citizens of the United States and of the state wherein they reside,' and that 'no state shall make or enforce any law which shall abridge the privileges or immunities of citizens of the United States; nor shall any state deprive any person of life, liberty or property without due process of law, nor deny to any person within its jurisdiction the equal protection of the laws.' These two amendments, if enforced according to their true intent and meaning, will protect all the civil rights that pertain to freedom and citizenship. Finally, and to the end that no citizen should be denied, on account of his race, the privilege of participating in the political control of his country, it was declared by the fifteenth amendment that 'the right of citizens of the United States to vote shall not be denied or abridged by the United States or by any state on account of race, color or previous condition of servitude.'

These notable additions to the fundamental law were welcomed by the friends of liberty throughout the world. They removed the race line from our governmental systems. They had, as this court has said, a common purpose, namely, to secure 'to a race recently emancipated, a race that through many generations have been held in slavery, all the civil rights that the superior race enjoy.' They declared, in legal effect, this court has further said, 'that the law in the states shall be the same for the black as for the white; that all persons, whether colored or white, shall stand equal before the laws of the states; and in regard to the colored race, for whose protection the amendment was primarily designed, that no discrimination shall be made against them by law because of their color.' We also said: 'The words of the amendment, it is true, are prohibitory, but they contain a necessary implication of a positive immunity or right, most valuable to the colored race, the right to exemption from unfriendly legislation against them distinctively as colored; exemption from legal discriminations, implying inferiority in civil society, lessening the security of their enjoyment of the rights which others enjoy; and discriminations which are steps towards reducing them to the condition of a subject race.' It was, consequently, adjudged that a state law that excluded citizens of the colored race from juries, because of their race, however well qualified in other respects to discharge the duties of jurymen, was repugnant to the fourteenth amendment. Strauder v. West Virginia, 100 U.S. 303, 306, 307 S.; Virginia v. Rives, Id. 313; Ex parte Virginia, Id. 339; Neal v. Delaware, 103 U.S. 370, 386; Bush v. Com., 107 U.S. 110, 116, 1 S. Sup. Ct. 625. At the present term, referring to the previous adjudications, this court declared that 'underlying all of those decisions is the principle that the constitution of the United States, in its present form, forbids, so far as civil and political rights are concerned, discrimination by the general government or the states against any citizen because of his race. All citizens are equal before the law.' Gibson v. State, 162 U.S. 565, 16 Sup. Ct. 904.

The decisions referred to show the scope of the recent amendments of the constitution. They also show that it is not within the power of a state to prohibit colored citizens, because of their race, from participating as jurors in the administration of justice.

It was said in argument that the statute of Louisiana does not discriminate against either race, but prescribes a rule applicable alike to white and colored citizens. But this argument does not meet the difficulty. Every one knows that the statute in question had its origin in the purpose, not so much to exclude white persons from railroad cars occupied by blacks, as to exclude colored people from coaches occupied by or assigned to white persons. Railroad corporations of Louisiana did not make discrimination among whites in the matter of commodation for travelers. The thing to accomplish was, under the guise of giving equal accommodation for whites and blacks, to compel the latter to keep to themselves while traveling in railroad passenger coaches. No one would be so wanting in candor as to assert the contrary. The fundamental objection, therefore, to the statute, is that it interferes with the personal freedom of citizens. 'Personal liberty,' it has been well said, 'consists in the power of locomotion, of changing situation, or removing one's person to whatsoever places one's own inclination may direct, without imprisonment or restraint, unless by due course of law.' 1 Bl. Comm. *134. If a white man and a black man

choose to occupy the same public conveyance on a public highway, it is their right to do so; and no government, proceeding alone on grounds of race, can prevent it without infringing the personal liberty of each.

It is one thing for railroad carriers to furnish, or to be required by law to furnish, equal accommodations for all whom they are under a legal duty to carry. It is quite another thing for government to forbid citizens of the white and black races from traveling in the same public conveyance, and to punish officers of railroad companies for permitting persons of the two races to occupy the same passenger coach. If a state can prescribe, as a rule of civil conduct, that whites and blacks shall not travel as passengers in the same railroad coach, why may it not so regulate the use of the streets of its cities and towns as to compel white citizens to keep on one side of a street, and black citizens to keep on the other? Why may it not, upon like grounds, punish whites and blacks who ride together in street cars or in open vehicles on a public road or street? Why may it not require sheriffs to assign whites to one side of a court room, and blacks to the other? And why may it not also prohibit the commingling of the two races in the galleries of legislative halls or in public assemblages convened for the consideration of the political questions of the day? Further, if this statute of Louisiana is consistent with the personal liberty of citizens, why may not the state require the separation in railroad coaches of native and naturalized citizens of the United States, or of Protestants and Roman Catholics?

The answer given at the argument to these questions was that regulations of the kind they suggest would be unreasonable, and could not, therefore, stand before the law. Is it meant that the determination of questions of legislative power depends upon the inquiry whether the statute whose validity is questioned is, in the judgment of the courts, a reasonable one, taking all the circumstances into consideration? A statute may be unreasonable merely because a sound public policy forbade its enactment. But I do not understand that the courts have anything to do with the policy or expediency of legislation. A statute may be valid, and yet, upon grounds of public policy, may well be characterized as unreasonable. Mr. Sedgwick correctly states the rule when he says that, the legislative intention being clearly ascertained, 'the courts have no other duty to perform than to execute the legislative will, without any regard to their views as to the wisdom or justice of the particular enactment.' Sedg. St. & Const. Law,

324. There is a dangerous tendency in these latter days to enlarge the functions of the courts, by means of judicial interference with the will of the people as expressed by the legislature. Our institutions have the distinguishing characteristic that the three departments of government are co-ordinate and separate. Each much keep within the limits defined by the constitution. And the courts best discharge their duty by executing the will of the law-making power, constitutionally expressed, leaving the results of legislation to be dealt with by the people through their representatives. Statutes must always have a reasonable construction. Sometimes they are to be construed strictly, sometimes literally, in order to carry out the legislative will. But, however construed, the intent of the legislature is to be respected if the particular statute in question is valid, although the courts, looking at the public interests, may conceive the statute to be both unreasonable and impolitic. If the power exists to enact a statute, that ends the matter so far as the courts are concerned. The adjudged cases in which statutes have been held to be void, because unreasonable, are those in which the means employed by the legislature were not at all germane to the end to which the legislature was competent.

The white race deems itself to be the dominant race in this country. And so it is, in prestige, in achievements, in education, in wealth, and in power. So, I doubt not, it will continue to be for all time, if it remains true to its great heritage, and holds fast to the principles of constitutional liberty. But in view of the constitution, in the eye of the law, there is in this country no superior, dominant, ruling class of citizens. There is no caste here. Our constitution is color-blind, and neither knows nor tolerates classes among citizens. In respect of civil rights, all citizens are equal before the law. The humblest is the peer of the most powerful. The law regards man as man, and takes no account of his surroundings or of his color when his civil rights as guaranteed by the supreme law of the land are involved. It is therefore to be regretted that this high tribunal, the final expositor of the fundamental law of the land, has reached the conclusion that it is competent for a state to regulate the enjoyment by citizens of their civil rights solely upon the basis of race.

In my opinion, the judgment this day rendered will, in time, prove to be quite as pernicious as the decision made by this tribunal in the Dred Scott Case.

It was adjudged in that case that the descendants of Africans who were imported into this country, and sold as slaves, were not included nor intended to be included under the word 'citizens' in the constitution, and could not claim any of the rights and privileges which that instrument provided for and secured to citizens of the United States; that, at time of the adoption of the constitution, they were 'considered as a subordinate and inferior class of beings, who had been subjugated by the dominant race, and, whether emancipated or not, yet remained subject to their authority, and had no rights or privileges but such as those who held the power and the government might choose to grant them.' 17 How. 393, 404. The recent amendments of the constitution, it was supposed, had eradicated these principles from our institutions. But it seems that we have yet, in some of the states, a dominant race,—a superior class of citizens,—which assumes to regulate the enjoyment of civil rights, common to all citizens, upon the basis of race. The present decision, it may well be apprehended, will not only stimulate aggressions, more or less brutal and irritating, upon the admitted rights of colored citizens, but will encourage the belief that it is possible, by means of state enactments, to defeat the beneficent purposes which the people of the United States had in view when they adopted the recent amendments of the constitution, by one of which the blacks of this country were made citizens of the United States and of the states in which they respectively reside, and whose privileges and immunities, as citizens, the states are forbidden to abridge. Sixty millions of whites are in no danger from the presence here of eight millions of blacks. The destinies of the two races, in this country, are indissolubly linked together, and the interests of both require that the common government of all shall not permit the seeds of race hate to be planted under the sanction of law. What can more certainly arouse race hate, what more certainly create and perpetuate a feeling of distrust between these races, than state enactments which, in fact, proceed on the ground that colored citizens are so inferior and degraded that they cannot be allowed to sit in public coaches occupied by white citizens? That, as all will admit, is the real meaning of such legislation as was enacted in Louisiana.

The sure guaranty of the peace and security of each race is the clear, distinct, unconditional recognition by our governments, national and state, of every right that inheres in civil freedom, and of the equality before the law of all citizens of the United States, without regard to race. State enactments regulating the enjoyment of civil rights upon the basis of race, and cunningly devised to defeat legitimate results of the war, under the pretense of recognizing equality of rights, can have no other result than to render permanent peace impossible, and to keep alive a conflict of races, the continuance of which must do harm to all concerned. This question is not met by the suggestion that social equality cannot exist between the white and black races in this country. That argument, if it can be properly regarded as one, is scarcely worthy of consideration; for social equality no more exists between two races when traveling in a passenger coach or a public highway than when members of the same races sit by each other in a street car or in the jury box, or stand or sit with each other in a political assembly, or when they use in common the streets of a city or town, or when they are in the same room for the purpose of having their names placed on the registry of voters, or when they approach the ballot box in order to exercise the high privilege of voting.

There is a race so different from our own that we do not permit those belonging to it to become citizens of the United States. Persons belonging to it are, with few exceptions, absolutely excluded from our country. I allude to the Chinese race. But, by the statute in question, a Chinaman can ride in the same passenger coach with white citizens of the United States, while citizens of the black race in Louisiana, many of whom, perhaps, risked their lives for the preservation of the Union, who are entitled, by law, to participate in the political control of the state and nation, who are not excluded, by law or by reason of their race, from public stations of any kind, and who have all the legal rights that belong to white citizens, are yet declared to be criminals, liable to imprisonment, if they ride in a public coach occupied by citizens of the white race. It is scarcely just to say that a colored citizen should not object to occupying a public coach assigned to his own race. He does not object, nor, perhaps, would he object to separate coaches for his race if his rights under the law were recognized. But he does object, and he ought never to cease objecting, that citizens of the white and black races can be adjudged criminals because they sit, or claim the right to sit, in the same public coach on a public highway. The arbitrary separation of citizens, on the basis of race, while they are on a public highway, is a badge of servitude wholly inconsistent with the civil freedom and the equality before the law established by the constitution. It cannot be justified upon any legal grounds.

If evils will result from the commingling of the two races upon public highways established for the benefit of all, they will be infinitely less than those that will surely come from state legislation regulating the enjoyment of civil rights upon the basis of race. We boast of the freedom enjoyed by our people above all other peoples. But it is difficult to reconcile that boast with a state of the law which, practically, puts the brand of servitude and degradation upon a large class of our fellow citizens,—our equals before the law. The thin disguise of 'equal' accommodations for passengers in railroad coaches will not mislead any one, nor atone for the wrong this day done.

The result of the whole matter is that while this court has frequently adjudged, and at the present term has recognized the doctrine, that a state cannot, consistently with the constitution of the United States, prevent white and black citizens, having the required qualifications for jury service, from sitting in the same jury box, it is now solemnly held that a state may prohibit white and black citizens from sitting in the same passenger coach on a public highway, or may require that they be separated by a 'partition' when in the same passenger coach. May it not now be reasonably expected that astute men of the dominant race, who affect to be disturbed at the possibility that the integrity of the white race may be corrupted, or that its supremacy will be imperiled, by contact on public highways with black people, will endeavor to procure statutes requiring white and black jurors to be separated in the jury box by a 'partition,' and that, upon retiring from the court room to consult as to their verdict, such partition, if it be a movable one, shall be taken to their consultation room, and set up in such way as to prevent black jurors from coming too close to their brother jurors of the white race. If the 'partition' used in the court room happens to be stationary, provision could be made for screens with openings through which jurors of the two races could confer as to their verdict without coming into personal contact with each other. I cannot see but that, according to the principles this day announced, such state legislation, although conceived in hostility to, and enacted for the purpose of humiliating, citizens of the United States of a particular race, would be held to be consistent with the constitution.

I do not deem it necessary to review the decisions of state courts to which reference was made in argument. Some, and the most important, of them, are wholly inapplicable, because rendered prior to the adoption of the last amendments of the constitution, when colored people had very few rights which the dominant race felt obliged to respect. Others were made at a time when public opinion, in many localities, was dominated by the institution of slavery; when it would not have been safe to do justice to the black man; and when, so far as the rights of blacks were concerned, race prejudice was, practically, the supreme law of the land. Those decisions cannot be guides in the era introduced by the recent amendments of the supreme law, which established universal civil freedom, gave citizenship to all born or naturalized in the United States, and residing ere, obliterated the race line from our systems of governments, national and state, and placed our free institutions upon the broad and sure foundation of the equality of all men before the law.

I am of opinion that the state of Louisiana is inconsistent with the personal liberty of citizens, white and black, in that state, and hostile to both the spirit and letter of the constitution of the United States. If laws of like character should be enacted in the several states of the Union, the effect would be in the highest degree mischievous. Slavery, as an institution tolerated by law, would, it is true, have disappeared from our country; but there would remain a power in the states, by sinister legislation, to interfere with the full enjoyment of the blessings of freedom, to regulate civil rights, common to all citizens, upon the basis of race, and to place in a condition of legal inferiority a large body of American citizens, now constituting a part of the political community, called the 'People of the United States,' for whom, and by whom through representatives, our government is administered. Such a system is inconsistent with the guaranty given by the constitution to each state of a republican form of government, and may be stricken down by congressional action, or by the courts in the discharge of their solemn duty to maintain the supreme law of the land, anything in the constitution or laws of any state to the contrary notwithstanding.

For the reason stated, I am constrained to withhold my assent from the opinion and judgment of the majority.

De Lôme Letter

(TRANSLATION OF LETTER WRITTEN BY SENOR DON ENRIQUE DUPUY DE LÔME TO SENOR DON JOSÉ CANELEJAS. UNDATED, BUT FROM INTERNAL EVIDENCE PROBABLY WRITTEN ABOUT THE MIDDLE OF DECEMBER, 1897.)

LEGACION DE ESPAÑA.
WASHINGTON.
His Excellency Don José Canalejas.

My distinguished and dear friend:

You have no reason to ask my excuses for not having written to me, I ought also to have written to you but I have put off doing so because overwhelmed with work and nous sommes quittes.

The situation here remains the same. Everything depends on the political and military outcome in Cuba. The prologue of all this, in this second stage (phase) of the war, will end the day when the colonial cabinet shall be appointed and we shall be relieved in the eyes of this country of a part of the responsibility for what is happening in Cuba while the Cubans, whom these people think so immaculate, will have to assume it.

Until then, nothing can be clearly seen, and I regard it as a waste of time and progress, by a wrong road, to be sending emissaries to the rebel camp, or to negotiate with the autonomists who have as yet no legal standing, or to try to ascertain the intentions and plans of this government. The (Cuban) refugees will keep on returning one by one and as they do so will make their way into the sheep-fold, while the leaders in the field will gradually come back. Neither the one nor the other class had the courage to leave in a body and they will not be brave enough to return in a body.

The Message has been a disillusionment to the insurgents who expected something different; but I regard it as bad (for us).

Besides the ingrained and inevitable bluntness (grosería) with which is repeated all that the press and public opinion in Spain have said about Weyler, it once more shows what McKinley is, weak and a bidder for the admiration of the crowd besides being a would-be politician (politicastro) who tries to leave a door open behind himself while keeping on good terms with the jingoes of his party.

Nevertheless, whether the practical results of it (the Message) are to be injurious and adverse depends only upon ourselves.

I am entirely of your opinions; without a military end of the matter nothing will be accomplished in Cuba, and without a military and political settlement there will always be the danger of encouragement being give to the insurgents, buy a part of the public opinion if not by the government.

I do not think sufficient attention has been paid to the part England is playing.

Nearly all the newspaper rabble that swarms in your hotels are Englishmen, and while writing for the Journal they are also correspondents of the most influential journals and reviews of London. It has been so ever since this thing began.

As I look at it, England's only object is that the Americans should amuse themselves with us and leave her alone, and if there should be a war, that would the better stave off the conflict which she dreads but which will never come about.

It would be very advantageous to take up, even if only for effect, the question of commercial relations and to have a man of some prominence sent hither, in order that I may make use of him here to carry on a propaganda among the seantors and others in opposition to the Junta and to try to win over the refugees.

So, Amblard is coming. I think he devotes himself too much to petty politics, and we have got to do something very big or we shall fail.

Adela returns your greeting, and we all trust that next year you may be a messenger of peace and take it as a Christmas gift to poor Spain.

Ever your attached friend and servant,
ENRIQUE DUPUY de LÔME.

Joint Resolution to Provide for Annexing the Hawaiian Islands to the United States

Fifty-fifth Congress of the United States of America; At the Second Session,

Begun and held at the City of Washington on Monday, the sixth day of December, one thousand eight hundred and ninety-seven.

JOINT RESOLUTION TO PROVIDE FOR ANNEXING THE HAWAIIAN ISLANDS TO THE UNITED STATES.

Whereas, the Government of the Republic of Hawaii having, in due form, signified its consent, in the manner provided by its constitution, to cede absolutely and without reserve to the United States of America, all rights of sovereignty of whatsoever kind in and over the Hawaiian Islands and their dependencies, and also to cede and transfer to the United States, the absolute fee and ownership of all public, Government, or Crown lands, public buildings or edifices, ports, harbors, military equipment, and all other public property of every kind and description belonging to the Government of the Hawaiian Islands, together with every right and appurtenance thereunto appertaining: Therefore,

Resolved by the Senate and House of Representatives of the United States of America in Congress assembled, That said cession is accepted, ratified, and confirmed, and that the said Hawaiian Islands and their dependencies be, and they are hereby, annexed as a part of the territory of the United States and are subject to the sovereign dominion thereof, and that all and singular the property and rights hereinbefore mentioned are vested in the United States of America.

The existing laws of the United States relative to public lands shall not apply to such lands in the Hawaiian Islands; but the Congress of the United States shall enact special laws for their management and disposition: *Provided,* That all revenue from or proceeds of the same, except as regards such part thereof as may be used or occupied for the civil, military, or naval purposes of the United States, or may be as-

signed for the use of the local government, shall be used solely for the benefit of the inhabitants of the Hawaiian Islands for educational and other public purposes.

Until Congress shall provide for the government of such islands all the civil, judicial, and military powers exercised by the officers of the existing government in said islands shall be vested in such person or persons and shall be exercised in such manner as the President of the United states shall direct; and the President shall have power to remove said officers and fill the vacancies so occasioned.

The existing treaties of the Hawaiian Islands with foreign nations shall forthwith cease and determine, being replaced by such treaties as may exist, or as may be hereafter concluded, between the United States and such foreign nations. The municipal legislation of the Hawaiian Islands, not enacted for the fulfillment of the treaties so extinguished, and not inconsistent with this joint resolution nor contrary to the Constitution of the United States nor to any existing treaty of the United States, shall remain in force until the Congress of the United States shall otherwise determine.

Until legislation shall be enacted extending the United States customs laws and regulations to the Hawaiian Islands the existing customs relations of the Hawaiian Islands with the United States and other countries shall remain unchanged.

The public debt of the Republic of Hawaii, lawfully existing at the date of the passage of this joint resolution, including the amounts due to depositors in the Hawaiian Postal Savings Bank, is hereby assumed by the Government of the United States; but the liability of the United States in this regard shall in no case exceed four million dollars. So long, however, as the existing Government and the present commercial relations of the Hawaiian Islands are continued as hereinbefore, provided said Government shall continue to pay the interest on said debt.

There shall be no further immigration of Chinese into the Hawaiian Islands, except upon such conditions as are now or may hereafter be allowed by the laws of the United States; and no Chinese, by reason of anything herein contained, shall be allowed to enter the United States from the Hawaiian Islands.

Sec. 1. The President shall appoint five commissioners, at least two of whom shall be residents of the Hawaiian Islands, who shall, as soon as reasonably practicable, recommend to Congress such legislation concerning the Hawaiian Islands as they shall deem necessary or proper.

Sec. 2. That the commissioners hereinbefore provided for shall be appointed by the President, by and with the advice and consent of the Senate.

Sec. 3. That the sum of one hundred thousand dollars, or so much thereof as may be necessary, is hereby appropriated, out of any money in the Treasury not otherwise appropriated, and to be immediately available, to be expended at the discretion of the President of the United States of America, for the purpose of carrying this joint resolution into effect.

LETTER OF PROTEST FROM QUEEN LILIUOKALANI OF HAWAII TO THE HOUSE OF REPRESENTATIVES

The House of Representatives of the United States:

I, Liliuokalani of Hawaii, named heir apparent on the 10th day of April, 1877, and proclaimed Queen of the Hawaiian Islands on the 29th day of January, 1891, do hereby earnestly and respectfully protest against the assertion of ownership by the United States of America of the so-called Hawaiian Crown Islands amounting to about one million acres and which are my property, and I especially protest against such assertion of ownership as a taking of property without due process of law and without just or other compensation.

Therefore, supplementing my protest of June 17, 1897, I call upon the President and the National Legislature and the People of the United States to do justice in this matter and to restore to me this property, the enjoyment of which is being withheld from me by your Government under what must be a misapprehension of my right and title.

Done at Washington, District of Columbia, United States of America, this nineteenth day of December, in the year one thousand eight hundred and ninety-eight.

[Endorsement]

The Platt Amendment

WHEREAS THE CONGRESS OF THE UNITED STATES OF AMERICA, BY AN ACT APPROVED MARCH 2, 1901, PROVIDED AS FOLLOWS:

Provided further, That in fulfillment of the declaration contained in the joint resolution approved April twentieth, eighteen hundred and ninety-eight, entitled "For the recognition of the independence of the people of Cuba, demanding that the Government of Spain relinquish its authority and government in the island of Cuba, and withdraw its land and naval forces from Cuba and Cuban waters, and directing the President of the United States to use the land and naval forces of the United States to carry these resolutions into effect," the President is hereby authorized to "leave the government and control of the island of Cuba to its people" so soon as a government shall have been established in said island under a constitution which, either as a part thereof or in an ordinance appended thereto, shall define the future relations of the United States with Cuba, substantially as follows:

"**I.** That the government of Cuba shall never enter into any treaty or other compact with any foreign power or powers which will impair or tend to impair the independence of Cuba, nor in any manner authorize or permit any foreign power or powers to obtain by colonization or for military or naval purposes or otherwise, lodgement in or control over any portion of said island."

"**II.** That said government shall not assume or contract any public debt, to pay the interest upon which, and to make reasonable sinking fund provision for the ultimate discharge of which, the ordinary revenues of the island, after defraying the current expenses of government shall be inadequate."

"**III.** That the government of Cuba consents that the United States may exercise the right to intervene for the preservation of Cuban independence, the maintenance of a government adequate for the protection of life, property, and individual liberty, and for discharging the obligations with respect to Cuba imposed by the treaty of Paris on the United States, now to be assumed and undertaken by the government of Cuba."

"**IV.** That all Acts of the United States in Cuba during its military occupancy thereof are ratified and validated, and all lawful rights acquired thereunder shall be maintained and protected."

"**V.** That the government of Cuba will execute, and as far as necessary extend, the plans already devised or other plans to be mutually agreed upon, for the sanitation of the cities of the island, to the end that a recurrence of epidemic and infectious diseases may be prevented, thereby assuring protection to the people and commerce of Cuba, as well as to the commerce of the southern ports of the United States and the people residing therein."

"**VI.** That the Isle of Pines shall be omitted from the proposed constitutional boundaries of Cuba, the title thereto being left to future adjustment by treaty."

"**VII.** That to enable the United States to maintain the independence of Cuba, and to protect the people thereof, as well as for its own defense, the government of Cuba will sell or lease to the United States lands necessary for coaling or naval stations at certain specified points to be agreed upon with the President of the United States."

"**VIII.** That by way of further assurance the government of Cuba will embody the foregoing provisions in a permanent treaty with the United States."

Theodore Roosevelt's Corollary to the Monroe Doctrine

EXCERPTED FROM THEODORE ROOSEVELT'S ANNUAL MESSAGE TO CONGRESS, DECEMBER 6, 1904

In treating of our foreign policy and of the attitude that this great Nation should assume in the world at large, it is absolutely necessary to consider the Army and the Navy, and the Congress, through which the thought of the Nation finds its expression, should keep ever vividly in mind the fundamental fact that it is impossible to treat our foreign policy, whether this policy takes shape in the effort to secure justice for others or justice for ourselves, save as conditioned upon the attitude we are willing to take toward our Army, and especially toward our Navy. It is not merely unwise, it is contemptible, for a nation, as for an individual, to use high-sounding language to proclaim its purposes, or to take positions which are ridiculous if unsupported by potential force, and then to refuse to provide this force. If there is no intention of providing and keeping the force necessary to back up a strong attitude, then it is far better not to assume such an attitude.

The steady aim of this Nation, as of all enlightened nations, should be to strive to bring ever nearer the day when there shall prevail throughout the world the peace of justice. There are kinds of peace which are highly undesirable, which are in the long run as destructive as any war. Tyrants and oppressors have many times made a wilderness and called it peace. Many times peoples who were slothful or timid or shortsighted, who had been enervated by ease or by luxury, or misled by false teachings, have shrunk in unmanly fashion from doing duty that was stern and that needed self-sacrifice, and have sought to hide from their own minds their shortcomings, their ignoble motives, by calling them love of peace. The peace of tyrannous terror, the peace of craven weakness, the peace of injustice, all these should be shunned as we shun unrighteous war. The goal to set before us as a nation, the goal which should be set before all mankind, is the attainment of the peace of justice, of the peace which comes when each nation is not merely safe-guarded in its own rights, but scrupulously recognizes and performs its duty toward others. Generally peace tells for righteousness; but if there is conflict between the two, then our fealty is due first to the cause of righteousness. Unrighteous wars are common, and unrighteous peace is rare; but both should be shunned. The right of freedom and the responsibility for the exercise of that right can not be divorced. One of our great poets has well and finely said that freedom is not a gift that tarries long in the hands of cowards. Neither does it tarry long in the hands of those too slothful, too dishonest, or too unintelligent to exercise it. The eternal vigilance which is the price of liberty must be exercised, sometimes to guard against outside foes; although of course far more often to guard against our own selfish or thoughtless shortcomings.

If these self-evident truths are kept before us, and only if they are so kept before us, we shall have a clear idea of what our foreign policy in its larger aspects should be. It is our duty to remember that a nation has no more right to do injustice to another nation, strong or weak, than an individual has to do injustice to another individual; that the same moral law applies in one case as in the other. But we must also remember that it is as much the duty of the Nation to guard its own rights and its own interests as it is the duty of the individual so to do. Within the Nation the individual has now delegated this right to the State, that is, to the representative of all the individuals, and it is a maxim of the law that for every wrong there is a remedy. But in international law we have not advanced by any means as far as we have advanced in municipal law. There is as yet no judicial way of enforcing a right in international law. When one nation wrongs another or wrongs many others, there is no tribunal before which the wrong-doer can be brought. Either it is necessary supinely to acquiesce in the wrong, and thus put a premium upon brutality and aggression, or else it is necessary for the aggrieved nation valiantly to stand up for its rights. Until some method is devised by which there shall be a degree of international control over offending nations, it would be a wicked thing for the most civilized powers, for those with most sense of international obligations and with keenest and most generous appreciation of the difference between right and wrong, to disarm. If the great civilized nations of the present day should completely disarm, the result would mean an immediate recrudescence of barbarism in one form or another. Under any circumstances a sufficient armament would have to be kept up to serve the purposes of international police; and until international cohesion and the sense of international duties and rights are far more advanced than at present, a nation desirous both of securing respect for itself and of doing good to others must have a force adequate for the work which it feels is allotted to it as its part of the general world duty. Therefore it follows that a self-respecting, just, and far-seeing nation should on the one hand endeavor by every means to aid in the development of the various movements which tend to provide substitutes for war, which tend to render nations in their actions toward one another, and indeed toward their own peoples, more responsive to the general sentiment of humane and civilized mankind; and on the other hand that it should keep prepared, while scrupulously avoiding wrongdoing itself, to repel any wrong, and in exceptional cases to take action which in a more advanced stage of international relations would come under the head of the exercise of the international police. A great free people owes it to itself and to all mankind not to sink into helplessness before the powers of evil.

We are in every way endeavoring to help on, with cordial good will, every movement which will tend to bring us into more friendly relations with the rest of mankind. In pursuance of this policy I shall shortly lay before the Senate treaties of arbitration with all powers which are willing to enter into these treaties with us. It is not possible at this period of the world's development to agree to arbitrate all matters, but there are many matters of possible difference between us and other nations which can be thus arbitrated. Furthermore, at the request of the Interparliamentary Union, an eminent body composed of practical statesmen from all countries, I have asked the Powers to join with this Government in a second Hague conference, at which it is hoped that the work already so happily begun at The Hague may be carried some steps further toward completion. This carries out the desire expressed by the first Hague conference itself.

It is not true that the United States feels any land hunger or entertains any projects as regards the other nations of the Western Hemisphere save such as are for their welfare. All that this country desires is to see the neighboring countries stable, orderly, and prosperous. Any country whose people conduct themselves well can count upon our hearty friendship. If a nation shows that it knows how to act with reasonable efficiency and decency in social and political matters, if it keeps order and pays its obligations, it need fear no interference from the United States. Chronic wrongdoing, or an impotence which results in a general loosening of the ties of civilized society, may in America, as elsewhere, ultimately require intervention by some civilized nation, and in the Western Hemisphere the adherence of the United States to the Monroe Doctrine may force the United States, however reluctantly, in flagrant cases of such wrongdoing or impotence, to the exercise of an international police power. If every country washed by the Caribbean Sea would show the progress in stable and just civilization which with the aid of the Platt Amendment Cuba has shown since our troops left the island, and which so many of the republics in both Americas are constantly and brilliantly showing, all question of interference by this Nation with their affairs would be at an end. Our interests and those of our southern neighbors are in reality identical. They have great natural riches, and if within their borders the reign of law and justice obtains, prosperity is sure to come to them. While they thus obey the primary laws of civilized society they may rest assured that they will be treated by us in a spirit of cordial and helpful sympathy. We would interfere with them only in the last resort, and then only if it became evident that their inability or unwillingness to do justice at home and abroad had violated the rights of the United States or had invited foreign aggression to the detriment of the entire body of American nations. It is a mere truism to say that every nation, whether in America or anywhere else, which desires to maintain its freedom, its independence, must ultimately realize that the right of such independence can not be separated from the responsibility of making good use of it.

In asserting the Monroe Doctrine, in taking such steps as we have taken in regard to Cuba, Venezuela, and Panama, and in endeavoring to circumscribe the theater of war in the Far East, and to secure the open door in China, we have acted in our own interest as well as in the interest of humanity at large. There are, however, cases in which, while our own interests are not greatly involved, strong appeal is made to our sympathies. Ordinarily it is very much wiser and more useful for us to concern ourselves with striving for our own moral and material betterment here at home than to concern ourselves with trying to better the condition of things in other nations. We have plenty of sins of our own to war against, and under ordinary circumstances we can do more for the general uplifting of humanity by striving with heart and soul to put a stop to civic corruption, to brutal lawlessness and violent race prejudices here at home than by passing resolutions and wrongdoing elsewhere. Nevertheless there are occasional crimes committed on so vast a scale and of such peculiar horror as to make us doubt whether it is not our manifest duty to endeavor at least to show our disapproval of the deed and our sympathy with those who have suffered by it. The cases must be extreme in which such a course is justifiable. There must be no effort made to remove the mote from our brother's eye if we refuse to remove the beam from our own. But in extreme cases action may be justifiable and proper. What form the action shall take must depend upon the circumstances of the case; that is, upon the degree of the atrocity and upon our power to remedy it. The cases in which we could interfere by force of arms as we interfered to put a stop to intolerable conditions in Cuba are necessarily very few. Yet it is not to be expected that a people like ours, which in spite of certain very obvious shortcomings, nevertheless as a whole shows by its consistent practice its belief in the principles of civil and religious liberty and of orderly freedom, a people among whom even the worst crime, like the crime of lynching, is never more than sporadic, so that individuals and not classes are molested in their fundamental rights—it is inevitable that such a nation should desire eagerly to give expression to its horror on an occasion like that of the massacre of the Jews in Kishenef, or when it witnesses such systematic and long-extended cruelty and oppression as the cruelty and oppression of which the Armenians have been the victims, and which have won for them the indignant pity of the civilized world.

16th Amendment to the U.S. Constitution: Federal Income Tax

Sixty-first Congress of the United States of America, At the First Session,

Begun and held at the City of Washington on Monday, the fifteenth day of March, one thousand nine hundred and nine.

JOINT RESOLUTION
Proposing an amendment to the Constitution of the United States.

Resolved by the Senate and House of Representatives of the United States of America in Congress assembled (two-thirds of each House concurring therein), That the following article is proposed as an amendment to the Constitution of the United States, which, when ratified by the legislature of three-fourths of the several States, shall be valid to all intents and purposes as a part of the Constitution:

"**ARTICLE XVI.** The Congress shall have power to lay and collect taxes on incomes, from whatever source derived, without apportionment among the several States, and without regard to any census or enumeration."

[Endorsements]

17th Amendment to the U.S. Constitution: Direct Election of U.S. Senators

Sixty-second Congress of the United States of America;
At the Second Session,

Begun and held at the City of Washington on Monday, the fourth day of December, one thousand nine hundred and eleven.

JOINT RESOLUTION

Proposing an amendment to the Constitution providing that Senators shall be elected by the people of the several States.

Resolved by the Senate and House of Representatives of the United States of America in Congress assembled (two-thirds of each House concurring therein), That in lieu of the first paragraph of section three of Article I of the Constitution of the United States, and in lieu of so much of paragraph two of the same section as relates to the filling of vacancies, the following be proposed as an amendment to the Constitution, which shall be valid to all intents and purposes as part of the Constitution when ratified by the legislatures of three-fourths of the States:

"The Senate of the United States shall be composed of two Senators from each State, elected by the people thereof, for six years; and each Senator shall have one vote. The electors in each State shall have the qualifications requisite for electors of the most numerous branch of the State legislatures.

"When vacancies happen in the representation of any State in the Senate, the executive authority of such State shall issue writs of election to fill such vacancies: *Provided*, That the legislature of any State may empower the executive thereof to make temporary appointments until the people fill the vacancies by election as the legislature may direct.

"This amendment shall not be so construed as to affect the election or term of any Senator chosen before it becomes valid as part of the Constitution. "

[Endorsements]

The Keating-Owen Child Labor Act of 1916

Sixty-fourth Congress of the United States of America; At the First Session,

Begun and held at the City of Washington on Monday, the sixth day of December, one thousand nine hundred and fifteen.

AN ACT To PREVENT INTERSTATE COMMERCE IN THE PRODUCTS OF CHILD LABOR, AND FOR OTHER PURPOSES.

Be it enacted by the Senate and House of Representatives of the United States of America in Congress assembled, That no producer, manufacturer, or dealer shall ship or deliver for shipment in interstate or foreign commerce, any article or commodity the product of any mine or quarry situated in the United States, in which within thirty days prior to the time of the removal of such product therefrom children under the age of sixteen years have been employed or permitted to work, or any article or commodity the product of any mill, cannery, workshop, factory, or manufacturing establishment, situated in the United States, in which within thirty days prior to the removal of such product therefrom children under the age of fourteen years have been employed or permitted to work, or children between the ages of fourteen years and sixteen years have been employed or permitted to work more than eight hours in any day, or more than six days in any week, or after the hour of seven o'clock postmeridian, or before the hour of six o'clock antemeridian: *Provided,* That a prosecution and conviction of a defendant for the shipment or delivery for shipment of any article or commodity under the conditions herein prohibited shall be a bar to any further prosecution against the same defendant for shipments or deliveries for shipment of any such article or commodity before the beginning of said prosecution.

SEC. 2. That the Attorney General, the Secretary of Commerce and the Secretary of Labor shall constitute a board to make and publish from time to time uniform rules and regulations for carrying out the provisions of this Act.

SEC. 3. That for the purpose of securing proper enforcement of this Act the Secretary of Labor, or any person duly authorized by him, shall have authority to enter and inspect at any time mines quarries, mills, canneries, workshops, factories, manufacturing establishments, and other places in which goods are produced or held for interstate commerce; and the Secretary of Labor shall have authority to employ such assistance for the purposes of this Act as may from time to time be authorized by appropriation or other law.

SEC. 4. That it shall be the duty of each district attorney to whom the Secretary of Labor shall report any violation of this Act, or to whom any State factory or mining or quarry inspector, commissioner of labor, State medical inspector or school-attendance officer, or any other person shall present satisfactory evidence of any such violation to cause appropriate proceedings to be commenced and prosecuted in the proper courts of the United States without delay for the enforcement of the penalties in such cases herein provided: *Provided,* That nothing in this Act shall be construed to apply to bona fide boys' and girls' canning clubs recognized by the Agricultural Department of the several States and of the United States.

SEC. 5. That any person who violates any of the provisions of section one of this Act, or who refuses or obstructs entry or inspection authorized by section three of this Act, shall for each offense prior to the first conviction of such person under the provisions of this Act, be punished by a fine of not more than $200, and shall for each offense subsequent to such conviction be punished by a fine of not more than $1,000, nor less than $100, or by imprisonment for not more than three months, or by both such fine and imprisonment, in the discretion of the court: *Provided,* That no dealer shall be prosecuted under the provisions of this Act for a shipment, delivery for shipment, or transportation who establishes a guaranty issued by the person by whom the goods shipped or delivered for shipment or transportation were manufactured or produced, resident in the United States, to the effect that such goods were produced or manufactured in a mine or quarry in which within thirty days prior to their removal therefrom no children under the age of sixteen years were employed or permitted to work, or in a mill, cannery, workshop, factory, or manufacturing establishment in which within thirty days prior to the removal of such goods therefrom no children under the ages of fourteen years were employed or permitted to work, nor children between the ages of fourteen years and sixteen years employed or permitted to work more than eight hours in any day or more than six days in any week or after the hour of seven o'clock postmeridian or before the hour of six o'clock antemeridian; and in such event, if the guaranty contains any false statement or a material fact the guarantor shall be amenable to prosecution and to the fine or imprisonment provided by this section for violation of the provisions of this Act. Said guaranty, to afford the protection above provided, shall contain the name and address of the person giving the same: And provided further, That no producer, manufacturer, or dealer shall be prosecuted under this Act for the shipment, delivery for shipment, or transportation of a product of any mine, quarry, mill, cannery, workshop, factory, or manufacturing establishment, if the only employment therein within thirty days prior to the removal of such product therefrom, of a child under the age of sixteen years has been that of a child as to whom the producer, or manufacturer has in; good faith procured, at the time of employing such child, and has since in good faith relied upon and kept on file a certificate, issued in such form, under such conditions, any by such persons as may be prescribed by the board, showing the child to be of such an age that the shipment, delivery for shipment, or transportation was not prohibited by this Act. Any person who knowingly makes a false statement or presents false evidence in or in relation to any such certificate or application therefor shall be amenable to prosecution and to the fine or imprisonment provided by this section for violations of this Act. In any State designated by the board, an employment certificate or other similar paper as to the age of the child, issued under the laws of that State and not inconsistent with the provisions of this Act, shall have the same force and effect as a certificate herein provided for.

SEC. 6. That the word "person" as used in this Act shall be construed to include any individual or corporation or the members of any partnership or other unincorporated association. The term "ship or deliver for shipment in interstate or foreign commerce" as used in this Act means to transport or to ship or deliver for shipment from any State or Territory or the District of Columbia to or through any other State or Territory or the District of Columbia or to any foreign country; and in the case of a dealer means only to transport or to ship or deliver for shipment from the State, Territory or district of manufacture or production.

SEC. 7. That this Act shall take effect from and after one year from the date of its passage.

Approved, September 1, 1916.

The Zimmermann Telegram

(DECODED MESSAGE TEXT OF THE ZIMMERMANN TELEGRAM)

FROM 2nd from London # 5747.

"We intend to begin on the first of February unrestricted submarine warfare. We shall endeavor in spite of this to keep the United States of America neutral. In the event of this not succeeding, we make Mexico a proposal or alliance on the following basis: make war together, make peace together, generous financial support and an understanding on our part that Mexico is to reconquer the lost territory in Texas, New Mexico, and Arizona. The settlement in detail is left to you. You will inform the President of the above most secretly as soon as the outbreak of war with the United States of America is certain and add the suggestion that he should, on his own initiative, invite Japan to immediate adherence and at the same time mediate between Japan and ourselves. Please call the President's attention to the fact that the ruthless employment of our submarines now offers the prospect of compelling England in a few months to make peace."

Signed, ZIMMERMANN.

Joint Address to Congress Leading to a Declaration of War Against Germany

ADDRESS:

GENTLEMEN OF THE CONGRESS:

I have called the Congress into extraordinary session because there are serious, very serious, choices of policy to be made, and made immediately, which it was neither right nor constitutionally permissible that I should assume the responsibility of making.

On the third of February last I officially laid before you the extraordinary announcement of the Imperial German Government that on and after the first day of February it was its purpose to put aside all restraints of law or of humanity and use its submarines to sink every vessel that sought to approach either the ports of Great Britain and Ireland or the western coasts of Europe or any of the ports controlled by the enemies of Germany within the Mediterranean. That had seemed to be the object of the German submarine warfare earlier in the war, but since April of last year the Imperial Government had somewhat restrained the commanders of its undersea craft in conformity with its promise then given to us that passenger boats should not be sunk and that due warning would be given to all other vessels which its submarines might seek to destroy when no resistance was offered or escape attempted, and care taken that their crews were given at least a fair chance to save their lives in their open boats. The precautions taken were meager and haphazard enough, as was proved in distressing instance after instance in the progress of the cruel and unmanly business, but a certain degree of restraint was observed. The new policy has swept every restriction aside. Vessels of every kind, whatever their flag, their character, their cargo, their destination, their errand, have been ruthlessly sent to the bottom: without warning and without thought of help or mercy for those on board, the vessels of friendly neutrals along with those of belligerents. Even hospital ships and ships carrying relief to the sorely bereaved and stricken people of Belgium, though the latter were provided with safe conduct through the proscribed areas by the German Government itself and were distinguished by unmistakable marks of identity, have been sunk with the same reckless lack of compassion or of principle. I was for a little while unable to believe that such things would in fact be done by any government that had hitherto subscribed to the humane practices of civilized nations. International law had its origin in the attempt to set up some law which would be respected and observed upon the seas, where no nation had right of dominion and where lay the free highways of the world.... This minimum of right the German Government has swept aside under the plea of retaliation and necessity and because it had no weapons which it could use at sea except these which it is impossible to employ as it is employing them without throwing to the winds all scruples of humanity or of respect for the understandings that were supposed to underlie the intercourse of the world. I am not now thinking of the loss of property involved, immense and serious as that is, but only of the wanton and wholesale destruction of the lives of noncombatants, men, women, and children, engaged in pursuits which have always, even in the darkest periods of modern history, been deemed innocent and legitimate. Property can be paid for; the lives of peaceful and innocent people cannot be. The present German submarine warfare against commerce is a warfare against mankind.

It is a war against all nations. American ships have been sunk, American lives taken, in ways which it has stirred us very deeply to learn of, but the ships and people of other neutral and friendly nations have been sunk and overwhelmed in the waters in the same way. There has been no discrimination. The challenge is to all mankind. Each nation must decide for itself how it will meet it. The choice we make for ourselves must be made with a moderation of counsel and a temperateness of judgment befitting our character and our motives as a nation. We must put excited feeling away. Our motive will not be revenge or the victorious assertion of the physical might of the nation, but only the vindication of right, of human right, of which we are only a single champion.

When I addressed the Congress on the twenty-sixth of February last I thought that it would suffice to assert our neutral rights with arms, our right to use the seas against unlawful interference, our right to keep our people safe against unlawful violence. But armed neutrality, it now appears, is impracticable. Because submarines are in effect outlaws when used as the German submarines have been used against merchant shipping, it is impossible to defend ships against their attacks as the law of nations has assumed that merchantmen would defend themselves against privateers or cruisers, visible craft giving chase upon the open sea. It is common prudence in such circumstances, grim necessity indeed, to endeavor to destroy them before they have shown their own intention. They must be dealt with upon sight, if dealt with at all. The German Government denies the right of neutrals to use arms at all within the areas of the sea which it has proscribed, even in the defense of rights which no modern publicist has ever before questioned their right to defend. The intimation is conveyed that the armed guards which we have placed on our merchant ships will be treated as beyond the pale of law and subject to be dealt with as pirates would be. Armed neutrality is ineffectual enough at best; in such circumstances and in the face of such pretensions it is worse than ineffectual: it is likely only to produce what it was meant to prevent; it is practically certain to draw us into the war without either the rights or the effectiveness of belligerents. There is one choice we cannot make, we are incapable of making: we will not choose the path of submission and suffer the most sacred rights of our Nation and our people to be ignored or violated. The wrongs against which we now array ourselves are no common wrongs; they cut to the very roots of human life.

With a profound sense of the solemn and even tragical character of the step I am taking and of the grave responsibilities which it involves, but in unhesitating obedience to what I deem my constitutional duty, I advise that the Congress declare the recent course of the Imperial German Government to be in fact nothing less than war against the government and people of the United States; that it formally accept the status of belligerent which has thus been thrust upon it, and that it take immediate steps not only to put the country in a more thorough state of defense but also to exert all its power and employ all its resources to bring the Government of the German Empire to terms and end the war.

What this will involve is clear. It will involve the utmost practicable cooperation in counsel and action with the governments now at war with Germany, and, as incident to that, the extension to those governments of the most liberal financial credit, in order that our resources may so far as possible be added to theirs. It will involve the organization and mobilization of all the material resources of the country to supply the materials of war and serve the incidental needs of the Nation in the most abundant and yet the most economical and efficient way possible. It will involve the immediate full equipment of the navy in all respects but particularly in supplying it with the best means of dealing with the enemy's submarines. It will involve the immediate addition to the armed forces of the United States already provided for by law in case of war at least five hundred thousand men, who should, in my opinion, be chosen upon the principle of universal liability to service, and also the authorization of subsequent additional increments of equal force so soon as they may be needed and can be handled in training. It will involve also, of course, the granting of adequate credits to the Government, sustained, I hope, so far as they can equitably be sustained by the present generation, by well conceived taxation. I say sustained so far as may be equitable by taxation because it seems to me that it would be most unwise to base the credits which will now be necessary entirely on money borrowed. It is our duty, I most respectfully urge, to protect our people so far as we may against the very serious hardships and evils which would be likely to arise out of the inflation which would be produced by vast loans.

In carrying out the measures by which these things are to be accomplished we should keep constantly in mind the wisdom of interfering as little as possible in our own preparation and in the equipment of our own military forces with the duty for it will be a very practical duty of supplying the nations already at war with Germany with the materials which they can obtain only from us or by our assistance. They are in the field and we should help them in every way to be effective there.

I shall take the liberty of suggesting, through the several executive departments of the Government, for the consideration of your committees, measures for the accomplishment of the several objects I have mentioned. I hope that it will be your pleasure to deal with them as having been framed after very careful thought by the branch of the Government upon which the responsibility of conducting the war and safeguarding the Nation will most directly fall.

While we do these things, these deeply momentous things, let us be very clear, and make very clear to all the world what our motives and our objects are.

My own thought has not been driven from its habitual and normal course by the unhappy events of the last two months, and I do not believe that the thought of the Nation has been altered or clouded by them. I have exactly the same things in mind now that I had in mind when I addressed the Senate on the twenty-second of January last, the same that I had in mind when I addressed the Congress on the third of February and on the twenty-sixth of February. Our object now, as then, is to vindicate the principles of peace and justice in the life of the world as against selfish and autocratic power and to set up amongst the really free and self-governed peoples of the world such a concert of purpose and of action as will henceforth insure the observance of those principles. Neutrality is no longer feasible or desirable where the peace of the world is involved and the freedom of its peoples, and the menace to that peace and freedom lies in the existence of autocratic governments backed by organized force which is controlled wholly by their will, not by the will of their people. We have seen the last of neutrality in such circumstances. We are at the beginning of an age in which it will be insisted that the same standards of conduct and of responsibility for wrong done shall be observed among nations and their governments that are observed among the individual citizens of civilized states.

We have no quarrel with the German people. We have no feeling towards them but one of sympathy and friendship. It was not upon their impulse that their government acted in entering this war. It was not with their previous knowledge or approval. It was a war determined upon as wars used to be determined upon in the old, unhappy days when peoples were nowhere consulted by their rulers and wars were provoked and waged in the interest of dynasties or of little groups of ambitious men who were accustomed to use their fellow men as pawns and tools.

Self-governed nations do not fill their neighbor states with spies or set the course of intrigue to bring about some critical posture of affairs which will give them an opportunity to strike and make conquest. Such designs can be successfully worked out only under cover and where no one has the right to ask questions. Cunningly contrived plans of deception or aggression, carried, it may be, from generation to generation, can be worked out and kept from the light only within the privacy of courts or behind the carefully guarded confidences of a narrow and privileged class. They are happily impossible where public opinion commands and insists upon full information concerning all the nation's affairs.

A steadfast concert for peace can never be maintained except by a partnership of democratic nations. No autocratic government could be trusted to keep faith within it or observe its covenants. It must be a league of honor, a partnership of opinion. Intrigue would eat its vitals away; the plottings of inner circles who could plan what they would and render account to no one would be a corruption seated at its very heart. Only free peonies can hold their purpose and their honor steady to a common end and prefer the interests of mankind to any narrow interest of their own.

Does not every American feel that assurance has been added to our hope for the future peace of the world by the wonderful and heartening things that have been happening within the last few weeks in Russia? Russia was known by those who knew it best to have been always in fact democratic at heart, in all the vital habits of her thought, in all the intimate relationships of her people that spoke their natural instinct, their habitual attitude towards life. The autocracy that crowned the summit of her political structure, long as it had stood and terrible as was the reality of its power, was not in fact Russian in origin, character, or purpose; and now it has been shaken off and the great, generous Russian people have been added in all their naive majesty and might to the forces that are fighting for freedom in the world, for justice, and for peace. Here is a fit partner for a League of Honor.

One of the things that has served to convince us that the Prussian, autocracy was not and could never be our friend is that from the very outset of the present war it has filled our unsuspecting communities and even our offices of government with spies and set criminal intrigues everywhere afoot against our national unity of counsel, our peace Within and without, our industries and our commerce. Indeed it is now evident that its spies were here even before the war began; and it is unhappily not a matter of conjecture but a fact proved in our courts of justice that the intrigues which have more than once come perilously near to disturbing the peace and dislocating the industries of the country have been carried on at the instigation, with the support, and even under the personal direction of official agents of the Imperial Government accredited to the Government of the United States. Even in checking these things and trying to extirpate them we have sought to put the most generous interpretation possible upon them because we knew that their source lay, not in any hostile feeling or purpose of the German people towards us (who were, no doubt, as ignorant of them as we ourselves were), but only in the selfish designs of a Government that did what it pleased and told its people nothing. But they have played their part in serving to convince us at last that that Government entertains no real friendship for us and means to act against our peace and security at its convenience. That it means to stir up enemies against us at our very doors the intercepted note to the German Minister at Mexico City is eloquent evidence.

We are accepting this challenge of hostile purpose because we know that in such a Government, following such methods, we can never have a friend; and that in the presence of its organized power, always lying in wait to accomplish we know not what purpose, there can be no assured security for the democratic Governments of the world. We are now about to accept gauge of battle with this natural foe to liberty and shall, if necessary, spend the whole force of the nation to check and nullify its pretensions and its power. We are glad, now that we see the facts with no veil of false pretense about them to fight thus for the ultimate peace of the world and for the liberation of its peoples, the German peoples included: for the rights of nations great and small and the privilege of men everywhere to choose their way of life and of obedience. The world must be made safe for democracy. Its peace must be planted upon the tested foundations of political liberty. We have no selfish ends to serve.

We desire no conquest, no dominion. We seek no indemnities for ourselves, no material compensation for the sacrifices we shall freely make. We are but one of the champions of the rights of mankind. We shall be satisfied when those rights have been made as secure as the faith and the freedom of nations can make them. Just because we fight without rancor and without selfish object, seeking nothing for ourselves but what we shall wish to share with all free peoples, we shall, I feel confident, conduct our operations as belligerents without passion and ourselves observe with proud punctilio the principles of right and of fair play we profess to be fighting for.

I have said nothing of the Governments allied with the Imperial Government of Germany because they have not made war upon us or challenged us to defend our right and our honor. The Austro-Hungarian Government has, indeed, avowed its unqualified endorsement and acceptance of the reckless and lawless submarine warfare adopted now without disguise by the Imperial German Government, and it has therefore not been possible for this Government to receive Count Tarnowski, the Ambassador recently accredited to this Government by the Imperial and Royal Government of Austria-Hungary; but that Government has not actually engaged in warfare against citizens of the United States on the seas, and I take the liberty, for the present at least, of postponing a discussion of our relations with the authorities at Vienna. We enter this war only where we are clearly forced into it because there are no other means of defending our rights.

It will be all the easier for us to conduct ourselves as belligerents in a high spirit of right and fairness because we act without animus, not in enmity towards a people or with the desire to bring any injury or disadvantage upon them, but only in armed opposition to an irresponsible government which has thrown aside all considerations of humanity and of right and is running amuck. We are, let me say again, the sincere friends of the German people, and shall desire nothing so much as the early reestablishment of intimate relations of mutual advantage between us,—however hard it may be for them, for the time being, to believe that this is spoken from our hearts. We have borne with their present Government through all these bitter months because of that friendship,—exercising a patience and forbearance which would otherwise have been impossible. We shall, happily, still have an opportunity to prove that friendship in our daily attitude and actions towards the millions of men and women of German birth and native sympathy who live amongst us and share our life, and we shall be proud to prove it towards all who are in fact loyal to their neighbors and to the Government in the hour of test. They are, most of them, as true and loyal Americans as if they had never known any other fealty or allegiance. They will be prompt to stand with us in rebuking and restraining the few who may be of a different mind and purpose. If there should be disloyalty, it will be dealt with with a firm hand of stern repression; but, if it lifts its head at all, it will lift it only here and there and without countenance except from a lawless and malignant few.

It is a distressing and oppressive duty, Gentlemen of the Congress, which I have performed in thus addressing you. There are, it may be many months of fiery trial and sacrifice ahead of us. It is a fearful thing to lead this great peaceful people into war, into the most terrible and disastrous of all wars, civilization itself seeming to be in the balance.

But the right is more precious than peace, and we shall fight for the things which we have always carried nearest our hearts,—for democracy, for the right of those who submit to authority to have a voice in their own Governments, for the rights and liberties of small nations, for a universal dominion of right by such a concert of free peoples as shall bring peace and safety to all nations and make the world itself at last free. To such a task we can dedicate our lives and our fortunes, every thing that we are and everything that we have, with the pride of those who know that the day has come when America is privileged to spend her blood and her might for the principles that gave her birth and happiness and the peace which she has treasured. God helping her, she can do no other.

President Woodrow Wilson's 14 Points

It will be our wish and purpose that the processes of peace, when they are begun, shall be absolutely open and that they shall involve and permit henceforth no secret understandings of any kind. The day of conquest and aggrandizement is gone by; so is also the day of secret covenants entered into in the interest of particular governments and likely at some unlooked-for moment to upset the peace of the world. It is this happy fact, now clear to the view of every public man whose thoughts do not still linger in an age that is dead and gone, which makes it possible for every nation whose purposes are consistent with justice and the peace of the world to avow nor or at any other time the objects it has in view. We entered this war because violations of right had occurred which touched us to the quick and made the life of our own people impossible unless they were corrected and the world secure once for all against their recurrence. What we demand in this war, therefore, is nothing peculiar to ourselves. It is that the world be made fit and safe to live in; and particularly that it be made safe for every peace-loving nation which, like our own, wishes to live its own life, determine its own institutions, be assured of justice and fair dealing by the other peoples of the world as against force and selfish aggression. All the peoples of the world are in effect partners in this interest, and for our own part we see very clearly that unless justice be done to others it will not be done to us. The programme of the world's peace, therefore, is our programme; and that programme, the only possible programme, as we see it, is this:

I. Open covenants of peace, openly arrived at, after which there shall be no private international understandings of any kind but diplomacy shall proceed always frankly and in the public view.

II. Absolute freedom of navigation upon the seas, outside territorial waters, alike in peace and in war, except as the seas may be closed in whole or in part by international action for the enforcement of international covenants.

III. The removal, so far as possible, of all economic barriers and the establishment of an equality of trade conditions among all the nations consenting to the peace and associating themselves for its maintenance.

IV. Adequate guarantees given and taken that national armaments will be reduced to the lowest point consistent with domestic safety.

V. A free, open-minded, and absolutely impartial adjustment of all colonial claims, based upon a strict observance of the principle that in determining all such questions of sovereignty the interests of the populations concerned must have equal weight with the equitable claims of the government whose title is to be determined.

VI. The evacuation of all Russian territory and such a settlement of all questions affecting Russia as will secure the best and freest cooperation of the other nations of the world in obtaining for her an unhampered and unembarrassed opportunity for the independent determination of her own political development and national policy and assure her of a sincere welcome into the society of free nations under institutions of her own choosing; and, more than a welcome, assistance also of every kind that she may need and may herself desire. The treatment accorded Russia by her sister nations in the months to come will be the acid test of their good will, of their comprehension of her needs as distinguished from their own interests, and of their intelligent and unselfish sympathy.

VII. Belgium, the whole world will agree, must be evacuated and restored, without any attempt to limit the sovereignty which she enjoys in common with all other free nations. No other single act will serve as this will serve to restore confidence among the nations in the laws which they have themselves set and determined for the government of their relations with one another. Without this healing act the whole structure and validity of international law is forever impaired.

VIII. All French territory should be freed and the invaded portions restored, and the wrong done to France by Prussia in 1871 in the matter of Alsace-Lorraine, which has unsettled the peace of the world for nearly fifty years, should be righted, in order that peace may once more be made secure in the interest of all.

IX. A readjustment of the frontiers of Italy should be effected along clearly recognizable lines of nationality.

X. The peoples of Austria-Hungary, whose place among the nations we wish to see safeguarded and assured, should be accorded the freest opportunity to autonomous development.

XI. Rumania, Serbia, and Montenegro should be evacuated; occupied territories restored; Serbia accorded free and secure access to the sea; and the relations of the several Balkan states to one another determined by friendly counsel along historically established lines of allegiance and nationality; and international guarantees of the political and economic independence and territorial integrity of the several Balkan states should be entered into.

XII. The turkish portion of the present Ottoman Empire should be assured a secure sovereignty, but the other nationalities which are now under Turkish rule should be assured an undoubted security of life and an absolutely unmolested opportunity of autonomous development, and the Dardanelles should be permanently opened as a free passage to the ships and commerce of all nations under international guarantees.

XIII. An independent Polish state should be erected which should include the territories inhabited by indisputably Polish populations, which should be assured a free and secure access to the sea, and whose political and economic independence and territorial integrity should be guaranteed by international covenant.

XIV. A general association of nations must be formed under specific covenants for the purpose of affording mutual guarantees of political independence and territorial integrity to great and small states alike.

In regard to these essential rectifications of wrong and assertions of right we feel ourselves to be intimate partners of all the governments and peoples associated together against the Imperialists. We cannot be separated in interest or divided in purpose. We stand together until the end.

For such arrangements and covenants we are willing to fight and to continue to fight until they are achieved; but only because we wish the right to prevail and desire a just and stable peace such as can be secured only by removing the chief provocations to war, which this programme does remove. We have no jealousy of German greatness, and there is nothing in this programme that impairs it. We grudge her no achievement or distinction of learning or of pacific enterprise such as have made her record very bright and very enviable. We do not wish to injure her or to block in any way her legitimate influence or power. We do not wish to fight her either with arms or with hostile arrangements of trade if she is willing to associate herself with us and the other peace- loving nations of the world in covenants of justice and law and fair dealing. We wish her only to accept a place of equality among the peoples of the world—the new world in which we now live—instead of a place of mastery.

19th Amendment to the U.S. Constitution: Women's Right to Vote

Sixty-sixth Congress of the United States of America; At the First Session,

Begun and held at the City of Washington on Monday, the nineteenth day of May, one thousand nine hundred and nineteen.

JOINT RESOLUTION

Proposing an amendment to the Constitution extending the right of suffrage to women.

Resolved by the Senate and House of Representatives of the United States of America in Congress assembled (two-thirds of each House concurring therein), That the following article is proposed as an amendment to the Constitution, which shall be valid to all intents and purposes as part of the Constitution when ratified by the legislature of three-fourths of the several States.

"ARTICLE ————.

"The right of citizens of the United States to vote shall not be denied or abridged by the United States or by any State on account of sex.

Congress shall have power to enforce this article by appropriate legislation."
[endorsements]

The Boulder Canyon Project Act

AN ACT To provide for the construction of works for the protection and development of the Colorado River Basin, for the approval of the Colorado River compact, and for other purposes.

Be it enacted by the Senate and House of Representatives of the United States of America in Congress assembled, That for the purpose of controlling the floods, improving navigation and regulating the flow of the Colorado River, providing for storage and for the delivery of the stored waters thereof for reclamation of public lands and other beneficial uses exclusively within the United States, and for the generation of electrical energy as a means of making the project herein authorized a self-supporting and financially solvent undertaking, the Secretary of the Interior, subject to the terms of the Colorado River compact hereinafter mentioned, is hereby authorized to construct, operate, and maintain a dam and incidental works in the main stream of the Colorado River at Black Canyon or Boulder Canyon adequate to create a storage reservoir of a capacity of not less than twenty million acre-feet of water and a main canal and appurtenant structures located entirely within the United States connecting the Laguna Dam, or other suitable diversion dam, which the Secretary of the Interior is hereby authorized to construct if deemed necessary or advisable by him upon engineering or economic considerations, with the Imperial and Coachella Valleys in California, the expenditures for said main canal and appurtenant structures to be reimbursable, as provided in the reclamation law, and shall not be paid out of revenues derived from the sale or disposal of water power or electric energy at the dam authorized to be constructed at said Black Canyon or Boulder Canyon, or for water for potable purposes outside of the Imperial and Coachella Valleys: Provided, however, That no charge shall be made for water or for the use, storage, or delivery of water for irrigation or water for potable purposes in the Imperial or Coachella Valleys; also to construct and equip, operate, and maintain at or near said dam, or cause to be constructed, a complete plant and incidental structures suitable for the fullest economic development of electrical energy from the water discharged from said reservoir; and to acquire by proceedings in eminent domain, or otherwise all lands, rights-of-way, and other property necessary for said purposes.

SEC. 2. (a) There is hereby established a special fund, to be known as the "Colorado River Dam fund" (hereinafter referred to as the "fund"), and to be available, as hereafter provided, only for carrying out the provisions of this Act. All revenues received in carrying out the provisions of this Act shall be paid into and expenditures shall be made out of the fund, under the direction of the Secretary of the Interior.

(b) The Secretary of the Treasury is authorized to advance to the fund, from time to time and within the appropriations therefor, such amounts as the Secretary of the Interior deems necessary for carrying out the provisions of this Act, except that the aggregate amount of such advances shall not exceed the sum of $165,000,000. Of this amount the sum of $25,000,000 shall be allocated to flood control and shall be repaid to the United States out of 62$^1/_2$ per centum of revenues, if any, in excess of the amount necessary to meet periodical payments during the period of amortization, as provided in section 4 of this Act. If said sum of $25,000,000 is not repaid in full during the period of amortization, then 62$^1/_2$ per centum of all net revenues shall be applied to payment of the remainder. Interest at the rate of 4 per centum per annum accruing during the year upon the amounts so advanced and remaining unpaid shall be paid annually out of the fund, except as herein otherwise provided.

(c) Moneys in the fund advanced under subdivision (b) shall be available only for expenditures for construction and the payment of interest, during construction, upon the amounts so advanced. No expenditures out of the fund shall be made for operation and maintenance except from appropriations therefor.

(d) The Secretary of the Treasury shall charge the fund as of June 30 in each year with such amount as may be necessary for the payment of interest on advances made under subdivision (b) at the rate of 4 per centum per annum accrued during the year upon the amounts so advanced and remaining unpaid, except that if the fund is insufficient to meet the payment of interest the Secretary of the Treasury may, in his discretion, defer any part of such payment, and the amount so deferred shall bear interest at the rate of 4 per centum per annum until paid.

(e) The Secretary of the Interior shall certify to the Secretary of the Treasury, at the close of each fiscal year, the amount of money in the fund in excess of the amount necessary for construction, operation, and maintenance, and payment of interest. Upon receipt of each such certificate the Secretary of the Treasury is authorized and directed to charge the fund with the amount so certified as repayment of the advances made under subdivision (b), which amount shall be covered into the Treasury to the credit of miscellaneous receipts.

SEC. 3. There is hereby authorized to be appropriated from time to time, out of any money in the Treasury not otherwise appropriated, such sums of money as may be necessary to carry out the purposes of this Act, not exceeding in the aggregate $165,000,000.

SEC. 4. (a) This Act shall not take effect and no authority shall be exercised hereunder and no work shall be begun and no moneys expended on or in connection with the works or structures provided for in this Act, and no water rights shall be claimed or initiated hereunder, and no steps shall be taken by the United States or by others to initiate or perfect any claims to the use of water pertinent to such works or structures unless and until (1) the States of Arizona, California, Colorado, Nevada, New Mexico, Utah, and Wyoming shall have ratified the Colorado River compact, mentioned in section 13 hereof, and the President by public proclamation shall have so declared, or (2) if said States fail to ratify the said compact within six months from the date of the passage of this Act then, until six of said States, including the State of California, shall ratify said compact and shall consent to waive the provisions of the first paragraph of Article XI of said compact, which makes the same binding and obligatory only when approved by each of the seven States signatory thereto, and shall have approved said compact without conditions, save that of such six-State approval, and the President by public proclamation shall have so declared, and, further, until the State of California, by act of its legislature, shall agree irrevocably and unconditionally with the United States and for the benefit of the States of Arizona, Colorado, Nevada, New Mexico, Utah, and Wyoming, as

an express covenant and in consideration of the passage of this Act, that the aggregate annual consumptive use (diversions less returns to the river) of water of and from the Colorado River for use in the State of California, including all uses under contracts made under the provisions of this Act and all water necessary for the supply of any rights which may now exist, shall not exceed four million four hundred thousand acre-feet of the waters apportioned to the lower basin States by paragraph (a) of Article III of the Colorado River compact, plus not more than one-half of any excess or surplus waters unapportioned by said compact, such uses always to be subject to the terms of said compact. The States of Arizona, California, and Nevada are authorized to enter into an agreement which shall provide (1) that of the 7,500,000 acre-feet annually apportioned to the lower basin by paragraph (a) of Article III of the Colorado River compact, there shall be apportioned to the State of Nevada 300,000 acre-feet and to the State of Arizona 2,800,000 acre-feet for exclusive beneficial consumptive use in perpetuity, and (2) that the State of Arizona may annually use one-half of the excess or surplus waters unapportioned by the Colorado River compact, and (3) that the State of Arizona shall have the exclusive beneficial consumptive use of the Gila River and its tributaries within the boundaries of said State, and (4) that the waters of the Gila River and its tributaries, except return flow after the same enters the Colorado River, shall never be subject to any diminution whatever by any allowance of water which may be made by treaty or otherwise to the United States of Mexico but if, as provided in paragraph (c) of Article III of the Colorado River compact, it shall become necessary to supply water to the United States of Mexico from waters over and above the quantities which are surplus as defined by said compact, then the State of California shall and will mutually agree with the State of Arizona to supply, out of the main stream of the Colorado River, one-half of any deficiency which must be supplied to Mexico by the lower basin, and (5) that the State of California shall and will further mutually agree with the States of Arizona and Nevada that none of said three States shall withhold water and none shall require the delivery of water, which cannot reasonably be applied to domestic and agricultural uses, and (6) that all of the provisions of said tri-State agreement shall be subject in all particulars to the provisions of the Colorado River compact, and (7) said agreement to take effect upon the ratification of the Colorado River compact by Arizona,

California, and Nevada. (b) Before any money is appropriated for the construction of said dam or power plant, or any construction work done or contracted for, the Secretary of the Interior shall make provision for revenues by contract, in accordance with the provisions of this Act, adequate in his judgment to insure payment of all expenses of operation and maintenance of said works incurred by the United States and the repayment, within fifty years from the date of the completion of said works, of all amounts advanced to the fund under subdivision (b) of section 2 for such works, together with interest thereon made reimbursable under this Act.

Before any money is appropriated for the construction of said main canal and appurtenant structures to connect the Laguna Dam with the Imperial and Coachella Valleys in California, or any construction work is done upon said canal or contracted for, the Secretary of the Interior shall make provision for revenues, by contract or otherwise, adequate in his judgment to insure payment of all expenses of construction, operation, and maintenance of said main canal and appurtenant structures in the manner provided in the reclamation law.

If during the period of amortization the Secretary of the Interior shall receive revenues in excess of the amount necessary to meet the periodical payments to the United States as provided in the contract, or contracts, executed under this Act, then, immediately after the settlement of such periodical payments, he shall pay to the State of Arizona $18^3/_4$ per centum of such excess revenues and to the State of Nevada $18^3/_4$ per centum of such excess revenues.

SEC. 5. That the Secretary of the Interior is hereby authorized, under such general regulations as he may prescribe, to contract for the storage of water in said reservoir and for the delivery thereof at such points on the river and on said canal as may be agreed upon, for irrigation and domestic uses, and generation of electrical energy and delivery at the switchboard to States, municipal corporations, political subdivisions, and private corporations of electrical energy generated at said dam, upon charges that will provide revenue which, in addition to other revenue accruing under the reclamation law and under this Act, will in his judgment cover all expenses of operation and maintenance incurred by the United States on account of works constructed under this Act and the payments to the United States under subdivision (b) of section 4. Contracts respecting water for irrigation

and domestic uses shall be for permanent service and shall conform to paragraph (a) of section 4 of this Act. No person shall have or be entitled to have the use for any purpose of the water stored as aforesaid except by contract made as herein stated. After the repayments to the United States of all money advanced with interest, charges shall be on such basis and the revenues derived therefrom shall be kept in a separate fund to be expended within the Colorado River Basin as may hereafter be prescribed by the Congress. General and uniform regulations shall be prescribed by the said Secretary for the awarding of contracts for the sale and delivery of electrical energy, and for renewals under subdivision (b) of this section, and in making such contracts the following shall govern:

(a) No contract for electrical energy or for generation of electrical energy shall be of longer duration than fifty years from the date at which such energy is ready for delivery. Contracts made pursuant to subdivision (a) of this section shall be made with a view to obtaining reasonable returns and shall contain provisions whereby at the end of fifteen years from the date of their execution and every ten years thereafter, there shall be readjustment of the contract, upon the demand of either party thereto, either upward or downward as to price, as the Secretary of the Interior may find to be justified by competitive conditions at distributing points or competitive centers and with provisions under which disputes or disagreements as to interpretation or performance of such contract shall be determined either by arbitration or court proceedings, the Secretary of the Interior being authorized to act for the United States in such readjustments or proceedings.

(b) The holder of any contract for electrical energy not in default thereunder shall be entitled to a renewal thereof upon such terms and conditions as may be authorized or required under the then existing laws and regulations, unless the property of such holder dependent for its usefulness on a continuation of the contract be purchased or acquired and such holder be compensated for damages to its property, used and useful in the transmission and distribution of such electrical energy and not taken, resulting from the termination of the supply.

(c) Contracts for the use of water and necessary privileges for the generation and distribution of hydroelectric energy or for the sale and delivery of electrical energy shall be made with responsible applicants therefor who will pay the price fixed by the said Secretary with a view to meeting the revenue requirements herein provided for. In case of conflicting applications, if any, such conflicts shall be resolved by the said Secretary, after hearing, with due regard to the public interest, and in conformity with the policy expressed in the Federal Water Power Act as to conflicting applications for permits and licenses, except that preference to applicants for the use of water and appurtenant works and privileges necessary for the generation and distribution of hydroelectric energy, or for delivery at the switchboard of a hydroelectric plant, shall be given, first, to a State for the generation or purchase of electric energy for use in the State, and the States of Arizona, California, and Nevada shall be given equal opportunity as such applicants.

The rights covered by such preference shall be contracted for by such State within six months after notice by the Secretary of the Interior and to be paid for on the same terms and conditions as may be provided in other similar contracts made by said Secretary: Provided, however, That no application of a State or a political subdivision for an allocation of water for power purposes or of electrical energy shall be denied or another application in conflict therewith be granted on the ground that the bond issue of such State or political subdivision, necessary to enable the applicant to utilize such water and appurtenant works and privileges necessary for the generation and distribution of hydroelectric energy or the electrical energy applied for, has not been authorized or marketed, until after a reasonable time, to be determined by the said Secretary, has been given to such applicant to have such bond issue authorized and marketed.

(d) Any agency receiving a contract for electrical energy equivalent to one hundred thousand firm horsepower, or more, may, when deemed feasible by the said Secretary, from engineering and economic considerations and under general regulations prescribed by him, be required to permit any other agency having contracts hereunder for less than the equivalent of twenty-five thousand firm horsepower, upon application to the Secretary of the Interior made within sixty days from the execution of the contract of the agency the use of whose transmission line is applied for, to participate in the benefits and use of any main transmission line constructed or to be constructed by the former for carrying such energy (not exceeding, however, one-fourth the capacity of

such line), upon payment by such other agencies of a reasonable share of the cost of construction, operation, and maintenance thereof. The use is hereby authorized of such public and reserved lands of the United States as may be necessary or convenient for the construction, operation, and maintenance of main transmission lines to transmit said electrical energy.

SEC. 6. That the dam and reservoir provided for by section 1 hereof shall be used: First, for river regulation, improvement of navigation, and flood control; second, for irrigation and domestic uses and satisfaction of present perfected rights in pursuance of Article VIII of said Colorado River compact; and third, for power. The title to said dam, reservoir, plant, and incidental works shall forever remain in the United States, and the United States shall, until otherwise provided by Congress, control, manage, and operate the same, except as herein otherwise provided: Provided, however, That the Secretary of the Interior may, in his discretion, enter into contracts of lease of a unit or units of any Government-built plant, with right to generate electrical energy, or, alternatively, to enter into contracts of lease for the use of water for the generation of electrical energy as herein provided, in either of which events the provisions of section 5 of this Act relating to revenue, term, renewals, determination of conflicting applications, and joint use of transmission lines under contracts for the sale of electrical energy, shall apply.

The Secretary of the Interior shall prescribe and enforce rules and regulations conforming with the requirements of the Federal Water Power Act, so far as applicable respecting maintenance of works in condition of repair adequate for their efficient operation, maintenance of a system of accounting, control of rates and service in the absence of State regulation or interstate agreement valuation for rate-making purposes, transfers of contracts, contracts extending beyond the lease period, expropriation of excessive profits, recapture and/or emergency use by the United States of property of lessees, and penalties for enforcing regulations made under this Act of penalizing failure to comply with such regulations or with the provisions of this Act. He shall also conform with other provisions of the Federal Water Power Act and of the rules and regulations of the Federal Power Commission, which have been devised or which may be hereafter devised, for the protection of the investor and consumer. The Federal Power Commission is hereby directed not to issue or approve any permits or licenses under said Federal Water Power Act upon or affecting the Colorado River or any of its tributaries, except the Gila River, in the States of Colorado, Wyoming, Utah, New Mexico, Nevada, Arizona, and California until this Act shall become effective as provided in section 4 herein.

SEC. 7. That the Secretary of the Interior may, in his discretion, when repayments to the United States of all money advanced, with interest, reimbursable hereunder, shall have been made, transfer the title to said canal and appurtenant structures, except the Laguna Dam and the main canal and appurtenant structures down to and including Syphon Drop, to the districts or other agencies of the United States having a beneficial interest therein in proportion to their respective capital investments under such form of organization as may be acceptable to him. The said districts or other agencies shall have the privilege at any time of utilizing by contract or otherwise such power possibilities as may exist upon said canal, in proportion to their respective contributions or obligations toward the capital cost of said canal and appurtenant structures from and including the diversion works to the point where each respective power plant may be located. The net proceeds from any power development on said canal shall be paid into the fund and credited to said districts or other agencies on their said contracts, in proportion to their rights to develop power, until the districts or other agencies using said canal shall have paid thereby and under any contract or otherwise an amount of money equivalent to the operation and maintenance expense and cost of construction thereof.

SEC. 8. (a) The United States, its permittees, licensees, and contractees, and all users and appropriators of water stored, diverted, carried, and/or distributed by the reservoir, canals, and other works herein authorized, shall observe and be subject to and controlled by said Colorado River compact in the construction, management, and operation of said reservoir, canals, and other works and the storage, diversion, delivery, and use of water for the generation of power, irrigation, and other purposes, anything in this Act to the contrary notwithstanding, and all permits, licenses, and contracts shall so provide.

(b) Also the United States, in constructing, managing, and operating the dam, reservoir, canals, and other works herein authorized, including the appropriation, delivery, and use of water for the generation of power, irrigation, or other uses, and all users of water thus delivered and all users and appropriators of waters stored by said reservoir and/or carried by said canal, including all permittees and licensees of the United States or any of its agencies, shall observe and be subject to and controlled, anything to the contrary herein notwithstanding, by the terms of such compact, if any, between the States of Arizona, California, and Nevada, or any two thereof, for the equitable division of the benefits, including power, arising from the use of water accruing to said States, subsidiary to and consistent with said Colorado River compact, which may be negotiated and approved by said States and to which Congress shall give its consent and approval on or before January 1, 1929; and the terms of any such compact concluded between said States and approved and consented to by Congress after said date: Provided, That in the latter case such compact shall be subject to all contracts, if any, made by the Secretary of the Interior under section 5 hereof prior to the date of such approval and consent by Congress.

SEC. 9. All lands of the United States found by the Secretary of the Interior to be practicable of irrigation and reclamation by the irrigation works authorized herein shall be withdrawn from public entry. Thereafter, at the direction of the Secretary of the Interior, such lands shall be opened for entry, in tracts varying in size but not exceeding one hundred and sixty acres, as may be determined by the Secretary of the Interior, in accordance with the provisions of the reclamation law, and any such entryman shall pay an equitable share in accordance with the benefits received, as determined by the said Secretary, of the construction cost of said canal and appurtenant structures; said payments to be made in such installments and at such times as may be specified by the Secretary of the Interior, in accordance with the provisions of the said reclamation law, and shall constitute revenue from said project and be covered into the fund herein provided for: Provided, That all persons who served in the United States Army, Navy, Marine Corps, or Coast Guard during World War II, the War with Germany, the War with Spain, or in the suppression of the insurrection in the Philippines, and who have been honorably separated or discharged therefrom or placed in the Regular Army or Naval Reserve, shall have the exclusive preference right for a period of three months to enter said lands, subject, however, to the provisions of subsection (c) of section 4 of the Act of December 5, 1924 (43 Stat.

672, 702; 43 U.S.C., sec. 433); and also, so far as practicable, preference shall be given to said persons in all construction work authorized by this chapter: Provided further, That the above exclusive preference rights shall apply to veteran settlers on lands watered from the Gila canal in Arizona the same as to veteran settlers on lands watered from the All-American canal in California: Provided further, That in the event such entry shall be relinquished at any time prior to actual residence upon the land by the entryman for not less than one year, lands so relinquished shall not be subject to entry for a period of sixty days after the filing and notation of the relinquishment in the local land office, and after the expiration of said sixty-day period such lands shall be open to entry, subject to the preference in the section provided.

SEC. 10. That nothing in this Act shall be construed as modifying in any manner the existing contract, dated October 23, 1918, between the United States and the Imperial Irrigation District, providing for a connection with Laguna Dam; but the Secretary of the Interior is authorized to enter into contract or contracts with the said district or other districts, persons, or agencies for the construction, in accordance with this Act, of said canal and appurtenant structures, and also for the operation and maintenance thereof, with the consent of the other users.

SEC. 11. That the Secretary of the Interior is hereby authorized to make such studies, surveys, investigations, and do such engineering as may be necessary to determine the lands in the State of Arizona that should be embraced within the boundaries of a reclamation project, heretofore commonly known and hereafter to be known as the Parker-Gila Valley reclamation project, and to recommend the most practicable and feasible method of irrigating lands within said project, or units thereof, and the cost of the same; and the appropriation of such sums of money as may be necessary for the aforesaid purposes from time to time is hereby authorized. The Secretary shall report to Congress as soon as practicable, and not later than December 10, 1931, his findings, conclusions, and recommendations regarding such project.

SEC. 12. "Political subdivision" or "political subdivisions" as used in this Act shall be understood to include any State, irrigation or other district, municipality, or other governmental organization.

"Reclamation law" as used in this Act shall be understood to mean that certain Act of the Congress of the United States approved June 17, 1902, entitled "An Act appropriating the receipts from the sale and disposal of public land in certain States and Territories to the construction of irrigation works for the reclamation of arid lands," and the Acts amendatory thereof and supplemental thereto.

"Maintenance" as used herein shall be deemed to include in each instance provision for keeping the works in good operating condition.

"The Federal Water Power Act," as used in this Act, shall be understood to mean that certain Act of Congress of the United States approved June 10, 1920, entitled "An Act to create a Federal Power Commission; to provide for the improvement of navigation; the development of water power; the use of the public lands in relation thereto; and to repeal section 18 of the River and Harbor Appropriation Act, approved August 8, 1917, and for other purposes," and the Acts amendatory thereof and supplemental thereto.

"Domestic" whenever employed in this Act shall include water uses defined as "domestic" in said Colorado River compact.

SEC. 13. (a) The Colorado River compact signed at Santa Fe, New Mexico, November 24, 1922, pursuant to Act of Congress approved August 19, 1921, entitled "An Act to permit a compact or agreement between the States of Arizona, California, Colorado, Nevada, New Mexico, Utah, and Wyoming respecting the disposition and apportionment of the waters of the Colorado River, and for other purposes," is hereby approved by the Congress of the United States, and the provisions of the first paragraph of article II of the said Colorado River compact, making said compact binding and obligatory when it shall have been approved by the legislature of each of the signatory States, are hereby waived, and this approval shall become effective when the State of California and at least five of the other States mentioned, shall have approved or may hereafter approve said compact as aforesaid and shall consent to such waiver, as herein provided.

(b) The rights of the United States in or to waters of the Colorado River and its tributaries howsoever claimed or acquired, as well as the rights of those claiming under the United States, shall be subject to and controlled by said Colorado River compact.

(c) Also all patents, grants, contracts, concessions, leases, permits, licenses, rights-of-way, or other privileges from the United States or under its authority, necessary or convenient for the use of waters of the Colorado River or its tributaries, or for the generation or transmission of electrical energy generated by means of the waters of said river or its tributaries, whether under this Act, the Federal Water Power Act, or otherwise, shall be upon the express condition and with the express covenant that the rights of the recipients or holders thereof to waters of the river or its tributaries, for the use of which the same are necessary, convenient, or incidental, and the use of the same shall likewise be subject to and controlled by said Colorado River compact.

(d) The conditions and covenants referred to herein shall be deemed to run with the land and the right, interest, or privilege therein and water right, and shall attach as a matter of law, whether set out or referred to in the instrument evidencing any such patent, grant, contract, concession, lease, permit, license, right-of-way, or other privilege from the United States or under its authority, or not, and shall be deemed to be for the benefit of and be available to the States of Arizona, California, Colorado, Nevada, New Mexico, Utah, and Wyoming, and the users of water therein or thereunder, by way of suit, defense, or otherwise, in any litigation respecting the waters of the Colorado River or its tributaries.

SEC. 14. This Act shall be deemed a supplement to the reclamation law, which said reclamation law shall govern the construction, operation, and management of the works herein authorized, except as otherwise herein provided.

SEC. 15. The Secretary of the Interior is authorized and directed to make investigation and public reports of the feasibility of projects for irrigation, generation of electric power, and other purposes in the States of Arizona, Nevada, Colorado, New Mexico, Utah, and Wyoming for the purpose of making such information available to said States and to the Congress, and of formulating a comprehensive scheme of control and the improvement and utilization of the water of the Colorado River and its tributaries. The sum of $250,000 is hereby authorized to be appropriated from said Colorado River Dam fund, created by section 2 of this Act, for such purposes.

SEC. 16. In furtherance of any comprehensive plan formulated hereafter for the control, improvement, and utilization of the resources of the Colorado River system and to the end that the project authorized by this Act may constitute and be administered as a unit in such control, improvement, and utilization, any commission or commissioner duly authorized under the laws of any ratifying State in that behalf shall have the right to act in an advisory capacity to and in cooperation with the Secretary of the Interior in the exercise of any authority under the provisions of sections 4, 5, and 14 of this Act, and shall have at all times access to records of all Federal agencies empowered to act under said sections, and shall be entitled to have copies of said records on request.

SEC. 17. Claims of the United States arising out of any contract authorized by this Act shall have priority over all others, secured or unsecured.

SEC. 18. Nothing herein shall be construed as interfering with such rights as the States now have either to the waters within their borders or to adopt such policies and enact such laws as they may deem necessary with respect to the appropriation, control, and use of waters within their borders, except as modified by the Colorado River compact or other interstate agreement.

SEC. 19. That the consent of Congress is hereby given to the States of Arizona, California, Colorado, Nevada, New Mexico, Utah, and Wyoming to negotiate and enter into compacts or agreements, supplemental to and in conformity with the Colorado River compact and consistent with this Act for a comprehensive plan for the development of the Colorado River and providing for the storage, diversion, and use of the waters of said river. Any such compact or agreement may provide for the construction of dams, headworks, and other diversion works or structures for flood control, reclamation, improvement of navigation, division of water, or other purposes and/or the construction of power houses or other structures for the purpose of the development of water power and the financing of the same; and for such purposes may authorize the creation of interstate commissions and/or the creation of corporations, authorities, or other instrumentalities.

(a) Such consent is given upon condition that a representative of the United States, to be appointed by the President, shall participate in the negotiations and shall make report to Congress of the proceedings and of any compact or agreement entered into.

(b) No such compact or agreement shall be binding or obligatory upon any of such States unless and until it has been approved by the legislature of each of such States and by the Congress of the United States.

SEC. 20. Nothing in this Act shall be construed as a denial or recognition of any rights, if any, in Mexico to the use of the waters of the Colorado River system.

SEC. 21. That the short title of this Act shall be "Boulder Canyon Project Act."
Approved, December 21, 1928.

The Tennessee Valley Authority Act

An Act to Improve the Navigability and to Provide for the Flood Control of the Tennessee River: To Provide for Reforestation and the Proper Use of Marginal Lands in the Tennessee Valley; to Provide for the Agricultural and Industrial Development of Said Valley; to Provide for the National Defense by the Creation of a Corporation for the Operation of Government Properties at and Near Muscle Shoals in the State of Alabama, and for Other Purposes May 18, 1933.

Be it enacted by the Senate and House of Representatives of the United States of America in Congress assembled, That for the purpose of maintaining and operating the properties now owned by the United States in the vicinity of Muscle Shoals, Alabama, in the interest of the national defense and for agriculture and industrial development, and to improve navigation in the Tennessee River and to control the destructive flood waters in the Tennessee River and Mississippi River Basins, there is hereby created a body corporate by the name of the "Tennessee Valley Authority" (hereinafter referred to as the "Corporation"). The board of directors first appointed shall be deemed the incorporators and the incorporation shall be held to have been effected from the date of the first meeting of the board. This Act may be cited as the "Tennessee Valley Authority Act of 1933."

Sec. 2. (a) The board of directors of the Corporation (hereinafter referred to as the "board") shall be composed of three members, to be appointed by the President, by and with the advice and consent of the Senate. In appointing the members of the board, the President shall designate the chairman. All other officials, agents, and employees shall be designated and selected by the board.

(b) The terms of office of the members first taking office after the approval of this Act shall expire as designated by the President at the time of nomination, one at the end of the third year, one at the end of the sixth year, and one at the end of the ninth year, after the date of approval of this Act. A successor to a member of the board shall be appointed in the same manner as the original members and shall have a term of office expiring nine years from the date of the expiration of the term for which his predecessor was appointed.

(c) Any member appointed to fill a vacancy in the board occurring prior to the expiration of the term for which his predecessor was appointed shall be appointed for the remainder of such term.

(d) Vacancies in the board so long as there shall be two members in office shall not impair the powers of the board to execute the functions of the Corporation, and two of the members in office shall constitute a quorum for the transaction of the business of the board.

(e) Each of the members of the board shall be a citizen of the United States, and shall receive a salary at the rate of $10,000 a year, to be paid by the Corporation as current expenses. Each member of the board, in addition to his salary, shall be permitted to occupy as his residence one of the dwelling houses owned by the Government in the vicinity of Muscle Shoals, Alabama, the same to be designated by the President of the United States. Members of the board shall be reimbursed by the Corporation for actual expenses (including traveling and subsistence expenses) incurred by them in the performance of the duties vested in the board by this Act. No member of said board shall, during his continuance in office, be engaged in other business, but each member shall devote himself to the work of the Corporation.

(f) No director shall have financial interest in any public utility corporation engaged in the business of distributing and selling power to the public nor in any corporation engaged in the manufacture, selling, or distribution of fixed nitrogen or fertilizer, or any ingredients thereof, nor shall any member have any interest in any business that may be adversely affected by the success of the Corporation as a producer of concentrated fertilizers or as a producer of electric power.

(g) The board shall direct the exercise of all the powers of the Corporation.

(h) All members of the board shall be persons who profess a belief in the feasibility and wisdom of this Act.

Sec. 3. The Board shall without regard to the provisions of Civil Service laws applicable to officers and employees of the United States, appoint such managers, assistant managers, officers, employees, attorneys, and agents, as are necessary for the transaction of its business, fix their compensation, define their duties, require bonds of such of them as the board may designate, and provide a system of organization to fix responsibility and promote efficiency. Any appointee of the board may be removed in the discretion of the board. No regular officer or employee of the Corporation shall receive a salary in excess of that received by the members of the board.

All contracts to which the Corporation is a party and which require the employment of laborers and mechanics in the construction, alteration, maintenance or repair of buildings, dams, locks, or other projects shall contain a provision that not less than the prevailing rate of wages for work of a similar nature prevailing in the vicinity shall be paid to such laborers or mechanics.

In the event any dispute arises as to what are the prevailing rates of wages, the question shall be referred to the Secretary of Labor for determination, and his decision shall be final. In the determination of such prevailing rate or rates, due regard shall be given to those rates which have been secured through collective agreement by representatives of employers and employees.

Where such work as is described in the two preceding paragraphs is done directly by the Corporation the prevailing rate of wages shall be paid in the same manner as though such work had been let by contract.

Insofar as applicable, the benefits of the Act entitled "An Act to provide compensation for employees of the United States suffering injuries while in the performance of their duties, and for other purposes," approved September 7, 1916, as amended, shall extend to persons given employment under the provisions of this Act.

Sec. 4. Except as otherwise specifically provided in this Act, the Corporation— (a) Shall have succession in its corporate name.

(b) May sue and be sued in its corporate name.

(c) May adopt and use a corporate seal, which shall be judicially noticed.

(d) May make contracts, as herein authorized.

(e) May adopt, amend, and repeal bylaws.

(f) May purchase or lease and hold such real and personal property as it deems necessary or convenient in the transaction of its business, and may dispose of any such personal property held by it.

The board shall select a treasurer and as many assistant treasurers as it deems proper, which treasurer and assistant treasurers shall give such bonds for the safe-keeping of the securities and moneys of the said Corporation as the board may require: Provided, That any member of said board may be removed from office at any time by a concurrent resolution of the Senate and the House of Representatives.

(g) Shall have such powers as may be necessary or appropriate for the exercise of the powers herein specifically conferred upon the Corporation.

(h) Shall have power in the name of the United States of America to exercise the right of eminent domain, and in the purchase of any real estate or the condemnation of real estate by condemnation proceedings, the title to such real estate shall be taken in the name of the United States of America, and thereupon all such real estate shall be entrusted to the Corporation as the agent of the United States to accomplish the purposes of this Act.

(i) Shall have power to acquire real estate for the construction of dams, reservoirs, transmission lines, power houses, and other structures, and navigation projects at any point along the Tennessee River, or any of its tributaries, and in the event that the owner or owners of such property shall fail and refuse to sell to the Corporation at a price deemed fair and reasonable by the board, then the Corporation may proceed to exercise the right of eminent domain, and to condemn all property that it deems necessary for carrying out the purposes of this Act, and all such condemnation proceedings shall be had pursuant to the provisions and requirements hereinafter specified, with reference to any and all condemnation proceedings.

(i) Shall have power to construct dams, reservoirs, power houses, power structures, transmission lines, navigation projects, and incidental works in the Tennessee River and its tributaries, and to unite the various power installations into one or more systems by transmission lines.

Sec. 5. The board is hereby authorized—(a) To contract with commercial producers for the production of such fertilizers or fertilizer materials as may be needed in the Government's program of development and introduction in excess of that produced by Government plants. Such contracts may provide either for outright purchase of materials by the board or only for the payment of carrying charges on special materials manufactured at the board's request for its program.

(b) To arrange with farmers and farm organizations for large scale practical use of the new forms of fertilizers under conditions permitting an accurate measure of the economic return they produce.

(c) To cooperate with National, State, district, or county experimental stations or demonstration farms, for the use of new forms of fertilizer or fertilizer practices during the initial or experimental period of their introduction.

(d) The board in order to improve and cheapen the production of fertilizer is authorized to manufacture and sell fixed nitrogen, fertilizer, and fertilizer ingredients at Muscle Shoals by the employment of existing facilities, by modernizing existing plants, or by any other process or processes that in its judgment shall appear wise and profitable for the fixation of atmospheric nitrogen or the cheapening of the production of fertilizer.

(e) Under the authority of this Act the board may make donations or sales of the product of the plant or plants operated by it to be fairly and equitably distributed through the agency of county demonstration agents, agricultural colleges, or otherwise as the board may direct, for experimentation, education, and introduction of the use of such products in cooperation with practical farmers so as to obtain information as to the value, effect, and best methods of their use.

(f) The board is authorized to make alterations, modifications, or improvements in existing plants and facilities, and to construct new plants.

(g) In the event it is not used for the fixation of nitrogen for agricultural purposes or leased, then the board shall maintain in stand-by condition nitrate plant numbered 2, or its equivalent, for the fixation of atmospheric nitrogen, for the production of explosives in the event of war or a national emergency until the Congress shall by joint resolution release the board from this obligation, and if any part thereof be used by the board for the manufacture or phosphoric acid or potash, the balance of nitrate plant numbered 2 shall be kept in stand-by condition.

(h) To establish, maintain, and operate laboratories and experimental plants, and to undertake experiments for the purpose of enabling the Corporation to furnish nitrogen products for military purposes, and nitrogen and other fertilizer products for agricultural purposes in the most economical manner and at the highest standard of efficiency.

(i) To request the assistance and advice of any officer, agent, or employee of any executive department or of any independent office of the United States, to enable the Corporation the better to carry out its powers successfully, and as far as practicable shall utilize the services of such officers, agents, and employees, and the President shall, if in his opinion, the public interest, service, or economy so require, direct that such assistance, advice, and service be rendered to the Corporation, and any individual that may be by the President directed to render such assistance, advice, and service shall be thereafter subject to the orders, rules, and regulations of the board: Provided, That any invention or discovery made by virtue of and incidental to such service by an employee of the Government of the United States serving under this section, or by any employee of the Corporation, together with any patents which may be granted thereon, shall be the sole and exclusive property of the Corporation, which is hereby authorized to grant licenses thereunder as shall be authorized by the board: Provided further, That the board may pay to such inventor such sum from the income from sale of licenses as it may deem proper.

(j) Upon the requisition of the Secretary of War or the Secretary of the Navy to manufacture for and sell at cost to the United States explosives or their nitrogenous content.

(k) Upon the requisition of the Secretary of War the Corporation shall allot and deliver without charge to the War Department so much power as shall be necessary in the judgment of said Department for use in operation of all locks, lifts, or other facilities in aid of navigation.

(l) To produce, distribute, and sell electric power, as herein particularly specified.

(m) No products of the Corporation shall be sold for use outside of the United States, its Territories and possessions, except to the United States Government for the use of its Army and Navy, or to its allies in case of war.

(n) The President is authorized, within twelve months after the passage of this Act, to lease to any responsible farm organization or to any corporation organized by it nitrate plant number 2 and Waco Quarry, together with the railroad connecting said quarry with nitrate plant number 2, for a term not exceeding fifty years at a rental of not less than $1 per year, but such authority shall be subject to the express condition that the lessee shall use said property during the term of said lease exclusively for the manufacture of fertilizer and fertilizer ingredients to be used only in the manufacture of fertilizer by said lessee and sold for use as fertilizer. The said lessee shall covenant to keep said property in first-class condition, but the lessee shall be authorized to modernize said plant numbered 2 by the installation of such machinery as may be necessary, and is authorized to amortize the cost of said machinery and improvements over the term of said lease or any part thereof. Said lease shall also provide that the board shall sell to the lessee power for the operation of said plant at the same schedule of prices that it charges all other customers for power of the same class and quantity. Said lease shall also provide that if the said lessee does not desire to buy power of the publicly owned plant it shall have the right to purchase power for the operation of said plant of the Alabama Power Company or any other publicly or privately owned corporation engaged in the generation and sale of electrical power, and in such case the lease shall provide further that the said lessee shall have a free right of way to build a transmission line over Government property to said plant paying the actual expenses and damages, if any, incurred by the Corporation on account of such line. Said lease shall also provide that the said lessee shall covenant that during the term of said lease the said lessee shall not enter into any illegal monopoly, combination, or trust with any privately owned corporation engaged in the manufacture, production, and sale of fertilizer with the object or effect of increasing the price of fertilizer to the farmer.

Sec. 6. In the appointment of officials and the selection of employees for said Corporation, and in the promotion of any such employees or officials, no political test or qualification shall be permitted or given consideration, but all such appointments and promotions shall be given and made on the basis of merit and efficiency. Any member of said board who is found by the President of the United States to be guilty of a violation of this section shall be removed from office by the President of the United States, and any appointee of said board who is found by the board to be guilty of a violation of this section shall be removed from office by said board.

Sec. 7. In order to enable the Corporation to exercise the powers and duties vested in it by this Act—

(a) The exclusive use, possession, and control of the United States nitrate plants numbered 1 and 2, including steam plants, located, respectively, at Sheffield, Alabama, and Muscle Shoals, Alabama, together with all real estate and buildings connected therewith, all tools and machinery, equipment, accessories, and materials belonging thereto, and all laboratories and plants used as auxiliaries thereto; the fixed-nitrogen research laboratory, the Waco limestone quarry, in Alabama, and Dam Numbered 2, located at Muscle Shoals, its power house, and all hydroelectric and operating appurtenances (except the locks), and all machinery, lands, and buildings in connection therewith, and all appurtenances thereof, and all other property to be acquired by the Corporation in its own name or in the name of the United States of America, are hereby intrusted to the Corporation for the purposes of the Act.

(b) The President of the United States is authorized to provide for the transfer to the Corporation of the use, possession, and control of such other real or personal property of the United States as he may from time to time deem necessary and proper for the purposes of the Corporation as herein stated.

Sec. 8. (a) The Corporation shall maintain its principal office in the immediate vicinity of Muscle Shoals, Alabama. The Corporation shall be held to be an inhabitant and resident of the northern judicial district of Alabama within the meaning of the laws of the United States relating to the venue of civil suits.

(b) The Corporation shall at all times maintain complete and accurate books of accounts.

(c) Each member of the board, before entering upon the duties of his office, shall subscribe to an oath (or affirmation) to support the Constitution of the United States and to faithfully and impartially perform the duties imposed upon him by this Act.

Sec. 9. (a) The board shall file with the President

and with the Congress, in December of each year, a financial statement and a complete report as to the business of the Corporation covering the preceding governmental fiscal year. This report shall include an itemized statement of the cost of power al each power station, the total number of employees and the names, salaries, and duties of those receiving compensation at the rate of more than $1,500 a year.

(b) The Comptroller General of the United States shall audit the transactions of the Corporation at such times as he shall determine, but not less frequently than once each governmental fiscal year, with personnel of his selection. In such connection he and his representatives shall have free and open access to all papers, books, records, files, accounts, plants, warehouses offices, and all other things, property and places belonging to or under the control of or used or employed by the Corporation, and shall be afforded full facilities for counting all cash and verifying transactions with and balance in depositaries. He shall make report of each such audit in quadruplicate, one copy for the President of the United States, one for the chairman of the board one for public inspection at the principal office of the Corporation, and the other to be retained by him for the uses of the Congress. The expenses for each such audit may be paid from moneys advanced therefor by the Corporation, or from any appropriation or appropriations for the General Accounting Office, and appropriations so used shall be reimbursed promptly by the Corporation as billed by the Comptroller General. All such audit expenses shall be charged to operating expenses of the Corporation. The Comptroller General shall make special report to the President of the United States and to the Congress of any transaction or condition found by him to be in conflict with the powers or duties intrusted to the Corporation by law.

Sec. 10. The board is hereby empowered and authorized to sell the surplus power not used in its operations, and for operation of locks and other works generated by it, to States, counties, municipalities, corporations, partnerships, or individuals, according to the policies hereinafter set forth and to carry out said authority, the board is authorized to enter into contracts for such sale for a term not exceeding twenty years, and in the sale of such current by the board it shall give preference to States, counties, municipalities, and cooperative organizations of citizens or farmers, not organized or doing business for profit, but primarily for the purpose of supplying electricity to its own citizens or members: Provided, That all contracts made with private companies or individuals for the sale of power, which is to be resold for a profit, shall contain a provision authorizing the board to cancel said contract upon five years' notice in writing, if the board needs said power to supply the demands of States, counties, or municipalities. In order to promote and encourage the fullest possible use of electric light and power on farms within reasonable distance of any of its transmission lines the board in its discretion shall have power to construct transmission lines to farms and small villages that are not otherwise supplied with electricity at reasonable rates, and to make such rules and regulations governing such sale and distribution of such electric power as in its judgment may be just and equitable: Provided further That the board is hereby authorized and directed to make studies, experiments, and determinations to promote the wider and better use of electric power for agricultural and domestic use, or for small or local industries, and it may cooperate with State governments, or their subdivisions or agencies with educational or research institutions, and with cooperatives or other organizations, in the application of electric power to the fuller and better balanced development of the resources of the region.

Sec. 11. It is hereby declared to be the policy of the Government so far as practical to distribute and sell the surplus power generated at Muscle Shoals equitably among the States, counties, and municipalities within transmission distance. This policy is further declared to be that the projects herein provided for shall be considered primarily as for the benefit of the people of the section as a whole and particularly the domestic and rural consumers to whom the power can economically be made available, and accordingly that sale to and use by industry shall be a secondary purpose, to be utilized principally to secure a sufficiently high load factor and revenue returns which will permit domestic and rural use at the lowest possible rates and in such manner as to encourage increased domestic and rural use of electricity. It is further hereby declared to be the policy of the Government to utilize the Muscle Shoals properties so far as may be necessary to improve, increase, and cheapen the production of fertilizer and fertilizer ingredients by carrying out the provisions of this Act.

Sec. 12. In order to place the board upon a fair basis for making such Contracts and for receiving bids for the sale of such power, it is hereby expressly authorized, either from appropriations made by Congress or from funds secured from the sale of such power, or from funds secured by the sale of bonds hereafter provided for, to construct, lease, purchase, or authorize the construction of transmission lines within transmission distance from the place where generated, and to interconnect with other systems. The board is also authorized to lease to any person, persons, or corporation the use of any transmission line owned by the Government and operated by the board, but no such lease shall be made that in any way interferes with the use of such transmission line by the board: Provided, That if any State, county, municipality, or other public or cooperative organization of citizens or farmers, not organized or doing business for profit, but primarily for the purpose of supplying electricity to its own citizens or members, or any two or more of such municipalities or organizations, shall construct or agree to construct and maintain a properly designed and built transmission line to the Government reservation upon which is located a Government generating plant, or to a main transmission line owned by the Government or leased by the board and under the control of the board, the board is hereby authorized and directed to contract with such State, county, municipality, or other organization, or two or more of them, for the sale of electricity for a term not exceeding thirty years; and in such case the board shall give to such State, county, municipality, or other organization ample time to fully comply with any local law now in existence or hereafter enacted providing for the necessary legal authority for such State, county, municipality, or other organization to contract with the board for such power: Provided further, That all contracts entered into between the Corporation and any municipality or other political subdivision or cooperative organization shall provide that the electric power shall be sold and distributed to the ultimate consumer without discrimination as between consumers of the same class, and such contract shall be voidable at the election of the board if a discriminatory rate, rebate, or other special concession is made or given to any consumer or user by the municipality or other political subdivision or cooperative organization: And provided further, That as to any surplus power not so sold as above provided to States, counties, municipalities, or other said organizations, before the board shall sell the same to any person or corporation engaged in the distribution and resale of electricity for profit, it shall require said person or corporation to agree that any resale of such electric power by said person or corporation shall be made to the ultimate consumer of

such electric power at prices that shall not exceed a schedule fixed by the board from time to time as reasonable, just, and fair; and in case of any such sale, if an amount is charged the ultimate consumer which is in excess of the price so deemed to be just, reasonable, and fair by the board the contract for such sale between the board and such distributor of electricity shall be voidable at the election of the board: And provided further, That the board is hereby authorized to enter into contracts with other power systems for the mutual exchange of unused excess power upon suitable terms, for the conservation of stored water, and as an emergency or breakdown relief.

Sec. 13. Five per centum of the gross proceeds received by the board for the sale of power generated at Dam Numbered 2, or from any other hydropower plant hereafter constructed in the State of Alabama, shall be paid to the State of Alabama; and 5 per centum of the gross proceeds from the sale of power generated at Cove Creek Dam, hereinafter provided for, or any other dam located in the State of Tennessee, shall be paid to the State of Tennessee. Upon the completion of said Cove Creek Dam the board shall ascertain how much additional power is thereby generated at Dam Numbered 2 and at any other dam hereafter constructed by the Government of the United States on the Tennessee River, in the State of Alabama, or in the State of Tennessee, and from the gross proceeds of the sale of such additional power two and a half per centum shall be paid to the State of Alabama and 2 and a half per centum to the State of Tennessee. These percentages shall apply to any other dam that may hereafter be constructed and controlled and operated by the board on the Tennessee River or any of its tributaries, the main purpose of which is to control flood waters and where the development of electric power is incidental to the operation of such flood-control dam. In ascertaining the gross proceeds from the sale of such power upon which a percentage is paid to the States of Alabama and Tennessee, the board shall not take into consideration the proceeds of any power sold or delivered to the Government of the United States, or any department or agency of the Government of the United States used in the operation of any locks on the Tennessee River or for any experimental purpose, or for the manufacture of fertilizer or any of the ingredients thereof, or for any other governmental purpose: Provided, That the percentages to be paid to the States of Alabama and Tennessee, as provided in this section, shall be subject to revision and change by the board, and any new percentages established by the board, when approved by the President, shall remain in effect until and unless again changed by the board with the approval of the President. No change of said percentages shall be made more often than once in five years, and no change shall be made without giving to the States of Alabama and Tennessee an opportunity to be heard.

Sec. 14. The board shall make a thorough investigation as to the present value of Dam Numbered 2, and the steam plants at nitrate plant numbered 1, and nitrate plant numbered 2, and as to the cost of Cove Creek Dam, for the purpose of ascertaining how much of the value or the cost of said properties shall be allocated and charged up to (1) flood control, (2) navigation, (3) fertilizer (4) national defense, and (5) the development of power. The findings thus made by the board, when approved by the President of the United States, shall be final, and such findings shall thereafter be used in all allocation of value for the purpose of keeping the book value of said properties. In a like manner, the cost and book value of any dams, steam plants, or other similar improvements hereafter constructed and turned over to said board for the purpose of control and management shall be ascertained and allocated.

Sec. 15. In the construction of any future dam, steam plant, or other facility, to be used in whole or in part for the generation or transmission of electric power the board is hereby authorized and empowered to issue on the credit of the United States and to sell serial bonds not exceeding $50,000,000 in amount, having a maturity not more than fifty years from the date of issue thereof, and bearing interest not exceeding $3^1/2$ per centum per annum. Said bonds shall be issued and sold in amounts and prices approved by the Secretary of the Treasury, but all such bonds as may be so issued and sold shall have equal rank. None of said bonds shall be sold below par, and no fee, commission, or compensation whatever shall be paid to any person, firm, or corporation for handling, negotiating the sale, or selling the said bonds. All of such bonds so issued and sold shall have all the rights and privileges accorded by law to Panama Canal bonds, authorized by section 8 of the Act of June 28, 1902, chapter 1302, as amended by the Act of December 21, 1905 (ch. 3, sec. 1, 34 Stat. 5), as now compiled in section 743 of title 31 of the United States Code. All funds derived from the sale of such bonds shall be paid over to the Corporation.

Sec. 16. The board, whenever the President deems it advisable, is hereby empowered and directed to complete Dam Numbered 2 at Muscle Shoals Alabama, and the steam plant at nitrate plant numbered 2, in the vicinity of Muscle Shoals, by installing in Dam Numbered 2 the additional power units according to the plans and specifications of said dam, and the additional power unit in the steam plant at nitrate plant numbered 2.

Sec. 17. The Secretary of War, or the Secretary of the Interior, is hereby authorized to construct, either directly or by contract to the lowest responsible bidder, after due advertisement, a dam in and across Clinch River in the State of Tennessee, which has by long custom become known and designates as the Cove Creek Dam, together with a transmission line from Muscle Shoals, according to the latest and most approved designs, including power house and hydroelectric installations and equipment for the generation of power, in order that the waters of the said Clinch River may be impounded and stored above said dam for the purpose of increasing and regulating the flow of the Clinch River and the Tennessee River below, so that the maximum amount of primary power may be developed at Dam Numbered 2 and at any and all other dams below the said Cove Creek Dam: Provided, however, That the President is hereby authorized by appropriate order to direct the employment by the Secretary of War, or by the Secretary of the Interior, of such engineer or engineers as he may designate, to perform such duties and obligations as he may deem proper, either in the drawing of plans and specifications for said dam, or to perform any other work in the building or construction of the same. The President may, by such order, place the control of the construction of said dam in the hands of such engineer or engineers taken from private life as he may desire: And provided further, That the President is hereby expressly authorized, without regard to the restriction or limitation of any other statute, to select attorneys and assistants for the purpose of making any investigation he may deem proper to ascertain whether, in the control and management of Dam Numbered 2, or any other dam or property owned by the Government in the Tennessee River Basin, or in the authorization of any improvement therein, there has been any undue or unfair advantage given to private persons, partnerships, or corporations, by any officials or employees of the Government, or whether in any such matters the Government has been injured or unjustly deprived of any of its rights.

Sec. 18. In order to enable and empower the Secretary of War, the Secretary of the Interior, or the board to carry out the authority hereby conferred, in the most economical and efficient manner, he or it is hereby authorized and empowered in the exercise of the powers of national defense in aid of navigation, and in the control of the flood waters of the Tennessee and Mississippi Rivers, constituting channels of interstate commerce, to exercise the right of eminent domain for all purposes of this Act, and to condemn all lands, easements, rights of way, and other area necessary in order to obtain a site for said Cove Creek Dam, and the flowage rights for the reservoir of water above said dam, and to negotiate and conclude contracts with States, counties, municipalities, and all State agencies and with railroads, railroad corporations, common carriers, and all public utility commissions and any other person, firm or corporation, for the relocation of railroad tracks, highways, highway bridges, mills, ferries, electric-light plants, and any and all other properties, enterprises, and projects whose removal may be necessary in order to carry out the provisions of this Act. When said Cove Creek Dam, transmission line, and power house shall have been completed, the possession, use, and control thereof shall be intrusted to the Corporation for use and operation in connection with the general Tennessee Valley project, and to promote flood control and navigation in the Tennessee River.

Sec. 19. The Corporation, as an instrumentality and agency of the Government of the United States for the purpose of executing its constitutional powers, shall have access to the Patent Office of the United States for the purpose of studying, ascertaining, and copying all methods, formulae, and scientific information (not including access to pending applications for patents) necessary to enable the Corporation to use and employ the most efficacious and economical process for the production of fixed nitrogen, or any essential ingredient of fertilizer, or any method of improving and cheapening the production of hydro-electric power, and any owner of a patent whose patent rights may have been thus in any way copied, used, infringed, or employed by the exercise of this authority by the Corporation shall have as the exclusive remedy a cause of action against the Corporation to be instituted and prosecuted on the equity side of the appropriate district court of the United States, for the recovery of reasonable compensation for such infringement. The Commissioner of Patents shall furnish to the Corporation, at its request and without payment of fees, copies of documents on file in his office: Provided, That the benefits of this section shall not apply to any art, machine, method of manufacture, or composition of matter, discovered or invented by such employee during the time of his employment or services with the Corporation or with the Government of the United States.

Sec. 20. The Government of the United States hereby reserves the right, in case of war or national emergency declared by Congress, to take possession of all or any part of the property described or referred to in this Act for the purpose of manufacturing explosives or for other war purposes; but, if this right is exercised by the Government, it shall pay the reasonable and fair damages that may be suffered by any party whose contract for the purchase of electric power or fixed nitrogen or fertilizer ingredients is hereby violated, after the amount of the damages has been fixed by the United States Court of Claims in proceedings instituted and conducted for that purpose under rules prescribed by the court.

Sec. 21. (a) All general penal statutes relating to the larceny, embezzlement, conversion, or to the improper handling, retention, use, or disposal of public moneys or property of the United States, shall apply to the moneys and property of the Corporation and to moneys and properties of the United States intrusted to the Corporation.

(b) Any person who, with intent to defraud the Corporation, or to deceive any director, officer, or employee of the Corporation or any officer or employee of the United States (1) makes any false entry in any book of the Corporation, or (2) makes any false report or statement for the Corporation, shall, upon conviction thereof, be fined not more than $10,000 or imprisoned not more than five years, or both.

(c) Any person who shall receive any compensation, rebate, or reward, or shall enter into any conspiracy, collusion, or agreement, express or implied, with intent to defraud the Corporation or wrongfully and unlawfully to defeat its purposes, shall, on conviction thereof, be fined not more than $5,000 or imprisoned not more than five years, or both.

Sec. 22. To aid further the proper use, conservation, and development of the natural resources of the Tennessee River drainage basin and of such adjoining territory as may be related to or materially affected by the development consequent to this Act, and to provide for the general welfare of the citizens of said areas, the President is hereby authorized, by such means or methods as he may deem proper within the limits of appropriations made therefor by Congress, to make such surveys of and general plans for said Tennessee basin and adjoining territory as may be useful to the Congress and to the several States in guiding and controlling the extent, sequence, and nature of development that may be equitably and economically advanced through the expenditure of public funds, or through the guidance or control of public authority, all for the general purpose of fostering an orderly and proper physical, economic, and social development of said areas; and the President is further authorized in making said surveys and plans to cooperate with the States affected thereby, or subdivisions or agencies of such States, or with cooperative or other organizations, and to make such studies, experiments, or demonstrations as may be necessary and suitable to that end.

Sec. 23. The President shall, from time to time, as the work provided for in the preceding section progresses, recommend to Congress such legislation as he deems proper to carry out the general purposes stated in said section, and for the especial purpose of bringing about in said Tennessee drainage basin and adjoining territory in conformity with said general purposes (1) the maximum amount of flood control; (2) the maximum development of said Tennessee River for navigation purposes; (3) the maximum generation of electric power consistent with flood control and navigation; (4) the proper use of marginal lands; (5) the proper method of reforestation of all lands in said drainage basin suitable for reforestation; and (6) the economic and social well-being of the people living in said river basin.

Sec. 24. For the purpose of securing any rights of flowage, or obtaining title to or possession of any property, real or personal, that may be necessary or may become necessary, in the carrying out of any of the provisions of this Act, the President of the United States for a period of three years from the date of the enactment of this Act, is hereby authorized to acquire title in the name of the United States to such rights or such property, and to provide for the payment for same by directing the board to contract to deliver power generated at any of the plants now owned or hereafter owned or constructed by the Government or by said Corporation, such future delivery of power to continue for a period not exceeding thirty years. Likewise, for one year after the enactment of this Act, the President is further authorized to sell or lease any parcel or part of any vacant real estate now owned by the Government in

said Tennessee River Basin, to persons, firms, or corporations who shall contract to erect thereon factories or manufacturing establishments, and who shall contract to purchase of said Corporation electric power for the operation of any such factory or manufacturing establishment. No contract shall be made by the President for the sale of any of such real estate as may be necessary for present or future use on the part of the Government for any of the purposes of this Act. Any such contract made by the President of the United States shall be carried out by the board: Provided, That no such contract shall be made that will in any way abridge or take away the preference right to purchase power given in this Act to States, counties, municipalities, or farm organizations: Provided further, That no lease shall be for a term to exceed fifty years: Provided further, That any sale shall be on condition that said land shall be used for industrial purposes only.

Sec. 25. The Corporation may cause proceedings to be instituted for the acquisition by condemnation of any lands, easements, or rights of way which, in the opinion of the Corporation, are necessary to carry out the provisions of this Act. The proceedings shall be instituted in the United States district court for the district in which the land, easement, right of way, or other interest, or any part thereof, is located, and such court shall have full jurisdiction to divest the complete title to the property sought to be acquired out of all persons or claimants and vest the same in the United States in fee simple, and to enter a decree quieting the title thereto in the United States of America.

Upon the filing of a petition for condemnation and for the purpose of ascertaining the value of the property to be acquired, and assessing the compensation to be paid, the court shall appoint three commissioners who shall be disinterested persons and who shall take and subscribe an oath that they do not own any lands, or interest or easement in any lands, which it may be desirable for the United States to acquire in the furtherance of said project and such commissioners shall not be selected from the locality wherein the land sought to be condemned lies. Such commissioners shall receive a per diem of not to exceed $15 for their services, together with an additional amount of $5 per day for subsistence for time actually spent in performing their duties as commissioners.

It shall be the duty of such commissioners to examine into the value of the lands sought to be condemned, to conduct hearings and receive evidence, and generally to take such appropriate steps as may be proper for the determination of the value of the said lands sought to be condemned, and for such purpose the commissioners are authorized to administer oaths and subpoena witnesses, which said witnesses shall receive the same fees as are provided for witnesses in the Federal courts. The said commissioners shall thereupon file a report setting forth their conclusions as to the value of the said property sought to be condemned, making a separate award and valuation in the premises with respect to each separate parcel involved. Upon the filing of such award in court the clerk of said court shall give notice of the filing of such award to the parties to said proceeding, in manner and form as directed by the judge of said court.

Either or both parties may file exceptions to the award of said commissioners within twenty days from the date of the filing of said award in court. Exceptions filed to such award shall be heard before three Federal district judges unless the parties, in writing, in person, or by their attorneys, stipulate that the exceptions may be heard before a lesser number of judges. On such hearing such judges shall pass de novo upon the proceedings had before the commissioners, may view the property, and may take additional evidence. Upon such hearings the said judges shall file their own award, fixing therein the value of the property sought to be condemned, regardless of the award previously made by the said commissioners.

At any time within thirty days from the filing of the decision of the district judges upon the hearing on exceptions to the award made by the commissioners, either party may appeal from such decision of the said judges to the circuit court of appeals, and the said circuit court of appeals shall upon the hearing on said appeal dispose of the same upon the record, without regard to the awards or findings theretofore made by the commissioners or the district judges, and such circuit court of appeals shall thereupon fix the value of the said property sought to be condemned.

Upon acceptance of an award by the owner of any property herein provided to be appropriated, and the payment of the money awarded or upon the failure of either party to file exceptions to the award of the commissioners within the time specified, or upon the award of the commissioners, and the payment of the money by the United States pursuant thereto, or the payment of the money awarded into the registry of the court by the Corporation, the title to said property and the right to the possession thereof shall pass to the United States, and the United States shall be entitled to a writ in the same proceeding to dispossess the former owner of said property, and all lessees, agents, and attorneys of such former owner, and to put the United States, by its corporate creature and agent, the Corporation, into possession of said property.

In the event of any property owned in Whole or in part by minors, or insane persons, or incompetent persons, or estates of deceased persons, then the legal representatives of such minors, insane persons, incompetent persons, or estates shall have power, by and with the consent and approval of the trial judge in whose court said matter is for determination, to consent to or reject the awards of the commissioners herein provided for, and in the event that there be no legal representatives, or that the legal representatives for such minors, insane persons, or incompetent persons shall fail or decline to act, then such trial judge may, upon motion, appoint a guardian ad litem to act for such minors, insane persons, or incompetent persons, and such guardian ad litem shall act to the full extent and to the same purpose and effect as his ward could act, if competent, and such guardian ad litem shall be deemed to have full power and authority to respond, to conduct, or to maintain any proceeding herein provided for affecting his said ward.

Sec. 26. The net proceeds derived by the board from the sale of power and any of the products manufactured by the Corporation, after deducting the cost of operation, maintenance, depreciation, amortization, and an amount deemed by the board as necessary to withhold as operating capital, or devoted by the board to new construction, shall be paid into the Treasury of the United States at the end of each calendar year.

Sec. 27. All appropriations necessary to carry out the provisions of this Act are hereby authorized.

Sec. 28. That all Acts or parts of Acts in conflict herewith are hereby repealed, so far as they affect the operations contemplated by this Act.

Sec. 29. The right to alter, amend, or repeal this Act is hereby expressly declared and reserved, but no such amendment or repeal shall operate to impair the obligation of any contract made by said Corporation under any power conferred in this Act.

Sec. 30. The sections of this Act are hereby declared to be separable, and in the event any one or more sections of this Act be held to be unconstitutional, the same shall not affect the validity of other sections of this Act. Approved, May 18, 1933.

The National Industrial Recovery Act

AN ACT

To encourage national industrial recovery, to foster fair competition, and to provide for the construction of certain useful public works, and for other purposes.

Be it enacted by the Senate and House of Representatives of the United States of America in Congress assembled,

TITLE I—INDUSTRIAL RECOVERY DECLARATION OF POLICY

SECTION 1. A national emergency productive of widespread unemployment and disorganization of industry, which burdens interstate and foreign commerce, affects the public welfare, and undermines the standards of living of the American people, is hereby declared to exist. It is hereby declared to be the policy of Congress to remove obstructions to the free flow of interstate and foreign commerce which tend to diminish the amount thereof; and to provide for the general welfare by promoting the organization of industry for the purpose of cooperative action among trade groups, to induce and maintain united action of labor and management under adequate governmental sanctions and supervision, to eliminate unfair competitive practices, to promote the fullest possible utilization of the present productive capacity of industries, to avoid undue restriction of production (except as may be temporarily required), to increase the consumption of Industrial and agricultural products by increasing purchasing power, to reduce and relieve unemployment, to improve standards of labor, and otherwise to rehabilitate industry and to conserve natural resources.

ADMINISTRATIVE AGENCIES

SEC. 2. (a) To effectuate the policy of this title, the President is hereby authorized to establish such agencies, to accept and utilize such voluntary and uncompensated services to appoint without regard to the provisions of the civil service laws, such officers and employees, and to utilize such Federal officers and employees, and, with the consent of the State, such State and local officers and employees,

as he may find necessary, to prescribe their authorities, duties, responsibilities, and tenure, and, without regard to the Classification Act of 1923, as amended, to fix the compensation of any officers and employees so appointed.

(b) The President may delegate any of his functions and powers under this title to such officers, agents, and employees as lie may designate or appoint, and may establish an industrial planning and research agency to aid in carrying out his functions under this title.

(c) This title shall cease to be in effect and any agencies established hereunder shall cease to exist at the expiration of two years after the date of enactment of this Act, or sooner if the President shall by proclamation or the Congress shall by joint resolution declare that the emergency recognized by section 1 has ended.

CODES OF FAIR COMPETITION

SEC. 3. (a) Upon the application to the President by one or more trade or industrial associations or groups the President may approve a code or codes of fair competition for the trade or industry or subdivision thereof, represented by the applicant or applicants, if the President finds (1) that such associations or groups impose no inequitable restrictions on admission to membership therein and are truly representative of such trades or industries or subdivisions thereof, and (2) that such code or codes are not designed to promote monopolies or to eliminate or oppress small enterprises and will not operate to discriminate against them, and will tend to effectuate the policy of this title: Provided, That such code or codes shall not permit monopolies or monopolistic practices: Provided further, That where such code or codes affect the services and welfare of persons engaged in other steps of the economic process, nothing in this section shall deprive such persons of the right to be heard prior to approval by the President of such code or codes. The President may, as a condition of his approval of any such code, impose such conditions (including requirements for the making of reports and the keeping of accounts) for the protection of consumers competitors, employees, and others, and in furtherance of the public interest, and may provide such exceptions to and exemptions from the provisions of such code, as the President in his discretion deems necessary to effectuate the policy herein declared.

(b) After the President shall have approved any such code, the provisions of such code shall be the standards of fair competition for such trade or industry or subdivision thereof. Any violation of such standards in any transaction in or affecting interstate or foreign commerce shall be deemed an unfair method of competition in commerce within the meaning of the Federal Trade Commission Act, as amended; but nothing in this title shall be construed to impair the powers of the Federal Trade Commission under such Act, as amended.

(c) The several district courts of the United States are hereby invested with jurisdiction to prevent and restrain violations of any code of fair competition approved under this title; and it shall be the duty of the several district attorneys of the United States, in their respective districts, under the direction of the Attorney General, to institute proceedings in equity to prevent and restrain such violations.

(d) Upon his own motion, or if complaint is made to the President that abuses inimical to the public interest and contrary to the policy herein declared are prevalent in any trade or industry or subdivision thereof, and if no code of fair competition therefor has theretofore been approved by the President, the President, after such public notice and hearing as he shall specify, may prescribe and approve a code of fair competition for such trade or industry or subdivision thereof, which shall have the same effect as a code of fair competition approved by the President under subsection (a) of this section.

(e) On his own motion, or if any labor organization, or any trade or industrial organization, association, or group, which has complied with the provisions of this title, shall make complaint to the President that any article or articles are being imported into the United States in substantial quantities or increasing ratio to domestic production of any competitive article or articles and on such terms or under such conditions as to render ineffective or seriously to endanger the maintenance of any code or agreement under this title, the President may cause an immediate investigation to be made by the United States Tariff Commission, which shall give precedence to inves-

tigations under this subsection, and if, after such investigation and such public notice and hearing as he shall specify, the President shall find the existence of such facts, he shall, in order to effectuate the policy of this title, direct that the article or articles concerned shall be permitted entry into the United States only upon such terms and conditions and subject to the payment of such fees and to such limitations in the total quantity which may be imported (in the course of any specified period or periods) as he shall find it necessary to prescribe in order that the entry thereof shall not render or tend to render ineffective any code or agreement made under this title. In order to enforce any limitations imposed on the total quantity of imports, in any specified period or periods, of any article or articles under this subsection, the President may forbid the importation of such article or articles unless the importer shall have first obtained from the Secretary of the Treasury a license pursuant to such regulations as the President may prescribe. Upon information of any action by the President under this subsection the Secretary of the Treasury shall, through the proper officers, permit entry of the article or articles specified only upon such terms and conditions and subject to such fees, to such limitations in the quantity which may be imported, and to such requirements of license, as the President shall have directed. The decision of the President as to facts shall be conclusive. Any condition or limitation of entry under this subsection shall continue in effect until the President shall find and inform the Secretary of the Treasury that the conditions which led to the imposition of such condition or limitation upon entry no longer exists.

(f) When a code of fair competition has been approved or prescribed by the President under this title, any violation of any provision thereof in any transaction in or affecting interstate, or foreign commerce shall be a misdemeanor and upon conviction thereof an offender shall be fined not more than $500 for each offense and each day such violation continues shall be deemed a separate offense.

AGREEMENTS AND LICENSES

SEC. 4. (a) The President is authorized to enter into agreement with, and to approve voluntary agreements between and among, persons engaged in a trade or industry, labor organizations, and trade or industrial organizations, associations, or groups, relating to any trade or industry, if in his judgment such agreements will aid in effectuating the policy of this title with respect to transactions in or affecting interstate or foreign commerce, and will be consistent with the requirements of clause (2) of subsection (a) of section 3 for a code of fair competition.

(b) Whenever the President shall find that destructive wage or price cutting or other activities contrary to the policy of this title are being practiced in any trade or industry or any subdivision thereof, and, after such public notice and hearing as he shall specify, shall find it essential to license business enterprises in order to make effective a code of fair competition or an agreement under this title or otherwise to effectuate the policy of this title, and shall publicly so announce, no person shall, after a date fixed in such announcement, engage in or carryon any business, in or affecting interstate or foreign commerce, specified in such announcement, unless he shall have first obtained a license issued pursuant to such relations as the President shall prescribe. The President may suspend or revoke any such license, after due notice and opportunity for hearing, for violations of the terms or conditions thereof. Any order of the President suspending or revoking any such license shall be final if in accordance with law. Any person who, without such a license or in violation of any condition thereof, carries on any such business for which a license is so required, shall, upon conviction thereof, be fined not more than $500, or imprisoned not more than six months, or both, and each day such violation continues shall be deemed a separate offense. Notwithstanding the provisions of section 2 (c) , this subsection shall cease to be in effect at the expiration of one year after the date of enactment of this Act or sooner if the President shall by proclamation or the Congress shall by joint resolution declare that the emergency recognized by section 1 has ended.

SEC. 5. While this title is in effect (or in the case of a license, while section 4 (a) is in effect) and for sixty days thereafter, any code, agreement, or license approved, prescribed, or issued and in effect under this title, and any action complying with the provisions thereof taken during such period, shall be exempt from the provisions of the antitrust laws of the United States.

Nothing in this Act, and no regulation thereunder, shall prevent an individual from pursuing the vocation of manual labor and selling or trading the products thereof; nor shall anything in this Act, or regulation thereunder, prevent anyone from marketing or trading the produce of his farm.

LIMITATIONS UPON APPLICATION OF TITLE

SEC. 6. (a) No trade or industrial association or group shall be eligible to receive the benefit of the provisions of this title until it files with the President a statement containing such information relating to the activities of the association or group as the President shall by regulation prescribe.

(b) The President is authorized to prescribe rules and regulations designed to insure that any organization availing itself of the benefits of this title shall be truly representative of the trade or industry or subdivision thereof represented by such organization. Any organization violating any such rule or regulation shall cease to be entitled to the benefits of this title.

(c) Upon the request of the President, the Federal Trade Commission shall make such investigations as may be necessary to enable the President to carry out the provisions of this title, and for such purposes the Commission shall have all the powers vested in it with respect of investigations under the Federal Trade Commission Act, as amended.

SEC. 7. (a) Every code of fair competition, agreement, and license approved, prescribed, or issued under this title shall contain the following conditions: (1) That employees shall have the right to organize and bargain collectively through representatives of their own choosing, and shall be free from the interference restraint, or coercion of employers of labor, or their agents, in the designation of such representatives or in self-organization or in other concerted activities for the purpose of collective bargaining or other mutual aid or protection; (2) that no employee and no one seeking employment shall be required as a condition of employment to join any company union or to refrain from joining, organizing, or assisting a labor organization of his own choosing; and (3) that employers shall comply with the maximum hours of labor, minimum rates of pay, and other conditions of employment, approved or prescribed by the President.

(b) The President shall, so far as practicable, afford every opportunity to employers and employees in any trade or industry or subdivision thereof with respect to which the conditions referred to in clauses (1) and (2) of subsection (a) prevail, to establish by mutual agreement, the standards as to the maximum hours of labor, minimum rates of pay, and such other conditions of employment as may be necessary in such trade or industry or subdivision thereof to effectuate the policy of this title; and the standards established in such agreements, when approved by the President, shall have the same effect as a code of fair competition, approved by the President under subsection (a) of section 3.

(c) Where no such mutual agreement has been approved by the President he may investigate the labor practices, policies, wages, hours of labor, and conditions of employment in such trade or industry or subdivision thereof; and upon the basis of such investigations, and after such hearings as the President finds advisable, he is authorized to prescribe a limited code of fair competition fixing such maximum hours of labor, minimum rates of pay, and other conditions of employment in the trade or industry or subdivision thereof investigated as he finds to be necessary to effectuate the policy of this title, which shall have the same effect as a code of fair competition approved by the President under subsection (a) of section 3. The President may differentiate according to experience and skill of the employees affected and according to the locality of employment; but no attempt shall be made to introduce any classification according to the nature of the work involved which might tend to set a maximum as well as a minimum wage.

(d) As used in this title, the term "person" includes any individual, partnership, association, trust, or corporation; and the terms "interstate and foreign commerce" and "interstate or foreign commerce" include, except where otherwise indicated, trade or commerce among the several States and with foreign nations, or between the District of Columbia or any Territory of the United States and any State, Territory or foreign nation, or between any insular possessions or other places under the jurisdiction of the United States, or between any such possession or place and any State or Territory of the United States or the District of Columbia or any foreign nation, or within the District of Columbia or any Territory or any insular possession or other place under the jurisdiction of the United States.

APPLICATION OF AGRICULTURAL ADJUSTMENT ACT

SEC. 8. (a) This title shall not be construed to repeal or modify any of the provisions of title I of the Act entitled "An Act to relieve the existing national economic emergency by increasing agricultural purchasing power, to raise revenue for extraordinary expenses incurred by reason of such emergency, to provide emergency relief with respect to agricultural indebtedness, to provide for the orderly liquidation of jointstock land banks, and for other purposes, approved May 12, 1933; and such title I of said Act approved May 12, 1933, may for all purposes be hereafter referred to as the "Agricultural Adjustment Act."

(b) The President may, in his discretion, in order to avoid conflicts in the administration of the Agricultural Adjustment Act and this title, delegate any of his functions and powers under this title with respect to trades, industries, or subdivisions thereof which are engaged in the handling of any agricultural commodity or product thereof, or of any competing commodity or product thereof, to the Secretary of Agriculture.

OIL REGULATION

SEC. 9. (a) The President is further authorized to initiate before the Interstate Commerce Commission proceedings necessary to prescribe regulations to control the operations of oil pipe lines and to fix reasonable, compensatory rates for the transportation of petroleum and its products by pipe lines, and the Interstate Commerce Commission shall grant preference to the hearings and determination of such cases.

(b) The President is authorized to institute proceedings to divorce from any holding company any pipe-line company controlled by such holding company which pipe-line company by unfair practices or by exorbitant rates in the transportation of petroleum or its products tends to create a monopoly.

(c) The President is authorized to prohibit the transportation in interstate and foreign commerce of petroleum and the products thereof produced or withdrawn from storage in excess of the amount permitted to be produced or withdrawn from storage by any State law or valid regulation or order prescribed thereunder, by any board, commission, officer, or other duly authorized agency of a State. Any violation of any order of the President issued under the provisions of this subsection shall be punishable by fine of not to exceed $1,000, or imprisonment for not to exceed six months, or both.

RULES AND REGULATIONS

SEC. 10. (a) The President is authorized to prescribe such rules and regulations as may be necessary to carry out the purposes of this title, and fees for licenses and for filing codes of fair competition and agreements, and any violation of any such rule or regulation shall be punishable by fine of not to exceed $500, or imprisonment for not to exceed six months, or both.

(b) The President may from time to time cancel or modify any order, approval, license, rule, or regulation issued under this title; and each agreement, code of fair competition, or license approved, prescribed, or issued under this title shall contain an express provision to that effect.

TITLE II—PUBLIC WORKS AND CONSTRUCTION PROJECTS

FEDERAL EMERGENCY ADMINISTRATION OF PUBLIC WORKS

SECTION 201. (a) To effectuate the purposes of this title, the President is hereby authorized to create a Federal Emergency Administration of Public Works, all the powers of which; shall be exercised by a Federal Emergency Administrator of Public Works (hereafter referred to as the "Administrator," and to establish such agencies, to accept and utilize such voluntary and uncompensated services, to appoint, without regard to the civil service laws, such officers and employees, and to utilize such Federal officers and employees, and, with the consent of the State, such State and local officers and employees as he may find necessary, to prescribe their authorities, duties, responsibilities, and tenure, and, without regard to the Classification Act of 1923, as amended, to fix the compensation of any officers and employees so appointed. The President may delegate any of his functions and powers under this title to such officers, agents, and employees as he may designate or appoint.

(b) The Administrator may, without regard to the civil service laws or the Classification Act of 1923, as amended, appoint and fix the compensation of such experts and such other officers and employees as are necessary to carry out the provisions of this title; and may make such expenditures (including expenditures for personal services and rent at the seat of government and elsewhere, for law books and books

of reference, and for paper, printing and binding) as are necessary to carry out the provisions of this title.

(c) All such compensation, expenses, and allowances shall be paid out of funds made available by this Act.

(d) After the expiration of two years after the date of the enactment of this Act, or sooner if the President shall by proclamation or the Congress shall by joint resolution declare that the emergency recognized by section 1 has ended, the President shall not make any further loans or grants or enter upon any new construction under this title, and any agencies established hereunder shall cease to exist and any of their remaining functions shall be transferred to such departments of the Government as the President shall designate: Provided, That he may issue funds to a borrower under this title prior to January 23, 1939, under the terms of any agreement, or any commitment to bid upon or purchase bonds, entered into with such borrower prior to the date of termination, under this section, of the power of the President to make loans.

SEC. 202. The Administrator, under the direction of the President, shall prepare a comprehensive program of public works, which shall include among other things the following: (a) Construction, repair, and improvement of public highways and park ways, public buildings, and any publicly owned instrumentalities and facilities; (b) conservation and development of natural resources, including control, utilization, and purification of waters, prevention of soil or coastal erosion, development of water power, transmission of electrical energy, and construction of river and harbor improvements and flood control and also the construction of any river or drainage improvement required to perform or satisfy any obligation incurred by the United States through a treaty with a foreign Government heretofore ratified and to restore or develop for the use of any State or its citizens water taken from or denied to them by performance on the part of the United States of treaty obligations heretofore assumed: Provided, That no river or harbor improvements shall be carried out unless they shall have heretofore or hereafter been adopted by the Congress or are recommended by the Chief of Engineers of the United States Army; (c) any projects of the character heretofore constructed or carried on either directly by public authority or with public aid to serve the interests of the general public; (d) construction, reconstruction, alteration, or repair under public regulation or control of low-cost housing and slum clearance projects; (e) any project (other than those included in the foregoing classes) of any character heretofore eligible for loans under subsection (a) of section 201 of the Emergency Relief and Construction Act of 1932, as amended, and paragraph (3) of such subsection (a) shall for such purposes be held to include loans for the construction or completion of hospitals the operation of which is partly financed from public funds, and of reservoirs and pumping plants and for the construction of dry docks; and if in the opinion of the President it seems desirable, the construction of naval vessels within the terms and/or limits established by the London Naval Treaty of 1930 and of aircraft required therefor and construction of heavier-than-air aircraft and technical construction for the Army Air Corps and such Army housing projects as the President may approve, and provision of original equipment for the mechanization or motorization of such Army tactical units as he may designate: Provided, however, that in the event of an international agreement for the further limitation of armament to which the United States is signatory, the President is hereby authorized and empowered to suspend, in whole or in part, any such naval or military construction or mechanization and motorization of Army units: Provided further, That this title shall not be applicable to public works under the jurisdiction or control of the Architect of the Capitol or of any commission or committee for which such Architect is the contracting and/or executive officer.

SEC. 203. (a) With a view to increasing employment quickly (while reasonably securing any loans made by the United States) the president is authorized and empowered, through the Administrator or through such other agencies as he may designate or create, (1) to construct, finance, or aid in the construction or financing of any public works project included in the program prepared pursuant to section 202; (2) upon such terms as the President shall prescribe, to make grants to States, municipalities, or other public bodies for the construction, repair, or improvement of any such project, but no such grant shall be in excess of 30 per centum of the cost of the labor and materials employed upon such project; (3) to acquire by purchase, or by exercise of the power of eminent domain, any real or personal property in connection with the construction of any such project, and to sell any security acquired or any property so constructed or acquired or to lease any such property with or without the privilege of purchase: Provided, That all moneys received from any such sale or lease or the repayment of any loan shall be used to retire obligations issued pursuant to section 209 of this Act, in addition to any other moneys required to be used for such purpose; (4) to aid in the financing of such railroad maintenance and equipment as may be approved by the Interstate Commerce Commission as desirable for the improvement of transportation facilities; and (5) to advance, upon request of the Commission having jurisdiction of the project, the unappropriated balance of the sum authorized for carrying out the provisions of the Act entitled "An Act to provide for the construction and equipment of an annex to the Library of Congress", approved June 13, 1930 (46 Stat. 583); such advance to be expended under the direction of such Commission and in accordance with such Act: Provided, That in deciding to extend any aid or grant hereunder to any State, county, or municipality the President may consider whether action is in process or in good faith assured therein reasonably designed to bring the ordinary current expenditures thereof within the prudently estimated revenues thereof. The provisions of this section and section 202 shall extend to public works in the several States, Hawaii, Alaska, the District of Columbia, Puerto Rico, the Canal Zone, and the Virgin Islands.

(b) All expenditures for authorized travel by officers and employees, including subsistence, required on account of any Federal public works projects, shall be charged to the amounts allocated to such projects, notwithstanding any other provisions of law; and there is authorized to be employed such personal services in the District of Columbia and elsewhere as may be required to be engaged upon such work and to be in addition to employees otherwise provided for, the compensation of such additional personal services to be a charge against the funds made available for such construction work.

(c) In the acquisition of any land or site for the purposes of Federal public buildings and in the construction of such buildings provided for in this title, the provisions contained in sections 305 and 306 of the Emergency Relief and Construction Act of 1932, as amended shall apply.

(d) The President, in his discretion, and under such terms as he may prescribe, may extend any of the benefits of this title to any State, county, or municipality notwithstanding any constitutional or legal restriction or limitation on the right or power of such State, county, or municipality to borrow money or incur indebtedness.

SEC. 204. (a) For the purpose of providing for emergency construction of public highways and related projects, the President is authorized to make grants to the highway departments of the several States in an amount not less than $400,000,000, to be expended by such departments in accordance with the provisions of the Federal Highway Act, approved November 9, 1921, as amended and supplemented, except as provided in this title, as follows:

(1) For expenditure in emergency construction on the Federal aid highway system and extensions thereof into and through municipalities. The amount apportioned to any State under this paragraph may be used to pay all or any part of the cost of surveys, plans, and of highway and bridge construction including the elimination of hazards to highway traffic, such as the separation of grades at crossing, the reconstruction of existing railroad grade crossing structures, the relocation of highways to eliminate railroad crossings the widening of narrow bridges and roadways, the building of footpaths, the replacement of unsafe bridges, the construction of routes to avoid congested areas, the construction of facilities to improve accessibility and the free flow of traffic, and the cost of any other construction that will provide safer traffic facilities or definitely eliminate existing hazards to pedestrian or vehicular traffic. No funds made available by this title shall be used for the acquisition of any land, right of way, or easement in connection with any railroad grade elimination project.

(2) For expenditure in emergency construction on secondary or feeder roads to be agreed upon by the State highway departments and the Secretary of Agriculture: Provided, That the State or responsible political subdivision shall provide for the proper maintenance of said roads. Such grants shall be available for payment of the full cost of surveys, plans, improvement, and construction of secondary or feeder roads, on which projects shall be submitted by the State highway department and approved by the Secretary of Agriculture.

(b) Any amount allocated by the President for grants under subsection (a) of this section shall be apportioned among the several States seven-eighths in accordance with the provisions of section 21 of the Federal Highway Act, approved November 9, 1921, as amended and supplemented (which Act is hereby further amended for the purposes of this title to include the District of Columbia), and one-eighth in the ratio which the population of each State bears to the total population of the United States, according to the latest decennial census and shall be available on July 1, 1933 and shall remain available until expended; but no part of the funds apportioned to any State need be matched by the State, and such funds may also be used in lieu of State funds to match unobligated balances of previous apportionments of regular Federal aid appropriations.

(c) All contracts involving the expenditure of such grants shall contain provisions establishing minimum rates of wages, to be predetermined by the State highway department, which contractors shall pay to skilled and unskilled labor, and such minimum rates shall be stated in the invitation for bids and shall be included in proposals for bids for the work.

(d) In the expenditure of such amounts, the limitations in the Federal Highway Act, approved November 9, 1921, as amended and supplemented, upon highway construction, reconstruction, and bridges within municipalities and upon payments per mile which may be made from Federal funds, shall not apply.

(e) As used in this section the term "State" includes the Territory of Hawaii and the District of Columbia. The term "highway" as defined in the Federal Highway Act approved November 9, 1921 "as amended and supplemented, for the purposes of this section, shall be deemed to include such main parkways as may be designated by the State and approved by the Secretary of Agriculture as part of the Federal aid highway system.

(f) Whenever, in connection with the construction of any highway project under this section or section 202 of this Act, it is necessary to acquire rights of way over or through any property or tracts of land owned and controlled by the Government of the United States, it shall be the duty of the proper official of the Government of the United States having control of such property or tracts of land with the approval of the President and the Attorney General of the United States, and without any expense whatsoever to the United States, to perform any acts and to execute any agreements necessary to grant the rights of way so required, but if at any time the land or the property the subject of the agreement shall cease to be used for the purposes of the highway, the title in and the jurisdiction over the land or property shall automatically revert to the Government of the United States and the agreement shall so provide.

(g) Hereafter in the administration of the Federal Highway Act, and Acts amendatory thereof or supplementary thereto, the first paragraph of section 9 of said Act shall not apply to publicly owned toll bridges or approaches thereto, operated by the highway department of any State, subject, however, to the condition that all tolls received from the operation of any such bridge, less the actual cost of operation and maintenance, shall be applied to the repayment of the cost of its construction or acquisition, and when the cost of its construction or acquisition shall have been repaid in full, such bridge thereafter shall be maintained and operated as a free bridge.

SEC. 205. (a) Not less than $50,000,000 of the amount made available by this Act shall be allotted for (A) national forest highways, (B) national forest roads, trails, bridges, and related projects, (C) national park roads and trails in national parks owned or authorized, (D) roads on Indian reservations, and (E) roads through public lands, to be expended in the same manner as provided in paragraph (2) of section 301 of the Emergency Relief and Construction Act of 1932, in the case of appropriations allocated for such purposes, respectively, in such section 301, to remain available until expended.

(b) The President may also allot funds made available by this Act for the construction, repair and improvement of public highways in Alaska, the Canal Zone, Puerto Rico, and the Virgin Islands.

SEC. 206. All contracts let for construction projects and all loans and grants pursuant to this title shall contain such provisions as are necessary to insure (1) that no convict labor shall be employed on any such project; (2) that (except in executive, administrative, and supervisory positions), so far as practicable and feasible, no individual directly employed on any such project shall be permitted to work more than thirty hours in any one week; (3) that all employees shall be paid just and reasonable wages which shall be compensation sufficient to provide, for the hours of labor as limited, a standard of living in decency and comfort; (4) that in the employment of labor in connection with any such project, preference shall be given, where they are qualified, to ex-service men with dependents, and then in the following order: (A) To citizens of the United States and aliens who have declared their intention of becoming citizens, who are bona fide resi-

dents of the political subdivision and/or county in which the work is to be performed, and (B) to citizens of the United States and aliens who have declared their intention of becoming citizens, who are bona fide residents of the State Territory, or district in which the work is to be performed: Provided, That these preferences shall apply only where such labor is available and qualified to perform the work to which the employment relates; and (5) that the maximum of human labor shall be used in lieu of machinery wherever practicable and consistent with sound economy and public advantage.

SEC. 207. (a) For the purpose of expediting the actual construction of public works contemplated by this title and to provide a means of financial assistance to persons under contract with the United States to perform such construction, the President is authorized and empowered through the Administrator or through such other agencies as he may designate or create to approve any assignment executed by any such contractor, with the written consent of the surety or sureties upon the penal bond executed in connection with his contract, to any national or State bank, or his claim against the United States, or any part of such claim, under such contract; and any assignment so approved shall be valid for all purposes, notwithstanding the provisions of sections 3737 and 3477 of the Revised Statutes as amended.

(b) The funds received by a contractor under any advances made in consideration of any such assignment are hereby declared to be trust funds in the hands of such contractor to be first applied to the payment of claims of subcontractors, architects, engineers, surveyors, laborers, and material men in connection with the project, to the payment of premiums on the penal bond or bonds, and premiums accruing during the construction of such project on insurance policies taken in connection therewith. Any contractor and any officer, director or agent of any such contractor, who applies, or consents to the application of, such funds for any other purpose and fails to pay any claim or premium hereinbefore mentioned, shall be deemed guilty of a misdemeanor and shall be punished by a fine of not more than $1,000 or by imprisonment for not more than one year, or by both such fine and imprisonment.

(c) Nothing in this section shall be considered as imposing upon the assignee any obligation to see to the proper application of the funds advanced by the assignee in consideration of such assignment.

SUBSISTENCE HOMESTEADS

SEC. 208. To provide for aiding the redistribution of the overbalance of population in industrial centers $25,000,000 is hereby made available to the President, to be used by him through such agencies as he may establish and under such regulations as he may make, for making loans for and otherwise aiding in the purchase of subsistence homesteads. The moneys collected as repayment of said loans shall constitute a revolving fund to be administered as directed by the President for the purposes of this section.

RULES AND REGULATIONS

SEC. 209. The President is authorized to prescribe such rules and regulations as may be necessary to carry out the purposes of this title, and any violation of any such rule or regulation shall be punishable by fine of not to exceed $500 or imprisonment not to exceed six months, or both.

ISSUE OF SECURITIES AND SINKING FUND

SEC. 210. (a) The Secretary of the Treasury is authorized to borrow, from time to time, under the Second Liberty Bond Act, as amended, such amounts as may be necessary to meet the expenditures authorized by this Act, or to refund any obligations previously issued under this section, and to issue therefor bonds, notes, certificates of indebtedness, or Treasury bills of the United States.

(b) For each fiscal year beginning with the fiscal year 1934 there is hereby appropriated, in addition to and as part of, the cumulative sinking fund provided by section 6 of the Victory Liberty Loan Act, as amended, out of any money in the Treasury not otherwise appropriated, for the purpose of such fund, an amount equal to $2\frac{1}{2}$ per centum of the aggregate amount of the expenditures made out of appropriations made or authorized under this Act as determined by the Secretary of the Treasury.

REEMPLOYMENT AND RELIEF TAXES

SEC. 211. (a) Effective as of the day following the date of the enactment of this Act, section 617 (a) of the Revenue Act of 1932 is amended by striking out "1 cent" and inserting in lieu thereof " $1\frac{1}{2}$ cents."

(b) Effective as of the day following the date of the enactment of this Act, section 617 (c) (2) of such: Act is amended by adding at the end thereof a new sentence to read as follows: "As used in this paragraph the term 'benzol' does not include benzol sold for use otherwise than as a fuel for the propulsion of motor vehicles, motor boats, or airplanes, and otherwise than in the manufacture or production of such fuel."

SEC. 212. Titles IV and V of the Revenue Act of 1932 are amended by striking out "1934" wherever appearing therein and by inserting in lieu thereof "1935." Section 761 of the Revenue Act of 1932 is further amended by striking out "and on July 1, 1933" and inserting in lieu thereof "and on July 1, 1933," and on July 1, 1934."

SEC. 213. (a) There is hereby imposed upon the receipt of dividends (required to be included in the gross income of the recipient under the provisions of the Revenue Act of 1932) by any person other than a domestic corporation, an excise tax equal to 5 per centum of the amount thereof, such tax to be deducted and withheld from such dividends by the payor corporation. The tax imposed by this section shall not apply to dividends declared before the date of the enactment of this Act.

(b) Every corporation required to deduct and withhold any tax under this section shall, on or before the last day of the month following the payment of the dividend, make return thereof and pay the tax to the collector of the district in which its principal place of business is located, or, if it has no principal place of business in the United States, to the collector at Baltimore, Maryland.

(c) Every such corporation is hereby made liable for such tax and is hereby indemnified against the claims and demands of any person for the amount of any payment made in accordance with the provisions of this section.

(d) The provisions of sections 115, 771 to 774, inclusive, and 1111 of the Revenue Act of 1932 shall be applicable with respect to the tax imposed by this section.

(e) The taxes imposed by this section shall not apply to the dividends of any corporation enumerated in section 103 of the Revenue Act of 1932.

SEC. 214. Section 104 of the Revenue Act of 1932 is amended by striking out the words "the surtax" wherever occurring in such section and inserting in lieu thereof "any internal revenue tax." The heading of such section is amended by striking out "surtaxes" and inserting in lieu thereof "internal revenue taxes." Section 13 (c) of such Act is amended by striking out "surtax" and inserting in lieu thereof "internal revenue tax."

SEC. 215. (a) For each year ending June 30 there is hereby imposed upon every domestic corporation with respect to carrying on or doing business for any part of such year an excise tax of $1 for each $1,000 of the adjusted declared value of its capital stock.

(b) For each year ending June 30 there is hereby imposed upon every foreign corporation with respect to carrying on or doing business in the United States for any part of such year an excise tax equivalent to $1 for each $1,000 of the adjusted declared value of capital employed in the transaction of its business in the United States.

(c) The taxes imposed by this section shall not apply—

(1) to any corporation enumerated in section 103 of the Revenue Act of 1932;

(2) to any insurance company subject to the tax imposed by section 201 or 204 of such Act;

(3) to any domestic corporation in respect of the year ending June 30, 1933, if it did not carry on or do business during a part of the period from the date of the enactment of this Act to June 30, 1933, both dates inclusive; or

(4) to any foreign corporation in respect of the year ending June 30, 1933, if it did not carry on or do business in the United States during apart of the period from the day of the enactment of this Act to June 30, 1933, both dates inclusive.

(d) Every corporation liable for tax under this section shall make a return under oath within one month after the close of the year with respect to which such tax is imposed to the collector for the district in which is located its principal place of business or, if it has no principal place of business in the United States, then to the collector at Baltimore, Maryland. Such return shall contain such information and be made in such manner as the Commissioner with the approval of the Secretary may by regulations prescribe. The tax shall, without assessment by the Commissioner or notice from the collector, be due and payable to the collector before the expiration of the period for filing the return. If the tax is not paid when due, there shall be added as part of the tax interest at the rate of 1 per centum a month from the time when the tax became due until paid. All provisions of law (including penalties) applicable in respect of the taxes imposed by section 600 of the Revenue Act of 1926 shall, in so far as not inconsistent with this section, be applicable in respect of the taxes imposed by this section. The Commissioner may extend the time for making the returns and paying the taxes imposed by this section, under such rules and regulations as he may prescribe with the approval of the Secretary, but no such extension shall be for more than sixty days.

(e) Returns required to be filed for the purpose of the tax imposed by this section shall be open to inspection in the same manner, to the same extent, and subject to the same provisions of law, including penalties, as returns made under title II of the Revenue Act of 1926.

(f) For the first year ending June 30 in respect of which a tax is imposed by this section upon any corporation, the adjusted declared value shall be the value, as declared by the corporation in its first return under this section (which declaration of value cannot be amended), as of the close of its last income tax taxable year ending at or prior to the close of the year for which the tax is imposed by this section (or as of the date of organization in the case of a corporation having no income tax taxable year ending at or prior to the close of the year for which the tax is imposed by this section). For any subsequent year ending June 30, the adjusted declared value in the case of a domestic corporation shall be the original declared value plus (1) the cash and fair market value of property paid in for stock or shares, (2) paid-in surplus and contributions to capital, and (3) earnings and profits, and minus (A) the value of property distributed in liquidation to shareholders, (B) distributions of earnings and profits, and (C) deficits, whether operating or nonoperating; each adjustment being made for the period from the date as of which the original declared value was declared to the close of its last income tax taxable year ending at or prior to the close of the year for which the tax is imposed by this section. For any subsequent year ending June 30, the adjusted declared value in the case of a foreign corporation shall be the original declared value adjusted, in accordance with regulations prescribed by the Commissioner with the approval of the Secretary, to reflect increases or decreases (for the period specified in the preceding sentence) in the capital employed in the transaction of its business in the United States.

(g) The terms used in this section shall have the same meaning as when used in the Revenue Act of 1932.

SEC. 216. (a) There is hereby imposed upon the net income of every corporation, for each income tax taxable year ending after the close of the first year in respect of which it is taxable under section 215, an excess profits tax equivalent to 5 per centum of such portion of its net income for such income tax taxable year as is in excess of $12^1/_2$ per centum of the adjusted declared value of its capital stock (or in the case of a foreign corporation the adjusted declared value of capital employed in the transaction of its business in the United States) as of the close of the preceding income-tax taxable year (or as of the date of organization if it had no preceding income-tax taxable year) determined as provided in section 215. The terms used in this section shall have the same meaning as when used in the Revenue Act of 1932.

(b) The tax imposed by this section shall be assessed, collected, and paid in the same manner, and shall be subject to the same provisions of law (including penalties), as the taxes imposed by title I of the Revenue Act of 1932.

SEC. 217. (a) The President shall proclaim the date of—

(1) the close of the first fiscal year ending June 30 of any year after the year 1933, during which the total receipts of the United States (excluding public-debt receipts) exceed its total expenditures (excluding public debt expenditures other than those chargeable against such receipts), or

(2) the repeal of the eighteenth amendment to the Constitution, whichever is the earlier.

(b) Effective as of the 1st day of the calendar year following the date so proclaimed section 617 (a) of the Revenue Act of 1932, as amended, is amended by striking out "$1^1/_2$ cents" and inserting in lieu thereof "1 cent".

(c) The tax on dividends imposed by section 213 shall not apply to any dividends declared on or after the 1st day of the calendar year following the date so proclaimed.

(d) The capital stock tax imposed by section 215 shall not apply to any taxpayer in respect of any year beginning on or after the 1st day of July following the date so proclaimed.

(e) The excess profits tax imposed by section 216 shall not apply to any taxpayer in respect of any taxable year after its taxable year during which the date so proclaimed occurs.

SEC. 218. (a) Effective as of January 1, 1933, sections 117, 23(i), 169, 187 and 205 of the Revenue Act of 1932 are repealed.

(b) Effective as of January 1,1933, section 23(r) (2) of the Revenue Act of 1932 is repealed.

(c) Effective as of January 1,1933, section 23(r) (3) of the Revenue Act of 1932 is amended by striking out all after the word "Territory" and inserting a period.

(d) Effective as of January 1,1933, section 182(a) of the Revenue Act of 1932 is amended by inserting at the end thereof a new sentence as follows: "No part of any loss disallowed to a partnership as a deduction by section 23(r) shall be allowed as a deduction to a member of such partnership in computing net income."

(e) Effective as of January 1, 1933, section 141(c) of the Revenue Act of 1932 is amended by striking out "except that for the taxable years 1932 and 1933 there shall be added to the rate of tax prescribed by sections 13(a), 201(b), and 204(a), a rate of three fourths of 1 per centum" and inserting in lieu thereof the following: "except that for the taxable years 1932 and 1933 there shall be added to the rate of tax prescribe by sections 13(a), 201(b), and 204(a), a rate of three fourths of 1 per centum and except that for the taxable years 1934 and 1935 there shall be added to the rate of tax prescribed by sections 13(a), 201(b), and 204(a), a rate of 1 per centum."

(f) No interest shall be assessed or collected for any period prior to September 15, 1933, upon such portion of any amount determined as a deficiency in income taxes as is attributable solely to the amendments made to the Revenue Act of 1932 by this section.

(g) In cases where the effect of this section is to require for a taxable year ending prior to June 30, 1933, the making of an income tax return not otherwise required by law, the time for making the return and paying the tax shall be the same as if the return was for a fiscal year ending June 30, 1933.

(h) Section 55 of the Revenue Act of 1932 is amended by inserting before the period at the end thereof a semicolon and the following: "and all returns made under this Act after the date of enactment of the National Industrial Recovery Act shall constitute public records and shall be open to public examination and inspection to such extent as shall be authorized in rules and regulations promulgated by the President."

SEC 219. Section 500 (a) (1) of the Revenue Act of 1926, as amended, is amended by striking out the period at the end of the second sentence thereof and inserting in lieu thereof a comma and the following: "except that no tax shall be imposed in the case of persons admitted free to any spoken play (not a mechanical reproduction), whether or not set to music or with musical parts or accompaniments, which is a consecutive narrative interpreted by a single set of characters, all necessary to the development of the plot, in two or more acts, the performance consuming more than 1 hour and 45 minutes of time."

APPROPRIATION

SEC. 220. For the purposes of this Act, there is hereby authorized to be appropriated, out of any money in the Treasury not otherwise appropriated, the sum of $3,300,000,000. The President is authorized to allocate so much of said sum, not in excess of $100,000,000, as he may determine to be necessary for expenditures in carrying out the Agricultural Adjustment Act and the purposes, powers, and functions heretofore and hereafter conferred upon the Farm Credit Administration.

SEC. 221. Section 7 of the Agricultural Adjustment Act, approved May 12, 1933, is amended by striking out all of its present terms and provisions and substituting therefor the following:

SEC. 7. The Secretary shall sell the cotton held by him at his discretion, but subject to the foregoing provisions: Provided, That he shall dispose of all cotton held by him by March 1, 1936: Provided further, That notwithstanding the provisions of section 6, the Secretary shall have authority to enter into option contracts with producers of cotton to sell to the producers such cotton held by him, in such amounts and at such prices and upon such terms and conditions as the Secretary may deem advisable, in combination with rental or benefit payments provided for in part 2 of this title.

"Notwithstanding any provisions of existing law, the Secretary of Agriculture may in the administration of the Agricultural Adjustment Act make public such information as he deems necessary in order to effec-

tuate the purposes of such Act."

TITLE III-AMENDMENTS TO EMERGENCY RELIEF AND CONSTRUCTION ACT AND MISCELLANEOUS PROVISIONS

SECTION 301. After the expiration of ten days after the date upon which the Administrator has qualified and taken office, (1) no application shall be approved by the Reconstruction Finance Corporation under the provisions of subsection (a) of section 201 of the Emergency Relief and Construction Act of 1932, as amended, and (2) the Administrator shall have access to all applications, files, and records of the Reconstruction Finance Corporation relating to loans and contracts and the administration of funds under such subsection: Provided, That the Reconstruction Finance Corporation may issue funds to a borrower under such subsection (a) prior to January 23, 1939, under the terms of any agreement or any commitment to bid upon or purchase bonds entered into with such borrower pursuant to an application approved prior to the date of termination, under this section, of the power of the Reconstruction Finance Corporation to approve applications.

DECREASE OF BORROWING POWER OF RECONSTRUCTION FINANCE CORPORATION

SEC. 302. The amount of notes, debentures, bonds, or other such obligations which the Reconstruction Finance Corporation is authorized and empowered under section 9 of the Reconstruction Finance Corporation Act, as amended, to have outstanding at anyone time is decreased by $400,000,000.

SEPARABILITY CLAUSE

SEC. 303. If any provision of this Act, or the application thereof to any person or circumstances, is held invalid, the remainder of the Act, and the application of such provision to other persons or circumstances, shall not be affected thereby.

SHORT TITLE

SEC. 304. This Act may be cited as the "National Industrial Recovery Act." Approved, June 16, 1933, 11:55 a.m.

The National Labor Relations Act

After the National Industrial Recovery Act was declared unconstitutional by the Supreme Court, organized labor was again looking for relief from employers who had been free to spy on, interrogate, discipline, discharge, and blacklist union members. In the 1930s, workers had begun to organize militantly, and in 1933 and 1934, a great wave of strikes occurred across the nation in the form of citywide general strikes and factory takeovers. Violent confrontations occurred between workers trying to form unions and the police and private security forces defending the interests of anti-union employers.

In a Congress sympathetic to labor unions, the National Labor Relations Act (NLRA) was passed in July of 1935. The broad intention of the act, commonly known as the Wagner Act after Senator Robert R. Wagner of New York, was to guarantee employees "the right to self-organization, to form, join, or assist labor organizations, to bargain collectively through representatives of their own choosing, and to engage in concerted activities for the purpose of collective bargaining or other mutual aid and protection." The NLRA applied to all employers involved in interstate commerce except airlines, railroads, agriculture, and government.

In order to enforce and maintain those rights, the act included provision for the National Labor Relations Board (NLRB) to arbitrate deadlocked labor-management disputes, guarantee democratic union elections, and penalize unfair labor practices by employers. To this day, the board of five members, appointed by the President, is assisted by 33 regional directors. The NLRB further determines proper bargaining units, conducts elections for union representation, and investigates charges of unfair labor practices by employers. Unfair practices, by law, include such things as interference, coercion, or restraint in labor's self-organizing rights; interference with the formation of labor unions; encouragement or discouragement of union membership; and the refusal to bargain collectively with a duly chosen employee representatives.

The constitutionality of the NLRA was upheld by the United States Supreme Court in *National Labor Relations Board v. Jones & Laughlin Steel Corp.* in 1937. The act contributed to a dramatic surge in union membership and made labor a force to be reckoned with both politically and economically. Women benefited from this shift to unionization as well. By the end of the 1930s, 800,000 women belonged to unions, a threefold increase from 1929. The provisions of the NLRA were later expanded under the Taft-Hartley Labor Act of 1957 and the Landrum-Griffin Act of 1959.

The Social Security Act

AN ACT to provide for the general welfare by establishing a system of Federal old-age benefits, and by enabling the several States to make more adequate provision for aged persons, blind persons, dependent and crippled children, maternal and child welfare, public health, and the administration of their unemployment compensation laws; to establish a Social Security Board; to raise revenue; and for other purposes.

Be it enacted by the Senate and House of Representatives of the United States of America in Congress assembled,

TITLE I-GRANTS TO STATES FOR OLD-AGE ASSISTANCE APPROPRIATION

SECTION 1. For the purpose of enabling each State to furnish financial assistance, as far as practicable under the conditions in such State, to aged needy individuals, there is hereby authorized to be appropriated for the fiscal year ended June 30, 1936, the sum of $49,750,000, and there is hereby authorized to be appropriated for each fiscal year thereafter a sum sufficient to carry out the purposes of this title. The sums made available under this section shall be used for making payments to States which have submitted, and had approved by the Social Security Board established by Title VII (hereinafter referred to as the Board), State plans for old-age assistance.

STATE OLD-AGE ASSISTANCE PLANS

SEC. 2. (a) A State plan for old-age assistance must

(1) provide that it shall be in effect in all political subdivisions of the State, and, if administered by them, be mandatory upon them;

(2) provide for financial participation by the State;

(3) either provide for the establishment or designation of a single State agency to administer the plan, or provide for the establishment or designation of a single State agency to supervise the administration of the plan;

(4) provide for granting to any individual, whose claim for old-age assistance is denied, an opportunity for a fair hearing before such State agency;

(5) provide such methods of administration (other than those relating to selection, tenure of office, and compensation of personnel) as are found by the Board to be necessary for the efficient operation of the plan;

(6) provide that the State agency will make such reports, in such form and containing such information, as the Board may from time to time require, and comply with such provisions as the Board may from time to time find necessary to assure the correctness and verification of such reports; and

(7) provide that, if the State or any of its political subdivisions collects from the estate of any recipient of old-age assistance any amount with respect to old-age assistance furnished him under the plan, one-half of the net amount so collected shall be promptly paid to the United States. Any payment so made shall be deposited in the Treasury to the credit of the appropriation for the purposes of this title.

(b) The Board shall approve any plan which fulfills the conditions specified in subsection (a), except that it shall not approve any plan which imposes, as a condition of eligibility for old-age assistance under the plan-

(1) An age requirement of more than sixty-five years, except that the plan may impose, effective until January 1, 1940, an age requirement of as much as seventy years; or

(2) Any residence requirement which excludes any resident of the State who has resided therein five years during the nine years immediately preceding the application for old-age assistance and has resided therein continuously for one year immediately preceding the application; or (3) Any citizenship requirement which excludes any citizen of the United States.

PAYMENT TO STATES

SEC. 3. (a) From the sums appropriated therefor, the Secretary of the Treasury shall pay to each State which has an approved plan for old-age assistance, for each quarter, beginning with the quarter commencing July 1, 1935,

(1) an amount, which shall be used exclusively as old-age assistance, equal to one-half of the total of the sums expended during such quarter as old-age assistance under the State plan with respect to each individual who at the time of such expenditure is sixty-five years of age or older and is not an inmate of a public institution, not counting so much of such expenditure with respect to any individual for any month as exceeds $30, and

(2) 5 per centum of such amount, which shall be used for paying the costs of administering the State plan or for old-age assistance, or both, and for no other purpose: Provided, That the State plan, in order to be approved by the Board, need not provide for financial participation before July 1, 1937, by the State, in the case of any State which the Board, upon application by the State and after reasonable notice and opportunity for hearing to the State, finds is prevented by its constitution from providing such financial participation.

(b) The method of computing and paying such amounts shall be as follows:

(1) The Board shall, prior to the beginning of each quarter, estimate the amount to be paid to the State for such quarter under the provisions of clause (1) of subsection (a), such estimate to be based on (A) a report filed by the State containing its estimate of the total sum to be expended in such quarter in accordance with the provisions of such clause, and stating the amount appropriated or made available by the State and its political subdivisions for such expenditures in such quarter, and if such amount is less than one-half of the total sum of such estimated expenditures, the source or sources from which the difference is expected to be derived,

(B) records showing the number of aged individuals in the State, and (C) such other investigation as the Board may find necessary.

(2) The Board shall then certify to the Secretary of the Treasury the amount so estimated by the Board, reduced or increased, as the case may be, by any

sum by which it finds that its estimate for any prior quarter was greater or less than the amount which should have been paid to the State under clause (1) of subsection (a) for such quarter, except to the extent that such sum has been applied to make the amount certified for any prior quarter greater or less than the amount estimated by the Board for such prior quarter.

(3) The Secretary of the Treasury shall thereupon, through the Division of Disbursement of the Treasury Department and prior to audit or settlement by the General Accounting Office, pay to the State, at the time or times fixed by the Board, the amount so certified, increased by 5 per centum.

OPERATION OF STATE PLANS

SEC. 4. In the case of any State plan for old-age assistance which has been approved by the Board, if the Board, after reasonable notice and opportunity for hearing to the State agency administering or supervising the administration of such plan, finds- (1) that the plan has been so changed as to impose any age, residence, or citizenship requirement prohibited by section 2 (b), or that in the administration of the plan any such prohibited requirement is imposed, with the knowledge of such State agency, in a substantial number of cases; or

(2) that in the administration of the plan there is a failure to comply substantially with any provision required by section 2 (a) to be included in the plan; the Board shall notify such State agency that further payments will not be made to the State until the Board is satisfied that such prohibited requirement is no longer so imposed, and that there is no longer any such failure to comply. Until it is so satisfied it shall make no further certification to the Secretary of the Treasury with respect to such State.

ADMINISTRATION

SEC. 5. There is hereby authorized to be appropriated for the fiscal year ending June 30, 1936, the sum of $250,000, for all necessary expenses of the Board in administering the provisions of this title.

DEFINITION

SEC. 6. When used in this title the term old age assistance means money payments to aged individuals.

TITLE II-FEDERAL OLD-AGE BENEFITS OLD-AGE RESERVE ACCOUNT

Section 201. (a) There is hereby created an account in the Treasury of the United States to be known as the Old-Age Reserve Account hereinafter in this title called the Account. There is hereby authorized to be appropriated to the Account for each fiscal year, beginning with the fiscal year ending June 30, 1937, an amount sufficient as an annual premium to provide for the payments required under this title, such amount to be determined on a reserve basis in accordance with accepted actuarial principles, and based upon such tables of mortality as the Secretary of the Treasury shall from time to time adopt, and upon an interest rate of 3 per centum per annum compounded annually. The Secretary of the Treasury shall submit annually to the Bureau of the Budget an estimate of the appropriations to be made to the Account. (b) It shall be the duty of the Secretary of the Treasury to invest such portion of the amounts credited to the Account as is not, in his judgment, required to meet current withdrawals. Such investment may be made only in interest-bearing obligations of the United States or in obligations guaranteed as to both principal and interest by the United States. For such purpose such obligations may be acquired (1) on original issue at par, or

(2) by purchase of outstanding obligations at the market price. The purposes for which obligations of the United States may be issued under the Second Liberty Bond Act, as amended, are hereby extended to authorize the issuance at par of special obligations exclusively to the Account. Such special obligations shall bear interest at the rate of 3 per centum per annum. Obligations other than such special obligations may be acquired for the Account only on such terms as to provide an investment yield of not less than 3 per centum per annum.

(c) Any obligations acquired by the Account (except special obligations issued exclusively to the Account) may be sold at the market price, and such special obligations may be redeemed at par plus accrued interest.

(d) The interest on, and the proceeds from the sale or redemption of, any obligations held in the Account shall be credited to and form a part of the Account.

(e) All amounts credited to the Account shall be available for making payments required under this title. (f) The Secretary of the Treasury shall include in his annual report the actuarial status of the Account.

OLD-AGE BENEFIT PAYMENTS

SEC. 202. (a) Every qualified individual (as defined in section 210) shall be entitled to receive, with respect to the period beginning on the date he attains the age of sixty-five, or on January 1, 1942, whichever is the later, and ending on the date of his death, an old-age benefit (payable as nearly as practicable in equal monthly installments) as follows:

(1) If the total wages (as defined in section 210) determined by the Board to have been paid to him, with respect to employment (as defined in section 210) after December 31, 1936, and before he attained the age of sixty-five, were not more than $3,000, the old-age benefit shall be at a monthly rate of one-half of 1 per centum of such total wages;

(2) If such total wages were more than $3,000, the old-age benefit shall be at a monthly rate equal to the sum of the following:

(A) One-half of 1 per centum of $3,000; plus

(B) One-twelfth of 1 per centum of the amount by which such total wages exceeded $3,000 and did not exceed $45,000; plus

(C) One-twenty-fourth of 1 per centum of the amount by which such total wages exceeded $45,000. (b) In no case shall the monthly rate computed under subsection (a) exceed $85.

(c) If the Board finds at any time that more or less than the correct amount has theretofore been paid to any individual under this section, then, under regulations made by the Board, proper adjustments shall be made in connection with subsequent payments under this section to the same individual.

(d) Whenever the Board finds that any qualified individual has received wages with respect to regular employment after he attained the age of sixty-five, the old-age benefit payable to such individual shall be reduced, for each calendar month in any part of which such regular employment occurred, by an amount equal to one month's benefit. Such reduction shall be made, under regulations prescribed by the Board, by deductions from one or more payments of old-age benefit to such individual.

PAYMENTS UPON DEATH

SEC. 203. (a) If any individual dies before attaining the age of sixty-five, there shall be paid to his estate an amount equal to 3 per centum of the total wages determined by the Board to have been paid to him, with respect to employment after December 31, 1936.

(b) If the Board finds that the correct amount of the old-age benefit payable to a qualified individual during his life under section 202 was less than 3 per centum of the total wages by which such old-age benefit was measurable, then there shall be paid to his estate a sum equal to the amount, if any, by which such 3 per centum exceeds the amount (whether more or less than the correct amount) paid to him during his life as old-age benefit.

(c) If the Board finds that the total amount paid to a qualified individual under an old-age benefit during his life was less than the correct amount to which he was entitled under section 202, and that the correct amount of such old-age benefit was 3 per centum or more of the total wages by which such old age benefit was measurable, then there shall be paid to his estate a sum equal to the amount, if any, by which the correct amount of the old age benefit exceeds the amount which was so paid to him during his life.

PAYMENTS TO AGED INDIVIDUALS NOT QUALIFIED FOR BENEFITS

SEC. 204. (a) There shall be paid in a lump sum to any individual who, upon attaining the age of sixty-five, is not a qualified individual, an amount equal to 3 per centum of the total wages determined by the Board to have been paid to him, with respect to employment after December 31, 1936, and before he attained the age of sixty-five.

(b) After any individual becomes entitled to any payment under subsection (a), no other payment shall be made under this title in any manner measured by wages paid to him, except that any part of any payment under subsection (a) which is not paid to him before his death shall be paid to his estate.

AMOUNTS OF $500 OR LESS PAYABLE TO ESTATES

SEC. 205. If any amount payable to an estate under section 203 or 204 is $500 or less, such amount may, under regulations prescribed by the Board, be paid to the persons found by the Board to be entitled thereto under the law of the State in which the deceased was domiciled, without the necessity of compliance with the requirements of law with respect to the administration of such estate.

OVERPAYMENTS DURING LIFE

SEC. 206. If the Board finds that the total amount paid to a qualified individual under an old-age benefit during his life was more than the correct amount to which he was entitled under section 202, and was 3 per centum or more of the total wages by which such old-age benefit was measurable, then upon his death there shall be repaid to the United States by his estate the amount, if any, by which such total amount paid to him during his life exceeds whichever of the following is the greater:

(1) Such 3 per centum, or

(2) the correct amount to which he was entitled under section 202.

METHOD OF MAKING PAYMENTS

SEC. 207. The Board shall from time to time certify to the Secretary of the Treasury the name and address of each person entitled to receive a payment under this title, the amount of such payment, and the time at which it should be made, and the Secretary of the Treasury through the Division of Disbursement of the Treasury Department, and prior to audit or settlement by the General Accounting Office, shall make payment in accordance with the certification by the Board.

ASSIGNMENT

SEC. 208. The right of any person to any future payment under this title shall not be transferable or assignable, at law or in equity, and none of the moneys paid or payable or rights existing under this title shall be subject to execution, levy, attachment, garnishment, or other legal process, or to the operation of any bankruptcy or insolvency law.

PENALTIES

SEC. 209. Whoever in any application for any payment under this title makes any false statement as to any material fact, knowing such statement to be false, shall be fined not more than $1,000 or imprisoned for not more than one year, or both.

DEFINITIONS

SEC. 210. When used in this title—(a) The term wages means all remuneration for employment, including the cash value of all remuneration paid in any medium other than cash; except that such term shall not include that part of the remuneration which, after remuneration equal to $3,000 has been paid to an individual by an employer with respect to employment during any calendar year, is paid to such employer with respect to employment during such calendar year.

(b) The term employment means any service, of whatever nature, performed within the United States by an employee for his employer, except-

(1) Agricultural labor;

(2) Domestic service in a private home;

(3) Casual labor not in the course of the employer's trade or business;

(4) Service performed as an officer or member of the crew of a vessel documented under the laws of the United States or of any foreign country;

(5) Service performed in the employ of the United States Government or of an instrumentality of the United States;

(6) Service performed in the employ of a State, a political subdivision thereof, or an instrumentality of one or more States or political subdivisions;

(7) Service performed in the employ of a corporation, community chest, fund, or foundation, organized and operated exclusively for religious, charitable, scientific, literary, or educational purposes, or for the prevention of cruelty to children or animals, no part of the net earnings of which inures to the benefit of any private shareholder or individual.

(c) The term qualified individual means any individual with respect to whom it appears to the satisfaction of the Board that

(1) He is at least sixty-five years of age; and

(2) The total amount of wages paid to him, with respect to employment after December 31, 1936, and before he attained the age of sixty-five, was not less than $2,000; and

(3) Wages were paid to him, with respect to employment on some five days after December 31, 1936, and before he attained the age of sixty-five, each day being in a different calendar year.

TITLE III-GRANTS TO STATES FOR UNEMPLOYMENT COMPENSATION ADMINISTRATION APPROPRIATION

SECTION 301. For the purpose of assisting the States in the administration of their unemployment compensation laws, there is hereby authorized to be appropriated, for the fiscal year ending June 30, 1936, the sum of $4,000,000, and for each fiscal year thereafter the sum of $49,000,000, to be used as hereinafter provided.

PAYMENTS TO STATES

SEC. 302. (a) The Board shall from time to time certify to the Secretary of the Treasury for payment to each State which has an unemployment compensation law approved by the Board under Title IX, such amounts as the Board determines to be necessary for the proper administration of such law during the fiscal year in which such payment is to be made. The Board s determination shall be based on

(1) the population of the State;

(2) an estimate of the number of persons covered by the State law and of the cost of proper administration of such law; and

(3) such other factors as the Board finds relevant. The Board shall not certify for payment under this section in any fiscal year a total amount in excess of the amount appropriated therefor for such fiscal year.

(b) Out of the sums appropriated therefor, the Secretary of the Treasury shall, upon receiving a certification under subsection

(a), pay, through the Division of Disbursement of the Treasury Department and prior to audit or settlement by the General Accounting Office, to the State agency charged with the administration of such law the amount so certified.

PROVISIONS OF STATE LAWS

SEC. 303. (a) The Board shall make no certification for payment to any State unless it finds that the law of such State, approved by the Board under Title IX, includes provisions for-

(1) Such methods of administration (other than those relating to selection, tenure of office, and compensation of personnel) as are found by the Board to be reasonably calculated to insure full payment of unemployment compensation when due; and

(2) Payment of unemployment compensation solely through public employment offices in the State or such other agencies as the Board may approve; and

(3) Opportunity for a fair hearing, before an impartial tribunal, for all individuals whose claims for unemployment compensation are denied; and

(4) The payment of all money received in the unemployment fund of such State, immediately upon such receipt, to the Secretary of the Treasury to the credit of the Unemployment Trust Fund established by section 904; and

(5) Expenditure of all money requisitioned by the State agency from the Unemployment Trust Fund, in the payment of unemployment compensation, exclusive of expenses of administration; and

(6) The making of such reports, in such form and containing such information, as the Board may from time to time require, and compliance with such provisions as the Board may from time to time find necessary to assure the correctness and verification of such reports; and

(7) Making available upon request to any agency of the United States charged with the administration of public works or assistance through public employment, the name, address, ordinary occupation, and employment status of each recipient of unemployment compensation, and a statement of such recipient's rights to further compensation under such law.

(b) Whenever the Board, after reasonable notice and opportunity for hearing to the State agency charged with the administration of the State law finds that in the administration of the law there is—

(1) a denial, in a substantial number of cases, of unemployment compensation to individuals entitled thereto under such law; or

(2) a failure to comply substantially with any provision specified in subsection (a); the Board shall notify such State agency that further payments will not be made to the State until the Board is satisfied that there is no longer any such denial or failure to comply. Until it is so satisfied it shall make no further certification to the Secretary of the Treasury with respect to such State.

TITLE IV-GRANTS TO STATES FOR AID TO DEPENDENT CHILDREN APPROPRIATION

SECTION 401. For the purpose of enabling each State to furnish financial assistance, as far as practicable under the conditions in such State, to needy dependent children, there is hereby authorized to be appropriated for the fiscal year ending June 30, 1936, the sum of $24,750,000, and there is hereby authorized to be appropriated for each fiscal year thereafter a sum sufficient to carry out the purposes of this title. The sums made available under this section shall be used for making payments to States which have submitted, and had approved by the Board, State plans for aid to dependent children.

STATE PLANS FOR AID TO DEPENDENT CHILDREN

SEC. 402. (a) A State plan for aid to dependent children must

(1) provide that it shall be in effect in all political subdivisions of the State, and, if administered by them, be mandatory upon them;

(2) provide for financial participation by the State;

(3) either provide for the establishment or designation of a single State agency to administer the plan, or provide for the establishment or designation of a single State agency to supervise the administration of the plan;

(4) provide for granting to any individual, whose claim with respect to aid to a dependent child is denied, an opportunity for a fair hearing before such State agency;

(5) provide such methods of administration (other than those relating to selection, tenure of office, and compensation of personnel) as are found by the Board to be necessary for the efficient operation of the plan; and

(6) provide that the State agency will make such reports, in such form and containing such information, as the Board may from time to time require, and comply with such provisions as the Board may from time to time find necessary to assure the correctness and verification of such reports.

(b) The Board shall approve any plan which fulfills the conditions specified in subsection (a) except that it shall not approve any plan which imposes as a condition of eligibility for aid to dependent children, a residence requirement which denies aid with respect to any child residing in the State

(1) who has resided in the State for one year immediately preceding the application for such aid or (2) who was born within the State within one year immediately preceding the application, if its mother has resided in the State for one year immediately preceding the birth.

PAYMENT TO STATES

SEC. 403. (a) From the sums appropriated therefor, the Secretary of the Treasury shall pay to each State which has an approved plan for aid to dependent children, for each quarter, beginning with the quarter commencing July 1, 1935, an amount, which shall be used exclusively for carrying out the State plan, equal to one-third of the total of the sums expended during such quarter under such plan, not counting so much of such expenditure with respect to any dependent child for any month as exceeds $18, or if there is more than one dependent child in the same home, as exceeds $18 for any month with respect to one such dependent child and $12 for such month with respect to each of the other dependent children. (b) The method of computing and paying such amounts shall be as follows:

(1) The Board shall, prior to the beginning of each quarter, estimate the amount to be paid to the State for such quarter under the provisions of subsection

(a), such estimate to be based on

(A) a report filed by the State containing its estimate of the total sum to be expended in such quarter in accordance with the provisions of such subsection and stating the amount appropriated or made available by the State and its political subdivisions for such expenditures in such quarter, and if such amount is less than two-thirds of the total sum of such estimated expenditures, the source or sources from which the difference is expected to be derived,

(B) records showing the number of dependent children in the State, and (C) such other investigation as the Board may find necessary.

(2) The Board shall then certify to the Secretary of the Treasury the amount so estimated by the Board, reduced or increased, as the case may be, by any sum by which it finds that its estimate for any prior quarter was greater or less than the amount which should have been paid to the State for such quarter, except to the extent that such sum has been applied to make the amount certified for any prior quarter greater or less than the amount estimated by the Board for such prior quarter.

(3) The Secretary of the Treasury shall thereupon, through the Division of Disbursement of the Treasury Department and prior to audit or settlement by the General Accounting Office, pay to the State, at the time or times fixed by the Board, the amount so certified.

OPERATION OF STATE PLANS

SEC. 404. In the case of any State plan for aid to dependent children which has been approved by the Board, if the Board, after reasonable notice and opportunity for hearing to the State agency administering or supervising the administration of such plan, finds

(1) that the plan has been so changed as to impose any residence requirement prohibited by section 402 (b), or that in the administration of the plan any such prohibited requirement is imposed, with the knowledge of such State agency, in a substantial number of cases; or

(2) that in the administration of the plan there is a failure to comply substantially with any provision required by section 402 (a) to be included in the plan; the Board shall notify such State agency that further payments will not be made to the State until the Board is satisfied that such prohibited requirement is no longer so imposed, and that there is no longer any such failure to comply. Until it is so satisfied it shall make no further certification to the Secretary of the Treasury with respect to such State.

ADMINISTRATION

SEC. 405. There is hereby authorized to be appropriated for the fiscal year ending June 30, 1936, the sum of $250,000 for all necessary expenses of the Board in administering the provisions of this title.

DEFINITIONS

SEC. 406. When used in this title (a) The term dependent child means a child under the age of sixteen who has been deprived of parental support or care by reason of the death, continued absence from the home, or physical or mental incapacity of a parent, and who is living with his father, mother, grandfather, grandmother, brother, sister, stepfather, stepmother, stepbrother, stepsister, uncle, or aunt, in a place of residence maintained by one or more of such relatives as his or their own home;

(b) The term aid to dependent children means money payments with respect to a dependent child or dependent children.

TITLE V-GRANTS TO STATES FOR MATERNAL AND CHILD WELFARE PART 1-MATERNAL AND CHILD HEALTH SERVICES

APPROPRIATION

SECTION 501. For the purpose of enabling each State to extend and improve, as far as practicable under the conditions in such State, services for promoting the health of mothers and children, especially in rural areas and in areas suffering from severe economic distress, there is hereby authorized to be appropriated for each fiscal year, beginning with the fiscal year ending June 30, 1936, the sum of $3,800,000. The sums made available under this section shall be used for making payments to States which have submitted, and had approved by the Chief of the Children's Bureau, State plans for such services.

ALLOTMENTS TO STATES

SEC. 502. (a) Out of the sums appropriated pursuant to section 501 for each fiscal year the Secretary of Labor shall allot to each State $20,000, and such part of $1,800,000 as he finds that the number of live births in such State bore to the total number of live births in the United States, in the latest calendar year for which the Bureau of the Census has available statistics.

(b) Out of the sums appropriated pursuant to section 501 for each fiscal year the Secretary of Labor shall allot to the States $980,000 (in addition to the allot-ments made under subsection (a)), according to the financial need of each State for assistance in carrying out its State plan, as determined by him after taking into consideration the number of live births in such State.

(c) The amount of any allotment to a State under subsection (a) for any fiscal year remaining unpaid to such State at the end of such fiscal year shall be available for payment to such State at the end of such fiscal year shall be available for payment to such State under section 504 until the end of the second succeeding fiscal year. No payment to a State under section 504 shall be made out of its allotment for any fiscal year until its allotment for the preceding fiscal year has been exhausted or has ceased to be available.

APPROVAL OF STATE PLANS

SEC. 503. (a) A State plan for maternal and child health services must (1) provide for financial participation by the State;

(2) provide for the administration of the plan by the State health agency or the supervision of the administration of the plan by the State health agency;

(3) provide such methods of administration (other than those relating to selection, tenure of office, and compensation of personnel) as are necessary for the efficient operation of the plan;

(4) provide that the State health agency will make such reports, in such form and containing such information, as the Secretary of Labor may from time to time require, and comply with such provisions as he may from time to time find necessary to assure the correctness and verification of such reports;

(5) provide for the extension and improvement of local maternal and child-health services administered by local child health units;

(6) provide for cooperation with medical, nursing, and welfare groups and organizations; and

(7) provide for the development of demonstration services in needy areas and among groups in special need.

(b) The Chief of the Children's Bureau shall approve any plan which fulfills the conditions specified in subsection (a) and shall thereupon notify the Secretary of Labor and the State health agency of his approval.

PAYMENT TO STATES

SEC. 504. (a) From the sums appropriate therefor and the allotments available under section 502 (a), the Secretary of the Treasury shall pay to each State which has an approved plan for maternal and child health services, for each quarter beginning with the quarter commencing July 1935, an amount, which shall be used exclusively for carrying out the State plan, equal to one-half of the total sum expended during such quarter for carrying out such plan.

(b) The method of computing and paying such amounts shall be as follows:

(1) The Secretary of Labor shall, prior the beginning of each quarter, estimate the amount to be paid to the State for such quarter under the provisions of subsection (a), such estimate to be based on (A) a report filed by the State containing its estimate of the total sum to be expended in such quarter in accordance with the provisions of such subsection and stating the amount appropriated or made available by the State and its political subdivisions for such expenditures in such quarter, and if such amount is less than one-half of the total sum of such estimated expenditures, the source or sources from which the difference is expected to be derived, and

(B) such investigation as he may find necessary.

(2) The Secretary of Labor shall then certify the amount so estimated by him to the Secretary of the Treasury, reduced or increased, as the case may be, by any sum by which the Secretary of Labor finds that his estimate for any prior quarter was greater or less than the amount, which should have been paid to the State for such quarter, except to the extent that such sum has been applied to make the amount certified for any prior quarter greater or less than the amount, estimated by the Secretary of Labor for such prior quarter.

(3) The Secretary of the Treasury shall thereupon, through the Division of Disbursement of the Treasury Department and prior to audit or settlement by the General Accounting Office, pay to the State, at the time or times fixed by the Secretary of Labor, the amount so certified.

(c) The Secretary of Labor shall from time to time certify to the Secretary of the Treasury the amounts to be paid to the States from the allotments available under section 502 (b), and the Secretary of the Trea-

sury shall, through the Division of Disbursement of the Treasury Department and prior to audit or settlement by the General Accounting Office, make payments of such amounts from such allotments at the time or times specified by the Secretary of Labor.

OPERATION OF STATE PLANS

SEC. 505. In the case of any State plan for maternal and child health services which has been approved by the Chief of the Children's Bureau, if the Secretary of Labor, after reasonable notice and opportunity for hearing to the State agency administering or supervising the administration of such plan, finds that in the administration of the plan there is a failure to comply substantially with any provision required by section 503 to be included in the plan, he shall notify such State agency that further payments will not be made to the State until he is satisfied that there is no longer any such failure to comply. Until he is so satisfied he shall make no further certification to the Secretary of the Treasury with respect to such State.

PART 2-SERVICES FOR CRIPPLED CHILDREN

APPROPRIATION

SEC. 511. For the purpose of enabling each State to extend and improve (especially in rural areas and in areas suffering from severe economic distress), as far as practicable under the conditions in such State, services for locating crippled children and for providing medical, surgical, corrective, and other services and care, and facilities for diagnosis, hospitalization, and aftercare, for children who are crippled or who are suffering from conditions which lead to crippling, there is hereby authorized to be appropriated for each fiscal year beginning with the fiscal year ending June 30, 1936, the sum of $2,850,000. The sums made available under this section shall be used for making payments to States which have submitted, and had approved by the Chief of the Children's Bureau, State plans for such services.

ALLOTMENTS TO STATES

SEC. 512. (a) Out of the sums appropriated pursuant to section 511 for each fiscal year the Secretary of Labor shall allot to each State $20,000, and the remainder to the States according to the need of each State as determined by him after taking into consideration the number of crippled children in such State in need of the services referred to section 511 and the cost of furnishing such service to them

(b) The amount of any allotment to a State under subsection (a) for any fiscal year remaining unpaid to such State at the end of such fiscal year shall be available for payment to such State under section 514 until the end of the second succeeding fiscal year. No payment to a State under section 514 shall be made out of its allotment for any fiscal year until its allotment for the preceding fiscal year has been exhausted or has ceased to be available.

APPROVAL OF STATE PLANS

SEC. 513. (a) A State plan for services for crippled children must

(1) provide for financial participation by the State;

(2) provide for the administration of the plan by a State agency or the supervision of the administration of the plan by a State agency;

(3) provide such methods of administration (other than those relating to selection, tenure of office, and compensation of personnel) as are necessary for the efficient operation of the plan;

(4) provide that the State agency will make such reports, in such form and containing such information, as the Secretary of Labor may from time to time require, and comply with such provisions as he may from time to time find necessary to assure the correctness and verification of such reports;

(5) provide for carrying out the purposes specified in section 511; and

(6) provide for cooperation with medical, health, nursing, and welfare groups and organizations and with any agency in such State charged with administering State laws providing for vocational rehabilitation of physically handicapped children.

(b) The Chief of the Children's Bureau shall approve any plan which fulfills the conditions specified in subsection (a) and shall thereupon notify the Secretary of Labor and the State agency of his approval.

PAYMENT TO STATES

SEC. 514. (a) From the sums appropriated therefor and the allotments available under section 512, the Secretary of the Treasury shall pay to each State which has an approved plan for services for crippled children, for each quarter, beginning the quarter commencing July 1, 1935, an amount which shall be used exclusively for carrying out the State plan, equal to one-half of the total sum expended during such quarter for carrying out such plan.

(b) The method of computing and paying such amounts shall be as follows:

(1) The Secretary of Labor shall, prior the beginning of each quarter, estimate the amount to be paid to the State for such quarter under the provisions of subsection (a), such estimate to be based on (A) a report filed by the State containing its estimate of the total sum to be expended in such quarter in accordance with the provisions of such subsection and stating the amount appropriated or made available by the State and its political subdivisions for such expenditures in such quarter and if such amount is less than one-half of the total sum of such estimated expenditures the source or sources from which the difference is expected to be derived, and

(B) such investigation as he may find necessary.

(2) The Secretary of Labor shall then certify the amount so estimated by him to the Secretary of the Treasury, reduced or increased as the case may be, by any sum by which the Secretary of Labor finds that his estimate for any prior quarter was greater or less than the amount which should have been paid to the State for such quarter, except to the extent that such sum has been applied to make the amount certified for any prior quarter greater or less than the amount estimated by the Secretary of Labor for such prior quarter.

(3) The Secretary of the Treasury shall thereupon, through the Division of Disbursement of the Treasury Department and prior to audit or settlement by the General Accounting Office, pay to the State, at the time or times fixed by the Secretary of Labor, the amount so certified.

OPERATION OF STATE PLANS

SEC. 515. In the case of any State plan for services for crippled children which has been approved by the Chief of the Children's Bureau, if the Secretary of Labor, after reasonable notice and opportunity for hearing to the State agency administering or supervising the administration of such plan finds that in the administration of the plan there a failure to comply substantially with any provision required by section 513 to be included in the plan, he shall notify such State agency that further payments will not be made to the State until he is satisfied that there is no longer any such failure to comply. Until he is so satisfied he shall make no further certification to the Secretary of the Treasury with respect to such State.

PART 3-CHILD WELFARE SERVICES

SEC. 521. (a) For the purpose of enabling the United States, through the Children's Bureau, to cooperate with State public welfare agencies establishing, extending, and strengthening, especially in predominantly rural areas, public welfare services (hereinafter in this section referred to as child welfare services) for the protection and care of homeless, dependent, and neglected children, and children in danger of becoming delinquent, there is hereby authorized to be appropriated for each fiscal year, beginning with the year ending June 30, 1936, the sum of $1,500,000. Such amount shall be allotted by the Secretary of Labor for use by cooperating State public welfare agencies on the basis of plans developed jointly by the State agency and the Children s Bureau, to each State, $10,000, and the remainder to each State on the basis of such plans, not to exceed such part of the remainder as the rural population of such State bears to the total rural population of the United States. The amount so allotted shall be expended for payment of part of the cost of district, county or other local child welfare services in areas predominantly rural, and for developing State services for the encouragement and assistance of adequate methods of community child welfare organization in areas predominantly rural and other areas of special need. The amount of any allotment to a State under this section for any fiscal year remaining unpaid to such State at the end of such fiscal year shall be available for payment to such State under this section until the end of the second succeeding fiscal year. No payment to a State under this section shall be made out of its allotment for any fiscal year until its allotment for the preceding fiscal year has been exhausted or has ceased to be available.

(b) From the sums appropriated therefor and the allotments available under subsection (a) the Secretary of Labor shall from time to time certify to the Secretary of the Treasury the amounts to be paid to the

States, and the Secretary of the Treasury shall, through the Division of Disbursement of the Treasury Department and prior to audit or settlement by the General Accounting Office, make payments of such amounts from such allotments at the time or times specified by the Secretary of Labor.

PART 4-VOCATIONAL REHABILITATION

SEC. 531. (a) In order to enable the United States to cooperate with the States and Hawaii in extending and strengthening their programs of vocational rehabilitation of the physically disabled, and to continue to carry out the provisions and purposes of the Act entitled An Act to provide for the promotion of vocational rehabilitation of persons disabled in industry or otherwise and their return to civil employment, approved June 2, 1920, as amended (U.S.C., title 29, ch. 4; U.S.C., Supp. VII title 29, secs. 31, 32, 34, 35, 37, 39, and 40), there is hereby authorized to be appropriated for the fiscal years ending June 30, 1936, and June 30, 1937, the sum of $841,000 for each such fiscal year in addition to the amount of the existing authorization, and for each fiscal year thereafter the sum of $1,938,000. Of the sums appropriated pursuant to such authorization for each fiscal year, $5,000 shall be apportioned to the Territory of Hawaii and the remainder shall be apportioned among the several States in the manner provided in such Act of June 2, 1920, as amended.

(b) For the administration of such Act of June 2, 1920, as amended, by the Federal agency authorized to administer it, there is hereby authorized to be appropriated for the fiscal years ending June 30, 1936, and June 30, 1937, the sum of $22,000 for each such fiscal year in addition to the amount of the existing authorization, and for each fiscal year thereafter the sum of $102,000.

PART 5-ADMINISTRATION

SEC. 541. (a) There is hereby authorized to be appropriated for the fiscal year ending June 30, 1936, the sum of $425,000, for all necessary expenses of the Children's Bureau in administering the provisions of this title, except section 531.

(b) The Children's Bureau shall make such studies and investigations as will promote the efficient administration of this title, except section 531.

(c) The Secretary of Labor shall include in his annual report to Congress a full account of the administration of this title, except section 531.

TITLE VI-PUBLIC HEALTH WORK APPROPRIATION

SECTION 601. For the purpose of assisting States, counties, health districts, and other political subdivisions of the States in establishing and maintaining adequate public health services, including the training of personnel for State and local health work, there is hereby authorized to be appropriated for each fiscal year, beginning with the fiscal year ending June 30, 1936, the sum of $8,000,000 to be used as hereinafter provided.

STATE AND LOCAL PUBLIC HEALTH SERVICES

SEC. 602. (a) The Surgeon General of the Public Health Service, with the approval of the Secretary of the Treasury, shall, at the beginning of each fiscal year, allot to the States the total of (1) the amount appropriated for such year pursuant to section 601; and (2) the amounts of the allotments under this section for the preceding fiscal year remaining unpaid to the States at the end of such fiscal year. The amounts of such allotments shall be determined on the basis of (1) the population; (2) the special health problems; and (3) the financial needs; of the respective States. Upon making such allotments the Surgeon General of the Public Health Service shall certify the amounts thereof to the Secretary of the Treasury. (b) The amount of an allotment to any State under subsection (a) for any fiscal year, remaining unpaid at the end of such fiscal year, shall be available for allotment to States under subsection (a) for the succeeding fiscal year, in addition to the amount appropriated for such year.

(c) Prior to the beginning of each quarter of the fiscal year, the Surgeon General of the Public Health Service shall, with the approval of the Secretary of the Treasury, determine in accordance with rules and regulations previously prescribed by such Surgeon General after consultation with a conference of the State and Territorial health authorities, the amount to be paid to each State for such quarter from the allotment to such State, and shall certify the amount so determined to the Secretary of the Treasury. Upon receipt of such certification, the Secretary of the Treasury shall, through the Division of Disbursement of the Treasury Department and prior to audit or settlement by the General Accounting Office, pay in accordance with such certification.

(d) The moneys so paid to any State shall be expended solely in carrying out the purposes specified in section 601, and in accordance with plans presented by the health authority of such State and approved by the Surgeon General of the Public Health Service.

INVESTIGATIONS

SEC. 603. (a) There is hereby authorized to be appropriated for each fiscal year, beginning with the fiscal year ending June 30, 1936, the sum of $2,000,000 for expenditure by the Public Health Service for investigation of disease and problems of sanitation (including the printing and binding of the findings of such investigations), and for the pay and allowances and traveling expenses of personnel of the Public Health Service, including commissioned officers, engaged in such investigations or detailed to cooperate with the health authorities of any State in carrying out the purposes specified in section 601: Provided, That no personnel of the Public Health Service shall be detailed to cooperate with the health authorities of any State except at the request of the proper authorities of such State.

(b) The personnel of the Public Health Service paid from any appropriation not made pursuant to subsection (a) may be detailed to assist in carrying out the purposes of this title. The appropriation from which they are paid shall be reimbursed from the appropriation made pursuant to subsection (a) to the extent of their salaries and allowances for services performed while so detailed.

(c) The Secretary of the Treasury shall include in his annual report to Congress a full account of the administration of this title.

TITLE VII-SOCIAL SECURITY BOARD ESTABLISHMENT

SECTION 701. There is hereby established a Social Security Board (in this Act referred to as the Board) to be composed of three members to be appointed by the President, by and with the advice and consent of the Senate. During his term of membership on the Board, no member shall engage in any other business, vocation, or employment. Not more than two of the members of the Board shall be members of the same political party. Each member shall receive a salary at the rate of $10,000 a year and shall hold office for a term of six years, except that

(1) any member appointed to fill a vacancy occurring prior to the expiration of the term for which his predecessor was appointed, shall be appointed for the remainder of such term; and

(2) the terms of office of the members first taking office after the date of the enactment of this Act shall expire, as designated by the President at the time of appointment, one at the end of two years, one at the end of four years, and one at the end of six years, after the date of the enactment of this Act. The President shall designate one of the members as the chairman of the Board.

DUTIES OF THE SOCIAL SECURITY BOARD

SEC. 702. The Board shall perform the duties imposed upon it by this Act and shall also have the duty of studying and making recommendations as to the most effective methods of providing economic security through social insurance, and as to legislation and matters of administrative policy concerning old-age pensions, unemployment compensation, accident compensation, and related subjects.

EXPENSES OF THE BOARD

SEC. 703. The Board is authorized to appoint and fix the compensation of such officers and employees, and to make such expenditures, as may be necessary for carrying out its functions under this Act. Appointments of attorneys and experts may be made without regard to the civil service laws.

REPORTS

SEC. 704. The Board shall make a full report to Congress, at the beginning of each regular session, of the administration of the functions with which it is charged.

TITLE VIII-TAXES WITH RESPECT TO EMPLOYMENT

INCOME TAX ON EMPLOYEES

SECTION 801. In addition to other taxes, there shall be levied, collected, and paid upon the income of every individual a tax equal to the following percentages of the wages (as defined in section 811) received by him after December 31, 1936, with respect to employment (as defined in section 811) after such date:

(1) With respect to employment during the calendar years 1937, 1938, and 1939, the rate shall be 1 per centum.

(2) With respect to employment during the calendar years 1940, 1941, and 1942, the rate shall 1 per centum.

(3) With respect to employment during the calendar years 1943, 1944, and 1945, the rate shall be 2 per centum.

(4) With respect to employment during the calendar years 1946, 1947, and 1948, the rate shall be 2 per centum.

(5) With respect to employment after December 31, 1948, the rate shall be 3 per centum.

DEDUCTION OF TAX FROM WAGES

SEC. 802. (a) The tax imposed by section 801 shall be collected by the employer of the taxpayer by deducting the amount of the tax from the wages as and when paid. Every employer required so to deduct the tax is hereby made liable for the payment of such tax, and is hereby indemnified against the claims and demands of any person for the amount of any such payment made by such employer.

(b) If more or less than the correct amount of tax imposed by section 801 is paid with respect to any wage payment, then, under regulations made under this title, proper adjustments, with respect both to the tax and the amount to be deducted, shall be made, without interest, in connection with subsequent wage payments to the same individual by the same employer.

DEDUCTIBILITY FROM INCOME TAX

SEC. 803. For the purposes of the income tax imposed by Title I of the Revenue Act of 1934 or by any Act of Congress in substitution therefor, the tax imposed by section 801 shall not be allowed as a deduction to the taxpayer in computing his net income for the year in which such tax is deducted from his wages.

EXCISE TAX ON EMPLOYERS

SEC. 804. In addition to other taxes, every employer shall pay an excise tax, with respect to having individuals in his employ, equal to the following percentages of the wages (as defined in section 811) paid by him after December 31, 1936, with respect to employment (as defined in section 811) after such date:

(1) With respect to employment during the calendar years 1937, 1938, and 1939, the rate shall be 1 per centum.

(2) With respect to employment during the calendar years 1940, 1941, and 1942, the rate shall be 1 per centum.

(3) With respect to employment during the calendar years 1943, 1944, and 1945, the rate shall be 2 per centum.

(4) With respect to employment during the calendar years 1946, 1947, and 1948, the rate shall be 2 per centum.

(5) With respect to employment after December 31, 1948, the rate shall be 3 per centum.

ADJUSTMENT OF EMPLOYERS TAX

SEC. 805. If more or less than the correct amount of tax imposed by section 804 is paid with respect to any wage payment, then, under regulations made under this title, proper adjustments with respect the tax shall be made, without interest, in connection with subsequent wage payments to the same individual by the same employer.

REFUNDS AND DEFICIENCIES

SEC. 806. If more or less than the correct amount of tax imposed by section 801 or 804 is paid or deducted with respect to any wage payment and the overpayment or underpayment of tax cannot be adjusted under section 802 (b) or 805 the amount of the overpayment shall be refunded and the amount of the underpayment shall be collected in such manner and at such times (subject to the statutes of limitations properly applicable thereto) as may be prescribed by regulations made under this title.

COLLECTION AND PAYMENT OF TAXES

SEC. 807. (a) The taxes imposed by this title shall be collected by the Bureau of Internal Revenue under the direction of the Secretary of the Treasury and shall be paid into the Treasury of the United States as internal revenue collections. If the tax is not paid when due, there shall be added as part of the tax interest (except in the case of adjustments made in accordance with the provisions of sections 802 (b) and 805) at the rate of one-half of 1 per centum per month from the date the tax became due until paid. (b) Such taxes shall be collected and paid in such manner, at such times, and under such conditions, not inconsistent with this title (either by making and filing returns, or by stamps, coupons, tickets, books, or other reasonable devices or methods necessary or helpful in securing a complete and proper collection and payment of the tax or in securing proper identification of the taxpayer), as may be prescribed by the Commissioner of Internal Revenue, with the approval of the Secretary of the Treasury.

(c) All provisions of law, including penalties, applicable with respect to any tax imposed by section 600 or section 800 of the Revenue Act of 1926 and the provisions of section 607 of the Revenue Act of 1934, shall, insofar as applicable and not inconsistent with the provisions of this title, be applicable with respect to the taxes imposed by this title.

(d) In the payment of any tax under this title a fractional part of a cent shall be disregarded unless it amounts to one-half cent or more, in which case it shall be increased to 1 cent.

RULES AND REGULATIONS

SEC. 808. The Commissioner of Internal Revenue, with the approval of the Secretary of the Treasury, shall make and publish rules and regulations for the enforcement of this title.

SALE OF STAMPS BY POSTMASTERS

SEC. 809. The Commissioner of Internal Revenue shall furnish to the Postmaster General without prepayment a suitable quantity of stamps, coupons, tickets, books, or other devices prescribed by the Commissioner under section 807 for the collection or payment of any tax imposed by this title, to be distributed to, and kept on sale by, all post offices of the first and second classes, and such post offices of the third and fourth classes as

(1) are located in county seats, or

(2) are certified by the Secretary of the Treasury to the Postmaster General as necessary to the proper administration of this title. The Postmaster General may require each such postmaster to furnish bond in such increased amount as he may from time to time determine, and each such postmaster shall deposit the receipts from the sale of such stamps, coupons, tickets, books, or other devices, to the credit of, and render accounts to, the Postmaster General at such times and in such form as the Postmaster General may by regulations prescribe. The Postmaster General shall at least once a month transfer to the Treasury, as internal revenue collections all receipts so deposited together with a statement of the additional expenditures in the District of Columbia and elsewhere incurred by the Post Office Department in performing the duties imposed upon said Department by this Act, and the Secretary of the Treasury is hereby authorized and directed to advance from time to time to the credit of the Post Office Department from appropriations made for the collection of the taxes imposed by this title, such sums as may be required for such additional expenditures incurred by the Post Office Department.

PENALTIES

SEC. 810. (a) Whoever buys, sells, offers for sale, uses, transfers, takes or gives in exchange, or pledges or gives in pledge, except as authorized in this title or in regulations made pursuant thereto, any stamp, coupon, ticket, book, or other device, prescribed by the Commissioner of Internal Revenue under section 807 for the collection or payment of any tax imposed by this title, shall be fined not more than $1,000 or imprisoned for not more than six months, or both.

(b) Whoever, with intent to defraud, alters, forges, makes, or counterfeits any stamp, coupon, ticket, book, or other device prescribed by the Commissioner of Internal Revenue under section 807 for the collection or payment of any tax imposed by this title, or uses, sells, lends, or has in his possession any such altered, forged, or counterfeited stamp, coupon, ticket, book, or other device, or makes, uses, sells, or has in his possession any material in imitation of the material used in the manufacture of such stamp, coupon, ticket, book, or other device, shall be fined not more than $5,000 or imprisoned not more than five years, or both.

DEFINITIONS

SEC. 811. When used in this title (a) The term wages means all remuneration for employment, including the cash value of all remuneration paid in any medium other than cash; except that such term shall not include that part of the remuneration which, after remuneration equal to $3,000 has been paid to an individual by an employer with respect to employment during any calendar year, is paid to such individual by such employer with respect to employment during such calendar year.

(b) The term employment means any service, of whatever nature, performed within the United States by an employee for his employer, except

(1) Agricultural labor;

(2) Domestic service in a private home;

(3) Casual labor not in the course of the employer's trade or business;

(4) Service performed by an individual who has attained the age of sixty-five;

(5) Service performed as an officer or member of the crew of a vessel documented under the laws of the United States or of any foreign country;

(6) Service performed in the employ of the United States Government or of an instrumentality of the United States;

(7) Service performed in the employ of a State, a political subdivision thereof, or an instrumentality of one or more States or political subdivisions;

(8) Service performed in the employ of a corporation, community chest, fund, or foundation, organized and operated exclusively for religious, charitable, scientific, literary, or educational purposes, or

for the prevention of cruelty to children or animals, no part of the net earnings of which inures to the benefit of any private shareholder or individual.

TITLE IX-TAX ON EMPLOYERS OF EIGHT OR MORE IMPOSITION OF TAX

SECTION 901. On and after January 1, 1936, every employer (as defined in section 907) shall pay for each calendar year an excise tax, with respect to having individuals in his employ, equal to the following percentages of the total wages (as defined in section 907) payable by him (regardless of the time of payment) with respect to employment (as defined in section 907) during such calendar year: (1) With respect to employment during the calendar year 1936 the rate shall be 1 per centum; (2) With respect to employment during the calendar year 1937 the rate shall be 2 per centum; (3) With respect to employment after December 31, 1937, the rate shall be 3 per centum.

CREDIT AGAINST TAX

SEC. 902. The taxpayer may credit against the tax imposed by section 901 the amount of contributions, with respect to employment during the taxable year, paid by him (before the date of filing of his return for the taxable year) into an unemployment fund under a State law. The total credit allowed to a taxpayer under this section for all contributions paid into unemployment funds with respect to employment during such taxable year shall not exceed 90 per centum of the tax against which it is credited, and credit shall be allowed only for contributions made under the laws of States certified for the taxable year as provided in section 903.

CERTIFICATION OF STATE LAWS

SEC. 903 (a) The Social Security Board shall approve any State law submitted to it, within thirty days of such submission, which it finds provides that-
(1) All compensation is to be paid through public employment offices in the State or such other agencies as the Board may approve;

(2) No compensation shall be payable with respect to any day of unemployment occurring within two years after the first day of the first period with respect to which contributions are required;

(3) All money received in the unemployment fund

shall immediately upon such receipt be paid over to the Secretary of the Treasury to the credit of the Unemployment Trust Fund established by section 904;

(4) All money withdrawn from the Unemployment Trust Fund by the State agency shall be used solely in the payment of compensation, exclusive of expenses of administration;

(5) Compensation shall not be denied in such State to any otherwise eligible individual for refusing to accept new work under any of the following conditions:

(A) If the position offered is vacant due directly to a strike, lockout, or other labor dispute;

(B) if the wages, hours, or other conditions of the work offered are substantially less favorable to the individual than those prevailing for similar work in the locality;

(C) if as a condition of being employed the individual would be required to join a company union or to resign from or refrain from joining any bona fide labor organization;

(6) All the rights, privileges, or immunities conferred by such law or by acts done pursuant thereto shall exist subject to the power of the legislature to amend or repeal such law at any time. The Board shall, upon approving such law, notify the Governor of the State of its approval.

(b) On December 31 in each taxable year the Board shall certify to the Secretary of the Treasury each State whose law it has previously approved, except that it shall not certify any State which, after reasonable notice and opportunity for hearing to the State agency, the Board finds has changed its law so that it no longer contains the provisions specified in subsection (a) or has with respect to such taxable year failed to comply substantially with any such provision.

(c) If, at any time during the taxable year, the Board has reason to believe that a State whose law it has previously approved, may not be certified under subsection (b), it shall promptly so notify the Governor of such State.

UNEMPLOYMENT TRUST FUND

SEC. 904. (a) There is hereby established in the Treasury of the United States a trust fund to be known as the Unemployment Trust Fund, hereinafter in this title called the Fund. The Secretary of the

Treasury is authorized and directed to receive and hold in the Fund all moneys deposited therein by a State agency from a State unemployment fund. Such deposit may be made directly with the Secretary of the Treasury or with any Federal reserve bank or member bank of the Federal Reserve System designated by him for such purpose.

(b) It shall be the duty of the Secretary of the Treasury to invest such portion of the Fund as is not, in his judgment, required to meet current withdrawals. Such investment may be made only in interest-bearing obligations of the United States or in obligations guaranteed as to both principal and interest by the United States. For such purpose such obligations may be acquired

(1) on original issue at par, or

(2) by purchase of outstanding obligations at the market price. The purposes for which obligations of the United States may be issued under the Second Liberty Bond Act, as amended, are hereby extended to authorize the issuance at par of special obligations exclusively to the Fund. Such special obligations shall bear interest at a rate equal to the average rate of interest, computed as of the end of the calendar month next preceding the date of such issue, borne by all interest-bearing obligations of the United States then forming part of the public debt; except that where such average rate is not a multiple of one eighth of 1 per centum, the rate of interest of such special obligations shall be the multiple of one-eighth of 1 per centum next lower than such average rate. Obligations other than such special obligations may be acquired for the Fund only on such terms as to provide an investment yield not less than the yield which would be required in the case of special obligations if issued to the Fund upon the date of such acquisition.

(c) Any obligations acquired by the Fund (except special obligations issued exclusively to the Fund) may be sold at the market price, and such special obligations may be redeemed at par plus accrued interest.

(d) The interest on, and the proceeds from the sale or redemption of, any obligations held in the Fund shall be credited to and form a part of the Fund.

(e) The Fund shall be invested as a single fund, but the Secretary of the Treasury shall maintain a separate book account for each State agency and shall credit quarterly on March 31, June 30, September 30, and December 31, of each year, to each account, on the basis of the average daily balance of such account, a proportionate part of the earnings of the Fund for the quarter ending on such date.

(f) The Secretary of the Treasury is authorized and directed to pay out of the Fund to any State agency such amount as it may duly requisition, not exceeding the amount standing to the account of such State agency at the time of such payment.

ADMINISTRATION, REFUNDS, AND PENALTIES

SEC. 905. (a) The tax imposed by this title shall be collected by the Bureau of Internal Revenue under the direction of the Secretary of the Treasury and shall be paid into the Treasury of the United States as internal revenue collections. If the tax is not paid when due, there shall be added as part of the tax interest at the rate of one-half of 1 per centum per month from the date the tax became due until paid. (b) Not later than January 31, next following the close of the taxable year, each employer shall make a return of the tax under this title for such taxable year. Each such return shall be made under oath, shall be filed with the collector of internal revenue for the district in which is located the principal place of business of the employer, or, if he has no principal place of business in the United States, then with the collector at Baltimore, Maryland, and shall contain such information and be made in such manner as the Commissioner of Internal Revenue, with the approval of the Secretary of the Treasury, may by regulations prescribe. All provisions of law (including penalties) applicable in respect of the taxes imposed by section 600 of the Revenue Act of 1926, shall, insofar as not inconsistent with this title, be applicable in respect of the tax imposed by this title. The Commissioner may extend the time for filing the return of the tax imposed by this title, under such rules and regulations as he may prescribe with the approval of the Secretary of the Treasury, but no such extension shall be for more than sixty days.

(c) Returns filed under this title shall be open to inspection in the same manner, to the same extent, and subject to the same provisions of law, including penalties, as returns made under Title II of the Revenue Act of 1926.

(d) The taxpayer may elect to pay the tax in four equal installments instead of in a single payment, in which case the first installment shall be paid not later than the last day prescribed for the filing of returns, the second installment shall be paid on or before the last day of the third month, the third installment on or before the last day of the sixth month, and the fourth installment on or before the last day of the ninth month, after such last day. If the tax or any installment thereof is not paid on or before the last day of the period fixed for its payment, the whole amount of the tax unpaid shall be paid upon notice and demand from the collector.

(e) At the request of the taxpayer the time for payment of the tax or any installment thereof may be extended under regulations prescribed by the Commissioner with the approval of the Secretary of the Treasury, for a period not to exceed six months from the last day of the period prescribed for the payment of the tax or any installment thereof. The amount of the tax in respect of which any extension is granted shall be paid (with interest at the rate of one-half of 1 per centum per month) on or before the date of the expiration of the period of the extension.

(f) In the payment of any tax under this title a fractional part of a cent shall be disregarded unless it amounts to one-half cent or more, in which case it shall be increased to 1 cent.

INTERSTATE COMMERCE

SEC. 906. No person required under a State law to make payments to an unemployment fund shall be relieved from compliance therewith on the ground that he is engaged in interstate commerce, or that the State law does not distinguish between employees engaged in interstate commerce and those engaged in intrastate commerce.

DEFINITIONS

SEC. 907. When used in this title — (a) The term employer does not include any person unless on each of some twenty days during the taxable year, each day being in a different calendar week, the total number of individuals who were in his employ for some portion of the day (whether or not at the same moment of time) was eight or more.

(b) The term wages means all remuneration for employment, including the cash value of all remuneration paid in any medium other than cash.

(c) The term employment means any service, of whatever nature, performed within the United States by an employee for his employer, except

(1) Agricultural labor;

(2) Domestic service in a private home;

(3) Service performed as an officer or member of a crew of a vessel on the navigable waters of the United States;

(4) Service performed by an individual in the employ of his son, daughter, or spouse, and service performed by a child under the age of twenty-one in the employ of his father or mother;

(5) Service performed in the employ of the United States Government or of an instrumentality of the United States;

(6) Service performed in the employ of a State, a political subdivision thereof, or an instrumentality of one or more States or political subdivisions;

(7) Service performed in the employ of a corporation, community chest, fund, or foundation, organized and operated exclusively for religious, charitable, scientific, literary, or educational purposes, or for the prevention of cruelty to children or animals, no part of the net earnings of which inures to the benefit of any private shareholder or individual.

(d) The term State agency means any State officer, board, or other authority, designated under a State law to administer the unemployment fund in such State.

(e) The term unemployment fund means a special fund, established under a State law and administered by a State agency, for the payment of compensation.

(f) The term contributions means payments required by a State law to be made by an employer into an unemployment fund, to the extent that such payments are made by him without any part thereof being deducted or deductible from the wages of individuals in his employ.

(g) The term compensation means cash benefits payable to individuals with respect to their unemployment.

RULES AND REGULATIONS

SEC. 908. The Commissioner of Internal Revenue, with the approval of the Secretary of the Treasury, shall make and publish rules and regulations for the enforcement of this title, except sections 903, 904, and 910.

ALLOWANCE OF ADDITIONAL CREDIT

SEC. 909. (a) In addition to the credit allowed under section 902, a taxpayer may, subject to the conditions imposed by section 910, credit against the tax imposed by section 901 for any taxable year after the taxable year 1937, an amount, with respect to each State law, equal to the amount, if any, by which the contributions, with respect to employment in such taxable year, actually paid by the taxpayer under such law before the date of filing his return for such taxable year, is exceeded by whichever of the following is the lesser (1) The amount of contributions which he would have been required to pay under such law for such taxable year if he had been subject to the highest rate applicable from time to time throughout such year to any employer under such law; or (2) Two and seven-tenths per centum of the wages payable by him with respect to employment with respect to which contributions for such year were required under such law.

(b) If the amount of the contributions actually so paid by the taxpayer is less than the amount which he should have paid under the State law, the additional credit under subsection (a) shall be reduced proportionately.

(c) The total credits allowed to a taxpayer under this title shall not exceed 90 per centum of the tax against which such credits are taken.

CONDITIONS OF ADDITIONAL CREDIT ALLOWANCE

SEC. 910. (a) A taxpayer shall be allowed the additional credit under section 909, with respect to his contribution rate under a State law being lower, for any taxable year, than that of another employer subject to such law, only if the Board finds that under such law—

(1) Such lower rate, with respect to contributions to a pooled fund, is permitted on the basis of not less than three years of compensation experience;

(2) Such lower rate, with respect to contributions to a guaranteed employment account, is permitted only when his guaranty of employment was fulfilled in the preceding calendar year, and such guaranteed employment account amounts to not less than 7 per centum of the total wages payable by him, in accordance with such guaranty, with respect to employ-

ment in such State in the preceding calendar year; (3) Such lower rate, with respect to contributions to a separate reserve account, is permitted only when (A) compensation has been payable from such account throughout the preceding calendar year, and (B) such account amounts to not less than five times the largest amount of compensation paid from such account within any one of the three preceding calendar years, and

(C) such account amounts to not less than 7 per centum of the total wages payable by him (plus the total wages payable by any other employers who may be contributing to such account) with respect to employment in such State in the preceding calendar year.

(b) Such additional credit shall be reduced, if any contributions under such law are made by such taxpayer at a lower rate under conditions not fulfilling the requirements of subsection (a), by the amount bearing the same ratio to such additional credit as the amount of contributions made at such lower rate bears to the total of his contributions paid for such year under such law.

(c) As used in this section

(1) The term reserve account means a separate account in an unemployment fund, with respect to an employer or group of employers, from which compensation is payable only with respect to the unemployment of individuals who were in the employ of such employer, or of one of the employers comprising the group.

(2) The term pooled fund means an unemployment fund or any part thereof in which all contributions are mingled and undivided, and from which compensation is payable to all eligible individuals, except that to individuals last employed by employers with respect to whom reserve accounts are maintained by the State agency, it is payable only when such accounts are exhausted.

(3) The term guaranteed employment account means a separate account, in an unemployment fund, of contributions paid by an employer (or group of employers) who

(A) guarantees in advance thirty hours of wages for each of forty calendar weeks (or more, with one weekly hour deducted for each added week guaranteed) in twelve months, to all the individuals in his employ in one or more distinct establishments, except that any such individual's guaranty may commence after a probationary period (included within twelve or less consecutive calendar weeks), and

(B) gives security or assurance, satisfactory to the State agency, for the fulfillment of such guaranties, from which account compensation shall be payable with respect to the unemployment of any such individual whose guaranty is not fulfilled or renewed and who is otherwise eligible for compensation under the State law.

(4) The term year of compensation experience, as applied to an employer, means any calendar year throughout which compensation was payable with respect to any individual in his employ who became unemployed and was eligible for compensation.

TITLE X-GRANTS TO STATES FOR AID TO THE BLIND APPROPRIATION

SECTION 1001. For the purpose of enabling each State to furnish financial assistance, as far as practicable under the conditions in such State, to needy individuals who are blind, there is hereby authorized to be appropriated for the fiscal year ending June 30, 1936, the sum of $3,000,000, and there is hereby authorized to be appropriated for each fiscal year thereafter a sum sufficient to carry out the purposes of this title. The sums made available under this section shall be used for making payments to States which have submitted, and had approved by the Social Security Board, State plans for aid to the blind.

STATE PLANS FOR AID TO THE BLIND

SEC. 1002. (a) A State plan for aid to the blind must

(1) provide that it shall be in effect in all political subdivisions of the State, and, if administered by them, be mandatory upon them;

(2) provide for financial participation by the State;

(3) either provide for the establishment or designation of a single State agency to administer the plan, or provide for the establishment or designation of a single State agency to supervise the administration of the plan;

(4) provide for granting to any individual, whose claim for aid is denied, an opportunity for a fair hearing before such State agency;

(5) provide such methods of administration (other than those relating to selection, tenure of office, and compensation of personnel) as are found by the Board to be necessary for the efficient operation of the plan;

(6) provide that the State agency will make such reports, in such form and containing such information, as the Board may from time to time require, and comply with such provisions as the Board may from time to time find necessary to assure the correctness and verification of such reports; and

(7) provide that no aid will be furnished any individual under the plan with respect to any period with respect to which he is receiving old-age assistance under the State plan approved under section 2 of this Act.

(b) The Board shall approve any plan which fulfills the conditions specified in subsection (a), except that it shall not approve any plan which imposes, as a condition of eligibility for aid to the blind under the plan

(1) Any residence requirement which excludes any resident of the State who has resided therein five years during the nine years immediately preceding the application for aid and has resided therein continuously for one year immediately preceding the application or

(2) Any citizenship requirement which excludes any citizen of the United States.

PAYMENT TO STATES

SEC. 1003. (a) From the sums appropriated therefor, the Secretary of the Treasury shall pay to each State which has an approved plan for aid to the blind, for each quarter, beginning with the quarter commencing July 1, 1935,

(1) an amount which shall be used exclusively as aid to the blind equal to one-half of the total of the sums expended during such quarter as aid to the blind under the State plan with respect to each individual who is blind and is not an inmate of a public institution not counting so much of such expenditure with respect to any individual for any month as exceeds $30, and

(2) 5 per centum of such amount, which shall be used for paying the costs of administering the State plan or for aid to the blind, or both, and for no other purpose.

(b) The method of computing and paying such amounts shall be as follows:

(1) The Board shall, prior to the beginning of each quarter, estimate the amount to be paid to the State for such quarter under provisions of clause (1) of subsection (a), such estimate to be based on

(A) a report filed by the State containing its estimate of the total sum to be expended in such quarter in accordance with the provisions of such clause, and stating the amount appropriated or made available by the State and its political subdivisions for such expenditures in such quarter, and if such amount is less than one-half of the total sum of such estimated expenditures, the source or sources from which the difference is expected to be derived,

(B) records showing the number of blind individuals in the State, and

(C) such other investigation as the Board may find necessary.

(2) The Board shall then certify to the Secretary of the Treasury the amount so estimated by the Board, reduced or increased, as the case may be, by any sum by which it finds that its estimate for any prior quarter was greater or less than the amount which should have been paid to the State under clause (1) of subsection (a) for such quarter, except to the extent that such sum has been applied to make the amount certified for any prior quarter greater or less than the amount estimated by the Board for such prior quarter.

(3) The Secretary of the Treasury shall thereupon, through the Division of Disbursement of the Treasury Department and prior to audit or settlement by the General Accounting Office, pay to the State, at the time or times fixed by the Board, the amount so certified, increased by 5 per centum.

OPERATION OF STATE PLANS

SEC. 1004. In the case of any State plan for aid to the blind which has been approved by the Board, if the Board, after reasonable notice and opportunity for hearing to the State agency administering or supervising the administration of such a plan, finds—
(1) that the plan has been so changed as to impose any residence or citizenship requirement prohibited by section 1002 (b), or that in the administration of the plan any such prohibited requirement is imposed, with the knowledge of such State agency, in a substantial number of cases; or

(2) that in the administration of the plan there is a failure to comply substantially with any provision required by section 1002 (a) be included in the plan; the Board shall notify such State agency that further payments will not be made to the State until the Board is satisfied that such prohibited requirement is no longer so imposed, and that there is no longer any such failure to comply. Until it is satisfied it shall make no further certification to the Secretary of the Treasury with respect to such State.

ADMINISTRATION

SEC. 1005. There is hereby authorized to be appropriated for the fiscal year ending June 30, 1936 the sum of $30,000, for all necessary expenses of the Board in administering the provisions of this title.

DEFINITION

SEC. 1006. When used in this title the term aid to the blind means money payments to blind individuals.

TITLE XI- GENERAL PROVISIONS

DEFINITIONS

SECTION 1101. (a) When used in this Act

(1) The term State (except when used in section 531) includes Alaska, Hawaii, and the District of Columbia.

(2) The term United States when used in a geographical sense means the States, Alaska, Hawaii, and the District of Columbia.

(3) The term person means an individual, a trust or estate, a partnership, or a corporation.

(4) The term corporation includes associations, joint-stock companies, and insurance companies.

(5) The term shareholder includes a member in an association, joint-stock company, or insurance company.

(6) The term employee includes an officer of a corporation.

(b) The terms includes and including when used in a definition contained in this Act shall not be deemed to exclude other things otherwise within the meaning of the term defined.

(c) Whenever under this Act or any Act of Congress, or under the law of any State, an employer is required or permitted to deduct any amount from the remuneration of an employee and to pay the amount deducted to the United States, a State, or any political subdivision thereof, then for the purposes of this Act the amount so deducted shall be considered to have been paid to the employee at the time of such deduction.

(d) Nothing in this Act shall be construed as authorizing any Federal official, agent, or representative, in carrying out any of the provisions of this Act, to take charge of any child over the objection of either of the parents of such child, or of the person standing in loco parentis to such child.

RULES AND REGULATIONS

SEC. 1102. The Secretary of the Treasury, the Secretary of Labor, and the Social Security Board respectively, shall make and publish such rules and regulations, not inconsistent with this Act, as may be necessary to the efficient administration of the functions with which each is charged under this Act.

SEPARABILITY

SEC. 1103. If any provision of this Act, or the application thereof to any person or circumstance is held invalid, the remainder of the Act, and the application of such provision to other persons or circumstances shall not be affected thereby.

RESERVATION OF POWER

SEC. 1104. The right to alter, amend, or repeal any provision of this Act is hereby reserved to the Congress.

SHORT TITLE

SEC. 1105. This Act may be cited as the Social Security Act.

Approved, August 14, 1935.

President Franklin Roosevelt's Radio Address unveiling the second half of the New Deal

Campaign Address at Madison Square Garden, New York City. "We Have Only Just Begun to Fight." October 31, 1936

(American desire for peace and security at home and abroad—What we have done to fulfill that desire—We shall continue in our fight to attain our objectives.)

Senator Wagner, Governor Lehman, ladies and gentlemen:

ON THE eve of a national election, it is well for us to stop for a moment and analyze calmly and without prejudice the effect on our Nation of a victory by either of the major political parties.

The problem of the electorate is far deeper, far more than the continuance in the Presidency of any individual. For the greater issue goes beyond units of humanity—it goes to humanity itself.

In 1932 the issue was the restoration of American democracy; and the American people were in a mood to win. They did win. In 1936 the issue is the preservation of their victory. Again they are in a mood to win. Again they will win.

More than four years ago in accepting the Democratic nomination in Chicago, I said: "Give me your help not to win votes alone, but to win in this crusade to restore America to its own people."

The banners of that crusade still fly in the van of a Nation that is on the march.

It is needless to repeat the details of the program which this Administration has been hammering out on the anvils of experience. No amount of misrepresentation or statistical contortion can conceal or blur or smear that record. Neither the attacks of unscrupulous enemies nor the exaggerations of overzealous friends will serve to mislead the American people.

What was our hope in 1932? Above all other things the American people wanted peace. They wanted peace of mind instead of gnawing fear.

First, they sought escape from the personal terror which had stalked them for three years. They wanted the peace that comes from security in their homes: safety for their savings, permanence in their jobs, a fair profit from their enterprise.

Next, they wanted peace in the community, the peace that springs from the ability to meet the needs of community life: schools, playgrounds, parks, sanitation, highways—those things which are expected of solvent local government. They sought escape from disintegration and bankruptcy in local and state affairs.

They also sought peace within the Nation: protection of their currency, fairer wages, the ending of long hours of toil, the abolition of child labor, the elimination of wild-cat speculation, the safety of their children from kidnappers.

And, finally, they sought peace with other Nations—peace in a world of unrest. The Nation knows that I hate war, and I know that the Nation hates war.

I submit to you a record of peace; and on that record a well-founded expectation for future peace—peace for the individual, peace for the community, peace for the Nation, and peace with the world.

Tonight I call the roll—the roll of honor of those who stood with us in 1932 and still stand with us today. Written on it are the names of millions who never had a chance—men at starvation wages, women in sweatshops, children at looms.

Written on it are the names of those who despaired, young men and young women for whom opportunity had become a will-o'-the-wisp.

Written on it are the names of farmers whose acres yielded only bitterness, business men whose books were portents of disaster, home owners who were faced with eviction, frugal citizens whose savings were insecure.

Written there in large letters are the names of countless other Americans of all parties and all faiths, Americans who had eyes to see and hearts to understand, whose consciences were burdened because too many of their fellows were burdened, who looked on these things four years ago and said, "This can be changed. We will change it."

We still lead that army in 1936. They stood with us then because in 1932 they believed. They stand with us today because in 1936 they know. And with them stand millions of new recruits who have come to know.

Their hopes have become our record.

We have not come this far without a struggle and I assure you we cannot go further without a struggle. For twelve years this Nation was afflicted with hear-nothing, see-nothing, do-nothing Government. The Nation looked to Government but the Government looked away. Nine mocking years with the golden calf and three long years of the scourge! Nine crazy years at the ticker and three long years in the breadlines! Nine mad years of mirage and three long years of despair! Powerful influences strive today to restore that kind of government with its doctrine that that Government is best which is most indifferent.

For nearly four years you have had an Administration which instead of twirling its thumbs has rolled up its sleeves. We will keep our sleeves rolled up.

We had to struggle with the old enemies of peace—business and financial monopoly, speculation, reckless banking, class antagonism, sectionalism, war profiteering.

They had begun to consider the Government of the United States as a mere appendage to their own affairs. We know now that Government by organized money is just as dangerous as Government by organized mob.

Never before in all our history have these forces been so united against one candidate as they stand today. They are unanimous in their hate for me—and I welcome their hatred.

I should like to have it said of my first Administration that in it the forces of selfishness and of lust for power met their match. I should like to have it said of my second Administration that in it these forces met their master.

The American people know from a four-year record that today there is only one entrance to the White House—by the front door. Since March 4, 1933, there has been only one pass-key to the White House. I have carried that key in my pocket. It is there tonight. So long as I am President, it will remain in my pocket.

Those who used to have pass-keys are not happy. Some of them are desperate. Only desperate men with their backs to the wall would descend so far below the level of decent citizenship as to foster the current pay-envelope campaign against America's working people. Only reckless men, heedless of con-

sequences, would risk the disruption of the hope for a new peace between worker and employer by returning to the tactics of the labor spy.

Here is an amazing paradox! The very employers and politicians and publishers who talk most loudly of class antagonism and the destruction of the American system now undermine that system by this attempt to coerce the votes of the wage earners of this country. It is the 1936 version of the old threat to close down the factory or the office if a particular candidate does not win. It is an old strategy of tyrants to delude their victims into fighting their battles for them.

Every message in a pay envelope, even if it is the truth, is a command to vote according to the will of the employer. But this propaganda is worse—it is deceit.

They tell the worker his wage will be reduced by a contribution to some vague form of old-age insurance. They carefully conceal from him the fact that for every dollar of premium he pays for that insurance, the employer pays another dollar. That omission is deceit.

They carefully conceal from him the fact that under the federal law, he receives another insurance policy to help him if he loses his job, and that the premium of that policy is paid 100 percent by the employer and not one cent by the worker. They do not tell him that the insurance policy that is bought for him is far more favorable to him than any policy that any private insurance company could afford to issue. That omission is deceit.

They imply to him that he pays all the cost of both forms of insurance. They carefully conceal from him the fact that for every dollar put up by him his employer puts up three dollars—three for one. And that omission is deceit.

But they are guilty of more than deceit. When they imply that the reserves thus created against both these policies will be stolen by some future Congress, diverted to some wholly foreign purpose, they attack the integrity and honor of American Government itself. Those who suggest that, are already aliens to the spirit of American democracy. Let them emigrate and try their lot under some foreign flag in which they have more confidence.

The fraudulent nature of this attempt is well shown by the record of votes on the passage of the Social Security Act. In addition to an overwhelming majority of Democrats in both Houses, seventy-seven Republican Representatives voted for it and only eighteen against it and fifteen Republican Senators voted for it and only five against it. Where does this last-minute drive of the Republican leadership leave these Republican Representatives and Senators who helped enact this law?

I am sure the vast majority of law-abiding businessmen who are not parties to this propaganda fully appreciate the extent of the threat to honest business contained in this coercion.

I have expressed indignation at this form of campaigning and I am confident that the overwhelming majority of employers, workers and the general public share that indignation and will show it at the polls on Tuesday next.

Aside from this phase of it, I prefer to remember this campaign not as bitter but only as hard-fought. There should be no bitterness or hate where the sole thought is the welfare of the United States of America. No man can occupy the office of President without realizing that he is President of all the people.

It is because I have sought to think in terms of the whole Nation that I am confident that today, just as four years ago, the people want more than promises.

Our vision for the future contains more than promises.

This is our answer to those who, silent about their own plans, ask us to state our objectives.

Of course we will continue to seek to improve working conditions for the workers of America—to reduce hours over-long, to increase wages that spell starvation, to end the labor of children, to wipe out sweatshops. Of course we will continue every effort to end monopoly in business, to support collective bargaining, to stop unfair competition, to abolish dishonorable trade practices. For all these we have only just begun to fight.

Of course we will continue to work for cheaper electricity in the homes and on the farms of America, for better and cheaper transportation, for low interest rates, for sounder home financing, for better banking, for the regulation of security issues, for reciprocal trade among nations, for the wiping out of slums. For all these we have only just begun to fight.

Of course we will continue our efforts in behalf of the farmers of America. With their continued co-operation we will do all in our power to end the piling up of huge surpluses which spelled ruinous prices for their crops. We will persist in successful action for better land use, for reforestation, for the conservation of water all the way from its source to the sea, for

drought and flood control, for better marketing facilities for farm commodities, for a definite reduction of farm tenancy, for encouragement of farmer cooperatives, for crop insurance and a stable food supply. For all these we have only just begun to fight.

Of course we will provide useful work for the needy unemployed; we prefer useful work to the pauperism of a dole.

Here and now I want to make myself clear about those who disparage their fellow citizens on the relief rolls. They say that those on relief are not merely jobless—that they are worthless. Their solution for the relief problem is to end relief—to purge the rolls by starvation. To use the language of the stock broker, our needy unemployed would be cared for when, as, and if some fairy godmother should happen on the scene.

You and I will continue to refuse to accept that estimate of our unemployed fellow Americans. Your Government is still on the same side of the street with the Good Samaritan and not with those who pass by on the other side.

Again—what of our objectives?

Of course we will continue our efforts for young men and women so that they may obtain an education and an opportunity to put it to use. Of course we will continue our help for the crippled, for the blind, for the mothers, our insurance for the unemployed, our security for the aged. Of course we will continue to protect the consumer against unnecessary price spreads, against the costs that are added by monopoly and speculation. We will continue our successful efforts to increase his purchasing power and to keep it constant.

For these things, too, and for a multitude of others like them, we have only just begun to fight.

All this—all these objectives—spell peace at home. All our actions, all our ideals, spell also peace with other nations.

Today there is war and rumor of war. We want none of it. But while we guard our shores against threats of war, we will continue to remove the causes of unrest and antagonism at home which might make our people easier victims to those for whom foreign war is profitable. You know well that those who stand to profit by war are not on our side in this campaign.

"Peace on earth, good will toward men"—democracy must cling to that message. For it is my deep conviction that democracy cannot live without that true religion which gives a nation a sense of justice and of moral purpose. Above our political forums, above our market places stand the altars of our faith—altars on which burn the fires of devotion that maintain all that is best in us and all that is best in our Nation.

We have need of that devotion today. It is that which makes it possible for government to persuade those who are mentally prepared to fight each other to go on instead, to work for and to sacrifice for each other. That is why we need to say with the Prophet: "What doth the Lord require of thee—but to do justly, to love mercy and to walk humbly with thy God." That is why the recovery we seek, the recovery we are winning, is more than economic. In it are included justice and love and humility, not for ourselves as individuals alone, but for our Nation.

That is the road to peace.

President Franklin Roosevelt's Annual Message (Four Freedoms) to Congress

Mr. President, Mr. Speaker, Members of the Seventy-seventh Congress:

I address you, the Members of the Seventy-seventh Congress, at a moment unprecedented in the history of the Union. I use the word "unprecedented," because at no previous time has American security been as seriously threatened from without as it is today.

Since the permanent formation of our Government under the Constitution, in 1789, most of the periods of crisis in our history have related to our domestic affairs. Fortunately, only one of these—the four-year War Between the States—ever threatened our national unity. Today, thank God, one hundred and thirty million Americans, in forty-eight States, have forgotten points of the compass in our national unity.

It is true that prior to 1914 the United States often had been disturbed by events in other Continents. We had even engaged in two wars with European nations and in a number of undeclared wars in the West Indies, in the Mediterranean and in the Pacific for the maintenance of American rights and for the principles of peaceful commerce. But in no case had a serious threat been raised against our national safety or our continued independence.

What I seek to convey is the historic truth that the United States as a nation has at all times maintained clear, definite opposition, to any attempt to lock us in behind an ancient Chinese wall while the procession of civilization went past. Today, thinking of our children and of their children, we oppose enforced isolation for ourselves or for any other part of the Americas.

That determination of ours, extending over all these years, was proved, for example, during the quarter century of wars following the French Revolution.

While the Napoleonic struggles did threaten interests of the United States because of the French foothold in the West Indies and in Louisiana, and while we engaged in the War of 1812 to vindicate our right to peaceful trade, it is nevertheless clear that neither France nor Great Britain, nor any other nation, was aiming at domination of the whole world.

In like fashion from 1815 to 1914—ninety-nine years—no single war in Europe or in Asia constituted a real threat against our future or against the future of any other American nation.

Except in the Maximilian interlude in Mexico, no foreign power sought to establish itself in this Hemisphere; and the strength of the British fleet in the Atlantic has been a friendly strength. It is still a friendly strength.

Even when the World War broke out in 1914, it seemed to contain only small threat of danger to our own American future. But, as time went on, the American people began to visualize what the downfall of democratic nations might mean to our own democracy.

We need not overemphasize imperfections in the Peace of Versailles. We need not harp on failure of the democracies to deal with problems of world reconstruction. We should remember that the Peace of 1919 was far less unjust than the kind of "pacification" which began even before Munich, and which is being carried on under the new order of tyranny that seeks to spread over every continent today. The American people have unalterably set their faces against that tyranny.

Every realist knows that the democratic way of life is at this moment being directly assailed in every part of the world—assailed either by arms, or by secret spreading of poisonous propaganda by those who seek to destroy unity and promote discord in nations that are still at peace.

During sixteen long months this assault has blotted out the whole pattern of democratic life in an appalling number of independent nations, great and small. The assailants are still on the march, threatening other nations, great and small.

Therefore, as your President, performing my constitutional duty to "give to the Congress information of the state of the Union," I find it, unhappily, necessary to report that the future and the safety of our country and of our democracy are overwhelmingly involved in events far beyond our borders.

Armed defense of democratic existence is now being gallantly waged in four continents. If that defense fails, all the population and all the resources of

Europe, Asia, Africa and Australasia will be dominated by the conquerors. Let us remember that the total of those populations and their resources in those four continents greatly exceeds the sum total of the population and the resources of the whole of the Western Hemisphere—many times over.

In times like these it is immature—and incidentally, untrue—for anybody to brag that an unprepared America, single-handed, and with one hand tied behind its back, can hold off the whole world.

No realistic American can expect from a dictator's peace international generosity, or return of true independence, or world disarmament, or freedom of expression, or freedom of religion—or even good business.

Such a peace would bring no security for us or for our neighbors. "Those, who would give up essential liberty to purchase a little temporary safety, deserve neither liberty nor safety."

As a nation, we may take pride in the fact that we are soft-hearted; but we cannot afford to be soft-headed.

We must always be wary of those who with sounding brass and a tinkling cymbal preach the "ism" of appeasement.

We must especially beware of that small group of selfish men who would clip the wings of the American eagle in order to feather their own nests.

I have recently pointed out how quickly the tempo of modern warfare could bring into our very midst the physical attack which we must eventually expect if the dictator nations win this war.

There is much loose talk of our immunity from immediate and direct invasion from across the seas. Obviously, as long as the British Navy retains its power, no such danger exists. Even if there were no British Navy, it is not probable that any enemy would be stupid enough to attack us by landing troops in the United States from across thousands of miles of ocean, until it had acquired strategic bases from which to operate.

But we learn much from the lessons of the past years in Europe—particularly the lesson of Norway, whose essential seaports were captured by treachery and surprise built up over a series of years.

The first phase of the invasion of this Hemisphere would not be the landing of regular troops. The necessary strategic points would be occupied by secret agents and their dupes—and great numbers of them are already here, and in Latin America.

As long as the aggressor nations maintain the offensive, they, not we—will choose the time and the place and the method of their attack.

That is why the future of all the American Republics is today in serious danger.

That is why this Annual Message to the Congress is unique in our history.

That is why every member of the Executive Branch of the Government and every member of the Congress faces great responsibility and great accountability.

The need of the moment is that our actions and our policy should be devoted primarily—almost exclusively—to meeting this foreign peril. For all our domestic problems are now a part of the great emergency.

Just as our national policy in internal affairs has been based upon a decent respect for the rights and the dignity of all our fellow men within our gates, so our national policy in foreign affairs has been based on a decent respect for the rights and dignity of all nations, large and small. And the justice of morality must and will win in the end.

Our national policy is this:

First, by an impressive expression of the public will and without regard to partisanship, we are committed to all-inclusive national defense.

Second, by an impressive expression of the public will and without regard to partisanship, we are committed to full support of all those resolute peoples, everywhere, who are resisting aggression and are thereby keeping war away from our Hemisphere. By this support, we express our determination that the democratic cause shall prevail; and we strengthen the defense and the security of our own nation.

Third, by an impressive expression of the public will and without regard to partisanship, we are committed to the proposition that principles of morality and considerations for our own security will never permit us to acquiesce in a peace dictated by aggressors and sponsored by appeasers. We know that enduring peace cannot be bought at the cost of other people's freedom.

In the recent national election there was no substantial difference between the two great parties in respect to that national policy. No issue was fought out on this line before the American electorate. Today it is abundantly evident that American citizens everywhere are demanding and supporting speedy and complete action in recognition of obvious danger.

Therefore, the immediate need is a swift and driving increase in our armament production.

Leaders of industry and labor have responded to our summons. Goals of speed have been set. In some cases these goals are being reached ahead of time; in some cases we are on schedule; in other cases there are slight but not serious delays; and in some cases— and I am sorry to say very important cases— we are all concerned by the slowness of the accomplishment of our plans.

The Army and Navy, however, have made substantial progress during the past year. Actual experience is improving and speeding up our methods of production with every passing day. And today's best is not good enough for tomorrow.

I am not satisfied with the progress thus far made. The men in charge of the program represent the best in training, in ability, and in patriotism. They are not satisfied with the progress thus far made. None of us will be satisfied until the job is done.

No matter whether the original goal was set too high or too low, our objective is quicker and better results. To give you two illustrations:

We are behind schedule in turning out finished airplanes; we are working day and night to solve the innumerable problems and to catch up.

We are ahead of schedule in building warships but we are working to get even further ahead of that schedule.

To change a whole nation from a basis of peacetime production of implements of peace to a basis of wartime production of implements of war is no small task. And the greatest difficulty comes at the beginning of the program, when new tools, new plant facilities, new assembly lines, and new ship ways must first be constructed before the actual materiel begins to flow steadily and speedily from them.

The Congress, of course, must rightly keep itself informed at all times of the progress of the program. However, there is certain information, as the Congress itself will readily recognize, which, in the interests of our own security and those of the nations that we are supporting, must of needs be kept in confidence.

New circumstances are constantly begetting new needs for our safety. I shall ask this Congress for greatly increased new appropriations and authorizations to carry on what we have begun.

I also ask this Congress for authority and for funds sufficient to manufacture additional munitions and war supplies of many kinds, to be turned over to those nations which are now in actual war with aggressor nations.

Our most useful and immediate role is to act as an arsenal for them as well as for ourselves. They do not need man power, but they do need billions of dollars worth of the weapons of defense.

The time is near when they will not be able to pay for them all in ready cash. We cannot, and we will not, tell them that they must surrender, merely because of present inability to pay for the weapons which we know they must have.

I do not recommend that we make them a loan of dollars with which to pay for these weapons—a loan to be repaid in dollars.

I recommend that we make it possible for those nations to continue to obtain war materials in the United States, fitting their orders into our own program. Nearly all their materiel would, if the time ever came, be useful for our own defense.

Taking counsel of expert military and naval authorities, considering what is best for our own security, we are free to decide how much should be kept here and how much should be sent abroad to our friends who by their determined and heroic resistance are giving us time in which to make ready our own defense.

For what we send abroad, we shall be repaid within a reasonable time following the close of hostilities, in similar materials, or, at our option, in other goods of many kinds, which they can produce and which we need.

Let us say to the democracies: "We Americans are vitally concerned in your defense of freedom. We are putting forth our energies, our resources and our organizing powers to give you the strength to regain and maintain a free world. We shall send you, in ever-increasing numbers, ships, planes, tanks, guns. This is our purpose and our pledge."

In fulfillment of this purpose we will not be intimidated by the threats of dictators that they will regard as a breach of international law or as an act of war our aid to the democracies which dare to resist their aggression. Such aid is not an act of war, even if a dictator should unilaterally proclaim it so to be.

When the dictators, if the dictators, are ready to make war upon us, they will not wait for an act of war on our part. They did not wait for Norway or Belgium or the Netherlands to commit an act of war.

Their only interest is in a new one-way international law, which lacks mutuality in its observance, and, therefore, becomes an instrument of oppression.

The happiness of future generations of Americans may well depend upon how effective and how immediate we can make our aid felt. No one can tell the exact character of the emergency situations that we may be called upon to meet. The Nation's hands must not be tied when the Nation's life is in danger.

We must all prepare to make the sacrifices that the emergency—almost as serious as war itself—demands. Whatever stands in the way of speed and efficiency in defense preparations must give way to the national need.

A free nation has the right to expect full cooperation from all groups. A free nation has the right to look to the leaders of business, of labor, and of agriculture to take the lead in stimulating effort, not among other groups but within their own groups.

The best way of dealing with the few slackers or trouble makers in our midst is, first, to shame them by patriotic example, and, if that fails, to use the sovereignty of Government to save Government.

As men do not live by bread alone, they do not fight by armaments alone. Those who man our defenses, and those behind them who build our defenses, must have the stamina and the courage which come from unshakable belief in the manner of life which they are defending. The mighty action that we are calling for cannot be based on a disregard of all things worth fighting for.

The Nation takes great satisfaction and much strength from the things which have been done to make its people conscious of their individual stake in the preservation of democratic life in America. Those things have toughened the fibre of our people, have renewed their faith and strengthened their devotion to the institutions we make ready to protect.

Certainly this is no time for any of us to stop thinking about the social and economic problems which are the root cause of the social revolution which is today a supreme factor in the world.

For there is nothing mysterious about the foundations of a healthy and strong democracy. The basic things expected by our people of their political and economic systems are simple. They are:

Equality of opportunity for youth and for others.

Jobs for those who can work.

Security for those who need it.

The ending of special privilege for the few.

The preservation of civil liberties for all.

The enjoyment of the fruits of scientific progress in a wider and constantly rising standard of living.

These are the simple, basic things that must never be lost sight of in the turmoil and unbelievable complexity of our modern world. The inner and abiding strength of our economic and political systems is dependent upon the degree to which they fulfill these expectations.

Many subjects connected with our social economy call for immediate improvement. As examples:

We should bring more citizens under the coverage of old-age pensions and unemployment insurance.

We should widen the opportunities for adequate medical care.

We should plan a better system by which persons deserving or needing gainful employment may obtain it.

I have called for personal sacrifice. I am assured of the willingness of almost all Americans to respond to that call.

A part of the sacrifice means the payment of more money in taxes. In my Budget Message I shall recommend that a greater portion of this great defense program be paid for from taxation than we are paying today. No person should try, or be allowed, to get rich out of this program; and the principle of tax payments in accordance with ability to pay should be constantly before our eyes to guide our legislation.

If the Congress maintains these principles, the voters, putting patriotism ahead of pocketbooks, will give you their applause.

In the future days, which we seek to make secure, we look forward to a world founded upon four essential human freedoms.

The first is freedom of speech and expression—everywhere in the world.

The second is freedom of every person to worship God in his own way—everywhere in the world.

The third is freedom from want—which, translated into world terms, means economic understandings which will secure to every nation a healthy peacetime life for its inhabitants—everywhere in the world.

The fourth is freedom from fear—which, translated into world terms, means a world-wide reduction of armaments to such a point and in such a thorough fashion that no nation will be in a position to commit an act of physical aggression against any neighbor—anywhere in the world.

That is no vision of a distant millennium. It is a definite basis for a kind of world attainable in our own time and generation. That kind of world is the very antithesis of the so-called new order of tyranny which the dictators seek to create with the crash of a bomb.

To that new order we oppose the greater conception—the moral order. A good society is able to face schemes of world domination and foreign revolutions alike without fear.

Since the beginning of our American history, we have been engaged in change—in a perpetual peaceful revolution—a revolution which goes on steadily, quietly adjusting itself to changing conditions—

without the concentration camp or the quick-lime in the ditch. The world order which we seek is the co-operation of free countries, working together in a friendly, civilized society.

This nation has placed its destiny in the hands and heads and hearts of its millions of free men and women; and its faith in freedom under the guidance of God. Freedom means the supremacy of human rights everywhere. Our support goes to those who struggle to gain those rights or keep them. Our strength is our unity of purpose. To that high concept there can be no end save victory.

The Lend-Lease Act

A BILL

Further to promote the defense of the United States, and for other purposes.

Be it enacted by the Senate add House of Representatives of the United States of America in Congress assembled, That this Act may be cited as "An Act to Promote the Defense of the United States."

SEC. 2. As used in this Act

(a) The term "defense article" means

(1) Any weapon, munition. aircraft, vessel, or boat;

(2) Any machinery, facility, tool, material, or supply necessary for the manufacture, production, processing, repair, servicing, or operation of any article described in this subsection;

(3) Any component material or part of or equipment for any article described in this subsection;

(4) Any agricultural, industrial or other commodity or article for defense.

Such term "defense article" includes any article described in this subsection: Manufactured or procured pursuant to section 3, or to which the United States or any foreign government has or hereafter acquires title, possession, or control.

(b) The term "defense information" means any plan, specification, design, prototype, or information pertaining to any defense article.

SEC. 3. (a) Notwithstanding the provisions of any other law, the President may, from time to time when he deems it in the interest of national defense, authorize the Secretary Of War, the Secretary of the Navy, or the bead of any other department or agency of the Government -

(1) To manufacture in arsenals, factories, and shipyards under their jurisdiction, or otherwise procure, to the extent to which funds are made available therefor, or contracts are authorized from time to time by the Congress, or both, any defense article for the government of any country whose defense the President deems vital to the defense of the United States.

(2) To sell, transfer title to, exchange, lease, lend, or otherwise dispose of, to any such government any defense article, but no defense article not manufactured or procured under paragraph (1) shall in any way be disposed of under this paragraph, except after consultation with the Chief of Staff of the Army or the Chief of Naval Operations of the Navy, or both. The value of defense articles disposed of in any way under authority of this paragraph, and procured from funds heretofore appropriated, shall not exceed $1,300,000,000. The value of such defense articles shall be determined by the head of the department or agency concerned or such other department, agency or officer as shall be designated in the manner provided in the rules and regulations issued hereunder. Defense articles procured from funds hereafter appropriated to any department or agency of the Government, other than from funds authorized to be appropriated under this Act. shall not be disposed of in any way under authority of this paragraph except to the extent hereafter authorized by the Congress in the Acts appropriating such funds or otherwise.

(3) To test, inspect, prove, repair, outfit, recondition, or otherwise to place in good working order, to the extent to which funds are made available therefor, or contracts are authorized from time to time by the Congress, or both, any defense article for any such government, or to procure any or all such services by private contract.

(4) To communicate to any such government any defense information pertaining to any defense article furnished to such government under paragraph (2) of this subsection.

(5) To release for export any defense article disposed of in any way under this subsection to any such government.

(b) The terms and conditions upon which any such foreign government receives any aid authorized under subsection (a) shall be those which the President deems satisfactory, and the benefit to the United States may be payment or repayment in kind or property, or any other direct or indirect benefit which the President deems satisfactory.

(c) After June 30, 1943, or after the passage of a concurrent resolution by the two Houses before June 30, 1943, which declares that the powers conferred by or pursuant to subsection (a) are no longer necessary to promote the defense of the United States, neither the President nor the head of any department or agency shall exercise any of the powers conferred by or pursuant to subsection (a) except that until July 1, 1946, any of such powers may be exercised to the extent necessary to carry out a contract or agreement with such a foreign government made before July 1, 1943, or before the passage of such concurrent resolution, whichever is the earlier.

(d) Nothing in this Act shall be construed to authorize or to permit the authorization of convoying vessels by naval vessels of the United States.

(e) Nothing in this Act shall be construed to authorize or to permit the authorization of the entry of any American vessel into a combat area in violation of section 3 of the neutrality Act of 1939.

SEC. 4. All contracts or agreements made for the disposition of any defense article or defense information pursuant to section 3 shall contain a clause by which the foreign government undertakes that it will not, without the consent of the President, transfer title to or possession of such defense article or defense information by gift, sale, or otherwise, or permit its use by anyone not an officer, employee, or agent of such foreign government.

SEC. 5. (a) The Secretary of War, the Secretary of the Navy, or the head of any other department or agency of the Government involved shall when any such defense article or defense information is exported, immediately inform the department or agency designated by the President to administer section 6 of the Act of July 2, 1940 (54 Stat. 714) of the quantities, character, value, terms of disposition and destination of the article and information so exported.

(b) The President from time to time, but not less frequently than once every ninety days, shall transmit to the Congress a report of operations under this Act except such information as he deems incompatible with the public interest to disclose. Reports provided for under this subsection shall be transmitted to the Secretary of the Senate or the Clerk of the House of representatives, as the case may be, if the Senate or the House of Representatives, as the case may be, is not in session.

SEC. 6. (a) There is hereby authorized to be appropriated from time to time, out of any money in the Treasury not otherwise appropriated, such amounts as may be necessary to carry out the provisions and accomplish the purposes of this Act.

(b) All money and all property which is converted into money received under section 3 from any government shall, with the approval of the Director of the Budget revert to the respective appropriation or appropriations out of which funds were expended with respect to the defense article or defense information for which such consideration is received, and shall be available for expenditure for the purpose for which such expended funds were appropriated by law, during the fiscal year in which such funds are received and the ensuing fiscal year; but in no event shall any funds so received be available for expenditure after June 30, 1946.

SEC. 7. The Secretary of War, the Secretary of the Navy, and the head of the department or agency shall in all contracts or agreements for the disposition of any defense article or defense information fully protect the rights of all citizens of the United States who have patent rights in and to any such article or information which is hereby authorized to he disposed of and the payments collected for royalties on such patents shall be paid to the owners and holders of such patents.

SEC. 8. The Secretaries of War and of the Navy are hereby authorized to purchase or otherwise acquire arms, ammunition, and implements of war produced within the jurisdiction of any country to which section 3 is applicable, whenever the President deems such purchase or acquisition to be necessary in the interests of the defense of the United States.

SEC. 9. The President may, from time to time, promulgate such rules and regulations as may be necessary and proper to carry out any of the provisions of this Act; and he may exercise any power or authority conferred on him by this Act through such department, agency, or officer as be shall direct.

SEC. 10. Nothing in this Act shall be construed to change existing law relating to the use of the land and naval forces of the United States, except insofar as such use relates to the manufacture, procurement, and repair of defense articles, the communication of information and other noncombatant purposes enumerated in this Act.

SEC 11. If any provision of this Act or the application of such provision to any circumstance shall be held invalid, the validity of the remainder of the Act and the applicability of such provision to other circumstances shall not be affected thereby.

Approved, March 11, 1941.

Executive Order 8802: Prohibition of Discrimination in the Defense Industry

Reaffirming Policy Of Full Participation In The Defense Program By All Persons, Regardless Of Race, Creed, Color, Or National Origin, And Directing Certain Action In Furtherance Of Said Policy

June 25, 1941

WHEREAS it is the policy of the United States to encourage full participation in the national defense program by all citizens of the United States, regardless of race, creed, color, or national origin, in the firm belief that the democratic way of life within the Nation can be defended successfully only with the help and support of all groups within its borders; and

WHEREAS there is evidence that available and needed workers have been barred from employment in industries engaged in defense production solely because of considerations of race, creed, color, or national origin, to the detriment of workers' morale and of national unity:

NOW, THEREFORE, by virtue of the authority vested in me by the Constitution and the statutes, and as a prerequisite to the successful conduct of our national defense production effort, I do hereby reaffirm the policy of the United States that there shall be no discrimination in the employment of workers in defense industries or government because of race, creed, color, or national origin, and I do hereby declare that it is the duty of employers and of labor organizations, in furtherance of said policy and of this order, to provide for the full and equitable participation of all workers in defense industries, without discrimination because of race, creed, color, or national origin;

And it is hereby ordered as follows:

1. All departments and agencies of the Government of the United States concerned with vocational and training programs for defense production shall take special measures appropriate to assure that such programs are administered without discrimination because of race, creed, color, or national origin;

2. All contracting agencies of the Government of the United States shall include in all defense contracts hereafter negotiated by them a provision obligating the contractor not to discriminate against any worker because of race, creed, color, or national origin;

3. There is established in the Office of Production Management a Committee on Fair Employment Practice, which shall consist of a chairman and four other members to be appointed by the President. The Chairman and members of the Committee shall serve as such without compensation but shall be entitled to actual and necessary transportation, subsistence and other expenses incidental to performance of their duties. The Committee shall receive and investigate complaints of discrimination in violation of the provisions of this order and shall take appropriate steps to redress grievances which it finds to be valid. The Committee shall also recommend to the several departments and agencies of the Government of the United States and to the President all measures which may be deemed by it necessary or proper to effectuate the provisions of this order.

Franklin D. Roosevelt
The White House,
June 25, 1941.

Joint Address to Congress Leading to a Declaration of War Against Japan

Mr. Vice President, and Mr. Speaker, and Members of the Senate and House of Representatives:

Yesterday, December 7, 1941—a date which will live in infamy—the United States of America was suddenly and deliberately attacked by naval and air forces of the Empire of Japan.

The United States was at peace with that Nation and, at the solicitation of Japan, was still in conversation with its Government and its Emperor looking toward the maintenance of peace in the Pacific. Indeed, one hour after Japanese air squadrons had commenced bombing in the American Island of Oahu, the Japanese Ambassador to the United States and his colleague delivered to our Secretary of State a formal reply to a recent American message. And while this reply stated that it seemed useless to continue the existing diplomatic negotiations, it contained no threat or hint of war or of armed attack.

It will be recorded that the distance of Hawaii from Japan makes it obvious that the attack was deliberately planned many days or even weeks ago. During the intervening time the Japanese Government has deliberately sought to deceive the United States by false statements and expressions of hope for continued peace.

The attack yesterday on the Hawaiian Islands has caused severe damage to American naval and military forces. I regret to tell you that very many American lives have been lost. In addition American ships have been reported torpedoed on the high seas between San Francisco and Honolulu.

Yesterday the Japanese Government also launched an attack against Malaya.

Last night Japanese forces attacked Hong Kong.

Last night Japanese forces attacked Guam.

Last night Japanese forces attacked the Philippine Islands.

Last night the Japanese attacked Wake Island. And this morning the Japanese attacked Midway Island.

Japan has, therefore, undertaken a surprise offensive extending throughout the Pacific area. The facts of yesterday and today speak for themselves. The people of the United States have already formed their opinions and well understand the implications to the very life and safety of our Nation.

As Commander in Chief of the Army and Navy I have directed that all measures be taken for our defense.

But always will our whole Nation remember the character of the onslaught against us.

No matter how long it may take us to overcome this premeditated invasion, the American people in their righteous might will win through to absolute victory. I believe that I interpret the will of the Congress and of the people when I assert that we will not only defend ourselves to the uttermost but will make it very certain that this form of treachery shall never again endanger us.

Hostilities exist. There is no blinking at the fact that our people, our territory, and our interests are in grave danger.

With confidence in our armed forces—with the unbounding determination of our people—we will gain the inevitable triumph—so help us God.

I ask that the Congress declare that since the unprovoked and dastardly attack by Japan on Sunday, December 7, 1941, a state of war has existed between the United States and the Japanese Empire.

Executive Order 9066:
Resulting in the Relocation of Japanese

Executive Order No. 9066

The President
Executive Order

Authorizing the Secretary of War to Prescribe Military Areas

Whereas the successful prosecution of the war requires every possible protection against espionage and against sabotage to national defense material, national defense premises, and national defense utilities as defined in Section 4, Act of April 20, 1918, 40 Stat. 533, as amended by the Act of November 30, 1940, 54 Stat. 1220, and the Act of August 21, 1941, 55 Stat. 655 (U.S.C., Title 50, Sec. 104);

Now, therefore, by virtue of the authority vested in me as President of the United States, and Commander in Chief of the Army and Navy, I hereby authorize and direct the Secretary of War, and the Military Commanders whom he may from time to time designate, whenever he or any designated Commander deems such action necessary or desirable, to prescribe military areas in such places and of such extent as he or the appropriate Military Commander may determine, from which any or all persons may be excluded, and with respect to which, the right of any person to enter, remain in, or leave shall be subject to whatever restrictions the Secretary of War or the appropriate Military Commander may impose in his discretion. The Secretary of War is hereby authorized to provide for residents of any such area who are excluded therefrom, such transportation, food, shelter, and other accommodations as may be necessary, in the judgment of the Secretary of War or the said Military Commander, and until other arrangements are made, to accomplish the purpose of this order. The designation of military areas in any region or locality shall supersede designations of prohibited and restricted areas by the Attorney General under the Proclamations of December 7 and 8, 1941, and shall supersede the responsibility and authority of the Attorney General under the said Proclamations in respect of such prohibited and restricted areas.

I hereby further authorize and direct the Secretary of War and the said Military Commanders to take such other steps as he or the appropriate Military Commander may deem advisable to enforce compliance with the restrictions applicable to each Military area hereinabove authorized to be designated, including the use of Federal troops and other Federal Agencies, with authority to accept assistance of state and local agencies.

I hereby further authorize and direct all Executive Departments, independent establishments and other Federal Agencies, to assist the Secretary of War or the said Military Commanders in carrying out this Executive Order, including the furnishing of medical aid, hospitalization, food, clothing, transportation, use of land, shelter, and other supplies, equipment, utilities, facilities, and services.

This order shall not be construed as modifying or limiting in any way the authority heretofore granted under Executive Order No. 8972, dated December 12, 1941, nor shall it be construed as limiting or modifying the duty and responsibility of the Federal Bureau of Investigation, with respect to the investigation of alleged acts of sabotage or the duty and responsibility of the Attorney General and the Department of Justice under the Proclamations of December 7 and 8, 1941, prescribing regulations for the conduct and control of alien enemies, except as such duty and responsibility is superseded by the designation of military areas hereunder.

Franklin D. Roosevelt
The White House,
February 19, 1942.

General Dwight D. Eisenhower's Order of the Day

SUPREME HEADQUARTERS
ALLIED EXPEDITIONARY FORCE

Soldiers, Sailors, and Airmen of the Allied Expeditionary Force!

You are about to embark upon the Great Crusade, toward which we have striven these many months. The eyes of the world are upon you. The hope and prayers of liberty-loving people everywhere march with you. In company with our brave Allies and brothers-in-arms on other Fronts, you will bring about the destruction of the German war machine, the elimination of Nazi tyranny over the oppressed peoples of Europe, and security for ourselves in a free world.

Your task will not be an easy one. Your enemy is will trained, well equipped and battle-hardened. He will fight savagely.

But this is the year 1944! Much has happened since the Nazi triumphs of 1940–41. The United Nations have inflicted upon the Germans great defeats, in open battle, man-to-man. Our air offensive has seriously reduced their strength in the air and their capacity to wage war on the ground. Our Home Fronts have given us an overwhelming superiority in weapons and munitions of war, and placed at our disposal great reserves of trained fighting men. The tide has turned! The free men of the world are marching together to Victory!

I have full confidence in your courage, devotion to duty and skill in battle. We will accept nothing less than full Victory!

Good luck! And let us beseech the blessing of Almighty God upon this great and noble undertaking.

[Endorsement]

The Servicemen's Readjustment Act

AN ACT

To provide Federal Government aid for the readjustment in civilian life of returning World War II veterans. Be it enacted by the Senate and House of Representatives of the United States of America in Congress assembled, That this Act may be cited as the "Servicemen's Readjustment Act of 1944."

TITLE I

CHAPTER I-HOSPITALIZATION, CLAIMS, AND PROCEDURES

SEC. 100. The Veterans' Administration is hereby declared to be an essential war agency and entitled, second only to the War and Navy Departments, to priorities in personnel, equipment, supplies, and material under any laws, Executive orders, and regulations pertaining to priorities, and in appointments of personnel from civil-service registers the Administrator of Veterans' Affairs is hereby granted the same authority and discretion as the War and Navy Departments and the United States Public Health Service: Provided, That the provisions of this section as to priorities for materials shall apply to any State institution to be built for the care or hospitalization of veterans.

SEC. 101. The Administrator of Veterans' Affairs and the Federal Board of Hospitalization are hereby authorized and directed to expedite and complete the construction of additional hospital facilities for war veterans, and to enter into agreements and contracts for the use by or transfer to the Veterans' Administration of suitable Army and Navy hospitals after termination of hostilities in the present war or after such institutions are no longer needed by the armed services; and the Administrator of Veterans Affairs is hereby authorized and directed to establish necessary regional offices, suboffices, branch offices, contact units, or other subordinate offices in centers of population where there is no Veterans' Administration facility, or where such a facility is not readily available or accessible: Provided, That there is hereby authorized to be appropriated the sum of $500,000,000 for the construction of additional hospital facilities.

SEC. 102. The Administrator of Veterans' Affairs and the Secretary of War and Secretary of the Navy are hereby granted authority to enter into agreements and contracts for the mutual use or exchange of use of hospital and domiciliary facilities, and such supplies, equipment, and material as may be needed to operate properly such facilities, or for the transfer, without reimbursement of appropriations, of facilities, supplies, equipment, or material necessary and proper for authorized care for veterans, except that at no time shall the Administrator of Veterans' Affairs enter into any agreement which will result in a permanent reduction of Veterans' Administration hospital and domiciliary beds below the number now established or approved, plus the estimated number required to meet the load of eligibles under laws administered by the Veterans' Administration, or in any way subordinate or transfer the operation of the Veterans' Administration to any other agency of the Government.

Nothing in the Selective Training and Service Act of 1940, as amended, or any other Act, shall be construed to prevent the transfer or detail of any commissioned, appointed or enlisted personnel from the armed forces to the Veterans Administration subject to agreements between the Secretary of War or the Secretary of the Navy and the Administrator of Veterans' Affairs: Provided, That no such detail shall be made or extend beyond six months after the termination of the war.

SEC.103. The Administrator of Veterans' Affairs shall have authority to place officials and employees designated by him in such Army and Navy installations as may be deemed advisable for the purpose of adjudicating disability claims of, and giving aid and advice to, members of the Army and Navy who are about to be discharged or released from active service.

SEC. 104. No person shall be discharged or released from active duty in the armed forces until his certificate of discharge or release from active duty and final pay, or a substantial portion thereof, are ready for delivery to him or to his next of kin or legal representative; and no person shall be discharged or released from active service on account of disability until and unless he has executed a claim for compensation, pension, or hospitalization, to be filed with the Veterans' Administration or has signed a statement that he has had explained to him the right to file such claim: Provided, That this section shall not preclude immediate transfer to a veterans' facility for necessary hospital care, nor preclude the discharge of any person who refuses to sign such claim or statement: And provided further, That refusal or failure to file a claim shall be without prejudice to any right the veteran may subsequently assert.

Any person entitled to a prosthetic appliance shall be entitled, in addition, to necessary fitting and training, including institutional training, in the use of such appliance, whether in a Service or a Veterans' Administration hospital, or by outpatient treatment, including such service under contract.

SEC. 105. No person in the armed forces shall be required to sign a statement of any nature relating to the origin, incurrence, or aggravation of any disease or injury he may have, and any such statement against his own interest signed at any time, shall be null and void and of no force and effect.

Manhattan Project Notebook

Eight months after the United States entered World War II, the Federal Government launched the Manhattan Project, an all-out, but highly secret, effort to build an atomic bomb—and to build one before the Germans did. The task was to translate the vast energy released by atomic fission into a weapon of unprecedented power. On December 2, 1942, a group of distinguished physicists, working under topsecret conditions in an unpretentious laboratory at the University of Chicago, took a crucial step towards this goal: they created the world's first controlled, self-sustaining nuclear chain reaction. Nobel prize winning physicist Enrico Fermi directed the experiment.

Fermi directed the construction of a pile of graphite and uranium bricks and wooden timbers, assembled in the precise arrangement necessary to start and stop a nuclear chain reaction. Cadmium rods inserted into the pile regulated the nuclear reaction to prevent it from "burning" itself out of control. Had it not been controlled, the experiment could have released a catastrophic amount of energy, wreaking havoc in the middle of the densely populated city of Chicago.

"We're cooking!" was the exuberant reaction recorded when the experiment succeeded. (The data shown on these notebook pages is the record of the nuclear reactor's response to the movement of the control rods.)

(Information excerpted from Stacey Bredhoff, *American Originals* [Seattle: University of Washington Press, 2001], pp. 94–95.)

The Surrender of Germany

Only this text in English is authoritative

ACT OF MILITARY SURRENDER

We the undersigned, acting by authority of the German High Command, hereby surrender unconditionally to the Supreme Commander, Allied Expeditionary Forces and simultaneously to the Soviet High Command all forces on land, sea and in the air who are at this date under German control.

The German High Command will at once issue orders to all German military, naval and air authorties and to all forces under German control to cease active operations at 2301 hours Central European time on 8 May and to remain in the positions occupied at that time. No ship, vessel, or aircraft is to be scuttled, or any damage done to their hull, machinery or equipment.

The German High Command will at once issue to the appropriate commander, and ensure the carrying out of any further orders issued by the Supreme Commander, Allied Expeditionary Force and by the Soviet High Command.

This act of military surrender is without prejudice to, and will be superseded by any general instrument of surrender imposed by, or on behalf of the United Nations and applicable to GERMANY and the German armed forces as a whole.

In the event of the German High Command or any of the forces under their control failing to act in accordance with this Act of Surrender, the Supreme Commander, Allied Expeditionary Force and the Soviet High Command will take such punitive or other action as they deem appropriate.

Signed at RHEIMS at 0241 on the 7th day of May, 1945. France On behalf of the German High Command.

JODL

IN THE PRESENCE OF

On behalf of the Supreme Commander,
Allied Expeditionary Force.
W. B. SMITH

On behalf of the Soviet High Command
SOUSLOPAROV

F SEVEZ
Major General, French Army
(Witness)

The United Nations Charter

WE THE PEOPLES OF THE UNITED NATIONS DETERMINED to save succeeding generations from the scourge of war, which twice in our lifetime has brought untold sorrow to mankind, and to reaffirm faith in fundamental human rights, in the dignity and worth of the human person, in the equal rights of men and women and of nations large and small, and to establish conditions under which justice and respect for the obligations arising from treaties and other sources of international law can be maintained, and to promote social progress and better standards of life in larger freedom, AND FOR THESE ENDS to practice tolerance and live together in peace with one another as good neighbours, and to unite our strength to maintain international peace and security, and to ensure, by the acceptance of principles and the institution of methods, that armed force shall not be used, save in the common interest, and to employ international machinery for the promotion of the economic and social advancement of all peoples, HAVE RESOLED TO COMBINE OUR EFFORTS TO ACCOMPLISH THESE AIMS Accordingly, our respective Governments, through representatives assembled in the city of San Francisco, who have exhibited their full powers found to be in good and due form, have agreed to the present Charter of the United Nations and do hereby establish an international organization to be known as the United Nations.

CHAPTER I
PURPOSES AND PRINCIPLES

ARTICLE 1

The Purposes of the United Nations are:

1. To maintain international peace and security, and to that end: to take effective collective measures for the prevention and removal of threats to the peace, and for the suppression of acts of aggression or other breaches of the peace, and to bring about by peaceful means, and in conformity with the principles of justice and international law, adjustment or settlement of international disputes or situations which might lead to a breach of the peace;

2. To develop friendly relations among nations based on respect for the principle of equal rights and self-determination of peoples, and to take other appropriate measures to strengthen universal peace;

3. To achieve international cooperation in solving international problems of an economic, social, cultural, or humanitarian character, and in promoting and encouraging respect for human rights and for fundamental freedoms for all without distinction as to race, sex, language, or religion; and

4. To be a centre for harmonizing the actions of nations in the attainment of these common ends.

ARTICLE 2

The Organization and its Members, in pursuit of the Purposes stated in Article 1, shall act in accordance with the following Principles.

1. The Organization is based on the principle of the sovereign equality of all its Members.

2. All Members, in order to ensure to all of them the rights and benefits resulting from membership, shall fulfil in good faith the obligations assumed by them in accordance with the present Charter.

3. All Members shall settle their international disputes by peaceful means in such a manner that international peace and security, and justice, are not endangered.

4. All Members shall refrain in their international relations from the threat or use of force against the territorial integrity or political independence of any state, or in any other manner inconsistent with the Purposes of the United Nations.

5. All Members shall give the United Nations every assistance in any action it takes in accordance with the present Charter, and shall refrain from giving assistance to any state against which the United Nations is taking preventive or enforcement action.

6. The Organization shall ensure that states which are not Members of the United Nations act in accordance with these Principles so far as may be necessary for the maintenance of international peace and security.

7. Nothing contained in the present Charter shall authorize the United Nations to intervene in matters which are essentially within the domestic

jurisdiction of any state or shall require the Members to submit such matters to settlement under the present Charter; but this principle shall not prejudice the application of enforcement measures under Chapter VII.

CHAPTER II
MEMBERSHIP

ARTICLE 3

The original Members of the United Nations shall be the states which, having participated in the United Nations Conference on International Organization at San Francisco, or having previously signed the Declaration by United Nations of 1 January 1942, sign the present Charter and ratify it in accordance with Article 110.

ARTICLE 4

1. Membership in the United Nations is open to a other peace-loving states which accept the obligations contained in the present Charter and, in the judgment of the Organization, are able and willing to carry out these obligations.

2. The admission of any such state to membership in the Nations will be effected by a decision of the General Assembly upon the recommendation of the Security Council.

ARTICLE 5

A Member of the United Nations against which preventive or enforcement action has been taken by the Security Council may be suspended from the exercise of the rights and privileges of membership by General Assembly upon the recommendation of the Security Council. The exercise of these rights and privileges may be restored by the Security Council.

ARTICLE 6

A Member of the United Nations which has persistently violated the Principles contained in the present Charter may be expelled from the Organization by the General Assembly upon the recommendation of the Security Council.

CHAPTER III
ORGANS

ARTICLE 7

1. There are established as the principal organs of the United Nations: a General Assembly, a Security Council, an Economic and Social Council, a Trusteeship Council, an International Court of Justice, and a Secretariat.

2. Such subsidiary organs as may be found necessary may be established in accordance with the present Charter.

ARTICLE 8

The United Nations shall place no restrictions on the eligibility of men and women to participate in any capacity and under conditions of equality in its principal and subsidiary organs.

CHAPTER IV
THE GENERAL ASSEMBLY

COMPOSITION
ARTICLE 9

1. The General Assembly shall consist of all the Members of the United Nations.

2. Each Member shall have not more than five representatives in the General Assembly.

FUNCTIONS AND POWERS
ARTICLE 10

The General Assembly may discuss any questions or any matters within the scope of the present Charter or relating to the powers and functions of any organs provided for in the present Charter, and, except as provided in Article 12, may make recommendations to the Members of the United Nations or to the Security Council or to both on any such questions or matters.

ARTICLE 11

1. The General Assembly may consider the general principles of cooperation in the maintenance of international peace and security, including the principles governing disarmament and the regulation of armaments, and may make recommendations with regard to such principles to the Members or to the Security Council or to both.

2. The General Assembly may discuss any questions relating to the maintenance of international peace and security brought before it by any Member of the United Nations, or by the Security Council, or by a state which is not a Member of the United Nations in accordance with Article 35, paragraph 2, and, except as provided in Article 12, may make recommendations with regard to any such questions to the state or states concerned or to the Security Council or to both. Any such question on which action is necessary shall be referred to the Security Council by the General Assembly either before or after discussion.

3. The General Assembly may call the attention of the Security Council to situations which are likely to endanger international peace and security.

4. The powers of the General Assembly set forth in this Article shall not limit the general scope of Article 10.

ARTICLE 12

1. While the Security Council is exercising in respect of any dispute or situation the functions assigned to it in the present Charter, the General Assembly shall not make any recommendation with regard to that dispute or situation unless the Security Council so requests.

2. The Secretary General, with the consent of the Security Council, shall notify the General Assembly at each session of any matters relative to the maintenance of international peace and security which are being dealt with by the Security Council and similarly notify the General Assembly, or the Members of the United Nations if the General Assembly is not in session, immediately the Security Council ceases to deal with such matters.

ARTICLE 13

1. The General Assembly shall initiate studies and make recommendations for the purpose of:

a. promoting international cooperation in the political field and encouraging the progressive development of international law and its codification;

b. promoting international cooperation in the economic, social, cultural, educational, and health fields, an assisting in the realization of human rights and fundamental freedoms for all without distinction as to race, sex, language, or religion.

2. The further responsibilities, functions and powers of the General with respect to matters mentioned in paragraph above are set forth in Chapters IX and X.

ARTICLE 14

Subject to the provisions of Article 12, the General Assembly may recommend measures for the peaceful adjustment of any situation, regardless of origin, which it deems likely to impair the general welfare or friendly relations among nations, including situations resulting from a violation of the provisions of the present Charter setting forth the Purposes and Principles of the United Nations.

ARTICLE 15

1. The General Assembly shall receive and consider annual and special reports from the Security Council; these reports shall include an account of the measures that the Security Council has decided upon or taken to maintain international peace and security.

2. The General Assembly shall receive and consider reports from the other organs of the United Nations.

ARTICLE 16

The General Assembly shall perform such functions with respect to the international trusteeship system as are assigned to it under Chapters XII and XIII, including the approval of the trusteeship agreements for areas not designated as strategic.

ARTICLE 17

1. The General Assembly shall consider and approve the budget of the Organization.

2. The expenses of the Organization shall be borne by the Members as apportioned by the General Assembly.

3. The Assembly shall consider and approve any financial and budgetary arrangements with specialize agencies referred to in Article 57 and shall examine the administrative budgets of such specialized agencies with a view to making recommendations to the agencies concerned.

VOTING
ARTICLE 18

1. Each member of the General Assembly shall have one vote.

2. Decisions of the General Assembly on important questions shall be made by a two-thirds majority of the members present and voting. These questions shall include: recommendations with respect to the maintenance of international peace and security, the election of the nonpermanent members of the Security Council, the election of the members of the Economic and Social Council, the election of members of the Trusteeship Council in accordance with paragraph 1 of Article 86, the admission of new Members to the United Nations, the suspension of the rights and privileges of membership, the expulsion of Members, questions relating to the operation of the trusteeship system, and budgetary questions.

3. Decisions on other questions, including the determination of additional categories of questions to be decided by a two-thirds majority, shall be made by a majority of the members present and voting.

Article 19

A Member of the United Nations which is in arrears in the payment of its financial contributions to the Organization shall have no vote in the General Assembly if the amount of its arrears equals or exceeds the amount of the contributions due from it for the preceding two full years. The General Assembly may, nevertheless, permit such a Member to vote if it is satisfied that the failure to pay is due to conditions beyond the of the Member.

Procedure
Article 20

The General Assembly shall meet in regular annual sessions and in such special sessions as occasion may require. Special sessions shall be convoked by the Secretary General at the request of the Security Council or of a majority of the Members of the United Nations.

Article 21

The General Assembly shall adopt its own rules of procedure. It shall elect its President for each session.

Article 22

The General Assembly may establish such subsidiary organs as it deems necessary for the performance of its functions.

CHAPTER V
THE SECURITY COUNCIL

Composition
Article 23

1. The Security Council shall consist of fifteen Members of the United Nations. The Republic of China, France, the Union of Soviet Socialist, the United Kingdom of Great Britain and Northern Ireland, and the United States of America shall be permanent members of the Security Council. The General Assembly shall elect ten other Members of the United Nations to be nonpermanent members of the Security Council, due regard being specially paid, in the first instance to the contribution of Members of the United Nations to the maintenance of international peace and security and to the other purposes of the Organization, and also to equitable geographical distribution.

2. The nonpermanent members of the Security Council shall be elected for a term of two years. In the first election of the nonpermanent members after the increase of the membership of the Security Council from eleven to fifteen, two of the four additional members shall be chosen for a term of one year. A retiring member shall not be eligible for immediate reelection.

3. Each member of the Security Council shall have one representative.

Functions and Powers
Article 24

1. In order to ensure prompt and effective action by the United Nations, its Members confer on the Security Council primary responsibility for the maintenance of international peace and security, and agree that in carrying out its duties under this responsibility the Security Council acts on their behalf.

2. In discharging these duties the Security Council shall act in accordance with the Purposes and Principles of the United Nations. The specific powers granted to the Security Council for the discharge of these duties are laid down in Chapters VI, VII, VIII, and XII.

3. The Security Council shall submit annual and, when necessary, special reports to the General Assembly for its consideration.

ARTICLE 25

The Members of the United Nations agree to accept and carry out the decisions of the Security Council in accordance with the present Charter.

ARTICLE 26

In order to promote the establishment and maintenance of international peace and security with the least diversion for armaments of the world's human and economic resources, the Security Council shall be responsible for formulating, with the assistance of the Military Staff Committee referred to in Article 47, plans to be submitted to the Members of the United Nations for the establishment of a system for the regulation of armaments.

VOTING
ARTICLE 27

1. Each member of the Security Council shall have one vote.
2. Decisions of the Security Council on procedural matters shall be made by an affirmative vote of nine members.
3. Decisions of the Security Council on all other matters shall be made by an affirmative vote of nine members including the concurring votes of the permanent members; provided that, in decisions under Chapter VI, and under paragraph 3 of Article 52, a party to a dispute shall abstain from voting.

PROCEDURE
ARTICLE 28

1. The Security Council shall be so organized as to be able to function continuously. Each member of the Security Council shall for this purpose be represented at times at the seat of the Organization.
2. The Security Council shall hold meetings at which each of its members may, if it so desires, be represented by a member of the government or by some other specially designated representative.
3. The Security Council may hold meetings at such places other than the seat of the Organization as in its judgment will best facilitate its work.

ARTICLE 29

The Security Council may establish such subsidiary organs as it deems necessary for the performance of its functions.

ARTICLE 30

The Security Council shall adopt its own rules of procedure, including the method of selecting its President.

ARTICLE 31

Any Member of the United Nations which is not a member of the Security Council may participate, without vote, in the discussion of any question brought before the Security Council whenever the latter considers that the interests of that Member are specially affected.

ARTICLE 32

Any Member of the United Nations which is not a member of the Security Council or any state which is not a Member of the United Nations, if it is a party to a dispute under consideration by the Security Council, shall be invited to participate, without vote, in the discussion relating to the dispute. The Security Council shall any down such conditions as it deems just for the participation of a state which is not a Member of the United Nations.

CHAPTER VI
PACIFIC SETTLEMENT OF DISPUTES

ARTICLE 33

1. The parties to any dispute, the continuance of which is likely to endanger the maintenance of international peace and security, shall, first of all, seek a solution by negotiation, enquiry, mediation, conciliation, arbitration, judicial settlement, resort to regional agencies or arrangements, or other peaceful means of their own choice.
2. The Security Council shall, when it deems necessary, call upon the parties to settle their dispute by such means.

ARTICLE 34

The Security Council may investigate any dispute, or any situation which might lead to international friction or give rise to a dispute, in order to determine whether the continuance of the dispute or situation is likely to endanger the maintenance of international peace and security.

ARTICLE 35

1. Any Member of the United Nations may bring any dispute, or any situation of the nature referred to in Article 34, to the attention of the Security Council or of the General Assembly.

2. A state which is not a Member of the United Nations may bring to the attention of the Security Council or of the General Assembly any dispute to which it is a party if it accepts in advance, for the purposes of the dispute, the obligations of pacific settlement provided in the present Charter.

3. The proceedings of the General Assembly in respect of matters brought to its attention under this Article will be subject to the provisions of Articles 11 and 12.

ARTICLE 36

1. The Security Council may, at any stage of a dispute of the nature referred to in Article 33 or of a situation of like nature, recommend appropriate procedures or methods of adjustment.

2. The Security Council should take into consideration any procedures for the settlement of the dispute which have already been adopted by the parties.

3. In making recommendations under this Article the Security Council should also take into consideration that legal disputes should as a general rule be referred by the parties to the International Court of Justice in accordance with the provisions of the Statute of the Court.

ARTICLE 37

1. Should the parties to a dispute of the nature referred to in Article 33 fail to settle it by the means indicated in that Article, they shall refer it to the Security Council.

2. If the Security Council deems that the continuance of the dispute is in fact likely to endanger the maintenance of international peace and security, it shall decide whether to take action under Article 36 or to recommend such terms of settlement as it may consider appropriate.

ARTICLE 38

Without prejudice to the provisions of Articles 33 to 37, the Security Council may, if all the parties to any dispute so request, make recommendations to the parties with a view to a pacific settlement of the dispute.

CHAPTER VII
ACTION WITH RESPECT TO THREATS TO THE PEACE, BREACHES OF THE PEACE, AND ACTS OF AGGRESSION

ARTICLE 39

The Security Council shall determine the existence of any threat to the peace, breach of the peace, or act of aggression and shall make recommendations, or decide what measures shall be taken in accordance with Articles 4 and 42, to maintain or restore international peace and security.

ARTICLE 40

In order to prevent an aggravation of the situation, the Security Council may, before making the recommendations or deciding upon the measures provided for in Article 39, call upon the parties concerned to comply with such provisional measures as it deems necessary or desirable. Such provisional measures shall be without prejudice to the rights, claims, or position of the parties concerned. The Security Council shall duly take account of failure to comply with such provisional measures.

ARTICLE 41

The Security Council may decide what measures not involving the use of armed force are to be employed to give effect to its decisions, and it may call upon the Members of the United Nations to apply such measures. These may include complete or partial interruption of economic relations and of rail, sea, air, postal, telegraphic, radio, and other means of communication, and the severance of diplomatic relations.

ARTICLE 42

Should the Security Council consider that measures provided for in Article 41 would be inadequate or have proved to be inadequate, it may take such action by air, sea, or land forces as may be necessary to maintain or restore international peace and security. Such action may include demonstrations, blockade, and other operations by air, sea, or land forces of Members of the United Nations.

ARTICLE 43

1. All Members of the United Nations, in order to contribute to the maintenance of international peace and security, undertake to make available to the Security Council, on its and in accordance with a special agreement or agreements, armed forces, assistance, and facilities, including rights of passage, necessary for the purpose of maintaining international peace and security.

2. Such agreement or agreements shall govern the numbers and types of forces, their degree of readiness and general location, and the nature of the facilities and assistance to be provided.

3. The agreement or agreements shall be negotiated as soon as possible on the initiative of the Security Council. They shall be concluded between the Security Council and Members or between the Security Council and groups of Members and shall be subject to ratification by the signatory states in accordance with their respective constitutional processes.

ARTICLE 44

When Security Council has decided to use force it shall, before calling upon a Member not represented on it to provide armed forces in fulfilment of the obligations assumed under Article 43, invite that Member, if the Member so desires, to participate in the decisions of the Security Council concerning the employment of contingents of that Member's armed forces.

ARTICLE 45

In order to enable the Nations to take urgent military measures, Members shall hold immediately available national air force contingents for combined international enforcement action. The strength and degree of readiness of these contingents and plans for their combined action shall be determined, within the limits laid down in the special agreement or agreements referred to in Article 43, by the Security Council with the assistance of the Military Committee.

ARTICLE 46

Plans for the application of armed force shall be made by the Security Council with the assistance of the Military Staff Committee.

ARTICLE 47

1. There shall be established a Military Staff Committee to advise and assist the Security Council on questions relating to the Security Council's military requirements for the maintenance of international peace and security, the employment and command of forces placed at its disposal, the regulation of armaments, and possible disarmament.

2. The Military Staff Committee consist of the Chiefs of Staff of the permanent members of the Security Council or their representatives. Any Member of the United Nations not permanently represented on the Committee shall be invited by the Committee to be associated with it when the efficient discharge of the Committee's responsibilities requires the participation of that Member its work.

3. The Military Staff Committee be responsible under the Security Council for the strategic direction of any armed forces paced at the disposal of the Security Council. Questions relating to the command of such forces shall be worked out subsequently.

4. The Military Staff Committee, with the authorization of the security Council and after consultation with appropriate regional agencies, may establish subcommittees.

ARTICLE 48

1. The action required to carry out the decisions of the Security Council for the maintenance of international peace and security shall be taken by all the Members of the United Nations or by some of them, as the Security Council may determine.

2. Such decisions shall be carried out by the Members of the United Nations directly and through their action in the appropriate international agencies of which they are members.

ARTICLE 49

The Members of the United Nations shall join in affording mutual assistance in carrying out the measures decided upon by the Security Council.

ARTICLE 50

If preventive or enforcement measures against any state are taken by the Security Council, any other state, whether a Member of the United Nations or not, which finds itself confronted with special economic problems arising from the carrying out of those measures shall have the right to consult the Security Council with regard to a solution of those problems.

ARTICLE 51

Nothing in the present Charter shall impair the inherent right of individual or collective self-defence if an armed attack occurs against a Member of the United Nations, until the Security Council has taken measures necessary to maintain international peace and security. Measures taken by Members in the exercise of this right of self-defence shall be immediately reported to the Security Council and shall not in any way affect the authority and responsibility of the Security Council under the present Charter to take at any time such action as it deems necessary in order to maintain or restore international peace and security.

CHAPTER VIII
REGIONAL ARRANGEMENTS

ARTICLE 52

1. Nothing in the present Charter the existence of regional arrangements or agencies for dealing with such matters relating to the maintenance of international peace and security as are appropriate for regional action, provided that such arrangements or agencies and their activities are consistent with the Purposes and Principles of the United Nations.

2. The Members of the United Nations entering into such arrangements or constituting such agencies shall make every effort to achieve pacific settlement of local disputes through such regional arrangements or by such regional agencies before referring them to the Security Council.

3. The Security Council shall encourage the development of pacific settlement of local disputes through such regional arrangements or by such regional agencies either on the initiative of the states concerned or by reference from the Security Council.

4. This Article in no way the application of Articles 34 and 35.

ARTICLE 53

1. The Security Council shall, where appropriate, utilize such regional arrangements or agencies for enforcement action under its authority. But no enforcement action shall be taken under regional arrangements or by regional agencies without the authorization of the Security Council, with the exception of measures against any enemy state, as defined in paragraph 2 of this Article, provided for pursuant to Article 107 or in regional arrangements directed against renewal of aggressive policy on the part of any such state, until such time as the Organization may, on request of the Governments concerned, be charged with the responsibility for preventing further aggression by such a state.

2. The term enemy state as used in paragraph 1 of this Article applies to any state which during the Second World War has been an enemy of any signatory of the present Charter.

ARTICLE 54

The Security Council shall at all times be kept fully informed of activities undertaken or in contemplation under regional arrangements or by regional agencies for the maintenance of international peace and security.

CHAPTER IX
INTERNATIONAL ECONOMIC AND SOCIAL COOPERATION

ARTICLE 55

With a view to the creation of conditions of stability and well-being which are necessary for peaceful and friendly relations among nations based on respect for the principle of equal rights and self-determination of peoples, the United Nations shall promote:

a. higher standards of living, fu employment, and conditions of economic and social progress and development;

b. solutions of international economic, social, health, and related problems; and international cultural and educational cooperation; and

c. universal respect for, and observance of, human rights and fundamental freedoms for all without distinction as to race, sex, language, or religion.

ARTICLE 56

All Members pledge themselves to take joint and separate action in cooperation with the Organization for the achievement of the purposes set forth in Article 55.

ARTICLE 57

1. The various specialized agencies, established by intergovernmental agreement and having wide international responsibilities, as defined in their basic instruments, in economic, social, cultural, educational, health, and related fields, shall be brought into relationship with the United Nations in accordance with the provisions of Article 63.

2. Such agencies thus brought into relationship with the United Nations are hereinafter referred to as specialized agencies.

ARTICLE 58

The Organization shall make recommendations for the coordination of the policies and activities of the specialized agencies.

ARTICLE 59

The Organization shall, where appropriate, initiate negotiations among the states concerned for the creation of any new specialized agencies required for the accomplishment of the purposes set forth in Article 55.

ARTICLE 60

Responsibility for the discharge of the functions of the Organization set forth in this Chapter shall be vested in the General Assembly and, under the authority of the General Assembly, in the Economic and Social Council, which shall have for this purpose the powers set forth in Chapter X.

CHAPTER X
THE ECONOMIC AND SOCIAL COUNCIL

COMPOSITION
ARTICLE 61

1. The Economic and Social Council shall consist of fifty-four Members of the United Nations elected by the General Assembly.

2. Subject to the provisions of paragraph 3, eighteen members of the Economic and Social Council shall be elected each year for a term of three years. A retiring member shall be eligible for immediate reelection.

3. At the first election after the increase in the membership of the Economic and Social Council from twenty-seven to fifty-four members, in addition to the members elected in place of the nine members whose term of office expires at the end of that year, twenty-seven additional members shall be elected. Of these twenty-seven additional members, the term of office of nine members so elected shall expire at the end of one year, and of nine other members at the end of two years, in accordance with arrangements made by the General Assembly.

4. Each member of the Economic and Social Council shall have one representative.

FUNCTIONS AND POWERS
ARTICLE 62

1. The Economic and Social Council may make or initiate studies and reports with respect to international economic, social, cultural, educational, health, and related matters and may make recommendations with respect to any such matters to the General Assembly, to the Members of the United Nations, and to the specialized agencies concerned.

2. It may make recommendations for the purpose of promoting respect for, and observance of, human rights and fundamental freedoms for all.

3. It may prepare draft conventions for submission to the General Assembly, with respect to matters falling within its competence.

4. It may call, in accordance with the rules prescribed by the United Nations, international conferences on matters falling within its competence.

ARTICLE 63

1. The Economic and Social Council may enter into agreements with any of the agencies referred to in Article 57, defining the terms on which the agency concerned shall be brought into relationship with the United Nations. Such agreements shall be subject to approval by the General Assembly.

2. It may coordinate the activities of the specialized agencies through consultation with and recommendations to such agencies and through recommendations to the General Assembly and to the Members of the United Nations.

ARTICLE 64

1. The Economic and Social Council may take appropriate steps to obtain regular reports from the specialized agencies may make arrangements with the Members of the United Nations and with the specialized agencies to obtain reports on the steps taken to give effect to its own recommendations and

to recommendations on matters falling within its competence made by the General Assembly.

2. It may communicate its observations on these reports to the General Assembly.

ARTICLE 65

The Economic and Social Council may furnish information to the Security Council and shall assist the Security Council upon its request.

ARTICLE 66

1. The Economic and Social Council shall perform such functions as fall within its competence in connexion with the carrying out of the recommendations of the General Assembly.

2. It may, with the approval of the General Assembly, perform services at the request of Members of the United Nations and at the request of specialized agencies.

3. It shall perform such other functions as are specified elsewhere in the present Charter or as may be assigned to it by the General Assembly.

VOTING
ARTICLE 67

1. Each member of the Economic and Social Council shall have one vote.

2. Decisions of the Economic and Social Council shall be made by a majority of the members present and voting.

PROCEDURE
ARTICLE 68

The Economic and Social Council shall set up commissions in economic and social fields and for the promotion of human rights, and such other commissions as may for the performance of its functions.

ARTICLE 69

The Economic and Social Council shall invite any Member of the United Nations to participate, without vote, in its deliberations on any matter of particular concern to that Member.

ARTICLE 70

The Economic and Social Council may make arrangements for representatives of the specialized agencies to participate, without vote, in its deliberations and in those of the commissions established by it, and for its representatives to participate in the deliberations of the specialized agencies.

ARTICLE 71

The Economic and Social Council may make suitable arrangements for consultation with nongovernmental organizations which are concerned with matters within its competence. Such arrangements may be made with international organizations and, where appropriate, with national organizations after consultation with the Member of the United Nations concerned.

ARTICLE 72

1. The Economic and Social Council shall adopt its own rules of procedure, including the method of selecting its President.

2. The Economic and Social Council shall meet as required in accordance with its rules, which shall include provision for the convening of meetings on the request of a majority of its members.

CHAPTER XI
DECLARATION REGARDING NON-SELF-GOVERNING TERRITORIES

ARTICLE 73

Members of the United Nations which have or assume responsibilities for the administration of territories whose peoples have not yet attained a full measure of self-government recognize the principle that the interests of the inhabitants of these territories are paramount, and accept as a sacred trust the obligation to promote to the utmost, within the system of international peace and security established by the present Charter, the well-being of the inhabitants of these territories, and, to this end:

a. to ensure, with due respect for the culture of the peoples concerned, their political, economic, social, and educational advancement, their just treatment, and their protection against abuses;

b. to develop self-government, to take due account of the political aspirations of the peoples, and to assist them in the progressive development of their free political institutions, according to the particular circumstances of each territory and its peoples and their varying stages of advancement;

c. to further international peace and security;

d. to promote constructive measures of development, to encourage research, and to cooperate with one another and, when and where appropriate, with specialized international bodies with a view to the practical achievement of the social, economic, and scientific purposes set forth in this Article; and

e. to transmit regularly to the Secretary General for information purposes, subject to such limitation as security and constitutional considerations may require, statistical and other information of a technical nature relating to economic, social, and educational conditions in the territories for which they are respectively responsible other than those territories to which Chapters XII and XIII apply.

ARTICLE 74

Members of the United Nations also agree that their policy in respect of the territories to which this Chapter applies, no less than in respect of their metropolitan areas, must be based on the general principle of good-neighbourliness, due account being taken of the interests and well-being of the rest of the world, in social, economic, and commercial matters.

CHAPTER XII
INTERNATIONAL TRUSTEESHIP SYSTEM

ARTICLE 75

The United Nations shall establish under its authority an international trusteeship system for the administration and supervision of such territories as may be placed thereunder by subsequent individual agreements. These territories are hereinafter referred to as trust territories.

ARTICLE 76

The basic objectives of the trusteeship system, in accordance with the Purposes of the United Nations laid down in Article 1 of the present Charter, shall be:

a. to further international peace and security;

b. to promote the political, economic, social, and educational advancement of the inhabitants of the trust territories, and their progressive development towards self-government or independence as may be appropriate to the particular circumstances of each territory and its peoples and the freely expressed wishes of the peoples concerned, and as may be provided by the terms of each trusteeship agreement;

c. to encourage respect for human rights and for fundamental freedoms for all without: as to race, sex, language, or religion, and to encourage recognition of the interdependence of the peoples of the world; and

d. to ensure equal treatment in social, economic, and commercial matters for all Members of the United Nations and their, and also equal treatment for the latter in the administration of justice, without prejudice to the attainment of the foregoing objectives and subject to the provisions of Article 80.

ARTICLE 77

1. The trusteeship system shall apply to such territories in the following categories as may be placed thereunder by means of trusteeship agreements:

a. territories now held under mandate;

b. territories which may be detached from enemy states as a result of the Second World War; and

c. territories voluntarily placed under the system by states responsible for their administration.

2. It will be a matter for subsequent agreement as to which territories in the foregoing categories will be brought under the trusteeship system and upon what terms.

ARTICLE 78

The trusteeship system shall not apply to territories which have become Members of the United Nations, relationship among which shall be based on respect for the principle of sovereign equality.

ARTICLE 79

The terms of trusteeship for each territory to be placed under the trusteeship system, including any alteration or amendment, shall be agreed upon by the states directly concerned, including the mandatory power in the case of territories held under mandate by a Member of the United Nations, and shall be approved as provided for in Articles 83 and 85.

ARTICLE 80

1. Except as may be agreed upon in individual trusteeship agreements, made under Articles 77, 79, and 81, placing each territory under the trusteeship

system, and until such agreements have been concluded, nothing in this Chapter shall be construed in or of itself to alter in any manner the rights whatsoever of any states or any peoples or the terms of existing international instruments to which Members of the United Nations may respectively be parties.

2. Paragraph 1 of this Article shall not be interpreted as giving grounds for delay or postponement of the negotiation and conclusion of agreements for placing mandated and other territories under the trusteeship system as provided for in Article 77.

ARTICLE 81

The trusteeship agreement shall in each case include the terms under which the trust territory will be administered and designate the authority which will exercise the administration of the trust territory. Such authority, hereinafter called the administering authority, may be one or more states or the Organization itself.

ARTICLE 82

There may be designated, in any trusteeship agreement, a strategic area or areas which may include part or all of the trust territory to which the agreement applies, without prejudice to any special agreement or agreements made under Article 43.

ARTICLE 83

1. All functions of the United Nations relating to strategic areas, including the approval of the terms of the trusteeship agreements and of their alteration or amendment, shall be exercised by the Security Council.

2. The basic objectives set forth in Article 76 shall be applicable to the people of each strategic area.

3. The Security Council shall, subject to the provisions of the trusteeship agreements and without prejudice to security considerations, avail itself of the assistance of the Trusteeship Council to perform those functions of the United Nations under the trusteeship system relating to political, economic, social, and educational matters in the strategic areas.

ARTICLE 84

It shall be the duty of the administering authority to ensure that the trust territory shall play its part in the maintenance of international peace and security. To this end the administering authority may make use of volunteer forces, facilities, and assistance from the trust territory in carrying out the obligations towards the Security Council undertaken in this regard by the administering authority, as well as for local defence and the maintenance of law and order within the trust territory.

ARTICLE 85

1. The functions of the United Nations with regard to trusteeship agreements for all areas not designated as strategic, including the approval of the terms of the trusteeship agreements and of their alteration or amendment, shall be exercised by the General Assembly.

2. The Trusteeship Council, operating under the authority of the General Assembly, shall assist the General Assembly in carrying out these functions.

CHAPTER XIII
THE TRUSTEESHIP COUNCIL

COMPOSITION
ARTICLE 86

1. The Trusteeship Council shall consist of the following Members of the United Nations:

a. those Members administering trust territories;

b. such of those Members mentioned by name in Article 23 as are not administering trust territories; and

c. as many other Members elected for three-year terms by the General Assembly as may be necessary to ensure that the total number of members of the Trusteeship Council is equally divided between those Members of the United Nations which administer trust territories and those which do not.

2. Each member of the Trusteeship Council shall designate one specially qualified person to represent it therein.

FUNCTIONS AND POWERS
ARTICLE 87

The General Assembly and, under its authority, the Trusteeship Council, in carrying out their functions, may:

a. consider reports submitted by the administering authority;

b. accept petitions and examine them in consultation with the administering authority;

c. provide for periodic visits to the respective trust territories at times agreed upon with the administering authority; and

d. take these and other actions in conformity with the terms of the trusteeship agreements.

ARTICLE 88

The Trusteeship Council shall formulate a questionnaire on the political, economic, social, and educational advancement of the inhabitants of each trust territory, and the administering authority for each trust territory within the competence of the General Assembly shall make an annual report to the General Assembly upon the basis of such questionnaire.

VOTING
ARTICLE 89

1. Each member of the Trusteeship Council shall have one vote.

2. Decisions of the Trusteeship Council shall be made by a majority of the members present and voting.

PROCEDURE
ARTICLE 90

1. The Trusteeship Council shall adopt its own rules of procedure, including the method of selecting its President.

2. The Trusteeship Council shall meet as required in accordance with its rules, which shall include provision for the convening of meetings on the request of a majority of its members.

ARTICLE 91

The Trusteeship Council shall, when appropriate, avail itself of the assistance of the Economic and Social Council and of the specialized agencies in regard to matters with which they are respectively concerned.

CHAPTER XIV
THE INTERNATIONAL COURT OF JUSTICE

ARTICLE 92

The International Court of Justice shall be the principal judicial organ of the United Nations. It shall function in accordance with the annexed Statute, which is based upon the Statute of the Permanent Court of International Justice and forms an integral part of the present Charter.

ARTICLE 93

1. All Members of the United Nations are facto parties to the Statute of the International Court of Justice.

2. A state which is not of the United Nations may become a party to the Statute of the International Court of Justice on to be determined in each case by the General Assembly upon the recommendation of the Security Council.

ARTICLE 94

1. Each Member of the United Nations undertakes to comply with the decision of the International Court of Justice in any case to which it is a party.

2. If any party to a case fails to perform the obligations incumbent upon it under a judgment rendered by the Court, the other party may have recourse to the Security Council, which may, if it deems necessary, make recommendations or decide upon measures to be taken to give to the judgment.

ARTICLE 95

Nothing in the present Charter shall prevent Members of the United Nations from entrusting the solution of their differences to other tribunals by virtue of agreements already in existence or which may be concluded in the future.

ARTICLE 96

1. The General Assembly or the Security Council may request the International Court of Justice to give an advisory opinion on any legal question.

2. Other organs of the United Nations and specialized agencies, which may at any time be so authorized by the General Assembly, may also request advisory opinions of the Court on legal questions arising within the scope of their activities.

CHAPTER XV
THE SECRETARIAT

ARTICLE 97

The Secretariat shall comprise a Secretary General and such staff as the Organization may require. The

Secretary General shall be appointed by the General Assembly upon the recommendation of the Security Council. He shall be the chief administrative officer of the Organization.

ARTICLE 98

The Secretary General shall act in that capacity in all meetings of the General Assembly, of the Security Council, of the Economic and Social Council, and of the Trusteeship Council, and shall perform such other functions as are entrusted to him by these organs. The Secretary-General shall make an annual report to the General Assembly on the work of the Organization.

ARTICLE 99

The Secretary General may bring to the attention of the Security Council any matter which in his opinion may threaten the maintenance of international peace and security.

ARTICLE 100

1. In the performance of their duties the Secretary General and the staff shall not seek or receive instructions from any government or from any other authority externa to the Organization. They shall refrain from any action which might on their position as international officials responsible only to the Organization.

2. Each Member of the United Nations undertakes to respect the exclusively international character of the responsibilities of the Secretary General and the staff and not to seek to influence them in the discharge of their responsibilities.

ARTICLE 101

1. The staff shall be appointed by the Secretary General under regulations established by the General Assembly.

2. Appropriate staffs shall be permanently assigned to the Economic and Social Council, the Trusteeship Council, and, as required, to other organs of the United Nations. These staffs shall form a part of the Secretariat.

3. The paramount consideration in the employment of the staff and in the determination of the conditions of service shall be the necessity of secur-

ing the highest standards of efficiency, competence, and integrity. Due regard shall be paid to the importance of recruiting the staff on as wide a geographical basis as possible.

CHAPTER XVI
MISCELLANEOUS PROVISIONS

ARTICLE 102

1. Every treaty and every international agreement entered into by any Member of the United Nations after the present Charter comes into force shall as soon as possible be registered with the Secretariat and published by it.

2. No party to any such treaty or international agreement which has not been registered in accordance with the provisions of paragraph I of this Article may invoke that treaty or agreement before any organ of the United Nations.

ARTICLE 103

In the event of a conflict between the obligations of the Members of the United Nations under the present Charter and their obligations under any other international agreement, their obligations under the present Charter shall prevail.

ARTICLE 104

The Organization shall enjoy in the territory of each of its Members such legal capacity as may be necessary for the exercise of its functions and the fulfilment of its purposes.

ARTICLE 105

1. The Organization shall enjoy in the territory of each of its Members such privileges and immunities as are necessary for the fulfilment of its purposes.

2. Representatives of the Members of the United Nations and officials of the Organization shall similarly enjoy such privileges and immunities as are necessary for the independent exercise of their functions in connexion with the Organization.

3. The General Assembly may make recommendations with a view to determining the details of the application of paragraphs 1 and 2 of this Article or may propose conventions to the Members of the United Nations for this purpose.

CHAPTER XVII
TRANSITIONAL SECURITY ARRANGEMENTS

ARTICLE 106

Pending the coming into force of such special agreements referred to in Article 43 as in the opinion of the Security Council enable it to begin the exercise of its responsibilities under Article 42, the parties to the Four-Nation Declaration, signed at Moscow, 30 October 1943, and France, shall, in accordance with the provisions of paragraph 5 of that Declaration, consult with one another and as occasion requires with other Members of the United Nations with a view to such joint action on behalf of the Organization as may be necessary for the purpose of maintaining international peace and security.

ARTICLE 107

Nothing in the present Charter shall invalidate or preclude action, in relation to any state which during the Second World War has been an enemy of any signatory to the present Charter, taken or authorized as a result of that war by the Governments having responsibility for such action.

CHAPTER XVIII
AMENDMENTS

ARTICLE 108

Amendments to the present Charter shall come into force for all Members of the United Nations when they have been adopted by a vote of two thirds of the members of the General Assembly and ratified in accordance with their respective constitutional processes by two thirds of the Members of the United Nations, including all the permanent members of the Security Council.

ARTICLE 109

1. A General Conference of the Members of the United Nations for the purpose of reviewing the present Charter may be held at a date and place to be fixed by a two-thirds vote of the members of the General Assembly and by a vote of any nine members of the Security Council. Each Member of the United Nations shall have one vote in the conference.

2. Any alteration of the present Charter recommended by a two-thirds vote of the conference shall take effect when ratified in accordance with their respective constitutional processes by two thirds of the Members of the United Nations including the permanent members of the Security Council.

3. If such a conference has not been held before the tenth annual session of the General Assembly following the coming into force of the present Charter, the proposal to call such a conference shall be placed on the agenda of that session of the General Assembly, and the conference shall be held if so decided by a majority vote of the members of the General Assembly and by a vote of any seven members of the Security Council.

CHAPTER XIX
RATIFICATION AND SIGNATURE

ARTICLE 110

1. The present Charter shall be ratified by the signatory states in accordance with their respective constitutional processes.

2. The shall be deposited with the Government of the United States of America, which shall notify all the signatory states of each deposit as well as the Secretary General of the Organization when he has been appointed.

3. The present Charter shall come into force upon the deposit of by the Republic of China, France, the Union of Soviet Socialist, the United Kingdom of Great Britain and Northern Ireland, and the United States of America, and by a majority of the other signatory states. A protocol of the deposited shall thereupon be drawn up by the Government of the United States of America which shall communicate copies thereof to all the signatory states.

4. The states signatory to the present Charter which ratify it after it has come into force will become original Members of the United Nations on the date of the deposit of their respective ratifications.

ARTICLE 111

The present Charter, of which the Chinese, French, Russian, English, and Spanish texts are equally authentic, shall remain deposited in the archives of the Government of the United States of America. Duly certified copies thereof shall be transmitted by that Government to the Governments of the other signatory states.

IN FAITH WHEREOF the representatives of the Governments of the United Nations have signed the present Charter.

DONE at the city of San Francisco the twenty-sixth day of June, one thousand nine hundred and forty-five.

The Surrender of Japan

INSTRUMENT OF SURRENDER

We, acting by command of and in behalf of the Emperor of Japan, the Japanese Government and the Japanese Imperial General Headquarters, hereby accept the provisions set forth in the declaration issued by the heads of the Governments of the United States, China, and Great Britain on 26 July 1945 at Potsdam, and subsequently adhered to by the Union of Soviet Socialist Republics, which four powers are hereafter referred to as the Allied Powers.

We hereby proclaim the unconditional surrender to the Allied Powers of the Japanese Imperial General Headquarters and of all Japanese armed forces and all armed forces under the Japanese control wherever situated.

We hereby command all Japanese forces wherever situated and the Japanese people to cease hostilites forthwith, to preserve and save from damage all ships, aircraft, and military and civil property and to comply with all requirements which may be imposed by the Supreme Commander for the Allied Powers or by agencies of the Japanese Government at his direction.

We hereby command the Japanese Imperial Headquarters to issue at once orders to the Commanders of all Japanese forces and all forces under Japanese control wherever situated to surrender unconditionally themselves and all forces under their control.

We hereby command all civil, military and naval officials to obey and enforce all proclamations, and orders and directives deemed by the Supreme Commander for the Allied Powers to be proper to effectuate this surrender and issued by him or under his authority and we direct all such officials to remain at their posts and to continue to perform their non-combatant duties unless specifically relieved by him or under his authority.

We hereby undertake for the Emperor, the Japanese Government and their successors to carry out the provisions of the Potsdam Declaration in good faith, and to issue whatever orders and take whatever actions may be required by the Supreme Commander for the Allied Powers or by any other designated representative of the Allied Powers for the purpose of giving effect to that Declaration.

We hereby command the Japanese Imperial Government and the Japanese Imperial General Headquarters at once to liberate all allied prisoners of war and civilian internees now under Japanese control and to provide for their protection, care, maintenance and immediate transportation to places as directed.

The authority of the Emperor and the Japanese Government to rule the state shall be subject to the Supreme Commander for the Allied Powers who will take such steps as he deems proper to effectuate these terms of surrender.

Signed at TOKYO BAY, JAPAN at 0904 I on the SECOND day of SEPTEMBER, 1945

MAMORU SHIGMITSU
By Command and in behalf of the Emperor
of Japan and the Japanese Government

YOSHIJIRO UMEZU
By Command and in behalf of the Japanese
Imperial General Headquarters

Accepted at TOKYO BAY, JAPAN at 0903 I on the SECOND day of SEPTEMBER, 1945, for the United States, Republic of China, United Kingdom and the Union of Soviet Socialist Republics, and in the interests of the other United Nations at war with Japan.

DOUGLAS MAC ARTHUR
Supreme Commander for the Allied Powers

C.W. NIMITZ
United States Representative

HSU YUNG-CH'ANG
Republic of China Representative

BRUCE FRASER
United Kingdom Representative

KUZMA DEREVYANKO
Union of Soviet Socialist Republics Representative

THOMAS BLAMEY
Commonwealth of Australia Representative

L. MOORE COSGRAVE
Dominion of Canada Representative

JACQUES LE CLERC
Provisional Government of the French Republic
Representative

C.E.L. HELFRICH
Kingdom of the Netherlands Representative

LEONARD M. ISITT
Dominion of New Zealand Representative

The Truman Doctrine

Mr. President, Mr. Speaker, Members of the Congress of the United States:

The gravity of the situation which confronts the world today necessitates my appearance before a joint session of the Congress. The foreign policy and the national security of this country are involved.

One aspect of the present situation, which I wish to present to you at this time for your consideration and decision, concerns Greece and Turkey.

The United States has received from the Greek Government an urgent appeal for financial and economic assistance. Preliminary reports from the American Economic Mission now in Greece and reports from the American Ambassador in Greece corroborate the statement of the Greek Government that assistance is imperative if Greece is to survive as a free nation.

I do not believe that the American people and the Congress wish to turn a deaf ear to the appeal of the Greek Government.

Greece is not a rich country. Lack of sufficient natural resources has always forced the Greek people to work hard to make both ends meet. Since 1940, this industrious and peace loving country has suffered invasion, four years of cruel enemy occupation, and bitter internal strife.

When forces of liberation entered Greece they found that the retreating Germans had destroyed virtually all the railways, roads, port facilities, communications, and merchant marine. More than a thousand villages had been burned. Eighty-five per cent of the children were tubercular. Livestock, poultry, and draft animals had almost disappeared. Inflation had wiped out practically all savings.

As a result of these tragic conditions, a militant minority, exploiting human want and misery, was able to create political chaos which, until now, has made economic recovery impossible.

Greece is today without funds to finance the importation of those goods which are essential to bare subsistence. Under these circumstances the people of Greece cannot make progress in solving their problems of reconstruction. Greece is in desperate need of financial and economic assistance to enable it to resume purchases of food, clothing, fuel and seeds. These are indispensable for the subsistence of its people and are obtainable only from abroad. Greece must have help to import the goods necessary to restore internal order and security, so essential for economic and political recovery.

The Greek Government has also asked for the assistance of experienced American administrators, economists and technicians to insure that the financial and other aid given to Greece shall be used effectively in creating a stable and self-sustaining economy and in improving its public administration.

The very existence of the Greek state is today threatened by the terrorist activities of several thousand armed men, led by Communists, who defy the government's authority at a number of points, particularly along the northern boundaries. A Commission appointed by the United Nations security Council is at present investigating disturbed conditions in northern Greece and alleged border violations along the frontier between Greece on the one hand and Albania, Bulgaria, and Yugoslavia on the other.

Meanwhile, the Greek Government is unable to cope with the situation. The Greek army is small and poorly equipped. It needs supplies and equipment if it is to restore the authority of the government throughout Greek territory. Greece must have assistance if it is to become a self-supporting and self-respecting democracy.

The United States must supply that assistance. We have already extended to Greece certain types of relief and economic aid but these are inadequate.

There is no other country to which democratic Greece can turn.

No other nation is willing and able to provide the necessary support for a democratic Greek government.

The British Government, which has been helping Greece, can give no further financial or economic aid after March 31. Great Britain finds itself under the necessity of reducing or liquidating its commitments in several parts of the world, including Greece.

We have considered how the United Nations might assist in this crisis. But the situation is an urgent one requiring immediate action and the United Nations and its related organizations are not in a position to extend help of the kind that is required.

It is important to note that the Greek Government has asked for our aid in utilizing effectively the financial and other assistance we may give to Greece, and in improving its public administration. It is of the utmost importance that we supervise the use of any funds made available to Greece; in such a manner that each dollar spent will count toward making Greece self-supporting, and will help to build an economy in which a healthy democracy can flourish.

No government is perfect. One of the chief virtues of a democracy, however, is that its defects are always visible and under democratic processes can be pointed out and corrected. The Government of Greece is not perfect. Nevertheless it represents eighty-five per cent of the members of the Greek Parliament who were chosen in an election last year. Foreign observers, including 692 Americans, considered this election to be a fair expression of the views of the Greek people.

The Greek Government has been operating in an atmosphere of chaos and extremism. It has made mistakes. The extension of aid by this country does not mean that the United States condones everything that the Greek Government has done or will do. We have condemned in the past, and we condemn now, extremist measures of the right or the left. We have in the past advised tolerance, and we advise tolerance now.

Greece's neighbor, Turkey, also deserves our attention.

The future of Turkey as an independent and economically sound state is clearly no less important to the freedom-loving peoples of the world than the future of Greece. The circumstances in which Turkey finds itself today are considerably different from those of Greece. Turkey has been spared the disasters that have beset Greece. And during the war, the United States and Great Britain furnished Turkey with material aid.

Nevertheless, Turkey now needs our support.

Since the war Turkey has sought financial assistance from Great Britain and the United States for the purpose of effecting that modernization necessary for the maintenance of its national integrity.

That integrity is essential to the preservation of order in the Middle East.

The British government has informed us that, owing to its own difficulties can no longer extend financial or economic aid to Turkey.

As in the case of Greece, if Turkey is to have the assistance it needs, the United States must supply it. We are the only country able to provide that help.

I am fully aware of the broad implications involved if the United States extends assistance to Greece and Turkey, and I shall discuss these implications with you at this time.

One of the primary objectives of the foreign policy of the United States is the creation of conditions in which we and other nations will be able to work out a way of life free from coercion. This was a fundamental issue in the war with Germany and Japan. Our victory was won over countries which sought to impose their will, and their way of life, upon other nations.

To ensure the peaceful development of nations, free from coercion, the United States has taken a leading part in establishing the United Nations, The United Nations is designed to make possible lasting freedom and independence for all its members. We shall not realize our objectives, however, unless we are willing to help free peoples to maintain their free institutions and their national integrity against aggressive movements that seek to impose upon them totalitarian regimes. This is no more than a frank recognition that totalitarian regimes imposed on free peoples, by direct or indirect aggression, undermine the foundations of international peace and hence the security of the United States.

The peoples of a number of countries of the world have recently had totalitarian regimes forced upon them against their will. The Government of the United States has made frequent protests against coercion and intimidation, in violation of the Yalta agreement, in Poland, Rumania, and Bulgaria. I must also state that in a number of other countries there have been similar developments.

At the present moment in world history nearly every nation must choose between alternative ways of life. The choice is too often not a free one.

One way of life is based upon the will of the majority, and is distinguished by free institutions, representative government, free elections, guarantees of individual liberty, freedom of speech and religion, and freedom from political oppression.

The second way of life is based upon the will of a minority forcibly imposed upon the majority. It relies upon terror and oppression, a controlled press and radio; fixed elections, and the suppression of personal freedoms.

I believe that it must be the policy of the United States to support free peoples who are resisting attempted subjugation by armed minorities or by outside pressures.

I believe that we must assist free peoples to work out their own destinies in their own way.

I believe that our help should be primarily through economic and financial aid which is essential to economic stability and orderly political processes.

The world is not static, and the status quo is not sacred. But we cannot allow changes in the status quo in violation of the Charter of the United Nations by such methods as coercion, or by such subterfuges as political infiltration. In helping free and independent nations to maintain their freedom, the United States will be giving effect to the principles of the Charter of the United Nations.

It is necessary only to glance at a map to realize that the survival and integrity of the Greek nation are of grave importance in a much wider situation. If Greece should fall under the control of an armed minority, the effect upon its neighbor, Turkey, would be immediate and serious. Confusion and disorder might well spread throughout the entire Middle East.

Moreover, the disappearance of Greece as an independent state would have a profound effect upon those countries in Europe whose peoples are struggling against great difficulties to maintain their freedoms and their independence while they repair the damages of war.

It would be an unspeakable tragedy if these countries, which have struggled so long against overwhelming odds, should lose that victory for which they sacrificed so much. Collapse of free institutions and loss of independence would be disastrous not only for them but for the world. Discouragement and possibly failure would quickly be the lot of neighboring peoples striving to maintain their freedom and independence.

Should we fail to aid Greece and Turkey in this fateful hour, the effect will be far reaching to the West as well as to the East.

We must take immediate and resolute action.

I therefore ask the Congress to provide authority for assistance to Greece and Turkey in the amount of $400,000,000 for the period ending June 30, 1948. In requesting these funds, I have taken into consideration the maximum amount of relief assistance which would be furnished to Greece out of the $350,000,000 which I recently requested that the Congress authorize for the prevention of starvation and suffering in countries devastated by the war.

In addition to funds, I ask the Congress to authorize the detail of American civilian and military personnel to Greece and Turkey, at the request of those countries, to assist in the tasks of reconstruction, and for the purpose of supervising the use of such financial and material assistance as may be furnished. I recommend that authority also be provided for the instruction and training of selected Greek and Turkish personnel.

Finally, I ask that the Congress provide authority which will permit the speediest and most effective use, in terms of needed commodities, supplies, and equipment, of such funds as may be authorized.

If further funds, or further authority, should be needed for purposes indicated in this message, I shall not hesitate to bring the situation before the Congress. On this subject the Executive and Legislative branches of the Government must work together.

This is a serious course upon which we embark.

I would not recommend it except that the alternative is much more serious. The United States contributed $341,000,000,000 toward winning World War II. This is an investment in world freedom and world peace.

The assistance that I am recommending for Greece and Turkey amounts to little more than 1 tenth of 1 per cent of this investment. It is only common sense that we should safeguard this investment and make sure that it was not in vain.

The seeds of totalitarian regimes are nurtured by misery and want. They spread and grow in the evil soil of poverty and strife. They reach their full growth when the hope of a people for a better life has died. We must keep that hope alive.

The free peoples of the world look to us for support in maintaining their freedoms.

If we falter in our leadership, we may endanger the peace of the world—and we shall surely endanger the welfare of our own nation.

Great responsibilities have been placed upon us by the swift movement of events.

I am confident that the Congress will face these responsibilities squarely.

The Marshall Plan

I need not tell you gentlemen that the world situation is very serious. That must be apparent to all intelligent people. I think one difficulty is that the problem is one of such enormous complexity that the very mass of facts presented to the public by press and radio make it exceedingly difficult for the man in the street to reach a clear appraisement of the situation. Furthermore, the people of this country are distant from the troubled areas of the earth and it is hard for them to comprehend the plight and consequent reaction of the long-suffering peoples, and the effect of those reactions on their governments in connection with our efforts to promote peace in the world.

In considering the requirements for the rehabilitation of Europe the physical loss of life, the visible destruction of cities, factories, mines, and railroads was correctly estimated, but it has become obvious during recent months that this visible destruction was probably less serious than the dislocation of the entire fabric of European economy. For the past 10 years conditions have been highly abnormal. The feverish maintenance of the war effort engulfed all aspects of national economics. Machinery has fallen into disrepair or is entirely obsolete. Under the arbitrary and destructive Nazi rule, virtually every possible enterprise was geared into the German war machine. Long-standing commercial ties, private institutions, banks, insurance companies and shipping companies disappeared, through the loss of capital, absorption through nationalization or by simple destruction. In many countries, confidence in the local currency has been severely shaken. The breakdown of the business structure of Europe during the war was complete. Recovery has been seriously retarded by the fact that 2 years after the close of hostilities a peace settlement with Germany and Austria has not been agreed upon. But even given a more prompt solution of these difficult problems, the rehabilitation of the economic structure of Europe quite evidently will require a much longer time and greater effort than had been foreseen.

There is a phase of this matter which is both interesting and serious. The farmer has always produced the foodstuffs to exchange with the city dweller for the other necessities of life. This division of labor is the basis of modern civilization. At the present time it is threatened with breakdown. The town and city industries are not producing adequate goods to exchange with the food-producing farmer. Raw materials and fuel are in short supply. Machinery is lacking or worn out. The farmer or the peasant cannot find the goods for sale which he desires to purchase. So the sale of his farm produce for money which he cannot use seems to him unprofitable transaction. He, therefore, has withdrawn many fields from crop cultivation and is using them for grazing. He feeds more grain to stock and finds for himself and his family an ample supply of food, however short he may be on clothing and the other ordinary gadgets of civilization. Meanwhile people in the cities are short of food and fuel. So the governments are forced to use their foreign money and credits to procure these necessities abroad. This process exhausts funds which are urgently needed for reconstruction. Thus a very serious situation is rapidly developing which bodes no good for the world. The modern system of the division of labor upon which the exchange of products is based is in danger of breaking down.

The truth of the matter is that Europe's requirements for the next 3 or 4 years of foreign food and other essential products—principally from America—are so much greater than her present ability to pay that she must have substantial additional help, or face economic, social, and political deterioration of a very grave character.

The remedy lies in breaking the vicious circle and restoring the confidence of the European people in the economic future of their own countries and of Europe as a whole. The manufacturer and the farmer throughout wide areas must be able and willing to exchange their products for currencies the continuing value of which is not open to question.

Aside from the demoralizing effect on the world at large and the possibilities of disturbances arising as a result of the desperation of the people concerned, the consequences to the economy of the United States should be apparent to all. It is logical that the United States should do whatever it is able to do to assist in the return of normal economic health in the world, without which there can be no political stability and no assured peace. Our policy is directed not against any country or doctrine but against hunger, poverty, desperation, and chaos. Its purpose should be the revival of working economy in the world so as to permit the emergence of political and social conditions in which free institutions can exist. Such assistance, I am convinced, must not be on a piecemeal basis as various crises develop. Any assistance that this Government may render in the future should provide a cure rather than a mere palliative. Any government that is willing to assist in the task of recovery will find full cooperation, I am sure, on the part of the United States Government. Any government which maneuvers to block the recovery of other countries cannot expect help from us. Furthermore, governments, political parties, or groups which seek to perpetuate human misery in order to profit therefrom politically or otherwise will encounter the opposition of the United States.

It is already evident that, before the United States Government can proceed much further in its efforts to alleviate the situation and help start the European world on its way to recovery, there must be some agreement among the countries of Europe as to the requirements of the situation and the part those countries themselves will take in order to give proper effect to whatever action might be undertaken by this Government. It would be neither fitting nor efficacious for this Government to undertake to draw up unilaterally a program designed to place Europe on its feet economically. This is the business of the Europeans. The initiative, I think, must come from Europe. The role of this country should consist of friendly aid in the drafting of a European program so far as it may be practical for us to do so. The program should be a joint one, agreed to by a number, if not all European nations.

An essential part of any successful action on the part of the United States is an understanding on the part of the people of America of the character of the problem and the remedies to be applied. Political passion and prejudice should have no part. With foresight, and a willingness on the part of our people to face up to the vast responsibilities which history has clearly placed upon our country, the difficulties I have outlined can and will be overcome.

The Press Release Announcing U.S. Recognition of Israel

This Government has been informed that a Jewish state has been proclaimed in Palestine, and recognition has been requested by the provisional Government thereof.

The United States recognizes the provision government as the de facto authority of the new State of Israel.

[Endorsement]

Approved, May 14, 1948.

Executive Order 9981: Desegregation of the Armed Forces

Establishing the President's Committee on Equality of Treatment and Opportunity In the Armed Forces.

WHEREAS it is essential that there be maintained in the armed services of the United States the highest standards of democracy, with equality of treatment and opportunity for all those who serve in our country's defense:

NOW THEREFORE, by virtue of the authority vested in me as President of the United States, by the Constitution and the statutes of the United States, and as Commander in Chief of the armed services, it is hereby ordered as follows:

1. It is hereby declared to be the policy of the President that there shall be equality of treatment and opportunity for all persons in the armed services without regard to race, color, religion or national origin. This policy shall be put into effect as rapidly as possible, having due regard to the time required to effectuate any necessary changes without impairing efficiency or morale.

2. There shall be created in the National Military Establishment an advisory committee to be known as the President's Committee on Equality of Treatment and Opportunity in the Armed Services, which shall be composed of seven members to be designated by the President.

3. The Committee is authorized on behalf of the President to examine into the rules, procedures and practices of the Armed Services in order to determine in what respect such rules, procedures and practices may be altered or improved with a view to carrying out the policy of this order. The Committee shall confer and advise the Secretary of Defense, the Secretary of the Army, the Secretary of the Navy, and the Secretary of the Air Force, and shall make such recommendations to the President and to said Secretaries as in the judgment of the Committee will effectuate the policy hereof.

4. All executive departments and agencies of the Federal Government are authorized and directed to cooperate with the Committee in its work, and to furnish the Committee such information or the services of such persons as the Committee may require in the performance of its duties.

5. When requested by the Committee to do so, persons in the armed services or in any of the executive departments and agencies of the Federal Governemt shall testify before the Committee and shall make available for use of the Committee such documents and other information as the Committee may require.

6. The Committee shall continue to exist until such time as the President shall terminate its existence by Executive order.

Harry Truman

The White House
July 26, 1948

The Armistice Agreement for the Restoration of the South Korean State

July 27, 1953

Agreement between the Commander-in-Chief, United Nations Command, on the one hand, and the Supreme Commander of the Korean People's Army and the Commander of the Chinese People's volunteers, on the other hand, concerning a military armistice in Korea.

PREAMBLE

The undersigned, the Commander-in-Chief, United Nations Command, on the one hand, and the Supreme Commander of the Korean People's Army and the Commander of the Chinese People's Volunteers, on the other hand, in the interest of stopping the Korean conflict, with its great toil of suffering and bloodshed on both sides, and with the objective of establishing an armistice which will insure a complete cessation of hostilities and of all acts of armed force in Korea until a final peaceful settlement is achieved, do individually, collectively, and mutually agree to accept and to be bound and governed by the conditions and terms of armistice set forth in the following articles and paragraphs, which said conditions and terms are intended to be purely military in character and to pertain solely to the belligerents in Korea:

ARTICLE I
MILITARY DEMARCATION LINE AND DEMILITARIZED ZONE

1. A military demarcation line shall be fixed and both sides shall withdraw two (2) kilometers from this line so as to establish a demilitarized zone between the opposing forces. A demilitarized zone shall be established as a buffer zone to prevent the occurrence of incidents which might lead to a resumption of hostilities.

2. The military demarcation line is located as indicated on the attached map.

3. This demilitarized zone is defined by a northern and southern boundary as indicated on the attached map.

4. The military demarcation line shall be plainly marked as directed by the Military Armistice Commission hereinafter established. The Commanders of the opposing sides shall have suitable markers erected along the boundary between the demilitarized zone and their respective areas. The Military Armistice Commission shall supervise the erection of all markers placed along the military demarcation line and along the boundaries of the demilitarized zone.

5. The waters of the Han River Estuary shall be open to civil shipping of both sides wherever one bank is controlled by one side and the other bank is controlled by the other side. The Military Armistice Commission shall prescribe rules for the shipping in that part of the Han River Estuary indicated on the attached map. Civil shipping of each side shall have unrestricted access to the land under the military control of that side.

6. Neither side shall execute any hostile act within, from, or against the demilitarized zone.

7. No person, military or civilian, shall be permitted to cross the military demarcation line unless specifically authorized to do so by the Military Armistice Commission.

8. No person, military of civilian, in the demilitarized zone shall be permitted to enter the territory under the military control of either side unless specifically authorized to do so by the Commander into whose territory entry is sought.

9. No person, military or civilian, shall be permitted to enter the demilitarized zone except persons concerned with the conduct of civil administration and relief and persons specifically authorized to enter by the Military Armistice Commission.

10. Civil administration and relief in that part of the demilitarized zone which is south of the military of the military demarcation line shall be the responsibility of the Commander-in-Chief, United Nations Command; and civil administration and relief in that part of the demilitarized zone which is north of the

military demarcation line shall be the joint responsibility of the Supreme Commander of the Korean People's Army and the Commander of the Chinese People's volunteers. The number of persons, military or civilian, from each side who are permitted to enter the demilitarized zone for the conduct of civil administration and relief shall be as determined by the respective Commanders, but in no case shall the total number authorized by either side exceed one thousand (1,000) persons at any one time. The number of civil police and the arms to be carried by them shall be a prescribed by the Military Armistice Commission. Other personnel shall not carry arms unless specifically authorized to do so by the Military Armistice Commission.

11. Nothing contained in this article shall be construed to prevent the complete freedom of movement to, from, and within the demilitarized zone by the Military Armistice Commission, its assistants, its Joint Observer Teams with their assistants, the Neutral Nations Supervisory Commission hereinafter established, its assistants, its Neutral Nations Inspection teams with their assistants, and of any other persons, materials, and equipment specifically authorized to enter the demilitarized zone by the Military Armistice Commission. Convenience of movement shall be permitted through the territory under the military control of either side over any route necessary to move between points within the demilitarized zone where such points are not connected by roads lying completely within the demilitarized zone.

ARTICLE II
CONCRETE ARRANGEMENTS FOR CEASE-FIRE AND ARMISTICE

A. GENERAL

12. The Commanders of the opposing sides shall order and enforce a complete cessation of all hostilities in Korea by all armed forces under their control, including all units and personnel of the ground, naval, and air forces, effective twelve (12) hours after this armistice agreement is signed. (See paragraph 63 hereof for effective date and hour of the remaining provisions of this armistice agreement.)/

13. In order to insure the stability of the military armistice so as to facilitate the attainment of a peaceful settlement through the holding by both sides of a political conference of a higher level, the Commanders of the opposing sides shall:

(a) Within seventy-two (72) hours after this armistice agreement becomes effective, withdraw all of their military forces, supplies, and equipment from the demilitarized zone except as otherwise provided herein. All demolitions, minefields, wire entanglements, and other hazards to the safe movement of personnel of the Military Armistice Commission or its Joint Observer Teams, known to exist within the demilitarized zone after the withdrawal of military forces therefrom, together with lanes known to be free of all such hazards, shall be reported to the MAC by the Commander of the side whose forces emplaced such hazards. Subsequently, additional safe lanes shall be cleared; and eventually, within forty-five (45) days after the termination of the seventy-two (72) hour period, all such hazards shall be removed from the demilitarized zone as directed by the under the supervision of the MAC. At the termination of the seventy-two (72) hour period, except for unarmed troops authorized forty-five (54) day period to complete salvage operations under MAC and agreed to by the MAC and agreed to by the Commanders of the opposing sides, and personnel authorized under paragraphs 10 and 11 hereof, no personnel of either side shall be permitted to enter the demilitarized zone.

(b) Within ten (10) days after this armistice agreement becomes effective, withdraw all of their military forces, supplies, and equipment from the rear and the coastal islands and waters of Korea of the other side. If such military forces are not withdrawn within the stated time limit, and there is no mutually agreed and valid reason for the delay, the other side shall have the right to take any action which it deems necessary for the maintenance of security and order. The term "coastal islands," as used above, refers to those islands, which, though occupied by one side at the time when this armistice agreement becomes effective, were controlled by the other side on 24 June 1950; provided, however, that all the islands lying to the north and west of the provincial boundary line between HWANGHAE-DO and KYONGGI-DO shall be under the military control of the Supreme Commander of the Korean People's Army and the Commander of the Chinese People's volunteers, except the island groups of PAENGYONG-DO (37 58' N, 124 40' E), TAECHONG-DO (37 50' N, 124 42' E), SOCHONG-DO (37 46' N, 124 46' E), YONPYONG-DO (37 38' N, 125 40' E), and U-DO (37 36'N, 125 58' E), which shall remain under the military control of the Commander-in-Chief, United

Nations Command. All the island on the west coast of Korea lying south of the above-mentioned boundary line shall remain under the military control of the Commander-in-Chief, United Nations Command. (See Map 3).

(c) Cease the introduction into Korea of Reinforcing military personnel; provided, however, that the rotation of units and personnel, the arrival in Korea of personnel on a temporary duty basis, and the return to Korea of personnel after short periods of leave or temporary duty outside of Korea shall be permitted within the scope prescribed below: "Rotation" is defined as the replacement of units or personnel by other units or personnel who re commencing a tour of duty in Korea. Rotation personnel shall be introduced into and evacuated from Korea only through the ports of entry enumerated in Paragraph 43 hereof. Rotation shall be conducted on a man-for-man basis; provided, however, that no more than thirty-five thousand (35,000) persons in the military service shall be admitted into Korea by either side in any calendar month under the rotation policy. No military personnel of either side shall be introduced into Korea if the introduction of such personnel will cause the aggregate of the military personnel of that side admitted into Korea since the effective date of this Armistice Agreement to exceed the cumulative total of the military personnel of that side who have departed from Korea since that date. Reports concerning arrivals in and departures from Korea of military personnel shall be made daily to the Military Armistice Commission and the Neutral Nations Supervisory Commission; such reports shall include places of arrival and departure and the number of persons arriving at or departing from each such place. The Neutral Nations Supervisory Commission, through its Neutral Nations Inspection Teams, shall conduct supervision and inspection of the rotation of units and personnel authorized above, at the ports of entry enumerated in Paragraph 43 hereof.

(d) Cease the introduction into Korea of reinforcing combat aircraft, armored vehicles, weapons, and ammunition; provided however, that combat aircraft, armored vehicles, weapons, and ammunition which are destroyed, damaged, worn out, or used up during the period of the armistice may be replaced on the basis piece-for-piece of the same effectiveness and the same type. Such combat aircraft, armored vehicles, weapons, and ammunition shall be introduced into Korea only through the ports of entry enumerated in paragraph 43 hereof. In order to justify the requirements for combat aircraft, armored vehicles, weapons, and ammunition to be introduced into Korea for replacement purposes, reports concerning every incoming shipment of these items shall be made to the MAC and the NNSC; such reports shall include statements regarding the disposition of the items being replaced. Items to be replace which are removed from Korea shall be removed only through the ports of entry enumerated in paragraph 43 hereof. The NNSC, through its Neutral Nations Inspection Teams, shall conduct supervision and inspection of the replacement of combat aircraft, armored vehicles, weapons, and ammunition authorized above, at the ports of entry enumerated in paragraph 43 hereof.

(e) Insure that personnel of their respective commands who violate any of the provisions of this armistice agreement are adequately punished.

(f) In those cases where places of burial are a matter of record and graves are actually found to exist, permit graves registration personnel of the other side to enter, within a definite time limit after this armistice agreement becomes effective, the territory of Korea under their military control, for the purpose of proceeding to such graves to recover and evacuate the bodies of the deceased military personnel of that side, including deceased prisoners of war. The specific procedures and the time limit for the performance of the above task shall be determined by the Military Armistice Commission. The Commanders of the opposing sides shall furnish to the other side all available information pertaining to the places of burial of the deceased military personnel of the other side.

(g) Afford full protection and all possible assistance and cooperation to the Military Armistice Commission, its Joint Observer Teams, the Neutral Nations Supervisory Commission, and its Neutral Nations Inspection Teams, in the carrying out of their functions and responsibilities hereinafter assigned; and accord to the Neutral Nations Inspection Teams, full convenience of movement between the headquarters of the Neutral Nations supervisory Commission and the ports of entry enumerated in Paragraph 43 hereof over main lines of communication agreed upon by both sides (see Map 4), and between the headquarters of the Neutral Nations Supervisory commission and the places where violations of this Armistice Agreement have been reported to have occurred. In order to prevent unnecessary delays, the use of alternate routes and means of transportation will be permitted whenever the main lines of communication are closed or impassable.

(h) Provide such logistic support, including communications and transportation facilities, as may be required by the military Armistice Commission and the Neutral Nations Supervisory Commission and their Teams.

(i) Each construct, operate, and maintain a suitable airfield in their respective parts of the Demilitarized Zone in the vicinity of the headquarters of the Military Armistice Commission, for such uses as the Commission may determine.

(j) Insure that all members and other personnel of the Neutral Nations Supervisory Commission and of the Neutral Nations Repatriation Commission hereinafter established shall enjoy the freedom and facilities necessary for the proper exercise of their functions, including privileges, treatment, and immunities equivalent to those ordinarily enjoyed by accredited diplomatic personnel under international usage.

14. This Armistice Agreement shall apply to all opposing ground forces under the military control of either side, which ground forces shall respect the Demilitarized Zone and the area of Korea under the military control of the opposing side.

15. This Armistice Agreement shall apply to all opposing naval forces, which naval forces shall respect the water contiguous to the Demilitarized Zone and to the land area of Korea under the military control of the opposing side, and shall not engage in blockade of any kind of Korea.

16. This Armistice Agreement shall apply to all opposing air forces, which air forces shall respect the air space over the Demilitarized Zone and over the area of Korea under the military control of the opposing side, and over the waters contiguous to both.

17. Responsibility for compliance with and enforcement of the terms and provisions of this Armistice Agreement is that of the signatories hereto and their successors in command. The Commanders of the opposing sides shall establish within their respective commands all measures and procedures necessary to insure complete compliance with all of the provisions hereof by all elements of their commands. They shall actively cooperate with one another and with the Military Armistice Commission and the Neutral nations supervisory Commission in requiring obser-

vance of both letter and the spirit of all of the provisions of this Armistice Agreement.

18. The costs of the operations of the Military Armistice Commission and of the Neutral Nations supervisory Commission and of their Teams shall be shared equally by the two opposing sides.

B. MILITARY ARMISTICE COMMISSION

1. Composition

19. A Military Armistice Commission is hereby established.

20. The Military Armistice commission shall be composed of ten (10) senior officers, five (5) of whom shall be appointed by the Commander-in-Chief, United Nations Command, and five (5) of whom shall be appointed jointly by the Supreme Commander of the Korean People's Army and the Commander of the Chinese People's Volunteers. Of the ten members, three (3) from each side shall be of general of flag rank. The two (2) remaining members on each side may be major generals, brigadier generals, colonels, or their equivalents.

21. Members of the Military Armistice Commission shall be permitted to use staff assistants as required.

22. The Military Armistice Commission shall able provided with the necessary administrative personnel to establish a Secretariat charged with assisting the Commission by performing record keeping, secretarial, interpreting, and such other functions as the Commission may assign to it. Each side shall appoint to the Secretariat a Secretary and an Assistant Secretary and such clerical and specialized personnel as required by the Secretariat. Records shall be kept in English, Korean, and Chinese, all of which shall be equally authentic.

23. (a) The Military Armistice Commission shall be initially provided with and assisted by ten (10) Joint Observer Teams, which number may be reduced by agreement of the senior members of both sides on the Military Armistice Commission.

(b) Each Joint Observer Team shall be composed of not less than four (4) nor mire than six (6) officers of field grade, half of whom shall be appointed by the Commander-in-Chief, United Nations Command, and half of whom shall be appointed by the Commander-in-Chief, United Nations Command, and half of whom shall be appointed jointly by the Supreme Commander of the Korean People's Army and the Commander of the Chinese People's Volunteers. Additional personnel such as drivers, clerks, and interpreters shall be furnished by each side as required for the functioning of the Joint Observer Teams.

24. The general mission of the Military Armistice Commission shall be to supervise the implementation of this Armistice Agreement and to settle through negotiations any violations of this Armistice Agreement.

25. The military Armistice Commission shall:

(a) Locate its headquarters in the vicinity of PANMUNJOM (37 57'29" n, 126 40'00" e). The Military Armistice Commission may relocate its headquarters at another point within the Demilitarized Zone by agreement of the senior members of both sides on the Commission.

(b) Operate as a joint organization without a chairman.

(c) Adopt such rules of procedure as it may, from time to time, deem necessary.

(d) Supervise the carrying out of the provisions of this Armistice Agreement pertaining to the Demilitarized Zone and to the Han River Estuary.

(e) Direct the operations of the Joint Observer Teams.

(f) Settle through negotiations any violations of this Armistice Agreement.

(g) Transmit immediately to the Commanders of the opposing sides all reports of investigations of violations of this Armistice Agreement and all other reports and records of proceedings received from the Neutral nations supervisory Commission.

(h) Give general supervision and direction to the activities of the Committee for Repatriation of Prisoners of War and the Committee for Assisting the Return of Displaced Civilians, hereinafter established.

(i) Act as intermediary in transmitting communications between the Commanders of the opposing sides; provided, however, that the foregoing shall not be construed to preclude the Commanders of both sides from Communicating with each other by any other means which they may desire to employ.

(j) Provide credentials and distinctive insignia for its staff and its Joint Observer Teams, and a distinctive marking for all vehicles, aircraft, and vessels, used in the performance of its mission.

26. The Mission of the Joint Observer Teams shall be to assist the Military Armistice Commission in supervising the carrying out of the provisions of this Armistice Agreement pertaining to the Demilitarized Zone and to the Han River Estuary.

27. The Military Armistice Commission, or the senior member of either side thereof, is authorized to dispatch Joint Observer Teams to investigate violations of this Armistice Agreement reported to have occurred in the Demilitarized Zone or in the Han River Estuary; provided, however, that not more than one half of the Joint Observer Teams which have not been dispatched by the Military Armistice Commission may be dispatched at any one time by the senior member of either side on the Commission.

28. The Military Armistice Commission, or the senior member of either side thereof, is authorized to request the Neutral Nations Supervisory Commission to conduct special observations and inspections at places outside the Demilitarized Zone where violations of this Armistice Agreement have been reported to have occurred.

29. When the Military Armistice Commission determines that a violation of this Armistice Agreement has occurred, it shall immediately report such violation to the Commanders of the opposing sides.

30. When the Military Armistice Commission determines that a violation of this Armistice Agreement has been corrected to its satisfaction, it shall so report to the Commanders of the opposing sides.

3. General

31. The Military Armistice Commission shall meet daily. Recesses of not to exceed seven (7) days may be agreed upon by the senior members of both sides; provided, that such recesses may be terminated on twenty-four (24) hour notice by the senior member of either side.

32. Copies of the record of the proceedings of all meetings of the Military Armistice Commission shall be forwarded to the Commanders of the opposing sides as soon as possible after each meeting.

33. The Joint Observer teams shall make periodic reports to the Military Armistice Commission as re-

quired by the Commission and, in addition, shall make such special reports as may be deemed necessary by them, or as may be required by the Commission.

34. The Military Armistice Commission shall maintain duplicate files of the reports and records of proceedings required by this Armistice Agreement. The Commission is authorized to maintain duplicate files of such other reports, records, etc., as may be necessary in the conduct of its business. Upon eventual dissolution of the Commission, one set of the above files shall be turned over to each side.

35. The Military Armistice Commission may make recommendations to the Commanders of the opposing sides with respect to amendments or additions to this Armistice Agreement. Such recommended changes should generally be those designed to insure a more effective armistice.

C. NEUTRAL NATIONS SUPERVISORY COMMISSION

1. Compositions

36. A Neutral Nations Supervisory Commission is hereby established.

37. The Neutral Nations supervisory Commission shall be composed of four (4) senior officers, two (2) of whom shall be appointed by neutral nations nominated by the Commander-in-Chief, United Nations Command, namely, SWEDEN and SWITZERLAND, and two (2) of whom shall be appointed by neutral nations nominated jointly by the Supreme Commander of the Korean People's Army and the Commander of the Chinese People's Volunteers, namely, POLAND and CZECHOSLOVAKIA. The term "neutral nations" as herein used is defined as those nations whose combatant forces have not participated in the hostilities in Korea. Members appointed to the Commission may be from the armed forces of the appointing nations. Each member shall designate an alternate member to attend those meetings which for any reason the principal member is unable to attend. Such alternate members shall be of the same nationality as their principals. The Neutral Nations supervisory Commission may take action whenever the number of members present from the neutral nations nominated by one side is equal to the number of members present from the neutral nations nominated by the other side.

38. Members of the Neutral nations Supervisory Commission shall be permitted to use staff assistants furnished by the neutral nations as required. These staff assistants may be appointed as alternate members of the Commission.

39. The neutral nations shall be requested to furnish the Neutral nations Supervisory Commission with the necessary administrative personnel to establish a Secretariat charged with assisting the Commission by performing necessary record keeping, secretarial, interpreting, and such other functions as the Commission may assign to it.

40. (a) The Neutral Nations supervisory Commission shall be initially provided with, and assisted by, twenty (20) neutral Nations Inspection Teams, which number may be reduced by agreement of the senior members of both sides on the Military Armistice Commission. The Neutral nations Inspection Teams shall be responsible to, shall report to, and shall be subject to the direction of, the Neutral Nations supervisory Commission only.

(b) Each Neutral Nations Inspection Team shall be composed of not less than four (4) officers, preferably of field grade, half of whom shall be from the neutral nations nominated by the Commander-in-Chief, United Nations Command, and half of whom shall be from the neutral nations nominated jointly by the Supreme Commander of the Korean People's Army, and the Commander of the Chinese People's Volunteers. Members appointed to the Neutral Nations Inspection Teams may be from the armed forces of the appointed. In order to facilitate the functioning of the Teams, subteams composed of not less than two (2) members, one of whom shall be from a neutral nation nominated by the Commander-in-Chief, United Nations Command, and one of whom shall be from a neutral nation nominated jointly by the Supreme Commander of the Korean People's Army and the Commander of the Chinese People's Volunteers, may be formed as circumstances require. Additional personnel such as drivers, clerks, interpreters, and communications personnel, and such equipment as may be required by the Teams to perform their missions, shall be furnished by the Commander of each side, as required, in the Demilitarized Zone and in the territory under his military control. The Neutral nations Supervisory Commission may provide itself and the Neutral Nations Inspection Teams with such of the above personnel shall be personnel of the same neutral nations of which the Neutral nations supervisory Commission is composed.

2. Functions and Authority

41. The mission of the Neutral Nations Supervisory Commission shall be to carry out the functions of supervision, observation, inspection, and investigation, as stipulated in Subparagraphs 13(c) and 13(d) and Paragraph 28 hereof, and to report the results of such supervision, observation, inspection, and investigation to the Military Armistice Commission.

42. The Neutral nations Supervisory Commission shall:

(a) Locate its headquarters in proximity to the to the headquarters of the Military Armistice Commission.

(b) Adopt such rules of procedure as it may, from time to time, deem necessary.

(c) Conduct, through its members and its Neutral nations Inspection teams, the supervision and inspection provided for in Subparagraphs 13(c) and 13(d) of this Armistice Agreement at the ports of entry enumerated in Paragraph 43 hereof, and the special observations and inspections provided for in paragraph 28 hereof at those places where violations of this Armistice Agreement have been reported to have occurred. The inspection of combat aircraft, armored vehicles, weapons, and ammunition by the Neutral Nations Inspection Teams shall be such as to enable them to properly insure that reinforcing combat aircraft, armored vehicles, weapons, and ammunition are not being introduced into Korea; but this shall not be construed as authorizing inspections or examinations of any secret designs of characteristics of any combat aircraft, armored vehicle, weapon, or ammunition.

(d) Direct and supervise the operations of the Neutral Nations Inspection Teams.

(e) Station five (5) neutral nations Inspection Teams at the ports of entry enumerated in Paragraph 43 hereof located in the territory under the military control of the Commander-in-Chief, United Nations Command; and five (5) Neutral nations Inspection Teams at the ports of entry enumerated in Paragraph 43 hereof located in the territory under the military control of the Supreme Commander of the Korean People's Army and the Commander of the Chinese People's Volunteers; and establish initially ten (10) mobile Neutral nations Inspection Teams in reserve, stationed in the general vicinity of the headquarters of the Neutral Nations supervisory Commission, which number may be reduced by agreement of the senior members of both sides on the Military Armistice Commission. Not more than half of the mobile Neutral Nations Inspection Teams shall be dispatched at any one time in accordance with requests of the senior member of either side on the Military Armistice Commission.

(f) Subject to the provisions of the preceding Subparagraphs, conduct without delay investigations of reported violations of this Armistice Agreement, including such investigations of reported violations of this Armistice Agreement as may be requested by the Military Armistice Commission or by the senior member of either side on the Commission.

(g) Provide credentials and distinctive insignia for its staff and its Neutral nations Inspection Teams, and a distinctive marking for all vehicles, aircraft, and vessels used in the Performance of this mission.

43. Neutral nations Inspection Teams shall be stationed at the following ports of entry.

Territory under the military contrail of the United Nations Command

INCHON	(37 28, 126 38'E)
TAEGU	(35 52'n, 128 36'E)
PUSAN	(35 45'N, 129 02'E)
KANGNUNG	(37 45'N, 128 54'E)
KUNSAN	(35 59'E, 126 43'E)

Territory under the military control of the Korean People's Army and the Chinese People's Volunteers

SINUJU	(40 06'n, 124 24E)
CHONGJIN	(41 46'N, 129 49E)
HUNGNAM	(39 50'N, 127 37'E)
MANPO	(41 46'N, 126 18'E)
SINANJU	(39 36'N, 125 36'E)

These Neutral Nations Inspection Teams shall be accorded full convenience of movement within the areas and over the routes of communication set forth on the attached map (Map 5).

3. General

44. The Neutral Nations Supervisory Commission shall meet daily. Recesses of not to exceed seven (7) days may be agreed upon by the members of the Neutral nations Supervisory Commission; provided, that such recesses may be terminated on twenty-four (24) hour notice by any member.

45. Copies of the record of the proceedings of all meetings of the Neutral Nations Supervisory com-

mission shall be forwarded to the Military Armistice commission as soon as possible after each meeting. Records shall be kept in English, Korean, and Chinese.

46. The Neutral Nations Inspection Teams shall make periodic reports concerning the results of their supervision observations, inspections, and investigations to the Neutral Nations supervisory Commission as required by the Commission and, in addition, shall make such special reports as may be deemed necessary by them, or as may be required by the Commission. Reports shall be submitted by a Team as a whole, but may also be submitted by one or more individual members thereof; provided, that the reports submitted by one or more individual members thereof shall be considered as information only.

47. Copies of the reports made by the Neutral Nations Inspection teams shall be forwarded to the Military Armistice Commission by the Neutral Nations Supervisory Commission without delay and in the language in which received. They shall not be delayed by the process of translation or evaluation. The Neutral Nations Supervisory Commission shall evaluate such reports at the earliest practicable time and shall forward their findings to the Military Armistice Commission as a matter of priority. The Military Armistice Commission shall not take final action with regard to any such report until the evaluation thereof has been received from the Neutral nations Supervisory Commission. Members of the Neutral nations Supervisory Commission and of its Teams shall be subject to appearance before the Military Armistice Commission, at the request of the senior member of either side on the Military Armistice Commission, for clarification of any report submitted.

48. The Neutral Nations Supervisory Commission shall maintain duplicate files of the reports and records of proceedings required by this Armistice Agreement. The Commission is authorized to maintain duplicate files of such other reports, records, etc., as may be necessary in the conduct of its business. Upon eventual dissolution of the Commission, one set of the above files shall be turned over to each side.

49. The Neutral Nations Supervisory Commission may make recommendations to the Military Armistice Commission with respect to amendments or additions to this Armistice Agreement. Such recommended changes should generally be those designed to insure a more effective armistice.

50. The Neutral Nations Supervisory Commission, or any member thereof, shall be authorized to communicated with any member of the Military Armistice Commission.

ARTICLE III
ARRANGEMENT RELATING TO PRISONERS OF WAR

51. The release and repatriation of all prisoners of war held in the custody of each side at the time this armistice agreement becomes effective shall be effected in conformity with the following provisions agreed upon by both sides prior to the signing of this armistice agreement.

(a) Within sixty (60) days after this agreement becomes effective each side shall, without offering any hindrance, directly repatriate and hand over in groups all those prisoners of war in its custody who insist on repatriation to the side to which they belonged at the time of capture. Repatriation shall be accomplished in accordance with the related provisions of this Article. In order to expedite the repatriation process of such personnel, each side shall, prior to the signing of the Armistice Agreement, exchange the total numbers, by nationalities, or personnel to be directly repatriated. Each group of prisoners of war delivered to the other side shall be accompanied by rosters, prepared by nationality, to include name, rank (if any) and internment or military serial number.

(b) Each side shall release all those remaining prisoners of war, who are not directly repatriated, from its military control and from its custody and hand them over to the Neutral Nations Repatriation Commission for disposition in accordance with the provisions in the Annex hereto, "Terms of Reference for Neutral Nations Repatriation Commission."

(c) So that there may be no misunderstanding owing to the equal use of three languages, the act of delivery of a prisoner of war by one side to other side shall, for the purposes of the Armistice Agreement, be called "repatriation" in English, ( ) "Song Hwan" in Korean and ( ) "Ch'ien Fan" in Chinese, notwithstanding the nationality or place of residence of such prisoner of war.

52. Each side insures that it will not employ in acts of war in the Korean conflict any prisoner of war released and repatriated incident to the coming into effect of this armistice agreement.

53. All the sick and injured prisoners of was who insist upon repatriation shall be repatriated with priority. Insofar as possible, there shall be captured medical personnel repatriated concurrently with the sick and injured prisoners of war, so as to provide medical care and attendance enroute.

54. The repatriation of all of the prisoners of war required by Subparagraph 51 (a) hereof shall be completed within a time limit of sixty (60) days after this Armistice Agreement becomes effective. Within this time limit each side undertakes to complete repatriation of the above-mentioned prisoners of war in its custody at the earliest practicable time.

55. PANMUNJOM is designated as the place where prisoners of war will be delivered and received by both sides. Additional place(s) of delivery and reception of prisoners of war in the Demilitarized Zone may be designated, if necessary, by the Committee for Repatriation of Prisoners of War.

56. (a) A committee for Repatriation of Prisoners of War is hereby established. It shall be composed of six (6) officers of field grade, three (3) of whom shall be appointed by the Commander-in-Chief, United Nations Command, and three (3) of whom shall be appointed jointly by the Supreme Commander of the Korean People's Army and the Commander of the Chinese People's Volunteers. This Committee shall, under the general supervision and direction of the Military Armistice Commission, be responsible for coordinating the specific plans of both sides for the repatriation of prisoners of war and for supervision the execution by both sides of all of the provisions of this Armistice Agreement relating to the repatriation of prisoners of war. It shall be the duty of this Committee to coordinate the timing of the arrival of prisoners of war at the place(s) of delivery and reception of prisoners of war from the prisoner of war camps of both sides; to make, when necessary, such special arrangements as may be required with regard to the transportation and welfare of sick and injured prisoners of war; to coordinate the work of the joint Red Cross teams, established in Paragraph 57 hereof, in assisting in the repatriation of prisoners of war; to supervise the implementation of the arrangements for the actual repatriation of prisoners of war stipulated in Paragraphs 53 and 54 hereof; to select, when necessary, additional place(s) of delivery and reception of prisoners of war; and to carry out such other related functions as are required for the repatriation of prisoners of war.

(b) When unable to reach agreement on any matter relating to its responsibilities, the committee for Repatriation of Prisoners of War shall immediately refer such matter to the Military Armistice Commission for decision. The Committee for Repatriation of Prisoners of War shall maintain its headquarters in proximity to the headquarters of the Military Armistice Commission.

(c) The Committee for Repatriation of Prisoners of War shall be dissolved by the Military Armistice Committee upon completion of the program of repatriation of prisoners of war.

57. (a) Immediately after this Armistice Agreement becomes effective, joint Red Cross teams composed of representatives of the national Red Cross Societies of countries contributing forces to the United Nations Command on the one hand, and representatives of the of the Red Cross Society of the Democratic People's Republic of Korea and representatives of the Red Cross Society of the People's Republic of China on the other hand, shall be established. The joint Red Cross teams shall assist in the execution by both sides of those provisions of this Armistice Agreement relating to the repatriation of all the prisoners of war specified in Subparagraph 51 (a) hereof, who insist upon repatriation, by the performance of such humanitarian services as are necessary and desirable for the welfare of the prisoners of war. To accomplish this task, the joint Red Cross teams shall provide assistance in the delivering and receiving of prisoners of war by both sides at the place(s) of delivery and reception of prisoners of war, and shall visit the prisoner-of-war camps of both sides to comfort the prisoners of war.

(b) The joint Red Cross teams shall be organized as set forth below:

(1) One team shall be composed of twenty (20) members, namely, ten (10) representatives from the national Red Cross Societies of each side, to assist in the delivering and receiving of prisoners of war by both sides at the place(s) of delivery and reception of prisoners of war. The chairmanship of this team shall alternate daily between representative from the Red Cross Societies of the two sides. The work and services of this team shall be coordinated by the Committee for Repatriation of Prisoners of War.

(2) One team shall be composed of sixty (60) members, namely, thirty (30) representatives from the national Red Cross Societies of each side, to visit the

prisoner-of-war camps under the administration of the Korean People's Army and the Chinese People's Volunteers. This team may provide services to prisoners of war while en route from the prisoner of war camps to the place(s) of delivery and reception of prisoners of war. A representative of a Red Cross Society of the Democratic People's Republic of Korea or of the Red Cross Society of the People's Republic of China shall serve as chairman of this team.

(3) One team shall be composed of sixty (60) members, namely, thirty (30) representatives from the national Red Cross Societies of each side, to visit the prisoner of war camps under the administration of the United Nations Command. This team may provide services to prisoners of war while en route from the prisoner of war camps to the place(s) of delivery and reception of prisoners of war. A representative of a Red Cross Society of a nation contributing to forces to the United Nations Command shall serve as chairman of this team.

(4) In order to facilitate the functioning of each joint Red Cross team, subteams composed of not less than two (2) members from this team, with an equal number of representatives from each side, may be formed as circumstances require.

(5) Additional personnel such as drivers, clerks, and interpreters, and such equipment as may be required by the joint Red Cross teams to perform their missions, shall be furnished by the Commander of each side to the team operating in the territory under his military control.

(6) Whenever jointly agreed upon by the representatives of both sides on any joint Red Cross team, the size of such team may be increased or decreased, subject to confirmation by the committee for Repatriation of Prisoners of War.

(c) The Commander of each side shall cooperate fully with the joint Red Cross teams in the performance of their functions, and undertakes to insure the security of the personnel of the Joint Red Cross team in the area under his military control. The Commander of each side shall provide such logistic, administrative, and communications facilities as may be required by the team operating in the territory under his military control.

(d) The joint Red Cross teams shall be dissolved upon completion of the program of repatriation of all of the prisoners of war specified in Sub-paragraph 51 (a) hereof, who insist upon repatriation.

58. (a) The Commander of each side shall furnish to the Commander of the other side as soon as practicable, but not later than ten (10) days after this Armistice Agreement becomes effective, the following information concerning prisoners of war:

(1) Complete data pertaining to the prisoners of war who escaped since the effective date of the data last exchanged.

(2) Insofar as practicable, information regarding name, nationality, rank, and other identification data, date and cause of death, and place of burial, of those prisoners of war who died while in his custody.

(b) If any prisoners of war escape or die after the effective date of the supplementary information specified above, the detaining side shall furnish to the other side, through the Committee for Repatriation of Prisoners of War, the data pertaining thereto in accordance with the provisions of Subparagraph 58 (a) hereof. Such data shall be furnished at ten-day intervals until the completion of the program of delivery and reception of prisoners of war.

(c) Any escaped prisoner of war who returns to the custody of the detaining side after the completion of the program of delivery and reception of prisoners of war shall be delivered to the Military Armistice Commission for disposition.

59. (a) All civilians who, at the time this Armistice Agreement become effective, are in territory under the military control of the Commander-in-Chief, United Nations Command, and who, on 24 June 1950, resided north of the Military Demarcation Line established in this Armistice Agreement shall, if they desire to return home, be permitted and assisted by the Commander-in-Chief, United Nations Command, to return to the area north of the military Demarcation Line; and all civilians who, at the time this Armistice Agreement becomes effective, are in territory under the military control of the Supreme Commander of the Korean People's Army and the Commander of the Chinese People's Volunteers, and who on 24 June 1950, resided south of the Military Demarcation Line established in this Armistice Agreement shall, if they desire to return home, be permitted and assisted by the Supreme Commander of the Korean People's Army and the Commander of the Chinese People's Volunteers to return to the area south Military Demarcation Line. The Commander of each side shall be responsible for publicizing widely throughout the territory under his military

control the contents of the provisions of this Sub-paragraph, and for calling upon the appropriate civil authorities to give necessary guidance and assistance to all such civilians who desire to return home.

(b) All civilians of foreign nationality who, at the time this Armistice Agreement becomes effective, are in territory under the military control of the Supreme Commander of the Korean People's Army and the Commander of the Chinese People's Volunteers shall if they desire to proceed to territory under the military control of the Commander-in-Chief, United Nations command, be permitted and assisted to do so; all civilians of foreign nationality who, at the time this Armistice Agreement becomes effective, are in territory under the military control of the Commander-in-Chief, United Nations Command, shall, if they desire to proceed to territory under the military Control of the Supreme Commander of the Korean People's Army and the Commander of the Chinese People's Volunteers, be permitted and assisted to do so. The Commander of each side shall be responsible for publicizing widely throughout the territory under his military control of contents of the provisions of this subparagraph, and for calling upon the appropriate civil authorizes to give necessary guidance and assistance to all such civilians of foreign nationality who desire to proceed to territory under the military control of the Commander of the other side.

(c) Measures to assist in the return of civilians provided for in Subparagraph 59 (a) hereof and the movement of civilians provided for in Subparagraph 59 (b) hereof shall be commenced by both sides as soon as possible after this Armistice Agreement becomes effective.

(d) (1) A Committee for Assisting the Return of Displace Civilians is hereby established. It shall be composed of four (4) officers of field grade, two (2) of whom shall be appointed jointly by the Commander-in-Chief, United Nations Command, and two (2) of whom shall be appointed jointly by the Supreme Commander of the Korean People's Army and the Commander of the Chinese People's Volunteers. This committee shall, under the general supervision and direction of the Military Armistice Commission, be responsible for coordinating the specific plans of both sides for assistance to the return of the above-mentioned civilians. It shall be the duty of this Committee to make necessary arrangements, in-cluding those of transportation, for expediting and coordinating the movement of the above-mentioned civilians; to select the crossing point(s) through which the above-mentioned civilians will cross the Military Demarcation Line; to arrange for security at the crossing point(s); and to carry out such other functions as are required to accomplish the return of the above-mentioned civilians.

(2) When unable to reach agreement on any matter relating to its responsibilities, the Committee for Assisting the return of Displaced Civilians shall immediately refer such matter to the Military Armistice Commission for decision. The Committee for assisting the Return of Displaced Civilians shall maintain its headquarters in proximity to the headquarters of the Military Armistice Commission.

(3) The Committee for Assisting the Return of Displaced Civilians shall be dissolved by the Military Armistice Commission upon fulfillment of its mission.

ARTICLE IV

Recommendations to the Governments Concerned on Both Sides

60. In order to insure the peaceful settlement of the Korean question, the military Commanders of both sides hereby recommend to the governments of the countries concerned on both sides that, within three (3) months after the Armistice Agreement is signed and becomes effective, a political conference of a higher level of both sides be held by representatives appointed respectively to settle through negotiation the questions of the withdrawal of all foreign forces from Korea, the peaceful settlement of the Korean question, etc.

ARTICLE V
MISCELLANEOUS

61. Amendments and additions to this Armistice Agreement must be mutually agreed to by the Commanders of the opposing sides.

62. The Articles and Paragraphs of this Armistice Agreement shall remain in effect until expressly superseded either by mutually acceptable amendments and additions or by provision in an appropriate agreement for a peaceful settlement at a political level between both sides.

63. All of the provisions of this Armistice Agreement, other than Paragraph 12, shall become effective at 2200 hours on 27 July 1953.

Done at Panmunjom, Korea at 10:00 hours on the 27th day of July 1953, in English, Korean and Chinese, all texts being equally authentic.

NAM IL
General, Korea People's Army
Senior Delegate,
Delegation of the Korean People's Army
and the Chinese People's Volunteers

WILLIAM K. HARRISON, JR.
Lieutenant General, United States Army
Senior Delegate,
United Nations Command Delegation

Senate Resolution 301:
Censure of Senator Joseph McCarthy

Resolved, That the Senator from Wisconsin, Mr. McCarthy, failed to cooperate with the Subcommittee on Privileges and Elections of the Senate Committee on Rules and Administration in clearing up matters referred to that subcommittee which concerned his conduct as a Senator and affected the honor of the Senate and, instead, repeatedly abused the subcommittee and its members who were trying to carry out assigned duties, thereby obstructing the constitutional processes of the Senate, and that this conduct of the Senator from Wisconsin, Mr. McCarthy, is contrary to senatorial traditions and is hereby condemned.

Sec 2. The Senator from Wisconsin, Mr. McCarthy, in writing to the chairman of the Select Committee to Study Censure Charges (Mr. Watkins) after the Select Committee had issued its report and before the report was presented to the Senate charging three members of the Select Committee with "deliberate deception" and "fraud" for failure to disqualify themselves; in stating to the press on November 4, 1954, that the special Senate session that was to begin November 8, 1954, was a "lynch-party"; in repeatedly describing this special Senate session as a "lynch bee" in a nationwide television and radio show on November 7, 1954; in stating to the public press on November 13, 1954, that the chairman of the Select Committee (Mr. Watkins) was guilty of "the most unusual, most cowardly things I've ever heard of" and stating further: "I expected he would be afraid to answer the questions, but didn't think he'd be stupid enough to make a public statement"; and in characterizing the said committee as the "unwitting handmaiden," "involuntary agent" and "attorneys-in-fact" of the Communist Party and in charging that the said committee in writing its report "imitated Communist methods—that it distorted, misrepresented, and omitted in its effort to manufacture a plausible rationalization" in support of its recommendations to the Senate, which characterizations and charges were contained in a statement released to the press and inserted in the Congressional Record of November 10, 1954, acted contrary to senatorial ethics and tended to bring the Senate into dishonor and disrepute, to obstruct the constitutional processes of the Senate, and to impair its dignity; and such conduct is hereby condemned.

Brown v. Board of Education

SUPREME COURT OF THE UNITED STATES
Brown v. Board of Education, 347 U.S. 483 (1954)
(USSC+)

Argued December 9, 1952

Reargued December 8, 1953

Decided May 17, 1954

APPEAL FROM THE UNITED STATES DIS-
TRICT COURT FOR THE DISTRICT OF KAN-
SAS*

Syllabus

Segregation of white and Negro children in the
public schools of a State solely on the basis of race,
pursuant to state laws permitting or requiring such
segregation, denies to Negro children the equal protection of the laws guaranteed by the Fourteenth
Amendment—even though the physical facilities
and other "tangible" factors of white and Negro
schools may be equal.

(a) The history of the Fourteenth Amendment is inconclusive as to its intended effect on public education.

(b) The question presented in these cases must
be determined not on the basis of conditions existing
when the Fourteenth Amendment was adopted, but
in the light of the full development of public education and its present place in American life throughout the Nation.

(c) Where a State has undertaken to provide an
opportunity for an education in its public schools,
such an opportunity is a right which must be made
available to all on equal terms.

(d) Segregation of children in public schools
solely on the basis of race deprives children of the
minority group of equal educational opportunities,
even though the physical facilities and other "tangible" factors may be equal.

(e) The "separate but equal" doctrine adopted in
Plessy v. Ferguson, 163 U.S. 537, has no place in the
field of public education.

(f) The cases are restored to the docket for further argument on specified questions relating to the
forms of the decrees.

Opinion

MR. CHIEF JUSTICE WARREN delivered the
opinion of the Court.

These cases come to us from the States of Kansas, South Carolina, Virginia, and Delaware. They
are premised on different facts and different local
conditions, but a common legal question justifies
their consideration together in this consolidated
opinion.

In each of the cases, minors of the Negro race,
through their legal representatives, seek the aid of
the courts in obtaining admission to the public
schools of their community on a nonsegregated basis.
In each instance, they had been denied admission to
schools attended by white children under laws requiring or permitting segregation according to race. This
segregation was alleged to deprive the plaintiffs of
the equal protection of the laws under the Fourteenth Amendment. In each of the cases other than
the Delaware case, a three-judge federal district court
denied relief to the plaintiffs on the so-called "separate but equal" doctrine announced by this Court in
Plessy v. Ferguson, 163 U.S. 537. Under that doctrine, equality of treatment is accorded when the
races are provided substantially equal facilities, even
though these facilities be separate. In the Delaware
case, the Supreme Court of Delaware adhered to that
doctrine, but ordered that the plaintiffs be admitted
to the white schools because of their superiority to
the Negro schools.

The plaintiffs contend that segregated public
schools are not "equal" and cannot be made "equal,"
and that hence they are deprived of the equal protection of the laws. Because of the obvious importance
of the question presented, the Court took jurisdiction. Argument was heard in the 1952 Term, and reargument was heard this Term on certain questions
propounded by the Court.

Reargument was largely devoted to the circumstances surrounding the adoption of the Fourteenth
Amendment in 1868. It covered exhaustively consideration of the Amendment in Congress, ratification
by the states, then-existing practices in racial segregation, and the views of proponents and opponents

of the Amendment. This discussion and our own investigation convince us that, although these sources cast some light, it is not enough to resolve the problem with which we are faced. At best, they are inconclusive. The most avid proponents of the post-War Amendments undoubtedly intended them to remove all legal distinctions among "all persons born or naturalized in the United States." Their opponents, just as certainly, were antagonistic to both the letter and the spirit of the Amendments and wished them to have the most limited effect. What others in Congress and the state legislatures had in mind cannot be determined with any degree of certainty.

An additional reason for the inconclusive nature of the Amendment's history with respect to segregated schools is the status of public education at that time. In the South, the movement toward free common schools, supported by general taxation, had not yet taken hold. Education of white children was largely in the hands of private groups. Education of Negroes was almost nonexistent, and practically all of the race were illiterate. In fact, any education of Negroes was forbidden by law in some states. Today, in contrast, many Negroes have achieved outstanding success in the arts and sciences, as well as in the business and professional world. It is true that public school education at the time of the Amendment had advanced further in the North, but the effect of the Amendment on Northern States was generally ignored in the congressional debates. Even in the North, the conditions of public education did not approximate those existing today. The curriculum was usually rudimentary; ungraded schools were common in rural areas; the school term was but three months a year in many states, and compulsory school attendance was virtually unknown. As a consequence, it is not surprising that there should be so little in the history of the Fourteenth Amendment relating to its intended effect on public education.

In the first cases in this Court construing the Fourteenth Amendment, decided shortly after its adoption, the Court interpreted it as proscribing all state-imposed discriminations against the Negro race. The doctrine of "separate but equal" did not make its appearance in this Court until 1896 in the case of Plessy v. Ferguson, supra, involving not education but transportation. American courts have since labored with the doctrine for over half a century. In this Court, there have been six cases involving the "separate but equal" doctrine in the field of public education. In Cumming v. County Board of Education, 175 U.S. 528, and Gong Lum v. Rice, 275 U.S. 78, the validity of the doctrine itself was not challenged. In more recent cases, all on the graduate school level, inequality was found in that specific benefits enjoyed by white students were denied to Negro students of the same educational qualifications. Missouri ex rel. Gaines v. Canada, 305 U.S. 337; Sipuel v. Oklahoma, 332 U.S. 631; Sweatt v. Painter, 339 U.S. 629; McLaurin v. Oklahoma State Regents, 339 U.S. 637. In none of these cases was it necessary to reexamine the doctrine to grant relief to the Negro plaintiff. And in Sweatt v. Painter, supra, the Court expressly reserved decision on the question whether Plessy v. Ferguson should be held inapplicable to public education.

In the instant cases, that question is directly presented. Here, unlike Sweatt v. Painter, there are findings below that the Negro and white schools involved have been equalized, or are being equalized, with respect to buildings, curricula, qualifications and salaries of teachers, and other "tangible" factors. Our decision, therefore, cannot turn on merely a comparison of these tangible factors in the Negro and white schools involved in each of the cases. We must look instead to the effect of segregation itself on public education.

In approaching this problem, we cannot turn the clock back to 1868, when the Amendment was adopted, or even to 1896, when Plessy v. Ferguson was written. We must consider public education in the light of its full development and its present place in American life throughout the Nation. Only in this way can it be determined if segregation in public schools deprives these plaintiffs of the equal protection of the laws.

Today, education is perhaps the most important function of state and local governments. Compulsory school attendance laws and the great expenditures for education both demonstrate our recognition of the importance of education to our democratic society. It is required in the performance of our most basic public responsibilities, even service in the armed forces. It is the very foundation of good citizenship. Today it is a principal instrument in awakening the child to cultural values, in preparing him for later professional training, and in helping him to adjust normally to his environment. In these days, it is doubtful that any child may reasonably be expected to succeed in life if he is denied the opportunity of an education. Such an opportunity, where the state has undertaken to provide it, is a right which must be made available to all on equal terms.

We come then to the question presented: Does segregation of children in public schools solely on the basis of race, even though the physical facilities and other "tangible" factors may be equal, deprive the children of the minority group of equal educational opportunities? We believe that it does.

In Sweatt v. Painter, supra, in finding that a segregated law school for Negroes could not provide them equal educational opportunities, this Court relied in large part on "those qualities which are incapable of objective measurement but which make for greatness in a law school." In McLaurin v. Oklahoma State Regents, supra, the Court, in requiring that a Negro admitted to a white graduate school be treated like all other students, again resorted to intangible considerations: ". . . his ability to study, to engage in discussions and exchange views with other students, and, in general, to learn his profession." Such considerations apply with added force to children in grade and high schools. To separate them from others of similar age and qualifications solely because of their race generates a feeling of inferiority as to their status in the community that may affect their hearts and minds in a way unlikely ever to be undone. The effect of this separation on their educational opportunities was well stated by a finding in the Kansas case by a court which nevertheless felt compelled to rule against the Negro plaintiffs:

Segregation of white and colored children in public schools has a detrimental effect upon the colored children. The impact is greater when it has the sanction of the law, for the policy of separating the races is usually interpreted as denoting the inferiority of the negro group. A sense of inferiority affects the motivation of a child to learn. Segregation with the sanction of law, therefore, has a tendency to [retard] the educational and mental development of negro children and to deprive them of some of the benefits they would receive in a racial[ly] integrated school system.

Whatever may have been the extent of psychological knowledge at the time of Plessy v. Ferguson, this finding is amply supported by modern authority. Any language in Plessy v. Ferguson contrary to this finding is rejected.

We conclude that, in the field of public education, the doctrine of "separate but equal" has no place. Separate educational facilities are inherently unequal. Therefore, we hold that the plaintiffs and others similarly situated for whom the actions have been brought are, by reason of the segregation complained of, deprived of the equal protection of the laws guaranteed by the Fourteenth Amendment. This disposition makes unnecessary any discussion whether such segregation also violates the Due Process Clause of the Fourteenth Amendment.

Because these are class actions, because of the wide applicability of this decision, and because of the great variety of local conditions, the formulation of decrees in these cases presents problems of considerable complexity. On reargument, the consideration of appropriate relief was necessarily subordinated to the primary question—the constitutionality of segregation in public education. We have now announced that such segregation is a denial of the equal protection of the laws. In order that we may have the full assistance of the parties in formulating decrees, the cases will be restored to the docket, and the parties are requested to present further argument on Questions 4 and 5 previously propounded by the Court for the reargument this Term The Attorney General of the United States is again invited to participate. The Attorneys General of the states requiring or permitting segregation in public education will also be permitted to appear as amici curiae upon request to do so by September 15, 1954, and submission of briefs by October 1, 1954.

It is so ordered.

* Together with No. 2, Briggs et al. v. Elliott et al., on appeal from the United States District Court for the Eastern District of South Carolina, argued December 9–10, 1952, reargued December 7–8, 1953; No. 4, Davis et al. v. County School Board of Prince Edward County, Virginia, et al., on appeal from the United States District Court for the Eastern District of Virginia, argued December 10, 1952, reargued December 7–8, 1953, and No. 10, Gebhart et al. v. Belton et al., on certiorari to the Supreme Court of Delaware, argued December 11, 1952, reargued December 9, 1953.

The National Interstate and Defense Highways Act

AN ACT

To amend and supplement the Federal-Aid Road Act approved July 11, 1916, to authorize appropriations for continuing the construction of highways; to amend the Internal Revenue Code of 1954 to provide additional revenue from the taxes on motor fuel, tires, and trucks and buses; and for other purposes.

Be it enacted by the Senate and House of Representatives of the United States of America in Congress assembled,

TITLE I—FEDERAL-AID HIGHWAY ACT OF 1956

SEC. 101.
SHORT TITLE FOR TITLE I.

This title may be cited as the "Federal-Aid Highway Act of 1956."

SEC. 102.
FEDERAL-AID HIGHWAYS.

(a) (1) AUTHORIZATION OF APPROPRIATIONS.—For the purpose of carrying out the provisions of the Federal-Aid Road Act approved July 11, 1916 (39 Stat. 355), and all Acts amendatory thereof and supplementary thereto, there is hereby authorized to be appropriated for the fiscal year ending June 30, 1957, $125,000,000 in addition to any sums heretofore authorized for such fiscal year; the sum of $850,000,000 for the fiscal year ending June 30, 1958; and the sum of $875,000,000 for the fiscal year ending June 30, 1959. The sums herein authorized for each fiscal year shall be available for expenditure as follows:

(A) 45 per centum for projects on the Federal-aid primary highway system.

(B) 30 per centum for projects on the Federal-aid secondary highway system.

(C) 25 per centum for projects on extensions of these systems within urban areas.

(2) APPORTIONMENTS.—The sums authorized by this section shall be apportioned among the several States in the manner now provided by law and in accordance with the formulas set forth in section 4 of the Federal-Aid Highway Act of 1944; approved December 20, 1944 (58 Stat. 838) : Provided, That the additional amount herein authorized for the fiscal year ending June 30, 1957, shall be apportioned immediately upon enactment of this Act.

(b) AVAILABILITY FOR EXPENDITURE.—Any sums apportioned to any State under this section shall be available for expenditure in that State for two years after the close of the fiscal year for which such sums are authorized, and any amounts so apportioned remaining unexpended at the end of such period shall lapse: Provided, That such funds shall be deemed to have been expended if a sum equal to the total of the sums herein and heretofore apportioned to the State is covered by formal agreements with the Secretary of Commerce for construction, reconstruction, or improvement of specific projects as provided in this title and prior Acts: Provided further, That in the case of those sums heretofore, herein, or hereafter apportioned to any State for projects on the Federal-aid secondary highway system, the Secretary of Commerce may, upon the request of any State, discharge his responsibility relative to the plans, specifications, estimates, surveys, contract awards, design, inspection, and construction of such secondary road projects by his receiving and approving a certified statement by the State highway department setting forth that the plans, design, and construction for such projects are in accord with the standards and procedures of such State applicable...

SEC. 108.
NATIONAL SYSTEM OF INTERSTATE AND DEFENSE HIGHWAYS.

(a) INTERSTATE SYSTEM.—It is hereby declared to be essential to the national interest to provide for the early completion of the "National System of Interstate Highways," as authorized and designated in accordance with section 7 of the Federal-Aid Highway Act of 1944 (58 Stat. 838). It is the intent of the Congress that the Interstate System be completed as nearly as practicable over a thirteen-year period and that the entire System in all the States be brought to simultaneous completion. Because of its primary importance to the national defense, the name of such system is hereby changed to the "National System of Interstate and Defense Highways." Such National System of Interstate and Defense Highways is hereinafter in this Act referred to as the "Interstate System."

(b) AUTHORIZATION OF APPROPRIATIONS.—For the purpose of expediting the construction, reconstruction, or improvement, inclusive of necessary bridges and tunnels, of the interstate System, including extensions thereof through urban areas, designated in accordance with the provisions of section 7 of the Federal-Aid Highway Act of 1944 (58 Stat. 838), there is hereby authorized to be appropriated the additional sum of $1,000,000,000 for, the fiscal year ending June 30, 1957, which sum shall be in addition to the authorization heretofore made for that year, the additional sum of $1,700,000,000 for the fiscal year ending June 30, 1958, the addi-

tional sum of $2,000,000,000 for the fiscal year ending June 30, 1959, the additional sum of $2,200,000,000 for the fiscal year ending June 30, 1960, the additional sum of $2,200,000,000 for the fiscal year ending June 30, 1961, the additional sum of $2,200,000,000 for the fiscal year ending June 30, 1962, the additional sum of $2,200,000,000 for the fiscal year ending June 30, 1963, the additional sum of $2,200,000,000 for the fiscal year ending June 30, 1964, the additional sum of $2,200,000,000 for the fiscal year ending June 30, 1965, the additional sum of $2,200,000,000 for the fiscal year ending June 30, 1966, the additional sum of $2,200,000,000 for the fiscal year ending June 30, 1967, the additional sum of $1,500,000,000 for the fiscal year ending June 30, 1968, and the additional sum of $1,025,000,000 for the fiscal year ending June 30, 1969.

(The first page of this document is provided. For the complete act, see The Federal Highway Act of 1956 (PL 627, 29 June 1956), 70 *United States Statutes At Large*, pp. 374–402.)

Executive Order 10730:
Desegregation of Central High School

EXECUTIVE ORDER 10730

PROVIDING ASSISTANCE FOR THE REMOVAL OF AN OBSTRUCTION OF JUSTICE WITHIN THE STATE OF ARKANSAS

WHEREAS on September 23, 1957, I issued Proclamation No. 3204 reading in part as follows:

"WHEREAS certain persons in the state of Arkansas, individually and in unlawful assemblages, combinations, and conspiracies, have wifully obstructed the enforcement of orders of the United States District Court for the Eastern District of Arkansas with respect to matters relating to enrollment and attendance at public schools, particularly at Central High School, located in Little Rock School District, Little Rock, Arkansas; and

"WHEREAS such wilful obstruction of justice hinders the execution of the laws of that State and of the United States, and makes it impracticable to enforce such laws by the ordinary course of judicial proceedings; and

"WHEREAS such obstruction of justice constitutes a denial of the equal protection of the laws secured by the Constitution of the United States and impedes the course of justice under those laws:

"NOW, THEREFORE, I, DWIGHT D. EISENHOWER, President of the United States, under and by virtue of the authority vested in me by the Constitution and Statutes of the United States, including Chapter 15 of Title 10 of the United States Code, particularly sections 332, 333 and 334 thereof, do command all persons engaged in such obstruction of justice to cease and desist therefrom, and to disperse forthwith;" and

WHEREAS the command contained in that Proclamation has not been obeyed and wilful obstruction of enforcement of said court orders still exists and threatens to continue:

NOW, THEREFORE, by virtue of the authority vested in me by the Constitution and Statutes of the United States, including Chapter 15 of Title 10, particularly sections 332, 333 and 334 thereof, and section 301 of Title 3 of the United States Code, It is hereby ordered as follows:

SECTION 1. I hereby authorize and direct the Secretary of Defense to order into the active military service of the United States as he may deem appropriate to carry out the purposes of this Order, any or all of the units of the National Guard of the United States and of the Air National Guard of the United States within the State of Arkansas to serve in the active military service of the United States for an indefinite period and until relieved by appropriate orders.

SEC. 2. The Secretary of Defense is authorized and directed to take all appropriate steps to enforce any orders of the United States District Court for the Eastern District of Arkansas for the removal of obstruction of justice in the State of Arkansas with respect to matters relating to enrollment and attendance at public schools in the Little Rock School District, Little Rock, Arkansas. In carrying out the provisions of this section, the Secretary of Defense is authorized to use the units, and members thereof, ordered into the active military service of the United States pursuant to Section 1 of this Order.

SEC. 3. In furtherance of the enforcement of the aforementioned orders of the United States District Court for the Eastern District of Arkansas, the Secretary of Defense is authorized to use such of the armed forces of the United States as he may deem necessary.

SEC. 4. The Secretary of Defense is authorized to delegate to the Secretary of the Army or the Secretary of the Air Force, or both, any of the authority conferred upon him by this Order.

DWIGHT D. EISENHOWER
THE WHITE HOUSE,
September 24, 1957.

President Dwight D. Eisenhower's Farewell Address

MY FELLOW AMERICANS:

Three days from now, after half a century in the service of our country, I shall lay down the responsibilities of office as, in traditional and solemn ceremony, the authority of the Presidency is vested in my successor.

This evening I come to you with a message of leave-taking and farewell, and to share a few final thoughts with you, my countrymen.

Like every other citizen, I wish the new President, and all who will labor with him, Godspeed. I pray that the coming years will be blessed with peace and prosperity for all.

Our people expect their President and the Congress to find essential agreement on issues of great moment, the wise resolution of which will better shape the future of the Nation.

My own relations with the Congress, which began on a remote and tenuous basis when, long ago, a member of the Senate appointed me to West Point, have since ranged to the intimate during the war and immediate post-war period, and, finally, to the mutually interdependent during these past eight years.

In this final relationship, the Congress and the Administration have, on most vital issues, cooperated well, to serve the national good rather than mere partisanship, and so have assured that the business of the Nation should go forward. So, my official relationship with the Congress ends in a feeling, on my part, of gratitude that we have been able to do so much together.

II

We now stand ten years past the midpoint of a century that has witnessed four major wars among great nations. Three of these involved our own country. Despite these holocausts America is today the strongest, the most influential and most productive nation in the world. Understandably proud of this preeminence, we yet realize that America's leadership and prestige depend, not merely upon our unmatched material progress, riches and military strength, but on how we use our power in the interests of world peace and human betterment.

III

Throughout America's adventure in free government, our basic purposes have been to keep the peace; to foster progress in human achievement, and to enhance liberty, dignity and integrity among people and among nations. To strive for less would be unworthy of a free and religious people. Any failure traceable to arrogance, or our lack of comprehension or readiness to sacrifice would inflict upon us grievous hurt both at home and abroad.

Progress toward these noble goals is persistently threatened by the conflict now engulfing the world. It commands our whole attention, absorbs our very beings. We face a hostile ideology—global in scope, atheistic in character, ruthless in purpose, and insidious in method. Unhappily the danger it poses promises to be of indefinite duration. To meet it successfully, there is called for, not so much the emotional and transitory sacrifices of crisis, but rather those which enable us to carry forward steadily, surely, and without complaint the burdens of a prolonged and complex struggle—with liberty at stake. Only thus shall we remain, despite every provocation, on our charted course toward permanent peace and human betterment.

Crises there will continue to be. In meeting them, whether foreign or domestic, great or small, there is a recurring temptation to feel that some spectacular and costly action could become the miraculous solution to all current difficulties. A huge increase in newer elements of our defense; development of unrealistic programs to cure every ill in agriculture; a dramatic expansion in basic and applied research—these and many other possibilities, each possibly promising in itself, may be suggested as the only way to the road we which to travel.

But each proposal must be weighed in the light of a broader consideration: the need to maintain balance in and among national programs—balance between the private and the public economy, balance between cost and hoped for advantage—balance between the clearly necessary and the comfortably desirable; balance between our essential requirements as a nation and the duties imposed by the nation upon the individual; balance between action of the moment and the national welfare of the future. Good judgment seeks balance and progress; lack of it eventually finds imbalance and frustration.

The record of many decades stands as proof that our people and their government have, in the main, understood these truths and have responded to them well, in the face of stress and threat. But threats, new in kind or degree, constantly arise. I mention two only.

IV

A vital element in keeping the peace is our military establishment. Our arms must be mighty, ready for instant action, so that no potential aggressor may be tempted to risk his own destruction.

Our military organization today bears little relation to that known by any of my predecessors in peace time, or indeed by the fighting men of World War II or Korea.

Until the latest of our world conflicts, the United States had no armaments industry. American makers of plowshares could, with time and as required, make swords as well. But now we can no longer risk emergency improvisation of national defense; we have been compelled to create a permanent armaments industry of vast proportions. Added to this, three and a half million men and women are directly engaged in the defense establishment. We annually spend on military security more than the net income of all United States corporations.

This conjunction of an immense military establishment and a large arms industry is new in the American experience. The total influence—economic, political, even spiritual—is felt in every city, every state house, every office of the Federal government. We recognize the imperative need for this development. Yet we must not fail to comprehend its grave implications. Our toil, resources and livelihood are all involved; so is the very structure of our society.

In the councils of government, we must guard against the acquisition of unwarranted influence, whether sought or unsought, by the military-industrial complex. The potential for the disastrous rise of misplaced power exists and will persist.

We must never let the weight of this combination endanger our liberties or democratic processes. We should take nothing for granted only an alert and knowledgeable citizenry can compel the proper meshing of huge industrial and military machinery of defense with our peaceful methods and goals, so that security and liberty may prosper together.

Akin to, and largely responsible for the sweeping changes in our industrial-military posture, has been the technological revolution during recent decades.

In this revolution, research has become central; it also becomes more formalized, complex, and costly. A steadily increasing share is conducted for, by, or at the direction of, the Federal government.

Today, the solitary inventor, tinkering in his shop, has been over shadowed by task forces of scientists in laboratories and testing fields. In the same fashion, the free university, historically the fountainhead of free ideas and scientific discovery, has experienced a revolution in the conduct of research. Partly because of the huge costs involved, a government contract becomes virtually a substitute for intellectual curiosity. For every old blackboard there are now hundreds of new electronic computers.

The prospect of domination of the nation's scholars by Federal employment, project allocations, and the power of money is ever present and is gravely to be regarded.

Yet, in holding scientific research and discovery in respect, as we should, we must also be alert to the equal and opposite danger that public policy could itself become the captive of a scientific-technological elite.

It is the task of statesmanship to mold, to balance, and to integrate these and other forces, new and old, within the principles of our democratic system—ever aiming toward the supreme goals of our free society.

V

Another factor in maintaining balance involves the element of time. As we peer into society's future, we—you and I, and our government—must avoid the impulse to live only for today, plundering, for our own ease and convenience, the precious resources of tomorrow. We cannot mortgage the material assets of our grandchildren without risking the loss also of their political and spiritual heritage. We want democracy to survive for all generations to come, not to become the insolvent phantom of tomorrow.

VI

Down the long lane of the history yet to be written America knows that this world of ours, ever growing smaller, must avoid becoming a community of dreadful fear and hate, and be, instead, a proud confederation of mutual trust and respect.

Such a confederation must be one of equals. The weakest must come to the conference table with the same confidence as do we, protected as we are by our moral, economic, and military strength. That table, though scarred by many past frustrations, cannot be abandoned for the certain agony of the battlefield.

Disarmament, with mutual honor and confidence, is a continuing imperative. Together we must learn how to compose difference, not with arms, but with intellect and decent purpose. Because this need is so sharp and apparent I confess that I lay down my official responsibilities in this field with a definite sense of disappointment. As one who has witnessed the horror and the lingering sadness of war—as one who knows that another war could utterly destroy this civilization which has been so slowly and painfully built over thousands of years—I wish I could say tonight that a lasting peace is in sight.

Happily, I can say that war has been avoided. Steady progress toward our ultimate goal has been made. But, so much remains to be done. As a private citizen, I shall never cease to do what little I can to help the world advance along that road.

VII

So—in this my last good night to you as your President—I thank you for the many opportunities you have given me for public service in war and peace. I trust that in that service you find somethings worthy; as for the rest of it, I know you will find ways to improve performance in the future.

You and I—my fellow citizens—need to be strong in our faith that all nations, under God, will reach the goal of peace with justice. May we be ever unswerving in devotion to principle, confident but humble with power, diligent in pursuit of the Nation's great goals.

To all the peoples of the world, I once more give expression to America's prayerful and continuing inspiration:

We pray that peoples of all faiths, all races, all nations, may have their great human needs satisfied; that those now denied opportunity shall come to enjoy it to the full; that all who yearn for freedom may experience its spiritual blessings; that those who have freedom will understand, also, its heavy responsibilities; that all who are insensitive to the needs of others will learn charity; that the scourges of poverty, disease and ignorance will be made to disappear from the earth, and that, in the goodness of time, all peoples will come to live together in a peace guaranteed by the binding force of mutual respect and love.

President John F. Kennedy's Inaugural Address

Vice President Johnson, Mr. Speaker, Mr. Chief Justice, President Eisenhower, Vice President Nixon, President Truman, Reverend Clergy, fellow citizens:

We observe today not a victory of party but a celebration of freedom—symbolizing an end as well as a beginning—signifying renewal as well as change. For I have sworn before you and Almighty God the same solemn oath our forbears prescribed nearly a century and three-quarters ago.

The world is very different now. For man holds in his mortal hands the power to abolish all forms of human poverty and all forms of human life. And yet the same revolutionary beliefs for which our forebears fought are still at issue around the globe—the belief that the rights of man come not from the generosity of the state but from the hand of God.

We dare not forget today that we are the heirs of that first revolution. Let the word go forth from this time and place, to friend and foe alike, that the torch has been passed to a new generation of Americans—born in this century, tempered by war, disciplined by a hard and bitter peace, proud of our ancient heritage—and unwilling to witness or permit the slow undoing of those human rights to which this nation has always been committed, and to which we are committed today at home and around the world.

Let every nation know, whether it wishes us well or ill, that we shall pay any price, bear any burden, meet any hardship, support any friend, oppose any foe to assure the survival and the success of liberty.

This much we pledge—and more.

To those old allies whose cultural and spiritual origins we share, we pledge the loyalty of faithful friends. United there is little we cannot do in a host of cooperative ventures. Divided there is little we can do—for we dare not meet a powerful challenge at odds and split asunder.

To those new states whom we welcome to the ranks of the free, we pledge our word that one form of colonial control shall not have passed away merely to be replaced by a far more iron tyranny. We shall not always expect to find them supporting our view. But we shall always hope to find them strongly supporting their own freedom—and to remember that, in the past, those who foolishly sought power by riding the back of the tiger ended up inside.

To those people in the huts and villages of half the globe struggling to break the bonds of mass misery, we pledge our best efforts to help them help themselves, for whatever period is required—not because the communists may be doing it, not because we seek their votes, but because it is right. If a free society cannot help the many who are poor, it cannot save the few who are rich.

To our sister republics south of our border, we offer a special pledge—to convert our good words into good deeds—in a new alliance for progress—to assist free men and free governments in casting off the chains of poverty. But this peaceful revolution of hope cannot become the prey of hostile powers. Let all our neighbors know that we shall join with them to oppose aggression or subversion anywhere in the Americas. And let every other power know that this Hemisphere intends to remain the master of its own house.

To that world assembly of sovereign states, the United Nations, our last best hope in an age where the instruments of war have far outpaced the instruments of peace, we renew our pledge of support—to prevent it from becoming merely a forum for invective—to strengthen its shield of the new and the weak—and to enlarge the area in which its writ may run.

Finally, to those nations who would make themselves our adversary, we offer not a pledge but a request: that both sides begin anew the quest for peace, before the dark powers of destruction unleashed by science engulf all humanity in planned or accidental self-destruction.

We dare not tempt them with weakness. For only when our arms are sufficient beyond doubt can we be certain beyond doubt that they will never be employed.

But neither can two great and powerful groups of nations take comfort from our present course—both sides overburdened by the cost of modern weapons, both rightly alarmed by the steady spread of the deadly atom, yet both racing to alter that uncertain balance of terror that stays the hand of mankind's final war.

So let us begin anew—remembering on both sides that civility is not a sign of weakness, and sincerity is always subject to proof. Let us never negotiate out of fear. But let us never fear to negotiate.

Let both sides explore what problems unite us instead of belaboring those problems which divide us.

Let both sides, for the first time, formulate serious and precise proposals for the inspection and control of arms—and bring the absolute power to destroy other nations under the absolute control of all nations.

Let both sides seek to invoke the wonders of science instead of its terrors. Together let us explore the stars, conquer the deserts, eradicate disease, tap the ocean depths and encourage the arts and commerce.

Let both sides unite to heed in all corners of the earth the command of Isaiah—to "undo the heavy burdens . . . (and) let the oppressed go free."

And if a beachhead of cooperation may push back the jungle of suspicion, let both sides join in creating a new endeavor, not a new balance of power, but a new world of law, where the strong are just and the weak secure and the peace preserved.

All this will not be finished in the first one hundred days. Nor will it be finished in the first one thousand days, nor in the life of this Administration, nor even perhaps in our lifetime on this planet. But let us begin.

In your hands, my fellow citizens, more than mine, will rest the final success or failure of our course. Since this country was founded, each generation of Americans has been summoned to give testimony to its national loyalty. The graves of young Americans who answered the call to service surround the globe.

Now the trumpet summons us again—not as a call to bear arms, though arms we need—not as a call to battle, though embattled we are— but a call to bear the burden of a long twilight struggle, year in and year out, "rejoicing in hope, patient in tribulation"—a struggle against the common enemies of man: tyranny, poverty, disease and war itself.

Can we forge against these enemies a grand and global alliance, North and South, East and West, that can assure a more fruitful life for all mankind? Will you join in that historic effort?

In the long history of the world, only a few generations have been granted the role of defending freedom in its hour of maximum danger. I do not shrink from this responsibility—I welcome it. I do not believe that any of us would exchange places with any other people or any other generation. The energy, the faith, the devotion which we bring to this endeavor will light our country and all who serve it—and the glow from that fire can truly light the world.

And so, my fellow Americans: ask not what your country can do for you—ask what you can do for your country.

My fellow citizens of the world: ask not what America will do for you, but what together we can do for the freedom of man.

Finally, whether you are citizens of America or citizens of the world, ask of us here the same high standards of strength and sacrifice which we ask of you. With a good conscience our only sure reward, with history the final judge of our deeds, let us go forth to lead the land we love, asking His blessing and His help, but knowing that here on earth God's work must truly be our own.

Executive Order 10924:
Establishment of the Peace Corps.

Executive Order 10924
ESTABLISHMENT AND ADMINISTRATION OF
THE PEACE CORPS IN THE DEPARTMENT OF
STATE

By virtue of the authority vested in me by the Mutual Security Act of 1954, 68 Stat. 832, as amended (22 U.S.C. 1750 et seq.), and as President of the United States, it is hereby ordered as follows:

SECTION 1. Establishment of the Peace Corps. The Secretary of State shall establish an agency in the Department of State which shall be known as the Peace Corps. The Peace Corps shall be headed by a Director.

SEC. 2. Functions of the Peace Corps. (a) The Peace Corps shall be responsible for the training and service abroad of men and women of the United States in new programs of assistance to nations and areas of the world, and in conjunction with or in support of existing economic assistance programs of the United States and of the United Nations and other international organizations.

(b) The Secretary of State shall delegate, or cause to be delegated, to the Director of the Peace Corps such of the functions under the Mutual Security Act of 1954, as amended, vested in the President and delegated to the Secretary, or vested in the Secretary, as the Secretary shall deem necessary for the accomplishment of the purposes of the Peace Corps.

SEC. 3. Financing of the Peace Corps. The Secretary of State shall provide for the financing of the Peace Corps with funds available to the Secretary for the performance of functions under the Mutual Security Act of 1954, as amended.

SEC. 4. Relation to Executive Order No. 10893. This order shall not be deemed to supersede or derogate from any provision of Executive Order No. 10893 of November 8, 1960, as amended, and any delegation made by or pursuant to this order shall, unless otherwise specifically provided therein, be deemed to be in addition to any delegation made by or pursuant to that order.

JOHN F. KENNEDY
THE WHITE HOUSE,
March 1, 1961.

John Glenn's Official Communication with the Command Center

04 36 56 0.4 CC   Roger.

04 37 00 9.6 P   There is quite a bit of cloud cover down in this area. I can, ah, right on track, I can only see certain areas. I can see quite a bit on up to the north, however.

04 37 18 2.4 P   This is Friendship 7, going to manual control.

04 37 21 1.3 CC   Ah, Roger, Friendship 7.

04 37 23 2.7 P   This is banging in and out here; I'll just control it manually.

04 37 25 0.4 CC   Roger.

04 37 48 3.1 CC   Friendship 7, Guaymas Cap Com, reading you loud and clear.

04 37 51 2.1 P   Roger, Guaymas, read you loud and clear also.

TEXAS

04 38 06 4.0 CT   Friendship 7, Friendship 7, this is Texas Com Tech. Do you read? Over.

04 38 10 1.3 P   Roger, Texas, go ahead.

04 38 13 3.9 CT   Ah, Roger. Reading you 5 square. Standby for Texas Cap Com.

04 38 16 0.4 P   Roger.

04 38 25 23.8 CC   This is Texas Cap Com, Friendship 7. We are recommending that you leave the retropackage on through the entire reentry. This means that you will have to override the 05g switch which is expected to occur at 04 43 _3. This also means that you will have to manually retract the scope. Do you read?

04 38 49 4.0 P   This is Friendship 7. What is the reason for this? Do you have any reason? Over.

04 38 53 3.6 CC   Not at this time; this is the judgement of Cape Flight.

04 38 58 2.6 P   Ah, Roger. Say again your instructions please. Over.

04 39 01 22.1 CC   We are recommending that the retropackage not, I say again, not be jettisoned. This means that you will have to override the 05g switch which is expected to occur at 04 43 53. This is approximately 4^1/$_2$ minutes from now. This also means that you will have to retract the scope manually. Do you understand?

04 39 25 9.7 P   Ah, Roger, understand. I will have to make a manual 05g entry when it occurs, and bring the scope in, ah, manually. Is that affirm?

04 39 35 2.5 CC   That is affirmative, Friendship 7.

04 39 39 0.6 P   Ah, Roger.

04 39 42 3.6 P   This is Friendship 7, going to reentry attitude, then, in that case.

04 40 00 3.8 CC   Friendship 7, Cape flight will give you the reasons for this action when you are in view.

04 40 06 2.6 P   Ah, Roger. Ah, Roger. Friendship 7.

04 40 09 2.5 CC   Everything down here on the ground looks okay.

04 40 12 1.5 P   Ah, Roger. This is Friendship 7.

04 40 14 1.4 CC   Confirm your attitudes.

04 40 16 0.4 P   Roger.

CANAVERAL

04 40 23 1.7 CC   Ah, Friendship 7, this is Cape. Over.

04 40 25 1.5 P   Go ahead, Cape. Friend 7.

04 40 27 4.9 CC   Ah, recommend you go to reentry attitude and retract the scope manually at this time.

04 40 32 1.9 P   Ah, Roger, retracting scope manually.

04 40 36 14.6 CC   While you're doing that, we are not sure whether or not your landing bag has deployed. We feel it is possible to reenter with the retropackage on. Ah, we see no difficulty at this time in that type of reentry. Over.

04 40 51 1.6 P   Ah, Roger, understand.

04 41 10 1.4 CC   Seven, this is Cape. Over.

04 41 12 1.5 P   Go ahead, Cape. Friendship 7.

04 41 15 5.4 CC   Estimating 05g at 04 44.

04 41 21 0.6 P   Ah, Roger.

04 41 23 3.0 CC   You override 05g at that time.

04 41 31 2.7 P   Ah, Roger. Friendship 7.

04 41 33 13.2 P   This is Friendship 7. I'm on straight manual control at present time. This was, ah, still kicking in and out of orientation mode, mainly in yaw, ah, following retrofire, so I am on straight manual now. I'll back it up —

04 41 45 0.8 CC   — on reentry.

04 41 47 0.9 P   Say again.

04 41 50 0.6 CC   Standby.

04 41 53 6.2 P   This is Friendship 7. Ah, going to fly-by-wire. I'm down to about 15 percent on manual.

04 42 00 8.9 CC   Ah, Roger. You're going to use fly-by-wire for reentry and we recommend that you do the best you can to keep a zero angle during reentry. Over.

04 42 09 1.2 P   Ah, Roger. Friendship 7.

04 42 13 3.4 P   This is Friendship 7. I'm on fly-by-wire, back-it up with manual. Over.

04 42 18 1.1 CC   Roger, understand.

04 42 29 9.2 CC   Ah, Seven, this is Cape. The weather in the recovery area is excellent, 3-foot waves, only one-tenth cloud coverage, 10 miles visibility.

04 42 39 1.2 P   Ah, Roger. Friendship 7.

04 42 47 1.4 CC   Ah, Seven, this is Cape. Over.

04 42 49 2.5 P   Go ahead, Cape, you're ground, you are going out.

04 42 52 1.8 CC   We recommend that you —-

04 43 16 2.9 P   This is Friendship 7. I think the pack just let go.

04 43 39 2.4 P   This is Friendship 7. A real fireball outside.

04 44 20 1.9 P   Hello, Cape. Friendship 7. Over.

04 45 18 1.9 P   Hello, Cape. Friendship 7. Over.

04 45 43 2.3 P   Hello, Cape. Friendship 7. Do you receive? Over.

04 46 20 2.0 P   Hello, Cape. Friendship 7. Do you receive? Over.

04 47 18 1.2 CC   — How do you read? Over.

04 47 20 1.5 P   Loud and clear; how me?

04 47 22 1.6 CC   Roger, reading you loud and clear. How are you doing?

04 47 25 1.0 P   Oh, pretty good.

04 47 30 3.8 CC   Roger. Your impact point is within one mile of the up-range destroyer.

04 47 34 0.5 P   Ah, Roger.

04 47 35 0.2 CC   — Over.

04 47 36 0.3 P   Roger.

04 47 44 3.4 CC   This is Cape, estimating 4 50. Over.

04 47 48 1.5 P   Roger, 04 50.

04 47 53 1.6 P   Okay, we're through the peak g now.

04 47 55 4.0 CC   Ah, Seven, this is Cape. What's your general condition? Are you feeling pretty well?

04 47 59 2.8 P   My condition is good, but that was a real fireball, boy.

04 48 05 3.2 P   I had great chunks of that retropack breaking off all the way through.

04 48 08 2.1 CC   Very good; it did break off, is that correct?

04 48 11 3.4 P   Roger. Altimeter off the peg indicating 80 thousand.

04 48 15 1.7 CC   Roger, reading you loud and clear.

04 48 17 0.3 P   Roger.

Aerial Photograph of Missiles in Cuba

Throughout 1962, in the midst of the Cold War, the movement of Soviet personnel and equipment to Cuba had aroused suspicions in the American intelligence community. In response, U.S. ships and planes began photographing every Cuba-bound Soviet vessel, and U-2 spy planes began regular reconnaissance flights over the island, just 90 miles off the coast of Florida. On September 13, Kennedy warned Soviet Premier Khrushchev: "If at any time the Communist build-up in Cuba were to endanger or interfere with our security in any way . . . or if Cuba should ever . . . become an offensive military base of significant capacity for the Soviet Union, then this country will do whatever must be done to protect its own security and that of its allies." Despite Kennedy's warnings, the Soviets continued to construct the bases, and the United States continued to monitor their activities and take pictures.

Bad weather in the Caribbean the week of October 7, 1962, prevented American U-2 surveillance planes from making more reconnaissance flights over Fidel Castro's Cuba. But Sunday morning, October 14, was cloudless, and the U-2 flight took photographs that, over the next few days, were analyzed and reanalyzed. They provided positive proof of what the United States had for months suspected: that the Soviet Union was installing medium-range nuclear weapons in Cuba, capable of striking major U.S. cities and killing tens of millions of Americans within minutes. With the October 14 photographs, the United States caught the Soviet Union building offensive nuclear missile bases in its backyard, and the two superpowers were now joined in the first direct nuclear confrontation in history.

In a televised address on October 22, 1962, President Kennedy informed the American people of the presence of missile sites in Cuba. When the United States put a naval blockade in place around Cuba, tensions mounted, and the world wondered if there could be a peaceful resolution to the crisis. Kennedy's speech drew wide support in Latin America and among United States' allies. The Pentagon continued plans for possible air strikes and a land invasion. Several Soviet vessels turned back from the quarantine line set by the navel blockade, and during a televised confrontation with the Soviet Union in the United Nations, the United States presented photographic proof of the missiles.

On Sunday, October 28, the Soviets agreed to remove the missiles from Cuba. Negotiations for final settlement of the crisis continued for several days, but the immediate threat of nuclear war had been averted. On November 20, Kennedy announced, "I have today been informed by Chairman Khrushchev that all of the IL-28 bombers in Cuba will be withdrawn in thirty days. . . . I have this afternoon instructed the Secretary of Defense to lift our naval quarantine." In addition, the United States agreed that it would never participate in an invasion of Cuba, and Kennedy ordered the dismantling of several obsolete American air and missile bases in Turkey.

Test Ban Treaty

TREATY

banning nuclear weapon tests in the atmosphere, in outer space and under water

The Governments of the United States of America, the United Kingdom of Great Britain and Northern Ireland, and the Union of Soviet Socialist Republics, hereinafter referred to as the "Original Parties,"

Proclaiming as their principal aim the speediest possible achievement of an agreement on general and complete disarmament under strict international control in accordance with the objectives of the United Nations which would put an end to the armaments race and eliminate the incentive to the production and testing of all kinds of weapons, including nuclear weapons,

Seeking to achieve the discontinuance of all test explosions of nuclear weapons for all time, determined to continue negotiations to this end, and desiring to put an end to the contamination of man's environment by radioactive substances,

Have agreed as follows:

ARTICLE I

1. Each of the Parties to this Treaty undertakes to prohibit, to prevent, and not to carry out any nuclear weapon test explosion, or any other nuclear explosion, at any place under its jurisdiction or control:

(a) in the atmosphere; beyond its limits, including outer space; or under water, including territorial waters or high seas; or

(b) in any other environment if such explosion causes radioactive debris to be present outside the territorial limits of the State under whose jurisdiction or control such explosion is conducted. It is understood in this connection that the provisions of this subparagraph are without prejudice to the conclusion of a Treaty resulting in the permanent banning of all nuclear test explosions, including all such explosions underground, the conclusion of which, as the Parties have stated in the Preamble to this Treaty, they seek to achieve.

2. Each of the Parties to this Treaty undertakes furthermore to refrain from causing, encouraging, or in any way participating in, the carrying out of any nuclear weapon test explosion, or any other nuclear explosion, anywhere which would take place in any of the environments described, or have the effect referred to, in paragraph 1 of this Article.

ARTICLE II

1. Any Party may propose amendments to this Treaty. The text of any proposed amendment shall be submitted to the Depositary Governments which shall circulate it to all Parties to this Treaty. Thereafter, if requested to do so by one-third or more of the Parties, the Depositary Governments shall convene a conference, to which they shall invite all the Parties, to consider such amendment.

2. Any amendment to this Treaty must be approved by a majority of the votes of all the Parties to this Treaty, including the votes of all of the Original Parties. The amendment shall enter into force for all Parties upon the deposit of instruments of ratification by a majority of all the Parties, including the instruments of ratification of all of the Original Parties.

ARTICLE III

1. This Treaty shall be open to all States for signature. Any State which does not sign this Treaty before its entry into force in accordance with paragraph 3 of this Article may accede to it at any time.

2. This Treaty shall be subject to ratification by signatory States. Instruments of ratification and instruments of accession shall be deposited with the Governments of the Original Parties—the United States of America, the United Kingdom of Great Britain and Northern Ireland, and the Union of Soviet Socialist Republics—which are hereby designated the Depositary Governments.

3. This Treaty shall enter into force after its ratification by all the Original Parties and the deposit of their instruments of ratification.

4. For States whose instruments of ratification or accession are deposited subsequent to the entry into force of this Treaty, it shall enter into force on the date of the deposit of their instruments of ratification or accession.

5. The Depositary Governments shall promptly inform all signatory and acceding States of the date of each signature, the date of deposit of each instrument of ratification of and accession to this Treaty, the date of its entry into force, and the date of receipt of any requests for conferences or other notices.

6. This Treaty shall be registered by the Depositary Governments pursuant to Article 102 of the Charter of the United Nations.

ARTICLE IV

This Treaty shall be of unlimited duration.

Each Party shall in exercising its national sovereignty have the right to withdraw from the Treaty if it decides that extraordinary events, related to the subject matter of this Treaty, have jeopardized the supreme interests of its country. It shall give notice of such withdrawal to all other Parties to the Treaty three months in advance.

ARTICLE V

This Treaty, of which the English and Russian texts are equally authentic, shall be deposited in the archives of the Depositary Governments. Duly certified copies of this Treaty shall be transmitted by the Depositary Governments to the Governments of the signatory and acceding States.

IN WITNESS WHEREOF the undersigned, duly authorized, have signed this Treaty.

DONE in triplicate at the city of Moscow the fifth day of August, one thousand nine hundred and sixty-three.

For the Government of the United States of America
DEAN RUSK

For the Government of the United Kingdom of Great Britain and Northern Ireland
SIR DOUGLAS HOME

For the Government of the Union of Soviet Socialist Republics
A. GROMYKO

Official Program for the March on Washington

MARCH ON WASHINGTON FOR JOBS AND FREEDOM AUGUST 28, 1963

LINCOLN MEMORIAL PROGRAM

1. The National Anthem
Led by Marian Anderson.

2. Invocation
The Very Rev. Patrick O'Boyle, *Archbishop of Washington.*

3. Opening Remarks
A. Philip Randolph, *Director March on Washington for Jobs and Freedom.*

4. Remarks
Dr. Eugene Carson Blake, *Stated Clerk, United Presbyterian Church of the U.S.A.; Vice Chairman, Commission on Race Relations of the National Council of Churches of Christ in America.*

5. Tribute to Negro Women Fighters for Freedom
Daisy Bates
Diane Nash Bevel
Mrs. Medgar Evers
Mrs. Herbert Lee
Rosa Parks
Gloria Richardson
Mrs. Medgar Evers

6. Remarks
John Lewis, *National Chairman, Student Nonviolent Coordinating Committee.*

7. Remarks
Walter Reuther, *President, United Automobile, Aerospace and Agricultural Implement Workers of America, AFL-CIO; Chairman, Industrial Union Department, AFL-CIO.*

8. Remarks
James Farmer, *National Director, Congress of Racial Equality.*

9. Selection
Eva Jessye *Choir*

10. Prayer
Rabbi Uri Miller, *President Synagogue Council of America.*

11. Remarks
Whitney M. Young, Jr., *Executive Director, National Urban League.*

12. Remarks
Matthew Ahmann, *Executive Director, National Catholic Conference for Interracial Justice.*

13. Remarks
Roy Wilkins, Executive Secretary, *National Association for the Advancement of Colored People.*

14. Selection
Miss Mahalia Jackson

15. Remarks
Rabbi Joachim Prinz, *President American Jewish Congress*.

16. Remarks
The Rev. Dr. Martin Luther King, Jr., *President, Southern Christian Leadership Conference*.

17. The Pledge
A. Philip Randolph

18. Benediction
Dr. Benjamin E. Mays, *President, Morehouse College*.

"WE SHALL OVERCOME"

The Civil Rights Act

AN ACT

To enforce the constitutional right to vote, to confer jurisdiction upon the district courts of the United States to provide injunctive relief against discrimination in public accommodations, to authorize the Attorney General to institute suits to protect constitutional rights in public facilities and public education, to extend the Commission on Civil Rights, to prevent discrimination in federally assisted programs, to establish a Commission on Equal Employment Opportunity, and for other purposes.

Be it enacted by the Senate and House of Representatives of the United States of America in Congress assembled, That this Act may be cited as the "Civil Rights Act of 1964."

TITLE I—VOTING RIGHTS

SEC. 101. Section 2004 of the Revised Statutes (42 U.S.C. 1971), as amended by section 131 of the Civil Rights Act of 1957 (71 Stat. 637), and as further amended by section 601 of the Civil Rights Act of 1960 (74 Stat. 90), is further amended as follows:

(a) Insert "1" after "(a)" in subsection (a) and add at the end of subsection (a) the following new paragraphs:

"(2) No person acting under color of law shall—
"(A) in determining whether any individual is qualified under State law or laws to vote in any Federal election, apply any standard, practice, or procedure different from the standards, practices, or procedures applied under such law or laws to other individuals within the same county, parish, or similar political subdivision who have been found by State officials to be qualified to vote;

"(B) deny the right of any individual to vote in any Federal election because of an error or omission on any record or paper relating to any application, registration, or other act requisite to voting, if such error or omission is not material in determining whether such individual is qualified under State law to vote in such election; or

"(C) employ any literacy test as a qualification for voting in any Federal election unless (i) such test is administered to each individual and is conducted wholly in writing, and (ii) a certified copy of the test and of the answers given by the individual is furnished to him within twenty-five days of the submission of his request made within the period of time during which records and papers are required to be retained and preserved pursuant to title III of the Civil Rights Act of 1960 (42 U.S.C. 1974—74e; 74 Stat. 88): Provided, however, That the Attorney General may enter into agreements with appropriate State or local authorities that preparation, conduct, and maintenance of such tests in accordance with the provisions of applicable State or local law, including such special provisions as are necessary in the preparation, conduct, and maintenance of such tests for persons who are blind or otherwise physically handicapped, meet the purposes of this subparagraph and constitute compliance therewith.

"(3) For purposes of this subsection— "(A) the term 'vote' shall have the same meaning as in subsection (e) of this section;

"(B) the phrase 'literacy test' includes any test of the ability to read, write, understand, or interpret any matter."

(b) Insert immediately following the period at the end of the first sentence of subsection (c) the following new sentence: "If in any such proceeding literacy is a relevant fact there shall be a rebuttable presumption that any person who has not been adjudged an incompetent and who has completed the sixth grade in a public school in, or a private school accredited by, any State or territory, the District of Columbia, or the Commonwealth of Puerto Rico where instruction is carried on predominantly in the English language, possesses sufficient literacy, comprehension, and intelligence to vote in any Federal election."

(c) Add the following subsection "(f)" and designate the present subsection "(f)" as subsection "(g)": "(f) When used in subsection (a) or (c) of this section, the words 'Federal election' shall mean any general, special, or primary election held solely or in part for the purpose of electing or selecting any candidate for the office of President, Vice President, presidential elector, Member of the Senate, or Member of the House of Representatives."

(d) Add the following subsection "(h)":

"(h) In any proceeding instituted by the United States in any district court of the United States under this section in which the Attorney General requests a finding of a pattern or practice of discrimination pursuant to subsection (e) of this section the Attorney General, at the time he files the complaint, or any defendant in the proceeding, within twenty days after service upon him of the complaint, may file with the clerk of such court a request that a court of three judges be convened to hear and determine the entire case. A copy of the request for a three-judge court shall be immediately furnished by such clerk to the chief judge of the circuit (or in his absence, the presiding circuit judge of the circuit) in which the case is pending. Upon receipt of the copy of such request it shall be the duty of the chief justice of the circuit or the presiding circuit judge, as the case may be, to designate immediately three judges in such circuit, of whom at least one shall be a circuit judge and another of whom shall be a district judge of the court in which the proceeding was instituted, to hear and determine such case, and it shall be the duty of the judges so designated to assign the case for hearing at the earliest practicable date, to participate in the hearing and determination thereof, and to cause the case to be in every way expedited.

An appeal from the final judgment of such court will lie to the Supreme Court.

"In any proceeding brought under subsection (c) of this section to enforce subsection (b) of this section, or in the event neither the Attorney General nor any defendant files a request for a three-judge court in any proceeding authorized by this subsection, it shall be the duty of the chief judge of the district (or in his absence, the acting chief judge) in which the case is pending immediately to designate a judge in such district to hear and determine the case. In the event that no judge in the district is available to hear and determine the case, the chief judge of the district, or the acting chief judge, as the case may be, shall certify this fact to the chief judge of the circuit (or, in his absence, the acting chief judge) who shall then designate a district or circuit judge of the circuit to hear and determine the case.

"It shall be the duty of the judge designated pursuant to this section to assign the case for hearing at the earliest practicable date and to cause the case to be in every way expedited."

TITLE II—INJUNCTIVE RELIEF AGAINST DISCRIMINATION IN PLACES OF PUBLIC ACCOMMODATION

SEC. 201. (a) All persons shall be entitled to the full and equal enjoyment of the goods, services, facilities, and privileges, advantages, and accommodations of any place of public accommodation, as defined in this section, without discrimination or segregation on the ground of race, color, religion, or national origin.

(b) Each of the following establishments which serves the public is a place of public accommodation within the meaning of this title if its operations affect commerce, or if discrimination or segregation by it is supported by State action:

(1) any inn, hotel, motel, or other establishment which provides lodging to transient guests, other than an establishment located within a building which contains not more than five rooms for rent or hire and which is actually occupied by the proprietor of such establishment as his residence;

(2) any restaurant, cafeteria, lunchroom, lunch counter, soda fountain, or other facility principally engaged in selling food for consumption on the premises, including, but not limited to, any such facility located on the premises of any retail establishment; or any gasoline station;

(3) any motion picture house, theater, concert hall, sports arena, stadium or other place of exhibition or entertainment; and

(4) any establishment (A)(i) which is physically located within the premises of any establishment otherwise covered by this subsection, or (ii) within the premises of which is physically located any such covered establishment, and (B) which holds itself out as serving patrons of such covered establishment.

(c) The operations of an establishment affect commerce within the meaning of this title if (1) it is one of the establishments described in paragraph (1) of subsection (b); (2) in the case of an establishment described in paragraph (2) of subsection (b), it serves or offers to serve interstate travelers or a substantial portion of the food which it serves, or gasoline or other products which it sells, has moved in commerce; (3) in the case of an establishment described in paragraph (3) of subsection (b), it customarily presents films, performances, athletic teams, exhibitions, or other sources of entertainment which move in commerce; and (4) in the case of an establishment described in paragraph (4) of subsection (b), it is physically located within the premises of, or there is physically located within its premises, an establishment the operations of which affect commerce within the meaning of this subsection. For purposes of this section, "commerce" means travel, trade, traffic, commerce, transportation, or communication among the several States, or between the District of Columbia and any State, or between any foreign country or any territory or possession and any State or the District of Columbia, or between points in the same State but through any other State or the District of Columbia or a foreign country.

(d) Discrimination or segregation by an establishment is supported by State action within the meaning of this title if such discrimination or segregation (1) is carried on under color of any law, statute, ordinance, or regulation; or (2) is carried on under color of any custom or usage required or enforced by officials of the State or political subdivision thereof; or (3) is required by action of the State or political subdivision thereof.

(e) The provisions of this title shall not apply to a private club or other establishment not in fact open to the public, except to the extent that the facilities of such establishment are made available to the customers or patrons of an establishment within the scope of subsection (b).

SEC. 202. All persons shall be entitled to be free, at any establishment or place, from discrimination or segregation of any kind on the ground of race, color, religion, or national origin, if such discrimination or segregation is or purports to be required by any law, statute, ordinance, regulation, rule, or order of a State or any agency or political subdivision thereof.

SEC. 203. No person shall (a) withhold, deny, or attempt to withhold or deny, or deprive or attempt to deprive, any person of any right or privilege secured by section 201 or 202, or (b) intimidate, threaten, or coerce, or attempt to intimidate, threaten, or coerce any person with the purpose of interfering with any right or privilege secured by section 201 or 202, or

(c) punish or attempt to punish any person for exercising or attempting to exercise any right or privilege secured by section 201 or 202.

SEC. 204. (a) Whenever any person has engaged or there are reasonable grounds to believe that any person is about to engage in any act or practice prohibited by section 203, a civil action for preventive relief, including an application for a permanent or temporary injunction, restraining order, or other order, may be instituted by the person aggrieved and, upon timely application, the court may, in its discretion, permit the Attorney General to intervene in such civil action if he certifies that the case is of general public importance. Upon application by the complainant and in such circumstances as the court may deem just, the court may appoint an attorney for such complainant and may authorize the commencement of the civil action without the payment of fees, costs, or security.

(b) In any action commenced pursuant to this title, the court, in its discretion, may allow the prevailing party, other than the United States, a reasonable attorney's fee as part of the costs, and the United States shall be liable for costs the same as a private person.

(c) In the case of an alleged act or practice prohibited by this title which occurs in a State, or political subdivision of a State, which has a State or local law prohibiting such act or practice and establishing or authorizing a State or local authority to grant or seek relief from such practice or to institute criminal proceedings with respect thereto upon receiving notice thereof, no civil action may be brought under subsection (a) before the expiration of thirty days after written notice of such alleged act or practice has been given to the appropriate State or local authority by registered mail or in person, provided that the court may stay proceedings in such civil action pending the termination of State or local enforcement proceedings.

(d) In the case of an alleged act or practice prohibited by this title which occurs in a State, or political subdivision of a State, which has no State or local law prohibiting such act or practice, a civil action may be brought under subsection (a): Provided, That the court may refer the matter to the Community Relations Service established by title X of this Act for as long as the court believes there is a reasonable possibility of obtaining voluntary compliance, but for not more than sixty days: Provided further, That upon expiration of such sixty-day period, the court may extend such period for an additional period, not to exceed a cumulative total of one hundred and twenty days, if it believes there then exists a reasonable possibility of securing voluntary compliance.

SEC. 205. The Service is authorized to make a full investigation of any complaint referred to it by the court under section 204(d) and may hold such hearings with respect thereto as may be necessary. The Service shall conduct any hearings with respect to any such complaint in executive session, and shall not release any testimony given therein except by agreement of all parties involved in the complaint with the permission of the court, and the Service shall endeavor to bring about a voluntary settlement between the parties.

SEC. 206. (a) Whenever the Attorney General has reasonable cause to believe that any person or group of persons is engaged in a pattern or practice of resistance to the full enjoyment of any of the rights secured by this title, and that the pattern or practice is of such a nature and is intended to deny the full exercise of the rights herein described, the Attorney General may bring a civil action in the appropriate district court of the United States by filing with it a complaint (1) signed by him (or in his absence the Acting Attorney General), (2) setting forth facts pertaining to such pattern or practice, and (3) requesting such preventive relief, including an application for a permanent or temporary injunction, restraining order or other order against the person or persons responsible for such pattern or practice, as he deems necessary to insure the full enjoyment of the rights herein described.

(b) In any such proceeding the Attorney General may file with the clerk of such court a request that a court of three judges be convened to hear and determine the case. Such request by the Attorney General shall be accompanied by a certificate that, in his opinion, the case is of general public importance. A copy of the certificate and request for a three-judge court shall be immediately furnished by such clerk to the chief judge of the circuit (or in his absence, the presiding circuit judge of the circuit) in which the case is pending. Upon receipt of the copy of such request it shall be the duty of the chief judge of the circuit or the presiding circuit judge, as the case may be, to designate immediately three judges in such circuit, of whom at least one shall be a circuit judge and another of whom shall be a district judge of the court in which the proceeding was instituted, to hear and

determine such case, and it shall be the duty of the judges so designated to assign the case for hearing at the earliest practicable date, to participate in the hearing and determination thereof, and to cause the case to be in every way expedited. An appeal from the final judgment of such court will lie to the Supreme Court.

In the event the Attorney General fails to file such a request in any such proceeding, it shall be the duty of the chief judge of the district (or in his absence, the acting chief judge) in which the case is pending immediately to designate a judge in such district to hear and determine the case. In the event that no judge in the district is available to hear and determine the case, the chief judge of the district, or the acting chief judge, as the case may be, shall certify this fact to the chief judge of the circuit (or in his absence, the acting chief judge) who shall then designate a district or circuit judge of the circuit to hear and determine the case.

It shall be the duty of the judge designated pursuant to this section to assign the case for hearing at the earliest practicable date and to cause the case to be in every way expedited.

SEC. 207. (a) The district courts of the United States shall have jurisdiction of proceedings instituted pursuant to this title and shall exercise the same without regard to whether the aggrieved party shall have exhausted any administrative or other remedies that may be provided by law.

(b) The remedies provided in this title shall be the exclusive means of enforcing the rights based on this title, but nothing in this title shall preclude any individual or any State or local agency from asserting any right based on any other Federal or State law not inconsistent with this title, including any statute or ordinance requiring nondiscrimination in public establishments or accommodations, or from pursuing any remedy, civil or criminal, which may be available for the vindication or enforcement of such right.

TITLE III—DESEGREGATION OF PUBLIC FACILITIES

SEC. 301. (a) Whenever the Attorney General receives a complaint in writing signed by an individual to the effect that he is being deprived of or threatened with the loss of his right to the equal protection of the laws, on account of his race, color, religion, or national origin, by being denied equal utilization of any public facility which is owned, operated, or managed by or on behalf of any State or subdivision thereof, other than a public school or public college as defined in section 401 of title IV hereof, and the Attorney General believes the complaint is meritorious and certifies that the signer or signers of such complaint are unable, in his judgment, to initiate and maintain appropriate legal proceedings for relief and that the institution of an action will materially further the orderly progress of desegregation in public facilities, the Attorney General is authorized to institute for or in the name of the United States a civil action in any appropriate district court of the United States against such parties and for such relief as may be appropriate, and such court shall have and shall exercise jurisdiction of proceedings instituted pursuant to this section. The Attorney General may implead as defendants such additional parties as are or become necessary to the grant of effective relief hereunder.

(b) The Attorney General may deem a person or persons unable to initiate and maintain appropriate legal proceedings within the meaning of subsection

(a) of this section when such person or persons are unable, either directly or through other interested persons or organizations, to bear the expense of the litigation or to obtain effective legal representation; or whenever he is satisfied that the institution of such litigation would jeopardize the personal safety, employment, or economic standing of such person or persons, their families, or their property.

SEC. 302. In any action or proceeding under this title the United States shall be liable for costs, including a reasonable attorney's fee, the same as a private person.

SEC. 303. Nothing in this title shall affect adversely the right of any person to sue for or obtain relief in any court against discrimination in any facility covered by this title.

SEC. 304. A complaint as used in this title is a writing or document within the meaning of section 1001, title 18, United States Code.

TITLE IV—DESEGREGATION OF PUBLIC EDUCATION DEFINITIONS

SEC. 401. As used in this title— (a) "Commissioner" means the Commissioner of Education.

(b) "Desegregation" means the assignment of students to public schools and within such schools without regard to their race, color, religion, or national origin, but "desegregation" shall not mean the assignment of students to public schools in order to overcome racial imbalance.

(c) "Public school" means any elementary or secondary educational institution, and "public college" means any institution of higher education or any technical or vocational school above the secondary school level, provided that such public school or public college is operated by a State, subdivision of a State, or governmental agency within a State, or operated wholly or predominantly from or through the use of governmental funds or property, or funds or property derived from a governmental source.

(d) "School board" means any agency or agencies which administer a system of one or more public schools and any other agency which is responsible for the assignment of students to or within such system.

SURVEY AND REPORT OF EDUCATIONAL OPPORTUNITIES

SEC. 402. The Commissioner shall conduct a survey and make a report to the President and the Congress, within two years of the enactment of this title, concerning the lack of availability of equal educational opportunities for individuals by reason of race, color, religion, or national origin in public educational institutions at all levels in the United States, its territories and possessions, and the District of Columbia.

TECHNICAL ASSISTANCE

SEC. 403. The Commissioner is authorized, upon the application of any school board, State, municipality, school district, or other governmental unit legally responsible for operating a public school or schools, to render technical assistance to such applicant in the preparation, adoption, and implementation of plans for the desegregation of public schools. Such technical assistance may, among other activities, include making available to such agencies information regarding effective methods of coping with special educational problems occasioned by desegregation, and making available to such agencies personnel of the Office of Education or other persons specially equipped to advise and assist them in coping with such problems.

TRAINING INSTITUTES

SEC. 404. The Commissioner is authorized to arrange, through grants or contracts, with institutions of higher education for the operation of short-term or regular session institutes for special training designed to improve the ability of teachers, supervisors, counselors, and other elementary or secondary school personnel to deal effectively with special educational problems occasioned by desegregation. Individuals who attend such an institute on a full-time basis may be paid stipends for the period of their attendance at such institute in amounts specified by the Commissioner in regulations, including allowances for travel to attend such institute.

GRANTS

SEC. 405. (a) The Commissioner is authorized, upon application of a school board, to make grants to such board to pay, in whole or in part, the cost of—
(1) giving to teachers and other school personnel inservice training in dealing with problems incident to desegregation, and

(2) employing specialists to advise in problems incident to desegregation.

(b) In determining whether to make a grant, and in fixing the amount thereof and the terms and conditions on which it will be made, the Commissioner shall take into consideration the amount available for grants under this section and the other applications which are pending before him; the financial condition of the applicant and the other resources available to it; the nature, extent, and gravity of its problems incident to desegregation; and such other factors as he finds relevant.

PAYMENTS

SEC. 406. Payments pursuant to a grant or contract under this title may be made (after necessary adjustments on account of previously made overpayments or underpayments) in advance or by way of reimbursement, and in such installments, as the Commissioner may determine.

SUITS BY THE ATTORNEY GENERAL

SEC. 407. (a) Whenever the Attorney General receives a complaint in writing— (1) signed by a parent or group of parents to the effect that his or their minor children, as members of a class of persons similarly situated, are being deprived by a school board of the equal protection of the laws, or

(2) signed by an individual, or his parent, to the effect that he has been denied admission to or not permitted to continue in attendance at a public college by reason of race, color, religion, or national origin, and the Attorney General believes the complaint is meritorious and certifies that the signer or signers of such complaint are unable, in his judgment, to initiate and maintain appropriate legal proceedings for relief and that the institution of an action will materially further the orderly achievement of desegregation in public education, the Attorney General is authorized, after giving notice of such complaint to the appropriate school board or college authority and after certifying that he is satisfied that such board or authority has had a reasonable time to adjust the conditions alleged in such complaint, to institute for or in the name of the United States a civil action in any appropriate district court of the United States against such parties and for such relief as may be appropriate, and such court shall have and shall exercise jurisdiction of proceedings instituted pursuant to this section, provided that nothing herein shall empower any official or court of the United States to issue any order seeking to achieve a racial balance in any school by requiring the transportation of pupils or students from one school to another or one school district to another in order to achieve such racial balance, or otherwise enlarge the existing power of the court to insure compliance with constitutional standards. The Attorney General may implead as defendants such additional parties as are or become necessary to the grant of effective relief hereunder.

(b) The Attorney General may deem a person or persons unable to initiate and maintain appropriate legal proceedings within the meaning of subsection

(a) of this section when such person or persons are unable, either directly or through other interested persons or organizations, to bear the expense of the litigation or to obtain effective legal representation; or whenever he is satisfied that the institution of such litigation would jeopardize the personal safety, employment, or economic standing of such person or persons, their families, or their property.

(c) The term "parent" as used in this section includes any person standing in loco parentis. A "complaint" as used in this section is a writing or document within the meaning of section 1001, title 18, United States Code.

SEC. 408. In any action or proceeding under this title the United States shall be liable for costs the same as a private person.

SEC. 409. Nothing in this title shall affect adversely the right of any person to sue for or obtain relief in any court against discrimination in public education.

SEC. 410. Nothing in this title shall prohibit classification and assignment for reasons other than race, color, religion, or national origin.

TITLE V—COMMISSION ON CIVIL RIGHTS

SEC. 501. Section 102 of the Civil Rights Act of 1957 (42 U.S.C. 1975a; 71 Stat. 634) is amended to read as follows:

"RULES OF PROCEDURE OF THE COMMISSION HEARINGS

"**SEC. 102.** (a) At least thirty days prior to the commencement of any hearing, the Commission shall cause to be published in the Federal Register notice of the date on which such hearing is to commence, the place at which it is to be held and the subject of the hearing. The Chairman, or one designated by him to act as Chairman at a hearing of the Commission, shall announce in an opening statement the subject of the hearing.

"(b) A copy of the Commission's rules shall be made available to any witness before the Commission, and a witness compelled to appear before the Commission or required to produce written or other matter shall be served with a copy of the Commission's rules at the time of service of the subpoena.

"(c) Any person compelled to appear in person before the Commission shall be accorded the right to be accompanied and advised by counsel, who shall have the right to subject his client to reasonable examination, and to make objections on the record and to argue briefly the basis for such objections. The Commission shall proceed with reasonable dispatch to conclude any hearing in which it is engaged. Due regard shall be had for the convenience and necessity of witnesses.

"(d) The Chairman or Acting Chairman may punish breaches of order and decorum by censure and exclusion from the hearings.

"(e) If the Commission determines that evidence or testimony at any hearing may tend to defame, degrade, or incriminate any person, it shall receive such evidence or testimony or summary of such evidence of testimony in executive session. The Commission shall afford any person defamed, degraded, or incriminated by such evidence or testimony an opportunity to appear and be heard in executive session, with a reasonable number of additional witnesses requested by him, before deciding to use such evidence or testimony. In the event the Commission determines to release or use such evidence or testimony in such manner as to reveal publicly the identity of the person defamed, degraded, or incriminated, such evidence or testimony, prior to such public release or use, shall be given at a public session, and the Commission shall afford such person an opportunity to appear as a voluntary witness or to file a sworn statement in his behalf and to submit brief and pertinent sworn statements of others. The Commission shall receive and dispose of requests from such person to subpoena additional witnesses.

"(f) Except as provided in sections 102 and 105 (f) of this Act, the Chairman shall receive and the Commission shall dispose of requests to subpoena additional witnesses.

"(g) No evidence or testimony or summary of evidence or testimony taken in executive session may be released or used in public sessions without the consent of the Commission. Whoever releases or uses in public without the consent of the Commission such evidence or testimony taken in executive session shall be fined not more than $1,000, or imprisoned for not more than one year.

"(h) In the discretion of the Commission, witnesses may submit brief and pertinent sworn statements in writing for inclusion in the record. The Commission shall determine the pertinency of testimony and evidence adduced at its hearings.

"(i) Every person who submits data or evidence shall be entitled to retain or, on payment of lawfully prescribed costs, procure a copy or transcript thereof, except that a witness in a hearing held in executive session may for good cause be limited to inspection of the official transcript of his testimony. Transcript copies of public sessions may be obtained by the public upon the payment of the cost thereof. An accurate transcript shall be made of the testimony of all witnesses at all hearings, either public or executive sessions, of the Commission or of any subcommittee thereof.

"(j) A witness attending any session of the Commission shall receive $6 for each day's attendance and for the time necessarily occupied in going to and returning from the same, and 10 cents per mile for going from and returning to his place of residence. Witnesses who attend at points so far removed from their respective residences as to prohibit return thereto from day to day shall be entitled to an additional allowance of $10 per day for expenses of subsistence including the time necessarily occupied in going to and returning from the place of attendance. Mileage payments shall be tendered to the witness upon service of a subpoena issued on behalf of the Commission or any subcommittee thereof.

"(k) The Commission shall not issue any subpoena for the attendance and testimony of witnesses or for the production of written or other matter which would require the presence of the party subpoenaed at a hearing to be held outside of the State wherein the witness is found or resides or is domiciled or transacts business, or has appointed an agent for receipt of service of process except that, in any event, the Commission may issue subpoenas for the attendance and testimony of witnesses and the production of written or other matter at a hearing held within fifty miles of the place where the witness is found or resides or is domiciled or transacts business or has appointed an agent for receipt of service of process.

"(l) The Commission shall separately state and currently publish in the Federal Register (1) descriptions of its central and field organization including the established places at which, and methods whereby, the public may secure information or make requests; (2) statements of the general course and method by which its functions are channeled and determined, and (3) rules adopted as authorized by law. No person shall in any manner be subject to or required to resort to rules, organization, or procedure not so published."

SEC. 502. Section 103(a) of the Civil Rights Act of 1957 (42 U.S.C. 1975b(a); 71 Stat. 634) is amended to read as follows:

"SEC. 103. (a) Each member of the Commission who is not otherwise in the service of the Government of the United States shall receive the sum of $75 per day for each day spent in the work of the Commission, shall be paid actual travel expenses, and per diem in lieu of subsistence expenses when away from his usual place of residence, in accordance with section 5 of the Administrative Expenses Act of 1946, as amended (5 U.S.C 73b-2; 60 Stat. 808)."

SEC. 503. Section 103(b) of the Civil Rights Act of 1957 (42 U.S.C. 1975(b); 71 Stat. 634) is amended to read as follows:

"(b) Each member of the Commission who is otherwise in the service of the Government of the United States shall serve without compensation in addition to that received for such other service, but while engaged in the work of the Commission shall be paid actual travel expenses, and per diem in lieu of subsistence expenses when away from his usual place of residence, in accordance with the provisions of the Travel Expenses Act of 1949, as amended

(5 U.S.C. 835—42; 63 Stat. 166)."

SEC. 504. (a) Section 104(a) of the Civil Rights Act of 1957 (42 U.S.C. 1975c(a); 71 Stat. 635), as amended, is further amended to read as follows:

"DUTIES OF THE COMMISSION

"**SEC. 104.** (a) The Commission shall— "(1) investigate allegations in writing under oath or affirmation that certain citizens of the United States are being deprived of their right to vote and have that vote counted by reason of their color, race, religion, or national origin; which writing, under oath or affirmation, shall set forth the facts upon which such belief or beliefs are based;

"(2) study and collect information concerning legal developments constituting a denial of equal protection of the laws under the Constitution because of race, color, religion or national origin or in the administration of justice;

"(3) appraise the laws and policies of the Federal Government with respect to denials of equal protection of the laws under the Constitution because of race, color, religion or national origin or in the administration of justice;

"(4) serve as a national clearinghouse for information in respect to denials of equal protection of the laws because of race, color, religion or national origin, including but not limited to the fields of voting, education, housing, employment, the use of public facilities, and transportation, or in the administration of justice;

"(5) investigate allegations, made in writing and under oath or affirmation, that citizens of the United States are unlawfully being accorded or denied the right to vote, or to have their votes properly counted, in any election of presidential electors, Members of the United States Senate, or of the House of Representatives, as a result of any patterns or practice of fraud or discrimination in the conduct of such election; and

"(6) Nothing in this or any other Act shall be construed as authorizing the Commission, its Advisory Committees, or any person under its supervision or control to inquire into or investigate any membership practices or internal operations of any fraternal organization, any college or university fraternity or sorority, any private club or any religious organization."

(b) Section 104(b) of the Civil Rights Act of 1957 (42 U.S.C. 1975c(b); 71 Stat. 635), as amended, is further amended by striking out the present subsection "(b)" and by substituting therefor:

"(b) The Commission shall submit interim reports to the President and to the Congress at such times as the Commission, the Congress or the President shall deem desirable, and shall submit to the President and to the Congress a final report of its activities, findings, and recommendations not later than January 31, 1968."

SEC. 505. Section 105(a) of the Civil Rights Act of 1957 (42 U.S.C. 1975d(a); 71 Stat. 636) is amended by striking out in the last sentence thereof "$50 per diem" and inserting in lieu thereof "$75 per diem."

SEC. 506. Section 105(f) and section 105(g) of the Civil Rights Act of 1957 (42 U.S.C. 1975d (f) and (g); 71 Stat. 636) are amended to read as follows:

"(f) The Commission, or on the authorization of the Commission any subcommittee of two or more members, at least one of whom shall be of each major political party, may, for the purpose of carrying out the provisions of this Act, hold such hearings and act at such times and places as the Commission or such authorized subcommittee may deem advisable. Subpoenas for the attendance and testimony of witnesses

or the production of written or other matter may be issued in accordance with the rules of the Commission as contained in section 102 (j) and (k) of this Act, over the signature of the Chairman of the Commission or of such subcommittee, and may be served by any person designated by such Chairman. The holding of hearings by the Commission, or the appointment of a subcommittee to hold hearings pursuant to this subparagraph, must be approved by a majority of the Commission, or by a majority of the members present at a meeting at which at least a quorum of four members is present.

"(g) In case of contumacy or refusal to obey a subpoena, any district court of the United States or the United States court of any territory or possession, or the District Court of the United States for the District of Columbia, within the jurisdiction of which the inquiry is carried on or within the jurisdiction of which said person guilty of contumacy or refusal to obey is found or resides or is domiciled or transacts business, or has appointed an agent for receipt of service of process, upon application by the Attorney General of the United States shall have jurisdiction to issue to such person an order requiring such person to appear before the Commission or a subcommittee thereof, there to produce pertinent, relevant and nonprivileged evidence if so ordered, or there to give testimony touching the matter under investigation; and any failure to obey such order of the court may be punished by said court as a contempt thereof."

SEC. 507. Section 105 of the Civil Rights Act of 1957 (42 U.S.C. 1975d; 71 Stat. 636), as amended by section 401 of the Civil Rights Act of 1960 (42 U.S.C. 1975d(h); 74 Stat. 89), is further amended by adding a new subsection at the end to read as follows:

"(i) The Commission shall have the power to make such rules and regulations as are necessary to carry out the purposes of this Act."

TITLE VI—NONDISCRIMINATION IN FEDERALLY ASSISTED PROGRAMS

SEC. 601. No person in the United States shall, on the ground of race, color, or national origin, be excluded from participation in, be denied the benefits of, or be subjected to discrimination under any program or activity receiving Federal financial assistance.

SEC. 602. Each Federal department and agency which is empowered to extend Federal financial assistance to any program or activity, by way of grant, loan, or contract other than a contract of insurance or guaranty, is authorized and directed to effectuate the provisions of section 601 with respect to such program or activity by issuing rules, regulations, or orders of general applicability which shall be consistent with achievement of the objectives of the statute authorizing the financial assistance in connection with which the action is taken. No such rule, regulation, or order shall become effective unless and until approved by the President. Compliance with any requirement adopted pursuant to this section may be effected (1) by the termination of or refusal to grant or to continue assistance under such program or activity to any recipient as to whom there has been an express finding on the record, after opportunity for hearing, of a failure to comply with such requirement, but such termination or refusal shall be limited to the particular political entity, or part thereof, or other recipient as to whom such a finding has been made and, shall be limited in its effect to the particular program, or part thereof, in which such noncompliance has been so found, or (2) by any other means authorized by law: Provided, however, That no such action shall be taken until the department or agency concerned has advised the appropriate person or persons of the failure to comply with the requirement and has determined that compliance cannot be secured by voluntary means. In the case of any action terminating, or refusing to grant or continue, assistance because of failure to comply with a requirement imposed pursuant to this section, the head of the federal department or agency shall file with the committees of the House and Senate having legislative jurisdiction over the program or activity involved a full written report of the circumstances and the grounds for such action. No such action shall become effective until thirty days have elapsed after the filing of such report.

SEC. 603. Any department or agency action taken pursuant to section 602 shall be subject to such judicial review as may otherwise be provided by law for similar action taken by such department or agency on other grounds. In the case of action, not otherwise subject to judicial review, terminating or refusing to grant or to continue financial assistance upon a finding of failure to comply with any requirement imposed pursuant to section 602, any person aggrieved (including any State or political subdivision thereof and any agency of either) may obtain judicial review

of such action in accordance with section 10 of the Administrative Procedure Act, and such action shall not be deemed committed to unreviewable agency discretion within the meaning of that section.

SEC. 604. Nothing contained in this title shall be construed to authorize action under this title by any department or agency with respect to any employment practice of any employer, employment agency, or labor organization except where a primary objective of the Federal financial assistance is to provide employment.

SEC. 605. Nothing in this title shall add to or detract from any existing authority with respect to any program or activity under which Federal financial assistance is extended by way of a contract of insurance or guaranty.

TITLE VII—EQUAL EMPLOYMENT OPPORTUNITY DEFINITIONS

SEC. 701. For the purposes of this title— (a) The term "person" includes one or more individuals, labor unions, partnerships, associations, corporations, legal representatives, mutual companies, joint-stock companies, trusts, unincorporated organizations, trustees, trustees in bankruptcy, or receivers.

(b) The term "employer" means a person engaged in an industry affecting commerce who has twenty-five or more employees for each working day in each of twenty or more calendar weeks in the current or preceding calendar year, and any agent of such a person, but such term does not include (1) the United States, a corporation wholly owned by the Government of the United States, an Indian tribe, or a State or political subdivision thereof, (2) a bona fide private membership club (other than a labor organization) which is exempt from taxation under section 501(c) of the Internal Revenue Code of 1954: Provided, That during the first year after the effective date prescribed in subsection (a) of section 716, persons having fewer than one hundred employees (and their agents) shall not be considered employers, and, during the second year after such date, persons having fewer than seventy-five employees (and their agents) shall not be considered employers, and, during the third year after such date, persons having fewer than fifty employees (and their agents) shall not be considered employers: Provided further, That it shall be the policy of the United States to insure equal employment opportunities for Federal employees without discrimination because of race, color, religion, sex or national origin and the President shall utilize his existing authority to effectuate this policy.

(c) The term "employment agency" means any person regularly undertaking with or without compensation to procure employees for an employer or to procure for employees opportunities to work for an employer and includes an agent of such a person; but shall not include an agency of the United States, or an agency of a State or political subdivision of a State, except that such term shall include the United States Employment Service and the system of State and local employment services receiving Federal assistance.

(d) The term "labor organization" means a labor organization engaged in an industry affecting commerce, and any agent of such an organization, and includes any organization of any kind, any agency, or employee representation committee, group, association, or plan so engaged in which employees participate and which exists for the purpose, in whole or in part, of dealing with employers concerning grievances, labor disputes, wages, rates of pay, hours, or other terms or conditions of employment, and any conference, general committee, joint or system board, or joint council so engaged which is subordinate to a national or international labor organization.

(e) A labor organization shall be deemed to be engaged in an industry affecting commerce if (1) it maintains or operates a hiring hall or hiring office which procures employees for an employer or procures for employees opportunities to work for an employer, or (2) the number of its members (or, where it is a labor organization composed of other labor organizations or their representatives, if the aggregate number of the members of such other labor organization) is (A) one hundred or more during the first year after the effective date prescribed in subsection (a) of section 716, (B) seventy-five or more during the second year after such date or fifty or more during the third year, or (C) twenty-five or more thereafter, and such labor organization—

(1) is the certified representative of employees under the provisions of the National Labor Relations Act, as amended, or the Railway Labor Act, as amended;

(2) although not certified, is a national or international labor organization or a local labor organization recognized or acting as the representative of employees of an employer or employers engaged in an industry affecting commerce; or

(3) has chartered a local labor organization or subsidiary body which is representing or actively seeking to represent employees of employers within the meaning of paragraph (1) or (2); or

(4) has been chartered by a labor organization representing or actively seeking to represent employees within the meaning of paragraph (1) or (2) as the local or subordinate body through which such employees may enjoy membership or become affiliated with such labor organization; or

(5) is a conference, general committee, joint or system board, or joint council subordinate to a national or international labor organization, which includes a labor organization engaged in an industry affecting commerce within the meaning of any of the preceding paragraphs of this subsection.

(f) The term "employee" means an individual employed by an employer.

(g) The term "commerce" means trade, traffic, commerce, transportation, transmission, or communication among the several States; or between a State and any place outside thereof; or within the District of Columbia, or a possession of the United States; or between points in the same State but through a point outside thereof.

(h) The term "industry affecting commerce" means any activity, business, or industry in commerce or in which a labor dispute would hinder or obstruct commerce or the free flow of commerce and includes any activity or industry "affecting commerce" within the meaning of the Labor Management Reporting and Disclosure Act of 1959.

(i) The term "State" includes a State of the United States, the District of Columbia, Puerto Rico, the Virgin Islands, American Samoa, Guam, Wake Island, The Canal Zone, and Outer Continental Shelf lands defined in the Outer Continental Shelf Lands Act.

EXEMPTION

SEC. 702. This title shall not apply to an employer with respect to the employment of aliens outside any State, or to a religious corporation, association, or society with respect to the employment of individuals of a particular religion to perform work connected with the carrying on by such corporation, association, or society of its religious activities or to an educational institution with respect to the employment of individuals to perform work connected with the educational activities of such institution.

DISCRIMINATION BECAUSE OF RACE, COLOR, RELIGION, SEX, OR NATIONAL ORIGIN

SEC. 703. (a) It shall be an unlawful employment practice for an employer—

(1) to fail or refuse to hire or to discharge any individual, or otherwise to discriminate against any individual with respect to his compensation, terms, conditions, or privileges of employment, because of such individual's race, color, religion, sex, or national origin; or

(2) to limit, segregate, or classify his employees in any way which would deprive or tend to deprive any individual of employment opportunities or otherwise adversely affect his status as an employee, because of such individual's race, color, religion, sex, or national origin.

(b) It shall be an unlawful employment practice for an employment agency to fail or refuse to refer for employment, or otherwise to discriminate against, any individual because of his race, color, religion, sex, or national origin, or to classify or refer for employment any individual on the basis of his race, color, religion, sex, or national origin.

(c) It shall be an unlawful employment practice for a labor organization—

(1) to exclude or to expel from its membership, or otherwise to discriminate against, any individual because of his race, color, religion, sex, or national origin;

(2) to limit, segregate, or classify its membership, or to classify or fail or refuse to refer for employment any individual, in any way which would deprive or tend to deprive any individual of employment opportunities, or would limit such employment opportunities or otherwise adversely affect his status as an employee or as an applicant for employment, because of such individual's race, color, religion, sex, or national origin; or

(3) to cause or attempt to cause an employer to discriminate against an individual in violation of this section.

(d) It shall be an unlawful employment practice for any employer, labor organization, or joint labor management committee controlling apprenticeship or other training or retraining, including on-the-job training programs to discriminate against any individual because of his race, color, religion, sex, or national origin in admission to, or employment in, any program established to provide apprenticeship or other training.

(e) Notwithstanding any other provision of this title, (1) it shall not be an unlawful employment practice for an employer to hire and employ employees, for an employment agency to classify, or refer for employment any individual, for a labor organization to classify its membership or to classify or refer for employment any individual, or for an employer, labor organization, or joint labor management committee controlling apprenticeship or other training or retraining programs to admit or employ any individual in any such program, on the basis of his religion, sex, or national origin in those certain instances where religion, sex, or national origin is a bona fide occupational qualification reasonably necessary to the normal operation of that particular business or enterprise, and (2) it shall not be an unlawful employment practice for a school, college, university, or other educational institution or institution of learning to hire and employ employees of a particular religion if such school, college, university, or other educational institution or institution of learning is, in whole or in substantial part, owned, supported, controlled, or managed by a particular religion or by a particular religious corporation, association, or society, or if the curriculum of such school, college, university, or other educational institution or institution of learning is directed toward the propagation of a particular religion.

(f) As used in this title, the phrase "unlawful employment practice" shall not be deemed to include any action or measure taken by an employer, labor organization, joint labor management committee, or employment agency with respect to an individual who is a member of the Communist Party of the United States or of any other organization required to register as a Communist-action or Communist-front organization by final order of the Subversive Activities Control Board pursuant to the Subversive Activities Control Act of 1950.

(g) Notwithstanding any other provision of this title, it shall not be an unlawful employment practice for an employer to fail or refuse to hire and employ any individual for any position, for an employer to discharge any individual from any position, or for an employment agency to fail or refuse to refer any individual for employment in any position, or for a labor organization to fail or refuse to refer any individual for employment in any position, if—

(1) the occupancy of such position, or access to the premises in or upon which any part of the duties of such position is performed or is to be performed, is subject to any requirement imposed in the interest of the national security of the United States under any security program in effect pursuant to or administered under any statute of the United States or any Executive order of the President; and

(2) such individual has not fulfilled or has ceased to fulfill that requirement.

(h) Notwithstanding any other provision of this title, it shall not be an unlawful employment practice for an employer to apply different standards of compensation, or different terms, conditions, or privileges of employment pursuant to a bona fide seniority or merit system, or a system which measures earnings by quantity or quality of production or to employees who work in different locations, provided that such differences are not the result of an intention to discriminate because of race, color, religion, sex, or national origin, nor shall it be an unlawful employment practice for an employer to give and to act upon the results of any professionally developed ability test provided that such test, its administration or action upon the results is not designed, intended or used to discriminate because of race, color, religion, sex or national origin. It shall not be an unlawful employment practice under this title for any employer to differentiate upon the basis of sex in determining the amount of the wages or compensation paid or to be paid to employees of such employer if such differentiation is authorized by the provisions of section 6(d) of the Fair Labor Standards Act of 1938, as amended (29 U.S.C. 206(d)).

(i) Nothing contained in this title shall apply to any business or enterprise on or near an Indian reservation with respect to any publicly announced employment practice of such business or enterprise under which a preferential treatment is given to any individual because he is an Indian living on or near a reservation.

(j) Nothing contained in this title shall be interpreted to require any employer, employment agency, labor organization, or joint labor management committee subject to this title to grant preferential treatment to any individual or to any group because of the race, color, religion, sex, or national origin of such individual or group on account of an imbalance which may exist with respect to the total number or percentage of persons of any race, color, religion, sex, or national origin employed by any employer, referred or classified for employment by any employment agency or labor organization, admitted to membership or classified by any labor organization, or admitted to, or employed in, any apprenticeship or other training program, in comparison with the total number or percentage of persons of such race, color, religion, sex, or national origin in any community, State, section, or other area, or in the available work force in any community, State, section, or other area.

OTHER UNLAWFUL EMPLOYMENT PRACTICES

SEC. 704. (a) It shall be an unlawful employment practice for an employer to discriminate against any of his employees or applicants for employment, for an employment agency to discriminate against any individual, or for a labor organization to discriminate against any member thereof or applicant for membership, because he has opposed, any practice made an unlawful employment practice by this title, or because he has made a charge, testified, assisted, or participated in any manner in an investigation, proceeding, or hearing under this title.

(b) It shall be an unlawful employment practice for an employer, labor organization, or employment agency to print or publish or cause to be printed or published any notice or advertisement relating to employment by such an employer or membership in or any classification or referral for employment by such a labor organization, or relating to any classification or referral for employment by such an employment agency, indicating any preference, limitation, specification, or discrimination, based on race, color, religion, sex, or national origin, except that such a notice or advertisement may indicate a preference, limitation, specification, or discrimination based on religion, sex, or national origin when religion, sex, or national origin is a bona fide occupational qualification for employment.

EQUAL EMPLOYMENT OPPORTUNITY COMMISSION

SEC. 705. (a) There is hereby created a Commission to be known as the Equal Employment Opportunity Commission, which shall be composed of five members, not more than three of whom shall be members of the same political party, who shall be appointed by the President by and with the advice and consent of the Senate. One of the original members shall be appointed for a term of one year, one for a term of two years, one for a term of three years, one for a term of four years, and one for a term of five years, beginning from the date of enactment of this title, but their successors shall be appointed for terms of five years each, except that any individual chosen to fill a vacancy shall be appointed only for the unexpired term of the member whom he shall succeed. The President shall designate one member to serve as Chairman of the Commission, and one member to serve as Vice Chairman. The Chairman shall be responsible on behalf of the Commission for the administrative operations of the Commission, and shall appoint, in accordance with the civil service laws, such officers, agents, attorneys, and employees as it deems necessary to assist it in the performance of its functions and to fix their compensation in accordance with the Classification Act of 1949, as amended. The Vice Chairman shall act as Chairman in the absence or disability of the Chairman or in the event of a vacancy in that office.

(b) A vacancy in the Commission shall not impair the right of the remaining members to exercise all the powers of the Commission and three members thereof shall constitute a quorum.

(c) The Commission shall have an official seal which shall be judicially noticed.

(d) The Commission shall at the close of each fiscal year report to the Congress and to the President concerning the action it has taken; the names, salaries, and duties of all individuals in its employ and the moneys it has disbursed; and shall make such further reports on the cause of and means of eliminating discrimination and such recommendations for further legislation as may appear desirable.

(e) The Federal Executive Pay Act of 1956, as amended (5 U.S.C. 2201-2209), is further amended—

(1) by adding to section 105 thereof (5 U.S.C. 2204) the following clause:

"(32) Chairman, Equal Employment Opportunity Commission"; and

(2) by adding to clause (45) of section 106(a) thereof (5 U.S.C. 2205(a)) the following: "Equal Employment Opportunity Commission (4)."

(f) The principal office of the Commission shall be in or near the District of Columbia, but it may meet or exercise any or all its powers at any other place. The Commission may establish such regional or State offices as it deems necessary to accomplish the purpose of this title.

(g) The Commission shall have power—

(1) to cooperate with and, with their consent, utilize regional, State, local, and other agencies, both public and private, and individuals;

(2) to pay to witnesses whose depositions are taken or who are summoned before the Commission or any of its agents the same witness and mileage fees as are paid to witnesses in the courts of the United States;

(3) to furnish to persons subject to this title such technical assistance as they may request to further their compliance with this title or an order issued thereunder;

(4) upon the request of (i) any employer, whose employees or some of them, or (ii) any labor organization, whose members or some of them, refuse or threaten to refuse to cooperate in effectuating the provisions of this title, to assist in such effectuation by conciliation or such other remedial action as is provided by this title;

(5) to make such technical studies as are appropriate to effectuate the purposes and policies of this title and to make the results of such studies available to the public;

(6) to refer matters to the Attorney General with recommendations for intervention in a civil action brought by an aggrieved party under section 706, or for the institution of a civil action by the Attorney General under section 707, and to advise, consult, and assist the Attorney General on such matters.

(h) Attorneys appointed under this section may, at the direction of the Commission, appear for and represent the Commission in any case in court.

(i) The Commission shall, in any of its educational or promotional activities, cooperate with other departments and agencies in the performance of such educational and promotional activities.

(j) All officers, agents, attorneys, and employees of the Commission shall be subject to the provisions of section 9 of the Act of August 2, 1939, as amended (the Hatch Act), notwithstanding any exemption contained in such section.

PREVENTION OF UNLAWFUL EMPLOYMENT PRACTICES

SEC. 706. (a) Whenever it is charged in writing under oath by a person claiming to be aggrieved, or a written charge has been filed by a member of the Commission where he has reasonable cause to believe a violation of this title has occurred (and such charge sets forth the facts upon which it is based) that an employer, employment agency, or labor organization has engaged in an unlawful employment practice, the Commission shall furnish such employer, employment agency, or labor organization (hereinafter referred to as the "respondent") with a copy of such charge and shall make an investigation of such charge, provided that such charge shall not be made public by the Commission. If the Commission shall determine, after such investigation, that there is reasonable cause to believe that the charge is true, the Commission shall endeavor to eliminate any such alleged unlawful employment practice by informal methods of conference, conciliation, and persuasion. Nothing said or done during and as a part of such endeavors may be made public by the Commission without the written consent of the parties, or used as evidence in a subsequent proceeding. Any officer or employee of the Commission, who shall make public in any manner whatever any information in violation of this subsection shall be deemed guilty of a misdemeanor and upon conviction thereof shall be fined not more than $1,000 or imprisoned not more than one year.

(b) In the case of an alleged unlawful employment practice occurring in a State, or political subdivision of a State, which has a State or local law prohibiting the unlawful employment practice alleged and establishing or authorizing a State or local authority to grant or seek relief from such practice or to institute criminal proceedings with respect thereto upon receiving notice thereof, no charge may be filed under subsection (a) by the person aggrieved before the expiration of sixty days after proceedings have been commenced under the State or local law, unless such proceedings have been earlier terminated, provided that such sixty-day period shall be extended to one hundred and twenty days during the first year after the effective date of such State or local law. If any requirement for the commencement of such proceedings is imposed by a State or local authority other than a requirement of the filing of a written and signed statement of the facts upon which the proceeding is based, the proceeding shall be deemed to have been commenced for the purposes of this subsection at the time such statement is sent by registered mail to the appropriate State or local authority.

(c) In the case of any charge filed by a member of the Commission alleging an unlawful employment practice occurring in a State or political subdivision of a State, which has a State or local law prohibiting the practice alleged and establishing or authorizing a State or local authority to grant or seek relief from such practice or to institute criminal proceedings with respect thereto upon receiving notice thereof, the Commission shall, before taking any action with respect to such charge, notify the appropriate State or local officials and, upon request, afford them a reasonable time, but not less than sixty days (provided that such sixty-day period shall be extended to one hundred and twenty days during the first year after the effective day of such State or local law), unless a shorter period is requested, to act under such State or local law to remedy the practice alleged.

(d) A charge under subsection (a) shall be filed within ninety days after the alleged unlawful employment practice occurred, except that in the case of an unlawful employment practice with respect to which the person aggrieved has followed the procedure set out in subsection (b), such charge shall be filed by the person aggrieved within two hundred and ten days after the alleged unlawful employment practice occurred, or within thirty days after receiving notice that the State or local agency has terminated the proceedings under the State or local, law, whichever is earlier, and a copy of such charge shall be filed by the Commission with the State or local agency.

(e) If within thirty days after a charge is filed with the Commission or within thirty days after expiration of any period of reference under subsection (c) (except that in either case such period may be extended to not more than sixty days upon a determination by the Commission that further efforts to secure voluntary compliance are warranted), the Commission has been unable to obtain voluntary compliance with this title, the Commission shall so notify the person aggrieved and a civil action may, within thirty days thereafter, be brought against the respondent named in the charge (1) by the person claiming to be aggrieved, or (2) if such charge was filed by a member of the Commission, by any person whom the charge alleges was aggrieved by the alleged unlawful employment practice. Upon application by the complainant and in such circumstances as the court may deem just, the court may appoint an attorney for such complainant and may authorize the commencement of the action without the payment of fees, costs, or security. Upon timely application, the court may, in its discretion, permit the Attorney General to intervene in such civil action if he certifies that the case is of general public importance. Upon request, the court may, in its discretion, stay further proceedings for not more than sixty days pending the termination of State or local proceedings described in subsection (b) or the efforts of the Commission to obtain voluntary compliance.

(f) Each United States district court and each United States court of a place subject to the jurisdiction of the United States shall have jurisdiction of actions brought under this title. Such an action may be brought in any judicial district in the State in which the unlawful employment practice is alleged to have been committed, in the judicial district in which the employment records relevant to such practice are maintained and administered, or in the judicial district in which the plaintiff would have worked but for the alleged unlawful employment practice, but if the respondent is not found within any such district, such an action may be brought within the judicial district in which the respondent has his principal office. For purposes of sections 1404 and 1406 of title 28 of the United States Code, the judicial district in which the respondent has his principal office shall in all cases be considered a district in which the action might have been brought.

(g) If the court finds that the respondent has intentionally engaged in or is intentionally engaging in an unlawful employment practice charged in the complaint, the court may enjoin the respondent from engaging in such unlawful employment practice, and order such affirmative action as may be appropriate, which may include reinstatement or hiring of employees, with or without back pay (payable by the employer, employment agency, or labor organization, as the case may be, responsible for the unlawful employment practice). Interim earnings or amounts earnable with reasonable diligence by the person or persons discriminated against shall operate to reduce the back pay otherwise allowable. No order of the court shall require the admission or reinstatement of an individual as a member of a union or the hiring, reinstatement, or promotion of an individual as an employee, or the payment to him of any back pay, if such individual was refused admission, suspended, or expelled or was refused employment or advancement or was suspended or discharged for any reason other than discrimination on account of race, color, religion, sex or national origin or in violation of section 704(a).

(h) The provisions of the Act entitled "An Act to amend the Judicial Code and to define and limit the jurisdiction of courts sitting in equity, and for other purposes," approved March 23, 1932 (29 U.S.C. 101-115), shall not apply with respect to civil actions brought under this section.

(i) In any case in which an employer, employment agency, or labor organization fails to comply with an order of a court issued in a civil action brought under subsection (e), the Commission may commence proceedings to compel compliance with such order.

(j) Any civil action brought under subsection (e) and any proceedings brought under subsection (i) shall be subject to appeal as provided in sections 1291 and 1292, title 28, United States Code.

(k) In any action or proceeding under this title the court, in its discretion, may allow the prevailing party, other than the Commission or the United States, a reasonable attorney's fee as part of the costs, and the Commission and the United States shall be liable for costs the same as a private person.

SEC. 707. (a) Whenever the Attorney General has reasonable cause to believe that any person or group of persons is engaged in a pattern or practice of resistance to the full enjoyment of any of the rights secured by this title, and that the pattern or practice is of such a nature and is intended to deny the full exercise of the rights herein described, the Attorney General may bring a civil action in the appropriate district court of the United States by filing with it a complaint (1) signed by him (or in his absence the Acting Attorney General), (2) setting forth facts pertaining to such pattern or practice, and (3) requesting such relief, including an application for a permanent or temporary injunction, restraining order or other order against the person or persons responsible for such pattern or practice, as he deems necessary to insure the full enjoyment of the rights herein described.

(b) The district courts of the United States shall have and shall exercise jurisdiction of proceedings instituted pursuant to this section, and in any such proceeding the Attorney General may file with the clerk of such court a request that a court of three judges be convened to hear and determine the case. Such request by the Attorney General shall be accompanied by a certificate that, in his opinion, the case is of general public importance. A copy of the certificate and request for a three-judge court shall be immediately furnished by such clerk to the chief judge of the circuit (or in his absence, the presiding circuit judge of the circuit) in which the case is pending. Upon receipt of such request it shall be the duty of the chief judge of the circuit or the presiding circuit judge, as the case may be, to designate immediately three judges in such circuit, of whom at least one shall be a circuit judge and another of whom shall be a district judge of the court in which the proceeding was instituted, to hear and determine such case, and it shall be the duty of the judges so designated to assign the case for hearing at the earliest practicable date, to participate in the hearing and determination thereof, and to cause the case to be in every way expedited. An appeal from the final judgment of such court will lie to the Supreme Court.

In the event the Attorney General fails to file such a request in any such proceeding, it shall be the duty of the chief judge of the district (or in his absence, the acting chief judge) in which the case is pending immediately to designate a judge in such district to hear and determine the case. In the event that no judge in the district is available to hear and determine the case, the chief judge of the district, or the acting chief judge, as the case may be, shall certify this fact to the chief judge of the circuit (or in his absence, the acting chief judge) who shall then designate a district or circuit judge of the circuit to hear and determine the case.

It shall be the duty of the judge designated pursuant to this section to assign the case for hearing at the earliest practicable date and to cause the case to be in every way expedited.

EFFECT ON STATE LAWS

SEC. 708. Nothing in this title shall be deemed to exempt or relieve any person from any liability, duty, penalty, or punishment provided by any present or future law of any State or political subdivision of a State, other than any such law which purports to require or permit the doing of any act which would be an unlawful employment practice under this title.

INVESTIGATIONS, INSPECTIONS, RECORDS, STATE AGENCIES

SEC. 709. (a) In connection with any investigation of a charge filed under section 706, the Commission or its designated representative shall at all reasonable times have access to, for the purposes of examination, and the right to copy any evidence of any person being investigated or proceeded against that relates to unlawful employment practices covered by this title and is relevant to the charge under investigation.

(b) The Commission may cooperate with State and local agencies charged with the administration of State fair employment practices laws and, with the consent of such agencies, may for the purpose of carrying out its functions and duties under this title and within the limitation of funds appropriated specifically for such purpose, utilize the services of such agencies and their employees and, notwithstanding any other provision of law, may reimburse such agencies and their employees for services rendered to assist the Commission in carrying out this title. In furtherance of such cooperative efforts, the Commission may enter into written agreements with such State or local agencies and such agreements may include provisions under which the Commission shall refrain from processing a charge in any cases or class of cases specified in such agreements and under which no person may bring a civil action under section 706 in any cases or class of cases so specified, or under which the Commission shall relieve any person or class of persons in such State or locality from requirements imposed under this section. The Commission shall rescind any such agreement whenever it determines that the agreement no longer serves the interest of effective enforcement of this title.

(c) Except as provided in subsection (d), every employer, employment agency, and labor organization subject to this title shall (1) make and keep such records relevant to the determinations of whether unlawful employment practices have been or are being committed, (2) preserve such records for such periods, and (3) make such reports therefrom, as the Commission shall prescribe by regulation or order, after public hearing, as reasonable, necessary, or appropriate for the enforcement of this title or the regulations or orders thereunder. The Commission shall, by regulation, require each employer, labor organization, and joint labor management committee subject to this title which controls an apprenticeship or other training program to maintain such records as are reasonably necessary to carry out the purpose of this title, including, but not limited to, a list of applicants who wish to participate in such program, including the chronological order in which such applications were received, and shall furnish to the Commission, upon request, a detailed description of the manner in which persons are selected to participate in the apprenticeship or other training program. Any employer, employment agency, labor organization, or joint labor management committee which believes that the application to it of any regulation or order issued under this section would result in undue hardship may (1) apply to the Commission for an exemption from the application of such regulation or order, or (2) bring a civil action in the United States district court for the district where such records are kept. If the Commission or the court, as the case may be, finds that the application of the regulation or order to the employer, employment agency, or labor organization in question would impose an undue hardship, the Commission or the court, as the case may be, may grant appropriate relief.

(d) The provisions of subsection (c) shall not apply to any employer, employment agency, labor organization, or joint labor management committee with respect to matters occurring in any State or political subdivision thereof which has a fair employment practice law during any period in which such employer, employment agency, labor organization, or joint labor management committee is subject to such law, except that the Commission may require such notations on records which such employer, employment agency, labor organization, or joint labor management committee keeps or is required to keep as are necessary because of differences in coverage or methods of enforcement between the State or local law and the provisions of this title. Where an employer is required by Executive Order 10925, issued March 6, 1961, or by any other Executive order prescribing fair employment practices for Government contractors and subcontractors, or by rules or regulations issued thereunder, to file reports relating to his employment practices with any Federal agency or committee, and he is substantially in compliance with such requirements, the Commission shall not require him to file additional reports pursuant to subsection (c) of this section.

(e) It shall be unlawful for any officer or employee of the Commission to make public in any manner whatever any information obtained by the Commission pursuant to its authority under this section prior to the institution of any proceeding under this title involving such information. Any officer or employee of the Commission who shall make public in any manner whatever any information in violation of this subsection shall be guilty of a misdemeanor and upon conviction thereof, shall be fined not more than $1,000, or imprisoned not more than one year.

INVESTIGATORY POWERS

SEC. 710. (a) For the purposes of any investigation of a charge filed under the authority contained in section 706, the Commission shall have authority to examine witnesses under oath and to require the production of documentary evidence relevant or material to the charge under investigation.

(b) If the respondent named in a charge filed under section 706 fails or refuses to comply with a demand of the Commission for permission to examine or to copy evidence in conformity with the provisions of section 709(a), or if any person required to comply with the provisions of section 709 (c) or (d) fails or refuses to do so, or if any person fails or refuses to comply with a demand by the Commission to give testimony under oath, the United States district court for the district in which such person is found, resides, or transacts business, shall, upon application of the Commission, have jurisdiction to issue to such person an order requiring him to comply with the provisions of section 709 (c) or (d) or to comply with the demand of the Commission, but the attendance of a witness may not be required outside the State where he is found, resides, or transacts business and the production of evidence may not be required outside the State where such evidence is kept.

(c) Within twenty days after the service upon any person charged under section 706 of a demand by the Commission for the production of documentary evidence or for permission to examine or to copy evidence in conformity with the provisions of section 709(a), such person may file in the district court of the United States for the judicial district in which he resides, is found, or transacts business, and serve upon the Commission a petition for an order of such court modifying or setting aside such demand. The time allowed for compliance with the demand in whole or in part as deemed proper and ordered by the court shall not run during the pendency of such petition in the court. Such petition shall specify each ground upon which the petitioner relies in seeking such relief, and may be based upon any failure of such demand to comply with the provisions of this title or with the limitations generally applicable to compulsory process or upon any constitutional or other legal right or privilege of such person. No objection which is not raised by such a petition may be urged in the defense to a proceeding initiated by the Commission under subsection (b) for enforcement of such a demand unless such proceeding is commenced by the Commission prior to the expiration of the twenty-day period, or unless the court determines that the defendant could not reasonably have been aware of the availability of such ground of objection.

(d) In any proceeding brought by the Commission under subsection (b), except as provided in subsection (c) of this section, the defendant may petition the court for an order modifying or setting aside the demand of the Commission.

SEC. 711. (a) Every employer, employment agency, and labor organization, as the case may be, shall post and keep posted in conspicuous places upon its premises where notices to employees, applicants for employment, and members are customarily posted a notice to be prepared or approved by the Commission setting forth excerpts from or, summaries of, the pertinent provisions of this title and information pertinent to the filing of a complaint.

(b) A willful violation of this section shall be punishable by a fine of not more than $100 for each separate offense.

VETERANS' PREFERENCE

SEC. 712. Nothing contained in this title shall be construed to repeal or modify any Federal, State, territorial, or local law creating special rights or preference for veterans.

RULES AND REGULATIONS

SEC. 713. (a) The Commission shall have authority from time to time to issue, amend, or rescind suitable procedural regulations to carry out the provisions of this title. Regulations issued under this section shall be in conformity with the standards and limitations of the Administrative Procedure Act.

(b) In any action or proceeding based on any alleged unlawful employment practice, no person shall be subject to any liability or punishment for or on account of (1) the commission by such person of an unlawful employment practice if he pleads and proves that the act or omission complained of was in good faith, in conformity with, and in reliance on any written interpretation or opinion of the Commission, or (2) the failure of such person to publish and file any information required by any provision of this title if he pleads and proves that he failed to publish and file such information in good faith, in conformity with the instructions of the Commission issued under this title regarding the filing of such information. Such a defense, if established, shall be a bar to the action or proceeding, notwithstanding that (A) after such act or omission, such interpretation or opinion is modified or rescinded or is determined by judicial authority to be invalid or of no legal effect, or (B) after publishing or filing the description and annual reports, such publication or filing is determined by judicial authority not to be in conformity with the requirements of this title.

FORCIBLY RESISTING THE COMMISSION OR ITS REPRESENTATIVES

SEC. 714. The provisions of section 111, title 18, United States Code, shall apply to officers, agents, and employees of the Commission in the performance of their official duties.

SPECIAL STUDY BY SECRETARY OF LABOR

SEC. 715. The Secretary of Labor shall make a full and complete study of the factors which might tend to result in discrimination in employment because of age and of the consequences of such discrimination on the economy and individuals affected. The Secretary of Labor shall make a report to the Congress not later than June 30, 1965, containing the results of such study and shall include in such report such recommendations for legislation to prevent arbitrary discrimination in employment because of age as he determines advisable.

EFFECTIVE DATE

SEC. 716. (a) This title shall become effective one year after the date of its enactment.

(b) Notwithstanding subsection (a), sections of this title other than sections 703, 704, 706, and 707 shall become effective immediately.

(c) The President shall, as soon as feasible after the enactment of this title, convene one or more conferences for the purpose of enabling the leaders of groups whose members will be affected by this title to become familiar with the rights afforded and obligations imposed by its provisions, and for the purpose of making plans which will result in the fair and effective administration of this title when all of its provisions become effective. The President shall invite the participation in such conference or conferences of (1) the members of the President's Committee on Equal Employment Opportunity, (2) the members of the Commission on Civil Rights, (3) representatives of State and local agencies engaged in furthering equal employment opportunity, (4) representatives of private agencies engaged in furthering equal employment opportunity, and (5) representatives of employers, labor organizations, and employment agencies who will be subject to this title.

TITLE VIII—REGISTRATION AND VOTING STATISTICS

SEC. 801. The Secretary of Commerce shall promptly conduct a survey to compile registration and voting statistics in such geographic areas as may be recommended by the Commission on Civil Rights. Such a survey and compilation shall, to the extent recommended by the Commission on Civil Rights, only include a count of persons of voting age by race, color, and national origin, and determination of the extent to which such persons are registered to vote, and have voted in any statewide primary or general election in which the Members of the United States House of Representatives are nominated or elected, since January 1, 1960. Such information shall also be collected and compiled in connection with the Nineteenth Decennial Census, and at such other times as the Congress may prescribe. The provisions of section 9 and chapter 7 of title 13, United States Code, shall apply to any survey, collection, or compilation of registration and voting statistics carried out under this title: Provided, however, That no person shall be compelled to disclose his race, color, national origin, or questioned about his political party affiliation, how he voted, or the reasons therefore, nor shall any penalty be imposed for his failure or refusal to make such disclosure. Every person interrogated orally, by written survey or questionnaire or by any other means with respect to such information shall be fully advised with respect to his right to fail or refuse to furnish such information.

TITLE IX—INTERVENTION AND PROCEDURE AFTER REMOVAL IN CIVIL RIGHTS CASES

SEC. 901. Title 28 of the United States Code, section 1447(d), is amended to read as follows:

"An order remanding a case to the State court from which it was removed is not reviewable on appeal or otherwise, except that an order remanding a case to the State court from which it was removed pursuant to section 1443 of this title shall be reviewable by appeal or otherwise."

SEC. 902. Whenever an action has been commenced in any court of the United States seeking relief from the denial of equal protection of the laws under the fourteenth amendment to the Constitution on account of race, color, religion, or national origin, the Attorney General for or in the name of the United States may intervene in such action upon timely application if the Attorney General certifies that the case is of general public importance. In such action the United States shall be entitled to the same relief as if it had instituted the action.

TITLE X—ESTABLISHMENT OF COMMUNITY RELATIONS SERVICE

SEC. 1001. (a) There is hereby established in and as a part of the Department of Commerce a Community Relations Service (hereinafter referred to as the "Service"), which shall be headed by a Director who shall be appointed by the President with the advice and consent of the Senate for a term of four years. The Director is authorized to appoint, subject to the civil service laws and regulations, such other personnel as may be necessary to enable the Service to carry out its functions and duties, and to fix their compensation in accordance with the Classification Act of 1949, as amended. The Director is further authorized to procure services as authorized by section 15 of the Act of August 2, 1946 (60 Stat. 810; 5 U.S.C. 55(a)), but at rates for individuals not in excess of $75 per diem.

(b) Section 106(a) of the Federal Executive Pay Act of 1956, as amended (5 U.S.C. 2205(a)), is further amended by adding the following clause thereto:

"(52) Director, Community Relations Service."

SEC. 1002. It shall be the function of the Service to provide assistance to communities and persons therein in resolving disputes, disagreements, or difficulties relating to discriminatory practices based on race, color, or national origin which impair the rights of persons in such communities under the Constitution or laws of the United States or which affect or may affect interstate commerce. The Service may offer its services in cases of such disputes, disagreements, or difficulties whenever, in its judgment, peaceful relations among the citizens of the community involved are threatened thereby, and it may offer its services either upon its own motion or upon the request of an appropriate State or local official or other interested person.

SEC. 1003. (a) The Service shall, whenever possible, in performing its functions, seek and utilize the cooperation of appropriate State or local, public, or private agencies.

(b) The activities of all officers and employees of the Service in providing conciliation assistance shall be conducted in confidence and without publicity, and the Service shall hold confidential any information acquired in the regular performance of its duties upon the understanding that it would be so held. No officer or employee of the Service shall engage in the performance of investigative or prosecuting functions of any department or agency in any litigation arising out of a dispute in which he acted on behalf of the Service. Any officer or other employee of the Service, who shall make public in any manner whatever any information in violation of this subsection, shall be deemed guilty of a misdemeanor and, upon conviction thereof, shall be fined not more than $1,000 or imprisoned not more than one year.

SEC. 1004. Subject to the provisions of sections 205 and 1003(b), the Director shall, on or before January 31 of each year, submit to the Congress a report of the activities of the Service during the preceding fiscal year.

TITLE XI—MISCELLANEOUS

SEC. 1101. In any proceeding for criminal contempt arising under title II, III, IV, V, VI, or VII of this Act, the accused, upon demand therefor, shall be entitled to a trial by jury, which shall conform as near as may be to the practice in criminal cases. Upon conviction, the accused shall not be fined more than $1,000 or imprisoned for more than six months.

This section shall not apply to contempts committed in the presence of the court, or so near thereto as to obstruct the administration of justice, nor to the mis-

behavior, misconduct, or disobedience of any officer of the court in respect to writs, orders, or process of the court. No person shall be convicted of criminal contempt hereunder unless the act or omission constituting such contempt shall have been intentional, as required in other cases of criminal contempt.

Nor shall anything herein be construed to deprive courts of their power, by civil contempt proceedings, without a jury, to secure compliance with or to prevent obstruction of, as distinguished from punishment for violations of, any lawful writ, process, order, rule, decree, or command of the court in accordance with the prevailing usages of law and equity, including the power of detention.

SEC. 1102. No person should be put twice in jeopardy under the laws of the United States for the same act or omission. For this reason, an acquittal or conviction in a prosecution for a specific crime under the laws of the United States shall bar a proceeding for criminal contempt, which is based upon the same act or omission and which arises under the provisions of this Act; and an acquittal or conviction in a proceeding for criminal contempt, which arises under the provisions of this Act, shall bar a prosecution for a specific crime under the laws of the United States based upon the same act or omission.

SEC. 1103. Nothing in this Act shall be construed to deny, impair, or otherwise affect any right or authority of the Attorney General or of the United States or any agency or officer thereof under existing law to institute or intervene in any action or proceeding.

SEC. 1104. Nothing contained in any title of this Act shall be construed as indicating an intent on the part of Congress to occupy the field in which any such title operates to the exclusion of State laws on the same subject matter, nor shall any provision of this Act be construed as invalidating any provision of State law unless such provision is inconsistent with any of the purposes of this Act, or any provision thereof.

SEC. 1105. There are hereby authorized to be appropriated such sums as are necessary to carry out the provisions of this Act.

SEC. 1106. If any provision of this Act or the application thereof to any person or circumstances is held invalid, the remainder of the Act and the application of the provision to other persons not similarly situated or to other circumstances shall not be affected thereby.

Approved July 2, 1964.

The Tonkin Gulf Resolution

Eighty-eighth Congress of the United States of America

AT THE SECOND SESSION

Begun and held at the City of Washington on Tuesday, the seventh day of January, one thousand nine hundred and sixty-four

Joint Resolution

To promote the maintenance of international peace and security in southeast Asia.

Whereas naval units of the Communist regime in Vietnam, in violation of the principles of the Charter of the United Nations and of international law, have deliberately and repeatedly attacked United Stated naval vessels lawfully present in international waters, and have thereby created a serious threat to international peace; and

Whereas these attackers are part of deliberate and systematic campaign of aggression that the Communist regime in North Vietnam has been waging against its neighbors and the nations joined with them in the collective defense of their freedom; and

Whereas the United States is assisting the peoples of southeast Asia to protest their freedom and has no territorial, military or political ambitions in that area, but desires only that these people should be left in peace to work out their destinies in their own way: Now, therefore be it

Resolved by the Senate and House of Representatives of the United States of America in Congress assembled, That the Congress approves and supports the determination of the President, as Commander in Chief, to take all necessary measures to repel any armed attack against the forces of the United States and to prevent further aggression.

Section 2. The United States regards as vital to its national interest and to world peace the maintenance of international peace and security in southeast Asia. Consonant with the Constitution of the United States and the Charter of the United Nations and in accordance with its obligations under the Southeast Asia Collective Defense Treaty, the United States is, therefore, prepared, as the President determines, to take all necessary steps, including the use of armed force, to assist any member or protocol state of the Southeast Asia Collective Defense Treaty requesting assistance in defense of its freedom.

Section 3. This resolution shall expire when the President shall determine that the peace and security of the area is reasonably assured by international conditions created by action of the United Nations or otherwise, except that it may be terminated earlier by concurrent resolution of the Congress.

[endorsements]

The Social Security Act Amendments

AN ACT

To provide a hospital insurance program for the aged under the Social Security Act with a supplementary medical benefits program and an extended program of medical assistance, to increase benefits under the Old-Age, Survivors, and Disability Insurance System, to improve the Federal-State public assistance programs, and for other purposes.

Be it enacted by the Senate and House of Representatives of the United States of America in Congress assembled, That this Act, with the following table of contents, may be cited as the "Social Security Amendments of 1965."

TABLE OF CONTENTS

TITLE I—HEALTH INSURANCE FOR THE AGED AND MEDICAL ASSISTANCE

SHORT TITLE
SEC. 100. This title may be cited as the "Health Insurance for the Aged Act."

PART 1—HEALTH INSURANCE BENEFITS FOR THE AGED

ENTITLEMENT TO HOSPITAL INSURANCE BENEFITS

SEC. 101. Title II of the Social Security Act is amended by adding at the end thereof the following new section:

"ENTITLEMENT TO HOSPITAL INSURANCE BENEFITS

"SEC. 226. (a) Every individual who—

"(1) has attained the age of 65, and

"(2) is entitled to monthly insurance benefits under section 202 or is a qualified railroad retirement beneficiary, shall be entitled to hospital insurance benefits under part A of title XVIII for each month for which he meets the condition specified in paragraph (2), beginning with the first month after June 1966 for which he meets the conditions specified in paragraphs (1) and (2).

"(b) For purposes of subsection (a)—

"(1) entitlement of an individual to hospital insurance benefits for a month shall consist of entitlement to have payment made under, and subject to the limitations in, part A of title XVIII on his behalf for inpatient hospital services, post-hospital extended care services, post-hospital home health services, and outpatient hospital diagnostic services (as such terms are defined in part C of title XVIII) furnished him in the United States (or outside the United States in the case of inpatient hospital services furnished under the conditions described in section 1814(f) during such months except that (A) no such payment may be made for post-hospital extended care services furnished before January 1967, and (B) no such payment may be made for post-hospital extended care services or post-hospital home health services unless the discharge from the hospital required to qualify such services for payment under part A of title XVIII occurred after June 30, 1966, or on or after the first day of the month in which he attains age 65, whichever is later; and

"(2) an individual shall be deemed entitled to monthly insurance benefits under section 202, or to be a qualified railroad retirement beneficiary, for the month in which he died if he would have been entitled to such benefits, or would have been a qualified railroad retirement beneficiary, for such month had he died in the next month.

" (c) For purposes of this section, the term 'qualified railroad retirement beneficiary' means an individual whose name has been certified to the Secretary by the Railroad Retirement Board under section 21 of the Railroad Retirement Act of 1937. An individual shall cease to be a qualified railroad retirement beneficiary at the close of the month preceding the month which is certified by the . . .

(The first page of the act is provided. For the remainder see "Social Security Amendments of 1965" (PL 89-97, 30 July 1965), 79 United States Statutes at Large, pp. 286–423.)

The Voting Rights Act

AN ACT To enforce the fifteenth amendment to the Constitution of the United States, and for other purposes.

Be it enacted by the Senate and House of Representatives of the United States of America in Congress assembled, That this Act shall be known as the "Voting Rights Act of 1965."

SEC. 2. No voting qualification or prerequisite to voting, or standard, practice, or procedure shall be imposed or applied by any State or political subdivision to deny or abridge the right of any citizen of the United States to vote on account of race or color.

SEC. 3. (a) Whenever the Attorney General institutes a proceeding under any statute to enforce the guarantees of the fifteenth amendment in any State or political subdivision the court shall authorize the appointment of Federal examiners by the United States Civil Service Commission in accordance with section 6 to serve for such period of time and for such political subdivisions as the court shall determine is appropriate to enforce the guarantees of the fifteenth amendment (1) as part of any interlocutory order if the court determines that the appointment of such examiners is necessary to enforce such guarantees or (2) as part of any final judgment if the court finds that violations of the fifteenth amendment justifying equitable relief have occurred in such State or subdivision: Provided, That the court need not authorize the appointment of examiners if any incidents of denial or abridgement of the right to vote on account of race or color (1) have been few in number and have been promptly and effectively corrected by State or local action, (2) the continuing effect of such incidents has been eliminated, and (3) there is no reasonable probability of their recurrence in the future.

(b) If in a proceeding instituted by the Attorney General under any statute to enforce the guarantees of the fifteenth amendment in any State or political subdivision the court finds that a test or device has been used for the purpose or with the effect of denying or abridging the right of any citizen of the United States to vote on account of race or color, it shall suspend the use of tests and devices in such State or

political subdivisions as the court shall determine is appropriate and for such period as it deems necessary.

(c) If in any proceeding instituted by the Attorney General under any statute to enforce the guarantees of the fifteenth amendment in any State or political subdivision the court finds that violations of the fifteenth amendment justifying equitable relief have occurred within the territory of such State or political subdivision, the court, in addition to such relief as it may grant, shall retain jurisdiction for such period as it may deem appropriate and during such period no voting qualification or prerequisite to voting, or standard, practice, or procedure with respect to voting different from that in force or effect at the time the proceeding was commenced shall be enforced unless and until the court finds that such qualification, prerequisite, standard, practice, or procedure does not have the purpose and will not have the effect of denying or abridging the right to vote on account of race or color: Provided, That such qualification, prerequisite, standard, practice, or procedure may be enforced if the qualification, prerequisite, standard, practice, or procedure has been submitted by the chief legal officer or other appropriate official of such State or subdivision to the Attorney General and the Attorney General has not interposed an objection within sixty days after such submission, except that neither the court's finding nor the Attorney General's failure to object shall bar a subsequent action to enjoin enforcement of such qualification, prerequisite, standard, practice, or procedure.

SEC. 4. (a) To assure that the right of citizens of the United States to vote is not denied or abridged on account of race or color, no citizen shall be denied the right to vote in any Federal, State, or local election because of his failure to comply with any test or device in any State with respect to which the determinations have been made under subsection (b) or in any political subdivision with respect to which such determinations have been made as a separate unit, unless the United States District Court for the District of Columbia in an action for a declaratory judgment brought by such State or subdivision against the United States has determined that no such test or device has been used during the five years preceding the filing of the action for the purpose or with the effect of denying or abridging the right to vote on account of race or color: Provided, That no such declaratory judgment shall issue with respect to any plaintiff for a period of five years after the entry of a final judgment of any court of the United States, other than the denial of a declaratory judgment under this section, whether entered prior to or after the enactment of this Act, determining that denials or abridgments of the right to vote on account of race or color through the use of such tests or devices have occurred anywhere in the territory of such plaintiff. An action pursuant to this subsection shall be heard and determined by a court of three judges in accordance with the provisions of section 2284 of title 28 of the United States Code and any appeal shall lie to the Supreme Court. The court shall retain jurisdiction of any action pursuant to this subsection for five years after judgment and shall reopen the action upon motion of the Attorney General alleging that a test or device has been used for the purpose or with the effect of denying or abridging the right to vote on account of race or color.

If the Attorney General determines that he has no reason to believe that any such test or device has been used during the five years preceding the filing of the action for the purpose or with the effect of denying or abridging the right to vote on account of race or color, he shall consent to the entry of such judgment

(b) The provisions of subsection (a) shall apply in any State or in any political subdivision of a state which (1) the Attorney General determines maintained on November 1, 1964, any test or device, and with respect to which (2) the Director of the Census determines that less than 50 percentum of the persons of voting age residing therein were registered on November 1, 1964, or that less than 50 percentum of such persons voted in the presidential election of November 1964.

A determination or certification of the Attorney General or of the Director of the Census under this section or under section 6 or section 13 shall not be reviewable in any court and shall be effective upon publication in the Federal Register.

(c) The phrase "test or device" shall mean any requirement that a person as a prerequisite for voting or registration for voting (1) demonstrate the ability to read, write, understand, or interpret any matter, (2) demonstrate any educational achievement or his

knowledge of any particular subject, (3) possess good moral character, or (4) prove his qualifications by the voucher of registered voters or members of any other class.

(d) For purposes of this section no State or political subdivision shall be determined to have engaged in the use of tests or devices for the purpose or with the effect of denying or abridging the right to vote on account of race or color if (1) incidents of such use have been few in number and have been promptly and effectively corrected by State or local action, (2) the continuing effect of such incidents has been eliminated, and (3) there is no reasonable probability of their recurrence in the future.

(e) (1) Congress hereby declares that to secure the rights under the fourteenth amendment of persons educated in American flag schools in which the predominant classroom language was other than English, it is necessary to prohibit the States from conditioning the right to vote of such persons on ability to read, write, understand, or interpret any matter in the English language.

(2) No person who demonstrates that he has successfully completed the sixth primary grade in a public school in, or a private school accredited by, any State or territory, the District of Columbia, or the Commonwealth of Puerto Rico in which the predominant classroom language was other than English, shall be denied the right to vote in any Federal, State, or local election because of his inability to read, write, understand, or interpret any matter in the English language, except that, in States in which State law provides that a different level of education is presumptive of literacy, he shall demonstrate that he has successfully completed an equivalent level of education in a public school in, or a private school accredited by, any State or territory, the District of Columbia, or the Commonwealth of Puerto Rico in which the predominant classroom language was other than English.

SEC. 5. Whenever a State or political subdivision with respect to which the prohibitions set forth in section 4(a) are in effect shall enact or seek to administer any voting qualification or prerequisite to voting, or standard, practice, or procedure with respect to voting different from that in force or effect on November 1, 1964, such State or subdivision may institute an action in the United States District Court for the District of Columbia for a declaratory judgment that such qualification, prerequisite, standard, practice, or procedure does not have the purpose and will not have the effect of denying or abridging the right to vote on account of race or color, and unless and until the court enters such judgment no person shall be denied the right to vote for failure to comply with such qualification, prerequisite, standard, practice, or procedure: Provided, That such qualification, prerequisite, standard, practice, or procedure may be enforced without such proceeding if the qualification, prerequisite, standard, practice, or procedure has been submitted by the chief legal officer or other appropriate official of such State or subdivision to the Attorney General and the Attorney General has not interposed an objection within sixty days after such submission, except that neither the Attorney General's failure to object nor a declaratory judgment entered under this section shall bar a subsequent action to enjoin enforcement of such qualification, prerequisite, standard, practice, or procedure. Any action under this section shall be heard and determined by a court of three judges in accordance with the provisions of section 2284 of title 28 of the United States Code and any appeal shall lie to the Supreme Court.

SEC. 6. Whenever (a) a court has authorized the appointment of examiners pursuant to the provisions of section 3(a), or (b) unless a declaratory judgment has been rendered under section 4(a), the Attorney General certifies with respect to any political subdivision named in, or included within the scope of, determinations made under section 4(b) that (1) he has received complaints in writing from twenty or more residents of such political subdivision alleging that they have been denied the right to vote under color of law on account of race or color, and that he believes such complaints to be meritorious, or (2) that, in his judgment (considering, among other factors, whether the ratio of nonwhite persons to white persons registered to vote within such subdivision appears to him to be reasonably attributable to violations of the fifteenth amendment or whether substantial evidence exists that bona fide efforts are being made within such subdivision to comply with the fifteenth amendment), the appointment of examiners is otherwise necessary to enforce the guarantees of the fifteenth amendment, the Civil Service Commission shall appoint as many examiners for such subdivision as it may deem appropriate to prepare and maintain lists of persons eligible to vote in Federal, State, and local elections. Such examiners, hearing officers provided for in section 9(a), and other persons deemed necessary by the Commission to carry out the provisions and purposes of this Act shall be appointed, compensated, and separated without regard to the provisions of any statute administered by the Civil Service Commission, and service under this Act shall not be considered employment for the purposes of any statute administered by the Civil Service Commission, except the provisions of section 9 of the Act of August 2, 1939, as amended (5 U.S.C. 118i), prohibiting partisan political activity: Provided, That the Commission is authorized, after consulting the head of the appropriate department or agency, to designate suitable persons in the official service of the United States, with their consent, to serve in these positions. Examiners and hearing officers shall have the power to administer oaths.

SEC. 7. (a) The examiners for each political subdivision shall, at such places as the Civil Service Commission shall by regulation designate, examine applicants concerning their qualifications for voting. An application to an examiner shall be in such form as the Commission may require and shall contain allegations that the applicant is not otherwise registered to vote.

(b) Any person whom the examiner finds, in accordance with instructions received under section 9(b), to have the qualifications prescribed by State law not inconsistent with the Constitution and laws of the United States shall promptly be placed on a list of eligible voters. A challenge to such listing may be made in accordance with section 9(a) and shall not be the basis for a prosecution under section 12 of this Act. The examiner shall certify and transmit such list, and any supplements as appropriate, at least once a month, to the offices of the appropriate election officials, with copies to the Attorney General and the attorney general of the State, and any such lists and supplements thereto transmitted during the month shall be available for public inspection on the last business day of the month and, in any event, not later than the forty-fifth day prior to any election. The appropriate State or local election official shall place such names on the official voting list. Any person whose name appears on the examiner's list shall be entitled and allowed to vote in the election district of his residence unless and until the appropriate election officials shall have been notified that such person has been removed from such list in accordance with subsection (d): Provided, That no person shall be entitled to vote in any election by virtue of this Act unless his name shall have been certified and transmitted on such a list to the offices of the appropriate election officials at least forty-five days prior to such election.

(c) The examiner shall issue to each person whose name appears on such a list a certificate evidencing his eligibility to vote.

(d) A person whose name appears on such a list shall be removed therefrom by an examiner if (1) such person has been successfully challenged in accordance with the procedure prescribed in section 9, or (2) he has been determined by an examiner to have lost his eligibility to vote under State law not inconsistent with the Constitution and the laws of the United States.

Sec. 8. Whenever an examiner is serving under this Act in any political subdivision, the Civil Service Commission may assign, at the request of the Attorney General, one or more persons, who may be officers of the United States, (1) to enter and attend at any place for holding an election in such subdivision for the purpose of observing whether persons who are entitled to vote are being permitted to vote, and (2) to enter and attend at any place for tabulating the votes cast at any election held in such subdivision for the purpose of observing whether votes cast by persons entitled to vote are being properly tabulated. Such persons so assigned shall report to an examiner appointed for such political subdivision, to the Attorney General, and if the appointment of examiners has been authorized pursuant to section 3(a), to the court.

SEC. 9.

(a) Any challenge to a listing on an eligibility list prepared by an examiner shall be heard and determined by a hearing officer appointed by and responsible to the Civil Service Commission and under such rules as the Commission shall by regulation prescribe. Such challenge shall be entertained only if filed at such office within the State as the Civil Service Commission shall by regulation designate, and within ten days after the listing of the challenged person is made available for public inspection, and if supported by (1) the affidavits of at least two persons having personal knowledge of the facts constituting grounds for the challenge, and (2) a certification that a copy of the challenge and affidavits have been served by mail or in person upon the person challenged at his place of residence set out in the application. Such challenge shall be determined within fifteen days after it has been filed. A petition for re-

view of the decision of the hearing officer may be filed in the United States court of appeals for the circuit in which the person challenged resides within fifteen days after service of such decision by mail on the person petitioning for review but no decision of a hearing officer shall be reversed unless clearly erroneous. Any person listed shall be entitled and allowed to vote pending final determination by the hearing officer and by the court.

(b) The times, places, procedures, and form for application and listing pursuant to this Act and removals from the eligibility lists shall be prescribed by regulations promulgated by the Civil Service Commission and the Commission shall, after consultation with the Attorney General, instruct examiners concerning applicable State law not inconsistent with the Constitution and laws of the United States with respect to (1) the qualifications required for listing, and (2) loss of eligibility to vote.

(c) Upon the request of the applicant or the challenger or on its own motion the Civil Service Commission shall have the power to require by subpoena the attendance and testimony of witnesses and the production of documentary evidence relating to any matter pending before it under the authority of this section. In case of contumacy or refusal to obey a subpoena, any district court of the United States or the United States court of any territory or possession, or the District Court of the United States for the District of Columbia, within the jurisdiction of which said person guilty of contumacy or refusal to obey is found or resides or is domiciled or transacts business, or has appointed an agent for receipt of service of process, upon application by the Attorney General of the United States shall have jurisdiction to issue to such person an order requiring such person to appear before the Commission or a hearing officer, there to produce pertinent, relevant, and nonprivileged documentary evidence if so ordered, or there to give testimony touching the matter under investigation, and any failure to obey such order of the court may be punished by said court as a contempt thereof.

SEC. 10. (a) The Congress finds that the requirement of the payment of a poll tax as a precondition to voting (i) precludes persons of limited means from voting or imposes unreasonable financial hardship upon such persons as a precondition to their exercise of the franchise, (ii) does not bear a reasonable relationship to any legitimate State interest in the conduct of elections, and (iii) in some areas has the purpose or effect of denying persons the right to vote because of race or color. Upon the basis of these findings, Congress declares that the constitutional right of citizens to vote is denied or abridged in some areas by the requirement of the payment of a poll tax as a precondition to voting.

(b) In the exercise of the powers of Congress under section 5 of the fourteenth amendment and section 2 of the fifteenth amendment, the Attorney General is authorized and directed to institute forthwith in the name of the United States such actions, including actions against States or political subdivisions, for declaratory judgment or injunctive relief against the enforcement of any requirement of the payment of a poll tax as a precondition to voting, or substitute therefor enacted after November 1, 1964, as will be necessary to implement the declaration of subsection (a) and the purposes of this section.

(c) The district courts of the United States shall have jurisdiction of such actions which shall be heard and determined by a court of three judges in accordance with the provisions of section 2284 of title 28 of the United States Code and any appeal shall lie to the Supreme Court. It shall be the duty of the judges designated to hear the case to assign the case for hearing at the earliest practicable date, to participate in the hearing and determination thereof, and to cause the case to be in every way expedited.

(d) During the pendency of such actions, and thereafter if the courts, notwithstanding this action by the Congress, should declare the requirement of the payment of a poll tax to be constitutional, no citizen of the United States who is a resident of a State or political subdivision with respect to which determinations have been made under subsection 4(b) and a declaratory judgment has not been entered under subsection 4(a), during the first year he becomes otherwise entitled to vote by reason of registration by State or local officials or listing by an examiner, shall be denied the right to vote for failure to pay a poll tax if he tenders payment of such tax for the current year to an examiner or to the appropriate State or local official at least forty-five days prior to election, whether or not such tender would be timely or adequate under State law. An examiner shall have authority to accept such payment from any person authorized by this Act to make an application for listing, and shall issue a receipt for such payment. The examiner shall transmit promptly any such poll tax payment to the office of the State or local official authorized to receive such payment under State law, together with the name and address of the applicant.

SEC. 11. (a) No person acting under color of law shall fail or refuse to permit any person to vote who is entitled to vote under any provision of this Act or is otherwise qualified to vote, or willfully fail or refuse to tabulate, count, and report such person's vote.

(b) No person, whether acting under color of law or otherwise, shall intimidate, threaten, or coerce, or attempt to intimidate, threaten, or coerce any person for voting or attempting to vote, or intimidate, threaten, or coerce, or attempt to intimidate, threaten, or coerce any person for urging or aiding any person to vote or attempt to vote, or intimidate, threaten, or coerce any person for exercising any powers or duties under section 3(a), 6, 8, 9, 10, or 12(e).

(c) Whoever knowingly or willfully gives false information as to his name, address, or period of residence in the voting district for the purpose of establishing his eligibility to register or vote, or conspires with another individual for the purpose of encouraging his false registration to vote or illegal voting, or pays or offers to pay or accepts payment either for registration to vote or for voting shall be fined not more than $10,000 or imprisoned not more than five years, or both: Provided, however, That this provision shall be applicable only to general, special, or primary elections held solely or in part for the purpose of selecting or electing any candidate for the office of President, Vice President, presidential elector, Member of the United States Senate, Member of the United States House of Representatives, or Delegates or Commissioners from the territories or possessions, or Resident Commissioner of the Commonwealth of Puerto Rico.

(d) Whoever, in any matter within the jurisdiction of an examiner or hearing officer knowingly and willfully falsifies or conceals a material fact, or makes any false, fictitious, or fraudulent statements or representations, or makes or uses any false writing or document knowing the same to contain any false, fictitious, or fraudulent statement or entry, shall be fined not more than $10,000 or imprisoned not more than five years, or both.

SEC. 12. (a) Whoever shall deprive or attempt to deprive any person of any right secured by section 2,

3, 4, 5, 7, or 10 or shall violate section 11(a) or (b), shall be fined not more than $5,000, or imprisoned not more than five years, or both.

(b) Whoever, within a year following an election in a political subdivision in which an examiner has been appointed (1) destroys, defaces, mutilates, or otherwise alters the marking of a paper ballot which has been cast in such election, or (2) alters any official record of voting in such election tabulated from a voting machine or otherwise, shall be fined not more than $5,000, or imprisoned not more than five years, or both

(c) Whoever conspires to violate the provisions of subsection (a) or (b) of this section, or interferes with any right secured by section 2, 3 4, 5, 7, 10, or 11(a) or (b) shall be fined not more than $5,000, or imprisoned not more than five years, or both.

(d) Whenever any person has engaged or there are reasonable grounds to believe that any person is about to engage in any act or practice prohibited by section 2, 3, 4, 5, 7, 10, 11, or subsection (b) of this section, the Attorney General may institute for the United States, or in the name of the United States, an action for preventive relief, including an application for a temporary or permanent injunction, restraining order, or other order, and including an order directed to the State and State or local election officials to require them (1) to permit persons listed under this Act to vote and (2) to count such votes.

(e) Whenever in any political subdivision in which there are examiners appointed pursuant to this Act any persons allege to such an examiner within forty-eight hours after the closing of the polls that notwithstanding (1) their listing under this Act or registration by an appropriate election official and (2) their eligibility to vote, they have not been permitted to vote in such election, the examiner shall forthwith notify the Attorney General if such allegations in his opinion appear to be well founded. Upon receipt of such notification, the Attorney General may forthwith file with the district court an application for an order providing for the marking, casting, and counting of the ballots of such persons and requiring the inclusion of their votes in the total vote before the results of such election shall be deemed final and any force or effect given thereto. The district court shall hear and determine such matters immediately after the filing of such application. The remedy provided in this subsection shall not preclude any remedy available under State or Federal law.

(f) The district courts of the United States shall have jurisdiction of proceedings instituted pursuant to this section and shall exercise the same without regard to whether a person asserting rights under the provisions of this Act shall have exhausted any administrative or other remedies that may be provided by law.

SEC. 13. Listing procedures shall be terminated in any political subdivision of any State (a) with respect to examiners appointed pursuant to clause (b) of section 6 whenever the Attorney General notifies the Civil Service Commission, or whenever the District Court for the District of Columbia determines in an action for declaratory judgment brought by any political subdivision with respect to which the Director of the Census has determined that more than 50 percentum of the nonwhite persons of voting age residing therein are registered to vote, (1) that all persons listed by an examiner for such subdivision have been placed on the appropriate voting registration roll, and (2) that there is no longer reasonable cause to believe that persons will be deprived of or denied the right to vote on account of race or color in such subdivision, and (b), with respect to examiners appointed pursuant to section 3(a), upon order of the authorizing court. A political subdivision may petition the Attorney General for the termination of listing procedures under clause (a) of this section, and may petition the Attorney General to request the Director of the Census to take such survey or census as may be appropriate for the making of the determination provided for in this section. The District Court for the District of Columbia shall have jurisdiction to require such survey or census to be made by the Director of the Census and it shall require him to do so if it deems the Attorney General's refusal to request such survey or census to be arbitrary or unreasonable.

SEC. 14.
(a) All cases of criminal contempt arising under the provisions of this Act shall be governed by section 151 of the Civil Rights Act of 1957 (42 U.S.C.1995).

(b) No court other than the District Court for the District of Columbia or a court of appeals in any proceeding under section 9 shall have jurisdiction to issue any declaratory judgment pursuant to section 4 or section 5 or any restraining order or temporary or permanent injunction against the execution or enforcement of any provision of this Act or any action of any Federal officer or employee pursuant hereto.

(c)(1) The terms "vote" or "voting" shall include all action necessary to make a vote effective in any primary, special, or general election, including, but not limited to, registration, listing pursuant to this Act, or other action required by law prerequisite to voting, casting a ballot, and having such ballot counted properly and included in the appropriate totals of votes cast with respect to candidates for public or party office and propositions for which votes are received in an election.

(2) The term "political subdivision" shall mean any county or parish, except that, where registration for voting is not conducted under the supervision of a county or parish, the term shall include any other subdivision of a State which conducts registration for voting.

(d) In any action for a declaratory judgment brought pursuant to section 4 or section 5 of this Act, subpoenas for witnesses who are required to attend the District Court for the District of Columbia may be served in any judicial district of the United States: Provided, That no writ of subpoena shall issue for witnesses without the District of Columbia at a greater distance than one hundred miles from the place of holding court without the permission of the District Court for the District of Columbia being first had upon proper application and cause shown.

SEC. 15. Section 2004 of the Revised Statutes (42 U.S.C.1971), as amended by section 131 of the Civil Rights Act of 1957 (71 Stat. 637), and amended by section 601 of the Civil Rights Act of 1960 (74 Stat. 90), and as further amended by section 101 of the Civil Rights Act of 1964 (78 Stat. 241), is further amended as follows:

(a) Delete the word "Federal" wherever it appears in subsections (a) and (c);

(b) Repeal subsection (f) and designate the present subsections (g) and (h) as (f) and (g), respectively.

SEC. 16. The Attorney General and the Secretary of Defense, jointly, shall make a full and complete study to determine whether, under the laws or practices of any State or States, there are preconditions to voting, which might tend to result in discrimination against citizens serving in the Armed Forces of the United States seeking to vote. Such officials shall, jointly, make a report to the Congress not later than June 30, 1966, containing the results of such study, together with a list of any States in which such preconditions exist, and shall include in such report such recommendations for legislation as they deem advisable to prevent discrimination in voting against citizens serving in the Armed Forces of the United States.

SEC. 17. Nothing in this Act shall be construed to deny, impair, or otherwise adversely affect the right to vote of any person registered to vote under the law of any State or political subdivision.

SEC. 18. There are hereby authorized to be appropriated such sums as are necessary to carry out the provisions of this Act.

SEC 19. If any provision of this Act or the application thereof to any person or circumstances is held invalid, the remainder of the Act and the application of the provision to other persons not similarly situated or to other circumstances shall not be affected thereby.

Approved August 6, 1965.

IMAGE FROM DEFENSE VISUAL INFORMATION CENTER

INDEX